INTERNATIONAL FINANCIAL REPORTING STANDARDS

International Accounting Standards (IAS)

Number	Topic
1	Presentation of Financial Statements
2	Inventories
7	Statement of Cash Flows
8	Accounting Policies, Changes in Accounting Estimates and Errors
10	Events after the Reporting Period
11	Construction Contracts
12	Income Taxes
16	Property, Plant, and Equipment
17	Leases
18	Revenue
19	Employee Benefits
20	Accounting for Government Grants and Disclosures of Government Assistance
21	The Effect of Changes in Foreign Exchange Rates
23	Borrowing Costs
24	Related Party Disclosures
26	Accounting and Reporting by Retirement Benefit Plans
27	Consolidated and Separate Financial Statements
28	Investments in Associates and Joint Ventures
29	Financial Reporting in Hyperinflationary Economies
31	Interests in Joint Ventures
32	Financial Instruments: Presentation
33	Earnings per Share
34	Interim Financial Reporting
36	Impairment of Assets
37	Provisions, Contingent Liabilities, and Contingent Assets
38	Intangible Assets
39	Financial Instruments: Recognition and Measurement
40	Investment Property
41	Agriculture

International Financial Reporting Standards (IFRS)

1	First-time Adoption of International Reporting Standards
2	Share-based Payment
3	Business Combinations
4	Insurance Contracts
5	Non-current Assets Held for Sale and Discontinued Operations
6	Exploration for and Evaluation of Mineral Resources
7	Financial Instruments: Disclosures
8	Operating Segments
9	Financial Instruments
10	Consolidated Financial Statements
11	Joint Arrangements
12	Disclosures of Interests in Other Entities
13	Fair Value Measurement

FINANCIAL REPORTING & ANALYSIS

6th EDITION

Lawrence Revsine
Late of Northwestern University

Daniel W. Collins
*Henry B. Tippie Research
Chair in Accounting
Tippie College of Business
The University of Iowa*

W. Bruce Johnson
*Sidney G. Winter
Professor of Accounting
Tippie College of Business
The University of Iowa*

H. Fred Mittelstaedt
*Deloitte Foundation
Professor of Accountancy
Mendoza College of Business
University of Notre Dame*

Leonard C. Soffer
*Clinical Professor of Accounting
Booth School of Business
University of Chicago*

Mc
Graw
Hill
Education

FINANCIAL REPORTING & ANALYSIS

Published by McGraw-Hill Education, 2 Penn Plaza, New York, NY 10121. Copyright © 2015 by McGraw-Hill Education. All rights reserved. Printed in the United States of America. Previous editions © 2012, 2009, and 2005. No part of this publication may be reproduced or distributed in any form or by any means, or stored in a database or retrieval system, without the prior written consent of McGraw-Hill Education, including, but not limited to, in any network or other electronic storage or transmission, or broadcast for distance learning.

Some ancillaries, including electronic and print components, may not be available to customers outside the United States.

This book is printed on acid-free paper.

1 2 3 4 5 6 7 8 9 0 DOW/DOW 1 0 9 8 7 6 5 4

ISBN   978-0-07-802567-9
MHID   0-07-802567-2

Senior Vice President, Products & Markets: *Kurt L. Strand*
Vice President, General Manager, Products & Markets: *Martin J. Lange*
Content Production & Technology Services: *Kimberly Meriwether David*
Managing Director: *Tim Vertovec*
Brand Manager: *James Heine*
Director of Development: *Ann Torbert*
Development Editor: *Gail Korosa*
Marketing Manager: *Kathleen Klehr*
Director, Content Production: *Terri Schiesl*
Content Project Manager: *Lisa Bruflodt*
Buyer: *Jennifer Pickel*
Media Project Manager: *Shawn Coenen*
Cover Designer: *Studio Montage, St. Louis, MO.*
Cover Image: © *Tetra Images/Getty*
Compositor: *Aptara®, Inc.*
Typeface: *10/13.5 Times*
Printer: *R. R. Donnelley*

All credits appearing on page or at the end of the book are considered to be an extension of the copyright page.

Library of Congress Cataloging-in-Publication Data

Revsine, Lawrence.
Financial reporting & analysis / Lawrence Revsine [and three others]. —6th edition.
    pages cm
    ISBN 978-0-07-802567-9 (alk. paper)
    1. Financial statements. 2. Financial statements—Case studies.
    3. Corporations—Accounting.
    I. Title. II. Title: Financial reporting and analysis.
HF5681.B2R398 2015
657'.3—dc23

                                                                                        2013050959

The Internet addresses listed in the text were accurate at the time of publication. The inclusion of a website does not indicate an endorsement by the authors or McGraw-Hill Education, and McGraw-Hill Education does not guarantee the accuracy of the information presented at these sites.

www.mhhe.com

The authors dedicate this work to:

Daniel W. Collins—Melissa, Theresa, Ann, and my late wife, Mary

W. Bruce Johnson—Diane and Cory

H. Fred Mittelstaedt—Laura and Grace

Leonard C. Soffer—Robin, Michael & Rachelli, Andy, and Leah

About the Authors

Lawrence Revsine

At the time of his passing in 2007, Lawrence Revsine was the *John and Norma Darling Distinguished Professor of Financial Accounting,* Kellogg Graduate School of Management, Northwestern University. A graduate of Northwestern University, he joined its accounting faculty in 1971.

Larry was a leading authority on various financial reporting issues and published more than 50 articles in top academic journals. He was a consultant to the American Institute of Certified Public Accountants, the Securities and Exchange Commission, and the Financial Accounting Standards Board and served on the Financial Accounting Standards Advisory Council. He was also a consultant to industry on external reporting issues and regulatory cases and taught extensively in management development and continuing education programs in the United States and abroad.

Larry was a master at making accounting come alive in the classroom. He had an uncommon knack for creating a sense of mystery and excitement about seemingly mundane accounting topics. Each class had a clear message that Larry delivered with great energy and enthusiasm. And each class was sprinkled with anecdotes conveyed with an element of wit that only Larry could pull off. It was his deep understanding of the subject matter and his dynamic delivery that endeared him to so many Kellogg students over the years. Among the many awards he received for teaching excellence are: the American Accounting Association's Outstanding Educator Award; the Illinois CPA Society's Outstanding Educator Award; the Sidney J. Levy Teaching Award, presented by the Kellogg Dean's Office; and the 1995 Reunion Class Alumni Choice Faculty Award, given to the Kellogg faculty member who has had the greatest impact on the professional and personal lives of Kellogg alums.

Larry was passionate about changing the way financial accounting is taught, and he was the driving force behind this book. As you read this book, listen carefully and you will hear his voice echo from every page.

Daniel W. Collins

Henry B. Tippie Research Chair in Accounting, Tippie College of Business, The University of Iowa; BBA 1968, Ph.D. 1973, The University of Iowa

Professor Collins was the recipient of the University of Iowa Board of Regents Award for Faculty Excellence in 2000 and the American Accounting Association (AAA) Outstanding Educator Award in 2001. His research focuses on the role of accounting numbers in equity valuation, earnings management, and the relation between firms' corporate governance mechanisms and cost of equity and debt financing. A frequent contributor to the top academic accounting journals, he has been recognized as one of the top 10 most highly cited authors in the accounting literature over the past 20 years.

Professor Collins has served on the editorial review boards of the *Journal of Accounting Research* and the *Journal of Accounting and Economics.* He has also served as associate editor of *The Accounting Review* and as director of publications for the AAA. Professor Collins has served on numerous AAA committees including the Financial Accounting Standards Committee and has chaired the Publications Committee, the National Program Committee, and the Doctoral Consortium Committee. He also served on the Financial Accounting Standards Advisory Council.

A member of the American Accounting Association, Professor Collins is a frequent presenter at research colloquia, conferences, and doctoral consortia in the United States, Australia, and Europe. He has also received outstanding teaching awards at both Michigan State University and The University of Iowa.

W. Bruce Johnson

Sidney G. Winter Professor of Accounting, Tippie College of Business, The University of Iowa; BS 1970, University of Oregon, MS 1973, Ph.D. 1975, The Ohio State University

W. Bruce Johnson joined the University of Iowa faculty in 1988 and has served as director of its McGladrey Institute for Accounting Education and Research, accounting group chairman, and associate dean for graduate programs. In the latter position, he was responsible for Iowa's MBA and Executive MBA programs.

Professor Johnson previously held faculty appointments at the University of Wisconsin, Northwestern University, the University of Chicago, and the China European International Business School (CEIBS).

His teaching and research interests include corporate financial reporting, financial analysis, value-driven management systems and investment strategies, executive compensation practices, and forensic accounting. He received the Gilbert P. Maynard Award for Excellence in Accounting Instruction and the Chester A. Phillips Outstanding Professor Award.

A well-respected author, Professor Johnson's articles have appeared in numerous scholarly publications and in academic and professional journals. He has served on the editorial boards of several academic journals and as a litigation consultant on financial reporting matters. He is a former member of the Financial Reporting Executive Committee (FinREC) of the American Institute of Certified Public Accountants and past president of the Financial Reporting and Accounting Section (FARS) of the American Accounting Association (AAA). He has also served as a research consultant to the Financial Accounting Standards Board and on the Research Advisory, Professional Practice Quality, and Outstanding Educator committees of the AAA. He is a member of the AAA and Financial Executives International. He was formerly senior vice president for Equity Strategy at SCI Capital Management, a money management firm.

H. Fred Mittelstaedt

Deloitte Foundation Professor of Accountancy, Mendoza College of Business, University of Notre Dame; BS 1979, MS 1982, Illinois State University, Ph.D. 1987, University of Illinois

Fred Mittelstaedt joined the University of Notre Dame faculty in 1992. He has served as the Department of Accountancy chairman since 2007. Prior to coming to Notre Dame, he held a faculty appointment at Arizona State University.

Professor Mittelstaedt has taught financial reporting courses to undergraduates, masters in accountancy students, MBAs, and Executive MBAs. While at Notre Dame, he has received the Kaneb Undergraduate Teaching Award and the Arnie Ludwig Executive MBA Outstanding Teacher Award.

His research focuses on financial reporting and retirement benefit issues and has been published in the *Journal of Accounting and Economics, The Accounting Review, Review of Accounting Studies,* the *Journal of Pension Economics and Finance,* and several other accounting and finance journals. He is a reviewer for numerous academic journals and has served on the Editorial Advisory and Review Board for *The Accounting Review.* In addition, he has testified on retiree health benefit issues before the U.S. House of Representatives Committee on Education and the Workforce.

Professor Mittelstaedt is a past president of the Federation of Schools of Accountancy and is a member of the American Accounting Association and the American Institute of Certified Public Accountants. Prior to joining academia, he was an auditor with Price Waterhouse & Co. and received an Elijah Watt Sells Award for exceptional performance on the May 1980 Uniform CPA Exam.

Leonard C. Soffer

Clinical Professor of Accounting, Booth School of Business, The University of Chicago; BS 1977, University of Illinois at Urbana, MBA 1981, Kellogg School of Management, Northwestern University, Ph.D. 1991, University of California at Berkeley.

Leonard Soffer rejoined the faculty of the University of Chicago in 2007. He was previously an Associate Professor of Accounting and Associate Dean of the Honors College at the University of Illinois at Chicago, where he was named the Accounting Professor of the Year. He also has served on the faculty of Northwestern University's Kellogg School of Management.

Professor Soffer has taught financial reporting, managerial accounting, and corporate valuation courses to both MBAs and Executive MBAs. He previously taught the consolidations and foreign currency translation modules of a nationally recognized CPA review course. He also teaches a financial reporting course to executive education students.

Professor Soffer's research focuses on the use of accounting information and analyst reports, particularly in the context of corporate valuation. His research has been published in *The Journal of Accounting Research, The Review of Accounting Studies, Contemporary Accounting Research, Accounting Horizons, Managerial Finance,* and *The Review of Accounting and Finance.* He is a co-author of the book *Financial Statement Analysis: A Valuation Approach.*

Professor Soffer is a member of the American Accounting Association, The American Institute of Certified Public Accountants, and the Illinois CPA Society. He served for 12 years on the Accounting Principles Committee of the Illinois CPA Society, and chaired or co-chaired the committee for three years. Before entering academia, Professor Soffer worked in accounting and finance positions, most recently in the Mergers and Acquisitions group of USG Corporation. He was a winner of the prestigious Elijah Watt Sells Award for his performance on the Uniform CPA Exam.

Preface

One of our objectives in writing this book is to help students become skilled preparers and informed consumers of financial statement information. The financial reporting environment today is particularly challenging. Accountants, auditors, and financial analysts must not only know the reporting practices that apply in the United States (U.S. GAAP), they must also be aware of the practices allowed in other countries under International Financial Reporting Standards (IFRS). Adding to this challenge is the fact that the Financial Accounting Standards Board (FASB) and its global counterpart—the International Accounting Standards Board (IASB)—have issued in the past few years an unprecedented number of proposed new standards intended to improve financial reporting practices worldwide and to achieve convergence of U.S. GAAP and IFRS. These proposed new standards will change in fundamental ways when revenue is recognized, how certain assets and liabilities are measured, and how information is presented in financial statements. We believe it is essential for students not only to comprehend the key similarities and differences between current U.S. GAAP and IFRS, but also to grasp the significant changes to those standards that are on the horizon.

Our other objective in writing this book is to change the way the second-level course in financial accounting is taught, both to graduate and undergraduate students. Typically this course—often called Intermediate Accounting—focuses on the details of GAAP with little emphasis placed on understanding the economics of business transactions or how financial statement readers use the resultant numbers for decision making. Traditional intermediate accounting texts are encyclopedic in nature and approach, lack a unifying theme, and emphasize the myriad of intricate accounting rules and procedures that could soon become outdated by new standards.

In contrast, we wrote *Financial Reporting & Analysis,* Sixth Edition, to foster a "critical thinking" approach to learning the subject matter. Our approach develops students' understanding of the environment in which financial reporting choices are made, what the options are, how accounting information is used for various types of decisions, and how to avoid misusing financial statement data. We convey the exciting nature of financial reporting in two stages. First, we provide a framework for understanding management's accounting choices, the effect those choices have on the reported numbers, and how financial statement information is used in valuation and contracting. Business contracts, such as loan agreements and management compensation agreements, are often linked to accounting numbers. We show how this practice creates incentives for managers to exploit the flexibility in financial reporting standards to "manage" the reported accounting numbers to benefit themselves or shareholders. Second, we integrate current real-world financial statements and events into our discussions to illustrate vividly how financial reporting alternatives and subjective accounting estimates give managers discretion in the timing of earnings and in reporting the components of financial position. We believe this approach—which focuses on the fundamental measurement and reporting issues that arise from both simple and complex business transactions, and how financial statements are used for decision making—better prepares students to adapt as business transactions and accounting standards continue to evolve.

An important feature of our approach is that it integrates the perspectives of accounting, corporate finance, economics, and critical analysis to help students grasp how business transactions get reported and understand the decision implications of financial statement numbers. We cover all of the core topics of intermediate accounting as well as several topics often found in advanced accounting courses, such as consolidations, joint venture accounting, and foreign currency translation. For each topic, we describe the underlying business transaction, the GAAP guidelines that apply, how the guidelines are implemented in practice, and how the financial statements are affected. We then go a step further and ask: What do the reported numbers mean? Does the accounting process yield numbers that faithfully present the underlying economic situation of a company? And, if not, what can financial statement users do to overcome this limitation in order to make more informed decisions? A Global Vantage Point discussion then summarizes the key similarities and differences between U.S. GAAP and IFRS, and previews potential changes to both.

Our book is aimed not only at those charged with the responsibility for preparing financial statements, but also those who will use financial statements for making decisions. Our definition of financial statement "users" is broad and includes lenders, equity analysts, investment bankers, boards of directors, and others charged with monitoring corporate performance and the behavior of management. As such, it includes auditors who establish audit scope and conduct analytical review procedures to spot problem areas in external financial statements. To be effective, auditors must understand the incentives of managers, how the flexibility of U.S. GAAP and IFRS accounting guidance can be exploited to conceal rather than reveal underlying economics, and the potential danger signals that should be investigated. Our intent is to help financial statement readers learn how to perform better audits, improve cash flow forecasts, undertake realistic valuations, conduct better comparative analyses, and make more informed evaluations of management.

Financial Reporting & Analysis, Sixth Edition, provides instructors with a teaching/learning approach for achieving goals stressed by professional accountants and analysts. Our book is designed to instill capacities for thinking in an abstract, logical manner; solving unstructured problems; understanding the determining forces behind management accounting choices; and instilling an integrated, cross-disciplinary view of financial reporting. Text discussions are written, and exercises, problems, and cases are carefully chosen, to help achieve these objectives without sacrificing technical underpinnings. Throughout, we explain in detail the source of the numbers, the measurement methods used, and how transactions are recorded and presented. We have strived to provide a comprehensive user-oriented focus while simultaneously helping students build a strong technical foundation.

Key Changes in the Sixth Edition

The first five editions of our book have been widely adopted in business schools throughout the United States, Canada, Europe, and the Pacific Rim. Our book has been used successfully at both the graduate and undergraduate levels, and in investment banking, commercial lending, and other corporate training programs. Many of our colleagues who used the first five editions have provided us with valuable feedback. Based on their input, we have made a number of changes in this edition of the book to achieve more effectively the objectives outlined above. Key changes include the following:

- Updated Global Vantage Point sections
  - Identify key differences between U.S. GAAP and IFRS.
  - Discuss financial statement excerpts of companies that follow IFRS.
  - Summarize proposed new accounting standards issued by the FASB and/or the IASB as part of their convergence project.
- Incorporation of all FASB and IASB standards, exposure drafts, and discussion papers released through July 2013.
- New Chapter 5 appendix on Segment Reporting.
- New or updated company examples throughout the book.
- New and revised end-of-chapter materials including exercises, problems, and cases tied to Global Vantage Points or to proposed new FASB and IASB standards.

Chapter Revision Highlights

Chapter 1: The Economic and Institutional Setting for Financial Reporting

- Streamlined discussion of how and why international accounting standards are developed.
- Explanation of the FASB Accounting Standards Codification™ project.
- Expanded description of the FASB Conceptual Framework.

Chapter 2: Accrual Accounting and Income Determination

- Revised discussion of alternative formats for presenting comprehensive income.
- Revised Global Vantage section that highlights key differences between other comprehensive income (OCI) components under IFRS versus U.S. GAAP.
- Updated exhibits from company reports throughout the chapter.
- Updated data displays on transitory earnings components (special or unusual items, discontinued operations, and extraordinary items).

Chapter 3: Additional Topics in Income Determination

- Revised Global Vantage Point section that discusses key differences between IFRS and U.S. GAAP on revenue recognition with examples.
- New discussion of FASB/IASB recent proposals on revenue recognition.
- Updated exhibits from company reports throughout the chapter.

Chapter 4: Structure of the Balance Sheet and Statement of Cash Flows

- Revised Global Vantage section that highlights key differences in where certain transactions are reported on the cash flow statement under IFRS versus U.S. GAAP.
- New problem material on IFRS versus U.S. GAAP cash flow statement items.
- Updated exhibits from company reports throughout the chapter.

Chapter 5: Essentials of Financial Statement Analysis

- Added new discussion of cause-of-change analysis.
- Updated exhibits from company reports throughout the chapter.
- Moved discussion of bankruptcy prediction models from appendix to chapter itself.
- Added new appendix on Segment Reporting.

Chapter 6: The Role of Financial Information in Valuation and Credit Risk Assessment

- Updated existing exhibits from company reports throughout the chapter.

Chapter 7: The Role of Financial Information in Contracting

- Updated examples throughout the chapter.

Chapter 8: Receivables

- Updated the Global Vantage Point section on IFRS similarities and differences, and the implications of the FASB Exposure Draft on Financial Instruments.
- Revised discussion on bad debt expense to be consistent with proposed ASU on Revenue Recognition.
- Introduced a new allowance for doubtful accounts analysis using Krispy Kreme.
- Updated the troubled debt restructuring discussion regarding what constitutes financial difficulties and concession under ASU 2011-02.
- Updated existing company examples throughout the chapter.

Chapter 9: Inventories

- Updated Global Vantage Point section on the differences between U.S. GAAP and IFRS and added new case materials.
- Updated inventory method and LIFO reserve statistics.
- Provided new examples of inventory write-offs and fraud.
- Added Whole Foods inventory disclosures to tie to Chapter 5 discussions.

Chapter 10: Long-Lived Assets

- Updated and expanded Global Vantage Point section on the differences between U.S. GAAP and IFRS.
- Expanded discussion of conceptual underpinnings of accounting for long-lived assets.
- New impairment example using Krispy Kreme.
- Streamlined discussion of difficulties associated with analyzing historical cost financial statements.
- New Whole Foods example to tie to Chapter 5 examples.
- Added and updated new problems and cases.
- Updated web appendix on current value accounting for IFRS issues; available on www.mhhe.com/revsine6e.

Chapter 11: Financial Instruments as Liabilities

- Updated Global Vantage Point sections on IFRS guidance for liability presentation, long-term debt, hedge accounting, and contingent liabilities.
- New section on loan guarantees and ASC 460.

Chapter 12: Financial Reporting for Leases

- Updated Global Vantage Point section on the differences between U.S. GAAP and IFRS and the Exposure Drafts jointly developed by the FASB and the IASB.
- Updated comparison of operating and capital lease obligations by industry.
- New Whole Foods example for illustrating constructive capitalization to tie to Chapter 5 examples.
- Added and updated problems and cases tied to FASB/IASB Exposure Draft and existing IFRS.

Chapter 13: Income Tax Reporting

- Added discussion of how the Patient Protection and Affordable Care Act affected many companies' deferred tax assets and resulted in earnings charges when the law was enacted.
- Added explanation of why deferred tax positions for a company never reverse even though individual items do reverse.
- Added discussion of deferred taxes and the cash flow statement.
- Updated exhibits from company reports throughout the chapter.

Chapter 14: Pensions and Postretirement Benefits

- Updated Global Vantage Point section on differences between U.S. GAAP and IFRS.
- Added new diagram of pension relationships.
- Updated and redesigned presention of statistics on plan assets by plan type, assumptions, and funded status.
- Revised analysis for GE by using 2012 information.
- Added discussion of immediate recognition of actuarial gains.
- Added new problems and cases.

Chapter 15: Financial Reporting for Owners' Equity

- New section on convertible debt that may be settled in cash.
- Added new examples and updated existing examples of company disclosures.
- Additional problem material on distinguishing equity from debt transactions.

Chapter 16: Intercorporate Equity Investments

- Reorganized material on debt investments so that it all appears together in the appendix.
- Reorganized material on purchase and pooling of interests methods so they appear together in the chapter itself.
- Updated exhibits from company reports throughout the chapter.

Chapter 17: Statement of Cash Flows

- Added appendix showing a simple way to use Excel to derive cash flow statements.
- Updated exhibits from company reports throughout the chapter.

Appendix: Time Value of Money

- Added discussion of Excel.

Acknowledgments

Colleagues at Iowa, Northwestern, and Notre Dame, as well other universities, have served as sounding boards on a wide range of issues over the past years, shared insights, and provided many helpful comments. Their input helped us improve this book. In particular, we thank: Jim Boatsman, Arizona State University; Brad Badertscher, Tom Frecka, Chao-Shin Liu, Bill Nichols, and Tom Stober, University of Notre Dame; Cristi Gleason and Ryan Wilson, University of Iowa; Tom Linsmeier, the Financial Accounting Standards Board; Larry Tomassini, The Ohio State University; Robert Lipe, University of Oklahoma; Don Nichols, Texas Christian University; Nicole Thibodeau, Willamette University; Paul Zarowin, New York University; and Stephen Zeff, Rice University.

We wish to thank the following professors who assisted in the Sixth Edition's development:

Stephen Brown, *University of Maryland-College Park*

Doug De Vidal, *University of Texas at Austin*

Barbara Durham, *University of Central Florida-Orlando*

Coby Harmon, *University of California-Santa Barbara*

Richard Houston, *University of Alabama-Tuscaloosa*

Frimette Kass-Schraibman, *Brooklyn College*

Adam Koch, *University of Virginia*

Bradley Lail, *Nc State University-Raleigh*

Kathryn Maxwell (Cordova), *University of Arizona*

Kevin Melendrez, *New Mexico State University-Las Cruces*

Brian Nagle, *Duquesne University*

Ramesh Narasimhan, *Montclair State University*

Sia Nassiripour, *William Paterson University*

Keith Patterson, *Brigham Young University-Idaho*

Bonita Peterson-Kramer, *Montana State University-Bozeman*

Maryann Prater, *Clemson University*

Atul Rai, *Wichita State University*

Eric Rothenburg, *Kingsborough Community College*

Lynn Saubert, *Radford University*

Mike Slaugbaugh, *Indiana University/Purdue University-Ft Wayne*

Sheldon Smith, *Utah Valley University Orem*

Robin Thomas, *Nc State University-Raleigh*

Terry Tranter, *University of Minnesota-Minneapolis*

Robert Trezevant, *University of Southern California*
Marcia R. Veit, *University of Central Florida-Orlando*
Kenton Walker, *University of Wyoming—Laramie*

Mike Wilkins, *Texas A & M University*
Michael Wilson, *Metropolitan State University*
Jennifer Winchel, *University of South Carolina*

We are grateful to the many users of prior editions whose constructive comments and suggestions have contributed to an improved Sixth Edition.

Lester Barenbaum, *La Salle University*
Gerhard Barone, *Gonzaga University*
John Bildersee, *New York University*
Sharon Borowicz, *Benedictine University*
John Brennan, *Georgia State University*
Philip Brown, *Harding University*
Shelly L. Canterbury, *George Mason University*
Jeffrey Decker, *University of Illinois—Springfield*
Ilia Dichev, *Emory University*
Timothy P. Dimond, *Northern Illinois University*
Joseph M. Donato, *Thomas College*
Michael T. Dugan, *University of Alabama*
David O. Fricke, *University of North Carolina—Pembroke*
Michael J. Gallagher, *Defiance College*
Lisa Gillespie, *Loyola University—Chicago*
Alan Glazer, *Franklin and Marshall College*
Cristi Gleason, *University of Iowa—Iowa City*
Patrick J. Griffin, *Lewis University*
Paul Griffin, *University of California—Davis*
Donald Henschel, *Benedictine University*
James Irving, *College of William & Mary*
Kurt Jesswein, *Sam Houston State University*
Gun Joh, *San Diego State University—San Diego*
J. William Kamas, *University of Texas at Austin*
Jocelyn Kauffunger, *University of Pittsburgh*
Robert Kemp, *University of Virginia*
Michael Kubik, *Johns Hopkins University*
Steve C. Lim, *Texas Christian University*
Chao-Shin Liu, *University of Notre Dame*
Don Loster, *University of California—Santa Barbara*
Troy Luh, *Webster University*
David Marcinko, *Skidmore College*
P. Michael McLain, *Hampton University*

Krish Menon, *Boston University*
Kyle S. Meyer, *Florida State University*
Stephen R. Moehrle, *University of Missouri—St. Louis*
Bruce Oliver, *Rochester Institute of Technology*
Erik Paulson, *Dowling College*
Chris Prestigiacomo, *University of Missouri—Columbia*
Richard Price, *Rice University*
Vernon Richardson, *University of Arkansas—Fayetteville*
Tom Rosengarth, *Bridgewater College*
Mike Sandretto, *University of Illinois—Champaign*
Paul Simko, *University of Virginia—Charlottesville*
Praveen Sinha, *California State University at Long Beach*
Greg Sommers, *Southern Methodist University*
Carolyn Spencer, *Dowling College*
Victor Stanton, *University of California—Berkeley*
Jack Stecher, *Carnegie Mellon University*
Thomas L. Stober, *University of Notre Dame*
Phillip Stocken, *Dartmouth College*
Ron Stunda, *Birmingham Southern College*
Kanaiyalal Sugandh, *La Sierra University*
Eric Sussman, *University of California—Los Angeles*
Nicole Thibodeau, *Willamette University*
Mark Trombley, *University of Arizona*
Suneel Udpa, *University of California—Berkeley*
Clark Wheatley, *Florida International University—Miami*
Colbrin Wright, *Central Michigan University*
Christian Wurst, *Temple University—Philadelphia*
Paul Zarowin, *New York University*

We are particularly grateful to Ilene Persoff, Long Island University/CW Post Campus, for her careful technical and editorial review of the manuscript, Solutions Manual, and Test Bank for the Sixth edition. Her insightful comments challenged our thinking and contributed to a much improved new edition.

Alan Jagolinzer, University of Colorado—Boulder, provided invaluable help in updating many of the Global Vantage Point sections of the book and related end-of-chapter materials. We are grateful to him for his work on this edition.

We are grateful to our supplements contributors for the Sixth edition: Barbara Muller, Arizona State University, who prepared the Test Bank; Peter Theuri, Northern Kentucky University, who prepared the Instructor's Manual; and Beth Woods, Accuracy Counts, who prepared the online quizzes and PowerPoints®.

We gratefully acknowledge the McGraw-Hill/Higher Education editorial and marketing teams for their encouragement and support throughout the development of the Sixth edition of this book.

Our goal in writing this book was to improve the way financial reporting is taught and mastered. We would appreciate receiving your comments and suggestions.

—Daniel W. Collins
—W. Bruce Johnson
—H. Fred Mittelstaedt
—Leonard C. Soffer

Walkthrough

Chapter Objectives

Each chapter opens with a **brief introduction and summary of learning objectives** to set the stage for the goal of each chapter and prepare students for the key concepts and practices.

Boxed Readings

Sidebar margin boxes call out key concepts in each chapter and provide additional information to reinforce concepts.

---

188   CHAPTER 4   Structure of the Balance Sheet and Statement of Cash Flows

defaulting on required interest and principal payments (see Chapter 5 for further discussion of capital structure ratios).

In addition to assessing the mix of debt versus equity financing, the balance sheet and related notes to the financial statements provide information for evaluating the **maturity structure** of the various obligations within the liability section. This information is critical to assessing the **liquidity** of an entity. Liquidity measures how readily assets can be converted to cash relative to how soon liabilities will have to be paid in cash. The balance sheet is the source of information for a variety of liquidity measures (detailed in Chapter 5) used by analysts and commercial loan officers to assess an entity's creditworthiness.

> *Maturity structure* refers to how far into the future the obligations will come due.

In addition to the liquidity measures that focus on short-term cash inflows and cash needs, balance sheets provide information for assessing long-term **solvency**—a company's ability to generate sufficient cash flows to maintain its productive capacity and still meet interest and principal payments on long-term debt. A company that cannot make debt payments when due is technically insolvent and may be forced to reorganize or liquidate.

Operating and financial flexibility refers to an entity's ability to adjust to unexpected downturns in the economic environment in which it operates or to take advantage of profitable investment opportunities as they arise. Balance...

> As part of a joint effort with the IASB, the FASB recently worked on a project on financial statement presentation that would require...

assessments. A firm that has most of its assets i... (for example, a foundry) has limited ability to... limited operating flexibility. Similarly, a firm... of high interest debt will have limited ability t...

Accrual Accounting and | 2
Income Determination

This chapter describes the key concepts and practices that govern the measurement of annual or quarterly income (or earnings) for financial reporting purposes. Income is the difference between **revenues** and **expenses**.[1] The cornerstone of income measurement is **accrual accounting**. Under accrual accounting, *revenues are recorded (recognized) in the period when they are "earned" and become "realized or realizable"*—that is, when the seller has performed a service or conveyed an asset to a buyer, which entitles the seller to the benefits represented by the revenues, and the value to be received for that service or asset is reasonably assured and can be measured with a high degree of reliability.[2] Revenues are considered realizable when the related assets received or held are readily convertible to known amounts of cash or claims to cash.[3] *Expenses are the expired costs or assets that are used up in producing those revenues. Expense recognition is tied to revenue recognition. Therefore, expenses are recorded in the same accounting period in which the revenues are recognized. The approach of tying expense recognition to revenue recognition is commonly referred to as the "matching principle."*

A natural consequence of accrual accounting is the decoupling of measured earnings from operating cash inflows and outflows. Reported revenues under accrual accounting generally do not correspond to cash receipts for the period; also, reported expenses generally do not correspond to cash outlays of the period. In fact, *accrual accounting can produce large differences between the firm's reported profit performance and the amount of cash generated from operations. Frequently, however, accrual accounting earnings provide a more accurate measure of the economic value added during the period than do operating cash flows.*[4]

[1] In this text, we use the terms *profit, earnings,* and *income* interchangeably.
[2] In "Elements of Financial Statements," *Statement of Financial Accounting Concepts (SFAC) No. 6,* the Financial Accounting Standards Board (FASB) defines revenues as "inflows or other enhancements of assets of an entity or settlements of its liabilities (or a combination of both) from delivering or producing goods, rendering services, or other activities that constitute the entity's ongoing major or central operations" (para. 78). Expenses are defined as "outflows or other using up of assets or incurrences of liabilities (or a combination of both) from delivering or producing goods, rendering services, or carrying out other activities that constitute the entity's ongoing major or central operations" (para. 80).
[3] "Recognition and Measurement in Financial Statements of Business Enterprises," *Statement of Financial Accounting Concepts No. 5* (Stamford, CT: FASB, 1984), para. 83. Assets that are readily convertible to cash have both the following characteristics: (a) interchangeable (fungible) units, and (b) quoted prices available in an active market that can rapidly absorb the quantity held by the entity without significantly affecting the price.
[4] *Economic value added* represents the increase in the value of a product or service as a consequence of operating activities. To illustrate, the value of an assembled automobile far exceeds the value of its separate steel, glass, plastic, rubber,

LEARNING OBJECTIVES
After studying this chapter, you will understand:

1. The distinction between cash-basis versus accrual income and why accrual-basis income generally is a better measure of operating performance.
2. The criteria for revenue recognition under accrual accounting and how they are used in selected industries.
3. The matching principle and how it is applied to recognize expenses under accrual accounting.
4. The difference between product and period costs.
5. The format and classifications for a multiple-step income statement and how the statement format is designed to differentiate earnings components that are more sustainable from those that are more transitory.
6. The distinction between special and unusual items, discontinued operations, and extraordinary items.
7. How to report a change in accounting principle, accounting estimate, and accounting entity.
8. The distinction between basic and diluted earnings per share (EPS) and required EPS disclosures.
9. What comprises comprehensive income and how it is displayed in financial statements.
10. Other comprehensive income differences between IFRS and U.S. GAAP.
11. The procedures for preparing

Why Financial Statements Are Important   **5**

NEWS CLIP

ACCOUNTING'S PERFECT STORM

WorldCom's revelation in June 2002 that it improperly hid $3.8 billion in expenses during the previous five quarters, or longer, set a low-water mark in a tide of accounting scandals among many firms. One of every 10 companies listed on the U.S. stock exchanges (or 845 companies in total) found flaws in past financial statements and restated earnings between 1997 and June 2002. Investors in those companies lost more than $100 billion when the restatements were announced. By comparison, only three companies restated earnings in 1981.

According to some observers, a confluence of events during the late 1990s created a climate in which accounting fraud wasn't just possible but was likely! This was accounting's perfect storm: the conjunction of unprecedented economic growth with inordinate incentive compensation, an extremely aggressive management culture, investors preoccupied with quarterly profits, and lax auditors. At companies that didn't make the Wall Street earnings number by even as little as a penny, the stock price tanked and put top management jobs at risk. Individually, some of these forces may have been good news. But when they all came together, it was a disaster waiting to happen.

Congress responded to the almost daily onslaught of accounting scandals by passing the **Sarbanes-Oxley Act** (SOX) in late July 2002. This legislation was hailed as the most groundbreaking corporate reform since the 1934 Securities and Exchange Commission. Key provisions of SOX are intended to strengthen auditor independence and improve financial statement transparency by:

- Requiring the CEO and CFO to certify in writing that the numbers in their company's financial reports are correct. Executives face potential civil charges of fraud or criminal charges of lying to the government if their company's numbers turn out to be bogus.
- Requiring each annual report of a public company to include a report by management on the company's internal control over financial reporting. Among other things, this report must disclose any material internal control weaknesses (i.e., deficiencies that result in more than a remote likelihood that a material accounting misstatement will not be prevented or detected).
- Banning outside auditors from providing certain nonaudit services—bookkeeping, financial system work, appraisals, actuarial work, internal audits, management and human resource consulting, investment-advisory work, and the auditors' other advocacy-related services—to their audit clients so that independence is not compromised. Fees paid to auditors for services must now be disclosed in the client's annual report.
- Requiring public companies to disclose whether the audit committee—comprising outside directors and charged with oversight of the annual audit—has a financial expert and if not, why not. Companies must also now reveal their off-balance-sheet arrangements (see Chapters 8 and 11) and reconcile reported "pro forma" earnings (see Chapter 5) with the audited earnings number.

In the words of one observer, "Our free market system does not depend on executives being saintly or altruistic. But markets do rely on institutional mechanisms, such as auditing and independent boards, to offset opportunistic, not to mention il-

---

News Clip boxes provide engaging news articles that capture real world financial reporting issues and controversies.

Recap boxes provide students a summary of each section, reminding them of the key points of what they just covered in small doses to reinforce what they just learned.

RECAP

Comprehensive income measures a company's change in equity (net assets) that results from all nonowner transactions and events. It is composed of both bottom-line accrual income that is reported on the income statement and other comprehensive income components. Other comprehensive income comprises selected unrealized gains and losses on incomplete (or open) transactions that bypass the income statement and are reported as direct increases or decreases to stockholders' equity. Firms are required to report comprehensive income in a statement that is displayed with the same promi-

---

xiii

Icons

Special "Getting Behind the Numbers" icons appear throughout the text to highlight and link discussions in chapters to the analysis, valuation, and contracting framework. Icons in the end-of-chapter materials signify a variety of exercises or direct students to the text website for materials such as Excel Templates.

Look for the International icon to read the new coverage of IFRS integrated throughout the text.

End-of-Chapter Elements

The text provides a variety of end-of-chapter materials to reinforce concepts. Learning objectives are included for each end-of-chapter item, making it easier than **ever** to tie your assignment back to the chapter material.

Exercises

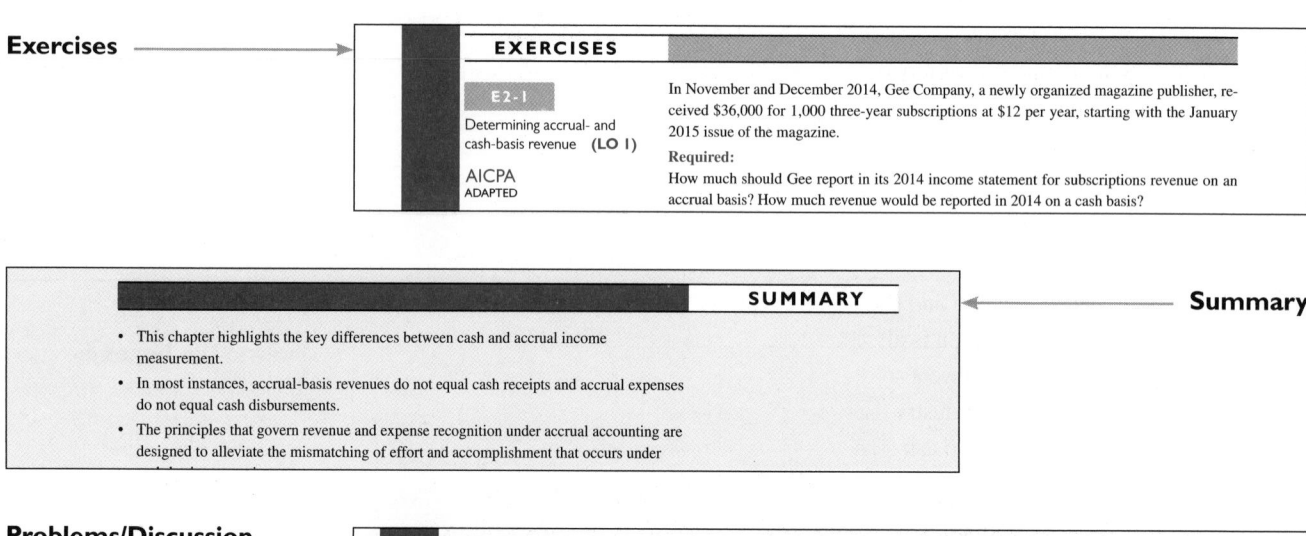

EXERCISES

E 2-1

Determining accrual- and cash-basis revenue   **(LO 1)**

AICPA
ADAPTED

In November and December 2014, Gee Company, a newly organized magazine publisher, received $36,000 for 1,000 three-year subscriptions at $12 per year, starting with the January 2015 issue of the magazine.

Required:

How much should Gee report in its 2014 income statement for subscriptions revenue on an accrual basis? How much revenue would be reported in 2014 on a cash basis?

SUMMARY

Summary

- This chapter highlights the key differences between cash and accrual income measurement.
- In most instances, accrual-basis revenues do not equal cash receipts and accrual expenses do not equal cash disbursements.
- The principles that govern revenue and expense recognition under accrual accounting are designed to alleviate the mismatching of effort and accomplishment that occurs under

Problems/Discussion Questions

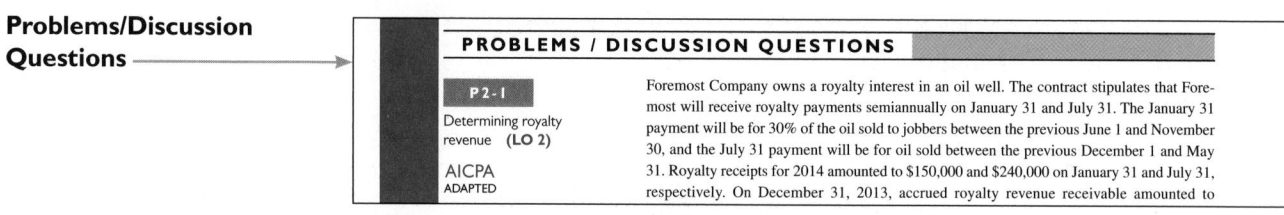

PROBLEMS / DISCUSSION QUESTIONS

P 2-1

Determining royalty revenue   **(LO 2)**

AICPA
ADAPTED

Foremost Company owns a royalty interest in an oil well. The contract stipulates that Foremost will receive royalty payments semiannually on January 31 and July 31. The January 31 payment will be for 30% of the oil sold to jobbers between the previous June 1 and November 30, and the July 31 payment will be for oil sold between the previous December 1 and May 31. Royalty receipts for 2014 amounted to $150,000 and $240,000 on January 31 and July 31, respectively. On December 31, 2013, accrued royalty revenue receivable amounted to

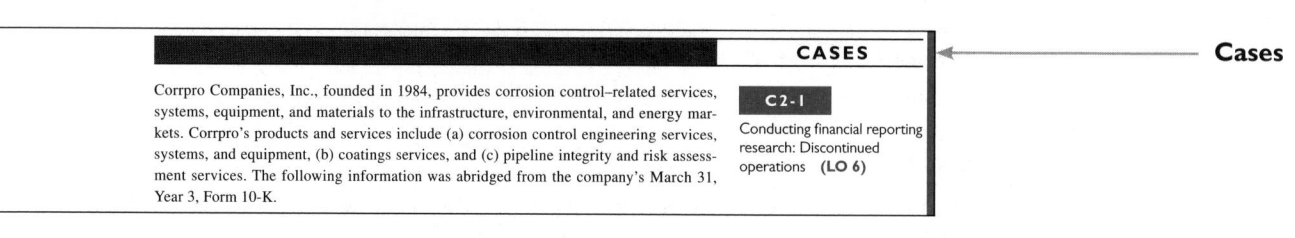

CASES

Cases

Corrpro Companies, Inc., founded in 1984, provides corrosion control–related services, systems, equipment, and materials to the infrastructure, environmental, and energy markets. Corrpro's products and services include (a) corrosion control engineering services, systems, and equipment, (b) coatings services, and (c) pipeline integrity and risk assessment services. The following information was abridged from the company's March 31, Year 3, Form 10-K.

C 2-1

Conducting financial reporting research: Discontinued operations   **(LO 6)**

Student Center

The text Online Learning Center at www.mhhe.com/revsine6e contains a variety of student study materials including:

- Online interactive quizzes include multiple-choice questions so students can quiz themselves. Grading occurs on the spot!
- Spreadsheet transparencies prepared by the authors are templates that provide students text data in Excel format.
- PowerPoint slides are included for students to review key lecture points.

Instructor Resource Center

The Instructor's Resource Center contains all of the instructor materials for your course in one convenient location at www.mhhe.com/revsine6e.

- Additional problem and case material for most chapters is provided for instructors in PDF form.
- The Solutions Manual prepared by the text authors is an extensive ancillary that provides detailed solutions for every end-of-chapter assignment.
- The Instructor's Resource Manual contains chapter overviews, outlines, and questions and answers. It also includes teaching tips and suggested readings to enhance your lectures and discussion groups.
- The new Test Bank includes a variety of examination questions to test students' grasp of chapter-by-chapter concepts and applications.
- The EZ Test Computerized Test Bank is the computerized version of the Test Bank that enables you to create your own exams.
- Powerpoint Lecture Slides include key lecture points as well as a variety of exhibits from the text.
- McGraw-Hill Higher Education and Blackboard have teamed up. What does this mean for you? Whether your institution is already using Blackboard or you just want to try Blackboard on your own, we have a solution for you. McGraw-Hill and Blackboard can now offer you easy access to industry leading technology and content, whether your campus hosts it, or we do. Be sure to ask your local McGraw-Hill representative for details.

To learn more about these supplements, visit the Revsine/Collins/Johnson/ Mittelstaedt/Soffer text website at www.mhhe.com/revsine6e or contact your McGraw-Hill sales representative.

AACSB Statement

The McGraw-Hill Companies is a proud corporate member of AACSB International. Understanding the importance and value of AACSB accreditation, *Financial Reporting & Analysis* recognizes the curricula guidelines detailed in the AACSB standards for business accreditation by connecting selected questions in the Test Bank to the six general knowledge and skill guidelines in the AACSB standards.

The statements contained in *Financial Reporting & Analysis* are provided only as a guide for the users of this textbook. The AACSB leaves content coverage and assessment within the purview of individual schools, the mission of the school, and the faculty. While *Financial*

Reporting & Analysis and the teaching package make no claim of any specific AACSB qualification or evaluation, we have within *Financial Reporting & Analysis* labeled selected questions according to the six general knowledge and skills areas.

Assurance of Learning Ready

Many educational institutions today are focused on the notion of *assurance of learning,* an important element of some accreditation standards. *Financial Reporting & Analysis* is designed specifically to support your assurance of learning initiatives with a simple, yet powerful solution. Each test bank question for *Financial Reporting & Analysis* maps to a specific chapter learning objective listed in the text. You can use our test bank software, EZ Test and EZ Test Online, to easily query for learning objectives that directly relate to the learning objectives for your course. You can then use the reporting features of EZ Test to aggregate student results in similar fashion, making the collection and presentation of assurance of learning data simple and easy.

Brief Contents

Contents

xviii

The Economic and Institutional Setting for Financial Reporting

"No one ever said accounting was an exact science."

I n late June 2002, WorldCom stunned investors by announcing that it intended to restate its financial statements for 2001 and the first quarter of 2002.[1] According to the company's press release, an internal audit of capital expenditures had uncovered $3.8 billion in improper bookkeeping transfers from line cost expense—an income statement item—to the balance sheet. Without those transfers, the company would have reported a loss for 2001 and the first quarter of 2002. The company's chief financial officer was fired, and its controller resigned. Trading in the company's stock was immediately halted. When trading resumed a few days later, the stock was worth only 6 cents per share, having lost more than 90% of its value.

The accounting scandal at WorldCom, along with those involving many other highly visible companies during the late 1990s and early 2000s, were watershed events. Investors, regulators, and politicians worldwide lost confidence in the soundness of U.S. accounting standards, the transparency of corporate financial reports, the expertise and independence of auditors, and the integrity of U.S. financial markets. Congress responded by passing the Sarbanes-Oxley Act, which contained sweeping reforms intended to restore public confidence. To understand why the reforms were needed, and how they have shaped today's financial reporting environment, let's step back in time to May 2002 and take a close look at the WorldCom scandal. After all, as the philosopher George Santayana has said: "Those who cannot learn from history are doomed to repeat it!"

LEARNING OBJECTIVES

After studying this chapter, you will understand:

1. Why financial statements are valuable sources of information about companies.

2. How the demand for financial information stems from its ability to improve decision making and monitor managers' activities.

3. How the supply of financial information is influenced by the costs of producing and disseminating it and by the benefits it provides.

4. How accounting rules are established, and why management can shape the financial information communicated to outsiders and still be within those rules.

5. Why financial reporting philosophies and detailed accounting practices sometimes differ across countries.

6. Why International Financial Reporting Standards (IFRS) influence the accounting practices of U.S. companies.

WorldCom's Curious Accounting

According to a report on the company from a highly regarded Wall Street analyst, WorldCom is doing surprisingly well despite tough times throughout the industry. The company is a global leader in the telecommunications industry, providing a complete package of communications services (voice, data, and Internet) to businesses and

Chapter

---

[1] This publication is designed to provide accurate and authoritative information in regard to the subject matter. It is sold with the understanding that the publishers and the authors are not engaged in rendering legal, accounting, investment, or other professional services. If legal advice or other expert assistance is required, the services of a competent professional person should be sought.

1

consumers. WorldCom grew very fast—an average of 58% each year from 1996 through 2000—as a result of a nearly insatiable demand for wireless communications and high-speed Internet access. Then, in March 2001, the dot-com bubble burst and Internet spending came to a screeching halt. Telecommunications companies suddenly faced excess capacity and shrinking demand for their services.

Despite the industry downturn, WorldCom reported better-than-expected 2002 first quarter results: sales of $8,120 million and pretax profits of $240 million. That's a 16% decline in sales and a 40% decline in profits, but other firms in the industry, including giants such as AT&T, are reporting even steeper sales and earnings decreases. WorldCom shares look incredibly cheap at the current price of $2 per share. As one stock analyst points out, "The company has $2.3 billion in cash, which translates into a $20.50 book value per share. And you have to pay only $2 a share for this gem! You cannot find a more attractive investment opportunity in the market." Perhaps investors have overreacted to the slump in wireless and Internet spending by penalizing WorldCom's stock too much. If so, now may be the ideal time to buy.

A closer look at WorldCom's financial statements confirms what the analyst is saying. Sales and earnings outpace the competition by a wide margin. Operating cash flows are positive and exceed the cash being spent for capacity expansion, and the balance sheet remains healthy. Overall, the company seems to be on a solid footing.

But what's this? An article in this morning's newspaper raises a new concern. The article says that WorldCom's "line costs," the rent WorldCom pays other companies for the use of their telecommunications networks, are holding steady at about 42% of sales. That's odd because line costs as a percentage of sales are rising at AT&T and other companies in the industry. WorldCom decided several years ago to lease large amounts of network capacity instead of building its own global communications network. These leases call for fixed rental payments each month without regard to message volume ("traffic"). This means that World-Com must still pay the same amount of rent even though its customers are not sending much traffic through the network these days. What seems odd to the news reporter is that the same rental payment each month combined with lower traffic revenue should produce an increase in line costs as a percent of sales. Higher line costs per dollar of revenue should translate into lower profits. That is what's happening at other companies, but at WorldCom, line costs haven't increased.

You call your broker, who confirms that WorldCom's stock is available at $1.75 per share in early trading. Should you take advantage of this investment opportunity and buy 10,000 shares? Should you avoid the stock because WorldCom's income statement may contain a line cost accounting torpedo that could potentially sink the share price? Should you take a closer look at company fundamentals—traffic volume, line costs, and other business aspects—before deciding whether to buy or avoid WorldCom shares? The unusual trend in line costs could indicate that WorldCom is successfully managing its excess capacity problems during a period of slack demand, or it could be a cautionary yellow flag warning of problems at the company.

What do you do?

WHY FINANCIAL STATEMENTS ARE IMPORTANT

This dilemma illustrates a fundamental point: Without adequate information, investors cannot properly judge the opportunities and risks of investment alternatives. To make informed decisions, investors use information about the economy, various industries, specific companies, and the products or services those companies sell. Complete information provided by reliable sources enhances the probability that the best decisions will be made. Of course, only later will you be able to tell whether your investment decision was a good one. What we can tell you now is that *if you want to know more about a company, its past performance, current health, and prospects for the future, the best source of information is the company's own financial statements.*

Why? Because the economic events and activities that affect a company and that can be translated into accounting numbers are reflected in the company's financial statements. Some financial statements provide a picture of the company at a moment in time; others describe changes that took place over a period of time. Both provide a basis for *evaluating* what happened in the past and for *projecting* what might occur in the future. For example, what is the annual rate of sales growth? Are accounts receivable increasing at an even greater rate than sales? How do sales and receivable growth rates compare to those of competitors? Are expenses holding steady? What rates of growth can be expected next year? These trends and relationships provide insights into a company's economic opportunities and risks including market acceptance, costs, productivity, profitability, and liquidity. Consequently, *a company's financial statements can be used for various purposes:*

- *As an analytical tool.*
- *As a management report card.*
- *As an early warning signal.*
- *As a basis for prediction.*
- *As a measure of accountability.*

As our prospective WorldCom stockholder knows, financial statements contain information that investors need to know to decide whether to invest in the company. Others need financial statement information to decide whether to extend credit, negotiate contract terms, or do business with the company. Financial statements serve a crucial role in allocating capital to the most productive and deserving firms. Doing so promotes the efficient use of resources, encourages innovation, and provides a liquid market for buying and selling securities and for obtaining and granting credit.

Periodic financial statements provide an economic history that is comprehensive and quantitative and, therefore, can be used to gauge company performance.[2] *For this reason, financial statements are indispensable for developing an accurate profile of ongoing performance and prospects.*

WorldCom stockholders learned an even more important lesson: Financial statements sometimes conceal more than they reveal.

Untangling the Web at WorldCom

In late May 2002, Cynthia Cooper, WorldCom's vice president of internal audit, and two of her employees discovered a series of questionable accounting entries made during 2001 and the first quarter of 2002. To Cooper's dismay, she realized that $3.8 billion of line cost expense had been shifted from the income statement to the balance sheet, a deceptive practice that made WorldCom look far more profitable than it actually was. In early June, she

---

[2] Published financial statements do not always contain the most up-to-date information about a company's changing economic fortunes. To ensure that important financial news reaches interested parties as soon as possible, companies send out press releases or hold meetings with analysts. Always check the company's investor relations website for any late-breaking news.

Figure 1.1

WORLDCOM'S
DISAPPEARING PROFITS

WorldCom improperly transferred a total of $3.8 billion in line cost expenses from the income statement to the balance sheet. This chart shows the company's profits (in millions) by quarter as reported originally and as later restated.

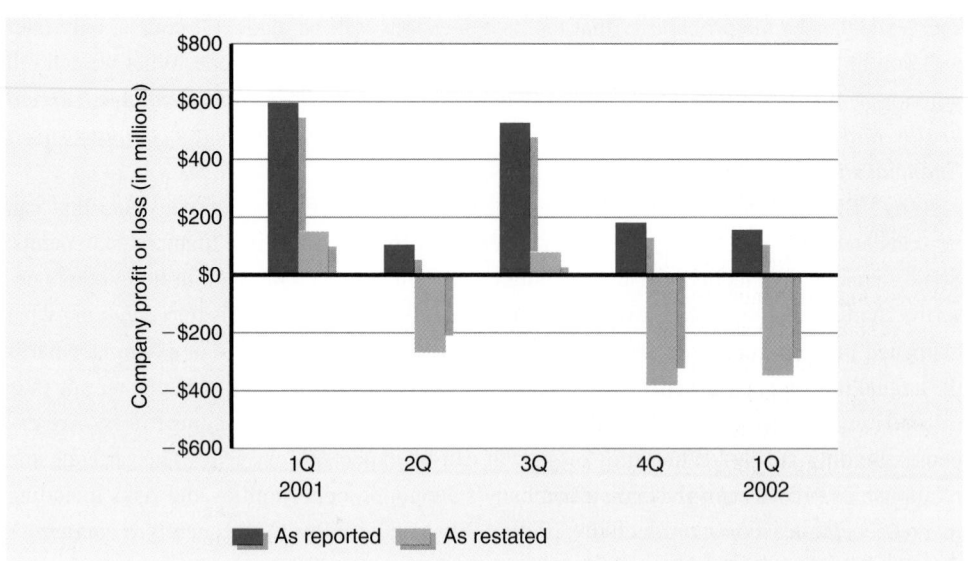

and a coworker discussed the line cost transfers with a WorldCom board member who chaired the audit committee. The committee then launched its own investigation. Based on its report, WorldCom's board decided in late June to restate the company's financial statements and to terminate the employment of two top executives. Figure 1.1 shows how WorldCom's profit picture for 2001 and early 2002 changed after the reported numbers were corrected.

The accounting rule that WorldCom violated is easy to understand. It says that when expenditures (think "money spent") provide a future benefit to the company, then and only then can the expenditures be recorded as balance sheet assets (Chapters 2 and 10 provide the details). This means that if the company spends a dollar today buying equipment that will be used for the next five years (the "future benefit"), the dollar spent should be shown as a balance sheet asset. But what if the dollar spent doesn't buy a *future* benefit? Then it cannot be shown as a balance sheet asset but instead must be shown on the income statement as a current period expense. That's the rule!

What did this accounting rule mean for the money WorldCom spent on line costs? Recall that these line costs were just the monthly rent WorldCom paid to other companies for the use of their communications networks and systems. Because the rent had to be paid each month, the money WorldCom spent wasn't buying a *future* benefit. So, all line costs should have been shown on the income statement as a current expense. Instead, WorldCom improperly "transferred" $3.8 billion of these costs from the income statement to the balance sheet where they were shown as an asset. This transfer violated the accounting rule for asset recognition and allowed WorldCom to appear more profitable than it actually was. The improper transfer also inflated WorldCom's operating cash flows.

Over the next few weeks, the situation at WorldCom grew far worse:

- Shareholder class action lawsuits were filed against the company and its management.
- The Securities and Exchange Commission (SEC) sued the company for accounting fraud and launched its own investigation.
- Five company executives were indicted on criminal charges, and four pleaded guilty.
- The company defaulted on a $4.25 billion credit line and was negotiating new payment terms with more than 30 banks.

NEWS CLIP

ACCOUNTING'S PERFECT STORM

WorldCom's revelation in June 2002 that it improperly hid $3.8 billion in expenses during the previous five quarters, or longer, set a low-water mark in a tide of accounting scandals among many firms. One of every 10 companies listed on the U.S. stock exchanges (or 845 companies in total) found flaws in past financial statements and restated earnings between 1997 and June 2002. Investors in those companies lost more than $100 billion when the restatements were announced. By comparison, only three companies restated earnings in 1981.

According to some observers, a confluence of events during the late 1990s created a climate in which accounting fraud wasn't just possible but was likely! This was accounting's perfect storm: the conjunction of unprecedented economic growth with inordinate incentive compensation, an extremely aggressive management culture, investors preoccupied with quarterly profits, and lax auditors. At companies that didn't make the Wall Street earnings number by even as little as a penny, the stock price tanked and put top management jobs at risk. Individually, some of these forces may have been good news. But when they all came together, it was a disaster waiting to happen.

Congress responded to the almost daily onslaught of accounting scandals by passing the **Sarbanes-Oxley Act** (SOX) in late July 2002. This legislation was hailed as the most groundbreaking corporate reform since the 1934 Securities Act that, among other things, had established the Securities and Exchange Commission. Key provisions of SOX are intended to strengthen auditor independence and improve financial statement transparency by:

- Creating the Public Companies Accounting Oversight Board (PCAOB) charged with establishing audit, independence, and ethical standards for auditors; investigating auditor conduct; and imposing penalties.

- Requiring the CEO and CFO to certify in writing that the numbers in their company's financial reports are correct. Executives face potential civil charges of fraud or criminal charges of lying to the government if their company's numbers turn out to be bogus.

- Requiring each annual report of a public company to include a report by management on the company's internal control over financial reporting. Among other things, this report must disclose any material internal control weaknesses (i.e., deficiencies that result in more than a remote likelihood that a material accounting misstatement will not be prevented or detected).

- Banning outside auditors from providing certain nonaudit services—bookkeeping, financial system work, appraisals, actuarial work, internal audits, management and human resource consulting, investment-advisory work, and the auditors' other advocacy-related services—to their audit clients so that independence is not compromised. Fees paid to auditors for services must now be disclosed in the client's annual report.

- Requiring public companies to disclose whether the audit committee—comprising outside directors and charged with oversight of the annual audit—has a financial expert and if not, why not. Companies must also now reveal their off-balance-sheet arrangements (see Chapters 8 and 11) and reconcile reported "pro forma" earnings (see Chapter 5) with the audited earnings number.

In the words of one observer, "Our free market system does not depend on executives being saintly or altruistic. But markets do rely on institutional mechanisms, such as auditing and independent boards, to offset opportunistic, not to mention illegal, behavior."* The Sarbanes-Oxley Act strengthens those important institutional mechanisms and, in so doing, calms the accounting storm.

* Robert Simmons as quoted in *CFO Magazine* (August 2002).

- In mid-July 2002, WorldCom filed for bankruptcy. The company was saddled with more than $40 billion in debt and had less than $10 billion in assets that could be readily converted into cash.

- In August of that year, the company acknowledged more than $7 billion in accounting errors over the previous several years.

The investigation would eventually uncover more than $11 billion in improper transfers and other accounting improprieties at the company. At least two dozen WorldCom employees were dismissed or resigned over the fraud. WorldCom—which now calls itself MCI and in 2006 became a subsidiary of Verizon—reached a settlement with the SEC to pay $750 million in penalties, then the largest fine ever levied against one company by the SEC. The company's former chief executive officer (CEO) and chief financial officer (CFO) were both sentenced to lengthy prison terms. In March 2004, after correcting hundreds of thousands of accounting entries, WorldCom restated profits by $74.4 billion for revenues, expenses, asset write-downs, and adjustments to liabilities including the $11 billion of fraudulent transactions first uncovered in 2002. Most experts agree that WorldCom's accounting improprieties were designed to meet the financial targets of Wall Street analysts and to sustain a high stock price despite diminished economic prospects for the industry.

Financial statement fraud is rare.[3] Most managers are honest and responsible, and their financial statements are free from the type of distortions that occurred at WorldCom. However, this example underscores the fact that investors and others should not simply accept the numbers in financial statements at face value. Instead, they must analyze the numbers in sufficient detail to assess the degree to which the financial statements faithfully represent the economic events and activities of the company.

Company data used by investors and analysts come primarily from published financial statements and from the company's willingness to provide additional financial and operating data voluntarily. Management has some latitude in deciding what financial information will be made available and when it will be released. For example, although financial statements must conform to accepted standards, management has discretion over the particular accounting procedures used in the statements and the details contained in supplemental notes and related disclosures. To further complicate matters, *accounting is not an exact science.* Some financial statement items, such as the amount of cash on deposit in a company bank account, are measured with a high degree of precision and reliability. Other items are more judgmental and uncertain in their measurement because they are derived from estimates of future events, such as product warranty liabilities.

Statement readers must:

- Understand current financial reporting standards.
- Recognize that management can shape the financial information communicated to outside parties.
- Distinguish between financial statement information that is highly reliable and information that is judgmental.

All three considerations weigh heavily in determining the quality of financial statement information—and thus the extent to which it should be relied on for decision-making purposes. By **quality of information,** we mean the degree to which the financial statements are grounded in facts and sound judgments and thus are free from distortion. The analytical tools and perspectives in this and later chapters will enable you to understand and better interpret the information in financial statements and accompanying disclosures as well as to appreciate fully the limitations of that information.

ECONOMICS OF ACCOUNTING INFORMATION

In the United States and other developed economies, the financial statements of business enterprises serve two key functions. First, they provide a way for company management to transfer information about business activities to people outside the company, which helps

---

[3] See *2012 Report to the Nation on Occupational Fraud & Abuse* (Austin TX: Association of Certified Fraud Examiners Inc., 2012). To learn more about accounting's "perfect storm" and the unprecedented wave of financial statement errors and irregularities uncovered at U.S. companies during the past two decades, see S. Scholz, *The Changing Nature and Consequences of Public Company Financial Restatements: 1997–2006* (Washington DC: The Department of the Treasury, April 2008).

solve an important problem known as **information asymmetry.** Second, financial statement information is often included in contracts between the company and other parties (such as lenders or managers) because doing so improves **contract efficiency.**

Information asymmetry just means that management has access to more and better information about the business than do people outside the company. The details vary from one business to another, but the idea is that information initially available only to management can help people outside the company form more accurate assessments of past economic performance, resource availability, future prospects, and risks. Financial statements are the primary formal mechanism for management to communicate some of this private information to outside parties.

Business enterprises enter into many different types of contracts. Examples include compensation contracts with managers who work for the company, debt contracts with bankers who loan money to the company, and royalty contracts with inventors who license products to the company for sale to consumers. Often these contracts contain language that refers to verifiable financial statement numbers such as "operating profit" for calculating managers' bonuses, "free cash flow" for determining loan compliance, and product "sales" for computing royalty payments. Contracts tied to financial statement numbers can restrict the range of decisions made by management and thereby align management's incentives with those of the other contracting parties (Chapter 7 explains how).

> Managers have a **stewardship** responsibility to investors and creditors. The company's resources belong to investors and creditors, but managers are "stewards" of those resources and are thus responsible for ensuring their efficient use and protecting them from adversity. To learn more about the stewardship role of accounting, see V. O'Connell, "Reflections on Stewardship Reporting," *Accounting Horizons* (June 2007): pp. 215–227.

Financial statements are demanded because of their value as a source of information about the company's performance, financial condition, and resource stewardship. People demand financial statements because the data reported in them improve decision making.

The supply of financial statement information is guided by the costs of producing and disseminating it and the benefits it will provide to the company. Firms weigh the benefits they may gain from financial disclosures against the costs they incur in making those disclosures.

To see financial statement demand and supply at work, consider a company that seeks to raise money by issuing common stock or debt securities. Here financial statements provide information that can reduce investor uncertainty about the company's opportunities and risks. Reduced uncertainty translates into a lower cost of capital (the price the company must pay for new money). Investors *demand* information about the company's past performance, opportunities, and risks so that the stock or debt securities can be properly priced at issuance. Because companies need to raise capital at the lowest possible cost, they have an economic incentive to *supply* the information investors want. In this section, you will see that the amount and type of financial accounting information provided by companies depend on demand and supply forces much like the demand and supply forces affecting any economic good. Of course, regulatory groups such as the SEC, the Financial Accounting Standards Board (FASB), and the International Accounting Standards Board (IASB) influence the amount and type of financial information companies disclose as well as when and how it is disclosed.

Demand for Financial Statements

The benefits of financial statement information stem from its usefulness to decision makers. People outside the company whose decisions demand financial statement information as a key input include:

1. Shareholders and investors.
2. Managers and employees.
3. Lenders and suppliers.
4. Customers.
5. Government and regulatory agencies.

Shareholders and Investors   Shareholders and investors, including investment advisors and securities analysts, use financial information to help decide on a portfolio of securities that meets their preferences for risk, return, dividend yield, and liquidity.

Financial statements are crucial in investment decisions that use **fundamental analysis** to identify mispriced securities: stocks or bonds selling for substantially more or less than they seem to be worth. Investors who use this approach consider past sales, earnings, cash flow, product acceptance, and management performance to predict future trends in these financial drivers of a company's economic success or failure. Then they assess whether a particular stock or group of stocks is undervalued or overvalued at the current market price. Fundamental investors buy undervalued stocks and avoid overvalued stocks.

Investors who believe in the **efficient markets hypothesis**—and who thus presume they have no insights about company value beyond the current security price—also find financial statement data useful. To efficient markets investors, financial statement data provide a basis for assessing risk, dividend yield, or other firm attributes that are important to portfolio selection decisions.

> The **efficient markets hypothesis** says a stock's current market price reflects the knowledge and expectations of all investors. Those who adhere to this theory consider it futile to search for undervalued or overvalued stocks or to forecast stock price movements using financial statements or other public data because any new development is quickly and correctly reflected in a firm's stock price.

Of course, shareholders and investors themselves can perform investment analysis as can professional securities analysts who may possess specialized expertise or some comparative advantage in acquiring, interpreting, and analyzing financial statements.

Shareholders and investors also use financial statement information when evaluating the performance of the company's top executives. This use is referred to as the stewardship function of financial reports. When earnings and share price performance fall below acceptable levels, disgruntled shareholders voice their complaints in letters and phone calls to management and outside directors. If this approach doesn't work, dissident shareholders may launch a campaign, referred to as a **proxy contest,** to elect their own slate of directors at the next annual meeting. New investors often see this as a buying opportunity. By purchasing shares of the underperforming company at a bargain price, these investors hope to gain by joining forces with existing shareholders, replacing top management, and "turning the company around."

The focal point of the proxy contest often becomes the company performance as described in its recent financial statements. Management defends its record of past accomplishments while perhaps acknowledging a need for improvement in some areas of the business. Dissident shareholders point to management's past failures and the need to hire a new executive team. Of course, both sides are pointing to the same financial statements. Where one side sees success, the other sees only failure, and undecided shareholders must be capable of forming their own opinion on the matter.

Managers and Employees   Although managers regularly make operating and financing decisions based on information that is much more detailed and timely than the information found in financial statements, they also need—and therefore demand—financial statement data. Their demand arises from contracts (such as executive compensation agreements) that are linked to financial statement variables.

Executive compensation contracts usually contain annual bonus and longer term pay components tied to financial statement results. Using accounting data in this manner increases the efficiency of executive compensation contracts. Rather than trying to determine firsthand whether a manager has performed capably during the year (and whether the manager deserves a bonus), the board of directors' compensation committee needs to look only at reported profitability or some other accounting measure that functions as a summary of the company's (and thus the manager's) performance.

Employees demand financial statement information for several reasons:

- To learn about the company's performance and its impact on employee profit sharing and employee stock ownership plans.
- To monitor the health of company-sponsored pension plans and to gauge the likelihood that promised benefits will be provided on retirement.
- To know about union contracts that may link negotiated wage increases to the company's financial performance.
- More generally, to help employees assess their company's current and potential future profitability and solvency.

Lenders and Suppliers   Financial statements play several roles in the relationship between the company and those who supply financial capital. Commercial lenders (banks, insurance companies, and pension funds) use financial statement information to help decide the loan amount, the interest rate, and the security (called **collateral**) needed for a business loan. Loan agreements contain contractual provisions (called **covenants**) that require the borrower to maintain minimum levels of working capital, debt to assets, or other key accounting variables that provide the lender a safety net. Violation of these loan provisions can result in technical default and allow the lender to accelerate repayment, request additional security, or raise interest rates. So, lenders monitor financial statement data to ascertain whether the covenants are being adhered to or violated.

Suppliers demand financial statements for many reasons. A steel company may sell millions of dollars of rolled steel to an appliance manufacturer on credit. Before extending credit, careful suppliers scrutinize the buyer's financial position in much the same way that a commercial bank does—and for essentially the same reason. That is, suppliers assess the financial strength of their customers to determine whether they will pay for goods shipped. Suppliers continuously monitor the financial health of companies with which they have a significant business relationship.

Customers   Repeat purchases and product guarantees or warranties create continuing relationships between a company and its customers. A customer needs to know whether the seller has the financial strength to deliver a high-quality product on an agreed-upon schedule and whether the seller will be able to provide replacement parts and technical support after the sale. You wouldn't buy a personal computer from a door-to-door vendor without first checking out the product and the company that stands behind it. Financial statement information can help current and potential customers monitor a supplier's financial health and thus decide whether to purchase that supplier's goods and services.

Government and Regulatory Agencies   Government and regulatory agencies demand financial statement information for various reasons. For example, the SEC requires publicly traded companies to compile annual financial reports (called *10-Ks*) and quarterly financial reports (called *10-Qs*). These periodic financial reports are filed with the SEC and then made available to investors and other interested parties. This process of **mandatory reporting** allows the SEC to monitor compliance with the securities laws and to ensure that investors have a "level playing field" with timely access to financial statement information.

Taxing authorities sometimes use financial statement information as a basis for establishing tax policies designed to enhance social welfare. For example, the U.S. Congress could point to widespread financial statement losses as justification for instituting a corporate income tax reduction during economic downturns.

> In the United States and most other industrialized countries, the accounting rules that businesses use for external financial reporting purposes differ from those required for income taxation purposes. As a consequence, corporate financial reporting choices in the United States are seldom influenced by the U.S. Internal Revenue Code. See Chapter 13 for details.

Government agencies are often customers of businesses. For example, the U.S. Army purchases weapons from suppliers whose contracts guarantee that they are reimbursed for costs and that they get an agreed-upon profit margin. So, financial statement information is essential to resolving contractual disputes between the Army and its suppliers and for monitoring whether companies engaged in government business are earning profits beyond what the contracts allow.

Financial statement information is used to regulate businesses—especially banks, insurance companies, and public utilities such as gas and electric companies. To achieve economies of scale in the production and distribution of natural gas and electricity, local governments have historically granted exclusive franchises to individual gas and electric companies serving a specified geographical area. In exchange for this monopoly privilege, the rates these companies are permitted to charge consumers are closely regulated. Accounting measures of profit and of asset value are essential because the accounting **rate of return**—reported profit divided by asset book value—is a key factor that regulators use in setting allowable charges.[4] If a utility company earns a rate of return that seems too high, regulators can decrease the allowable charge to consumers and thereby reduce the company's profitability.

Banks, insurance companies, and savings and loan associations are subject to regulation aimed at protecting individual customers and society from insolvency losses—for example, a bank's inability to honor deposit withdrawal requests or an insurance company's failure to provide compensation for covered damages as promised. Financial statements aid regulators in monitoring the health of these companies so that corrective action can be taken when needed.

Regulatory intervention (in the form of antitrust litigation, protection from foreign imports, government loan guarantees, price controls, etc.) by government agencies and legislators constitutes another source of demand for financial statement information.

Financial statement information has value either because it reduces uncertainty about a company's future profitability or economic health or because it provides evidence about the quality of its management, about its ability to fulfill its obligations under supply agreements or labor contracts, or about other facets of the company's business activities. Financial statements are demanded because they provide information that helps improve decision making or makes it possible to monitor managers' activities.

Disclosure Incentives and the Supply of Financial Information

Commercial lenders sometimes possess enough bargaining power to allow them to compel companies to deliver the financial information they need for analysis. For example, a cash-starved company applying for a bank loan has a strong incentive to provide all of the data the lender requests. Most financial statement users are less fortunate, however. They must rely on mandated reporting (for example, SEC 10-K filings), voluntary company disclosures that go beyond the minimum required reporting (for example, corporate "fact" books), and sources outside the company (for example, analysts and reporters) for the financial information needed to make decisions.

---

[4] This regulation process is intended to enhance economic efficiency by precluding the construction of duplicate facilities that might otherwise occur in a competitive environment. Eliminating redundancies presumably lowers the ultimate service cost to consumers. Regulatory agencies specify the accounting practices and disclosure policies that must be followed by companies under their jurisdiction. As a result, the accounting practices that utility companies use in preparing financial statements for regulatory agencies sometimes differ from those used in their shareholder reports.

What forces induce managers to supply information? Browse through several corporate financial reports and you will notice substantial differences across companies—and perhaps over time—in the quality and quantity of the information provided. Some companies routinely disclose operating profits, production levels, and order backlogs by major product category so analysts and investors can quickly spot changes in product costs and market acceptance. Other companies provide detailed descriptions of their outstanding debt and their efforts to hedge interest rate risk or foreign currency risk. Still other companies seem to disclose only the bare minimum required. What explains this diversity in the quality and quantity of financial information?

If the financial reporting environment were unregulated, disclosure would occur *voluntarily* as long as the incremental benefits to the company and its management from supplying financial information exceeded the incremental costs of providing that information. In other words, management's decisions about the scope, timing, and content of the company's financial statements and notes would be guided solely by the same cost and benefit considerations that influence the supply of any commodity. Managers would assess the benefits created by voluntary disclosures and weigh those benefits against the costs of making the information available. Any differences in financial disclosures across companies and over time would then be due to differences in the benefits or costs of voluntarily supplying financial information.

In fact, however, financial reporting in the United States and other developed countries is regulated by public agencies such as the SEC and by private agencies such as the FASB. The various public and private sector regulatory agencies establish and enforce financial reporting requirements *designed to ensure that companies meet certain minimum levels of financial disclosure.* Nevertheless, companies frequently communicate financial information that exceeds these minimum levels. They apparently believe that the benefits of the "extra" disclosures outweigh the costs. What are the potential benefits from voluntary disclosures that exceed minimum requirements?

> The SEC passed Regulation Fair Disclosure, known as "Reg FD," to prevent selective disclosure by companies to market professionals and certain shareholders. Reg FD helps to level the playing field between individual investors and institutional investors by limiting what management can say in private conversations with an analyst or investor, or in meetings and conference calls where public access is restricted.

Disclosure Benefits   Companies compete with one another in capital, labor, and product markets. This competition creates incentives for management to reveal "good news" financial information about the firm. The news itself may be about a successful new product introduction, increased consumer demand for an existing product, an effective quality improvement, or other matters favorable to the financial perception of the company. By voluntarily disclosing otherwise unknown good news, the company may be able to obtain capital more cheaply or get better terms from suppliers.

To see how these incentives work, consider the market for raising financial capital. Companies seek capital at the lowest possible cost. They compete with one another in terms of both the return they promise to capital suppliers and the characteristics of the financial instrument they offer. The capital market has two important features:

1. Investors are uncertain about the quality (that is, the riskiness) of each debt or equity instrument offered for sale because the ultimate return from the security depends on future events.

2. It is costly for a company to be mistakenly perceived as offering investors a low-quality ("high-risk") stock or debt instrument—a "lemon."[5]

---

[5] "Lemon," when describing an automobile, refers to an auto with hidden defects. In financial capital markets, "lemon" refers to a financial instrument (for example, stock or debt securities) with hidden risks. See, G. Akerlof, "The Market for 'Lemons': Quality Uncertainty and the Market Mechanism," *Quarterly Journal of Economics,* August 1970, pp. 488–500.

This lemon cost has various forms. It could be lower proceeds received from issuing stock, a higher interest rate that will have to be paid on a commercial loan, or more stringent conditions, such as borrowing restrictions, placed on that loan.

These market forces mean that owners and managers have an economic incentive to supply the amount and type of financial information that will enable them to raise capital at the lowest cost. A company offering attractive, low-risk securities can avoid the lemon penalty by voluntarily supplying financial information that enables investors and lenders to gauge the risk and expected return of each instrument accurately. Of course, companies offering higher risk securities have incentives to mask their true condition by supplying overly optimistic financial information. However, other forces partially offset this tendency. Examples include requirements for audited financial statements and legal penalties associated with issuing false or misleading financial statements. Managers also want to maintain access to capital markets and establish a reputation for supplying credible financial information to investors and analysts.

Financial statement disclosures can convey economic benefits to firms—and thus to their owners and managers. However, firms often cannot obtain these benefits at zero cost.

Disclosure Costs   Four costs can arise from informative financial disclosures:

1. Information collection, processing, and dissemination costs.
2. Competitive disadvantage costs.
3. Litigation costs.
4. Political costs.

The costs associated with **financial information collection, processing, and dissemination** can be high. Determining the company's obligation for postretirement employee health care benefits provides an example. This disclosure requires numerous complicated actuarial computations as well as future health care cost projections for existing or anticipated medical treatments. Whether companies compile the data themselves or hire outside consultants to do it, the cost of generating a reasonable estimate of the company's postretirement obligation can be considerable. The costs of developing and presenting financial information also include the cost incurred to audit the accounting statement item (if the information is audited). Owners—who are the shareholders—ultimately pay all of these costs, just as they ultimately bear all other company costs.

> Many firms promise to pay some of the health care costs employees incur after retirement. See Chapter 14 for details.

Another financial disclosure cost is the possibility that competitors may use the information to harm the company providing the disclosure. Several disclosures—financial and nonfinancial—might create a **competitive disadvantage:**

- Details about the company's strategies, plans, and tactics, such as new products, pricing strategies, or new customer markets.
- Information about the company's technological and managerial innovations, such as new manufacturing and distribution systems, successful process redesign and continuous quality improvement methods, or uniquely effective marketing approaches.
- Detailed information about company operations, such as sales and cost figures for individual product lines or narrow geographical markets.[6]

---

[6] R. B. Stevenson, Jr., *Corporations and Information: Secrecy, Access, and Disclosure* (Baltimore, MD: Johns Hopkins University Press, 1994).

Disclosing sales and profits by individual product line or geographical area may highlight opportunities previously unknown to competitors, thereby undermining a company's market-place advantage. For example, Uniroyal Inc., an automobile tire manufacturer, objected to disclosing its financial data by geographical area because:

> this type of data would be more beneficial to our competition than to the general users of financial data. This is especially true in those countries or geographical areas where we might not be as diversified as we are in the United States. In these cases, the data disclosed could be quite specific, thereby jeopardizing our competitive situation.[7]

Labor unions, major suppliers, or key customers may also use the company's financial information to improve their bargaining power, which would increase the company's costs and possibly weaken its competitive advantage.

Litigation costs result when shareholders, creditors, and other financial statement users initiate court actions against the company and its management for alleged financial misrepresentations. For example, it's common for shareholders to initiate litigation when there's a sudden drop in stock price soon after the company has released new financial information. Shareholders who sue will claim that they would not have purchased company shares if they had known then (back when they bought the stock) what they know now (after the company's disclosure).

The costs of defending against suits, even those without merit, can be substantial. Beyond legal fees and settlement costs is the damage to corporate and personal reputations and the distraction of executives from productive activities that otherwise would add value to the company.

There are potential **political costs** of financial reporting, especially for companies in highly visible industries such as oil and pharmaceuticals. Politically vulnerable firms with high earnings are often attacked in the financial and popular press, which alleges that those earnings constitute evidence of anticompetitive business practices. Politicians sometimes respond to (or exploit) heightened public opinion. They propose solutions to the "crisis" that is causing high earnings, thereby gaining media exposure for themselves and improving their chances for reelection or reappointment. These "solutions" are often political initiatives designed to impose taxes on unpopular companies or industries. The windfall profits tax levied on U.S. oil companies in the early 1980s is one example. This tax was prompted, in part, by the large profit increases that oil companies reported during several years prior to enactment of the legislation.[8]

Antitrust litigation, environmental regulations, and the elimination of protective import quotas are other examples of the costs politicians and government bureaucrats can impose on unpopular companies and industries. Financial reports are one source of information that politicians and bureaucrats can use to identify target firms or industries. For this reason, astute managers carefully weigh political considerations when choosing what financial information to report and how best to report it. As a result, some highly profitable—but politically vulnerable—firms may make themselves appear less profitable than they really are.[9]

---

[7] Uniroyal Inc. correspondence as reported in G. Foster, *Financial Statement Analysis* (Upper Saddle River, NJ: Prentice Hall, 1986), p. 185.

[8] There is another side to this "excessive profits" story. Politicians sometimes respond to public concern over record losses at highly visible companies by providing subsidies in the form of government loan guarantees (for example, Chrysler Corporation), import tariffs (for example, Harley-Davidson), and restrictions on the activities of competitors.

[9] To learn more about the costs and benefits of accounting disclosures, see A. Beyer, D. Cohen, T. Lys, and B. Walther, "The Financial Reporting Environment: Review of Recent Literature," *Journal of Accounting and Economics* (2010).

A company's financial reporting decisions are driven by economic considerations and thus by cost-benefit trade-offs. Companies that confront distinctly different competitive pressures in the marketplace and that face different financial reporting costs and benefits are likely to choose different accounting and reporting practices. A clear understanding of the economic factors that influence a company's financial reporting choices can help you to assess more keenly the quality of the provided information. That's what we'll help you do in this textbook.

A CLOSER LOOK AT PROFESSIONAL ANALYSTS

Financial statement users have diverse information needs because they face different decisions or may use different approaches to making the same kind of decision. For example, a retail customer deciding which brand of automobile to purchase needs far less financial information about each automotive manufacturer than does a long-term equity investor who is planning to purchase stock in one of those companies. Similarly, a commercial banker engaged in asset-based lending—meaning the borrower's inventory or receivables are pledged to repay the loan—needs far different financial information about the business than does a banker who lends solely on the basis of the borrower's projected future cash flows.

> "To perform good audits, we need more skills than just forensic accounting . . . general accounting skills, tax planning, risk management, and securities analysis are all vital competencies for auditors to possess." Samuel DiPiazza, Jr., former global CEO of PricewaterhouseCoopers.

It would be difficult (maybe impossible!) to frame our examination of corporate financial reporting and analysis around the diverse information needs of all potential users—investors, lenders, customers, suppliers, managers, employees, regulators, and so on—and the varied decisions they might possibly confront. Instead, we focus attention on professional analysts. But we define *analyst* broadly to include investors, creditors, financial advisors, and auditors—anyone who uses financial statements to make decisions as part of their job. Let's see what professional analysts do.

Analysts' Decisions

The task confronting **equity investors** is first to form an educated opinion about the value of the company and its equity securities—common and preferred stock—and then to make investment decisions based on that opinion. Investors who follow a *fundamental analysis approach* estimate the value of a stock by assessing the amount, timing, and uncertainty of future cash flows that will accrue to the company issuing the stock (Chapter 6 shows how). The company's financial statements and other data are used to develop projections of its future cash flows. These cash flow estimates are then discounted for risk and the time value of money. The discounted cash flow estimate or **fundamental value** (say, $25 per share) is then compared to the current price of the company's stock (say, $18 per share). This comparison allows the investor to make decisions about whether to buy, hold, or sell the stock. *Financial statement information is essential, in one way or another, to this and other equity investment strategies.*

Creditors' decisions require an assessment of the company's ability to meet its debt-related financial obligations through the timely payment of interest and principal or through asset liquidation in the event interest and principal cannot be repaid. Creditors include commercial banks, insurance companies and other lenders, suppliers who sell to the company on credit, and those who invest in the company's publicly traded debt securities. Creditors form educated opinions about the company's **credit risk** by comparing required principal and interest payments to estimates of the company's current and future cash flows (Chapter 5 explains how). Companies that are good credit risks have projected operating cash flows that are more than sufficient to meet these debt payments, or they possess **financial flexibility:** the ability to raise additional cash by selling assets, issuing stock, or borrowing more.

Companies judged to be high credit risks are charged higher rates of interest and may have more stringent conditions—referred to as **covenants**—placed on their loan agreements. These loan covenants may restrict the company from paying dividends, selling assets, buying other companies, forming joint ventures, or borrowing additional funds without the lender's prior approval. Other types of covenants, particularly those based on reported accounting figures, protect the lender from deterioration in the borrower's credit risk. This is why creditors must monitor the company's ongoing ability to comply with lending agreement covenants. *Financial statement information is indispensable for assessing credit risk and monitoring loan covenant compliance.*

Financial advisors include securities analysts, brokers, credit rating agencies, portfolio managers, and others who provide information and advice to investors and creditors. They are often able to gather, process, and evaluate financial information more economically and accurately than individual investors and creditors can because they possess specialized skills or knowledge (for example, industry expertise) or because they have access to specialized resources provided by their organizations. As a consequence, financial advisors can play a crucial role in the decision-making process of investors and creditors. Securities analysts and credit rating agencies, in particular, are among the most important and influential users of financial statements.

Independent auditors carefully examine financial statements prepared by the company prior to conducting an audit of those statements. An understanding of management's reporting incentives coupled with detailed knowledge of accounting rules enables auditors to recognize vulnerable areas where financial reporting abuses are likely to occur. Astute auditors choose audit procedures designed to ensure that major improprieties can be detected.

But the Treadway Commission believes that independent auditors can (and should) do more:

> The potential of analytical review procedures for detecting fraudulent financial reporting has not been realized fully. Unusual year-end transactions, deliberate manipulations of estimates or reserves, and misstatements of revenues and assets often introduce aberrations in otherwise predictable amounts, ratios, or trends that will stand out to a skeptical auditor.[10]

Current auditing standards require independent auditors to use analytical review procedures on each engagement. Why? Because they can help auditors avoid the embarrassment and economic loss from accounting "surprises," such as the one uncovered at WorldCom.

Independent auditors need to be well versed in the techniques of financial analysis to design effective audits. That's why auditors are included among those people we call "analysts." Current auditing standards echo the lessons of past audit failures: *You can't build a bulletproof audit unless you know how the game is played.* That means understanding the incentives of managers and being a skilled financial analyst.

> "Consideration of Fraud in a Financial Statement Audit," *Statement of Auditing Standards No. 99* (New York: AICPA, 2002)—also known as AU Section 240—provides examples of **fraud risk factors** that auditors must be aware of in designing audit procedures: rapid growth or unusual profitability compared to other firms in the same industry; unduly aggressive financial targets; a significant portion of management pay tied to accounting numbers; an excessive interest by management in maintaining or increasing the firm's stock price or earnings trend; and ineffective board of directors or audit committee oversight of the financial reporting process.

> **Analytical review procedures** are the tools auditors use to illuminate relationships among the data. These procedures range from simple ratio and trend analysis to complex statistical techniques—a tool kit not unlike that used by any financial analyst. The auditor's goal is to assess the general reasonableness of the reported numbers in relation to the company's activities, industry conditions, and business climate. Astute auditors are careful to "look behind the numbers" when the reported figures seem unusual.

---

[10] *Report of the National Commission of Fraudulent Financial Reporting* (Washington, DC: 1987), p. 48. The "Treadway Commission"—officially the National Commission on Fraudulent Financial Reporting—was formed in 1985 to study the causal factors that can lead to fraudulent financial reporting and to develop recommendations for public companies and their independent auditors, for the SEC and other regulators, and for educational institutions.

Financial statement information helps investors assess the value of a firm's debt and equity securities, creditors assess the company's ability both to meet its debt payments and to abide by loan terms, financial advisors and securities analysts to do their job of providing information and advice to investors and creditors, and auditors both to recognize potential financial reporting abuses and to choose audit procedures to detect them.

THE RULES OF THE FINANCIAL REPORTING GAME

"There's virtually no standard that the FASB has ever written that is free from judgment in its application."

—D. R. Beresford, chairman of the FASB (1987–1997)[11]

Professional analysts are forward looking. Their goal is to predict what will happen in the future to the value of a company and its ability to repay debt. Financial statements and notes depict the past: an economic history of transactions and other events that have affected the company. These past data provide analysts a jumping-off point for forecasting future events, especially future earnings and cash flows.

To extrapolate into the future from financial statement data, investors, creditors, and their financial advisors must first understand the accounting measurement rules, estimates, and judgments used to produce the data. Financial statements present a picture of the company at a point in time, a picture that translates many (but not all) of the economic events affecting the business into financial terms. For example, the company's accounting system translates the act of providing goods and services to customers in exchange for promised future cash payments into financial statement amounts known as "sales revenue" and "accounts receivable." This linkage between economic events and how those events are depicted in a financial statement can sometimes seem mysterious or confusing. For example, some companies record sales revenue *before* goods are actually delivered to customers. Other companies record revenue at the date of customer delivery. And still others record revenue only when payment for the goods is received from the customer, which can be long *after* delivery (Chapter 3 explains why). We'll now look more closely at the rules that govern accounting and financial reporting practices.

Generally Accepted Accounting Principles

Over time, the accounting practitioners and standards setters have developed a network of conventions, rules, and procedures, collectively referred to as **generally accepted accounting principles (GAAP).** The principles and rules that govern financial reporting continue to develop and evolve in response to changing business conditions. Consider, for example, the lease of retail store space at a shopping mall. As people moved from the city to the suburbs, shopping malls emerged as convenient and accessible alternatives to traditional urban retail stores. Leasing became a popular alternative to ownership because it enabled retailing companies to gain access to store space without having to bear the burden of the large dollar outlay necessary to buy or build the store. Leasing was also attractive because it shared risks—such as the risk of competition from a new mall opening nearby—between the retailer and shopping mall owner. As leasing increased in popularity, the accounting profession developed

---

[11] As quoted by F. Norris, "From the Chief Accountant, a Farewell Ledger," *The New York Times,* June 1, 1997.

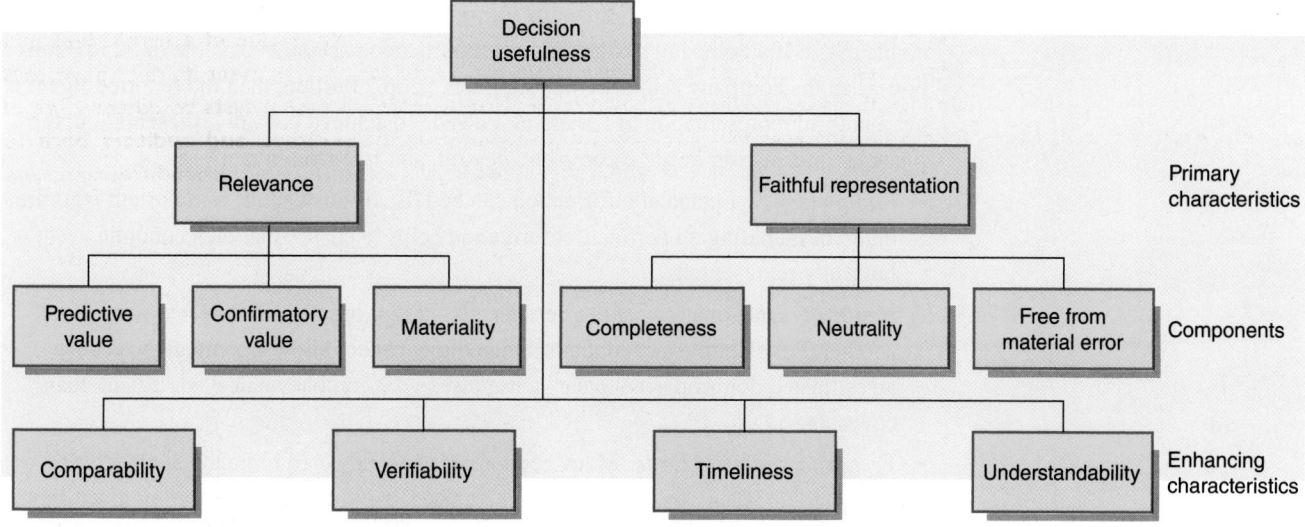

Figure 1.2 DESIRABLE CHARACTERISTICS OF ACCOUNTING INFORMATION

Source: "Conceptual Framework for Financial Reporting: Chapter 1, *The Objective of General Purpose Financial Reporting,* and Chapter 3, *Qualitative Characteristics of Useful Financial Information,*" Statement of Financial Accounting Concepts No. 8 (Norwalk, CT: FASB, September 2010).

practices, some complex, that are followed when accounting for leases. The practices that evolved are now part of GAAP and are discussed in detail in Chapter 12.

The goal of GAAP is to ensure that a company's financial statements clearly represent its economic condition and performance. To achieve this goal, financial statements should possess certain qualitative characteristics (summarized in Figure 1.2) that make the reported information useful:[12]

- ***Relevance:*** The financial information is capable of making a difference in a decision. Relevant information helps users form more accurate predictions about the future (*predictive value*), or it allows them to better understand how past economic events have affected the business (*confirmatory value*).

  - ***Predictive value:*** The information improves the decision maker's ability to forecast the future outcome of past or present events. For example, suppose a company's balance sheet lists accounts receivable of $200,000 and an allowance for doubtful accounts of $15,000. This information has value for predicting future cash collections— management is saying that only $185,000 ($200,000 − $15,000) of the receivables will be collected.

  - ***Confirmatory value:*** The information confirms or alters the decision maker's earlier beliefs. For example, suppose we learn next year that the company mentioned above collected $190,000 of its accounts receivable instead of the $185,000 originally forecasted. This information has confirmatory value and indicates that management's earlier estimate of doubtful accounts was too high.

  - ***Materiality:*** Omission or misstatement of the information could influence the decisions that financial statement users make about a specific reporting entity.

> Since the 1960s, accounting standards setters in the United States have been building a **conceptual framework** for financial reporting—a coherent system of objectives and fundamentals intended to guide the evolution of GAAP. These *Statements of Financial Accounting Concepts* establish the basics, such as why general purpose financial reports are produced and what kinds of information they should provide but they are not actual accounting rules.

---

[12] See "Conceptual Framework for Financial Reporting: Chapter 1, *The Objective of General Purpose Financial Reporting,* and Chapter 3, *Qualitative Characteristics of Useful Financial Information,*" Statement of Financial Accounting Concepts No. 8 (Norwalk, CT: FASB, September 2010). This concept statement replaces SFAC No.1 and No. 2.

- *Faithful Representation:* The financial information actually depicts the underlying economic event. If a company's balance sheet reports trade accounts payable of $254.3 million when the company actually owes suppliers $266.2 million, then the reported figure is not a faithful representation of the amount owed. To achieve faithful representation, the financial information must be complete, neutral, and free from material error.

  - *Completeness:* Financial information can be false or misleading if important facts are omitted. Including all pertinent information helps to ensure that the economic event is faithfully represented.

  - *Neutrality:* Information cannot be selected to favor one set of interested parties over another. For example, accountants and auditors cannot allow a company to reduce an estimated doubtful accounts expense just so the company can evade a bank loan covenant.

  - *Free from material error:* Many economic events depicted in financial reports are measured under uncertainty. Because estimates and judgments are common, we should not expect all accounting measurements to be error-free. However, some minimum level of accuracy is also necessary for an estimate to be a faithful representation of an economic event.

Materiality plays a critical role, first in management's judgments in preparing the financial statements, and then in the judgments of independent accountants who audit the statements. Suppose management unintentionally fails to record a $100,000 expense and the bookkeeping error is discovered shortly after the end of the quarter. Unless this error is corrected, quarterly earnings will be overstated by, say, 2.4%, but the overstatement will reverse out next quarter when the expense is eventually recorded. Is the misstatement material? Should the quarterly financial statements be corrected now? Or is the self-correcting misstatement immaterial and unimportant?

According to both the FASB and the SEC, the answer depends on both *quantitative* (the amount of the misstatement) and *qualitative* (the possible impact of the misstatement) considerations. Financial statements are materially misstated when they contain omissions or misstatements that would alter the judgment of a reasonable person.[13] Quantitative materiality thresholds, such as "an item is material if it exceeds 5% of pre-tax income," are inadequate because they fail to recognize how even small misstatements can impact users' perceptions. For example, a small percentage misstatement can be material if it allows the company to avoid a loan covenant violation, reverses an earnings trend, or transforms a loss into a profit.

Figure 1.2 also identifies four qualitative characteristics—comparability, verifiability, timeliness, and understandability—that enhance the decision usefulness of relevant and representationally faithful financial information. **Comparability** across companies allows analysts to identify real economic similarities in and differences between underlying economic events because those similarities or differences are not obscured by accounting methods or disclosure practices. *Consistency,* another facet of comparability, occurs when the same accounting methods and disclosure practices are used to describe similar events from period to period. Consistency allows trends—and turning points—in economic performance or condition to be identified because the trends are not masked by changes in accounting methods or disclosure practices.

---

[13] Material misstatements can result either from errors, which are unintentional, or fraud, which is intentional and meant to deceive financial statement users. See "Materiality," *SEC Staff Accounting Bulletin No. 99* (Washington, DC: SEC, August 12, 1999) and the FASB's Accounting Standards Codification (ASC) 250-10-S99-1 Accounting Changes and Error Corrections—Overall—SEC Materials—Materiality.

Verifiability means that independent measurers should get similar results when using the same yardstick. For example, the 2012 net sales of $11,699 million reported by Whole Foods Market, the organic grocery chain, is verifiable to the extent that knowledgeable accountants and auditors would agree on this amount after examining the company's sales transactions for the year. So, verifiability refers to the degree of consensus among measurers. Financial information that lacks verifiability is less reliable for decision purposes. **Timeliness** refers to information that is available to decision makers while it is still fresh and capable of influencing their decisions. An example is sales to customers made during the current quarter as opposed to sales made a distant quarter ago. **Understandability** is the characteristic of information that enables users to comprehend its meaning. Management has a responsibility to ensure that the company's financial information is properly assembled, classified, characterized, and presented clearly and concisely. Professional analysts also have a responsibility. They must not only possess a reasonable understanding of the business and economic events, they must also be able to read financial reports and be willing to study the information.

> **Conservatism** in accounting strives to ensure that business risks and uncertainties are adequately reflected in the financial reports. For example, it is prudent to record possible losses from product liability litigation as soon as those losses become probable and measurable. Doing so helps statement readers assess the potential cash flow implications of the litigation even though an exact dollar amount has not yet been determined. Unfortunately, conservatism is sometimes used to defend poor accounting judgments such as overstated provisions for "big bath" restructuring costs or "cookie-jar" reserves described in Chapter 3.[14]

No single accounting method has all of these characteristics all of the time. In fact, GAAP frequently requires financial statement users to accept a compromise that favors some qualitative characteristics over others. For example, GAAP financial statements would show a real estate company's office building investment at its historical cost (original purchase price) minus accumulated depreciation. The most *relevant* measure of the office building is often the discounted present value of its expected future rental revenues, but this measure is not as *representationally faithful* or *verifiable* as historical cost because future vacancy rates are unpredictable and must be estimated. GAAP's use of historical cost trades off increased representational faithfulness and verifiability for decreased relevance. Qualitative trade-offs such as this arise frequently and make it difficult to identify what are the "best" accounting methods and disclosure practices. Of course, **cost** also is a pervasive constraint on the information that financial statements can provide. GAAP recognizes that financial reporting costs must be justified by the benefits of reporting that information.

Who Determines the Rules?

The U.S. federal government, through the SEC, has the ultimate authority to determine the rules to be followed in preparing financial statements by companies whose securities are sold to the general public in the United States. This authority was given to the SEC when it was established in 1934 by Congress in response to the severe stock market decline of 1929. The SEC requires companies to file both annual *and* quarterly financial statements as well as other types of reports. The SEC's Electronic Data Gathering and Retrieval (EDGAR) system receives, processes, and disseminates more than 500,000 financial statements every year. In 2009 alone, the EDGAR website logged over 1 billion searches.

> Prior to the establishment of the FASB, the **American Institute of Certified Public Accountants (AICPA)** had the primary responsibility for setting accounting standards in the United States. The AICPA's Auditing Standards Board still sets standards for private company audits.

Although the SEC has the ultimate legal authority to set accounting principles in the United States, it has looked to private-sector organizations to establish these principles. (The SEC retains enforcement authority.) The FASB, or simply "the Board," is the organization that currently sets accounting standards in the United States. The SEC monitors the FASB's

---

[14] See R. Watts, "Conservatism in Accounting, Part I: Explanations and Implications," *Accounting Horizons*, September 2003, pp. 207–21; and R. Watts, "Conservatism in Accounting, Part II: Evidence and Research Opportunities," *Accounting Horizons*, December 2003, pp. 287–301.

activities and works closely with the FASB in formulating reporting rules. Although the FASB is funded through accounting support fees levied against issuers of securities (as provided for by the Sarbanes-Oxley Act of 2002), it exists as an independent group with seven full-time members and a large staff. Board members are appointed to five-year terms and are required to sever all ties with the companies and institutions they served prior to joining the Board.

Auditing standards for public companies are set by the **Public Company Accounting Oversight Board (PCAOB),** a private-sector, nonprofit corporation created by the Sarbanes-Oxley Act of 2002. The PCAOB has two central roles: (1) to establish standards for auditing and ethics at public accounting firms under its jurisdiction and (2) to inspect and investigate the auditing practices of public accounting firms. The PCAOB can bar a person from participating in audits of public companies in the United States. The Sarbanes-Oxley Act (SOX) prohibits accounting firms that are not registered with the PCAOB from auditing public companies in the United States. The SOX act also requires foreign accounting firms that audit U.S. companies to comply with PCAOB rules. Currently, about 2,400 U.S. and foreign accounting firms are registered with the PCAOB.

How are financial reporting standards determined outside the United States? In some countries, it's by professional accounting organizations akin to the FASB, and in other countries, it's by commercial law and/or tax law requirements. The growth of global investing has spurred the development of worldwide accounting standards. These standards are now written by the **International Accounting Standards Board (IASB).** The IASB works to formulate accounting standards, promote their worldwide acceptance, and achieve greater convergence of financial reporting regulations, standards, and procedures across countries. The IASB has issued 13 International Financial Reporting Standards (IFRS), and still retains many of the 41 International Accounting Standards (IAS) issued by the IASB's predecessor body, the International Accounting Standards Committee (IASC). The IASB reviews existing IAS and often issues revised guidance as IFRS.

The Politics of Accounting Standards

Standards setting in the United States and most other countries is a political as well as technical process. FASB members make choices among financial reporting alternatives, and the particular alternative selected is unlikely to satisfy everyone. In making these choices, FASB is expected to serve a diverse constituency that includes preparers, auditors, and users of financial statements as well as the public interest. The preference of any one constituent may differ substantially from that of some other constituent, and those divergent viewpoints can be difficult (if not impossible) to reconcile. To ensure that their voice is heard in the standards-setting process, professional associations, industry trade groups, regulatory agencies, individual companies (e.g., Apple) and even prominent individuals (e.g., Warren Buffett) can and do exert pressure on the FASB as new accounting rules are being deliberated. Disgruntled constituents lobby FASB, the SEC, and Congress, and sometimes take more direct action:

- Claiming irreparable injury because of an adverse effect to its debt-to-equity ratio, the country's largest electric power company sued in the 1950s to block mandatory recognition of deferred tax liabilities (Chapter 13). The U.S. Supreme Court ruled against the company.
- Congress enacted the **investment tax credit (ITC)** in 1962 as part of an economic stimulus package. Under the ITC, businesses were permitted to reduce their income tax payable in the year in which a qualifying asset (think "equipment") is purchased and put to use. A newly established accounting standard spread GAAP recognition of the ITC benefit over several years instead of recording it immediately. Many companies were not pleased by

this approach because it presented a less favorable near-term earnings picture. Under pressure from industry, accounting firms, and the Kennedy administration, the SEC stepped in and allowed immediate recognition, thus forcing a change to established GAAP.

- As part of the Energy Policy and Conservation Act of 1975, Congress instructed the SEC to require all oil and gas companies to use the same accounting method in their financial statements. At the time, companies could choose between two alternatives—successful efforts or full costing. The issue was added to the FASB agenda and the Board later allowed only successful efforts. Most small and medium-sized oil and gas producers were using full costing. They vigorously protested FASB's decision and enlisted support in Congress, the Departments of Energy and Justice, and the Federal Trade Commission. Those agencies believed that successful efforts would cause many producers to curtail their exploration activities (thus contributing to an oil shortage) or drive them into mergers with big oil companies (thus reducing the number of competitors in the industry). Once again, the SEC stepped in and overruled FASB's position.[15]

- By the 1990s, employee stock options were a popular form of compensation especially among cash-starved high-technology firms. One reason was that GAAP did not require firms to record an expense when stock options were doled out. FASB was increasingly uncomfortable with this approach and moved to require a recorded expense. An unprecedented lobbying campaign by small, high-technology firms secured congressional support and prevented FASB from requiring recognition of the stock option expense in companies' financial statements. Chapter 15 tells you more of the story.

> Chapter 7 describes fair value accounting and the role it may have played in the crisis.

Political pressure exerted by interested parties continues to shape the debates surrounding sensitive and controversial U.S. accounting standards. Some industry representatives and politicians blamed a type of **fair value accounting** (called *mark-to-market accounting*) for contributing to the global financial crisis and the ensuing collapse of many banks. Although the intensity and frequency of political influence on financial reporting practices is unlikely to diminish in the future, it is important to remember that accounting standards reflect both:

1. Sound concepts coupled with independent and objective decision making by standards setters such as FASB.
2. Compromises necessary to ensure that proposed standards are generally acceptable.[16]

FASB Accounting Standards Codification™

Over the years, the FASB and its predecessors in the United States have published a seemingly endless stream of pronouncements—concept statements, standards, opinions, interpretations, bulletins, and so on—that collectively constitute GAAP. Financial statement preparers (company accountants) and their independent auditors struggled to determine where to look for answers to financial accounting and reporting questions. For instance, at one time more than 200 pronouncements described GAAP revenue recognition rules. Many of the pronouncements were industry specific and some produced conflicting results for economically similar transactions.

---

[15] A chronology of the events surrounding this oil and gas accounting controversy can be found in G. Foster, "Accounting Policy Decisions and Capital Markets," *Journal of Accounting and Economics*, March 1980, pp. 29–62.

[16] To learn more about the politics of U.S. accounting standards, see Z. Palmrose, "Science, Politics, and Accounting: A View from the Potomac," *The Accounting Review*, March 2009, pp. 281–98 and S. Zeff "The Evolution of U.S. GAAP: The Political Forces behind Professional Standards," *The CPA Journal*, January 2005, pp. 19–27 and February 2005, pp. 19–29.

Because the pronouncements were not equally authoritative, eventually the need arose to establish a pecking order among them. Responding to this need in 1975, the AICPA defined the phrase *generally accepted accounting principles* and established a GAAP hierarchy in *Statement on Auditing Standards No. 69.*[17] According to the AICPA, GAAP is:

> . . . a technical accounting term that encompasses the conventions, rules, and procedures necessary to define accepted accounting practice at a particular time. It includes not only broad guidelines of general application, but also detailed practices and procedures. (para. 2.02)

The GAAP hierarchy provided preparers and auditors with guidance about where to look for answers to financial accounting and reporting questions such as how to value convertible debt securities or when to record asset impairment charges. The hierarchy also provided guidance on how to resolve matters when the underlying pronouncements suggested different accounting approaches for the same business transaction. But it did not eliminate conflicting guidance or the need to search a voluminous GAAP literature for answers.

> ASC includes some authoritative rules issued by the SEC but it is not the official source of SEC guidance on accounting and financial reporting matters and does not contain all SEC rules, regulations, interpretive releases, and staff guidance.

In 2009, the FASB completed a five-year effort to distill the existing GAAP literature into a single database by creating the **Accounting Standards Codification** (or **ASC**), an online filing cabinet that groups all authoritative rules into roughly 90 topics.[18] ASC is now the authoritative source of U.S. accounting and reporting standards for nongovernmental entities, in addition to guidance issued by the Securities and Exchange Commission (SEC). Accounting Standards Updates (or ASUs) modify the codification, provide background information about the revised guidance, and provide the basis for conclusions on changes made to ASC.

ASC Topical Structure and Referencing   The ASC uses a structure in which the FASB's authoritative accounting guidance is organized into topics, subtopics, sections, subsections, and paragraphs. *Topics,* the broadest categorization of related guidance, are grouped into four areas: *presentation* matters relating to financial statements or notes; *financial statement accounts* such as Receivables, Inventory, or Revenue; *broad transactions* including business combinations and derivatives; and *industries* where specialized GAAP unique to an industry (airlines or gaming) or type of activity (software development) is described. *Subtopics* represent subdivisions of a topic and are generally distinguished by type or scope. For example, Operating Leases and Capital Leases are two subtopics of the Lease topic. *Sections* are subdivisions such as Recognition, Measurement, or Disclosure that denote the nature of the content in a subtopic. *Subsections* and *paragraphs* allow further segregation and navigation of content.

> Throughout this book, we use ASC numerical references when mentioning current U.S. GAAP but we use the original pronouncement reference (e.g., *SFAS No. 162*) when tracing the evolution of U.S. accounting practices.

Topics, subtopics, and sections are numerically referenced and correlate very closely to International Financial Reporting Standards (IFRS). An example of the numerical referencing is ASC 305-10-05 where 305 is the "Cash and Cash Equivalents" topic, 10 denotes the "Overall" subtopic, and 05 is the "Overview and Background" section.

---

[17] "The Meaning of Present Fairly in Conformity with Generally Accepted Accounting Principles," *Statement of Auditing Standards No. 69* (New York: AICPA, 1975).

[18] "The FASB Accounting Standards Codification™ and the Hierarchy of Generally Accepted Accounting Principles—a Replacement of *FASB Statement No. 162,*" *Statement of Financial Accounting Standards No. 168* (Norwalk, CT: FASB, 2009), which is codified as FASB ASC 105, *Generally Accepted Accounting Principles.*

ADVERSARIAL NATURE OF FINANCIAL REPORTING

GAAP permits alternatives (such as LIFO versus FIFO for inventory valuation), requires estimates (for example, the useful life of depreciable assets), and incorporates management judgments (are assets impaired?). Managers have a degree of flexibility in choosing specific accounting techniques and reporting procedures, and the resulting financial statements are sometimes open to interpretation.

Managers have reasons to exploit this flexibility. Their interests may conflict with the interests of shareholders, lenders, and others who rely on financial statement information. Some companies adopt exemplary reporting standards while others tend to be less forthright. Analysts who understand these conflicting incentives as well as the flexibility available under GAAP will see that a decision based on uncritical acceptance of financial statement data may turn out to be naïve—and financially dangerous.

The flexibility of GAAP financial reporting standards provides opportunities to use accounting tricks that make the company seem less risky than it really is. For instance, some real liabilities such as equipment leases can be transformed into off-balance-sheet (and thus less visible) items. The company would then appear, from the balance sheet data alone, to have less debt and more borrowing capacity than is really the case. Commercial lenders who fail to spot off-balance-sheet liabilities of this sort can understimate the credit risk lurking in their loan portfolios.

Companies can also smooth reported earnings by strategically timing the recognition of revenues and expenses to dampen the normal ups and downs of business activity. This strategy projects an image of a stable company that can easily service its debt even in a severe business downturn. The benefits of such deceptions can be large if lenders are fooled.[19] Furthermore, once the loan is granted, the company has additional incentives to report its financial results in ways that avoid default on loan covenants tied to accounting numbers.

Self-interest sometimes drives managers to manipulate the reported financial statement numbers to earn bonuses linked to sales or earnings targets. For example, if earnings are down late in the fiscal year, product deliveries may be accelerated to increase recognized revenues and income before year-end. Managers may also delay until next year discretionary expenses such as building repairs and maintenance if earnings this year are expected to be too low. On the other hand, if earnings are comfortably above the bonus goal, managers may write off obsolete equipment and inventory or increase allowances for uncollectible trade receivables, whereas those same accounting adjustments are often postponed when earnings are inadequate.

> Manville Corporation's 1982 bankruptcy changed the way analysts view legal contingencies. Although some people had been asking questions about the company's exposure to asbestos-related litigation for quite some time, Manville's bankruptcy announcement caught most analysts and investors by surprise. That's because the company's last quarterly report prior to bankruptcy estimated the total cost of settling asbestos-related claims at about $350 million, less than half of Manville's $830 million of shareholders' equity. Manville's bankruptcy announcement put the potential damages at no less than $2 billion, and the company's stock plunged by 35% the next day.

Another way in which financial reporting practices can be molded to suit management's interests is to downplay the significance of contingent liabilities, such as unresolved product liability lawsuits, that may affect firm value. For many reasons, management is likely to understate the true significance of a major legal contingency. In a lawsuit, candid disclosure could compromise the company's legal strategy. Similarly, public disclosure of impending financial hardships may harm the company if creditors respond by accelerating loan repayment schedules, curtailing trade credit, or seeking to liquidate the business.

This discussion states the case boldly and may portray the motives underlying financial reporting practices in an unflattering light. In reality, most companies strive to provide fair

---

[19] Lenders are fooled when they mistakenly assign too little risk (thus charging too low an interest rate) to the borrowing. An interest cost savings of one-half of a percentage point on $1 billion of borrowings equates to $5 million (pre-tax) per year. If the company is in a 34% tax bracket and its stock trades at 15 times earnings, the payoff for concealing credit risk on financial statements is $49.5 million in share value. This value increase represents a wealth transfer to shareholders from creditors.

and reasonable disclosure of their financial affairs. Some of these companies are undoubtedly motivated as much by honor and integrity as by the knowledge that they will be rewarded for being forthright. Other companies take full advantage of the leeway available under GAAP.

The SEC and the FASB provide constraints that limit the range of financial statement discretion. Auditors, sound corporate governance practices, and the courts further counterbalance opportunistic financial reporting practices. Nevertheless, the analyst should recognize the adversarial nature of financial reporting, maintain a healthy skepticism, and understand that financial disclosures sometimes conceal more than they reveal. The flexibility inherent in GAAP can have dire consequences for those caught unaware.

Aggressive Financial Reporting: A Case Study

"We're not saying they're cooking the books, but there's ample evidence to wonder if everything is on the up-and-up."

—Arthur Russell, equity analyst at the investment firm of Edward Jones[20]

As the information technology sector ballooned during the 1990s, Computer Associates International Inc. (CA) emerged as the world's third-largest software company. In the business of software for managing mainframes and computer networks, CA was king. It offered business customers more than 1,200 software products that operated and connected large computers, storage technology, wireless products, and high-tech security systems. Annual revenues hit nearly $7 billion by fiscal 2000, net profits approached $700 million, and the company's 40% operating margin rivaled that of Microsoft Corporation.

Investors were well rewarded for the company's success. An investor who bought CA stock for $5 a share in January 1990 could have sold the stock for $75 in January 2000 when the tech bubble peaked. That's a whopping 1,400% investment return, or about 31% each year for 10 straight years. As for CA's management team, in 1998, the company's top three officers took home stock grants collectively worth $1.1 billion, the largest award of this sort ever paid to U.S. executives. Outraged by the sheer size of the awards, investors sued the company and a judge later reduced the awards by almost half, but even $500 million is a princely sum.

CA and other software companies faced a vicious downturn in customer sales once the dot-com bubble burst in 2000. As customers cut back their software spending, CA's stock price tumbled (see Figure 1.3). CA changed its revenue accounting policies in May 2000 and sliced a hefty $2.56 billion off the total for the previous five years. Then in July 2000, CA said that quarterly revenues would fall short of analysts' estimates. Investors ran for cover, and the stock plunged 42% that day.

CA revamped its software license contracts in October 2000 and began offering customers more flexible payment terms. Rather than making a single upfront payment, customers could opt for a "subscription" plan and pay the multiyear license fee in equal installments over time. CA also radically changed the way it reported its financial results. In addition to the required GAAP financial statements where all contract revenue was booked immediately, CA provided "pro forma" results that recalculated past revenue and earnings as if they were based on the new subscription approach. The difference between the two sets of numbers, GAAP and "pro forma," was often quite startling. In the first quarter after adopting the new approach, CA reported pro forma profits of $247 million while under GAAP it suffered a $342 million loss. Analysts didn't entirely trust the pro formas numbers, in part because revenue was being double counted.

Aggressive accounting concerns continued to dog CA for several years. In February 2002, the company announced that the SEC had launched an investigation into CA's accounting

---

[20] As quoted in S. Hamm, "Getting to the Bottom of Computer Associates," *BusinessWeek,* September 30, 2002.

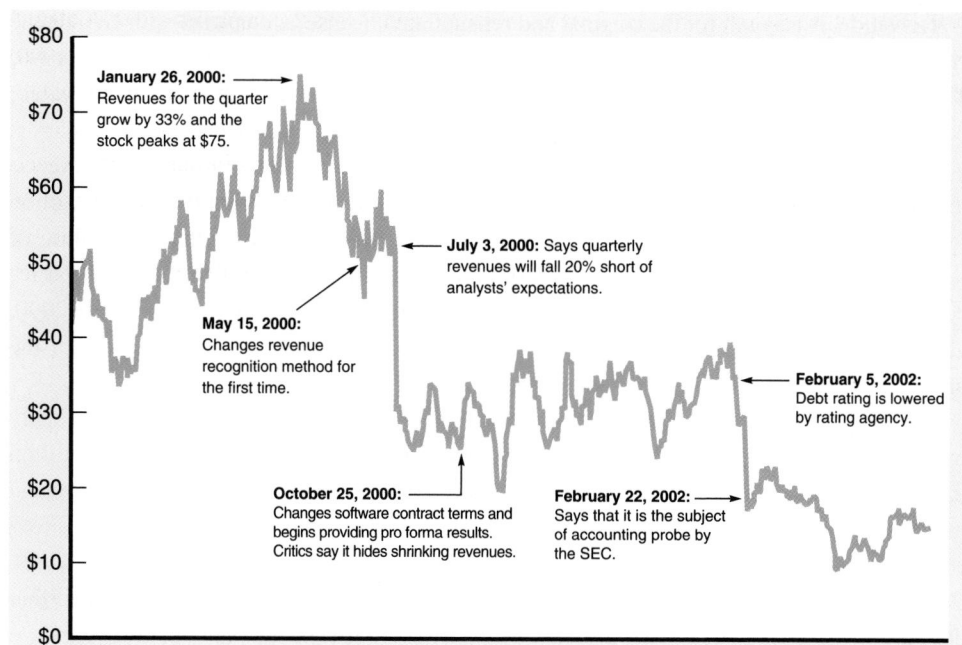

Figure 1.3

COMPUTER ASSOCIATES
INTERNATIONAL

Daily Stock Price from
January 4, 1999, through
December 31, 2002.

practices. The announcement followed on the heels of an investment rating downgrade of CA debt. News articles in the financial press described the company's accounting woes and questioned whether there was anything improper or illegal about the way CA kept its books.

The Accounting Issues   The first accounting controversy surfaced in May 2000 when CA changed how it booked revenues from software licenses that were renegotiated during the licensing period. Here's an example to illustrate the issue. Suppose that CA sells a one-year software license on July 1, 1999, for $20 million to a business customer who pays the full amount in cash upfront. On January 2, 2000, the customer renegotiates the license, adding several more software products and extending the licensing period for another six months. The new license bundle is priced at $25 million, but the customer pays only $15 million cash after deducting a $10 million credit for the unused portion of the original (July 1999) license. The following diagram shows the licensing period and payment associated with the original and renegotiated contract.

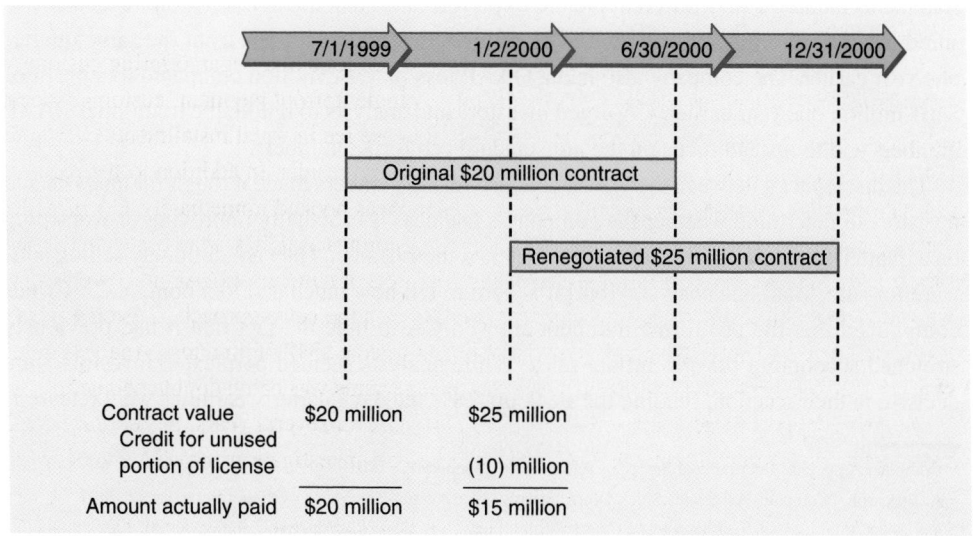

How did CA account for the original and renegotiated license? Consistent with GAAP, the company booked the entire $20 million of revenue from the original contract on July 1, 1999. That's when the customer signed the licensing agreement, the software product was delivered, payment occurred, and CA's obligation to the customer ended.

What about the renegotiated license? Well, prior to May 2000, CA would book as revenue the entire value of the contract ($25 million) even though the customer paid only $15 million for the added software and extended license. In effect, CA double counted $10 million of revenue associated with the original license agreement, first as part of the $20 million recorded in 1999 and then again as part of the $25 million in 2000. To square its books in 2000, CA would deduct as a "cost of sales" the $10 million credit the customer received for the unused portion of the original license.

Investors and analysts who were unaware of the double counting at CA would mistakenly presume that software revenue increased over time, from $20 million in 1999 to $25 million in 2000 in our example. However, the reality of our example is that both software revenue and cash receipts from customers instead declined from $20 million to $15 million.

CA stopped double-counting revenue on renegotiated software licenses in May 2000. When the company announced this accounting change, investors and analysts learned that double counting had added $2.56 billion to software revenue over the previous five years.

The second accounting controversy at CA stemmed from the company's decision in October 2000 to roll out a new subscriptions-based business model and begin reporting results using nonstandard pro forma accounting in its press releases. Here's an excerpt from the quarterly earnings press release issued just after CA launched the new business model and revamped accounting:

> Reaping the benefits of an innovative business model designed to provide greater flexibility to customers, to improve revenue predictability, and to unlock shareholder value, Computer Associates International, Inc. (NYSE: CA) today reported financial results for its third fiscal quarter. The results, reported on a ***pro forma pro rata basis,*** beat analysts' consensus earnings per share estimates of $0.40 by $0.02.[21] [Emphasis added]

The press release also stated that pro forma software revenue increased 13% to $1.284 billion compared to the same quarter the previous year and that pro forma operating income increased 28% to $247 million. CA touted the pro forma numbers as providing more clarity to investors and analysts because they presented sales as if all revenues—past, present, and future—were based on the company's new subscription business model.

Also disclosed in the quarterly earnings press release, the company's GAAP financial statements painted a very different picture of performance that quarter. Software revenue measured according to GAAP was only $783 million, down almost 53% from the same quarter one year earlier. The company also had a GAAP loss of $342 million compared to a profit of $401 million one year earlier. CA urged investors and analysts to ignore the traditional GAAP numbers and to instead focus on the nonstandard pro forma numbers.

The discrepancy between the GAAP and pro forma numbers made it tough for analysts and investors to determine whether the company's business was actually improving or worsening on a quarter-to-quarter basis. Some just scratched their heads. "They are definitely selling software for sure," said one analyst, "[but] it is hard to tell how much and to whom. . . ."[22] Critics complained that the pro forma numbers allowed CA to hide the fact that it had previously stretched accounting rules to inflate sales. While analysts seemed perplexed, investors were decisive in their reaction, sending the stock up 5.8% the day quarterly earnings were released.

You'll learn more about GAAP revenue recognition rules in Chapters 2 and 3.

---

[21] Computer Associates International Inc. press release issued January 22, 2001.

[22] A. Berenson, "Computer Associates Stock Drops Sharply Once Again," *The New York Times,* February 22, 2002.

Questions to Consider This scenario raises several intriguing questions about corporate financial reporting practices, managerial behavior, and the influence of accounting information on the decisions of investors, creditors, and others:

- How flexible is GAAP, and how much latitude is available to managers in the choice of "acceptable" accounting practices?

- What factors influence the accounting methods managers use? Why do firms change accounting methods? Does a change in accounting imply that previously reported figures (those produced using the old method) were incorrect?

- Do company disclosures make clear what accounting methods are used? Do those disclosures enable analysts to adjust reported figures when a company's accounting method either deviates from industry norms or changes through time?

- Can firms use one accounting method in their GAAP financial statements and some other nonstandard (pro forma) method when reporting results in press releases?

- How do analysts and investors use reported earnings and balance sheet numbers when valuing a firm's common stock?

- How does an accounting change alter creditors' opinions about a company's future cash flows and credit risk?

Perhaps the most provocative question, however, centers on the allegations raised in 2002 by an SEC investigation into Computer Associate's accounting practices. Did the company violate GAAP and mislead investors by using accounting procedures that failed to provide an accurate and timely portrayal of historical profit performance, current financial condition, and future prospects? Subsequent chapters of this book help you formulate answers to these and related questions about financial reporting practices in the United States and other countries.

Epilog Computer Associates admitted in October 2003 that some software license contracts had been backdated, a practice known internally as "the 35-day month," to mask declining performance and meet Wall Street forecasts for quarterly sales and profits. An internal investigation was launched, and CA restated $2.2 billion in sales that had been improperly booked during 1999 and 2000. The company spent $30 million on the investigation and reviewed tens of thousands of internal e-mail messages and 1,000 license agreements with customers. Employees who did not cooperate with the investigation were fired.

The Justice Department and the SEC sued CA and several top executives. CA agreed in 2004 to pay $225 million in restitution to shareholders and submit its accounting to an independent monitor. Seven former executives pleaded guilty to civil charges of securities fraud and obstruction of justice in connection with the company's accounting scandal. Two other top executives, the company's former chief executive and the former top salesman, confessed to a wide-ranging conspiracy to inflate sales and interfere with the subsequent federal inquiry. They are serving prison sentences of up to 12 years each.

> *Backdating* occurs when someone intentionally alters the contract signing date so that revenue can be booked in an earlier period. For example, suppose a customer and seller sign a $20 million software license agreement on January 3, 2000, but then backdate it to December 30, 1999. Unless the backdating is discovered, the seller would mistakenly record the $20 million as revenue in 1999 rather than in 2000.

> Accounting scandals are not unique to U.S. firms. Prominent foreign firms where accounting irregularities have been uncovered include Livedoor (Japan), Royal Ahold (the Netherlands), Parmalat (Italy), and Satyam Computer Systems (India).

AN INTERNATIONAL PERSPECTIVE

Because financial reporting practices vary widely in countries outside the United States and because international business transactions are now more frequent and complex, the professional life of an analyst—in any country—has become more difficult. Multinational companies are regularly shifting resources throughout the world. These shifts cannot be accomplished efficiently without reliable financial information that permits careful analysis of investment opportunities and continuous control over how resources are deployed. Multinational companies must also resolve differences in national currencies and accounting rules when combining the financial statements of all their foreign and domestic businesses into consolidated reports.

The Coca-Cola Company, for example, conducts business in more than 200 countries, hedges foreign currency cash flows, and uses foreign loans to finance investments outside the United States. Sales in North America (Canada and United States) represented 44.2% of 2011 worldwide revenues and generated 22.8% of worldwide operating income. By contrast, Latin America sales were only 9.4% of 2011 operating revenues, but this region produced 27.7% of Coca-Cola's worldwide operating income.

Understanding the economic, political, and cultural factors that contribute to regional differences in operating performance is daunting even for the most experienced financial analyst. Yet assessing a multinational company's current performance and future prospects requires experience, knowledge, and skill with these factors.

Global competition is prevalent in most industries today as companies facing mature domestic markets look outside their home borders for new customers and growth. Exhibit 1.1 presents sales, net income, and assets for three automobile manufacturers that compete on a worldwide basis: Ford Motor Company, Fiat S.A., and Honda Motor Company. Honda, a Japanese firm, reports financial statements in Japanese yen, Ford uses U.S. dollars, and Fiat, an Italian company, uses the euro for financial reporting purposes. Which company was the most profitable?

In the upper part of Exhibit 1.1, the financial statement amounts reported by these three companies are not directly comparable because each firm uses a different currency. For example, Honda had sales of 10,011,241 million yen but how does this yen-denominated amount compare to Ford's revenue of $129,166 million? The yen/dollar exchange rate averaged 110.10 for the year. This means that each U.S. dollar was worth about 110.10 yen. In the case of Fiat, the euro/dollar exchange rate averaged about 0.68 for the year. The lower part of the

EXHIBIT 1.1	Ford, Fiat, and Honda		

Revenue, Net Income, and Assets (in millions)

	Ford Motor Co. (United States)	Fiat S.A. (Italy)	Honda Motor Co. (Japan)
As reported in local currency			
Revenue	129,166	59,380	10,011,241
Net income	(14,672)	1,721	137,005
Assets	218,328	61,722	11,818,917
U.S. dollar equivalents			
Revenue	129,166	87,368	100,012
Net income	(14,672)	2,532	1,369
Assets	218,328	87,009	121,510
Local currency	U.S. dollar	Euro	Yen
Accounting methods	U.S. GAAP	IFRS	U.S. GAAP
Fiscal year-end	December 31	December 31	March 31

Note: Sales and net income in the lower part of the table are restated into U.S. dollars using the average exchange rate for the fiscal year because the flows occur throughout the year. Year-end assets are restated into U.S. dollars using the exchange rate as of the end of fiscal year.

Source: Company financial statements.

exhibit shows each company's sales, net income, and assets expressed in U.S. dollars. Here, you can see that Ford has the largest sales ($129,166 million), but Fiat is the most profitable ($2,532 million).

Another factor complicates our analysis. Financial statement comparisons of this type become less meaningful when accounting standards and measurement rules vary from one country to another. Both Ford and Honda use U.S. GAAP, but Fiat prepares its financial statements using IFRS. As a result, Fiat's lower reported sales and net income might not be attributable to economic factors if IFRS income recognition rules are more conservative than U.S. rules. Analysts must be aware of potential differences in accounting standards and guard against the tendency to assume that financial statements are readily comparable across national borders.

International Financial Reporting

Stock exchanges around the world now offer domestic investors the opportunity to purchase securities (primarily common stock) issued by foreign companies. Foreign companies comprise roughly 14% of the stocks listed on the New York Stock Exchange (NYSE) and over 20% of those listed on the London Stock Exchange (LSE). Clearly, investors who choose to concentrate on a specific industrial or commercial sector are compelled to think globally these days.

Before the early 1990s—when cross-border investing was nascent— accounting standards for use by domestic companies were developed by home-country organizations (e.g., Accounting Standards Board in the United Kingdom and the French Conseil National de la Comptabilité in France).[23] The resulting diversity of financial reporting recognition, measurement, and disclosure rules used in different countries complicated global investment decisions. Even the philosophy and objective of financial reporting varied considerably between nations.

> This approach originated and evolved in both the United Kingdom and the United States. In turn, this Anglo-American accounting perspective influenced financial reporting practices in most British Commonwealth countries and many others. The phrase **true and fair view** is central to this perspective because it expresses the notion that a company's financial statements must reflect the underlying economic performance and conditions experienced by the company.

Two widely divergent financial reporting approaches existed. First was a group of countries whose financial statements were intended (at least in principle) to capture and reflect the underlying economic performance and condition of the reporting entity. Financial reporting rules in those countries were designed to achieve this goal and thereby help investors and creditors make informed decisions. We'll call this reporting philosophy the **economic performance approach.**

The second group of countries had financial accounting and reporting rules that did not necessarily try to capture "economic reality." Instead, financial statements in those countries simply conformed to mandated laws or detailed tax rules designed to achieve purposes such as raising tax revenues to fund government activities or stimulate capital investment. We'll call this other reporting philosophy the **commercial and tax law approach.** Because this approach was widespread, investors reading foreign financial statements were often confronted with unfamiliar reporting rules, unique tax-driven financial statement items, and country-specific nuances. Happily, this confusing array of cross-border financial reporting options has been greatly simplified in recent years.

> Examples include France, Italy, and Belgium, where national tax laws still heavily influence financial statements prepared for domestic distribution. In Germany, Japan, and Switzerland, both commercial and tax laws influence the accounting and reporting standards. For example, to qualify for the extra depreciation tax deduction allowed by German tax law, a company's financial statements must show the same depreciation charges shown on the tax return. Conformity requirements of this sort greatly restrict the ability of financial statements to reflect economic performance.

---

[23] To learn more about differences in accounting practices around the globe and the evolution of international accounting standards, see C. Nobes and R. Parker, *Comparative International Accounting* (Edinburgh Gate, England: Prentice Hall, 2008); F. Choi and G. Meek, *International Accounting* (Upper Saddle River, NJ: Prentice Hall, 2008); and M. Plumlee, *International Financial Reporting Standards* (Upper Saddle River, NJ: Prentice Hall, 2010).

Why Do Reporting Philosophies Differ Across Countries?   A country's financial reporting philosophy does not exist in a vacuum. Instead, it evolves from and reflects the specific legal, political, and financial institutions within the country as well as social customs. As one example, German workers have been entitled to representation on the governing boards of German companies since the early 1950s. Understandably, these labor representatives championed accounting practices that would ensure firm continuity—and thus future employment opportunities. Partially as a consequence of labor's active board participation, Germany developed ultraconservative accounting rules and dividend guidelines designed to protect companies' survival prospects and workers' jobs. So, financial reporting differences across countries sometimes mirror societal differences.

Cross-country differences in financial reporting practices also arise from differences in how companies obtain financial capital. In countries where the bulk of capital is attracted from a broad base of external investors, those investors understandably want comprehensive data to help them select appropriate securities. So, external investors who provide capital demand a reporting system that accurately depicts a company's past economic performance and its future prospects. The United States, United Kingdom, and Canada are examples of this type of broad-based ownership because an exceedingly large portion of firms' capital requirements in these countries are provided by individual debt and equity investors—either through direct investment in companies or indirectly through pension plans and mutual funds. *The financial reporting environment in these countries has evolved to meet this public financial market demand for information.*

By contrast, in countries such as Japan and Germany, only a small amount of firms' financial capital has historically been provided by individual investors. The primary capital providers in Germany have been several large banks—and the government itself. The German stock market is small. Similarly, large banks provide much of the financing in Japan; in addition, companies there also raise capital from members of their associated corporate group. Individual investors were relatively unimportant in Japan. In countries such as Germany and Japan, these few important capital providers wield great power including the ability to acquire information directly from the firm seeking capital. *Because of this concentrated power and the insignificance of the public financial market, the demand for economically realistic reporting standards was low.* Instead, financial reporting standards conformed to income tax rules or commercial law.

But sources of financing do shift over time. When this happens in a country, changes in the financial reporting environment occur as well.

Globalization and the Rise of IFRS   As cross-border barriers in markets for goods, labor, and capital relaxed in the mid-1990s, international competitiveness increased. Companies throughout the world sought new global buyers for their goods and services by expanding and investing in new facilities and technologies. This expansion fueled a need for companies to access new and ever-larger sources of capital to finance these initiatives. But in countries that used the commercial and tax law approach to financial reporting such as France, Germany, and Japan, companies faced a severe disadvantage in raising capital. Foreign investors and other potential capital providers demanded transparent financial reports prepared using familiar reporting standards that reflected underlying firm economic performance. Statements based on narrow, national commercial law or tax rules, which companies in these countries normally provided, were deemed unsuitable. Consequently, many firms in countries where financial reports used the commercial and tax law approach felt compelled to provide foreign investors with supplemental financial statements prepared using U.S. GAAP

These loosely interconnected corporate associations are called *keiretsu.* Keiretsu members typically own shares of other member firms, an arrangement that provides a source of capital and further aligns the group's incentives toward mutual benefits. Cross-ownership in the 20% to 30% range is not unusual.

IFRS—like U.S. GAAP—embrace the economic performance approach to financial reporting. Statements prepared using IFRS are designed to provide a "fair presentation" of the underlying economic conditions experienced by the company.

or international standards called IFRS. The hope was that the financial statements would be more understandable to foreign investors if they were prepared using procedures required by potential investors' home countries. Daimler-Benz began issuing U.S. GAAP financial statements in 1996, and Hoechst AG issued IFRS reports beginning in 1995. These two German companies apparently believed that U.S. GAAP- or IFRS-based financial reports would help attract more capital from investors outside their home country.

As this trend accelerated, a two-tiered financial report system emerged in many countries that previously had used the commercial and tax law approach to financial reporting. In the first financial reporting tier, rigid **book/tax conformity** is maintained in **parent company** financial statements. The parent is an amalgamation that corresponds to the tax-paying and statutory entities comprising the firm—often (but not always) in the form of a holding company. Because the parent company statements conform to the commercial or tax law, they satisfy national legal rules. In the second financial reporting tier, separate statements directed to potential foreign investors are prepared. They are called **consolidated financial statements** (or **group statements** in foreign accounting terminology). These group statements include all of the company's various operating subsidiaries. Firms hoped that these group statements— prepared using more investor-friendly and familiar U.S. GAAP or IFRS rules—would facilitate access to foreign capital.

> Consolidated financial statements are described in Chapter 16.

In 2001 and 2002, accounting scandals at companies such as Enron, WorldCom, Health-South, and Global Crossing tarnished the reputation of U.S. financial reporting practices and lowered the appeal of U.S. GAAP for some foreign firms. Many believed this tipped the scale in favor of IFRS rather than U.S. GAAP as companies began to cope with the financial reporting demands of globalization. In June 2002, the Council of the European Union (EU) required all publicly traded EU companies to adopt by 2005 IFRS for financial reporting in consolidated statements. In the words of the European Commission:

> The regulation will help eliminate barriers to cross-border trading in securities by ensuring that company accounts throughout the EU are more reliable and transparent and that they can be more easily compared.[24]

The regulation affected approximately 8,000 companies in the EU and dramatically enhanced the visibility of IFRS.

International Accounting Standards Board (IASB)

International Financial Reporting Standards are established by the IASB, an organization formed in 2001. Its predecessor, the International Accounting Standards Committee (IASC), was created in July 1973 following an agreement by professional accounting organizations in Australia, Canada, France, Germany, Japan, Mexico, the Netherlands, Ireland, the United Kingdom, and the United States. The IASB has four stated goals:

1. To develop a single set of high-quality, understandable, enforceable, and globally accepted international financial reporting standards (IFRS).
2. To promote the use and rigorous application of those standards.
3. To take account of the financial reporting needs of emerging economies and small and medium-sized entities.
4. To promote and facilitate the adoption of IFRS through the convergence of national accounting standards and IFRS.

---

[24] European Commission Press Release, June 7, 2002.

The European Commission, in conjunction with the Accounting Regulatory Committee (a group composed of representatives of the Member State governments), must "endorse" IFRS for required use by EU companies. The Economic and Monetary Affairs Committee of the European Parliament can initiate delaying actions, and the Parliament has veto power over Commission endorsement.

There are exceptions. For example, IFRS does not permit use of the last-in, first-out (LIFO) method of inventory accounting (described in Chapter 9).

The IASB and its predecessor committee have issued 54 standards and 54 interpretations of those standards. The accounting practices set forth in these international standards are now in use by some, or all, domestic-listed companies in 125 countries worldwide, although jurisdictional variations persist. These variations arise because each country still has its own accounting standards-setting organization that must approve IFRS for use by domestic companies, and approval is not automatic. For example, financial institutions in Europe are not required to follow one provision of the international hedge accounting standards in *IAS 39,* "Financial Instruments: Recognition and Measurement," because the provision was not sanctioned in the EU.

Compared to U.S. GAAP, IASB standards allow firms more latitude. IFRS often permit different accounting treatments for similar business transactions and events. Some critics contend that this latitude is a natural result of the diversity of the IASB's membership and constituencies.

IFRS differ from U.S. GAAP in another important way—the level of detail they encompass. IFRS frequently follow a more generalized overview approach than do U.S. GAAP standards. This difference in the level of standards-setting detail has generated a strong debate about which of the two approaches is preferable. Critics of the **principles-based** IASB approach contend that IFRS are so general and the implementation guidance so ambiguous that company managers have excessive latitude in choosing accounting practices. This latitude makes it easier for them to evade debt covenant restrictions, realize bonus targets, reach earnings goals, and/or achieve other contracting incentives. Critics of IFRS contend that because U.S. GAAP contains more detailed rules and implementation guidance, similar transactions tend to result in more similar accounting treatments.

Supporters of the IASB approach counter that IFRS are built on broad principles and are not narrowly defined, detailed standards such as those found in **rules-based** U.S. GAAP. They further assert that under a broad principles approach, the standard's financial reporting objective is made clear. This leads to closer conformity between the financial statement numbers and the underlying economic reality. By contrast, they argue that narrow U.S. GAAP rules allow managers to invent loopholes that conform to the letter of the standard but simultaneously violate its spirit. These critics point to examples like Enron's use of off-balance-sheet special purpose entities (SPEs) to mask corporate profitability and hide corporate liabilities. Provided that certain narrow guidelines were satisfied, U.S. GAAP did not require SPE consolidation, thereby allowing Enron's consolidated financial statements to conceal its deteriorating real business condition from investors and creditors.[25]

The SEC and FASB both admit that certain GAAP standards provide too much detailed guidance and too many scope exceptions.[26] Since 2004, the FASB has endeavored to draft standards that clearly identify the accounting objective, explain the accounting principle(s) being applied, avoid bright-line rules, and provide enough implementation guidance for consistent application.[27] In recent years, the FASB has also worked jointly with the IASB to draft new pronouncements, which has helped move GAAP closer to principles-based guidance.

---

[25] This loophole is now mostly closed in U.S. GAAP. See the Variable Interest Entities Subsections under ASC Topic 810: Consolidation (pre-Codification *FASB Interpretation No. 46*). SPEs are discussed in Chapters 8 and 16.

[26] See Securities and Exchange Commission (SEC), *Study Pursuant to Section 108(d) of the Sarbanes-Oxley Act of 2002 on the Adoption by the United States Financial Reporting System of a Principles-Based Accounting System* (Washington, DC: SEC, July 2003) and FASB, *Proposal: Principles-Based Approach to U.S. Standard Setting* (Norwalk, CT: FASB, October 2002).

[27] See "On the Road to an Objectives-Oriented Accounting System," *The FASB Report* (Norwalk, CT: FASB, August 2004).

The March toward Convergence   Consider the financial reporting choice faced by Toyota Motor Company, the Japanese automobile manufacturer. The company's stock is traded on the Tokyo Stock Exchange and on the New York Stock Exchange. Investors world-wide can buy or sell Toyota shares on either exchange. Which set of presently available country-specific accounting standards—Japanese GAAP or U.S. GAAP—should Toyota use to prepare its financial statements?

Perhaps the best answer is neither! Suppose there is a third choice, a single set of accounting standards accepted worldwide and one that more fairly presents Toyota's economic performance and condition to global investors. This is the goal of the growing movement toward international convergence of accounting standards.

The arguments favoring convergence are both clear and compelling. Differences in accounting practices and reporting systems make cross-border comparisons difficult and costly and impose an increasing burden on economic efficiency. Without convergence, some countries might be tempted to reduce the quality of their accounting standards in a short-sighted attempt to attract foreign firms to list on their local stock exchanges. As a first step toward achieving convergence, more and more countries outside the United States are requiring their listed companies to adopt IFRS rather than domestic GAAP.

The FASB and IASB have also worked toward eliminating differences between U.S. GAAP and IFRS. The process began with the October 2002 Norwalk Agreement that focused on short-term projects aimed at convergence improvements in accounting for nonmonetary exchanges, business combinations, and changes in accounting policies. In 2006, the FASB and IASB signed a memorandum of understanding, endorsed by the SEC and European Commission, which outlined a process for achieving even greater convergence.[28] These efforts have achieved some success, in part because U.S. GAAP and IFRS are grounded in the same economic performance philosophy. However, important differences between U.S. GAAP and IFRS remain. Here are three examples:

1. *Reversal of inventory write-downs.* Both IFRS and U.S. GAAP require companies to write down inventory if its market value declines below what the company paid for it (Chapter 9 tells you why and how). Under IFRS, the inventory value is also written back up to the higher initial figure if its market value recovers but U.S. GAAP does not permit "loss reversals."

2. *Extraordinary items.* IFRS does not let companies segregate onetime events from normal income and designate them as extraordinary, as does U.S. GAAP (Chapter 2). This means that Gold Reserve Inc.'s $86 million GAAP extraordinary loss stemming from the 2008 government expropriation of its Venezuelan mining properties would be included in normal income under IFRS rules.

3. *Research and development costs.* U.S. GAAP requires R&D expenditures to be charged to expense in the period when they are made (Chapter 10). IFRS is more lenient and allows "development phase" expenditures to be capitalized if technical feasibility and other criteria demonstrating value creation are attained.

In late 2009, the IASB and FASB agreed to redouble their convergence efforts with an aim of achieving solutions by June 2011 on several major projects that address consolidation, fair value measurement, revenue recognition, leases, and financial statement presentation among other topics. Working together, the IASB and FASB have sought to develop a single set of high-quality, compatible accounting standards that can be used for both domestic and cross-border financial reporting. The path to achieving this goal may be long.

---

[28] See *A Roadmap for Convergence between IFRSs and U.S. GAAP—2006 Memorandum of Understanding between the FASB and the IASB* (Norwalk, CT: FASB, 2006).

Meanwhile, the SEC has been considering whether it might allow U.S. firms to adopt IFRS. While acknowledging that IFRS use may benefit some U.S. companies, the SEC also has expressed concern that (1) the transition to IFRS might be prohibitively expensive; (2) the United States may not have sufficient influence over IASB standards setting; and (3) that the U.S. legal environment relies heavily contract language that refers to "U.S. GAAP." As a result, the SEC staff is exploring other (more time-consuming) approaches such as standard-by-standard GAAP revisions aimed toward convergence.[29]

The SEC already permits foreign businesses to list their securities on a U.S. stock exchange as long as certain procedures are followed. Foreign businesses that do not use U.S. GAAP or IFRS to prepare their financial statements must file a **Form 20-F** each year with the SEC. This form is designed for the convenience of U.S. financial statement readers because it reconciles the company's reported financial results—specifically, earnings and shareholders' equity—as shown in foreign GAAP or IFRS to what those numbers would have been under U.S. GAAP. This presumably allows investors to evaluate the performance of foreign issuers relative to U.S. companies using a common reporting basis—U.S. GAAP. However, the Form 20-F reconciliation may not fully achieve this goal. The reason is that SEC rules do not require foreign firms to prepare complete financial statements on a U.S. GAAP basis. It requires only that Form 20-F identify the differences between the company's home-country financial statements and U.S. GAAP. When no "finalized" financial statements in U.S. GAAP are provided by the foreign firm, the burden of constructing financial statements comparable to those provided by U.S. companies falls on the analyst. This task is often not straightforward.

> All companies listed on the London Stock Exchange are required to use IFRS.

> Foreign issuers are given six months to file the Form 20-F reconciliation, a substantial delay after the issuance of current home-country financial statements.

RECAP

The diversity in international accounting practices has narrowed in recent years as more countries around the globe embrace IFRS. The FASB and IASB have been working toward eliminating differences between U.S. GAAP and IFRS, and the SEC has shown some (albeit cautious) interest in potentially adopting IFRS in the United States. Nonetheless, diversity in accounting practice remains a fact of life. Readers of financial statements must never lose sight of this diversity.

SUMMARY

Financial statements are an extremely important source of information about a company, its economic health, and its prospects. They help improve decision making and make it possible to monitor managers' activities.

- Equity investors use financial statements to form opinions about the value of a company and its stock.
- Creditors use statement information to gauge a company's ability to repay its debt and to check whether the company is complying with loan covenants.
- Stock analysts, brokers, and portfolio managers use financial statements as the basis for their recommendations to investors and creditors.
- Auditors use financial statements to help design more effective audits by spotting areas of potential reporting abuses.

---

[29] *Final Staff Report: Work Plan for the Consideration of Incorporating International Financial Reporting Standards into the Financial Reporting System for U.S. Issuers* (Washington DC: SEC, July 2012).

Investors, creditors, and other interested parties demand financial statements because the information is useful. But what governs the supply of financial information?

- Mandatory reporting is a partial answer. Most companies in the United States and other developed countries are required to compile and distribute financial statements to shareholders and to file a copy with a government agency (in the United States, that agency is the SEC). This requirement allows all interested parties to view the statements.

- The advantages of voluntary disclosure are the rest of the answer. Financial information that goes beyond the minimum requirements can benefit the company, its managers, and its owners. For example, voluntary financial disclosures can help the company obtain capital more cheaply or negotiate better terms from suppliers. But benefits like these come with potential costs: information collection, processing, and dissemination costs; competitive disadvantage costs; litigation costs; and political costs. This means that two companies with different financial reporting benefits and costs are likely to choose different accounting policies and reporting strategies.

Different companies choose different accounting policies and reporting strategies because financial reporting standards are often imprecise and open to interpretation. This imprecision gives managers an opportunity to shape financial statements in ways that allow them to achieve specific reporting goals.

- Most managers use their accounting flexibility to paint a truthful economic picture of the company.
- Other managers mold the financial statements to mask weaknesses and to hide problems.
- Analysts who understand financial reporting, managers' incentives, and the accounting flexibility available to managers will maintain a healthy skepticism about the numbers and recognize that financial statements sometimes conceal more than they reveal.

The accountant's and analyst's job is made more difficult when financial reporting measurement and disclosure rules differ across national boundaries. Reporting rules in some countries such as Canada, the United Kingdom, and the United States evolved to reflect firms' underlying economic performance. But reporting rules in many other countries—France, Germany, and Japan, for example—merely complied with taxation or other statutory requirements.

- Globalization forced many firms in countries using a commercial or tax law approach to seek foreign capital. In turn, this has led countries around the world to move to IFRS, making it easier for firms in their countries to raise capital in domestic and foreign financial markets.
- The FASB and IASB are working together to converge U.S. GAAP and IFRS but the road may be long and bumpy.

GAAP IN THE UNITED STATES

This is a brief, historical overview of the public and private sector organizations that have influenced the development of financial accounting practices in the United States. As you shall see, some organizations have explicit legal authority to decide what constitutes U.S. GAAP. Other organizations lack that authority but remain influential.[30]

---

[30] We gratefully acknowledge the substantial contributions of Professor Stephen A. Zeff to the material in this appendix.

Early Developments

Corporate financial reporting practices in the United States prior to 1900 were primarily intended to provide accounting information for management's use. Financial statements were made available to shareholders, creditors, or other interested external parties on a limited basis. The **New York Stock Exchange (NYSE),** established in 1792, was the primary mechanism for trading ownership in corporations. As such, it could establish specific requirements for the disclosure of financial information and thereby dictate accounting standards for corporations whose shares it listed. Beginning in 1869, the NYSE attempted to persuade listed companies to make their financial statements public. Few companies complied. The prevailing view of corporate management was that financial information was a private concern of the company and that public disclosure would harm the company's competitive advantage.

> The library archive at the University of California at Berkeley contains examples of public company annual reports dating back to the 1850s. The archive includes General Electric (1892), National Biscuit Company (Nabisco, 1898), and Procter & Gamble (1891).

Passage of the Sixteenth Amendment to the U.S. Constitution in 1913 and subsequent legislation allowing the federal government to tax corporate profits set the stage for expanded corporate financial disclosure. This legislation required companies to maintain accurate financial recordkeeping systems; the goal of this legislation was to ensure proper tax accounting and to facilitate collection. However, corporate financial disclosures to outsiders were still limited.

The stock market crash of 1929 and the Great Depression that followed provoked widespread concern about financial disclosure. Some observers alleged that the collapse of the stock market was due largely to the lack of meaningful requirements for reporting corporate financial information to investors and creditors.[31] Many also believed that economic conditions would not improve until investors regained confidence in the financial markets.

When Franklin D. Roosevelt was sworn in as president in March 1933, the economy was still paralyzed, unemployment was rampant, and the nation's banking system was on the verge of collapse. In the Senate, public hearings exposed a pattern of financial abuse by such distinguished banking institutions as J.P. Morgan, National City Bank, and Chase National Bank that included insider trading, market manipulation, reckless speculation, and special favors to influential friends.

In an effort to bolster public confidence and restore order to the securities market, Congress enacted the Securities Act of 1933, which required companies selling capital stock or debt in interstate commerce to provide financial information pertinent to establishing the value and risk associated with those securities. One year later, the act was amended to establish the SEC as an independent agency of the government, an agency whose function was to regulate both the securities sold to the public and the exchanges where those securities were traded. Companies issuing stock or debt listed on organized exchanges were required to file annual audited reports with the SEC.[32] The SEC was also empowered to establish and enforce the accounting policies and practices followed by registered companies.

> In January 1933, the NYSE began requiring all companies seeking exchange listing to submit independently audited financial statements and to agree to audits of all future reports.

These powers are given to the SEC in Section 19(a) of the Securities Act of 1933 as amended:

> . . . the Commission shall have authority, for the purposes of this title, to prescribe the form or forms in which required information shall be set forth, the items or details to be shown in the balance sheet and earning statement, and the methods to be followed in the preparation of

---

[31] See E. R. Willet, *Fundamentals of Securities Markets* (New York: Appleton-Century-Crofts, 1968), pp. 208–14.

[32] Security registration statements and other reports filed under the 1934 amendments to the Securities Act are public information and are available for inspection at the SEC and at the securities exchange where the company's securities are listed.

accounts, in the appraisal or valuation of assets and liabilities, in the determination of deprecia- tion and depletion, in the differentiation of recurring and nonrecurring income, in the differenti- ation of investment and operating income, and in the preparation, where the Commission deems it necessary or desirable, of consolidated balance sheets or income accounts of any person di- rectly or indirectly controlling or controlled by the issuer, or any person under direct or indirect common control with the issuer. The rules and regulations of the Commission shall be effective upon publication in the manner which the Commission shall prescribe.

In addition to its primary pronouncement—*Regulation S-X,* which describes the principal formal financial disclosure requirements for companies—the SEC issues *Financial Reporting Releases, Staff Accounting Bulletins,* and other publications stating positions on accounting and auditing matters.

The SEC's Division of Corporation Finance (DCF) reviews the financial statements in both periodic filings and prospectuses to ensure compliance with SEC requirements. The DCF writes deficiency letters to companies when it has questions about their accounting and dis- closure practices. If a company cannot satisfy the DCF's concerns, it must revise and reissue its financial statements accordingly. Companies that fail to do so risk an SEC-imposed trading suspension or offering curtailment. No other securities commission in the world has such extensive authority to regulate financial reporting practices.

Accounting Series Release No. 4, issued in April 1938, first expressed the SEC's position that generally accepted accounting principles for which there is "substantial authoritative sup- port" constitute the SEC standard for financial reporting and disclosure. The release further indicated that a company filing financial statements reflecting an accounting principle that had been formally disapproved by the SEC or for which there was no substantial authoritative sup- port would be presumed to be filing misleading financial statements even though there was full disclosure of the accounting principles applied. However, the release did not provide guidance as to what the SEC meant by *substantial authoritative support.* This void was later filled.

Emergence of GAAP

The Securities Exchange Act of 1934 required the financial statements of all publicly traded firms to be audited by independent accountants but only if so stipulated by the SEC, which soon did so. This requirement elevated the role of the independent accoun- tants' professional organizations. These organizations were active in influenc- ing accounting policy prior to the 1930s, but the securities acts accentuated the need for more formal accounting standards and for systematic public an- nouncement of those standards.

> In 1938 and 1939, Congress permitted compa- nies to use a new inventory method—LIFO or last-in, first-out described in Chapter 9—for in- come tax purposes, but only if LIFO is also used in corporate annual reports to shareholders. This is one of the very few instances in which tax policy has influenced GAAP.

During the years immediately following passage of the 1933 and 1934 secu- rities acts, the SEC relied primarily on the American Institute of Certified Public Accountants (AICPA), the national professional organization of certi- fied public accountants, to develop and enforce accounting standards.[33] In response to the SEC and to the growing need to report reliable financial information, the AICPA created the Com- mittee on Accounting Procedure in 1939 to establish, review, and evaluate accepted accounting procedures. This committee began the practice of developing U.S. financial accounting and reporting standards in the private sector. The SEC, by a narrow vote, expressed its support for this private-sector approach to establishing U.S. accounting standards. The SEC did not delegate its standards-setting authority to the committee—by law, it cannot delegate that authority.

---

[33] The American Association of Public Accountants was established in 1887 and represented the core of the accounting pro- fession in the United States. The name of the organization was changed to the American Institute of Accountants in 1917, and it became the AICPA in 1957.

Until its demise in 1959, the AICPA's Committee on Accounting Procedure was responsible for narrowing the differences and inconsistencies in accounting practice. The committee issued 51 Accounting Research Bulletins (ARBs) and four Accounting Terminology Bulletins that set forth what the committee believed GAAP should be. These pronouncements were not binding on companies or their auditors.

In 1959, the AICPA established the Accounting Principles Board (APB) to replace the Committee on Accounting Procedure. The APB's basic charge was to develop a statement of accounting concepts—that is, a conceptual foundation for accounting—and to issue pronouncements resolving current accounting controversies. During its existence from 1959 to 1973, the APB issued 31 Opinions and four Statements designed to improve financial accounting and disclosure. (Opinions were mandatory accounting standards, Statements were not.) At the outset, the force of these pronouncements, as with earlier ARBs, depended on general acceptance and persuasion. The APB sought compliance with financial reporting standards by attempting to persuade corporations and independent auditors that the standards improved the quality of financial reporting. By 1964, many accounting professionals and business leaders were convinced that persuasion alone could neither reduce the tremendous latitude available under then-existing accounting and reporting practices nor eliminate inconsistencies in the application of those practices. Critics cited instances in which identical transactions could be accounted for by any one of several different methods and net income could be manipulated by selecting a particular accounting approach from among several considered to be "generally accepted."

A turning point in the development of corporate financial reporting standards occurred in October 1964 when the Council (or governing body) of the AICPA adopted a requirement that was later incorporated into the rules of ethics for independent CPAs:

Rule 203—Accounting Principles:
A member shall not (1) express an opinion or state affirmatively that the financial statements or other financial data of any entity are presented in conformity with generally accepted accounting principles or (2) state that he or she is not aware of any material modifications that should be made to such statements or data in order for them to be in conformity with generally accepted accounting principles, if such statements or data contain any departure from an accounting principle promulgated by bodies designated by Council to establish such principles that has a material effect on the statements or data taken as a whole. If, however, the statements or data contain such a departure and the member can demonstrate that due to unusual circumstances the financial statements or data would otherwise have been misleading, the member can comply with the rule by describing the departure, its approximate effects, if practicable, and the reasons why compliance with the principle would result in a misleading statement. [As amended.][34]

This requirement provided further impetus to corporations and their auditors to implement the accounting standards prescribed in APB opinions and in earlier pronouncements not superseded by these opinions. (Of course, the SEC's DCF is responsible for ensuring GAAP compliance.) This in turn caused greater attention to be focused on the APB's activities.

Complaints about the process used to develop financial reporting and accounting standards surfaced in the 1960s and early 1970s. Corporate management, government regulators, and other interested external parties voiced concern about the lack of participation by organizations other than the AICPA, the quality of the opinions issued, the failure of the APB to develop a coherent conceptual foundation for external financial reporting, the insufficient

---

[34] The Special Bulletin approved by the Council in 1964 referred to departures from APB Opinions, not GAAP, and did not mention the term *misleading*. In 1973, the Council approved the inclusion of language from the Special Bulletin as Rule 203. The GAAP "override" provision described in the last sentence of Rule 203 is rarely seen these days in the financial statements of companies subject to SEC oversight, and most observers believe the SEC will not accept departures from GAAP.

output by the APB, and the APB's failure to act promptly to correct alleged accounting and reporting abuses.

The APB was not immune to criticism from politicians, government regulators, and the business community. One example occurred in the early 1960s when the APB attempted to resolve the question of accounting for the **investment tax credit.** The APB initially required the tax credit to be treated as a balance sheet item, a reduction in the asset's purchase cost, rather than as an immediate increase to earnings. This decision met with strong resistance from government, business, and several major accounting firms who argued that the APB's approach would impede economic growth. After the SEC said it would allow both methods in filings with the Commission, the APB had no alternative but to rescind its earlier pronouncement (*Opinion No. 2*) and to permit the earnings increase (*Opinion No. 4*).[35] This change in the accounting standard enabled firms to use the accounting methods they preferred for the investment tax credit. This disagreement over the accounting treatment for the investment tax credit epitomized the political interference inherent in the establishment of GAAP.

The 1971 Study Group on Establishment of Accounting Principles (or "Wheat Committee") was formed by the AICPA to review and evaluate the private-sector standard-setting process as well as to recommend improvements where possible. This committee was created because of growing concern among accounting professionals over the APB's ability to withstand pressure from the business community. The committee recommended that a new and independent, full-time standards-setting organization be established in the private sector to replace the APB. This recommendation, which the AICPA approved and which became effective in July 1973, created the FASB. The FASB was the first full-time accounting standards-setting body in the world.

> During the transition period between the APB and FASB, the SEC took a more active and aggressive role in policy making. During its last nine months of operation (October 1972 through June 1973), the APB issued seven opinions in an attempt to complete its agenda of in-process accounting policy considerations. The SEC issued eight releases on accounting matters during this same period and another nine during the first year of the FASB.

The FASB differed from its predecessors in several ways:

1. Board membership consisted of 7 voting members, in contrast to the 18 members on the APB.
2. Autonomy and independence were enhanced by requiring members to sever all ties with their prior employers and by dictating that the FASB directly pay member salaries.
3. Broader representation was achieved by not requiring board members to hold a CPA license.
4. Staff and advisory support was increased substantially.

Accounting Series Release No. 150, issued by the SEC in December 1973, formally acknowledged that financial accounting pronouncements of the FASB (and its predecessor organizations) are ordinarily considered by the SEC as having "substantial authoritative support" and thus are the SEC standards for financial reporting and disclosure. Accounting practices that are contrary to FASB pronouncements are considered to not have such support. This release also reaffirmed the SEC's private-sector approach to standards setting. It said,

> the Commission intends to continue its policy of looking to the private sector for leadership in establishing and improving accounting principles and standards through the FASB with the expectation that the body's conclusions will promote the interests of investors.

---

[35] In fact, Congress passed legislation in December 1971 permitting the investment tax credit to "flow through" to reported earnings in the year the credit was taken against the company's federal tax obligation. This situation illustrates the ultimate power of the Congress over the establishment of financial reporting and accounting standards in the United States. See "Accounting for the Investment Credit," *APB Opinion No. 2* (New York: AICPA, 1962); "Accounting for the Investment Credit," *APB Opinion No. 4* (New York: AICPA, 1964).

Current Institutional Structure in the United States

The SEC still retains broad statutory powers to define accounting terms, prescribe the methods to be followed in preparing financial reports, specify the details to be presented in financial statements, and enforce financial accounting and reporting rules. Under the Securities Act of 1933, companies wanting to issue securities interstate must file a **prospectus** with the SEC. The prospectus is a public document prepared for each new security offering containing information about the company, its officers, and its financial affairs. The financial section of the prospectus must be audited by an independent CPA who is registered to practice before the SEC. Once securities have been sold to the public, the company is required to file publicly accessible, audited financial statements with the SEC each year. These annual statements are known as the *10-K filing.* In addition, unaudited quarterly financial reports (called *10-Q filings*) are required. The annual 10-K disclosure requirements closely overlap the information in the company's published financial statements but are more extensive.[36]

Although the SEC has wide statutory authority to impose financial reporting rules, it continues to rely on private sector organizations (currently the FASB) to set accounting standards. The SEC has occasionally forced these organizations to tackle critical problems, and it once rejected an accounting standard issued by the FASB.[37] Such situations occur rarely.

Since July 1973, the FASB has been responsible for establishing accounting standards in the United States. The FASB has issued more than 70 Accounting Standards Updates (ASUs), 168 Statements of Financial Accounting Standards, eight Statements of Financial Accounting Concepts, and numerous interpretations. FASB Technical Bulletins, Staff Implementation Guides, Staff Announcements, and Staff Positions provide clarification and interpretation guidance, but they represent the views of staff, not the Board. In 2009, the FASB distilled this voluminous GAAP literature into a single authoritative database called the Accounting Standards Codification (ASC).

The FASB has neither the authority nor the responsibility to enforce compliance with GAAP. That responsibility rests with company management, the accounting profession, the SEC, and the courts. Some observers believe that compliance is the weak link in the private-sector standards-setting chain. These critics point to frequent litigation on financial reporting matters in the courts, the escalating cost of liability insurance premiums paid by audit firms, and criticism by the SEC's chief accountant regarding the independence of external auditors.[38]

---

[36] The financial reporting and accounting requirements pertaining to SEC registrants are described in the following publications: Regulation S-X, the original and comprehensive document issued by the commission that prescribes financial reporting rules and the forms to be filed with the SEC; Accounting Series Releases, which are amendments, extensions, and additions to Regulation S-X; Special SEC Releases that relate to current issues as they arise; Accounting and Auditing Enforcement Releases (AAERs), which document the SEC response to accounting and auditing irregularities; and Financial Reporting Releases (FRRs). The FRRs and AAERs are the successors to Accounting Series Releases. Staff Accounting Bulletins are issued by Office of the Chief Accountant and DCF and serve as interpretations of Regulation S-X and its amendments, extensions, and additions; they do not carry the legal weight of SEC releases.

[37] "Financial Accounting and Reporting by Oil and Gas Producing Companies," *Statement of Financial Accounting Standards (SFAS) No. 19* (Stamford, CT: FASB, 1977). This statement was issued after protracted deliberation, and it identified a single method of accounting that was to be followed by all affected companies. In August 1978, the SEC ruled that a new method of accounting for oil and gas reserves needed to be developed and that in the meantime, companies could use any method that had been generally accepted prior to *SFAS No. 19.* This directly contradicted the FASB and required the issuance of both a statement suspending *SFAS No. 19* and a second FASB statement finally bringing the SEC and FASB into conformity with one another. SEC involvement was, in part, due to enactment of a public law requiring an investigation into and action on the state of oil and gas accounting rules by December 25, 1977. Such legal deadlines in connection with the accounting standards-setting process are rare.

[38] W. P. Schuetze, "A Mountain or a Molehill?" *Accounting Horizons,* March 1994, pp. 69–75.

The FASB follows a "due process" procedure in developing Accounting Standards Updates. This process is designed to ensure public input in the decision process. Most updates issued by the FASB go through three steps:

1. *Discussion-memorandum stage:* After the Board and its staff have considered a topic on its agenda and perhaps consulted with experts and other interested parties, it issues a discussion memorandum. This memorandum outlines the key issues involved and the Board's preliminary views on those issues. The public is invited to comment in writing on the memorandum, and public hearings are sometimes held to permit interested individuals to express their views in person.

2. *Exposure-draft stage:* After further deliberation and modification by the Board and its staff, an exposure draft of the proposed update is issued. During this stage, a period of not less than 30 days, further public comment is requested and evaluated.

3. *Voting stage:* Finally, the Board votes on whether to issue an ASU describing amendments to the Accounting Standards Codification or to revise the proposed update and reissue a new exposure draft. For a proposed update to become official and a part of GAAP, a majority of Board members must approve it.

Influential groups and organizations use the FASB's due process to plead for alternative solutions. The arguments often include cost-benefit considerations, claims that the proposed accounting treatment is not theoretically sound or will not be understood by users, implementation issues, and concerns that the proposed update will be economically harmful to specific companies, industries, or the country.[39] Government agencies, preparer organizations such as the Business Roundtable, and industry trade organizations such as Financial Executives International create substantial pressures on the Board. Some contend that the interests of investors, creditors, and other financial statement users are not always well represented in this political forum. Others disagree.

What does the future hold? According to one keen observer of the process by which accounting principles are established in the United States, history is destined to repeat itself:

> When a highly prescriptive standards setter is coupled with a rigorous enforcement process used by a government regulator to secure compliance with accounting standards, especially in a confrontational society such as the United States, companies and even branches of government will lobby the standards setter not to approve standards that interfere with their business plans and strategies. This is what has happened increasingly in the United States since the 1970s, and there is no sign that, on sensitive and controversial issues, it will diminish in intensity or frequency.[40]

Public Company Accounting Oversight Board When Congress gave the task of setting accounting standards to the newly created SEC in 1934, it left the job of overseeing auditing standards and individual audit firms to the accounting profession. For nearly seven decades, the AICPA and its predecessor organization have performed the job. In the late 1970s, the AICPA formed the Public Oversight Board to monitor the conduct of auditors. The Board was funded by the dues paid by members of the AICPA's SEC Practice Section, but it had little power to enforce auditing standards or discipline wayward audit firms.

---

[39] For example, SEC reversal of *SFAS No. 19* was justified on the grounds that implementation of the proposed accounting standard would sharply inhibit petroleum exploration and development activities.

[40] S. A. Zeff, "The Evolution of U.S. GAAP: The Political Forces Behind Professional Standards," *The CPA Journal,* February 2005.

The Public Company Accounting Oversight Board (PCAOB), the successor to the old Board, is funded by mandatory fees from public companies and operates under the SEC's oversight. The new Board was created by the Sarbanes-Oxley Act (SOX) of 2002. The PCAOB is empowered to establish auditing standards, including standards for independence and ethics, and to conduct periodic quality reviews ("inspections") of auditors' work. It can also investigate alleged audit failures and impose penalties on auditors and their firms. The PCAOB can fine, censure, suspend, or bar from practice auditors and audit firms for wrongdoing.

SOX Compliance The groundbreaking SOX was enacted to rein in earlier accounting abuses by strengthening auditor independence and improving financial reporting transparency. In addition to establishing the PCAOB, SOX requires company compliance in a number of areas. For most companies, Sections 302 and 404 represent the bulk of SOX compliance work. The following is a brief overview of each section.

> **Section 302: Corporate Responsibility for Financial Reports.** This section requires CEOs and CFOs to personally certify the accuracy of financial statements and related disclosures in the annual and quarterly reports. CEOs and CFOs must certify that those statements fairly present in all material aspects the results of operations and financial condition of the company.
>
> **Section 404: Management Assessment of Internal Controls.** This section requires an annual evaluation of internal controls and procedures for financial reporting. CEOs and CFOs must periodically assess and certify the effectiveness of internal controls and procedures. Companies are obliged to include an internal control report in their annual report. Among other things, this report:
>
> - Acknowledges management's responsibility for establishing and maintaining internal control over financial reporting.
> - Contains an assessment of the effectiveness of the company's internal control over financial reporting as of the end of the most recent fiscal year.
> - Discloses any material weaknesses uncovered in the company's internal controls.

Section 404 also requires a company's external auditor to examine and report on management's assessment of internal controls as well as the effectiveness of the controls themselves.

In addition to these provisions, SOX **Section 906** requires CEOs and CFOs to sign and certify that the company's financial statements comply with SEC reporting requirements and fairly represent the company's financial condition and results. Willful failure to comply with this requirement can result in fines of up to $5 million and imprisonment for up to 20 years.

The accounting profession and SEC have long recognized that sound internal controls are essential to ensure financial statement credibility. For example, in December 1977, after hundreds of public companies disclosed bribes, kickbacks, and political payoffs, Congress amended the Securities Exchange Act of 1934 to require issuers to have reasonable internal controls. In 1981, the U.S. Senate attempted to delete this section of the law but failed. Over the years, several professional groups have urged the SEC to require management reporting to shareholders on the effectiveness of internal control. Among these are the *Report of the National Commission on Fraudulent Financial Reporting* (the Treadway Commission) in 1987, the Public Accounting Oversight Board in 1993, and the General Accounting Office in 1996. In the end, a crisis of confidence and congressional action rather than a proactive SEC resulted in legislation requiring that corporations have adequate internal controls to ensure complete and accurate financial reporting.

PROBLEMS / DISCUSSION QUESTIONS

Required:

1. Explain why each of the following groups might want financial accounting information. What type of financial information would each group find most useful?

    a. The company's existing shareholders.

    b. Prospective investors.

    c. Financial analysts who follow the company.

    d. Company managers.

    e. Current employees.

    f. Commercial lenders who have loaned money to the company.

    g. Current suppliers.

    h. Debt-rating agencies such as Moody's or Standard and Poor's.

    i. Regulatory agencies such as the Federal Trade Commission.

2. Identify at least one other group that might want financial accounting information about the company, and describe how it would use the information.

P1-1

Demand for accounting information **(LO 1)**

Required:

1. Describe how the following market forces influence the supply of financial accounting information:

    a. Debt and equity financial markets.

    b. Managerial labor markets.

    c. The market for corporate control (for example, mergers, takeovers, and divestitures).

2. What other forces might cause managers to voluntarily release financial information about the company?

3. Identify five ways managers can voluntarily provide information about the company to outsiders. What advantages do these voluntary approaches have over the required financial disclosures contained in annual and quarterly reports to shareholders?

P1-2

Incentives for voluntary disclosure **(LO 3)**

Required:

1. Define each of the following disclosure costs associated with financial accounting information, and provide an example of each cost:

    a. Information collection, processing, dissemination costs.

    b. Competitive disadvantage costs.

    c. Litigation costs.

    d. Political costs.

2. Identify at least one other potential disclosure cost.

P1-3

Costs of disclosure **(LO 3)**

Allocating resources in the most efficient manner maximizes the wealth of any country. It is generally acknowledged that financial information plays an important role in efficient resource allocation.

Required:

Given that both of the preceding statements are correct, why are the financial reporting rules in some countries (e.g., Canada and the United States) designed to be very helpful to external investors whereas in other countries (e.g., Germany and Japan) they are intended to be less helpful?

P1-4

Determining why financial reporting rules differ **(LO 5)**

P1-5

Generally accepted accounting principles (GAAP) **(LO 4)**

A friend of yours sent an e-mail asking about generally accepted accounting principles (GAAP). It seems your friend was browsing through Whirlpool Corporation's recent annual report and she spotted the following statement:

> The financial statements have been audited by Ernst & Young LLP, an independent registered public accounting firm, whose report, based upon their audits, expresses the opinion that these financial statements present fairly the consolidated financial position, statements of income and cash flows of Whirlpool and its subsidiaries in accordance with accounting principles generally accepted in the United States.

She asks you what generally accepted accounting principles are, in what ways they are important to independent auditors and external users (investors or creditors), and where they come from.

Required:

1. What are generally accepted accounting principles (GAAP)?
2. Why is GAAP important to independent auditors and to external users?
3. Describe the FASB organization and how it establishes new accounting rules.
4. Describe the IASB organization and its role in establishing new accounting standards.
5. How does the Securities Exchange Commission (SEC) influence the financial reporting practices of U.S. companies?

P1-6

Relevant versus faithful representation **(LO 1)**

You have decided to buy a new automobile and have been gathering information about the purchase price. The manufacturer's website shows a "list price" of $24,500, which includes your preferred options: leather trim and digital audio player. You have also consulted the "Blue Book" guide to car prices and found that the average price paid for a similar new vehicle is $19,500. However, the guide also indicates that recent selling prices have ranged from $18,000 up to $22,000.

Required:

1. Which price quote, the "list price" or the "Blue Book" average price, is the more relevant for your decision? Why?
2. Which price quote is more representationally faithful? Why?

P1-7

Accounting information characteristics **(LO 1)**

Farmers State Bank is considering a $500,000 loan to Willard Manufacturing. Three items appearing on Willard's balance sheet are:

a. Cash on hand and in the bank, $20,000.
b. Accounts receivable of $60,000, less an allowance for uncollectibles of $15,000.
c. Accumulated depreciation of $36,000.

Required:

1. Which of the balance sheet items—cash, net accounts receivable, or accumulated depreciation—is the most relevant for the bank's loan decision? Why?
2. Which of the balance sheet items is the most representationally faithful? Why?

P1-8

Accounting conservatism **(LO 1)**

Suppose your company purchased land and a warehouse for $5 million. The price was steep, but you were told that a new interstate highway was going to be built nearby. Two months later, the highway project is canceled and your property is now worth only $3 million.

Required:

1. How does the concept of accounting conservatism apply to this situation?
2. Suppose instead that you paid $3 million and later learned that the property is worth $5 million because a new highway is going to be built nearby. How does the conservatism concept apply to this new situation? Why?

Required:

Provide a two- or three-sentence response that argues for or against (indicate which) each of these statements:

P 1 - 9

Your position on the issues
(LO 4)

1. Accounting is an exact science.
2. Managers choose accounting procedures that produce the most accurate picture of the company's operating performance and financial condition.
3. U.S. accounting standards are influenced more by politics than by science or economics.
4. If the FASB and SEC were not around to require and enforce minimum levels of financial disclosure, most companies would provide little (if any) information to outsiders.
5. When managers possess good news about the company (that is, information that will increase the stock price), they have an incentive to disclose the information as soon as possible.
6. When managers possess bad news about the company (that is, information that will decrease the stock price), they have an incentive to delay disclosure as long as possible.
7. Managers who disclose only the minimum information required to meet FASB and SEC requirements may be doing a disservice to shareholders.

In the early 1990s, the FASB issued new rules that dramatically altered the way in which many companies recorded their obligations for postretirement health care benefits. The Board found that most companies used "cash basis" accounting and waited until expenditures for benefits were actually made before recording any expense. This meant that no liability to pay future benefits appeared on the companies' balance sheets even though an obligation to pay future health care benefits clearly existed. The FASB concluded that this approach was inappropriate and instead required companies to record the cost of future health care benefits as incurred.

P 1 - 1 0

Economic consequences of accounting standards
(LO 3)

The affected companies and their trade organizations argued that having to record a liability and an expense equal to the extremely large dollar amounts of these health care benefit commitments would cause employers to substantially reduce their promised benefits to employees and perhaps curtail the benefits entirely.

Required:

1. Why were companies concerned about suddenly reporting a large liability (and corresponding expense) for postretirement health care benefits? What economic consequences might this accounting change have on the affected companies?
2. Some affected companies said they would reduce or eliminate promised benefits to avoid recording the liability and expense. This action harms employees who will then have to bear the burden of future health care costs. Should the FASB consider economic consequences of this sort when updating accounting standards? Why or why not?

"It's time for the government to stop enabling accounting fraud. The Internal Revenue Service and the SEC let companies keep two sets of books, one for tax reporting and the other for financial reporting. There should be no difference in the figures corporations report to the IRS and the SEC. The combined surveillance and enforcement by these agencies of one set of books and identical tax and financial reports should give the investing public a clearer picture of corporate performance." Letter to the Editor, *BusinessWeek,* August 12, 2002.

P 1 - 1 1

Two sets of books   **(LO 1)**

Required:

1. Why do companies keep two sets of accounting books, one for tax reporting and the other for shareholder financial reports?
2. Why might it *not* be a good idea to force companies to issue the same financial statements for both IRS and SEC purposes?

<table>
<tr><td>

P1-12

Accounting quality and the audit committee **(LO 4)**

</td><td>

The New York Stock Exchange (NYSE) and the National Association of Securities Dealers (NASD) require that listed firms have audit committees of independent (that is, outside) company directors. Audit committees review the firm's audited financial statements with management and with the outside auditor and recommend to the full board of directors that the statements be included in the company's annual report. As a committee member, you might ask management about the following:

</td></tr>
</table>

1. What are the key business and financial risks the company has to deal with in its financial reporting?
2. What financial reporting areas involved subjective judgments or estimates, and how are those judgments made and estimates determined?
3. Are there significant areas where the company's accounting policies were difficult to determine?
4. How do the company's accounting practices compare with those of others in the industry?
5. Are the financial statements and underlying accounting methods consistent with those used last year?
6. Are alternative accounting practices being proposed or considered that should be brought to the committee's attention?
7. Were there serious problems in preparing the financial statements?
8. Have outside parties including the SEC, major investors, analysts, and the news media voiced concern about the company's accounting practices?
9. Were there disagreements between management and the auditor regarding accounting practices and, if so, how were they resolved?

Source: Audit Committee Update 2000, PricewaterhouseCoopers LLP.

Required:

Explain for each question why the audit committee and investors might be interested in the answer.

<table>
<tr><td>

P1-13

Worldwide convergence of accounting standards **(LO 6)**

</td><td>

The IASB and its predecessor organization have as a stated objective to narrow worldwide differences in accounting practices and the presentation of financial information. In February 2006 at a ceremony in Beijing, People's Republic of China, the Chinese Ministry of Finance announced the adoption of new Chinese accounting standards that bring about substantial convergence between them and the IASB's IFRS. These are excerpts from a statement made during the ceremony by Sir David Tweedie, chairman of the IASB:

</td></tr>
</table>

> I am honoured to be here today to mark what I believe is an important step for the development of the Chinese economy and its place in the world's increasingly integrated capital markets. The adoption of the new Chinese accounting standards system brings about substantial convergence between Chinese standards and International Financial Reporting Standards (IFRSs), as set by the International Accounting Standards Board (IASB). Like the United States and Japan, China is committed to convergence with IFRS. . . .
>
> The benefits of these accounting reforms for China are clear. The new Chinese standards that incorporate accounting principles familiar to investors worldwide will encourage investor confidence in China's capital markets and financial reporting and will be an additional spur for investment from both domestic and foreign sources of capital. For Chinese companies that are increasingly playing a global role, the acceptance of the new standards should also reduce the cost of complying with the accounting regimes of the different jurisdictions in which they operate. . . .

Required:

1. Why might it be beneficial to narrow worldwide differences in accounting practices? Are there any disadvantages associated with convergence?

2. Explain how the convergence of Chinese accounting standards and IFRS can benefit the Chinese investor who invests only in Chinese companies.

3. Explain how the convergence of Chinese accounting standards and IFRS can benefit the U.S. investor who sometimes invests in Chinese companies.

Friedman's Inc. is a leading fine jewelry retailer. In November 2004, the company said that it might default on certain of the financial covenants contained in one of the company loan agreements. Here is an excerpt from the company's press release:

P1-14

Debt covenants and aggressive accounting practices   **(LO 4)**

> In particular, Friedman's expects that it will fail to meet cumulative EBITDA requirements for the period ending October 30, 2004, constituting a default under its term loan, and it will fail to meet a minimum ratio of Accounts Payable to Inventory as of October 30, 2004, constituting a default under both its term loan and its revolving loan. Friedman's is currently in discussions with its senior lenders under the credit facility regarding the amendment of its covenants to eliminate the default.

EBITDA stands for earnings before interest, taxes, depreciation, and amortization. Apparently, Friedman's term loan contained a provision that required the company to maintain a minimum level of profitability (measured using EBITDA) over several periods (hence, the use of "cumulative," meaning summed over the periods in question).

Required:

1. What will happen to the company if it violates these two covenants and is unsuccessful in obtaining a waiver or amendment from senior lenders?

2. Explain how the EBITDA covenant creates an incentive for Friedman's to engage in aggressive accounting practices. Provide one or more examples of aggressive accounting that Friedman's might use to avoid violating the EBITDA covenant.

3. Explain how the accounts payable to inventory covenant also creates an incentive for Friedman's to engage in aggressive accounting practices.

Both U.S. GAAP and International Financial Reporting Standards (IFRS) require firms to record lease contracts as the purchase of a leased asset and the incurrence of a liability when the contract terms meet certain established characteristics.

P1-15

Rules versus Principles in Lease Accounting   **(LO 6)**

Among other things, U.S. GAAP currently requires this "capital lease" treatment when:

> "(t)he lease term . . . is equal to 75 percent or more of the estimated economic life of the leased property" or where "(t)he present value at the beginning of the lease term of the minimum lease payments . . . equals or exceeds 90 percent of the . . . fair value of the leased property." (ASC Topic 840)

IFRS currently requires this treatment when:

> "the lease term is for the major part of the economic life of the asset" or where "at the inception of the lease the present value of the minimum lease payments amounts to at least substantially all of the fair value of the leased asset." (IAS 17)

Required:

1. Which lease standard—U.S. GAAP or IFRS—is more rules-based? Which is more principles-based? What specific language identifies the distinction?

2. As the Chief Financial Officer (CFO) of an airline company that leases air frames and jet engines, which standard would you prefer? Why?

3. As an outside auditor who is legally and professionally responsible for attesting to the validity of the choices made by the airline company CFO, which standard would you prefer? Why?

P1-16 Toshiba Corporation **(LO 6)**	Locate the most recent annual report of Toshiba Corporation, the large Japanese electronics company, on the company's website: www.toshiba.co.jp. You will find an electronic copy of the annual report in the "Investor Relations" section of the website. **Required:** 1. Besides the financial statements and related notes, what other types of information are contained in the annual report? 2. What types of financial statements are included in the annual report? 3. What country's GAAP rules does Toshiba follow in preparing its annual report? 4. Toshiba's common stock is traded on the New York Stock Exchange. How can you determine if there are differences between Toshiba's reported net income and the net income that would have been reported under U.S. GAAP?
P1-17 Carrefour Group **(LO 5)**	Locate the most recent annual report of Carrefour Group, the French retail company and the second largest retailer in the world, on the company's website: www.carrefour.com. You will find an electronic copy of the annual report in the "Finance: Publications and Presentations" section of the website. The report is in two parts: a summary "annual" report, and the more detailed "financial" report. **Required:** 1. What types of financial information are contained in the "annual" report? 2. Besides the financial statements and related notes, what other types of information are contained in the "financial" report? 3. What types of financial statements are included in the "financial" report? 4. What country's GAAP rules does Carrefour's follow in preparing its financial statements? 5. How does the Carrefour's statement of financial position (balance sheet) differ from those of U.S. companies?

CASES

C1-1 Novartis AG: Form 20-F Reconciliation **(LO 6)**	Novartis AG is a Swiss company that develops, manufactures, and markets pharmaceuticals and vaccines. As of January 2005, European firms, including Novartis, were required to compile their financial reports in accordance with International Financial Reporting Standards (IFRS). In 2006, Novartis filed with the U.S. Securities and Exchange Commission a Form 20-F that, among other things, included a reconciliation of "net income from continuing operations under IFRS" to "net income under U.S. GAAP." A copy of that reconciliation follows.

	2006	2005	2004
	($ millions)	($ millions)	($ millions)
Net income from continuing operations under IFRS	**7,019**	**6,072**	**5,365**
US GAAP adjustments:			
Available-for-sale securities	(114)	278	(183)
Inventory	103	20	(43)
Associated companies		(6)	179
Intangible assets	(1,743)	(1,238)	(590)
Property, plant and equipment	58	53	77
Pensions and other post-employment benefits	(198)	(181)	(82)
Deferred taxes	125	178	423
Share-based compensation	(5)	(44)	(61)
Currency translation			(301)
Minority interests	(27)	(11)	(15)
Others	(68)		9
Net income from continuing operations under US GAAP	**5,150**	**5,121**	**4,778**
Net income from discontinuing operations under US GAAP	114	69	15
Net income under US GAAP	**5,264**	**5,190**	**4,793**

Required:

1. What is the magnitude (in $ millions) of the difference between IFRS net income and U.S. GAAP net income?

2. Which net income number would Novartis managers prefer to report to stakeholders? Why?

3. As an investor who is considering buying shares of a pharmaceutical company, how would your decision be influenced if a candidate company reported $7,019 million of net income rather than $5,264 million?

4. Why are Form 20-F reconciliations helpful to investors who plan to buy or sell shares of a foreign company traded on a U.S. stock exchange?

5. Why might Form 20-F reconciliations also be helpful to investors who plan to buy or sell shares of a foreign company traded on a foreign stock exchange?

As your first week at Henley Manufacturing Inc. draws to a close, you find a memorandum on your desk from the company's CEO. The memo outlines sales and earnings goals for next year: Sales are expected to increase 15% with net income growing by 20%.

The memo says that these goals are ambitious in light of the company's performance over the past two years—ambitious but attainable if "everyone remains focused and committed to our business strategy."

As you finish the memo, your boss, the vice president of finance, steps into your office. She asks you what you think about the memo. You reply that it is important to have clear financial goals but that you would need to know more before making any comments on whether the goals will be easy or difficult to achieve. As she leaves your office, you ask if the CEO will be announcing these goals at next week's annual shareholders' meeting. Your boss answers, "We've never disclosed our sales and earning goals in the past." When you ask why, she says, "We aren't required to under U.S. securities regulations."

Two days later, your boss stops by again and tells you that she raised the issue of disclosing to shareholders the firm's net income and sales goals at this morning's executive committee meeting. The CEO was intrigued but requested that someone identify the costs and benefits of doing so. As she leaves your office, your boss asks you to prepare a briefing document for presentation at the next executive committee meeting.

C1-2

Henley Manufacturing Inc.: Announcing sales and earnings goals **(LO 3)**

Required A:

1. What are the potential costs and benefits to Henley Manufacturing of announcing its sales and earnings goals at the shareholders' meeting?

2. Would you recommend that the CEO announce both, one, or neither goal? Why?

3. If the company's sales and earnings goals covered three years rather than just next year, would your recommendation change? Why or why not?

Required B:

Suppose the memo was more detailed and described the following financial goals for next year: annual sales growth of 15%; annual earnings growth of 20%; a return on net tangible assets of 16%; a return on common equity of 20%; a minimum current ratio of 2.4; a minimum interest coverage ratio of 7.0; a minimum profit margin of 5%; a dividend payout ratio (dividends/net income) of 35% to 40%; a maximum long-term debt to common equity ratio of 40% to 45%; a minimum increase of 15% in annual capital expenditures; and a minimum inventory turnover ratio of 4.5.

Would you recommend that the CEO disclose all, some, or none of these goals at the shareholders' meeting? Which ones and why?

C I - 3

Fortress International:
Disclosing major customers
(LO 2)

The following excerpt is from Fortress International Group's 2012 10-K report filed with the SEC and is a required disclosure:

> [W]e earned approximately 46% of our total revenue from two customers for the year ended December 31, 2012, and 43% from three customers for the year ended December 31, 2011.

Required:

1. Why does the SEC require companies like Fortress International to alert financial statement readers to the existence of major customers?
2. How might this information be of use to a financial analyst?
3. Why might these two substantial customers want to monitor the financial performance and health of Fortress? What specific information about Fortress would be of most interest to the customers?
4. Why might Fortress want to monitor the financial performance and health of these two customers? What information about the customers would be of most interest to Fortress?

C I - 4

The gap in GAAP   **(LO 4)**

It is often alleged that the value of financial statement information is compromised by the latitude that GAAP gives to management. Companies can use different accounting methods to summarize and report the outcome of otherwise similar transactions. Inventory valuation and depreciation are examples in which GAAP allows several alternative accounting methods.

At one extreme, the FASB and the SEC could limit accounting flexibility by establishing a single set of accounting methods and procedures that all companies would apply. At the other extreme, the FASB and the SEC could simply require companies to provide relevant and reliable financial information to outsiders without placing any restrictions on the accounting methods used.

Required:

1. Why should managers be allowed some flexibility in their financial accounting and reporting choices?
2. Of the two approaches to accounting standards setting that are mentioned, which better describes the current financial reporting environment in the United States?
3. Describe the advantages and disadvantages of these two approaches to accounting standards setting, and tell how these advantages and disadvantages vary across different groups of financial statement users.

C I - 5

Federal Express: Making
sense of an earnings
announcement   **(LO I)**

Returning home from your job as a financial analyst covering the airline industry, you find a message from your father, a retired Federal Express (FedEx) pilot. He will be in town this evening and would like you to join him for dinner. He needs your investment advice. Having been with FedEx, he is ecstatic over an article he spotted on Business-Week Online.

FedEx announced first quarter net income of $1.53 per share, up 39% from the $1.10 per share the company earned in the same quarter last year. FedEx also raised its forecasted earnings for the year from $6.30 to $6.65 per share. Despite this good earnings news, the stock price fell nearly 2%.

Required:

Explain to your father why the price of FedEx shares might have fallen on the earnings announcement date.

FEDEX DIPS AFTER REPORTING STRONGER EARNINGS

FedEx Corp. (NYSE: FDX) on Sept. 21 reported stronger than expected quarterly earnings results, while expressing confidence in both its own and the U.S. economy's growth prospects. However, its stock fell after the company issued guidance that was below consensus analyst forecasts.

The Memphis (Tenn.) package deliverer earned $1.53 per diluted share for the first quarter ended Aug. 31, compared to $1.10 per diluted share a year ago. The company, which is seen as a bellwether for the U.S. economy, said revenue surged 11% to $8.54 billion year over year.

"We remain confident in our ability to achieve solid profitable growth by taking advantage of strong international trade trends, increased demand for fast-cycle logistics and the expansion of online purchasing," said Frederick W. Smith, chairman, president and chief executive officer, in a press release. "The global economy is growing at a healthy pace with the U.S. economy growing at a moderate, sustainable rate."

The company also revised its earnings forecasts after reaching a tentative agreement on a new labor contract with its pilots. The agreement, which is between FedEx Express and the Air Line Pilots Association, Int'l (ALPA), the collective bargaining representative for FedEx Express pilots, will be subject to ratification vote during the fiscal second quarter.

FedEx now expects second quarter earnings to be $1.45 to $1.60 per diluted share, and earnings for the year to be $6.30 to $6.65 per diluted share, reflecting a 20-cents charge for costs related to the new pilot contract if ratified. Excluding the impact of the up-front pilot compensation, the fiscal 2007 earnings guidance range was increased by 5 cents per share from the company's initial guidance.

FedEx's stock price fell 1.7% to $105.70, erasing early gains.

Standard & Poor's Corp. analyst Jim Corridore said FedEx beat his expectations for August quarter earnings per share by a penny. In a research note Sept. 21, he reiterated a strong buy on the stock. But he also slashed his fiscal year 2007 EPS estimate to $6.65 from $6.80., noting an expected slowing of the U.S. economy.

Source: BusinessWeek Online (September 22, 2006).

COLLABORATIVE LEARNING CASES

You have been asked to attend a hastily called meeting of Landfil's senior executives. The meeting was called to formulate a strategy for responding to questions from shareholders, analysts, and the media about Landfil's accounting for site development costs. A major competitor, Chambers Development, announced yesterday that it would no longer capitalize site development costs but instead would expense those costs as they were incurred. Stock market reaction to the Chambers announcement was swift and negative, with the stock down 57% at this morning's opening of the NYSE.

Landfil Inc. acquires, operates, and develops nonhazardous solid waste disposal facilities. Landfil is the third largest waste management company of its type in the United States with 37 disposal sites. Sales have been growing at the rate of 30% annually for the last five years, and the company has established a solid record of earnings and operating cash flow performance.

C1-6

Landfil's accounting change **(LO 4)**

Accounting Policy

Landfil capitalizes site development costs in much the same way that Chambers Development did prior to its announcement yesterday. Under the old accounting method at Chambers Development, when the firm spent $20 million on landfill site development, it would book the entire amount as a deferred asset. Then Chambers would spread the cost over 10 years by charging $2 million to earnings each year. Under the new accounting method, all $20 million is expensed in the first year.

Landfil has included the following description of its site development accounting in all annual reports issued during the last five years:

> The Company capitalizes landfill acquisition costs, including out-of-pocket incremental expenses incurred in connection with the preacquisition phase of a specific project (for example, engineering, legal, and accounting due-diligence fees); the acquisition purchase price, including future guaranteed payments to sellers; and commissions. If an acquisition is not consummated, or a development project is abandoned, all of such costs are expensed. Salaries, office expenses, and similar administrative costs are not capitalized. Landfill development and permitting costs, including the cost of property, engineering, legal, and other professional fees, and interest are capitalized and amortized over the estimated useful life of the property upon commencement of operations.

The Meeting

Discussion at the meeting became rather heated as several different points of view emerged. Some members of the executive team argued that Landfil should do nothing but reaffirm its capitalization policy, informing shareholders and others who contacted the company that this policy was consistent with GAAP and disclosed fully in the annual report. Other members of the team argued for a more proactive response involving both direct communication with shareholders and analysts as well as press releases to the media. These communications would also reaffirm the company's capitalization policy but in a more strident manner. Still other members of the executive team argued that Landfil should immediately announce that it too was discontinuing capitalization in favor of immediate expensing. No clear consensus emerged as the meeting progressed, and the group decided to take a 10-minute break before resuming discussion.

As the meeting was about to reconvene, the CEO stopped by your chair and said, "I've been handed a phone message indicating that our largest shareholder has just called. She wants to know our reaction to the events at Chambers Development. I have to call her back in 15 minutes with an answer. When the meeting starts, I'd like you to summarize the major issues we face and to state how you think we should proceed."

Required:

Prepare your summary.

**Remember to check the book's companion website
for additional study material.**

Accrual Accounting and Income Determination | 2

This chapter describes the key concepts and practices that govern the measurement of annual or quarterly income (or earnings) for financial reporting purposes. Income is the difference between **revenues** and **expenses.**[1] The cornerstone of income measurement is **accrual accounting.** Under accrual accounting, *revenues are recorded (recognized) in the period when they are "earned" and become "realized or realizable"*—that is, when the seller has performed a service or conveyed an asset to a buyer, which entitles the seller to the benefits represented by the revenues, and the value to be received for that service or asset is reasonably assured and can be measured with a high degree of reliability.[2] Revenues are considered realizable when the related assets received or held are readily convertible to known amounts of cash or claims to cash.[3] *Expenses are the expired costs or assets that are used up in producing those revenues. Expense recognition is tied to revenue recognition. Therefore, expenses are recorded in the same accounting period in which the revenues are recognized. The approach of tying expense recognition to revenue recognition is commonly referred to as the "matching principle."*

A natural consequence of accrual accounting is the decoupling of measured earnings from operating cash inflows and outflows. Reported revenues under accrual accounting generally do not correspond to cash receipts for the period; also, reported expenses generally do not correspond to cash outlays of the period. In fact, *accrual accounting can produce large differences between the firm's reported profit performance and the amount of cash generated from operations. Frequently, however, accrual accounting earnings provide a more accurate measure of the economic value added during the period than do operating cash flows.*[4]

LEARNING OBJECTIVES

After studying this chapter, you will understand:

1. The distinction between cash-basis versus accrual income and why accrual-basis income generally is a better measure of operating performance.

2. The criteria for revenue recognition under accrual accounting and how they are used in selected industries.

3. The matching principle and how it is applied to recognize expenses under accrual accounting.

4. The difference between product and period costs.

5. The format and classifications for a multiple-step income statement and how the statement format is designed to differentiate earnings components that are more sustainable from those that are more transitory.

6. The distinction between special and unusual items, discontinued operations, and extraordinary items.

7. How to report a change in accounting principle, accounting estimate, and accounting entity.

8. The distinction between basic and diluted earnings per share (EPS) and required EPS disclosures.

9. What comprises comprehensive income and how it is displayed in financial statements.

10. Other comprehensive income differences between IFRS and U.S. GAAP.

11. The procedures for preparing financial statements and how to analyze T-accounts.

---

[1] In this text, we use the terms *profit, earnings,* and *income* interchangeably.

[2] In "Elements of Financial Statements," *Statement of Financial Accounting Concepts (SFAC) No. 6,* the Financial Accounting Standards Board (FASB) defines revenues as "inflows or other enhancements of assets of an entity or settlements of its liabilities (or a combination of both) from delivering or producing goods, rendering services, or other activities that constitute the entity's ongoing major or central operations" (para. 78). Expenses are defined as "outflows or other using up of assets or incurrences of liabilities (or a combination of both) from delivering or producing goods, rendering services, or carrying out other activities that constitute the entity's ongoing major or central operations" (para. 80).

[3] "Recognition and Measurement in Financial Statements of Business Enterprises," *Statement of Financial Accounting Concepts No. 5* (Stamford, CT: FASB, 1984), para. 83. Assets that are readily convertible to cash have both the following characteristics: (a) interchangeable (fungible) units, and (b) quoted prices available in an active market that can rapidly absorb the quantity held by the entity without significantly affecting the price.

[4] *Economic value added* represents the increase in the value of a product or service as a consequence of operating activities. To illustrate, the value of an assembled automobile far exceeds the value of its separate steel, glass, plastic, rubber, and electronics components. The difference between the aggregate cost of the various parts utilized in manufacturing the automobile and the price at which the car is sold to the dealer represents economic value added (or lost) by production.

The following example illustrates this point; it highlights the basic distinction between cash and accrual accounting measures of performance.

EXAMPLE: CASH VERSUS ACCRUAL INCOME MEASUREMENT

> The entries to record the initial borrowing and repayment of the loan principal are ignored because they are financing activities that do not affect the determination of cash-basis income.

In January 2014, Canterbury Publishing sells three-year subscriptions to its quarterly publication, *Windy City Living,* to 1,000 subscribers. The subscription plan requires prepayment by the customers, so Canterbury received the full subscription price of $300 (12 issues × $25 per issue) from each of the subscribers ($300 × 1,000 = $300,000) at the beginning of 2014. To help finance the purchase of newsprint and other printing supplies, Canterbury takes out a $100,000 three-year loan from a local bank on January 1, 2014. The loan calls for interest of 10% of the face amount of the loan each year (10% × $100,000 = $10,000), but the interest is not payable until the loan matures on December 31, 2016. The cost of publishing and distributing the magazine amounts to $60,000 each year ($60 per subscriber), which is paid in cash at the time of publication. The entries to record the **cash-basis** revenues and expenses for each year follow:

Cash-basis entries for 2014

> Throughout this book, **DR** represents the debit side and **CR** represents the credit side of the accounting entry to record the transaction being discussed. See the appendix to this chapter for a review of how these transactions are recorded.

DR Cash		$300,000	
CR Subscription revenue			$300,000

To record collection of 1,000 three-year subscriptions at $300 each for *Windy City Living.*

DR Publishing and distribution expense		$ 60,000	
CR Cash			$ 60,000

To record publishing and distribution expenses paid in cash.

Cash-basis entries for 2015

DR Publishing and distribution expense		$ 60,000	
CR Cash			$ 60,000

To record publishing and distribution expenses paid in cash.

Cash-basis entries for 2016

DR Publishing and distribution expense		$ 60,000	
CR Cash			$ 60,000

To record publishing and distribution expenses paid in cash.

DR Interest expense		$ 30,000	
CR Cash			$ 30,000

To record interest expense paid on the three-year loan ($100,000 × 0.10 × 3 years = $30,000).

A schedule of operating cash inflows and outflows and cash-basis income would look as follows:

Cash-Basis Income Determination

($000 omitted)	2014	2015	2016
Cash inflows	$300	$ —	$ —
Cash outflows for production and distribution	(60)	(60)	(60)
Cash outflow for interest on loan	—	—	(30)
Net income (loss)—cash basis	$240	$(60)	$(90)

Publishing the magazine and servicing the subscriptions require economic effort in each of the years 2014 through 2016, as indicated by the $60,000 of operating cash outflows each period. However, under cash-basis accounting, the entire $300,000 of cash inflow from subscription receipts would be treated as revenue in 2014, the year in which the subscriptions are sold and cash is collected with no revenue recognized in the remaining two years of the subscription period. Likewise, the $30,000 of interest ($10,000 per year $\times$ 3 years) paid on December 31, 2016, would be recorded as an expense in year 2016 under the cash basis of accounting with no interest expense recognized in the first two years. Consequently, on a cash basis, Canterbury Publishing would report a relatively high "profit" of $240,000 in 2014 when the subscriptions are sold and collected, and this 2014 profit would be followed by operating "losses" of $60,000 in 2015 and $90,000 in 2016 when the costs associated with publishing the remaining issues and financing the operations are paid.

Clearly, cash-basis accounting distorts our view of Canterbury's operating performance on a year-by-year basis. Moreover, none of the annual cash-basis profit figures provide a reliable benchmark for predicting future operating results. This distortion is due to differences in the timing of when cash inflows and outflows occur. Recognizing cash inflows as revenue and cash outflows as expenses results in a cash-basis income number that fails to properly match effort and accomplishment.

> Revenues are "earned" as a consequence of publishing magazines and servicing subscriptions—economic activities that span a three-year period. Canterbury's obligation to subscribers is fulfilled gradually over these three years as each issue is delivered, not just in 2014 when cash is collected.

The principles that govern revenue and expense recognition under accrual accounting are designed to alleviate the mismatching problems that exist under cash-basis accounting, making accrual earnings a more useful measure of a firm's performance. Accrual accounting allocates $100,000 of subscription revenue to each of the years 2014, 2015, and 2016 as the magazine is delivered to subscribers and the revenues are "earned." Likewise, accrual accounting recognizes $10,000 of interest expense in each year the bank loan is outstanding, not just in year 2016 when the interest is paid. These modifications to the cash-basis results to obtain accrual earnings are accomplished by means of the following series of "deferral" and "accrual" **adjusting entries,** which are made at the end of each year under accrual accounting (see the appendix for details).

Adjusting entries on December 31, 2014

DR	Subscription revenue	$200,000	
	CR Deferred subscription revenue		$200,000

To adjust the Subscription revenue account for subscriptions received but not yet earned. ($300,000 was initially credited to Subscription revenue. Only $100,000 was earned in 2014. Therefore, Subscription revenue must be debited for $200,000.) Deferred subscription revenue is a liability account reflecting Canterbury's obligation to provide subscribers with future issues of *Windy City Living.*

DR	Interest expense	$ 10,000	
	CR Accrued interest payable		$ 10,000

To adjust for interest expense incurred but not yet paid, and to set up a liability for interest accrued during the period that will be paid on December 31, 2016.

Adjusting entries on December 31, 2015

DR	Deferred subscription revenue	$100,000	
	CR Subscription revenue		$100,000

To adjust Deferred subscription revenue and Subscription revenue for subscriptions earned during the year by providing customers four issues of *Windy City Living.*

DR	Interest expense	$ 10,000	
	CR Accrued interest payable		$ 10,000

To adjust for interest expense incurred but not yet paid, and to set up a liability for interest accrued during the period that will be paid on December 31, 2016.

On December 31, 2016, the accrued interest is paid and the following entry made:

DR Accrued interest payable ... $30,000

    CR Cash ... $30,000

Adjusting entries on December 31, 2016

DR Deferred subscription revenue $100,000

    CR Subscription revenue $100,000

To adjust Deferred subscription revenue and Subscription revenue for subscriptions earned during the year by providing customers with four issues of *Windy City Living*.

DR Interest expense .... $ 10,000

    CR Accrued interest payable .... $ 10,000

To adjust for interest expense incurred during the year. After this adjusting entry, the Accrued interest payable account will have a balance of $30,000.

After these adjustments, the diagram of accrual-basis income looks like this:

Accrual-Basis Income Determination

($000 omitted)	2014	2015	2016	
Cash received	$300			
Deferred to future years	−$200			
Revenue recognized as earned each year	$100	$100	$100	
Expenses				
Publication and distribution (paid in cash)	(60)	(60)	(60)	
			(30)	Interest paid in cash
Interest accrued	(10)	(10)	20	Add: Amounts accrued in prior years
Net income—accrual basis	$ 30	$ 30	$ 30	

From this example, note that accrual accounting revenue for a period does not correspond to cash receipts for the same period ($100,000 of accrual-basis revenue in 2014 does not correspond to the $300,000 of cash received in that year, nor does the $100,000 of recorded accrual revenue in 2015 and 2016 correspond to $0 cash received in those years). Likewise, the reported accrual-basis expenses in a period do not correspond to cash outflows in that period ($10,000 of interest expense recorded under accrual accounting in 2014 and 2015 does not correspond to the $0 of interest paid in those periods, and the $10,000 of interest expense in 2016 does not correspond to the $30,000 of interest paid in cash in that year). As you can see, ***accrual accounting decouples earnings measurement from operating cash flows.*** Indeed, accrual accounting can result in large differences between the firm's reported accrual-basis earnings and the amount of cash generated from operations (cash-basis earnings) year by year, as shown in Figure 2.1.

As this example illustrates, ***accrual accounting better matches economic benefit*** (revenue from subscriptions) ***with economic effort*** (magazine publication and distribution expenses and interest costs), ***thereby producing a measure of operating performance—accrual earnings—that provides a more realistic picture of past economic activities.*** Many believe that accrual accounting numbers also provide a better basis for predicting future performance of an enterprise.

The view that accrual earnings dominate cash flow measures of performance is asserted in *Statement of Financial Accounting Concepts No. 1* issued by the Financial Accounting Standards Board (FASB) in 1978. It stated:

> Information about enterprise earnings and its components measured by accrual accounting generally provides a better indication of enterprise performance than does information about current cash receipts and payments.[5]

---

[5] "Objectives of Financial Reporting by Business Enterprises," *Statement of Financial Accounting Concepts No. 1* (Stamford, CT: FASB, 1978), para. 44.

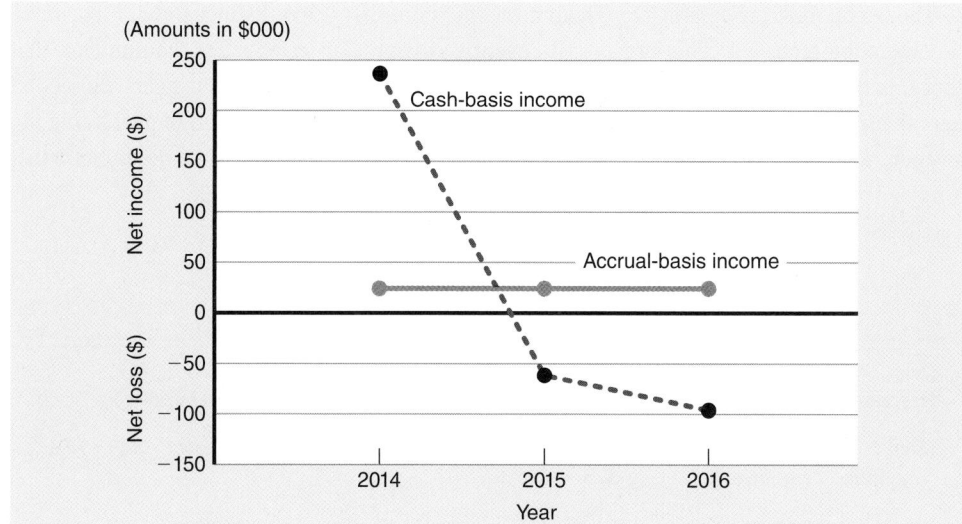

Figure 2.1

CANTERBURY PUBLISHING

Comparison of Accrual- and Cash-Basis Income

Despite the assertions of the FASB and others regarding the superiority of accrual earnings over net cash flows as a measure of a firm's performance, it is important to recognize that reported accrual accounting income for a given period may not always provide an accurate picture of underlying economic performance for that period. One of our objectives is to help you, as a user of accounting information, understand not only the benefits of accrual accounting numbers but also their limitations. Throughout the book, we contrast accounting measurements and their earnings impact with the underlying economic circumstances, highlighting those situations in which the two may diverge.

MEASUREMENT OF PROFIT PERFORMANCE: REVENUES AND EXPENSES

We have introduced the concept of accrual accounting income and contrasted it with cash-basis earnings in a simplified setting. Now, in more realistic (and complex) settings, we review some of the mechanics associated with measuring accrual accounting revenues and expenses.

For virtually all firms, income is not earned as a result of just one activity. A manufacturing firm, for example, earns income as a result of these separate and diverse activities:

1. Marketing the product.
2. Receiving customers' orders.
3. Negotiating and signing production contracts.
4. Ordering materials.
5. Manufacturing the product.
6. Delivering the product.
7. Collecting the cash from customers.

> The sequence of activities comprising the **operating cycle** that is presented here is only one of several possible sequences. The activities comprising the operating cycle can vary across firms or even across products for a given firm. Some companies manufacture the product for inventory prior to identifying a particular buyer and perhaps even in advance of launching a marketing campaign intended to stimulate product demand (for example, Apple manufacturing a new model of laptop computer). In other cases, the product is manufactured to customer order (for example, Boeing manufacturing a new airplane for one of the airlines).

Because income is earned as a result of complex, multiple-stage processes, some guidelines are needed to determine at which stage income is to be recognized in the financial statements. The key issue is the *timing* of income recognition: *When,* under generally accepted accounting principles (GAAP), are revenues and expenses—and thus income—to be recognized?

The accounting process of recognizing income comprises two distinct steps. First, revenues must be recorded. This process of **revenue recognition** establishes the numbers that appear at the top of the income statement. The recognition of revenue then triggers the second step: the **matching** against revenue of the costs that expired (were used up) in generating the revenue. The difference between revenues and expired costs (expenses) is the **net income** that is recognized for the period.

This two-step process is illustrated in the following journal entries:

		Accounting entry	Effect on income (+ or −)
(*Step* 1) **Revenue recognition**	**DR**	Cash or accounts receivable	
	CR	Sales revenue	Sales revenues (+)
(*Step* 2) **Matching of expense**	**DR**	Cost of goods sold	Cost of goods sold (−)
	CR	Inventory	
Income recognition			Net income

Income recognition is a by-product of revenue recognition and expense matching. It is not a separate step that is independent of the other two steps. Once revenue has been recognized and expenses have been matched against the revenue, net income is simply the net difference that results.

The process of revenue recognition and matching expenses against revenue has an obvious effect on the income statement: The excess of recognized revenues over expired costs increases the bottom-line net income number. But accrual accounting affects more than income statement accounts. Due to the double-entry, self-balancing nature of accounting, important changes also occur in **net assets** (that is, assets minus liabilities) on the balance sheet. To understand the effect that accrual accounting has on net assets, consider the following example.

ABC Company has only one asset, inventory, with a $100 cost. Its balance sheet appears as:

ABC Company

INITIAL BALANCE SHEET

Assets		Liabilities + Owners' equity	
Inventory	$100	Initial equity	$100

Assume that all of the inventory is sold for $130, which is immediately received in cash. Clearly, income should be recognized as a result of this transaction. We focus on the balance sheet effects and analyze the transaction using the basic accounting equation:

Assets	=	Liabilities	+	Owners' equity

First, we record the inflow of the asset (cash) and the source of the inflow (sales revenue):

Step 1: **Revenue recognition**

Assets	=	Liabilities	+	Owners' equity
+$130 Cash				+$130 Sales revenue

Next, we record the outflow of the asset (inventory) and match this expired cost against recognized revenue:

Step 2: **Expense matching**

Assets	=	Liabilities	+	Owners' equity
−$100 Inventory				−$100 Cost of goods sold

After recording these transactions, the balance sheet shows:

ABC Company

SUBSEQUENT BALANCE SHEET

Assets		Liabilities + Owners' equity	
Cash	$130	Liabilities	$ —
Inventory	—	Initial equity	$100
		+ increase in equity:	
		Income (+$130 − $100)	30
	$130		$130

Comparing the initial and subsequent balance sheets shows that equity has increased by $30, the amount of income recognized from the transaction. Equally important, net assets have also increased by $30 (that is, $130 of cash inflow minus $100 of inventory outflow = net asset increase of $30). The point of this example is that when income is recognized in the financial statements, two things happen:

1. Owners' equity increases by the amount of the income.
2. Net assets (that is, gross assets minus gross liabilities) increase by an identical amount.

Thus, there are two equivalent ways of thinking about the financial statement effects of income recognition. One perspective is that when income is recognized, the bottom-line net income number (and thus, owners' equity) increases. The other is that when net income is recognized, net assets are increased.

The two approaches to thinking about income recognition merely focus on different aspects of the same transaction. The approach that focuses on the net asset effect on the balance sheet provides a means for understanding the *total* financial statement effects of net income recognition. This approach reminds us that net income recognition simultaneously triggers an increase in the book value (carrying value) of net assets; ***that is, net asset valuation and net income determination are inextricably intertwined.*** When income is recognized in the financial statements, the accountant is acknowledging that the company's net assets have increased in value.[6] The real issue in net income recognition is this: At what point in the cycle of operating activities is it appropriate to recognize that a firm's net assets have increased in value? The next section addresses this.

As noted, net income recognition has two separate steps:

1. Revenue recognition
2. Recognition of expired costs associated with revenue that is recognized (Expense matching).

Let's consider each step separately.

> **Book value** or **carrying value** refers to the amount at which an account (or set of related accounts) is reported on a company's financial statements. For example, the cost of property, plant, and equipment may be reported at $1,000,000 with accumulated depreciation of $300,000. The net book value or carrying value of property, plant, and equipment is the cost minus accumulated depreciation, or $700,000.

---

[6] Notice that the accounting concept of income recognition is really a specific application of the economic concept of value added.

Criteria for Revenue Recognition

According to GAAP, revenue is recognized at the *earliest* moment in time that *both* of the following conditions are satisfied:

Condition 1: The **critical event** in the process of earning the revenue has taken place.

Condition 2: The amount of revenue that will be collected is reasonably assured and is **measurable** with a reasonable degree of reliability.

U.S. GAAP Revenue Recognition Criteria

U.S. GAAP uses different words to describe these two revenue recognition conditions. Condition 1, rephrased using the FASB's terminology, says revenues are not recognized until **earned.** The Board defines *earned* as:

". . . [R]evenues are considered to have been earned when the entity has substantially accomplished what it must do to be entitled to the benefits represented by the revenues."*

The FASB's terminology for Condition 2 says revenues must also be **realizable.** The Board defines *realizable* as (para. 83):

Revenues and gains are realizable when related assets received or held are readily convertible to known amounts of cash or claims to cash. Readily convertible assets have (i) interchangeable (fungible) units and (ii) quoted prices available in an active market that can rapidly absorb the quantity held by the entity without significantly affecting the price.

While the concepts embodied in "earned" and "realizable" are identical to "critical event" and "measurable," we believe that the latter terms are more easily understood and accordingly use them throughout this book.

* "Recognition and Measurement in Financial Statements of Business Enterprises," *Statement of Financial Accounting Concepts No. 5* (Stamford, CT: FASB, 1984), para. 83.

IASB Revenue Recognition Criteria

The International Accounting Standards Board (IASB) uses the following criteria to determine when an entity should recognize revenue.

1. Significant risks and rewards of ownership have been transferred from the seller to the buyer.
2. Managerial involvement and control over the asset being transferred has passed from the seller to the buyer.
3. The seller can reliably measure the amount of revenue or consideration received in the exchange.
4. It is probable that the seller will receive economic benefits.
5. The seller can reliably measure the costs (both past and future) of the transaction.*

* "Revenue," *IAS 18,* Revised and Reissued 1993 (London: IASB, 1993).

 **International**

Condition 1: The Critical Event (Revenue has been "earned")   While the earnings process is the result of many separate activities, it is generally acknowledged that there is usually one critical event or key stage considered to be absolutely essential to the ultimate increase in the firm's net asset value. The exact nature of this critical event varies from industry to industry, as we show in subsequent examples. Unless the critical event takes place, no increase in value is added to the firm's net assets. Thus, the occurrence of the critical event is a first step that must be satisfied before revenue can be recognized. It is a necessary, but not sufficient, condition for revenue to be recognized.

Condition 2: Measurability (Amounts to be received are readily convertible into known amounts of cash)   Accountants do not immediately recognize revenue just because the critical event has taken place. There must be something else: It must be possible to measure the amount of revenue that has been earned with a reasonable degree of assurance. Condition 2 indicates that revenue cannot be recognized merely on the basis of an intuitive "feel" that certain events have added value to the firm's assets. Objective, verifiable evidence as to the amount of value that has been added must exist. Unless the amount of value added can be reliably quantified, GAAP does not allow an increase in asset values to be recorded. Generally, this translates into having a readily determinable price for the goods or service, a price established in the marketplace where buyers and sellers are free to negotiate the terms of trade. So-called "list prices" assigned to the good or service by the seller often do not satisfy the measurability condition because they can deviate from the market-clearing price paid by the buyer.

Only after Conditions 1 and 2 are *both* met can revenue be recognized under GAAP. To illustrate how these revenue recognition conditions are applied, let's return to the example of the three-year subscriptions sold by Canterbury Publishing in January 2014. Recall that accrual accounting would not recognize the $300,000 as revenue when the cash is received because the subscriptions revenue will be earned only as each magazine issue is published and delivered to the customers. If the publisher were to discontinue the magazine before all 12 issues were published, a refund would be owed to subscribers. ***In this magazine example, the critical event in earning subscription revenue is actually providing the product to the customers.*** Thus, $100,000 of revenue will be recorded in each of the three years as the magazine is published and sent to subscribers. Stated somewhat differently, while revenue recognition Condition 2 is met in this example on initial receipt of the subscription order (that is, the amount of ultimate revenue, $300,000, is measurable with a high degree of assurance and reliability), Condition 1 is not met at that time and, therefore, no revenue is recognized because the critical event has not yet occurred. Canterbury has not *earned* the revenue that has been collected because the company has not delivered the magazines promised to subscribers.

To further illustrate how the revenue recognition conditions are applied, let's consider another example. On January 2, 2014, Gigantic Motors Corporation assembles 1,000 automobiles, each with a sticker price of $18,000. These cars have not yet been sold to dealers, so they are parked in a lot adjacent to the plant. Let's examine how revenue recognition Conditions 1 and 2 operate in this setting.

Most observers would agree that the critical event in adding value in automobile manufacturing is production itself.[7] Accordingly, the critical event occurred as the automobiles rolled off the production line. However, no revenue would be recognized at that time. Although revenue recognition Condition 1 is satisfied, Condition 2 is *not* satisfied merely on completion of production. ***This revenue recognition condition is not satisfied because the ultimate sale price of the automobiles is still unknown.*** While Gigantic Motors has established a suggested list price of $18,000 per vehicle, the ultimate amount of cash to actually be received in the future depends on general economic conditions, consumer tastes and preferences, and the availability and asking price of competing automobile models. Thus, the specific amount of value that has been added by production is not yet measurable with a reasonable degree of assurance. Revenue is recognized only when the cars are sold to dealers at a known price (i.e., amount becomes realizable). Only then is revenue recognition Condition 2 satisfied.

The magazine subscription and automobile production examples illustrate that revenue recognition takes place only when revenue recognition Conditions 1 and 2 are *both* met. When Canterbury Publishing receives the cash subscriptions to the magazine, Condition 2 (measurability) is satisfied but not Condition 1: No revenue is recognized until Canterbury provides the magazines to the customers and earns the revenue. When automobile production takes place at Gigantic Motors, Condition 1 (critical event) is satisfied but not Condition 2: No revenue is recognized until the sale takes place, which determines with reasonable assurance the amount that Gigantic will receive from the customer.

The financial reporting rules governing revenue recognition are often misunderstood. Because revenue is usually recognized at the time of sale in most industries, some observers erroneously conclude that the sale is itself the sole criterion for recognizing revenue, but this is not correct. The financial reporting rule for recognizing revenue is more complicated and subtle. Specifically, revenue is recognized as soon as Condition 1 (critical event) *and* Condition 2

---

[7] Automobile manufacturers eventually sell all units produced, although not always immediately following production or always at the sticker price.

(measurability) are *both* satisfied. ***In most instances the time of sale turns out to be the earliest moment at which both Conditions 1 and 2 are satisfied, which is why revenue is most frequently recognized at the time of sale of the product or service.***

However, Conditions 1 and 2 are occasionally satisfied even before a legal sale (that is, transfer of title) occurs. The following example illustrates when revenue can be recognized prior to sale:

> Weld Shipyards has been building oceangoing oil tankers since 1981. In January 2014, Weld signs a contract to build a standard-design tanker for Humco Oil. The contract price is $60 million, and construction costs are estimated to total approximately $45 million. The tanker is expected to be completed by December 31, 2015. Weld intends to account for the project using the **percentage-of-completion** method.

Under the percentage-of-completion method (discussed in Chapter 3), revenue and expenses are recognized as production takes place rather than at the time of completion (the sale). For example, if the tanker is 40% complete at the end of 2014 and finished in 2015, revenue and expenses would be recognized according to the following percentage-of-completion schedule:

($ in millions)	2014	2015	Two-Year Total
Percentage	40%	60%	100%
Revenue	$24	$36	$60
Expenses	(18)	(27)	(45)
Net income	$ 6	$ 9	$15

GAAP permits this method when certain conditions—as in the Weld Shipyards example—are met. Condition 1 (critical event) is satisfied over time as the tanker is built, just as it was in the Gigantic automotive production example. Unlike the Gigantic Motors example, however, revenue recognition Condition 2 is satisfied for Weld Shipyards because a firm contract with a known buyer at a set price of $60 million exists. Thus, the tanker example satisfies *both* of the two conditions necessary for revenue to be recognized. Additionally, expenses are measurable with a reasonable degree of assurance because the tanker is of a standard design that Weld has built repeatedly in past years. This example provides an overview of why the percentage-of-completion method, when used properly, meets revenue recognition Conditions 1 and 2.

In other circumstances, Conditions 1 and 2 may not both be satisfied until *after* the time of sale—for instance, until the cash is collected. In these cases, it would be inappropriate to recognize income when the sale is made; instead, income recognition is deferred and is ultimately recognized in proportion to cash collections. Chapter 3 discusses the **installment-sales method,** an example in which revenue and expenses are recognized at the time of cash collection rather than at the time of sale.

Figure 2.2 is a time-line diagram depicting the activities comprising the revenue recognition process for some selected industries.

To justify recognizing revenue during the **production phase,** the following conditions must be met:

1. A specific customer must be identified and an exchange price agreed on. In most cases, a formal contract must be signed.

2. A significant portion of the services to be performed has been performed, and the expected costs of future services can be reliably estimated.

3. An assessment of the customer's credit standing permits a reasonably accurate estimate of the amount of cash that will be collected.

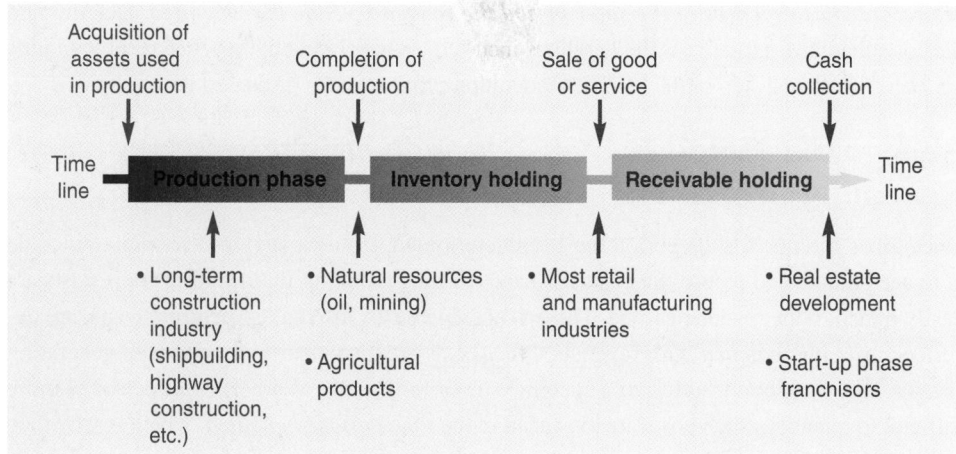

Figure 2.2

THE REVENUE
RECOGNITION PROCESS

Industries Recognizing
Revenue at Indicated Phases

Situations in which these conditions may be satisfied include long-term contracts for the construction of ships, bridges, and office buildings as well as, for example, special-order government contracts for the production of military equipment.

As depicted in Figure 2.2, in some industries revenue may be recognized on **completion of production.** This is justified under the following conditions:

1. The product is immediately saleable at quoted market prices.
2. Units are homogeneous.
3. No significant uncertainty exists regarding the costs of distributing the product.

Examples where these circumstances exist include mining of natural resources and harvesting agricultural crops. These commodities are traded in active, organized markets, and thus a reliable market price can be determined at production even though the eventual buyer's identity is unknown at that time. Although GAAP permits mining and other natural resource companies to recognize revenue at completion of production, few actually do so. Instead, most delay revenue recognition until the time of sale.

Revenue recognition *at the time of sale* is the dominant practice in most retail and manufacturing industries. Occasionally, revenue is not recognized until *after the time of sale.* To justify postponing recognition of revenues, one or more of the following conditions must generally be present:

1. Extreme uncertainty exists regarding the amount of cash to be collected from customers. This uncertainty may be attributable to various factors:
   - The customer's precarious financial condition.
   - Contingencies in the sales agreement that allow the buyer or seller to terminate the exchange.
   - Customers have the right to return the product and this right is frequently exercised.
2. Future services to be provided are substantial, and their costs cannot be estimated with reasonable precision.

These conditions exist in circumstances such as real estate sales, when collection of the sale price occurs in protracted installments, and in sales of franchises for new or unproved concepts or products.

Regardless of which basis of revenue recognition is used, the recognition of expenses generally adheres to the matching principle: That is, all costs incurred in generating the revenue are recorded as expenses in the same period the related revenue is recognized. Determining the costs that have expired (or the liabilities incurred) in generating the revenue recorded in the period is the second step of the income recognition process and is discussed next.

Recognizing Expenses Associated with the Revenue Earned (Matching)

Once gross revenue for the period has been determined, the next step in determining income is to accumulate and record the costs associated with generating the revenue. Some costs are easily traced to the revenue earned. These **traceable costs,** also called **product costs,** are described as being *matched* with revenue. Other costs are also clearly important in generating revenue, but their contribution to a specific sale or to revenue of a particular period is more difficult to quantify. Such costs are expensed in the *time periods benefited,* which is why they are called **period costs.** Let's see how the matching principle is applied to traceable or product costs and to period costs.

Traceable or Product Costs   This next example illustrates how product costs are matched with revenue under GAAP income measurement rules.

> Cory TV and Appliance, a retailer, sells one 50-inch color television set on the last day of February for $500 cash. The TV set was purchased from the manufacturer for $240 cash in January of that same year. Cory provides a 60-day parts and labor warranty to the customer. A typical 50-inch color TV requires $10 of warranty service during the first month following the sale and another $15 of service in the second month.

The expected (as well as the actually experienced) cash flows associated with this single transaction are depicted in Figure 2.3.

GAAP revenue recognition criteria are satisfied by the cash sale in February, so $500 of revenue is recorded in that month. The current and expected future costs of generating that revenue are $265 ($240 + $10 + $15), and these costs are recorded as expenses in the same month (February) that the revenue is recognized. Thus, accrual accounting transforms the cash flow diagram of Figure 2.3 into the revenue recognition and expense matching diagram shown in Figure 2.4.

Figure 2.3

CASH FLOW DIAGRAM

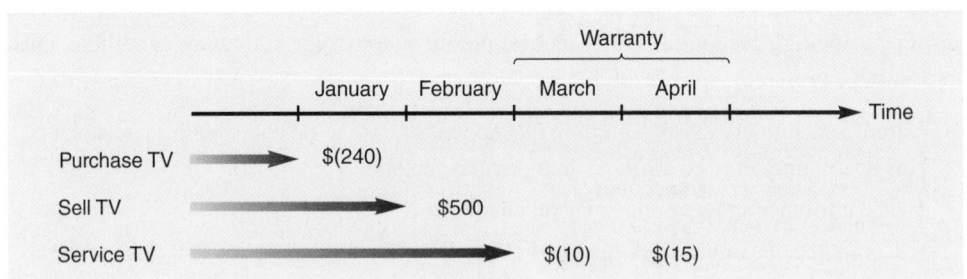

Figure 2.4

REVENUE RECOGNITION AND EXPENSE MATCHING

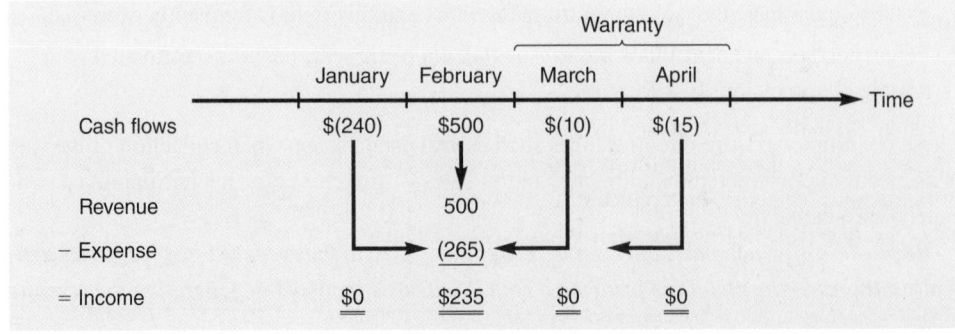

Period Costs   Cory TV and Appliance incurs other types of costs that also are crucial in generating revenue. However, the linkage between these costs and individual sales is difficult to establish. One example of costs of this nature is advertising expenditure.

Assume that Cory TV buys five minutes of advertising time on a local radio station each month for a cost of $700. Obviously, the purpose of advertising is to generate sales. However, it is virtually impossible to associate any month's advertising expenditure with any specific sale because consumer behavior is the result of diverse influences and repeated advertising exposure. Consequently, GAAP does not try to match advertising expenditures with specific sales. Instead, the cost of advertising is charged as an expense in the period in which the ads run. Such costs are called *period costs.* No effort is made to link any particular advertising campaign with particular sales because no objective means for establishing this linkage exists.

The distinction between traceable (product) costs and period costs is discussed further in Chapter 9. At this point, it is important to understand that in applying the matching concept, some costs are directly matched against revenue while others are associated with time periods.

Revenue is recognized at the point when it is (1) earned and (2) realized or realizable. These two conditions can be satisfied at different points in time in different industries. Matching associates expired costs (expenses) with the revenues recognized in a period or with the passage of time. Costs directly matched against revenues are called *product costs;* **costs matched with the passage of time are called** *period costs.*

RECAP

INCOME STATEMENT FORMAT AND CLASSIFICATION

Virtually all decision models in modern corporate finance are based on future cash flows. Recognizing this, the FASB stated:

> Thus, financial reporting should provide information to help investors, creditors, and others assess the amounts, timing, and uncertainty of prospective net cash inflows to the related enterprise.[8]

One way to provide users with information about prospective future cash flows is to present them with cash flow forecasts prepared by *management.* Traditional financial reporting rejects presenting *forecasted* cash flow information because such numbers are considered to be too "soft"—that is, too speculative or manipulable.

Another way to satisfy users' needs for assessing future cash flows is to provide financial information based on past and current events in a format that gives statement users reliable and representative baseline numbers for generating *their own* (user) forecasts of future cash flows. To accomplish this, an income statement format that segregates components of income has evolved. The intent of this format is to classify separately income components that are "transitory" and to clearly differentiate them from income components believed to be "sustainable" or likely to be repeated in future reporting periods.

As we survey the existing format and classification rules, you will see that the rationale behind the rules for multiple-step income statements is intended to subdivide income in a manner that facilitates forecasting. Our discussion is based on the comparative income statements of

 **Valuation**

---

[8] *Statement of Financial Accounting Concepts No. 1,* op. cit., para. 37.

EXHIBIT 2.1	**Mythical Corporation**

Income Statements for the Years Ended December 31,

($ in millions)	2014	2013	2012
Net sales	$3,957	$3,478	$3,241
Costs of goods sold	(1,364)	(1,189)	(1,096)
Gross profit	2,593	2,289	2,145
Selling, general and administrative expenses	(1,093)	(949)	(922)
② **Special or unusual charges (Note 1)**	(251)	—	—
Income from continuing operations before income taxes	1,249	1,340	1,223
Income tax expense	(406)	(436)	(411)
① **Income from continuing operations**	843	904	812
③ **Discontinued operations (Note 2)**			
Income from operation of discontinued			
business segment, net of tax	203	393	528
Gain on disposal of discontinued			
business segment, net of tax	98	—	—
Income before extraordinary item	1,144	1,297	1,340
④ **Extraordinary loss, net of income tax effect (Note 3)**	—	(170)	—
Net income	$1,144	$1,127	$1,340

Note 1: Special or Unusual Charges—A strike closed operations in the Pleasant Grove manufacturing facility for five months in mid-2014. The fixed costs incurred at the idle plant totaled $251 million.

Note 2: Discontinued Operations—The Company discontinued a business segment in 2014. The 2014 operating income and gain on disposal of this segment, net of tax, were $203 million and $98 million, respectively.

Note 3: Extraordinary Loss—The extraordinary loss arose as a consequence of a fire that partially destroyed the chemical plant in River City. The Company had no insurance coverage for such losses due to its long-standing policy of self-insurance.

Mythical Corporation for 2012–2014, presented in Exhibit 2.1. This exhibit illustrates how existing disclosure rules are designed to help users predict future events.

The top line of Mythical's income statement is Net sales. This line represents the revenue generated from sales of products earned during the period less any discounts, provisions for uncollectible accounts, and returns of damaged or defective goods. The next line is Cost of goods sold. This line represents the costs (both direct and indirect) of producing the goods or services that were sold during the period. Examples of the direct costs would be the material and direct labor costs of manufacturing a product. An example of an indirect cost would be manufacturing overhead such as the depreciation charges on the plant used to manufacture the product.[9] The Gross profit (or Gross margin) line is a key number for assessing the performance of an enterprise and for predicting future profitability. Because this number is the difference between the revenue from selling a product or service and the related costs of producing that product or service (product costs), it is a useful number for understanding how competitive pressures affect profit margins. Selling, general, and administrative expenses include marketing costs like advertising and sales commissions, accounting and legal costs, depreciation on corporate offices, and salaries of corporate management.

Mythical's income statement isolates a key figure called **Income from continuing operations.** (See ① in Exhibit 2.1.) This component of income should include only *the normal, recurring, (presumably) more sustainable, ongoing operating activities* of the organization.

---

[9] See Chapter 9 for further discussion of direct and indirect product costs associated with the production of manufactured goods.

As we discuss shortly, this intermediate income number can sometimes include gains and losses that occur infrequently—which we refer to as **Special or unusual items** (item ② in Exhibit 2.1)—but nevertheless arise from a firm's ongoing, continuing operations. With the possible exception of some of these special or unusual items, Income from continuing operations summarizes the wealth effects of recurring transactions or activities that are expected to continue into the future. Therefore, this figure is intended to serve as the anchor or jumping-off point for forecasting future profits.

> "Special" is a street term often used to refer to any type of nonrecurring item reported as part of income from continuing operations.

There are other components of income that are not recurring and, hence, do not form a good basis for projecting future income. These other, more transitory components of income are isolated and disclosed separately so that statement users can place less weight on these earnings components when forecasting the future profitability of an enterprise (see discussion in Chapter 6). These transitory earnings components fall into three categories:

- Special or unusual items (item ②).
- Discontinued operations (item ③).
- Extraordinary items (item ④).

The rules governing the classification and placement of these three categories of transitory items within the income statement are discussed in the following sections. These classification rules provide detailed guidance regarding what qualifies for inclusion in each statement category. As you will see, the rules standardize the format of disclosures as well as prevent certain abuses or distortions that might occur if firms were allowed to commingle these nonrecurring components of earnings with more sustainable, recurring revenue and expense items.

> As used in the authoritative accounting literature, an item is considered material if it is of sufficient magnitude or importance to make a difference in a statement user's decision.

Special or Unusual Items (Item ②)

Material events that arise from a firm's ongoing, continuing activities but that are either unusual in nature or infrequent in occurrence, but not both, must be disclosed as a separate line item as part of income from continuing operations (or in notes to the financial statements). For example, the Mythical Corporation income statement presented in Exhibit 2.1 includes special or unusual charges for losses incurred in conjunction with a labor strike, which is disclosed as a separate line item and discussed in a statement note (see item ② and Note 1 in Exhibit 2.1).

Other examples of special or unusual items include:[10]

1. Write-downs or write-offs of receivables, inventories, equipment leased to others, and intangibles.
2. Gains or losses from the exchange or translation of foreign currencies.
3. Gains or losses from the sale or abandonment of property, plant, or equipment.
4. Special one-time charges resulting from corporate restructurings.
5. Gains or losses from the sale of investments.

> Some companies tend to designate as "special" items that are in fact nonrecurring but are reported on a regular basis, perhaps hoping that investors will discount or ignore these frequent large charges to earnings. For example, Motorola was cited for reporting special, nonrecurring items for *15 consecutive quarters*.*
>
> * J. Drucker, "Motorola's Profit: 'Special' Again?" *The Wall Street Journal,* October 15, 2002.

Including special or unusual items as a component of income from continuing operations complicates financial forecasting and analysis. These special items are treated as a part of income from continuing operations because collectively they represent events that arise repeatedly as a normal part of ongoing business activities.[11] However, some special items occur often while others recur sporadically. For example, some firms are continuously

---

[10] FASB Accounting Standards Codification (ASC) Paragraph 225-20-45-4: Income Statement—Extraordinary and Unusual Items—Other Presentation Matters—Criteria for Presentation as Extraordinary Items and FASB ASC Paragraph 420-10-45-3 Exit or Disposal Cost Obligations—Overall—Other Presentation Matters—Income from Continuing Operations.

[11] Evidence that special items are likely to recur in the aggregate is provided by P. M. Fairfield, R. J. Sweeney, and T. L. Yohn, "Accounting Classification and the Predictive Content of Earnings," *The Accounting Review,* July 1996, pp. 337–55.

selling or disposing of obsolete manufacturing assets as well as taking write-downs on inventory or selling investment securities. However, other special items such as strikes and reorganizations occur less frequently. Consequently, the persistence of special or unusual items is likely to vary from period to period and from item to item. As a result, separate disclosure is provided for these items to assist users in forecasting future results. Because these items are included as part of income from continuing operations before tax (sometimes referred to as being reported "above the line"), they are not disclosed net of tax effects.

Discontinued Operations (Item ③)

Because a primary objective of financial reporting is to assist users in generating estimates of future cash flows, transactions related to operations that the firm intends to discontinue or has already discontinued must be separated from other income items.[12] The reason is straight-forward because, by definition, discontinued operations will not generate *future* operating cash flows.

In Exhibit 2.1, Mythical Corporation discontinued a component of its business in 2014 (item ③). Notice that the operating results of this recently discontinued business segment are not included in income from continuing operations in the current period (2014) when the decision to discontinue was made; nor are they included in any of the prior years (2013 and 2012) for which comparative data are provided.[13] That is, the revenue and expenses of this component of Mythical Corporation that was disposed of in 2014 are removed from the corresponding numbers reflecting 2013 and 2012 results (highlighted). This makes the Income from continuing operations number of $843 million in 2014, the year of the discontinued operations, truly comparable with the Income from continuing operations numbers of $904 million and $812 million in 2013 and 2012, respectively. Restating the 2013 and 2012 results to make them comparable to the 2014 results means that all the numbers from the Net sales line through the Income from continuing operations line reported in the 2013 and 2012 columns of the 2014 annual report will be different from the corresponding numbers originally reported in the 2013 and 2012 statements. While initially confusing to analysts who wish to review the past sequence of earnings numbers to detect trends in a company's financial performance (often referred to as **time-series analysis**), this adjustment to the numbers is essential for valid year-to-year comparisons.

Under U.S. GAAP, a discontinued operation is a **component of an entity,**[14] which comprises operations and cash flows that can be clearly distinguished, operationally and for financial reporting purposes, from the rest of the entity. A component of an entity may be a reportable segment or operating segment, a reporting unit, a subsidiary, or an asset group. An asset group represents the lowest level for which identifiable cash flows are largely independent of the cash flows of other groups of assets and liabilities within the entity.

> IFRS rules use the notion of a **disposal group** for identifying discontinued operations. A disposal group is a group of assets (and liabilities directly associated with those assets) that a firm will dispose of in a single transaction. The group includes goodwill acquired in a business combination if the group is a cash-generating unit of the firm to which goodwill has been allocated. The disposal group notion under IFRS rules envisions a larger unit than the component of an entity notion under U.S. GAAP. [See "Non-current Assets Held for Sale and Discontinued Operations," *IFRS 5* (London, UK: International Accounting Standards Board [IASB]), 2004.]

International

---

[12] FASB ASC Paragraph 205-20-45-3: Presentation of Financial Statements—Discontinued Operations—Other Presentation Matters—Reporting Discontinued Operations.

[13] Securities and Exchange Commission (SEC) rules (Regulation S-X, Article 3) require that comparative income statement data for at least three years and comparative balance sheet data for two years be provided in filings with the Commission. For this reason, most publicly held corporations provide these comparative income statement and balance sheet data in their annual report to shareholders.

[14] FASB ASC Master Glossary.

If a component of an entity has either been sold during the period or is classified as **held for sale,** its results of operations are to be reported as discontinued operations ("below the line") if the following two conditions are met:

1. The operations and cash flows of the component have been (or will be) eliminated from the firm's ongoing operations.
2. The firm will not have any significant continuing involvement in the operations of the component after the disposal transaction.

If either of these two conditions is not met, then the component's operating results are reported as part of income from continuing operations and prior years' results are not restated for comparative purposes.

Amounts Reported When Assets (Disposal Group) Have Been Sold

When the discontinued component is sold before the end of the reporting period, companies are required to report two elements as part of discontinued operations:

1. Operating income or loss (that is, revenue minus expenses) from operating the component from the beginning of the reporting period to the disposal date, net of related tax effects.
2. Gain or loss on disposal computed as the net sale price minus book value of net assets disposed of, net of related tax effects.

Panel (a) of Exhibit 2.2 illustrates a typical income statement disclosure for this situation whose disposal date is September 5, 2014.

> Current U.S. GAAP, sets forth six conditions for an asset group to be considered "held for sale." The most important of these are:
>
> - Management has adopted a formal plan to sell the asset group.
> - An active program to locate a buyer has been initiated.
> - The sale of the asset group is probable and the sale is expected to be completed within one year.
>
> *Source:* FASB ASC Paragraph 360-10-45-9: Property, Plant, and Equipment—Overall—Other Presentation Matters—Initial Criteria for Classification as Held for Sale.

EXHIBIT 2.2   Alternative Disclosure for Discontinued Operations

Partial Income Statement Format for Discontinued Operations

Panel (a): When Assets Have Been Sold on September 5, 2014

Income from continuing operations	$800,000
Income tax expense	(280,000)
Income from continuing operations after tax	520,000
Discontinued operations	
Operating income (net of taxes of $35,000) from	
January 1, 2014, through September 5, 2014	65,000
Loss on disposal of discontinued operations	
(net of $21,000 tax benefit)	(39,000)
Net income	$546,000

Panel (b): When Assets Are "Held for Sale" at Year-End

Income from continuing operations	$800,000
Income tax expense	(280,000)
Income from continuing operations after tax	520,000
Discontinued operations	
Operating income (net of taxes of $42,000) from	
January 1, 2014, through December 31, 2014	78,000
Impairment loss (net of $17,500 tax benefit)	
on assets held for sale	(32,500)
Net income	$565,500

Amounts Reported When Assets (Disposal Group) Are Considered "Held for Sale"   If a company has decided to discontinue a component of its business but has not sold it by the end of the reporting period, the income effects of the discontinued operations are reported in two elements:

1. Operating income or loss (that is, revenue minus expenses) from operating the component from the beginning of the reporting period to the end of the reporting period, net of tax effects.
2. An impairment loss[15] (net of tax effects) if the book value of the net assets in the disposal group is more than the net assets' fair value minus cost to sell.

Panel (b) of Exhibit 2.2 illustrates a typical income statement disclosure for this situation with an after-tax impairment loss on assets "held for sale" of $32,500.

It is important to note that both the income (loss) from operating the discontinued component and any gain (loss) from disposal or impairment are reported net of tax effects. This "net of tax" treatment is called **intraperiod income tax allocation.** The reason for this net of tax treatment is the belief that the income tax burden or benefit should be matched with the item giving rise to it. The allocation of the tax burden or benefit across components of income is believed to make the income figures more informative to users.

Here's why: If income tax were not matched with the item giving rise to it, total reported income tax expense would combine taxes arising both from items that were transitory as well as from other items that were more sustainable. Mixing together the tax effect of continuing activities with the tax effect of single occurrence events would make it difficult for statement readers to forecast future tax outflows arising from ongoing events. Under intraperiod income tax allocation, the income tax associated with the (presumably) transitory items ③ and ④ are not included in Mythical's $406 million income tax expense figure for 2014 (Exhibit 2.1) related to income from continuing operations, thus facilitating forecasts of expected future flows after tax.

Proposed Changes for Reporting Discontinued Operations

The FASB recently issued a new Exposure Draft on reporting of discontinued operations that would make it harder for a disposition of a major business component to qualify as a discontinued operation.[16] The revised definition of a discontinued operation is a component of a business that has either been disposed of, or is classified as held for sale, and

- represents a separate major line of business or major geographical area of operations,
- is part of a single coordinated plan to dispose of a separate major line of business or geographical area of operations, or
- is a business that meets the criteria for classification as held for sale upon acquisition.

The proposal would no longer preclude presentation as a discontinued operation if (a) there are operations and cash flows that have not been eliminated from the entities' ongoing operations, or (b) there is continuing significant involvement with the component after the disposal transaction.

---

[15] See Chapter 10 for further details on determining whether an asset has become impaired and, if so, the amount of the loss.
[16] FASB, Proposed Accounting Standards Update, *Presentation of Financial Statements (Topic 205): Reporting Discontinued Operations,* April 2, 2013, Norwalk, CT.

Because the proposed accounting standards update would raise the bar for reporting a disposal as a discontinued operation, the board decided to require additional disclosures about disposals of individual material business components that are *not* classified as discontinued operations. The new disclosures would include:

- Pre-tax profit or loss attributable to the disposed component for the current and prior periods.
- If there is a noncontrolling interest (see Chapter 16), the profit or loss attributable to the parent.
- In notes to the financial statements, the firm must report a reconciliation of the component's major classes of assets and liabilities classified as held for sale to the amounts presented on the face of the balance sheet for the current period.

Under the proposal, for those dispositions that are treated as a discontinued operation, the firm would be required to disclose in notes to the financial statements a reconciliations of a component's major income and expense items to the after-tax income or loss from the discontinued operations on the face of the income statement, as well as a reconciliation of the major classes of assets and liabilities to the amounts that are presented on the face of the balance sheet. These proposed new disclosure requirements are aimed at enhancing the interperiod comparability of financial statement amounts and to enhance the predictive usefulness of current period numbers with respect the future ongoing activities of an entity. The proposed new standard would also better align the threshold for determining whether a component should be presented as a discontinued operation with the guidance in IFRS 5 (Noncurrent Assets Held for Sale and Discontinued Operations).

 **International**

Extraordinary Items (Item ④)

Another category of transitory items reported separately on the income statement is extraordinary items (item ④ in Exhibit 2.1). To be treated as an extraordinary item, the event or transaction must meet *both* of the following criteria:[17]

> IFRS rules require separate disclosure of gains (losses) resulting from unusual or infrequent events but does not permit the use of the label *extraordinary.*

1. *Unusual nature:* The underlying event or transaction possesses a high degree of abnormality, and considering the environment in which the company operates, that event or transaction is unrelated to the business's ordinary activities.
2. *Infrequent occurrence:* The underlying event or transaction is a type that would not reasonably be expected to recur in the foreseeable future, again considering the environment in which the business operates.[18]

 **International**

The justification for defining extraordinary items so precisely and for requiring separate disclosure of special or unusual items is to prevent statement manipulation. Without such requirements, management might, in a "down" earnings year, be tempted to treat nonrecurring gains as part of income from continuing operations and nonrecurring losses as extraordinary. Precise guidelines preclude this.

---

[17] FASB ASC Section 225-20-45: Income Statement—Extraordinary and Unusual Items—Other Presentation Matters: Criteria for Presentation as Extraordinary Items.

[18] The business environment in which an enterprise operates is a primary consideration in determining whether an underlying event or transaction is unusual in nature and infrequent in occurrence. The environment of an enterprise includes such factors as the characteristics of the industry or industries in which it operates, the geographical location of its operations, and the nature and extent of government regulation. For example, a plant explosion that results in uninsured losses would be considered an extraordinary loss by most businesses. But for a company that manufactures explosive materials (for example, dynamite), losses from such an event may not be considered unusual in nature or infrequent in occurrence given the environment in which the entity conducts its operations.

Like discontinued operations, extraordinary items are reported net of tax. Given the stringency of the criteria, few events qualify as extraordinary items. Examples of qualifying items include losses resulting from catastrophic events (for example, an oil rig explosion resulting in large cleanup costs) or losses arising from new laws or edicts (for example, an expropriation by a foreign government), and in some cases, gains and losses on early debt retirement.

Current GAAP calls for gains and losses from early debt retirement to be classified as extraordinary only if they meet the two criteria enumerated above.[19] Accordingly, firms that use early debt retirement on a recurring basis as part of their ongoing risk management practices report the associated gains and losses as part of income from continuing operations with separate line-item disclosure. Other firms, for which early debt retirement is an unusual and infrequent occurrence, are required to report associated gains and losses as an extraordinary item.

RECAP

To be categorized as extraordinary and to appear below the Income from continuing operations line, an item must be unusual in nature *and* occur infrequently. Special or unusual items that do not meet both criteria, but are considered material, must be disclosed separately as part of pre-tax income from continuing operations.

Frequency and Magnitude of Various Categories of Transitory Income Statement Items

As Exhibit 2.1 illustrates, financial reporting rules for presenting operating results are designed to isolate transitory and nonsustainable components of earnings to assist users in predicting future earnings and cash flows. Research evidence confirms that the GAAP income statement classification framework we have discussed is useful to statement users. Specifically, subdividing earnings into three transitory components—special or unusual items, discontinued operations, and extraordinary items—and disclosing these amounts separately so that they are distinguished from the income that comes from continuing operations improves forecasts of future earnings.[20]

Figure 2.5(a) reveals that the proportion of firms reporting one or more of the types of transitory earnings components highlighted in the previous discussion has hovered around 60% for the 10-year period from 2002 to 2011. Clearly, material, separately disclosed gains and losses are quite common elements of firms' earnings statements in recent years.

Figure 2.5(b) displays the proportion of firms reporting (1) Special or unusual items, (2) Discontinued operations, or (3) Extraordinary items on their income statement from 2002–2011. The most common category of separately disclosed earnings components is special or unusual items reported as part of income from continuing operations. Roughly 57% of the sample firms reported such items in 2011, compared to 52.5% in 2002. Discontinued operations is the next most common separately disclosed item, appearing on approximately 13.5% of the earnings statements of firms in 2011 compared to 12% in 2002. The proportion of firms disclosing extraordinary items decreased from 13% in 2002 to less than 0.2% in 2011.

---

[19] FASB ASC Paragraph 470-50-45-1: Debt—Modifications and Extinguishments—Other Presentation Matters.

[20] For evidence that predictive ability is improved when transitory components of earnings are identified, see P.M. Fairfield, R.J. Sweeney, and T.L. Yohn, "Accounting Classification and the Predictive Content of Earnings," *The Accounting Review,* July 1996, pp. 337–55.

Panel (a)

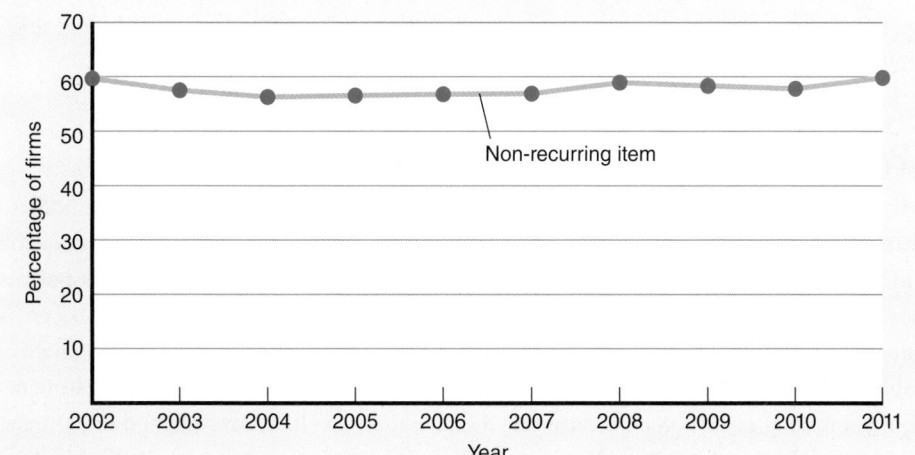

Figure 2.5

PROPORTION OF
FIRMS REPORTING
NONRECURRING
ITEMS (2002–2011)

*Source: Standard and Poor's Compustat®
Annual Industrial File* as data source;
methodology not verified or controlled
by *Standard & Poor's*.

Panel (b)

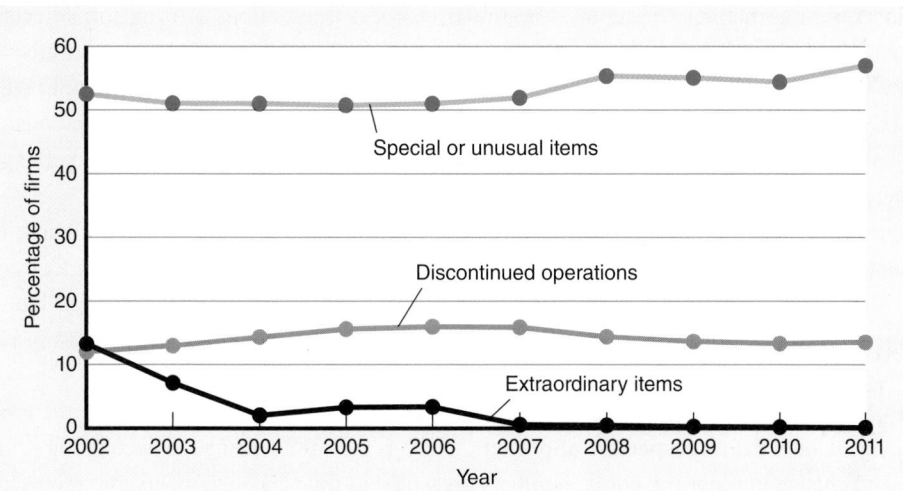

Exhibit 2.3 shows that over the 2002–2011 period, the majority of special or unusual items and extraordinary items were losses (for example, 75.9% of special items in 2011 as highlighted). The preponderance of losses for special or unusual items reflects two things:

1. The conservative bias of accrual accounting rules encourages early recognition of declines in asset values below cost or book value but tends to delay recognition of increases in value until the asset is sold.

EXHIBIT 2.3	**Percentage of Nonrecurring Items That Are Losses (2002–2011)**								
	2002	**2003**	**2004**	**2005**	**2006**	**2007**	**2008**	**2009**	**2010**	**2011**
Special or unusual items	76.8%	71.4%	72.6%	72.3%	69.9%	73.0%	78.6%	74.4%	74.5%	75.9%
Discontinued operations	56.0	51.0	47.3	44.2	43.5	43.1	51.1	54.9	50.5	48.3
Extraordinary items	80.3	64.4	53.5	71.4	33.7	38.9	17.8	21.4	33.3	9.1
Any nonrecurring item (net)	78.7	72.3	72.1	71.8	69.3	72.1	78.3	75.3	75.1	76.0

Source: Compustat Annual Industrial File.

2. Firms have a stronger incentive to separately disclose and clearly label losses than they do gains. To include (undisclosed) nonrecurring losses as part of the income from continuing operations line would cause statement users to underestimate future income. To avoid this understatement firms opt for separate line-item disclosure of losses.

REPORTING ACCOUNTING CHANGES

Consistency, as the term is used in accounting, is using the same accounting methods to describe similar economic events from period to period. It enhances accounting's decision usefulness by allowing users to identify trends or turning points in a company's performance over time. However, because we live in a dynamic and ever-changing business environment, consistency in application of accounting standards over time is not always possible. Firms sometimes voluntarily switch methods of accounting or revise estimates used in computing net income because they believe that the alternative method or estimate better reflects the firm's underlying economics. Also, accounting standards-setting bodies, such as the FASB, frequently issue new standards in response to changes in the business environment that require companies to change accounting methods. When firms use different accounting principles to account for similar business transactions or events in adjacent periods, the period-to-period consistency of the reported numbers can be compromised. Below we describe how accounting method changes are recorded and disclosed under current U.S. GAAP.[21] These disclosures are designed to enhance the comparability and consistency of the numbers over time and to alert statement users about the effects of the change on the current period results.

Accounting changes fall into one of three categories as shown in Exhibit 2.4: change in accounting principle, change in accounting estimate, and change in reporting entity. Correction of an accounting error is not considered a true accounting change but is treated like a change in accounting principle. We discuss and illustrate the accounting and disclosure requirements for accounting error corrections in Chapter 3.

GAAP specifies two approaches for reporting accounting changes depending on the type of change. Under the **retrospective approach,** which is used for a change in accounting principle and change in reporting entity, numbers presented in financial statements that represent amounts in previous years are revised to reflect the impact of the change. The advantage of this approach is that all financial statement numbers—those for the change year and those for years prior to the change—are presented on the same basis of accounting. This enhances the comparability and consistency of the accounting numbers over time. The downside of this approach is that firms may use an aggressive accounting method in earlier years that overstates income and asset values in an effort to lower new debt or equity financing costs and subsequently change to a more appropriate (conservative) method. In such instances, public confidence in the integrity of accounting data may suffer when numbers previously reported and relied on for decision making are later revised.

A second approach to account for accounting changes is the **prospective approach,** which is used for changes in accounting estimates. This approach requires no adjusting entry to modify prior years' financial statements, and prior years' numbers presented for comparative purposes are not restated. Instead, the new estimate is used in determining the income for the year of the change (i.e., the current year) and is applied to all future years. The effect of using the new estimate versus the old estimate on the current period income is disclosed in the note to the financial statements that explains the change in estimate.

---

[21] FASB ASC Topic 250: Accounting Changes and Error Corrections.

EXHIBIT 2.4	Types of Accounting Changes	
Type of Change	**Description**	**Examples**
Change in accounting principle	Change from one generally accepted accounting principle to another. This change can be voluntary (initiated by the firm) or mandatory (required by a standards-setting body such as the FASB).	Voluntary • Change in methods of inventory costing • Change from completed-contract to percentage-of-completion method for recognizing revenue and profits on long-term construction contracts Mandatory • Adoption of a new FASB standard
Change in accounting estimate	Revision of an estimate because of new information or new experience.	• Change in estimated percentage of uncollectible accounts (bad debts) • Change in depreciation method (e.g., straight line to accelerated method)* • Change in estimated service life or salvage value of depreciable assets
Change in accounting entity	Change in the economic units that comprise the reporting entity.	• Reporting consolidated financial statements in place of financial statements for individual entities • Adding a subsidiary not previously included in prior years' consolidated financial statements

* Under U.S. GAAP, a change in depreciation methods is treated as a change in estimate that is achieved by a change in accounting principle.

We now provide a more detailed discussion of these two approaches that are selectively applied to the three types of accounting changes that are summarized in Exhibit 2.4.

Change in Accounting Principle   A change in an accounting principle occurs when (1) a firm *voluntarily* changes from one generally accepted accounting principle to another generally accepted accounting principle or (2) when the accounting principle that was formerly used is made obsolete because the accounting standards-setting body (FASB) revises GAAP to require firms to follow a new approach or method (*mandatory* change). An example of a voluntary change is a firm switching from using the completed-contract to percentage-of-completion method of accounting for long-term construction contracts or switching from the first-in, first-out (FIFO) to last-in, first out (LIFO) method for valuing inventories. A mandatory accounting change is illustrated by a GAAP change that requires firms to expense employee stock option grants on the income statement rather than just disclosing the value of such grants only in financial statements notes as was previously allowed.[22]

As indicated, GAAP requires firms to use the *retrospective approach* to account for changes in accounting principles unless it is impracticable to do so.[23] Under this approach, prior years' financial statements (balance sheet, income statement, cash flow statement, and statement of stockholders' equity) that are presented for comparative purposes are revised in

[22] FASB ASC Topic 718: Compensation—Stock Compensation.

[23] Changes in principles that are deemed to be impracticable to apply retrospectively occur when information needed to do so is not available or would require assumptions about management's intent in a prior period that cannot be independently verified [FASB ASC Paragraph 250-10-45-9: Accounting Changes—Overall—Other Presentation Matters—Impracticability].

the year of the change to reflect the impact of the accounting principle change. This means that for each year in the comparative statements reported, the revised balance of each account shows what that balance would have been under the new principle. The income statement, cash flow statement, and balance sheet amounts for the year of the change are based on the application of the new accounting principle.

Besides reporting revised amounts in the comparative financial statements, a journal entry is made to adjust all account balances to reflect what those amounts would have been under the new method as of the beginning of the current year (i.e., the change year). In addition to adjusting existing asset or liability accounts, the entry to record the accounting principle change typically requires an adjustment to the firm's beginning Retained earnings balance to reflect the **cumulative effect** of the accounting principle change on all prior periods' reported income. This cumulative effect is the difference between what reported earnings would have been in prior years if the new method had always been used versus the earnings previously reported under the old method.[24]

> Like many retailers, Abercrombie & Fitch's fiscal year-end is the end of January. So the 2012 fiscal year ends on February 2, 2013. Abercrombie & Fitch's 2012 10-K report was filed with the SEC on April 4, 2013, which is after the effective date of this accounting change.

Exhibit 2.5 illustrates how apparel retailer Abercrombie & Fitch Co. used the retrospective approach for its change from the lower of cost or market (LCM) utilizing the retail method to the weighted average cost method to account for its inventories that was made effective February 3, 2013. Panel (a) provides an explanation for why the change was made. Panel (b) shows the effect of the change on various income statement line items for the 2011 and 2010 fiscal years (ended January 28, 2012 and January 29, 2011, respectively), the two years for which Abercrombie & Fitch provided comparative income statement data in its 2012 10-K report. Because the 2012 fiscal year income statement is based on the newly adopted average cost method, having the restated income statement line items for 2011 and 2010 fiscal years allows statement users to compare operating results over these three years using a consistent basis of inventory accounting. Panel (c) shows the effect of the change on the ending balance sheet values for fiscal 2011, the only year for which comparative balance sheet information was provided in Abercrombie & Fitch's 2012 fiscal year annual report. Note that the $68.879 million (net of deferred tax effects) increase in the January 28, 2012 (fiscal 2011 year-end) inventory values is offset by a $69.043 million increase in Retained earnings. This offset arises because prior years' income would have been higher if Abercrombie & Fitch had been using the weighted average cost method rather than the LCM retail method in those years (Chapter 9 explains why).

Retroactive Effect Indeterminable   In some cases, it is impracticable to determine the cumulative effect of applying a change in accounting principle to prior periods. For example, a firm may switch its method of determining inventory costs from the average cost method to the LIFO method (see Chapter 9) and may not have the detailed records to retroactively restate prior periods' results under the new method of inventory accounting. Exhibit 2.6 on pg. 78 illustrates the disclosure of a change in the method of determining inventory costs implemented by Big Lots Inc. in January of 2012 for which the retroactive effect was indeterminable.

Change in Accounting Estimate   Estimates are used extensively in accounting. Examples of items for which estimates are necessary include percentage-of-completion accounting for long-term contracts, uncollectible receivables, inventory obsolescence, service lives and salvage values of depreciable assets, and warranty obligations. Changes in accounting

---

[24] The cumulative effect on beginning retained earnings reflects only the direct effects on earnings, which includes related tax effects. Indirect effects (e.g., profit sharing or royalty payments based on reported income) are not included under the retrospective application [FASB ASC Paragraph 250-10-45-8: Accounting Changes—Overall—Other Presentation Matters—Change in Accounting Principle].

EXHIBIT 2.5	Abercrombie & Fitch Co.

**Disclosures for Change in Accounting Principle (Retrospective Method)
Abercrombie & Fitch Co. 2012 10-K**

4. Change in Accounting Principle

Panel (a):

The Company elected to change its method of accounting for inventory from the lower of cost or market utilizing the retail method to the weighted average cost method effective February 2, 2013. In accordance with generally accepted accounting principles, all periods have been retroactively adjusted to reflect the period-specific effects of the change to the weighted average cost method. The Company believes that accounting under the weighted average cost method is preferable as it better aligns with the Company's focus on realized selling margin and improves the comparability of the Company's financial results with those of its competitors. Additionally, it will improve the matching of cost of goods sold with the related net sales and reflect the acquisition cost of inventory outstanding at each balance sheet date. The cumulative adjustment as of January 30, 2010, was an increase in its inventory of $73.6 million and an increase in retained earnings of $47.3 million.

Panel (b):

As a result of the retroactive application of the change in accounting for inventory, the following items in the Company's Consolidated Statements of Operations have been restated:

	Fiscal Year Ended January 28, 2012		
($ in thousands, except per share data)	**As Reported**	**Effect of Change**	**As Restated**
Cost of goods sold	$1,639,188	$(31,354)	$1,607,834
Tax expense from continuing operations	59,591	15,078	74,669
Net income	127,658	16,276	143,934

	Fiscal Year Ended January 29, 2011		
($ in thousands, except per share data)	**As Reported**	**Effect of Change**	**As Restated**
Cost of goods sold	$1,256,596	$(5,248)	$1,251,348
Tax expense from continuing operations	78,287	(178)	78,109
Net income	150,283	5,426	155,709

Panel (c):

As a result of the retroactive application of the change in accounting for inventories, the following items in the Company's Consolidated Balance Sheets have been restated:

	January 28, 2012		
($ in thousands)	**As Reported**	**Effect of Change**	**As Restated**
Inventories	$ 569,818	$110,117	$ 679,935
Deferred income taxes	77,120	(41,238)	35,882
Total assets	3,048,153	68,879	$3,117,032
Retained earnings	2,320,571	69,043	2,389,614
Total stockholders' equity	1,862,456	68,879	1,931,335
Total liabilities and stockholders' equity	3,048,153	68,879	3,117,032

estimates come about because new information indicates the previous estimate is no longer valid. In some cases, a change in accounting estimate results from a change in accounting principle. For example, a change from using straight-line depreciation to an accelerated depreciation method may occur because management concludes that the pattern of consumption of an asset's expected benefits has changed and that a new depreciation method better reflects

EXHIBIT 2.6	Big Lots Inc.

Accounting Change—Retroactive Effect Indeterminable (Prospective Method)

Big Lots Inc.—Accounting Change—Retroactive Effect Indeterminable

Excerpt from 2012 10-K report

Merchandise Inventories

Merchandise inventories are valued at the lower of cost or market using the average cost retail inventory method. Under our previous inventory management system, which was used through the end of 2011, we calculated average cost at the department level, which constituted 50 inventory cost pools. On January 29, 2012, the first day of 2012, we completed the implementation of our new inventory management systems, which has allowed us to more precisely determine our inventory cost under the average cost retail inventory method. We now calculate average cost at the class level, which constitutes approximately 350 inventory cost pools.

This change in accounting principle, to include approximately 350 class inventory cost pools in the retail method calculation instead of approximately 50 departments in the calculation's inventory cost pools, is preferable as it provides us with a more precise estimate of the average cost of our merchandise inventories.

Accounting Standards Codification ("ASC") 250, "Accounting Changes and Error Corrections" requires that unless it is impracticable to do so, the voluntary adoption of a new accounting principle should be done retrospectively. Prior to January 29, 2012, the date we completed our implementation of SAP® for Retail, our accounting systems did not capture merchandise inventory costs with class level detail needed for us to recognize, measure, and disclose amounts for prior periods under the retrospective application. In particular, the previous inventory system did not track or reconcile stock ledger information by class, but rather by department. Specifically, key items such as freight and shrink costs were aggregated at the department level, with no data identifier to the class, which made it impractical to retrospectively account for the change. Therefore, we have adopted this change in accounting principle prospectively from the beginning of the current year, as we can determine the cumulative effect in inventory cost as of that date.

As the impact of the accounting change in the beginning of the current year inventory is immaterial, we have recognized the cumulative effect of the change in accounting principle as a current year expense by recording a reduction in inventory and a corresponding increase to cost of sales of approximately $5.6 million in the first quarter of 2012. This non-cash charge reduced the 2012 income from continuing operations and net income by approximately $3.4 million.

that new pattern. Changes in accounting estimates that result from a change in accounting principle are accounted for as a change in estimate.

When accounting estimates are changed, prior year income is never adjusted; instead, the income effects of the changed estimate are accounted for in the period of the change and in future periods if the change affects both. This is called the *prospective approach* to reporting an accounting change.[25] If the change in estimate has a material effect on current and future income, the dollar amount of the effect must be disclosed. Exhibit 2.7 shows Computer Sciences Corporation's disclosure for handling of changes in estimates related to contract revenue recognized under its fixed-price software development contracts.

We use another example to illustrate how current and future period numbers are adjusted when a change in an accounting estimate is made. Miles Corporation purchases a production machine on January 1, 2012, for $6 million. The machine has no salvage value, an expected useful life of 10 years, and is being depreciated on a straight-line basis. On January 1, 2014, the machine's book value is $4.8 million (that is, $6 million of original

---

[25] FASB ASC Paragraphs 250-10-45-17 to 20: Accounting Changes—Overall—Other Presentation Matters—Change in Accounting Estimate.

EXHIBIT 2.7	Computer Sciences Corporation

Change in Accounting Estimate (Prospective Method)

Excerpt from 2012 10-K Report

Under the percentage-of-completion method, progress toward completion is measured based on either achievement of specified contract milestones, costs incurred as a proportion of estimated total costs, or other measures of progress when available. Profit in a given period is reported at the estimated profit margin to be achieved on the overall contract. This method can result in the recognition of unbilled receivables, the deferral of costs as work in process, or deferral of profit on these contracts. Contracts that require estimates at completion using the percentage-of-completion method accounted for approximately 17.9% of the Company's revenues for fiscal 2013. Management regularly reviews project profitability and underlying estimates. Revisions to the estimates at completion are reflected in results of operations as a change in accounting estimate in the period in which the facts that give rise to the revision become known by management. Provisions for estimated losses at completion, if any, are recognized in the period in which the loss becomes evident. The provision includes estimated costs in excess of estimated revenue and any profit margin previously recognized.

cost minus two years of accumulated depreciation at $0.6 million per year). At that date, it becomes evident that due to changes in demand for the machine's output, its *remaining* useful life is six years, not eight years. If Miles Corporation had perfect foresight, the annual depreciation charge should have been $0.75 million ($6 million divided by eight years), amounting to $1.5 million over the first two years. Consequently, there is $0.3 million too little accumulated depreciation ($1.5 million minus $1.2 million) as of January 1, 2014, and pre-tax income for the previous two years is overstated by $0.3 million. Rather than forcing Miles to retroactively adjust reported prior year income, the GAAP disclosure rules require the change in estimate to be reflected in higher depreciation charges over the new remaining life of the asset; in this case, from 2014 to 2019. Depreciation in those years will be $0.8 million per year (that is, the remaining book value of $4.8 million divided by the remaining useful life of six years). Over the eight-year life of the asset, depreciation will appear as follows:

2012–2013	2 years × $0.6 million per year	=	$1.2 million
2014–2019	6 years × $0.8 million per year	=	4.8 million
Total cost of the asset			$6.0 million

From the perspective of perfect foresight in which depreciation would have been $0.75 million per year, depreciation in the first two years is understated by $0.15 million annually. In each of the last six years, it is overstated by $0.05 million annually. Obviously, over the asset's eight-year life, depreciation totals $6.0 million.

Why are changes in estimates "corrected" in this peculiar fashion? The reason is that accrual accounting requires many estimates; because the future is highly uncertain, a high proportion of actual results turn out to be different from estimated amounts. If prior years' income were corrected for each misestimate, income statements would be cluttered with numerous retroactive adjustments. The approach illustrated by this example provides an expedient way to deal with the uncertainty in financial statements by just going forward with a new estimate, without generating burdensome corrections.

Change in Reporting Entity   A different type of accounting change arises when a company acquires another company. In such circumstances, the newly combined entity presents consolidated financial statements in place of the previously separate statements of each party to the merger. Such combinations result in what is called a **change in reporting entity.**

When a change in a reporting entity occurs, comparative financial statements for prior years must be restated for comparative purposes to reflect the new reporting entity as if it had been in existence during all the years presented.[26] In addition, the effect of the change on income before extraordinary items, net income, other comprehensive income, and any related per share amounts are disclosed for all periods presented.

Comparative financial statements represent an important resource for analysts because they provide potentially valuable data for assessing trends and turning points. However, under current GAAP, not all business combinations or spin-offs result in a change in the reporting entity. Consequently, analysts must understand the circumstances under which retroactive restatement takes place (and when it does not) to ensure that the data being used are indeed comparable. These matters are discussed in more detail in Chapter 16.

RECAP

Accounting changes can dramatically affect reported earnings and distort year-to-year comparisons. For these reasons, GAAP requires special disclosures to improve interperiod comparability and to help statement users understand what effect the accounting change has had on the current period's reported profits.

Thompson Financial (First Call) is a leading provider of analyst EPS forecasts in the United States. The EPS forecasts reported by Thompson are typically basic EPS for income from continuing operations excluding the effects of special, nonrecurring gains or losses. These items are excluded because they are nonrecurring and difficult to forecast. Sometimes analysts also exclude from forecasted basic EPS certain other noncash charges (for example, depreciation and goodwill amortization). Such earnings are frequently referred to as pro forma or "Street" earnings because they do not strictly correspond to a GAAP earnings number.

EARNINGS PER SHARE

One of the most commonly reported measures of a company's operating performance is **earnings per share** (**EPS**). All publicly traded companies must report EPS numbers on the face of their income statement.[27] Exhibit 2.8 illustrates the EPS disclosures for Enpro Industries. Note that two sets of numbers are reported: one set for **basic EPS** and another set for **diluted EPS.** Basic EPS is computed by dividing income available to common shareholders (that is, net income minus dividends to preferred shareholders) by the weighted average common shares outstanding for the period. Diluted EPS reflects the EPS that would result if all potentially dilutive securities were converted into common shares. It is reported for firms with complex capital structures; that is, firms with convertible debt, convertible preferred stock, options, or warrants outstanding. The calculations involved for diluted EPS are complex and are covered in detail in Chapter 15. Here we simply illustrate the financial statement presentation of EPS.

Note that each set of EPS numbers includes separately reported numbers for income from continuing operations, discontinued operations, extraordinary items, and bottom-line net income. Therefore, it is important for the statement user to be aware of how the number being reported in companies' earnings announcements is defined. This caution applies both to announcements in the financial press and to analysts' forecasts of firms' performance.

---

[26] FASB ASC Paragraph 250-10-45-21; Accounting Changes and Error Corrections—Overall—Other Presentation Matters—Change in Reporting Entity.

[27] FASB ASC Topic 260: Earning per Share.

EXHIBIT 2.8	Enpro Industries, Inc.—EPS Presentation

Consolidated Statements of Operations

	Years Ended December 31,		
($ in millions, except per share data)	Year 3	Year 2	Year 1
Net sales	$ 803.0	$993.8	$873.8
Cost of sales	523.8	635.4	560.2
Gross profit	279.2	358.4	313.6
Operating expenses:			
Selling, general and administrative expenses	224.3	241.6	209.1
Asbestos-related expenses	135.5	52.1	68.4
Goodwill impairment charge	113.1	—	—
Other operating expense (income), net	10.5	(0.3)	6.0
	483.4	293.4	283.5
Operating income (loss)	(204.2)	65.0	30.1
Interest expense	(12.3)	(12.7)	(12.5)
Interest income	0.9	2.7	8.3
Other income (expense), net	17.4	(5.4)	0.6
Income (loss) from continuing operations before income taxes	(198.2)	49.6	26.5
Income tax benefit (expense)	54.6	(16.8)	(9.3)
Income (loss) from continuing operations	(143.6)	32.8	17.2
Income from discontinued operations, net of taxes	4.3	17.8	17.9
Income (loss) before extraordinary item	(139.3)	50.6	35.1
Extraordinary item, net of taxes	—	—	2.5
Net income (loss)	$(139.3)	$ 50.6	$ 37.6
Basic earnings (loss) per share:			
Continuing operations	$ (7.19)	$ 1.62	$ 0.81
Discontinued operations	0.22	0.88	0.84
Extraordinary item	—	—	0.12
Net income (loss) per share	$ (6.97)	$ 2.50	$ 1.77
Diluted earnings (loss) per share:			
Continuing operations	$ (7.19)	$ 1.56	$ 0.77
Discontinued operations	0.22	0.84	0.80
Extraordinary item	—	—	0.11
Net income (loss) per share	$ (6.97)	$ 2.40	$ 1.68

COMPREHENSIVE INCOME AND OTHER COMPREHENSIVE INCOME

GAAP defines **comprehensive income** as a change in equity (net assets) of a business entity that occurs during a reporting period from transactions or events from nonowner sources.[28] So it includes all changes in equity during a period except those resulting from investments by owners (e.g., purchase of common stock) and distributions to owners (e.g., dividend payments). Obviously, a major source of change in equity is net income, determined by the general rules outlined earlier in this chapter. Therefore, net income is part of comprehensive income. Recollect that income recognition automatically triggers a corresponding change in

---

[28] FASB ASC Topic 220: Comprehensive Income.

the carrying amount of net assets (equity). Generally, items included in net income result from **completed** or **closed transactions** with outside parties. A closed transaction is one whose ultimate payoff results from events (1) that have already occurred and (2) whose dollar flows can be predicted fairly accurately.

> Fair value is the price that would be received to sell an asset or the price paid to transfer or settle a liability in an orderly transaction between market participants at the settlement date (FASB ASC Master Glossary).

Sometimes the carrying amounts of net assets on a firm's balance sheet change even though the transaction is not yet completed or closed and, therefore, is not reported as part of net income. These types of events or transactions give rise to **other comprehensive income** (OCI).[29] OCI comprises revenues, expenses, gains, and losses that, under GAAP, are included in comprehensive income (thus, that cause changes in equity) but are *excluded* from net income. Other comprehensive income components frequently arise from using **fair value** measurements for selected assets or liabilities reported on firms' balance sheets. This section provides an overview of the major items that constitute other comprehensive income (which are described in greater detail in later chapters of the book) and the alternative ways that firms can report comprehensive income under current GAAP.

> See Chapter 16 for a more complete discussion of using fair value measurements for marketable securities held in an available-for-sale portfolio.

Let's consider a specific example of an other comprehensive income component that affects equity but is not reported as part of net income. Banks and other financial institutions (e.g., insurance companies) often hold investments in stocks or bonds of other entities with readily determinable fair values. Assume that these securities are held in the firm's available-for-sale portfolio and that the fair values have increased over the current reporting period. To recognize the fair value increases, GAAP requires that the following accounting entry be made:

DR Marketable securities—Available-for-sale securities	XXX	
CR Other comprehensive income (OCI)—unrealized		
holding gain on available-for-sale securities		XXX

At fiscal year-end, the OCI account would be closed out to Accumulated other comprehensive income (AOCI), which is a separate account shown in the stockholders' equity section of the balance sheet. The closing entry would be as follows:

DR OCI—unrealized holding gain on available-for-sale securities	XXX	
CR Accumulated other comprehensive income		
(AOCI)—stockholders' equity		XXX

Note that through this series of entries, equity (net assets) is increased without an effect on net income. Comprehensive income is increased through an OCI component.

Under current GAAP, other comprehensive income components fall into the following general categories (see FASB ASC paragraph 220-10-55-2):

1. Foreign currency translation adjustments and gains and losses on intra-entity foreign currency transactions that are of a long-term-investment nature (see Chapter 16).
2. Gains and losses on foreign currency transactions that are designated as, and are effective as, economic hedges of a net investment in a foreign entity.

---

[29] FASB ASC Section 220-10-20: Comprehensive Income—Overall—Glossary.

3. Unrealized holding gains and losses on available-for-sale securities and on a debt security being transferred into the available-for-sale category from the held-to-maturity category (see Chapter 16).

4. Amounts recognized in other comprehensive income for debt securities classified as available-for-sale and held-to-maturity related to an other-than-temporary impairment if a portion of the impairment was not recognized in earnings (see Chapter 16).

5. Subsequent decreases (if not an other-than-temporary impairment) or increases in the fair value of available-for-sale securities previously written down as impaired (see Chapter 16).

6. Gains or losses associated with pension or other postretirement benefits (that are not recognized immediately as a component of net periodic benefit cost) (see Chapter 14).

7. Prior service costs or credits associated with pension or other postretirement benefits (see Chapter 14).

8. Transition assets or obligations associated with pension or other postretirement benefits (that are not recognized immediately as a component of net periodic benefit cost) (see Chapter 14).

Current GAAP requires firms to report comprehensive income in a statement that is displayed with equal prominence as other financial statements. Firms are permitted to display the components of other comprehensive income in one of two formats:[30]

1. In a single-statement format, one in which net income and other comprehensive income are added to disclose total comprehensive income.

2. In a two-statement format, one in which the components of net income constitute one statement and a second statement of comprehensive income that begins with net income and shows the individual other comprehensive income components.

Exhibit 2.9 from Arden Group's 2012 annual report illustrates the single-statement format. Exhibit 2.10 shows the two-statement approach for Exxon Mobil.

RECAP

Comprehensive income measures a company's change in equity (net assets) that results from all nonowner transactions and events. It is composed of both bottom-line accrual income that is reported on the income statement and other comprehensive income components. Other comprehensive income comprises selected unrealized gains and losses on incomplete (or open) transactions that bypass the income statement and that are reported as direct increases or decreases to stockholders' equity. Firms are required to report comprehensive income in a statement that is displayed with the same prominence as other financial statements. But firms are free to choose the presentation format, either as a separate statement or as part of a statement that is combined with the income statement.

---

[30] FASB ASC Section 220-10-65-1: Comprehensive Income-Overall-Transition and Open Effective Date Information (Transition Related to Accounting Standards Update No. 2011-05—Presentation of Comprehensive Income).

EXHIBIT 2.9	Arden Group—Comprehensive Income Disclosure: Single-Statement Approach

Arden Group, Inc. and Consolidated Subsidiaries
Consolidated Statements of Operations and Comprehensive Income

($ in Thousands, Except Share and Per Share Date)	Fifty-Two Weeks Ended December 29, 2012	Fifty-Two Weeks Ended December 31, 2011	Fifty-Two Weeks Ended January 1, 2011
Sales	$439,038	$429,483	$417,066
Cost of sales	271,164	268,544	257,506
Gross profit	167,874	160,939	159,560
Selling, general and administrative expense	134,387	134,817	129,416
Loss from exitactivity	1,912	0	0
Operating income	31,575	26,122	30,144
Interest and dividend income	167	134	338
Other income (expense), net	0	2,243	(66)
Interest expense	(83)	(76)	(84)
Income before income taxes	31,659	28,423	30,332
Income tax provision	12,740	11,418	12,245
Net income	$ 18,919	$ 17,005	$ 18,087
Other comprehensive gain (loss), net of tax:			
Unrealized gain (loss) from available-for-sale securities:			
Net unrealized holding gain (loss) arising during the period	7	5	(45)
Reclassification adjustment for realized loss included in net income	0	0	38
Net unrealized gain (loss), net of income tax expense (benefit) of $5 for 2012, $3 for 2011 and ($4) for 2010	7	5	(7)
Comprehensive income	$ 18,926	$ 17,010	$ 18,080

EXHIBIT 2.10	Exxon Mobil Corporation—Two-Statement Approach

Consolidated Statement of Income

($ in millions)	2012	2011	2010
Revenues and other income			
Sales and other operating revenue	$453,123	$467,029	$370,125
Income from equity affiliates	15,010	15,289	10,677
Other income	14,162	4,111	2,419
Total revenues and other income	482,295	486,429	383,221
Costs and other deductions			
Crude oil and product purchases	265,149	266,534	197,959
Production and manufacturing expenses	38,521	40,268	35,792
Selling, general and administrative expenses	13,877	14,983	14,760
Depreciation and depletion	15,888	15,583	14,760
Exploration expenses, including dry holes	1,840	2,081	2,144
Interest expense	327	247	259
Sales-based taxes	32,409	33,503	28,547
Other taxes and duties	35,558	39,973	36,118
Total costs and other deductions	403,569	413,172	330,262
Income before income taxes	78,726	73,257	52,959
Income taxes	31,045	31,051	21,561
Net income including noncontrolling interests	47,681	42,206	31,398
Net income attributable to noncontrolling interests	2,801	1,146	938
Net income attributable to ExxonMobil	$ 44,880	$ 41,060	$ 30,460

(continued)

EXHIBIT 2.10	Exxon Mobil Corporation—Two-Statement Approach *(continued)*

Consolidated Statement of Comprehensive Income

($ in millions)	2012	2011	2010
Net income including noncontrolling interests	$47,681	$42,206	$31,398
Other comprehensive income (net of income taxes)			
Foreign exchange translation adjustment	920	(867)	1,034
Adjustment for foreign exchange translation (gain)/loss included in net income	(4,352)	—	25
Postretirement benefits reserves adjustment (excluding amortization)	(3,574)	(4,907)	(1,161)
Amortization and settlement of postretirement benefits reserves adjustment included in net periodic benefit costs	2,395	1,217	1,040
Change in fair value of cash flow hedges	—	28	184
Realized (gain)/loss from settled cash flow hedges included in net income	—	(83)	(129)
Total other comprehensive income	(4,611)	(4,612)	993
Comprehensive income including noncontrolling interests	43,070	37,594	32,391
Comprehensive income attributable to noncontrolling interests	1,251	834	1,293
Comprehensive income attributable to Exxon Mobil	$41,819	$36,760	$31,098

GLOBAL VANTAGE POINT

The previous section discusses the concept of other comprehensive income (OCI) and notes that OCI often arises from changes to the carrying amounts of net assets on the firm's balance sheet even though transactions have not actually occurred. Because the firm has not yet sold or unwound its positions in these balance sheet items, carrying amount value fluctuations remain unrealized and are therefore frequently reported as a component of OCI.

U.S. GAAP financial reporting standards and IFRS still differ in many respects. One can look more carefully at the components within OCI to see at least some examples of where these two reporting standards still differ considerably. IFRS allows, in some cases, more opportunities for managers to change the balance sheet valuation of certain assets even when managers have no intention to sell or dispose of these assets. Because this practice generates unrealized gains or losses, the effect will typically be found as a component of OCI. As we discuss further in Chapter 10, for example, IFRS allows (but U.S. GAAP does not allow) managers to choose to periodically revalue property, plant, and equipment assets at an appraised fair value. This might enable a company that owns land to adjust the carrying value of the land on its balance sheet as changes occur to the land's appraised fair value. This IFRS-specific option seems to provide more relevant and timely information with regard to asset values reported on the balance sheet. It also, however, introduces unrealized gains and losses (assuming the land is not sold or transferred) that are typically reported in OCI. As discussed in more detail in Chapters 4 and 10, increases (or decreases) in the appraised value of property, plant, and equipment under this particular rule are often reflected in stockholders' equity account called Revaluation surplus. Exhibit 2.11 shows such revaluations for WorkCover Queensland, a government-related provider of workers' compensation insurance in Queensland, Australia, from its 2010–2011 Annual Report. Note 26 from WorkCover Queensland's annual report shows the changes in OCI (i.e., changes in the Revaluation surplus account) associated with "annual valuations (for land and buildings) by an external independent valuer." You will not observe a similar note from any company that files its financial statements under U.S. GAAP.

IFRS also differs considerably from U.S. GAAP with respect to how firms report their periodic expense associated with defined benefit pension obligations. Recent changes to *IAS 19,* which became effective in January 2013, could introduce differences in OCI between entities that file their reports under IFRS relative to entities that file under U.S.

EXHIBIT 2.11   WorkCover Queensland

26. Asset revaluation surplus by class

(Amounts reported in $000 Australian)	Land	Building	Total
Carrying amount at the beginning of the prior year	$8,820	$13,931	$22,751
Movements for the prior year revaluation:			
Revaluation of land and building	(3,000)	(2,285)	(5,285)
Income tax effect on revaluation of land and building	900	686	1,586
	(2,100)	(1,599)	(3,699)
Carrying amount at the end of the prior year	6,720	12,332	19,052
Carrying amount at the beginning of the current year	6,720	12,332	19,052
Movements for the current year revaluation:			
Revaluation of land and building	—	(898)	(898)
Income tax effect on revaluation of land and building	—	269	269
	—	(629)	(629)
Carrying amount at the end of the current year	$6,720	$11,703	$18,423

The asset revaluation surplus is used to record increments and decrements on the revaluation of land and building to fair value.

GAAP. Chapter 14 discusses, in detail, current reporting guidance for U.S. firms that offer employees defined benefit pension plans. Because defined benefit pensions typically guarantee retirement payments to employees until their death, both U.S. GAAP and IFRS require firms to hire actuaries (i.e., statisticians often employed in the insurance industry) to make estimates regarding elements that could materially affect the magnitude of the company's expected liability to its retired employees. Actuarial estimates, such as employee life expectancy, are often adjusted each period, which directly affects the reported balance sheet value of the net pension obligation. Both U.S. GAAP and IFRS require companies to report these valuation changes in OCI each period. However, as of January 2013, U.S. GAAP is now alone in requiring some firms to periodically recategorize a portion of these OCI changes into periodic net income. Exhibit 2.12 shows such a recategorization for Boeing Company, a company that reports under U.S. GAAP. Exhibit 2.12 shows that Boeing recategorized $2.272 billion of actuarial adjustment losses relating to pensions from OCI into net income (by including it as a "net periodic benefit cost" in the income statement). After January 2013, you will not observe a similar note for companies that file financial statements under IFRS.

Recently, both the FASB (through Accounting Standards Update 2011-05) and the IASB (through an amendment to IAS 1 *Presentation of Financial Statements*) enacted changes

---

EXHIBIT 2.12   Boeing Company

Excerpt from 2012 annual report—pension note

The estimated amount that will be amortized from Accumulated other comprehensive loss into net periodic benefit cost during the year ended December 31, 2013 is as follows:

($ in millions)	Pensions	Other Postretirement Benefits
Recognized net actuarial loss	$2,272	$102
Amortization of prior service costs/(credits)	195	(180)
Total	$2,467	($78)

regarding the presentation of comprehensive income to improve consistency and clarity. *IAS 1* allows firms to present a single statement of comprehensive income or alternatively present separately a net income statement and a statement of comprehensive income. If two separate statements are presented, *IAS 1* requires the net income statement to immediately precede the statement of comprehensive income. The main change within the amendment to *IAS 1* is that entities are now required to group items within OCI based on whether they will not be reclassified subsequently into net income (e.g., actuarial estimate changes to defined benefit pension plans) or they will be reclassified subsequently to net income when specific conditions are met (e.g., when cash flows are realized, fair value changes to derivatives assigned as cash flow hedge instruments are reclassified from OCI to net income, as discussed further in Chapter 11). The main changes under U.S. GAAP are the elimination of the option to report components of OCI as part of the statement of changes in stockholders' equity, and a requirement for entities to show reclassification adjustments from OCI to net income on the face of the financial statements that are associated with OCI. [31] The first of the two main U.S. GAAP changes would likely make the presentation of OCI more consistent with the presentation required by IFRS.

SUMMARY

- This chapter highlights the key differences between cash and accrual income measurement.
- In most instances, accrual-basis revenues do not equal cash receipts and accrual expenses do not equal cash disbursements.
- The principles that govern revenue and expense recognition under accrual accounting are designed to alleviate the mismatching of effort and accomplishment that occurs under cash-basis accounting.
- Revenue is recognized when *both* the critical event and measurability conditions are satisfied.
- The critical event establishes when the entity has done something to earn the asset being received, and measurability is established when the revenue can be measured with a reasonable degree of assurance.
- The critical event and measurability conditions may be satisfied before or after the point of sale.
- The matching principle determines how and when the assets that are used up in generating the revenue or that expire with the passage of time are expensed.
- Relative to current operating cash flows, accrual earnings generally provide a more useful measure of firm performance and serve as a more useful benchmark for predicting future cash flows.
- Predicting future cash flows and earnings is critical to assessing the value of a firm's shares and its creditworthiness.
- Multiple-step income statements are designed to facilitate this forecasting process by isolating the more recurring or sustainable components of earnings from the nonrecurring or transitory earnings components.

---

[31] FASB Accounting Standards Update 2011-12 delayed the implementation of the second requirement to show reclassification adjustments from OCI to net income on the face of the statements that are associated with OCI. To support the decision to delay implementation, the FASB noted stakeholder concerns that the net income statement, for example, would become overly cluttered and therefore more difficult to understand with these disclosures (BC11b.). Stakeholders also noted that they did not have processes and controls in place to collect and summarize the level of detailed information required (BC11a.).

- GAAP disclosure requirements for various types of accounting changes also facilitate the analysis of company performance over time.

- All publicly traded companies must report EPS numbers on the face of their income statement. All firms are required to report basic EPS based on the weighted average number of shares actually outstanding during the period, while firms with complex capital structures are required to disclose diluted EPS, which reflects the EPS that would result if all potentially dilutive securities were converted into common shares.

- Occasionally, changes in assets and liabilities resulting from incomplete or open transactions bypass the income statement and are reported as direct adjustments to stockholders' equity. These direct adjustments are called *other comprehensive income components*. Under U.S. GAAP, firms are required to report the components of other comprehensive income in either a single-statement format or a two-statement format.

APPENDIX

REVIEW OF ACCOUNTING PROCEDURES AND T-ACCOUNT ANALYSIS

The basic accounting equation is the foundation of financial reporting:

$$A = L + OE$$

The basic accounting equation says that at all times, the dollar sum of a firm's assets (A) must be equal to the dollar sum of the firm's liabilities (L) plus its owners' equity (OE). To understand why this equality must always hold, keep two things in mind:

1. Assets don't materialize out of thin air; they have to be financed from somewhere.
2. Only two parties can provide financing for a firm's assets:
   a. Creditors of the company—for example, when a supplier ships inventory to a firm on credit (an asset—inventory—is received).
   b. Owners of the company—for example, when owners buy newly issued shares directly from the firm (an asset—cash—is received).

> For simplicity, we ignore nuances of the par value of the stock, etc., and simply treat the entire amount as "common stock." The details of stock transactions are explored further in Chapter 15.

Putting these two things together explains why the two sides of the basic accounting equation must be equal. The equation says the total resources a firm owns or controls (its assets) must, by definition, be equal to the total of the financial claims against those assets held by either creditors or owners.

We'll now use the basic accounting equation to show how various transactions affect its components. Notice that each transaction maintains the basic equality; for example, any increase in an asset must be offset by (1) a corresponding increase in a liability or owners' equity account or (2) a decrease in some other asset.

Assume that Chicago Corporation sells office furniture and provides office design consulting services. It is incorporated on January 1, 2014, and issues $1 million of stock to investors for cash. Here's how this and subsequent transactions will affect the basic accounting equation:

Transaction 1

Assets	=	Liabilities	+	Owners' equity
+$1,000,000 Cash				+$1,000,000 Common stock

On the next day, Chicago Corporation buys a combination office building and warehouse for $330,000, paying $30,000 in cash and taking out a $300,000 loan at 8% interest per year.

Transaction 2

Assets	=	Liabilities	+	Owners' equity
−$30,000 Cash		+$300,000 Loan payable		
+$330,000 Building				

Suppliers ship a wide assortment of inventory costing $97,000 to the firm on credit on January 11.

Transaction 3

Assets	=	Liabilities	+	Owners' equity
+$97,000 Inventory		+$97,000 Accounts payable		

On January 15, Chicago Corporation sells a portion of its inventory costing $50,000 to several customers for $76,000 on account.

Transaction 4

Assets	=	Liabilities	+	Owners' equity
+$76,000 Accounts receivable				+$76,000 Sales revenue
−$50,000 Inventory				−$50,000 Cost of goods sold

A sale causes assets to flow into the company. Who benefits from this inflow of assets? The owners do. That's why owners' equity is increased by $76,000 in Transaction 4. The source of this increase is labeled; in this case, the source of the increase is Sales revenue. But in making a sale, the firm must relinquish an asset, Inventory. Whose claims are reduced as a result of this outflow of assets? The owners'. That's why owners' equity is decreased by $50,000 in the second part of Transaction 4. Again, the reason for the decrease in owners' equity is labeled; in this case, the need to deliver inventory to the customer reduces owners' equity claims on the firm's assets by $50,000, the Cost of goods sold.

In addition to the balance sheet (which follows the balancing format of the basic accounting equation), there is another financial statement called the income statement. Recollect that Sales revenue is the top line of the income statement and that Cost of goods sold is deducted from revenues. So Transaction 4, which was illustrated in a basic accounting equation (that is, balance sheet) format, really includes income statement accounts. *Another way to say the same thing is that the revenue and expense accounts that appear on the income statement are really owners' equity accounts. Revenues are owners' equity increases; expenses are owners' equity decreases.* (Later in this appendix, we'll show how these accounts are closed into Retained earnings, a component of owners' equity, as part of the adjusting and closing process.)

Understanding Debits and Credits

Keeping track of transactions using the basic accounting equation as we did in Transaction 1–4 is cumbersome. For this reason, a streamlined approach is used to record how transactions either increase or decrease financial statement accounts. Increases and decreases in accounts are based on the convention of *debits* and *credits*. Debit (abbreviated DR) means left side of accounts, and credit (abbreviated CR) means right side of accounts.

We now depict the basic accounting equation in T-account form and show the rules for how debits and credits operate to reflect increases or decreases to various accounts.

Asset accounts	=	Liability accounts	+	Owners' equity accounts

Debits	Credits	Debits	Credits	Debits	Credits
(DR) **increase** the account balance	**(CR)** **decrease** the account balance	**(DR)** **decrease** the account balance	**(CR)** **increase** the account balance	**(DR)** **decrease** the account balance	**(CR)** **increase** the account balance

Because Transaction 4 showed us that revenue accounts increase owners' equity and expense accounts decrease it, the DR and CR rules treat revenue and expense accounts just like any other owners' equity accounts. The rules can be summarized as follows:

Revenues (that is, OE increases)		Expenses (that is, OE decreases)	
Debits	Credits	Debits	Credits
(DR) **decrease** the account balance	**(CR)** **increase** the account balance	**(DR)** **increase** the account balance	**(CR)** **decrease** the account balance

Let's elaborate on the debit and credit rules for expense accounts. Expense accounts are increased by debits. An increase in an expense *decreases* owners' equity. Owners' equity is decreased by debits. That's why increases in an expense account (which decrease owners' equity) are debits.

The basic accounting equation must always be "in balance"—that is, the total of the assets must always equal the total of the liabilities plus owners' equity. ***Similarly, for each transaction, the dollar total of the debits must equal the dollar total of the credits.*** Adherence to the debit and credit rules for each transaction automatically keeps the basic accounting equation in balance. To help you visualize how this happens, we redo Transactions 1–4 in debit and credit format and show (in brackets to the right of the account name) what happens to the basic accounting equation:

Transaction 1:   **Stock issued for cash**

DR	Cash [+A]	$1,000,000	
	CR Common stock [+OE]		$1,000,000

Transaction 2: **Purchase of building**

DR	Building [+A]	$330,000	
	CR Cash [−A]		$ 30,000
	CR Loan payable [+L]		300,000

Transaction 3: **Purchase of inventory on credit**

DR	Inventory [+A]	$97,000	
	CR Accounts payable [+L]		$97,000

Transaction 4: **Sale of inventory on account**

DR	Accounts receivable [+A]	$76,000	
DR	Cost of goods sold [−OE]	50,000	
	CR Sales revenue [+OE]		$76,000
	CR Inventory [−A]		50,000

As the pluses and minuses to the right of the account names show, adherence to the DR/CR rules automatically maintains the balance of the basic accounting equation.

We next introduce four additional transactions for Chicago Corporation. Assume that the company purchases a one-year fire and theft insurance policy on the building and its contents on January 15, 2014, for $6,000. It makes the following journal entry upon purchasing the policy:

Transaction 5: **Purchase of prepaid insurance**

DR	Prepaid insurance [+A]	$6,000	
	CR Cash [−A]		$6,000

Prepaid insurance is an asset account because the policy provides a valuable benefit to the company: insurance coverage for the ensuing 12 months.

Next, assume that the company receives a $10,000 fee in advance from a law firm to help the firm design its new office space. The fee is received on January 17, and the consulting/design services are to be provided over the next month. Chicago Corporation makes the following journal entry:

Transaction 6:   **Receipt of consulting fees in advance**

DR	Cash [+A]	$10,000	
	CR Fee received in advance [+L].		$10,000

The credit is to the liability account, Fee received in advance, because the firm has an obligation to provide the consulting services (or return the fee). Until the critical event of providing those services occurs, no revenue can be recognized.

Further assume that Chicago pays certain suppliers $37,000 for inventory recorded in Transaction 3. Other suppliers will be paid in ensuing periods.

Transaction 7: Payment on account

DR	Accounts payable [−L].	$37,000	
	CR Cash [−A].		$37,000

Finally, $30,000 is received from one of the customers to whom inventory was sold in Transaction 4.

Transaction 8: Collections on account

DR	Cash [+A]	$30,000	
	CR Accounts receivable [−A]		$30,000

Adjusting Entries

Before financial statements are prepared (either monthly, quarterly, or annually), a firm's financial accounts must be reviewed to determine whether all economic events that have occurred are reflected in the accounts. It is usually the case that certain readily identifiable types of events will *not* be reflected in the accounts. To include these events in the accounts, **adjusting entries** must be made. These adjusting entries fall into four categories:

1. Adjustments for prepayments.
2. Adjustments for unearned revenues.
3. Adjustments for accrued expenses.
4. Adjustments for accrued revenues.

We now assume that Chicago is preparing financial statements for the month ended January 31, 2014. Adjusting entries in each of the four categories are necessary and discussed next.

Adjustments for Prepayments The insurance policy acquired for $6,000 on January 15 in Transaction 5 has partially expired. One-half of one month's coverage has now elapsed; consequently, 1/24 of the original *annual* premium payment is no longer an asset. The passage of time means that *past* insurance coverage has no future value. So, the following adjusting entry is made:

Adjusting Entry A1:

DR	Insurance expense [−OE]	$250	
	CR Prepaid insurance [−A]		$250
	($6,000/12 months = $500; $500 × 1/2 month = $250)		

After this entry is made, the balance in the Prepaid insurance account is $5,750; this is the original $6,000 balance minus the $250 credit in Adjusting Entry A1. The $5,750 represents the remaining asset, insurance coverage for the ensuing 11½ months. The adjusting entry has *simultaneously* accomplished two things:

1. The DR recognizes that portion of the premium that has expired, that is, the portion that is a January expense. This is the matching principle in action because the expense is matched against January revenues.
2. The CR reduces the carrying amount in the asset account by $250. As a result of this reduction, the Prepaid insurance account is shown at $5,750; this is the portion of the original $6,000 insurance premium that has not yet expired.

The building acquired in Transaction 2 also represents a prepayment. Chicago paid for the building in early January 2014, and this building is expected to be used in operations over a series of *future* years. As the building is used, a portion of its future service potential declines. This decline in service potential value is an expense of the period called **depreciation.** Assume that Chicago estimates building depreciation for January totaled $1,250. The following adjusting entry is then made:

> We will discuss the various methods for estimating depreciation in Chapter 10.

Adjusting Entry A2:

    DR   Depreciation expense [−OE] $1,250

           CR   Accumulated depreciation [−A] $1,250

(The Accumulated depreciation account represents a contra-asset account that is deducted from the cost of the building, as we shall see later.)

> A **contra** account is an account that is *subtracted* from another account to which it relates. Contra-asset accounts carry credit balances because they are subtracted from asset accounts that carry debit balances.

Adjustments for Unearned Revenues

By the end of January, let's assume that 60% of the design work for the law firm has been completed. Consequently, the following adjusting entry is made:

Adjusting Entry A3:

    DR   Fee received in advance [−L] $6,000

           CR   Consulting fees revenue [+OE] $6,000

Notice that this entry also accomplishes two things. First, the debit lowers the balance in the liability account, Fee received in advance, to $4,000 (that is, the original $10,000 minus the $6,000 liability reduction arising from the debit). Second, the credit properly recognizes that 60% of the $10,000 advance has been earned in January and thereby increases owners' equity.

Adjustments for Accrued Expenses

Salaries and wages for the month of January totaled $16,000. The paychecks will not be issued to employees until Monday, February 3. Because the expense arose in January, a liability exists for money owed to the employees and the following entry must be made:

Adjusting Entry A4:

    DR   Salary and wages expense [−OE] $16,000

           CR   Salary and wages payable [+L] $16,000

Adjusting entries such as this one must be made for a wide range of expenses that *accrue* over the reporting period. ***Accrual accounting recognizes expenses as the underlying real*** *economic event occurs, not necessarily when the cash flows out.* Consequently, adjusting entries for accrued expenses must be made not only for accrued wages payable but also for items such as heat, light, and power used during the month and for interest on amounts borrowed that has accumulated during the period but has not yet been paid. Assume that the utility bill arrives on January 31 but will not be paid until February 9, its due date. If the utility bill for January totaled $9,000, the following additional adjusting entry is necessary:

Adjusting Entry A5:

DR	Heat, light, and power expense [−OE]	$9,000
CR	Accounts payable [+L]	$9,000

Furthermore, interest of $2,000 has accrued on the loan principal that was used to buy the building. (The accrued interest is determined as follows: $300,000 × 8% per year = $24,000 × 1/12 of year = $2,000.) The following entry is made:

Adjusting Entry A6:

DR	Interest expense [−OE]	$2,000
CR	Accrued interest payable [+L]	$2,000

Adjustments for Accrued Revenues

During the last week in January, Chicago Corporation provides design consulting services to a physician who is remodeling her office. The physician is billed for the $2,100 due. The adjusting entry is:

Adjusting Entry A7:

DR	Accounts receivable [+A]	$2,100
CR	Consulting fees revenue [+OE]	$2,100

Again, the adjusting entry simultaneously accomplishes two things:

1. The DR reflects the asset that the firm expects to collect as a result of consulting services rendered in January.
2. The CR shows the corresponding increase in owners' equity that arises when the asset (Accounts receivable) is recognized.

Posting Journal Entries to Accounts and Preparing Financial Statements

Throughout this book, we use journal entries as a streamlined mechanism for showing you how economic events affect financial statement accounts. In this section of the appendix, we provide a terse overview of how professional accountants use journal entries as the building blocks for preparing financial statements. We use T-accounts to demonstrate this. We also show how analysis of T-accounts can be used to infer what transactions (and dollar amounts) a firm entered into between two balance sheet dates.

The DRs and CRs in each journal entry that is made are posted to T-accounts. **Posting** means the DR or CR is entered in the appropriate left (or right) side of the affected T-account. A separate T-account is maintained for each asset, liability, and owners' equity account. (Remember: Revenue and expense accounts are effectively owners' equity accounts, too. The balances accumulated in these accounts for a particular reporting period will be closed out, or transferred to owners' equity at the end of the period.)

EXHIBIT 2.13	Posting to T-accounts

| Assets | = | Liabilities | + | Owners' equity |

Cash

(1) $1,000,000	(2)	$30,000
(6)	10,000	(5)	6,000
(8)	30,000	(7)	37,000

Bal. $967,000

Accounts payable

| (7) | $37,000 | (3) | $97,000 |
| | | (A5) | 9,000 |

Bal. $69,000

Common stock

| | (1) $1,000,000 |

Bal. $1,000,000

Retained earnings

(Revenue and expense account balances will be closed out to this account at end of the accounting period.)

Accounts receivable

| (4) | $76,000 | (8) | $30,000 |
| (A7) | 2,100 | | |

Bal. $48,100

Salary and wages payable

| | (A4) $16,000 |

Bal. $16,000

Consulting fees revenue

| | (A3) | $6,000 |
| | (A7) | 2,100 |

Bal. $8,100

Sales revenue

| | (4) | $76,000 |

Bal. $76,000

Inventory

| (3) | $97,000 | (4) | $50,000 |

Bal. $47,000

Accrued interest payable

| | (A6) | $2,000 |

Bal. $2,000

Cost of goods sold

| (4) | $50,000 |

Bal. $50,000

Insurance expense

| (A1) | $250 |

Bal. $250

Prepaid insurance

| (5) | $6,000 | (A1) | $250 |

Bal. $5,750

Loan payable

| | (2) | $300,000 |

Bal. $300,000

Depreciation expense

| (A2) | $1,250 |

Bal. $1,250

Salary and wages expense

| (A4) | $16,000 |

Bal. $16,000

Building

| (2) | $330,000 |

Bal. $330,000

Fee received in advance

| (A3) | $6,000 | (6) | $10,000 |

Bal. $4,000

Heat, light, and power expense

| (A5) | $9,000 |

Bal. $9,000

Interest expense

| (A6) | $2,000 |

Bal. $2,000

Accumulated depreciation

| | (A2) | $1,250 |

Bal. $1,250

Exhibit 2.13 shows all T-accounts that arise from Chicago's transactions during January 2014. The journal entry DR or CR that gave rise to the amount posted in the T-account is indicated by a number to the left of each item. For example, in the Cash T-account, the (1) to the left of the DR of $1,000,000 indicates that this item arose from the $1,000,000 DR in Transaction 1. The (1) to the left of the $1,000,000 credit to common stock indicates that this item resulted from the balancing CR in Transaction 1. Posting *both* the DR and CR to the T-accounts reflected in the original entry maintains the equality of the basic accounting equation.

The adjusting entries are also posted to the T-accounts shown in those entries. For example, in Exhibit 2.13, the (A1) to the left of the $250 DR to the Insurance expense T-account tells us that this item arose from adjusting entry A1. (Notice the CR from that entry was posted as a credit to the Prepaid insurance account, with the A1 designation to the left of the posting.)

The accountant preparing the financial statements would use the balances in the revenue and expense accounts (highlighted in Exhibit 2.13) to prepare the January 2014 income statement. As shown in Exhibit 2.14, income for January (ignoring taxes) is $5,600. This amount represents the **net** increase in owners' equity for the month arising from operations. Consequently, the $5,600 appears again *in the balance sheet* as an owners' equity increase labeled Retained earnings (shown by the arrows). The asset, liability, and common stock T-accounts (entered in black) compose the other balance sheet accounts. (Notice that the credit balance in Accumulated depreciation is deducted from the Building account. That's why this is a contra-asset account.)

This is true because revenues increase owners' equity and expenses decrease owners' equity (review Transaction 4). So, the excess of revenues over expenses represents the *net* increase in owners' equity.

EXHIBIT 2.14   **Chicago Corporation**

Income Statement for the Month Ended January 31, 2014

Revenues

Sales revenue		$76,000
Consulting fees revenue		8,100
Total revenue		84,100

Expenses

Cost of goods sold	$ 50,000	
Salary and wages expense	16,000	
Heat, light, and power expense	9,000	
Depreciation expense	1,250	
Insurance expense	250	
Interest expense	2,000	
Total expense		78,500
Pretax income		$ 5,600 —————————————→

Statement of Financial Position, January 31, 2014

Assets			Liabilities and Equity	
Cash		$ 967,000	Liabilities	
Accounts receivable		48,100	Accounts payable	$ 69,000
Inventory		47,000	Fees received in advance	4,000
Prepaid insurance		5,750	Salary and wages payable	16,000
Building	$330,000		Accrued interest payable	2,000
Less: Accumulated			Loan payable	300,000
depreciation	(1,250)	328,750	Equity	
			Common stock	1,000,000
			Retained earnings	5,600 ←—
Total assets		$1,396,600	Total liabilities and equity	$1,396,600

Closing Entries

After the income statement for the month of January 2014 has been prepared, the revenue and expense accounts have served their purpose. So, balances in these accounts are "zeroed out" (or closed) to get them ready to reflect February transactions. To get the revenue and expense account balances to zero, a **closing journal entry** is made. All revenue account balances (which are credits) are *debited* (to get them to zero); all expense account balances (which are debits) are *credited* (to get them to zero). The difference between the closing entry debits and credits—in this case, a credit of $5,600—is made to Retained earnings. Here's the entry:

DR	Sales revenue	$76,000	
DR	Consulting fees revenue	8,100	
	CR Cost of goods sold		$50,000
	CR Salary and wages expense		16,000
	CR Heat, light, and power expense		9,000
	CR Depreciation expense		1,250
	CR Insurance expense		250
	CR Interest expense		2,000
	CR Retained earnings		5,600

After this entry has been posted to the accounts, all revenue and expense accounts will have zero balances. The accounts are now clear to receive February income statement transactions.

T-accounts Analysis as an Analytical Technique

Understanding the various events or transactions that affect individual account balances is critical to analyzing financial statements. Users of financial statements can't "see" the individual transactions that underlie various account balances and changes in account balances in comparative balance sheets. Nevertheless, it's often possible to "get behind the numbers" and deduce the aggregate amount of certain common events or transactions that have taken place during the reporting period. Armed with the following knowledge, one can reconstruct transactions that have occurred during a given reporting period.

- Start with beginning and ending balances in various balance sheet T-accounts (which are always available from comparative balance sheets).
- Know the major types of transactions or events that cause increases or decreases in individual T-accounts.
- Know how various accounts and financial statement items articulate with one another.

T-account analysis also can be used to gain insights into why accrual-basis earnings and cash-basis earnings (that is, cash flows from operations) differ.

Let's use a new example, Trevian Corporation, to illustrate how T-account analysis can be used to infer or deduce unknown or unobservable transactions. Consider the following analysis of Accounts receivable (net of the Allowance for doubtful accounts):

Accounts receivable—net

Beginning Balance	$1,000,000	Collections on account	(B)
Sales on account	(A)		
Ending Balance	$1,200,000		

> A comparative balance sheet reflects the asset, liability, and owners' equity account balances as of the end of the current reporting period (typically a quarter or year) and for one previous reporting period. Firms are required by the SEC to show two years of comparative balance sheet data and three years of comparative income statement data in annual 10-K reports.

Note that the major transaction that increases Accounts receivable (debits to this account) is sales on account, and the major transaction causing a decrease in Accounts receivable (credits to this account) is the collections on account. Assuming that these are the only events that affected Accounts receivable during the period, we can infer from the $200,000 increase in Trevian's Accounts receivable that sales on account exceeded collections on account during the period by $200,000. Can we go a step further and deduce the aggregate amounts of the debits (A) and credits (B) to this account? Yes, we can. However, to do so, we need to understand how parts of the income statement and balance sheet articulate with one another.

Recall that the first line of the income statements of most companies is Sales revenue. Typically, when one business sells a product or service to another company, the sale is a credit sale, meaning that the sale is "on account" and will be collected within 30, 60, or 90 days, depending on industry credit terms. Suppose Trevian's sales revenue was $3,500,000 and all sales were credit sales. We can re-create the following entry that summarizes the credit sales for the period and shows directly how income statement and balance sheet accounts reflect opposite sides of the same transaction and, thus, articulate with one another.

> Other transactions that can affect the Accounts receivable account include write-offs of specific accounts determined to be uncollectible, sales returns and allowances, and customers that take advantage of sales discounts by paying off their account balance within the discount period. Typically, these events have a minimal effect on the Accounts receivable balance for the period.

DR	Accounts receivable	$3,500,000	
	CR Sales revenue		$3,500,000

Knowing that all sales on account are reflected in an offsetting debit to Accounts receivable allows us to deduce the amount (A) = $3,500,000 in the Accounts receivable T-account just presented. Next, we can combine this information with the fact that the net increase in Accounts receivable was $200,000 to deduce that the collections on account during the period—unknown amount (B)—must have been $3,300,000. In other words,

Beginning accounts receivable balance	$1,000,000
+ Sales on account	3,500,000
− Collections on account	(3,300,000) ← (Plug to balance = B)
= Ending accounts receivable balance	$1,200,000

Analysis of the Accounts receivable T-account also provides information for understanding differences between accrual-basis income and cash from operations. The important insight from the analysis of the Accounts receivable T-account is that sales on account (reflected as revenue in accrual-basis income) are recorded on the debit side of this account while collections on account (reflected as revenue in cash-basis income measurement—that is, cash flow from operations) are recorded on the credit side of this account. Knowing that Trevian's Accounts receivable has increased by $200,000 tells us that accrual-basis revenue exceeded cash-basis revenue for the period by $200,000. Therefore, we would need to *subtract* this increase in Accounts receivable from the accrual-basis income number to convert accrual earnings to cash flow from operations. Conversely, if collections on account had exceeded sales on account by $200,000, this *decrease* in Accounts receivable would have to be *added* to accrual-basis net income to arrive at cash flow from operations.

Analogous reasoning can be used to gain insights into transactions that affect Accounts payable and the differences between accrual-basis expenses and cash-basis expenses. The following T-account summarizes the key events that cause changes in Trevian's Accounts payable for a period:

Accounts payable

		Beginning balance	$2,000,000
Payments on account	(B)		
		Purchases of inventory on account	(A)
		Ending balance	$1,500,000

Here we can see that payments on account exceeded purchases of inventory on account by $500,000, resulting in a decrease in the Accounts payable T-account for the period. We can deduce the amount of purchases on account by again referring to the income statement and recalling the components that constitute the cost of goods sold computation for a merchandising firm. For purposes of this illustration, assume that Trevian's cost of goods sold is $2,100,000, and the beginning and ending inventory from its comparative balance sheets are $1,500,000 and $1,800,000, respectively. Purchases of inventory for the period can be deduced as follows:

Beginning inventory	$1,500,000
+ Purchases of inventory	2,400,000 ← (Plug to balance = A)
− Ending inventory	(1,800,000)
= Cost of goods sold	$2,100,000

Assuming that all purchases of merchandise inventory were purchased on credit (generally the case for most businesses), we can determine through T-account analysis that payments on account must have been $2,900,000 determined as follows:

Beginning accounts payable balance	$2,000,000
+ Purchases on account (see above)	2,400,000
− Payments on account	(2,900,000) ← (Plug to balance = B)
= Ending accounts payable balance	$1,500,000

Changes in the Accounts payable and Inventory T-accounts help us understand the differences between accrual accounting's cost of goods sold expense and the cash-basis expense for inventory purchases. We'll use the preceding schedules for Trevian's cost of goods sold and accounts payable to demonstrate this point:

Accrual accounting cost of goods sold deduction included in determining income	$2,100,000
+ Inventory increase	300,000
= Total inventory purchases in 2014	2,400,000
+ Accounts payable decrease	500,000
= Cash basis expense for inventory purchases	$2,900,000

As shown, two adjustments are required to convert accrual-basis cost of goods sold ($2,100,000) to cash-basis expense for inventory purchases ($2,900,000). The first adjustment for the inventory increase is because beginning inventory is a *noncash addition* to cost of goods sold, while ending inventory is a *noncash deduction* in arriving at cost of goods sold (see cost of goods sold schedule above). Therefore, to remove the net noncash effects of beginning and ending inventory from cost of goods sold, we must add the increase in inventory. (If inventory had declined, we would subtract the decrease.) Making this adjustment to cost of goods sold gives us the total inventory purchased in 2014. (We've assumed that all inventory purchases are on account. Consequently, all inventory purchases during the year would be credited to Accounts payable.)

The second adjustment, for the decrease in Accounts payable, is made because Trevian's cash *payments* for inventory purchased on account exceeded new inventory *purchases* on account in the current period (see Accounts payable schedule on page 98). Thus, Trevian's cash payments for inventory actually exceeded the credit purchases of inventory that are included in the accrual-basis cost of goods sold number. Accordingly, to convert the accrual-basis cost of goods sold expense to a cash-basis expense, the decrease in Accounts payable must be added. (If Accounts payable had increased, this change would have been subtracted.)

Note that in the previous discussion, the adjustments made are to convert accrual-basis *expense* to cash-basis *expense*. To adjust accrual-basis *income* to obtain cash-basis *income* (cash flow from operations), the adjustment for the changes in Inventory and Accounts payable would be in the opposite direction. That is, the increase in Inventory and the decrease in Accounts payable would be *subtracted* from accrual income to obtain cash flow from operations. This is so because adjustments to expense have the opposite effect on income.

In general, analyses similar to that used for Accounts receivable and Accounts payable can be carried out for Accrued revenue, Accrued expense, Deferred (unearned) revenue, and Deferred (prepaid) expense accounts to deduce other differences between accrual-basis income and cash-basis income. Understanding that differences between accrual-basis and cash-basis income can be gleaned from most working capital accounts (that is, current asset and current liability accounts reported on the balance sheet) is one of the key lessons in financial statement analysis that we will return to repeatedly throughout later chapters in this book.

EXERCISES

E2-1

Determining accrual- and cash-basis revenue   **(LO 1)**

AICPA
ADAPTED

In November and December 2014, Gee Company, a newly organized magazine publisher, received $36,000 for 1,000 three-year subscriptions at $12 per year, starting with the January 2015 issue of the magazine.

Required:

How much should Gee report in its 2014 income statement for subscriptions revenue on an accrual basis? How much revenue would be reported in 2014 on a cash basis?

E2-2

Determining unearned subscription revenue   **(LO 2)**

AICPA
ADAPTED

Jerry's Jellies sells one- and two-year mail-order subscriptions for its jelly-of-the-month business. Subscriptions are collected in advance and credited to sales. An analysis of the recorded sales activity revealed the following:

	2013	2014
Sales	$520,000	$650,000
Less cancellations	(10,000)	(30,000)
Net sales	$510,000	$620,000
Subscription expirations		
2013	$230,000	
2014	195,000	$190,000
2015	85,000	250,000
2016		180,000
	$510,000	$620,000

Required:

What amount of unearned subscription revenue should Jerry's Jellies report on its December 31, 2014, balance sheet?

E2-3

Determining unearned revenue   **(LO 2)**

AICPA
ADAPTED

Regal Department Store sells gift certificates redeemable for store merchandise that expire one year after their issuance. Regal has the following information pertaining to its gift certificates sales and redemptions:

Unredeemed at 12/31/13	$ 75,000
2014 sales	250,000
2014 redemptions of prior year sales	25,000
2014 redemptions of current year sales	175,000

Regal's experience indicates that 10% of gift certificates sold will not be redeemed.

Required:

In its December 31, 2014, balance sheet, what amount should Regal report as unearned revenue?

E2-4

Determining when to recognize revenue   **(LO 2)**

AICPA
ADAPTED

On October 1, 2014. Bullseye Company sold 250,000 gallons of diesel fuel to Schmidt Co. at $3 per gallon. On November 8, 2014, 150,000 gallons were delivered; on December 27, 2014. another 50,000 gallons were delivered; and on January 15, 2015, the remaining 50,000 gallons were delivered. Payment terms are: 10% due on October 1, 2014, 50% due on first delivery; 20% due on the next delivery; and the remaining 20% due on final delivery.

Required:

What amount of revenue should Bullseye recognize from this sale during 2014 on an accrual basis?

In its accrual-basis income statement for the year ended December 31, 2014, Dart Company reported revenue of $1,750,000. Additional information follows:

Accounts receivable 12/31/13	$375,000
Uncollectible accounts written off during 2014	20,000
Accounts receivable 12/31/14	505,000

Required:

Under the cash basis of income determination, how much should Dart report as revenue for 2014?

E2-5

Converting from accrual- to cash-basis revenue **(LO 1)**

AICPA
ADAPTED

Joel Hamilton, D.D.S., keeps his accounting records on the cash basis. During 2014, he collected $200,000 in fees from his patients. At December 31, 2013, Dr. Hamilton had accounts receivable of $18,000. At December 31, 2014, he had accounts receivable of $25,000 and unearned fees of $8,000.

Required:

On the accrual basis, what was Dr. Hamilton's patient service revenue for 2014?

E2-6

Converting from cash- to accrual-basis revenue **(LO 1)**

AICPA
ADAPTED

Under Hart Company's accounting system, all insurance premiums paid are debited to Prepaid insurance. For interim financial reports, Hart makes monthly estimated charges to Insurance expense with credits to Prepaid insurance. Additional information for the year ended December 31, 2014, follows:

Prepaid insurance at December 31, 2013	$210,000
Charges to Insurance expense during 2014, including	
a year-end adjustment of $35,000	875,000
Unexpired insurance premiums at December 31, 2014	245,000

Required:

What was the total amount of insurance premiums Hart paid during 2014?

E2-7

Converting from accrual- to cash-basis expense **(LO 1, 3)**

AICPA
ADAPTED

Munnster Corporation's income statements for the years ended December 31, 2014, and 2013 included the following information before adjustments:

	2014	2013
Operating income	$ 900,000	$750,000
Gain on sale of division	350,000	—
	$1,250,000	$750,000
Provision for income taxes	(375,000)	(225,000)
Net income	$ 875,000	$525,000

On January 1, 2014, Munnster Corporation agreed to sell the assets and product line of one of its operating divisions for $2,000,000. The sale was consummated on December 31, 2014, and it resulted in a gain on disposition of $350,000. This division's pre-tax net losses were $505,000 in 2014 and $170,000 in 2013. The income tax rate for both years was 30%.

Required:

Starting with operating income (before tax), prepare revised comparative income statements for 2014 and 2013 showing appropriate details for gain (loss) from discontinued operations.

E2-8

Determining gain (loss) from discontinued operations **(LO 5, 6)**

AICPA
ADAPTED

E2-9

Determining loss on discontinued operations (LO 6)

On September 1, 2014, Revsine Co. approved a plan to dispose of a segment of its business. Revsine expected that the sale would occur on March 31, 2014, at an estimated gain of $350,000. The segment had actual and estimated operating profits (losses) as follows:

Realized loss from 8/1/14 to 8/31/14	$(300,000)
Realized loss from 9/1/14 to 12/31/14	(200,000)
Expected profit from 1/1/15 to 3/30/15	400,000

Assume that the marginal tax rate is 30%.

Required:

In its 2014 income statement, what should Revsine report as profit or loss from discontinued operations (net of tax effects)?

E2-10

Determining period versus product costs (LO 4)

Required:

Classify the following costs as period or product costs. If a product cost, indicate which will be matched with sales as part of cost of goods sold and which will be shown as a direct deduction from sales.

Depreciation on office building	Depreciation on factory
Insurance expense for factory building	Bonus to factory workers
Product liability insurance premium	Salary to marketing staff
Transportation charges for raw materials	Administrative expenses
Factory repairs and maintenance	Bad debt expense
Rent for inventory warehouse	Advertising expenses
Cost of raw materials	Research and development
Factory wages	Warranty expense
Salary to chief executive officer	Electricity for plant

E2-11

Converting from cash to accrual basis (LO 1, 3)

The following information is provided for Kelly Plumbing Supply.

Cash received from customers during December 2014	$387,000
Cash paid to suppliers for inventory during December 2014	131,000

Cash received from customers includes November accounts receivables of $139,000. Sales totaling $141,000 were made on account during December and are expected to be collected in January 2015. Cash paid to suppliers in December included payments of $19,000 for inventory purchased and used in November. All inventory purchased in December and $39,000 of inventory purchased in November was used in December.

Required:

What is gross profit for the month of December under accrual accounting?

E2-12

Determining effect of omitting year-end adjusting entries (LO 1, 2, 3, 11)

Hentzel Landscaping commenced its business on January 1, 2014.

1. During the first year of its operations, Hentzel purchased supplies in the amount of $12,000 (debited to Supplies inventory), and of this amount, $3,000 were unused as of December 31, 2014.

2. On March 1, 2014, Hentzel received $18,000 for landscaping services to be rendered for 18 months (beginning July 1, 2014). This amount was credited to Unearned landscaping revenue.

3. The company's gasoline bill for $2,500 for the month of December 2014 was not received until January 15, 2015.

4. The company had borrowed $50,000 from HomeTown Financing on April 1, 2014, at a 12% interest rate per annum. The principal, along with all the interest, is due on April 1, 2015.

5. On January 1, 2014, the company purchased 10 lawnmowers at $3,000 per unit. They are expected to last for three years with no salvage value.

On December 31, 2014, Hentzel did not record any adjusting entries with respect to these transactions.

Required:
Using the following table format, show the effect of the *omission* of each year-end adjusting entry on the following. (Indicate both the amount and the direction of the effect.) Use OS for overstated, US for understated, and NE for no effect.

Item Number	Assets	Liabilities	Net Income
Direction of effect			
Dollar amount of effect			

Presented below is a combined single-step income and retained earnings statement for Hardrock Mining Co. for 2014.

Statement of Income and Retained Earnings for the Year Ended December 31, 2014

E2-13

Preparing a multiple-step income statement
(LO 5, 6)

($ in 000)	
Net sales	$5,281,954
Costs and expenses	
Cost of products sold	4,765,505
Marketing, administrative, and other expenses	193,147
Interest expense	17,143
Other, net	54,529
Total expenses before taxes	5,030,324
Earnings before income taxes	251,630
Provision for income taxes	(75,489)
Net income	176,141
Retained earnings at 1/1/14	3,046,660
Dividends on common stock	(100,000)
Retained earnings at 12/31/14	$3,122,801

Additional facts gleaned from notes to Hardrock's financial statement follow (amounts in $000):

a. Other, net for 2014 included a corporate restructuring charge of $8,777 and a gain of $12,000 resulting from compensation paid by the U.S. government for company property taken under the right of eminent domain. The remainder of the category is composed of investment losses.

b. Marketing, administrative, and other expenses for 2014 included a loss on currency translation of $55.

c. All of these transactions were subject to Hardrock's income tax rate of 30%.

d. Hardrock disclosed earnings per share data only in the notes to the financial statements. The company had 10,000,000 shares of common stock outstanding throughout 2014.

Required:
Recast this single-step combined income statement and retained earnings statement as a multiple-step income statement in appropriate form. Include appropriate per share amounts.

<table>
<tr><td>

E2-14

Preparing an income statement with irregular items **(LO 5, 6)**

</td><td>

KEW Corp. has 500,000 shares of common stock outstanding. In 2014, KEW reports income from continuing operations before taxes of $4,350,000. Additional transactions from 2014—and not considered in the $4,350,000—are as follows:

1. The company reviewed its notes receivable and discovered that a note carried at $16,000 was 18 months past due. The note was not likely to be collected.
2. KEW sold machinery for $85,000 that originally cost $300,000. Accumulated depreciation at the time of the sale amounted to $225,000. KEW sells unneeded machinery occasionally when retooling one of its production processes.
3. KEW sold a division during 2014 resulting in a pre-tax loss of $890,000. The operating loss incurred by the discontinued division prior to its sale was $650,000; the loss from its disposal was $240,000. This transaction meets the criteria for discontinued operations.
4. KEW lost $395,000 (pre-tax) when a plant it operated in a third-world country was expropriated following a revolution. There was no prior history of the government expropriating assets of companies operating in that country.

Required:

Based on this information, prepare an income statement for the year ended December 31, 2014, starting with income from continuing operations before income taxes; include proper earnings per share disclosures. KEW's total effective tax rate on all items was 35%.

</td></tr>
<tr><td>

E2-15

Change in inventory methods **(LO 7)**

</td><td>

Jones Corporation switched from the LIFO method of costing inventories to the FIFO method at the beginning of 2014. The LIFO inventory at the end of 2013 would have been $80,000 higher using FIFO. Reported retained earnings at the end of 2013 were $1,750,000. Jones's tax rate is 30%.

Required:

1. Calculate the balance in retained earnings at the time of the change (beginning of 2014) as it would have been reported had FIFO been previously used.
2. Prepare the journal entry to record the change in accounting principle at the beginning of 2014.

</td></tr>
<tr><td>

E2-16

Income statement presentation **(LO 5, 6, 7)**

</td><td>

Krewatch, Inc., is a vertically integrated manufacturer and retailer of golf clubs and accessories (gloves, shoes, bags, etc.). Krewatch maintains separate financial reporting systems for each of its facilities. The company experienced the following events in 2014:

1. After several years of production problems at the accessories manufacturing plant, Krewatch sold the plant to an investor group headed by a former manager at the plant.
2. Krewatch incurred restructuring costs of $12,562,990 when it eliminated a layer of middle management.
3. Krewatch extinguished $200 million in 30-year bonds issued 18 years ago. These bonds were the only ones issued in the company's history. Krewatch recognized a gain on this transaction.
4. Krewatch changed its method of accounting for inventory from FIFO to the average cost method. Sufficient information was available to determine the effect of this change on prior years' earnings numbers.
5. Due to technological advances in golf club manufacturing, management determined that production equipment would need to be upgraded more frequently than in the past. Consequently, the useful lives of equipment for depreciation purposes were reduced.
6. The company wrote off inventory that was not salable.
7. Equipment was sold at a loss.

</td></tr>
</table>

Required:

For each event, (1) identify the appropriate reporting treatment from the following list (consider each event to be material), and (2) indicate whether it would be included in income from continuing operations, would appear on the income statement below that subtotal, or would require retrospective application.

a. Change in accounting estimate.

b. Change in accounting principle.

c. Discontinued operation.

d. Special or unusual item.

e. Extraordinary item.

JDW Corporation reported the following for 2014: net sales $2,929,500; cost of goods sold $1,786,995; selling and administrative expenses $585,900; an unrealized holding loss on available-for-sale securities $22,000; a gain from foreign currency translation $26,250 (no tax effect); and an unrealized loss from pension adjustment $7,000. JDW's tax rate was 30%.

Required:

Prepare a multiple-step income statement and a statement of comprehensive income using the two-statement format. Ignore earnings per share.

E2-17

Preparing comprehensive income statement
(LO 5, 9)

Wellington International Airport Limited is a for-profit company domiciled in New Zealand that manages the Wellington Airport and files its financial statements in compliance with IFRS. For the period ending September 30, 2012, Wellington reported the following data:

E2-18

Wellington International Airport Limited—Reporting of asset revaluations in OCI **(LO 10)**

WELLINGTON INTERNATIONAL AIRPORT LIMITED
STATEMENT OF COMPREHENSIVE INCOME
FOR THE PERIOD ENDED 30 SEPTEMBER 2012

($ in 000)	6 months 30 Sep 2012 Unaudited	Consolidated 6 months 30 Sep 2011 Unaudited	12 months 31 Mar 2012 Unaudited
Net (loss)/surplus for the period	$(5,571)	$(6,650)	$ 8,981
Other comprehensive income			
Revaluation of land	—	—	74,270
Revaluation of property, plant, and equipment	—	—	9,338
Amortisation of fair value of ineffective hedges transferred to profit or loss	626	2,736	4,380
Income tax relating to components of other comprehensive income	(175)	(766)	(3,840)
Other comprehensive income, net of tax	451	1,970	84,148
Total comprehensive income	$(5,120)	$(4,680)	$93,129

Required:

1. Why do you think the revaluations of both land and property, plant, and equipment are reported in other comprehensive income instead of in net income?

2. Over the 12 months ending March 31, 2012, did the values of land and property, plant, and equipment go up or down?

3. If Wellington International Airport Limited were located in the United States or if the company chose to file its financial reports under U.S. GAAP, how much revaluation would the company report for both land and property, plant, and equipment?

E2-19 Calculating EPS **(LO 8)**	An analyst gathered the following information about a company whose fiscal year-end is December 31: • Net income for the year was $10.5 million. • Preferred stock dividends for $2 million were declared and paid for the year. • Common stock dividends of $3.5 million were paid for the year. • There were 20 million shares of common stock outstanding on January 1, 2014. • The company issued 6 million new shares of common stock on April 1, 2014. • The capital structure does not include any potentially dilutive convertible securities, options, warrants, or other contingent securities. **Required:** What would be the company's basic earnings per share for 2014?

PROBLEMS / DISCUSSION QUESTIONS

P2-1 Determining royalty revenue **(LO 2)** **AICPA** ADAPTED	Foremost Company owns a royalty interest in an oil well. The contract stipulates that Foremost will receive royalty payments semiannually on January 31 and July 31. The January 31 payment will be for 30% of the oil sold to jobbers between the previous June 1 and November 30, and the July 31 payment will be for oil sold between the previous December 1 and May 31. Royalty receipts for 2014 amounted to $150,000 and $240,000 on January 31 and July 31, respectively. On December 31, 2013, accrued royalty revenue receivable amounted to $40,000. Production reports show the following oil sales:

June 1, 2013–November 30, 2013	$500,000
December 1, 2013–May 31, 2014	800,000
June 1, 2014–November 30, 2014	600,000
December 1, 2014–December 31, 2014	100,000

Required:
What amount should Foremost report as royalty revenue for 2014?

P2-2 Preparing journal entries and statement **(LO 3, 11)**	a. On January 1, 2014, Frances Corporation started doing business and the owners contributed $200,000 capital in cash. b. The company paid $24,000 to cover the rent for the office space for the 24-month period from January 1, 2014, to December 31, 2015. c. On March 1, 2014, MSK Inc. entered into a consulting contract under which Frances Corporation promised to provide consulting to MSK Inc. for the 10-month period from March 1, 2014, to December 31, 2014. In return, MSK promised to pay a monthly consulting fee of $15,000, which was to be paid in January 2015. Frances fulfilled its contractual obligation during 2014. d. On July 1, 2014, Frances purchased office equipment for $100,000 cash. The equipment has an estimated useful life of five years and no salvage value. The equipment was immediately placed into use. Frances uses the straight-line method of depreciation. It records depreciation expense in proportion to the number of months' usage. e. Through November 30, 2014, the company had paid $66,000 to its employees for 11 months of salaries. Accrued salaries on December 31, 2014, were $6,000. f. On December 31, 2014, Norbert Corporation advanced $20,000 to Frances Corporation for consulting services to be provided during 2015.

Required:

1. Provide journal entries for each of these transactions.

2. Provide adjusting entries at the end of the year.

3. Prepare an income statement for the year ended December 31, 2014.

4. Prepare a balance sheet as of December 31, 2014.

The following information pertains to Stein Flowers, a calendar-year sole proprietorship, which maintained its books on the cash basis during the year.

Unadjusted Trial Balance as of December 31, 2014

P 2-3

Converting accounting records from cash basis to accrual basis   (LO 1, 11)

AICPA
ADAPTED

e**X**cel

mhhe.com/revsine6e

	DR	CR
Cash	$ 23,200	
Accounts receivable 12/31/13	16,200	
Inventory 12/31/13	58,000	
Furniture and fixtures	128,500	
Land improvements	50,000	
Accumulated depreciation 12/31/13		$ 32,400
Accounts payable 12/31/13		21,000
Stein, drawings		–0–
Stein, capital 12/31/13		124,900
Sales		660,000
Purchases	307,300	
Salaries	174,000	
Payroll taxes	12,400	
Insurance	9,000	
Rent	34,200	
Utilities	12,500	
Living expenses	13,000	
	$838,300	$838,300

The Stein, drawings account is used to record any distributions to Mark Stein. The Stein capital account is used to record any capital contributions that Stein makes to the business and any profits or losses retained in the business.

Stein has developed plans to expand into the wholesale flower market and is in the process of negotiating a bank loan to finance the expansion. The bank is requesting 2014 financial statements prepared on the accrual basis of accounting from Stein. During the course of a review engagement, Sue Crook, Stein's accountant, obtained the following additional information:

1. Amounts due from customers totaled $27,500 at December 31, 2014.

2. An analysis of the receivables revealed that an allowance for uncollectible accounts of $2,800 should be provided.

3. Unpaid invoices for flower purchases totaled $33,500 and $21,000 at December 31, 2014, and December 31, 2013, respectively.

4. A physical count of the goods at December 31, 2014, determined that the inventory totaled $71,900. The inventory was priced at cost, which approximates market value.

5. On May 1, 2014, Stein paid $9,000 to renew its comprehensive insurance coverage for one year. The premium on the previous policy, which expired on April 30, 2014, was $8,700.

6. On January 2, 2014, Stein entered into a 25-year operating lease for the vacant lot adjacent to his retail store, which was to be used as a parking lot. As agreed to in the lease, Stein paved and fenced in the lot at a cost of $50,000. The improvements were completed on April 1, 2014, and have an estimated useful life of 20 years. No provision for depreciation or amortization has been recorded. Depreciation on furniture and fixtures was $13,000 for 2014.

7. Accrued expenses at December 31, 2013 and 2014, follow:

	2013	2014
Utilities	$ 900	$1,500
Payroll taxes	1,100	1,600
	$2,000	$3,100

8. Stein was notified late in the year of a lawsuit filed against his business for an injury to a customer. His attorney believes that an unfavorable outcome is probable and that a reasonable estimate of the settlement exclusive of amounts covered by insurance is $40,000.

9. The Salaries account includes $5,000 per month paid to the proprietor. He also receives $250 per week for living expenses. These amounts should have been charged to Stein's drawing account.

Required:

1. Determine the adjustments required to convert Stein Flowers' unadjusted trial balance to the correct accrual basis of accounting for the year ended December 31, 2014. Prepare formal journal entries to support your adjustments.

2. Write a brief memo to Stein explaining why the bank would require financial statements prepared on the accrual basis instead of the cash basis.

P2-4

Making adjusting entries and statement preparation (LO 11)

mhhe.com/revsine6e

The following is the preclosing trial balance of Ralph Retailers, Inc.:

Preclosing Trial Balance as of December 31, 2014

	DR	CR
Cash	$ 38,700	
Accounts receivable	71,600	
Prepaid rent	12,000	
Inventory	125,000	
Equipment	50,000	
Building	125,000	
Allowance for doubtful accounts		$ 3,000
Accumulated depreciation—equipment		40,000
Accumulated depreciation—building		12,000
Advance from customers		18,000
Accounts payable		26,000
Salaries payable		5,500
Capital stock		70,000
Retained earnings 1/1/14		264,850
Sales revenue		425,000
Cost of goods sold	275,250	
Salaries expense	60,000	
Bad debt expense	18,300	
Rent expense	40,000	
Insurance expense	15,000	
Depreciation expense—building	6,000	
Depreciation expense—equipment	3,000	
Dividends	23,500	
Totals	$864,350	$864,350

The following additional information is provided:

a. The company paid a salary advance of $5,000 to one of its employees, a total that was debited to the Salaries expense account. This was an advance against the employee's salary for the year 2015.

b. On January 1, 2014, the company paid an insurance premium of $15,000, which was debited to the Insurance expense account. The premium provided insurance coverage for 18 months beginning on January 1, 2014.

c. The company decided to revise its estimate of bad debts expense by calculating it at 5% of its sales revenue.

d. On January 1, 2015, the company's board of directors declared an additional dividend of $20,000 for the year 2014.

Required:

1. Prepare the necessary adjusting entries for the year ended December 31, 2014.

2. Prepare an income statement for the year ended December 31, 2014.

3. Prepare a balance sheet as of December 31, 2014.

Required:

Following is selected information from the balance sheet for Flaps Inc. Solve for the missing amounts for each of the five years.

P2-5

Understanding the accounting equation **(LO 11)**

	Year				
	2013	**2014**	**2015**	**2016**	**2017**
Total liabilities and stockholders' equity	$13,765	F	K	P	U
Current liabilities	A	$3,420	$3,467	$3,517	V
Common stock	138	139	L	142	$ 144
Contributed capital	2,340	G	2,387	2,422	W
Noncurrent assets	8,667	8,721	M	8,968	X
Retained earnings	2,795	2,813	2,851	Q	Y
Total assets	B	H	14,040	R	14,351
Noncurrent liabilities	5,231	I	5,335	S	5,454
Additional paid-in capital	C	2,216	2,247	T	2,296
Current assets	D	J	5,200	5,275	5,315
Total liabilities	8,630	8,683	N	8,929	Z
Total stockholders' equity	E	5,168	O	5,314	5,354

The following is selected information from Bob Touret, Inc.'s financial statements. Solve for the missing amounts for each of the five years. You may have to use some numbers from the year before or the year after to solve for certain current year numbers. (NA = not available.)

P2-6

Understanding the accounting equation **(LO 11)**

	Year				
	2013	**2014**	**2015**	**2016**	**2017**
Current assets (CA)	A	$2,736	L	$2,778	X
Noncurrent assets	$4,002	F	$3,900	R	$4,805
Total assets	6,748	G	M	7,008	Y
Current liabilities (CL)	1,536	H	N	S	1,463
Noncurrent liabilities	B	2,345	O	2,206	2,252
Contributed capital	1,250	I	P	1,300	Z
Retained earnings (ending)	1,750	J	1,756	T	1,924
Total stockholders' equity	C	3,091	3,056	U	AA
Total liabilities and stockholders' equity	D	K	6,916	7,008	BB
Working capital (CA − CL)	E	935	1,331	V	771
Net income (loss)	NA	105	Q	55	135
Dividends	NA	14	9	W	12

P 2 - 7

Converting from cash to accrual basis   (LO 1)

During August 2014, Packer Manufacturing had the following cash receipts and disbursements:

Cash received from customers	$319,000
Cash received from selling equipment	11,200
Cash paid for salaries	47,000
Cash paid to suppliers for inventory purchases	130,000

In addition, the following balance sheet account balances were shown on Packer's books:

	July 31	August 31
Accounts receivable	$128,000	$135,000
Inventory	33,000	25,000
Accounts payable	21,000	25,000
Salaries payable	8,000	5,000

Assume all sales and purchases are on account.

Required:

1. Determine sales for August 2014.

2. Determine salary expense for August 2014.

3. Determine cost of goods sold for August 2014.

P 2 - 8

Journal entries and statement preparation   (LO 11)

Bob's Chocolate Chips and More, a bakery specializing in gourmet pizza and chocolate chip cookies, started business October 1, 2014. The following transactions occurred during the month.

a. Common stock of $90,000 was sold at par to start the business.

b. Equipment consisting of mixers and ovens was acquired October 1 for $30,000 cash. The equipment is expected to last five years and can be sold at that time for $5,000. Management uses the straight-line method to calculate depreciation expense.

c. Ingredients costing $15,000 were purchased on account during the month and all but $5,000 was paid for by the end of the month.

d. Rent is $500 a month. October, November, and December's rent was paid October 5.

e. A payment of $800 for utilities was made during the month.

f. Sixty percent of the ingredients purchased in part c were prepared and sold for $35,000 on account; $26,000 was collected on accounts receivable during the month.

g. Wages of $5,200 were paid during the month. Moreover, wages for the last three days of the month amounted to $400 and will be paid during the first week of November.

h. Borrowed $12,000 from the bank for additional working capital requirements, and $3,000 was repaid by month-end. Interest on the unpaid loan balance amounted to $450 at the end of October and was paid on November 5.

Required:

Prepare the required journal entries and adjusting entries as well as an income statement and a balance sheet for Bob's Chocolate Chips and More as of October 31, 2014. (*Hint:* You may want to consider using T-accounts to classify and accumulate the preceding transactions before preparing the statements.)

P 2 - 9

Determining missing amounts on income statement (LO 5, 6)

The following information was taken from the income statement of AJAX Corporation for the year ended December 31, 2014.

AJAX is a holding company with subsidiaries providing research, development, manufacturing, and marketing of brand name household products.

	($ in 000)
Amortization of intangible assets	$?
Cost of goods sold	?
Extraordinary gain on extinguishment of debt, net of taxes	2,242
General and administrative expenses	176,868
Gross profit	482,342
Net income	149,284
Income before extraordinary item	?
Income from continuing operations	?
Income from continuing operations before income taxes	69,328
Income from discontinued operations, net of taxes	97,808
Interest expense	?
Interest income	23,944
Net revenues	?
Operating income	?
Other income, net	41,660
Provision for income taxes	20,094
Research and development	97,230
Restructuring costs and asset write-downs	24,444
Selling expenses	159,016
Gross profit as percent of sales	37.81%
Total operating expenses	$464,904

Required:

1. Recast AJAX's income statement and present it in good form. Fill in the missing data.

2. Consider the item called Restructuring costs and asset write-downs. What impact did this charge have on AJAX's cash flows?

3. AJAX's income statements over the last three years report research and development expenses averaging $51.3 million per year. AJAX incurred these expenses to enhance current products and to develop new products in the hope of generating higher future sales. GAAP requires that all such costs be expensed in the year incurred. Consider the following statement:

   > Research and development expenditures are really assets because they will benefit the future operations of the firm (that is, lead to higher sales).

   If you agree, suggest an alternative way to account for research and development expenditures rather than expensing them in the year incurred. If you disagree, what are your reasons?

4. Assume that you are a financial analyst for AJAX. Your boss has asked you to project next year's net earnings. What earnings number from the information provided here would you use as the basis for your projection? Why?

The following condensed statement of income of Helen Corporation, a diversified company, is presented for the two years ended December 31, 2014 and 2013:

P2-10

Determining income from continuing operations and gain (loss) from discontinued operations   **(LO 5, 6)**

AICPA
ADAPTED

	2014	2013
Net sales	$10,000,000	$9,600,000
Cost of sales	(6,200,000)	(6,000,000)
Gross profit	3,800,000	3,600,000
Operating expenses	(2,200,000)	(2,400,000)
Operating income	1,600,000	1,200,000
Gain on sale of division	900,000	—
Net income before taxes	2,500,000	1,200,000
Provision for income taxes	(1,250,000)	(600,000)
Net income	$ 1,250,000	$ 600,000

On January 1, 2014, Helen entered into an agreement to sell for $3,200,000 the assets and product line of one of its separate operating divisions. The sale was consummated on December 31, 2014, and resulted in a gain on disposition of $900,000. This division's contribution to Helen's reported income before taxes for each year was as follows:

2014	$640,000 loss
2013	$500,000 loss

Assume an income tax rate of 50%.

Required:

1. In preparing a revised comparative statement of income, Helen should report income from continuing operations after income taxes for 2014 and 2013, respectively, amounting to how much?

2. Starting with the revised income from continuing operations numbers you obtained in requirement 1, prepare the revised comparative income statements for 2014 and 2013 showing appropriate details for gain (loss) from discontinued operations.

P2-11

Preparing an income statement with irregular items **(LO 5, 6)**

Jordan Wing, Inc., a sporting goods retailer, began operations on January 2, 2012. It reported net income of $3,091,660 during 2014. Additional information about transactions occurring in 2014 follows:

1. Jordan Wing realized $175,000 from settling a trademark infringement lawsuit.

2. The corporation disposed of its catalog sales component at a pre-tax loss of $345,000. This transaction meets the criteria for discontinued operations.

3. Sale of 10,000 shares of Xerox stock held as a short-term investment resulted in a gain of $23,450.

4. The firm changed its method of depreciating fixed assets from the straight-line method to the declining balance method, which was used to determine income in 2014.

5. Jordan Wing suffered a $23,000 impairment loss in 2013, which it failed to record.

6. The firm experienced an (extraordinary) uninsured tornado pre-tax loss in the amount of $83,500.

Required:

Prepare an income statement for the year ended December 31, 2014, starting with income from continuing operations before taxes; include proper earnings per share disclosures. Jordan Wing had 150,000 common shares outstanding for the year. Assume a 35% tax rate on all items.

P2-12

Discontinued operations components held for sale **(LO 5, 6, 8)**

For 2014, Silvertip Construction, Inc., reported income from continuing operations (after tax) of $1,650,000 before considering the following information. On November 15, 2014, the company adopted a plan to dispose of a component of the business. This component qualifies for discontinued operations treatment. During 2014, the component had pre-tax operating losses of $95,000. The component's assets have a book value of $760,000 on December 31, 2014. A recent market value analysis of these assets placed their estimated selling price at $735,000, less a 6% brokerage commission. Management appropriately determines that these assets are impaired and expects to find a buyer for the component and complete the sale early in 2015.

Required:

Prepare a partial income statement for Silvertip including EPS disclosures for the year ended December 31, 2014. Begin at income from continuing operations. Assume a 35% income tax rate and 1,000,000 shares of outstanding common stock.

The following information was taken from the records of Liz's Theatrical Supplies for 2014. In addition to selling theatrical supplies, Liz owned and operated a theater until October 15, 2014, when Liz sold this component of the business. All listed amounts are pre-tax, but are subject to a 38% income tax rate.

P2-13

Preparing comprehensive income under single-step format **(LO 9)**

Cost of goods sold	$490,823
Extraordinary loss	50,000
Income from discontinued operations	70,000
Interest income	4,650
Loss from disposal of discontinued component	95,000
Loss on write-off of obsolete inventory	23,500
Net sales	791,650
Rent revenue	16,000
Selling and administrative expenses	158,330
Unrealized holding loss on available-for-sale securities	15,000

Required:

Prepare a single-step income statement and statement of comprehensive income for 2014 using a single-statement format.

The income statement of Smithfield Beverage, Inc., that follows does not include any required reporting related to a $62,000 pre-tax gain that was realized in 2014 when Smithfield repurchased and retired $1 million of its 8% term bonds (scheduled to mature in 2018). Smithfield's income tax rate is 35%; 250,000 shares of common stock were outstanding during 2014.

P2-14

Extinguishing debt early **(LO 6)**

Income Statement for the Year Ended December 31, 2014

Sales	$3,512,000
Cost of goods sold	(2,177,440)
Gross profit	1,334,560
Selling and administrative expenses	(772,640)
Income from operations, before income taxes	561,920
Income taxes	(196,672)
Net income	$ 365,248
Earnings per share	$ 1.46

Required:

Discuss any modifications to Smithfield's income statement necessitated by this gain under each of the following independent assumptions (do not produce "corrected" income statements):

1. Such early debt retirements are part of Smithfield's risk management strategy.

2. Smithfield has been in business for 65 years. The company occasionally issues term bonds, but has not previously retired bonds prior to normal maturity.

Roger's Plumbing, Inc., operates two segments: (1) a division that installs residential and commercial plumbing in buildings being constructed and (2) a service division that has both residential and commercial components. A recent construction boom has kept Roger's so busy that it has been unable to handle all of the service work on a timely basis. Growing tired of phone messages from irritated customers who wanted their leak fixed yesterday (and unable to hire additional qualified employees), management decides in October to sell the service business, begins to advertise its availability, and has the division's assets appraised. Ted Roger, CEO, believes the service business will be easier to sell if it is split into residential and commercial components. The appraisal results in the following information. Goodwill is the appraiser's estimate of the value of the company's customer base as Roger's Plumbing plans to forward all service calls for a period of three years to whoever buys each component of the

P2-15

Reporting discontinued operations **(LO 5, 6)**

service business. Roger's Plumbing has income before taxes of $2,756,000 for 2014 (the year management decides to sell the service division). This amount includes $185,400 residential service income and $215,000 commercial service income. Roger's Plumbing is subject to an income tax rate of 35%.

Assets	Book Value	Fair Value
Residential service component:		
Service vehicles	$ 40,000	$ 45,000
Repair parts inventory	25,000	22,000
Tool and equipment	9,500	8,000
Goodwill	—	20,000
Total—Residential service	$ 74,500	$ 95,000
Commercial service component:		
Service vehicles	55,000	53,500
Repair parts inventory	21,000	21,000
Tool and equipment	14,500	12,000
Goodwill	—	25,000
Total—Commercial service	$ 90,500	$111,500
Total for service division	$165,000	$206,500

Required:

Assume that Roger's Plumbing sells the residential service component on December 5, 2014, for $99,500 (less disposal costs of $2,000). By year-end, the company has received three firm offers for the commercial service component that ranged from $82,500 to $87,000. Management is still actively seeking a better offer, but if none is obtained plans to sell the component to the highest bidder before the end of January 2015. The company's auditors tell management that the consistency of the bids to date indicates an error in the appraisal and that an impairment loss should be recognized. Assume estimated costs of $2,500 to sell the commercial service component. Prepare an income statement for Roger's Plumbing, Inc. (for 2014), beginning with income from continuing operations. For purposes of working this problem, report the various components of the gains/losses for discontinued operations separately for actual sales versus assets held for sale. Ignore per share disclosures.

P2-16

Reporting a change in accounting principle   **(LO 7)**

Barden, Inc., operates a retail chain that specializes in baby clothes and accessories that are made to its specifications by a number of overseas manufacturers. Barden began operations in 2005 and has always employed the FIFO method to value its inventory. Since 2005, prices have generally declined as a result of intense competition among Barden's suppliers. In 2013, however, prices began to rise significantly as these suppliers succumbed to international pressure and addressed sweatshop conditions in their factories. The improved working conditions and benefits led to increased costs that are being passed on to Barden. In turn, Barden's management believes that FIFO no longer is the best method to value its inventories and thus switched to LIFO on January 1, 2014. This accounting change was justified because of LIFO's better matching of current costs with current revenues. Barden judges it impractical to apply the LIFO method on a retrospective basis because the company never maintained records on a LIFO basis. As a result of this change, ending inventory was reported at $275,000 instead of its $345,000 FIFO value. Barden reported 2014 net income of $825,000; the company's income tax rate is 35%. Barden has 10,000 shares of stock outstanding.

Required:

1. How should Barden's 2014 comparative financial statements reflect this change in accounting principle?
2. Prepare whatever disclosure is required under current GAAP as a result of this change.

During the fourth quarter of 2014, ABBA Fabrics, Inc., elected to change its method of valuing inventory to the weighted average cost ("WAC") method, whereas in all prior years inventory was valued using the last-in, first-out (LIFO) method. The company determined that the WAC method of accounting for inventory is preferable as the method better reflects ABBA's inventory at current costs and enhances the comparability of its financial statements by changing to the predominant method utilized in its industry. Condensed financial statements for 2014 (using WAC) and 2013 (as originally reported) appear below. Inventory as originally reported at December 31, 2013 ($77,907), and December 31, 2012 ($127,574), increases by $36,382 and $37,432 respectively under WAC.

P2-17

Disclosures for change in accounting principle **(LO 7)**

ABBA Fabrics, Inc., Balance Sheets December 31, (in thousands)

	2014 (Under WAC)	2013 (Under LIFO)
Current assets:		
Cash and cash equivalents	$ 2,338	$ 2,280
Receivables, less allowance for doubtful accounts	3,380	4,453
Inventories, net	104,156	77,907
Other current assets	1,735	9,866
Total current assets	111,609	94,506
Long-term assets	53,065	56,438
Total assets	164,674	150,944
Total liabilities	117,325	123,888
Common stock	88,348	75,650
Retained earnings	124,907	100,953
Treasury stock	(153,684)	(153,622)
Other comprehensive income	(12,222)	4,075
Total liabilities and shareholders' equity	$ 164,674	$ 150,944

ABBE Fabrics, Inc., Statements of Operations
Years Ended December 31, (in thousands)

	2014 (Under WAC)	2013 (Under LIFO)
Sales	$ 276,381	$ 276,247
Cost of goods sold	156,802	157,617
Gross profit	119,579	118,630
Selling, general, and administrative expenses	112,106	117,815
Depreciation and amortization	4,409	3,815
Operating income (loss)	$ 3,064	$ (3,000)

Required:

1. Restate the 2013 financial statements as they should appear for comparative purposes in the 2014 annual report.
2. Draft the disclosures required by current GAAP related to this restatement.

Other comprehensive income (OCI) is an account that recognizes items that accounting standard-setters believe should not be accrued in Net income. Some examples of items that are typically reported in OCI include:

P2-18

Isolating OCI components from normal income components **(LO 9, 10)**

- Changes in the value of equity investments in other companies that are held for intermediate periods of time (under both U.S. GAAP and IFRS).
- Changes in the value of property, plant, and equipment holdings if the company chooses to have regular appraisals (under IFRS only).
- Changes in pension obligation estimates made by an actuary (under both U.S. GAAP and IFRS).

Assume you are analyzing an automobile dealer business that has car sales lots located in multiple geographic locations. Revenue earned on car sales for the year ending December 31, 2014, is $1,200,000. Cost of automobiles sold is $750,000. Sales support and administrative expense for the year is $150,000. Also assume the company holds a temporary investment in the shares of Apple Inc. that it plans to sell in six months to pay for a new car sales lot. The value of the Apple Inc. investment increased by $50,000 during 2014. Assume that the appraised value of the land on which all the car dealerships are located increased by $300,000 during 2014. Finally, assume that an actuary has determined that the company's retired employees will likely live longer, thereby increasing the company's estimated pension liability (a loss) by $100,000.

Required:

1. How much is income from operations during 2014?

2. How much would the company report for income if it were to include the change in the value of the Apple Inc. investment (instead of reporting this value in OCI)?

3. How much would the company report for income if it were to include the change in the appraised value of the land (instead of reporting this value in OCI)?

4. How much would the company report for income if it were to include the change in actuarial estimates regarding the pension obligation (instead of reporting this value in OCI)?

5. How much would the company report for income if it were to include all of the value changes?

6. Which of the income computations above best represent the fundamental operational performance of the automobile sales business?

7. Why do you think standards-setters require some items to be included in OCI instead of in Net income?

P2-19

Change in accounting policy   **(LO 7)**

In its 2012 annual report, UPS, a global package delivery company, reported the following performance data:

Financial Highlights

	2012	2011	2010
Revenue	$54,127	$53,105	$49,545
Operating expenses	52,784	47,025	43,904
Net income	807	3,804	3,338

As an analyst, you are trying to determine whether the significant drop in Net income between the end of 2011 and the end of 2012 is due to fundamental changes in business operations or the business environment.

At the beginning of 2012, UPS reported it was changing its accounting relating to its employee pension plans.

Historically, UPS would:

- Accrue losses that relate to underperforming pension plan investments into Accumulated other comprehensive income (AOCI).
- When accrued losses in AOCI became too high, UPS would spread a portion of these losses into net income over a period of several years.

Under the new policy, UPS would:

- Accrue losses that relate to underperforming pension plan investments into Accumulated other comprehensive income (AOCI).
- When accrued losses in AOCI become too high, UPS would recognize a portion of these losses all in the current period.

Required:

1. What are the implications of UPS' change in accounting policy on its reported Net income?

2. Why might an analyst care about this change in accounting policy if she is trying to assess potential fundamental changes in business operations or the business environment?

CASES

C2-1

Conducting financial reporting research: Discontinued operations **(LO 6)**

Corrpro Companies, Inc., founded in 1984, provides corrosion control–related services, systems, equipment, and materials to the infrastructure, environmental, and energy markets. Corrpro's products and services include (a) corrosion control engineering services, systems, and equipment, (b) coatings services, and (c) pipeline integrity and risk assessment services. The following information was abridged from the company's March 31, Year 3, Form 10-K.

Assets and Liabilities Held for Sale

In July Year 2, the Company's Board of Directors approved a formal business restructuring plan. The multi-year plan includes a series of initiatives to improve operating income and reduce debt. The Company intends to sell non-core business units and use the proceeds to reduce debt. The Company has engaged outside professionals to assist in the disposition of the domestic and international non-core business units. Prior to the quarter ended September 30, Year 2, the Company's non-core domestic and international units were reported as the Other Operations and International Operations reporting segments. Effective for the quarter ended September 30, Year 2, the Other Operations and the International Operations reporting segments have been eliminated and the non-core domestic and international units are reported as Discontinued operations. Prior year financial statements have been reclassified to reflect these non-core units as Discontinued operations, which are also referred to as "assets and liabilities held for sale."

Corrpro, Inc.

Consolidated Statements of Operations for the Years Ended March 31,

($ in 000s)	Year 3	Year 2	Year 1
Revenues	$104,220	$123,058	$120,489
Operating costs and expenses			
Cost of sales	71,607	87,326	85,325
Selling, general, and administrative	29,788	32,327	35,535
Operating income (loss)	2,825	3,405	(371)
Interest expense	5,907	5,055	4,401
Loss from continuing operations before income taxes	(3,082)	(1,650)	(4,772)
Provision (benefit) for income taxes	(331)	10,669	(934)
Loss from continuing operations	(2,751)	(12,319)	(3,838)
Discontinued operations			
Loss from operations, net of taxes	(9,931)	(5,898)	(4,443)
Gain on disposals, net of taxes	2,095	—	—
Net loss	$(10,587)	$(18,217)	$ (8,281)

Required:

1. What criteria must be met to warrant reclassifying the noncore business units as discontinued operations effective with the quarter ending September 30, Year 2?

2. Suppose that in March Year 3 a buyer signed a purchase commitment for Corrpro's Rohrback Cosasco Systems division. This sale requires regulatory approval that is expected to take at least 18 months to obtain. Should Corrpro's Year 3 financial statements include this division in assets and liabilities held for sale? Explain.

3. Assume that in February Year 3 a potential buyer of another of the domestic noncore business units insisted on a site assessment prior to signing a purchase commitment. The assessment's purpose was to determine whether the site was environmentally impaired. Unfortunately for Corrpro, trace amounts of a suspected carcinogen were discovered, causing the buyer to terminate the purchase. The buyer is willing to reconsider its decision if the site is remediated. While the site can be remediated using existing technology, doing so will be costly enough to negate the purpose of the sale, which is to raise funds to reduce debt. Management believes that employing new remediation methods currently being tested will make this sale economically feasible and thus places the sale of this business unit on hold. Should Corrpro's Year 3 financial statements include this division in Assets and liabilities held for sale?

4. Is there any reason for management to prefer discontinued operations treatment for these noncore business units?

C 2-2

McDonald's Corporation: Identifying critical events for revenue recognition **(LO 2)**

The following information is taken from the Year 2 10-K statement of McDonald's Corporation.

The Company franchises and operates McDonald's restaurants. Of the 32,478 restaurants in 117 countries at year-end Year 2, 26,216 were operated by franchisees [including 19,020 operated by conventional franchisees, 3,160 operated by developmental licensees, and 4,036 operated by foreign affiliated markets (affiliates)—primarily in Japan] and 6,262 were operated by the Company. Under our conventional franchise arrangement, franchisees provide a portion of the capital required by initially investing in the equipment, signs, seating and décor of their restaurant businesses, and by reinvesting in the business over time. The Company owns the land and building or secures long-term leases for both Company-operated and conventional franchised restaurant sites. This maintains long-term occupancy rights, helps control related costs, and assists in alignment with franchisees. In certain circumstances, the Company participates in reinvestment for conventional franchised restaurants. Under our developmental license arrangement, licensees provide capital for the entire business, including the real estate interest, and the Company has no capital invested. In addition, the Company has an equity investment in a limited number of affiliates that invest in real estate and operate or franchise restaurants within a market.

The Company's revenues consist of sales by Company-operated restaurants and fees from franchised restaurants operated by conventional franchisees, developmental licensees and affiliates. Sales by Company-operated restaurants are recognized on a cash basis. The Company presents sales net of sales tax and other sales-related taxes. Revenues from conventional franchised restaurants include rent and royalties based on a percent of sales with minimum rent payments, and initial fees. Revenues from restaurants licensed to affiliates and developmental licensees include a royalty based on a percent of sales, and may include initial fees. Continuing rent and royalties are recognized in the period earned. Initial fees are recognized upon opening of a restaurant or granting of a new franchise term, which is when the Company has performed substantially all initial services required by the franchise arrangement.

Required:

1. McDonald's uses different critical events to recognize revenue for its different business activities. Identify the critical events and rank them from the most to the least conservative policy based on your judgment of the circumstances. For each source of revenue, does the chosen revenue recognition method satisfy both the critical event and the measurability criteria? If you don't have enough information, discuss what additional information is needed to form a judgment on this issue.

2. McDonald's believes that locally owned and operated restaurants help the Company maximize brand performance and are at the core of its competitive advantage, making McDonald's not just a global brand but also a locally relevant one. To that end, for Year 1 and Year 2 combined, the Company refranchised (i.e., sold company-owned stores to franchisees) about 1,100 restaurants, increasing the percent of restaurants franchised worldwide to 81%. Briefly discuss the expected impacts of refranchising on McDonald's financial statements.

Neville Company decides at the beginning of 2014 to adopt the FIFO method of inventory valuation. It had used the LIFO method for financial and tax reporting since its inception on January 1, 2012, and had maintained records that are sufficient to retrospectively apply the FIFO method. Neville concluded that the FIFO method is the preferable inventory valuation method for its inventory (it was the lone member of its industry that used LIFO; its competitors all valued inventory using FIFO).

C 2-3

Retrospectively applying a change in accounting principle   **(LO 7)**

The effects of the change in accounting principle on inventory and cost of sales are presented in the following table:

Date	Inventory Determined By		Cost of Sales Determined By	
	LIFO Method	**FIFO Method**	**LIFO Method**	**FIFO Method**
1/1/2012	$ —	$ —	$ —	$ —
12/31/2012	200	160	1,600	1,640
12/31/2013	400	480	2,000	1,880
12/31/2014	640	780	2,260	2,200

For each year presented, assume that sales are $6,000 and selling, general, and administrative expenses are $1,800. Neville Company's effective income tax rate for all years is 35% (there are no permanent or temporary differences under *FASB ASC Section 740—Income Taxes* prior to the change). Neville's annual report provides two years of financial results. The company's income statements as originally reported under the LIFO method follow.

Income Statements	2013	2012
Sales	$6,000	$6,000
Cost of goods sold	2,000	1,600
Selling, general, & administrative expenses	1,800	1,800
Income before income taxes	2,200	2,600
Income taxes	770	910
Net income	$1,430	$1,690

Required:

1. Prepare Neville Company's 2014 and 2013 income statements reflecting the retrospective application of the accounting change from the LIFO method to the FIFO method.

2. Prepare Neville Company's disclosure related to the accounting change; limit disclosure of financial statement line items affected by the change in accounting principle to those appearing on the company's income statements for the years presented.

COLLABORATIVE LEARNING CASE

C2-4

Baldwin Piano and Organ
Analyzing and interpreting the
income statement (LO 5, 6)

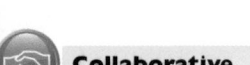
Collaborative

Consider the following information provided from the annual report and 10-K statement of Baldwin Piano and Organ Company.

Income Statements for the Years Ended December 31,

	Year 3	Year 2	Year 1
Net sales	$120,657,455	$110,076,904	$103,230,431
Cost of goods sold	(89,970,702)	(79,637,060)	(74,038,724)
Gross profit	30,686,753	30,439,844	29,191,707
Income on the sale of installment receivables	5,746,125	5,256,583	4,023,525
Interest income on installment receivables	443,431	308,220	350,058
Other operating income, net	3,530,761	3,803,228	3,768,760
	40,407,070	39,807,875	37,334,050
Operating expenses			
Selling, general, and administrative expense	(26,187,629)	(25,118,465)	(23,970,568)
Provision for doubtful accounts	(1,702,234)	(2,053,189)	(2,131,644)
Operating profit	12,517,207	12,636,221	11,231,838
Interest expense	(2,232,258)	(2,610,521)	(3,932,830)
Income before income taxes	10,284,949	10,025,700	7,299,008
Income taxes	(4,120,000)	(4,090,000)	(2,884,000)
Net income	$ 6,164,949	$ 5,935,700	$ 4,415,008

Interest income on installment receivables represents interest on receivables not sold to the independent financial institution.

The following summary table was prepared on the basis of the business segment data reported by Baldwin:

Business	Segment Revenue as a Percentage of Total Revenue		Segment Profit as a Percentage of Segment Revenue	
	Year 3	Year 2	Year 3	Year 2
Musical products	72.70%	81.50%	5.00%	7.60%
Electronic	22.20	13.30	14.80	13.90
Financing services	5.20	5.10	52.80	49.20

The cash flow statement indicates that the company has repaid long-term debt of about $8.6 million, $5.6 million, and $8.3 million during Year 1, Year 2, and Year 3, respectively. The balance sheet indicates that the book value of the company's finished goods inventory decreased by about 8% from Year 2 to Year 3.

In March Year 3, the contents of one of the company's finished goods warehouses were damaged by exposure to smoke from a fire adjacent to the warehouse. The company has received insurance proceeds equal to the wholesale value of the destroyed inventory. Accordingly, a gain of approximately $1,412,000 on the insurance settlement is included in the Year 3 consolidated statements of earnings in the component labeled Other operating income, net.

On January 27, Year 3, the company entered into an agreement in principle whereby Peridot Associates, Inc. (Peridot), would acquire all outstanding shares of the company's common stock at a per share price of $18.25, subject to certain contingencies. The agreement expired on May 16, Year 3. Under the agreement, the company was obligated to reimburse Peridot $800,000 for certain expenses incurred by Peridot. Additionally, the company incurred other expenses of approximately $305,000 related to the proposed acquisition. These combined expenses are included in the Year 3 consolidated statements of earnings as the component labeled Other operating income, net.

Required:

Identify and explain the sources of the change in Baldwin's profitability from Year 2 to Year 3 with a view to evaluating its current earnings quality and future prospects. To what extent can this change be attributed to changes in the management's estimates?

(*Hint:* Preparing a common-size income statement and/or year-to-year percentage change analysis of income statement items will help you formulate your response.)

Remember to check the book's companion website for additional study material.

Additional Topics in 3
Income Determination

This chapter covers special topics in income determination. The first part of the chapter outlines the conditions and describes the accounting procedures for recognizing revenue and profit either before a sale occurs or after a sale occurs. We also discuss selected transactions or circumstances when the timing and amount of revenue recognition presents significant challenges. The second part of the chapter looks at earnings management and how firms can sometimes exploit the flexibility in GAAP to manage annual earnings up or down. We next discuss accounting errors and irregularities and how these are corrected and reported once they are discovered. We conclude this chapter with a discussion of key differences between IFRS and U.S. GAAP for recognizing revenues and how revenue recognition would change under a recent joint IASB/FASB exposure draft on revenue recognition.

Because revenue is usually recognized at the time of sale in most industries, some people erroneously conclude that the sale is itself the *sole* criterion in recognizing revenue. This is not correct! The correct rule for recognizing revenue is more complicated and subtle. As noted in Chapter 2, revenue is recognized at the earliest moment in time that Condition 1 (the "critical event" or being earned) *and* Condition 2 ("measurability" or being realized or realizable) are *both* satisfied. That is, at what point in the earnings process is the revenue earned and when do the benefits received become realized or realizable? ***The earliest moment at which Conditions 1 and 2 are both satisfied is usually the time of sale.*** That is why revenue is usually recognized when the sale is made.

In some cases Conditions 1 and 2 are satisfied *before* the sale, for example, as production takes place on a long-term construction contract. When this happens and when expenses are *also* measurable with a reasonable degree of assurance, GAAP allows income to be recognized before the sale.

In other circumstances, Conditions 1 and 2 may not both be satisfied until *after* the time of sale, for instance, not until the cash is received on installment sales when considerable uncertainty exists regarding ultimate collection. In these cases, GAAP disallows revenue recognition when the sale occurs; instead, revenue (and profit) recognition is deferred until cash is received.

LEARNING OBJECTIVES

After studying this chapter, you will understand:

1. The conditions under which it is appropriate to recognize revenues and profits either before or after the point of sale.

2. The procedures for recognizing revenue and adjusting associated asset values in three specific settings: long-term construction contracts, agricultural commodities, and installment sales.

3. Specialized application of revenue recognition principles for franchise sales, sales with right of return, and "bundled" sales with multiple deliverable elements.

4. How the flexibility in GAAP for income determination invites managers to manipulate or manage earnings.

5. The various techniques used to manage earnings.

6. SEC guidance on revenue recognition designed to curb earnings management.

7. How error corrections and restatements of prior period financial statements are reported.

8. Key differences between IFRS and U.S. GAAP rules for revenue recognition.

9. Proposed changes that IASB and FASB are considering for contract-based revenue recognition.

Chapter

REVENUE RECOGNITION PRIOR TO SALE
Percentage-of-Completion Method

Long-term construction projects—such as roads and bridges, military hardware, and costly items such as oil tankers—frequently satisfy both revenue recognition conditions prior to the time of sale.

These types of projects are usually begun only after a formal contract with a purchaser has been signed. Because a buyer for the completed project is assured, the critical event in the earning of revenue is the actual construction; that is, revenue recognition Condition 1 is satisfied as construction progresses. Furthermore, because the contract price is specified, the amount of the revenue that has been earned is measurable with a reasonable degree of assurance, thus satisfying revenue recognition Condition 2.

In many construction projects, it is also possible to estimate with reasonable accuracy the cost of the project and to measure its stage of completion. Furthermore, construction contracts usually require purchasers to make progress payments to the contractor as construction progresses. These interim payment requirements help ensure that the contractor will receive payment for the work performed.

When long-term construction contracts possess all of these attributes, revenue recognition Conditions 1 and 2 are both satisfied as construction progresses, and expenses can be matched against revenues to determine income. This is called the **percentage-of-completion method.**[1] Here's how it works.

Solid Construction Corporation signs a contract with the City of Springfield on January 1, 2014, to build a highway bridge over Stony Creek. The contract price is $1,000,000; construction costs are estimated to be $800,000, and the project is scheduled to be completed by December 31, 2016. Periodic cash payments are to be made by the City of Springfield as construction progresses. Here is a summary of the Stony Creek project's progress each year:

	Actual Experience on the Project as of December 31,		
	2014	**2015**	**2016**
Costs incurred to date	$240,000	$544,000	$ 850,000
Estimated future costs	560,000	306,000	—
Billings to date	280,000	650,000	1,000,000
Cash collections to date	210,000	600,000	1,000,000

Under the percentage-of-completion method, the profit to be recognized in any year is based on the ratio of incurred contract costs divided by estimated total contract costs. Using the data in the example, we compute the profit for 2014 using the following steps:

Step 1: **Compute the percentage-of-completion ratio by dividing costs incurred to date by estimated total costs.**

This is done to estimate the percentage of completion at any given point during the project. At the end of 2014, estimated total costs on the project are $800,000, comprising $240,000 of costs incurred in 2014 plus $560,000 of estimated future costs. The cost ratio is:

$$\frac{\$240,000}{\$800,000} = 0.30 \text{ or } 30\%$$

In this example, we use costs incurred to date divided by the total estimated cost of the project to estimate the percentage of completion. Output measures are sometimes used as we discuss below.

---

[1] FASB Accounting Standards Codification (ASC) Section 910-605: Contractors—Construction—Revenue Recognition.

Step 2: **Determine the estimated total profit on the contract by comparing the contract price with the estimated total costs.**

At the end of 2014, the estimated profit on the contract is still $200,000, that is, the difference between the contract price of $1,000,000 and estimated total costs of $800,000.

Step 3: **Compute the estimated profit earned to date.**

The estimated profit earned to date is the cost ratio (or percentage of completion) computed in Step 1 multiplied by the estimated profit computed in Step 2, that is, 0.30 × $200,000 = $60,000.

Notice that 30% of the total estimated costs of $800,000 has been incurred by the end of 2014, so 30% of the total estimated profit of $200,000 can be recognized in that same year. That is, profit is recognized in proportion to costs incurred. Because no profit has been recognized prior to 2014, all of the $60,000 is recognizable in 2014.

Because cost estimates and completion stages change, these computations must be repeated in each subsequent year. Furthermore, the profit computation for each subsequent contract year must incorporate an additional step. The computation for 2015 illustrates this.

Step 1: **Compute the percentage-of-completion ratio, determined by dividing incurred costs to date by estimated total costs.**

At the end of 2015, estimated total costs on this contract have risen to $850,000: $544,000 of costs incurred through 2015 plus $306,000 of estimated future costs. The cost ratio (or percentage of completion) is:

$$\frac{\$544,000}{\$850,000} = 0.64 \text{ or } 64\%$$

Step 2: **Determine the estimated profit on the contract.**

The estimated profit on the contract has now dropped to $150,000—the difference between the contract price of $1,000,000 and the newly estimated total costs of $850,000 as of the end of 2015:

Step 3: **Compute the estimated profit earned to date.**

Because 64% of the total estimated costs has already been incurred (Step 1), 64% of the revised estimated profit of $150,000 (Step 2), or $96,000, has been earned through December 31, 2015.

Be sure to notice that a portion of the profit on this contract—$60,000—has already been recognized in 2014. Therefore, only the *incremental profit* earned in 2015 should be recognized. This requires an additional computation.

Step 4: **Compute the incremental profit earned in the current year.**

The estimated total profit earned through December 31, 2015, is $96,000 (Step 3). Because $60,000 of the estimated profit was recognized on this contract in 2014, only $36,000 ($96,000 − $60,000) of additional profit can be recognized in 2015.

These four steps can be expressed succinctly using the following profit computation formula:

$$\underbrace{\left[\frac{\text{Cost incurred to date}}{\text{Estimated total costs}} \times \frac{\text{Estimated}}{\text{total profit}} \right]}_{\text{Profit earned to date}} - \underbrace{\frac{\text{Profit recognized}}{\text{in previous years}}}_{\substack{\text{Previously recognized} \\ \text{profit}}} = \frac{\text{Profit recognized}}{\text{in current year}} \quad \textbf{(3.1)}$$

The previously recognized profit is the sum of all profits (or losses) recognized on the contract in prior years, that is, the sum of all profits (or losses) that were determined by multiplying the cost-completion ratio by the total profit estimated at those earlier dates. Again, the reason for subtracting this amount from the profit-earned-to-date figure is to avoid double counting profits recognized in prior years.

Repeating the computations for 2014 and 2015 using the formula in equation (3.1) gives the following results:

Profit Computation

$$
\textbf{2014:} \quad \left[\frac{\$240,000}{\$800,000} \times \$200,000 \right] - 0 = \$60,000
$$

| | Profit earned to date | Previously recognized profit | Profit recognized in 2014 |

$$
\textbf{2015:} \quad \left[\frac{\$544,000}{\$850,000} \times \$150,000 \right] - \$60,000 = \$36,000
$$

| | Profit earned to date | Previously recognized profit | Profit recognized in 2015 |

Of course, these results are identical to those derived using the multiple-step approach illustrated previously. The computation for 2016 would be:

$$
\textbf{2016:} \quad \left[\frac{\$850,000}{\$850,000} \times \$150,000 \right] - \$96,000 = \$54,000
$$

| | Profit earned to date | Previously recognized profit | Profit recognized in 2016 |

Using the percentage-of-completion method, the cumulative profit recognized over the three years totals $150,000 ($60,000 + $36,000 + $54,000). This total equals the difference between the contract price of $1,000,000 and the actual costs of $850,000.

The journal entries shown in Exhibit 3.1 would be used to record these events on the books of Solid Construction Corporation.

Entries (2) and (3) of Exhibit 3.1 require elaboration. In entry (2), the amount debited to the Construction expense account each period is for the actual construction costs incurred in that period. The credit to Construction revenue is determined by multiplying the total contract price by the completion percentage and then subtracting any revenue recognized in prior periods. For example, the revenue recognized in 2015 is determined by multiplying the contract price of $1,000,000 times the completion percentage as of the end of 2015 (64%), giving total revenue earned to date of $640,000. Subtracting the $300,000 of revenue recognized in 2014 yields Construction revenue of $340,000 recognized in 2015. An alternative to entry (2) is to recognize income (profit) on the construction project as a net amount without showing the revenue and expense amounts separately. This net amount is determined by using the formula in equation (3.1).

Consistent with linking asset valuation and income determination together, as discussed in Chapter 2, the carrying value of net assets is increased as income is recognized. This is why the entry (2) debit increases the Inventory: Construction in progress account, which is a part of inventory. Thus, entry (2) reflects the dual financial statement impact of income recognition: *both net assets and income increase.*

EXHIBIT 3.1	Solid Construction Corporation

Journal Entries
Percentage-of-Completion Method

	2014	2015	2016
(1) To record costs incurred			
DR Inventory: Construction in progress	$240,000	$304,000	$ 306,000
CR Accounts payable, cash, etc.	$240,000	$304,000	$ 306,000
(2) To record revenue and expense separately			
DR Inventory: Construction in progress	$ 60,000[a]	$ 36,000[a]	$ 54,000[a]
DR Construction expense	240,000[b]	304,000[b]	306,000[b]
CR Construction revenue	$300,000[c]	$340,000[c]	$ 360,000[c]
Alternative entry: To record income as a net amount			
DR Inventory: Construction in progress	$ 60,000	$ 36,000	$ 54,000
CR Income on long-term construction contract	$ 60,000	$ 36,000	$ 54,000
(3) To record customer billings			
DR Accounts receivable	$280,000	$370,000	$ 350,000
CR Billings on construction in progress	$280,000	$370,000	$ 350,000
(4) To record cash received			
DR Cash	$210,000	$390,000	$ 400,000
CR Accounts receivable	$210,000	$390,000	$ 400,000
(5) To record completion and acceptance of the project			
DR Billings on construction in progress			$1,000,000
CR Inventory: Construction in progress			$1,000,000

	2014	2015	2016
[a] Gross profit earned in current period	30% × ($1,000,000 − $800,000)	64% × ($1,000,000 − $850,000) − $60,000	($1,000,000 − $850,000) − $96,000
[b] Actual construction costs incurred in current period	$240,000	$544,000 − $240,000	$850,000 − $544,000
[c] Revenues earned in current period	30% × $1,000,000	(64% × $1,000,000) − $300,000	$1,000,000 − $300,000 − $340,000

In entry (3), Billings on construction in progress is a contra account, which is subtracted from the account Inventory: Construction in progress. The net of these two accounts is shown as a current asset (if there is a debit balance) or as a current liability (if there is a credit balance). In our example, the balance sheet presentation for Solid Construction Corporation would be as follows for 2014 and 2015:

2014

Current Assets		
Accounts receivable		$70,000
Inventory: Construction in progress	$300,000	
Less: Billings on construction in progress	(280,000)	
Inventory in excess of contract billings		20,000

2015

Current Assets		
Accounts receivable		$50,000
Current Liabilities		
Inventory: Construction in progress	$(640,000)	
Less: Billings on construction in progress	650,000	
Contract billings in excess of inventory		$10,000

The reason Billings on construction in progress is treated as a contra-inventory account (that is, shown as a deduction from inventory) is to avoid balance sheet double counting. Here's why. Typically, a sale results in an asset (Accounts receivable) being increased for the selling price of the goods with a simultaneous decrease in another asset, Inventory, for the cost of goods sold. However, inventory is not reduced at the time the receivable is recorded under long-term construction accounting. Rather, the Inventory: Construction in progress account remains on the company's books until the project is complete and the sale is finalized. Treating the Billings on construction in progress account as an offset (contra) to the Inventory: Construction in progress account avoids including certain costs and profits twice on the balance sheet—once in Inventory: Construction in progress and a second time in the Accounts receivable account.

In our example, cumulative income to date is determined by using the ratio of incurred costs to date divided by estimated total costs. This cost ratio is widely used because it provides a simple index of progress toward completion, that is, work done to date. However, there are situations in which this cost ratio may not accurately reflect construction progress. For example, consider a case in which raw materials to be used in construction are stockpiled in advance of use. In such situations, costs are being incurred as the raw materials are received and recorded on the books, yet these costs do not increase the stage of completion until the raw materials are actually *used*. In projects in which this stockpiling is significant, some other means for measuring progress toward completion would be preferable. Possibilities include labor hours worked or various output measures (such as miles of roadway completed).

Finally, although profits are recognized in proportion to percentage of completion as construction progresses, ***estimated losses on a contract are recognized in their entirety as soon as it becomes known that a loss will ensue.*** To illustrate, suppose that in the Solid Construction example above it becomes known in 2015 that total contract costs will be $1,050,000, implying a loss of $50,000. The entries and supporting calculations to report the expected loss in 2015 and the entries for 2016 would be as follows:[2]

---

[2] We thank Steve Zeff for suggesting this example to us.

2015[a]

DR	Inventory: Construction in progress	$304,000	
	CR Cash (Accounts payable)		$304,000
DR	Accounts receivable	$370,000	
	CR Billings on construction in progress		$370,000
DR	Construction expense	$328,100	
	CR Inventory: Construction in progress (*loss* recognized) ..		$110,000
	CR Construction revenue		218,100

2016[b]

DR	Inventory: Construction in progress	$506,000	
	CR Cash (Accounts payable)		$506,000
DR	Accounts receivable	$350,000	
	CR Billings on construction in progress		$350,000
DR	Construction expense	$481,900	
	CR Construction revenue		$481,900

[a] Supporting calculations:

Costs to date (12/31/15) ($240,000 + $304,000)	$ 544,000
Estimated costs to complete	506,000
Estimated total costs	$1,050,000
Percent complete ($544,000 ÷ $1,050,000)	51.81%
Revenue recognized in 2015	
($1,000,000 × 51.81% = $518,100 − $300,000)	$ 218,100
Costs recognized in 2015 (see schedule below)*	(328,100)
Loss recognized in 2015	$ (110,000)

* Loss on contract (estimated)		$ 50,000
Add:		
Remaining total project cost, not including loss		
($1,050,000 − $50,000)	$1,000,000	
Multiplied by percent complete (see above)	51.81%	
		518,100
Total		568,100
Less: Cost of construction recognized in 2014		(240,000)
Cost of construction recognized in 2015		$ 328,100

[b] Supporting calculations:

Total revenue recognized	$1,000,000
Less: Revenue recognized in 2014 and 2015	
($300,000 + $218,100)	(518,100)
Revenue recognized in 2016	481,900
Costs of construction ($1,050,000 − $240,000 − $328,100)	(481,900)
Loss on contract (full loss was recognized in 2015)	$ –0–

Completed-Contract Method[3]

In some cases, it is not possible to determine expected costs with a high degree of reliability under long-term construction contracts (for example, building underground street tunnels in Boston), making the use of the percentage-of-completion method inappropriate. In these situations, the **completed-contract method** is used instead.

The completed-contract method postpones recognition of income until the project is completed. Journal entries under the completed-contract method are identical to the journal entries illustrated previously for the percentage-of-completion method except that entry (2) in

---

[3] We discuss the completed-contract method here for convenience although it is *not* a method that recognizes revenue and profits prior to sale.

EXHIBIT 3.2	Yearly Income Comparison of Two Long-Term Contract Accounting Methods

Year	Completed-Contract Method	Percentage-of-Completion Method
2014	–0–	$ 60,000
2015	–0–	36,000
2016	$150,000	54,000
Total income	$150,000	$150,000

Exhibit 3.1, which records income as construction progresses, is omitted. Instead, all of the income on the contract is recognized when the contract is completed. The entry for recognizing income under the completed-contract method in 2016 follows:

DR Billings on construction in progress	$1,000,000	
CR Inventory: Construction in progress		$850,000
CR Income on long-term construction contract		150,000

Although income is recognized only on completion, losses are recognized in their entirety as soon as their probable existence is known.

Exhibit 3.2 illustrates that total income for the three years is the same under both the completed-contract method and the percentage-of-completion method ($150,000). However, the timing of income recognition differs considerably.

The net asset balance at intermediate construction stages will also differ with the two methods. As shown in column (g) of Exhibit 3.3, *the amount of this net asset balance difference in any year is precisely equal to the difference in cumulative profit recognized on each basis.* This difference in net asset balances exists because the recognition of income has a corresponding effect on net asset balances.

Revenue Recognition on Commodities

The timing of revenue recognition for producers of agricultural and mining commodities raises some interesting issues. There is general agreement that in both mining and farming,

EXHIBIT 3.3	Comparative Account Balances

Percentage-of-Completion versus Completed-Contract Method

December 31, Year-End Account Balances

	Completed-Contract Method			Percentage-of-Completion Method			
	(a) Inventory: Construction in Progress	(b) Billings	(c) Net Asset (Liability) Balance Col. (a) − Col. (b)	(d) Inventory: Construction in Progress	(e) Billings	(f) Net Asset (Liability) Balance Col. (d) − Col. (e)	(g) Difference in Net Asset Balances Between Methods Col. (f) − Col. (c)
2014	$240,000	$280,000	$ (40,000)	$300,000	$280,000	$ 20,000	$60,000*
2015	544,000	650,000	(106,000)	640,000	650,000	(10,000)	96,000†
2016	–0–	–0–	–0–	–0–	–0–	–0–	–0–

* Also equals difference between cumulative profit on percentage-of-completion method ($60,000) and the completed-contract method ($0) from Exhibit 3.2.

† Also equals difference between cumulative profit on percentage-of-completion method ($60,000 + $36,000 = $96,000) and the completed-contract method ($0 + $0) from Exhibit 3.2.

the critical event in adding value usually comes *before* the actual sale. The critical event in mining is extracting the resource from the ground. In agriculture, the critical event is harvesting the crop. (The critical event is harvest because prior to harvest, the crop may still be lost because of drought, hail, insects, or disease. Only after the crop is safely out of the field have these income-threatening possibilities been avoided.) Thus, revenue recognition Condition 1 is satisfied prior to the sale itself.

However, the precise time at which revenue recognition Condition 2 (measurability) is satisfied for commodities producers is open to some dispute. The following example explores the issues.

A farmer harvests 110,000 bushels of corn on September 30, 2014. On this date, the posted market price per bushel was $3.50. The total cost of growing the crop was $220,000, or $2.00 per bushel. The farmer decides to sell 100,000 bushels for cash on September 30 at the posted price of $3.50 and stores the remaining 10,000 bushels. On January 2, 2015, the market price drops to $3.00. Fearing further price declines, the farmer immediately sells the bushels in storage at a price of $3.00 per bushel.

Completed-Transaction (Sales) Method   The timing of revenue recognition on the 100,000 bushels of corn that were sold on September 30 is straightforward. Revenue recognition Conditions 1 and 2 are both satisfied at September 30, and income would be recognized at the time of sale. The income statement would show:

2014 Income Statement
Completed-transaction (sales) method

Revenues (sale of 100,000 bushels at a market price of $3.50 per bushel)	$350,000
Expenses (costs of $2.00 per bushel for 100,000 bushels sold)	(200,000)
Income from sale	$150,000

> As costs are incurred during the year, the direct costs of crop production—things such as seed, fertilizer, fuel, and depreciation on machinery—are charged to a Production in process or Crop inventory account with offsetting credits to Cash, Accounts payable, or Accumulated depreciation.

Under the traditional view, which we call the **completed-transaction (sales) method,** no income would be recognized at September 30 on the 10,000 bushels that were harvested but not sold. For these 10,000 bushels, revenue recognition Condition 2 is considered not to have been met because the eventual selling price is unknown: That is, the sale transaction is not yet completed. The bushels in storage would be reflected on the farmer's balance sheet at their *cost* of $20,000 ($2.00 per bushel × 10,000 bushels).

When the bushels in storage are sold in 2015, the income statement would show the profit on the sale of the 10,000 bushels:

2015 Income Statement
Completed-transaction (sales) method

Revenues (sale of 10,000 bushels at a market price of $3.00 per bushel)	$30,000
Expenses (costs of $2.00 per bushel for 10,000 bushels sold)	(20,000)
Income from sale	$10,000

Note that the traditional approach avoids recognizing any income on the 10,000 unsold bushels until the sales transaction is completed in 2015.

The International Accounting Standards Board (IASB) requires agricultural produce harvested by an enterprise to be measured at its fair value at time of harvest less estimated cost to transport the grain to the local elevator. The difference is referred to as **net realizable value.** Any gain or loss arising from initial recognition of harvested assets and from the change in fair value less estimated transportation costs of harvested assets are to be included in net profit or loss for the period in which it arises. See "Agriculture," *IAS 41* (London: International Accounting Standards Board [IASB], 2002).

Market Price (Production) Method

There is another way for measuring income in the previous example. This alternative recognizes that well-organized liquid markets exist for most agricultural and many mining commodities. In addition, the quantities offered for sale by any individual producer are usually very small in relation to the total size of the market. Producers face an established price for as many units as they choose to sell. These factors mean that a readily determinable market price at which output *could be sold* is continuously available. In this view, revenue recognition Condition 2 (measurability) is satisfied prior to the actual sale of actively traded commodities.

Because revenue recognition Condition 1 (critical event) occurs at harvest, both conditions necessary to recognize revenue are satisfied as soon as the crop is safely out of the field (that is, at the point of production or harvest). Thus, farming income on all 110,000 bushels is recognized under this approach on September 30 (when grain is harvested):

 **International**

2014 Income Statement
Market price (production) method

Revenues (100,000 bushels sold at a market price of $3.50)	$350,000
Expenses (costs of $2.00 per bushel for 100,000 bushels sold)	(200,000)
Market gain on unsold inventory (10,000 bushels times the difference between the $3.50 market price at the date of harvest and the $2.00 cost per bushel)	15,000
Total income from farming activities	$165,000

The market price used in this calculation is the **net realizable value**—that is, the market price at point of delivery less any delivery costs. Thus, if it costs the farmer $0.10 per bushel to transport the grain from the farm to the local elevator, the net realizable value would be $3.40 ($3.50 − $0.10). This would be the price used to compute the gain on the unsold inventory.

This **market price (production) method** recognizes farming income on the 10,000 unsold bushels as well as on the 100,000 bushels sold. This view emphasizes the fact that the farmer *could have sold* these 10,000 bushels at the time of harvest for a readily determinable price of $3.50 per bushel. Because the critical event in farming is harvest and the potential sales price at the time of harvest is known, both revenue recognition conditions relating to farming are deemed to be satisfied on September 30. Therefore, farming income of $165,000 is immediately determinable.

Under the market price method, the farmer's balance sheet reflects the bushels in storage at $35,000 ($3.50 market price at harvest times 10,000 bushels). If the corn was initially carried at its *cost* of $20,000 ($2.00 per bushel times 10,000 bushels), the entry necessary to reflect the value added by farming is:

DR	Crop inventory	$15,000
CR	Market gain on unsold inventory	$15,000

The credit would appear as shown on the income statement for 2014.

After the corn is harvested, the activity called *farming* has ended. However, the farmer is actually engaged in another business in addition to farming. By withholding 10,000 bushels from the market, the farmer is also pursuing a separate (nonfarming) activity called **speculation.** This speculation is undertaken in the hope that prices will rise above their September 30 level of $3.50 per bushel. Subsequent changes in the market price of corn will thus give rise to speculative gains or losses—also called **inventory holding gains and losses.**

To illustrate, recollect that at the start of 2015, the market price of corn drops from $3.50 to $3.00 per bushel. This decline in price gives rise to a speculative (holding) loss in 2015 of

$5,000 (a decline of $0.50 per bushel times 10,000 bushels). The inventory is **marked-to-market,** and the journal entry to reflect the loss is:

DR Inventory (holding) loss on speculation	$5,000	
CR Crop inventory		$5,000

After this entry is posted, the inventory's carrying value is now reduced to $30,000 (10,000 bushels times $3.00 per bushel).

Fearing further price declines, the farmer immediately sells the remaining 10,000 bushels at $3 on January 2. The entry is:

DR Cost of goods sold	$30,000	
CR Crop inventory		$30,000
DR Cash	$30,000	
CR Crop revenue		$30,000

Comparison: Completed-Transaction (Sales) and Market Price (Production) Methods

Although total income over the two periods is the same under each approach, the income recognized in each period is *not* the same, and the activities to which the income is attributed also differ:

Completed-Transaction (Sales) Method			Market Price (Production) Method	
Income from sales	$150,000	2014	Income from farming activities	$165,000
Income from sales	10,000	2015	Holding loss on speculation	(5,000)
Total income	$160,000		Total income	$160,000

The completed-transaction (sales) method avoids recognizing any income on the 10,000 unsold bushels until the transaction is completed (when the grain is sold). However, in emphasizing completed transactions, this traditional approach—the completed-transaction method—merges the results of the farmer's speculative and farming (operating) activities and does not reflect the separate results of either.

This example illustrates why income recognition can be controversial: Should the farmer recognize market-price changes on agricultural commodities prior to sale? In practice, the completed-transaction method is far more prevalent. However, the market price method is deemed to be in conformity with generally accepted accounting principles when readily determinable market values are continuously available. The market price method has the dual advantages of:

1. Explicitly recognizing the separate results arising from the farming and speculative activities that the farmer is engaged in.

2. Conforming more closely to the income recognition conditions introduced in Chapter 2.

RECAP

For long-term construction contracts and commodities (natural resources and agricultural products), the two conditions for revenue recognition—critical event (being earned) and measurability (being realized or realizable)—are frequently satisfied prior to sale. The percentage-of-completion method recognizes revenue and profits (losses) on long-term construction contracts as work progresses. The market price (production) method recognizes the difference between the cost of the natural resource or agricultural commodity and its prevailing market price as income at the time of production or harvest. In both cases, an inventory account—Inventory: Construction in progress (for long-term construction contracts) and Crop inventory (for commodities)—is debited to reflect the increase in value recognized on the income statement, thereby maintaining the linkage between income determination and asset valuation.

REVENUE RECOGNITION SUBSEQUENT TO SALE

Installment Sales Method

Sometimes revenue is not recognized at the point of sale even though a valid sale has taken place. This accounting treatment is acceptable only under highly unusual circumstances. One instance in which revenue recognition might be delayed beyond the point of sale is when sales are made under very extended cash collection terms. Examples include installment sales of consumer durables and retail land sales of vacation or retirement property. A lengthy collection period considerably increases the risk of nonpayment. ***When the risk of noncollection is unusually high and when there is no reasonable basis for estimating the proportion of installment accounts likely to prove uncollectible, then revenue recognition may be deferred.***

When these extreme risk situations exist, neither of the two revenue recognition conditions is satisfied. Specifically, when it's highly uncertain whether customers will make the cash payments called for in the contract, then the sale itself is not the critical event in creating value. In such circumstances, the actual cash collection is the critical event, and revenue recognition Condition 1 is satisfied only as the amounts due from customers are received. Similarly, revenue recognition Condition 2 is not satisfied because the amount ultimately collectible from customers is not measurable with a reasonable degree of assurance at the time of sale.

Because Conditions 1 and 2 are both satisfied only over time as cash collections take place, a revenue recognition method tied to cash collections has been devised to deal with such situations. This revenue recognition approach is called the **installment sales method.**

Installment Sales Method Illustrated The installment sales method recognizes revenue and gross profit proportionately as cash is collected. The amount recognized in any period is based on two factors:

1. The installment sales gross-profit percentage (gross profit/sales).
2. The amount of cash collected on installment accounts receivable.

Here's an example of revenue and gross profit recognition under the installment sales method:

	2014	2015
Installment sales	$1,200,000	$1,300,000
Cost of installment goods sold	840,000	884,000
Gross profit	$ 360,000	$ 416,000
Gross-profit percentage	30%	32%
Cash collections		
On 2014 installment sales	$ 300,000	$ 600,000
On 2015 installment sales		340,000

During 2014, installment sales of $1,200,000 were made. The potential gross profit on these sales is $360,000. The installment contracts call for cash payments over each of the next four years. Because of the extreme uncertainties regarding ultimate collectibility, this gross profit will be recognized only as customers pay on their accounts. Because $300,000 of cash is collected in 2014, the gross profit recognized in 2014 will be $90,000—that is, $300,000 multiplied by 30%, the gross-profit percentage (gross profit/sales) on 2014 installment sales. This $90,000 is shown on the 2014 income statement. The difference between the total potential gross profit of $360,000 and the $90,000 of recognized gross profit, or $270,000, is deferred gross profit (see entries [4] and [5] in Exhibit 3.4).

EXHIBIT 3.4	**Installment Sales Method**

Journal Entries

	2014		2015	
(1) To record installment sales				
DR Accounts receivable—2014 installment sales	$1,200,000			
DR Accounts receivable—2015 installment sales			$1,300,000	
CR Installment sales revenue.		$1,200,000		$1,300,000
(2) To record cost of goods sold				
DR Cost of installment goods sold.	$ 840,000		$ 884,000	
CR Inventory		$ 840,000		$ 884,000
(3) To record cash collections				
DR Cash.	$ 300,000		$ 940,000	
CR Accounts receivable—2014 installment sales . . .		$ 300,000		$ 600,000
CR Accounts receivable—2015 installment sales . . .				340,000
(4) To defer gross profit on portion of current-period sales that are not yet collected				
DR Deferred gross profit (income statement)	$ 270,000		$ 307,200	
CR Deferred gross profit—Adjustment to accounts receivable		$ 270,000		$ 307,200
(5) To recognize realized gross profit on installment sales of prior periods				
DR Deferred gross profit—Adjustment to accounts receivable.			$ 180,000	
CR Recognized gross profit on installment sales—prior year				$ 180,000

The gross profit recognized in 2015 from installment sales is comprised of two components:

1. A component relating to 2015 cash collections on 2014 installment sales.
2. A component relating to 2015 cash collections on 2015 installment sales.

The computation for installment sales gross profit recognized in 2015 is:

Total Gross Profit Recognized in 2015—Installment Sales Method

	Gross Profit Recognized
Component relating to 2014 sales:	
Cash collections in 2015 from 2014 sales	$600,000
Multiplied by 2014 gross-profit percentage	30%
	$180,000
Component relating to 2015 sales:	
Cash collections in 2015 from 2015 sales	$340,000
Multiplied by 2015 gross-profit percentage	32%
	$108,800
Total installment sales gross profit recognized in 2015	$288,800

See Exhibit 3.4 for journal entries to record these facts for years 2014 and 2015.

The income statement would appear as follows:

	2014	2015
Installment sales	$1,200,000	$1,300,000
Cost of installment goods sold	(840,000)	(884,000)
Gross profit	360,000	416,000
Less: Deferred gross profit on installment sales of current year	(270,000)	(307,200)
Gross profit recognized on current year's sales	90,000	108,800
Plus: Gross profit recognized on installment sales of prior years	—	180,000
Total gross profit recognized this year	$ 90,000	$ 288,800

Some additional internal recordkeeping is necessary when applying the installment sales method. Installment sales and the related cost of goods sold must be tracked by individual year in order to compute the gross-profit percentage that applies to each year. In addition, the accounting system must match cash collections with the specific sales year to which the cash collections relate. This matching is needed to apply the correct gross-profit percentage to cash receipts.

On the balance sheet, the Accounts receivable—installment sales components are classified as current assets if they are due within 12 months of the balance sheet date. Amounts not expected to be collected within the next year may also be classified as current assets if installment sales are a normal part of the company's operations because the company's operating cycle would include the installment collection period. Existing practice typically classifies the Deferred gross-profit account as a contra-asset, which is shown as a reduction to Accounts receivable.

Selling, general, and administrative expenses relating to installment sales are treated as period costs—that is, as costs that are expensed in the period in which they are incurred—because they provide no future benefits. This treatment is consistent with the manner in which period costs are handled for normal (noninstallment) sales.

Interest on Installment Contracts   The essence of an installment sales contract is that the cash payments arising from the sale are spread over multiple periods. Because of this delay in receiving the sales proceeds, sellers charge interest on installment sales contracts. Consequently, the required monthly or quarterly installment payments include both interest and principal. This complication was omitted from the example we just illustrated. GAAP requires that the interest component of the periodic cash proceeds must be recorded separately as interest revenue. This means that interest payments are not considered when computing the recognized gross profit on installment sales. Chapter 8 outlines the procedures for differentiating between principal and interest payments on customer receivables.

Cost Recovery Method

When collections on installment sales occur over an extended period and there is no reasonable basis for estimating collectibility, GAAP allows companies to use the **cost recovery method** for recognizing profits on such sales.[4] This method is commonly used when a high degree of uncertainty exists regarding the collection of receivables (for example, for retail land development sales). Under this method, no profit is recognized until cash payments received from the buyer exceed the seller's cost of goods sold. After the cost of the merchandise

---

[4] FASB ASC Section 605-10-25: Revenue Recognition—Overall—Recognition.

has been recovered, any cash collected in excess of this amount is recorded as recognized gross profit on the seller's income statement.

The following example illustrates the accounting treatment under the cost recovery method.

In 2014, Florida Swamp Land Development Company sells 100 one-acre lots for $12,000 each. One-third of the sales price, $4,000 per lot, or $400,000 total, is collected when the contract is signed and the remainder is to be collected in two equal installments in the following two years. The cost of acquiring and developing the land was $600,000. Because most of the sales are made to individuals who reside outside the State of Florida, there tends to be a high rate of default on collections, which is difficult to estimate.

If the cost recovery method is applied to these sales and the cash is collected on schedule, the accounting entries would be as follows:

2014

DR	Installment receivables		$1,200,000	
	CR	Land inventory		$600,000
	CR	Deferred gross profit		600,000

To record sale of 100 lots at $12,000 each.

DR	Cash		$ 400,000	
	CR	Installment receivables		$400,000

To record collections on account.

2015

DR	Cash		$ 400,000	
	CR	Installment receivables		$400,000

To record collections on account.

DR	Deferred gross profit		$ 200,000	
	CR	Realized gross profit		$200,000

To record realized gross profit equal to cumulative cash collections in excess of cost of land sold = $800,000 − $600,000 = $200,000.

2016

DR	Cash		$ 400,000	
	CR	Installment receivables		$400,000

To record collections on account.

DR	Deferred gross profit		$ 400,000	
	CR	Realized gross profit		$400,000[a]

[a] To record realized gross profit determined as follows:

Cumulative cash collections	$1,200,000
Cost of land sold	(600,000)
Gross profit recognized in prior periods	(200,000)
Amount recognized in 2016	$ 400,000

Note that the cost recovery method is more conservative than the regular installment sales method because the regular installment method recognizes gross profit on each dollar collected while the cost recovery method recognizes profit only when the cumulative cash collections exceed the total cost of land sold.

RECAP The installment sales method of revenue recognition is used when the risk of noncollection is high or when it is impractical to estimate the amount of uncollectibles. Under the installment sales method, the gross profit on sales is deferred and recognized as income in subsequent periods, that is, when the installment receivables are collected in cash. The linkage between income determination and asset valuation is maintained by showing Deferred gross profit as a contra account (reduction) to Installment accounts receivable.

REVENUE RECOGNITION FOR SPECIALIZED SALES TRANSACTIONS

In this section, we briefly review accounting requirements for industries or transactions that have specialized applications of revenue recognition principles. Specifically, we consider the unique revenue recognition issues for the following areas:

- Franchise sales.
- Sales with right of return.
- Bundled (multiple-element) sales.

Franchise Sales

Franchising is a popular way to expand sales of products and services in a variety of industries. In 2012, franchise operations accounted for more than $1.25 trillion of sales in the United States. Exhibit 3.5 identifies the 10 fastest growing franchise operations for 2013 and the industries in which they operate.

In franchise arrangements, the franchisor (seller) gives the franchisee (buyer) the exclusive right to sell a product or service in a given locale or area and use the franchisor's name for a specified period of time. Typically, franchise agreements call for both of the following two types of payments:

1. An initial franchise fee, all or part of which is paid to the franchisor when the franchise agreement is signed, with the remainder due in installments (with interest) over a specified period; and
2. Continuing or periodic fees generally based on a percentage of sales generated by the franchisee.

EXHIBIT 3.5	Ten Fastest Growing Franchise Operations for 2013
Franchise	**Industry**
Hampton Hotels	Midprice hotels
Subway	Restaurants/Fast food
Jiffy Lube International, Inc.	Auto servicing (service)
7-Eleven Inc.	Convenience store
Supercuts	Hair salon (service)
Anytime Fitness	Personal fitness (service)
Servpro	Insurance/Disaster restoration and cleaning
Denny's Inc.	Restaurants
McDonald's	Restaurants/Fast food
Pizza Hut Inc.	Restaurants/Fast food

Source: www.entreprenuer.com/franchise500.

Accounting for continuing periodic fees received by the franchisor poses little difficulty. These fees are recorded as revenue in the period they are earned and received. Accounting for the initial franchise fee, however, raises some challenging revenue recognition issues as you will see.

The initial franchise fee typically comprises two elements:

1. Payment for the right to operate a franchise in a given area.
2. Payment for services to be performed by the franchisor.

Examples of initial services include:

- Finding and securing a site for the franchise.
- Overseeing construction of the facilities.
- Training employees.
- Setting up and maintaining a recordkeeping system.
- Sales promotion and advertising.

Occasionally, initial franchise fees may also include payment for tangible property such as signs, equipment, inventory, land, and buildings. Fees received for tangible assets are recognized when title to the property passes to the franchisee.

The key issue in franchise fee accounting centers on when and how much of the initial franchise fee should be recognized up front as revenue by the franchisor. GAAP specifies that revenue from initial franchise fees should be recognized when all material services or conditions relating to the sale have been substantially performed or satisfied by the franchisor.[5] Essentially, the question is—when are the initial franchise fees earned by the franchisor? The answer is not always easily discernable, opening the way for possible abuses from recognizing revenue before it is earned.

The following example illustrates the key measurement and recognition issues related to franchise fee revenue.

On January 1, 2014, Diet Right sells a dieting/weight loss franchise for an initial fee of $25,000 with $10,000 due at the signing of the franchise agreement and the remainder due in three annual installments (due December 31) of $5,000 each plus interest at 8% on the unpaid balance. The $10,000 up-front payment gives the franchisee the right to use Diet Right's name and sell prepackaged healthy meals prepared at Diet Right's corporate headquarters. In return for the initial franchise fee, Diet Right agrees to train employees, set up a recordkeeping system, maintain a website with online dietary counseling by a registered dietician, and provide advertising and various promotional materials. In addition to the initial franchise fee, Diet Right will receive 2% of the franchise's annual sales for allowing the franchisee to purchase prepackaged meals at below market prices.

Recording Initial Franchise Fees Assuming that the deferred payments under the franchise agreement are for services not yet performed (for example, training employees, maintaining the website, and advertising), Diet Right would record the following entry for the initial franchise fee when the franchise agreement is signed.

[5] FASB ASC Section 952-605-25: Franchisors—Revenue Recognition—Recognition.

January 1, 2014:

DR Cash	$10,000	
DR Note receivable	15,000[a]	
CR Earned franchise fee revenue		$10,000[b]
CR Unearned franchise fees		15,000

[a] Initial fee of $25,000 minus $10,000 received at signing of franchise agreement
[b] Amount received for right to use Diet Right name and to sell Diet Right's prepackaged meals

The unearned franchise fees will be recognized as earned when the initial services are performed. These services could be performed evenly over time or at one point in time.

Assuming that one-half of the deferred payment ($7,500) is for employee training and recordkeeping system installation completed by Diet Right before the franchise opens, the following entry would be made on Diet Right's books when the franchise commences operations on March 1, 2014.

March 1, 2014:

DR Unearned franchise fees	$7,500	
CR Earned franchise fees		$7,500

Note that this portion of the initial franchise fee is recognized even though the amount has not been received in cash. This treatment is appropriate assuming that the collectibility of the note receivable from the franchisee is reasonably assured.

If the remaining $7,500 of the initial franchise fee is for services provided by Diet Right on an ongoing basis over the term of the note (for example, maintenance of the website and advertising), the following adjusting entry would be made at the end of each year to record franchise fee revenue earned during the period.

December 31, 2014 (2015 and 2016):

DR Unearned franchise fees	$2,500	
CR Earned franchise fee revenue		$2,500

In addition, the entry to record the receipt of payment on the note receivable and interest earned at 8% on the outstanding note balance would be as follows at December 31:

	2014		2015		2016	
DR Cash	$5,000		$5,000		$5,000	
CR Notes receivable		$5,000		$5,000		$5,000
DR Cash	$1,200[a]		$ 800[b]		$ 400[c]	
CR Interest revenue		$1,200		$ 800		$ 400

[a] 0.08 × $15,000 = $1,200   [b] 0.08 × $10,000 = $800   [c] 0.08 × $5,000 = $400

Recording Continuing Franchise Fees

If the franchisee sales were $100,000 in 2014, the entry for the continuing or periodic fee (0.02 × $100,000 = $2,000) would be:

DR	Cash	$2,000	
	CR Earned franchise fee revenue		$2,000

Costs incurred by the franchisor to provide initial and continuing services (for example, counseling by a registered dietician or advertising) are expensed in the same periods as the franchise revenue following the matching principle.

> These returns may be made by the ultimate customer or by a party who resells the product to the final customer (that is, a distributor).

Sales with Right of Return

Due to the nature of their products, certain companies such as book publishers, packaged software companies, and semiconductor manufacturers experience high rates of return of their products. For example, book publishers commonly have rates of return in excess of 25% for hardcover books. Because of rapid obsolescence of their product, semiconductor manufacturers such as Motorola Solutions and Intel grant distributors the right to return semiconductors they are unable to sell.

When the frequency and magnitude of returns are high, a question arises as to whether an entity should recognize revenue at the time of sale or defer recognition until the uncertainty regarding product returns is resolved. GAAP specifies that for a seller to record revenue at time of sale when **right of return** exists, all the following criteria must be met:[6]

- The seller's price to the buyer is substantially fixed or determinable at the date of sale.
- The buyer has paid the seller or the buyer is obligated to pay the seller and the obligation is not contingent on the resale of the product.
- The buyer's obligation to the seller does not change in the event of theft or physical destruction or damage of the product.
- The buyer acquiring the product for resale has economic substance and exists separate and distinct from the seller. That is, the buyer cannot be a **special purpose entity** established by the seller for the sole purpose of buying and reselling the seller's product and thus allowing the seller to recognize revenue.
- The seller does not have significant obligations for future performance to directly bring about resale of the product to the buyer.
- The amount of future returns can be reasonably estimated.

> This is perhaps the most important of these criteria and the one subject to greatest uncertainty. Because estimation of future product returns entails considerable judgment, it can lead to manipulation and revenue overstatement. Statement users need to be particularly wary of unusual patterns in return provisions for those entities that operate in industries with high levels and variability of product returns.

When all six of these conditions are met, an entity will debit Sales returns and credit Allowance for sales returns for the estimated returns from sales made during the period. The Sales returns account is netted against (shown contra to) the gross sales figure for the period to avoid overstatement of sales revenue, and the Allowance for sales returns account is shown contra to Accounts receivable to avoid overstating this asset account.

When any of these conditions is not met, then sales revenue and the related cost of sales are deferred and recognized either when the return privilege has substantially expired or when the conditions listed above are met, whichever comes first.

---

[6] FASB ASC Section 605-15-25: Revenue Recognition—Products—Recognition.

Bundled (Multiple-Element) Sales

Software vendors such as Microsoft and Oracle often package their products in "bundles" of more than one product or service ("multiple deliverables") that are sold for a lump-sum contract price. In addition to the software itself (or the license to use the software), other deliverables include items that are not essential to the principal functionality of the product such as training in the use of the software, upgrades and enhancements, and postcontract customer support. The key accounting issue related to bundled sales transactions is the timing of revenue recognition. That is, how much of the lump-sum contract price should be recognized up front when the product is delivered to the customer, and how much should be deferred and recognized as the seller satisfies its commitment for other deliverables specified in the contract?

Authoritative guidance states that if a software sales arrangement includes multiple, distinct elements, the revenue from the arrangement should be allocated to the various elements based on vendor-specific objective evidence (VSOE) of the elements' relative fair value.[7] As a practical matter, vendor-specific objective evidence is obtained from observed prices charged when the elements are sold separately.

To illustrate how revenue is allocated with multiple deliverables, assume that Oracle sells its database management software system to a corporate client for $1 million. The contract stipulates that in addition to the software, Oracle will provide staff training on the use of the software, a free upgrade on a when-and-if-available basis, and customer support over the five years of the licensing agreement. Objective evidence of relative fair values, based on what Oracle would charge for these individual elements if sold separately, is as follows:

	Fair Value	Percentage of Total Fair Value
Database management software	$ 600,000	40%
Training	450,000	30
Upgrades	300,000	20
Customer support	150,000	10
Total estimated fair values if sold separately	$1,500,000	100%

In this example, Oracle would recognize $400,000 (0.40 × $1 million) of revenue when the software is delivered and installed for the client, $300,000 (0.30 × $1 million) when the training is complete, $200,000 (0.20 × $1 million) when upgrades are installed and $100,000 (0.10 × $1 million) recognized evenly over the five years of the contract as the customer service is provided.

Exhibit 3.6 is an excerpt from Oracle's note on significant accounting policies that explains its revenue recognition policies for software licensing revenues and service revenues. The amount of sales revenue that Oracle deferred and reported as unearned revenue amounted to $7.331 billion as of May 31, 2012.

For multiple-element sales that lack vendor-specific or objective third-party evidence for one of more elements in the contract, companies are allowed to estimate the selling price of those elements. The overall arrangement fee (selling price) is allocated to each element based on their relative selling prices regardless of how those estimated selling prices are determined and revenue is recognized as each element is delivered.[8]

---

[7] FASB ASC Section 985-605-25: Software—Revenue Recognition—Recognition.

[8] FASB ASC Section 605-25: Revenue Recognition—Multiple-Element Arrangements.

EXHIBIT 3.6	Oracle Corporation Excerpts from Significant Accounting Policies Note—Fiscal Year 2012 10-K Report

Revenue Recognition

Our sources of revenues include: (1) software, which includes new software license revenues earned from granting licenses to use our software products and fees from cloud software subscription offerings, and software license updates and product support revenues; (2) hardware systems, which includes the sale of hardware systems products including computer servers and storage products, and hardware systems support revenues; and (3) services, which includes software and hardware related services including consulting, managed cloud services and education revenues.

For software license arrangements that do not require significant modification or customization of the underlying software, we recognize new software license revenues when: (1) we enter into a legally binding arrangement with a customer for the license of software; (2) we deliver the products; (3) the sale price is fixed or determinable and free of contingencies or significant uncertainties; and (4) collection is probable. Revenues that are not recognized at the time of sale because the foregoing conditions are not met, are recognized when those conditions are subsequently met.

The vast majority of our software license arrangements include software license updates and product support contracts, which are entered into at the customer's option and are recognized ratably over the term of the arrangement, typically one year.

We often enter into arrangements with customers that purchase both software related products and software related services from us at the same time, or within close proximity of one another (referred to as software related multiple-element arrangements). Such software related multiple-element arrangements include the sale of our software products, software license updates and product support contracts and other software related services whereby software license delivery is followed by the subsequent or contemporaneous delivery of the other elements. For those software related multiple-element arrangements, we have applied the residual method to determine the amount of software license revenues to be recognized pursuant to ASC 985-605. Under the residual method, if fair value exists for undelivered elements in a multiple-element arrangement, such fair value of the undelivered elements is deferred with the remaining portion of the arrangement consideration recognized upon delivery of the software license or services arrangement. We allocate the fair value of each element of a software related multiple-element arrangement based upon its fair value as determined by our vendor specific objective evidence (VSOE—described further below), with any remaining amount allocated to the software license.

Revenues from the sales of our nonsoftware elements are recognized when: (1) persuasive evidence of an arrangement exists; (2) we deliver the products and passage of the title to the buyer occurs; (3) the sale price is fixed or determinable; and (4) collection is reasonably assured. Revenues that are not recognized at the time of sale because the foregoing conditions are not met are recognized when those conditions are subsequently met. When applicable, we reduce revenues for estimated returns or certain other incentive programs where we have the ability to sufficiently estimate the effects of these items.

We establish VSOE of selling price for deliverables in nonsoftware multiple-element arrangements using the price charged for a deliverable when sold separately and for software license updates and product support and hardware systems support, based on the renewal rates offered to customers.

Source: 2012 Oracle 10-K Report.

Because the determination of relative fair values of multiple deliverables requires considerable judgment on the part of companies' management, there is potential for premature revenue recognition and/or arbitrary income shifting from period to period. Accordingly, statement users need to be particularly vigilant when assessing companies' revenue and profits with significant amounts of bundled or multiple-element sales arrangements.

EARNINGS MANAGEMENT

"Executives rarely have to violate the law to put a gloss on dreary earnings. Accepted accounting principles leave ample room for those who want to fudge the numbers."[9]

The criteria for revenue and expense recognition outlined in Chapter 2 provide general guidelines for accrual accounting income determination. Applying these rules in specific settings still leaves room, however, for considerable latitude and judgment. For example, determining when revenue has been earned (critical event) and is realizable (measurability)—the two conditions for revenue recognition—are often judgment calls. Managers can sometimes exploit the flexibility in GAAP to manipulate reported earnings in ways that mask the company's underlying performance. Some managers have even resorted to outright financial fraud to inflate reported earnings, but this is relatively rare.

The increasing propensity of managers to bolster earnings by exploiting the flexibility in GAAP or by resorting to financial fraud led former SEC Chairman Arthur Levitt to warn:

> Increasingly, I have become concerned that the motivation to meet Wall Street earnings expectations may be overriding commonsense business practices. Too many corporate managers, auditors, and analysts are participating in a game of nods and winks. In the zeal to satisfy consensus earnings estimates and project a smooth earnings path, wishful thinking may be winning the day over faithful representation. As a result, I fear that we are witnessing an erosion in the quality of earnings, and therefore, the quality of financial reporting. Managing may be giving way to manipulation; integrity may be losing to illusion.[10]

Earnings management is not new. But the perception is that it has become increasingly common in today's marketplace because of pressure to meet analysts' earnings forecasts. Companies that miss analysts' earnings per share estimates by even a few pennies frequently experience significant stock price declines. Several highly publicized examples of alleged accounting "irregularities"[11] and several research studies[12] lend support to Chairman Levitt's concerns about earnings management.

One way to avoid a decline in stock price for reporting a loss is to make sure to report an accounting profit. Ideally, this should be accomplished through real economic events that are accounted for correctly. When all else fails, however, managers sometimes resort to various sorts of accounting "tricks" (described more fully later) to artificially inflate earnings. Results from a recent research study suggest that artificially inflating earnings

---

[9] F. S. Worthy, "Manipulating Profits: How It's Done," *Fortune,* June 25, 1984, pp. 50–54.

[10] Statements made by Arthur Levitt, chairman of the Securities and Exchange Commission, in a speech entitled, "The Numbers Game," delivered at the New York University Center for Law and Business, September 28, 1998.

[11] D. Bank, "Informix Says Accounting Problems Were More Serious Than First Disclosed," *The Wall Street Journal,* September 23, 1997; T. O'Brien, "KnowledgeWare Accounting Practices Are Questioned," *The Wall Street Journal,* September 7, 1994; M. Maremont, "Anatomy of a Fraud: How Kurzweil's Straight-Arrow CEO Went Awry," *BusinessWeek,* September 16, 1996, pp. 90–93; S. Lipin, "How Telxon Corp. Came to Restate Earnings," *The Wall Street Journal,* December 23, 1998; J. Laing, "Dangerous Games: Did 'Chainsaw Al' Dunlap Manufacture Sunbeam's Earnings Last Year?" *Barron's Online,* June 8, 1998, pp. 1–8; and E. Nelson and J. Lublin, "Whistle-Blowers Set Off Cendant Probe," *The Wall Street Journal,* August 13, 1998.

[12] D. Burgstahler and I. Dichev, "Earnings Management to Avoid Earnings Decreases and Losses," *Journal of Accounting and Economics,* December 1997, pp. 99–126; F. Degeorge, J. Patel, and R. Zeckhauser, "Earnings Management to Exceed Thresholds," *Journal of Business,* January 1999, pp. 1–33; and P. Dechow, S. Richardson, and A. Tuna, "Why Are Earnings Kinky? A Reexamination of the Earnings Management Explanation," *Review of Accounting Studies,* vol. 8, 2003, pp. 335–84.

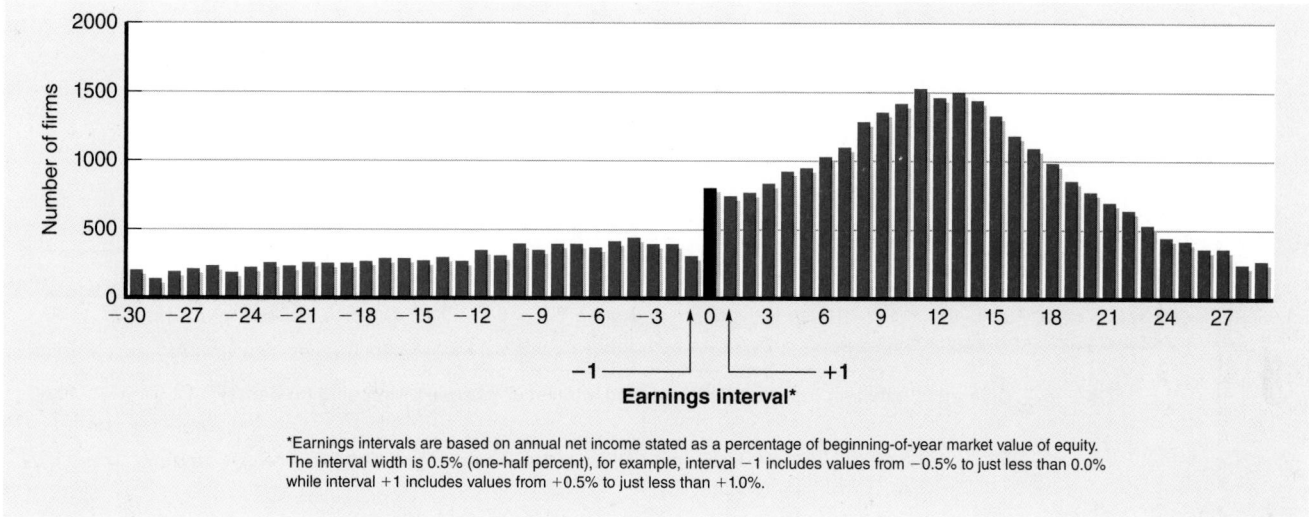

Figure 3.1 DISTRIBUTION OF ANNUAL NET INCOME

Source: P. Dechow, S. Richardson, and A. Tuna, "Why Are Earnings Kinky? A Reexamination of the Earnings Management Explanation," *Review of Accounting Studies,* Vol. 8, 2003, pp. 335–84.

is a common occurrence, especially for firms that would otherwise report small losses.[13] Figure 3.1 is a frequency distribution of annual reported earnings for a large number of firms over a 20-year period. The horizontal axis represents groupings of individual firms' reported earnings stated as a percentage of their beginning-of-year market value of equity. The interval width of each grouping (that is, the interval width for each bar on the graph) is 0.5%, or half of 1 percent. Thus, the grouping labeled −1 includes firms whose earnings stated as a percentage of beginning-of-year market value of equity falls in the range from −0.5% to just less than the negative side of 0.00%. Grouping 0 contains values from 0.00% to just less than +0.5% while grouping +1 contains values from +0.5% to just less than 1.0%. The vertical axis measures the number of firms whose reported earnings fall into the various categories.

> Let's use a numerical example for clarity. Assume Hong Company reports 2014 earnings of $500,000 and the market value of its equity on January 1, 2014, was $62,500,000. Thus, $500,000/$62,500,000 = .008 or 0.8%. Since 0.8% is within the interval of 0.5% to 1.0%, Hong Company would appear in interval +1.

The striking feature of this graph is the discontinuity in the number of firms reporting slightly negative earnings versus slightly positive earnings. Substantially fewer firms fall just below zero (grouping −1) while a substantially higher number of firms report earnings at or just above zero (groupings 0 and +1). What appears to be happening is that managers of firms that would otherwise report small losses (group −1) are finding ways to prop up earnings to move the firm's reported profits into the group 0 or group 1 range (that is, slightly positive range). One way of doing so, even in troubled times, is to exploit the flexibility in GAAP or to resort to a variety accounting gimmicks to push earnings into the positive range.

As has been noted, investors often penalize companies that fail to meet analysts' earnings expectations. Figure 3.2 provides indirect evidence on the strong incentive managers have to meet or beat analysts' earnings estimates. This graph shows the distribution of analysts' annual earnings per share (EPS) forecast errors, that is, actual EPS minus analysts' consensus EPS

---

[13] Dechow et al., Ibid.

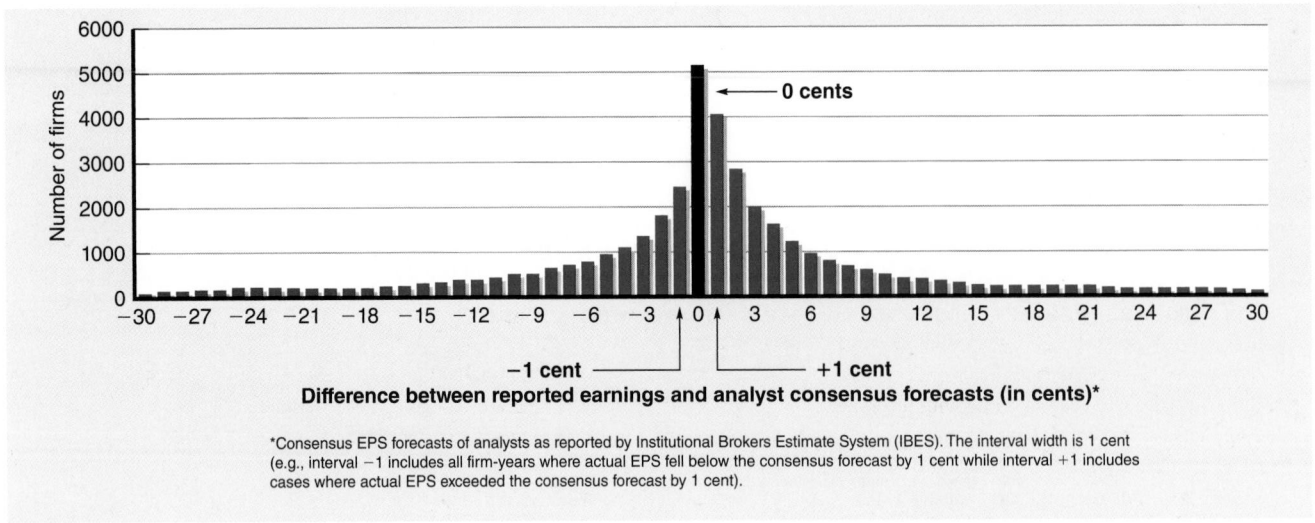

Figure 3.2 DISTRIBUTION OF ANNUAL FORECAST ERRORS (IN CENTS) AS REPORTED BY I/B/E/S

Source: P. Dechow, S. Richardson, and I. Tuna, "Are Benchmark Beaters Doing Anything Wrong?" Working Paper. Copyright © 2000 Irem Tuna. Reprinted by permission of the author. July 2000.

estimate. The interval width of each bar is 1 cent. Thus, the forecast error bar labeled −1 cent (+1 cent) reflects the number of firm-years when actual earnings per share falls below (above) the analysts' consensus forecasts by 1 cent. Note the large number of observations clustered in the zero forecast error interval where actual EPS equals the consensus estimate. Also note the much smaller number of forecast errors that fall in the bar just below zero (−1 cent) compared to the number that fall just above zero (+1 cent). One explanation of this result is that some companies are managing earnings upward to "meet or beat" analysts' earnings projections.

> The analysts' consensus EPS estimates come from Institutional Brokers Estimate System (I/B/E/S) which provides analyst earnings per share forecasts (both annual and quarterly) for more than 18,000 companies in more than 50 countries.

A survey of more than 400 chief financial officers (CFOs) and treasurers of major U.S. companies provides evidence that corroborates the data displayed in Figures 3.1 and 3.2.[14] More than 65% of the financial executives surveyed indicated that reporting a profit was an important earnings benchmark while approximately 74% indicated that meeting or beating analysts' consensus EPS forecasts for the current quarter was an important benchmark.

When asked why their company tries to meet earnings benchmarks, more than 86% of the financial executives surveyed indicated that they did so to help build credibility with the capital market. In addition, 82% indicated that benchmark beating was important to maintain or increase stock price while 74% indicated that beating benchmarks helped to convey future growth prospects to investors. Managers say they willingly sacrifice firm value to appease Wall Street analysts: more than 80% of the CFOs surveyed indicted that they would delay research and development, advertising, and maintenance spending; 55% acknowledged that they would delay the start of positive net present value projects to achieve earnings targets. Earnings can also be managed with

> "For years, Wall Street has known that companies manage earnings. Academic studies have found that actual earnings do not fall randomly around the consensus estimate. Instead, they tend to come in at or above the forecast. Some companies . . . almost always seem to beat estimates by a penny or two a share, no matter what the economic conditions. . . . Managements try to give investors what they want, and companies whose earnings are predictable are prized on Wall Street, which does not like unhappy surprises."
>
> *Source:* A. Berenson, "Tweaking Numbers to Meet Goals Comes Back to Haunt Executives," *The New York Times,* June 29, 2002.

---

[14] J. Graham, C. Harvey, and S. Rajgopal, "The Economic Implications of Corporate Financial Reporting," *Journal of Accounting & Economics,* December 2005, pp. 3–73.

a variety of accrual estimates and year-end adjustments. Clearly, real transaction management or accrual management seems more consistent with managing earnings to disguise the firm's true underlying economic performance than with managing earnings to convey value-relevant private information to investors about the firm's future growth prospects.

Overvaluation of a firm's stock price provides a strong incentive for managers to use accounting gimmicks to meet or beat analysts' earnings forecasts. A highly regarded financial economist explains why:

> Because compensation is tied to budgets and targets, people are paid not for what they do but for what they do relative to some target. And this leads people to game the system by manipulating both the setting of the targets and how they meet their targets. These counterproductive target-based budget and compensation systems provide the fertile foundation for the damaging effects of the earnings management game with the capital markets. Corporate managers and the financial markets have been playing a game similar to the budgeting game. Just as managers' compensation suffers if they miss their internal targets, CEOs and CFOs know that capital markets will punish the entire firm if they miss analysts' [earnings] forecasts by as much as a penny. And just as managers who meet or exceed their internal targets receive a bonus, the capital markets reward a firm with a premium for meeting or beating analysts' [earnings] expectations during the quarter. . . . Generally, the only way for managers to meet those expectations year in and year out is to cook their numbers to mask the inherent uncertainty in their business. And that cannot be done without sacrificing value.[15]

Collectively, the survey results and the conjectures in the preceding quote suggest that when capital market-based incentives to manage earnings to meet or beat analysts' forecasts are present, the representational faithfulness and predictive usefulness of the resultant accounting numbers may be compromised.[16] As a user of financial statements, you should be aware of managements' incentives to distort reported earnings and the ways in which this is done, a subject to which we turn in the next section and throughout the remainder of the book.

Popular Earnings Management Devices

What are some of the more popular techniques firms use to manage earnings? Former Chairman Levitt singled out the following areas that are particularly troublesome and pervasive.[17]

- *"Big Bath" restructuring charges:* To remain competitive and become more efficient, hundreds of companies have closed plants, consolidated operations, reduced their labor force, and sold off noncore business units. Once a decision to restructure is made, GAAP requires companies to estimate the future costs they expect to incur to carry out the restructuring for such things as employee severance payments and plant closings.[18] These estimated restructuring costs are then charged to an expense account with an offsetting credit to a liability account (Restructuring reserve) in the current period. In

---

[15] M. Jensen, "Agency Costs of Overvalued Equity," *Financial Management,* Spring 2005, p. 5–19. Copyright © 2005 Wiley-Blackwell. Used with permission.

[16] For empirical evidence consistent with this concern, see B. Badertscher, "Overvaluation and the Choice of Alternative Earnings Management Mechanisms," *The Accounting Review,* September 2011, pp. 1491–1518; B. Badertscher, C. Collins, and T. Lys, "Discretionary Accounting Choices and the Predictive Ability of Accruals with Respect to Future Cash Flows," *Journal of Accounting & Economics,* February–April, 2012, pp. 330–52; and J. Efendi, A. Srivastava, and E. Swanson, "Why Do Corporate Managers Misstate Financial Statements? The Role of In-the-Money Options and Other Incentives," *Journal of Financial Economics,* September 2007, pp. 667–708.

[17] Levitt, "The Numbers Game," op. cit.

[18] FASB ASC Section 420: Exit or Disposal Cost Obligations.

A report prepared by outside investigators for the Board of Freddie Mac, a big mortgage financier, highlights how management used a variety of cookie jar reserves to artificially smooth earnings.

Freddie Mac, which for most of the last few years has faced the uncommon problem of having profits that substantially exceeded Wall Street forecasts, did not want to deviate too much from those expectations, the report said. So it used techniques to make its underlying business of insuring and buying mortgages seem less profitable and to create a reserve of earnings for later years. . . . Freddie Mac said it had understated its pre-tax profits by as much as $6.9 billion in 2002 and previous years as a result of serious accounting problems, and the company ousted its three top executives. The report offers more evidence of what regulators and many investors say is a culture of earnings management in corporate America. Like many other big publicly traded companies, Freddie Mac put a premium on meeting analysts' forecasts of its profits and providing consistent growth in reported earnings.

Source: A. Berenson, "Report Says Freddie Mac Misled Investors," *The New York Times,* July 24, 2003. Copyright © 2003. Used by permission of The New York Times Co., Inc.

an effort to "clean up" company balance sheets, managers have often taken excessive restructuring write-offs and overstated estimated charges for future expenditures. Examples of questionable items that the SEC has found in restructuring charges include services to be provided in some future period by lawyers, accountants, and investment bankers; special bonuses for officers; and expenses for retraining and relocating people. Amazingly, some companies even took charges for training people not yet hired!

Why are companies tempted to overstate restructuring charges? The conventional wisdom is that investors look beyond one-time special charges and write-offs and, instead, value a company's stock based on sustainable operating earnings (see Chapter 6). So, many believe that taking "big bath" charges does not adversely affect stock price.[19] Moreover, these restructuring charges and associated liability reserves are sometimes reversed in future years when earnings fall short of targets, thereby providing a boost to the bottom line at opportune times.

- *Miscellaneous "cookie jar reserves":* Accrual accounting allows companies to estimate and accrue for obligations that will be paid in *future periods* as a result of transactions or events in the *current period.* Similar reserves are allowed for estimated declines in asset values. Examples include provisions for bad debts and loan losses, warranty costs, sales returns, and reserves for various future expenditures related to corporate restructuring. Some companies use unrealistic assumptions to arrive at these estimated charges. They overreserve in good times and cut back on estimated charges, or even reverse previous charges, in bad times. As a result, these "cookie jar reserves" become a convenient income smoothing device. One critique of IFRS is that it might offer more opportunities for "cookie jar reserves" accrual accounting than U.S. GAAP. As discussed in Chapter 10, IFRS allows companies to reverse prior period asset impairments. This might allow a company to impair assets in good times and reverse these impairments later.

- *Intentional errors deemed to be "immaterial" and intentional bias in estimates:* Materiality thresholds are another way of using financial reporting flexibility to inflate earnings. Sometimes, companies intentionally misapply GAAP, for example, capitalizing an expenditure that should be expensed. If the auditor subsequently catches this incorrect treatment, management might justify the error by arguing that the earnings effect is "immaterial" and, therefore, not worth correcting. The problem, of course, is that a series of these "immaterial" errors spread across several accounts can, in the aggregate, have a material effect on bottom-line earnings.

    Intentional misstatement of estimates is another area of abuse. Estimates abound in accrual accounting. Examples include estimated useful lives and salvage values for fixed assets, estimates of bad debts, and the amount of write-down for obsolete inventory. Management can often shade these estimates in one direction or the other to achieve a desired earnings target. As long as these estimates fall within "acceptable" ranges, the biased estimate is unlikely to draw attention from the external auditor.

---

[19] J. Elliott and D. Hanna, "Repeated Accounting Write-Offs and the Information Content of Earnings," *Journal of Accounting Research, Supplement,* 1996, pp. 135–55.

- *Premature or aggressive revenue recognition:* Another common abuse is to recognize revenues before they have been "earned" (the critical event criterion) or become "realized" (the measurability criterion). The next section discusses this important earnings management device.

Revenue Recognition Abuses   The SEC says that revenue is earned (critical event) and is realized or realizable (measurability)—and, therefore, can be recognized—when all of the following criteria are met:

1. Persuasive evidence of an exchange arrangement exists.
2. Delivery has occurred or services have been rendered.
3. The seller's price to the buyer is fixed or determinable.
4. Collectibility is reasonably assured.

> "Arrangement" means there is a final understanding between the parties as to the specific nature and terms of the agreed-upon transaction.

The following scenarios taken from *SEC Staff Accounting Bulletin (SAB) No. 104* illustrate some troublesome areas of revenue recognition as well as the SEC's recommendation regarding the appropriate treatment.[20]

- *Scenario 1—Goods shipped on consignment:* A software manufacturer (seller) ships 100,000 copies of a new video game to distributors, charging $50 per copy. Under terms of the signed agreement, distributors have the right (a) to return unsold copies of the video game and (b) not to pay the seller until they resell the product to final customers through their retail outlets. The software manufacturer wants to recognize $5,000,000 of revenue upon delivery of the video games to the distributors. Can the company do this?

    SEC interpretive response: No revenue can be recognized on delivery. The reason is that the seller retains the risks and rewards of ownership of the product. Title does not pass to the distributor when the goods are shipped. Also, under criterion 4 in the preceding list, there is considerable uncertainty as to ultimate collectibility of the sales price on the goods shipped.

- *Scenario 2—Sales with delayed delivery:* Prior to the close of its September 30 fiscal quarter, a manufacturer (seller) completes production of 50,000 specialized gas valves. The valves sell for $60 each and were ordered by customers that assemble and sell gas fireplaces. The customers are unable to take delivery by September 30 for reasons that include (1) lack of available storage space, (2) having ample inventory on hand to cover production for the next month, and (3) delayed production schedules. The seller segregates the valves awaiting shipment from other unsold products in its own warehouse and wishes to recognize $3,000,000 of revenue in the current quarter from these goods produced but not shipped.

    SEC interpretive response: Without evidence of an exchange being spelled out in the sales agreement (criterion 1), the seller cannot recognize revenue until delivery has taken place (criterion 2). Generally, delivery is *not* considered to have occurred unless the customer (1) takes title and (2) assumes the risks and rewards of ownership of the products. Typically, these conditions are met when a product is received at the customer's place of business or when the product is shipped to the customer and the customer assumes responsibility for the product once it leaves the seller's premises. If the buyer requests in the sales agreement that the transaction be on a "bill and hold" basis and has a substantial business purpose for doing so, the seller may recognize revenue when the production of the goods is complete.

- *Scenario 3—Goods sold on layaway:* Company R, a retailer, offers layaway sales to its customers. It collects an initial cash deposit from the customer but retains the merchandise

---

[20] FASB ASC Section 605-10-S25: Revenue Recognition—Overall—(SEC) Revenue Recognition [also located in "Revenue Recognition," *Staff Accounting Bulletin No. 104* (Washington, DC: SEC, December 17, 2003)].

and sets it aside in its inventory. Although a date may be specified within which the customer must finalize the purchase, Company R does not require the customer to sign a fixed payment agreement. The merchandise is not released to the customer until full payment is received. Company R wants to recognize revenue equal to a pro rata portion of the merchandise sales price as cash is collected.

SEC interpretive response: Company R should postpone recognizing revenue until merchandise is delivered to the customer (criterion 2 delivery has not occurred). Until then, the cash received to date should be recognized as a liability such as Deposits from layaway customers. Because Company R retains the risks of ownership, receives only deposits, and does not have an enforceable right to the remainder of the purchase price, it is not entitled to recognize revenue until the sales price is received in full.

- *Scenario 4—Nonrefundable up-front fees:* Increasingly, service providers negotiate agreements with customers that require the customer to pay a nonrefundable up-front "initiation" or service "activation" fee. For example, companies that provide telecommunications services typically charge each new customer a nonrefundable activation fee. Once enrolled for service, customers then pay monthly usage fees that just cover the company's operating costs. The costs to activate the telecommunications service are minimal. Thus, the up-front fee customers pay more than covers these costs. The key question here involves when revenue from nonrefundable up-front activation fees should be recognized.

    SEC interpretive response: Unless the up-front fee is in exchange for products delivered or services performed that represent the culmination of a separate earnings process, deferral of revenue is appropriate because service has not been rendered (criterion 2, delivery). In such circumstances, the up-front fees, even if nonrefundable, are deemed to be earned as the services are delivered over the service agreement's full term. This means that the up-front fees should be deferred and recognized pro rata over the periods when services are provided because that's when the fees are earned.

- *Scenario 5—Gross versus net basis for Internet resellers:* Another troublesome area is the method used to record sales by certain Internet companies that simply act as an agent or broker in a transaction. For example, assume that Dot-com Company operates an Internet site from which it sells airline tickets. Customers place orders by selecting a specific flight from Dot-com's website and providing a credit card number for payment. Dot-com receives the order and credit card authorization and passes this information along to the airline. The airline sends the tickets directly to the customer. Dot-com does not take title to the tickets and, therefore, has no ownership risk or other responsibility for the tickets. The airline is fully responsible for all returned tickets and disputed credit card charges. (So, Dot-com is just an agent or broker that facilitates the transaction between the customer and the airline.) The average ticket price is $500, of which Dot-com receives a $25 commission. In the event a credit card sale is rejected, Dot-com loses its $25 commission on sale. Because its management believes that revenue growth is what drives its share price, it seeks to report the revenue from this transaction on a "gross" basis at $500, along with cost of sales of $475.

    SEC interpretive response: Dot-com should report the revenue from this transaction on a "net" basis: $25 as commission revenue and $0 for cost of sales. In determining whether revenue should be reported gross (with separate display of cost of sales) or on a net basis, the SEC stipulates that the following factors be considered:

1. Is Dot-com acting as a principal or as an agent/broker in the transaction?
2. Does Dot-com take title to the ticket?
3. Does Dot-com assume the risks of ownership such as possible losses from bad debts or returns?

If Dot-com acts as a principal in the transaction, takes title to the tickets or assumes the ownership risks, then the gross method is deemed appropriate. Otherwise, the net method must be used.

- *Scenario 6—Capacity swaps:* Over the past decade, revenue growth has been a major factor that affects the value of telecommunications companies. In an effort to bolster quarter-over-quarter revenue growth and build capacity for future expected customer demand, several telecommunication companies entered into a series of **"capacity swap"** transactions exchanging access to each other's networks. As an example, assume that on January 1, 2014, San Francisco Telecom agrees to exchange $150 million worth of capacity over its fiber optic network between San Francisco and Asia for $175 million of capacity on Boston Telecom's communications network between New York and Europe. Company engineers estimate that current customer demand would have to increase five-fold (not a likely outcome for the foreseeable future) before the capacity being acquired would be needed. On signing the agreement, each company seeks to book revenue equal to the capacity rights being sold while booking the capacity bought as a capital expenditure that will be written off on a straight-line basis over the 10-year term of the swap agreement. As a consequence, San Francisco Telecom plans to book $150 million of revenue and $17.5 million per year ($175 million/10 years) of expenses resulting in increased pre-tax profits of $132.5 million in the year the swap agreement is signed. Boston Telecom would book $175 million of revenue, $15 million of expenses, and $160 million in pre-tax profits. Thus, both companies stand to report substantially higher revenues and profits in the current period despite the fact that none, or very little, of the capacity exchanged is likely to be used by paying customers in the current period.

    SEC interpretive response:[21] The SEC position is that rather than recognize the entire amount of the swapped capacity as revenue up front when the contract is signed, revenues should be deferred and recognized over the term of the swap agreement as the capacity is brought on line and used by the acquiring firm's customers. Capacity acquired is to be charged against earnings over the life of the swap agreement as indicated earlier.

    It is important to note that *SAB 104* was not meant to change GAAP. Instead, it is intended to close some loopholes and eliminate gray areas in how GAAP is being applied in practice. A survey of annual reports indicates that the SEC guidelines have diminished abuses.[22] However, aggressive revenue recognition still occurs, so analysts must be vigilant for firms that overstate true earnings performance by bending revenue recognition rules.

The criteria for revenue and expense recognition are intended to provide general guidance for accrual accounting income determination. However, these general criteria leave ample room for judgment and interpretation that create flexibility in GAAP. Analysts and investors must be alert for management's attempts to exploit this flexibility in ways that push the boundaries of acceptable revenue and expense recognition.

---

[21] This interpretative response was issued subsequent to *SAB 104* (FASB ASC Section 605-10-S25, op.cit.) as part of enforcement actions brought against companies deemed to have violated GAAP. The SEC publishes details of major enforcement actions against firms with accounting irregularities in a series called Accounting and Auditing Enforcement Releases.

[22] P. McConnell, J. Pegg, and D. Zion, "Revenue Recognition 101," *Accounting Issues* (New York: Bear, Stearns & Co. Inc., March 10, 2000).

ACCOUNTING ERRORS, EARNINGS RESTATEMENTS, AND PRIOR PERIOD ADJUSTMENTS

Accounting errors or irregularities[23] can occur for a variety of reasons. Sometimes they occur because of simple oversight. For example, a buyer may fail to include in its ending inventory the cost of merchandise in transit for which title transfers at the time goods are shipped by the seller (see Chapter 9). Errors can also occur because different parties disagree on how to account for a given transaction, resulting in misapplication of GAAP. For example, practicing accountants looking at a given set of facts can sometimes disagree on when the critical event and measurability conditions have been satisfied for revenue recognition. Finally, errors sometimes occur because management attempts to exploit the flexibility in GAAP or commits outright financial fraud to inflate earnings and overstate net assets. The Enron and WorldCom restatements in 2001 and 2002 that led to the largest corporate failures in U.S. history provide examples.

Several different parties are charged with the responsibility for discovering accounting errors and irregularities:

- The company's internal audit staff and audit committee of the board of directors are charged with the responsibility for evaluating internal controls, overseeing the preparation of the financial statements, and ensuring that their content fully and accurately depicts the company's financial condition and results of operations. As part of their ongoing review of control systems and financial reporting process, the audit committee and the company's internal audit staff provide the first-line defense against accounting errors/irregularities.

- External auditors provide an additional safeguard in identifying and correcting accounting errors and irregularities. Although the company's management is responsible for the preparation and content of the published financial statements, the independent external auditor is charged with the responsibility for auditing the financial statements to ensure that they are fairly presented in all material respects in accordance with GAAP. As part of the interim review and year-end audit, the external auditor will occasionally uncover accounting errors and irregularities that require correction of current period results or restatement of prior period financial statements.

- The Securities Act of 1933 and the Securities Exchange Act of 1934 require companies that sell securities in the United States to register with the SEC and make periodic financial filings with the Commission. As part of its oversight of the registration and filing process, the SEC staff reviews selected issuers' filings to ensure compliance with SEC accounting and disclosure requirements. Through this process, the SEC staff sometimes identifies accounting irregularities that require correction.

A report issued by the U.S. Department of Treasury demonstrates a dramatic increase in the incidence of accounting irregularities leading to earnings restatements over the decade from 1997 to 2006.[24] Figure 3.3 shows that the number of financial statement restatements grew nearly eighteen-fold from 90 in 1997 to 1,577 in 2006. Companies listed on the major exchanges (NYSE, AMEX and NASDAQ) accounted for 3,310 of the restatement, or nearly half

---

[23] Some characterize an *accounting error* as an unintentional mistake in applying GAAP, while an *accounting irregularity* is an accounting choice that management knowingly makes that is subsequently determined to have gone beyond the boundaries of acceptable GAAP. In this section, we use the terms *accounting error* and *irregularity* without making a distinction because they both have the same reporting consequence in terms of required restatements.

[24] "The Changing Nature and Consequences of Public Company Financial Restatements: 1997–2006," by Susan Scholz (Washington, DC, U.S. Department of the Treasury, April 2008).

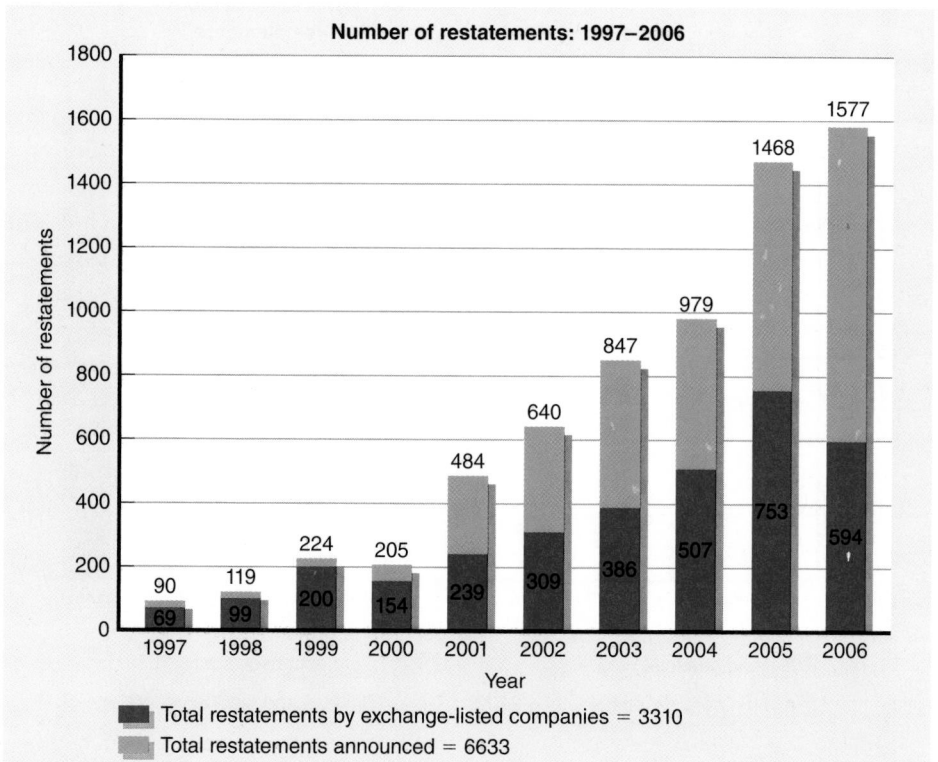

Number of restatements: 1997–2006

■ Total restatements by exchange-listed companies = 3310
■ Total restatements announced = 6633

Figure 3.3

TOTAL NUMBER OF FINAN-
CIAL STATEMENT RESTATE-
MENTS FROM 1997 TO 2006.

Source: U.S. Department of Treasury,
"The Changing Nature and Conse-
quences of Public Company Financial
Restatements: 1997–2006," by Susan
Scholz, 2008.

of the 6,633 total restatements during this 10-year period. Restatements began to accelerate in 2001 prior to high profile corporate accounting scandals like Enron and Worldcom and the passage of the Sarbanes-Oxley (SOX) Act in 2002. The implementation of the internal control reporting provisions under SOX Section 404, which took effect in 2005 for most firms, appears to be associated with the big jump in restatements beginning in 2005, particularly among larger companies. In addition, two specific accounting issues—leases in 2005 and stock options backdating in 2006—contribute to the rather large jump in restatements that took place in 2005 and 2006.

Figure 3.4 on the following page summarizes the major reasons for the restatements. Revenue recognition accounts for 1,314 (roughly 20%) of the restatements. Restatements due to revenue recognition irregularities include recognizing revenue sooner or later than is allowed under GAAP, or recognizing questionable or fictitious revenue. Restatements related to core expense issues account for 2,639 (roughly 40%) of the restatements. This category includes improper recognition of costs or expenses and improperly capitalizing as assets expenditures that should be expensed on the income statement. These restatements involve cost of sales, compensation (including stock-based grants), lease and depreciation costs, selling, general, and administrative costs, and research and development costs. Non-core expense issues account for 2,202 (33.5%) of the restatements. This category includes misstatements of asset impairment charges, improper restructuring charges, tax expense issues, improper accounting for interest on convertible debt, and improper accounting for acquisitions and mergers including under- or overstatement of gains/losses related to acquisitions, and improper valuations of in-process R&D at acquisition. Reclassification and disclosure issues account for the remaining 478 (7.2%) of the restatements. Most of these do not affect net income but involve repositioning balance sheet, income statement, or cash flow statement line items.

> WorldCom provides an example of this type of accounting irregularity. During 2001 and the first quarter of 2002, it improperly capitalized more than $3.8 billion of operating line costs. After announcing this improper accounting treatment, WorldCom's market value plummeted nearly $29 billion, and the company was forced into bankruptcy.

Figure 3.4

ACCOUNTING ISSUES
ASSOCIATED WITH
RESTATEMENTS 1997–2006

Source: U.S. Department of Treasury,
"The Changing Nature and Consequences
of Public Company Financial Restatements:
1997–2006," by Susan Scholz, 2008.

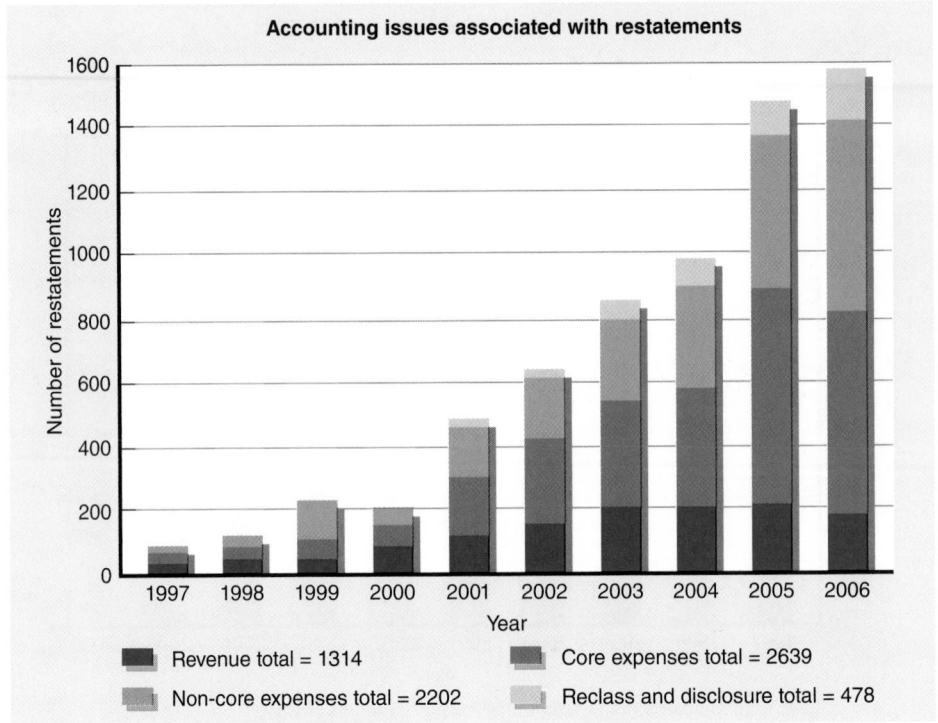

Once discovered, accounting errors and irregularities must be corrected and disclosed. Material errors discovered after the year in which the error is made are corrected through a **prior period adjustment.**[25] This adjustment results in an addition to, or subtraction from, the company's beginning Retained earnings balance (for the year the error is detected) and correction of related asset or liability balances. In addition to making the prior period adjustment to Retained earnings, previous years' financial statements that are presented for comparative purposes are retroactively restated to reflect the specific accounts that are corrected, and the impact of the error on current and prior period reported net income is disclosed in the notes to the financial statements.

Studies find that firms forced to restate earnings suffer a dramatic decline in stock prices.[26] Figure 3.5 on the following page plots the average and median two-day market-adjusted abnormal return estimated over the restatement announcement date and the following day for the 6,633 restatements summarized in Figure 3.3. The average market-adjusted returns are negative each year and statistically less than zero in every year except 2003. Clearly, earnings restatements are important events. Firms caught manipulating their accounting numbers suffer a significant loss in market value, and lawsuits against firms' management and their auditors often ensue. That's why it's so important you understand the rules for proper revenue and expense recognition and the various methods that management sometimes uses to circumvent these rules to manipulate earnings.

---

[25] FASB ASC Paragraphs 250-10-45-23 and -24: Accounting Changes and Error Corrections—Overall—Other Presentation Matters—Correction of an Error in Previously Issued Financial Statements.

[26] S. Richardson, I. Tuna, and M. Wu, "Predicting Earnings Management: The Case of Earnings Restatements," Working Paper, University of Pennsylvania, 2002; Z. Palmrose, V. Richardson, and S. Scholz, "Determinants of Market Reactions to Restatement Announcements," *Journal of Accounting and Economics*, February 2004, pp. 59–90.

Restatements can also affect the share prices of nonrestating firms as well. See C. Gleason, N. Jenkins, and B. Johnson, "The Contagion Effects of Accounting Restatements," *The Accounting Review,* January 2008, pp. 83–110.

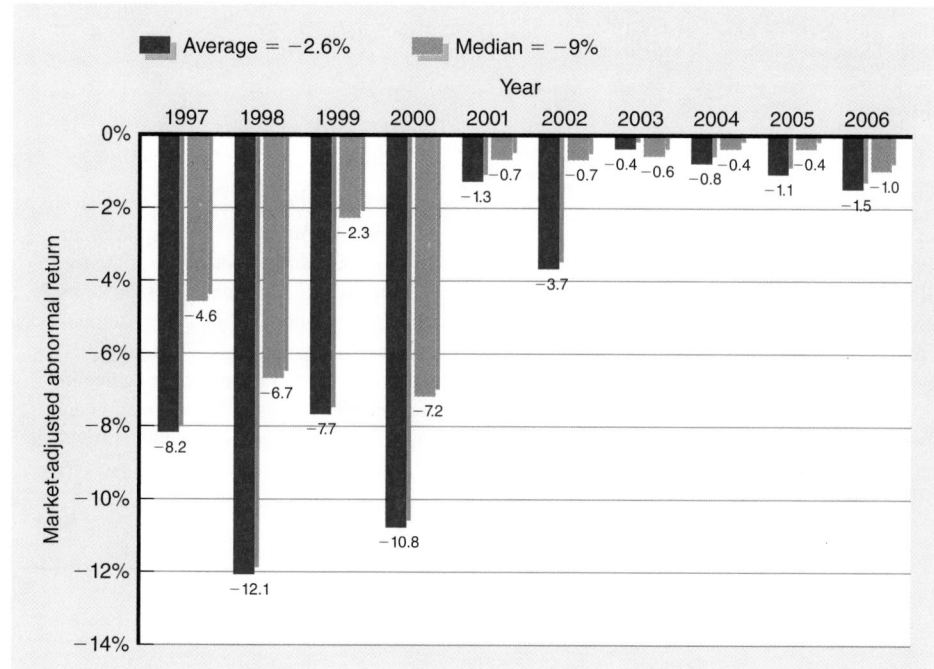

Figure 3.5

AVERAGE AND MEDIAN
TWO-DAY ANNOUNCE-
MENT PERIOD RETURNS
FOR RESTATEMENTS FROM
1997–2006

Source: Scholz, op. cit.

Exhibit 3.7 provides an example of a restatement disclosure for Universal Hospital Services, Inc. (UHS), a provider of medical equipment outsourcing, technical services, and medical equipment sales and remarketing. UHS's restatement was prompted by discovery of certain accounting irregularities related to improper recording of gains from both nonmonetary and cash refunds received on recalled infusion pumps. These irregularities led to an overstatement of revenues and an understatement of cost of sales. The company also corrected certain deferred tax asset and liability items and goodwill recorded in conjunction with a 2011 acquisition of another company. As explained in Exhibit 3.7, most of these adjustments involve reclassifications of amounts across line items on UHS's 2011 and 2010 fiscal year financial statements.

Panel (a) of Exhibit 3.7 describes the nature of the accounting irregularities leading to the restatement. Panel (b) shows the effect of the restatement on the company's consolidated balance sheet as of December 31, 2011. Panel (c) shows the restatements to various revenue and expense line items on Universal Hospital Services's consolidated income statement for 2011 and 2010. The 2011 balance sheet adjustments include a $1.339 million adjustment to the ending Accumulated deficit (think retained earnings). As shown in Panel (b), this entire adjustment to the Accumulated deficit resulted from understatement of the net loss in fiscal 2011 due to the overstatement of the tax benefit from the reported loss for the year. The entry that Universal Hospital Services made in 2012 to correct the 2011 ending balance sheet accounts is as follows ($ in thousands):

DR	Accumulated deficit	$1,339	
DR	Deferred income tax liability	2,368	
	CR	Deferred income tax asset	$2,368
	CR	Goodwill	707
	CR	Other accrued expense liabilities	632

| **EXHIBIT 3.7** | **Universal Hospital Services, Inc.** |

Accounting Restatement Disclosure

Panel (a)

For the years ended December 31, 2011 and 2010, the Company recorded $15.8 million and $5.3 million, respectively, of gains from both nonmonetary and cash refunds on recalled infusion pumps within revenues. Noncash gains result from receiving a replacement pump for a recalled pump. The gains are a result of the fair market value of the replacement pump less the net book value of the recalled pump. The infusion pump recall program began in 2010 and ended in July 2012. The Company has determined that the gains should have been presented as a reduction of cost of sales. As a result, the Company is restating its consolidated financial statements and related disclosures to recognize a reduction of both revenue and costs of sales for the years ended December 31, 2011 and 2010, for this item. In addition, the Company also chose to correct certain tax items that were immaterial individually and in the aggregate. These other tax corrections related to a $1.0 million adjustment to deferred taxes recorded in connection with a 2011 acquisition and the corresponding impact on the goodwill and valuation allowance balances; a $0.3 million increase to taxes payable and the provision for income taxes; and a $2.4 million reclassification between the deferred income tax asset and deferred income tax liability.

Panel (b)

	As of December 31, 2011		
	Previously Reported	Adjustments	Restated
Assets			
Deferred income taxes	$ 12,328	$(2,368)	$ 9,960
Total current assets	94,496	(2.368)	92.128
Goodwill	326,618	(707)	325,911
Total assets	940,007	(3,075)	936,932
Liabilities and Shareholders' Equity			
Other accrued expenses	9,720	632	10,352
Total current liabilities	72,354	632	72.986
Deferred income taxes	75,657	(2,368)	73,289
Accumulated deficit	(108,327)	(1,339)	(109,666)
Total Universal Hospital Services, Inc. equity	94,140	(1,339)	92,801
Total equity	94,526	(1,339)	93,187
Total liabilities and equity	940,007	(3,075)	936,932

Panel (c)

The following table presents the impact of the restatement adjustments on the Company's Consolidated Statements of Operations for the years ended December 31, 2011 and 2010:

	For the twelve months ended December 31, 2011		
	Previously Reported	Adjustments	Restated
Revenue			
Medical equipment outsourcing	$291,753	$(15,843)	$275,910
Technical and professional services	54,058	—	54,058
Medical equipment sales and remarketing	25,188	—	25,188
Total revenues	370,999	(15,843)	355,156
Cost of Sales			
Cost of medical equipment outsourcing	113,546	(15,843)	97,703
Cost of technical and professional services	40,518	—	40,518
Cost of medical equipment sales and remarketing	19,734	—	19,734
Medical equipment depreciation	68,032	—	68,032
Total costs of medical equipment outsourcing, technical and professional services, and medical equipment sales and remarketing	241,830	(15,843)	225,987
Gross margin	129,169	—	129,169
Provision (benefit) for income taxes	(9,682)	(1,339)	(8,343)
Consolidated net loss	(20,600)	(1,339)	(21,939)
Net loss attributable to Universal Hospital Services, Inc.	(21,051)	(1,339)	(22,390)

(continued)

EXHIBIT 3.7	Universal Hospital Services, Inc. (*continued*)

	For the twelve months ended December 31, 2010		
	Previously Reported	Adjustments	Restated
Revenue			
Medical equipment outsourcing	$250,455	$ (5,310)	$245,145
Technical and professional services	44,426	—	44,426
Medical equipment sales and remarketing	22,541	—	22,541
Total revenues	317,422	(5,310)	312,112
Cost of Sales			
Cost of medical equipment outsourcing	91,520	(5,310)	86,210
Cost of technical and professional services	31,690	—	31,690
Cost of medical equipment sales and remarketing	16,342	—	16,342
Medical equipment depreciation	69,496	—	69,496
Total costs of medical equipment outsourcing, technical and professional services, and medical equipment sales and remarketing	209,048	(5,310)	203,738
Gross margin	$108,374	—	$108,374

Source: Universal Hospital Services revised 10-K for 2011.

GLOBAL VANTAGE POINT

 International

IFRS and U.S. GAAP for revenue recognition and measurement largely overlap, although U.S. GAAP is much more voluminous and detailed. There are, however, important areas of difference. This section provides a brief overview of revenue recognition and measurement under IFRS rules and highlights important differences between IFRS and U.S. GAAP in two areas: (1) long-term construction contracts, and (2) installment sales. We also briefly discuss a recent exposure draft on revenue recognition jointly issued by the IASB and FASB. Key changes in revenue recognition that are being considered by the Boards in this joint project are highlighted.

IFRS Revenue Recognition and Measurement

International Accounting Standard (IAS) 18, "Revenue," prescribes the general requirements for recognizing and measuring revenue from the sale of goods, rendering of services, and use of an entity's assets that yield interest, dividends, or royalties.[27] *IAS 18* requires that the following five conditions be met before an entity can recognize revenue on the *sale of goods:*

1. The seller has transferred significant risks and rewards of ownership of the goods to the buyer.
2. The seller retains neither continuing management involvement associated with ownership nor effective control over the goods being sold.
3. The amount of revenue can be measured reliably.
4. It is probable that the entity will obtain economic benefits associated with the transaction.
5. The costs incurred for the transaction can be measured reliably.

With respect to revenue generated by providing *services* (like a long-term service contract), *IAS 18* prescribes that revenue should be recognized using the percentage-of-completion

[27] "Revenue," *International Accounting Standards (IAS) 18,* (London: IASC, 1993).

method. That is, revenue is recognized when it is probable that future economic benefits will be received and the entity can reliably measure all of the following:

- Amount of revenue
- Stage of completion
- Cost incurred
- Costs to complete the project

The IFRS rules allow surveys of work performed, services performed to date, and the percentage of costs incurred over total estimated costs as acceptable methodologies for measuring the stage of completion. When the outcome of a transaction for services cannot be reliably measured, IFRS rules call for entities to recognize revenue only up to the amount of recoverable costs incurred to that point. Examples of the cost-recovery method of revenue recognition are illustrated in the next two sections. Unlike IFRS accounting, U.S. GAAP does not require use of the percentage-of-completion method for service contracts.

> An example of when the outcome for services cannot be reliably measured is when the cost of completing the contracted work is highly uncertain.

Both U.S. GAAP and IFRS call for revenue to be measured at the fair value of the consideration received or receivable. The fair value should take into account any trade discounts or volume rebates. When a transaction is effectively a financing arrangement, *IAS 18* requires an entity to determine the fair value by discounting future cash flows using an imputed interest rate, which is either the prevailing rate on similar instruments issued by firms with similar credit ratings or the rate that discounts the nominal amount of the cash flows to be received to the cash sales price of the goods or services provided. This is the same approach used under U.S. GAAP.

Long-Term Construction Accounting

IFRS rules for revenue recognition on long-term construction contracts distinguish two types of contracts: cost-plus and fixed-price.[28] **Cost-plus contracts** are those for which the contractor is reimbursed for allowable or otherwise defined costs plus a profit mark-up. A **fixed-price contract** is one in which the contractor agrees to a fixed contract price or fixed rate per unit of output, which in some cases may be subject to cost escalation clauses. The examples provided earlier in the chapter are for fixed-price contracts. Like U.S. GAAP, when the outcome of a contract can be reliably estimated, IFRS rules allow firms to recognize contract revenue and expenses using the percentage-of-completion method with reference to the stage of completion at the end of each reporting period.[29] For fixed-price contracts, a firm is deemed to be able to reliably estimate a contract outcome when it can measure: (1) total contract revenue; (2) costs to complete the contract; (3) and the stage of completion at the end of the reporting period. For a cost-plus contract, a contractor can reliably estimate the contract outcome when it is probable that future economic benefits will flow to the contractor from the construction contract and contract costs can be clearly identified and reliably measured so that accrued costs can be compared to prior estimates.

When the contract outcome cannot be reliably estimated, IFRS rules do not permit firms to use the completed contract method. (Recall that under this method, revenue and expense

---

[28] The IFRS rules for long-term construction contract accounting are set forth in "Construction Contracts," *International Accounting Standard (IAS) 11* (London: IASC, 1993), and in "Agreements for the Construction of Real Estate," *International Financial Reporting Interpretive Comment (IFRIC)* 15 (London: IASB, 2008).

[29] As is the case for U.S. GAAP, when it is probable that total contract costs will exceed total contract revenue, IFRS rules require firms to recognize the expected loss immediately.

recognition is postponed until the contract is completed.) Rather, IFRS calls for firms to recognize contract costs as an expense in the period incurred and recognize contract revenue only to the extent that contract costs have been incurred and cost recovery is probable. Thus, this is a variant of the cost recovery method illustrated earlier in the chapter. To illustrate the application of this method, assume that Bridge Builders, Ltd., agrees to build a bridge for a highway construction project in Iceland for €10 million (Euros). The contract is a fixed-price contract over a three-year period beginning in 2014. The cost of constructing the bridge is expected to range between €6.5 million and €8.5 million, depending on the weather conditions. Because of uncertainty about weather conditions, the estimated future costs to complete the project at any point in time prior to completion are deemed too uncertain to reliably estimate (assume collection of all billings and recovery of costs are probable, however):

(€ in 000)	Actual Experience on the Project As of December 31,		
	2014	**2015**	**2016**
Cost incurred to date	€2,800	€5,400	€ 8,300
Estimated future costs	Too uncertain to reliably estimate		–0–
Billings to date	2,700	6,500	10,000
Cash collections to date	2,200	6,200	10,000

Under the cost recovery method of revenue recognition for long-term contracts, IFRS rules would result in the following revenues, expenses, and profits being recognized over the three-year contract period:

(€ in 000)	**2014**	**2015**	**2016**
Expenses recognized equal to costs incurred in year	€2,800	€2,600[a]	€2,900[b]
Revenues recognized	2,800*	2,600*	4,600[c]
Profit recognized	–0–	–0–	1,700[d]

* Revenues recognized equal to costs incurred in year

[a] €5,400 (costs incurred to date) − €2,800 (costs incurred in prior periods)

[b] €8,300 (costs incurred to date) − €5,400 (costs incurred in prior periods)

[c] €10,000 (contract price) − [€2,800 + €2,600] (revenue previously recognized)

[d] €10,000 − €8,300 or €4,600 − €2,900

Exhibit 3.8 shows disclosures provided by Brookfield Multiplex Group, Ltd., related to its long-term construction contracts for the six months ended December 31, Year 1. Brookfield follows IFRS reporting rules and is one of Australia's largest integrated diversified property construction and management companies. Panel (a) summarizes Brookfield's significant revenue and expense recognition policies related to its long-term construction contracts for fixed-price contracts, cost-plus contracts, and contracts for which fees are charged for managing the project (fee-generating contracts). Note that when the outcome of a contract cannot be reliably estimated, costs are expensed as incurred and contract revenue is recognized on a cost-recovery basis. Panel (b) provides Brookfield's note detailing the amount of consolidated revenue from construction projects (highlighted) recognized in each reporting period. Panel (c) shows details on the costs and profits (losses) that constitute Brookfield's Contract work in progress inventory account.

EXHIBIT 3.8	**Brookfield Multiplex Group, Ltd.** **Illustration of IFRS Disclosures for Long-Term Construction Contracts**

Excerpts from Notes to the Financial Statements

Panel (a)

1. Summary of significant accounting policies

Revenue and expenses are recognised for the major business activities as follows:

Construction contracts

For fixed price contracts, construction contract revenues and expenses are recognised on an individual contract basis using the percentage of completion method. Once the outcome of a construction contract can be estimated reliably, contract revenues and expenses are recognised in the Income Statement in proportion to the stage of completion of the contract. The stage of completion is measured by reference to actual costs incurred to date as a percentage of estimated total costs for each contract. Where the outcome of a contract cannot be reliably determined, contract costs are expensed as incurred. Where it is probable that the costs will be recovered, revenue is recognised to the extent of costs incurred. Where it is probable that a loss will arise from a construction contract the excess of total expected costs over revenue is recognised as an expense immediately.

For cost plus contracts, construction contract revenue is recognised by reference to the recoverable costs incurred during the reporting period plus the margin entitled to be charged on those recoverable costs.

For fee generating contracts, construction contract revenue is measured by the proportion that cost incurred to date compare to the estimated total cost of the contract multiplied by the expected total fee to be earned on the contract. Early completion bonuses are recognised only when construction projects are substantially complete.

Contract costs comprise:

- costs that relate directly to the contract;
- costs that are related to construction activities in general and can be allocated to the contract on a reasonable basis (such as insurance, costs of design and technical assistance);
- other costs that are specifically chargeable to a customer in accordance with the terms of a contract; and
- costs expected to be incurred under penalty clauses and rectification provisions are also included.

Panel (b)

2a. Revenue and expenses, Continuing operations

($ in millions)	6 Months Ended 31 Dec Year I	Consolidated 12 Months Ended 30 Jun Year I
1 Revenues		
Revenue from the sale of development properties	$ 248.9	$ 407.0
Construction revenue	895.3	1,684.8
Property rental revenue	153.7	272.6
Property funds management revenue	57.9	104.5
Infrastructure revenue	0.3	1.1
Interest revenue—loans and receivable	8.6	32.3
Total revenues	$1,364.7	$2,502.3

(continued)

EXHIBIT 3.8   **Brookfield Multiplex Group, Ltd.**
Illustration of IFRS Disclosures for Long-Term
Construction Contracts *(continued)*

Panel (c)

24. Contract work in progress (balance sheet asset)

($ in millions)	31 Dec Year 1	Consolidated 30 Jun Year 1
24 Contract work in progress		
Contract costs incurred to date	$6,693.7	$9,257.6
Profit/(losses) recognised to date (less recognised losses)	395.4	(57.2)
	7,089.1	9,200.4
Less: Progress billings	(7,353.1)	(9,419.4)
Net contract work in progress	$ (264.0)	$ (219.0)
Net contract work in progress comprises:		
Amounts due to customers—contract work in progress[1]	$ (339.3)	$ (390.2)
Amounts due from customers—inventories[2]	75.3	171.2
	$ (264.0)	$ (219.0)
Advances on construction projects in progress included in trade creditors	$ (66.7)	$ (44.7)
Retentions on construction projects in progress included in progress billings	$ 124.1	$ 114.1

[1] Represents billings raised to clients in excess of costs and profits recognised on these projects.

[2] Represents construction costs incurred on projects in excess of that billed to clients.

Installment Sales

Earlier in the chapter, we illustrated the installment sales method of revenue recognition, which U.S. GAAP allows when the risk of noncollection is high or when there is no reasonable basis for estimating the uncollectibles. The installment sales method allowed by U.S. GAAP is not permitted by IFRS. Rather, the cost recovery method is required. Because the majority of the costs related to an installment sale have been incurred prior to or at the time of sale, the only uncertainty is whether the cash received from the customer will be sufficient to cover the seller's costs. As installment receivables are collected, cost recovery takes place. The cost recovery method recognizes revenues and expenses equal to the amount of *cash collected* each period up to the point where costs have been fully recovered.[30] Only after the cumulative amount of cash collected exceeds the cost of the installment sale will the entity recognize any profits.

The following example illustrates the differences between the amount of revenue and profit recognized under U.S. GAAP using the installment sales method and under IFRS accounting using the cost recovery method.

> In 2014, Alpine Land Development Company sells 100 lots in the French Alps for €120,000 each or €12,000,000 total. The cost of acquiring the land and building the infrastructure is €9,000,000. (Thus, the gross margin percentage is $1 - 9/12 = 25\%$.) The sales price is to be

---

[30] Notice that the illustration here differs somewhat from how the cost recovery method was illustrated in the previous section for long-term construction contracts. In that example, the major uncertainty related to the amount of costs to be *incurred* rather than to the amount of costs that would be *recovered* by collection from the customer. So in the previous example, revenues are recognized equal to the costs incurred each period up to the point where all costs have been recovered.

collected in equal installments over a three-year period, with the first payment made at the time of sale. There is considerable uncertainty as to the future collectability of the installment receivable. Actual payments collected over the ensuing three years are: 2014—€4 million; 2015—€3 million; 2016—€3 million.

The amount of revenue, expenses, and profits recognized each year under the installment sales method (U.S. GAAP) and under the cost recovery (IFRS) would be as follows:

(in € millions)	2014	2015	2016
Installment sales method (U.S. GAAP):			
Revenues recognized[1]	€4.0	€ 3.0	€ 3.0
Costs recognized as expenses[2]	3.0	2.25	2.25
Profits recognized[3]	1.0	0.75	0.75
Cost recovery method (IFRS):			
Revenues recognized[1]	€4.0	€ 3.0	€ 3.0
Costs recognized as expenses[4]	4.0	3.0	2.0
Profits recognized	0	0	1.0

[1] Revenues recognized equal to cash collections.
[2] Expenses recognized = 9/12 × revenues recognized.
[3] Gross margin percentage (25%) times cash collected.
[4] Costs recognized as expenses to extent recovered through cash collections.

Note that the cost recovery method prescribed by IFRS rules is more conservative than the installment sales method allowed under U.S. GAAP. This is because the cost recovery method recognizes profit only when cumulative cash collections exceed the total cost of the goods sold on an installment basis, while the installment method recognizes profit on each dollar collected equal to the gross margin percentage.

Joint IASB/FASB Project on Revenue Recognition

In December 2008, the IASB and FASB jointly issued a discussion paper on revenue recognition.[31] The aim of this project is to create a joint revenue recognition standard for IFRS and U.S. GAAP that companies can apply consistently across various industries and transactions rather than the piecemeal and sometimes disjointed rules that currently apply. By developing a common standard that clarifies the principles for recognizing revenue, the two standards setting boards hope to:

- Remove inconsistencies and weaknesses in existing revenue recognition standards and practices.
- Provide a more robust and coherent framework for addressing revenue recognition issues that may arise going forward.
- Simplify the preparation of financial statements by reducing the number of standards to which companies must refer.
- Improve comparability of revenue across companies and across geographical boundaries.

As we go to press, the two Boards have jointly issued a once-revised exposure document and staff papers that address *when* and *how much* revenue should be recognized in contracts to

---

[31] "Preliminary Views on Revenue Recognition in Contracts with Customers," *Financial Accounting Series Discussion Paper* (Norwalk, CT: FASB, 2008).

provide goods or services to customers.[32] When an entity enters into a contract with a customer, it obtains rights to payment from the customer and it assumes obligations to provide goods or services to the customer—otherwise known as **performance obligations.** The combination of rights and obligations arising out of a contract give rise to a **net contract position** that can be a net asset, net liability, or net nil position for the company selling the good or service. Revenues arise from increases in that net contract position over the life of the contract.

The revenue recognition model proposed in the ED reflects this performance obligation viewpoint. Five steps that entities would apply to determine the appropriate timing and amount of revenue recognition are:

1. Identify the contract(s) with the customer. The proposed guidance indicates that the contracts may be written, oral, or implied.
2. Identify the separate performance obligations in the contract.
3. Determine the transaction price.
4. Allocate the transaction price to the separate performance obligations.
5. Recognize revenue when each performance obligation is satisfied.

Addressing the "When" Question   The ED proposes that a company should recognize revenue when it satisfies the performance obligation in the contract; that is, when it fulfills the promise to provide a good or service to the customer. This is accomplished when the selling company has transferred the promised good or service to the customer. For a good, like the construction of a building, the transfer typically takes place when the customer takes physical possession of the property. For a service, transfer occurs when the customer has received the promised service. If a company promises to transfer more than one good or service, as in a multiple-element (bundled) sales arrangement, the ED proposed that revenue be recognized as each promised good or service is transferred to the customer.

Companies following current authoritative guidance for recognizing revenue under multiple-element arrangements will likely not see a significant change in the timing of revenue recognition. However, companies that use the percentage-of-completion method for construction or production-based contracts may see a significant change in the timing of revenue recognition. The percentage of completion method is considered an "Input method" in the ED for measuring progress toward complete satisfaction of a performance obligation. The ED notes that "a shortcoming of input methods is that there may not be a direct relationship between the entity's inputs and the transfer of control of goods or services to the customer." Currently, these entities frequently identify the *entire contract as a single unit of accounting.* Under the proposed new revenue recognition model, this could result in delaying revenue recognition until all of the performance obligations are satisfied and the product (e.g., the building being constructed) is transferred to the buyer. Essentially, this means that revenue would be recognized under the completed-contract method outlined earlier in the chapter. Under the proposed model, firms would need to identify more than one performance obligation (for example, separate obligations for completing the foundation and each floor of a multistory building) within a contract in order to recognize revenue on a percentage-of-completion basis. To address concerns from the building and construction industries about the potential loss of the percentage-of-completion method,

---

[32] "Revenue Recognition (Topic 605)—Revenue Contracts with Customers," *Exposure Draft of Proposed Accounting Standards Update* (Norwalk, CT: FASB, June 2010, revised November 14, 2011). As of February 2013, the boards have completed their substantive redeliberations of the 2011 Exposure Draft. The staff is now planning to begin drafting the final revenue standard. (FASB and IASB Staff Paper, "Effects of joint IASB and FASB redeliberations on the November 2011 Exposure Draft Revenue from Contracts with Customers", February 2013.)

the revised ED (paragraph BC 90) notes that a performance obligation is satisfied over time as the entity creates or enhances an asset that the customer controls throughout. This revised guidance may allow for the continued use of the percentage-of-completion method.

What Amount to Recognize   The ED proposes that the amount of revenue that a company should recognize is the payment (consideration) received from the customer in exchange for transferring the good or service. In some instances, a customer pays for a bundle of goods and services. In this case, a determination must be made as to how much of the total consideration should be allocated to each performance obligation. The ED proposes that a company should allocate the consideration received in proportion to the company's stand-alone selling price for the promised good or service underlying each performance obligation. If the stand-alone selling price cannot be observed, then it must be estimated. As each performance obligation is satisfied (i.e., as each good or service is transferred to the customer), the amount allocated to that performance obligation is then recognized as revenue. This is the approach illustrated in the Oracle bundled sales example provided earlier in the chapter (pp. 142–143).

Remeasurement of Performance Obligations   The ED discusses how the measurement of performance obligations affects not only how much revenue to recognize each reporting period, but also how the company's net contract position is depicted in the statement of financial position each period. Because circumstances may change significantly after the start of a contract, companies may need to update (i.e., remeasure) the carrying amount of a performance obligation in order to accurately reflect its net contract position. The ED provides guidance on when and how the remeasurement should occur, but this guidance is beyond the scope of the current discussion.

Product Warranties and Contingent Consideration   The accounting for common components of revenue transactions will also be affected by the proposed guidance in the ED, including product warranties and contingent consideration. All product warranties will result in a portion of the product selling being deferred and recognized over the warranty period. Additionally, the amount of revenue recorded will include any contingent consideration that an entity expects to receive, even if the company does not yet have the right to collect that contingent consideration.

RECAP

IFRS and U.S. GAAP rules for revenue recognition and measurement largely overlap. However, important differences exist for long-term construction contracts and installment sales contracts. **IFRS** rules call for the use of alternative versions of the cost recovery method when the outcome of these contracts, either in terms of the amount of contract costs or the recovery of those costs, cannot be reliably determined. Generally, this results in **IFRS** revenue recognition being more conservative than **U.S. GAAP.**

As an outgrowth of their joint project on revenue recognition, the **IASB** and **FASB** have recently issued an exposure draft calling for a contract-based approach to determining the timing and amount of revenue recognition. The proposals made in this document may substantially change how many companies currently recognize revenue, particularly under long-term construction contracts treated as single unit of accounting. The proposed changes appear intended to constrain management discretion over the timing and perhaps amount of revenue to be recognized. Unfortunately, some of the proposed changes raise the possibility that financial statements will provide less timely information about a firm's economic performance, which we view as a negative unintended consequence of the new proposal.

SUMMARY

- This chapter outlines the special accounting procedures used when revenue recognition doesn't occur at the point of sale.

- The "critical event" and "measurability" conditions for revenue recognition are typically satisfied at point of sale.

- In some circumstances—long-term construction contracts, production of natural resources and agricultural commodities—it is appropriate to recognize revenue prior to sale.

- Revenue recognition may also be delayed until after the sale, specifically, when cash is collected. The installment sales method or cost recovery method is used when considerable uncertainty exists about the collectibility of the sales price or when significant costs that are difficult to predict will be incurred after the sale.

- Franchise sales, sales with right of return, and multiple-element sales pose particularly challenging revenue recognition issues and statement users need to be aware of potential accounting abuses.

- The broad criteria for revenue and expense recognition leave room for considerable latitude and judgment. This flexibility in GAAP can sometimes be exploited by management to hide or misrepresent the underlying economic performance of a company.

- This chapter outlines some of the more common ways to manage earnings that have come under SEC scrutiny. Later chapters provide further examples of how earnings can be manipulated.

- Auditors and financial statement users must be aware of management's incentives to manage earnings and the ways in which this is accomplished. Armed with this knowledge, you will be in a much better position to spot potential "accounting irregularities" and to avoid their unpleasant consequences.

- Once discovered, accounting errors or irregularities must be corrected and disclosed. Errors discovered after the year in which they occur are corrected through a prior period adjustment to Retained earnings.

- IFRS and U.S. GAAP rules for revenue recognition and measurement largely overlap. But important differences do exist for long-term construction contracts and the installment method of revenue recognition.

- The IASB and FASB have recently issued an exposure draft on revenue recognition. If adopted, certain proposals made in this document would substantially change current revenue recognition practices, particularly percentage-of-completion for long-term construction contracts and multiple-element sales arrangements.

EXERCISES

In 2014, Keefer Construction began construction work under a three-year contract. The contract price was $500,000. Keefer Construction uses the percentage-of-completion method for financial reporting purposes and applies it by basing recognized income each year on the proportion of cost incurred to date to total estimated costs for the contract. Trial balance information related to this contract at December 31, 2014, was as follows:

E3-1

Percentage of completion method **(LO 1, 2)**

AICPA
ADAPTED

	DR	CR
Accounts receivable	$ 7,500	
Inventory: Construction in progress	125,000	
Billings on construction contract		$110,000
Construction revenue		125,000
Construction expenses	100,000	

Required:

1. What was the initial estimated total profit before tax on this contract?

2. How much cash was collected on this contract in 2014?

<table>
<tr><td>

E3-2

Determining gross profit under percentage of completion　**(LO 1, 2)**

AICPA
ADAPTED

</td><td>

Haft Construction Company has consistently applied the percentage-of-completion method. On January 10, 2014, Haft began work on a $3,000,000 construction contract. At the inception date, the estimated cost of construction was $2,250,000. The following data relate to the progress of the contract:

Gross profit recognized at 12/31/14	$ 300,000
Costs incurred 1/01/14 through 12/31/15	1,800,000
Estimated cost to complete at 12/31/15	600,000

Required:

In its income statement for the year ended December 31, 2015, what amount of gross profit should Haft report?

</td></tr>
</table>

<table>
<tr><td>

E3-3

Determining gross profit using the installment sales method and cost recovery method　**(LO 1, 2)**

AICPA
ADAPTED

</td><td>

KC Music Corporation sells pipe organs on a deferred-payment plan. Summary information appears below:

	2014	**2015**	**2016**
Sales	$160,000	$220,000	$300,000
Cost of goods sold	(112,000)	(165,000)	(219,000)
Gross profit	$ 48,000	$ 55,000	$ 81,000
Customer collections on:			
2014 sales	$ 60,000	$ 80,000	$ 20,000
2015 sales		100,000	80,000
2016 sales			140,000

Required:

1. Calculate the amount of gross profit that would be recognized each year under the installment sales method.

2. Calculate the amount of gross profit that would be recognized each year under the cost recovery method.

</td></tr>
</table>

<table>
<tr><td>

E3-4

Determining realized gross profit using the installment method　**(LO 1, 2)**

AICPA
ADAPTED

</td><td>

On January 2, 2014, Yardley Company sold a plant to Ivory Inc. for $1,500,000. On that date, the plant's carrying cost was $1,000,000. Ivory gave Yardley $300,000 cash and a $1,200,000 note, payable in four annual installments of $300,000 cash plus 12% interest. Ivory made the first principal and interest payment of $444,000 on December 31, 2014. Yardley uses the installment method of revenue recognition.

Required:

In its 2014 income statement, what amount of realized gross profit should Yardley report?

</td></tr>
</table>

<table>
<tr><td>

E3-5

Determining installment accounts receivable　**(LO 2)**

AICPA
ADAPTED

</td><td>

Taft Corporation, which began business on January 1, 2014, appropriately uses the installment sales method of accounting. The following data are available for December 31, 2014 and 2015:

	2014	**2015**
Balance of deferred gross profit on sales on account for:		
2014	$300,000	$120,000
2015		440,000
Gross profit on sales	30%	40%

</td></tr>
</table>

Required:

The Installment accounts receivable balances at December 31, 2014 and 2015 would be how much?

On December 31, 2014, Simmons, Inc., authorized Jensen to operate a franchise for an initial franchise fee of $300,000. Of this amount, $50,000 was received upon signing the agreement and the balance, represented by a note, is due in five annual payments of $50,000 each, beginning December 31, 2015. The present value on December 31, 2014, of the five annual payments appropriately discounted is $190,000. According to the agreement, the nonrefundable down payment represents the fair value of the services already performed by Simmons; however, substantial future services are required of Simmons. Collectibility of the note is reasonably certain.

Required:

In Simmons's December 31, 2014, balance sheet, at what amount should the unearned franchise fees from Jensen's franchise be reported?

> **E3-6**
> Determining deferred franchise fee revenue
> **(LO 3)**
> AICPA
> ADAPTED

For $50 a month, Rawl Company visits its customers' premises and performs insect control services. If customers experience problems between regularly scheduled visits, Rawl makes service calls at no additional charge. Instead of paying monthly, customers may pay an annual fee of $540 in advance.

Required:

For a customer who pays the annual fee in advance, Rawl should recognize the related revenue in what amounts and when?

> **E3-7**
> Determining revenue recognized with advanced fees **(LO 1)**
> AICPA
> ADAPTED

Baker Company is a real estate developer that began operations on January 2, 2014. It appropriately uses the installment method of revenue recognition. Baker's sales are made on the basis of a 10% down payment with the balance payable over 30 years. Baker's gross profit percentage is 40%. Relevant information for Baker's first two years of operations follows:

	2015	2014
Sales	$16,000,000	$14,000,000
Cash collections	2,020,000	1,400,000

Required:

1. At December 31, 2014, Baker's deferred gross profit was how much?
2. Baker's realized gross profit for 2015 was how much?

> **E3-8**
> Determining gross profit and deferred gross profit under the installment method
> **(LO 1, 2)**
> AICPA
> ADAPTED

Each of Potter Pie Co.'s 21 new franchisees contracted to pay an initial franchise fee of $30,000. By December 31, 2014, each franchisee had paid a nonrefundable $10,000 fee and signed a note to pay $10,000 principal plus the market rate of interest on December 31, 2015, and December 31, 2016. Experience indicates that one franchisee will default on the additional payments. Services for the initial fee will be performed in 2015.

Required:

What amount of net unearned franchise fees would Potter report at December 31, 2014?

> **E3-9**
> Determining unearned franchise fees **(LO 3)**
> AICPA
> ADAPTED

	E3-10

**Cost recovery method
(LO 1, 2)**

AICPA
ADAPTED

Several of Fox, Inc.'s, customers are having cash flow problems. Information pertaining to these customers for the year ended December 31, 2013 and 2014, follows:

	12/31/13	12/31/14
Sales	$10,000	$15,000
Cost of sales	8,000	9,000
Cash collections		
on 2013 sales	7,000	3,000
on 2014 sales	—	12,000

Required:

If the cost recovery method is used, what amount would Fox report as gross profit from sales for the year ended December 31, 2014?

E3-11

Income determination for various methods of revenue recognition (LO 1, 2)

AICPA
ADAPTED

The following information relates to a three-year period for Fulda Corporation, a manufacturer and distributor of satellite phones made to sell for $1,000 each.

2014   Produced 2,000 phones and incurred costs of $600 per phone. Sold 800 phones on account; collected $650,000 in cash from customers.

2015   Sold 600 phones on account; collected cash from customers as follows: on 2014 sales, $150,000; on 2015 sales, $450,000.

2016   Sold the remaining 600 phones for cash; collected the remaining cash due on previous years' sales.

Required:

Calculate the amount of gross profit to be recognized each year under each of the following methods of revenue recognition:

1. Gross profit recognized when production is complete.
2. Gross profit recognized at point of sale.
3. Gross profit recognized using the installment sales method.
4. Gross profit recognized using the cost recovery method.

E3-12

Franchise sales: Revenue recognition (LO 3)

On April 1, 2014, Oversized Burrito Company entered into a 10-year franchise agreement with a group of individuals. The company receives a $300,000 initial franchise fee and agrees to assist in the design of the building, help secure financing, and provide management advice over the first half of the franchise agreement. A down payment of 20% of the franchise fee is due on April 1, 2014. The remaining 80% is to be payable in eight equal installments beginning on April 1, 2015. With each installment, the franchisee also remits interest of 7% of the unpaid note balance.

Assume that services to be performed by Oversized Burrito between April 1, 2014, and August 15, 2015, the date that the franchise opened, are substantial and that the installment receivable is reasonably collectible. Also assume that substantial performance of the initial services has occurred as of August 15, 2014.

Required:

1. Prepare the necessary journal entries for Oversized Burrito for April 1, 2014, when the franchise agreement is signed.

2. Prepare the necessary journal entries for August 15, 2014 (ignore any interest accruals).

E3-13

Franchise sales (LO 3)

Indoor Golf Centers, Inc., sells franchises. The initial franchise fee is $50,000, payable 20% down with the balance in five equal annual installments plus interest at 10% on the unpaid balance. In return for the initial fee, the corporation agrees to assist in designing and constructing an indoor golf driving range, help the franchisee obtain financing, help train a club pro, and provide management advice to the franchisee over a five-year period.

Required:

Prepare the franchisor's entry to record the initial franchise fee, the first annual installment, and interest revenue under each of the following independent assumptions:

1. At the time the franchise is signed, none of the services promised have been provided; however, at least 80 percent of the services have been provided on the date of the first installment. Collectibility of the franchise fee is reasonably assured.

2. Same scenario as requirement 1, except that collectibility of the remaining installments cannot be estimated.

3. At the time the franchise is signed, the value of the services rendered is estimated to be at least $10,000. The remaining services are performed equally over the five-year period, and collectibility of the franchise fee is assured.

4. At the time the franchise is signed, all the services promised have been provided, and collection of the franchise fee is assured.

5. Same scenario as requirement 4, except that collectibility of the remaining installments cannot be estimated.

Megabyte Software Developers shipped its tax return preparation product to a customer on September 15, 2014. In addition to the software, Megabyte's contract requires the company to provide (1) training to the customer's accounting staff during October of 2014, (2) technical product support for one year starting October 1, 2014, and (3) an upgrade early in 2015 to the software that reflects last-minute changes in tax laws affecting tax returns for 2014. The customer paid the total contract price of $85,000 prior to product shipment. Megabyte would charge the following if these individual contract elements were sold separately:

E3-14

Revenue recognition:
Bundled sales   **(LO 3)**

	Fair Value
Tax return preparation software	$ 70,000
Training customer's staff	10,000
Customer support	15,000
Software upgrade	5,000
Total fair value	$100,000

Required:

1. Prepare a journal entry to record receipt of the cash payment.

2. Determine the amount of revenue to be recognized in 2014 and prepare the necessary journal entry.

York's Rustic Furniture began operations on January 1, 2014. To build its customer base, the company permitted customers, regardless of their credit history, to pay in installments when they made a major purchase. Installment sales amounted to $750,000 in 2014; these items cost York's Rustic Furniture $400,000. Given the questionable credit histories of many of its customers and its inability to use past history to estimate collection rates, the company adopted the cost recovery method and accordingly recognized $75,000 in gross profit.

E3-15

Installment sales and cost recovery methods
(LO 1, 2)

AICPA
ADAPTED

Required:

1. How much cash did the company collect on installment sales in 2014?

2. Assume that York's Rustic Furniture had instead used the installment sales method. What amount of gross profit would it have deferred in 2014?

E3-16

Error correction/Prior period adjustment **(LO 7)**

Bettner, Inc., is a calendar year corporation whose financial statements for 2012 and 2013 included errors as follows:

Year	Ending Inventory	Depreciation Expense
2012	$12,000 overstated	$22,300 overstated
2013	8,000 understated	6,000 understated

Assume that purchases were recorded correctly and that no correcting entries were made at December 31, 2012, or December 31, 2013.

Required:

1. Ignoring income taxes, what amount should Bettner report as a prior period adjustment to the beginning retained earnings in its statement of retained earnings at January 1, 2014?

2. Prepare the journal entries that Bettner would make in 2014 to correct the errors.

E3-17

Error correction/Prior period adjustment **(LO 7)**

Tack, Inc., reported a Retained earnings balance of $150,000 at December 31, 2013. In June 2014, Tack's internal audit staff discovered two errors that were made in preparing the 2013 financial statements that are considered material:

a. Merchandise costing $40,000 was mistakenly omitted from the 2013 ending inventory.

b. Equipment purchased on July 1, 2013, for $70,000 was mistakenly charged to a repairs expense account. The equipment should have been capitalized and depreciated using straight-line depreciation, a 10-year useful life, and $10,000 salvage value.

Required:

1. What amount should Tack report as a prior period adjustment to beginning Retained earnings at January 1, 2014? (Ignore taxes.)

2. Prepare the journal entries that Tack would make in June 2014 to correct the errors made in 2013. Assume that depreciation for 2014 is made as a year-end adjusting entry. (Ignore taxes.)

E3-18

Correction of errors/Prior period adjustment **(LO 7)**

Krafty Kris, Inc., discovered the following errors after the 2014 financial statements were issued:

a. A major supplier shipped inventory valued at $8,550 to Krafty Kris on consignment. This merchandise was mistakenly included in the inventory taken by Krafty Kris on December 31, 2013. (Goods shipped on consignment are the property of the consignor and should be included in its inventory.)

b. Krafty Kris renewed its liability insurance policy on October 1, 2013, paying a $36,000 premium and debiting Insurance expense. No further entries have been made. The premium purchased insurance coverage for a period of 36 months.

c. Repair expense was debited at the time equipment was purchased for $100,000 on January 8, 2014. The equipment has a life of five years; its salvage value is considered immaterial. Krafty uses straight-line depreciation method.

Required:

1. Prepare journal entries to correct these errors. Ignore income taxes.

2. Assuming that these errors remain uncorrected, explain their effects on the 2015 financial statements issued by Krafty Kris, Inc.

Boeing Corporation is one of the world's largest airplane manufacturing companies that often builds airplanes for military use. On March 13, 2012, Diana L. Sands, Boeing's vice president of finance and corporate controller, wrote a comment letter addressed to the FASB that raised concerns about some of the proposed guidance written in the joint revised IASB/FASB Exposure Draft for Revenue Recognition.[32] Specifically, she wrote that Boeing

> "recommend(s) further clarity around when a bundle of goods or services should be considered a single performance obligation versus multiple performance obligations. We understand that there are conflicting interpretations of the proposed criteria of highly interrelated, significant integration services and significantly modified or customized (contracts). Generally we believe that production units such as military airplanes that are bid, negotiated and managed as a single arrangement should be accounted for as a single performance obligation rather than considering each airplane to represent a separate performance obligation. We recommend providing additional indicators to help determine when to bundle goods or services into a single performance obligation and providing examples of common goods and services that would be expected to represent single versus multiple performance obligations."

Required:

1. Why would the controller for Boeing care whether military contracts are considered a single performance obligation (where delivery of the entire set of aircraft is considered the performance obligation) or a multiple performance obligation (where delivery of each individual aircraft is considered a performance obligation)? What are the revenue recognition implications for each of these criteria under the joint IASB/FASB Revised Exposure Draft for Revenue Recognition?

2. Further assume the following set of data applies to an order from the U.S. Armed Forces for 20 Boeing aircraft.

Total contract price: $200,000,000

Actual experience on the project as of December 31,

	2013	2014	2015
Costs incurred to date	$ 30,000,000	$120,000,000	$183,000,000
Estimated future costs	$150,000,000	$ 62,000,000	$ 0
Aircraft delivered	0	5	15

How much revenue would Boeing report for 2013, 2014, and 2015 if it complies with the ED guidance under the following scenarios?

a. Completed contract method, where the contract is considered a single performance obligation

b. Completed contract method, where the contract is considered to include multiple performance obligations (i.e., where delivery of each individual aircraft is considered a performance obligation)

c. Percentage of completion method, where the contract is considered a single performance obligation

---

[32] http://www.fasb.org/cs/BlobServer?blobkey=id&blobwhere=1175823808224&blobheader=application%2Fpdf&blobcol=urldata&blobtable=MungoBlobs.

PROBLEMS / DISCUSSION QUESTIONS

P3-1

Income determination under alternative revenue recognition rules **(LO 1, 2)**

On January 1, 2014, Heinkel Corporation's balance sheet consisted of $900,000 in cash and $900,000 in equity. On this date, Heinkel began production of an electronic device for improving the sound quality of CDs. During 2014, Heinkel produced 100,000 devices at a unit cost of $12. These devices had a selling price of $20 each and were to be sold on account to various dealers in the northeastern United States. Commissions and other selling costs incurred at the time of sale were $1.00 per unit. During 2014, 2015, and 2016, the 100,000 units produced were sold and cash was collected as follows:

	2014	2015	2016
Units sold	60,000	40,000	0
Cash collections	$1,000,000	$800,000	$200,000

Required:

1. Calculate the amount of Heinkel's net income each year, assuming that revenue and gross profit are recognized:

   a. At the completion of production.

   b. At the point of sale.

   c. As cash is collected (installment method).

2. Prepare Heinkel's journal entries for 2014 under each of the methods in requirement 1.

P3-2

Income determination under alternative bases of revenue recognition **(LO 1, 2)**

AgriPro, a farm corporation, produced 20,000 bushels of corn in its first year of operations. During the year, it sold 15,000 bushels of the corn produced for $3.00 per bushel and collected 80% of the selling price on the corn sold; the balance is to be collected in equal amounts during each of the two following years. The local feed mill is quoting a year-end market price of $3.50 per bushel. Additional data for the first year are as follows:

Depreciation on equipment	$ 5,000
Other production costs (cash)—per bushel	0.60
Miscellaneous administrative costs (cash)	3,000
Selling and delivery costs (incurred and paid at time of sale), per bushel	0.15
Dividends paid to stockholders during year	10,000
Interest on borrowed money (1/2 paid in cash)	8,000

AgriPro is enthusiastic about the accountant's concept of matching product costs with revenues.

Required:

Compute net income under each of the following methods and determine the carrying (book) value of inventory and accounts receivable at the end of the first year of operation for each of these methods.

1. Recognize revenue when production is complete.

2. Recognize revenue at point of sale.

3. Recognize revenue on an installment (cash collection) basis.

P3-3

Determining pre-tax income, inventory carrying value, and accounts receivable under sales and production basis **(LO 1, 2)**

Howe, Inc., a Texas crude oil producer, started business on May 1, 2014. It sells all of its production to a single customer at the current spot price for West Texas crude. The customer pays Howe 60% of the selling price on delivery with the remainder to be paid in 10 months. Throughout 2014, the oil spot market price was $28 per barrel; however, on December 31, 2014, the market price jumped to $31 per barrel, where it is expected to remain. Howe's direct production costs are $12 per barrel, drilling equipment depreciation expense totaled $180,000 for the eight-month period ending December 31, and property taxes of $75,000 were paid during the year. Howe produced 30,000 barrels of oil of which 6,000 barrels were included in January 1, 2015, opening inventory.

Required:

Compute Howe's 2014 pre-tax income and determine its inventory carrying value and Accounts receivable balance at December 31, 2014, under the following:

1. Production basis.

2. Sales (completed transaction) basis.

3. Installment (cash collection) basis.

Cornwell Construction Company has been operating in Pennsylvania for a number of years. During 2014, the firm contracted with the Borough of Lewisburg to build a domed sports complex. Cornwell estimated that it would take three years to complete the facility at a total cost of $25 million. The total contract price was $30 million. During 2014, construction costs of $8.5 million were incurred related to the sports complex, including $500,000 in materials purchased in 2014 but not yet used; estimated additional costs to complete the project were $15.5 million as of December 31, 2014. Contract billings through December 31, 2014, were $9 million of which the Borough of Lewisburg had paid $7.5 million.

P 3 - 4
Income recognition on long-term contracts **(LO 1, 2)**
AICPA ADAPTED

Required:

1. Prepare schedules to calculate the amount of income to be recognized by Cornwell Construction on the sports complex for the year ended December 31, 2014, using each of the following methods:

   a. Completed-contract method.

   b. Percentage-of-completion method.

2. Prepare all necessary journal entries related to the project for 2014 assuming:

   a. The percentage-of-completion method is appropriate.

   b. The completed-contract method is appropriate.

MSK Construction Company contracted to construct a factory building for $525,000. Construction started during 2014 and was completed in 2015. Information relating to the contract follows:

P 3 - 5
Long-term construction contract accounting **(LO 1, 2)**

	2014	2015
Costs incurred during the year	$290,000	$150,000
Estimated additional cost to complete	145,000	—
Billings during the year	260,000	265,000
Cash collections during the year	240,000	285,000

Required:

Record the preceding transactions in MSK's books under the completed-contract and the percentage-of-completion methods. Determine amounts that will be reported on the balance sheet at the end of 2014.

P3-6

Determining income under
installment sales
method   **(LO 1, 2)**

AICPA
ADAPTED

Maple Corporation sells farm machinery on the installment plan. On July 1, 2014, it entered into an installment sale contract with Agriculture, Inc., for an eight-year period. Equal annual payments under the installment sale are $100,000 and are due on July 1. The first payment was made on July 1, 2014. Additional information follows:

- The amount that would be realized on an outright sale of similar farm machinery is $556,000.

- The cost of the farm machinery sold to Agriculture is $417,000.

- The finance charges relating to the installment period are $244,000 based on a stated interest rate of 12%, which is appropriate.

- Circumstances are such that the collection of the installments due under the contract is reasonably assured.

Required:

What income or loss before income taxes should Maple record for the year ended December 31, 2014, as a result of this transaction? Show supporting computations in good form.

P3-7

Construction accounting
under both U.S. GAAP and
IFRS   **(LO 8, 9)**

At the beginning of 2014, the Jensen Construction Company signed a contract with the state of Florida to build a highway for $6 million. The project is estimated to be completed by the end of 2016. Jensen will bill the state in installments over the construction period per a schedule in the contract. Information related to the contract is as follows:

	2014	**2015**	**2016**
Actual construction costs incurred during the year	$1,800,000	$1,255,000	$1,945,000
Actual construction costs incurred in prior years		1,800,000	3,055,000
Cumulative actual construction costs	1,800,000	3,055,000	5,000,000
Estimated costs to complete at end of year	2,700,000	1,645,000	—
Total construction costs	$4,500,000	$4,700,000	$5,000,000
Billings made over the course of the year	$1,750,000	$1,800,000	$2,450,000
Cash collections during the year	$1,700,000	$1,600,000	$2,700,000

For each of the following independent requirements, assume collection of all billings and recovery of costs are probable.

Required:

1. Because the highway is being built in an area with very stable soils, Jensen believes it is able to reasonably estimate the contract's completion costs and thus uses the percentage-of-completion method of accounting for this contract. Prepare the journal entry that Jensen would make at the *end* of each year to appropriately recognize the revenue, expense, and profit on the project for that year.

2. Because the highway is being built in an area with very unstable soils, Jensen believes it is not able to reasonably estimate the contract's completion costs and thus uses the completed-contract method of accounting (U.S. GAAP) for this contract. Prepare the journal entry that Jensen would make at the *end* of each year to appropriately recognize the revenue, expense, and profit on the project for that year.

3. Because the highway is being built in an area with very unstable soils, Jensen believes it is not able to reasonably estimate the contract's completion costs and thus uses the cost-recovery method of accounting (IFRS) for this contract. Prepare the journal entry that Jensen would make at the *end* of each year to appropriately recognize revenue, expense, and profit on the project for that year.

4. How would the solution to the three requirements above change if the contract-based revenue recognition principles proposed in the recent IASB/FASB exposure draft on revenue recognition are adopted? Assume that the entire contract is viewed as a single unit of accounting.

Refer to the data in problem P3-7 for Jensen Construction Company. Assume Jensen uses the percentage-of-completion method of accounting for this project.

Required:

Prepare the journal entry that Jensen would make at the *end* of 2015 and 2016 to appropriately recognize the revenue, expense, and profit (loss) on the project for these two years if the estimated costs to complete the project were $3,045,000 instead of $1,645,000 as of the end of 2015 as previously estimated. Assume that during 2016 actual costs incurred were as previously estimated (i.e., $3,045,000) at the end of 2015.

P3-8

Construction accounting under both U.S. GAAP and IFRS when a contract loss occurs **(LO 2, 8)**

STRETCH

On July 1, 2014, the Miller Company held an inventory clearance sale to rid itself of a sizeable amount of rapidly obsolescing inventory. To ensure the success of the sale, Miller offered generous credit terms: customers—with no minimum credit score required—could purchase up to $5,000 worth of Miller's products, paying 25% down with the balance due in three equal annual installments. Interest at a market rate of 10% of the unpaid balance was to be remitted with each installment. Miller was quite pleased with the event as the company sold inventory costing $300,000 for $500,000. Assume that installment payments occur on July 1 each year and the following principal amounts are collected after the initial down payment: 2015, $125,000; 2016, $100,000; 2017, $75,000. Due to the generally poor credit scores of the purchasers of this merchandise, Miller believes it appropriate to not recognize revenue at the time of sale.

Required:

1. Prepare Miller's journal entries each year if Miller adopts the installment sales accounting method under U.S. GAAP. (Ignore any presumed interest collections.)

2. Prepare Miller's journal entries each year if Miller adopts the cost-recovery accounting method under IFRS. (Ignore any presumed interest collections.)

3. Prepare Miller's journal entry under each method at December 31, 2017, if the company believes it will not collect any more of these installment receivables.

P3-9

Accounting for installment sales under U.S. GAAP and IFRS **(LO 2, 8)**

STRETCH

On July 1, 2014, Quincy Company sold a piece of industrial equipment to Tana Company for $200,000. The equipment cost Quincy $80,000 to manufacture. Per the sales agreement, Tana made a 20% down payment and paid the remaining balance in four equal quarterly installments plus 10% on the unpaid balance, starting October 1, 2014.

Required:

1. Identify and explain three alternative methods for revenue and cost recognition available to Quincy in this scenario.

2. Calculate the amount of gross profit recognized in 2014 under each of the alternatives identified in requirement 1.

3. Elaborate on what circumstances would have to exist for each alternative to be employed.

P3-10

Alternative bases of revenue recognition **(LO 1, 2)**

Founded in 1989, Brio Software, Inc., helps Global 3000 companies improve business performance by creating new value from existing information systems and, ultimately, aligning everyone in the enterprise with key corporate goals. Brio's business intelligence software lets companies access, analyze, and share information, offering users relevant, accurate, and timely insight into the variables that impact their business. With this insight, companies can make superior business decisions.

P3-11

Bundled services **(LO 3)**

The following information appears in Brio Software's 10-K report regarding its revenue recognition policies:

Revenue Recognition

Brio derives revenues from two sources, perpetual license fees and services. Services include software maintenance and support, training and consulting, and system implementation services. Maintenance and support consist of technical support and software upgrades and enhancements. Significant management judgments and estimates are made and used to determine the revenue recognized in any accounting period. Material differences may result in the amount and timing of Brio's revenue for any period if different conditions were to prevail.

Brio applies the provisions of FASB ASC Section 985-605-25: Software—Revenue Recognition—Recognition to account for software revenue and FASB ASC Section 605-25: Revenue recognition—Multiple-element arrangements.

Brio recognizes product revenue when persuasive evidence of an arrangement exists, the product has been delivered, the fee is fixed or determinable, and collection of the resulting receivable is probable. In software arrangements that include rights to multiple elements, such as software products and services, Brio uses the residual method under which revenue is allocated to the undelivered elements based on vendor-specific objective evidence (VSOE) of the fair value of such undelivered elements. VSOE of the undelivered elements is determined based on the price charged when such elements are sold separately. The residual amount of revenue is allocated to delivered elements and recognized as revenue. Such undelivered elements in these arrangements typically consist of services.

Brio uses a purchase order or a signed contract as persuasive evidence of an arrangement for sales of software, maintenance renewals, and training. Sales through Brio's value added resellers, private label partners, resellers, system integrators, and distributors (collectively "resellers") are evidenced by a master agreement governing the relationship with binding purchase orders on a transaction-by-transaction basis. Brio uses a signed statement of work to evidence an arrangement for consulting and system implementation services.

Software is delivered to customers electronically or on a CD-ROM. Brio assesses whether the fee is fixed or determinable based on the payment terms associated with the transaction. Brio's standard payment terms are generally less than 90 days. When payments are subject to extended payment terms, revenue is deferred until payments become due, which is generally when the payment is received. Brio assesses collectibility based on a number of factors, including the customer's past payment history and its current creditworthiness. If Brio determines that collection of a fee is not probable, it defers the revenue and recognizes it when collection becomes probable, which is generally on receipt of cash payment. If an acceptance period is other than in accordance with standard user documentation, revenue is recognized on the earlier of customer acceptance or the expiration of the acceptance period.

When licenses are sold with consulting and system implementation services, license fees are recognized upon shipment provided that (1) the preceding criteria have been met, (2) payment of the license fees does not depend on the performance of the consulting and system implementation services, (3) the services are not essential to the functionality of the software, and (4) VSOE exists for the undelivered elements. For arrangements that do not meet these criteria, both the product license revenues and services revenues are recognized in accordance with the provisions of FASB ASC Section 985-605-25. Brio accounts for the arrangements under the completed-contract method pursuant to FASB ASC Section 605-35: Revenue recognition-Construction-type and production-type contracts because reliable estimates are typically not available for the costs and efforts necessary to complete the consulting and system implementation services.

The majority of Brio's consulting and system implementation services qualify for separate accounting. Brio uses VSOE of fair value for the services and maintenance to account for the arrangement using the residual method, regardless of any separate prices stated within the contract for each element. Brio's consulting and system implementation service contracts are bid either on a fixed-fee basis or on a time-and-materials basis. For a fixed-fee contract, Brio recognizes revenue using the completed-contract method. For time-and-materials contracts, Brio recognizes revenue as services are performed.

Maintenance and support revenue is recognized ratably over the term of the maintenance contract, which is typically one year. Training revenue is recognized when the training is provided.

Assume that Brio enters into a contract with a customer for deliverable software and services as follows. The prices listed are those quoted in the contract.

Perpetual license fee	$ 650,000
Elements undelivered at contract signing:	
Technical support	120,000
Training	80,000
System implementation services	100,000
Software upgrades and enhancements	50,000
Total contract price	$1,000,000

These contract elements, if purchased separately, would be priced as follows:

Perpetual license fee	$ 840,000
Elements undelivered at contract signing:	
Technical support	120,000
Training	72,000
System implementation services	108,000
Software upgrades and enhancements	60,000
Total contract price	$1,200,000

Required:

1. Following Brio's stated revenue recognition policies, how much revenue would it recognize on this contract?

2. Prepare the journal entry to record receipt of the signed contract and electronic delivery of the software. Assume that the sale conforms to Brio's normal billing terms and that collectibility is not an issue.

3. How much revenue would Brio recognize on this contract if the various elements included in the contract were not sold separately?

Roxio, Inc., is a leading provider of digital media software and services for the consumer market. The company provides software that enables individuals to record digital content onto CDs and DVDs and offers photo and video editing products. Roxio's Form 10-K for the year ended March 31, Year 3, reported the following information:

P3-12

Sales with right of return **(LO 3, 4, 5)**

Roxio, Inc.

	Selected Financial Data for the Years Ended March 31		
($ in 000s)	**YR1**	**YR2**	**YR3**
Net revenues	$121,908	$142,521	$120,408
Net income	3,570	2,349	(9,944)
Allowance for sales returns and certain sales incentives:			
Balance at beginning of period	2,186	4,602	5,492
Additions	8,351	16,286	18,333
Deductions	5,935	15,396	16,749
Balance at the end of period	4,602	5,492	7,076

Business Risks

We rely on distributors and retailers to sell our products. If our distributors attempt to reduce their levels of inventory or if they do not maintain sufficient levels to meet customer demand, our sales could be negatively impacted. If we reduce the prices of our products to our distributors, we may have to compensate them for the difference between the higher price they paid to buy their inventory and the new lower prices. In addition, we are exposed to the risk of product returns from distributors through their exercise of contractual return rights.

Revenue Recognition

For software product sales to distributors, revenues are recognized on product shipment to the distributors or receipt of the products by the distributor, depending on the shipping terms, provided that all fees are fixed or determinable, evidence of an arrangement exists, and collectibility is probable. Our distributor arrangements provide distributors certain product rotation rights. Additionally, we permit our distributors to return products in certain circumstances, generally during periods of product transition. End users additionally have the right to return their product within 30 days of the purchase. We establish allowances for expected product returns in accordance with FASB ASC Section 605-15-25. These allowances are recorded as a direct reduction of revenues and accounts receivable. Management applies significant judgment and relies on historical experience in establishing these allowances. If future return patterns differ from past return patterns due to reduced demand for our product or other factors beyond our control, we may be required to increase these allowances in the future and may be required to reduce future revenues. If at any point in the future we become unable to estimate returns reliably, we could be required to defer recognizing revenues until the distributor notifies us that the product has been sold to an end user. We provide for estimated product returns and pricing adjustments in the period in which the revenues are recognized.

Required:

1. Re-create (in summary form) the journal entries Roxio made in the Allowance for sales returns and certain sales incentives account for fiscal years Year 1–Year 3. Explain the rising balance in this account.

2. Are opportunities for "earnings management" present in Roxio's stated accounting policies for expected product returns? Is there any evidence in the data presented that Roxio's management has availed themselves of any of the opportunities you identify?

3. Determine Roxio's gross revenues for fiscal years Year 1–Year 3.

P3-13

Manipulation of receivables
(LO 4, 5)

Holman Electronics manufactures audio equipment, selling it through various distributors. Holman's days sales outstanding (Accounts receivable / Average daily credit sales) figures increased steadily in 2014 and then spiked dramatically in 2015, peaking at 120 days in the second quarter. In the third quarter of 2015, Holman's days sales outstanding figure dropped to 90 days. Its chief financial officer engineered this drop by artificially reducing the amount of outstanding accounts receivable. Channel partners with large outstanding receivables were pressured into signing notes for those amounts. Once sales personnel secured the notes, the CFO directed a reclassification entry to the general ledger converting more than $30 million in trade receivables into notes receivable, which are not included in the days sales outstanding calculation. This reclassification was not disclosed in the Form 10-Q that Holman filed for that quarter.

Required:

What might be the motive for the CFO's actions? Explain your answer.

P3-14

Correction of errors and
worksheet preparation
(LO 7)

KEW Enterprises began operations in January 2012 to manufacture a hand sanitizer that promised to be more effective and gentler on the skin than existing products. Family members, one of whom was delegated to be the office manager and bookkeeper, staffed the company. Although conscientious, the office manager lacked formal accounting training, which became apparent when the growing company was forced in March 2015 to hire a CPA as controller. Although ostensibly brought in to relieve some of the office manager's stress, management made it clear to the new controller that they had some concerns about the quality of information they were receiving. Accordingly, the controller made it a priority to review the records of prior years, looking for ways to improve the accounting system. From this review, the following errors were uncovered.

1. The office manager expensed rent on equipment and facilities when paid. Amounts paid in 2012, 2013, and 2014 that represent prepaid rent are $5,000, $4,500, and $4,900, respectively.

2. No adjusting entries were ever made to reflect accrued salaries. The amounts $12,000, $13,500, and $8,300 should have been accrued in each of the three prior years, respectively.

3. Errors occurred in the depreciation calculations that resulted in depreciation expense being overstated by $3,500 in 2012, understated by $7,000 in 2013, and understated by $6,000 in 2014.

4. In February 2015 some surplus production equipment that originally had cost $14,000 was sold for $4,000; $12,000 in depreciation had correctly been taken on this equipment. The office manager made this entry to record the sale:

To record sale of surplus equipment

DR	Cash	$ 4,000	
DR	Accumulated depreciation	10,000	
	CR Equipment		$14,000

5. Supplies expenses in the amount of $2,400 were incorrectly classified as administrative expenses in 2014.

Required:
Complete the worksheet shown below to assist in preparing the correcting entry. (By way of example, the first required entry on the worksheet has been made.)

Error Corrections Worksheet

	Effect on Income				Accounts to be Adjusted	
Description	2012	2013	2014	2015	Dr.	Cr.
Reported income	$(24,000)	$43,000	$40,000	N/A		
Item 1:						
Prepaid rent—2012	5,000	(5,000)			Counterbalancing error	
Prepaid rent—2013						
Prepaid rent—2014						
Item 2:						
Accrued wages—2012						
Accrued wages—2013						
Accrued wages—2014						
Item 3:						
Depreciation						
Item 4:						
Gain on machinery						
Item 5:						
Classification						
Adjusted income						

P3-15

Correcting errors/Prior
period adjustment **(LO 7)**

In 2014, the new CEO of Watsontown Electric Supply became concerned about the company's apparently deteriorating financial position. Wishing to make certain that the grim monthly reports he was receiving from the company's bookkeeper were accurate, the CEO engaged a CPA firm to examine the company's financial records. The CPA firm discovered the following facts during the course of the engagement, which was completed prior to any adjusting or closing entries being prepared for 2014.

1. A new digital imaging system was acquired on January 5, 2013, at a cost of $5,000. Although this asset was expected to be in use for the next four years, the purchase was inadvertently charged to office expense. Per the company's accounting manual, office equipment of this type should be depreciated using the straight-line method with no salvage value assumed.

2. A used truck, purchased on November 18, 2014, was recorded with this entry:

    To record truck expenditure:

DR	Vehicle Expense.....................................	$18,000	
	CR Cash..		$18,000

    Management plans to use this truck for three years and then trade it in on a new one. Salvage is estimated at $3,000. Watsontown has always used straight-line depreciation for fixed assets, recording a half-year of depreciation in the year the asset is acquired.

3. On July 1, 2014, the company rented a warehouse for three years. The lease agreement specified that each year's rent be paid in advance, so a check for the first year's rent of $18,000 was issued and recorded as an addition to the Buildings account.

4. Late in 2013, Watsontown collected $23,500 from a customer in full payment of his account. The cash receipt was credited to revenue. Two months before the audit, Watsontown's bookkeeper was reviewing outstanding receivables and noticed the outstanding balance. Knowing the customer in question had recently died, she wrote off the account. Because Watsontown seldom has bad debts, the company uses the direct write-off method whereby it charges Bad debts expense and credits Accounts receivable when an account is deemed uncollectible.

5. A three-year property and casualty insurance policy was purchased in January 2013 for $30,000. The entire amount was recorded as an insurance expense at the time.

6. On October 1, 2013, Watsontown borrowed $100,000 from a local bank. The loan terms specified annual interest payments of $8,000 on the anniversary date of the loan. The first interest payment was made on October 1, 2014, and expensed in its entirety.

Required:

Prepare any journal entry necessary to correct each error as well as any year-end adjusting entry for 2014 related to the described situation. Ignore income tax effects.

P3-16

General Motors restatement
(LO 7)

General Motors (GM) disclosed in a Form 8-K filed in November Year 2, that it would restate its financial statements to correct the accounting for credits and other lump-sum payments from suppliers. Typically, suppliers offer an up-front payment in exchange for the customer's promise to purchase certain quantities of merchandise over time. Per GAAP, such "rebates" cannot be recognized until after the promised purchases occur.

As GM noted,

GM erroneously recorded as a reduction to cost of sales certain payments and credits received from suppliers prior to completion of the earnings process. GM concluded that the payments and credits received were associated with agreements for the award of future services or products or other rights and privileges and should be recognized when subsequently earned.

Assume that GM signed a procurement contract on January 2, Year 1, that obligated it to purchase 1 million tires each year for the next three years from one of its suppliers. As part of this agreement, GM received a cash payment of $75 million on January 5, Year 1.

Required:

1. Given GM's past accounting practices for such rebates, what journal entry did the company make when it received the payment?

2. Had GM followed GAAP, what would the appropriate journal entry have been? Where would the account credited be shown on GM's financial statements?

3. Assume that GM made the entry you suggested in requirement 2. What adjusting entry, if any, would have been required at December 31, Year 1? (Assume that GM reports on a calendar year basis and makes annual adjusting entries.)

4. Assume that GM "discovered" the error in its approach to recording supplier rebates on November 1, Year 2. What entry would be necessary to restate GM's Year 1 balance sheet? (Ignore income tax effects.)

5. What impact did GM's past accounting practices related to supplier credits and rebates have on reported net income in the year in which the rebate was received and in subsequent years?

The joint revised IASB/FASB Exposure Document (ED) for Revenue Recognition includes guidance for reporting "onerous performance obligations." Specifically, the ED proposes that

> "an entity shall recognize a liability and a corresponding expense if the performance obligation is onerous" when the performance obligation is satisfied over time and the entity expects, at contract inception, that the time to complete the obligation is greater than one year. "A performance obligation is onerous if the lowest cost of settling the performance obligation exceeds the amount of the transaction price allocated to that performance obligation."

P3-17

Onerous performance obligations **(LO 9)**

Assume Software Developer LTD shipped its product to a customer on September 1, 2013. In addition to the software, the contract requires the company to provide service support through December 31, 2015, for the software. The customer paid the total contract price of $85,000 prior to product shipment. The company would charge the following if these individual contract elements were sold separately:

Software	$ 80,000
Support	$ 20,000
Total Fair Value	$100,000

To settle the service support performance obligation, the company estimates it will cost between $17,500 and $20,000 in development and labor costs.

Required:

1. Prepare a journal entry to record receipt of the cash payment on September 1, 2013.

2. Determine the amount of revenue to be recognized in 2013 and prepare any necessary end of year adjusting journal entries.

3. If the company had to follow the proposed guidance from the ED, show the journal entry on September 1, 2013, to recognize any "onerous performance obligation" liability and expense.

CASES

C3-1

Criswell's Farm: Alternative bases of income determination   **(LO 1, 2)**

Bill Criswell owns and operates a farm in Pennsylvania. During 2014, he produced and harvested 60,000 bushels of soybeans. He had no inventory of soybeans at the start of the year. Immediately after harvesting the soybeans in fall of 2014, Criswell sold 45,000 bushels to a local grain elevator operator. As of December 31, 2014, he had received payment for 30,000 bushels. Additional information relating to the farm follows:

Price:	
Market price per bushel at the time of harvest and sale to the grain elevator operator	$ 3.60
Market price per bushel at December 31, 2014	3.60
Costs:	
Variable production costs per bushel	0.50
Delivery costs per bushel	0.20
Annual fixed cost of operating the farm that are unrelated to the volume of production	$50,000

Required:

1. Prepare a 2014 income statement for Criswell's farm under each of the following assumptions regarding what constitutes the "critical event" in the process of recognizing income:

   a. Assuming that production is the critical event.

   b. Assuming that the sale is the critical event.

   c. Assuming that cash collection is the critical event.

   (For simplicity, treat the fixed operating costs as period rather than product costs.)

2. Determine the December 31, 2014, balances for Soybeans inventory and Accounts receivable under each of the three income recognition methods in requirement 1.

3. Assume that the farm is left idle during 2015. With no harvest, Criswell's only transaction consists of an October 2015 sale of the 15,000 bushels in inventory at $2.80 per bushel. Further assume that no fixed costs are incurred while the farm is idle. Compute income during 2015 on both the sale and production basis. Discuss the causes for any profit or loss reported under each income determination alternative.

C3-2

London, Inc.: Determining gross profit under the percentage-of-completion method   **(LO 1, 2)**

AICPA
ADAPTED

London, Inc., began operation of its construction division on October 1, 2014, and entered into contracts for two separate projects. The Beta project contract price was $600,000 and provided for penalties of $10,000 per week for late completion. Although during 2015 the Beta project had been on schedule for timely completion, it was completed four weeks late in August 2016. The Gamma project's original contract price was $800,000. Change orders during 2016 added $40,000 to the original contract price. The following data pertain to the separate long-term construction projects in progress:

	Beta	Gamma
As of September 30, 2015:		
Costs incurred to date	$360,000	$410,000
Estimated costs to complete	40,000	410,000
Billings	315,000	440,000
Cash collections	275,000	365,000
As of September 30, 2016:		
Cost incurred to date	450,000	720,000
Estimated costs to complete	—	180,000
Billings	560,000	710,000
Cash collections	560,000	625,000

Additional Information

London accounts for its long-term construction contracts using the percentage-of-completion method for financial reporting purposes and the completed-contract method for income tax purposes.

Required:

1. Prepare a schedule showing London's gross profit (loss) recognized for the years ended September 30, 2015 and 2016, under the percentage-of-completion method.

2. Prepare a schedule showing London's balances in the following accounts at September 30, 2015, under the percentage-of-completion method:

   - Accounts receivable
   - Costs and estimated earnings in excess of billings
   - Billings in excess of costs and estimated earnings

3. Determine how much income would be recognized if London used the completed-contract method for the 2015 and 2016 fiscal years.

ClearOne Communications, Inc., is a provider of end-to-end video and audio conferencing services, including the manufacture and sale of video and audio conferencing products. From its inception as a manufacturer of this equipment through 2001, ClearOne sold its products through a nationwide network of manufacturer's representatives. Sometime in early 2001, ClearOne decided to alter its business model and instead of utilizing manufacturer's representatives, began selling its products through a nationwide network of distributors complemented by a direct sales force. Through early 2001, ClearOne experienced robust growth and increased product sales every quarter. From the selected financial data extracted from ClearOne's Form 10-Ks that follow, this growth appeared to continue through fiscal 2002. However, a complaint filed by the SEC against ClearOne alleges that things may not be as rosy as they seem.

C3-3

Channel stuffing **(LO 5)**

ClearOne Communications

	Selected Financial Data Years Ended June 30,		
	2002	**2001**	**2000**
Product sales	$37,215,161	$28,189,612	$22,226,504
Service sales	17,327,525	11,688,793	5,891,909
Cost of goods sold—products	15,057,167	10,633,956	8,033,867
Cost of goods sold—services	7,942,952	5,869,106	2,974,456
Operating expenses	20,809,281	14,904,460	10,568,861
Pre-tax operating income	10,733,286	8,470,883	6,541,229
Income from continuing operations	7,410,752	5,525,185	4,301,742
Net accounts receivable at June 30	$20,316,730	$ 7,212,970	$ 4,153,677
Cost of goods sold %—products	40.5%	37.7%	36.1%

Required:

1. Retrieve the SEC's complaint against ClearOne Communications, Inc. (www.sec.gov/litigation/litreleases/lr17934.htm). Describe management's scheme for inflating revenue.

2. The SEC alleges that by the end of fiscal 2002, ClearOne had stuffed approximately $11.5 million of inventory into the distribution channel. On the basis of this assertion, what was the approximate amount of its alleged revenue overstatement by the end of 2002?

3. Does the financial statement data presented support your estimate? Why, or why not?

C3-4

Financial reporting case:
Revenue recognition—
Software sales   (LO 3)

Indus International, Inc. (the Company), develops, markets, implements, and supports a proprietary line of Enterprise Asset Management (EAM) software and service solutions for capital-intensive industries (for example, the utilities and energy industry) worldwide. The following was extracted from Forms 10-Q and 10-K filed by the company for Year 1.

Revenue Recognition

The Company provides its software to customers under contracts, which provide for both software license fees and system implementation services. Revenues from system implementation services, which generally are time and material-based, are recognized as direct contract costs are incurred. The revenues from software license fees have been recognized as earned revenue in accordance with FASB ASC Section 985-605-25: Software—Revenue Recognition relating to software revenue recognition, when persuasive evidence of arrangement exists, delivery has occurred, the license fee is fixed and determinable, and collection is probable. Prior to Year 0, the Company began to report applicable new license fees on standard software products not requiring substantial modification or customization as earned revenue upon shipment to customers. Previously, because substantial modification and customization of software products was expected by customers, The Indus Group, Inc., had deferred the applicable license fees initially and recognized those fees as earned over the period of modification, customization and other installation services. Maintenance and support services are subject to separate contracts for which revenue is recognized ratably over the contract period. Unbilled accounts receivable represent amounts related to revenue which has been recorded either as deferred revenue or earned revenue but which has not been billed. Generally, unbilled amounts are billed within 60 to 90 days of the sale of product or performance of services. Deferred revenue represents primarily unearned maintenance and support fees and unearned license fees, for which future performance obligations remain.

Indus International, Inc.

Condensed Consolidated Statements of Operations

	Three Months Ended September 30	
($ in 000s, except per share amounts)	Year 1	Year 0
Revenues:		
Software license fees	$ 9,935	$13,042
Service and maintenance	40,945	37,291
Total revenues	50,880	50,333
Cost of revenues	25,292	25,994
Gross profit	25,588	24,339
Operating expenses:		
Research and development	8,874	8,171
Sales and marketing	7,232	8,778
General administrative	4,930	4,379
Total operating expenses	21,036	21,328
Income from operations	4,552	3,011
Interest and other income (expense), net	1,126	(206)
Income before income taxes	5,678	2,805
Income taxes	2,158	—
Net income	$ 3,520	$ 2,805
EPS (basic)	$ 0.11	$ 0.09
EPS (diluted)	$ 0.10	$ 0.08
Shares used in computing EPS (basic)	32,196	30,990
Shares used in computing EPS (diluted)	34,750	34,739

Required:

1. Reported third quarter income includes more than $2 million in revenue from two contracts for which the CEO had "side letters" written to the customers giving each a right to cancel its contracts. Should this revenue have been recognized at that time? Cite appropriate authoritative literature in support of your answer.

2. On October 28, Year 1, Indus issued a press release announcing its third quarter Year 1 financial results. The company reported that it had met quarterly targets with revenues of $50.88 million and earnings of $3.52 million, or 10 cents per share on a diluted basis. What would be the approximate effect on reported EPS of not including revenue from the two contracts referred to in requirement 1?

Mystery Technologies, Inc., a hypothetical company, is a leading manufacturer of bar code scanners and related information technology whose stock is traded on the New York Stock Exchange. In Year 3, the SEC filed allegations that during the previous five-year period, the company manipulated millions of dollars in revenue, net income, and other measures of financial performance. These manipulations were designed to meet financial projections driven by Wall Street expectations and were allegedly engineered and/or facilitated by the company's chief accounting officer (a CPA).

An example of the various ploys used by Mystery Technologies occurred in Year 1 when an officer and other employees created an excessive reserve of $10 million for obsolete inventory. This $10 million cushion was a "cookie jar" reserve designed for use when the company failed to meet its quarterly forecast, and it exceeded any reasonable estimate of the company's exposure for obsolete inventory. This reserve was released into earnings in the fourth quarter of Year 1. By making this and other adjustments that quarter, Mystery Technologies reported net income of $13.4 million rather than a $2.4 million loss and hit the quarterly forecast right on the nose. The reversal of this "cookie jar" inventory reserve and the favorable impact on reported earnings were not disclosed to the public.

Required:

Identify the ethical issues involved with the "cookie jar" reserves and the economic consequences for parties affected by the chief accounting officer's actions. (*Hint:* Reference the AICPA's Code of Professional Conduct for CPAs.)

> **C3-5**
>
> Ethical issues: Earnings management (LO 4, 5)

Big Daddy's BBQ, Inc. (Big Daddy's), franchises restaurants. The company currently has approximately 215 franchisees operating Big Daddy's restaurants in 22 states.

Big Daddy's standard franchise agreement has a 10-year term, with one 10-year renewal option. It provides for a one-time payment of an initial franchise fee and a continuing royalty fee based on gross sales. Sales reports and financial statements are regularly collected from franchisees.

Each franchisee is responsible for selecting the location for its restaurant, subject to Big Daddy's approval (based on demographics, competition, traffic volume, etc.). Each franchised restaurant must have a designated manager and assistant manager who have completed Big Daddy's six-week manager training program or who have been otherwise approved by the company. For the opening of a restaurant, Big Daddy's provides consultation and makes company personnel generally available to a franchisee. In addition, the company sends a team of personnel to the restaurant for up to two weeks to assist the franchisee and its managers in the opening, the initial marketing and training effort, as well as the overall operation of the restaurant.

Initial franchise fees are recognized when the company has substantially performed all material services and the restaurant has opened for business. Franchise royalties, which are

> **C3-6**
>
> Franchise sales (LO 3)

based on a percentage of monthly sales, are recognized as income on the accrual basis. Costs associated with franchise operations are recognized on the accrual basis.

Assume that:

1. Big Daddy's entered into a standard franchise agreement on July 1, 2014, with Linda Bundy to open a Big Daddy's BBQ in Lewisburg, PA.

2. The agreement called for an initial franchise fee of $300,000 and a 2.0% royalty. $75,000 of the fee is payable immediately; the remainder is to be paid in equal annual installments each July 1 over the life of the franchise agreement.

3. Interest of 5% on the unpaid franchise fee balance is also payable each July 1.

4. Royalty payments are to be submitted with accompanying financial statements 15 days after the end of each quarter.

5. The restaurant opened on September 30, 2014. Big Daddy's management sent a team to assist with the opening. Because Bundy felt that this assistance would be more valuable if rendered primarily after the restaurant opened, the team scheduled its arrival in Lewisburg for September 26, 2014, and was on site until October 10. Management estimated that $28,000 in costs was incurred to provide the entire package of "restaurant opening" services.

6. In keeping with the agreement, the restaurant reported the following gross sales in 2014 and 2015 and made the required payments:

		Quarter		
	First	Second	Third	Fourth
2014				$215,000
2015	$245,000	$210,000	$218,000	263,000

Required:

1. Should Big Daddy's recognize revenue from the initial franchise fee in their quarter ending September 30, 2014? Explain.

2. For Big Daddy's, prepare summary journal entries for 2014 and 2015 necessitated by this franchise agreement.

 **.mhhe.com/revsine6e**

Remember to check the book's companion website for additional study material.

Structure of the Balance Sheet and Statement of Cash Flows

T he **balance sheet**—sometimes called the *statement of financial position*—contains a summation of the assets owned by the firm, the liabilities incurred to finance these assets, and the shareholders' equity representing the amount of financing provided by owners at a specific date.

The Financial Accounting Standards Board (FASB) defines the three basic elements of the balance sheet:[1]

1. *Assets:* Probable future economic benefits obtained or controlled by an entity as a result of past transactions or events.

2. *Liabilities:* Probable future sacrifices of economic benefits arising from an entity's *present* obligations to transfer assets or provide services to other entities in the *future* as a result of *past* transactions or events.

3. *Equity:* The residual interest in an entity's assets that remains after deducting its liabilities. For a corporate form of organization, this interest is referred to as *shareholders'* or *stockholders' equity.*

The balance sheet tells us how management has invested the firm's assets and where the financing for those assets came from. It provides information for assessing rates of return, capital structure, liquidity, solvency, and financial flexibility of an enterprise.

Two **rate of return** measures for evaluating operating efficiency and profitability of an enterprise are return on assets (ROA) and return on common equity (ROCE). (The precise calculation of these two performance measures is detailed in Chapter 5.) By comparing ROA to ROCE, statement users can see whether the use of debt financing enhances the return earned by shareholders.

The balance sheet provides critical information for understanding an entity's **capital structure (debt/equity ratio),** which refers to how much of an entity's assets are financed from debt versus equity sources. An important decision in corporate finance is determining the proper mix of debt and equity financing. Management must weigh the benefits of using debt financing (with tax-deductible interest) against the dangers of becoming overleveraged (that is, having too much debt) and the possibility of

LEARNING OBJECTIVES

After studying this chapter, you will understand:

1. How the various asset, liability, and stockholders' equity accounts on a typical corporate balance sheet are measured and classified.

2. How to use balance sheet information to understand key differences in the nature of firms' operations and how those operations are financed.

3. Differences in balance sheet terminology and presentation format in countries outside the United States.

4. The information provided in notes to the financial statements on significant accounting policies, subsequent events, and related-party transactions.

5. How successive balance sheets and the income statement can be used to determine cash inflows and outflows for a period.

6. How information provided in the cash flow statement can be used to explain changes in noncash accounts on the balance sheet.

7. The distinction between operating, investing, and financing sources and uses of cash.

8. How changes in current asset and current liability accounts can be used to adjust accrual earnings to obtain cash flows from operations.

9. Subtle differences between IFRS and U.S. GAAP regarding where certain items are shown on the statement of cash flows.

---

[1] "Elements of Financial Statements of Business Enterprises," *Statement of Financial Accounting Concepts No. 6* (Stamford, CT: Financial Accounting Standards Board [FASB] 1985), para. 25, 35, 49.

defaulting on required interest and principal payments (see Chapter 5 for further discussion of capital structure ratios).

In addition to assessing the mix of debt versus equity financing, the balance sheet and related notes to the financial statements provide information for evaluating the **maturity structure** of the various obligations within the liability section. This information is critical to assessing the **liquidity** of an entity. Liquidity measures how readily assets can be converted to cash relative to how soon liabilities will have to be paid in cash. The balance sheet is the source of information for a variety of liquidity measures (detailed in Chapter 5) used by analysts and commercial loan officers to assess an entity's creditworthiness.

In addition to the liquidity measures that focus on short-term cash inflows and cash needs, balance sheets provide information for assessing long-term **solvency**—a company's ability to generate sufficient cash flows to maintain its productive capacity and still meet interest and principal payments on long-term debt. A company that cannot make debt payments when due is technically insolvent and may be forced to reorganize or liquidate.

Operating and financial flexibility refers to an entity's ability to adjust to unexpected downturns in the economic environment in which it operates or to take advantage of profitable investment opportunities as they arise. Balance sheets provide information for making these assessments. A firm that has most of its assets invested in specialized manufacturing facilities (for example, a foundry) has limited ability to adjust to economic downturns and, thus, has limited operating flexibility. Similarly, a firm with minimal cash reserves and large amounts of high interest debt will have limited ability to take advantage of profitable investment opportunities that may arise.

Now that we have outlined the information contained in balance sheets and how it is used, we turn our attention to how various balance sheet accounts are measured and classified.

CLASSIFICATION CRITERIA AND MEASUREMENT CONVENTIONS FOR BALANCE SHEET ACCOUNTS

We will use Motorola Solutions's financial statements to illustrate the classification criteria and measurement methods used in a typical balance sheet. While many people characterize generally accepted accounting principles (GAAP) balance sheet carrying amounts as **historical costs,** what they really represent is more complicated. In fact, carrying amounts in a GAAP balance sheet are a mixture of historical costs, **current replacement costs, fair value, net realizable value,** and **discounted present values.**

Exhibit 4.1 shows Motorola Solutions's consolidated balance sheet, which uses a typical U.S. disclosure format. In the Assets section, cash and any other assets expected to be converted into cash within the next 12 months (or within the **operating cycle,** if the operating cycle is longer than 12 months) are classified as current assets. Assets not expected to be converted into cash within this period are categorized separately. Within the current assets category, items are disclosed in descending order of liquidity—how quickly the items will be converted into cash through the normal course of business. In the Liabilities section of the balance sheet, items expected to be settled from current assets within the next 12 months (or within the operating cycle, if longer) are categorized as current liabilities. All other liabilities appear in a separate section as noncurrent or long-term obligations. Equity claims also appear in their own separate section of the balance sheet, which is often referred to as the Stockholders' equity section.

Maturity structure refers to how far into the future the obligations will come due.

As part of a joint effort with the IASB, the FASB recently worked on a project on financial statement presentation that would require firms to use the term "statement of financial position" in place of "balance sheet" and to report selected line items and subtotals that are typically not currently provided. Further details on proposed changes to the format of the statement of financial position (balance sheet) are not discussed here, because the project has been tabled indefinitely by both standard setting agencies.

A firm's **operating cycle** is the elapsed time beginning with the initiation of production and ending with the cash collection of the receivables from the sale of the product.

EXHIBIT 4.1	Motorola Solutions, Inc. Consolidated Balance Sheets		

		December 31	
(In millions, except per share amounts)		**2012**	**2011**
Assets			
Cash and cash equivalents		$ 1,468	$ 1,881
Sigma Fund and short-term investments		2,135	3,210
Accounts receivable, net		1,881	1,866
Inventories, net		513	512
Deferred income taxes		604	613
Other current assets		800	686
Total current assets		7,401	8,768
Property, plant, and equipment, net		839	896
Investments		144	166
Deferred income taxes		2,416	2,375
Goodwill		1,510	1,428
Other assets		369	296
Total assets		$12,679	$13,929
Liabilities and Stockholders' Equity			
Current portion of long-term debt		$ 4	$ 405
Accounts payable		705	677
Accrued liabilities		2,626	2,733
Total current liabilities		3,335	3,815
Long-term debt		1,859	1,130
Other liabilities		4,195	3,710
Stockholders' Equity			
Preferred stock, $100 par value		—	—
Common stock: 12/31/12—$.01 par value; 12/31/11—$.01 par value		3	3
Authorized shares: 12/31/12—600.0; 12/31/11—600.0			
Issued shares: 12/31/12—277.3; 12/31/11—320.0			
Outstanding shares: 12/31/12—276.1; 12/31/11—318.8			
Additional paid-in capital		4,937	7,071
Retained earnings		1,625	1,016
Accumulated other comprehensive loss		(3,300)	(2,876)
Total Motorola Solutions, Inc. stockholders' equity		3,265	5,214
Noncontrolling interests		25	60
Total stockholders' equity		3,290	5,274
Total liabilities and stockholders' equity		$12,679	$13,929

To convey a feeling for the diversity of the measurement bases used in a typical balance sheet, we will discuss selected accounts from Motorola Solutions's 2012 comparative balance sheet (see Exhibit 4.1). Many of the measurement issues discussed below are explored in greater depth in subsequent chapters.

Cash and Cash Equivalents
The balance sheet carrying amount for this account reflects the amount of money or currency the firm has on hand in bank accounts or in certificates of deposit. If cash consists exclusively of U.S. dollar amounts, the balance sheet Cash account reflects the *historical* amount of net dollar units arising from past transactions. Due to the unique liquidity of cash, however, this historical amount of net dollar units is identical to the current market value of the cash.

Monetary assets are fixed in dollar amounts regardless of price changes. A $300,000 cash deposit remains fixed at $300,000 even if the general level of prices goes up and the purchasing power of that $300,000 declines. **Nonmonetary assets** such as inventory and buildings are *not* fixed in dollar amounts; that is, inventory purchased for $300,000 can conceivably increase in value if prices go up. While not assured, this potential for changing value is the distinguishing characteristic of nonmonetary items—their value is *not* measured in a fixed number of monetary units.

If some of the cash amounts are denominated in foreign currency units (likely for Motorola Solutions, a multinational firm), those amounts in foreign currency units must be *translated* into U.S. dollar equivalents. For **monetary assets** such as cash, accounts receivable, and notes receivable, the current rate of exchange in effect at the balance sheet date is used to translate foreign currency units into dollars. As a consequence of using the current rate of exchange (rather than the historical rate of exchange that was in effect at the time of the foreign currency cash inflows), this portion of the Cash account is carried at its **current market price,** *not* at its historical transaction amount. For these foreign currency deposits, current market exchange values are used regardless of whether they are higher or lower than the historical rate. Consequently, the GAAP measurement convention for cash is, in reality, current market price rather than historical cost.

A U.S. company with 1 million pesos in the bank account of its Mexican manufacturing subsidiary would value the cash at $58,501 U.S. dollars on December 31, 2012, when the exchange rate was 17.0936 pesos to the dollar. This same bank account (with 1 million pesos) would have been valued at $55,326 U.S. dollars on December 31, 2011, when the exchange rate was 18.0748 pesos to the dollar.

Sigma Fund

As described in Motorola Solutions's notes, this account represents a portfolio of investments in certificates of deposit, commercial paper, government bonds, and high-quality corporate debt obligations that are carried at fair value on Motorola Solutions's balance sheet. The portion of these investments that Motorola Solutions does not intend to convert to cash within the next year is reported in the noncurrent asset section of the balance sheet.

When the balance sheet carrying amount of the securities investment is written up or down to current fair value, the offsetting gain or loss appears on the income statement if the securities are **trading securities** for which the intent is to generate profits on short-term differences in price. When less actively traded securities (termed **available-for-sale securities**) are marked to fair value, the offsetting gain or loss goes directly to Other comprehensive income rather than being part of Net income. (These accounting rules are discussed further in Chapter 16.)

Short-Term Investments

This category of assets comprises items such as U.S. Treasury bills, notes, equity securities, or other financial assets that companies use to earn a return on funds not currently needed in operations. The GAAP measurement rules for investments in debt and equity securities distinguish between debt securities, which the reporting company intends to hold to maturity, and all other securities (both debt and equity), which an entity intends to hold only for short periods of time.[2]

The rules are:

1. Debt securities the company intends to hold to maturity are carried at amortized cost. (When debt securities are sold at a premium or discount, the premium or discount is amortized over time, hence, the term **amortized cost.)**

2. Debt and equity securities held for short-range investment purposes are carried at fair value at each balance sheet date (generally, the price at which these securities can be bought and sold), regardless of whether that price is above or below cost.

How long the company intends to hold the debt securities determines how they are measured on the balance sheet. Some will be carried at amortized cost and others at fair value. Equity securities held for the short term are always measured at fair value.

---

[2] FASB Accounting Standards Codification (ASC) Section 320-10-25: Investments—Debt and Equity Securities—Overall—Recognition.

Accounts Receivable, Net
This account reflects credit sales that have not yet been collected. The balance sheet carrying amount for gross accounts receivable equals the face amount due that arises from past credit sales transactions. Thus, if a company sold goods with a $100,000 sales price on November 15, 2014, the following entry would be made:

DR	Accounts receivable	$100,000	
	CR Sales revenue		$100,000

If the receivable is still outstanding at December 31, 2014, it would be shown on the balance sheet at $100,000. However, accrual accounting requires that any future costs be matched against the revenues recognized in the period of sale. When sales are made for credit (on account), some sales may unknowingly be made to customers who will be incapable of making the required payment. The expense associated with these uncollectible accounts must be recognized—on an estimated basis—in the period in which the sales arise. This compels companies to prepare an estimate of the proportion of existing accounts receivable balances that they reasonably believe will ultimately not be collected. In Motorola Solutions's case, the 2012 accounts receivable note disclosure shows the details behind the Accounts receivable, net balance shown on its balance sheet as follows:

> The accounting entry to recognize estimated uncollectible accounts is:
>
> | | | | |
> |---|---|---|---|
> | **DR** | Bad debt expense | $XXX | |
> | | **CR** Allowance for doubtful accounts | | $XXX |
>
> The debited account reduces income in the current period, but the account credited appears as a deduction from gross accounts receivable. Such deductions from asset accounts are called **contra-asset** accounts. (Estimating and recognizing bad debt expense is discussed in Chapter 8.)

($ in millions)	
Gross accounts receivable	$1,932
Less: Allowance for doubtful accounts	(51)
Net accounts receivable reported on balance sheet	$1,881

Notice that as a consequence of this "netting" of accounts, the total for net accounts receivable $1,881 million) is carried at expected **net realizable value** as of the balance sheet date, not at original historical cost ($1,932 million).

Inventories
The inventory account for a manufacturing firm such as Motorola Solutions comprises three components: (1) raw materials, (2) work-in-process, and (3) finished goods. In the notes to its financial statements, Motorola Solutions discloses that inventories are carried at **lower of cost or market,** where cost is computed using the weighted average method (discussed in Chapter 9). Therefore, the measurement basis for inventories depends on the comparison between historical cost and current market price.

> For a wholesale or retail company, this account reflects only finished goods, that is, merchandise held for resale.

- When costs are lower than market price, the carrying amounts for inventory conform to the historical cost convention.

- When cost exceeds market, inventories on the balance sheet are carried at current market price, where that market price is the cost to replace the item (subject to GAAP rules described in Chapter 9).

Deferred Income Taxes
In the United States, and many other industrialized countries, the rules used to determine income for financial reporting purposes (called **book income**) frequently do not conform to the rules used to determine income for taxation purposes (called **taxable income**). Income determination rules for financial reporting differ from rules for determining income for taxation purposes because of the very different objectives of the

two computations. The objective in measuring book income is to reflect a firm's underlying economic success: Was the firm profitable during the period? The objective in measuring taxable income is to conform to laws designed to provide a basis for funding government operations. Because the rules that govern income determination for tax purposes result from a national political process, these rules do not necessarily measure changes in firms' underlying economic condition.

Because the rules for determining book income differ from the rules used to determine taxable income, revenues or expenses are frequently reported in a different period for book purposes than for tax purposes. These differences are referred to as **temporary** or **timing differences.** The amount of the difference in the revenue or expense item times the marginal tax rate (currently 35% in the United States) determines the amount of deferred tax. Deferred tax assets arise when a revenue (expense) is reported in an earlier (later) period for tax purposes than for book purposes. Deferred tax liabilities arise when the opposite occurs—that is, when a revenue (expense) is reported in a later (earlier) period for tax purposes than for book purposes. (The measurement and reporting rules for deferred taxes are covered in Chapter 13.)

Notice that Motorola Solutions reports Deferred income taxes in both the current and noncurrent portion of the asset section of its balance sheet. This is because U.S. GAAP requires firms to classify net deferred tax assets (or liabilities) according to whether the asset or liability giving rise to the temporary difference is classified as current or noncurrent. For example, a deferred tax asset for a temporary difference related to the allowance for doubtful accounts on accounts receivable (a current asset) would be classified in the current asset section of the balance sheet, while a deferred tax asset for temporary differences on employee pension benefits (a noncurrent liability) would be reported in the noncurrent section of the balance sheet.

The current amount of Deferred income taxes ($604 million) and the noncurrent amount ($2,416 million) reported on Motorola Solutions's balance sheet are due to temporary differences that caused taxable income to exceed book income in the current or prior years. Because the temporary differences giving rise to these net deferred tax assets will reverse in subsequent years, book income will exceed taxable income in *future years*. Even though these reversals may be expected to take place several years into the future, GAAP reports the related tax effects at their *undiscounted amounts*. In other words, GAAP ignores the time value of money in reporting deferred tax assets or liabilities and treats expected reversals one year into the future the same as reversals ten years into the future.

> There are other reasons why book income may differ from taxable income—called **permanent differences**—but they do *not* give rise to deferred taxes. For example, U.S. income tax law does not tax interest on state and municipal bonds. Consequently, if a firm owns municipal bonds and receives interest income from these bonds, the interest is tax free. Book income will include the interest income, but taxable income will not.

Property, Plant, and Equipment—Net

This account reflects the tangible long-lived assets that Motorola Solutions uses in its operations. This item appears on the balance sheet at its net amount: historical cost minus accumulated depreciation. Motorola Solutions, like most companies, provides information about the components of this figure in the financial statement notes.

	December 31,	
($ in millions)	2012	2011
Land	$ 38	$ 69
Buildings	739	774
Machinery and equipment	1,932	2,052
	2,709	2,895
Less: Accumulated depreciation	(1,870)	(1,999)
Property, plant, and equipment—net	$ 839	$ 896

When a long-lived asset becomes impaired—that is, when its carrying amount may no longer be recoverable—the fixed asset account is reduced to its lower **fair value.**[3] If available, quoted current market prices represent the best measure of fair value. However, market prices for long-lived assets are not always readily available. So, fair value may need to be estimated by discounting expected future net operating cash flows. (This topic is covered in Chapter 10.)

> The FASB defines *fair value* of an asset as "the amount at which the asset could be bought or sold in a current transaction between willing parties, that is, other than a forced or liquidation sale." (ASC 820-10-20 Glossary.)

Investments   This account consists of U.S. government and agency obligations and corporate debt and equity securities that are held in Motorola Solutions's available-for-sale portfolio (see Chapter 16), which are not expected to be sold in the near term. These securities are reported at fair value at the balance sheet date.

Goodwill   This is an **intangible asset** recognized as part of a business combination. It is initially measured as the difference between the consideration given by Motorola Solutions to acquire another business entity and the fair value of the identifiable net assets (assets minus liabilities) of that entity on the date of acquisition. The amount reported on Motorola Solutions's balance sheet is adjusted for any amounts that have been written off since acquisition due to impairment (see Chapter 16 for further discussion of measurement of goodwill and Chapter 10 for discussion of asset impairments).

Other Assets   A note to Motorola Solutions's financial statements indicates that this account is composed primarily of intangible assets, net of accumulated amortization, and royalty licensing agreements. Thus, the assets in this account are carried at historical cost less amounts amortized to date (see Chapter 10).

Current Portion of Long-Term Debt   The current portion of long-term debt represents the portion of long-term borrowings that fall due within one year of the balance sheet date. Because these amounts will be paid within a relatively short period of time (within one year), they are reported at their (undiscounted) face amount, that is, the amount due at the payment date.

Accounts Payable and Accrued Liabilities   Accounts payable represent amounts owed to suppliers of merchandise or services purchased on open account (that is, for credit). Payment is typically due within 30 to 90 days. Accrued liabilities represent expenses that have been incurred, but not yet paid. Examples include accrued wages and accrued interest expense. These items are reflected on the balance sheet at the amount of the original liability, that is, at the amount arising at the transaction's inception. Consequently, the numbers are shown at historical cost.

Long-Term Debt   This account represents obligations that fall due beyond one year from the balance sheet date. Examples include notes, bonds, and lease obligations. When long-term debt (typically, notes or bonds) is issued, the initial balance sheet carrying amount is determined by computing the **discounted present value** of the sum of (1) the future principal repayment *plus* (2) the periodic interest payments. The rate used for discounting these

---

[3] FASB ASC Paragraph 360-10-35-17: Property, Plant, and Equipment—Overall—Subsequent Measurement—Measurement of Impairment Loss.

amounts is the **effective yield** on the notes or bonds at the date they were issued. Here, we'll simply provide a brief overview of the general measurement rules for long-term debt. More on bonds and other long-term debt instruments is presented in Chapter 11.

When bonds are sold at par, the amount received equals the recorded face amount of the debt. For example, if Motorola Solutions sells $100,000,000 of 15-year, 10% bonds for $100,000,000, the accounting entry is:

DR Cash	$100,000,000	
CR Bonds payable.		$100,000,000

The $100,000,000 carrying amount equals the present value of the principal *and* interest payments over the life of the bond discounted at 10%, the effective yield at the time of issue. The effective yield is 10% because the effective yield on bonds sold at par equals the rate stated on the face of the bond (referred to as "stated rate"). (We'll show why in Chapter 11.) When bonds are sold at a premium (say, $105 million) or at a discount (say, $95 million), the initial carrying amount is again equal to the present value of the future interest and principal payments discounted at the effective yield on the bonds. In general, at balance sheet dates after the bonds' issuance date, the subsequent carrying amount of *all* bonds outstanding equals the present value of the future principal and interest flows discounted at the *original effective yield rate.* This carrying amount will differ from the bonds' current market price whenever interest rates have changed subsequent to issuance.

Other Liabilities   Notes to Motorola Solutions's financial statements indicate this account is composed primarily of obligations to employees arising from Motorola Solutions's defined benefit pension and postretirement health care plans (see Chapter 14 for discussion of how these obligations are measured).

Common Stock   This account represents the **par value** of shares issued and outstanding. The par value is determined by the company's articles of incorporation. Par values were originally established to ensure that a corporation would maintain a minimum level of investment by shareholders to protect the interests of creditors. For example, some states preclude companies from paying dividends to shareholders that would result in a reduction of stockholders' equity below the par value of shares issued and outstanding. As a practical matter, debt covenant provisions in the borrower's lending agreements generally place restrictions on firms' distributions to shareholders that are more stringent than the statutory par-value restrictions. Therefore, the par value of shares has limited economic significance, as discussed in Chapter 15.

Additional Paid-in Capital   This account reflects the amounts in excess of par or stated value that the corporation received when the shares were originally issued. For example, if Motorola Solutions issued 100,000 shares of $3 par-value stock for $15 per share, the Additional paid-in capital component would be credited for

$$(\$15 - \$3) \times 100,000 = \$1,200,000$$

Thus, additional paid-in capital is also shown at historical cost (that is, the amount above par value paid to the firm when the shares were originally issued).

Retained Earnings   This account measures the net of cumulative earnings less cumulative dividend distributions of the company since inception. Therefore, it represents the cumulative earnings that have been reinvested in the business. The Retained earnings account is increased (decreased) by the net income (net loss) for the period and is decreased for dividends that are declared in the period. For many firms, like Motorola Solutions, retained earnings represents the major portion of stockholders' equity. Thus, the book value of equity is largely determined by the past earnings that have been retained and reinvested in the business. As we will see in Chapters 5 and 6, book value of equity is a key element of many performance measures—such as return on common equity (ROCE)—and it plays an important role in equity valuation.

Different measurement bases pervade the balance sheet, and since these different measurements impact related revenue or expense amounts that at some time will appear on the income statement, income is a mixture of historical costs, current values, and present values. This means that retained earnings is also a mixture of many different measurement bases.

Accumulated Other Comprehensive Income   This account measures the cumulative unrealized gains and losses from components of comprehensive income (see Chapter 2) recognized in current and prior years. As noted in Chapter 2, the most common components of other comprehensive income are:

1. Fair value adjustments made to securities classified as "available-for-sale" (see Chapter 16).
2. Fair value changes on derivatives that meet certain conditions for hedge accounting (see Chapter 11).
3. Foreign currency translation adjustments (see Chapter 16).
4. Unrealized actuarial gains and losses on pension assets and liabilities and increases (decreases) in pension obligations due to prior service cost adjustments (see Chapter 14).
5. Losses on certain investments that are other than temporary (see Chapter 16).

Unrealized gains are credited to this account and unrealized losses are debited to this account. All amounts included in this account are net of tax effects. Because the balance in this account is shown in parentheses on Motorola Solutions's balance sheet, it represents a cumulative loss (debit balance). For Motorola Solutions the balance in this account increased from a $2,876 million debit balance at the end of 2011 to a $3,300 million debit balance at the end of 2012, representing an additional unrealized loss of $424 million for 2012. Motorola Solutions's consolidated statement of stockholders' equity (not shown) explains the components of this change (all shown net of tax effects), which are the components of other comprehensive income for 2012:

($ in millions)	Unrealized Gain (Loss)	
1. Unrealized gain on available-for-sale securities	$ 1	**CR**
2. Foreign currency translation adjustment gain	14	**CR**
3. Pension and retirement-related adjustments	(443)	**DR**
4. Unrealized gain on derivative instruments	4	**CR**
Net unrealized loss for period	$(424)	**DR**

Noncontrolling Interests   The consolidated balance sheet includes the assets and liabilities (net assets) of Motorola Solutions and all of its subsidiaries. Subsidiaries are companies that Motorola Solutions controls by owning more than 50 percent of the outstanding voting stock of those companies. If Motorola Solutions owns less than 100 percent of one (or more) of its subsidiaries, then a **noncontrolling interest** in the net assets of the subsidiary is held by investors other than Motorola Solutions. The noncontrolling interest reported in the stockholders' equity section of Motorola Solutions's consolidated balance sheet is measured at the fair value of the subsidiary at the time that Motorola Solutions acquired its controlling interest plus (minus) the noncontrolling interest in subsidiary earnings (losses) subsequent to Motorola Solutions's acquisition (see Chapter 16 for further discussion of noncontrolling interests and how they are measured).

Analytical Insights: Understanding the Nature of a Firm's Business

One tool for gaining insights into the nature of a company's operations and for analyzing its asset and financial structure is to prepare a **common-size balance sheet.** In it, each balance sheet account is expressed as a percentage of total assets or, equivalently, as a percentage of total liabilities plus shareholders' equity. Exhibit 4.2 presents common-size balance sheets for four companies operating in four distinctly different industries: E-Trade Group, an Internet company specializing in online investing services; Deere & Company, a manufacturer of agricultural and heavy construction equipment with a large finance subsidiary; Wal-Mart, a well-known discount retailer; and Potomac Electric Power Company, an electrical utility providing service to Washington, D.C., and the surrounding area. Can you match up the common-size statements with each of these companies? Think about the industry in which each firm operates and about the economic activities the firms might engage in. Then try to figure out how these activities might impact a typical balance sheet.

Note that Company C has a very large proportion of its assets in cash, marketable securities, and accounts receivable with no inventory, and a relatively small amount of property, plant, and equipment (PP&E). Most of Company C's debt financing comes from short-term liabilities, because the company carries no long-term debt. Finally, note that Retained earnings is negative (a deficit), indicating that the company has suffered cumulative losses since it was formed. The lack of inventory rules out Deere and Wal-Mart as the source of Company C's data because both would hold significant inventories. Also, the relatively low amount of PP&E further rules out these two firms as well as Potomac Power because all three need significant amounts of fixed assets to conduct business. This leaves E-Trade Group as the obvious match. A corroborating piece of evidence is the deficit in retained earnings. Because of heavy start-up costs, many of the relatively young Internet companies such as E-Trade fail to turn a profit in the early years of their existence.

Both Company A and Company B have relatively high amounts of current assets, but the mix of current assets is quite different. For Company A, current receivables represent nearly 57% of total assets while Company B has no current receivables, but 27% of its assets are in inventory. Because many of Deere's agricultural and heavy construction equipment products sell for well in excess of $100,000, dealers and customers often need to finance their purchases. Deere offers this financing through its wholly owned finance subsidiary whose operations are included in the consolidated numbers. Thus, the large receivables balance for Company A coupled with significant amounts invested in inventories and PP&E provide strong clues that Deere is Company A.

Like most national discount retailers, Wal-Mart would be expected to have large amounts of inventory. Because most sales are for cash or paid through bank credit cards (for example, Visa or MasterCard), Wal-Mart would likely have little or no current receivables on its balance sheet. Moreover, with a large number of store facilities either purchased or leased under capital lease arrangements, we would expect to see relatively large investments in PP&E. This profile seems to match up well with Company B's data.

This leaves Potomac Power as Company D. Note the relatively low amount of current assets and the large investment in PP&E to generate electricity. The large amount of long-term debt financing is also quite common for utilities. Regulated utilities are allowed to build a "reasonable and fair return" to stockholders into the energy rates charged customers. Therefore, they have a relatively steady and predictable earnings and cash flow stream. This allows utilities such as Potomac Power to use proportionately more long-term debt to finance their operations relative to companies with more volatile earnings patterns.

The preceding exercise demonstrates how statement readers can extract useful information from common-size balance sheets to learn about the underlying economics of an industry and the nature of the firm's operations. Chapter 5 will introduce additional analytical tools for conducting in-depth analyses of companies.

EXHIBIT 4.2 Common-Size Balance Sheet Comparison

	Company A		Company B		Company C		Company D	
	$ in Millions	%	$ in Millions	%	$ in Millions	%	$ in Millions	%
Assets								
Current assets								
Cash and marketable securities	$ 1,206.2	5.3	$ 2,161.0	2.6	$ 5,157.5	28.4	$ 676.7	12.8
Current receivables	12,826.9	56.6	2,000.0	2.4	10,149.7	55.8	401.2	7.6
Inventories	1,505.7	6.6	22,614.0	27.1	—	—	37.8	0.7
Other current assets	1,939.3	8.6	1,471.0	1.8	—	—	24.2	0.5
Total current assets	17,478.1	77.1	28,246.0	33.9	15,307.2	84.2	1,139.9	21.6
Noncurrent assets								
Property, plant, and equipment, net	2,052.3	9.0	45,750.0	54.8	331.7	1.8	2,753.4	52.1
Goodwill and intangibles, net	874.0	3.9	8,595.0	10.3	684.4	3.8	—	—
Other assets, net	2,258.7	10.0	860.0	1.0	1,849.1	10.2	1,392.6	26.3
Total assets	$22,663.1	100.0%	$83,451.0	100.0%	$18,172.4	100.0%	$5,285.9	100.0%
Liabilities and Stockholders' Equity								
Current liabilities								
Total current liabilities	$ 9,456.6	41.7	$27,282.0	32.7	$16,532.0	91.0	$ 965.4	18.2
Long-term liabilities	9,214.3	40.7	21,067.0	25.2	—	—	2,287.5	43.3
Total liabilities	18,670.9	82.4	48,349.0	57.9	16,532.0	91.0	3,252.9	61.5
Redeemable preferred stock	—	—	—	—	69.5	0.4	209.8	4.0
Stockholders' equity								
Contributed capital and other equity items	157.4	0.7	661.0	0.8	1,818.0	10.0	849.1	16.1
Retained earnings (deficit)	3,834.8	16.9	34,441.0	41.3	(247.1)	(1.4)	974.1	18.4
Total liabilities and stockholders' equity	$22,663.1	100.0%	$83,451.0	100.0%	$18,172.4	100.0%	$5,285.9	100.0%

International Differences in Balance Sheet Presentation

The account titles and format of balance sheets prepared in other countries can sometimes differ rather dramatically from those prepared under U.S. GAAP.[4] U.S. firms' balance sheets list assets from most liquid to least liquid, where *liquid* refers to the ease of converting the asset into cash. Similarly, current liabilities are reported before noncurrent or long-term liabilities. Firms that use International Financial Reporting Standards (IFRS) are allowed, but not required, to reverse the ordering of assets from least liquid to most liquid, with the same ordering for displaying liabilities.[5] This format is illustrated in Exhibit 4.3, which presents the fiscal 2011 balance sheet of Burberry PLC, a British company that designs, manufactures, and distributes luxury apparel throughout the world.

Note that the noncurrent assets are presented first followed by the current assets. Within the noncurrent assets category, Intangible assets are presented first followed by tangible assets (that is, Property, plant, and equipment), Investment properties, Deferred tax assets, and finally Trade and other receivables and Derivative financial assets. Burberry's balance sheet format is presented in a way that emphasizes the firm's liquidity by placing current assets and current liabilities in close proximity to one another.

Balance sheets prepared in the United Kingdom also introduce some account titles that can be confusing to the unwary. For example, inventory is sometimes referred to using the account title, Stocks. Although Burberry uses familiar terminology for Trade and other receivables, some British companies use the term Debtors for this account. The Equity section of Burberry's balance sheet contains several account titles that reflect unique British terminology in applying IFRS. Exhibit 4.4 on pg. 200 shows the accounts under U.S. GAAP that correspond to these British accounts. One of the British equity accounts that requires brief elaboration since it has no U.S. counterpart is the Capital reserve. In the United Kingdom, when a company repurchases its own shares, these shares are canceled. When the repurchase is paid for from profits, an amount equivalent to the par or stated value of the shares repurchased is transferred from the Ordinary share capital account to a Capital reserve account, which is not available for dividend distribution. The Hedging reserve and Foreign currency translation reserve are equivalent to Other comprehensive income accounts under U.S. GAAP. Although not shown on Burberry's balance sheet, some British companies report a Revaluation reserve as part of shareholders' equity. IFRS rules allow companies to periodically revalue both tangible and intangible long-lived assets upward. The offsetting credit when assets are written up to fair value is the Revaluation reserve (see Chapter 10 for further details).[6]

Finally, note that Burberry reports the numbers on its balance sheet for the "Group." The Group numbers reflect the financial position of Burberry and all of its subsidiaries. This is equivalent to the "consolidated" financial statement numbers of a parent and its subsidiaries under U.S. GAAP.

This example provides a brief glimpse of how balance sheet format and terminology used in other countries differ from those used under U.S. GAAP. Examples of differences in U.S. versus IFRS accounting appear elsewhere throughout the book.

---

[4] In addition, the measurement bases used for various accounts can sometimes be quite different from country to country. Throughout the book, we will alert you to these important differences as we discuss the recognition, measurement, and disclosure rules that govern financial reporting.

[5] "Presentation of Financial Statements," *International Accounting Standard (IAS) 1* (revised 2005) (London: IASB, 2005).

[6] "Property, Plant and Equipment," *IAS 16* (London: International Accounting Standards Board [IASB], revised 2003). "Intangible Assets," *IAS 38* (London: IASB, 2004).

| EXHIBIT 4.3 | Burberry Group Balance Sheet Fiscal 2011/2012 |

(Amounts reported in millions of BritishSterling)	As at 31 March 2012 £m	As at 31 March 2011 £m
Assets		
Noncurrent assets		
Intangible assets	133.1	114.7
Property, plant, and equipment	328.8	281.8
Investment properties	2.8	3.0
Deferred tax assets	84.1	70.4
Trade and other receivables	22.3	15.2
Derivative financial assets	14.7	9.2
	585.8	494.3
Current assets		
Inventories	311.1	247.9
Trade and other receivables	145.2	132.5
Derivative financial assets	3.2	1.6
Income tax receivables	10.1	8.3
Cash and cash equivalents	546.9	466.3
	1,016.5	856.6
Assets classified as held for sale	8.3	13.5
	1,024.8	870.1
Total assets	1,610.6	1,364.4
Liabilities		
Noncurrent liabilities		
Trade and other payables	(104.9)	(84.4)
Deferred tax liabilities	(1.4)	(1.8)
Derivative financial liabilities	(0.2)	—
Retirement benefit obligations	(0.8)	(0.6)
Provisions for other liabilities and charges	(15.1)	(9.6)
	(122.4)	(96.4)
Current liabilities		
Bank overdrafts and borrowings	(208.6)	(168.4)
Derivative financial liabilities	(1.9)	(3.9)
Trade and other payables	(324.4)	(283.4)
Provisions for other liabilities and charges	(8.2)	(18.6)
Income tax liabilities	(53.7)	(60.0)
	(596.8)	(534.3)
Total liabilities	(719.2)	(630.7)
Net assets	891.4	733.7
Equity		
Capital and reserves attributable to the Company's equity holders		
Ordinary share capital	0.2	0.2
Share premium account	202.6	192.5
Capital reserve	33.9	28.9
Hedging reserve	4.9	2.4
Foreign currency translation reserve	118.6	123.2
Retained earnings	507.1	366.4
	867.3	713.6
Noncontrolling interest in equity	24.1	20.1
Total equity	891.4	733.7

Source: Burberry Group Annual Report 2011/2012

EXHIBIT 4.4	Comparison of U.K. and U.S. Account Titles

U.K. Equity Accounts	Equivalent U.S. Accounts
Ordinary share capital	Common stock—par
Share premium	Capital in excess of par
Capital reserve	No equivalent in U.S. GAAP
Hedging reserve	Accumulated other comprehensive income account
Foreign currency translation reserve	Accumulated other comprehensive income account
Revaluation reserve	No equivalent in U.S. GAAP

RECAP

The balance sheet provides a snapshot of a company's financial position at a given point in time. It shows the various types of assets held at the balance sheet date and the claims against those assets (that is, how those assets have been financed).

Balance sheet accounts reflect a variety of measurement bases, including historical cost, current costs (also called fair value), net realizable value, and discounted present value. Therefore, users of balance sheet information must be careful to recognize the effects that these different measurement bases can have both when aggregating numbers across accounts as well as when computing ratios that are used in making intercompany comparisons.

With the tremendous growth in international business and the increased frequency of cross-border financing, it is likely that you will encounter financial statements prepared under non–U.S. GAAP sometime during your career. When you do, you must be aware of differences in recognition and measurement criteria, statement format, and terminology to properly interpret and analyze those statements.

NOTES TO FINANCIAL STATEMENTS

Notes are an integral part of companies' financial reports. Financial statement notes provide a wealth of information that allows statement users to better understand and interpret the numbers presented in the body of the financial statements. In some instances, notes contain important information not found in the financial statements themselves. For example, the lease note shows a firm's future commitments under noncapitalized operating leases, which is useful in assessing a firm's future cash flow needs and creditworthiness. Throughout the remainder of the book, we illustrate the type of information typically found in notes, which includes various disclosures required by GAAP. We discuss how this information can be used to evaluate a company's future prospects and creditworthiness.

Here we briefly discuss and illustrate three important notes typically found in companies' financial reports:

> FASB Accounting Standards Codification uses the term, *notes to financial statements*. We sometimes use the term *footnotes* because it is a common term used in practice, and many firms still refer to their financial statement notes as footnotes.

1. Summary of significant accounting policies.
2. Disclosure of important subsequent events.
3. Related-party transactions.

Summary of Significant Accounting Policies As you will see in later chapters, in many areas of accounting, management is free to choose from equally acceptable alternative accounting methods. Examples include different cost flow assumptions for valuing inventory (FIFO versus LIFO), different methods for determining depreciation expense (straight-line versus accelerated), and different methods of accounting for long-term construction contracts (percentage-of-completion versus completed contract). To make valid intercompany comparisons, it is important for statement users to recognize and understand the alternative accounting methods that a reporting entity has selected to account for its economic activities.

EXHIBIT 4.5 Motorola Solutions, Inc. and Subsidiaries
Excerpts from 2012 Accounting Policies Note

1. Summary of Significant Accounting Policies

Investments: Investments in equity and debt securities classified as available-for-sale are carried at fair value. Debt securities classified as held-to-maturity are carried at amortized cost. Equity securities that are restricted for more than one year or that are not publicly traded are carried at cost. Certain investments are accounted for using the equity method if the Company has significant influence over the issuing entity. The Company assesses declines in the fair value of investments to determine whether such declines are other-than-temporary. This assessment is made considering all available evidence, including changes in general market conditions, specific industry and individual company data, the length of time and the extent to which the fair value has been less than cost, the financial condition and the near-term prospects of the entity issuing the security, and the Company's ability and intent to hold the investment until recovery. Other-than-temporary impairments of investments are recorded to Other within Other income (expense) in the Company's consolidated statements of operations in the period in which they become impaired.

    Inventories: Inventories are valued at the lower of average cost (which approximates cost on a first-in, first-out basis) or market (net realizable value or replacement cost).

    Property, Plant, and Equipment: Property, plant, and equipment are stated at cost less accumulated depreciation. Depreciation is recorded using straight-line, based on the estimated useful lives of the assets (buildings and building equipment, 5 to 40 years; machinery and equipment, 2 to 10 years) and commences once the assets are ready for their intended use.

EXHIBIT 4.6 Pfizer Inc.
2012 Annual Report

Note 19: Subsequent Event

Also on January 28, 2013, we transferred to Zoetis substantially all of the assets and liabilities of our Animal Health business in exchange for all of the Class A and Class B common stock of Zoetis, $1.0 billion of the $3.65 billion senior notes and an amount of cash equal to substantially all of the cash proceeds received by Zoetis from the remaining $2.65 billion senior notes issued. The $1.0 billion of senior notes received by Pfizer were exchanged by Pfizer for the retirement of Pfizer commercial paper issued in December 2012, and the cash proceeds received by Pfizer of approximately $2.5 billion are restricted to debt repayment, dividends, and/or stock buybacks, in all cases to be completed by mid-2014.

    The **Summary of Significant Accounting Policies** explains the important accounting choices that the reporting entity uses to account for selected transactions and accounts.[7] Exhibit 4.5 shows excerpts from the accounting policy note in Motorola Solutions's 2012 annual report explaining how it accounts for Investments; Inventories; and Property, plant, and equipment.

Subsequent Events   Events or transactions that have a significant effect on a company's financial position or results of operations sometimes occur after the close of its fiscal year-end but before the financial statements are issued. Disclosure of these **subsequent events** is required if they are material and are likely to influence investors' appraisal of the risk and return prospects of the reporting entity.[8] Examples of such events include loss of a major customer, a business combination, issuance of debt or equity securities, or a catastrophic loss. Exhibit 4.6 illustrates a subsequent event disclosure provided by Pfizer Inc. in its 2012 annual

---

[7] FASB ASC Topic 235: Notes to Financial Statements.

[8] FASB ASC Topic 855: Subsequent Events.

EXHIBIT 4.7	**Independent Film Development Corporation**

Note 7: Related Party Transaction (Excerpts)

As of March 31, 2013, the Company owed its CEO $9,209. The money was advanced to the company to cover certain operating expenses. Amount is due on demand and accrues interest at 8% per year.

During the year ended September 30, 2012, the Company authorized the issuance of 75,000 common shares to Rachel Boulds, the Company's CFO, for compensation of services. The shares were issued based on the value of the common stock on the date of authorization for total compensation expense of $25,713.

On or about February 4, 2013, the Company authorized the issuance of 75,000 common shares to Rachel Boulds, the Company's CFO, for compensation of services. The shares were issued at $0.0369 based on the value of the common stock on the date of authorization for total compensation expense of $2,767. The shares were not issued by the transfer agent as of March 31, 2013, so therefore have been recorded as a stock payable.

report related to its transfer of substantially all of the assets and liabilities of its Animal Health business to Zoetis Corp., a wholly owned subsidiary of Pfizer. Note that the transfer took place on January 28, 2013, after Pfizer's fiscal year-end closing date of December 31, but before the 2012 financial statements were issued.

Related-Party Transactions   A **related-party transaction** occurs when a company enters into a transaction with individuals or other businesses that are in some way connected with it or its management or board of directors. Examples include transactions between:

1. The reporting entity and its principal owners, management or members of their immediate families, and members of the board of directors.
2. Subsidiaries of a common parent.
3. The reporting entity and nonconsolidated affiliates in which it holds a significant ownership stake.

> Enron's dealings with several special purpose entities set up as limited partnerships that were headed up by Andrew Fastow, Enron's chief financial officer, provide an example of this type of related-party transaction.

Because related-party transactions are not entered into at arm's length, these events pose greater risks. Therefore, companies are required to disclose in a financial statement note any related-party transactions, including the nature of the relationship, a description of the transaction, and any dollar amounts involved.[9] Exhibit 4.7 illustrates a related-party note disclosure from Independent Film Development Corporation's March 31, 2013, quarterly report detailing transactions that the company entered into with its CEO and CFO.

STATEMENT OF CASH FLOWS

The balance sheet shows a firm's investment (assets) and financial structure (liabilities and stockholders' equity) at a given *point in time.* By contrast, the **statement of cash flows** shows the user why a firm's investments and financial structure have *changed* between two balance sheet dates. The connection between successive balance sheet positions and the statement of

---

[9] FASB ASC Topic 850: Related Party Disclosures.

cash flows can be demonstrated through simple algebraic manipulation of the basic accounting equation:

$$\text{Assets} = \text{Liabilities} + \text{Stockholders' equity} \qquad (4.1)$$

Partitioning the assets into cash and all other assets yields:

$$\text{Cash} + \text{Noncash assets} = \text{Liabilities} + \text{Stockholders' equity} \qquad (4.2)$$

Rearranging yields:

$$\text{Cash} = \text{Liabilities} - \text{Noncash assets} + \text{Stockholders' equity} \qquad (4.3)$$

From basic algebra, we know that an equality like this must also hold for the algebraic sum of the changes on both sides of the equation. Representing equation (4.3) in the form of the change (Δ) in each term results in

$$\Delta\text{Cash} = \Delta\text{Liabilities} - \Delta\text{Noncash assets} + \Delta\text{Stockholders' equity} \qquad (4.4)$$

Thus, the cash flow statement, which provides an explanation of why a firm's cash position has changed between successive balance sheet dates, simultaneously explains the changes that have taken place in the firm's noncash asset, liability, and stockholders' equity accounts over the same time period.

The change in a firm's cash position between successive balance sheet dates will *not* equal the reported earnings for that period for three reasons:

1. Reported net income usually will not equal cash flow from **operating activities** because under accrual accounting (a) noncash revenues and expenses are often recognized as part of net income, and (b) certain operating cash inflows and outflows are not recorded as revenues or expenses in the same period the cash flows occur.

2. Changes in cash are also caused by nonoperating **investing activities** such as the purchase or sale of fixed assets.

3. Additional changes in cash are caused by **financing activities** such as the issuance of stock or bonds, the repayment of a bank loan, or dividends paid to stockholders.

Cash flows are critical to assessing a company's liquidity and creditworthiness. Firms with cash flows that are insufficient to cover currently maturing obligations can be forced into bankruptcy or liquidation. Because cash flows and accrual earnings can differ dramatically, current reporting standards mandate that firms prepare a statement of cash flows as well as an income statement and balance sheet. The cash flow statement is designed to explain the causes for year-to-year changes in the balance of cash and cash equivalents.[10] We provide a brief introduction to the statement of cash flows here, focusing on the format of the statement and on the nature of some of the basic adjustments that are needed to convert accrual earnings to cash flow from operations. Later, after you have reviewed the accrual and cash flow effects of the transactions that affect various balance sheet and income statement accounts in the intervening chapters, you will find a more detailed explanation of the cash flow statement in Chapter 17.

> **Cash equivalents** include short-term, highly liquid investments that are readily convertible to cash such as demand deposits, savings accounts, certificates of deposit, money market funds, and U.S. treasury bills.

---

[10] The format for preparing the cash flow statement is specified in FASB ASC Topic 230: Statement of Cash Flows.

The cash flow statement summarizes the cash inflows and outflows of a company broken down into its three principal activities:

- *Operating activities:* Cash flows from operating activities result from the cash effects of transactions and events that affect operating income at some point: both production and delivery of goods and services.
- *Investing activities:* Cash flows from investing activities include making and collecting loans; investing in and disposing of debt or equity securities of other companies; and purchasing and disposing of assets, such as equipment, that are used by a company in the production of goods or services.
- *Financing activities:* Cash flows from financing activities include obtaining cash from new issues of stock or bonds, paying dividends or buying back a company's own shares (treasury stock), borrowing money, and repaying amounts borrowed.

Companies that are able to satisfy most of their cash needs from operating cash flows are generally considered to be in stronger financial health and better credit risks.

Exhibit 4.8 presents Wal-Mart Stores' 2012 fiscal year (ended January 31, 2013) cash flow statement segregated into operating, investing, and financing activities. Note that operating activities generated $25.591 billion in cash flows, investing activities used $12.611 billion, and financing activities used $11.972 billion of cash, resulting in a net cash increase of $1.231 billion after adjusting for a $223 million foreign currency exchange rate change on cash. Wal-Mart uses the **indirect method** to calculate cash flows from operations by adjusting accrual-basis earnings for differences between accrual revenues and expenses and cash inflows and outflows related to operating activities during the period.[11] The rationale for the depreciation and amortization adjustment and why changes in various working capital accounts capture the differences between accrual earnings and operating cash flows is explained with a simplified example in the following section.

Wal-Mart's major investing cash outflow ($12.611 billion) was for purchase of property and equipment. In the financing section, short-term borrowings provided $2.754 billion of cash. Major financing cash outflows were used for repayment of long-term debt ($1.478 billion), dividend payments ($5.361 billion), and purchase of company stock ($7.6 billion).

Cash Flows versus Accrual Earnings

The following example illustrates the major differences between cash flows and accrual earnings, why a cash flow statement is needed to fully understand the distinction between the two, and why certain adjustments are made to accrual earnings to obtain cash flows from operations.

HRB Advertising Company opened for business on April 1, 2014. The corporation's activities and transactions for the remainder of 2014 are summarized as follows:

1. Herb Wilson, Robin Hansen, and Barbara Reynolds each contributed $3,500 cash on April 1 for shares of the company's common stock.
2. HRB rented office space beginning April 1, and paid the full year's rental of $2,000 per month, or $24,000, in advance.

---

[11] An alternative for preparing cash flows from operations is called the **direct method.** Under this approach, individual sources of operating cash inflows (e.g., collections from customers) and cash outflows (e.g., payments to suppliers and employees) are reported. See Chapter 17 for further discussion of the direct method.

EXHIBIT 4.8 — Wal-Mart Stores, Inc. Consolidated Statements of Cash Flows

(Amounts in millions)	Fiscal Years Ended January 31,		
	2013	2012	2011
Cash flows from operating activities:			
Consolidated net income	$17,756	$16,387	$16,993
Loss from discontinued operations, net of income taxes	—	67	(1,034)
Income from continuing operations	17,756	16,454	15,959
Adjustments to reconcile income from continuing operations to net cash provided by operating activities:			
Depreciation and amortization	8,501	8,130	7,641
Deferred income taxes	(133)	1,050	651
Other operating activities	527	398	1,087
Changes in certain assets and liabilities, net of effects of acquisitions:			
Receivables, net	(614)	(796)	(733)
Inventories	(2,759)	(3,727)	(3,205)
Accounts payable	1,061	2,687	2,676
Accrued liabilities	271	(935)	(280)
Accrued income taxes	981	994	(153)
Net cash provided by operating activities	25,591	24,255	23,643
Cash flows from investing activities:			
Payments for property and equipment	(12,898)	(13,510)	(12,699)
Proceeds from the disposal of property and equipment	532	580	489
Investments and business acquisitions, net of cash acquired	(316)	(3,548)	(202)
Other investing activities	71	(131)	219
Net cash used in investing activities	(12,611)	(16,609)	(12,193)
Cash flows from financing activities:			
Net change in short-term borrowings	2,754	3,019	503
Proceeds from issuance of long-term debt	211	5,050	11,396
Payments of long-term debt	(1,478)	(4,584)	(4,080)
Dividends paid	(5,361)	(5,048)	(4,437)
Purchase of Company stock	(7,600)	(6,298)	(14,776)
Other financing activities	(498)	(597)	(634)
Net cash used in financing activities	(11,972)	(8,458)	(12,028)
Effect of exchange rates on cash and cash equivalents	223	(33)	66
Net increase (decrease) in cash and cash equivalents	1,231	(845)	(512)
Cash and cash equivalents at beginning of year	6,550	7,395	7,907
Cash and cash equivalents at end of year	$ 7,781	$ 6,550	$ 7,395
Supplemental disclosure of cash flow information:			
Income taxes paid	$ 7,304	$ 5,899	$ 6,984
Interest paid	2,262	2,346	2,163

Source: Wal-Mart Stores 2012 Annual Report.

3. The company borrowed $10,000 from a bank on April 1. The principal plus accrued interest is payable January 1, 2015, with interest at the rate of 12% per year.

4. HRB purchased office equipment with a five-year life for $15,000 cash on April 1. Salvage value is zero and the equipment is being depreciated using the straight-line method.

5. HRB sold and billed customers for $65,000 of advertising services rendered between April 1 and December 31. Of this amount, $20,000 was still uncollected by year-end.

6. By year-end, the company incurred and paid the following operating costs: (a) utilities, $650; (b) salaries, $36,250; and (c) supplies, $800.

7. The company had accrued (unpaid) expenses at year-end as follows: (a) utilities, $75; (b) salaries, $2,400; and (c) interest, $900.

8. Supplies purchased on account and unpaid at year-end amounted to $50. When supplies are purchased, they are charged to an asset account.

9. Supplies inventory on hand at year-end amounted to $100.

10. Annual depreciation on office equipment is $15,000/5 = $3,000. Because the equipment was acquired on April 1, the depreciation expense for 2014 is $3,000 × 9/12 = $2,250.

Herb, Robin, and Barbara were delighted to discover that the company earned a profit (before taxes) of $3,725 in 2014. However, they were shocked to learn that the company's checking account was overdrawn by $11,200 at year-end. This overdraft was particularly disconcerting because the bank loan had come due.

Is HRB Advertising Company profitable, or is it about to go bankrupt? What are its prospects for the future? Exhibit 4.9 helps us examine these issues.

While HRB Advertising generated *positive* accrual accounting earnings of $3,725 during 2014, its operating cash flow was a *negative* $16,700. Columns (b) and (c) show the causes for the divergence between the components of accrual income (Column [a]) and operating cash flows (Column [d]). Because of a net infusion of cash from financing activities (Column [d]), the net change in cash (a negative $11,200) was much smaller than the negative cash flow of $16,700 from operating activities.

EXHIBIT 4.9	HRB Advertising Company Analysis of Accrual Income versus Change in Cash		

		For Year Ended December 31, 2014		
Item	(a) Accrual Income	(b) Noncash Accruals: Revenue Earned (or Expenses Incurred)	(c) Prepayments and Supplies Buildup	(d) a + b + c Cash Received (or Paid) During 2014
Operating activities				
Advertising revenues	$65,000	−$20,000[5]		$45,000
Salaries	−38,650	+2,400[7b]		−36,250
Rent	−18,000		−$6,000[2]	−24,000
Utilities	−725	+75[7a]		−650
Supplies	−750	+50[8]	−100[9]	−800
Interest	−900	+900[7c]		−0−
Depreciation	−2,250	+2,250[10]		−0−
Operating cash flow				−$16,700
Net income	$ 3,725			
Investing activities				
Equipment purchase				−$15,000[4]
Financing activities				
Stock issuance				$10,500[1]
Bank borrowing				10,000[3]
				$20,500
Change in cash				−$11,200

Note: Numbers in parentheses refer to numbered transactions on pages 204–206.

We now discuss the rationale behind the adjustments in Columns (b) and (c). We examine each adjustment in terms of how it affects bottom-line *accrual-basis net income,* not how the adjustment affects revenues or expenses that compose net income. Because expenses are treated as negative amounts in computing net income, an adjustment that reduces (increases) an expense is treated as a plus (negative) amount in Columns (b) and (c). This way of designating positive and negative amounts will facilitate our discussion of the adjustments to accrual-basis income needed to arrive at operating cash flows.

- Advertising revenues recognized under accrual accounting totaled $65,000. However, $20,000 of this remains as uncollected accounts receivable at year-end. Thus, the ending balance in the Accounts receivable account must be *subtracted* from the accrual-basis revenues to derive the cash received during the year for advertising services.

- The salaries expense of $38,650 for the year includes the $36,250 of salaries incurred and paid in cash plus the $2,400 of salary expense accrued at year-end. Therefore, the accrued (unpaid) salaries, which is the ending balance in the Accrued salaries payable (liability) account, must be *added back* to total salaries expense to derive the salaries paid in cash.

- HRB recognized rent expense of $2,000 × 9 months = $18,000 in 2014. The difference between the amount paid out in cash and the amount recognized as expense under accrual accounting ($24,000 − $18,000, or $6,000) would be the ending balance in the Prepaid rent (asset) account. This amount is shown as a negative adjustment (*subtraction*) in Column (c) because the cash outflow for rent was higher than the amount of rent expense recognized.

- The utilities expense of $725 for the year includes the $650 of utilities paid in cash plus $75 of utilities expense accrued at year-end. The utilities expense incurred but not yet paid, which is the ending balance in the Accrued utilities payable (liability) account, must be *added back* to the total utilities expense to obtain the cash payments for utilities in 2014.

- Total supplies purchased during the year included $800 paid in cash and $50 purchased on account (Accounts payable). Of the amount purchased, $100 of supplies remains on hand in the Supplies inventory account at year-end. So, supplies expense under accrual accounting is $800 + $50 − $100 = $750. To adjust the accrual-basis expense to derive the cash outflow for supplies requires that we *add back* the ending balance in Accounts payable (which was a noncash increase to the supplies expense) and *subtract* the $100 ending balance in Supplies inventory (which was a noncash decrease to the supplies expense).

- Accrued interest expense for the year is $10,000 × 12% × 9/12 = $900. Because none of this has been paid in cash, the ending balance in the Accrued interest payable (liability) account must be *added back* to the Interest expense account to obtain the cash paid out for interest in 2014.

- Depreciation is a noncash expense under accrual accounting. So this amount, which is reflected in the increase in the Accumulated depreciation (contra-asset) account, must be *added back* to depreciation expense.

Except for depreciation, each of the adjustments we just outlined uses the ending balance (which is also the *change* in the account balance in the first year of a company's life) of a current asset account (for example, Accounts receivable, Supplies inventory, or Prepaid rent) or a current liability account (for example, Accounts payable, Salaries payable, Utilities payable, or Interest payable) to adjust accrual-basis revenues or expenses to derive cash flows from operations. The adjustments to accrual-basis income (revenues − expenses) for

> Remember, for a start-up company, beginning account balances are zero.

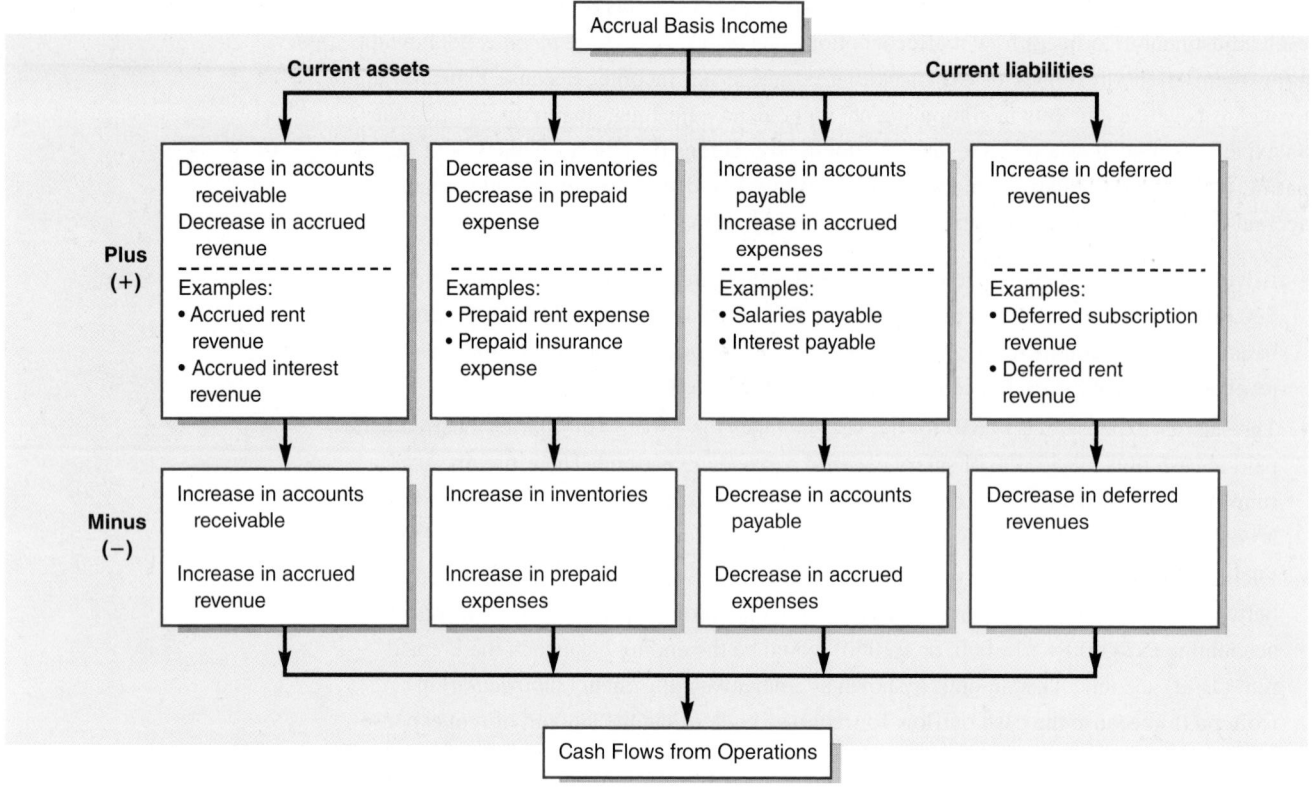

Figure 4.1   ADJUSTMENTS TO ACCRUAL EARNINGS FOR CHANGES IN WORKING CAPITAL ACCOUNTS TO OBTAIN CASH FLOWS FROM OPERATIONS

changes in current asset and current liability accounts that represent accrued revenues, deferred (unearned) revenues, accrued expenses, or deferred (prepaid) expenses are summarized in Figure 4.1.

Exhibit 4.10 on the following page illustrates how the adjustments to accrual earnings due to *changes* in various current asset and liability accounts would be reflected in a GAAP statement of cash flows. The item numbers appearing next to each element in the cash flow statement correspond to the numbers in Columns (b), (c), and (d) of Exhibit 4.9. The presentation format illustrated is the indirect method (described previously) because it does not show the individual operating cash inflows and outflows *directly*. (The **direct method,** which shows the revenues collected in cash and the expenses paid in cash, is shown in Column [d] of Exhibit 4.9.) In Exhibit 4.10, net cash flows from operations is arrived at indirectly by adjusting earnings for the differences between accrual-basis revenues and expenses and cash inflows and outflows during the period.

> Only adjustments for changes in working capital accounts are summarized in Figure 4.1. Other adjustments (such as depreciation and gains/losses on asset sales) will be discussed in Chapter 17.

The cash flow statement in Exhibit 4.10 will help Herb, Robin, and Barbara understand the causes for their overdrawn checking account. While the business was profitable from an accrual accounting standpoint, total cash flows were negative. This should not be surprising since start-up companies often spend a large portion of their available cash on equipment purchases, inventory buildup, and the production of goods and services that are frequently sold on account—and, therefore, that generate no cash immediately. Although the company is profitable, it may be forced into bankruptcy unless quick action is taken to resolve the cash flow deficit. To remain in business, the owners must infuse more equity capital, arrange for an extension of their bank loan, and/or speed up cash collections from customers.

EXHIBIT 4.10	HRB Advertising Company Statement of Cash Flows	

	For Year Ended December 31, 2014	
Operating cash flows		
Net income		$ 3,725
Plus		
Depreciation[10]	$ 2,250	
Increase in salaries payable[7b]	2,400	
Increase in accounts payable[8]	50	
Increase in utilities payable[7a]	75	
Increase in interest payable[7c]	900	5,675
Minus		
Increase in receivables[5]	(20,000)	
Increase in prepaid rent[2]	(6,000)	
Increase in supplies inventory[9]	(100)	(26,100)
Cash flows from operations		$(16,700)
Investing cash flows		
Equipment purchase[4]		$(15,000)
Financing cash flows		
Stock issuance[1]		$ 10,500
Bank borrowing[3]		10,000
		$ 20,500
Change in cash		$(11,200)

Note: Numbers in parentheses refer to numbered transactions on pages 204–206.

Deriving Cash Flow Information

The three owners were able to convince their banker to refinance the loan but only after they each agreed to contribute another $2,000 to the company, a total of $6,000. The loan was replaced by a three-year note, but the interest rate was increased to 13.50% to reflect the additional risk associated with the refinanced borrowing. Herb, Robin, and Barbara felt confident that with careful attention to both earnings and cash flow, they could successfully grow the business and repay the note before its maturity.

During 2015, the second year of business, revenues increased and operating cash flows were positive, but the company recorded a loss for the year. Exhibit 4.11 contains HRB Advertising's comparative balance sheets for 2014 and 2015, and Exhibit 4.12 presents the company's income and cash flow statements for the two years.

We can see from the balance sheet that the $10,000 bank loan was refinanced as a Note payable (Exhibit 4.11) and that additional common stock of $6,000 was issued during 2015. Also notice that the company's Cash account ended the year with a positive balance of $500.

Highlights from the income statement [Exhibit 4.12(a)] include substantial growth in advertising revenues from $65,000 to $92,000, a 41.5% increase. At the same time, the company was able to speed up its collection of credit sales and reduce its Accounts receivable balance, as shown in Exhibit 4.11. Unfortunately, salary expense increased nearly 63% from $38,650 to $62,875, which seems to be the major factor contributing to the company's $1,725 loss for the year. From the cash flow statement [see Exhibit 4.12(b)], we see that 2015 cash flows from operations totaled a positive $7,200 even though the business sustained a loss for the year. The company's overall cash balance increased by $11,700 during the year with $6,000

EXHIBIT 4.11	HRB Advertising Company Comparative Balance Sheets		
		December 31,	
		2014	**2015**
Assets			
Cash		$(11,200)	$ 500
Accounts receivable		20,000	15,775
Supplies inventory		100	225
Prepaid rent		6,000	6,000
Office equipment		15,000	16,500
Less: Accumulated depreciation		(2,250)	(5,500)
Total assets		$ 27,650	$33,500
Liabilities and Equities			
Utilities payable		$ 75	$ 50
Interest payable		900	675
Accounts payable (supplies)		50	75
Salaries payable		2,400	4,200
Bank loan		10,000	—
Note payable		—	10,000
Total liabilities		13,425	15,000
Common stock		10,500	16,500
Retained earnings		3,725	2,000
Total liabilities and stockholders' equity		$ 27,650	$33,500

of that amount representing cash contributed by the owners in exchange for additional common stock.

U.S. companies must include a cash flow statement similar to Exhibit 4.12(b) in their annual report to shareholders: Quarterly cash flow statements are not required, although most companies voluntarily make them available to shareholders. Companies that don't provide quarterly cash flow statements challenge the analyst. How can cash flow information be derived from a company's balance sheet and income statement when the cash flow statement itself is not available?

The answer is not very complicated, as we will see. Deriving information about a company's cash receipts and disbursements from balance sheet and income statement information involves little more than a careful and systematic analysis of the changes in individual balance sheet accounts and their corresponding income statement effects. From this analysis, you can deduce individual cash flows and construct a summary schedule of cash receipts (inflows) and disbursements (outflows) that closely resembles the cash flow statement presented in Exhibit 4.12(b).

The starting point for this analysis is the Cash account itself. Notice from the balance sheet (Exhibit 4.11) that the company's cash position increased by $11,700 during 2015 from the $11,200 deficit at the beginning of the year to a $500 positive balance at year-end. Consequently, we know that total cash receipts for the year must have been $11,700 higher than total cash payments. Now let's uncover some individual cash flow items.

Exhibit 4.13 illustrates the general T-account analysis that can be used to derive cash flow information from selected balance sheet accounts of HRB Advertising for 2015. From the comparative balance sheet in Exhibit 4.11, the beginning and ending balances can be obtained for each *balance sheet* account that is affected when a revenue or expense item is recorded. The accrual-basis revenue or expense that results in a debit or credit to the related balance sheet account can then be entered (see circled items in Exhibit 4.13). The cash received or

EXHIBIT 4.12	HRB Advertising Company Comparative Income and Cash Flow Statements		

| | | For Years Ended December 31, | |
		2014	**2015**
Panel (a)			
Income Statement			
Revenue from advertising services		$ 65,000	$ 92,000
Less			
Salaries expense		(38,650)	(62,875)
Supplies expense		(750)	(1,200)
Rent expense		(18,000)	(24,000)
Utilities expense		(725)	(1,050)
Interest expense		(900)	(1,350)
Depreciation		(2,250)	(3,250)
Net income		$ 3,725	$ (1,725)
Panel (b)			
Cash Flow Statement			
Net income		$ 3,725	$ (1,725)
Depreciation		2,250	3,250
		5,975	1,525
Changes in current assets and liabilities:			
Accounts receivable decrease (increase)		(20,000)	4,225
Supplies inventory (increase)		(100)	(125)
Prepaid rent decrease (increase)		(6,000)	—
Utilities payable increase (decrease)		75	(25)
Accounts payable (supplies) increase		50	25
Interest payable increase (decrease)		900	(225)
Salaries payable increase		2,400	1,800
Cash flow from operating activities		$(16,700)	$ 7,200
Equipment purchases		$(15,000)	$ (1,500)
Cash flow from investing activities		$(15,000)	$ (1,500)
Bank loan proceeds (repayment)		$ 10,000	$(10,000)
Note payable issued		—	10,000
Common stock issued		10,500	6,000
Cash flow from financing activities		$ 20,500	$ 6,000
Change in cash balance		$(11,200)	$ 11,700

cash paid, which results in an offsetting entry to each of these accounts, is the "plug" figure (in blue) that is needed to arrive at the ending balance that is given. We now illustrate this analysis for selected accounts in Exhibit 4.13.

The company's only source of operating cash inflows is customer receipts, so we begin with an analysis of the Accounts receivable account. As shown in Exhibit 4.13, the balance in Accounts receivable declined by $4,225 during 2015 from a beginning balance of $20,000 to a year-end balance of $15,775. Because billings for advertising services performed during 2015 totaled $92,000 [that is, Advertising revenues in the income statement of Exhibit 4.12(a)], HRB must have collected $96,225 from its customers. To see this, note that collections must have been $4,225 higher than new billings because the Accounts receivable balance decreased by this amount during the year. Another way to think about this calculation is to assume that all customers pay on a timely basis. In this case, HRB would have collected

EXHIBIT 4.13   HRB Advertising Company

Analysis of Income Statement and Balance Sheet Accounts for Year Ended December 31, 2015

INCOME STATEMENT	BALANCE SHEET

Advertising revenues | ### Accounts receivable

		Beginning balance	$20,000		
	$92,000	Advertising revenues (accrual basis)	$92,000	$96,225	Collections (cash basis)
		Ending balance	$15,775		

Salaries expense | ### Salaries payable

				$ 2,400	Beginning balance
$62,875		Salaries paid (cash basis)	$61,075	$62,875	Salaries expense
		(accrual basis)		$ 4,200	Ending balance

Rent expense | ### Prepaid rent

Rent expense from 1/1/15 to 3/31/15

| $ 6,000 | | Beginning balance | $ 6,000 | | Expensed from beginning balance |
| | | Rent paid in advance on 4/1/15 (cash basis) | $24,000 | $ 6,000 | Rent expense from 1/1/15 to 3/31/15 |

Rent expense from 4/1/15 to 12/31/15

| $18,000 | | (accrual basis) | | $18,000 | Expensed from 4/1/15 payment: For the period from 4/1/15 to 12/31/15 |
| Total expense $24,000 | | Ending balance | $ 6,000 | | |

Utilities expense | ### Accounts payable (utilities)

				$ 75	Beginning balance
$ 1,050		Payments (cash basis)	$ 1,075	$ 1,050	Utilities expense
		(accrual basis)		$ 50	Ending balance

Accounts payable (supplies)

Payments (cash basis)	$ 1,300	$ 50	Beginning balance
		$ 1,325	Purchases on accounts
		$ 75	Ending balance

Supplies expense | ### Supplies inventory

		Beginning balance	$ 100		
$ 1,200		Purchases on account $ 1,325 (accrual basis)		$ 1,200	Supplies used
		Ending balance	$ 225		

Interest expense | ### Accrued interest payable

				$ 900	Beginning balance
$ 1,350		Payments (cash basis)	$ 1,575	$ 1,350	Accrued expense
		(accrual basis)		$ 675	Ending balance

Depreciation expense | ### Accumulated depreciation

				$ 2,250	Beginning balance
$ 3,250				$ 3,250	Depreciation expense
		(accrual basis)		$ 5,500	Ending balance

$20,000 cash from customers billed in 2014 and another $76,225 from customers billed in 2015 (or $92,000 billings minus the $15,775 that was uncollected at year-end).

Salary payments represent the company's largest operating cash outflow. Exhibit 4.13 shows that Salaries payable increased by $1,800 during the year, from a beginning balance of $2,400 to $4,200 at year-end. Consequently, salary payments must have been $61,075 for the year, or $1,800 less than the total salaries expense of $62,875 that shows up in the income statement in Exhibit 4.12(a).

Some cash inflows and outflows involve more than one balance sheet account. Exhibit 4.13 shows this for supplies. As shown there, Accounts payable (supplies) increased $25 during the year, from a beginning balance of $50 to $75 at year-end. This means that payments for supplies must have been $25 less than purchases. But where can we find information about purchases? Certainly not from the income statement [Exhibit 4.12(a)] because it reports the cost of supplies *used* during the year regardless of when they were purchased. Because purchases increase the total supplies on hand, we turn our attention to the Supplies inventory account. As we see in Exhibit 4.13, Supplies inventory increased by $125 during the year, from $100 at the start to $225 at year-end. Purchases must therefore have been $125 more than the amount of supplies used during the year [that is, the supplies expense from Exhibit 4.12(a)]. In other words, purchases must have totaled $1,325 (or the $1,200 supplies expense plus the $125 Supplies inventory increase), and consequently, supplier payments must have totaled $1,300 (or $1,325 purchases minus the $25 Accounts payable increase).

The same type of analysis just outlined is illustrated for the Prepaid rent, Accounts payable (utilities), and Accrued interest payable accounts in Exhibit 4.13. The process continues until all balance sheet accounts are fully reconciled and the company's cash receipts and disbursements are identified. In addition, analysis of changes in the Notes payable, Common stock, and Equipment accounts (not shown) can identify cash inflows and outflows from investing and financing activities.

> These investing and financing activities will be discussed in Chapters 10 and 11.

The derived cash inflows and outflows for HRB Advertising are listed in Exhibit 4.14, by major sources: operating, investing, and financing activities. This schedule explains why the

---

EXHIBIT 4.14   **HRB Advertising Company**
Schedule of Cash Receipts and Disbursements

	For the Years Ended December 31,		
	2014	2015	
Operating activities			
Advertising services	$ 45,000	$ 96,225	← *from Accounts receivable*
Salaries	(36,250)	(61,075)	← *from Salaries payable*
Rent	(24,000)	(24,000)	← *from Prepaid rent*
Utilities	(650)	(1,075)	← *from Utilities payable*
Supplies	(800)	(1,300)	← *from Supplies payable*
Interest	—	(1,575)	← *from Interest payable*
Operating cash flow	$(16,700)	$ 7,200	
Investing activities			
Equipment purchase	$(15,000)	$ (1,500)	← *from Office equipment*
Financing activities			
Bank borrowing	$ 10,000	$(10,000)	← *from Notes payable*
Note issuance	—	10,000	← *from Notes payable*
Stock issuance	10,500	6,000	← *from Common stock*
	20,500	6,000	
Change in cash	$(11,200)	$ 11,700	← *from Cash*

company's cash balance increased by $11,700 during the year. Operating activities contributed $7,200 of cash, $1,500 was spent on new equipment, and financing activities added another $6,000. These are precisely the cash inflows and outflows listed in the company's cash flow statement in Exhibit 4.12(b).

The analysis in Exhibit 4.14 has focused on the adjustments to accrual earnings that are required as a result of changes in various working capital (current assets minus current liabilities) accounts to derive operating cash flows under the indirect method. Obviously, many other adjustments are required to fully reconcile accrual earnings and cash flows from operations. These will be discussed in Chapter 17 after you have had a chance to review in some detail the accrual accounting entries related to noncurrent asset and liability accounts.

RECAP

Accrual earnings and cash flows capture different aspects of a firm's performance and often differ by a wide margin from year to year. Cash flows are critical to assessing a company's liquidity and creditworthiness. The cash flow statement provides a detailed summary of the cash inflows and outflows that are derived from a company's three primary activities: operations, investing, and financing. This section has outlined the basic techniques for deriving operating cash flows from an analysis of comparative balance sheets and income statement information. To do this, you must analyze changes in current asset and current liability accounts (as well as other noncash revenues and expenses such as depreciation) that capture differences between the cash flow effects and accrual earnings effects of revenue and expense transactions.

GLOBAL VANTAGE POINT

IFRS (IAS 7) encourages, but does not require, entities to report cash flows from operating activities using the direct method. This is because the direct method is believed to provide information that may be useful in estimating future cash flows that is not available under the indirect method. Both FASB and IASB recently tabled a proposal to mandate the use of the direct method for reporting operating cash flows. Very few companies opt to report under the direct method perhaps because companies' computer information systems are not set up to efficiently process the requisite data.[12]

One example of a company that does prepare the cash flow statement using the direct method is EMC Corporation, which files under U.S. GAAP. EMC's Consolidated Cash Flow Statement for 2012 is presented in Exhibit 4.15. We can notice here that the direct method provides more detail about the sources of cash inflows and cash outflows. EMC Corporation's 2012 Consolidated Statement of Cash Flows provides a nice way to compare the two approaches because it shows the direct method approach in the top half of the statement and an indirect method reconciliation of accrual earnings and net cash flows from operating activities in the bottom half. Notice that EMC reported almost $22.585 billion of cash received from customers in 2012, which contributed to their net cash provided by operating activities of just over $6.26 billion. If one only looks at the indirect method reconciliation, it is likely not plausible to determine how much cash was received from customers. It seems clear that analysts who are evaluating EMC Corporation's financial health would

---

[12] Marie Leone, "Nothing Direct about the Direct Cash-flow Method, *CFO.com,* November 19, 2009, http://www.cfo.com/blogs/index.cfm/l_detail/14456437.

EXHIBIT 4.15   EMC Corporation Cash Flow Statement

EMC CORPORATION
Consolidated Statements of Cash Flows
(in thousands)

	For the Year Ended December 31,		
	2012	**2011**	**2010**
Cash flows from operating activities:			
Cash received from customers	$ 22,584,805	$ 21,144,690	$ 17,585,447
Cash paid to suppliers and employees	(16,018,457)	(15,218,678)	(12,830,684)
Dividends and interest received	103,174	135,971	102,912
Interest paid	(32,751)	(70,071)	(76,711)
Income taxes paid	(374,352)	(323,097)	(232,121)
Net cash provided by operating activities	6,262,419	5,668,815	4,548,843
Cash flows from investing activities:			
Additions to property, plant, and equipment	(819,159)	(801,375)	(745,412)
Capitalized software development costs	(419,079)	(442,341)	(362,956)
Purchases of short- and long-term available-for-sale securities	(6,346,580)	(7,180,169)	(6,329,894)
Sales of short- and long-term available-for-sale securities	4,982,790	5,121,454	3,625,260
Maturities of short- and long-term available-for-sale securities	1,048,979	1,130,321	437,297
Business acquisitions, net of cash acquired	(2,135,758)	(536,624)	(3,194,611)
Purchases of strategic and other related investments	(117,103)	(329,483)	(24,946)
Sales of strategic and other related investments	70,623	29,007	148,813
Joint venture funding	(227,881)	(383,211)	(29,600)
Proceeds from divestiture of business	58,100	—	—
Purchase of leasehold interest	—	(151,083)	—
Net cash used in investing activities	(3,905,068)	(3,543,504)	(6,476,049)
Cash flows from financing activities:			
Issuance of EMC's common stock from the exercise of stock options	560,275	673,389	780,732
Issuance of VMware's common stock from the exercise of stock options	253,159	337,618	431,306
EMC repurchase of EMC's common stock	(684,559)	(1,999,968)	(999,924)
EMC purchase of VMware's common stock	(290,294)	(399,984)	(399,224)
VMware repurchase of VMware's common stock	(467,534)	(526,203)	(338,527)
Excess tax benefits from stock-based compensation	260,747	361,632	281,872
Payment of short-term and long-term obligations	(15,629)	(27,089)	(4,128)
Proceeds from short-term and long-term obligations	4,604	3,096	4,066
Payment of convertible debt	(1,699,816)	—	—
Interest rate contract settlement	(69,905)	(140,993)	—
Net cash used in financing activities	(2,148,952)	(1,718,502)	(243,827)
Effect of exchange rate changes on cash and cash equivalents	14,625	5,089	(12,328)
Net increase (decrease) in cash and cash equivalents	223,024	411,898	(2,183,361)
Cash and cash equivalents at beginning of period	4,531,036	4,119,138	6,302,499
Cash and cash equivalents at end of period	$ 4,754,060	$ 4,531,036	$ 4,119,138
Reconciliation of net income to net cash provided by operating activities:			
Net income	$ 2,886,017	$ 2,608,885	$ 1,969,686
Adjustments to reconcile net income to net cash provided by operating activities:			
Depreciation and amortization	1,527,748	1,421,598	1,167,550
Noncash interest expense on convertible debt	46,178	102,907	105,649
Noncash restructuring and other special charges	12,974	(1,484)	6,861
Stock-based compensation expense	895,384	822,576	667,728
Provision for doubtful accounts	39,313	20,255	18,965
Deferred income taxes, net	(117,573)	(19,423)	(49,787)
Excess tax benefits from stock-based compensation	(260,747)	(361,632)	(281,872)
Gain on XtremIO common stock	(31,599)	—	—
Other, net	20,337	4,573	(21,250)

(*continued*)

EXHIBIT 4.15	EMC Corporation Cash Flow Statement *(continued)*		
	For the Year Ended December 31,		
	2012	**2011**	**2010**
Changes in assets and liabilities, net of acquisitions:			
Accounts and notes receivable	(535,371)	(391,672)	(405,758)
Inventories	(458,663)	(393,156)	(114,111)
Other assets	174,386	(61,830)	(54,469)
Accounts payable	89,299	34,871	154,496
Accrued expenses	(64,238)	5,147	4,162
Income taxes payable	660,819	336,711	455,964
Deferred revenue	1,366,961	1,508,520	957,114
Other liabilities	11,194	31,969	(32,085)
Net cash provided by operating activities	$ 6,262,419	$ 5,668,815	$ 4,548,843
Noncash investing and financing activity:			

find this specific cash flow information much more informative than simply learning that the balance of accounts and notes receivable went down over the year by approximately $0.535 billion.

There are also some subtle but important differences between IFRS and U.S. GAAP regarding where certain items are reported in the statement of cash flows. U.S. GAAP, for example, requires entities to report cash interest from investments as part of operating cash flows. *IAS 7* allows the option for entities to report these in-flows as cash flows from investing activities. Investment analysts often compare cash flows from operations across two or more companies. Therefore, this choice under IFRS may affect the ability to make valid comparisons of operating cash flows of firms with large amounts of debt investments, particularly if one company reports under U.S. GAAP and another under IFRS. Further differences between IFRS and U.S. GAAP regarding where certain items are reported within a cash flow statement are discussed in Chapter 17.

SUMMARY

- The balance sheet and statement of cash flows are two of the primary financial statements required under GAAP.
- The balance sheet shows the assets owned by a company at a given point in time and how those assets are financed (debt versus equity). A variety of measurement bases are used to report the various asset, liability, and stockholders' equity accounts.
- When making intercompany comparisons, financial statement users must be careful to recognize how the different measurement bases affect key financial ratios and how account titles and statement formats vary across countries.
- Financial statement notes are an integral part of companies' financial reports and provide a wealth of information that allows statement users to better understand and interpret the numbers presented in the body of the financial statements.
- The statement of cash flows shows the change in cash for a given period broken down into operating, investing, and financing activities.

- Successive balance sheets and the statement of cash flows articulate with one another meaning changes in noncash balance sheet accounts can be used to explain changes in cash for a period.

- Analysis of changes in selected balance sheet accounts also can be used to explain why operating cash flows differ from accrual income.

- Conversely, the statement of cash flows provides information that enables users to understand changes in balance sheet accounts that have occurred over the reporting period.

- Understanding the interrelationships between successive balance sheets and the statement of cash flows and being able to exploit these interrelationships to derive unknown account balances are important skills for analysts and lending officers.

- Understanding the basic differences between the direct and indirect approach to presenting cash flows from operations, and differences between where certain items are reported on a cash flow statement under IFRS versus U. S. GAAP.

EXERCISES

The following classification scheme typically is used in the preparation of a balance sheet:

E4-1

Analyzing balance sheet classification **(LO 1)**

a. Current assets
b. Investments and funds
c. Property, plant, and equipment
d. Intangible assets
e. Other assets

f. Current liabilities
g. Long-term liabilities
h. Contributed capital
i. Retained earnings

Using the letters above and the format below, indicate the balance sheet category in which an entity typically would place each of the following items. Indicate a contra account by placing your answer in parentheses.

1. _____ Long-term receivables
2. _____ Accumulated amortization
3. _____ Current maturities of long-term debt
4. _____ Notes payable (short term)
5. _____ Accrued payroll taxes
6. _____ Leasehold improvements
7. _____ Retained earnings appropriated for plant expansion
8. _____ Machinery
9. _____ Donated capital
10. _____ Short-term investments
11. _____ Deferred tax liability (long term)
12. _____ Allowance for uncollectible accounts
13. _____ Premium on bonds payable
14. _____ Supplies inventory
15. _____ Additional paid-in capital
16. _____ Work-in-process inventory
17. _____ Notes receivable (short-term)
18. _____ Copyrights
19. _____ Unearned revenue (long-term)
20. _____ Inventory

E4-2

Preparing a balance
sheet   (LO 1)

The following balance sheet, which has some weaknesses in terminology and classification, has been prepared by an inexperienced accountant and submitted to you for review:

Mikeska Company

Balance Sheet as of December 31, 2014

($ in thousands)

Assets		
Fixed assets—tangible		
Land	$500	
Buildings and equipment	200	
Less: Reserve for depreciation	(50)	$ 650
Factory supplies		20
Current assets		
Inventory	163	
Accounts receivable	102	
Cash	68	333
Fixed assets—intangibles		
Patents	51	
Goodwill	49	100
Deferred charges		
Discount on bonds payable	12	
Returnable containers	32	44
Total assets		$1,147
Liabilities		
Current liabilities		
Accounts payable	140	
Allowance for doubtful accounts	7	
Wages payable	195	$ 342
Long-term liabilities		
Bonds payable	400	
Reserve for contingencies	50	450
Equity		
Capital stock, $10 par, 5,000 shares issued and outstanding	50	
Capital surplus	75	
Earned surplus	270	
Dividends paid	(40)	355
Total liabilities		$1,147

Required:

Prepare a classified balance sheet in proper form. Make any necessary corrections.

E4-3

Making financial disclosures
(LO 4)

IMA
ADAPTED

The preliminary draft of the balance sheet at the end of the current fiscal year for Eagle Industries follows. The statement will be incorporated into the annual report to stockholders and will present the dollar amounts at the end of both the current and prior years on a comparative basis. The accounts in the statement are properly classified, and the dollar amounts have been determined in accordance with generally accepted accounting principles. The company does not intend to provide any more detailed information in the body of the statement.

Eagle Industries

Balance Sheet as of December 31, 2014

($ in millions)

Assets		
Current assets		
Cash	$	13.5
Short-term investments		6.8
Accounts receivable (net)		113.0
Inventories		228.0
Prepayments and other		4.8
Total current assets		366.0
Investments in equity securities (available for sale)		55.2
Property, plant, and equipment (net)		787.1
Total assets		$1,208.3
Liabilities and Stockholders' Equity		
Current liabilities		
Current maturities on long-term debt	$	36.5
Notes payable		79.5
Accounts payable		139.8
Accrued taxes		42.3
Accrued interest		11.0
Other		4.4
Total current liabilities		313.4
Long-term liabilities		477.2
Total liabilities		790.5
Stockholders' equity		
Preferred stock		30.0
Common stock		77.0
Additional paid-in capital on common stock		65.4
Retained earnings—appropriated		40.8
Retained earnings—unappropriated		204.6
Total stockholders' equity		417.8
Total liabilities and stockholders' equity		$1,208.3

Required:

Identify the accounts that most likely would require further disclosure in the notes to the financial statements and describe what information would have to be disclosed in those notes by Eagle Industries before the statement can be included as part of the annual report for presentation to its stockholders.

Following is a list of items taken from the December 31, 2014, balance sheet of Reagan Company (amounts omitted):

Accounts payable	Goodwill
Accrued expenses	Income taxes payable
Accumulated depreciation—buildings	Land
Accumulated depreciation—machinery	Machinery and equipment
and equipment	Notes payable to banks (short term)
Bonds payable	Preferred stock
Buildings	Prepaid expenses
Cash	Raw materials
Common stock	Retained earnings
Contributed capital in excess of par	Short-term investments
Current portion of long-term debt	Trade accounts receivable
Deferred tax liability (noncurrent)	Trademarks
Finished products inventory	Work-in-process inventory

E 4 - 4

Balance sheet classification
(LO 1)

Required:

Using the above information, prepare a classified balance sheet in good form.

E 4-5

Determining collections on account   **(LO 5)**

AICPA
ADAPTED

During 2014, Kew Company, a service organization, had $200,000 in cash sales and $3,000,000 in credit sales. The accounts receivable balances were $400,000 and $485,000 at December 31, 2013 and 2014, respectively.

Required:
What was Kew Company's cash receipts from sales in 2014?

E 4-6

Determining cash from operations   **(LO 5)**

AICPA
ADAPTED

The following information is available from Sand Corporation's accounting records for the year ended December 31, 2014:

Cash received from customers	$870,000
Rent received	10,000
Cash paid to suppliers and employees	510,000
Taxes paid	110,000
Cash dividends paid	30,000

Required:
Compute cash flow provided by operations for 2014.

E 4-7

Determining cash payments to suppliers   **(LO 5)**

Dunnsmore Company reported cost of goods sold of $318,450 on its 2014 income statement. Other information for Dunnsmore is as follows:

	1/1/2014	12/31/2014
Inventories	$37,200	$43,400
Accounts payable	23,100	29,900

Required:
Prepare a schedule showing the amount of cash Dunnsmore paid to suppliers in 2014.

E 4-8

Determining cash disbursements   **(LO 5)**

AICPA
ADAPTED

Serven Corporation has estimated its accrual-basis revenue and expenses for June 2014 and would like your help in estimating cash disbursements. Selected data from these estimated amounts are as follows:

Sales	$700,000
Gross profit (based on sales)	30%
Increase in trade accounts receivable for the month	$ 20,000
Change in accounts payable during month	0
Increase in inventory during month	$ 10,000
Variable selling, general, and administrative expenses include a charge for uncollectible accounts of 1% of sales.	
Total selling, general, and administrative expenses are $71,000 per month plus 15% of sales.	
Depreciation expense of $40,000 per month is included in fixed selling, general, and administrative expense.	

Required:
On the basis of the preceding data, what are the estimated cash disbursements from operations for June?

E 4-9

Determining cash collections on account   **(LO 5)**

AICPA
ADAPTED

The following information was taken from the 2014 financial statement of Planet Corporation:

Accounts receivable, January 1, 2014	$ 21,600
Accounts receivable, December 31, 2014	30,400
Sales on accounts and cash sales	438,000
Uncollectible accounts (bad debts)	1,000

No accounts receivable were written off or recovered during the year.

Required:
Determine the cash collected from customers by Planet Corporation in 2014.

The following information was taken from the 2014 financial statements of Eiger Corporation, a maker of equipment for mountain and rock climbers:

Determining cash from operations and reconciling with accrual net income **(LO 5, 7, 8)**

Net income	$100,000
Depreciation	30,000
Increase (decrease) in	
Accounts receivable	110,000
Inventories	(50,000)
Prepaid expenses	15,000
Accounts payable	(150,000)
Salaries payable	15,000
Other current liabilities	(70,000)

Required:

1. Calculate Eiger's cash flow from operating activities for 2014.

2. Explain the reasons for the difference between the firm's net income and its cash flow from operating activities in 2014.

The following information was taken from the 2014 financial statements of Zurich Corporation, a maker of fine Swiss watches:

Determining cash from operations and reconciling with accrual net income **(LO 5, 8)**

Net income	$(200,000)
Depreciation	50,000
Increase (decrease) in	
Accounts receivable	(140,000)
Inventories	25,000
Other current assets	10,000
Accounts payable	120,000
Accrued payables	(25,000)
Interest payable	50,000

Required:

1. Calculate Zurich's cash flow from operating activities for 2014.

2. Explain the reasons for the difference between the firm's net income and its cash flow from operating activities in 2014.

An income statement for the first year of operations for Patti Company appears below:

Cash provided (used) by operations **(LO 5)**

Sales	$ 390,000
Dividend revenue	39,000
Interest revenue	24,050
Cost of goods sold	(208,000)
Salary expense	(26,000)
Depreciation expense	(70,200)
Income tax expense	(109,200)
Net income	$ 39,650

Additional information:

a. Accounts payable, end of year, $13,000.

b. Salaries payable, end of year, $8,450.

c. Inventories, end of year, $26,000.

d. Accounts receivable, end of year, $32,500.

e. Customers' accounts with credit balances (included in item *d*), end of year, $2,600.

Required:

Use the direct approach to calculate the cash provided (used) by operating activities for Patti Company.

PROBLEMS / DISCUSSION QUESTIONS

P 4 - 1

Preparing a balance sheet
(LO 1)

Ricky Corporation had the following alphabetical account balance listing at December 31, 2014 (in thousands of dollars).

	Debit	Credit
Accounts payable		$ 9,224
Accounts receivable	$ 3,248	
Accrued liabilities		12,226
Accumulated depreciation—buildings		6,028
Accumulated depreciation—furniture and office equipment		322
Accumulated depreciation—land improvements		862
Accumulated depreciation—machinery and equipment		19,664
Additional paid-in capital		1,584
Allowance for uncollectible accounts		14
Bonds payable		1,358
Buildings	19,950	
Cash	354	
Common stock		960
Furniture and office equipment	634	
Income taxes payable		1,888
Inventories	15,152	
Investment (noncurrent)	10,816	
Land	536	
Land improvements	1,438	
Leasehold improvements (net of amortization)	44	
Machinery and equipment	28,868	
Notes payable (long-term)		600
Notes receivable (Due June 15, 2015)	8,014	
Preferred stock		566
Prepaid expenses	1,458	
Retained earnings		?
Short-term investments	7,754	
Special tools	1,984	
Unearned revenues (current)		188
Unearned revenues (long-term)		2,768

Required:

Prepare a balance sheet for Ricky Corporation at December 31, 2014.

P 4 - 2

Preparation of a statement of cash flows and a balance sheet **(LO 1, 5, 7)**

Kay Wing, Inc., prepared the following balance sheet at December 31, 2013.

Kay Wing, Inc.

Balance Sheet as of December 31, 2013

Cash	$ 65,000
Accounts receivable	37,000
Inventory	70,000
Long-term investments	20,000
Land	39,000
Plant and equipment (net)	109,000
Total assets	$340,000

(continued)

Accounts payable	$ 33,000	
Taxes payable	4,000	
Bonds payable	80,000	
Capital stock	90,000	
Retained earnings	133,000	
Total liabilities and stockholders' equity	$340,000	

The following occurred during 2014.

1. $15,000 in cash and a $35,000 note payable were exchanged for land valued at $50,000.

2. Bonds payable (maturing in 2018) in the amount of $30,000 were retired by paying $28,000 cash.

3. Capital stock in the amount of $40,000 was issued at par value.

4. The company sold surplus equipment for $10,000. The equipment had a book value of $14,000 at the time of the sale.

5. Net income was $35,500.

6. Cash dividends of $5,000 were paid to the stockholders.

7. 100 shares of stock (considered short-term investments) were purchased for $8,300.

8. A new building was acquired through the issuance of $75,000 in bonds.

9. $12,000 of depreciation was recorded on the plant and equipment.

10. At December 31, 2014, Cash was $93,200, Accounts receivable had a balance of $41,500, Inventory had increased to $73,000, and Accounts payable had fallen to $25,500. Long-term investments and Taxes payable were unchanged from 2013.

Required:

1. Prepare a statement of cash flows for 2014.

2. Prepare the December 31, 2014, balance sheet for Kay Wing, Inc.

A December 31, 2014, post-closing trial balance for Short Erin Company follows.

P4-3

Preparing a balance sheet
(LO 1)

Account Title	Debits	Credits
Cash	$ 61,500	
Short-term investments	47,000	
Accounts receivable	95,600	
Inventory	175,000	
Prepaid expenses	13,500	
Land	241,800	
Buildings	584,900	
Accumulated depreciation—buildings		$ 132,500
Production equipment	$ 477,700	
Accumulated depreciation—production equipment		$ 239,600
Patents	50,000	
Leasehold	7,000	
Accounts payable		38,400
Accrued salaries		3,400
Taxes payable		65,800
Notes payable		200,000
Installment note payable		84,200
Bonds payable		250,000
Common stock		300,000
Retained earnings		440,100
Totals	$1,754,000	$1,754,000

Additional information about Short Erin's account balances:

1. Cash includes $12,000 in U.S. treasury bills purchased on December 21, 2014, that mature in January 2015. The account also includes $8,500 in stock purchased just before year-end that the company plans to sell in a few days.

2. The Accounts receivable balance consists of:

Trade receivables	$84,700
Allowance for doubtful trade accounts	(4,600)
Note receivable from Short Erin's president due in 2015	15,500
	$95,600

Trade receivables includes $1,400 of customer accounts with credit balances.

3. Notes payable consists of two notes. One, in the amount of $50,000, is due on March 19, 2015. The other note matures on October 27, 2017.

4. The Taxes payable account contains deferred income taxes amounting to $61,250.

5. The installment note payable bears an annual interest rate of 10%. Semiannual payments of $6,756.43 are due each June 30 and December 31 and include principal and accrued interest. These payments will reduce the Installment note balance by $5,220 in 2015.

6. Of the 1,000,000 authorized shares of no par common stock, 300,000 shares are issued and outstanding.

7. The company recently announced plans to sell its operating facility in Katy, Texas, consisting of land (cost $82,000) and a building (cost $175,000; book value $110,000). Production equipment has already been removed from the Katy plant and is being used in other company facilities.

Required:

Prepare a classified balance sheet for the Short Erin Company at December 31, 2014.

P4-4

Preparing the income statement and statement of cash flows   **(LO 5, 8)**

Consider the following transactions pertaining to Retail Traders Company. Amounts in parentheses indicate a decrease in the account.

Explanation	Assets		=	Liabilities	+	Owners' Equity	
	Cash	Inventory		Accounts Payable		Common Stock	Retained Earnings
Beginning balance		$ 10,000		$ 5,000		$3,000	$ 2,000
Credit purchases		100,000		100,000			
Cash sales	$115,000						115,000
Cost of goods sold		(90,000)					(90,000)
Cash paid to suppliers	(85,000)			(85,000)			
Ending balance	$ 30,000	$ 20,000		$ 20,000		$3,000	$ 27,000

Required:

1. Based on this information, prepare an income statement and statement of cash flows.

2. Provide an intuitive explanation of how the adjustments made to net income in the cash flow statement convert the accrual numbers to cash flow numbers.

P4-5

Analyzing common-size financial statements   **(LO 2)**

The common-size balance sheets from four companies follow: Amazon.com, an Internet book retailer; Alcoa, a major producer of aluminum products; Wendy's, a fast-food services organization; and Delta Air Lines, a major supplier of air transportation.

Required:

Based on your general business knowledge, the economic activities of these four firms, and information derived from the following balance sheet analysis, match the company with its respective balance sheet. Explain your reasoning for the choices that you make.

Common-Size Balance Sheet Comparisons

	Company			
	A	**B**	**C**	**D**
Assets				
Current assets				
Cash and marketable securities	1.84%	6.91%	28.57%	11.19%
Current receivables	13.85	3.64	—	4.22
Inventories	9.48	—	8.93	2.14
Other current assets	2.95	5.60	3.45	1.02
Total current assets	28.12%	16.15%	40.95%	18.57%
Noncurrent assets				
Property, plant, and equipment, net	53.52%	69.32%	12.85%	73.76%
Goodwill and intangibles, net	7.78	9.56	29.55	2.56
Other assets, net	10.58	4.97	16.65	5.11
Total assets	100.00%	100.00%	100.00%	100.00%
Liabilities and Stockholders' Equity				
Current liabilities				
Total current liabilities	17.60%	32.20%	29.90%	15.09%
Long-term liabilities	36.84	39.73	59.33	17.73
Total liabilities	54.44	71.93	89.23	32.82
Minority interest	8.53	—	—	—
Redeemable preferred stock	—	—	—	10.62
Stockholders' Equity				
Contributed capital and other equity items	1.51	11.41	46.46	(0.18)
Retained earnings (deficit)	35.52	16.66	(35.69)	56.74
Total liabilities and stockholders' equity	100.00%	100.00%	100.00%	100.00%

Following are the common-size balance sheets from four companies: Pfizer, Inc., a global research-driven pharmaceutical company; JCPenney, a national retailer; TimeWarner, a global media and entertainment company; and Duke Energy, a leading energy company focused on electric power and gas distribution.

P 4-6

Analyzing common-size financial statements **(LO 2)**

Required:

Based on your general business knowledge, the environments in which the above firms operate, and information derived from the balance sheet analysis, match the company with its respective balance sheet. Explain the reasoning for the choices that you make.

Common-Size Balance Sheet Comparisons

	Company			
	A	**B**	**C**	**D**
Assets				
Current assets				
Cash and marketable securities	23.93%	12.19%	2.70%	7.30%
Current receivables	0.00	6.88	3.05	7.78
Inventories	24.04	5.82	2.66	2.71
Other current assets	4.90	4.06	1.70	2.00
Total current assets	52.87%	28.96%	10.11%	19.79%

(continued)

	Company			
	A	**B**	**C**	**D**
Noncurrent assets				
Property, plant, and equipment	42.58%	10.70%	66.53%	6.03%
Goodwill and intangibles, net	0.00	51.84	8.67	61.92
Other assets, net	4.55	8.50	14.69	12.26
Total assets	100.00%	100.00%	100.00%	100.00%
Liabilities and Stockholders' Equity				
Current liabilities				
Total current liabilities	25.82%	17.48%	7.17%	13.33%
Long-term liabilities	36.20	40.05	54.46	35.36
Total liabilities	62.02	57.53	61.63	48.69
Stockholders' equity				
Contributed capital and other equity items*	21.90	23.49	35.84	199.11
Retained earnings (deficit)	16.08	18.98	2.56	(147.80)
Total liabilities and stockholders' equity	100.00%	100.00%	100.00%	100.00%

* Net of cost of shares repurchased for treasury and other comprehensive income items.

P4-7

Determining cash flows from operating and investing activities   **(LO 5, 6, 7)**

AICPA
ADAPTED

Karr, Inc., reported net income of $300,000 for 2014. Changes occurred in several balance sheet accounts as follows:

Equipment	$25,000 increase	Inventories	$20,000 decrease
Accumulated depreciation	40,000 increase	Accounts receivable	15,000 increase
Note payable	30,000 increase	Accounts payable	5,000 decrease

Additional Information:

a. During 2014, Karr sold equipment costing $25,000, with accumulated depreciation of $12,000, for a gain of $5,000.

b. In December 2014, Karr purchased equipment costing $50,000, with $20,000 cash and a 12% note payable of $30,000.

c. Depreciation expense for the year was $52,000.

Required:

1. In Karr's 2014 statement of cash flows, calculate net cash provided by operating activities.

2. In Karr's 2014 statement of cash flows, calculate net cash used in investing activities.

P4-8

Determining operating cash flow components   **(LO 5)**

AICPA
ADAPTED

The following data have been extracted from the financial statements of Prentiss, Inc., a calendar-year merchandising corporation:

	December 31,	
Balance Sheet Data	**2014**	**2015**
Trade accounts receivable—net	$ 84,000	$ 78,000
Inventory	150,000	140,000
Accounts payable—merchandise (credit)	(95,000)	(98,000)

- Total sales for 2015 were $1,200,000 and for 2014 were $1,100,000. Cash sales were 20% of total sales each year.

- Cost of goods sold was $840,000 for 2015.

- Variable general and administrative (G&A) expenses for 2015 were $120,000. These expenses have varied in proportion to sales and have been paid at the rate of 50% in the year incurred and 50% the following year. Unpaid G&A expenses are *not* included in accounts payable.

- Fixed G&A expenses, including $35,000 depreciation and $5,000 bad debt expense, totaled $100,000 each year. The amount of such expenses involving cash payments was paid at the rate of 80% in the year incurred and 20% the following year. In each year, there was a $5,000 bad debt estimate and a $5,000 write-off. Unpaid G&A expenses are *not* included in accounts payable.

Required:

Compute the following:

1. The amount of cash collected during 2015 that resulted from total sales in 2014 and 2015.

2. The amount of cash disbursed during 2015 for purchases of merchandise.

3. The amount of cash disbursed during 2015 for variable and fixed G&A expenses.

The following cash flow information pertains to the 2014 operations of Matterhorn, Inc., a maker of ski equipment:

P 4-9

Understanding the relation between the income statement, cash flow statement, and changes in balance sheet accounts **(LO 5, 6)**

Cash collections from customers	$ 16,670
Cash payments to suppliers	19,428
Cash payments for various operating expenses	7,148
Cash payments for current income taxes	200
Cash provided (used) by operating activities	(10,106)

The following additional information comes from Matterhorn's 2014 income statement:

Net income	$ 609
Depreciation of equipment	2,256
Amortization of patents	399
Loss on sale of equipment	169

The following additional information comes from Matterhorn's 2013 and 2014 comparative balance sheets (decreases are in parentheses):

Change in accounts receivable	$ 3,630
Change in inventory	3,250
Change in accounts payable	(3,998)
Change in accrued operating expenses	(2,788)
Change in deferred taxes payable	127

Required:

1. Use the preceding information to derive Matterhorn's 2014 income statement.

2. Use the same information to compute Matterhorn's 2014 cash flow from operating activities under the indirect method (that is, derive cash flow from operating activities by making the necessary adjustments to net income).

3. Provide a brief explanation for the difference observed between net income and cash provided by operating activities.

P4-10

Understanding the relation between income statement, cash flow statement, and changes in balance sheet accounts   **(LO 5, 6, 8)**

The following cash flow information pertains to the 2014 operations of Fishmaster, Inc., a maker of fishing equipment.

Cash collections from customers	$79,533
Cash payments to suppliers	64,097
Cash payments for selling and administrative expenses	11,166
Cash payments for interest	1,548
Cash payments for current income taxes	2,350
Cash provided by operating activities	372

The following additional information comes from Fishmaster's 2014 income statement:

Net income	$3,728
Depreciation of equipment	6,380
Gain on sale of equipment	1,327

The following additional information comes from Fishmaster's 2013 and 2014 comparative balance sheets (decreases are in parentheses):

Change in accounts receivable	$ 1,850
Change in inventory	5,299
Change in accounts payable	(1,711)
Change in accrued selling and administrative expenses	910
Change in deferred taxes payable	(342)
Change in accrued interest payable	(117)

Required:

1. Use the preceding information to derive Fishmaster's 2014 income statement.

2. Use the same information to compute Fishmaster's 2014 cash flow from operating activities under the indirect method (that is, derive cash flow from operating activities by making the necessary adjustments to net income).

3. Provide a brief explanation for the difference observed between net income and cash provided by operating activities.

P4-11

Understanding the relation between operating cash flows and accrual earnings
(LO 5, 6, 8)

The following information is taken from the operating section of the statement of cash flows (direct method) of Battery Builders, Inc.:

Collections from customers	$28,000
Payments to suppliers for purchases	(13,000)
Payments for operating expenses	(9,000)
Payments for current period income taxes	(4,000)
Cash provided by operating activities	2,000

The following information is obtained from the income statement of Battery Builders:

Net income	$4,000
Depreciation expense	4,000
Gain on sale of equipment	2,000
Write-off of intangibles	1,000

In addition, the following information is obtained from the comparative balance sheets of Battery Builders (decreases in parentheses):

Change in accounts receivable	$ 3,000
Change in inventory	3,000
Change in accounts payable	2,000
Change in accrued payable (related to operating expense)	(2,000)
Change in deferred income taxes payable	1,000

Required:

1. Prepare a complete accrual-basis income statement for the current year.

2. Compute the cash flows from operations using the indirect approach (that is, start with accrual-basis net income and adjust for various items to obtain cash flows from operations).

The following information was taken from Royal Caribbean's Year 2 balance sheet. Royal Caribbean is one of the largest cruise lines in the world.

P 4-12

Finding missing values on a classified balance sheet and analyzing balance sheet changes **(LO 1, 2)**

($ in thousands)	December 31, Year 2
Accounts payable	$ 264,554
Accrued expenses and other liabilities	487,764
Accrued interest	147,547
Accumulated other comprehensive income (loss)	182,733
Cash and cash equivalents	284,619
Common stock	2,243
Current portion of long-term debt	756,215
Customer deposits	?
Derivative financial instruments	114,094
Goodwill	?
Hedged firm commitments	33,426
Inventories	107,877
Long-term debt	7,663,555
Other assets	1,146,677
Other long-term liabilities	321,192
Paid-in capital	?
Preferred stock	—
Prepaid expenses and other assets	?
Property and equipment, net	15,268,053
Retained earnings	4,754,950
Total assets	?
Total current assets	1,026,391
Total current liabilities	2,749,030
Total liabilities and shareholders' equity	18,233,494
Total shareholders' equity	?
Trade and other receivables, net	338,804
Treasury stock	(413,704)

The following is Royal Caribbean's Year 1 balance sheet.

Consolidated Balance Sheets

($ in thousands)	December 31, Year 1
Assets	
Current assets	
Cash and cash equivalents	$ 402,878
Trade and other receivables, net	271,287
Inventories	96,077
Prepaid expenses and other assets	125,160
Derivative financial instruments	81,935
Total current assets	977,337
Property and equipment, net	13,878,998
Goodwill	779,246
Other assets	827,729
Total assets	$16,463,310
Liabilities and Shareholders' Equity	
Current liabilities	
Current portion of long-term debt	$ 471,893
Accounts payable	245,225
Accrued interest	128,879
Accrued expenses and other liabilities	687,369
Customer deposits	968,520
Hedged firm commitments	172,339
Total current liabilities	2,674,225
Long-term debt	6,539,510
Other long-term liabilities	446,563
Shareholders' equity	
Preferred stock	—
Common stock	2,239
Paid-in capital	2,952,540
Retained earnings	4,592,529
Accumulated other comprehensive income (loss)	(319,936)
Treasury stock	(424,360)
Total shareholders' equity	6,803,012
Total liabilities and shareholders' equity	$16,463,310

Required:

1. Solve for the missing values and present Royal Caribbean's Year 2 balance sheet in good form.

2. Royal Caribbean has recently become a customer of your firm. In fact, its accounts receivable is one of your firm's largest current assets. The amount is so large that the chief executive officer (CEO) of your firm is concerned because if Royal Caribbean doesn't pay in a timely fashion, your firm could experience severe cash flow problems. Use Royal Caribbean's balance sheet to assess Royal Caribbean's ability to make timely payments of its current liabilities.

3. Using your Year 2 and the Year 1 balance sheets provided, compare and contrast the firm's financial position at the end of these two years. For example, were there any changes in Royal Caribbean's financial position from the end of Year 1 to the end of Year 2? In what ways did the firm's financial position improve or deteriorate over this time period?

4. Assume you are a financial analyst. Based on the financial position of Royal Caribbean as portrayed in the Year 1 and Year 2 balance sheets, would you advise your clients to invest in the firm's common stock? Why or why not?

5. Before advising your clients about whether or not to purchase the common stock of Royal Caribbean, what information beyond the Year 1 and Year 2 balance sheets would you seek?

The statement of cash flows for the year ended December 31, 2014, and other data for Bradley Corporation are shown below:

P4-13

Conversion of statement of cash flows to accrual-basis income statement
(LO 5, 6, 8)

Cash flows from operating activities:		
Cash collections from customers	$ 375,000	
Dividends received	10,000	
Cash outflows for:		
Merchandise	(120,000)	
Salaries	(55,000)	
Taxes	(25,000)	
Other operating expenses	(25,000)	
Net cash provided by operating activities		$ 160,000
Cash flows from investing activities:		
Sales of investments	40,000	
Purchased machinery	(150,000)	
Net cash used by investing activities		(110,000)
Cash flows from financing activities:		
Issue of capital stock		50,000
Net increase in cash		$ 100,000

Additional data:

a. Bradley's Dividends receivable account decreased by $2,000 during the year.

b. The Machinery account, net of accumulated depreciation, increased by $100,000 during the year. The only other transaction, exclusive of depreciation, was the write-off on May 15, 2014, of obsolete machinery that had a book value of $8,000.

c. Accounts receivable increased by $40,000 during 2014. The Allowance account increased by $4,000. There were no write-offs of uncollectible accounts.

d. Salaries payable at the beginning of the year were $6,000; at the end of the year, $10,000.

e. Inventories decreased $12,000 during 2014.

f. Taxes payable increased $6,000 during the year.

g. The investments that were sold had a book value of $30,000.

Required:

On the basis of the above data, prepare Bradley Corporation's single-step income statement for the year ended December 31, 2014.

Vanguard Corporation is a distributor of food products. The corporation has approximately 1,000 stockholders, and its stock, which is traded "over-the-counter," is sold throughout 2014 at about $7 a share with little fluctuation. The corporation's balance sheet at December 31, 2013, follows.

P4-14

Preparing the balance sheet and income statement
(LO 5, 8)

AICPA
ADAPTED

mhhe.com/revsine6e

Balance Sheet as of December 31, 2013

Assets		
Current assets		
Cash		$ 4,386,040
Accounts receivable	$ 3,150,000	
Less allowance for doubtful accounts	(94,500)	3,055,500
Inventories—at the lower of cost (FIFO) or market		2,800,000
Total current assets		10,241,540
Fixed assets—at cost	3,300,000	
Less accumulated depreciation	(1,300,000)	2,000,000
Total assets		$12,241,540

(continued)

Liabilities and Stockholders' Equity

Current liabilities

Notes payable due within one year		$ 1,000,000
Accounts payable and accrued liabilities		2,091,500
Federal income taxes payable		300,000
Total current liabilities		3,391,500
Notes payable due after one year		4,000,000

Stockholders' equity

Capital stock—authorized 2,000,000 shares of $1 par value; issued and outstanding 1,000,000 shares	$1,000,000	
Additional paid-in capital	1,500,000	
Retained earnings	2,350,040	
Total stockholders' equity		4,850,040
Total liabilities and stockholders' equity		$12,241,540

Information concerning the corporation and its activities during 2014 follows:

1. Sales for the year were $15,650,000. The gross profit percentage for the year was 30% of sales. Merchandise purchases and freight-in totaled $10,905,000. Depreciation and other expenses do not enter into cost of goods sold.

2. Administrative, selling, and general expenses (including provision for state taxes) other than interest, depreciation, and provision for doubtful accounts amounted to $2,403,250.

3. The December 31, 2014, accounts receivable amounted to $3,350,000, and the corporation maintains an allowance for doubtful accounts equal to 3% of the accounts receivable outstanding. During the year $50,000 of 2013 receivables were deemed uncollectible and charged off to the allowance account.

4. The rate of depreciation of fixed assets is 13% per annum, and the corporation consistently follows the policy of taking one-half year's depreciation in the year of acquisition. The depreciation expense for 2014 was $474,500.

5. The notes are payable in 20 equal quarterly installments commencing March 31, 2014, with interest at 5% per annum also payable quarterly.

6. Accounts payable and accrued liabilities at December 31, 2014, were $2,221,000.

7. The balance of the 2013 federal income tax paid in 2014 was in exact agreement with the amount accrued on the December 31, 2013, balance sheet.

8. The 2014 estimated tax payments made in 2014 totaled $400,000. Income tax expense for 2014 on an accrual accounting basis was $530,000.

9. During the second month of each quarter of 2014, dividends of $0.10 a share were declared and paid. In addition, in July 2014, a 5% stock dividend was declared and paid.

Required:

Prepare the following statements in good form and support them by well-organized and developed computations for the year ending December 31, 2014:

a. Balance sheet

b. Income statement

P4-15

Positioning of items within cash flow statement—IFRS vs. U.S. GAAP   **(LO 9)**

Lend Corp. has a primary business model of borrowing funds at low interest rates and lending them out at higher interest rates. Lend Corp's ending balance sheet for December 31, 2014, is as follows:

Assets		Liabilities	
Cash	$300,000	Accounts payable	$ 40,000
Land	$300,000	Notes payable	$ 800,000
Building	$800,000		
Accum depr: Building	$160,000	**Owner's Equity**	
Accounts receivable	$ 20,000	Retained earnings	$ 320,000
Notes receivable	$900,000	Contributed capital	$1,000,000

During 2015, Lend Corp. has the following transactions:

- Received $45,000 in cash interest on notes receivable.
- Paid $16,000 of cash interest on notes payable.
- Collected $10,000 cash from accounts receivable.
- Paid $40,000 cash to reduce accounts payable.
- Owes $3,000 at the end of the year to administrative employees for work performed.
- Building depreciation is an additional $20,000.

Required:

1. Compute Lend Corp's 2015 net income.
2. Show Lend Corp's 12/31/2015 balance sheet.
3. Report Lend Corp's 12/31/2015 statement of cash flows using the indirect method under U.S. GAAP.
4. Report Lend Corp's 12/31/2015 statement of cash flows using the indirect method under IFRS. Record cash flows from interest received in the cash flows from investing section. Record cash flows from interest paid in the cash flows from financing section.
5. Compare your net cash flows from operations computed from requirement 3 vs. requirement 4. Which do you think better reflects Lend Corp's fundamental operating cash flows?

Sell Corp. has a primary business model of buying and selling merchandise inventory. Sell Corp's ending balance sheet for December 31, 2014, is as follows:

P 4-16

Positioning of items within cash flow statement—IFRS vs. U.S. GAAP **(LO 9)**

Assets		Liabilities	
Cash	$300,000	Accounts payable	$ 40,000
Land	$300,000	Notes payable	$ 800,000
Building	$800,000		
Accum depr: Building	$160,000		
Inventory	$800,000	**Owner's Equity**	
Accounts receivable	$ 20,000	Retained earnings	$ 320,000
Notes receivable	$100,000	Contributed capital	$1,000,000

During 2015, Sell Corp. has the following transactions:

- Received $5,000 in cash interest on notes receivable.
- Paid $16,000 of cash interest on notes payable.
- Collected $10,000 cash from Accounts receivable.
- Paid $40,000 cash to reduce Accounts payable.
- Owes $30,000 at the end of the year to employees for work performed.
- Building depreciation is an additional $20,000.
- Sold $200,000 of inventory at a retail price of $400,000. Received $350,000 in cash but $50,000 is still due from customers.

Required:

1. Compute Sell Corp's 2015 net income.

2. Show Sell Corp's 12/31/2015 balance sheet.

3. Report Sell Corp's 12/31/2015 statement of cash flows using the indirect method under U.S. GAAP.

4. Report Sell Corp's 12/31/2015 statement of cash flows using the indirect method under IFRS. Record cash flows from interest received in the cash flows from investing section. Record cash flows from interest paid in the cash flows from financing section.

5. Compare your net cash flows from operations computed from requirement 3 vs. requirement 4. Which do you think better reflects Sell Corp's fundamental operating cash flows?

CASES

C4-1

Subsequent events   **(LO 4)**

The following events and transactions related to David Company occurred after the balance sheet date of December 31, 2014, and before the financial statements were issued in 2015. None of the items is reflected in the financial statements as of December 31, 2014.

1. In order to secure a bank loan of $200,000, David pledged as collateral certain fixed assets with a net book value of $300,000. David applied for the loan on December 18, 2014, and the bank approved the loan on January 8, 2015.

2. On November 21, 2014, David initiated a lawsuit seeking $500,000 in damages from a firm that David claims infringed on its trademark. David's attorneys have stated that the chances of winning and of getting the $500,000 are excellent.

3. On March 1, 2015, the IRS assessed David an additional $125,000 for the 2013 tax year. However, both the tax attorneys for David and the tax accountants have indicated that it is likely that the IRS will settle the government's claim for $75,000.

4. On February 22, 2015, David issued bonds at an interest rate 2 percentage points above the LIBOR (London Interbank Offered Rate). This is the average interest rate estimated by leading banks in London that they would be charged if borrowing from other banks.

5. A warehouse containing a significant portion of David's inventory was destroyed by fire on January 30, 2015.

6. A supplier to whom David owes $15,000 declared bankruptcy on February 3, 2015.

Required:
Indicate whether the item would be reported in David Company's 2014 financial statements or in the notes to the financial statements, and what information would be reported. Assume that each of these events is considered material.

C4-2

Conducting financial reporting research: Related-party matters   **(LO 4)**

John Rigas founded Adelphia Communications Corporation with a $300 license in 1952, took the company public in 1986, and built it into the sixth largest cable television operator by acquiring other systems in the 1990s. As the company grew, it also expanded into other fields. It operated a telephone business, a sports radio station, a sports cable channel, and many other smaller subsidiaries. Despite being a publicly held firm, the company remained a family-run business; five of the firm's nine board members were Rigas family members who also held various executive posts. John was the CEO and chairman of the board. His sons, Tim (CFO), Michael (VP of operations), and James (VP of strategic planning), made up much of the firm's leadership team. In addition, John Rigas's son-in-law sat on Adelphia's board of directors. The company filed for bankruptcy in June 2002 after it disclosed $2.3 billion in off-balance-sheet debt. The Rigases are among a number of former corporate executives who have faced criminal charges since Enron's fall in 2001 touched off a series of white-collar scandals.

At John's trial, prosecutors said the Rigases used complicated cash management systems (CMS) to spread money around to various family-owned entities to cover stealing about $100 million for themselves. Rigas Entities consisted of approximately 63 different entities organized as partnerships, corporations, or limited liability companies exclusively owned or controlled by members of the Rigas family. Adelphia managed and maintained virtually every aspect of the approximately 14 companies comprising the Rigas Cable Entities, including maintaining their books and records on a general ledger system shared with Adelphia and its subsidiaries. Adelphia and Rigas Entities participated jointly in a CMS operated by Adelphia, which resulted in commingling funds among the participants and greatly facilitating the fraud at Adelphia.

A complaint filed by the SEC stated:

> The commission charges that Adelphia, at the direction of the individual defendants: (1) fraudulently excluded billions of dollars in liabilities from its consolidated financial statements by hiding them in off-balance sheet affiliates; (2) falsified operations statistics and inflated Adelphia's earnings to meet Wall Street's expectations; and (3) concealed rampant self-dealing by the Rigas Family, including the undisclosed use of corporate funds for Rigas Family stock purchases and the acquisition of luxury condominiums in New York and elsewhere. The Commission seeks a final judgment ordering the defendants to account for and disgorge all ill-gotten gains including . . . all property unlawfully taken from Adelphia through undisclosed related-party transactions.[13]

The SEC also alleges that since at least 1986, Adelphia improperly netted, or offset, related-party payables and related-party receivables as of year-end. As a result of this offset, gross related-party receivables of $1.351 billion and gross related-party payables of $1.348 billion were reported as a mere $3 million net receivable.[14]

Required:

1. Review FASB ASC Topic 850: Related Party Disclosures (available on the FASB's website: www.FASB.org).
2. Use EDGAR (www.SEC.gov) to access the 2000 Form 10-K for Adelphia Communications Corporation. Examine Adelphia's balance sheet and locate a line item called Related-party receivables—net. Next, look up and read the "related-party" note (note 13). Do you believe that this note adequately explains the nature of these related-party receivables or meets the disclosure requirement for related-party transactions? Justify your answer.
3. What is the significance of Adelphia's treatment of related-party receivables and payables and the company's failure to adequately disclose its related-party transactions?
4. Why is it important that companies disclose related-party transactions?

C4-3

Analyzing international reporting **(LO 3)**

A recent balance sheet for Pittards, PLC, a British company, follows. The company's principal activities are the design, production, and procurement of technically advanced leather. The Group financial statements consolidate the accounts of Pittards, PLC, and all its subsidiary undertakings. (References to financial statement notes that appear on the original balance sheet have been omitted.)

Required:

1. Examine the Pittards balance sheet and identify at least three differences between balance sheets as presented in the United Kingdom and the United States.
2. Compare the Pittards balance sheet with the Burberry Group balance sheet in Exhibit 4.3 and identify at least three differences between them.
3. Review Pittards' balance sheet and discuss how its format provides useful information to investors and creditors.

---

[13] Securities and Exchange Commission, *Accounting and Auditing Enforcement Release No. 1599,* July 24, 2002.

[14] Securities and Exchange Commission, *Accounting and Auditing Enforcement Release No. 2326,* September 30, 2005.

Pittards, PLC

Balance Sheet as at 31 December Year 1

(£ in 000)	Group	Company
Fixed assets		
Tangible fixed assets	£ 6,235	£ 631
Investments	—	3,368
	6,235	3,999
Current assets		
Stocks	6,086	—
Debtors	3,509	11,943
Cash at bank and in hand	21	—
	9,616	11,943
Creditors—amounts falling due within one year		
Bank loans and overdrafts	(971)	(971)
Trade creditors	(3,137)	—
Other creditors	(3,733)	(13,889)
	(7,841)	(14,860)
Net current assets (liabilities)	1,775	(2,917)
Total assets less current liabilities	8,010	1,082
Creditors—amounts falling due after more than one year	(3,004)	(428)
Provisions for liabilities and charges	(520)	(13)
Net assets before pension scheme liability	4,486	641
Pension scheme liability	—	—
Net assets (liabilities) after pension scheme liability	4,486	641
Capital and reserves		
Called up share capital	2,233	2,233
Share premium account	4,214	4,214
Capital redemption reserve	8,158	8,158
Revaluation reserve	2,335	—
Capital reserve	6,475	—
Profit and loss account	(18,434)	(13,469)
Own shares	(495)	(495)
Shareholders' funds	4,486	641

C 4-4

Bertha's Bridal Boutique: Determining cash flow amounts from comparative balance sheets and income statements **(LO 5, 7, 8)**

AICPA
ADAPTED

The balance sheet and income statement for Bertha's Bridal Boutique are presented along with some additional information about the accounts. You are to answer the questions that follow concerning cash flows for the period.

Balance Sheet

	December 31,	
	2014	**2013**
Assets		
Current assets		
Cash	$ 450,000	$ 364,000
Accounts receivable—net	692,000	625,000
Inventory	723,000	610,000
Prepaid expenses	50,000	70,000
Total current assets	1,915,000	1,669,000
Long-term investments	150,000	20,000
Property, plant, and equipment	1,622,000	815,000
Less: Accumulated depreciation	(100,000)	(75,000)
	1,522,000	740,000
Total assets	$3,587,000	$2,429,000

(continued)

	December 31,	
	2014	**2013**
Liabilities and Stockholders' Equity		
Current liabilities		
Accounts payable	$ 399,000	$ 451,000
Accrued expenses	185,000	179,000
Dividends payable	50,000	—
Total current liabilities	634,000	630,000
Notes payable—due 2017	750,000	—
Stockholders' Equity		
Common stock	1,400,000	1,300,000
Retained earnings	803,000	499,000
Total stockholders' equity	2,203,000	1,799,000
Total liabilities and stockholders' equity	$3,587,000	$2,429,000

Income Statements

	Years Ended December 31,	
	2014	**2013**
Net credit sales	$7,200,000	$6,500,000
Cost of goods sold	4,320,000	3,900,000
Gross profit	2,880,000	2,600,000
Operating expenses (including income taxes)	2,376,000	2,145,000
Net income	$ 504,000	$ 455,000

a. All accounts receivable and accounts payable are related to trade merchandise. Accounts payable are recorded net and always are paid to take all the discounts allowed. The allowance for doubtful accounts at the end of 2014 was the same as at the end of 2013; no receivables were charged against the allowance during 2014.

b. The proceeds from the note payable were used to finance a new warehouse. Capital stock was sold to provide additional working capital.

Required:

1. Calculate the cash collected during 2014 from accounts receivable.
2. Calculate the cash payments during 2014 on accounts payable to suppliers.
3. Calculate the cash provided from operations for 2014.
4. Calculate the cash inflows during 2014 from financing activities.
5. Calculate the cash outflows from investing activities during 2014.

Following is Crash Zone Corporation's balance sheet at the end of 2013 and its cash flow statement for 2014. Crash zone manufactures safety equipment for race cars.

Balance Sheet as of December 31, 2013

Assets	
Current assets	
Cash	$ 8,250
Accounts receivable—net	7,110
Inventory	14,221
Prepaid assets	1,850
Total current assets	31,431
Land	30,278
Building and equipment	222,665
Less: Accumulated depreciation, building and equipment	(41,115)
Total assets	$243,259

C4-5

Crash Zone Corporation: Understanding the relation between successive balance sheets and the cash flow statement **(LO 5, 6, 8)**

mhhe.com/revsine6e

(continued)

Balance Sheet as of December 31, 2013

Liabilities and Stockholders' Equity

Current liabilities	
Accounts payable	$ 13,500
Accrued expenses	4,888
Total current liabilities	18,388
Long-term debt	31,500
Stockholders' equity	
Common stock, $10.00 par value	21,552
Paid-in capital	45,002
Retained earnings	146,872
Less: Treasury stock	(20,005)
Total liabilities and stockholders' equity	$243,259

Statement of Cash Flows for Year Ended December 31, 2014

Operating activities	
Net income	$ 15,750
Plus (minus) noncash items	
+Depreciation expense	6,210
Plus (minus) changes in current asset and liability accounts	
−Increase in inventory	(350)
+Decrease in prepaid assets	102
−Decrease in accrued expenses	(655)
−Increase in accounts receivable	(3,178)
−Decrease in accounts payable	(1,230)
Cash provided by operating activities	16,649
Investing activities	
Purchase of equipment	(27,910)
Proceeds from the sale of land	6,555
Cash used by investing activities	$(21,355)
Financing activities	
Issuance of long-term debt	8,900
Issuance of common stock	23,000
Cash dividends paid	(12,200)
Purchase of treasury stock	(7,513)
Cash provided by financing activities	12,187
Net cash flow	$ 7,481

Additional Information:

a. During 2014, 500 shares of common stock were sold to the public.

b. Land was sold during 2014 at an amount equal to its original cost.

Required:

Use the preceding information to derive Crash Zone's balance sheet at the end of 2014.

 **.mhhe.com/revsine6e**

**Remember to check the book's companion website
for additional study material.**

Essentials of Financial Statement Analysis | 5

> *"Investors would be well advised to shut out all the yammering about earnings expectations, consensus forecasts, and whisper numbers and focus instead on the financial information reported by companies themselves."* [1]

LEARNING OBJECTIVES

After studying this chapter, you will understand:

1. How cause-of-change analysis and common-size and trend statements illuminate complex financial statement patterns and shed light on business activities.
2. How competitive forces and business strategies affect a company's profitability and financial position.
3. How return on assets (ROA) can be used to analyze a company's profitability, and what insights are gained from disaggregating ROA into its profit margin and asset turnover components.
4. How return on common equity (ROCE) can be used to assess the effect of financial leverage on profitability.
5. How short-term liquidity risk differs from long-term solvency risk, and what financial ratios are helpful in assessing these two dimensions of credit risk.
6. How to use cash flow statement information when assessing credit risk.
7. How to interpret the results of an analysis of profitability and risk.
8. How to prepare and analyze business segment disclosures.

A firm's financial statements are like an optical lens. If you know how to look through them, you can see more clearly what is going on at the firm. Has profitability improved? Are customers paying their bills promptly? How was the new manufacturing plant financed? Financial statements hold the answers to these and other questions. They can tell us how the company got to where it is today, and they can help us forecast where the company might be tomorrow.

This chapter provides an overview of four financial analysis tools—**cause-of-change analysis, common-size statements, trend statements,** and **financial ratios.** We show how to use each tool to analyze profitability and credit risk, and we explain how to interpret the results from each. An important message in this chapter is that all financial analysis tools are built around reported accounting data, and no financial analysis is better than the data on which it relies. *What financial data a company chooses to report and how the data are reported affect not only the financial statements themselves but also the ratios and other statistics derived from those statements.*

Introducing financial analysis tools at this early point prepares you for later chapters in which we describe various financial reporting alternatives and their effects on ratios, trends, and other comparisons.

BASIC APPROACHES

Analysts use financial statements and financial data in many ways and for many different purposes. Two purposes you should know are time-series analysis and cross-sectional analysis.

Time-series analysis helps identify trends for a *single* company or business unit. For example, an analyst studying Intel might be interested in determining the rate of growth in the company's sales or the degree to which its earnings have fluctuated historically

---

[1] G. Morgenson, "Flying Blind in a Fog of Data," *The New York Times,* June 18, 2000.

with inflation, business cycles, foreign currency exchange rates, or changes in economic growth in domestic or foreign markets.

Cross-sectional analysis helps identify similarities and differences *across* companies or business units at a single point in time. The analyst might compare the 2014 profitability of one company in an industry to a competitor's profitability in the same year. A related analytic tool—**benchmark comparison**—measures a company's performance or condition against some predetermined standard. For example, commercial lending agreements often require the borrowing company to maintain minimum dollar levels of working capital or tangible net worth. Once the loan has been granted, the lender—a bank or insurance company—monitors compliance by comparing the borrower's reported financial amounts and ratios to those specified in the loan agreement.

> **Tangible net worth** is usually defined as total *tangible* assets minus total liabilities; tangible assets exclude intangibles such as goodwill, patents, and trademarks.

Financial Statement Analysis and Accounting Quality

Cause-of-change analysis, common-size statements, trend statements, and financial ratios are powerful tools for understanding how a company got where it is today and where the company might be heading tomorrow. But because these tools are built around reported accounting data, they are no better than the data on which they rely. A company that uses aggressive accounting methods to appear more profitable will also present a more favorable picture in a financial analysis. Analysts need a thorough understanding of accounting rules and a keen eye for information in the financial statement notes so they are aware of how accounting rules and choices have affected the reported results. Only then can they use financial analysis tools to their full advantage.

Analysts use financial statement information to "get behind the numbers"—that is, to see more clearly the economic activities and condition of a company and its prospects (see Figure 5.1). However, financial statements do not always provide a complete and faithful picture of a company's activities and condition. The raw data needed for a complete and faithful picture do not always reach the financial reports because the information is filtered by generally accepted accounting principles (GAAP) and by management's accounting discretion. Both factors can distort the reported information and the analyst's view of the company.

Let's see how the financial reporting "filter" works with equipment leases. GAAP requires each lease to be classified as either a **capital lease** or an **operating lease,** and it requires only

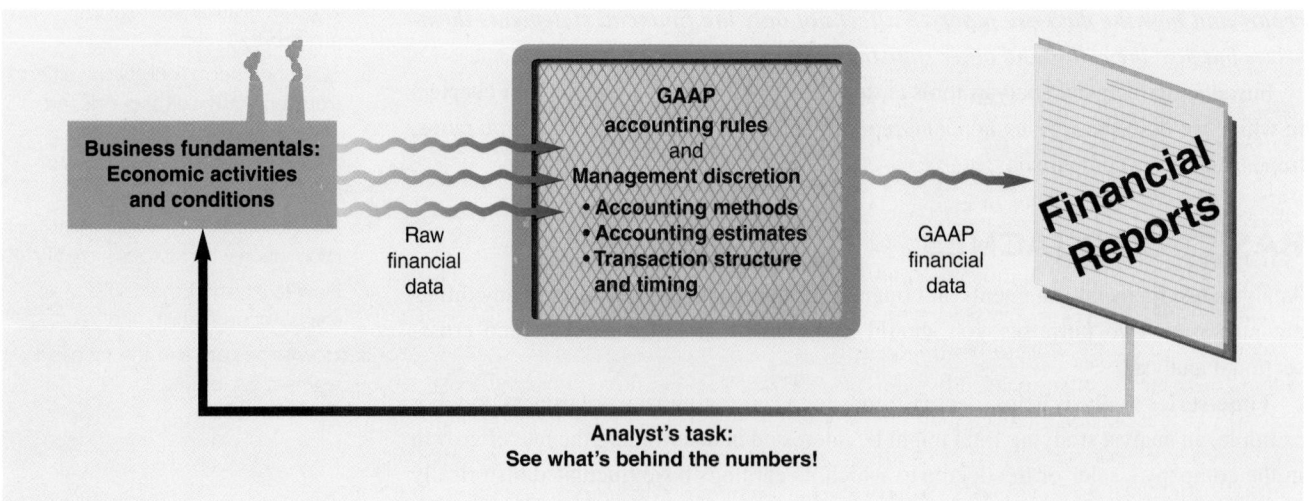

Figure 5.1 THE FINANCIAL REPORTING FILTER AND THE ANALYST'S TASK

capital leases to be reported in the balance sheet. Operating leases are "off-balance-sheet" items—meaning they are not included in the reported asset and liability numbers but are instead disclosed in notes that accompany the financial statements. (We'll see how and why this is so in Chapter 12.) So GAAP requires that capital leases "pass through the filter" to the balance sheet, but it filters out operating leases, sending them to the notes. Analysts can—and do—use these notes to recast the balance sheet so that all equipment leases are treated the same way, and the GAAP filter is overcome.

Management discretion can cloud financial analysis in several ways. For example, managers who understand GAAP can structure transactions to achieve particular financial reporting results. Do you, as a manager, want to keep equipment leases off the balance sheet? If so, then structure your company's lease contracts to meet the GAAP rules for an operating lease. Doing so keeps the leases off your balance sheet and lowers reported debt, as well as financial ratios intended to measure the degree of financial leverage.

Management discretion can also complicate an analyst's task in areas where GAAP allows managers to choose freely from among alternative reporting methods. For example, some companies account for inventory using the first-in first-out (FIFO) method; others use last-in first-out (LIFO). These alternative methods can produce very different balance sheet and income statement figures and, as a result, numerous financial ratios and comparisons can be affected (Chapter 9). Here, too, the analyst can sometimes use information disclosed in the notes to recast the reported financial results and thereby eliminate the filtering effect of management discretion.

Management also has discretion over accounting estimates and the timing of business transactions. Consider estimated bad debts, management's forecast of the amount of current credit sales that will never be collected from customers. A reduction in estimated bad debts could mean that customer credit quality has improved—that is, more credit customers are now expected to pay their bills. Or it could mean the bad debt estimate was reduced to meet a quarterly earnings goal. Similar questions arise over the timing of discretionary expenditures for advertising, research and development (R&D), or information technology. Did advertising expense decline because the current ad program was a resounding success or because management curtailed spending this quarter to meet an earnings goal? In other words, have business fundamentals improved, or is the appearance of improvement due simply to "earnings management"?

> GAAP and management discretion can sometimes make the analyst's task easier by illuminating aspects of the company's activities and condition. For example, GAAP requires companies to disclose sales and operating income by business segment—information that few companies would otherwise make available. Similarly, management sometimes goes far beyond GAAP's minimum reporting requirements by disclosing financial and nonfinancial operating details that are invaluable to analysts.

Conflicts of interest pose another potential threat to the quality of financial reports. Conflicts of interest arise when what is good for one party (for example, management) isn't necessarily good for another party (say, lenders or outside investors). Take the case of Adelphia Communications, a provider of cable entertainment and communication services. In March 2002, Adelphia revealed for the first time the existence of $2.6 billion in previously unreported off-balance-sheet liabilities. Over the next several months, lenders and investors learned that Adelphia's top executives—including the company's founder and his family members—had deliberately shifted bank loans totaling $2.6 billion from Adelphia's books to the books of unconsolidated affiliates controlled by the family. What happened to the $2.6 billion that was originally borrowed? Family members used it to buy Adelphia stock, construct a golf course, pay off personal loans, and purchase luxury condominiums in Colorado, Mexico, and New York City—uses unrelated to the original business purpose of the bank loans. By June 2002, Adelphia and more than 200 of its subsidiaries and affiliates had filed for bankruptcy.

When related-party transactions occur, GAAP requires companies to disclose the nature of the relationship, provide a description of the transactions, and report the dollar amount of the transactions and any amounts due to or from related parties. A high level of disclosure is required because related-party transactions do not result from "arm's-length" negotiations between independent parties in a competitive marketplace. See FASB Accounting Standards Codification Topic 850: Related-Party Disclosures.

Companies have an obligation to disclose business transactions that involve potential conflicts of interest. Adelphia concealed from lenders and investors that billions of dollars had been given to affiliates controlled by the founder's family and how the money was being spent. Adelphia violated GAAP by systematically hiding the debt on the books of the affiliates. The company also violated Securities and Exchange Commission (SEC) guidelines by reporting misleading information. Lenders and investors were caught unaware.

 **RECAP**

The message here is simply that analysts must always be vigilant about the possibility that accounting distortions are present and complicate the interpretation of financial ratios, percentage relations, and trend indices. That's why each chapter of this book alerts you to potential accounting distortions and then shows you how to eliminate those distortions. Only then can you reliably assess a company's profitability and credit risk. So, remember that the first step to informed financial statement analysis is a careful evaluation of the quality of the company's reported accounting numbers. No tool of financial statement analysis is completely immune to distortions caused by GAAP or by management's reporting choices.

A CASE IN POINT: GETTING BEHIND THE NUMBERS AT WHOLE FOODS MARKET

In 1978, twenty-five year old college dropout John Mackey and twenty-one year old Rene Lawson Hardy, borrowed $45,000 from family and friends to open the doors of a small natural foods store called SaferWay in Austin, Texas (the name being a spoof of Safeway, which operated grocery stores under their own name in Austin at that time). When the couple got booted out of their apartment for storing food products there, they decided to simply live at the store. Since it was zoned commercial, there was no shower stall. Instead, they bathed in the Hobart dishwasher, which had an attached water hose.

Two years later, John and Rene partnered with Craig Weller and Mark Skiles to merge SaferWay with their Clarksville Natural Grocery, resulting in the opening of the original Whole Foods Market on September 20, 1980.[2]

Natural and organic food is one of the fastest growing segments of food retailing today, and Whole Foods Market is the dominant player with 335 stores in the United States, Canada, and the United Kingdom as of September 30, 2012. The company's stores offer an extensive selection of high-quality food products that promote a healthy lifestyle, and high levels of customer service. Flagship Whole Foods stores combine an old-fashioned neighborhood grocery with an organic farmers' market, a European bakery, a New York deli, and a modern supermarket.[3] Patrons select from among more than 30,000 natural and organic items that include an extensive selection of fruits, vegetables, cheese, fish, and seafood as well as meat and poultry. Perishable foods account for about 67% of sales.

Because competition in the grocery business is local, each Whole Foods store offers a customized product mix. For example, the Austin, Texas, store carries products from small local producers and vendors—from salsas to tofu to tabbouleh to humus, to hundreds of other items

---

[2] Whole Foods Market, Inc., corporate website.

[3] In addition to its signature banner, the company also operates stores under the trade names of Bread & Circus, Fresh Fields, Wellspring Grocery, Merchant of Vino, and Wild Oats Markets, among others.

unique to that store. Some stores also offer special services such as massage, valet parking, and home delivery. The retail stores are supported by regional offices and distribution centers, bake house facilities, commissary kitchens, seafood processing facilities, produce procurement centers, a national meat purchasing office, a confectionary, and a specialty coffee and tea procurement and brewing operation.

New store openings, acquisitions of competitors, and organic growth—more customers spending more dollars at existing stores—have all contributed to the company's rapid growth. Sales increased at a 26% compound annual growth rate between 1991 and 2012. Sales in 2012 were $11.7 billion, up 15.7% from 2011. Net income in 2012 was $466 million, up almost 36% from 2011, and operating cash flows were strong at $920 million.

Food retailing was once an intensely personalized business. People bought food directly from local farmers or neighborhood shops. Owners of the early mom-and-pop stores often lived in the same neighborhood where their businesses were located. They were "close to the customer" and knew their customers' names and ages, where they lived and worked, and their grocery likes and dislikes. In the 1950s, large numbers of people began to migrate from cities to suburbs. Merchants followed them, leading to explosive growth in shopping centers and, eventually, to the formation of giant grocery chains. Large supermarkets came to dominate the retail landscape.

Today, retail grocery chains act as intermediaries, bringing producers and consumers together. They buy products from many suppliers and transport those products to retail stores where customers can choose among them. Store hours are often long to suit the varying schedules of a complex society.

The grocery industry remains one of the most fragmented U.S. retail sectors. According to *Progressive Grocer,* the grocery industry had 2011 sales of $584 billion, up 3.8% from 2010. According to Plunkett Research, which also included nontraditional grocery stores such as wholesale clubs in its definition of the grocery industry, 2011 sales exceeded $1 trillion. And, according to *Supermarket News,* every company in its 2012 "Top 75" achieved sales in excess of $1 billion.

According to *Natural Foods Merchandiser*, 2011 sales within the narrower natural foods product category were $73 billion, a 10% increase over 2010. Whole Foods attributes this growth to heightened awareness of healthy eating, a better-educated and aging population, and increasing concerns for food safety and the environment. However, grocery retailing has always been a low-margin business, characterized by intense price competition. As a result, cost control is imperative in the industry.

Now that you have an understanding of the business and the industry—an essential starting point for financial statement analysis—let's take a look at Whole Foods' financial statements.

Examining Whole Foods Market's Financial Statements

Exhibit 5.1 provides comparative income statements for Whole Foods Market. It shows that sales increased from $8.0 billion in 2009 to $11.7 billion in 2012, a compound annual growth rate of 13.4%. These figures reflect revenue from natural and organic grocery products and other items sold at the company's retail stores. But sales growth is only part of the story at Whole Foods. Net income also grew over this period, from $147 million to $466 million.

Cause-of-Change Analysis   There are many reasons why Whole Foods' net income grew so much from 2009 to 2012. As we have already seen, sales were up over the period. But Whole Foods' operating margin (operating income divided by sales) was higher as well. And, Whole Foods' effective income tax rate (income tax provision divided by income before income taxes) was lower. To what extent did each of these components account for the net income change?

EXHIBIT 5.1	Whole Foods Market			

Comparative Income Statements

($ in thousands)	2012	2011	2010	2009
Sales	$11,698,828	$10,107,787	$9,005,794	$8,031,620
Cost of goods sold and occupancy costs	7,543,054	6,571,238	5,869,519	5,276,493
Gross profit	4,155,774	3,536,549	3,136,275	2,755,127
Direct store expenses	2,983,419	2,628,811	2,376,590	2,146,626
General and administrative expenses	372,065	310,920	272,449	243,749
Pre-opening expenses	46,899	40,852	38,044	49,218
Relocation, store closure and lease termination costs	9,885	8,346	11,217	31,185
Operating income	743,506	547,620	437,975	284,349
Interest expense	(354)	(3,882)	(33,048)	(36,856)
Investment and other income	8,892	7,974	6,854	3,449
Income before income taxes	752,044	551,712	411,781	250,942
Provision for income taxes	286,471	209,100	165,948	104,138
Net income	$ 465,573	$ 342,612	$ 245,833	$ 146,804

One way to quantify the components of change is with a "cause-of-change analysis." The idea is to show the effects of individual changes on the change in net income. We do this by creating a simple model that describes net income and then by changing one component of the model at a time from the 2009 value to the 2012 value. With each change, we observe the effect on net income until we have changed every component of the model from the 2009 value to the 2012 value.

Here is the model we will use:

$$\text{Operating income} = \text{Sales} \times \text{Operating margin }\%$$

$$\text{Income before income taxes} = \text{Operating income} + \text{Interest and investment income (expense), net}$$

$$\text{Net income} = \text{Income before income taxes} \times (1 - \text{Effective income tax rate})$$

Using this model, we can describe 2009 and 2012 net income as shown in Exhibit 5.2. Note that this is not a traditional income statement. Rather, it shows a computation of net income based on the inputs to the model we have developed.

EXHIBIT 5.2	Whole Foods Market	

Simple Financial Model Representation of Net Income

($ in thousands)	2009	2012
Sales	$8,031,620	$11,698,828
× Operating margin %	3.540369%	6.355389%
Operating income	284,349	743,506
Interest and investment income (expense), net	(33,407)	8,538
Income before income taxes	250,942	752,044
× [1 − effective income tax rate]	0.585012	0.619077
Net income	$ 146,804	$ 465,573

EXHIBIT 5.3	Whole Foods Market

Cause-of-Change Analysis

($ in thousands)	2009	Change Sales	Change Margin	Change Int./Inv.	Change Tax Rate
Sales	$8,031,620	$11,698,828	$11,698,828	$11,698,828	$11,698,828
× Operating margin %	3.540369%	3.540369%	6.355389%	6.355389%	6.355389%
Operating income	284,349	414,182	743,506	743,506	743,506
Interest and investment income (expense), net	(33,407)	(33,407)	(33,407)	8,538	8,538
Income before income taxes	250,942	380,775	710,099	752,044	752,044
× [1 − effective income tax rate]	0.585012	0.585012	0.585012	0.585012	0.619077
Net income	$ 146,804	$ 222,758	$ 415,416	$ 439,955	$ 465,573
Effect of change		$ 75,954	$ 192,658	$ 24,538	$ 25,618

Cause-of-Change Analysis:

2009 net income	$ 146,804
Effect of sales growth	75,954
Effect of margin expansion	192,658
Effect of change in interest and investment income	24,539
Effect of decrease in income tax rate	25,618
2012 net income	$ 465,573

Now suppose we were to change sales from the 2009 level to the 2012 level, *holding all other inputs to the model constant at the 2009 level*. As the "Change Sales" column of Exhibit 5.3 shows, operating income would be $11,698,828,000 times 3.540369%, or $414,182,000. This is not an actual operating income amount for any period. Rather, it is the hypothetical operating income that would have been achieved if sales had grown as they did, but operating margin percentage remained unchanged. Subtracting 2009 interest and investment expense, net, would give $380,775,000 of income before taxes. Multiplying that amount by one minus the 2009 effective tax rate would result in net income of $222,758,000. In other words, given Whole Foods' roughly $3.7 billion increase in sales, had the company maintained the same operating margin percentage, the same interest and investment income and expense, and the same effective income tax rate, net income would have been about $222.8 million. So, the sales increase from 2009 to 2012 accounted for $76.0 million ($222.8 million minus $146.8 million) of the increase in net income over that period.

Continuing with Exhibit 5.3, we next change the operating margin percentage from its 2009 level to its 2012 level, holding sales constant at the 2012 level of $11.7 billion and all other parameters at their 2009 levels. The resulting additional change is attributable to operating margin expansion. That is, margin expansion accounted for about $193 million of the increase in net income. Then we change the interest and investment income (expense), net and finally the effective income tax rate. When we are done, we will have explained the entirety of the change in net income from 2009 to 2012.

Cause-of-change analysis is a useful tool because it allows us to understand which factors most influenced the change in net income. Despite Whole Foods' excellent sales growth over the three-year period, only about 24% of the increase in net income was a direct result of sales growth. About 60% of the profit increase was attributable to operating margin expansion, with the remainder due to changes in interest and investment income and a decline in the effective income tax rate. A forecaster might use this information and, believing that substantial additional margin expansion is unlikely, temper earnings growth forecasts for future years to be more in line with growth rates in sales.

Note that a cause-of-change analysis is not just a simple line-by-line comparison of income statement amounts in two years. We determined the effect of sales growth by considering all the other income statement changes that would follow naturally from an increase in sales. That is, operating earnings would increase when sales increase, but not dollar-for-dollar due to the increased operating costs and income tax provision that would go hand in hand with a sales increase.

Common-Size and Trend Analysis Income Statements

Financial analysts use common-size and trend statements of net income to help spot changes in a company's cost structure and profit performance. **Common-size income statements** (top of Exhibit 5.4) recast each statement item as a percentage of sales. Common-size income statements show you how much of each sales dollar the company spent on operating expenses and other business costs and how much of each sales dollar hit the bottom line as profit. For example, Whole Foods Market's direct store expenses for 2012 are shown as 25.5% of 2012 sales ($25.5\% = \$2,983,419$ direct store expenses$_{2012}$/$\$11,698,828$ sales$_{2012}$) instead of the dollar amount. This means 25.5 cents of each 2012 sales dollar was spent on direct store costs. That leaves 74.5 cents of each 2012 sales dollar to cover the wholesale cost of grocery products sold and other business costs and to provide a profit for the year.

The trend statements (bottom of Exhibit 5.4) also recast each statement item in percentage terms, but they do so using a base year number rather than sales. Trend statements help you spot increases and decreases over time in each income statement item. For instance, the trend statements of income show Whole Foods Market's 2012 net income as 317.1% of base year 2009 net income. This means net income in 2012 was more than three times what it was in 2009 ($465.6 million versus $146.8 million). The trend statements of income also show 2012 sales were 145.7% of base year 2009 sales, which translates into a 45.7% cumulative rate of sales growth over three years.

The common-size and trend statements of net income reveal several interesting aspects of the company's profit performance:

- The trend statements indicate that sales increased substantially over the three-year period and that this growth occurred roughly evenly across the three years.

- The trend statements also indicate that net income growth greatly exceeded sales growth. These results are consistent with the margin expansion we quantified in the cause-of-change analysis.

- According to the common-size statements, over time there were only small fluctuations in operating expense items such as direct store expenses, and cost of goods sold and occupancy costs. But in the low margin grocery business, these small fluctuations can have a large effect on profit margins. The main reasons net income jumped to 4.0% of sales in 2012 from 1.8% in 2009 were the 1.2 percentage-point decreases in both cost of goods sold and occupancy costs and direct store expenses. While a 2.2 percentage point increase in profit margin may seem small, the result was that net income, as a percent of sales, more than doubled.

The trend statements show that sales increased 45.7% over three years. What factors contributed to this growth? Whole Foods' Form 10-K discloses information about the number of stores open at the beginning and end of each year. We can use this information to understand

EXHIBIT 5.4 Whole Foods Market

Common-Size and Trend Analysis of Income

Common-Size Statements

(% of sales)	2012	2011	2010	2009
Sales	100.0%	100.0%	100.0%	100.0%
Cost of goods sold and occupancy costs	64.5	65.0	65.2	65.7
Gross profit	35.5	35.0	34.8	34.3
Direct store expenses	25.5	26.0	26.4	26.7
General and administrative expenses	3.2	3.1	3.0	3.0
Pre-opening expenses	0.4	0.4	0.4	0.6
Relocation, store closure and lease termination costs	0.1	0.1	0.1	0.4
Operating income	6.4	5.4	4.9	3.5
Interest expense	(0.0)	(0.0)	(0.4)	(0.5)
Investment and other income	0.1	0.1	0.1	0.0
Income before income taxes	6.4	5.5	4.6	3.1
Provision for income taxes	2.4	2.1	1.8	1.3
Net income	4.0%	3.4%	2.7%	1.8%

Trend Statements (2009 = 100%)

(% of sales)	2012	2011	2010	2009
Sales	145.7%	125.8%	112.1%	100.0%
Cost of goods sold and occupancy costs	143.0	124.5	111.2	100.0
Gross profit	150.8	128.4	113.8	100.0
Direct store expenses	139.0	122.5	110.7	100.0
General and administrative expenses	152.6	127.6	111.8	100.0
Pre-opening expenses	95.3	83.0	77.3	100.0
Relocation, store closure and lease termination costs	31.7	26.8	36.0	100.0
Operating income	261.5	192.6	154.0	100.0
Interest expense	1.0	10.5	89.7	100.0
Investment and other income	257.8	231.2	198.7	100.0
Income before income taxes	299.7	219.9	164.1	100.0
Provision for income taxes	275.1	200.8	159.4	100.0
Net income	317.1%	233.4%	167.5%	100.0%

Note: Percentages are rounded.

better the extent to which the sales growth has been driven by additional stores or by growth in sales per store. Exhibit 5.5 indicates the number of stores open at the beginning and end of each year since 2009. Assuming that store openings occur approximately evenly throughout the year, we can estimate the average number of stores open during each year by taking a simple average of the beginning and ending numbers. We can then compute average sales per store. The exhibit shows that both the number of stores and the sales per store were growing from 2009 to 2012. From the beginning of 2009 to the end of 2012, Whole Foods added 60 new stores (335−275), net of closures, a 22% increase in the number of stores open in four years. And, sales per store grew 26%, from $28.7 million to $36.2 million. We can also use a cause-of-change analysis to quantify each of these effects on sales. Exhibit 5.5 shows that $1.25 billion of the increase in sales since 2009 was attributable to new store openings, while $2.42 billion was due to growth in sales per store.

EXHIBIT 5.5   Whole Foods Market

Store Analysis	2012	2011	2010	2009
Stores open at beginning of year	311	299	284	275
Stores open at end of year	335	311	299	284
Average number of stores open during year	323.0	305.0	291.5	279.5
($ in thousands)				
Sales	$11,698,828	$10,107,787	$9,005,794	$8,031,620
Sales per store	$ 36,219	$ 33,140	$ 30,895	$ 28,736
Cause-of-change analysis for sales:				
2009 sales	$ 8,031,620			
Sales growth due to new store openings	1,250,002			
Sales assuming 2009 sales per store and 2012 number of stores(*)	9,281,622			
Sales growth due to increase in sales per store	**2,417,206**			
2012 sales	$11,698,828			

(*) 323.0 x $28,735.671 (unrounded average store sales in 2009)

Common-Size and Trend Analysis Balance Sheets

Exhibit 5.6 shows Whole Foods Market's comparative balance sheets. Historically, the company's assets have been concentrated in the stores themselves, represented by the Property and equipment, Goodwill, and Merchandise inventories accounts. However, due to its strong cash flow in recent years, Whole Foods has built up substantial investments in "available-for-sale" securities, which are discussed in Chapter 16. By the end of fiscal 2012, Whole Foods had accumulated more than $1.3 billion in investments (of which $1.1 billion was classified as current and $0.2 billion was classified as noncurrent). To finance its various operating assets, the company has relied on a combination of vendor payables (in Accounts payable), long-term debt, and common stock along with internally generated resources represented by Retained earnings.

The common-size balance sheets and trend analyses provided in Exhibit 5.7 (Assets) and Exhibit 5.8 (Liabilities and Shareholders' Equity) highlight changes in asset mix and financial structure, respectively. Consider the composition of Whole Foods' assets in 2012. According to the common-size statements in Exhibit 5.7, Property and equipment made up 41.4% of that year's total assets compared to 50.2% in 2009. Exhibit 5.8 provides the liabilities and shareholders' equity sections of the common-size balance sheet and trend analysis. It shows a substantial reduction in the use of debt by Whole Foods, or a "de-levering" of the company, as long-term debt has fallen from 19.5% of total assets in 2009 to 0.4% in 2012. This drop indicates that Whole Foods has paid down debt using its strong operating cash flow. As a result, shareholders' equity has increased from 43.0% of total assets in 2009 to 71.8% in 2012.

Why was there such a large decrease in Property and equipment as a percentage of total assets? Did the company somehow become less capital intensive? And is the decline in Property and equipment somehow related to the de-levering of the company? In a common-size financial statement, all balance sheet items are rescaled so that total assets are shown as 100.0. So, a decrease in Property and equipment must correspond to an increase in some other asset. We see that other asset is the available-for-sale securities we mentioned earlier, which grew from zero in 2009 to 25.6% of total assets in 2012. The company did not really become less capital intensive. In fact, Property and equipment

EXHIBIT 5.6	Whole Foods Market

Comparative Balance Sheets

($ in thousands)	2012	2011	2010	2009
Assets				
Current assets:				
Cash and cash equivalents	$ 89,016	$ 212,004	$ 131,996	$ 430,130
Short-term investments—available for sale securities	1,131,213	442,320	329,738	
Restricted cash	102,873	91,956	86,802	71,023
Accounts receivable	196,503	175,310	133,346	104,731
Merchandise inventories	374,269	336,799	323,487	310,602
Prepaid expenses and other current assets	76,511	73,579	54,686	51,137
Deferred income taxes	132,246	121,176	101,464	87,757
Total current assets	2,102,631	1,453,144	1,161,519	1,055,380
Property and equipment, net	2,192,683	1,997,212	1,886,130	1,897,853
Long-term investments—available for sale securities	221,426	52,815	96,146	
Goodwill	662,938	662,938	665,224	658,254
Intangible assets, net	62,399	67,234	69,064	73,035
Deferred income taxes	42,834	50,148	99,156	91,000
Other assets	9,305	8,584	9,301	7,866
Total assets	$5,294,216	$4,292,075	$3,986,540	$3,783,388
Liabilities and Shareholders' Equity				
Current liabilities:				
Current installments of long-term debt and capital lease obligations	$ 1,012	$ 466	$ 410	$ 389
Accounts payable	247,089	236,913	213,212	189,597
Accrued payroll, bonus and other benefits due team members	307,164	281,587	244,427	207,983
Dividends payable	25,959	17,827		8,217
Other current liabilities	395,964	342,568	289,823	277,838
Total current liabilities	977,188	879,361	747,872	684,024
Long-term debt and capital lease obligations, less current installments	23,110	17,439	508,288	738,848
Deferred lease liabilities	440,822	353,776	294,291	250,326
Other long-term liabilities	50,627	50,194	62,831	69,262
Total liabilities	1,491,747	1,300,770	1,613,282	1,742,460
Series A redeemable preferred stock				413,052
Shareholders' Equity:				
Common stock, no par value	2,592,369	2,120,972	1,773,897	1,283,028
Common stock in treasury, at cost	(28,599)			
Accumulated other comprehensive income (loss)	5,266	(164)	791	(13,367)
Retained earnings	1,233,433	870,497	598,570	358,215
Total shareholders' equity	3,802,469	2,991,305	2,373,258	1,627,876
Total liabilities and shareholders' equity	$5,294,216	$4,292,075	$3,986,540	$3,783,388

grew by 15.5% from 2009 to 2012 (2012 balance is 115.5% of the 2009 balance, from Exhibit 5.7 trend analysis). Property and equipment is a smaller portion of total assets because cash generated by operations has been used to purchase investments rather than distributed to shareholders, thus inflating the level of total assets beyond what Whole Foods requires to operate its business. Had Whole Foods declared larger dividends or repurchased stock rather than making these investments, Property and equipment would have been 55.6% of total assets [41.4/(100.0 − (21.4 + 4.2))], an increase from the 50.2%

EXHIBIT 5.7	Whole Foods Market

Common-Size and Trend Analysis of Assets

(% of total assets)	2012	2011	2010	2009
Assets				
Current assets:				
Cash and cash equivalents	1.7%	4.9%	3.3%	11.4%
Short-term investments—available for sale securities	21.4	10.3	8.3	0.0
Restricted cash	1.9	2.1	2.2	1.9
Accounts receivable	3.7	4.1	3.3	2.8
Merchandise inventories	7.1	7.8	8.1	8.2
Prepaid expenses and other current assets	1.4	1.7	1.4	1.4
Deferred income taxes	2.5	2.8	2.5	2.3
Total current assets	39.7	33.9	29.1	27.9
Property and equipment, net	41.4	46.5	47.3	50.2
Long-term investments—available for sale securities	4.2	1.2	2.4	0.0
Goodwill	12.5	15.4	16.7	17.4
Intangible assets, net	1.2	1.6	1.7	1.9
Deferred income taxes	0.8	1.2	2.5	2.4
Other assets	0.2	0.2	0.2	0.2
Total assets	100.0%	100.0%	100.0%	100.0%

Trend Statements (2009 = 100%)

	2012	2011	2010	2009
Assets				
Current assets:				
Cash and cash equivalents	20.7%	49.3%	30.7%	100.0%
Short-term investments—available for sale securities	—	—	—	—
Restricted cash	144.8	129.5	122.2	100.0
Accounts receivable	187.6	167.4	127.3	100.0
Merchandise inventories	120.5	108.4	104.1	100.0
Prepaid expenses and other current assets	149.6	143.9	106.9	100.0
Deferred income taxes	150.7	138.1	115.6	100.0
Total current assets	199.2	137.7	110.1	100.0
Property and equipment, net	115.5	105.2	99.4	100.0
Long-term investments—available for sale securities	—	—	—	—
Goodwill	100.7	100.7	101.1	100.0
Intangible assets, net	85.4	92.1	94.6	100.0
Deferred income taxes	47.1	55.1	109.0	100.0
Other assets	118.3	109.1	118.2	100.0
Total assets	139.9%	113.4%	105.4%	100.0%

Note: Percentages are rounded. The — denotes a trend percentage that cannot be computed because the 2009 base-year value is zero.

reported in 2009. In fact, other than the effects of the large increase in investments held, Whole Foods' 2012 asset mix was similar to what it was in 2009.

For the reason illustrated above, many analysts think of investments that are not integral to the company's core business operations as "negative debt," and when such investments are substantial, that treatment does give a better sense for how the mix of operating assets might have changed over time. This treatment would result in the common-size balance sheets

EXHIBIT 5.8 **Whole Foods Market**

Common-Size and Trend Analysis of Liabilities and Shareholders' Equity

Common-Size Statements

(% of total assets)	2012	2011	2010	2009
Liabilities and Shareholders' Equity				
Current liabilities:				
Current installments of long-term debt and capital lease obligations	0.0%	0.0%	0.0%	0.0%
Accounts payable	4.7	5.5	5.3	5.0
Accrued payroll, bonus and other benefits due team members	5.8	6.6	6.1	5.5
Dividends payable	0.5	0.4	0.0	0.2
Other current liabilities	7.5	8.0	7.3	7.3
Total current liabilities	18.5	20.5	18.8	18.1
Long-term debt and capital lease obligations, less current installments	0.4	0.4	12.8	19.5
Deferred lease liabilities	8.3	8.2	7.4	6.6
Other long-term liabilities	1.0	1.2	1.6	1.8
Total liabilities	28.2	30.3	40.5	46.1
Series A redeemable preferred stock	0.0	0.0	0.0	10.9
Shareholders' Equity:	0.0	0.0	0.0	0.0
Common stock, no par value	49.0	49.4	44.5	33.9
Common stock in treasury, at cost	(0.5)	0.0	0.0	0.0
Accumulated other comprehensive income (loss)	0.1	(0.0)	0.0	(0.4)
Retained earnings	23.3	20.3	15.0	9.5
Total shareholders' equity	71.8	69.7	59.5	43.0
Total liabilities and shareholders' equity	100.0%	100.0%	100.0%	100.0%

Trend Statements (2009 = 100%)

	2012	2011	2010	2009
Liabilities and Shareholders' Equity				
Current liabilities:				
Current installments of long-term debt and capital lease obligations	260.2%	119.8%	105.4%	100.0%
Accounts payable	130.3	125.0	112.5	100.0
Accrued payroll, bonus and other benefits due team members	147.7	135.4	117.5	100.0
Dividends payable	315.9	217.0	0.0	100.0
Other current liabilities	142.5	123.3	104.3	100.0
Total current liabilities	142.9	128.6	109.3	100.0
Long-term debt and capital lease obligations, less current installments	3.1	2.4	68.8	100.0
Deferred lease liabilities	176.1	141.3	117.6	100.0
Other long-term liabilities	73.1	72.5	90.7	100.0
Total liabilities	85.6	74.7	92.6	100.0
Series A redeemable preferred stock	0.0	0.0	0.0	100.0
Shareholders' Equity:				
Common stock, no par value	202.1	165.3	138.3	100.0
Common stock in treasury, at cost	—	—	—	—
Accumulated other comprehensive income (loss)	(39.4)	1.2	(5.9)	100.0
Retained earnings	344.3	243.0	167.1	100.0
Total shareholders' equity	233.6	183.8	145.8	100.0
Total liabilities and shareholders' equity	139.9%	113.4%	105.4%	100.0%

Note: Percentages are rounded. The — denotes a trend percentage that cannot be computed because the 2006 base year value is zero.

provided in Exhibit 5.9. When we treat the investments as negative debt, we see that Property and equipment has actually grown in terms of percentage of assets and most other asset categories have remained relatively stable. We also see that Whole Foods has greatly de-levered since 2009 and it is now in a position where nearly all its liabilities could be satisfied simply by liquidating its noncore investments. When viewed this way, virtually all of the company's financing is now coming from equity.

Note that no values were shown in the trend analysis for the available-for-sale investments (Exhibit 5.7). Because there were no such investments in 2009, the base year for the analysis, it is not possible to compute the trend data for that item. It is also possible that a base year could have a nonzero, but very small, amount for a particular item. When that is the case, the values in the trend analysis may be unusually large. For example, Whole Foods reported $2.252 million in cash on its

---

EXHIBIT 5.9	Whole Foods Market

Common-Size Balance Sheets with Investments Treated as "Negative Debt"

(% of total assets)	2012	2011	2010	2009
Assets				
Current assets:				
Cash and cash equivalents	2.3%	5.6%	3.7%	11.4%
Restricted cash	2.6	2.4	2.4	1.9
Accounts receivable	5.0	4.6	3.7	2.8
Merchandise inventories	9.5	8.9	9.1	8.2
Prepaid expenses and other current assets	1.9	1.9	1.5	1.4
Deferred income taxes	3.4	3.2	2.8	2.3
Total current assets	24.6	26.6	23.4	27.9
Property and equipment, net	55.6	52.6	53.0	50.2
Goodwill	16.8	17.5	18.7	17.4
Intangible assets, net	1.6	1.8	1.9	1.9
Deferred income taxes	1.1	1.3	2.8	2.4
Other assets	0.2	0.2	0.3	0.2
Total assets	100.0%	100.0%	100.0%	100.0%
Liabilities and Shareholders' Equity				
Current liabilities:				
Current installments of long-term debt and capital lease obligations	0.0%	0.0%	0.0%	0.0%
Accounts payable	6.3	6.2	6.0	5.0
Accrued payroll, bonus and other benefits due team members	7.8	7.4	6.9	5.5
Dividends payable	0.7	0.5	0.0	0.2
Other current liabilities	10.0	9.0	8.1	7.3
Total current liabilities	24.8	23.2	21.0	18.1
Long-term debt and capital lease obligations, less current installments	0.6	0.5	14.3	19.5
Available for sale securities (negative debt)	(34.3)	(13.0)	(12.0)	0.0
Deferred lease liabilities	11.2	9.3	8.3	6.6
Other long-term liabilities	1.3	1.3	1.8	1.8
Total liabilities	3.5	21.2	33.3	46.1
Series A redeemable preferred stock	0.0	0.0	0.0	10.9
Shareholders' Equity:				
Common stock, no par value	65.8	55.9	49.8	33.9
Common stock in treasury, at cost	(0.7)	0.0	0.0	0.0
Accumulated other comprehensive income (loss)	0.1	(0.0)	0.0	(0.4)
Retained earnings	31.3	22.9	16.8	9.5
Total shareholders' equity	96.5	78.8	66.7	43.0
Total liabilities and shareholders' equity	100.0%	100.0%	100.0%	100.0%

balance sheet at the end of fiscal 2006, which was an unusually low amount relative to most years. In 2009 it reported $430.130 million in cash. A trend analysis using 2006 as a base year would report the 2009 value as being 19,099.9% of the base year amount. So, a trend analysis helps you spot changes over time, but these changes could be because the base year is an aberration.

Common-Size and Trend Analysis Cash Flow Statements   Exhibit 5.10

provides comparative cash flow statements. Some line items are combined for the sake of brevity. Common-size statements and trends for selected line items are in Exhibit 5.11. The common-size statements are constructed by dividing each cash flow item by sales for the year. For example, Whole Foods Market's operating activities generated $919.7 million cash (Exhibit 5.10) in 2012, or 7.9% (Exhibit 5.11) of $11.7 billion in sales that year, up from 7.3% in 2009 (Exhibit 5.11).

How does Whole Foods use these operating cash flows? Like most growing retail companies, it devotes some financial resources to expanding the store base. Therefore, a major use of its cash went for new store location development costs and capital expenditures for property, plant, and equipment. These two activities used $456.2 million ($261.7 + $194.5 from Exhibit 5.10) in 2012, or 3.9 cents per sales dollar (2.2% + 1.7% from Exhibit 5.11). Notice that the cash generated that year by operating activities (7.9 cents per sales dollar) was more than enough to fund retail store expansion. This fact is largely what enabled Whole Foods to purchase the available-for-sale securities it built up over the last three years.

EXHIBIT 5.10	Whole Foods Market			

Comparative Cash Flow Statements

($ in thousands)	2012	2011	2010	2009
Net income	$ 465,573	$ 342,612	$ 245,833	$ 146,804
Adjustments to reconcile net income to net				
cash provided by operating activities	454,142	412,233	339,452	440,917
Net cash provided by operating activities	919,715	754,845	585,285	587,721
Development costs of new locations	(261,710)	(203,457)	(171,379)	(247,999)
Other property and equipment expenditures	(194,539)	(161,507)	(85,414)	(66,616)
Purchases of available for sale securities	(3,009,503)	(1,228,920)	(1,072,243)	
Sales and maturities of available for sale securities	2,138,221	1,155,795	646,594	
Increase in restricted cash	(10,917)	(5,154)	(15,779)	(70,406)
Payment for purchase of acquired entities,				
net of cash acquired		(1,972)	(14,470)	
Other investing activities	(2,901)	(5,509)	(2,715)	(1,262)
Net cash used in investing activities	(1,341,349)	(450,724)	(715,406)	(386,283)
Common stock dividends paid	(94,505)	(52,620)		
Preferred stock dividends paid			(8,500)	(19,833)
Issuance of common stock	370,226	296,719	46,962	4,286
Purchase of treasury stock	(28,599)			
Issuance of redeemable preferred stock				413,052
Proceeds from long-term borrowing				123,000
Excess tax benefit related to exercise of team				
member stock options	50,349	22,741	2,982	
Payments on long-term debt and capital lease obligations	(305)	(490,394)	(210,350)	(318,370)
Other				(2,680)
Net cash provided by (used in) financing activities	297,166	(223,554)	(168,906)	199,455
Effect of exchange rate changes on cash and cash equivalents	1,480	(559)	893	(1,297)
Net change in cash and cash equivalents	$ (122,988)	$ 80,008	$ (298,134)	$ 399,596

EXHIBIT 5.11   Whole Foods Market

Common-Size and Trend Analysis of Selected Cash Flow Items

Common-Size Statements

(% of sales)	2012	2011	2010	2009
Selected Items				
Net cash provided by operating activities	7.9%	7.5%	6.5%	7.3%
Development costs of new locations	(2.2)	(2.0)	(1.9)	(3.1)
Other property and equipment expenditures	(1.7)	(1.6)	(0.9)	(0.8)

Trend Statements (2009 = 100%)

	2012	2011	2010	2009
Selected Items				
Net cash provided by operating activities	156.5%	128.4%	99.6%	100.0%
Development costs of new store locations	105.5	82.0	69.1	100.0
Other property and equipment expenditures	292.0	242.4	128.2	100.0

But this was not always the situation. Back in 2007, cash generated by operating activities was 5.9 cents per sales dollar, which was insufficient to fund retail store expansion of 8.0 cents per sales dollar. Also in that year, Whole Foods paid $596 million to acquire Wild Oats Markets. Where did Whole Foods find the cash in 2007 to fund its retail store expansion, the Wild Oats acquisition, and a dividend payment? Some of the funds came from issuing common stock ($54.4 million) and some from liquidating short-term investments ($198.3 million), but the bulk of it was provided by the issuance of long-term debt ($717.0 million).

The years 2012 and 2007 illustrate the nature of the cash flows in various sections of the cash flow statement and how they interact. The financing section, as well as purchases and sales of noncore investments in the investing section, are largely "facilitating transactions." These transactions facilitate the needs of the core business operations. A company whose operating cash flow, net of reinvestment requirements such as store expansion, is positive, must redeploy its funds, and it will do so by some combination of dividends, debt repayments, stock repurchases, and purchases of noncore investments. That is what Whole Foods did in 2012. In contrast, when a firm's cash flow from operations, net of reinvestment requirements, is negative, the firm must obtain the necessary funds to offset the negative cash flow. It does so by a combination of debt issuances, stock issuances, and sales of noncore investments. That is what Whole Foods did in 2007. The end result is often that there is little net change in cash from year to year, despite large amounts of cash flow from operations, investing, and financing, as Exhibits 5.10 and 5.11 illustrate.

 RECAP

From our analysis of **Whole Foods Market** and its financial statements, we can come to three conclusions:

- Financial statements help the analyst gain a sharper understanding of the company's economic condition and its prospects for the future.

- Informed financial statement analysis begins with knowledge of the company and its industry.

- Cause-of-change analysis helps identify the various reasons a particular quantity, such as net income, changed from one period to another.

- Common-size and trend statements provide a convenient way to organize financial statement information so that major financial components and changes can be easily recognized.

PROFITABILITY, COMPETITION, AND BUSINESS STRATEGY

"The mechanics of running a business are not really very complicated when you get down to essentials. You have to make some stuff and sell it to somebody for more than it cost you. That's about all there is, except for a few million details."

—John L. McCaffey

Financial Ratios and Profitability Analysis

Financial ratios provide other powerful tools analysts use to evaluate profit performance and to assess credit risk. Most evaluations of profit performance begin with the **return on assets (ROA)** ratio,

$$ROA = \frac{\text{Earnings before interest (EBI)}}{\text{Average assets}}$$

where *EBI* refers to the company's *earnings before interest* for a particular period (such as a year), and *average assets* represents the average book value of total assets over that same time period. Before computing ROA, analysts may adjust the company's reported earnings and asset figures. These adjustments fall into three broad categories:

1. Adjustments aimed at *isolating a company's sustainable profits* by removing nonrecurring items—analysts sometimes call these "special" items—from reported income.
2. An adjustment that *eliminates after-tax interest expense* from the profit calculation so that profitability comparisons over time or across companies are not affected by differences in financial structure.[4]
3. Adjustments for *distortions related to accounting quality concerns,* which involve potential adjustments to both earnings and assets for items such as LIFO liquidations and off-balance-sheet operating leases, which were mentioned earlier.

Exhibit 5.12 summarizes the ROA calculations for Whole Foods using the company's earnings and balance sheet information from Exhibits 5.1 and 5.6. The adjustments made to reported earnings each year eliminate interest expense ($354 thousand in 2012) on an after-tax basis. ROA for 2012 thus becomes:

$$ROA_{2012} = \frac{\text{Net income} + \text{Interest expense} \times (1 - \text{Tax rate})}{\text{Average assets}}$$

$$= \frac{\$465,573 + [\$354 \times (1 - 0.40)]}{(\$5,294,216 + \$4,292,075)/2} = 0.097 \text{ or } 9.7\%$$

Whole Foods' ROA grew from 4.7% in 2009 to 9.7% in 2012. Here's why:

Analysts sometimes make income statement and balance sheet adjustments intended to isolate core operating activities—think of selling grocery products at Whole Foods Market—from nonoperating activities. The resulting profit performance measure is return on operating net assets, or RONA. Whole Foods Market's short-term investments and the income produced by those investments would not be included in a RONA computation.

Accounting quality adjustments are ignored for brevity because the underlying details are not described until later chapters.

---

[4] Later in this chapter we illustrate how financial leverage affects profitability measures that do not exclude interest and debt as the ROA calculation does.

EXHIBIT 5.12   **Whole Foods Market**

Return on Assets

	2012	2011	2010	2009
Net income as reported	$ 465,573	$ 342,612	$ 245,833	$ 146,804
Interest expense (after tax)	212	2,329	19,829	22,114
Earnings before interest (EBI)	$ 465,785	$ 344,941	$ 265,662	$ 168,918
Assets at end of year	$5,294,216	$4,292,075	$3,986,540	$3,783,388
Assets at beginning of year	4,292,075	3,986,540	3,783,388	3,380,736
Average assets	$4,793,146	$4,139,308	$3,884,964	$3,582,062
Return on assets (EBI/Average assets)	9.7%	8.3%	6.8%	4.7%

Note: An estimated marginal income tax rate of 40% is used to compute the after-tax effect of interest expense.

A company can increase its ROA in two ways:

1. By increasing the profit margin. For example, a large manufacturing company might use its bargaining power to negotiate price reductions from raw material suppliers, increasing the company's profit margin.

2. By increasing the intensity of asset utilization. For example, a restaurant that was previously open only for lunch and dinner might decide to stay open 24 hours a day. Doing so would not require substantial additional investment, so the restaurant could generate more sales per dollar invested in restaurant assets, thus yielding an increase in asset utilization.

By disaggregating ROA into profit margin and asset turnover, we can see how each of these elements affects ROA:

$$\text{ROA} = \frac{\text{EBI}}{\text{Average assets}} = \left(\frac{\text{EBI}}{\text{Sales}}\right) \times \left(\frac{\text{Sales}}{\text{Average assets}}\right)$$

$$= \text{Profit margin} \times \text{Asset turnover}$$

Consider a company that earns $9 million of EBI on sales of $100 million and has an average asset base of $50 million. The ROA for this company is:

$$\text{ROA} = \left(\frac{\text{EBI}}{\text{Sales}}\right) \times \left(\frac{\text{Sales}}{\text{Average assets}}\right)$$

$$= \left(\frac{\$9}{\$100}\right) \times \left(\frac{\$100}{\$50}\right) = 0.09 \times 2 = 0.18, \text{ or } 18\%$$

Suppose the firm could increase its profit margin from 9% to 10% through improved pricing or aggressive expense reductions. Sales are unchanged and asset turnover stays at 2, but ROA is now:

$$\text{ROA} = \left(\frac{\text{EBI}}{\text{Sales}}\right) \times \left(\frac{\text{Sales}}{\text{Average assets}}\right)$$

$$= \left(\frac{\$10}{\$100}\right) \times \left(\frac{\$100}{\$50}\right) = 0.10 \times 2 = 0.20, \text{ or } 20\%$$

Alternatively, suppose that management is able to reduce average assets to $45 million without sacrificing any sales. Asset turnover will increase to 2.22, and ROA will rise to 20%:

$$\text{ROA} = \left(\frac{\text{EBI}}{\text{Sales}}\right) \times \left(\frac{\text{Sales}}{\text{Average assets}}\right)$$

$$= \left(\frac{\$9}{\$100}\right) \times \left(\frac{\$100}{\$45}\right) = 0.09 \times 2.22 = 0.20, \text{ or } 20\%$$

In both cases, the firm increased ROA from 18% to 20%, but in different ways.

Exhibit 5.13 extends the ROA analysis of Whole Foods by presenting profit margin and asset turnover figures for each of the four years. Here we learn that the company's increased ROA stems mostly from higher profit margins, although asset turnover increased slightly. The profit margin nearly doubled from 2.1% to 4.0%, while asset turnover increased about 9%, from 2.24 to 2.44. The result was that ROA more than doubled in three years.

Part of the explanation for the increase in Whole Foods Market's profitability over our analysis period is the base year we used: 2009. As the economy slid into recession in late 2007, some of the company's customers began to shop at less expensive grocery stores. This situation coincided with an increased asset base following Whole Foods' acquisition of Wild Oats in 2007. So, relative to the base year, 2012 looks much better. However, if we used a longer time frame, we would get a different picture. For example, in 2006, ROA was 10.3%. It bottomed at 4.1% in 2008 and has climbed steadily ever since. By 2012, Whole Foods' ROA had returned to roughly its prerecession level.

Many analysts find it helpful to decompose ROA further by isolating individual factors that contribute to a company's profit margin and asset turnover. For example, Whole Foods' profit margin can be expressed as:

$$\text{Profit margin} = \frac{\text{EBI}}{\text{Sales}} = \frac{(\text{Sales} - \text{COGS} - \text{OpEx} + \text{Other} - \text{Taxes})}{\text{Sales}}$$

$$= \left(\frac{\text{Sales}}{\text{Sales}}\right) - \left(\frac{\text{COGS}}{\text{Sales}}\right) - \left(\frac{\text{OpEx}}{\text{Sales}}\right) + \left(\frac{\text{Other}}{\text{Sales}}\right) - \left(\frac{\text{Taxes}}{\text{Sales}}\right)$$

$$= 100\% - \left(\frac{\text{COGS}}{\text{Sales}}\right) - \left(\frac{\text{OpEx}}{\text{Sales}}\right) + \left(\frac{\text{Other}}{\text{Sales}}\right) - \left(\frac{\text{Taxes}}{\text{Sales}}\right)$$

EXHIBIT 5.13	Whole Foods Market			

ROA Decomposition

	2012	2011	2010	2009
Sales	$11,698,828	$10,107,787	$9,005,794	$8,031,620
Earnings before interest (Exhibit 5.12)	465,785	344,941	265,662	168,918
Average assets (Exhibit 5.12)	4,793,146	4,139,308	3,884,964	3,582,062
Profit margin (EBI/Sales)	4.0%	3.4%	2.9%	2.1%
Asset turnover (Sales/Average assets)	2.44	2.44	2.32	2.24
ROA = Margin × Asset turnover	9.7%	8.3%	6.8%	4.7%

Note: Amounts are rounded. 9.7% ROA is the product of *unrounded* profit margin and asset turnover amounts.

where, from Exhibit 5.1, *COGS* is the company's cost of goods sold and occupancy costs; *OpEx* is Whole Foods' other operating expenses (direct store expenses, general and administrative expenses, and preopening and relocating costs); *Other* is nonoperating investment and other income, and *Taxes* is *adjusted* income tax expense. (Some income statement items are combined for brevity.) These margin components (which happen to correspond to the common-size income statement items we've already described) can help the analyst identify areas where cost reductions have been achieved or where cost improvements are needed.

It is a bit more complicated to decompose the asset turnover component of ROA because we must disaggregate the denominator of the ratio:

$$
\begin{aligned}
\text{Asset turnover} &= \frac{\text{Sales}}{\text{Average assets}} \\[2mm]
&= \left(\frac{\text{Sales}}{\text{Average current assets} + \text{Average long-term assets}} \right) \\[2mm]
&= \frac{1}{\left(\dfrac{\text{Average current assets}}{\text{Sales}} \right) + \left(\dfrac{\text{Average long-term assets}}{\text{Sales}} \right)} \\[2mm]
&= \frac{1}{\left(\dfrac{1}{\text{Current asset turnover}} \right) + \left(\dfrac{1}{\text{Long-term asset turnover}} \right)}
\end{aligned}
$$

Exhibit 5.14 shows that Whole Foods' modest asset turnover improvement is due to gains in long-term asset turnover, partially offset by reduced current asset turnover. The **current asset turnover** ratio helps the analyst spot efficiency gains from improved accounts receivable and inventory management; the **long-term asset turnover** ratio captures information about property, plant, and equipment utilization. We have much more to say about these and other asset utilization ratios later.

ROA and Competitive Advantage

Our analysis of Whole Foods' profit performance has thus far revealed that the company's ROA for 2012 was 9.7%, up from 4.7% in 2009. This profitability increase was traced to a much higher profit margin and a slightly higher asset turnover. Now we want to know how Whole Foods' profit performance compares with that of other firms in the industry.

> EBI represents earnings before interest but after taxes. Thus, it consists of earnings before interest and taxes (EBIT) less taxes pertaining to EBIT. The taxes pertaining to EBIT, which we call adjusted taxes, are the reported income tax expense plus the income tax effect of the interest expense. Because we use a pretax earnings number that excludes interest, we must use an income tax expense that excludes the tax savings related to that interest expense. Using the information in the Whole Foods' 2012 income statement to illustrate the income tax expense adjustment, we find that adjusted taxes would be $286,612 instead of the reported income tax expense of $286,471. The $141 adjustment is equal to the $354 pretax interest expense that was added back to arrive at EBIT times the estimated marginal income tax rate of 40%.

EXHIBIT 5.14	**Whole Foods Market**			
Asset Turnover Decomposition				
	2012	**2011**	**2010**	**2009**
Sales	11,698,828	10,107,787	9,005,794	8,031,620
Average current assets	1,777,887.5	1,307,331.5	1,108,449.5	838,993.0
Current asset turnover	6.58	7.73	8.12	9.57
Average long-term assets	3,015,258.0	2,831,976.0	2,776,514.5	2,743,069.0
Long-term asset turnover	3.88	3.57	3.24	2.93
Reciprocal of current asset turnover	0.1520	0.1293	0.1231	0.1045
Reciprocal of long-term asset turnover	0.2577	0.2802	0.3083	0.3415
Sum of reciprocals	0.4097	0.4095	0.4314	0.4460
Reciprocal of sum = Asset turnover	2.44	2.44	2.32	2.24

EXHIBIT 5.15	Whole Foods Market and Benchmarks

2012 ROA Decomposition

	Whole Foods Market	SUPERVALU	Grocery Industry
Profit margin (EBI/Sales)	4.0%	(2.0)%	1.9%
Asset turnover (Sales/Average assets)	2.44	2.80	2.39
ROA = Margin × Asset turnover	9.7%	(5.7)%	4.6%

Note: Amounts are rounded. 9.7% ROA is the product of *unrounded* profit margin and asset turnover amounts.

One of Whole Foods' most important direct competitors was Wild Oats Market, a company Whole Foods acquired in 2007. There are no other natural and organic food grocery chains that operate as public companies, so we will instead benchmark Whole Foods' profit performance against that of the traditional grocery chain SUPERVALU.

Exhibit 5.15 presents a decomposition of ROA for Whole Foods and SUPERVALU.[5] Also shown are the average ROA and component values for the industry—grocery stores[6]—to which these two companies belong. Industry data such as these are available from a variety of sources, including Standard & Poor's *Industry Survey,* Robert Morris and Associates' *Annual Statement Studies,* and many online financial information services.

Whole Foods was more profitable than both SUPERVALU and the average grocery chain in 2012, earning an ROA of 9.7% compared to −5.7% for SUPERVALU and 4.6% for the industry. The ROA decomposition reveals that the company's profit margin was 4.0 cents per sales dollar—better than the industry average profit margin of 1.9% and far superior to the −2.0% margin at SUPERVALU. Asset utilization at Whole Foods was, however, only average. It generated $2.44 in sales per asset dollar compared to $2.80 at SUPERVALU and $2.39 for the industry. So, the key to the company's success lay in its profit margin. Whole Foods outperformed the competition by earning a higher profit margin on each sales dollar even though it generated only average sales per asset dollar. Given Whole Foods' strategy, a higher margin with only average turnover is not surprising.

Can Whole Foods maintain this level of performance? This question can be addressed only by identifying the company's competitive advantage—that is, the source of its superior ROA—and determining whether that competitive advantage is sustainable. Several factors can explain why companies operating in the same industry—and therefore confronting similar economic conditions—can earn markedly different rates of return on their assets. Some companies gain a competitive advantage over rivals by developing unique products or services. Others do so by providing consistent quality or exceptional customer service and convenience. Still others excel because of innovative production technologies, distribution channels, or sales and marketing efforts. The sustainability of these advantages, however, varies.

Competition in an industry continually works to drive down the rate of return on assets toward the competitive floor—that is, the rate of return that would be earned in the economist's "perfectly competitive" industry. Companies that consistently earn rates of return above the floor are said to have a **competitive advantage.** However, rates of return that are higher than the industry floor stimulate more competition as existing companies innovate and expand

---

[5] Whole Foods data is for the year ended September 30, 2012, and SUPERVALU data is for the year ended February 25, 2012.

[6] Based on the 4-digit SIC code 5411. Results are for the most recent full year reported by each company.

Figure 5.2

ILLUSTRATION OF HOW
MARGIN AND TURNOVER
AFFECT RETURN ON
ASSETS (ROA)

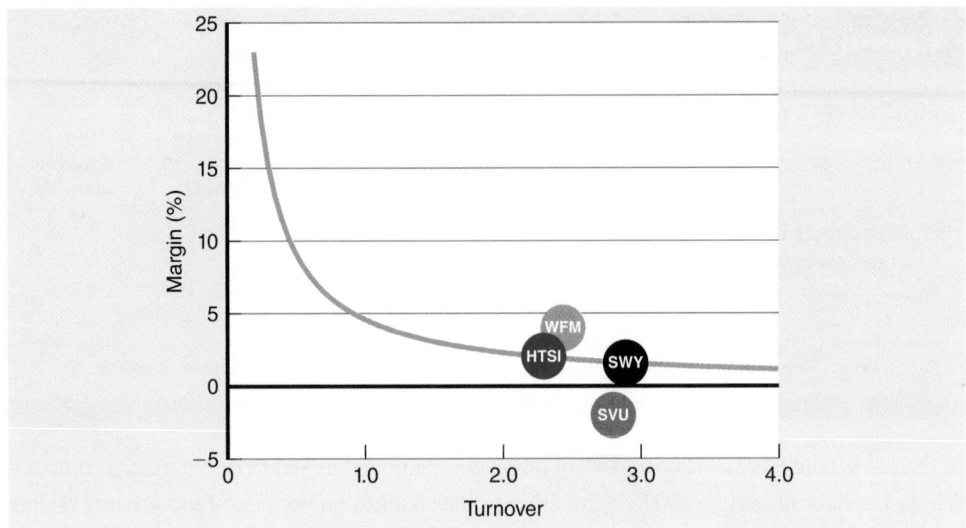

their market reach or as new companies enter the industry. These developments lead to an eventual erosion of profitability and advantage.

To see how these forces work, consider the simplified representation of the grocery industry in Figure 5.2.

The average ROA in the grocery industry is 4.6%, a return that could be earned in many ways. Any point on the curve in Figure 5.2 represents a 4.6% ROA, but different points on the curve achieve that return with a different combination of margin and turnover. For example, Harris Teeter Supermarkets (HTSI) and Safeway, Inc. (SWY) both earned approximately the average industry return of 4.6%. Harris did it with higher margins and lower turnover than Safeway. Whole Foods (WFM) was well above the industry average ROA, while SUPER-VALU (SVU) was well below it.

The competitive advantage Whole Foods now enjoys may not persist. Other groceries with similar formats will attempt to take market share from Whole Foods. In addition, traditional groceries will stock products that compete with Whole Foods' most successful products, moving into Whole Foods' "space" where it is attractive to do so. As rivals become more successful, they will attract sales dollars that would otherwise have gone to Whole Foods, prompting a reduction in Whole Foods' asset turnover, shifting Whole Foods leftward in Figure 5.2 toward the industry average ROA. Of course, Whole Foods' management is unlikely to ignore its rivals' actions. Faced with a threatened loss of competitive advantage, Whole Foods could respond by reducing prices, by increasing advertising expenditures, or by introducing new products, just to name a few possible strategies. These responses could stimulate additional sales and increase asset turnover, causing a shift back to the right. However, price reductions and increased advertising costs lower the company's profit margin, so there would also be a downward shift. Whether a price-reduction strategy was successful would depend on whether the net effect on ROA of the higher turnover and lower margin was positive.

In contrast to Whole Foods, SUPERVALU's challenge is to improve its profit margins. Obviously, a firm cannot stay in business very long when it is operating at a loss, regardless of its asset turnover. The company needs to generate additional sales or contain costs so that it can push itself upward in Figure 5.2, above breakeven and hopefully closer to the industry average ROA. Unless it is able to rectify its profitability problem, the company will be unable to attract additional capital to expand. If the situation continues for an extended period, bankruptcy would also be a possibility.[7]

According to many observers, there are two key strategies for achieving superior performance in any business. One strategy is product and service differentiation, the other is low-cost leadership.[8] A differentiation strategy focuses on "unique" products or services to gain brand loyalty and attractive margins. The idea is simple: People are willing to pay premium prices for things they value and can't get elsewhere.

Differentiation can take several forms. Examples include advanced technology and performance capabilities, consistent quality, availability in multiple colors and sizes, prompt delivery, technical support services, customer financing, distribution channels, or some other feature of importance to customers. A restaurant chain, for example, might focus on superior taste and nutritional benefits when introducing new menu items. Retailers like Bloomingdale's, Neiman Marcus, and Nordstrom achieve differentiation by emphasizing customer service, merchandise quality, and a unique shopping experience.

A low-cost leadership strategy focuses on operating efficiencies, which permit the company to underprice the competition, achieve high sales volumes, and still make a profit on each sale. Companies can attain a low-cost position in various ways. Examples include making quantity discount purchases, having a lean administrative structure, and using production efficiencies from outsourcing or vigorous cost containment. Large retailing companies such as Home Depot are able to negotiate steep quantity discounts with manufacturers because their size gives them more bargaining power; such discounts allow the retailer to offer merchandise to customers at comparatively low prices.

Few companies pursue one strategy to the exclusion of the other. Most companies try to do both—developing customer loyalty while controlling costs. Understanding the relative emphasis a company places on differentiation versus low-cost leadership can be important for competitive analysis. ***Differences in the business strategies companies adopt give rise to economic differences, which are reflected as differences in profit margins, asset utilization, and profitability.*** That is why we cannot look at profit margins or asset turnovers alone as a sign of success. In Figure 5.2 we saw that Harris Teeter and Safeway had similar ROAs with different strategies and therefore different combinations of margin and turnover. Success is measured by distance to the "northeast" away from the average ROA curve, which can be achieved with higher margins or higher turnover. How management chooses to try to move in that direction is based on its assessment of opportunities in the industry and the company's competitive advantage.

Not every company in an industry earns the same rate of return on its assets. Some earn more than the industry average ROA while others earn less. Companies that fall below the industry average ROA strive to grow sales, improve operating efficiency, and better manage assets so that they can become competitive again. Those fortunate enough to earn more than the industry average ROA struggle to maintain their competitive advantage—through differentiation or low-cost leadership—and to stay on top. This ebb and flow of competition show up as differences in ROA and in its profit margin and asset turnover components.

---

[7] In January 2013, Cerberus Capital Management, a private equity firm, agreed to acquire 30% of SUPERVALU for $3.3 billion, which includes the assumption of $3.2 billion of SUPERVALU debt. Under the terms of the deal, Cerberus will have 3 of 11 seats on the board of directors and SUPERVALU will appoint a new chairman, the chief executive officer of Albertson's LLC, which is owned by Cerberus. See "Private-Equity Investors Show Supervalu Who's the Boss," *The Wall Street Journal*, January 11, 2013.

[8] See W. K. Hall, "Survival Strategies in a Hostile Environment," *Harvard Business Review*, September–October 1980, pp. 78–85; and M. E. Porter, *Competitive Strategy* (New York: Free Press, 1980). Porter also describes a "niche" or "focused" strategy by which companies achieve uniqueness within a narrowly defined market segment.

RETURN ON COMMON EQUITY AND FINANCIAL LEVERAGE

If you want to gauge a company's profit performance from its shareholders' viewpoint, use ROCE. *ROCE measures a company's performance in using capital provided by common shareholders to generate earnings.*[9] It explicitly considers how the company finances its assets. Interest charged on loans and dividends on preferred stock are both subtracted in arriving at net income available to common shareholders. So too is the portion of earnings attributable to noncontrolling interests, the net income earned by consolidated subsidiaries but allocable to minority investors, if any, in those subsidiaries. The capital provided by common shareholders during the period can be computed by averaging total common shareholders' equity at the beginning and end of the period. For example, using the data in Exhibit 5.1 and Exhibit 5.6, the ROCE for Whole Foods Market in 2012 was:

$$\text{ROCE} = \frac{\text{Net income} - \text{Preferred dividends}}{\text{Average common shareholders' equity}}$$

$$\text{ROCE}_{2012} = \frac{\$465,573 - \$0}{\dfrac{\$3,802,469 + \$2,991,305}{2}} = \frac{\$465,573}{\$3,396,887} = .137 \text{ or } 13.7\%$$

Whole Foods' ROCE was substantially above the 8.1% ROCE it achieved in 2009.

ROCE is affected by both ROA and the degree of financial leverage employed by the company. These two factors interact in the following way: For firms with more financial leverage, the ups and downs in ROA are exaggerated in the ROCE metric. That is, when ROA is low at a highly levered firm, ROCE will be *very* low, perhaps even negative. When ROA is high at a highly levered firm, ROCE will be *very* high. In contrast, for firms that do not employ much financial leverage, ROCE is not much more volatile than ROA.[10]

To illustrate the relationship between ROA and ROCE, consider two companies—NoDebt and HiDebt—each with $2 million in assets. NoDebt raised all its capital from common shareholders; HiDebt borrowed $1 million at 10% interest. Both companies pay income taxes at a combined federal and state rate of 40%. The two companies have identical operations, so their earnings before interest and taxes (EBIT) and assets employed are always identical.

Exhibit 5.16 shows how the two companies compare in different earnings years. Let's start with a good earnings year, one in which both companies earn $400,000 before interest and taxes. The numerator in the ROA calculation is earnings before interest but after taxes, so it is $400,000 \times (1 - 40\%$ tax rate$) = \$240,000$ for both firms. And both firms have $2 million in assets, the denominator in the calculation. So, ROA is 12% for both firms, as is ROCE for NoDebt Company. HiDebt's ROCE is 18% because $180,000 of earnings is available to common shareholders, who have $1 million of equity. Leverage increased the return to HiDebt's shareholders because the capital contributed by lenders earned 12% but required an after-tax interest payment of only 6%—that is, a 10% rate of interest $\times (1 - 40\%$ tax rate$)$. The extra 6% earned on each borrowed asset dollar increased the return to common shareholders.

Exercise 5.12 explores the ROCE performance of Whole Foods Markets.

---

[9] If the analyst's goal is to isolate *sustainable* ROCE, Net income available to common shareholders must be purged of nonoperating and nonrecurring items and corrected for accounting quality distortions. These adjustments are discussed in later chapters.

[10] To learn about alternative approaches to disaggregating ROCE into various components, see K. Palepu and P. Healy, *Business Analysis and Valuation,* 5ed (Mason, OH: Thomson South-Western, 2013) or S. Penman, *Financial Statement Analysis and Security Valuation,* 5ed. (New York: McGraw-Hill, 2013).

EXHIBIT 5.16 • NoDebt and HiDebt

Profitability and Financial Leverage

	Total Assets	Shareholders' Equity	Earnings before Interest and Taxes (EBIT)	Interest Expense	Earnings before Taxes (EBT)	Net Income	ROA	ROCE
Good earnings year								
HiDebt	$2 million	$1 million	$400,000	$100,000	$300,000	$180,000	12.0%	18.0%
NoDebt	2 million	2 million	400,000	—	400,000	240,000	12.0	12.0
Neutral earnings year								
HiDebt	2 million	1 million	200,000	100,000	100,000	60,000	6.0	6.0
NoDebt	2 million	2 million	200,000	—	200,000	120,000	6.0	6.0
Bad earnings year								
HiDebt	2 million	1 million	100,000	100,000	0	0	3.0	0.0
NoDebt	2 million	2 million	100,000	—	100,000	60,000	3.0	3.0

What happens when earnings are low? That situation is illustrated by the bad earnings year in Exhibit 5.16. Both companies earn $100,000 before interest and taxes and a 3% ($100,000 × 60%/$2 million) ROA. All of these earnings are available to NoDebt shareholders, so ROCE for that company is also 3%. At HiDebt, after-tax interest charges wipe out earnings, and ROCE becomes 0% because there's nothing left for shareholders. HiDebt earns 3% on each asset dollar but must pay 6% to lenders for each dollar borrowed. In this case, leverage decreases the return to common equity and harms shareholders.

In the neutral year, leverage neither helps nor harms shareholders. That's because the 6% return earned on each asset dollar just equals the 6% after-tax cost of borrowing. Figure 5.3 illustrates the key results from this example.

Financial leverage works two ways. It makes good years better by increasing the shareholders' return, but it also makes bad years worse by decreasing the shareholders' return. Whether a year is "good" or "bad" in this context depends on whether the company earns more on each borrowed dollar than it pays out in interest, net of taxes.

RECAP

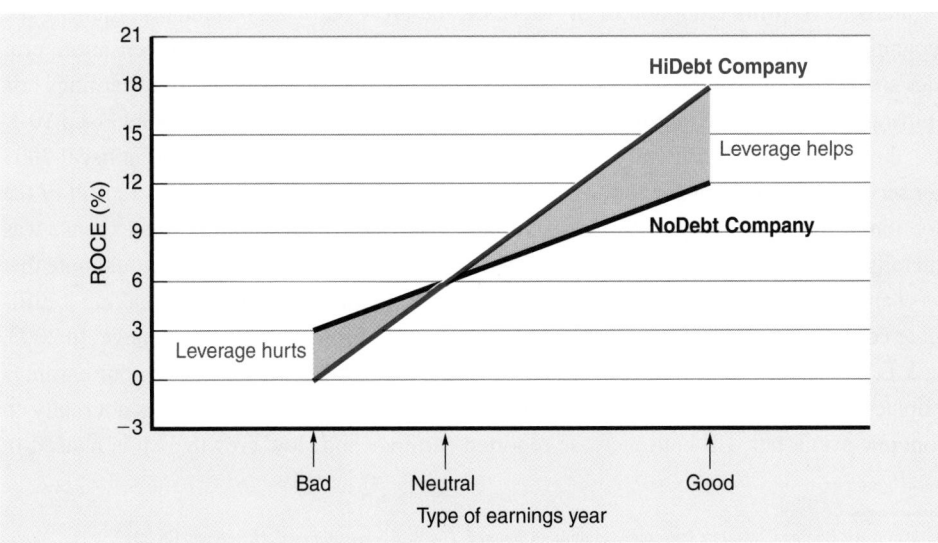

Figure 5.3

FINANCIAL LEVERAGE AND ROCE

GLOBAL VANTAGE POINT

The previous sections discussed how to compute and interpret ratios that rely on earnings measures in the numerator (e.g., ROA, ROCE). However, how earnings are determined may be different for firms using U.S. GAAP than for firms that follow IFRS. This only adds to the comparability issues that arise because firms, whether they follow U.S. GAAP or IFRS, can choose from a menu of acceptable accounting treatments, and their choices can affect materially how earnings are measured. Firms may even change how they determine earnings, making it difficult to analyze trends through time. Some of those changes may be because standards setters (e.g., FASB and IASB) revise standards. A well-trained analyst recognizes potential differences across firms and over time in how earnings are calculated, and makes adjustments to make comparisons more informative.

Novartis, a Swiss company known internationally for its pharmaceutical business, provides one example. In its 2012 annual report, Novartis notes that it includes in 2012 net income a $3 million (USD) "Reversal of prior year impairment charges" relating to its intangible assets. As we discuss in Chapter 10, U.S. GAAP does not permit reversals of impairment charges. However, as a Swiss company, Novartis follows IFRS, which allows such reversals. A well-trained analyst would note that Novartis's ROA and ROCE would have "head starts" on similar metrics for their competitors because Novartis availed itself of an income-increasing option that is not available under U.S. GAAP.

Boeing, a U.S.–based airplane manufacturer, provides another example of how accounting choices can materially affect the computation of net income, which influences the interpretation of ROA and ROCE. A November 13, 2012, *Wall Street Journal* article notes that Boeing was considering changing its accounting for defined benefit pension plans to a method that introduces "more volatility in earnings' reports" by recognizing, each period, certain gains and losses that are generally smoothed across periods.[11] This option is available under U.S. GAAP, but it is not widely used. Note that if Boeing goes forward with this change to its pension accounting, then the numerator of ROA or ROCE will be determined by the market performance of the firms' pension plan assets to a larger extent than for its competitors, making it more difficult to draw inferences from ROA or ROCE about Boeing's fundamental operational performance. The analyst should also expect that Boeing would likely restate its prior earnings history as if it had adopted this accounting choice from the beginning. Changing the historical trend in Boeing's ROA and ROCE would provide a different picture of Boeing's earnings performance through time.

Finally, U.S. firms' adoption of SFAS 123R, the pre-Codification standard requiring the recognition of compensation expense by firms that grant employee stock compensation, provides another example of how standards changes can make most reporting firms' earnings less comparable to their own prior history. Morgan Stanley noted in its 2003 amended Form 10-K that "the Company will recognize the fair value of stock-based awards granted in fiscal 2003 over service periods of three and four years, including the year of the grant" as a result of the adoption of the new standard. As we discuss in Chapter 15, recognition of this expense was generally not required before SFAS 123R was adopted. A well-trained analyst would note that this change in standard could materially alter the computation of net income, making it difficult to compare the values of most firms' ROA or ROCE before and after the change. In 2003, Mark L. Constant, an analyst for Lehman Brothers, noted "that the increase in our earnings estimates primarily reflects the change in accounting for compensation (which is not really an economic event, but will both increase reported earnings and slow growth as it is phased-in

---

[11] J. Ostrower, "Boeing Considers Pension Accounting Change," *The Wall Street Journal,* November 13, 2012.

over the next 3–4 years). This change does not, however, affect our estimates of economic Return on Invested Capital, nor our resulting valuation, because it is really cosmetic."

LIQUIDITY, SOLVENCY, AND CREDIT ANALYSIS

Credit risk refers to the risk of nonpayment by the borrower. A borrower's ability to pay its debts affects the likelihood the lender (typically a bank or insurance company) will receive the promised principal and interest payments when due. The borrower's ability to pay is driven by its capacity to generate cash from operations, asset sales, or external financial markets.

Numerous and interrelated risks influence a company's ability to generate cash. Multinational companies, for example, must cope with possible changes in host government regulations, potential political unrest, and fluctuating currency exchange rates. Domestic companies are exposed to the risks of political or demographic changes, recession, inflation, and interest rate fluctuations. Companies within a particular industry confront risks related to technological change, shifting competition, regulation, and availability of raw materials and labor. Management competency, litigation, and the company's strategic direction are additional sources of risk. Each of these risks ultimately affects a company's operating performance, net income, and cash flows. In fact, the statement of cash flows—which reports the net amount of cash generated or used by operating, investing, and financing activities—is an important source of information for analyzing a company's credit risk. Figure 5.4 illustrates the components of the cash flow statement.

For example, the comparative cash flow statements for Whole Foods Market in Exhibit 5.10 reveal strong and growing operating cash flows. In fact, cash generated by operating activities was more than sufficient to fund the company's store expansion and property and equipment purchases. This strong cash flow position allowed the company to purchase nearly $1 billion of marketable securities, net of its security sales ($3.0 billion − $2.1 billion).

What about the company's debt burden and its credit risk? The comparative balance sheets (Exhibit 5.6) reveal that Whole Foods had only $23 million of long-term debt outstanding at the end of 2012, having paid off most of its debt in 2011. Its remaining debt is a small fraction of its operating cash flow. Moreover, more than $1 billion of cash and short-term investments could be tapped if the company needed money. So, Whole Foods is characterized by minimal credit risk: annual operating cash flows are substantial relative to the balance owed lenders, and other highly liquid assets are available to service the debt.

Although cash flow statements contain information enabling a user to assess a company's credit risk, financial ratios are also useful for this purpose. *Credit risk analysis using financial ratios typically involves an assessment of liquidity and solvency.* **Liquidity** refers to the company's *short-term* ability to generate cash for working capital needs and

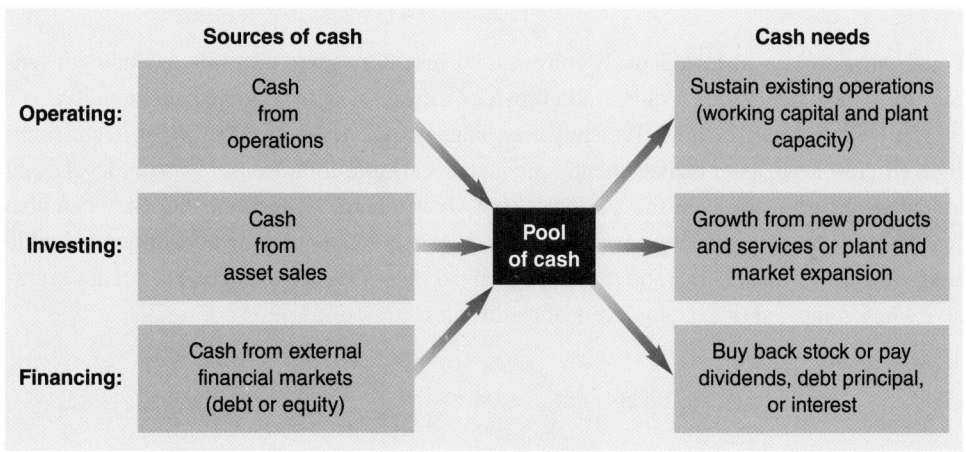

Figure 5.4

BALANCING CASH SOURCES AND NEEDS

immediate debt repayment needs. **Solvency** refers to the *long-term* ability to generate cash internally or from external sources to satisfy plant capacity needs, fuel growth, and repay debt when due. Our discussion of financial ratios as an analytical tool for assessing credit risk is based on the distinction between concerns for short-term liquidity and for long-term solvency.

Short-Term Liquidity

Short-term liquidity problems can arise when operating cash inflows don't match outflows. To illustrate the mismatching problem, consider the **operating cycle** of a retailer such as Walmart. It acquires merchandise from suppliers on credit, promising to pay within 30 or 60 days. The merchandise is first shipped to Walmart warehouses. Later it is sent on to Walmart stores where it is displayed for purchase and promoted through in-store and media advertising. Walmart pays for some transportation, labor, and advertising costs immediately and delays payment of other costs. Eventually, Walmart sells the merchandise to customers, who pay by cash or charge card; receivables (if any) are collected some time later; and the company then pays the remaining amounts owed to suppliers and others. Liquidity problems can arise when cash inflows from customers lag behind the cash outflows to employees, suppliers, and others, because the company does not have sufficient funds to make the payments on a timely basis.

The operating cycle must not only generate sufficient cash to supply working capital needs, but also provide cash to service debt as payments become due. For some companies, operating cash flows are sufficient to cover periodic interest payments, but the need to repay loan principal causes a liquidity problem. Companies that are not liquid—and are therefore not able to pay obligations as they come due—may be forced into bankruptcy.

One index of a company's short-term liquidity is its **current ratio:**

$$\text{Current ratio} = \frac{\text{Current assets}}{\text{Current liabilities}}$$

Current assets include cash and "near cash" items. For example, receivables become cash as they are collected, so they are only one step removed from cash. Inventories are converted into cash in two steps. First they must be sold. Then, if they were sold on credit, the resulting receivable must be collected.

By including receivables and inventory in current assets, the current ratio reflects existing cash as well as amounts to be converted to cash in the normal operating cycle.

A more short-run reflection of liquidity is the **quick ratio:**

$$\text{Quick ratio} = \frac{\text{Cash} + \text{Short-term investments} + \text{Receivables}}{\text{Current liabilities}}$$

Few businesses can instantaneously convert their inventories into cash. By excluding inventory from the numerator, the quick ratio provides a measure of *very* immediate liquidity.

Activity ratios tell us how efficiently the company uses its assets. Activity ratios can highlight efficiencies in asset management—accounts receivable collections, inventory levels, and vendor payment—and help the company spot areas needing improvement. They can also highlight causes for operating cash flow mismatches. For example, the **accounts receivable turnover** ratio is an activity ratio that helps analysts determine whether receivables are excessive when compared to existing levels of credit sales:

$$\text{Accounts receivable turnover} = \frac{\text{Net credit sales}}{\text{Average accounts receivable}}$$

To illustrate how to interpret this ratio, suppose annual credit sales totaled $10 million and customer accounts receivable were $2 million at the beginning of the year and $3 million at year-end. The accounts receivable turnover ratio value is then:

$$\frac{\$10}{(\$2 + \$3)/2} = 4 \text{ times per year}$$

The average annual balance of receivables ($2.5 million) represents one-fourth of yearly credit sales ($2.5/$10 = 1/4), so receivables must turn over four times per year.

The analyst can also use the accounts receivable turnover ratio to spot changing customer payment patterns. For example, if we divide the accounts receivable turnover ratio into 365 days, the result tells us the number of days that the average customer receivable is "on the books" before it is collected:

$$\text{Days accounts receivable outstanding} = \frac{365 \text{ days}}{\text{Accounts receivable turnover}}$$

$$= \frac{365 \text{ days}}{4} = 91.25 \text{ days}$$

> Most companies just report a single "sales" number that is the sum of cash plus credit sales. Using total sales instead of "credit sales" in the accounts receivable turnover calculation produces misleading results if cash sales are a substantial portion of the total, although cash sales are rare in a large number of businesses today because of credit and debit cards. In certain industries such as discount retailing (Walmart) and groceries (Whole Foods Market), however, substantial cash sales are still the rule rather than the exception.

In our example, the average account receivable is collected about 91 days after the credit sale occurs. This is the same as saying accounts receivable "turn over" four times per year. An accounts receivable turnover ratio of 4 (91 days) is quite acceptable for a company where the terms of sale allow customers to delay payment by 90 days or more. This same turnover ratio would, however, cause great concern for a business where customers are expected to pay within 30 days.

Another activity ratio is the **inventory turnover ratio,** which tells us how effectively inventories are managed:

$$\text{Inventory turnover} = \frac{\text{Cost of goods sold}}{\text{Average inventory}}$$

Assume beginning inventory was $8 million, year-end inventory was $9 million, and cost of goods sold was $43.35 million. The inventory turnover is:

$$\frac{\$43.35}{(\$8 + \$9)/2} = 5.1 \text{ times per year}$$

The inventory turnover ratio can be used to determine the average **days inventory held** as follows:

$$\text{Days inventory held} = \frac{365 \text{ days}}{\text{Inventory turnover}}$$

$$= \frac{365 \text{ days}}{5.1} = 71.57 \text{ days}$$

In our example, it takes about 72 days for inventory to move from the company to its customers. In other words, average inventory is sufficient to cover almost 72 days of customer sales.

> Calculating inventory turnover and days inventory held for a manufacturing firm is more complicated than for the merchandising firm illustrated here. That's because inventory in a manufacturing firm must pass through three stages of the operating cycle:
>
> 1. As *raw material,* from purchase to the start of production.
> 2. As *work in process,* over the length of the production cycle.
> 3. As *finished goods,* from completion of production until it is sold.
>
> To calculate how long inventory is held at each stage, analysts use the following activity ratios:
>
> Raw materials: $365 \text{ days} \times \dfrac{\text{Average raw materials inventory}}{\text{Raw materials used}}$
>
> Work in process: $365 \text{ days} \times \dfrac{\text{Average work-in-process inventory}}{\text{Cost of goods manufactured}}$
>
> Finished goods: $365 \text{ days} \times \dfrac{\text{Average finished goods inventory}}{\text{Cost of goods sold}}$
>
> Cost of goods sold and the breakdown of inventory into raw materials, work in process, and finished goods is reported in the financial statements. Cost of goods manufactured can be calculated as cost of goods sold *plus* ending finished goods inventory *minus* beginning finished goods inventory. However, the amount of raw materials used in production is rarely disclosed in financial statements. It may be available in the company's fact book or obtained by contacting the company's investor relations group.

Consider the inventory turnover ratio for Dell Inc., the personal computer manufacturer. The business models used by lean manufacturing companies like Dell reduce the need to stock inventory at production facilities, distribution warehouses, or retail stores. Dell builds its PCs and related equipment "on demand" using component parts delivered "just-in-time" by vendors. PCs are shipped to customers as soon as they are assembled. As a result, inventory turnover is quite high. Dell's inventory turnover ratio for the fiscal year ended February 3, 2012 (29.3) has a large numerator ($39,689 million) relative to the denominator ($1,353 million). Dell's inventory is held on average for only about 12 days (365 days divided by 29.3).

The **accounts payable turnover** ratio—and its **days payable outstanding** counterpart—helps analysts understand the company's pattern of payments to suppliers:

$$\text{Accounts payable turnover} = \frac{\text{Inventory purchases}}{\text{Average accounts payable}}$$

$$\text{Days accounts payable outstanding} = \frac{365 \text{ days}}{\text{Accounts payable turnover}}$$

Suppose trade accounts payable averaged $7.3 million and inventory purchases totaled $44.35 million during the year. The accounts payable turnover ratio would be about 6, and the days accounts payable outstanding would be about 60 days. (You should verify both calculations!) ***More timely payment of accounts payable would lead to a lower average payable balance, a higher turnover ratio, and fewer days outstanding.***

> For retail companies such as Amazon.com and Walmart, inventory purchases equal cost of goods sold expense plus the year's inventory increase— that is, $44.35 = $43.35 + ($9 − $8) in our example.

Let's piece these activity ratios together to get a picture that will help us analyze the financial condition of our company.

- Inventory remains on hand for about 72 days.
- Inventory is sold, and another 91 days elapse before cash is collected from the customer.
- Suppliers are paid about 60 days after inventory is purchased.

Figure 5.5 illustrates the timeline of events beginning with an inventory purchase. It shows that cash outflows and inflows are dangerously mismatched. The company's **operating cycle** spans 163 days—that is how long it takes to sell inventory (72 days) and collect cash from the customers (91 days). But the company pays for inventory purchases in just 60 days, so its **cash conversion cycle** is 103 days, meaning suppliers are paid 103 days before the company has received cash from product sales. This hypothetical company may face a short-term liquidity problem because of the cash flow mismatch. It must rely on other cash sources—for example, bank loans—to sustain its operating working capital requirements over the 103-day gap.

Exhibit 5.17 reports the operating cycle and cash conversion cycle for three retailers: Amazon.com, Walmart, and Nordstrom. Each company employs a different business model, resulting in differences in working capital activity ratios, operating cycles, and cash conversion cycles. Amazon.com is an e-commerce retailer that doesn't stock inventory on store shelves, although its distribution centers do stock inventory. Amazon's inventories have been low historically. However, inventories have grown in recent years, both in absolute terms and

Figure 5.5

TIMELINE OF EVENTS

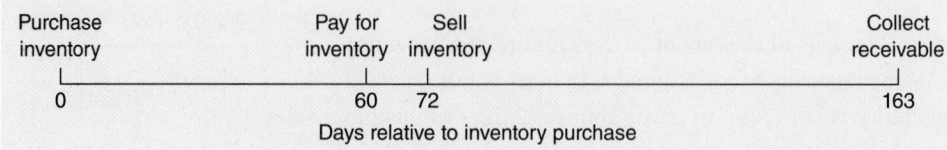

Purchase inventory	Pay for inventory	Sell inventory	Collect receivable
0	60	72	163

Days relative to inventory purchase

EXHIBIT 5.17 — Amazon.com, Walmart, and Nordstrom

Comparison of Operating and Cash Conversion Cycles

	Amazon.com	Walmart	Nordstrom
Working capital and activity ratios:			
1. Days inventory held	40.1	42.0	58.8
2. Days accounts receivable outstanding	18.1	4.5	70.6
3. Days accounts payable outstanding	89.6	37.8	47.6
Operating cycle (1 + 2)	58.2	46.5	129.4
Cash conversion cycle (1 + 2 − 3)	(31.5)	8.8	81.8

Note: Amounts are rounded.

in terms of days inventory held. At December 31, 2011, inventory days stood at 40.1. Amazon's customers pay by bank credit card so Amazon gets cash (from the customer's credit card company) very quickly after a sale. The operating cycle at Amazon.com is 58 days, but the cash conversion cycle is *minus* 31 days. That's because Amazon waits 90 days after buying inventory to pay its suppliers.

> The cash conversion cycle at Dell is −55 days.

Walmart and Nordstrom are traditional brick-and-mortar retailers that target different market segments. Walmart carries a broad line of merchandise and emphasizes low prices. Most of its customers pay cash or use a credit card. Nordstrom is known for its fashion apparel and shoes. The company emphasizes product quality and customer service and promotes its in-store credit card. Walmart has a 47-day operating cycle compared to 129 days at Nordstrom. It takes Nordstrom longer to sell inventory (59 days compared to 42 days at Walmart) and longer to collect cash from customers once the sale has been made (71 days, compared to 5 days at Walmart). However, Walmart pays suppliers in about 38 days while Nordstom's suppliers wait 48 days for payment. So, the difference in cash conversion cycles at the two companies—9 days at Walmart compared to 82 days at Nordstrom—can be attributed to Nordstrom's emphasis on slower-to-sell fashion apparel and its in-store credit card, which slows the collection of cash. Both companies must carefully manage their short-term liquidity because cash outflows and inflows are mismatched.

> The company's restricted cash is excluded from the current and quick ratio computations because these dollars cannot be used to pay short-term creditors. Of course, that's why the cash is restricted. Similarly, the company's short-term investments are included in the quick ratio computation because these dollars can be used to pay creditors. Analytical adjustments of this type are common in credit risk analysis.

Let's return to our analysis of Whole Foods Market. See Exhibit 5.18 for data on the company's short-term liquidity ratios. Whole Foods' current ratio was 2.05 in 2012, up from 1.44

EXHIBIT 5.18 — Whole Foods Market

Credit Risk Analysis: Short-Term Liquidity

	2012	2011	2010	2009
Current ratio	2.05	1.55	1.44	1.44
Quick ratio	1.45	0.94	0.80	0.78
Working capital activity ratios:				
1. Days inventory held	17.2	18.3	19.7	22.1
2. Days accounts receivable outstanding	5.8	5.6	4.8	5.0
3. Days accounts payable outstanding	11.7	12.5	12.5	12.9
Operating cycle (1 + 2)	23.0	23.9	24.5	27.1
Cash conversion cycle (1 + 2 − 3)	11.4	11.4	12.0	14.1

Note: The current and quick ratio excludes the company's restricted cash whereas short-term investments are included in the quick ratio.

three years earlier. The quick ratio was 1.45, which was also more than the 2009 level of 0.78. The quick ratio indicates that Whole Foods' cash, short-term investments, and accounts receivable covered more than 100% of the company's current liabilities at the end of fiscal 2012. Adding inventories and other current assets further improves the picture—a current ratio of 2.05 means that total current assets (adjusted to exclude restricted cash) cover more than double Whole Foods Market's current liabilities.

Inventory levels were down from 22 days in 2009 to 17 days in 2012. Several factors may have contributed to this inventory turnover improvement: a more appealing merchandise mix, warehouse distribution efficiencies, or reduced inventory levels. There was little change in the apparent payment pattern of Whole Foods' credit customers. Days receivable outstanding in 2012 was just 5.8 days, compared to 5.0 days in 2009. Of course, this unusually prompt payment pattern—credit customers paying their bills within 6 days—is distorted by our inability to break out credit sales from cash sales at the company. In effect, we treat cash sales as if they were credit sales that were collected immediately. Days payable outstanding decreased modestly: 11.7 days in 2012, compared to 12.9 days in 2009.[12]

Some misalignment of operating cash flows exists because payments to suppliers occurred about 12 days after inventory was purchased but it took about 23 days (17.2 + 5.8) to generate a sale and collect cash from credit customers. In view of the company's overall level of positive operating cash flow, this misalignment is unlikely to cause concerns.

Long-Term Solvency   Solvency refers to a company's ability to generate a stream of cash inflows sufficient to maintain its productive capacity and still meet the interest and principal payments on its long-term debt. A company that cannot make timely debt service payments becomes insolvent and may be compelled to reorganize or liquidate.

Debt ratios provide information about the amount of long-term debt in a company's financial structure. The more a company relies on long-term borrowing to finance its business activities, the higher is its debt ratio and the greater is the long-term solvency risk. There are several variations in debt ratios. Two commonly used ratios are **long-term debt to assets** and **long-term debt to tangible assets:**

$$\text{Long-term debt to assets} = \frac{\text{Long-term debt}}{\text{Total assets}}$$

$$\text{Long-term debt to tangible assets} = \frac{\text{Long-term debt}}{\text{Total tangible assets}}$$

Suppose a company has $20 million of outstanding long-term debt and $100 million of total assets, of which $35 million are intangibles such as goodwill or purchased patents, trademarks, or copyrights. The two debt ratios would be:

$$\text{Long-term debt to assets} = \frac{\$20}{\$100} = 0.200 \text{ or } 20.0\%$$

$$\text{Long-term debt to tangible assets} = \frac{\$20}{\$100 - \$35} = 0.308 \text{ or } 30.8\%$$

---

[12] As you may recall from Whole Foods Market's comparative income statement (Exhibit 5.1), the company presents cost of goods sold and occupancy costs as a single line item. This creates distortions in both inventory turnover and accounts payable turnover in that the resulting figures reflect too few days of actual activity.

These results tell us that 20 cents of each asset dollar were financed using long-term debt. The remaining 80 cents came from other sources—internally generated resources, short-term borrowing, or equity capital in the form of common and preferred stock.

Debt ratios vary by industry. For example, a 20% long-term debt-to-assets ratio would be high for a discount retailer such as Walmart but unusually low for an electric utility company. Retailers use short-term debt and trade credit to finance inventory purchases, and they often lease (but don't own) their retail stores. Electric utilities, on the other hand, rely on long-term debt to support their sizable investments in power-generating facilities and transmission lines. Electric utilities also have relatively predictable operating cash flows because energy demand is reasonably stable and competition is limited by regulators. Companies whose sales fluctuate widely due to changing economic conditions generally employ less debt because the fixed interest charges can be difficult to meet during bad times. These cyclical companies tend to have smaller debt-to-asset ratios.

Analysts devote considerable attention to refining both the numerator and denominator of debt ratios. For example, some analysts include in the numerator "hybrid" securities, or obligations that have the cash flow characteristics of balance sheet debt although they may not be classified as such on the balance sheet. Operating leases and other off-balance-sheet obligations are routinely included as debt "equivalents" in the numerator. The exclusion of intangible assets from the solvency ratio denominator is also common. This adjustment is intended to remove "soft" assets—those difficult to value reliably—from the analysis.

Comparative debt ratios for Whole Foods Market are shown in Exhibit 5.19. The company's long-term debt-to-assets ratio was 0.005 in 2012, meaning that each total asset dollar supported 0.5 cents of long-term debt. This represented a sharp decline from the 0.195 debt-to-assets level in 2009. A similar picture emerges when Whole Foods' solvency is measured using tangible (rather than total) assets. The company's debt-to-tangible-assets ratio was 0.005 in 2012, down from 0.242 in 2009. These two debt ratios moved in the same direction and were consistent with a financially sound company that paid off most of its debt, after taking on about $700 million of debt in 2007 when it acquired Wild Oat Markets.

Most analysts add the current portion of long-term debt to the numerator in long-term debt solvency ratios, although this debt is classified as a current liability on the balance sheet. Some analysts go so far as to include *all* short-term interest-bearing debt (such as notes payable) in their solvency ratio calculations. Several arguments favor this approach: (1) Long-term debt repayable over several years will always have some portion shown as a current liability, and this current portion should not be ignored; (2) long-term debt is shown as a current liability when loan covenants have been violated, but this does not mean that the firm's solvency risk has improved; (3) a firm with significant short-term debt but no long-term debt is not necessarily less risky than one with only long-term debt outstanding. Adding short-term debt to the ratio numerator overcomes distortions that can affect the interpretation of solvency risk. Some analysts will treat the company's redeemable preferred stock as long-term debt. Chapter 15 explains why.

Although debt ratios are useful for understanding a company's financial structure, they provide no information about its ability to generate a stream of inflows sufficient to make

---

EXHIBIT 5.19   Whole Foods Market

Credit Risk Analysis: Long-Term Solvency

	2012	2011	2010	2009
Long-term debt to assets ratio	0.005	0.004	0.128	0.195
Long-term debt to tangible assets ratio	0.005	0.005	0.156	0.242
Interest coverage ratio	2,100.3	141.1	13.3	7.7
Operating cash flow to total liabilities	0.970	0.701	0.437	0.389

Note: Current installments are included in long-term debt for purposes of these ratios.

principal and interest payments. One financial ratio commonly used for this purpose is the **interest coverage ratio:**

$$\text{Interest coverage} = \frac{\text{Operating income before taxes and interest}}{\text{Interest expense}}$$

This ratio indicates how many times interest expense is covered by operating profits before taxes and interest are factored in. It reflects the cushion between operating profit inflows and required interest payments. If the company must also make periodic principal payments, the analyst could include those amounts in the calculation.

> Many analysts use an *adjusted* operating income figure that removes nonrecurring items and corrects for accounting quality distortions.

Suppose a company has $200 million of operating income before taxes and interest and $50 million of interest expense. The company's interest coverage ratio is $200/$50 = 4. This shows that operating profit is four times larger than interest expense—a substantial cushion for the lender. But now suppose that the company is also required to make a $100 million debt principal payment. The revised interest coverage ratio is $200/($50 + $100) = 1.33. When required debt payments are factored in, the lender's cushion looks thin.

A criticism of the traditional interest coverage ratio is that it uses earnings rather than operating cash flows in the numerator. Some analysts prefer to compute a **cash flow coverage ratio** in which the numerator is operating cash flows before interest payments are factored in. When operating profits and cash flows move in tandem, both versions of the ratio will yield similar results. However, when the two measures diverge—for example, during a period in which the company experiences rapid growth—income may be a poor substitute for cash flow. In that case, the cash flow coverage ratio is preferable as a solvency measure. After all, real cash (not just operating profits) is what the company needs to make its required interest payments.

Another useful measure of long-term solvency compares a company's **operating cash flow** to its **total liabilities** (excluding deferred taxes):

$$\frac{\text{Operating cash flow}}{\text{to total liabilities}} = \frac{\text{Cash flow from continuing operations}}{\text{Average current liabilities plus long-term debt}}$$

This ratio shows a company's ability to generate cash from operations to service both short-term and long-term borrowings.

Exhibit 5.19 shows that Whole Foods' interest coverage ratio was greater than 2,000 in 2012. When the interest coverage is so high, it usually means debt, and therefore interest expense, is very close to zero. In 2009, Whole Foods' interest coverage ratio was 7.7, indicating ample cushion at the time.

Whole Foods' operating cash flow to total liabilities ratio clearly demonstrates why most analysts view the company as financially sound and a low credit risk. Operating cash flows in 2012 were alone sufficient to repay nearly all (97%) of the company's total liabilities.

Cash Flow Analysis

Although a company's earnings are important, an analysis of its cash flows is central to credit evaluations and lending decisions. This is because a company's earnings and cash flow may diverge. Obviously, a company cannot make interest and principal payments with its receivables or inventories. Rather, the company must pay its lenders with cold, hard cash!

Consider the situation confronting your client, G. T. Wilson Company. Wilson has been a client of your bank for more than 40 years. The company owns and operates nearly 850 retail

EXHIBIT 5.20   G. T. Wilson Company

Comparative Statements of Cash Flow

	Years Ended January 31,						
($ in thousands)	2008	2009	2010	2011	2012	2013	2014
Operating:							
Net income	$ 38,200	$ 41,900	$ 36,400	$ 31,600	$ 34,950	$ 10,900	$(145,400)
Depreciation	8,400	9,000	9,600	10,600	12,000	13,600	14,600
Other adjustments to income	(1,100)	(1,600)	(2,500)	(1,800)	(1,700)	(1,350)	(17,000)
(Increase) Decrease in receivables	(40,300)	(55,500)	(12,000)	(49,900)	(60,300)	(72,200)	9,600
(Increase) in inventories	(24,900)	(13,500)	(38,400)	(38,200)	(100,850)	(51,100)	(4,350)
(Increase) Decrease in prepayments	(400)	(650)	(200)	(150)	(1,250)	(650)	700
Increase (Decrease) in accounts payable	22,400	2,050	13,900	6,900	(12,100)	(8,000)	42,400
Increase (Decrease) in other current liabilities	8,500	15,400	(21,900)	13,900	14,950	15,650	(1,500)
Cash flow from operations	10,800	(2,900)	(15,100)	(27,050)	(114,300)	(93,150)	(100,950)
Investing:							
Acquisition of property, plant, and equipment	(10,600)	(14,400)	(16,100)	(25,900)	(26,250)	(23,150)	(15,500)
Acquisition of investments	—	—	(450)	(6,000)	(2,200)	(5,700)	(5,300)
Cash flow from investing	(10,600)	(14,400)	(16,550)	(31,900)	(28,450)	(28,850)	(20,800)
Financing:							
Increase (Decrease) in short-term borrowing	18,900	64,000	64,300	(8,650)	152,300	63,050	147,600
Increase (Decrease) in long-term borrowing	(1,500)	(1,650)	(1,500)	98,450	(1,600)	93,900	(4,000)
Increase (Decrease) in capital stock	850	(17,900)	(8,900)	7,400	(8,200)	1,800	850
Dividends	(17,700)	(19,700)	(20,800)	(21,100)	(21,150)	(21,100)	(4,500)
Cash flow from financing	550	24,750	33,100	76,100	121,350	137,650	139,950
Other	(100)	—	(400)	(1,350)	2,450	(650)	(700)
Change in cash	$ 650	$ 7,450	$ 1,050	$ 15,800	$ (18,950)	$ 15,000	$ 17,500

furniture stores throughout the United States and has more than 38,000 employees. Sales and earnings growth have exceeded the industry average until recently, and the company has paid dividends consistently for almost 100 years. Prior to 2008, Wilson built its reputation on sales of moderately priced upholstered furniture, case goods (wooden tables, chairs, and bookcases), and decorative accessories. The company's stores were located in large urban centers where occupancy costs were quite low. Increased competition and changing consumer tastes caused Wilson to alter its strategy beginning in 2008. One aspect of this strategic shift involved expanding the company's product line to include higher quality furniture, consumer electronics, and home entertainment systems. To complement its expanded product line, Wilson also introduced a credit card system so customers could more easily pay for their purchases. Wilson used commercial paper, bank loans, and trade credit to finance the growth of receivables and inventories. The company's strategy also focused on closing unprofitable downtown stores; at the same time, it expanded by opening new stores in suburban shopping centers.

Your bank has extended two loans to Wilson, a $50 million secured construction loan that matures in 2018 and a $200 million revolving credit line that is currently up for renewal. Wilson has always complied with the terms of the revolving line of credit, but the company's borrowing has been at or near the maximum amount allowed for the past two years. See Exhibit 5.20 for the company's comparative cash flow statements and Exhibit 5.21 for selected

---

EXHIBIT 5.21 | G. T. Wilson Company

Selected Financial Statistics

	Years Ended January 31,						
	2008	2009	2010	2011	2012	2013	2014
Operations							
Sales ($ millions)	$1,095	$1,210	$1,250	$1,375	$1,665	$1,850	$1,762
Number of new stores (net of closures)	13	21	52	40	37	41	21
Gross profit/sales	32.8%	33.0%	36.5%	35.8%	35.3%	35.1%	30.1%
Selling, general, and administrative/Sales	25.2%	25.2%	29.9%	30.7%	30.6%	30.4%	41.3%
Net income/Sales	3.5%	3.5%	2.9%	2.3%	2.1%	0.6%	(8.3)%
Dividends/net income	46.3%	47.0%	57.1%	66.8%	60.5%	193.6%	(3.1)%
Short-Term Liquidity							
Current assets/Current liabilities	3.3	3.4	3.7	4.6	4.5	5.0	6.2
Operating cash flows as a % of sales	1.0%	(0.2)%	(1.2)%	(2.0)%	(6.9)%	(5.0)%	(5.7)%
Days receivable	104.1	115.1	126.2	131.1	130.5	140.0	142.5
Allowance for uncollectibles (%)	3.8%	4.0%	3.6%	3.2%	2.8%	3.0%	3.3%
Days inventory	102.7	104.3	112.8	117.1	129.6	131.2	130.5
Days payable	48.6	45.7	48.9	47.1	33.6	30.7	42.6
Long-Term Solvency							
Total debt as a % of assets	25.9%	30.8%	37.3%	41.8%	49.8%	56.4%	75.7%
Interest coverage	8.7	6.4	4.7	4.5	3.9	1.2	(2.4)
Short-term debt as a % of total debt	59.4%	70.8%	81.6%	64.0%	75.8%	70.0%	78.3%

financial statistics. What do these cash flow statements and summary statistics tell us about the company's credit risk?

Cash Flow from Operations

A company's cash flow from operations refers to the amount of cash it is able to generate from ongoing core business activities. Generating cash from operations is essential to any company's long-term economic viability. However, not every company can be expected to produce positive operating cash flows every year. Even financially healthy companies must sometimes spend more cash on their operating activities than they receive from customers.

The comparative cash flow statements in Exhibit 5.20 show that Wilson produced positive operating cash flows in 2008. Since then, its operating cash flows have been consistently negative and increasing in magnitude, with the average level for the last three years equal to about *minus* $100 million. This view contrasts sharply with the company's sales and earnings performance as shown in Exhibit 5.21. Sales have increased steadily from $1.095 billion in 2008 to $1.85 billion in 2013 with a small decline in 2014. Net income (Exhibit 5.20) increased from $38.2 million in 2008 to a peak of $41.9 million in 2009 followed by three years of relative stability where earnings averaged about $34 million per year. Net income declined in 2013 to $10.9 million, and the company reported a $145.4 million loss in 2014.

What aspects of Wilson's operations consumed cash during the company's profitable years? Exhibit 5.20 shows the primary factors contributing to the company's negative operating cash flows were increases in accounts receivable and increases in inventories. Some increase in receivables and inventories is to be expected because of the company's decision to expand its product line and introduce a customer credit card. However, increases in receivables or inventories can sometimes signal unfavorable business conditions. For example, the average collection period for customer accounts (days receivables in Exhibit 5.21) increased from 104.1 days in 2008 to 142.5 days in 2014. This trend could reflect expanded credit card use, more lenient credit policies offered to customers, or a deterioration in customers' ability to pay. Similarly, the increase in days inventory (Exhibit 5.21) from 102.7 in 2008 to 130.5 in 2014 could be due to product line extensions, escalating merchandise costs, or slack consumer demand. The analyst must evaluate each possible explanation to discover what economic forces are responsible for the company's negative operating cash flows and whether positive cash flows from operating activities are likely to be generated in the future.

> It is interesting to note that Wilson's allowance for uncollectibles actually declined in percentage terms after 2009 (Exhibit 5.21) even though the average collection period increased. So, bad debt expense accruals apparently fell.

A business such as G. T. Wilson that spends more cash on its operating activities than it generates must find ways to finance the operating cash flow shortfall. Typically, this means using up cash reserves, borrowing additional cash, issuing additional equity, or liquidating investments such as real estate and other fixed assets. None of these options can be sustained indefinitely. For example, Wilson could finance the company's operating cash flow deficit by selling some retail stores. However, this action might jeopardize the company's ability to generate positive operating cash flows in the future. Similarly, creditors are unlikely to keep lending to a business that continually fails to generate an acceptable level of cash flow from operations. In this regard, Wilson's inability to generate positive operating cash flows in recent years is troublesome.

Investing Activities   In the investing section of the cash flow statement, companies present cash flows related to expansion or contraction of fixed assets, as well as cash flows related to nonoperating investments. These cash flows include capital expenditures and asset sales, acquisitions and divestitures, and purchases and sales or maturities of securities classified as available for sale.

Wilson Company's cash flow statements (Exhibit 5.20) show sustained investment in property, plant, and equipment that is consistent with the company's expansion (Exhibit 5.21). Analysts should investigate carefully a company's capital expenditures and fixed asset retirements in light of the company's business strategy and growth opportunities. For example, consider the following scenarios:

- *Emerging companies* require substantial investments in property, plant, and equipment at a stage when operating cash flows are often negative.
- *Established growth companies* also require substantial fixed asset investments to further expand their market presence. Operating cash flows for established growth companies can be positive or negative depending on the pace of expansion, the degree to which expansion also requires working capital investment, and the ability of the company to generate a positive operating cash flow from markets in which it is established.
- *Mature companies'* capital expenditures are limited to the amount needed to sustain current levels of operations, usually at a time when operating cash flows are significantly positive.

Consequently, changes in a company's capital expenditures or fixed asset sales over time must be analyzed carefully. For example, a sharp reduction in capital expenditures for an emerging growth company may indicate that the company is suffering from a temporary cash shortage. Decreased capital expenditures may also signal a more fundamental change in management's expectations about the company's growth opportunities and its competitive environment. Similarly, an increase in fixed asset sales could mean that management needs to raise cash quickly or that it is eliminating excess production capacity. The analyst needs to evaluate each of these possibilities because they have very different implications for the company's future operating cash flows.

Financing Activities   The most significant source of external financing for most companies is debt. A large amount of research has been conducted that explores the "optimal" amount of debt financing that companies should include in their capital structures. Determining this optimal debt level involves a trade-off between two competing economic forces—taxes and costs of financial distress.[13] Unlike dividends, interest on debt is tax deductible, creating an advantage for debt financing over equity financing. However, highly-levered firms have a greater risk of financial distress and perhaps even bankruptcy. This risk is costly, not just because investors could lose their investments, but because distressed firms' operations suffer. For example, customers may be reluctant to do business with a firm that may not survive and suppliers may not offer trade credit, making it more difficult to operate. The precise point at which these two forces counterbalance one another varies from company to company and over time. One way analysts can assess the optimal debt level is to evaluate the company's historical and estimated future ability to meet scheduled debt payments. In this regard, Wilson Company's situation appears bleak.

The financing section of Wilson's cash flow statements (Exhibit 5.20) reveals a heavy reliance on short-term debt to finance the company's capital expenditures and operating cash flow deficits. The company issued $98.45 million of long-term debt in 2011 and $93.9 million in 2013. But the vast majority of Wilson's external financing has been in the form of short-term debt. Total debt as a percentage of assets (Exhibit 5.21) increased from 25.9% in 2008 to 75.7% in 2014; short-term debt as a percentage of total debt increased from 59.4% in 2008 to 78.3% in 2014, and over the same period the company's interest coverage ratio deteriorated from 8.7 times to *minus* 2.4 times.

Wilson's cash flow needs and growing debt burden raise questions about the wisdom of its dividend policy. Recall that Wilson has paid cash dividends to shareholders for almost 100 years and continued to do so during 2014 when the company reported a $145.4 million loss. Cash dividend payments totaled $17.7 million in 2008, increased to $20.8 million in 2010, and then held steady at approximately that level until falling to $4.5 million in 2014. These cash flows could instead have been used to finance the company's operating deficits and capital expenditures—or to pay down debt.[14]

Why was management so reluctant to curtail dividends? The payment of a cash dividend is viewed as an important signal by many financial analysts and investors. Management presumably "signals" its expectations about the future through its dividend policy. A cash dividend increase is viewed as an indication that management expects future operating cash flows to be favorable—to the extent it can sustain the higher dividend. A reduction in cash dividends is interpreted as an indication that management expects future operating cash flows to decrease and remain at this decreased level. Research tends to corroborate dividend signaling. Increases and decreases in cash dividend payments are (on average) associated with subsequent earnings and operating cash flow changes in the same direction. Of course, the degree of association between dividend changes and future earnings or operating cash flow performance is less than perfect. So, financial analysts and investors must carefully evaluate the specific circumstances confronting each company.

Recommendation   Wilson's use of short-term debt financing coupled with its inability to generate positive cash flows from operations places the company in a precarious position. Unless other external financing sources are identified or unless operating activities start to

---

[13] See Ross, Westerfield, and Jaffe, op. cit. These and other authors identify a third economic force that influences firms' capital structure decisions—that is, agency costs. These costs are considered in more detail in Chapter 7.

[14] Some might argue the dividend payments expose failures by creditors. The dividend payments moved assets beyond the reach of creditors, who risked being left with debt that could not be repaid. The lenders could have protected themselves with appropriate debt covenants. (See Chapter 7 for more on that topic.)

generate positive cash flows, the company will be forced to declare bankruptcy if (and when) short-term creditors demand payment on existing loans. Wilson Company is a serious credit risk to the bank, and renewal of the $200 million revolving credit line is probably not justified. In fact, the bank may consider taking immediate steps to improve the likelihood of loan repayment and to protect its creditor position in the event of bankruptcy.

> This illustration is based loosely on the financial statements of a real company, W. T. Grant, for the years 1969 through 1975. At the time that it filed for bankruptcy in late 1975, Grant was the seventeenth largest retailer in the United States. The company's collapse has been traced to a failed business strategy that involved rapid store expansion, product line extensions, and customer credit terms that contributed to delayed payment and increased customer default risk.
>
> *Source:* J. Largay and C. Stickney, "Cash Flows, Ratio Analysis and the W. T. Grant Company Bankruptcy," *Financial Analysts Journal,* July–August 1980, pp. 51–84.

RECAP

Timing differences between cash inflows and cash outflows create the need to borrow money. Cash flow analysis helps lenders identify why cash flow imbalances occur and whether the imbalance is temporary. Commercial banks, insurance companies, pension funds, and other lenders will lend the needed cash only if there is a high probability that the borrower's future cash inflows will be sufficient to repay the loan. Credit analysts rely on their understanding of the company, its business strategy and the competitive environment, and the adequacy of its past cash flows as a basis for forecasting future cash flows and assessing the company's financial flexibility under stress.

Financial Ratios and Default Risk

A company is in **default** when it fails to make a required loan payment on time. Lenders can respond to a default in several ways. At one end of the spectrum, lenders may simply adjust the loan payment schedule to better suit the company's anticipated operating cash flows. This response is appropriate when the default stems from a temporary cash flow shortfall and the borrower is fundamentally sound. If the borrower has a serious cash flow problem, lenders may modify the payment schedule in exchange for an increased interest rate or additional collateral, such as receivables, inventory, or equipment. If the borrower's cash flow problem is extreme, lenders may petition a court to judge the borrower insolvent. The court-appointed trustee may either liquidate or reorganize the business—and restructure its loans—in an effort to settle all obligations in an orderly and equitable manner. Insolvency (or *bankruptcy,* as it is more commonly known) thus becomes the ultimate form of default.

Credit analysis is intended to help lenders assess a borrower's default risk or the likelihood of loan default. Financial ratios play two crucial roles in credit analysis. First, they help lenders quantify a potential borrower's default risk before a loan decision is finalized. Second, after a loan is granted, financial ratios serve as an early warning device that alerts lenders to changes in the borrower's credit risk. But which specific financial ratios are most useful for these purposes? In other words, which particular financial ratios best predict default risk and how well do they do so?

Figure 5.6 shows the 1-year, 5-year, and 15-year default rates for 1981 to 2008 among public companies covered by Standard & Poor's, a credit-rating agency. S&P assigns a credit rating to each of several thousand companies. Because most public companies are financially sound and thus earn a relatively high credit rating, there are actually relatively few defaults in a given year, and this rarity makes predicting defaults difficult. Although about one in four of the firms in the highest risk category (CCC/C) default within a year, a relatively small portion

Figure 5.6

DEFAULT RATES AMONG
PUBLIC COMPANIES BY S&P
CREDIT RATING: 1981–2008

Source: Investor Fact Book 2009/2010,
The McGraw Hill Companies.

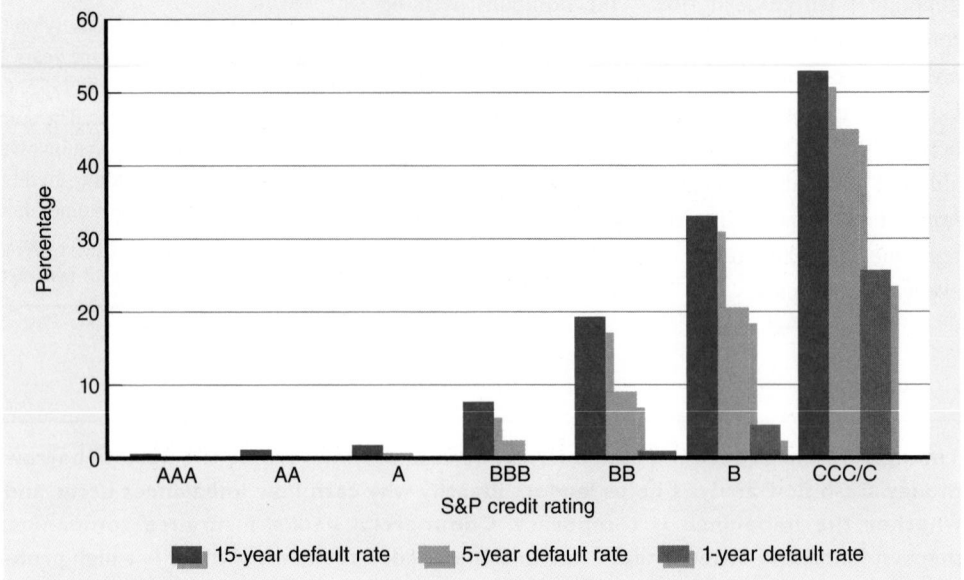

of the population of firms is in this group. Nonetheless, the ability of S&P's ratings to sort companies by default rates is immediately clear from Figure 5.6. Companies assigned the top rating (AAA) are very unlikely to default, even over long periods of time, and default rates over any time horizon are clearly increasing with lower ratings.

Financial ratios also relate to future default rates and, in fact, are generally incorporated in the credit analysis that leads to a firm's credit rating, which we have already seen relates to the probability of future default. Figure 5.7 plots default frequency for four common financial ratios: return on assets (ROA), debt to tangible assets, interest coverage, and the quick ratio. Each curve was estimated using financial data from public companies in Moody's loan default database over the 1980–1999 period. For each variable, the data were divided into 50 groups that ranged from very low values of the variable to very high values. The companies in each group were examined to determine whether a default occurred within five years of the financial statement date. Default frequencies were compiled for each group and statistically smoothed to aid interpretation.

The pattern of default frequencies in Figure 5.7 confirms basic intuition. Default risk decreases as ROA, interest coverage, and the quick ratio increase and it increases as the debt to tangible assets ratio increases. So, we see that given data about default frequencies, one could estimate the probability of default by finding where a firm's financial ratio falls on a particular curve. For example, a firm at the 40th percentile for ROA would appear to have a 5% five-year default risk.

Of course, these graphs show the relationships between default risk and a single variable at a time. If a firm whose ROA suggested a 5% default risk was in the 80th percentile for interest coverage, that statistic would suggest the default risk was below 2%. Which value is correct? Ideally, we would like to consider the effects of many variables simultaneously. One popular approach to doing so is the Altman Z-score. It combines a set of five financial ratios using multiple discriminant analysis to estimate a company's default risk conditional on all five variables.[15]

---

[15] E. Altman, "Financial Ratios, Discriminant Analysis and the Prediction of Corporate Bankruptcy," *Journal of Finance,* September 1968, pp. 589–609.

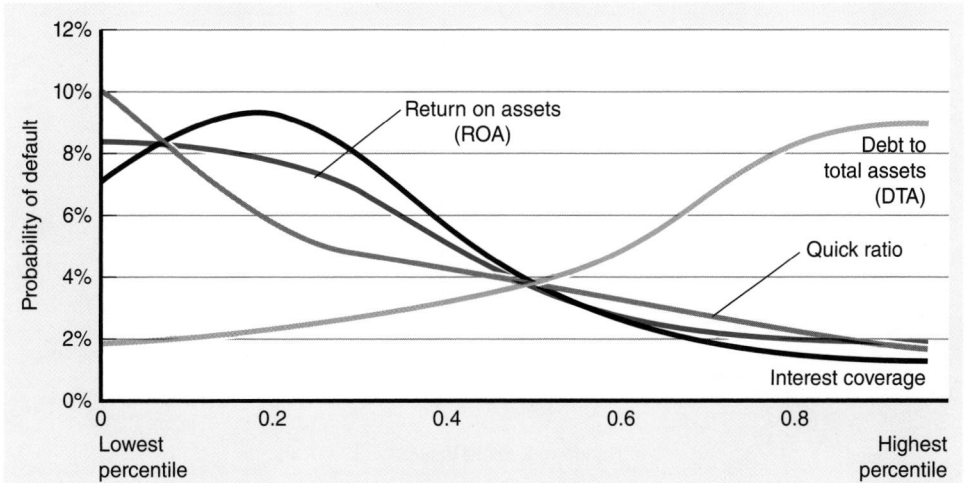

Figure 5.7

PROBABILITY OF DEFAULT
WITHIN FIVE YEARS
AMONG PUBLIC
COMPANIES: 1980–1999

Source: RiskCalc for Private Companies:
Moody's Default Model Rating
Methodology, Moody's Investors Service
(May 2000).

The Z-score model is:

$$
\begin{aligned}
\text{Z-score} = \; & 1.2 \times \text{Working capital/Total assets} \\
& + 1.4 \times \text{Retained earnings/Total assets} \\
& + 3.3 \times \text{EBIT/Total assets} \\
& + 0.6 \times \text{Market value of equity/Book value of debt} \\
& + 1.0 \times \text{Sales/Total assets}
\end{aligned}
$$

where EBIT is earnings before interest and taxes. Notice how the model combines information about a company's current profitability (EBIT/Total assets), long-term profitability (Retained earnings/Total assets), liquidity (Working capital/Total assets), solvency (Market value of equity/Book value of debt), and asset turnover (Sales/Total assets) into a single measure of bankruptcy risk. Notice also that the five surviving ratios are not simply added together to form the overall Z-score value. Instead, each ratio has its own unique weight in the final calculation.

Now suppose you applied the Z-score formula to a company and got 2.4 as your answer. As you can probably guess by looking carefully at the formula, high Z-scores are good and low Z-scores are bad. What does a Z-score of 2.4 mean? Is a value of 2.4 above or below the cutoff for predicted bankruptcy? Before we see how Altman answered this question, let's look at some hypothetical data so that we can better understand the problem Altman faced.

Suppose your company sells merchandise on credit and that it has only two types of credit customers: "deadbeats" who fail to pay their bills and "prompt payers" who always pay the full amount on time. Of course, you can't know for certain which customer types you are dealing with until it comes time for them to pay their bills. You can, however, use historical information about your customers and their payment patterns to identify characteristics that seem to predict whether a customer will be a deadbeat or prompt payer. If your customers are companies, financial ratios might do the trick, especially if those ratios are combined according to the Z-score formula. Refer to Figure 5.8 for the historical frequency distribution of Z-score values for the deadbeats and prompt-paying customers. As you might suspect, deadbeats tend to have low Z-scores (high default risk) while prompt-paying customers tend to have high Z-scores (low default risk).

Now suppose that you were to set the cutoff point at Z_1, meaning customers with Z-score values below that point would be denied credit. Almost all your prompt-paying customers

Figure 5.8

FREQUENCY DISTRIBUTION
OF Z-SCORES FOR TWO
TYPES OF CREDIT
CUSTOMER

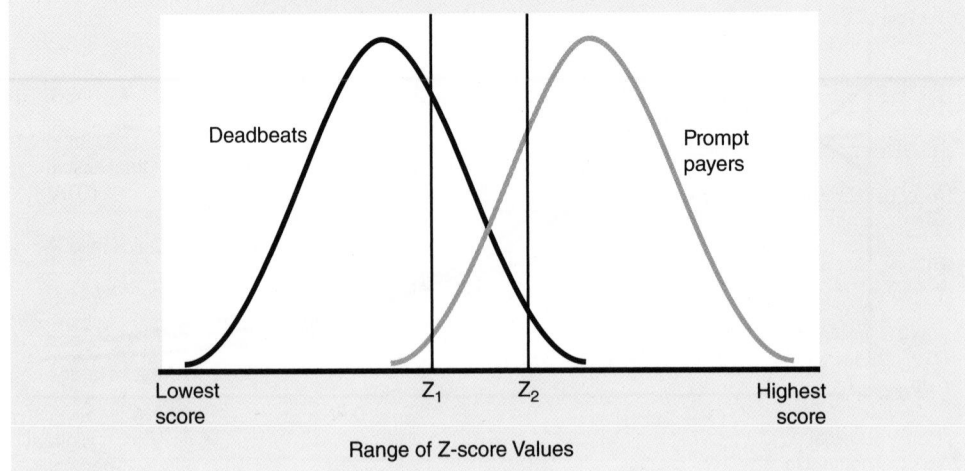

Range of Z-score Values

would qualify for credit because the vast majority of these customers have Z-scores above Z_1. Unfortunately, so do many deadbeats. If you want to deny credit to more deadbeats, you need to set the cutoff higher. The value Z_2 in Figure 5.8 is one possibility. Using this cutoff, fewer deadbeats will qualify for credit, but you will also be denying credit to a larger number of prompt-paying customers.

The research evidence led Altman to conclude that firms having a Z-score higher than 2.99 (think Z_2) clearly fell into the "prompt payer" category—our label, not his—and were predicted to remain solvent. Firms having a Z-score of less than 1.81 (think Z_1) clearly fell into the deadbeat category and were predicted to go bankrupt. Firms with Z-scores that fell between these two cutoff points landed in a gray area, where classification mistakes can be large (because the two distributions overlap) and costly. Altman recommends that these firms be given additional, in-depth scrutiny using conventional financial analysis tools and information beyond just that contained in the published financial statements.

The original Z-score model was designed for publicly traded manufacturing firms. Altman has since developed models for private companies and public service–sector firms.[16] Credit-rating agencies like Dun and Bradstreet have used a similar approach to develop their credit-rating scores, although these agencies are often silent about the specific factors they consider and how much weight each factor is given in the composite score.

Other researchers have developed bankruptcy prediction models as well using other statistical techniques. Two of the more well know models are by Ohlson (1980) and Zmijewski (1984).[17]

RE CAP

When lenders want to know about a company's ability to pay debts on time, they assess its credit risk. Credit risk assessment often begins with a cash flow statement because it shows the company's operating cash flows along with its financing and investment needs. A low credit risk company generates operating cash flows substantially in excess of what are required to sustain its business activities. The lender also can use liquidity and solvency ratios to assess credit risk.

[16] See E. Altman, *Corporate Financial Distress and Bankruptcy* (New York: Wiley, 1993).

[17] See J. Ohlson, "Financial Ratios and the Probabilistic Prediction of Bankruptcy," *Journal of Accounting Research,* Spring 1980, pp. 109–31, and M. Zmijewski, "Methodological Issues Related to the Estimation of Financial Distress Prediction Models," *Journal of Accounting Research*, Supplement 1984, pp. 59–82.

SUMMARY

Financial ratios, along with common-size and trend statements, provide analysts powerful tools for tracking a company's performance over time, for making comparisons among different companies, and for assessing compliance with contractual benchmarks. Here are some things to remember about those tools:

- **There is no single "correct" way to compute many financial ratios.** In this chapter, we have shown you how to compute common financial ratios using widely accepted methods. But not every analyst calculates these ratios in exactly the same way. Why? Sometimes it's a matter of personal taste or industry practice (for example, operating profit ratios for retail companies often exclude depreciation and rent). At other times, it's because the analyst is attempting to make the numbers more comparable across companies or over time.

- **Financial ratios don't provide the answers, but they can help you ask the right questions.** It's useful to know that a company's profitability or credit risk has improved (or declined), but it's even more important to know *why* the change occurred. Did consumer demand increase, or was the company stealing market share from competitors? Were operating costs reduced and, if so, which ones? Use the financial ratios and the other tools in this chapter to guide your analysis. They can help you to ask the right questions and tell you where to look for answers.

- **Is it the economics of the business or is it the accounting?** Watch out for accounting distortions that can complicate your interpretation of financial ratios and other comparisons. Remember that the analyst's task is to "get behind the numbers"—that is, to develop a solid understanding of the company's economic activities and how industry fundamentals have shaped where the company is today and where it will be tomorrow.

APPENDIX

SEGMENT REPORTING

Whereas Whole Foods operates in one industry, most public companies have operations in multiple industries that may have very different operating characteristics and risks. To inform investors and creditors about these differences, U.S. GAAP requires **public entities** with multiple business segments to disclose limited financial information for each segment.[18] The 2012 AICPA survey of 2011 annual reports shows that 84% of the 500 companies surveyed report separate information for business segments.[19]

Definition of a Reportable Segment

The standards do not mandate the basis (e.g., product type or geography) for segment disclosure. Instead, they require a **management approach** where the information is disclosed in the same manner that it is organized internally for "making operating decisions and assessing

---

[18] The guidance is contained under Financial Accounting Standards Board (FASB) Accounting Standards Codification (ASC) Topic 280: Segment Reporting. The guidance for segment reporting under *International Financial Reporting Standards (IFRS) 8—"Operating Segments"* is very similar to the FASB guidance discussed in this appendix. The FASB Codification defines a **public entity** as a business or not-for-profit entity that has publicly traded debt or equity securities, is required to file financial statements with the Securities and Exchange Commission (SEC), or makes financial statements public in anticipation of issuing publicly traded securities (see FASB ASC 280-10-20: Segment Reporting—Overall—Glossary.

[19] See R. J. Petrino, D. J. Cohen, A. V. Patel, and K. A. Kraft (eds.), *Accounting Trends and Techniques* (New York: American Institute of Certified Public Accountants, Inc., 2012), p. 45.

performance."[20] The standards define an **operating segment** as a component of a public entity that earns revenue and incurs expenses within or outside the entity and produces discrete financial information that is reviewed and used by the **chief operating decision maker** (CODM). The CODM may be the chief executive officer (CEO), chief operating officer (COO), president, or group of officers responsible for reviewing entity activities and allocating resources.[21]

An entity could have hundreds of operational units that meet the above definition of an operating segment. Disclosing separate financial information for so many segments would be onerous for the reporting entity and overly detailed for investors and creditors. Therefore, U.S. GAAP provides criteria for aggregating operating segments. An entity may combine operating segments into one segment when the segments have similar economic characteristics (e.g., gross margin) and are similar with regard to *all* of the following:

a. Product and service,

b. Production process,

c. Type or class of customer,

d. Product and service distribution methods, and

e. Regulatory environment.[22]

After the operating segments are aggregated using the above criteria, the firm must disclose information for segments meeting any of the following **quantitative thresholds:**

a. Revenue equals or exceeds 10% of total revenue from internal and external parties.

b. The absolute value of operating profit or loss equals or exceeds 10% of the greater of (in absolute value terms) combined segment operating profit of those segments with profits and combined segment operating losses of those segments with losses.

c. Assets equal or exceed 10% of total segment assets.

When operating segments do not meet the 10% thresholds, management may disclose information at lower thresholds if it believes the information meets the objective of the standard or may further aggregate operating segments if the **majority** of the five aggregation criteria from above are met. **Reportable segments** (segments for which management provides separate disclosure) must represent at least 75% of the revenue reported on the income statement. To meet this requirement, a firm may have to report segment information for a segment with revenue, profit, or assets that represent less than 10% of the total amounts.[23]

To illustrate the interaction of the aggregation and quantitative guidelines, we use the following example and focus on revenue.[24] A similar approach would be used for operating profit and assets to determine whether their magnitude would make the segment reportable.

[20] See FASB ASC Paragraph 280-10-05-3: Segment Reporting—Overall—Overview and Background—General.

[21] See FASB ASC Paragraphs 280-10-50-1 to 9: Segment Reporting—Overall—Disclosure—General.

[22] See FASB ASC Paragraphs 280-10-50-10 to 11: Segment Reporting—Overall—Disclosure—General.

[23] See FASB ASC Paragraphs 280-10-50-12 to 14: Segment Reporting—Overall—Disclosure—General.

[24] We base this example on illustrations contained in FASB ASC Paragraphs 280-10-55-31 to 42: Segment Reporting—Overall—Implementation Guidance and Illustrations—General.

Castle Company has seven operating segments with the following revenue. All revenue amounts represent sales to external customers. In other words, there are no sales between segments.

Operating Segment	Revenue
A	$ 23
B	31
C	19
D	9
E	7
F	5
G	6
Total	$100

Assume that the economic environments of Segments A and C are similar. Both segments have similar products, production processes, customers, distribution methods, and regulatory environment. Segments D and F have similar products, production processes, and regulatory environments. Segments E and G are not similar to any of the other segments.

Step 1 in determining the reportable segments is to aggregate the segments with similar economic environments. Therefore, Castle would aggregate segments **A** and **C** to form a combined **AC** reportable segment. **Step 2** is to determine which segments exceed the 10% of revenue threshold. **AC** $42 ($23 from **A** + $19 from **C**) and **B** exceed the 10% threshold. **Step 3** allows Castle to combine segments with revenue below the 10% threshold if the segments meet the **majority** of the aggregation criteria. In this case, segments **D** and **F** may be combined to form a combined **DF** reportable segment with revenue of $14 ($9 from **D** and $5 from **F**). The sum of the revenue for the three reportable segments is $87 ($42 from **AC** + $31 from **B** + $14 from **DF**), which is greater than 75% of total revenue. Castle would combine segments **E** and **G** in an "Other" category when reconciling to the revenue reported on the income statement.

In this case, Castle moved from seven *operating* segments to three *reportable* segments. Firms with tens or hundreds of segments would follow the same process. The accounting standards suggest that a firm would generally limit disclosures to 10 reportable segments. Often managers resist identifying additional segments because they fear that competitors could use the resulting disclosures.

Required Disclosures

GAAP requires companies to explain how they determine their reportable segments and to describe the products or services generating revenue for each segment.[25] In addition, it requires for each segment the following income statement data:

a. Revenue from customers outside the company,

b. Revenue from other segments within the company,

c. Interest revenue,

---

[25] See FASB ASC Paragraphs 280-10-50-20 to 42: Segment Reporting—Overall—Disclosure—General.

   d. Interest expense,

   e. Depreciation, depletion, amortization, and other significant noncash expenses,

   f. Unusual gains and losses, such as restructuring charges or gains on sales of subsidiaries,

   g. Equity method income (see Chapter 16, pages 961–966),

   h. Income tax expense,

   i. Extraordinary items, and

   j. Profit or loss.

A company also must report for each segment the following balance sheet data:

   a. Total assets,

   b. Equity method investments (see Chapter 16, pages 961–966), and

   c. Additions to long-lived assets.

The above segment information must be reconciled to the amounts reported in the financial statements for the full company. We discuss the reconciliations in conjunction with the Harley-Davidson example in the next section of the appendix.

   As mentioned earlier in the appendix, companies report segments according to how they are managed internally. To improve comparability, U.S. GAAP requires minimal **enterprise-wide disclosures** related to industry and geographic location if it is *not* included in the disclosures based on the management approach. These requirements also apply to companies that have only one business segment. Under these requirements, the company must report revenues from external customers for each group of similar products or services. The geographic disclosures include:

   a. Revenues from external customers derived from the entity's country of domicile,

   b. Revenues from external customers derived from all foreign sources, with disclosure by individual country when the revenues from that country are material,

   c. Long-lived assets located in the entity's country of domicile, and

   d. Long-lived assets located in foreign countries, with disclosure by individual country when the long-lived assets located in the country are material.

To provide additional information on risk, GAAP requires a public entity to make additional disclosures when one external customer accounts for 10% or more of its revenues. This disclosure includes the total amount from each such customer and the segments affected. For example, The Boeing Company's 2012 Form 10-K reported that 33% of its 2012 revenue came from the United States government. The Defense, Space & Security segment generated the revenue. Actions to reduce the U.S. deficit could threaten this revenue in future years.

Case Study: Harley-Davidson, Inc.

To illustrate and analyze segment disclosures, we use excerpts from Harley-Davidson's 2012 Form 10-K (see Exhibit 5.22). We number the schedules to make it easier to follow our explanations. Harley-Davidson (hereafter, HD) operates in two segments, Motorcycles and Financial Services. Manufacturers of expensive, long-lived equipment often have finance subsidiaries, which can make some ratios similar to banks instead of manufacturing firms.

   Schedule 1 of Exhibit 5.22 provides income statement information. We can isolate each segment's contribution to total company revenue (a common-size approach), compute an operating profit margin (that is, operating income divided by revenue), and growth for each segment. Total revenue for 2012 is $5,580.5 million (Motorcycles net revenue of

$4,942.6 million + Financial services revenue of $637.9 million). Motorcycles revenue represents 88.6% ($4,942.6 million/$5,580.5 million), and Financial services represents the remaining 11.4%. The operating profit margin for each segment is considerably different. The 2012 operating profit margin for Motorcycles is 14.5% (Operating income of $715.5 million/ Revenue of $4,942.6 million), whereas the ratio for Financial services is 44.6% (Operating income of $284.7 million/Revenue of $637.9 million).

The growth rates for each segment also differ. The 2012 growth rates for Motorcycle revenue and operating profit are 6.0% (2012 Motorcycles revenue of $4,942.6 million/2011

EXHIBIT 5.22	Harley-Davidson, Inc. Business Segment and Geographic Disclosures

Business Segments:

The Company operates in two business segments: Motorcycles and Financial Services. The Company's reportable segments are strategic business units that offer different products and services. They are managed separately based on the fundamental differences in their operations.

The Motorcycles segment designs, manufactures and sells at wholesale heavyweight (engine displacement of 651+cc) cruiser and touring motorcycles as well as a line of motorcycle parts, accessories, general merchandise and related services.

The Financial Services segment provides wholesale and retail financing and provides insurance and insurance-related programs primarily to Harley-Davidson dealers and their retail customers. HDFS conducts business principally in the United States and Canada.

Schedule 1: Income Statement Information

Information by segment is set forth below for the years ended December 31 (in thousands):

	2012	2011	2010
Motorcycles net revenue	$4,942,582	$4,662,264	$4,176,627
Gross profit	1,720,188	1,555,976	1,427,403
Selling, administrative and engineering expense	976,224	926,808	885,137
Restructuring expense and other impairments	28,475	67,992	163,508
Operating income from Motorcycles	$ 715,489	$ 561,176	$ 378,758
Financial services revenue	$ 637,924	$ 649,449	$ 682,709
Financial services expense	353,237	380,658	500,836
Operating income from Financial Services	$ 284,687	$ 268,791	$ 181,873

Schedule 2: Asset Information

Information by industry segment is set forth below as of December 31 (in thousands):

	Motorcycles	Financial Services	Consolidated
2012			
Total assets	$2,751,018	$6,419,755	$9,170,773
Depreciation	$ 162,659	$ 6,319	$ 168,978
Capital expenditures	$ 180,416	$ 8,586	$ 189,002
2011			
Total assets	$2,959,333	$6,714,831	$9,674,164
Depreciation	$ 173,959	$ 6,449	$ 180,408
Capital expenditures	$ 179,988	$ 9,047	$ 189,035
2010			
Total assets	$2,701,965	$6,728,775	$9,430,740
Depreciation	$ 248,246	$ 6,925	$ 255,171
Capital expenditures	$ 167,730	$ 3,115	$ 170,845

(continued)

EXHIBIT 5.22 Harley-Davidson, Inc. Business Segment and Geographic Disclosures *(continued)*

Schedule 3: Geographic Information

Included in the consolidated financial statements are the following amounts relating to geographic locations for the years ended December 31 (in thousands):

	2012	2011	2010
Revenue from Motorcycles[a]:			
United States	$3,363,640	$3,155,608	$2,818,032
Europe	710,861	781,432	699,492
Japan	244,907	229,427	234,247
Canada	186,550	154,314	157,606
Australia	186,674	141,392	136,172
Other foreign countries	249,950	200,091	131,078
	$4,942,582	$4,662,264	$4,176,627
Revenue from Financial Services[a]:			
United States	$ 607,909	$ 619,214	$ 652,849
Europe	5,483	4,471	3,497
Canada	24,532	25,764	26,363
	$ 637,924	$ 649,449	$ 682,709
Long-lived assets[b]:			
United States	$ 825,509	$ 822,089	$ 842,461
International	56,143	59,571	62,192
	$ 881,652	$ 881,660	$ 904,653

[a] Revenue is attributed to geographic regions based on location of customer.

[b] Long-lived assets include all long-term assets except those specifically excluded under ASC Topic 280, "Segment Reporting," such as deferred income taxes and finance receivables.

Motorcycles revenue of $4,662.3 million minus 1) and 27.5% (2012 Motorcycles operating income of $715.5 million/2011 Motorcycles operating income of $561.2 million minus 1), respectively. In contrast, the growth rates for Financial services are much lower. The 2012 growth rates for Financial services revenue and operating profit are −1.8% (2012 Financial services revenue of $637.9 million/2011 Financial services revenue of $649.4 million minus 1) and 5.9% (2012 Financial services operating income of $284.7 million/2011 Financial services operating income of $268.8 million minus 1), respectively.

Segment notes provide three years of income statement data, and analysts can ascertain how the segment contributions to revenue and profit change over time. The growth rates and margins also provide insights into how well managers are running the various segments. When growth rates, margins, or mix of income changes, the analyst should critically examine management explanations for the changes found in the **Management Discussion and Analysis (MD&A)** section of Form 10-K. The analyst may have to revise forecasts upward or downward depending on the explanations and the analyst's view of the future business environment.

Schedule 2 provides Total assets, Depreciation, and Capital expenditures for both segments. Note that the Motorcycles segment has most of the Capital expenditures and Depreciation. However, the Financial services segment has more than twice the total assets. As we stated earlier, the Financial services segment financial statements are similar to those of banks. Whereas the Motorcycles segment has most of the physical assets, the Financial services segment holds primarily financial assets.

Schedule 3 provides geographic information. Both segments derive most of their revenues from the United States. However, Motorcycles revenue also is disclosed separately for Europe, Japan, Canada, and Australia. The currency rate changes, business cycles, regulations, and risks differ across these geographic areas. The vast majority of Financial services revenue comes from the United States, but HD discloses separate amounts for Europe and Canada. Finally, most long-lived assets reside in the United States.

Usually, companies with finance subsidiaries provide detailed income statement and balance sheet information for the finance subsidiary and the remainder of the company. These schedules also may be used to reconcile the segment amounts to the company's total (consolidated) financial statement amounts. Exhibit 5.23 provides HD's detailed income statement and balance sheet information for Motorcycles, Financial services, reconciling items (eliminations), and Consolidated (total) amounts.

Note that the Motorcycles and Financial services segments have different categories of revenue and expense items on its income statement. We also see different captions for the segments on the balance sheet. As mentioned previously, the Motorcycles segment has most of the physical assets, and the Financial services segment has most of the financial assets. This additional detail allows an analyst to compute separately most of the ratios discussed earlier in the chapter for both the finance and nonfinance segments. In addition, this type of information and the segment information presented in Exhibit 5.22 allows more accurate forecasting (see Chapter 6, Appendix B, page 347). The Eliminations column removes the effects of transactions between the Motorcycles and Financial services segments so that only transactions with external parties are included in the Consolidated column. Chapter 16 (page 972) discusses intercompany transactions and their eliminations in detail.

EXHIBIT 5.23 Harley-Davidson, Inc. Supplemental Business Segment Income Statement and Balance Sheet Information

	Motorcycles & Related Products Operations	Financial Services Operations	Eliminations	Consolidated
Revenue:				
Motorcycles and related products	$4,952,748	$ —	$ (10,166)	$4,942,582
Financial services	—	639,482	(1,558)	637,924
Total revenue	4,952,748	639,482	(11,724)	5,580,506
Costs and expenses:				
Motorcycles and related products cost of goods sold	3,222,394	—	—	3,222,394
Financial services interest expense	—	195,990	—	195,990
Financial services provision for credit losses	—	22,239	—	22,239
Selling, administrative and engineering expense	977,782	145,174	(11,724)	1,111,232
Restructuring expense	28,475	—	—	28,475
Total costs and expenses	4,228,651	363,403	(11,724)	4,580,330
Operating income	724,097	276,079	—	1,000,176
Investment income	232,369	—	(225,000)	7,369
Interest expense	46,033	—	—	46,033
Income before provision for income taxes	910,433	276,079	(225,000)	961,512
Provision for income taxes	233,385	104,202	—	337,587
Income from continuing operations	677,048	171,877	(225,000)	623,925
Income from discontinued operations, net of tax	—	—	—	—
Net income	$ 677,048	$171,877	$(225,000)	$ 623,925

(continued)

Year Ended December 31, 2012

| EXHIBIT 5.23 | Harley-Davidson, Inc. Supplemental Business Segment Income Statement and Balance Sheet Information (continued) | | | |

| | December 31, 2012 | | | |
	Motorcycles & Related Products Operations	Financial Services Operations	Eliminations	Consolidated
ASSETS				
Current assets:				
Cash and cash equivalents	$ 727,716	$ 340,422	$ —	$1,068,138
Marketable securities	135,634	—	—	135,634
Accounts receivable, net	781,642	—	(551,563)	230,079
Finance receivables, net	—	1,743,045	—	1,743,045
Inventories	393,524	—	—	393,524
Restricted cash	—	188,008	—	188,008
Deferred income taxes	84,486	26,367	—	110,853
Other current assets	146,419	31,242	3,994	181,655
Total current assets	2,269,421	2,329,084	(547,569)	4,050,936
Finance receivables, net	—	4,038,807	—	4,038,807
Property, plant and equipment, net	783,068	32,396	—	815,464
Goodwill	29,530	—	—	29,530
Deferred income taxes	175,839	—	(3,994)	171,845
Other long-term assets	116,925	19,468	(72,202)	64,191
	$3,374,783	$6,419,755	$(623,765)	$9,170,773
LIABILITES AND SHAREHOLDERS' EQUITY				
Current liabilities:				
Accounts payable	$ 221,064	$ 587,885	$(551,563)	$ 257,386
Accrued liabilities	439,144	74,447	—	513,591
Short-term debt	—	294,943	—	294,943
Current portion of long-term debt	—	437,162	—	437,162
Total current liabilities	660,208	1,394,437	(551,563)	1,503,082
Long-term debt	303,000	4,067,544	—	4,370,544
Pension liability	330,294	—	—	330,294
Postretirement healthcare liability	278,062	—	—	278,062
Other long-term liabilities	114,476	16,691	—	131,167
Commitments and contingencies (Note 16)				
Total shareholders' equity	1,688,743	941,083	(72,202)	2,557,624
	$3,374,783	$6,419,755	$(623,765)	$9,170,773

EXERCISES

E5-1

Calculating Profitability Ratios **(LO 3)**

AICPA
ADAPTED

The following information is from the 2014 annual report of Weber Corporation, a company that supplies manufactured parts to the household appliance industry.

Average total assets	$24,500,000
Average interest-bearing debt	10,000,000
Average other liabilities	2,250,000
Average shareholders' equity	12,250,000
Sales	49,000,000
Interest expense	800,000
Net income	2,450,000

Required:

1. Compute Weber Corporation's return on assets (ROA) for 2014 using a combined federal and state income tax rate of 40% where needed.

2. Compute the profit margin and asset turnover components of ROA for 2014.

3. Weber's management believes that various business initiatives will produce an asset turn-over rate of 2.25 next year. If the profit margin next year is unchanged from 2014, what will be the company's ROA?

On January 1, 2014, River Company's inventory was $400,000. During 2014, the company purchased $1,900,000 of additional inventory, and on December 31, 2014, its inventory was $500,000.

Required:
What is the inventory turnover for 2014?

E 5-2

Determining inventory turnover **(LO 3)**

AICPA
ADAPTED

Utica Company's net accounts receivable was $250,000 at December 31, 2013, and $300,000 at December 31, 2014. Net cash sales for 2014 were $100,000. The accounts receivable turn-over for 2014 was 5.0, which was computed from net credit sales for the year.

Required:
What was Utica's total net sales for 2014?

E 5-3

Determining receivable turnover **(LO 3)**

AICPA
ADAPTED

Selected data of Islander Company follow:

E 5-4

Assessing receivable and inventory turnover **(LO 3)**

AICPA
ADAPTED

	As of December 31,	
Balance Sheet Data	**2014**	**2013**
Accounts receivable	$500,000	$470,000
Allowance for doubtful accounts	(25,000)	(20,000)
Net accounts receivable	$475,000	$450,000
Inventories—lower of cost or market	$600,000	$550,000

	Year Ended December 31,	
Income Statement Data	**2014**	**2013**
Net credit sales	$2,500,000	$2,200,000
Net cash sales	500,000	400,000
Net sales	$3,000,000	$2,600,000
Cost of goods sold	$2,000,000	$1,800,000
Selling, general, and administrative expenses	300,000	270,000
Other	50,000	30,000
Total operating expenses	$2,350,000	$2,100,000

Required:

1. What is the accounts receivable turnover for 2014?

2. What is the inventory turnover for 2014?

E5-5 Analyzing current and quick ratios **(LO 5)** AICPA ADAPTED	Todd Corporation wrote off $100,000 of obsolete inventory at December 31, 2014. **Required:** What effect did this write-off have on the company's December 31, 2014, current and quick ratios?
E5-6 Analyzing effects on current ratio **(LO 5)** AICPA ADAPTED	Gil Corporation has current assets of $90,000 and current liabilities of $180,000. **Required:** Compute the effect of each of the following independent transactions on Gil's current ratio: 1. Refinancing a $30,000 long-term mortgage with a short-term note. 2. Purchasing $50,000 of merchandise inventory with short-term accounts payable. 3. Paying $20,000 of short-term accounts payable. 4. Collecting $10,000 of short-term accounts receivable.

E5-7

Calculating interest coverage **(LO 5)**

AICPA
ADAPTED

The following data were taken from the financial records of Glum Corporation for 2014:

Sales	$3,600,000
Bond interest expense	120,000
Income taxes	600,000
Net income	800,000

Required:
How many times was bond interest earned in 2014?

E5-8

Analyzing why inventory turnover increased **(LO 7)**

AICPA
ADAPTED

A comparison of 2014 to 2013 performance shows that Neir Company's inventory turnover increased substantially although sales and inventory amounts were essentially unchanged.

Required:
Which of the following statements best explains the increased inventory turnover ratio?

1. Cost of goods sold decreased.
2. Accounts receivable turnover increased.
3. Total asset turnover increased.
4. Gross profit percentage decreased.

E5-9

Calculating days sales outstanding **(LO 3)**

AICPA
ADAPTED

Selected information taken from the accounting records of Vigor Company follows:

Net accounts receivable at December 31, 2013	$ 900,000
Net accounts receivable at December 31, 2014	$1,000,000
Accounts receivable turnover	5 to 1
Inventories at December 31, 2013	$1,100,000
Inventories at December 31, 2014	$1,200,000
Inventory turnover	4 to 1

Required:

1. What was Vigor's gross profit for 2014?
2. Suppose that there are 360 business days in the year. What were the number of days sales outstanding in average receivables and the number of days sales outstanding in average inventories, respectively, for 2014?

The Hershey Co. is famous worldwide for its chocolate confections—the Hershey bar and those delightful Hershey Kisses. Tootsie Roll Industries is equally famous for its chewy Tootsie Roll and those flavorful Tootsie Roll Pops. Selected financial information about each company's performance in 2011 follows:

	Hershey Co.	Tootsie Roll Indus.
Sales	$6,080 mil.	$533 mil.
Net income	$629 mil.	$44 mil.
Return on assets (ROA)	15.8%	5.1%
Profit margin	11.3%	8.3%
Asset turnover	1.40	0.62

Required:

1. Why is Tootsie Roll so much less profitable than Hershey?

2. The industry-average ROA for confectioners is around 10%. Which company has the more valuable brand?

Mentor Graphics Corporation, a supplier of electronic design automation systems, just announced its second quarter results. According to the earnings press release, the company reported "revenues of $182.6 million, non-GAAP earnings per share of $0.02, and a GAAP loss per share of $0.22." Elsewhere in the press release the company says that non-GAAP earnings excludes the following items incurred during the quarter: equity-based (noncash) employee compensation; severance and related employee "rebalancing" costs; fees paid to consultants; losses related to the abandonment of excess facility space and to a facility fire; interest expense; along with other assorted items.

There is no standard definition of non-GAAP earnings. Each firm is permitted to construct its own definition for press release purposes. As a result, the Securities and Exchange Commission requires firms such as Mentor Graphics to provide a reconciliation of GAAP and non-GAAP earnings any time a non-GAAP measure is presented.

Required:

1. Which of the excluded items represent ongoing costs of running the business and which are one-time "special" costs?

2. How might analysts and investors benefit when firms call attention to their non-GAAP earnings?

3. How might analysts and investors be harmed?

This exercise is built around Whole Foods Market's financial statements from the chapter. Several items of additional information are needed: there were no dividends on redeemable preferred stock in 2012, the preferred stock having been redeemed in 2010; preferred dividends were $19,833 in 2009; average common shareholders' equity for 2009 was $1,566,950; and a 40% income tax rate should be used as needed.

Required:

1. Whole Foods earned an ROA of 4.7% in 2009. What was ROCE that year?

2. ROA at the company grew to 9.7% in 2012. What was ROCE that year?

3. Did financial leverage help or hurt Whole Foods Market in 2012? How can you tell?

E5-13

Cause-of-change analysis
(LO 1)

Following are income statements for Hossa Corporation for 2014 and 2013. Percentage of sales amounts are also shown for each operating expense item. Hossa's income tax rate was 38% in 2013 and 40% in 2014.

($ in millions)	2013		2014	
	$ in millions	**% of sales**	**$ in millions**	**% of sales**
Sales	$5,500		$6,500	
Cost of sales	(2,475)	45%	(3,055)	47%
Other operating expenses	(825)	15%	(1,040)	16%
Operating income	2,200		2,405	
Provision for income taxes	(836)		(962)	
Net income	$1,364		$1,443	
Income tax rate	38%		40%	

Hossa's management was pleased that 2014 net income was up 5.8% from the prior year. Although you are also happy with the increase in net income, you are not so sure the news is all positive. You have modeled Hossa's income as follows:

$$\text{NET INCOME} = \text{SALES} \times (1 - \text{COGS\%} - \text{OPEX\%}) \times (1 - \text{TAX RATE})$$

Using this model, net income in 2013 is computed as $5,500 \times (1 - 45\% - 15\%) \times (1 - 38\%) = \$1,364$. Net income in 2014 is computed as $6,500 \times (1 - 47\% - 16\%) \times (1 - 40\%) = \$1,443$.

Required:

1. Prepare a cause-of-change analysis to show the extent to which each of the following items contributed to the $79 million increase in Hossa's net income from 2013 to 2014:

   - Increase in sales (SALES)

   - Increase in cost of sales as a percent of sales (COGS%)

   - Increase in other operating expenses as a percent of sales (OPEX%)

   - Increase in income tax rate (TAX RATE)

2. Interpret the results for Hossa's management.

PROBLEMS / DISCUSSION QUESTIONS

P5-1

Comparing profitablity
(LO 3)

The following table presents ROA calculations for three companies in the retail grocery industry using earnings before interest (EBI) and balance sheet data for each company. The Kroger Company operates more than 2,400 supermarkets and multi-department stores. Publix Super Markets operates about 1,000 supermarkets in the Southeastern United States. Stater Brothers Holdings operates 167 supermarkets in Southern California.

The Kroger Co.				
Year Ending	**01/31/09**	**01/30/10**	**01/29/11**	**01/28/12**
Sales (in millions of dollars)	$76,063	$76,609	$82,049	$90,374
Profit margin (EBI/sales)	2.03%	0.47%	1.71%	0.95%
Asset turnover (Sales/Average assets)	3.27	3.31	3.49	3.85
ROA = Margin × Asset turnover	6.62%	1.55%	5.96%	3.65%

(continued)

Publix Super Markets

Year Ending	12/27/08	12/26/09	12/25/10	12/31/11
Sales (in millions of dollars)	$23,929	$24,320	$25,134	$26,967
Profit margin (EBI/sales)	4.55%	4.78%	5.32%	5.53%
Asset turnover (Sales/Average assets)	2.96	2.70	2.47	2.39
ROA = Margin × Asset turnover	13.47%	12.90%	13.17%	13.24%

Stater Brothers Holdings

Year Ending	09/27/09	09/26/10	09/25/11	09/30/12
Sales (in millions of dollars)	$3,766	$3,607	$3,693	$3,873
Profit margin (EBI/sales)	2.01%	1.82%	1.61%	1.72%
Asset turnover (Sales/Average assets)	2.86	2.73	3.00	3.21
ROA = Margin × Asset turnover	5.76%	4.97%	4.83%	5.50%

Note: Amounts are rounded. ROA = EBI/Average assets. ROA is also equal to the product of Profit margin and Asset turnover computed using the *unrounded* values for those amounts.

Required:

1. Which company has shown the strongest sales growth over the past three years?

2. Which company was the most profitable in its most recent fiscal year? What was the source of that superior profitability—a profit margin advantage or better turnover?

P5-2

Assessing short-term liquidity **(LO 5)**

The following table reports the operating cycle, cash conversion cycle, and current ratio for three apparel retailers all having year-ends at January 28, 2012. Aeropostale, which was originally owned by Macy's, is a specialty retailer of casual apparel and accessories targeting 14- to 17-year olds. The GAP built its brand name on basic, casual clothing and expanded its market by opening Banana Republic and Old Navy Stores. Ross Stores operates over 1,000 Ross Dress for Less® stores, which primarily target middle-income households.

	Aeropostale	GAP	Ross Stores
Days inventory held	33.7	63.7	64.8
Days accounts receivable outstanding	0.0	0.0	2.0
Days accounts payable outstanding	21.6	41.6	44.4
Operating cycle (1 + 2)	33.7	63.7	66.9
Cash conversion cycle (1 + 2 − 3)	12.0	22.0	22.5
Current ratio	2.29	2.02	1.43

All three companies follow the industry practice of including occupancy costs in cost of goods sold.

Required:

1. Do any of these companies appear to have a short-term liquidity problem?

2. How does the industry practice of including occupancy costs in cost of goods sold affect the statistics presented in the above table?

3. What is the most likely explanation for Ross Stores' 2.0 days accounts receivable outstanding?

4. What is the most likely explanation for 0.0 days accounts receivable outstanding at Aeropostale and The GAP?

P5-3

Analyzing credit risk and long-term solvency **(LO 5)**

AK Steel Holding Corporation is a fully integrated producer of steel operating seven manufacturing and finishing plants in Indiana, Kentucky, Ohio, and Pennsylvania. These plants produce cold-rolled and hot-rolled steel products as well as specialty stainless and electrical steels that are sold to the domestic automotive, appliance, industrial machinery and equipment, and construction markets. Comparative debt ratios for AK Steel are shown in the following table.

AK Steel Holding Corporation

	2008	2009	2010	2011
Long-term debt-to-assets ratio	0.14	0.14	0.16	0.15
Long-term debt-to-tangible-assets ratio	0.14	0.14	0.16	0.15
Interest coverage ratio	0.86	(1.65)	(4.29)	(4.35)
Cash flow coverage ratio	2.79	2.59	(3.01)	(2.80)
Operating cash flow to total liabilities	0.02	0.02	(0.04)	(0.05)

Required:

1. Does AK Steel appear to be able to make its interest payments? How can you tell?

2. Does AK Steel rely heavily on debt to finance asset purchases? Has the company's reliance on debt changed significantly over the past several years?

3. Does AK Steel have significant amounts of intangible assets? How can you tell?

P 5-4

Decomposing return on common shareholders' equity (ROCE) **(LO 4)**

The following table provides ROA and ROCE for Best Buy, a retailer of consumer electronics.

Best Buy

	Year Ended		
	February 27, 2010	**February 26, 2011**	**March 3, 2012**
ROA	0.080	0.074	(0.068)
ROCE	0.217	0.179	(0.211)

Required:

1. How did Best Buy's performance change over the period shown?

2. What is the most likely reason the change in ROCE was so much greater than the change in ROA?

P 5-5

Interpreting accounts receivable turnover **(LO 7)**

Boise, Inc., manufactures packaging and paper products, including corrugated containers, protective packaging, and newsprint. KapStone Paper and Packaging Corporation manufactures unbleached kraft paper products and corrugated products. Financial statement data for these two companies follow:

Boise, Inc.

(in thousands of dollars)	2008	2009	2010	2011
Sales		$1,935,410	$2,058,132	$2,364,024
Accounts receivable at December 31	$220,204	185,110	188,589	228,838

KapStone Paper and Packaging Corporation

Sales		$632,478	$782,676	$906,119
Accounts receivable at December 31	$71,489	58,408	66,640	108,320

Required:

1. Determine the receivables turnover ratios for both companies for 2009, 2010, and 2011.

2. Which company collected its accounts receivable more quickly in 2011?

3. Which company showed more improvement in accounts receivable collection over the period presented?

4. What factors might explain why these two companies, which operate in similar markets, have different accounts receivable turnover ratios?

5. How does the way we compute average accounts receivable—by averaging the beginning and ending balances—potentially distort the accounts receivable turnover ratio? How could this potential distortion be mitigated?

Danaher Corporation manufactures a variety of products, including electronic measurement instruments and network communications products, water quality measurement systems, and medical and dental instruments. Selected financial statement data and related performance indicators follow.

P 5 - 6

Analyzing inventories
(LO 7)

Danaher Corporation

($ in thousands)	**2009**	**2010**	**2011**
Sales	$11,184,938	$13,202,602	$16,090,540
Cost of goods sold	5,904,718	6,575,812	7,913,876
Average inventory	1,067,663	1,109,084	1,473,488
Selected performance measures:			
Gross profit (%)	47.2%	50.2%	50.8%
Inventory turnover ratio	5.53	5.93	5.37

Required:
How well did Danaher manage its inventories over the three-year period?

Lennox International Inc. makes air conditioning, heating, and fireplace systems for residential and commercial uses, as well as commercial refrigeration equipment. Tecumseh Products Company manufactures air conditioning and refrigeration compressors, condensing units, heat pumps, and complete refrigeration systems. Select financial statement data and asset utilization ratios for each company follow.

P 5 - 7

Analyzing fixed asset
turnover   **(LO 7)**

Lennox International

($ in millions)	**2009**	**2010**	**2011**
Sales	$2,847.5	$3,096.4	$3,303.6
ROA	0.035	0.077	0.058
Current assets turnover	3.22	3.48	3.57
Fixed (long-term) assets turnover	3.97	4.26	4.27
Total assets turnover	1.78	1.91	1.94

Tecumseh Products Company

($ in millions)	**2009**	**2010**	**2011**
Sales	$735.9	$933.8	$864.4
ROA	(0.111)	0.083	(0.101)
Current assets turnover	1.93	2.31	2.24
Fixed (long-term) assets turnover	1.84	2.59	3.13
Total assets turnover	0.94	1.22	1.30

Required:
1. Compare the asset utilization effectiveness of the two companies. Which company seems to be doing a better job?

2. How do the companies' operating profit margins compare?

P5-8

Determining accounting quality **(LO 2)**

Electronic Arts develops, markets, publishes, and distributes interactive software games. The "lease commitments" section of the Commitments and Contingencies note from the company's annual report for the year ended March 31, 2012, includes the following:

> As of March 31, 2012, we leased certain of our current facilities, furniture and equipment under non-cancelable operating lease agreements. We were required to pay property taxes, insurance and normal maintenance costs for certain of these facilities and any increases over the base year of these expenses on the remainder of our facilities.

Operating leases are "off-balance sheet" obligations, meaning that under GAAP the lease obligations are not recognized in a company's balance sheet. Operating lease obligations are only disclosed in the financial statement notes. In contrast, capital leases are recognized in the balance sheet, resulting in the recording of both an asset (representing "economic ownership" of the asset, even though the company does not have legal ownership) and a liability (representing the obligation to make the promised payments). (Chapter12 provides the details.)

Required:
1. Suppose Electronic Arts had accounted for the leases described in the note as capital leases rather than operating leases. Describe qualitatively the effect this change would have had on Electronic Arts' long-term debt-to-assets ratio.
2. Should credit analysts consider operating leases when they evaluate a firm's creditworthiness?

P5-9

Comparing profitability for three companies **(LO 1)**

The following table shows four ratios derived from the financial statements of three real companies, labeled A, B, and C in the table. (They are not listed in the table in any particular order.) The real companies are:

- Brunswick Corporation, a leader in the leisure products industry that manufactures boats and marine engines, bowling and billiard products, as well as fitness equipment.
- Consolidated Edison, an electricity and natural gas company whose nonutility operations include energy marketing and fiber-optic telecommunications.
- Foot Locker, a shoe retailer with about 3,400 specialty stores in North America, Australia, and Europe. It also operates Champs Sports, an athletic wear retail chain, and a direct-to-customers business that sells through catalogs, mobile devices, and the Internet.

	A	B	C
Operating profit margin	0.12	0.04	0.04
Asset turnover ratio	0.47	1.13	1.88
ROA	0.06	0.04	0.07
ROCE	0.12	0.09	0.15

Required:
Which company is which? Explain how you identified each company from the data in the table.

P5-10

Determining profitability **(LO 4)**

Nucor Corporation produces steel and steel products at its eight mills and is a major recycler of scrap metal. The following data relate to Nucor for four years.

Nucor Corporation				
($ in thousands)	**Year 1**	**Year 2**	**Year 3**	**Year 4**
Total assets	$3,729,848	$3,721,788	$3,759,348	$4,381,001
Common stockholders' equity	2,262,248	2,130,952	2,201,460	2,322,989
Sales		4,756,521	4,333,707	4,801,776
Net income		310,908	112,961	162,080
Interest expense		22,449	22,002	22,918
Income tax rate		0.37	0.37	0.296

Required:

1. Calculate Nucor's ROA for Year 2, Year 3, and Year 4. Decompose ROA into operating profit margin and asset turnover components.

2. Has Nucor's profitability changed over the three years? If so, how?

3. Calculate the rate of return on common stockholders' equity for Year 2, Year 3, and Year 4.

4. What seem to be the reasons for the change in ROCE over the three years?

Tiffany & Company is a luxury jeweler and specialty retailer that sells timepieces, sterling silverware, china, crystal, fragrances, and accessories through its retail stores worldwide. Signet Jewelers Ltd. operates a number of well-known retail stores (Belden Jewelers and Kay Jewelers, among them) that sell moderately priced jewelry and other items. Selected financial information about each company follows:

P5-11

Business strategy and profit performance **(LO 2)**

	Tiffany & Co.	Signet Jewelers
Sales	$2,826 mil.	$3,338 mil.
Net income	$305 mil.	$190 mil.
Return on assets (ROA)	9.1%	6.7%
Profit margin	10.8%	5.7%
Asset turnover	0.84	1.18

Required:

1. The profit margin at Tiffany & Co. is higher than at Signet Jewelers. What is it about each company's strategy and positioning that might explain the profit margin difference? You may want to visit each company's website before answering this question.

2. The asset turnover at Signet Jewelers is higher than at Tiffany & Company. What is it about each company's strategy and positioning that might explain the asset turnover difference?

3. Suppose Tiffany management found a way to increase sales to the point where the company's asset turnover ratio exactly equaled that of Signet Jewelers. Calculate the dollar amount of sales and net income that would result if expenses only increased in proportion to sales.

4. At its current asset turnover rate, how high must the profit margin at Signet Jewelers be for the company to earn an ROA equal to Tiffany's 9.1%?

Blockbuster Inc. provides home movie and game entertainment. At the end of 2009, Blockbuster operated more than 5,000 stores and franchisees operated another 1,300. Nine months later the company filed for bankruptcy protection. By the end of 2010, Blockbuster had closed nearly 1,000 company-operated and 300 franchised stores. As part of its bankruptcy reorganization, Blockbuster was acquired by Dish Network in 2011. Dish Network continues to downsize Blockbuster's operations. Selected financial information about Blockbuster prior to its bankruptcy filing follow.

P5-12

Blockbuster Inc. **(LO 6)**

($ in millions)	2009	2008	2007
Revenue	$4,062	$5,065	$5,314
Operating income (pre-tax)	(355)	(304)	27
Net income	(558)	(374)	(73)
Cash flow provided by operations	29	51	(56)
Cash flow provided by (used in) investing activities	(75)	(116)	77
Cash flow from financing activities:			
Debt repayments	(864)	(164)	(329)

Required:

1. Explain why the amount shown for Cash flow provided by (used in) investing activities in 2007 is a positive number ($77 million) rather than a negative number. You may need to refer back to Chapter 4 and its Statement of Cash Flow discussion.

2. Blockbuster repaid $329 million of debt in 2007. Based only on the information provided, what were the likely sources of cash for this debt repayment?

3. Blockbuster repaid $864 million of debt in 2009 as part of a refinancing completed in October of that year. What were the likely sources of cash for this debt repayment?

4. A financial statement note in the company's 2009 annual report reveals the following scheduled debt payments: $112.5 million in 2010; $90 million in 2011; $390 million in 2012; $90 million in 2013; and $292 million in 2014. Explain why most observers at the time said Blockbuster was characterized by high credit risk.

P5-13

Analyzing why financial ratios change   **(LO 7)**

AICPA
ADAPTED

Daley, Inc., is consistently profitable. Its normal financial statement relationships are as follows:

Current ratio	3 to 1
Inventory turnover	4 times
Long-term debt/total assets ratio	0.5 to 1

Required:
Determine whether each transaction or event that follows increased, decreased, or had no effect on each ratio. Consider each transaction independently of the others.

1. Daley declared but did not pay a cash dividend.

2. Customers returned invoiced goods for which they had not paid.

3. Accounts payable were paid at year-end.

4. Daley recorded both a receivable from an insurance company and a loss from fire damage to a factory building.

5. Early in the year, Daley increased the selling price of one of its products because customer demand far exceeded production capacity. The number of units sold this year was the same as last year.

P5-14

Explaining changes in financial ratios   **(LO 7)**

AICPA
ADAPTED

Audit engagement partners were comparing notes about changes in clients' financial statement ratios or amounts from the prior year's figures. Here is what the partners had discovered.

Client 1. Inventory turnover increased substantially from the prior year. (Select three explanations.)

Client 2. Accounts receivable turnover decreased substantially from the prior year. (Select three explanations.)

Client 3. Allowance for doubtful accounts increased in dollars from the prior year but decreased from the prior year as a percentage of accounts receivable. (Select three explanations.)

Client 4. Long-term debt increased from the prior year, but interest expense increased more than the percentage increase in long-term debt. (Select one explanation.)

Client 5. Operating income increased from the prior year although the company was less profitable than in the prior year. (Select two explanations.)

Client 6. Gross margin percentage was unchanged from the prior year although gross profit increased from the prior year. (Select one explanation.)

Required:
Select from the following list the most likely explanation(s) for each audit client.

a. Items shipped on consignment during the last month of the year were recorded as sales.

b. A significant number of credit memos for returned merchandise issued during the last month of the year were not recorded.

c. Year-end inventory purchases were overstated because items received in the first month of the subsequent year were incorrectly included.

d. Year-end inventory purchases were understated because items received before year-end were incorrectly excluded.

e. A larger percentage of sales occurred during the last month of the year compared to the prior year.

f. A smaller percentage of sales occurred during the last month of the year compared to the prior year.

g. The same percentage of sales occurred during the last month of the year compared to the prior year.

h. Sales increased at the same percentage as cost of goods sold compared to the prior year.

i. Sales increased at a lower percentage than cost of goods sold increased compared to the prior year.

j. Sales increased at a higher percentage than cost of goods sold increased compared to the prior year.

k. Interest expense decreased compared to the prior year.

l. The effective income tax rate increased compared to the prior year.

m. The effective income tax rate decreased compared to the prior year.

n. Short-term borrowing was refinanced on a long-term basis at the same interest rate.

o. Short-term borrowing was refinanced on a long-term basis at lower interest rates.

p. Short-term borrowing was refinanced on a long-term basis at higher interest rates.

Griffin and Lasky, Inc. (G&L), supplies industrial automation equipment and machine tools to the automotive industry. G&L uses the percentage of completion method for recognizing revenue on its long-term contracts. Customer orders have long lead times because they involve multiyear capital investment programs. Sometimes orders are canceled. Selected items from the company's financial statements follow.

P5-15.

EBITDA and revenue recognition **(LO 7)**

($ in millions)	2012	2013	2014
Sales	$571.5	$619.5	$730.6
Accounts receivable—billed	141.6	94.5	147.9
Accounts receivable—unbilled	104.5	249.4	202.7
Total accounts receivable	246.1	343.9	350.6
Inventory	57.4	74.8	102.3
Earnings before interest and taxes (EBIT)	74.8	75.8	38.1
Depreciation and amortization	14.8	15.4	19.3
Plant write-down	–0–	–0–	30.3

Required:

1. Compute earnings before interest, taxes, depreciation, and amortization (EBITDA) and adjusted EBITDA—after excluding the plant write-down—for each year in the schedule.

2. Are profits at G&L keeping pace with sales?

3. Compute the days receivables outstanding using year-end receivables for each year in the schedule.

4. Why might analysts be concerned about earnings quality at G&L?

Margaret O'Flaherty, a portfolio manager for MCF Investments, is considering investing in Alpine Chemical 7% bonds, which mature in 10 years. She asks you to analyze the company to determine the riskiness of the bonds.

Alpine Chemical Company Financial Statements

	Years Ended December 31,					
($ in millions)	**2009**	**2010**	**2011**	**2012**	**2013**	**2014**
Assets						
Cash	$ 190	$ 55	$ 0	$ 157	$ 249	$ 0
Accounts receivable	1,637	2,087	1,394	2,143	3,493	3,451
Inventories	2,021	945	1,258	1,293	1,322	1,643
Other current assets	17	27	55	393	33	171
Current assets	3,865	3,114	2,707	3,986	5,097	5,265
Gross fixed assets	4,650	5,038	5,619	5,757	6,181	7,187
Less: Accumulated depreciation	2,177	2,543	2,841	3,138	3,465	3,893
Net fixed assets	2,473	2,495	2,778	2,619	2,716	3,294
Total assets	$ 6,338	$ 5,609	$ 5,485	$ 6,605	$ 7,813	$ 8,559
Liabilities and net worth						
Notes payable	$ 525	$ 750	$ 0	$ 1,300	$ 1,750	$ 1,900
Accounts payable	673	638	681	338	743	978
Accrued liabilities	303	172	359	359	483	761
Current liabilities	1,501	1,560	1,040	1,997	2,976	3,639
Long-term debt	1,985	1,044	1,401	1,457	1,542	1,491
Deferred tax credits	352	347	363	336	345	354
Total liabilities	3,838	2,951	2,804	3,790	4,863	5,484
Common stock	50	50	100	100	100	100
Capital surplus	100	100	0	0	0	0
Retained earnings	2,350	2,508	2,581	2,715	2,850	2,975
Net worth	2,500	2,658	2,681	2,815	2,950	3,075
Total liabilities and net worth	$ 6,338	$ 5,609	$ 5,485	$ 6,605	$ 7,813	$ 8,559
Income statement	**2009**	**2010**	**2011**	**2012**	**2013**	**2014**
Net sales	$14,100	$15,508	$13,875	$14,750	$19,133	$19,460
Cost of goods sold	10,200	11,220	9,366	10,059	13,400	13,117
Gross profit	3,900	4,288	4,509	4,691	5,733	6,343
Operating expense	2,065	2,203	2,665	2,685	3,472	3,885
Operating income	1,835	2,085	1,844	2,006	2,261	2,458
Interest expense	275	465	275	319	376	318
Depreciation expense	475	477	479	478	495	511
Profit before tax	1,085	1,143	1,090	1,209	1,390	1,629
Income taxes	193	115	265	145	192	150
Net income	$ 892	$ 1,028	$ 825	$ 1,064	$ 1,198	$ 1,479

Required:

1. Using the data provided in the accompanying financial statements, calculate the following ratios for Alpine Chemical for 2014:

   a. EBIT/Interest expense

   b. Long-term debt/Total capitalization

   c. Funds from operations/Total debt

   d. Operating income/Sales

Use the following conventions: EBIT is earnings before interest and taxes; Total capital-ization is interest-bearing long-term debt plus net worth; Funds from operations means net income plus depreciation expense; and Total debt includes interest-bearing short-term and long-term debt.

2. Briefly explain the significance of each ratio calculated in requirement 1 to the assess-ment of Alpine Chemical's creditworthiness.

3. Insert your answers to requirement 1 into Table 1 that follows. Then from Table 2, select an appropriate credit rating for Alpine Chemical.

TABLE I	Alpine Chemical Company					
	2009	**2010**	**2011**	**2012**	**2013**	**2014**
EBIT/Interest expense	4.95	3.46	4.96	4.79	4.70	?
Long-term debt/Total capitalization	44%	28%	34%	34%	34%	?
Funds from operations/Total debt	54%	84%	93%	56%	51%	?
Operating income/Sales	13%	13%	13%	14%	12%	?

TABLE 2	Industry Data					
Three-Year Medians (2012–2014) by Credit-Rating Category						
	Aaa	**Aa**	**A**	**Bbb**	**Bb**	**B**
EBIT/Interest expense	11.0	9.5	4.5	3.0	2.0	1.0
Long-term debt/Total capitalization	13.0	16.5	29.5	39.0	45.5	63.5
Funds from operations/Total debt	83.0	74.0	45.5	31.5	18.5	8.0
Operating income/Sales	21.5	16.0	15.0	12.0	11.0	9.0

The following income statement and balance sheet information is available for the operating segments of Bogart, Inc.

P5-17

Determining reportable segments (LO 8)

mhhe.com/revsine6e

Operating Segments

(In millions of dollars)	Grant	Stewart	Kelly	Flynn	Cagney	Total
Revenue	2,076.0	350.0	304.0	195.0	1,375.0	4,300.0
Cost of goods sold	(626.8)	(104.5)	(174.1)	(104.5)	(731.2)	(1,741.1)
Gross profit	1,449.2	245.5	129.9	90.5	643.8	2,558.9
Depreciation expense	(193.8)	(45.9)	(61.2)	(25.5)	(183.6)	(510.0)
Administrative expense	(174.3)	(93.5)	(34.0)	(12.8)	(110.5)	(425.1)
Operating profit before taxes	1,081.1	106.1	34.7	52.2	349.7	1,623.8
Total assets	3,000.0	430.0	945.0	325.0	2,300.0	7,000.0

The segments do not sell goods or services to one another. The Flynn and Cagney segments have similar economic characteristics, products, processes, customers, distribution method, and regulatory environments.

Required:

1. Explain why U.S. GAAP requires a company to disclose information about its business segments.

2. How does a firm define an operating segment under U.S. GAAP?

3. Identify Bogart's reportable segments. Aggregate segments where possible. Explain your logic for determining the reportable segments.

CASES

C5-1

McDonald's and Buffalo Wild Wings: Comparing two restaurant chains (LO 1)

McDonald's Corporation franchises and operates more than 30,000 fast-service restaurants in 119 countries. Buffalo Wild Wings franchises and operates more than 500 restaurants in the United States. Buffalo Wild Wings features chicken wings and a full bar in its restaurants.

Financial information for each company follows. EBI denotes after-tax earnings before interest expense.

Selected Financial Data

	Buffalo Wild Wings					McDonald's				
	2007	**2008**	**2009**	**2010**	**2011**	**2007**	**2008**	**2009**	**2010**	**2011**
Number of stores operating at year-end:										
Company-owned	161	197	232	259	319	6,906	6,502	6,262	6,399	6,435
Franchised	332	363	420	473	498	24,471	25,465	26,216	26,338	27,075
Revenues ($ in millions):										
Company-owned stores		379.7	488.7	555.2	717.4		16,560.9	15,458.5	16,233.3	18,292.8
Franchise fees		42.7	50.2	58.1	67.1		6,961.5	7,286.2	7,841.3	8,713.2
Total		422.4	538.9	613.3	784.5		23,522.4	22,744.7	24,074.6	27,006.0

Required:

1. Determine the amounts of sales revenue per company-owned store and franchise fees per franchised store for each year and each company. In these computations, use the average number of stores open during the year.

2. Assume that for both companies sales at company-owned stores are the same (on a per store basis) as sales for the same company's franchised stores. Estimate each company's franchise fee rate, which is stated as a percentage of each franchisee's sales revenue.

3. Perform a cause-of-change analysis from 2008 to 2011 for each company to disaggregate the increase in revenues from company-owned stores between growth in the average number of average stores open and growth in revenues per store.

4. Perform a similar analysis for franchise fee revenues.

5. What do your analyses from requirements 4 and 5 tell you about the companies' growth strategies?

C5-2

Crocs and Deckers Outdoor: Comparing footwear manufacturers (LO 1)

Crocs designs, develops, and manufactures consumer products from specialty resins. The company's primary product line is Crocs-branded footwear for men, women, and children. It sells its products through traditional retail channels, including specialty footwear stores. Deckers Outdoor designs and produces sport sandals as well as sheepskin and sustainable footwear. The company's products are marketed under three proprietary brands: Teva, Simple, and UGG. It sells its products through domestic retailers and global distributors and directly to consumers via the Internet.

Financial ratios for each company follow. EBI denotes after-tax earnings before interest expense and excluding nonoperating gains or losses.

Selected Financial Ratios

	Crocs			Deckers Outdoor		
	2009	**2010**	**2011**	**2009**	**2010**	**2011**
Annual growth rate						
Sales	(10.5%)	22.3%	26.7%	17.9%	23.1%	37.6%
Operating earnings (before taxes)	(72.8%)	(258.3%)	68.5%	55.0%	37.4%	14.4%
Assets	(10.1%)	34.1%	26.6%	23.8%	35.0%	41.7%
Profitability						
EBI/Sales margin	(0.064)	0.086	0.113	0.143	0.158	0.145
Asset turnover	1.49	1.65	1.61	1.50	1.42	1.41
Return on Assets (ROA)	(0.095)	0.142	0.182	0.215	0.225	0.204
Selected expense items (% of sales)						
Cost of goods sold	52.3%	46.2%	46.4%	54.4%	49.8%	50.7%
Selling, general, and administrative	48.3%	43.3%	40.2%	23.3%	25.4%	28.6%
Selected asset utilization ratios						
Days receivables outstanding	24.2	26.5	27.2	41.4	35.2	41.1
Days inventory held	127.8	107.4	98.5	73.5	77.1	98.9
Days payables outstanding	37.1	27.5	39.4	37.9	38.8	39.3

Required:

1. Which company was the more profitable in 2011?

2. What was the likely source of that company's superior profit performance in 2011?

3. Which company was the more profitable in 2009? What seems to have been the problem at the underperforming company that year?

4. Which company better manages its receivables, inventories, and payables?

It's late Tuesday evening, and you've just received a phone call from Dennis Whiting, your boss at GE Capital. Dennis wants to know your reaction to the Argenti loan request before tomorrow's loan committee meeting. Here's what he tells you:

> We've provided seasonal loans to Argenti for the past 20 years, and they've always been a first-rate customer, but I'm troubled by several recent events. For instance, the company just reported a $141 million loss for the first quarter of 2014. This loss comes on top of a $237 million loss in 2013 and a $9 million loss in 2012. What's worse, Argenti changed inventory accounting methods last year, and this change reduced the 2013 loss by $22 million. I can't tell if the company's using other accounting tricks to prop up earnings, but I doubt it.
>
> I believe Argenti's problem lies in its core business—customers just aren't buying its merchandise these days. Management's aggressive price discount program in the fourth quarter of 2013 helped move inventory, but Argenti doesn't have the cost structure needed to be competitive as a discounter. Take a look at the financials I'm sending over, and let me know what you think.

Argenti Corporation operates a national chain of retail stores (Argenti's) selling appliances and electronics, home furnishings, automotive parts, apparel, and jewelry. The company's first store opened in New York City in 1904. Today, the company owns or leases more than 900 stores located in downtown areas of large cities and in suburban shopping malls. Customer purchases are financed in house using ArgentiCredit cards. The company employs more than 58,000 people.

C 5-3

Argenti Corporation: Evaluating credit risk   **(LO 7)**

mhhe.com/revsine6e

The Seasonal Credit Agreement with GE Capital—dated October 4, 2013—provides a revolving loan facility in the principal amount of $165 million. The purpose of this facility is to provide backup liquidity as Argenti reduces its inventory levels. Under the credit agreement, Argenti may select among several interest rate options, which are based on market rates. Unless GE Capital agrees, loans may be made under the seasonal credit facility only after the commitments under the company's other debt agreements are fully used.

Argenti Corporation

Balance Sheets and Selected Other Data

($ in millions)	2013	2012	2011	2010	2009
Assets					
Cash and securities	$ 35	$ 38	$ 36	$ 117	$ 92
Receivables	213	166	112	62	47
Inventories	1,545	1,770	1,625	1,242	1,038
Other current assets	13	22	6	4	312
	1,806	1,996	1,779	1,425	1,489
Property, plant, and equipment—net	1,308	1,366	1,396	1,263	1,222
Investments	317	345	314	296	277
Other assets	1,448	1,177	1,048	851	445
	$4,879	$4,884	$4,537	$3,835	$3,433
Liabilities and shareholders' equity					
Notes payable	$1,028	$ 160	$ 144	$ 0	$ 0
Accounts payable	1,812	2,040	1,955	1,595	1,399
Accrued expenses	1,232	1,201	1,248	1,204	1,148
	4,072	3,401	3,347	2,799	2,547
Long-term debt	87	423	228	213	125
Other liabilities	112	185	203	216	208
Preferred stock	175	175	75	0	0
Common stock	54	46	23	19	16
Retained earnings	518	768	750	661	583
Less: Treasury stock	(139)	(114)	(89)	(73)	(46)
	$4,879	$4,884	$4,537	$3,835	$3,433
Selected earnings and cash flow data					
Sales	$6,620	$7,085	$7,029	$6,023	$5,806
Cost of goods sold	4,869	5,211	5,107	4,258	4,047
Gross margin	1,751	1,874	1,922	1,765	1,759
Net income	(237)	(9)	137	101	60
Operating cash flow	(356)	(182)	153	132	157
Dividends	9	4	24	23	19

Argenti management has asked GE Capital for a $1.5 billion refinancing package that would be used to pay off all or a substantial portion of its outstanding debt. Excerpts from the company's financial statement notes follow.

Management Discussion and Analysis (2013 Annual Report)
The company has obtained waivers under the Long-Term Credit Agreement and the Short-Term Credit Agreement with respect to compliance for the fiscal quarter ending March 29, 2013—with covenants requiring maintenance of minimum consolidated shareholders' equity, a maximum ratio of debt to capitalization, and minimum earnings before interest, taxes, depreciation, amortization, and rent (EBITDAR). These waivers and amendments reduce the

maximum amount of debt permitted to be incurred, and the maturity of the Long-Term Agreement was changed from February 28, 2015, to August 29, 2013.

The company is currently in discussions with financing sources with a view toward both a longer term solution to its liquidity problems and obtaining refinancing for all or a substantial portion of its outstanding indebtedness, including a total of $1,008 million, which will mature on or about August 29, 2013. This would include repayment of the current bank borrowings and amounts outstanding under the Note Purchase Agreements. The company's management is highly confident that the indebtedness can be refinanced. Its largest shareholder, GE Capital, also expects the company to be able to refinance such indebtedness. However, there can be no assurance that such refinancing can be obtained or that amendments or waivers required to maintain compliance with the previous agreements can be obtained.

Note to Financial Statements (2013 Annual Report)

The company intends to improve its financial condition and reduce its dependence on borrowing by slowing expansion, controlling expenses, closing certain unprofitable stores, and continuing to implement its inventory reduction program. Management is in the process of reevaluating the company's merchandising, marketing, store operations, and real estate strategies. The company is also considering the sale of certain operating units as a means of generating cash. Future cash is also expected to continue to be provided by ongoing operations, sale of receivables under the Accounts Receivable Purchase Agreement with GE capital, borrowings under revolving loan facilities, and vendor financing programs.

Quarterly Income

	Mar. 14	Dec. 13	Sep. 13	Jun. 13	Mar. 13
Sales	$ 1,329	$ 2,084	$ 1,567	$ 1,534	$ 1,435
Cost of goods sold	997	1,525	1,096	1,210	1,038
Gross profit	332	559	471	324	397
Net income	(141)	(165)	(35)	11	(48)
Gross profit (% sales)	25.0%	26.8%	30.1%	21.1%	27.7%
Net income (% sales)	(10.6)%	(7.9)%	(2.2)%	0.7%	(3.3)%

Required:

1. Why did Argenti need to increase its notes payable borrowing to more than $1 billion in 2013?

2. What recommendation would you make regarding the company's request for a $1.5 billion refinancing package?

Excerpts from IBM's 2012 segment disclosures are given below.

C5-4

Analyzing reportable segment disclosures **(LO 8)**

Business Segments and Capabilities

The company's major operations consist of five business segments: Global Technology Services and Global Business Services, which the company collectively calls Global Services, Software, Systems and Technology and Global Financing. **Global Technology Services (GTS)** primarily provides IT infrastructure and business process services, creating business value for clients through unique technology and IP integrated services within its global delivery model. **Global Business Services (GBS)** has the mission to deliver predictable business outcomes to the company's clients across two primary business areas: Consulting and

Application Management Services. **Software** consists primarily of middleware and operating systems software. **Systems and Technology (STG)** provides clients with business solutions requiring advanced computing power and storage capabilities. **Global Financing** facilitates clients' acquisition of IBM systems, software and services. Global Financing invests in financing assets, leverages with debt and manages the associated risks with the objective of generating consistently strong returns on equity.

The segments represent components of the company for which separate financial information is available that is utilized on a regular basis by the chief executive officer in determining how to allocate resources and evaluate performance. The segments are determined based on several factors, including client base, homogeneity of products, technology, delivery channels and similar economic characteristics.

Segment revenue and pre-tax income include transactions between the segments that are intended to reflect an arm's-length, market-based transfer price.

The following tables reflect the results of operations of the company's segments consistent with the management and measurement system utilized within the company. Performance measurement is based on pre-tax income. These results are used, in part, by senior management, both in evaluating the performance of, and in allocating resources to, each of the segments.

Management System Segment View

($ in millions)

For the year ended December 31:	Global Services Segments		Software	Systems and Technology	Global Financing	Total Segments
	Global Technology Services	Global Business Services				
2012						
External revenue	$40,236	$18,566	$25,448	$17,667	$2,013	$103,930
Internal revenue	1,166	719	3,274	676	2,060	7,896
Total revenue	$41,402	$19,286	$28,722	$18,343	$4,073	$111,826
Pre-tax income	$ 6,961	$ 2,983	$10,810	$ 1,227	$2,034	$ 24,015
Revenue year-to-year change	(1.7)%	(4.0)%	1.8%	(7.5)%	(2.9)%	(2.3)%
Pre-tax income year-to-year change	10.8%	(0.8)%	8.4%	(24.9)%	1.1%	4.8%
Pre-tax income margin	16.8%	15.5%	37.6%	6.7%	49.9%	21.5%
2011						
External revenue	$40,879	$19,284	$24,944	$18,985	$2,102	$106,194
Internal revenue	1,242	797	3,276	838	2,092	8,246
Total revenue	$42,121	$20,081	$28,219	$19,823	$4,195	$114,440
Pre-tax income	$ 6,284	$ 3,006	$ 9,970	$ 1,633	$2,011	$ 22,904
Revenue year-to-year change	6.6%	5.6%	10.9%	5.6%	2.8%	7.1%
Pre-tax income year-to-year change	14.3%	18.1%	5.3%	12.2%	2.8%	9.5%
Pre-tax income margin	14.9%	15.0%	35.3%	8.2%	47.9%	20.0%
2010						
External revenue	$38,201	$18,223	$22,485	$17,973	$2,238	$ 99,120
Internal revenue	1,313	798	2,950	804	1,842	7,707
Total revenue	$39,514	$19,021	$25,436	$18,777	$4,080	$106,827
Pre-tax income	$ 5,499	$ 2,546	$ 9,466	$ 1,456	$1,956	$ 20,923
Revenue year-to-year change	2.0%	2.6%	5.7%	9.8%	0.1%	4.2%
Pre-tax income year-to-year change	0.3%	1.8%	13.8%	12.1%	13.5%	8.3%
Pre-tax income margin	13.9%	13.4%	37.2%	7.8%	48.0%	19.6%

Management System Segment View

($ in millions)

For the year ended December 31:	Global Services Segments		Software	Systems and Technology	Global Financing	Total Segments
	Global Technology Services	Global Business Services				
2012						
Assets	$15,884	$8,022	$26,291	$8,232	$38,882	$97,310
Depreciation/amortization of intangibles*	1,597	75	1,157	786	853	4,470
Capital expenditures/investments in intangibles	1,760	42	618	1,106	708	4,233
Interest income	—	—	—	—	1,942	1,942
Interest expense	—	—	—	—	410	410
2011						
Assets	$15,475	$8,078	$23,926	$7,649	$36,427	$91,557
Depreciation/amortization of intangibles*	1,713	83	1,062	737	1,145	4,739
Capital expenditures/investments in intangibles	1,838	56	469	1,032	930	4,325
Interest income	—	—	—	—	2,139	2,139
Interest expense	—	—	—	—	538	538
2010						
Assets	$15,560	$8,007	$22,625	$7,287	$35,813	$89,292
Depreciation/amortization of intangibles*	1,632	75	992	784	1,417	4,900
Capital expenditures/investments in intangibles	1,511	52	463	1,163	1,246	4,434
Interest income	—	—	—	—	2,116	2,116
Interest expense	—	—	—	—	548	548

* Segment pre-tax Income does not include the amortization of intangible assets.

Major Clients

No single client represented 10 percent or more of the company's total revenue in 2012, 2011, or 2010.

Geographic Information

The following provides information for those countries that are 10% or more of the specific category.

Revenue*

($ in millions)

For the year ended December 31:	2012	2011	2010
United States	$ 36,270	$ 37,041	$35,581
Japan	10,697	10,968	10,701
Other countries	57,540	58,906	53,589
Total IBM consolidated revenue	**$104,507**	**$106,916**	**$99,870**

* Revenues are attributed to countries based on the location of the client.

Plant and Other Property—Net

($ in millions)

At December 31:	2012	2011	2010
United States	$ 6,555	$ 6,271	$ 6,134
Other countries	6,299	6,186	6,298
Total	$12,854	$12,457	$12,432

Required:

All questions relate to 2012 unless stated otherwise.

1. IBM refers to its segment reports as the "Management System Segment View." What does IBM mean by this and how does it relate to the disclosure requirements under U.S. GAAP?

2. Which business segment contributes the most (least) external revenue for IBM? Compute the percentage of segment external revenue to total segments external revenue for these two segments.

3. Which business segment contributes the most (least) pre-tax income for IBM? Compute the percentage of segment pre-tax income to total segments pre-tax income for these two segments.

4. Which business segment had the highest (lowest) percentage growth (year-to-year change) in total revenue from 2011 to 2012? Show how the growth percentage was computed for the Software segment.

5. Which business segment had the highest (lowest) percentage growth (year-to-year change) in pre-tax income from 2011 to 2012?

6. Which segment had the highest (lowest) pre-tax income margin? Show how IBM computes the pre-tax income margin for these segments.

7. How would analysts use the business segment data related to the income statement?

8. Why would the Global Financing segment hold 40% ($38,882/$97,310) of the segment assets, but generate only 3.6% ($4,073/$111,826) of total segment revenue?

9. What percentage of IBM's revenue is earned in the United States?

The Role of Financial Information in Valuation and Credit Risk Assessment | 6

The previous chapter introduced the key financial ratios used to assess a company's operating performance, liquidity, and solvency. In this chapter, we examine the role financial accounting information plays in valuation and credit risk assessment. We also describe the expanding use of fair value accounting in financial statements and explain why accountants and auditors must be skilled at valuation. Along the way, we will build a framework for understanding what academic and professional research says about the usefulness of accounting numbers to investors and creditors.

Business valuation involves estimating the worth—or intrinsic value—of a company, one of its operating units, or its ownership shares. Although several valuation methods are used in practice, we focus on the **fundamental valuation** approach because it is comprehensive and rigorous and uses basic accounting measures (or "fundamentals") to assess the amount, timing, and uncertainty of a firm's *future* operating cash flows or earnings. Data from a firm's financial statements, along with industry and economywide data, are used to develop projections of future earnings or cash flows. These projected cash flows are discounted at a risk-adjusted cost of capital to arrive at a valuation estimate, which becomes the basis for the analyst's recommendation (buy, hold, or sell) and investment decision.

Cash flow assessment also plays a central role in gauging a company's **credit risk.** Lenders and credit analysts use the firm's financial statements and other information to estimate its *future* cash flows. They compare these cash flow projections to the firm's future debt-service requirements. Companies with projected operating cash flows that comfortably exceed required future debt principal and interest payments are deemed good credit risks. Less favorable operating cash flow prospects may suggest the firm is a high credit risk, in which case the firm may be charged higher rates of interest, have more stringent conditions placed on its loans, or be refused credit.

LEARNING OBJECTIVES

After studying this chapter, you will understand:

1. The basic steps in business valuation using free cash flows and abnormal earnings.

2. Why *current* earnings are considered more useful than *current* cash flows for assessing *future* cash flows.

3. The expanding use of *fair value* measurements in financial statements.

4. What factors contribute to variation in price-earnings multiples.

5. The notion of earnings quality and what factors influence the quality of earnings.

6. How stock returns relate to "good news" and "bad news" earnings surprises.

7. The importance of credit risk assessment in lending decisions and how credit ratings are determined.

8. How to forecast a company's financial statements.

Chapter

BUSINESS VALUATION

Valuing an entire company, an operating division of that company, or its ownership shares involves three steps:

1. **Forecasting** future amounts of some financial attribute—what we call a **value-relevant attribute**—that ultimately determine how much a company is worth. Common value-relevant attributes include:
   - Distributable or free cash flows (defined and discussed in the next section).
   - Accounting earnings.
   - Balance sheet book values.
2. Determining the **risk** or **uncertainty** associated with the forecasted future amounts.
3. Determining the **discounted present value** of the expected future amounts using a discount rate that reflects the risk or uncertainty from Step 2.

> Dividends are another value-relevant attribute discussed in finance texts. However, the dividend discount valuation approach is of limited practical use despite its intuitive appeal because dividends represent the *distribution* of wealth. The accounting-based attributes considered here focus on wealth *creation,* which is what permits dividends to be distributed.

The Discounted Free Cash Flow Approach to Valuation

The **distributable—or free—cash flow valuation approach** combines the elements in these three steps to express what a stock is worth—its intrinsic value—as the discounted present value of expected future distributable cash flows. **Free cash flow**—a term popular among analysts—is often defined as the company's operating cash flows (before interest) minus cash outlays for routine operating capacity replacement such as equipment and furnishings. It's the amount available to finance further expansion of operating capacity, to reduce debt, to pay dividends, or to repurchase stock. This is the best way to measure free cash flows if you are interested in valuing the company as a whole without regard to its capital structure.

But what if you want to value just the company's common stock? Then you would need to refine the free cash flow measure by also subtracting cash interest payments, debt repayments, and preferred dividends. What's left is the free cash flow (denoted *CF*) that's available to common stockholders.[1] Of course, *CF* can be used to pay common dividends, buy back common stock, or expand operating capacity. The free cash flow equity valuation model can be written as:[2]

$$
\underbrace{V_0 = \frac{E_0(\widetilde{CF}_1)}{(1+r)^1} + \frac{E_0(\widetilde{CF}_2)}{(1+r)^2} + \frac{E_0(\widetilde{CF}_3)}{(1+r)^3}}_{\text{Discount factor each period}\ \longrightarrow\ \infty} + \cdots (\text{continuing to infinity}) = \sum_{t=1}^{\infty} \frac{E_0(\widetilde{CF}_t)}{(1+r)^t} \quad \textbf{(6.1)}
$$

Expected free cash flow each period $\longrightarrow \infty$

The math may look complex, but the intuition is straightforward. The free cash flow valuation model says that today's (at time $t = 0$) estimate of the value (V_0) of a company's stock equals the sum (Σ) of the stream of *expected future free cash flows* (the various $E_0[\widetilde{CF}]$ terms)

---

[1] One of the earliest accounting treatments of this concept appeared in L. Revsine, *Replacement Cost Accounting* (Upper Saddle River, NJ: Prentice Hall, 1973), pp. 33–35 and 95–100. There, free cash flow was defined as "the portion of net operating flows that can be distributed as a dividend without reducing the level of future physical operations" (p. 34).

[2] See E. F. Fama and M. H. Miller, *The Theory of Finance* (New York: Holt, Rinehart & Winston, 1972); R. Brealey and S. Myers, *Principles of Corporate Finance* (New York: McGraw-Hill, 2006); S. A. Ross, R. W. Westerfield, and J. F. Jaffee, *Corporate Finance* (New York: McGraw-Hill, 2005); as well as the books referenced in footnote 7.

per share of stock *discounted back to the present* (the $[1 + r]^t$ terms).[3] Each periodic expected future free cash flow has its own unique discount factor $(1/[1 + r]^t)$, which reflects the risk (r) and timing (t) of the free cash flow. The E_0 signifies that the expected future cash flows are based on investors' *current assessment* (at time $t = 0$) of the company's future business activities.

The valuation model's cash flow stream begins one period from now at $t = 1$, and it continues over an infinite horizon to $t = \infty$. Each future free cash flow is uncertain.[4] Consequently, valuation practitioners devote considerable effort to ensuring that the cash flow forecasts used are reliable.

The discount rate (r), commonly referred to as the **equity cost of capital,** is adjusted to reflect the uncertainty or riskiness of the expected cash flow stream.[5] Streams that are more risky are discounted at a higher rate.

Simply put, the free cash flow valuation model in equation (6.1) says that today's intrinsic value (and market price) of each common share depends on investors' current *expectations* about the firm's future economic prospects as measured by free cash flows available to common shareholders. These future cash flows are discounted by a factor that reflects the risk (or uncertainty) and timing of the anticipated flows.[6]

Here's an illustration of the discounted free cash flow approach to valuation.

> Judy Choi is thinking about starting a truck rental business. She plans to buy four trucks now and to add a fifth truck in two years. Each truck will cost $20,000. Judy has carefully evaluated the local market for rental trucks and believes that each truck will generate $5,000 of net operating cash flows each year. At the end of five years, she believes the trucks can be sold for $30,000 in total. How much is the business worth?

Exhibit 6.1 shows each step in the valuation process. First, Choi forecasts the expected future free cash flows associated with the truck rental business. These forecasted cash flows include the expected net operating cash flows of $5,000 per truck or $20,000 in the first two years (from four trucks) and $25,000 in the final three years (when the fifth truck is added). Then there's the additional $30,000 cash flow she expects to receive when the trucks are sold at the end of Year 5, and the $20,000 she must spend at the end of Year 2 to buy the final truck.

Next, Choi must assess the cash flow risk associated with the truck rental business and determine the appropriate discount rate. For now, let's just say it's 10%.

Actual market prices may deviate from fundamental intrinsic values when markets are inefficient. This possibility is what motivates some investors to use intrinsic value estimates (V_0) as the basis for investment decisions. The hope is to buy a stock at a price (P_0) today that is less than the stock is currently worth $(P_0 < V_0)$, and then sell it later at a higher price when the stock's true value is recognized by other investors.

Of course, analysts must be careful because when $V_0 \neq P_0$, it is possible the analyst's valuation, not the market price, is incorrect due to an unreliable cash flow forecast or an erroneous discount rate.

To learn more about present values, see the Appendix to this book.

---

[3] We denote uncertain future amounts with a tilde ($\tilde{\ }$). Thus, $E_0(\tilde{CF}_3)$ indicates the currently expected but uncertain free cash flow for Period 3 in the future. By contrast, the already known past Period 0 cash flow would be shown without the tilde (that is, as CF_0).

[4] An alternative representation of the discounted cash flow valuation model presumes that the future cash flow stream continues only through some finite terminal period, T, at which point the company is liquidated and a liquidating or terminal cash distribution $(\tilde{CF}_T)$ is paid to stockholders:

$$V_0 = \sum_{t=1}^{T-1} \frac{E_0(\tilde{CF}_t)}{(1 + r)^t} + \frac{E_0(\tilde{CF}_T)}{(1 + r)^T}$$

[5] The most popular approach to estimating the cost of equity is the **capital asset pricing model** (CAPM), which expresses the equity cost of capital as the sum of the return on a riskless asset (r_f) plus an equity risk premium $(E[r_M] - r_f)$ multiplied by the company's systematic (beta) risk:

$$r_e = r_f + \beta(E[r_M] - r_f)$$

See J. Pettit, "Corporate Capital Costs: A Practitioners' Guide," *Journal of Applied Corporate Finance,* Spring 1999, pp. 115–20.

[6] Some finance textbooks adopt a slightly different cash flow approach to business valuation. This alternative approach uses a *weighted average cost of capital* (WACC) to discount the expected future free cash flows available to all capital providers—both lenders and equity investors. The WACC discount rate is a blended rate that combines the equity cost of capital and the debt cost of capital. When enterprise value has been determined, it is apportioned into the value of debt and the value of equity. When equivalent assumptions are used, this alternative approach yields the same intrinsic value estimate as the equity cash flow approach in equation (6.1).

EXHIBIT 6.1	Illustration of the Discounted Free Cash Flow Approach to Valuation

Step 1: Forecast expected future free cash flows

	Year 1	Year 2	Year 3	Year 4	Year 5
Net cash flows from operations	$20,000	$20,000	$25,000	$25,000	$25,000
Cash flow from selling all trucks					30,000
Capital expenditure in Year 2 for the fifth truck		(20,000)			
Future free cash flows	20,000	0	25,000	25,000	55,000

Step 2: Determine the discount rate (10%)

Step 3: Determine the discounted present value of future free cash flows

		Year 1	Year 2	Year 3	Year 4	Year 5
Future free cash flows		20,000	0	25,000	25,000	55,000
$\times$ Present value factor $1/(1.10)^t$		0.90909	0.82645	0.75131	0.68301	0.62092
Present values		$18,182	$ 0	$18,783	$17,075	$34,151

Total present value of future free cash flows	$88,191
Cost to launch business	(80,000)
Net present value of business opportunity	$ 8,191

The final step is to determine the discounted present value of the future free cash flows. The discount factors in Exhibit 6.1 are computed as $1/(1 + 0.10)^t$ and thus capture information about the risk of the business opportunity (10%, or 0.10) and about the timing of each cash flow (the exponent t). The present value of the entire free cash flow stream (the sum of the free cash flow present values for Years 1 through 5) is $88,191. Because Choi must initially invest $80,000 in Year 0, the net present value of the venture is $8,191.

> For example, we assumed that Choi sold all the trucks at the end of Year 5 and ceased doing business.

The above example was simplified in that it involved a finite number of years. In fact, most businesses are going concerns; they are expected to operate indefinitely. To apply the discounted free cash flow valuation approach represented in equation (6.1) to a going concern, we need to estimate free cash flows for every future period *forever*. Obviously this task would be daunting. In practice, some simplifying assumptions are made to facilitate the valuation process.[7]

One simplification for a mature firm with a stable cash flow pattern is to assume the *current level* of cash flows (CF_0) will continue unchanged forever—a zero-growth perpetuity. This means the *expected* free cash flows in each future period will equal the *known* current period cash flow so that equation (6.1) becomes:

Expected free cash flow in each future year set
equal to the actual free cash flow realized in Year 0 $\longrightarrow \infty$

$$V_0 = \frac{CF_0}{(1 + r)^1} + \frac{CF_0}{(1 + r)^2} + \frac{CF_0}{(1 + r)^3} + \cdots \text{(continuing to infinity)} \qquad (6.2)$$

Discount factor each year $\longrightarrow \infty$

---

[7] These simplifying assumptions and other detailed aspects of the valuation process are described in T. Koller, M. Goedhart, and D. Wessels, *Valuation: Measuring and Managing the Value of Companies* (New York: Wiley, 2005); A. Damadoran, *Investment Valuation* (New York: Wiley, 2002); S. Penman, *Financial Statement Analysis and Security Valuation* (New York: McGraw-Hill/Irwin, 2007); and L. Soffer and R. Soffer, *Financial Statement Analysis: A Valuation Approach* (Upper Saddle River, NJ: Prentice Hall, 2003).

The present value of the same dollar cash flow each period over an infinite horizon—called a **constant perpetuity**—simplifies the business valuation model to:[8]

$$V_0 = \frac{CF_0}{r} \tag{6.3}$$

Thus, if a company is currently generating a free cash flow of $5 per share that is expected to continue indefinitely, and if the discount rate is 10%, the per share intrinsic value estimate is $5/0.10 = $50.

The details of free cash flow valuation are important not only to stock analysts and investors, but also to accountants. Because of financial reporting practices for goodwill, accountants and auditors must know how to use the discounted cash flow valuation approach. For example, here's an excerpt from News Corporation's fiscal 2012 annual report to shareholders. News Corporation operates the FOX Network and publishes *The Wall Street Journal*.

Note 9: Goodwill and other Intangible Assets

Annual Impairment Review

The Company's goodwill impairment reviews are determined using a two-step process. The first step of the process is to compare the fair value of a reporting unit with its carrying amount, including goodwill. In performing the first step, the Company determines the fair value of a reporting unit by primarily using a discounted cash flow analysis and market-based valuation approach methodologies. Determining fair value requires the exercise of significant judgments, including judgments about appropriate discount rates, long-term growth rates, relevant comparable company earnings multiples and the amount and timing of expected future cash flows. The cash flows employed in the analyses are based on the Company's estimated outlook and various growth rates have been assumed for years beyond the long-term business plan period. Discount rate assumptions are based on an assessment of the risk inherent in the future cash flows of the respective reporting units. In assessing the reasonableness of its determined fair values, the Company evaluates its results against other value indicators, such as comparable public company trading values. If the fair value of a reporting unit exceeds its carrying amount, goodwill of the reporting unit is not impaired and the second step of the impairment review is not necessary. If the carrying amount of a reporting unit exceeds its fair value, the second step of the goodwill impairment review is required to be performed to estimate the implied fair value of the reporting unit's goodwill. The implied fair value of goodwill is determined in the same manner as the amount of goodwill recognized in a business combination. That is, the estimated fair value of the reporting unit is allocated to all of the assets and liabilities of that unit (including any unrecognized intangible assets) as if the reporting unit had been acquired in a business combination and the estimated fair value of the reporting unit was the purchase price paid. The implied fair value of the reporting unit's goodwill is compared with the carrying amount of that goodwill. If the carrying amount of the reporting unit's goodwill exceeds the implied fair value of that goodwill, an impairment loss is recognized in an amount equal to that excess.

Fiscal 2012

During the fourth quarter of fiscal 2012, the Company completed its annual impairment review of goodwill and indefinite-lived intangible assets. As a result of the impairment review performed, the Company recorded non-cash impairment charges of approximately $2.8 billion ($2.4 billion, net of

---

[8] A constant perpetuity is a stream of equal, periodic cash flows without end. To see why the present value (V_0) of a constant perpetuity reduces to $V_0 = CF_0/r$, note that

$$V_0 = \frac{CF_0}{(1+r)^1} + \frac{CF_0}{(1+r)^2} + \cdots \text{ Multiplying both sides of this equation by } (1+r) \text{ gives}$$

$$V_0 \cdot (1+r) = CF_0 + \frac{CF_0}{(1+r)^1} + \frac{CF_0}{(1+r)^2} + \cdots \text{ Now, subtracting the first equation from the second}$$

gives $V_0 \cdot r = CF_0$, so $V_0 = CF_0/r$.

tax) for the fiscal year ended June 30, 2012. The charges consisted of a write-down of the Company's goodwill of approximately $1.5 billion and a write-down of the indefinite-lived intangible assets (primarily newspaper mastheads and distribution networks) of approximately $1.3 billion. These impairment charges were primarily the result of adverse trends affecting several businesses in the Company's Publishing segment, including secular declines in the economic environment in Australia, a decline in in-store advertising spend by consumer packaged goods manufacturers in the U.S. and lower forecasted revenues from certain businesses utilizing various trade names owned by the Company's newspaper operations. Australia, in particular, has experienced weakness in newspaper advertising reflecting a combination of a softening economy and declines in paid circulation. During the fourth quarter, the business announced a number of major new initiatives to extend the business into multi-platforms and to address these challenges. The charges also reflected the pending sale of certain businesses at values below their respective carrying values.

Source: News Corp. Form 10-K for the year ended June 30, 2012. Edited for brevity.

Goodwill arises when one company buys another company for more than the acquired company's individual net assets are worth. (You will learn more about goodwill in Chapter 16.) For example, suppose News Corporation pays $800 million for another publisher. If the acquired company's identifiable net assets (cash, receivables, office supplies, equipment, buildings, and so on *minus* liabilities) have a **fair value** of only $50 million, then News Corporation must record the $750 million excess as goodwill.

> *Fair value* is the price that would be received on selling each asset in an orderly market transaction. We will have more to say about fair value later in this chapter.

Accounting Standards Codification (ASC) 350, "Goodwill and other Intangibles," requires companies to "test" for impairment of goodwill at least once a year. That's what News Corporation's accountants and auditors did using the free cash flow valuation approach. Continuing our example, suppose that a year later News Corporation estimated the expected future free cash flows associated with its reporting unit (the acquired company) to be worth only $400 million. Why? Because a downturn in demand for newspapers has lowered News Corporation's forecast of the acquired company's future revenues, earnings, and free cash flows from what they were when News Corporation bought the unit.

If the reporting unit's fair value of identifiable net assets is still $50 million, then News Corporation can show only $350 million of goodwill. The original goodwill ($750 million) has become impaired and it must be written down by $400 million—a direct charge to net income for the year. (We've skipped certain details of *ASC 350* but they are described in Chapter 10.)

How common are goodwill impairments? According to one study, about 300 publicly traded U.S. firms recognized a goodwill impairment charge in 2008, and the total amount booked that year was $340 billion.[9] The very next year, goodwill impairments totaling $92 billion were recognized by more than 200 U.S. companies.

Goodwill impairment accounting can result in dramatic earnings hits—$1.5 billion in fiscal 2012 for News Corporation—and impairment tests must be performed each year. That's one reason accountants and auditors must understand discounted cash flow valuation.

The Role of Earnings in Valuation

We have just described a free cash flow approach to valuation. *But what role does earnings play in valuation?* If investors are interested in knowing a company's future cash flows, why do they care about current earnings? The answer hinges on the belief that *current* accrual

---

[9] M. Leone, "Goodwill Charges Sink Like a Rock," *CFO.com,* June 8, 2010.

accounting earnings are more useful than *current* cash flows in predicting *future* cash flows. The Financial Accounting Standards Board (FASB), for example, makes this assertion:

> Information about enterprise earnings and its components measured by accrual accounting generally provides a better indication of enterprise performance than information about current cash receipts and payments.[10]

The Board stresses that the primary objective of financial reporting is to provide information useful to investors and creditors in assessing the *amount, timing,* and *uncertainty* of future net cash flows.[11] The FASB contends that users pay attention to firms' accounting earnings because this accrual measure of periodic performance improves their ability to forecast future cash flows.

The FASB's belief that *current* earnings outperform *current* cash flows in predicting *future* cash flows stems from the *forward-looking* nature of accrual accounting. To illustrate, consider this example. Under generally accepted accounting principles (GAAP), a $100,000 cash expenditure for production equipment is not expensed when purchased. Instead, the expenditure is charged to an asset account, and the asset is depreciated over future years as it is used in the production process. Both the depreciable life and depreciation method are chosen to reflect the *expected future benefit pattern* that arises from the use of the asset. Accrual accounting automatically incorporates this long-horizon, multiple-period view for capital expenditure transactions.

Consider another example. Under accrual accounting, an up-front cash advance from a customer is recognized as income not when the cash is received but rather over a series of future periods as the advance is earned (recall the Canterbury Publishing example from Chapter 2).

Cash flows are "lumpy." But as these examples illustrate, accrual accounting earnings measurement takes a long-horizon perspective that smooths out the "lumpiness" in year-to-year cash flows. This explains why the FASB contends that current earnings provide a much better measure of long-run expected operating performance than do current cash flows.

The FASB's contention is supported by empirical research that shows two results:

- Current earnings are a better forecast of future cash flows than are current cash flows.[12]
- Stock returns correlate better with accrual earnings than with realized operating cash flows.[13]

These results imply that investors are better able to predict a company's future free cash flows using the company's accrual earnings than by using realized cash flows.

The following quote from the "Intrinsic Value" column of *The Wall Street Journal* underscores the importance of accrual earnings as an indicator of future free cash flows:

> As per usual, this column values stocks by their expected future free cash flow, discounted back to the present. Earnings are a proxy—imperfect but the best we have—for free cash flow, which is the spare change that the underlying business throws off to their owners after paying for salaries, interest, capital maintenance, taxes and Danish for their chief executives, in addition to their eight-figure bonuses.

Source: R. Lowenstein, "S&P 500: Cheap, Fair, Going, Gone. . . . ," *The Wall Street Journal,* June 19, 1997. Copyright © 1997 Dow Jones & Company, Inc. All rights reserved worldwide. Reprinted with permission.

---

[10] "Objectives of Financial Reporting by Business Enterprises," *Statement of Financial Accounting Concepts (SFAC) No. 1* (Stamford, CT: FASB, 1978), para. 44.

[11] Ibid., para. 37. The term **net cash flows** refers to the difference between cash receipts (inflows) and cash payments (outflows).

[12] See M. Barth, C. Cram, and K. Nelson, "Accruals and the Prediction of Future Cash Flows," *The Accounting Review,* January 2001, pp. 27–58; and P. Dechow, S. P. Kothari, and R. Watts, "The Relation between Earnings and Cash Flows," *Journal of Accounting and Economics,* May 1998, pp. 133–68. Additional evidence on the usefulness of *current earnings* in predicting *future cash flows* is provided by R. Greenberg, G. Johnson, and K. Ramesh, "Earnings versus Cash Flow as a Predictor of Future Cash Flow," *Journal of Accounting, Auditing and Finance,* Fall 1986, pp. 266–77; and C. Finger, "The Ability of Earnings to Predict Future Earnings and Cash Flow," *Journal of Accounting Research,* Autumn 1994, pp. 210–23.

[13] B. Lev and P. Zarowin, "The Boundaries of Financial Reporting and How to Extend Them," *Journal of Accounting Research,* Autumn 1999, pp. 353–85; J. Callen and D. Segal, "Do Accruals Drive Stock Returns? A Variance Decomposition Analysis," *Journal of Accounting Research,* June 2004, pp. 527–60; J. Watson and P. Wells, "The Association between Various Earnings and Cash Flow Measures of Firm Performance and Stock Returns: Some Australian Evidence," Working Paper, University of Technology, Sydney, AU, 2005; P. Dechow, "Accounting Earnings and Cash Flows as Measures of Firm Performance: The Role of Accounting Accruals," *Journal of Accounting and Economics,* July 1994, pp. 3–42.

Figure 6.1

LINKAGE BETWEEN STOCK
PRICE AND ACCRUAL
EARNINGS

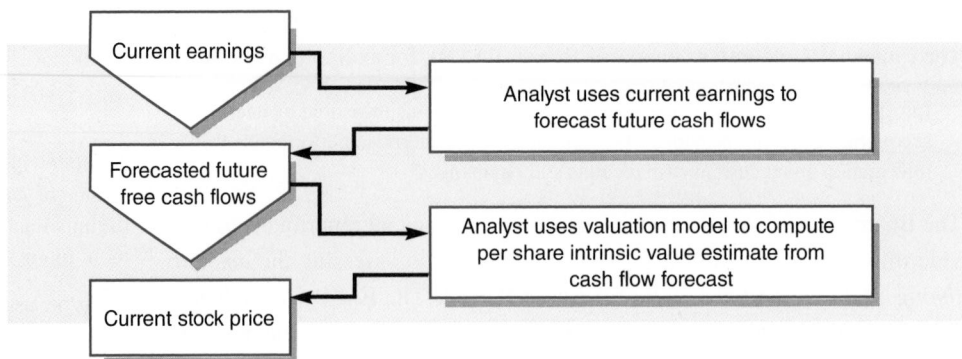

Figure 6.1 illustrates the linkage between a company's current earnings, future free cash flows, and current stock price, as suggested by the FASB and by the empirical evidence.[14] As Figure 6.1 shows, the analyst combines information about the company's current earnings, its business strategy, and the industry's competitive dynamics to forecast future free cash flows. ***Through the use of accruals and deferrals, accrual accounting produces an earnings number that smooths out the unevenness or "lumpiness" in year-to-year cash flows, and it provides an estimate of sustainable long-run future free cash flows.***

The final step in this process involves using the free cash flow estimate together with the risk-adjusted discount rate to arrive at an estimated intrinsic value for the firm's shares.

To appreciate the implications of these linkages, let's revisit the simplified zero-growth perpetuity setting and our free cash flow valuation model. Assuming zero growth means that one way to estimate a firm's equity value (or stock price) is to use its current period's free cash flow (CF_0) as our forecast for each future period free cash flow. But according to the FASB's assertion, the current period's accrual income is a better proxy for sustainable future cash flows than is the current period's free cash flow. So, we replace the current period's cash flow (CF_0) in equation (6.3) with the current period's earnings (denoted X_0). In this case, the free cash flow valuation equation simplifies to:

$$V_0 = \frac{X_0}{r} \qquad (6.4)$$

Note that equation (6.4) can be rewritten as $\frac{V_0}{X_0} = \frac{1}{r}$, indicating that $1/r$ is the *implied* **price/earnings (P/E) ratio**—also called the **earnings multiple**—which is a measure of the relation between a firm's current earnings and its intrinsic share value (V_0). Under the assumption of zero growth, the P/E ratio is the reciprocal of the equity cost of capital (risk-adjusted interest rate) used to discount future earnings. If the equity cost of capital is 8%, the earnings multiple for a zero-growth firm is $1/0.08 = 12.5$, which is the rate at which $1 of current earnings is capitalized into share price. If the company reports current earnings of $5 per share and if investors believe this earnings level will persist forever as a perpetuity of $5 per share, then the present value of the future earnings stream implies a share price of $5 × 12.5 = $62.50.

CAP

In theory, business valuation involves discounting the expected value of some measure of wealth creation—such as free cash flow or earnings—over an infinite horizon using a risk-adjusted discount rate that reflects the equity cost of capital. In practice, simplifying

---

[14] For a slightly different discussion of these linkages, see W. Beaver, *Financial Reporting: An Accounting Revolution* (Upper Saddle River, NJ: Prentice Hall, 1981), Ch. 4.

assumptions are made to facilitate the valuation process. One simplification is to assume that future periods' free cash flows will be a perpetuity equal to the current period's accrual earnings. Accrual accounting produces an earnings number that smooths out the unevenness in year-to-year cash flows, thereby providing a measure of firm performance that is generally a better indicator of a company's long-run sustainable free cash flows.

The Abnormal Earnings Approach to Valuation

In the previous section, we found that the role of accounting earnings information in valuation is *indirect*—earnings are useful because they help generate forecasts of future free cash flows. These future free cash flow estimates were discounted to arrive at an estimated value for the company and its shares. Another valuation approach has emerged that uses earnings and equity book value numbers themselves as *direct* inputs in the valuation process. Given equivalent assumptions about future performance, this approach leads to valuation estimates that are equivalent to the free cash flow approach. So, why is it important to learn about this approach? Because it helps us understand the economic forces that influence share prices over time and across firms.

This approach is based on the notion that a company's value (and its share price) is driven not by the level of earnings per se but by the level of earnings *relative to a fundamental economic benchmark*. That benchmark is the cost of capital expressed in dollars, and it reflects the level of earnings investors demand from the company as compensation for the risks of investment. Investors willingly pay a premium only for those firms that earn more than the cost of capital—meaning firms that produce **positive abnormal earnings.** For firms whose earnings are "ordinary" or "normal"—that is, have an earnings rate equal to the cost of capital—investors are willing to pay only an amount equal to the underlying book value of net assets. Firms that earn less than the cost of capital—that is, that produce **negative abnormal earnings**—sell at a discount to book value. This relationship among share prices, book value, and abnormal earnings performance is expressed mathematically as:[15]

> In theory, the abnormal earnings approach and the free cash flow approach *always* produce the same valuation estimate. In practice, however, the two approaches sometimes produce different valuation estimates. When this occurs, it's because the analyst has made assumptions in one model that are not equivalent to those in the other.

$$
\underset{\substack{\uparrow \\ \text{Share value at} \\ \text{Time 0}}}{V_0} = \underset{\substack{\uparrow \\ \text{Book value of} \\ \text{equity at Time 0}}}{BV_0} + \overset{\substack{\text{Expected future abnormal} \\ \text{earnings} \\ \downarrow}}{\underset{\substack{\uparrow \\ \text{Discount factors for each} \\ \text{future period}}}{\sum_{t=1}^{\infty} \frac{E_0(\text{Abnormal earnings}_t)}{(1 + r)^t}}} \tag{6.5}
$$

where *BV* denotes the book value of the firm's equity (assets minus liabilities, or net assets) per share, E_0 denotes the expectation about future abnormal EPS formed at Time 0, and *r* is the equity cost of capital.

---

[15] Several variations of the abnormal earnings valuation model have appeared in the literature. Examples include J. Ohlson, "Earnings, Book Values, and Dividends in Equity Valuation," *Contemporary Accounting Research,* Spring 1995, pp. 661–87; T. Koller, M. Goedhart, and D. Wessels, *Valuation: Measuring and Managing the Value of Companies, 5 ed.* (New York: Wiley, 2010); R. Lundholm and R. Sloan, *Equity Valuation and Analysis, 3 ed.* (New York: McGraw-Hill, 2012); B. Madden, *CFROI Valuation* (Boston, MA: Butterworth-Heinemann, 1999); S. Penman, *Financial Statement Analysis and Security Valuation, 5 ed.* (New York: McGraw-Hill, 2013); L. Soffer and R. Soffer, *Financial Statement Analysis: A Valuation Approach* (Upper Saddle River, NJ: Prentice Hall, 2003); and G. B. Stewart III, *The Quest for Value* (New York: Harper Business, 1991).

The cost of equity capital, r, also corresponds to the risk-adjusted return stockholders *require* from their investment. So, the earnings level the company must generate in period t to satisfy stockholders is $r \times BV_{t-1}$, or stockholders' required rate of return multiplied by the beginning of period $(t - 1)$ invested capital. Any difference between actual earnings for the period (X_t) and stockholders' required dollar return on invested capital for the period $(r \times BV_{t-1})$ represents **abnormal earnings.**

$$
\text{Abnormal earnings}_t = \overset{\overset{\text{Actual earnings}}{\downarrow}}{X_t} - \overset{\overset{\text{Required earnings}}{\downarrow}}{(r \times BV_{t-1})} \tag{6.6}
$$

To illustrate, suppose a company's equity book value (BV) at the beginning of the year is $100 per share and the cost of equity (r) is 15%. Stockholders therefore require earnings of at least $100 \times 15\%$, or $15 per share. If investors expect the company to report earnings equal to the benchmark earnings of $15 per share, but the company does even better and earns $20 per share—thus exceeding the benchmark—its stock price will increase to reflect its superior performance. If actual earnings are only $10—thus falling short of the benchmark expected earnings—the stock price will fall. The amount of the stock price increase (or decline) depends on the degree to which stockholders believe that abnormal earnings (earnings above *or* below the benchmark) are permanent rather than temporary.

Exhibit 6.2 shows how the abnormal earnings approach can be used to assign a value to Judy Choi's truck rental business. You remember Choi? Recall that she plans to buy four trucks now and to add a fifth truck in two years. Each truck will cost $20,000, and she believes each will generate $5,000 of net operating cash flows every year. At the end of five years, she believes the trucks can be sold for $30,000 in total.

Additional information:

- Choi will put $80,000 cash into the business. This amount represents beginning equity.
- The company will pay out all excess cash as dividends each year. The cash needed to buy the last truck in Year 2 will come from operating cash flows that year. No new investment will be required.
- Truck depreciation is $3,043.48 per truck per year, which results in the trucks having a book value of $30,000, the expected salvage value, at the end of Year 5.

Step 1 of Exhibit 6.2 shows the computations of forecasted net income, dividends paid (assuming no net change in cash), and book value of equity. Equity book value increases by net income for the year and decreases when dividends are paid to shareholders. Notice that Choi's company does not pay a dividend in Year 2. Why? Because the entire $20,000 of operating cash flows generated that year (4 trucks $\times$ $5,000 operating cash flow per truck) is needed to buy the fifth truck.

Step 2 of Exhibit 6.2 illustrates the computation of expected future abnormal earnings. Each year the beginning book value of equity is multiplied by the 10% rate of return required by investors to arrive at required or "normal" earnings. For example, the required earnings threshold in Year 1 is $8,000 ($80,000 of initial equity capital $\times$ 10%). The $8,000 required earnings is subtracted from the $7,826 of forecasted earnings for the year to arrive at expected abnormal earnings of $-$174.

EXHIBIT 6.2	Illustration of the Abnormal Earnings Approach to Valuation

Step 1: Forecast earnings and equity book value

	Year 1	Year 2	Year 3	Year 4	Year 5
Operating cash flows (= earnings before depreciation)	$20,000	$20,000	$25,000	$25,000	$25,000
Depreciaton ($3,043.48 per truck per year)	(12,174)	(12,174)	(15,217)	(15,218)	(15,217)
Net income	$ 7,826	$ 7,826	$ 9,783	$ 9,782	$ 9,783
Operating cash flows	$20,000	$20,000	$25,000	$25,000	$25,000
Capital expenditures	0	(20,000)	0	0	0
Proceeds on sale of trucks					30,000
Cash available to pay dividends	20,000	0	25,000	25,000	55,000
Dividends	(20,000)	0	(25,000)	(25,000)	(55,000)
Net change in cash	$ 0	$ 0	$ 0	$ 0	$ 0
Beginning book value of equity	$80,000	$67,826	$75,652	$60,435	$45,217
Net income	7,826	7,826	9,783	9,782	9,783
Dividends	(20,000)	0	(25,000)	(25,000)	(55,000)
Ending book value of equity	$67,826	$75,652	$60,435	$45,217	$ 0

Step 2: Forecast future abnormal earnings

	Year 1	Year 2	Year 3	Year 4	Year 5
Net income	$ 7,826	$ 7,826	$ 9,783	$ 9,782	$ 9,783
Beginning book value of equity	80,000	67,826	75,652	60,435	45,217
Cost of equity capital	10%	10%	10%	10%	10%
Normal earnings	8,000	6,783	7,565	6,044	4,522
Abnormal earnings	($174)	$ 1,043	$ 2,218	$ 3,738	$ 5,261

Step 3: Determine the present value of expected future abnormal earnings

	Year 1	Year 2	Year 3	Year 4	Year 5
Abnormal earnings	($174)	$ 1,043	$ 2,218	$ 3,738	$ 5,261
Present value factor	0.90909	0.82645	0.75131	0.68301	0.62092
Present value of future abnormal earnings	($158)	$ 862	$ 1,666	$ 2,553	$ 3,267

Sum of all present values	$ 8,190
Beginning equity book value	80,000
Value of business	$88,190

← Difference versus Exhibit 6.1 is due to rounding.

Step 3 of Exhibit 6.2 shows the present value of expected future abnormal earnings over the life of the business. The discount factors shown are the same ones used in the discounted free cash flow approach in Exhibit 6.1. The individual present values are summed, and this amount ($8,190) is added to the beginning book value of equity ($80,000) to arrive at the estimated value of $88,190. This is the same value estimate (within rounding) we developed using the free cash flow approach!

Financial statements and related notes provide a wealth of information for assessing the relationships expressed by abnormal earnings valuation equations (6.5) and (6.6). The balance sheet provides detailed information on the book value of equity (assets minus liabilities). The income statement provides detailed information for assessing a firm's earnings. These financial statement numbers and their forecasted amounts are the ingredients used in the abnormal earnings approach.

Figure 6.2

RELATIONSHIP BETWEEN
ROCE PERFORMANCE
AND MARKET-TO-BOOK
(M/B) RATIOS FOR
48 RESTAURANT
COMPANIES

Regression Result:

$$M/B = 1.31 + 0.13\,ROCE$$
$$R^2 = 59.1\%$$

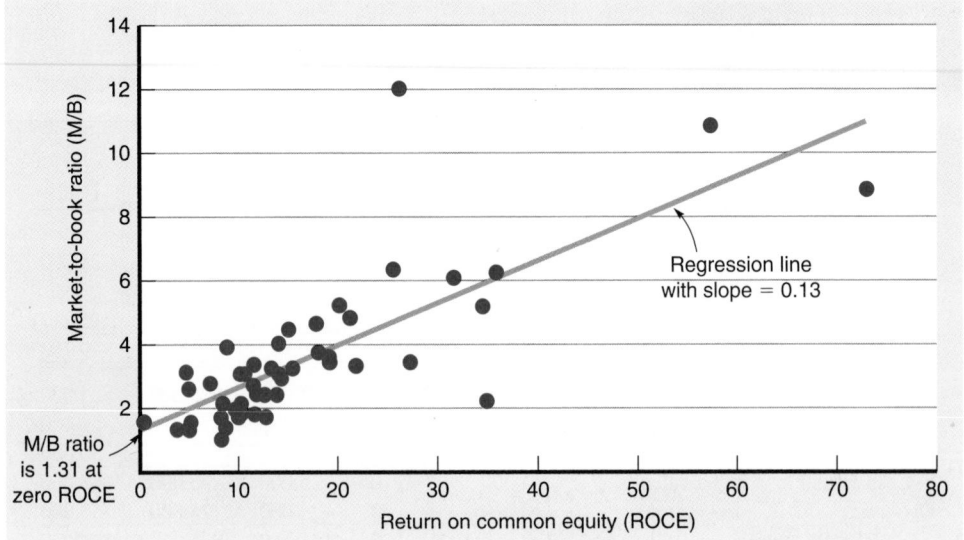

Abnormal Earnings and ROCE ROCE combines information about earnings and equity book value—two financial statement items essential to the abnormal earnings valuation approach. A firm's ROCE can be compared to its required rate of return on common equity (cost of equity capital) or to the ROCEs of other companies in the industry to evaluate its prospects for generating "abnormal earnings." Companies with ROCEs that consistently exceed the industry average generally have shares that sell for a premium relative to book value (that is, a higher market-to-book ratio).

Figure 6.2 plots the relationship between the ROCE and the year-end market-to-book ratios of 48 restaurant companies. The upward-sloping line represents the estimated regression line of market-to-book ratio versus ROCE for these companies. The regression line has an intercept estimate of 1.31 and a slope coefficient estimate of 0.13. According to the regression line, a restaurant company that earns an ROCE of 20% should have a market-to-book ratio of 3.91 (or 1.31 + [0.13 × 20]). A market-to-book ratio of 3.91 means that the company's shares sell for almost four times their equity book value.

In making comparisons across firms, the analyst must gauge the quality and comparability of the accounting policies or methods used. For example, does the company being analyzed tend to select liberal accounting methods (those that may increase earnings and net asset values) or more conservative methods (those that may decrease earnings and net asset values)? The degree of conservatism associated with a firm's accounting choices has a direct bearing on the relationship among share price, earnings, and equity book value components of equation (6.5). To see this, consider a company that has a $10 share price and an $8 per share equity book value. Analysts who understand the accounting complexities described later in this book know there are two reasons why this company's stock may be valued at a $2 premium to equity book value. One reason is that shareholders believe the company will be very profitable in the future, resulting in abnormal earnings worth—according to equation (6.5)—$2 today. A second possibility, however, is that the company's conservative accounting methods result in an unusually low equity book value, and the low book value results in abnormal earnings whose present value is $2 per share.[16] Note that in this case, a lower book value is associated

---

[16] For a further discussion of these points and the implications of the abnormal earnings valuation model, see G. Feltham and J. Ohlson, "Valuation and Clean Surplus Accounting for Operating and Financial Assets," *Contemporary Accounting Research,* Spring 1995, pp. 689–731; V. Bernard. "The Feltham-Ohlson Framework: Implications for Empiricists," *Contemporary Accounting Research,* Spring 1995, pp. 733–47; Lundholm and Sloan, ibid.; Penman, ibid.; Soffer and Soffer, ibid.; and Stewart, ibid.

with greater abnormal earnings, so that more conservative accounting will not reduce a firm's value, which combines the book value and abnormal earnings.

Much of the information needed for assessing the quality and value relevance of a company's reported accounting numbers appears in notes to its financial statements. These notes describe accounting policies for matters such as revenue recognition (completed contract versus percentage of completion), depreciation (straight line versus accelerated), and inventory valuation (LIFO versus FIFO). Later chapters will clarify the important differences in these and other accounting methods and their effects on earnings and balance sheet book values. In certain instances, we show how you can adjust reported numbers to put firms that use different methods on a more equal footing before using those numbers for valuation purposes.

RECAP

The abnormal earnings approach to valuation says a company's future earnings are determined by (1) the resources (net assets) available to management and (2) the rate of return or profitability earned on those net assets. If a firm can earn a return on net assets (common equity book value) that *exceeds* its cost of equity capital, it will generate positive abnormal earnings. Its stock will then sell at a premium relative to book value. However, if the firm earns a return on net assets that falls *below* its cost of equity capital, it will generate negative abnormal earnings. Its stock will then sell at a discount relative to book value. A key feature of this valuation approach is that it explicitly takes into account a cost for the capital (net assets) provided by the owners of the business. Value is added only if the earnings generated from those net assets exceed the equity cost of capital benchmark. Appendix A to this chapter illustrates how to use this valuation model for a real company.

FAIR VALUE ACCOUNTING

For decades, GAAP balance sheet carrying amounts were based primarily on **historical cost,** or what had been paid for a particular asset. But over the last 25 years, more and more **fair value** measurements have been introduced. As you may recall from Chapter 4, today's balance sheet contains a mixture of historical cost and other measurements, including fair value. One example, already mentioned in this chapter, is the requirement that fair value be used to assess goodwill impairment. Others are described throughout the book. In some ways, the growing use of fair value accounting parallels a shift in the United States from a manufacturing to a financial services economy in which financial assets and liabilities are increasingly important.

Before 2006, accountants and auditors had no consensus on how to determine fair values. Consider, for example, an investment in a truck rental firm. Should the fair value of that investment be measured by the **exit price** (the amount the firm would *receive* if it sold its investment) or by the **entry price** (the amount the firm would *pay* if it bought an identical investment)? And what if there are no readily ascertainable **market prices** to determine an asset's fair value? If there is no active market for an asset, then fair value could be determined either (a) by using market values for similar, albeit not identical, assets and adjusting for the ways in which the reference asset differs from the asset being valued, or (b) by using a valuation model such as those described in the chapter. So, at least three different approaches could be used to measure the investment's exit or entry price, resulting in a total of six (3 × 2) distinct ways to measure fair value.

In September 2006, the FASB issued *SFAS No. 157,* "Fair Value Measurements," to increase consistency and comparability in the way fair values are determined for financial reporting purposes. *ASC Topic 820,* "Fair Value Measurement and Disclosures," which is based on *SFAS No. 157,* defines fair value, establishes a framework for measuring fair value, and

> Carrying amounts in a GAAP balance sheet are measured using historical cost, net realizable value, discounted present value, and fair value.

requires expanded disclosures about fair value measurements. However, it does not establish any new instances that require fair value measurement.

ASC Topic 820 defines fair value as "the price that would be received to sell an asset or paid to transfer a liability in an orderly transaction between market participants at the measurement date."[17] This means that, for accounting purposes, fair value is an exit price, not an entry price. *ASC Topic 820* also states that the hypothetical transaction of selling the asset or transferring the liability is presumed to occur in the ordinary course of business (i.e., not a forced sale or transfer) and in the item's principal market. Transaction costs do not reduce fair value. *ASC Topic 820* further states that a nonfinancial asset's fair value must reflect its "highest and best use," which is not necessarily how the company uses it. This distinction can be important when, for example, valuable California ocean-front real estate is used as a company parking lot. *ASC Topic 820* also states that a liability's fair value must incorporate the company's credit risk.

GAAP provides a hierarchy of approaches to be used in measuring fair values. The hierarchy differentiates between assets and liabilities that trade in an active market (e.g., a share of stock in Ford Motor) and those that do not (e.g., a grain silo). The hierarchy has three levels of fair value estimates:

- A *Level 1* estimate uses *quoted prices* from active markets for *identical* assets or liabilities to determine fair value.

- A *Level 2* estimate uses *observable* inputs other than Level 1 quoted prices. These inputs include quoted prices from active markets for similar (but not identical) assets or liabilities, quoted prices from less-than-active markets, and observable inputs other than quoted prices (such as interest rate yield curves or stock price volatility measures).

- A *Level 3* estimate uses a valuation model, together with *unobservable* inputs such as management's estimates or expected future cash flows or abnormal earnings. Level 3 estimates are often referred to as mark-to-model valuation inputs.

Firms must use the highest level estimate possible when determining a fair value. That is, if a Level 1 estimate is feasible, it must be used. If not, a Level 2 estimate must be used if feasible. Level 3 estimates are permitted only when it is not possible to obtain either a Level 1 or a Level 2 estimate.

Firms must disclose at each reporting date the hierarchy level at which the fair values were determined, transfers between levels, a reconciliation of beginning Level 3 inputs to ending inputs, and the amount of unrealized fair value gains or losses that are included in earnings for the period, among other related disclosures. The Level 3 reconciliation alerts financial statement readers to any changes in management forecasts and valuation model assumptions. Research evidence supports the FASB's emphasis on observable market inputs (Levels 1 and 2) and the importance of disclosing the extent to which fair values rely on management judgment and discretion (Level 3).[18]

ASC Topic 820 gives companies, auditors, and investors much needed guidance on how to measure fair values. It also reopens the door to potential accounting abuses. The accounting irregularities uncovered at Enron in late 2001 led the FASB to ban the use of mark-to-model fair value accounting for most energy contracts. Why? Because the use of subjective, internal valuation models invited Enron and other energy companies to inflate their earnings through

---

[17] "Fair Value Measurements," *SFAS No. 157* (Norwalk, CT: FASB, 2006), para. 5. This definition is retained in FASB Accounting Standards Codification (ASC) Master Glossary: Fair Value and in *ASC Topic 820-10.*

[18] See AAA Financial Accounting Standards Committee, "Response to the FASB's Exposure Draft on Fair Value Measurements," *Accounting Horizons,* September 2005, pp. 187–96.

unreasonably optimistic assumptions. Critics then and now claim that mark-to-model fair value accounting is "a license for management to invent the financial statements to be whatever they want them to be."[19] Level 3 fair values add an additional layer of uncertainty and subjectivity as well as risk of material misstatement to financial reports.

Fair value accounting poses a significant challenge for auditors who must evaluate how companies came up with their numbers. Expanded use of fair value accounting means that auditors must have technical knowledge of the valuation tools described in this chapter and how the tools are used in practice. That is one reason why valuation is an important component of this book.

GLOBAL VANTAGE POINT

Recently, the International Accounting Standards Board (IASB) and FASB concluded a joint convergence project on fair value measurement and disclosure. The aim was to ensure that U.S. GAAP and IFRS reflect a shared view about fundamental principles such as what fair value means and how best to measure it. The IASB issued IFRS 13 "Fair Value Measurement" in May 2011 (effective for fiscal years that begin after January 1, 2013) that fundamentally agrees with U.S. GAAP on the definition of fair value as an exit price, the three-level measurement hierarchy, and most disclosure requirements. As part of the convergence project, FASB released Accounting Standards Update No. 2011-04 in May 2011, revising *ASC 820-10* to bring U.S. fair value disclosure rules more in line with recent IFRS.

A number of people mistakenly believe that GAAP balance sheet carrying amounts are based on historical cost, but many of these carrying amounts are now shown at fair value. *ASC Topic 820* provides fair value guidance for companies, their auditors, and investors. It also serves as a wake-up call to accountants and auditors about the need to become more skilled in valuing balance sheet assets and liabilities.

RESEARCH ON EARNINGS AND EQUITY VALUATION

For nearly 40 years, researchers have investigated the **value-relevance** of financial accounting information.[20] This research seeks to further our understanding of the relation between stock prices and earnings.

To illustrate, recall equation (6.4), which says that intrinsic share value (V_0) is related to current earnings (X_0) in the sense that a perpetual earnings stream of $5 per share gives rise to an intrinsic share value of $62.50 (when the discount rate is 8%). If stock prices (P_0) approximate

[19] Damon Silvers, associate general counsel for the AFL-CIO, as quoted in D. Reilly, "FASB to Issue Retooled Rule for Valuing Corporate Assets," *The Wall Street Journal,* September 15, 2006.

[20] For an overview of this research, see B. Lev and J. Ohlson, "Market-Based Empirical Research in Accounting: A Review, Interpretation, and Extension," *Journal of Accounting Research,* Supplement 1982, pp. 249–322; B. Lev, "On the Usefulness of Earnings and Earnings Research: Lessons and Directions from Two Decades of Empirical Research," *Journal of Accounting Research,* Supplement 1989, pp. 153–92; S. Kothari, "Capital Markets Research in Accounting," *Journal of Accounting and Economics,* September 2001, pp. 105–232; R. Holthausen and R. Watts, "The Relevance of the Value-Relevance Literature for Financial Accounting Standard Setting," *Journal of Accounting and Economics,* September 2001, pp. 3–76; and A. Beyer, D. Cohen, T. Lys, and B. Walther, "The Financial Reporting Environment: Review of the Recent Literature," *Journal of Accounting and Economics,* December 2010, pp. 296–343.

intrinsic share values (V_0), as they will when markets are efficient, then equation (6.4) also describes how stock prices and current earnings would be related, assuming all future cash flows are perpetuities. It immediately follows that *differences* in current earnings across firms should help explain *differences* in stock prices across firms. ***That is, if investors view accounting earnings as an important piece of information for assessing firm value, then earnings differences across firms should help explain differences in firms' stock prices.*** This is just another way of saying that earnings are value-relevant.

One way to test whether reported earnings are value-relevant is to examine the statistical association between stock prices and earnings across many firms at a given point in time. Researchers have explored this statistical association using the following simple valuation equation:

$$P_i = \alpha + \beta X_i + e_i \qquad (6.7)$$

where P_i is the end-of-period closing stock price for firm i, and X_i is the firm's reported earnings per share for the same period; the intercept (α) and slope (β) terms represent coefficients to be estimated using standard regression analysis; e_i denotes a random error that reflects the variation in stock prices that cannot be explained by earnings.[21]

If accounting earnings are relevant for determining stock prices, then the estimated slope coefficient β, which measures the relationship between earnings and prices, should be positive. A statistically positive β means that differences in earnings across firms explain a significant portion of the variation in firms' share prices.

Figure 6.3 plots year-end stock prices (shown on the vertical axis) against annual EPS (shown on the horizontal axis) for 48 restaurant companies. The upward-sloping line represents the estimated price-earnings relation for the regression equation (6.7) for this group of

> For now, earnings per share (EPS) can be taken to mean a company's net income divided by its number of outstanding common shares. As you will discover in Chapter 15, EPS calculations are actually more complicated than this.

Figure 6.3

STOCK PRICE AND ACTUAL EPS FOR 48 RESTAURANT COMPANIES

Regression Result:

$P_i = \$9.57 + 14.28X_i$
$R^2 = 61.7\%$

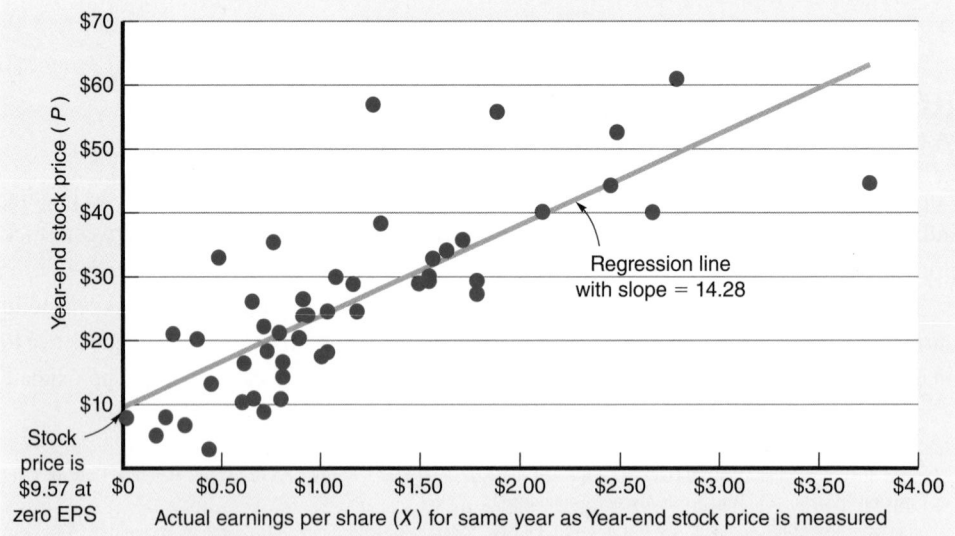

---

[21] This specification is not perfect because it implies that stock prices could be negative, given sufficiently negative earnings. However, for a wide range of data, the specification is a useful analytical tool.

companies. The regression line has a vertical axis intercept (α) estimate of $9.57 per share and a slope (β) coefficient estimate of 14.28—that is:

$$P_i = \underset{\substack{\uparrow \\ \text{Implied stock} \\ \text{price at} \\ \$0 \text{ EPS}}}{\overset{\substack{\text{Intercept} \\ \downarrow}}{\$9.57}} + \underset{\substack{\uparrow \\ \text{Earnings} \\ \text{multiple}}}{\overset{\substack{\text{Slope} \\ \downarrow}}{14.28}} \times \underset{\substack{\uparrow \\ \text{EPS}}}{(\$X_i)} \qquad (6.8)$$

A restaurant firm that reported EPS of $X_i = \$1$ would be predicted to have a stock price of $23.85 = [\$9.57 + (14.28 \times \$1)]$. The estimated slope coefficient ($\beta = 14.28$) is positive and statistically significant, indicating that reported earnings explains some of the variation in stock prices of restaurant companies. In fact, the proportion of variation in share prices explained by earnings (the R^2 for the regression) is 61.7%. However, some points lie well above the average price-earnings relation in Figure 6.3 while others fall far below the regression line.[22] The next section discusses reasons why current earnings do not explain all of the variation in current prices and why some firms' P/E ratios are well above (or below) average.

> Figure 6.3 dots that are above the regression line denote firms that *seem* to be "over-valued" by investors—P/E is too high—whereas *seemingly* "undervalued" firms fall below the line.

Sources of Variation in P/E Multiples

Current Earnings, a Poor Forecast of Future Expected Earnings

Two firms with identical current earnings can have very different stock prices if investors believe that the firms' future earnings will not be the same. Investors care most about where a firm is headed (future earnings and free cash flows), not where it has been (past earnings and cash flows). To illustrate, suppose that Firms A and B both earn $1.50 per share in the current year. However, investors expect Firm A to earn $2.50 per share next year (and every year thereafter) whereas they expect Firm B to earn only $1.50 in perpetuity. If the equity cost of capital for both firms is 10% and we apply equation (6.4), Firm A will command a stock price of $25 (= $2.50/0.10), but Firm B will sell for only $15 (= $1.50/0.10) per share. Even though both firms earn $1.50 per share this year, Firm A has a higher stock price because its expected future earnings are higher. As a result, Firm A's P/E multiple will be 16.7 (= $25/$1.50) while Firm B's will be only 10.0 (= $15/$1.50).

What happens when *expected* future earnings replace current earnings in Figure 6.3? The answer can be found in Figure 6.4, which plots the relation between year-end stock prices (shown on the vertical axis) and professional stock analysts' consensus forecasts of next year's EPS (shown on the horizontal axis) for 43 restaurant firms where analysts' forecasts are available. Stock prices and EPS forecasts are both from December. The upward-sloping regression line in Figure 6.4 now has an intercept (α) estimate of $6.65 and a slope ($\beta$) coefficient estimate of 14.83. This means that a restaurant firm forecasted to earn $1 per share next year would be predicted to have a stock price of $21.48 = [$6.65 + (14.83 \times \$1)]$. Although using *expected* future earnings still does not explain all of the

---

[22] The error term (e_i) in equation (6.7) does not show up in equation (6.8). That's because equation (6.8) is the expression for the *fitted regression line*. The vertical distances between the fitted regression line and the data points for individual firms in Figure 6.3 are the e_i error terms in equation (6.7).

Figure 6.4

STOCK PRICE AND
FORECASTED EPS FOR
43 RESTAURANT
COMPANIES

Regression Result:

$$P_i = \$6.65 + 14.83\,X_i$$
$$R^2 = 74.4\%$$

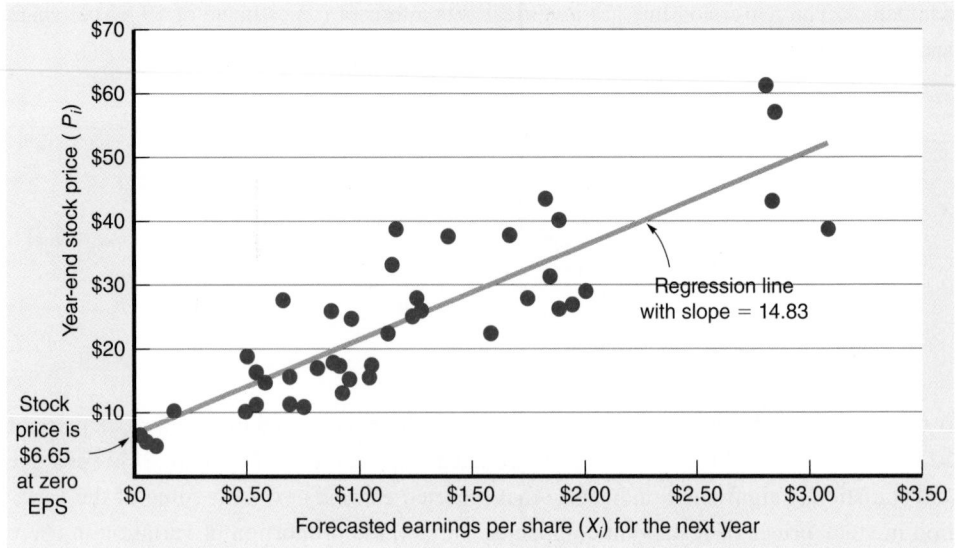

variation in share price, it explains 74.4% (the regression R^2), which is more than actual earnings explained (61.7%).

Risk Differences   Two firms with the same level of current *and* future expected earnings can sell for different prices because of differences in the risk or uncertainty associated with those earnings. Riskier firms have a higher risk-adjusted cost of capital, which means that the discount rate for capitalizing their earnings (and free cash flows, for that matter) will be *higher,* resulting in *lower* share prices.

To illustrate, suppose Firm A and Firm B both report current earnings of $10 per share, and investors expect these earnings will, on average, persist into the future forever. However, Firm A's earnings exhibit greater volatility over time—and therefore, greater risk—which equates to a 15% cost of equity capital for Firm A. Firm B's earnings are more stable—that is, they represent a lower risk—so Firm B's cost of equity capital is only 10%.

The estimated share price for each firm would be:

Firm A	Firm B
$\dfrac{\$10}{0.15} = \$66.67$	$\dfrac{\$10}{0.10} = \$100$

Thus, despite having equal earnings, Firm A's share price will be one-third less than Firm B's ($66.67 versus $100) because Firm A is riskier and its cost of capital is higher.

Growth Opportunities   Most firms' P/E ratios range between 10 and 30. However, it is not uncommon to find young technology-based companies such as Facebook trading at share prices 100 times current EPS or more. What explains these exceptionally high P/E ratios?

In addition to valuing earnings generated from existing assets, the market values **growth opportunities**—that is, the firm's *potential earnings* from reinvesting current earnings in new projects that will eventually earn a rate of return in excess of the cost of equity capital. The net present value of growth opportunities (NPVGO) adds a positive increment to the firm's stock price, resulting in above average P/E multiples. For a firm with positive growth opportunities, the pricing equation (6.4) can be rewritten as:

$$P_0 = \underbrace{\frac{X_0}{r}}_{\substack{\text{Present value of earnings} \\ \text{from assets in place}}} + \underbrace{\text{NPVGO}}_{\substack{\text{Net present value of future} \\ \text{growth opportunities}}} \qquad \textbf{(6.9)}$$

The first term is the value of current operations for a firm that has no growth opportunities. Current earnings (X_0) are viewed as a level perpetuity; that is, earnings next year are expected also to be X_0. The second term (NPVGO) is the future growth value of a firm—the *additional* share value created (or lost) if the firm retains its earnings to fund new investment projects. For example, Facebook had a stock price (P_0) of about \$30 per share in early 2013 and trailing 12-month EPS (X_0) of only \$0.19. Using an equity cost of capital (r) of 10%, the present value of earnings from assets in place was \$1.90 (=\$0.19/0.10). This means that NPVGO for Facebook was \$28.10. Growth opportunities thus comprise 94% of the company's stock price.

> If on the one hand, investors believe the firm will put money into worthwhile projects (that is, those with a *positive* net present value), NPVGO will be positive. On the other hand, if investors believe the firm will invest in unprofitable projects (that is, those with a *negative* net present value), NPVGO will be negative.

Permanent, Transitory, and Valuation-Irrelevant Components of Earnings

If investors view firms' current earnings levels as likely to persist in perpetuity, then the slope coefficient (β) in equation (6.7) should equal the average earnings multiple for the particular companies and time period being examined. This prediction follows directly from the equity valuation model in equation (6.4), in which current earnings are translated into share price using an earnings multiple based on the risk-adjusted cost of equity capital. For example, if the average cost of capital is 8%, then β should be 1/0.08, or 12.5. However, for many firms, the earnings multiple falls well below this value.[23] Why?

> Equation (6.7) is our simple earnings valuation equation: $P_i = \alpha + \beta X_i + e_i$ where P is stock price, X is earnings per share, α and β are regression coefficients, and e is the error term.

One explanation is that reported earnings numbers often contain three distinctly different components, each subject to a different earnings capitalization rate:

1. A **permanent earnings** component, which is expected to persist into the future and is therefore valuation-relevant. In theory, the multiple for this component should approach $1/r$.

2. A **transitory earnings** component, which is valuation-relevant but is not expected to persist into the future. Because transitory earnings result from one-time events or transactions, the multiple for this component should approach 1.0.

3. A **value-irrelevant earnings** (or **noise**) component, which is unrelated to future free cash flows or future earnings and, therefore, is *not* pertinent to assessing current share price. Such earnings components should carry a multiple of zero.[24]

---

[23] Notice that the slope coefficient of 14.28 for restaurants in Figure 6.3 suggests an earnings capitalization rate of about 7% because 1/0.07 = 14.29.

[24] For a more formal discussion of these three earnings components and their valuation implication, see R. Ramakrishnan and J. Thomas, "Valuation of Permanent, Transitory, and Price-Irrelevant Components of Reported Earnings," *Journal of Accounting, Auditing and Finance,* Summer 1998, pp. 301–36.

These three earnings components correspond roughly to elements of the multiple-step income statements described in Chapter 2. For example:

- **Income from continuing operations** (with the possible exception of certain so-called special items) is generally regarded as a recurring, sustainable component of a company's profit performance, and thus it would fall into the permanent earnings category.

- **Income (loss) from discontinued operations and extraordinary gains and losses** are nonrecurring. These items are more likely to be viewed as transitory components of earnings and, therefore, to be valued at a much lower multiple than those items associated with permanent earnings components.

- **The current-year impact of a change in accounting principles,** which has no future cash flow consequences to shareholders, may be viewed as "noise" that is valuation-irrelevant.

> Investors may view some items that comprise income from continuing operations as highly transitory and/or value-irrelevant and, accordingly, those items would be capitalized at lower multiples. Analysts call these "special" items. Examples include inventory holding gains and losses embedded in first-in, first-out (FIFO) earnings and last-in, first-out (LIFO) liquidation profits that result when old LIFO inventory layers are sold. Later chapters discuss the value-relevance of these and other earnings and balance sheet items in considerable detail.

To illustrate the importance of distinguishing between permanent, transitory, and value-irrelevant earnings components, let's suppose that two companies report identical bottom-line earnings of $10 per share. Would they necessarily sell for the same price? Perhaps not, as Exhibit 6.3 illustrates.

Exhibit 6.3 disaggregates each firm's earnings into permanent, transitory, and value-irrelevant components. For Firm A, 60% of its earnings is judged to be permanent, 30% is transitory, and 10% is value-irrelevant.[25] For Firm B, 50% is permanent, 20% is transitory, and 30% is value-irrelevant.

Using a 10% cost of capital, the implied stock prices are $63 and $52 for Firm A and Firm B, respectively. Firm A's stock price is 21% higher, even though the two companies report the same EPS. Firm A's stock sells for a higher multiple because, in the vernacular of the analyst community, investors perceive its **earnings quality** to be superior to that of Firm B.

EXHIBIT 6.3	**Applying P/E Multiples to Earnings Components**	
	Firm A	**Firm B**
EPS as reported	$10	$10
Analyst's EPS decomposition:		
Permanent component	60% of $10 = $6	50% of $10 = $5
Transitory component	30% of $10 = $3	20% of $10 = $2
Value-irrelevant component	10% of $10 = $1	30% of $10 = $3
Earnings multiple (β) applied to each earnings component at cost of capital of $r = 10\%$		
Permanent component ($\beta_P = 10 = 1/0.10$)	$10 \times \$6 = \$60$	$10 \times \$5 = \$50$
Transitory component ($\beta_T = 1$)	$1 \times \$3 = \$3$	$1 \times \$2 = \$2$
Value-irrelevant component ($\beta_{VI} = 0$)	$0 \times \$1 = \$0$	$0 \times \$3 = \$0$
Implied share price	$63	$52
Implied total earnings multiple (share price/EPS as reported)	6.3	5.2

---

[25] In theory, permanent (sustainable) earnings should have a higher earnings multiple than transitory earnings because we expect the former to persist longer into the future. Lipe presents evidence consistent with this conjecture. He finds a greater stock price reaction to earnings components that exhibit greater permanence than to those components that are more transitory in nature. See R. Lipe, "The Information Contained in the Components of Earnings," *Journal of Accounting Research,* Supplement 1986, pp. 33–64.

The Concept of Earnings Quality

The Concept of Earnings Quality   A *Wall Street Journal* article described earnings quality and its implications for stock prices:

> Quality of earnings measures how much the profits companies publicly report diverge from their true operating earnings. Low quality means the bottom line is padded with paper gains—such as the profit-fattening effect of inflation on a company's reported inventory values, or gains produced by "underdepreciation," when a company doesn't write off plant and equipment as fast as their real value is falling.
>
> Because a decline in quality means companies' reported earnings are weaker and less sustainable than they appear, it indicates likely trouble for future earnings—whether or not a recession arrives. If history is any guide, those lower quality earnings also will come home to roost in lower stock prices. . . .[26]

The notion of earnings quality is multifaceted, and there is no consensus on how best to measure it.[27] Under the definition illustrated in Exhibit 6.3, earnings are considered to be high quality when they are *sustainable*. For example, earnings that are generated from repeat customers and from high-quality products that enjoy steady consumer demand would be considered high quality. Examples of *un*sustainable earnings items include gains or losses from debt retirement; asset write-offs from corporate restructuring and plant closings; or profit increases traceable to temporary reductions in discretionary expenditures for advertising, research and development, or employee training. GAAP treats these discretionary expenditures as expenses, so a firm can boost earnings temporarily by cutting back on the amount spent for these activities. However, earnings increases of this type are not sustainable because the expenditures are critical to creating future demand for the firm's products and to creating new products or developing competent management—all important determinants of long-run sustainable earnings.

Some analysts define earnings quality in terms of the accounting methods management chooses to describe routine, ongoing business activities (such as using LIFO rather than FIFO for inventory accounting) and by the other accounting choices firms make through estimates (for example, the allowance for future uncollectibles).

Does earnings quality matter? One study finds that when reported earnings are adjusted for quality differences—for example, subtracting (or adding back) transitory gains (or losses) or adjusting for differences in inventory methods (FIFO versus LIFO)—the "quality-adjusted" earnings numbers better explain why firms' stocks sell for different prices.[28] These results suggest that differences in earnings quality are associated with differences in the overall earnings capitalization rate (earnings multiple) that investors assign to reported earnings when determining share prices. Notice carefully that as transitory or value-irrelevant components become a larger part of a firm's reported earnings:

- The quality of those reported earnings is eroded.
- Reported earnings become a less reliable indicator of the company's long-run sustainable cash flows.
- Hence, earnings are a less reliable indicator of fundamental value.

---

[26] B. Donnelly, "Profits' 'Quality' Erodes, Making Them Less Reliable," *The Wall Street Journal,* October 18, 1990.

[27] See L. Bernstein and J. Siegel, "The Concept of Earnings Quality," *Financial Analysts Journal,* July–August 1979, pp. 72–75; and J. Siegel, "The 'Quality of Earnings' Concept—A Survey," *Financial Analysts Journal,* March–April 1982, pp. 60–68.

[28] See B. Lev and R. Thiagarajan, "Fundamental Information Analysis," *Journal of Accounting Research,* Autumn 1993, pp. 190–215. To arrive at "quality-adjusted" earnings the researchers start with reported earnings and then eliminate revenue or expense items thought to be transitory or value-irrelevant. Additional research insights about earnings quality can be found in P. Dechow, W. Ge, and C. Schrand, "Understanding Earnings Quality: A Review of the Proxies, Their Determinants, and Their Consequences," *Journal of Accounting and Economics,* December 2010, pp. 344–401; K. Schipper and L. Vincent, "Earnings Quality," *Accounting Horizons,* Supplement 2003, pp. 97–110; and S. Whisenant and P. Fairfield, "Using Fundamental Analysis to Assess Earnings Quality: Evidence from the Center for Financial Research and Analysis," *Journal of Accounting, Auditing and Finance,* Fall 2001, pp. 273–95.

This phenomenon is illustrated in Exhibit 6.3, where we see that Firm B (with a higher proportion of transitory or value-irrelevant components of earnings) has an overall earnings multiple of 5.2 compared to 6.3 for Firm A. In contrast, the stock of a firm whose entire reported earnings were considered permanent would sell for $10/0.10 = $100, and the earnings multiple would be 10. Low-quality earnings will be assigned a lower overall earnings multiple and capitalized at a lower rate.

The research to date suggests that the capital market is rather sophisticated—it does not react naively to reported earnings, but instead it appears to distinguish among permanent, transitory, and value-irrelevant earnings components. Investors recognize differences in the quality of reported earnings numbers and consider these differences when assessing the implications of earnings reports for share prices. From time to time throughout this book, we will come back to this idea as we discuss alternative accounting treatments both for ongoing events and for specialized transactions and as we review the academic and professional research literature on the valuation-relevance of alternative accounting methods and financial notes disclosures.

RE**CAP**

Firms' shares usually sell at prices that differ from multiplying current reported earnings by the average earnings multiple for their industry. A variety of factors contribute to variation in P/E multiples. These include differences in risk; in growth opportunities; and in what proportions of current earnings are considered to be permanent, transitory, and value-irrelevant. The persistence of earnings is related to earnings quality—higher quality earnings are more persistent and sustainable. Assessing earnings quality involves using information from a multiple-step income statement, a balance sheet, a cash flow statement, financial notes, and Management's Discussion and Analysis (MD&A) to identify components of current earnings that are likely to be sustainable in contrast to those that are transitory or price irrelevant.

Earnings Surprises

The earnings capitalization model and the abnormal earnings model both require estimates of future earnings. But estimates can (and usually do) prove to be incorrect. When this happens, an "earnings surprise" results.

Two examples follow, both occurring on January 16:

- eBay Inc., the online auction site, reported fourth-quarter EPS of $0.70, one penny more than analysts were forecasting. The announcement occurred after the stock market had closed for the day. eBay shares rose 2.4% the next day.

- Northern Trust Corporation, the Chicago-based bank, reported fourth-quarter EPS of $0.69 when analysts had been expecting $0.75. Northern's announcement came in the morning before the market opened and by the end of the day, the company's stock had fallen 5.7%.

If securities markets are rational and efficient in the sense that they fully and correctly impound all available information into a company's stock price, the price will reflect investors' *unbiased* expectations about the company's future earnings and cash flows. Financial reports are an important source of information investors use to form and update their expectations, but they are only one source. Investors' expectations take into account a vast array of other publicly available information, including information about the company's earnings and cash flow history, product market conditions, competitor actions, and other factors. For example, the stock prices of Ford and Toyota incorporate information about unit sales figures published weekly in the financial press as well as expectations about changes in interest rates

Unbiased means that, on average, the market's earnings expectations will be correct—neither too high nor too low.

because interest rates influence consumers' carbuying behavior. Stock prices move up or down as investors receive new information and revise their expectations about the future earnings and cash flow prospects of the company.

Consider a typical quarterly earnings announcement that is released through major financial wire services. If reported quarterly earnings correspond exactly to the earnings investors expected before the announcement, the investors have no reason to alter their expectations about future earnings or cash flows. The reported quarterly earnings simply *confirm* the market's expectations. In other words, although the earnings release may resolve market uncertainty about current earnings, it does not provide new information to investors. On the other hand, if reported quarterly earnings deviate from investors' expectations, this **earnings surprise** represents new information that investors will use to revise their expectations about the company's future earnings and cash flow prospects. In turn, this change in investor expectations will cause the company's stock price to change following the earnings announcement. That's what happened at eBay and Northern Trust.

Figure 6.5 illustrates the typical behavior of stock returns leading up to and following quarterly earnings announcements for three different scenarios:

1. Reported earnings are viewed as a *good news* earnings surprise because they exceed market expectations (think eBay).

2. Reported earnings contain *no news* because they correspond exactly to market expectations.

3. Reported earnings are viewed as a *bad news* earnings surprise because they fall below market expectations (think Northern Trust).

Companies that report good news earnings (a positive earnings surprise) tend to have an upward movement in stock price before the actual earnings announcement date (Day 0 in Figure 6.5), followed by another stock price increase on announcement. The stock returns of companies reporting bad news earnings surprises exhibit negative returns before the

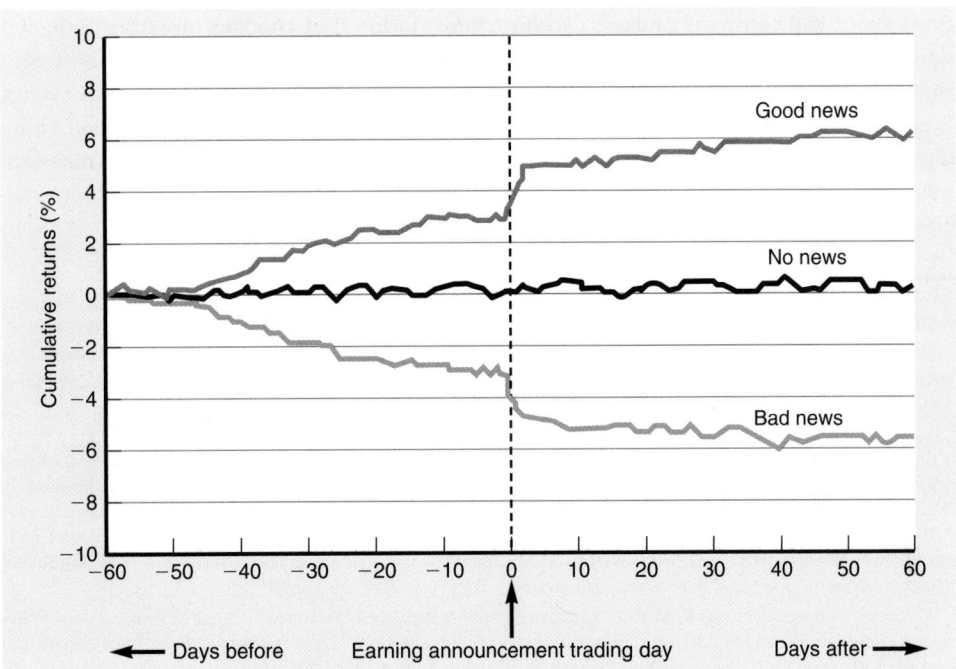

Figure 6.5

STOCK RETURNS AND QUARTERLY EARNINGS "SURPRISES"

announcement followed by another decrease in stock price at the announcement date.[29] Modest postannouncement drifts in stock returns are also not uncommon, especially when the earnings surprise is quite large.[30] Quarterly earnings announcements that contain "no news" lead to stock returns that hover around zero both before and after announcement.

It's easy to explain why stock prices sometimes exhibit a positive or negative movement *before* the earnings announcement date. Consider Ford Motor Company. Investors learn about automobile sales on a weekly basis and therefore can anticipate fairly well the actual quarterly earnings number prior to its formal announcement by Ford. The fact that Ford's stock price sometimes changes at the announcement date indicates that not all of the information contained in the earnings release is fully anticipated by investors. Small companies—and those followed by just a few securities analysts—tend to exhibit smaller preannouncement stock returns because investors often have very limited information about those companies and their earnings prospects for the quarter. Large companies, whose performance is tracked by many analysts, are more likely to exhibit the preannouncement stock return behavior illustrated in Figure 6.5.

You should understand one more feature of quarterly earnings surprises. Sometimes the earnings surprise and its associated stock return are in opposite directions. Here is an example.

- *October 23:* Coach Inc., the leather goods and accessories company, reported first quarter EPS of $0.41, up 21% from the same quarter a year earlier. Sales increased 28%. Coach shares fell 12% on the New York Stock Exchange.

Why did the stock price fall despite the apparent good news about sales and earnings performance for the quarter? The answer can be found in the company's earnings press release. In addition to reporting strong performance for the quarter, Coach said it was becoming "more conservative" in its outlook and thus lowering its sales and earnings forecasts for the rest of the fiscal year. Investors revised their expectations accordingly, and the share price fell.

How common is this phenomenon? Quarterly earnings surprises and their associated stock returns are in the opposite direction roughly 40% of the time, although the reasons why are not well understood.[31]

RECAP

A company's stock price at any given point in time reflects investors' aggregate expectations about the company's future earnings. Information that changes investors' expectations about future earnings will cause the stock price to rise or fall. Research demonstrates that quarterly and annual earnings announcements are important information events. Stock prices tend to increase (or decrease) when the reported earnings turn out to be higher (or lower) than expected. The degree of the surprise conveyed by an earnings announcement depends on the amount of pre-earnings announcement information available in the financial press and from other public sources.

[29] For early research on the association between earnings surprises and stock returns, *see* R. Ball and P. Brown, "An Empirical Evaluation of Accounting Income Numbers," *Journal of Accounting Research,* Autumn 1968, pp. 159–78; and G. Foster, C. Olsen, and T. Shevlin, "Earnings Releases, Anomalies, and the Behavior of Security Returns," *The Accounting Review,* October 1984, pp. 574–603. Recent research is summarized in S. Kothari, "Capital Market Research in Accounting," *Journal of Accounting and Economics,* September 2001, pp. 105–232.

[30] A number of studies investigate whether postearnings announcement drift is a profit opportunity for investors. For a review of this literature, see V. Bernard, "Stock Price Reactions to Earnings Announcements: A Summary of Recent Anomalous Evidence and Possible Explanations," in R. Thaler (ed.), *Advances in Behavioral Finance* (New York: Russell Sage Foundation, 1992); and V. Bernard, J. Thomas, and J. Abarbanell, "How Sophisticated Is the Market in Interpreting Earnings News?" *Journal of Applied Corporate Finance,* Summer 1993, pp. 54–63. A comprehensive review of this and related research is provided by S. Richardson, I. Tuna, and P. Wysoki, "Accounting Anomalies and Fundamental Analysis: A Review of Recent Research Advances," *Journal of Accounting and Economics,* December 2010, pp. 410–54.

[31] W. Kinney, D. Burgstahler, and R. Martin, "Earnings Surprise Materiality as Measured by Stock Returns," *Journal of Accounting Research,* December 2002, pp. 1297–1329; and W. B. Johnson and R. Zhou, "Contrarian Share Price Reactions to Earnings Surprises," *Journal of Accounting, Auditing and Finance*, April 2012, pp. 236–66.

CREDIT RISK ASSESSMENT

Equity investors analyze financial statements to determine the value of a firm's shares. In contrast, creditors are concerned primarily with assessing a firm's ability to meet its debt obligations through timely payments of principal and interest. Commercial banks, insurance companies, pension funds, and other lenders form opinions about a company's **credit risk** by comparing current and future debt-service requirements to estimates of the company's current and expected future cash flows.

Traditional Lending Products

Commercial bank loans are a common source of financing for many companies. These loans can be structured either as short-term or long-term, fixed or floating rate, payable on demand or with fixed maturity, and secured or unsecured.

Short-Term Loans   Loans with maturities of one year or less, called *short-term loans,* comprise more than half of all commercial bank loans. **Seasonal lines of credit** and special purpose loans are the most common short-term borrowing. Short-term loans are used primarily to finance working capital needs when inventory or receivables increase temporarily. They may be **secured** by the inventories or receivables themselves, or they may be **unsecured.** Cash flow to facilitate loan repayment usually comes from the routine generation of cash as inventories are sold and receivables are collected.

Long-Term Loans   Called **term lending agreements,** long-term loans have maturities of more than one year with maturities ranging from two to five years being most common. The principal and interest repayment schedule, along with other conditions of the loan, are detailed in a contractual agreement between the borrower and the bank. Term loans are often used to finance the purchase of fixed assets, the acquisition of another company, the refinancing of existing long-term debt, or permanent working capital needs. They are frequently secured by pledging the assets acquired with the loan proceeds, although lenders rarely look to asset liquidation as the primary source of funds for loan repayment. Scheduled principal and interest payments are generally presumed to come from the borrower's future operating cash flows.

> Companies with sales cycles that are seasonal (e.g., lawn and garden equipment retailers) commonly use seasonal lines of credit. These loans provide the cash to support increases in current assets during the peak selling period. The borrower draws on the seasonal credit line as funds are required and later repays as seasonal sales produce net cash inflows.

Revolving Loans   Revolving loans are a variation on the seasonal credit line. They allow borrowing up to a maximum level at any time over the life (usually more than one year) of the loan commitment. Revolving loans are often used to finance cash flow imbalances that arise in day-to-day operations, seasonal needs, or permanent working capital needs when normal trade credit is inadequate to support a company's sales volume. Borrowers can *prepay* the revolving loan and later reborrow those funds, but they must comply with the terms and conditions specified in the loan agreement. The interest rate on the revolving line of credit is usually the bank's prime lending rate plus an additional percentage, and the rate will usually change (or "float") as the prime rate rises or falls over the life of the credit line. In addition to interest, the borrower often pays a "commitment fee" that is based on the total amount of the credit extended.

Commercial Paper   Commercial banks are not the only source of debt financing for businesses. Another source of financing is **commercial paper**—short-term notes sold directly to investors by large and financially sound companies. These notes usually mature in 270 days or less and carry a fixed interest rate. Because commercial paper is issued directly to institutional investors (such as insurance companies) and is usually secured by a bank credit line, the interest rate the borrowing company pays is often significantly below the rate a bank would charge for a comparable direct loan.

Public Debt   Long-term forms of public (that is, nonbank) debt financing include bonds, debentures, and notes. Long-term debt securities are promises the issuing company makes to pay principal when due and to make timely interest payments on the unpaid balance. Bonds can have numerous special features. For example, **secured bonds** specify collateral that protects the bondholder if the borrower defaults. Other bonds contain **seniority** features that specify the order in which bondholders will be paid in the event of bankruptcy. Some may contain **sinking fund provisions** that require the borrowing company to make annual payments to a trustee (usually a bank), who uses the funds to retire a portion of the debt prior to its maturity. Still others may contain **call provisions** that allow the borrowing company to "call" (meaning repurchase) part or all of the debt at stated prices over a specific period.

> The word **bond** is commonly used to refer to all types of secured and unsecured debt although, strictly speaking, a bond is a secured debt. A **debenture** is an *unsecured* debt, meaning no specific pledge of property is made, although the debenture holder does have a claim on property not otherwise pledged as collateral or security. The term **note** is generally used for unsecured debt instruments issued with a maturity of 10 years or less.

Regardless of the special features attached, virtually all bonds or notes contain numerous **protective covenants** designed to protect the lender's interests. These covenants place restrictions on the borrower's activity and are described in the **indenture,** a written agreement between the borrowing company and its lenders. The role that accounting numbers play in these debt covenants is described in Chapter 7.

Credit Analysis

Before approving a loan to a company, a commercial loan officer evaluates the prospective borrower's ability to repay the proposed loan at maturity. This evaluation typically involves financial analysis and includes the preparation of forecasted financial statements, "due diligence" (a qualitative assessment of the business, its customers and suppliers, and management's character and capability), and analysis of credit risk.

Financial analysis of a potential borrower begins with an understanding of the firm, its business, its key risks and success factors, and the competitive dynamics of its industry. Next, an evaluation of the quality of its accounting earnings and financial reporting choices is made to determine whether traditional ratios and statistics derived from the financial statements can be relied on to measure the company's economic performance and financial condition. However, lenders and credit analysts frequently adjust a company's reported financial statement numbers. For example, nonrecurring gains and losses are often removed from the reported bottom-line earnings number to arrive at a measure of operating performance that is more representative of a firm's long-run sustainable profitability. Off-balance-sheet obligations (such as operating lease commitments) are frequently added to a firm's reported debt. Finally, other adjustments are made to improve the comparability of the financial data across potential loan candidates.

The next step is evaluating the company's profit performance and balance sheet strength. Financial, operating, and leverage ratios (discussed in Chapter 5) as well as trends in revenues and expenses are examined and compared to industry averages. This phase of the analysis identifies positive and negative changes in the prospective borrower's profitability, financial health, and industry position. However, the historical performance and condition of the borrower is only one indication of creditworthiness. Loan approval is largely determined by the borrower's ability to repay the proposed loan from *future* operating cash flows. ***Consequently, an estimate of the company's future financial condition is indispensable to most lending***

decisions. Analysts accomplish this assessment by constructing pro forma financial statement projections (forecasts) of borrower cash flows.

The credit analyst prepares pro forma or "as if" financial statement projections to assess the borrower's ability to generate sufficient cash flows to make interest and principal payments when due. These projections incorporate the analyst's understanding of the company's plans and business strategy, the likely responses of rival companies, and other factors that shape the prospective borrower's economic environment. The pro forma financial statements and their underlying assumptions are then tested to establish the borrower's vulnerability to changing economic circumstances. This testing involves examining plausible "worst-case" scenarios that indicate just how poorly the company could perform before it defaults. It enables the analyst to gauge the company's **financial flexibility**—that is, the degree to which the company could satisfy its cash needs during periods of fiscal stress by drawing on existing credit lines, accessing financial markets, curtailing discretionary cash expenditures, or selling assets.

> Appendix B shows how you can construct pro forma financial statement projections.

A **due diligence** evaluation is like "kicking the tires" of the prospective borrower. The analyst conducts plant tours, checks for pending litigation and promptness of bill payment, and interviews competitors, suppliers, customers, and employees. Comprehensive due diligence may also include asset appraisals; reviews of the company's other debt obligations, internal controls, planned capital expenditures, and potential environmental liabilities; and analysis of other matters that bear on the company's future success and ability to repay debt at maturity.

The final step of credit analysis is a **comprehensive risk assessment** that involves evaluating and summarizing the various individual risks associated with the loan. Some risks are unique to the specific borrower (for example, a pharmaceutical company may run the risk that a new drug it has developed may ultimately prove ineffective during clinical test trials); other risks are associated with potential changes in the economy or industry, new regulations, or unanticipated events. The credit analyst evaluates the severity of each risk in terms of (1) its probability of occurrence, (2) how it could affect the borrower's ability to repay, and (3) the bank's estimated costs if the borrower defaults.[32]

If the prospective borrower is judged to be creditworthy, the lender negotiates the terms and conditions of the loan with the borrower. Obviously, a lender is compensated for *anticipated* credit risks by the interest rate it charges on the loan. The interest rate must be sufficient to cover the lender's (1) cost of borrowing funds, (2) costs of administering, monitoring, and servicing the loan, (3) normal (competitive) return on the capital needed to support the bank's lending operations, and (4) premium for exposure to default risk. Collateralized loans or loans with personal guarantees lower credit risk and enable lenders to lower the borrower's cost of debt.

Comprehensive credit analysis of the type we have just described is an expensive and time-consuming activity. Sometimes lenders find it more cost effective to use less rigorous and detailed approaches to assessing borrower creditworthiness. For example, manufacturers such as Xerox routinely provide equipment lease financing to business customers. Because the dollar amount involved in any one lease is often small (say less than $25,000 per copier) and Xerox retains ownership of the equipment during the lease period, the lender (Xerox) has minimal risk exposure. Lenders such as Xerox adopt more streamlined approaches to credit analysis to avoid costly scrutiny of financial statement details, ratios, and cash flow projections for each potential business customer. One streamlined approach is to rely on credit reports issued by companies such as Dun & Bradstreet. These third-party reports include financial statements for the business along with information about existing loans, payment histories, pending litigation, other pertinent data, and a **credit score** that predicts future payment

---

[32] For additional insights about the tools and techniques of credit analysis, see B. Ganguin and J. Bilardello, *Fundamentals of Corporate Credit Analysis* (New York: McGraw-Hill, 2005).

habits and financial stability. Lenders such as Xerox can then use the Dun & Bradstreet credit score to set the price, terms, and condition of the equipment lease contract.

Credit-Rating Agencies

Large companies often borrow money by selling commercial paper, notes, bonds, or debentures to individual and institutional investors. Investors' beliefs about borrower credit risk influence the price paid—and thus the amount borrowed. The riskier the borrower is perceived to be, the less investors are willing to pay for the security. How do these investors assess credit risk? One way is to rely on the opinion of a credit-rating agency.

In the United States, three agencies (Moody's Investors Service, Standard & Poor's Corp., and Fitch Inc.) assess and grade the creditworthiness of companies and public entities—individual states, counties, municipalities—that sell debt to investors. Credit ratings are letter-based grades (e.g., AAA) that express the rating agency's opinion about default risk or the borrower's capacity and willingness to meet its financial commitments on time and in accordance with the terms of the debt security. The higher the credit rating, the lower is the default risk as judged by the rating agency.

> Standard & Poor's, for example, now rates more than $32 trillion in bonds and other financial obligations of borrowers in more than 50 countries.

John Moody invented credit ratings in 1909 when he first published the *Manual of Railroad Securities,* which rated 200 U.S. railroad companies and their debt securities. The Standard Company began grading bonds in 1916. Poor's and Fitch followed in the 1920s. Poor's and Standard merged in 1941. Initially, all rating agencies charged investors for their ratings. They began charging borrowers instead in the 1970s because photocopiers made it easy for nonpaying investors to obtain the ratings. Credit-rating agencies are independent of any investment banking company, commercial bank, and similar organization.

Credit Ratings and Default Risk Exhibit 6.4 describes the credit-rating levels used by Standard & Poor's, along with a credit quality description and historical default rate

---

EXHIBIT 6.4 | **Standard & Poor's Credit Ratings**

Rating	Credit Quality	Historical Default Rate (%)
Investment grade		
AAA	Extremely strong	0.52%
AA	Very strong	1.13
A	Strong	2.32
BBB	Adequate protection	6.64
Speculative (or "junk") grade		
BB	Less vulnerable	19.52
B	More vulnerable	35.76
CCC	Currently vulnerable	54.38
CC	Highly vulnerable	
C	Currently highly vulnerable	
D	In default	

Note: Historical default rates are the percentages of defaults by issuers rated by Standard & Poor's during 1987–2002 based on the rating they were initially assigned. Defaults on investment grade bonds—those rated BBB or better—seldom happen.

Source: See A. Borrus, "The Credit Rates: How They Work and How They Might Work Better," *BusinessWeek,* April 8, 2002; and D. Henry, "Anatomy of a Ratings Downgrade," *BusinessWeek,* October 1, 2007.

for each level. The default rates in Exhibit 6.4 refer to the percentage of borrowers that failed to make all promised debt payments based on the credit rating initially assigned. If credit ratings predict default risk, borrowers whose debt is highly rated should default less often than those with low-rated debt. This is indeed the case.

Standard & Poor's highest rating (AAA), for example, means that the borrower's capacity to meet its financial commitment on the debt is judged to be "extremely strong." Less than 1% of AAA borrowers default. In contrast, a BBB rating means that the debt has "adequate protection" against nonpayment but that adverse economic conditions or changing circumstances could weaken the borrower's capacity to meet its debt repayment obligation. In other words, BBB-rated debt is presumed to be riskier than AAA debt. And this presumption is correct! The historical default rate on BBB debt is more than 6%. Even riskier is debt rated CCC—meaning "currently vulnerable" to nonpayment—for which the historical default rate is about 54%.

The Credit-Rating Process The ratings process involves much more than just a detailed examination of financial statements, notes, and ratios:[33]

> Credit ratings often are identified with financial analysis, and especially ratios. But it is critical to realize that ratings analysis starts with the assessment of the business and competitive profile of the company. Two companies with identical financial metrics are rated very differently, to the extent that their business challenges and prospects differ.[34]

> Credit-rating agencies have been criticized for their alleged role in the subprime mortgage debacle and global financial crisis. Critics claim that flawed rating methodologies caused the agencies to assign overly optimistic ratings to residential mortgage-backed securities (RMBS) during the U.S. housing boom. For example, roughly 90% of the RMBS rated AAA at issuance in 2006 and 2007 were down-graded to "speculative" by 2010. See R. Myers, "Rating Disaster," *CFO Magazine,* June 2010, pp. 50–54. Chapter 7 has more to say about the global financial crisis.

Each rating agency has teams of analysts who grill corporate executives about operating and financial plans, management policies, risk tolerance, and the firm's competitiveness within the industry. They also conduct a thorough review of business fundamentals, including an assessment of industry prospects for growth, patterns of business cycles, and vulnerability to technological change, labor unrest, and regulatory action.

Organizational considerations can also adversely affect credit risk. Standard & Poor's credit analysts, for example, regard the following situations as involving increased default risk:

- The company has a highly aggressive business model and is growing through large acquisitions or expanding into unproven markets.
- The company has made frequent and significant changes to its strategy or has excessive management turnover.
- The organization relies significantly on an individual, especially one who may be nearing retirement.
- Management compensation is excessive or poorly aligned with stakeholders' interests.
- The company has an excessively complex legal structure, perhaps employing intricate off-balance-sheet structures.

Credit risk also increases when firms are deemed to be aggressive in their application of accounting standards or when their financial statements lack transparency to business fundamentals.

At Standard & Poor's, the financial statement analysis phase of the credit-rating process begins with an assessment of accounting quality. The purpose is to determine whether ratios and statistics derived from the statements reliably indicate economic performance and financial

---

[33] For a more detailed description of the credit-rating process at Standard & Poor's, see *Corporate Ratings Criteria 2005* (New York: Standard & Poor's Corp.).

[34] Ibid., p. 19.

condition. High-quality financial statements help credit analysts see what's really going on at the company; low-quality statements mask the company's performance and condition. Among the accounting quality issues that credit analysts at Standard & Poor's routinely review are revenue and expense recognition (Chapters 2 and 3 of this book); receivables and the provision for doubtful accounts (Chapter 8); LIFO inventory (Chapter 9); fixed asset depreciation methods and asset lives (Chapter 10); operating leases (Chapter 12); environmental liabilities and contingent obligations not yet recognized on the balance sheet (Chapter 11); research and development or interest costs that are capitalized rather than expensed (Chapter 10); derivatives and hedges (Chapter 11); and nonrecurring items that affect operating cash flow (Chapter 17).

To the extent possible, analytical financial statement adjustments are made to portray economic reality more faithfully and to eliminate accounting-induced differences among companies. At Standard & Poor's, nonrecurring gains and losses are eliminated from earnings. Unusual cash flow items similar in origins to nonrecurring gains and losses are also reversed. Operating leases are added to the balance sheet so that companies that buy all of their plant and equipment are put on a more comparable basis with those that lease part or all of their operating assets. Although it is rarely possible to completely recast a company's financial statements, it is important for credit analysts to have at least some notion of the extent to which different financial metrics are overstated or understated.

The financial statement analysis phase of the credit-rating process then proceeds using the tools and techniques described in Chapter 5. When this phase has been completed, analytical team members meet with the rating committee to discuss their recommendation and pertinent facts supporting the rating. The committee votes on the rating recommendation. The borrower is notified of the rating and can appeal. When a final rating is assigned, it is disseminated to the public through the news media.

All ratings are monitored after they have been assigned. Surveillance is intended to spot changes in the borrower's credit risk. The surveillance process includes continually reviewing new financial or economic information and possibly meeting with management. When it becomes necessary to reassess a rating, the analytical team undertakes an initial review. The borrower may then be placed on Standard & Poor's *CreditWatch* listing if the likelihood of a rating change is sufficiently high. A comprehensive credit rating analysis—including, if warranted, a meeting with management—is presented to the rating committee. The committee then decides whether to confirm the existing rating, or to issue a downgrade or an upgrade. Rating downgrades and upgrades thus signal changes in borrower credit risk.

In most markets outside the United States, ratings are assigned only on the borrower's request, so the borrower can choose to make the rating public or keep it confidential. In the United States, Standard & Poor's assigns and publishes ratings regardless of borrower request if the debt security is to be sold publicly. In the case of private placements, the borrower retains publication rights.

Financial Ratios and Debt Ratings

Exhibit 6.5 describes the key financial statement ratios that credit analysts at Standard & Poor's track, along with each ratio's median value for U.S. corporate borrowers in each rating level. These key financial ratios measure profitability (return on capital); the extent to which operating earnings exceed interest costs (EBIT interest coverage and EBITDA interest coverage); financial structure (Total debt/ Capital); and cash flow capacity (Funds from operations/Total debt, Free operating cash flow/Total debt, and Total debt/EBITDA). Each ratio has a precise Standard & Poor's definition so that every credit analyst at the rating agency is computationally consistent.

Notice how the median ratio values in Exhibit 6.5 rise or fall across credit-rating levels. For example, the median borrower assigned a AAA rating is quite profitable (return on capital of 35.1%) with little debt (Total debt/Capital of 6.2%) and sizeable operating cash flow (Free operating cash flow/Total debt of 104.1%). By comparison, the median BB speculative-grade borrower is substantially less profitable (return on capital of 10.3%) with much more debt

EXHIBIT 6.5	Standard & Poor's Key Financial Ratios and Ratings of Corporate Debt						
	Three-Year Medians						
	AAA	**AA**	**A**	**BBB**	**BB**	**B**	**CCC**
EBIT interest coverage	23.8	13.6	6.9	4.2	2.3	0.9	0.4
EBITDA interest coverage	25.3	17.1	9.4	5.9	3.1	1.6	0.9
FFO/Total debt (%)	167.8	77.5	43.2	34.6	20.0	10.1	2.9
Free operating cash flow/Total debt (%)	104.1	41.1	25.4	16.9	7.9	2.6	(0.9)
Total debt/EBITDA	0.2	1.1	1.7	2.4	3.8	5.6	7.4
Return on capital (%)	35.1	26.9	16.8	13.4	10.3	6.7	2.3
Total debt/Capital (%)	6.2	34.8	39.8	45.6	57.2	74.2	101.2

Formulas

EBIT interest coverage	Earnings from continuing operations* before interest and taxes/Gross interest incurred before subtracting capitalized interest and interest income
EBITDA interest coverage	Adjusted earnings from continuing operations† before interest, taxes, depreciation, and amortization/Gross interest incurred before subtracting capitalized interest and interest income
Funds from operations (FFO)/Total debt	Net income from continuing operations, depreciation, and amortization, deferred income taxes, and other noncash items/Long-term debts + Current maturities + Commercial paper and other short-term borrowings
Free operating cash flow/Total debt	FFO − Capital expenditures +(−) increase (decrease) in working capital (excluding changes in cash, marketable securities, and short-term debt)/Long-term debts + Current maturities, commercial paper, and other short-term borrowings
Total debt/EBITDA	Long-term debt + Current maturities, commercial paper, and other short-term borrowings/Adjusted earnings from continuing operations before interest, taxes, and depreciation and amortization
Return on capital	EBIT/Average of beginning-of-year and end-of-year capital, including short-term debt, current maturities, long-term debt, noncurrent deferred taxes, minority interest, and equity (common and preferred stock)
Total debt/Capital	Long-term debt + Current maturities, commercial paper, and other short-term borrowings/ Long-term debt + Current maturities, commercial paper, and other short-term borrowings + Shareholder's equity (including preferred stock) + Nonparticipating interests

Note: Standard & Poor's uses different ratios to rate debt issued by utilities and financial services companies. The universe of rated companies includes about 1,000 industrial firms. See *Corporate Ratings Criteria 2005* (New York: Standard & Poor's Corp.), pp. 43–44.

* Including interest income and equity earnings; excluding nonrecurring items.

† Excludes interest income, equity earnings, and nonrecurring items; also excludes rental expense that exceeds the interest component of capitalized operating leases. Includes amounts for operating lease debt equivalent, and debt associated with accounts receivable sales/securitization programs.

(Total debt/Capital of 57.2%) and significantly less operating cash flow (Free operating cash flow/Total debt of only 7.9%). These patterns are consistent with the idea, discussed in Chapter 5, that certain financial statement ratios are quite useful in predicting loan default.[35]

Commercial banks, insurance companies, pension funds, and others lend money only if the probability of repayment is high. Consequently, the central question facing the credit analyst is whether the borrower's future cash inflows will be sufficient to repay the loan. Credit analysts rely on their understanding of the company, its business strategy, and the competitive environment when they apply the tools and techniques of financial statement analysis and cash flow forecasting to assess credit risk and the company's financial flexibility under stress.

[35] To learn more about how accounting information affects bond market activity, see P. Easton, S. Monahan, and F. Vasvari, "Initial Evidence on the Role of Accounting Earnings in the Bond Market," *Journal of Accounting Research,* June 2009, pp. 721–66.

SUMMARY

In *Concepts Statement No. 1,* the FASB sets forth the primary objectives of financial reporting. One of those objectives states:

> Financial reporting should provide information to help present and potential investors and creditors and others in assessing the amounts, timing and uncertainty of prospective cash receipts from dividends or interest and the proceeds from the sale, redemption, or maturity of securities or loans. Since investors' and creditors' cash flows are related to enterprise cash flows, financial reporting should provide information to help investors, creditors, and others assess the amounts, timing, and uncertainty of prospective net cash inflows to the related enterprise.[36]

This chapter provides a framework for understanding how financial reporting meets this important objective. Specifically,

- We show how accounting numbers are used in business valuation and credit risk assessment, and then illustrate in Appendix A what it means to "assess the amounts, timing, and uncertainty of prospective net cash inflows" of a business.

- A critical part of understanding the **decision-usefulness** of accounting information—a major focus of this book—is understanding *which* accounting numbers are used, *why* they are used, and *how* they are used when making investment and credit decisions.

- Knowing how earnings, book values, and cash flows are used in investment and credit decisions will help you to evaluate the alternative accounting measures discussed in subsequent chapters of this book—not only those recognized directly in the financial statements but also those disclosed in the financial statement notes.

APPENDIX A

DISCOUNTED CASH FLOW AND ABNORMAL EARNINGS VALUATION APPLICATIONS

This appendix illustrates how the discounted free cash flow and abnormal earnings valuation methods are used to value a business opportunity and to determine the value of a company's common stock.

Valuing a Business Opportunity

Allen Ford's passion for coffee motivated him to consider opening a neighborhood coffee shop. Ford convinced a colleague who was an expert in market research to look at the economic viability of such a shop. His analysis fueled Ford's enthusiasm: The market demographics were favorable, and there was little competition. Annual sales were projected ultimately to reach $350,000.

Ford rejected the idea of opening his own independent coffee shop and instead focused on several opportunities. By affiliating with a national or regional company, he would enjoy immediate brand-name recognition, economies of scale in purchasing and advertising, and employee training and support programs. After investigating several possibilities, Allen settled on By the Cup, an expanding regional chain of franchised coffee shops specializing in "pour over" brewing, whereby each cup is brewed individually. Each store had comfortable seating, abundant natural light, and a layout that encouraged patrons to stay and chat (and perhaps

---

[36] "Objectives of Financial Reporting by Business Enterprises," *SFAC No. 1* (Stamford, CT: FASB, 1978), CON 1–2.

have a second cup). The franchise had a proven record of success in similar communities, and it appealed to Ford's tastes.

Ford learned that a By the Cup store could be established for $100,000, which included the initial franchise fee of $21,000, store fixtures of $25,000, and an inventory cost of $54,000. The inventory and fixtures would be purchased from the corporate parent. Corporate staff would conduct a site location study, assist in negotiating lease terms for retail space, help with store layout and renovation, train employees on operating policies and procedures, and provide all grand opening advertising and promotional materials. Once a new By the Cup franchise opened, the corporate parent received royalties (typically as a percentage of sales) determined in accordance with a 15-year renewable franchise contract.

The prospectus Ford obtained from the parent company contained selected financial data for a typical By the Cup franchise store. It indicated that franchise royalties are 5% of sales, and other operating expenses, excluding depreciation and amortization, are 85% of sales. The original store fixtures are depreciated over 10 years, but after five years, the franchisee should expect to make capital expenditures equal to the amount of depreciation to maintain the facility, resulting in depreciation continuing indefinitely at the same level. The original franchise fee of $21,000 is amortized over five years. Finally, the franchisee should expect to increase inventories in any year that sales increase. The increase in inventory is to be 10% of the sales increase. Income taxes have been ignored because they are owner specific, thus making them highly variable across locations.

With these financial projections and his understanding of the marketplace, Ford had to decide whether to invest $100,000 in a By the Cup franchise. Influencing the decision were several nonfinancial considerations, such as his confidence in By the Cup's corporate staff and whether the ambiance of the shop would attract customers. However, viewed through the stark lens of economics, Ford's decision problem simplified to the standard net present value rule— invest if the estimated value of the franchise (adjusted for the risk of investment) exceeds its $100,000 cost. From trade sources, Ford learned that 16% was a reasonable estimate of the cost of equity capital for franchised neighborhood coffee shops. He used two different approaches to estimate the value of the coffee shop, relying on predictions contained in the information provided by the franchisor whenever possible. The first approach, based on expected future free cash flows, is summarized in Exhibit 6.6.

Sales are based on the amounts provided by the franchisor and royalties are 5% of that amount in each year. Depreciation is computed as $25,000 divided by the 10-year depreciation period, or $2,500 per year. Note that depreciation continues indefinitely even after the 10-year period ends because additional capital expenditures will also be depreciated. Amortization of the franchise fee is $4,200 per year ($21,000/5). As the exhibit shows, pre-tax income grows to $32,500 by Year 6. Note that in all years beyond Year 6, pre-tax income will be the same amount as in Year 6 because (1) sales are constant; (2) royalties and other operating expenses are a percent of sales, so those will be constant; and (3) depreciation is also constant.

To determine the amount of free cash flow, we begin with the pre-tax income amount and add back depreciation and amortization, which are noncash expenses, and subtract capital expenditures and additions to inventory. Because sales are constant after five years, there are no inventory additions after that point. And, because pre-tax income is flat and capital expenditures are equal to depreciation in every year after Year 5, Year 6 and all subsequent years will have the same level of free cash flow: $32,500, which is also equal to the amount of pre-tax income.

We now take the present value of the free cash flow stream. Note that even though the cash flows go on indefinitely, we can still determine the present value without literally summing an infinite number of individual present values. The $32,500 per year to be received forever

EXHIBIT 6.6	By the Cup Franchise

Valuation of Expected Future Free Cash Flows

	Year 1	Year 2	Year 3	Year 4	Year 5	Year 6+
Sales	$200,000	$250,000	$300,000	$325,000	$350,000	$350,000
Royalties	(10,000)	(12,500)	(15,000)	(16,250)	(17,500)	(17,500)
Depreciation	(2,500)	(2,500)	(2,500)	(2,500)	(2,500)	(2,500)
Amortization	(4,200)	(4,200)	(4,200)	(4,200)	(4,200)	
Other operating expenses	(170,000)	(212,500)	(255,000)	(276,250)	(297,500)	(297,500)
Pre-tax income	13,300	18,300	23,300	25,800	28,300	32,500
Pre-tax income	13,300	18,300	23,300	25,800	28,300	32,500
Depreciation and amortization	6,700	6,700	6,700	6,700	6,700	2,500
Working capital (inventory additions)		(5,000)	(5,000)	(2,500)	(2,500)	0
Capital expenditures						(2,500)
Free cash flow	20,000	20,000	25,000	30,000	32,500	32,500
Perptuity factor						6.25000
Present value of perpetual flows as of Year 5						203,125
Present value factors	0.86207	0.74316	0,64066	0.55229	0.47611	0.47611
Present value	17,241	14,863	16,016	16,569	15,474	96,710
Total present value	$176,873					

beginning in Year 6 has a present value of $32,500/0.16 = $203,125 as of Year 5. (The perpetuity factor is 6.25 = 1/0.16.) Discounting that value an additional five years gives a present value of this perpetuity value, or a terminal value, of $203,125/1.16^5 = $96,710. When this terminal value is added to the present values of the free cash flows in Years 1 through 5, we obtain a total present value of $176,873. As this greatly exceeds the investment of $100,000, the project is quite attractive financially.

To illustrate that Ford would get exactly the same result using an abnormal earnings approach, we illustrate that approach in Exhibit 6.7. We take care to ensure that the assumptions we make in this exhibit, which are formulated in terms of earnings and book values, are consistent with the cash flows we obtained in Exhibit 6.6. First we determine the investment's book value of equity each year. For each year, we can take beginning book value, add pre-tax income, and subtract dividends. We have already determined pre-tax income for each period. Dividends are set to the amount of free cash flow generated during the year, because this represents the amount of cash that could be taken out of the business without affecting its ability to generate the future cash flows in the forecast. So, for example, in Year 1, equity book value declines by $6,700 because the dividend exceeds pre-tax income by that amount. The resulting book value of $93,700 becomes the beginning book value for the next year, and the process is repeated.

> The free cash flow valuation approach and the abnormal earnings approach will always produce the same value estimate when the analyses use equivalent assumptions.

We multiply the beginning book value in each period by 16% (the cost of capital) to determine the level of normal earnings for the year. When we subtract that amount from actual pre-tax income we have abnormal earnings. Note that abnormal earnings also settle at a constant level—$19,460—allowing us once again to compute the present value of an infinite series. The present value of the abnormal earnings is $76,874, resulting in an investment value of $176,874. Because we used assumptions that are equivalent in the approaches, the results were identical, except for a $1 difference due to rounding.

Another word about valuations is appropriate here. Valuation professionals often treat cash flows as if they occur at midyear, in order to approximate more closely cash flows that occur

EXHIBIT 6.7 By the Cup Franchise

Valuation of Expected Abnormal Earnings

	Year 1	Year 2	Year 3	Year 4	Year 5	Year 6+
Beginning book value	$100,000	$ 93,300	$ 91,600	$ 89,900	$ 85,700	$ 81,500
Pre-tax income	13,300	18,300	23,300	25,800	28,300	32,500
Dividend (=FCF)	(20,000)	(20,000)	(25,000)	(30,000)	(32,500)	(32,500)
Ending book value	93,300	91,600	89,900	85,700	81,500	81,500
Pre-tax income	13,300	18,300	23,300	25,800	28,300	32,500
Normal earnings	16,000	14,928	14,656	14,384	13,712	13,040
Abnormal earnings	(2,700)	3,372	8,644	11,416	14,588	19,460
Perptuity factor						6.25000
Present value of perpetual abnormal earnings as of Year 5						121,625
Present value factors	0.86207	0.74316	0.64066	0.55229	0.47611	0.47611
Present value of abnormal earnings	(2,328)	2,506	5,538	6,305	6,946	57,907
Total present value of abnormal earnings	76,874					
Initial investment	100,000					
Total value of investment	$176,874					

throughout the year. This treatment is accomplished by discounting cash flows for 0.5 years, 1.5 years, . . . , or by use of a "midyear adjustment" to the present value as it is computed in Exhibit 6.6. The midyear adjustment is to multiply the present value in the exhibit by the square root of one plus the discount rate. In our example, the adjustment results in a present value of $176,873 · $\sqrt{1.16}$ = $190,498.

Financing the By the Cup Franchise

After careful review, Allen Ford decided to purchase a By the Cup franchise. The evaluation process was lengthy. It included interviews with 10 current franchise owners. These interviews helped Ford gain a deeper understanding of the business and its key risks and success factors. He was able to identify several proven marketing and promotion strategies for launching the franchise. With this information and an assessment of local market conditions, Ford refined the financial projections supplied by the parent company, performed a valuation analysis, and concluded that the franchise was likely to earn an acceptable risk-adjusted rate of return. There was still one hurdle—financing a portion of the $100,000 franchise purchase price.

> Before investing, Ford should perform a **sensitivity analysis** of the free cash flow and abnormal earnings valuation estimates. Sensitivity analysis involves constructing "best-case" and "worst-case" scenarios for the business that incorporate alternative assumptions about sales, costs, and competitor behavior. Each scenario produces financial forecasts that become the basis for revised free cash flow and abnormal earnings valuation estimates. In this way, Ford could learn how alternative economic conditions might affect the coffee shop's value and his return on investment.

Ford needed a bank loan for two reasons. First, his personal investment portfolio was worth only $50,000. Second, his interviews with other franchise owners revealed that a $100,000 initial investment might not provide an adequate cash cushion during the first year of operation.

Ford described the business opportunity to a local banker and said his cash needs would be in the $50,000 to $100,000 range. The banker said a loan of this size would not be a problem because ample funds were currently available at attractive interest rates. Ford had to complete a detailed loan application, including a personal credit history and business plan, and to prepare monthly earnings and cash flow projections for the first two years of franchise operations. Filled with optimism, Ford began assembling the financial and other information required and thinking about the kind of loan he would request from the bank.

> You will learn more about Ford's bank loan in Chapter 7.

Valuing Whole Foods Market's Shares

This section illustrates how to use published earnings forecasts along with the abnormal earnings valuation model to produce an **intrinsic stock price estimate** for a company. We use Whole Foods Market, Inc., and rely on the analysts' earnings forecasts that were available in January 2013 when the company's common stock was trading at $90 per share.

Share Price Valuation The five steps to deriving a share price estimate using analysts' earnings forecasts and the abnormal earnings valuation model are:

1. Obtain analysts' EPS forecasts for some finite horizon, say the next five years.
2. Combine the EPS forecasts with projected dividends to forecast common equity book value over the horizon.
3. Compute yearly *abnormal* earnings by subtracting *normal* earnings (that is, beginning equity book value multiplied by the equity cost of capital) from analysts' EPS forecasts.
4. Forecast the perpetual (terminal year) *abnormal* earnings flow that will occur beyond the explicit forecast horizon.
5. Add the current book value and the present value of the two abnormal earnings components—the first five years and for years beyond the terminal period—to obtain an intrinsic value estimate of the company's share price.

Each of these steps is illustrated in the Whole Foods Market valuation in Exhibit 6.8.

Our forecast horizon—and the one used by analysts covering the company—is the five-year period from 2013 through 2017. Analysts focus on a short- to intermediate-term forecast horizon in valuing a company for at least three reasons. First, competitive pressures make it difficult for the company to sustain growth in sales, profits, and cash flows in the long run. Thus, it is unrealistic to forecast a company to maintain high growth rates indefinitely. Second, long-range projections are more uncertain and, therefore, subject to greater error. Simply put, projected earnings and dividend payouts become less and less reliable the further removed they are from the current forecast date. And third, because of the time value of money, the discounted present values of future abnormal earnings (or free cash) flows become smaller as the forecast horizon increases. In other words, longer range forecasts often do not matter very much in terms of determining current share price. For example, the present value of a dollar received 25 years from now discounted at 15% is $1/(1 + 0.15)^{25} = 0.03.

In January 2013, securities analysts covering Whole Foods were forecasting EPS of $2.89 in fiscal 2013 and $3.43 in fiscal 2014, after the company had earned $1.93 and $2.52 in fiscal 2011 and 2012, respectively. These same analysts were forecasting annual EPS growth of 18.7% through 2017. The resulting EPS forecasts through 2017 appear at the top of Exhibit 6.8.

Next we need to compute the book value of common equity for each year of the forecast horizon. We begin with book value of $20.51 per share at the beginning of 2013. We incorporate forecasted earnings each year and assume dividends grow in proportion to EPS growth, resulting in a constant dividend payout as a percent of EPS. To simplify matters, we assume net stock issuances and comprehensive income adjustments are zero over the forecast horizon.

The abnormal earnings calculations for each of the five years in our forecast horizon are shown in part (c) of Exhibit 6.8. Here, normal earnings are subtracted from the annual EPS forecasts. Normal earnings are Whole Foods Market's common equity book value at the *beginning* of each year—as computed in part (b)—multiplied by the company's cost of equity

EXHIBIT 6.8	Whole Foods Market, Inc.

Abnormal Earnings Valuation

	Actual Results		Forecasted Results					
	2011	2012	2013	2014	2015	2016	2017	Beyond 2017
(a) Earnings per share	$1.93	$2.52	$2.89	$3.43	$4.07	$4.83	$5.73	
(b) Equity Book Value (per share amounts) and ROE								
Equity book value at beginning of year	$13.80	$16.72	$20.51	$22.76	$25.43	$28.60	$32.36	
Earnings per share			2.89	3.43	4.07	4.83	5.73	
Dividends			(0.64)	(0.76)	(0.90)	(1.07)	(1.27)	
Equity book value at end of year			$22.76	$25.43	$28.60	$32.36	$36.82	
Return on Equity	14.0%	15.1%	14.1%	15.1%	16.0%	16.9%	17.7%	
(c) Abnormal Earnings								
Equity book value at beginning of year	$13.80	$16.72	$20.51	$22.76	$25.43	$28.60	$32.36	
Equity cost of capital	0.0845	0.0845	0.0845	0.0845	0.0845	0.0845	0.0845	
Normal earnings	1.17	1.41	1.73	1.92	2.15	2.42	2.73	
Actual or forecasted earnings	1.93	2.52	2.89	3.43	4.07	4.83	5.73	
Less normal earnings	1.17	1.41	1.73	1.92	2.15	2.42	2.73	
Abnormal earnings	0.76	1.11	1.16	1.51	1.92	2.41	3.00	
(d) Valuation								
Future abnormal earnings in forecast horizon			1.16	1.51	1.92	2.41	3.00	
Discount factor at 8.45%			0.92208	0.85024	0.78399	0.72291	0.66658	
Present value of abnormal earnings in forecast horizon			1.07	1.28	1.51	1.74	2.00	
Abnormal earnings in 2017								3.00
One plus long-term growth factor								1.045
Abnormal earnings in 2018								3.14
Divide by discount rate minus long-term growth rate								0.0395
Present value of abnormal earnings in perpetuity as of 2017								79.49
Present value factor to discount to 2012								0.66658
Present value of abnormal earnings in perpetuity								52.99
(e) Estimated share price								
Sum of present values of abnormal earnings over forecast horizon			7.60					
Present value of abnormal earnings in perpetuity			52.99					
Present value of abnormal earnings			60.59					
Current equity book value			20.51					
Estimated current share price at end of fiscal 2012			$81.10					
Actual share price			$90.00					

capital, which is 8.45%.[37] For example, Whole Foods Market's normal earnings for 2013 would be calculated by multiplying its equity book value at the beginning of the year, which is $20.51, by the equity cost of capital, which is 0.0845. The result is $1.73. These normal earnings are subtracted from forecasted earnings of $2.89. The difference of $1.16 is Whole Foods Market's abnormal earnings for 2013.

The abnormal earnings forecasts from part (c) become the basic inputs to the valuation calculation in part (d), where abnormal earnings are discounted at the company's equity cost of capital. A *terminal value* calculation intended to represent the value of the company's abnormal earnings flow beyond our five-year forecast horizon is also shown in part (d). To arrive at this terminal value estimate, we assume that Whole Foods Market's abnormal earnings of $3.00 in 2017 will continue to grow by 4.5% each year for the foreseeable future. The present value of this growing perpetual flow at the end of 2017 is $79.49.[38] This quantity is discounted using the present value factor for five periods at 8.45% (0.66658), resulting in a present value of $52.99 at the end of fiscal 2012. Part (e) shows that the sum of all discounted abnormal earnings flows ($60.59) plus the company's 2012 year-end equity book value ($20.51) produces an estimated share price of $81.10; this contrasts with Whole Foods Market's actual $90 share price in January 2013.

What does this tell us? For one thing, Whole Foods Market's $90 per share stock price in January 2013 was considerably higher than that implied by securities analysts' five-year EPS forecasts coupled with our own predictions about earnings growth beyond the forecast horizon (2017). In this regard, Whole Foods Market's stock may appear to be somewhat overpriced in the marketplace. However, the market may have been anticipating abnormal earnings to increase even faster and for a longer time period than our projections would indicate. Or, our estimate of the market premium may be incorrect. The rub, of course, is that we cannot know at the time which of the forecasts will prove correct in the future.

The abnormal earnings valuation model in Exhibit 6.8 can be used to value almost any publicly traded company. It's easy to implement because it requires just a handful of data items—earnings forecasts from analysts, a beginning book value of equity, forecasts of dividends and stock repurchases, an equity cost of capital (discount rate), and a long-term growth rate for abnormal earnings beyond the terminal year. But how well does it work?

This question has several answers. One approach compares the accuracy of stock price estimates from several different valuation models—for example, the abnormal earnings model versus the free cash flow valuation model. A study did just that using a sample of nearly 3,000 firm-year observations from 1989 through 1993.[39] Earnings, dividends, and cash flow forecasts were gathered from *Value Line* for each sample firm and year. These forecasts were then used as inputs to an abnormal earnings valuation model (like the one in Exhibit 6.8) and as inputs to a separate free cash flow valuation model. The two value estimates—one based on abnormal earnings and the other based on free cash flows—were then compared to actual stock prices. Which valuation model was better? Abnormal earnings value estimates were more accurate and explained more of the variation in actual stock prices than did free cash flow value estimates. Of course, the study must have used different assumptions in the two models

---

[37] This figure was derived from the CAPM using the then-current risk-free rate of 3.2% for 30-year Treasury bonds, Whole Foods Market's equity beta of 1.05, which was estimated using the most recent five years of daily returns data, and a long-term market risk premium of 5%. The CAPM formula applied to Whole Foods Market is:

$$3.2\% + (1.05 \times 5\%) = 8.45\%$$

[38] This perpetuity discount factor is equal to 1 divided by the difference between the equity cost of capital (8.45%) and the abnormal earnings growth rate (4.5%).

[39] J. Francis, P. Olsson, and D.R. Oswald, "Comparing the Accuracy and Explainability of Dividends, Free Cash Flow, and Abnormal Earnings Equity Value Estimates," *Journal of Accounting Research,* Spring 2000, pp. 45–70.

because the models are equivalent. The different assumptions, not the different models per se, explain the results.

A related study asked if money can be made from the abnormal earnings valuation model in Exhibit 6.8.[40] Using a sample of nearly 18,000 firm-year observations covering 1979 to 1991, the researchers computed valuation estimates for each firm and year. These estimates were then used to construct a *value index*—the estimated value divided by the actual share price—for each company and year. (The value index for Whole Foods Market would be 0.901 ($81.10/$90). The simulated trading strategy involved "buying" the most undervalued companies (high value index) and "selling short" the most overvalued companies (low value index). This strategy produced a three-year portfolio return of 35%, which suggests investors can profit from using the abnormal earnings valuation model.

> In theory, both valuation models should produce the same stock price estimate. But in practice, the two valuation models often do not produce the same stock price estimate because analysts make different assumptions when using the two models.

FINANCIAL STATEMENT FORECASTS

Financial statement forecasts (or projections) are essential ingredients of business valuation and credit risk analyses. This appendix illustrates the construction of *comprehensive* financial statement forecasts.[41] Our approach uses information about the company's complete operating, investing, and financing activities to yield a forecast of each individual financial statement item. As a result, it ensures that the forecasted financial statements—sometimes called *pro forma projections*—are internally consistent. Nothing is overlooked, and the projected financial statements fit together, or articulate, as they should.

The starting point for developing comprehensive financial statement forecasts is a detailed understanding of the company, its recent financial performance, and health. (Chapter 5 shows you how!) Obtaining this detailed understanding requires learning about the company and its industry, competitors, customers, and suppliers. Armed with this knowledge, the analyst can develop plausible predictions about future economic conditions in the industry and about how the company and its competitors will respond to those conditions. The analyst incorporates these predictions into the forecasted financial statements.

> Sometimes the analyst is interested in forecasting only a single financial statement item, such as EPS. Shortcuts that circumvent the need to construct comprehensive financial statement forecasts are often used in such cases, but the resulting single-item forecasts may prove highly unreliable.

Preparing comprehensive financial statement forecasts involves six steps:

1. Project sales revenue for each period in the forecast horizon (say, two years).
2. Forecast operating expenses such as cost of goods sold (but not depreciation, interest, or tax expense, which are handled separately), and derive projected pre-tax operating income before depreciation and amortization. Expense margins—for example, cost of goods sold as a percentage of sales—are useful for this purpose.
3. Forecast the level of balance sheet operating assets and liabilities—cash, inventories, accounts receivable, accounts payable, and the like—needed to support the projected

[40] R. Frankel and C. Lee, "Accounting Valuation, Market Expectation, and Cross-Sectional Stock Returns," *Journal of Accounting and Economics,* June 1998, pp. 283–320.

[41] Techniques for constructing financial statement forecasts are described in T. Koller et al., op. cit.; R. Lundholm and R. Sloan, op. cit.; P. Healy and K. Palepu, *Business Analysis and Valuation* (Cincinnati, OH: South-Western Publishing, 2013); L. Soffer and R. Soffer, op. cit.; and C. Stickney and P. Brown, *Financial Statement Analysis: A Strategic Perspective* (Fort Worth, TX: Dryden Press, 1999).

operations in Steps 1 and 2. Turnover ratios (also called *utilization ratios*) can help guide these projections.

4. Forecast depreciation expense and tax expense each period. These are two of the last three items needed to construct projected income statements.

5. Forecast the company's financial structure (mix of debt and equity financing) and dividend policy each period. Then use this information, along with an estimate of the interest rate charged on debt financing, to project interest expense and complete the income statement.

6. Derive projected cash flow statements from the forecasted income statements and balance sheets.

Illustration of Comprehensive Financial Statement Forecasts

Veto Equipment Supply Company manufactures original equipment parts for the U.S. automobile industry. The company has been in business more than 50 years. Although sales rise and fall with the ebb and flow of consumer demand for U.S. automobiles, the company has remained profitable throughout most of its history. In 2013, Veto reported sales of $25.2 million, an increase of 5% from the previous year. Net income that year was $1.056 million, an increase of 20% from 2012.

The company has a $2.5 million revolving credit loan with Commerce First Bank. At the end of 2013, Veto had drawn only $2.077 million of the available credit, but management is still concerned about its borrowing needs over the next two years. The reason for this concern is that Veto has developed a successful new product that is expected to increase its sales significantly. However, the new product will require Veto to expand its operations. Management wants to know whether Veto will need a higher credit limit to support the planned expansion.

Exhibit 6.9 shows the company's income statements and balance sheets for the past two years. An abbreviated statement of retained earnings is included to provide an explicit link between income statement and balance sheet amounts. Our task is to "fill in the blanks" by preparing forecasted financial statements for 2014 and 2015 using the six-step process described above.

Although we will be using historical data to guide us, we do not necessarily assume forecast data, such as sales growth, are the same as the historical levels. Our understanding of the company and its industry help us to determine when future performance is likely to differ from historical results. That part of the analysis is beyond our scope here. Instead, we focus on the construction of the projections, given a set of assumptions about future performance. Let's get started!

Step 1: **Project sales revenue.** Management forecasts sales growth of 10% in 2014 and another 15% in 2015, versus 4% in 2012 and 5% in 2013. We will use management's sales growth estimates to compute projected sales revenue for the next two years. So, sales in 2014 are expected to be $27.720 million, or $25.200 million × 1.10. Similarly, sales in 2015 are projected to be $31.878 million, or $27.720 × 1.15.

	Historical		Projected	
	2012	**2013**	**2014**	**2015**
Sales growth	4.0%	5.0%	10.0%	15.0%

EXHIBIT 6.9	Veto Equipment Supply Company

Historical Financial Statements

	Historical		Projected	
($ in thousands)	2012	2013	2014	2015
Income Statement				
Sales	$24,000	$25,200		
Cost of goods sold	15,760	16,380		
Research and development expense	—	—		
Selling, general, and administrative expense	5,600	5,796		
Depreciation expense	1,080	1,147		
Pre-tax operating income	1,560	1,877		
Interest expense	240	277		
Nonoperating income (loss)	—	—		
Pre-tax earnings	1,320	1,600		
Tax expense	440	544		
Net income	$ 880	$ 1,056		
Balance Sheet				
Operating cash and equivalents	$ 1,160	$ 1,134		
Accounts receivable	2,120	2,016		
Inventories	3,240	3,528		
Other current assets	—	—		
Current assets	6,520	6,678		
Property, plant, and equipment (gross)	16,600	17,640		
Accumulated depreciation	(10,080)	(11,227)		
Other assets	600	756		
Total assets	$13,640	$13,847		
Current portion of long-term debt	$ 180	$ 208		
Accounts payable	2,820	2,520		
Other payables	160	252		
Current liabilities	3,160	2,980		
Long-term debt	1,800	1,869		
Other liabilities	800	504		
Shareholders' equity				
Contributed capital	5,000	5,358		
Retained earnings	2,880	3,136		
Total shareholders' equity	7,880	8,494		
Total liabilities and equity	$13,640	$13,847		
Retained Earnings				
Beginning retained earnings	$ 2,800	$ 2,880		
+ Net income	880	1,056		
− Dividends	(800)	(800)		
= Ending retained earnings	$ 2,880	$ 3,136		

Step 2: **Forecast operating expenses (except depreciation and interest expense, and taxes).** A good jumping-off point for this step is to assemble information about the company's historical expense margins. These data provide a basis for projecting future expense amounts.

The historical expense margins and our projected margins follow.

	Historical (%)		Projected (%)	
	2012	**2013**	**2014**	**2015**
Expense margins:				
Cost of goods sold	65.7%	65.0%	65.0%	65.0%
Research and development expense	0.0	0.0	0.0	0.0
Selling, general, and administrative expense	23.3	23.0	23.0	23.0
Nonoperating income (loss)	0.0	0.0	0.0	0.0

Cost of goods sold was 65.7% of sales in 2012 but declined to only 65.0% in 2013. We are projecting a continuation of this lower margin for the next two years. Consequently, cost of goods sold is expected to be $18.018 million in 2014, or 65.0% of the $27.720 million in projected sales for that year. The 2015 cost of goods sold forecast ($20.721 million) is constructed in a similar manner.

Research and development expenses are projected to remain at zero for the next two years, as are nonoperating items. Selling, general, and administrative expenses are projected to be 23.0% of sales. In other words, our expense forecasts presume that management will continue to operate the business over the next two years in the same manner it did in 2013.

> To simplify the forecasting task, utilization ratios are computed using year-end balance sheet amounts.

Step 3: **Forecast the level of balance sheet operating assets and liabilities.** Here, too, information about the company's historical asset and liability utilization ratios—for example, operating cash or accounts receivable as a percent of sales—is helpful as a starting point. Here are the historical (and projected) utilization ratios for each operating asset and liability.

	Historical (%)		Projected (%)	
	2012	**2013**	**2014**	**2015**
Operating asset and liability utilization:				
Operating cash and equivalents/Sales	4.8%	4.5%	4.5%	4.5%
Accounts receivable/Sales	8.8	8.0	8.0	8.0
Inventory/Sales	13.5	14.0	17.0	17.0
Other current assets/Sales	0.0	0.0	0.0	0.0
Property, plant, and equipment (gross)/Sales	69.2	70.0	65.0	70.0
Other assets/Sales	2.5	3.0	3.0	3.0
Accounts payable/Sales	11.8	10.0	10.0	10.0
Other payables/Sales	0.7	1.0	1.0	1.0
Other liabilities/Sales	3.3	2.0	2.0	2.0

For example, accounts receivable at the end of 2012 were 8.8% of sales that year. However, accounts receivable were only 8.0% of sales at the end of 2013. We are projecting that receivables will maintain their current 8.0% level over the next two years. As a result, accounts receivable are forecasted to be $2.218 million at the end of 2014 (or 8.0% of the $27.720 in expected 2014 sales). A similar computation determines the forecasted balance of accounts receivable at the end of 2015.

Most of the operating assets and liabilities are forecasted to remain at their 2013 utilization ratios for the next two years. However, there are two exceptions. Inventory levels are expected to increase from 14.0% of sales in 2013 to 17.0% of sales in 2014 and 2015. At the same time,

Veto's investment in gross property, plant, and equipment is expected to decline from 70.0% of sales in 2013 to 65.0% of sales in 2014 and then rise back again to 70.0% in 2015.

Step 4: **Forecast Depreciation expense and Tax expense.** Historical and projected information about Depreciation expense (as a percent of the year-end cost of property, plant, and equipment) and Tax expense (as a percent of pre-tax earnings) is shown in the following table.

	Historical (%)		Projected (%)	
	2012	**2013**	**2014**	**2015**
Depreciation expense/PP&E gross cost	6.5%	6.5%	6.5%	6.5%
Tax expense/Pre-tax earnings	33.3	34.0	34.0	34.0

Depreciation expense has been running at 6.5% of the company's year-end investment in property, plant, and equipment. Depreciation is expected to remain at this level for the next two years. So, Depreciation expense is forecasted to be $1.171 million in 2014 (or 6.5% of the $18.018 million invested in property, plant, and equipment at the end of that year). This amount of Depreciation expense is shown on the company's 2014 income statement, and as an increase to the Accumulated depreciation balance sheet account at December 31, 2014. Tax expense is projected to be 34.0% of pre-tax earnings for the next two years, a level equal to that in 2013. So, tax expense is forecasted to be $0.634 million in 2014 (or 34% of the $1.864 million in pre-tax earnings that year including interest expense from Step 5).

Step 5: **Forecast the company's financial structure.** This forecasting step develops projections for dividends, debt, and interest expense. Here's an historical snapshot of each financial statement component and our projections for 2014 and 2015.

	Historical (%)		Projected (%)	
	2012	**2013**	**2014**	**2015**
Financial structure:				
Debt/Assets	14.5%	15.0%	15.0%	15.0%
Current portion of long-term debt/Debt	9.1	10.0	10.0	10.0
Interest rate on beginning debt	12.1	14.0	14.0	14.0
Dividends ($ in thousands)	$800	$800	$800	$800

The debt (current portion plus long-term portion) to asset ratio at Veto Equipment Supply was 14.5% in 2012, and 9.1% of the company's debt that year was listed as a current liability on the balance sheet. The debt to asset ratio increased to 15% in 2013 and is projected to remain at that percentage level over the next two years. The current portion of long-term debt is projected to stay at 10%. This means that Veto is projected to have debt of $2.194 million in 2014 (or 15.0% of the $14.629 in forecasted total assets). Of that amount, $0.219 (or 10%) is classified as a current liability.

Interest expense as a percent of beginning debt was 12.1% in 2012 but then increased to 14.0% in 2013. We are projecting interest expense to remain at this percentage level over the next two years. So, interest expense in 2014 is projected to be $0.291 million (or 14.0% of the $2.077 million in *beginning* debt that year). Dividends have been $0.800 million each year and are expected to remain so for the next two years.

We have now completed the forecasting steps necessary to construct projected income statements and balance sheets for Veto Equipment Supply Company. See Exhibit 6.10 for our detailed forecasts.

We did not forecast one financial statement item—Contributed capital—directly. Instead, we used the balance sheet equation that requires total assets to equal total liabilities plus shareholders' equity. The projected contributed capital figure was set equal to an amount that ensured that the balance sheet equation held for each forecast year. We are implicitly assuming that Veto issues or repurchases stock as necessary.

EXHIBIT 6.10	Veto Equipment Supply Company

Historical and Projected Income Statements and Balance Sheets

	Historical		Projected	
($ in thousands)	2012	2013	2014	2015
Income Statement				
Sales	$24,000	$25,200	$27,720	$31,878
Cost of goods sold	15,760	16,380	18,018	20,721
Research and development expense	—	—	—	—
Selling, general, and administrative expense	5,600	5,796	6,376	7,332
Depreciation expense	1,080	1,147	1,171	1,450
Pre-tax operating income	1,560	1,877	2,155	2,375
Interest expense	240	277	291	307
Nonoperating income (loss)	—	—	—	—
Pre-tax earnings	1,320	1,600	1,864	2,068
Tax expense	440	544	634	703
Net income	$ 880	$ 1,056	$ 1,230	$ 1,365
Balance Sheet				
Operating cash and equivalents	$ 1,160	$ 1,134	$ 1,247	$ 1,435
Accounts receivable	2,120	2,016	2,218	2,550
Inventories	3,240	3,528	4,712	5,419
Other current assets	—	—	—	—
Current assets	6,520	6,678	8,177	9,404
Property, plant, and equipment (gross)	16,600	17,640	18,018	22,315
Accumulated depreciation	(10,080)	(11,227)	(12,398)	(13,848)
Other assets	600	756	832	956
Total assets	$13,640	$13,847	$14,629	$18,827
Current portion of long-term debt	$ 180	$ 208	$ 219	$ 282
Accounts payable	2,820	2,520	2,772	3,188
Other payables	160	252	277	319
Current liabilities	3,160	2,980	3,268	3,789
Long-term debt	1,800	1,869	1,975	2,541
Other liabilities	800	504	554	638
Shareholders' equity				
Contributed capital	5,000	5,358	5,266	7,728
Retained earnings	2,880	3,136	3,566	4,131
Total shareholders' equity	7,880	8,494	8,832	11,859
Total liabilities and equity	$13,640	$13,847	$14,629	$18,827
Retained Earnings				
Beginning retained earnings	$ 2,800	$ 2,880	$ 3,136	$ 3,566
+ Net income	880	1,056	1,230	1,365
− Dividends	(800)	(800)	(800)	(800)
= Ending retained earnings	$ 2,880	$ 3,136	$ 3,566	$ 4,131

In 2015, the company is projected to have sales of $31.878 million and net income of $1.365 million. However, the revolving credit line needs are expected to reach $2.823 million (or $0.282 in current debt plus another $2.541 million in long-term debt). This amount exceeds the credit limit on the Commerce First Bank loan. Let's take a look at Veto's projected cash flow statements to learn the reason for this projected increase in borrowing.

Step 6: **Derive projected cash flow statements.** Projected cash flow statements can now be derived directly from the company's projected income statements and balance sheets. See Exhibit 6.11 for the company's historical and projected cash flows.

The historical cash flow statements reveal that Veto enjoyed positive free cash flows—Cash from operations *minus* Cash used in investing activities—in both 2012 and 2013. The statements also indicate the company paid dividends and increased its long-term debt in both years, suggesting the company is borrowing money to maintain a stable dividend payout, which should concern creditors.

The projected cash flow statements indicate Veto will face a significant cash flow problem in 2015. Even though operating cash flows that year are projected to be $2.234 million, free cash flows are expected to be in a deficit position of $2.187 million (or $2.234 million in operating cash flows minus $4.421 million in required investment). Add the dividend payment of $800,000, and the cash flow deficit approaches $3 million.

According to our forecasts, Veto will make up this deficit by borrowing $0.629 million, as shown by the increase in long-term debt, and by raising another $2.462 million from stockholders as the increase in contributed capital shows. But what if stockholders are unwilling to buy more shares from the company? Then management must either scale back the company's operating plans to free up more cash or negotiate a substantially larger credit line with Commerce First Bank.

EXHIBIT 6.11	**Veto Equipment Supply Company**			

Historical and Projected Cash Flow Statements

	Historical		Projected	
($ in thousands)	2012	2013	2014	2015
Cash Flow Statement				
Net income	$ 880	$ 1,056	$ 1,230	$ 1,365
Noncash expense				
Depreciation	1,080	1,147	1,171	1,450
Changes in noncash working capital accounts				
Accounts receivable decrease (increase)	65	104	(202)	(332)
Inventory decrease (increase)	(158)	(288)	(1,184)	(707)
Accounts payable increase (decrease)	100	(300)	252	416
Other payables increase (decrease)	(20)	92	25	42
Cash from operations	1,947	1,811	1,292	2,234
Increase in property, plant, and equipment	(985)	(1,040)	(378)	(4,297)
Increase in other assets	(67)	(156)	(76)	(124)
Cash used in investing activities	(1,052)	(1,196)	(454)	(4,421)
Increase in long-term debt	200	97	117	629
Increase (decrease) in other liabilities	(50)	(296)	50	84
Increase (decrease) in contributed capital	—	358	(92)	2,462
Dividends paid	(800)	(800)	(800)	(800)
Cash from financing activities	(650)	(641)	(725)	2,375
Net increase (decrease) in cash	$ 245	$ (26)	$ 113	$ 188

EXERCISES

E6-1

Free cash flow valuation
(LO 1)

Required:
1. What are *free cash flows*?
2. Explain the difference between a company's operating cash flow and its free cash flow.
3. Briefly describe the key features of the free cash flow approach to valuation.

E6-2

Abnormal earnings
valuation **(LO 1)**

Required:
1. What does the phrase *sustainable earnings* mean? What types of earnings are not sustainable?
2. What are abnormal earnings?
3. Briefly describe the key features of the abnormal earnings approach to valuation.

E6-3

Predicting future cash flow
(LO 2)

Shelter Products sells portable livestock shelters to hog producers in the Central and Midwest regions of the United States. The terms of sale require cash payment within 30 days, and most customers take full advantage of this payment option. Sales are somewhat seasonal as indicated by the following table of monthly sales, accounts receivable, and cash receipts information. Accounts receivable figures are as of the month end, and December credit sales and cash collections are omitted for brevity.

	Dec	Jan	Feb	Mar	Apr	May	June
Credit sales		$38,000	$24,000	$45,000	$56,000	$63,000	$42,000
Accounts receivable	$15,000	36,000	23,000	42,000	55,500	61,000	41,000
Cash collections		17,000	37,000	26,000	42,500	57,500	62,000

Required:
1. Which accounting attribute—current month's credit sales or cash collections—seems to do the better job of predicting future (i.e., next month's) cash collections? Why?
2. Briefly explain why current period accrual earnings may be a better predictor of future operating cash flow than is current period operating cash flow.

E6-4

Explaining differences in
P/E ratios **(LO 4)**

The price/earnings ratios of four companies from different industries are:

Company	P/E Ratio
Amazon.com	2,763
Microsoft	16
Toyota Motors	13
Whole Foods Market	41

Required:
What factors might explain the difference in the P/E ratios of these companies?

E6-5

Why P/E ratios vary **(LO 4)**

The price/earnings ratios of four companies from the same industry are:

Company	P/E Ratio
Fresh Market	49
Kroger	23
Safeway	9
Whole Foods Market	41

Required:
What factors might explain the difference in the P/E ratios of these companies?

Required:

1. Why is fair value accounting so important to companies such as News Corporation (mentioned in the chapter) that have substantial investments in goodwill recorded on their balance sheets?

2. News Corporation uses a discounted free cash flow valuation approach when assessing goodwill impairment. This valuation approach corresponds to which level of the FASB's fair value measurement hierarchy?

3. Why doesn't News Corporation use a Level 1 fair value measurement to assess goodwill impairment?

E 6-6

Fair Value Accounting and Goodwill **(LO 3)**

Required:

1. Define the term *quality of earnings.*

2. List the techniques that management can use to improve a company's *reported* earnings performance in the short run.

3. Give examples of low-quality earnings components.

E 6-7

Earnings quality **(LO 5)**

Halifax Products has a $1 million bank loan that comes due next year. Management has prepared cash flow forecasts for each of the next six quarters as shown in the table below. Planned capital expenditures are intended to replace failing manufacturing equipment, upgrade computer systems, and refurbish the company president's office. These forecasts have been shared with the bank loan officer responsible for overseeing the Halifax loan.

E 6-8

Cash Flow and Credit Risk **(LO 7)**

	Y1Q1	Y1Q2	Y1Q3	Y1Q4	Y2Q1	Y2Q2
Scheduled loan payments					$500,000	$500,000
Forecasted cash flows:						
Cash from operations	$200,000	$250,000	$300,000	$240,000	200,000	220,000
Capital expenditures	(150,000)		(150,000)		(175,000)	
Dividends to owners					(50,000)	

Required:

1. Explain why the loan officer might consider the Halifax loan to be of high credit risk.

2. What steps can company management take to reduce the loan's credit risk?

3. What steps can the bank loan officer take to reduce the loan's credit risk?

In October 2010, Moody's Investors Services reduced the credit rating assigned to Greece's government bonds from investment grade to a speculative (junk-level) rating. At the time, Greece was considered by many to be the epicenter of the European debt crisis. The debt-laden country had already received financial support packages from the European Union and the International Monetary Fund, and had agreed to a three-year austerity and reform program intended to help the country meet its debt commitments. However, the Greek economy was experiencing a lengthy recession and many economists predicted economic contraction to worsen as governmental austerity measures began to take hold.

E 6-9

Moody's Slashes Greek Bond Rating **(LO 7)**

Required:

1. Why do agencies such as Moody's assign credit risk ratings to government bonds?

2. Briefly explain how Moody's analysts might go about the task of assigning a credit risk rating to Greek government debt.

3. What message should current and potential investors take from the Greek debt ratings downgrade?

<table>
<tr><td>**E6-10**</td><td colspan="6">The quarterly cash flows from operations for two software companies are</td></tr>
</table>

Credit risk and cash flow
volatility   **(LO 7)**

	2013				2014
	Q1	**Q2**	**Q3**	**Q4**	**Q1**
Firm A	$406.1	$204.2	$729.1	$440.2	$ 587.8
Firm B	136.7	243.1	708.2	(87.9)	(161.4)

Required:

1. Explain why Firm B has more credit risk than Firm A.

2. Suppose that Firm B's cash flow was $200 higher each quarter (e.g., $336.7 in Q1 of 2013). Explain why Firm B might still be judged to have higher credit risk than Firm A.

PROBLEMS / DISCUSSION QUESTIONS

P6-1

Interpreting stock price
changes   **(LO 6)**

On July 10, 2012, Advanced Micro Devices (AMD) announced that it expected its revenues for the second quarter to be about $1.4 billion. At the time of the announcement, financial analysts expected AMD's second quarter revenue to be about $1.6 billion.

Required:

1. Would AMD's announcement cause a change in the company's stock price on the date of the announcement? Explain why or why not. (Assume the announcement was made while the market was open.)

2. Consider the following two scenarios:

   a. The $200 million difference between AMD's management forecast and analysts' forecast is completely attributable to a previously reported monthlong labor strike at one of AMD's manufacturing facilities.

   b. The $200 million difference between AMD's management forecast and analysts' forecast is attributable to AMD's previously undisclosed decision to cut prices to meet those of a competitor.

   Do you expect the magnitude of the stock price change to be greater under scenario (a) or scenario (b)?

P6-2

Assessing credit risk using
cash flow forecasts   **(LO 7)**

Randall Manufacturing has requested a $2 million, four-year term loan from Farmers State Bank. It will use the money to expand its warehouse and to upgrade its assembly line. Randall supplied the following cash flow forecasts as part of the loan application.

($ in thousands)	**2014**	**2015**	**2016**	**2017**
Cash provided by operations	$ 685	$715	$720	$735
Cash used for investing activities	(2,590)	(50)	(50)	(50)
Cash used for financing activities	2,000	(100)	(100)	(100)
Net change in cash	$ 95	$565	$570	$585

The forecasts assume that the loan is granted in 2014 and that $2.590 million will be spent that year on the expansion and upgrade. Randall plans to spend $50,000 each year to replace worn-out manufacturing equipment and $100,000 each year for dividends.

Required:

1. As the bank's chief loan officer, what is your opinion about the degree of credit risk associated with this $2 million loan?

2. How can Randall Manufacturing lower its credit risk?

As shown in equation (6.9), the price equation for a firm with positive growth opportunities is

P6-3

Valuing growth opportunities
(LO 4)

$$P_0 = \frac{X_0}{r} + \text{NPVGO}$$

where P_0 is the current stock price, X_0 is current reported earnings per share, r is the cost of equity capital, and NPVGO is the net present value of future growth opportunities. Recent values of P_0, X_0, and r for several companies are:

	P_0	X_0	r
Brunswick	$36.19	$0.54	0.121
eBay	57.21	1.99	0.081
Home Depot	67.30	2.81	0.075
Walmart	70.49	4.86	0.055
Walgreen	40.31	2.21	0.063

Required:

1. Why does eBay have a higher cost of equity capital (r) than Wal-Mart?

2. Compute NPVGO for each company.

3. Compute NPVGO as a percent of stock price for each company.

4. Why is eBay's NPVGO as a percent of stock price greater than Home Depot's?

5. Why is Walmart's NPVGO negative?

Swiss Valley Veterinary Products distributes animal health care products to commercial live-stock producers throughout the United States and Europe. Its terms of sale require cash payment within 30 days, and most customers take full advantage of this payment option. Swiss Valley buys health care products on credit from multinational pharmaceutical companies. The credit purchase terms require cash payment within 60 days. Sales are somewhat seasonal.

P6-4

Predicting future cash flow   **(LO 2)**

The following table shows monthly activities for one of Swiss Valley's most important business segments—swine health care products. Cash collections are from customers and cash payments are to suppliers of swine health care products. The figures shown for Accounts receivable, Inventories, and Accounts payable represent month-end amounts. Some December amounts have been omitted for brevity.

Dollar amounts in thousands	**Dec**	**Jan**	**Feb**	**Mar**	**Apr**	**May**	**June**
Sales		$620	$ 650	$ 800	$ 880	$ 940	$ 850
Cost of goods sold		500	520	640	700	750	680
Gross profit		120	130	160	180	190	170
Accounts receivable	$ 500	610	630	790	865	925	830
Inventories	600	625	770	840	900	820	660
Accounts payable	1,100	985	1,130	1,315	1,410	1,370	1,113
Cash collections		510	630	640	805	880	945
Cash payments		640	480	525	665	710	760
Net cash flow		(130)	150	115	140	170	185

Required:

1. In March, customers purchased $800,000 of swine health care products. Of this amount, how much did March customers still owe at month-end?

2. Cash collections totaled $640,000 in March. Explain how this figure was determined.

3. What was the amount of swine health care products purchased in March from pharmaceutical suppliers?

4. March cash payments to suppliers totaled $525,000. Explain how this figure was determined.

5. Which accounting attribute—current month's gross profits or current month's net cash flow—does a better job of predicting future (i.e., the next month's) net cash flow? Why?

6. Briefly explain why current period accrual earnings may be a better predictor of future operating cash flow than is current period operating cash flow.

P6-5

Tail O' the Dog: Fair Value
Measurement   **(LO 3)**

Tail O' the Dog operates a chain of seven gourmet hot dog stands in southern California. The firm's first stand, built in 1948, was shaped like (what else?) a giant hot dog, in a giant hot dog bun, and with mustard, of course. Over the years, this humble counter has served the public over 5 million hot dogs—everything from the *Mexican Ole* (with chili, cheese, and onions) to the *Boston Celtic* (with baked beans). The company's other six outlets maintain the original stand's architectural kitsch.

Yesterday, Tail O' the Dog was acquired by Conover Corporation in a stock-for-stock deal valued at $28 million based on the market value of Conover stock. Conover must now determine the fair value of each identifiable Tail O' the Dog asset and liability, consistent with the requirements of applicable accounting standards.

There is a Tail O' the Dog stand on the edge of Carlsbad, California, just north of San Diego. The stand sits on the east side of the Pacific Coast Highway, the state route that runs along the California coastline from Mexico to Oregon. Across the highway is a one-acre, paved parking lot also owned by Tail O' the Dog (and now Conover). The beachfront parcel is zoned for commercial or residential use and has majestic coastline views. In attempting to determine the fair value of this parcel, Conover has learned that:

- The parking lot is carried on the books of Tail O' the Dog at its 1962 historical cost of $12,000. Improvements made to the parcel over the years are now fully depreciated.

- Tail O' the Dog allows free use of the parking lot by its customers, other businesses, neighborhood residents, and tourists seeking beach access. A local developer contacted the company last year and proposed converting the lot into monthly paid parking. According to the developer's estimates, doing so would produce an income stream of $60,000 each year (net of improvements and annual operating costs) for Tail O' the Dog. The developer's offer was declined but Conover has calculated the capitalized value of this potential income stream to be $600,000.

- Because Tail O' the Dog receives no income from the parcel, it is currently assessed for property tax purposes as an "unimproved commercial lot" at $200,000.

- A parking lot of similar size but located several blocks east of the highway and closer to downtown Carlsbad sold for $500,000 last year.

- An unimproved residential beachfront lot of similar size sold for $1.2 million last year. That lot was also located several blocks closer to city center than is the Tail O' the Dog lot. In speaking with several real estate professionals, Conover has learned that property values in the area are down slightly from a year ago.

Required:

1. Conover Corporation's financial reporting problem is to determine the parking lot's fair value in a manner consistent with GAAP. Which of the five measurements is the least relevant for this purpose? Why?

2. Which measurement is the most relevant for determining the parking lot's fair value? Why?

3. Which of the five measurements (if any) correspond to Level 2 in the fair value measurement hierarchy? Which measurements (if any) correspond to Level 3?

4. Why might auditors be more challenged by a Level 3 fair value measurement than by a Level 2 fair value measurement?

Sonic Solutions develops digital media products, services, and technologies for consumers and content development professionals. In June 2010, a team of analysts at J.P. Morgan issued a research report that valued Sonic's stock at $13 per share, compared to the then current market price of $8.71. The research report's discounted cash flow valuation table is reproduced below (slightly edited for improved clarity). The 2009 figures are as reported by Sonic but the 2010 through 2017 figures are J.P. Morgan analysts' forecasts. Key assumptions include a weighted-average cost of capital (WACC) of 12% and a perpetual growth rate of 5%. All dollar amounts are in millions except share value.

P 6 - 6

Sonic Solutions: Discounted Cash Flow Valuation **(LO 1)**

	Actual 2009	J.P. Morgan Forecast							
		2010	2011	2012	2013	2014	2015	2016	2017
Total revenues:	110.3	137.4	234.5	347.2	600.5	690.6	794.2	913.4	1050.4
EBITDA	6.7	9.4	15.9	31.3	59.2	69.1	87.4	114.2	136.5
Capital expenditures	−0.2	−1.7	−1.9	−2.3	−2.9	−3.0	−3.1	−3.3	−3.5
Cash taxes	−2.6	−3.1	−5.6	−11.6	−22.5	−26.4	−33.7	−44.3	−53.2
Free cash flow	3.9	4.6	8.4	17.4	33.8	39.7	50.6	66.6	79.8
Discount factor:		0.89286	0.79719	0.71178	0.63552	0.56743	0.50663	0.45235	0.40388
Present value:		4.11	6.70	12.38	21.48	22.53	25.64	30.13	32.23
Present value beyond 2017		460.43							
Present value 2010–2017		155.19							
		615.61							
Less net debt		−56.50							
Equity value		672.11							
Shares outstanding		51.69							
Share value		$ 13.00							

Required:

1. Comment on how the Free Cash Flow spreadsheet calculation compares with how accountants and auditors might compute free cash flow directly from the company's financial statements.

2. Compute the annual rate of growth in forecasted sales and free cash flow for each year (2010 through 2017). Comment on the relative rates of sales and free cash flow growth.

3. What role does the 12% weighted average cost of capital assumption play in the discounted cash flow valuation analysis?

4. Write a brief paragraph explaining to someone unfamiliar with present value calculations how the figure $155.19 for Present value 2010–2017 is computed.

5. Explain how the figure $460.43 for Present value beyond 2017 is computed.

6. Why does the analyst team subtract an amount for net debt in arriving at Equity value? (Note: The term *net debt* is defined for spreadsheet purposes as financial liabilities (e.g., loans) minus any financial assets (e.g., money market investments) and is negative in the spreadsheet because Sonic's financial assets exceed its financial liabilities.)

7. What share value estimate would the J.P. Morgan team have calculated if they had used an abnormal earnings value approach rather than a discounted cash flow approach and had developed forecasts of abnormal earnings and book values that were consistent with the cash flow forecast in the above worksheet? Why?

8. Sometimes analysts' research reports contain inadvertent computational errors. What would the estimated value of Sonic's stock have been if the J.P. Morgan team mistakenly used 34.60 million shares outstanding rather than the correct 51.69 million share count?

9. Rovi Corporation announced on December 22, 2010, that it had agreed to acquire Sonic Solutions for a combination of cash and stock worth $14 per Sonic share. Sonic shareholders could choose between receiving $14 cash for each Sonic share they owned, or Rovi shares having a value of $14.

Here is a summary of the trading in Rovi's stock in the days surrounding the announcement. What does this information suggest about how Rovi shareholders viewed the transaction?

Date	Volume	Closing Price	S&P 500 Closing
December 20, 2010	759,800	$57.04	1247.08
December 21, 2010	444,200	57.76	1254.60
December 22, 2010	664,600	58.36	1258.84
December 23, 2010	3,234,600	57.26	1256.77
December 27, 2010	1,018,800	57.60	1257.54
December 28, 2010	1,844,000	58.25	1258.51
December 29, 2010	1,621,900	59.84	1259.78

P6-7

Determining abnormal earnings—Some examples **(LO 1)**

As discussed in the chapter, abnormal earnings (AE) are

$$AE_t = \text{Actual earnings}_t - \text{Required or "normal" earnings}_t$$

which may be expressed as

$$AE_t = \text{NOPAT}_t - (r \times BV_{t-1})$$

where NOPAT is the firm's net operating profit after taxes, r is the cost of equity capital, and BV_{t-1} is the book value of equity at time $t - 1$.

Required:
Solve the following problems:

1. If NOPAT is $5,000, $r = 15\%$, and BV_{t-1} is $50,000, what is AE?
2. If NOPAT is $25,000, $r = 18\%$, and BV_{t-1} is $125,000, what is AE?
3. Assume the firm in requirement 2 can increase NOPAT to $30,000 by instituting some cost-cutting measures. What is the new AE?
4. Assume the firm in requirement 2 can divest $25,000 of unproductive capital with NOPAT falling by only $2,000. What is the new AE?
5. Assume the firm in requirement 2 can add a new division at a cost of $40,000, which will increase NOPAT by $7,600 per year. Would adding the new division increase AE?
6. Assume the firm in requirement 1 can add a new division at a cost of $25,000, which will increase NOPAT by $3,500 per year. Would adding the new division increase AE?

P6-8

Assigning credit ratings using financial ratios **(LO 7)**

Exhibit 6.5 describes the key financial ratios Standard & Poor's analysts use to assess credit risk and assign credit ratings to industrial companies. The same financial ratios for three firms follow.

	Firm 1	Firm 2	Firm 3
EBIT interest coverage	2.7	12.8	16.7
EBITDA interest coverage	3.7	18.7	24.6
FFO/Total debt	19.8	80.2	135.1
Free operating cash flow/Total debt	8.2	40.6	87.9
Total debt/EBITDA	4.0	1.0	0.3
Return on capital	9.9	29.2	32.7
Total debt/Capital	54.8	30.2	8.1

Required:

1. What credit rating would be assigned to Firm 1?

2. What credit rating would be assigned to Firm 2?

3. Does Firm 3 have more or less credit risk than Firm 2? How can you tell?

As discussed in the chapter, abnormal earnings (AE) are

$$AE_t = \text{Actual earnings}_t - \text{Required earnings}_t$$

which may be expressed as

$$AE_t = \text{NOPAT}_t - (r \times BV_{t-1})$$

where NOPAT is the firm's net operating profit after taxes, r is the cost of equity capital, and BV_{t-1} is the book value of equity at $t - 1$.

Following are NOPAT, BV_{t-1}, and cost of equity capital for two firms.

P6-9

Calculating value creation by two companies **(LO 1)**

e**X**cel

mhhe.com/revsine6e

Company A	2010	2011	2012	2013	2014
NOPAT	$ 66,920	$ 79,632	$ 83,314	$ 89,920	$ 92,690
BV_{t-1}	478,000	504,000	541,000	562,000	598,000
Cost of equity capital	0.152	0.167	0.159	0.172	0.166

Company B	2010	2011	2012	2013	2014
NOPAT	$192,940	$176,341	$227,700	$ 198,900	$ 282,964
BV_{t-1}	877,000	943,000	989,999	1,020,000	1,199,000
Cost of equity capital	0.188	0.179	0.183	0.175	0.186

Required:

1. Calculate each firm's AE each year from 2010 to 2014.

2. Which firm was better managed over the 2010–2014 period? Why?

3. Which firm is likely to be the better stock investment in 2015 and beyond? Why?

Exhibit 6.5 describes the key financial ratios Standard & Poor's analysts use to assess credit risk and assign credit ratings to industrial companies. Those same financial ratios for a single company over time follow. The company was assigned a AAA credit rating at the beginning of 2010.

P6-10

Making credit-rating changes **(LO 7)**

	2013				2014	
	Q1	Q2	Q3	Q4	Q1	Q2
EBIT interest coverage	23.8	22.1	21.6	20.8	20.6	12.4
EBITDA interest coverage	25.3	26.4	25.6	23.2	22.9	16.5
FFO/Total debt	167.8	150.8	130.7	128.4	80.2	76.2
Free operating cash flow/Total debt	104.1	107.3	103.7	98.6	61.5	45.3
Total debt/EBITDA	0.2	0.2	0.2	0.6	0.8	1.0
Return on capital	35.1	34.3	30.6	28.1	25.9	24.7
Total debt/Capital	6.2	6.8	7.5	15.4	27.2	35.6

Required:

1. Did the company's credit risk increase or decrease over these six quarters?

2. What credit rating should be assigned to the company as of Q2 in 2014?

3. In what quarter should the company's credit rating be downgraded from AAA?

P6-11

Enron: Fair Value Accounting
(LO 3)

In mid-2000, Enron Corporation and Blockbuster (a division of Viacom) set up a pilot project, streaming videos to a few dozen apartments in Portland, Oregon, from servers set up in the basement of the building. With that tiny beginning, Enron opened up a partnership, called Braveheart, which later that year would pump $110 million of fair value accounting profit onto Enron's books. Here's how the deal worked:

- Enron signed a 20-year exclusive agreement with Blockbuster to provide on-demand videos over Enron's broadband network. Enron's CEO boasted the venture would be a "killer app" that would help create demand for Enron's coast-to-coast fiber-optic network. Enron hoped to make millions of dollars off the deal.

- Enron then created a partnership called EBS Content Systems LLC—but known inside the company as Braveheart—whose purpose was to get someone to advance Enron the money it expected to make on the deal with Blockbuster. To capitalize Braveheart, a small amount of money came from outside investors while Enron contributed the Blockbuster agreement and lent the partnership some stock. Braveheart thus became one of Enron's infamous off-balance-sheet entities: consolidation was not required by GAAP and Enron recorded the Braveheart capitalization as a financial asset called "Investment in EBS Content Systems."

- Next, an outside investment bank gave Braveheart $115 million in return for a promise that most of the earnings from the Blockbuster deal would go directly to the bank. In essence, Braveheart "securitized" its future earnings from the Enron–Blockbuster venture by selling its rights to the future earnings stream to the investment bank. If the earnings were not enough for the bank to recoup its investment, Enron promised that it would repay the bank.

- Enron then "marked-to-market" its Braveheart investment—Braveheart now had millions in cash from the investment bank—and booked the $110 million fair value increase as profit. Enron did not count all $115 million because, under an accounting rule, it had to estimate the fair value of its guarantee to pay back the bank and reduce its Braveheart investment fair value estimate by that amount.

In the end, the Blockbuster venture never made it beyond the pilot stage before Enron pulled the plug. At its peak, the service was provided to a few thousand households in four cities. Enron later reversed the entire $110 million of profits in 2001. Some Enron employees said that while the arrangement existed, it helped Enron executives hit earnings targets that served both to pump up the value of the company's stock and to inflate their bonuses.

Required:

1. What features of the Braveheart structure enabled Enron to bolster its 2000 profits using fair value accounting?

2. Describe how someone might determine the bank guarantee's fair value (estimated to be $5 million by Enron).

3. Suppose the fair value of the bank guarantee was estimated to be $100 million. What impact would this new fair value estimate have on the amount of profit to be recorded by Enron in 2000 on the Braveheart deal?

4. What steps might an auditor take to assess the reliability of Enron's $5 million fair value estimate for the bank guarantee?

P6-12

Calculating sustainable
earnings   **(LO 5)**

Colonel Electric Company is one of the largest and most diversified industrial corporations in the world. From the time of its incorporation in 1892, the company has engaged in developing, manufacturing, and marketing a wide variety of products for the generation, transmission, distribution, control, and utilization of electricity.

Appearing in the following table are the 2011–2013 income statements of Colonel Electric Company.

mhhe.com/revsine6e

Comparative Income Statement for Years Ended December 31,

($ in millions)	2013	2012	2011
Revenues			
Sales of goods	$54,196	$53,177	$52,767
Sales of services	11,923	10,836	8,863
Royalties and fees	1,629	753	783
Total revenues	67,748	64,766	62,413
Costs and expenses			
Cost of goods sold	(24,594)	(24,308)	(22,775)
Cost of services sold	(8,425)	(6,785)	(6,274)
Restructuring (charges) reversals	1,000	—	(2,500)
Interest charges	(595)	(649)	(410)
Other costs and expenses	(6,274)	(5,743)	(5,211)
Litigation charges (income)	550	—	(250)
(Losses) gains on sales of investments	(75)	—	25
(Losses) gains on asset sales	25	55	(35)
Inventory write-offs	—	(18)	—
Asset impairment write-offs	—	—	(24)
Special item charges	(34)	—	(8)
Loss from labor strike	—	(20)	—
Total costs and expenses	(38,422)	(37,468)	(37,462)
Earnings from continuing operations before income taxes	29,326	27,298	24,951
Provision for income taxes (34%)	(9,971)	(9,281)	(8,483)
Earnings from continuing operations	19,355	18,017	16,468
Income (loss) from discontinued operations (net of tax)	—	(250)	1,100
Gain (loss) on sale of discontinued operations (net of tax)	750	—	—
Extraordinary gain (loss) on early debt retirement (net of tax)	(50)	—	10
Net earnings	$20,055	$17,767	$17,578

In 2013, the company earned Royalties and fees revenue of $1 billion from a one-time, six-month contract with the U.S. government. The company does not expect to do any further business with the U.S. government in the future.

Required:

1. Calculate Colonel Electric's sustainable earnings for each year. (Although there is no consensus on how best to measure sustainable earnings, one common approach is to start with GAAP reported earnings and then eliminate unsustainable earnings items.)

2. How do Colonel Electric's sustainable earnings compare to its reported net earnings in each year?

In August 2003, Krispy Kreme's common stock was trading at $44 per share. Several analysts and investors believed at the time that its shares were worth considerably less. They appear to have been right because by November 2007, the stock was trading below $3 per share.

This problem illustrates how the abnormal earnings valuation model described in Appendix A of this chapter can be combined with security analysts' published earnings forecasts and used to spot potentially overvalued stocks.

P6-13

Krispy Kreme Doughnuts: Valuing abnormal earnings **(LO 1)**

Required:

1. Use the abnormal earnings valuation model from Exhibit 6.8 of Appendix A of this chapter to derive an estimate of Krispy Kreme's stock price as of August 2003. A spreadsheet template is available on the textbook website. You will need this additional information:

   - Actual EPS for 2001 and 2002 were $0.49 and $0.70, respectively.

   - The per share amount of stock issued in 2001 and 2002 was $0.65 and $0.39, respectively. No stock was expected to be issued or bought back during the next five years (2003–2007).

   - Other comprehensive income per share was $0.32 in 2002 and zero in 2001. Analysts were forecasting other comprehensive income to be zero each year during the next five years.

   - Krispy Kreme does not pay dividends.

   - Return on equity, calculated using the beginning-of-year equity book value, was 21.1% and 20.2% in 2001 and 2002, respectively.

   - Analysts were forecasting EPS to be $0.70 and $0.89 in 2003 and 2004, respectively. The estimated long-term EPS growth rate was 13.25% for 2005 through 2007.

   - Krispy Kreme's equity cost of capital is 11%, and the long-term growth rate (beyond 2007) is assumed to be 3%.

2. Why might your value estimate from requirement 1 differ from the company's $44 stock price in August 2003?

CASES

C6-1

Illinois Tool Works: Valuing
abnormal earnings   **(LO 1)**

As described in the chapter, the abnormal earnings approach for estimating common share value is

$$P_0 = BV_0 + \sum_{t=1}^{\infty} \frac{E_0(X_t - r \times BV_{t-1})}{(1 + r)^t}$$

where P_0 is the total value of all outstanding shares, BV_0 is the current book value of stockholders' equity, BV_{t-1} is the book value of shareholders' equity at the beginning of period t, r is the cost of equity capital, E_0 is the expectations operator, and X_t is period t net income. The model says that share value equals the book value of stockholders' equity plus the present value of future expected abnormal earnings (where abnormal earnings is net income minus the cost of equity capital multiplied by the beginning-of-period book value of stockholders' equity).

The model is silent on how one comes up with expected net income for future years (and therefore future expected abnormal earnings) and just how many future years should be used. Because of the way present value is calculated, abnormal earnings amounts expected for years in the distant future have a small present value and are essentially irrelevant to valuation, especially if abnormal earnings are close to zero in the long run, as many analysts assume. Thus, professional analysts rarely use more than 15 years, often fewer than 10.

Comparative income statements and retained earnings statements for Illinois Tool Works (ITW) for Year 1–Year 3 follow.

Required:

1. Assume a 10-year forecasting horizon. Also assume that ITW's Year 3 return on beginning stockholders' equity (net income without extraordinary items divided by beginning Year 3 stockholders' equity) of 9.5% is expected to persist throughout the forecasting

horizon (that is, that expected net income is always equal to 0.095 multiplied by beginning-of-the-year stockholders' equity). Also assume that no additional stock issuances or repurchases are made and that dividends equal 25% of net income in each year. (This is ITW's approximate historical dividend payout ratio.) Given these assumptions, the book value of stockholders' equity at the *end* of Year 4 equals book value at the *beginning* of Year 4 plus $(1 - 0.25)$ times Year 4 net income. Finally assume that the cost of equity capital is 9%. (This is ITW's approximate cost of equity capital.) With these relatively simple assumptions, use the abnormal earnings model to estimate the total value of Illinois Tool Works' common shares as of the end of Year 3. Ignore terminal values at the end of the 10-year forecast horizon in your calculations.

2. As of the end of Year 3, 307 million common shares were outstanding. Convert your estimate in requirement 1 to a per share estimate. For purposes of comparison, the actual market value of ITW's common shares ranged from $56 to $64 during the first quarter of Year 4.

3. Now assume that ITW will maintain a 20% return on beginning stockholders' equity over the 10-year forecast horizon. What would the company's shares then be worth?

Illinois Tool Works
Consolidated Statement of Income

($ in millions)	Year 3	Year 2	Year 1
Sales	$9,468	$9,293	$9,984
Cost of goods sold	5,936	5,910	6,192
Gross profit	3,532	3,383	3,792
Selling and administrative expenses	1,720	1,691	1,814
Depreciation and amortization	306	385	414
Operating profit	1,506	1,307	1,564
Interest expense	68	68	72
Nonoperating income (expense)	(4)	(7)	(13)
Special items	0	3	0
Pre-tax income	1,434	1,235	1,479
Total income taxes	502	429	521
Extraordinary items	(219)	0	0
Net income	$ 713	$ 806	$ 958

Illinois Tool Works
Consolidated Statement of Shareholders' Equity

($ in millions)	Year 3	Year 2	Year 1
Balance at beginning of year	$ 9,823	$9,604	$9,061
Net income (loss)	713	806	958
Stock issued (repurchased)	361	(337)	(192)
Common stock dividends	(273)	(250)	(223)
Balance at end of year	$10,624	$9,823	$9,604

Sunny Day Stores operates convenience stores throughout much of the United States. The industry is highly competitive, with low profit margins. The company's competition includes national, regional, and local supermarkets; oil companies; and convenience store operators.

C6-2

Sunny Day Stores: Analyzing debt covenants and financial distress **(LO 7)**

A note to the 2014 financial statements described the company's long-term debt:

Note payable to the Prudential Insurance Company of America ("Prudential") with annual principal payments of $900,000, interest at 8.93%. Amount outstanding: $5,700,000 in 2014 and $6,600,000 in 2013.

Term note payable to First Florida Bank ("First Florida") maturing in September 2019, with quarterly principal payments of $125,000 through June 30, 2015, and $250,000 thereafter, with interest at 1% in excess of prime (5.5% at December 26, 2014). Amount outstanding $3,563,956 in 2014 and $3,000,000 in 2013.

Revolving note payable to First Florida with interest at 1% in excess of prime (5.5% at December 26, 2014). Amount outstanding: $7,400,000 in 2014 and 2013.

Certain of the Company's loan agreements pertaining to the borrowings from Prudential and First Florida require the Company to maintain minimum interest coverage ratio, working capital, and net worth levels, impose restrictions on additional borrowings, and prohibit the payment of dividends. Specifically, at the end of fiscal 2014, Sunny Day must have a net worth of at least $22,850,000, working capital (on a FIFO inventory basis) must be at least $1,300,000, and the interest coverage ratio must be at least 1.6.

The company's 2014 financial statements that follow show that Sunny Day Stores was not in compliance with these loan covenants at year-end.

Sunny Day Stores, Inc.
Comparative Balance Sheets

	2014	2013		2014	2013
Cash and cash equivalents	$ 1,451,688	$ 2,971,457	Accounts payable		
Accounts receivable less			Trade	$ 9,237,416	$ 6,208,733
allowances for doubtful			Money orders	1,637,255	1,442,811
accounts of $82,000			Fuel taxes	1,106,713	635,556
and $63,000 in 2014			Accrued liabilities		
and 2013, respectively	985,987	705,923	Salaries and wages	774,519	846,131
Refundable income taxes	400,000	135,831	Self-insurance reserves	1,186,613	966,770
Inventories—FIFO basis	10,640,125	8,690,734	State and local taxes	1,136,241	569,160
Less: LIFO reserve	(3,057,715)	(2,845,703)	Current portion of long-		
Total inventories	7,582,410	5,845,031	term debt	1,956,369	1,082,429
Prepaid expenses and			Total current liabilities	17,035,126	11,751,590
other assets	764,627	547,705			
Refundable deposits	700,000	380,522			
Total current assets	11,884,712	10,586,469			
Property and equipment			Deferred income taxes	400,000	1,477,323
Land	11,016,168	13,603,304	Unearned revenue	111,426	179,224
Buildings	19,673,636	19,801,221			
Fixtures and equipment	32,232,643	32,749,133	Long-term debt, less		
Leaseholds and			current portion	13,969,745	16,693,772
improvements	5,084,679	4,929,748			
	68,007,126	71,083,406			
Less: Allowances for					
depreciation and					
amortization	(31,008,778)	(28,988,173)	Stockholders' equity		
	36,998,348	42,095,233	Common stock	170,165	170,165
Other assets			Additional paid-in capital	5,124,245	5,124,245
Land held for sale	2,641,735		Retained earnings	15,171,001	17,735,240
Other	456,913	449,857		20,465,411	23,029,650
			Total liabilities and		
Total assets	$51,981,708	$53,131,559	stockholders' equity	$51,981,708	$53,131,559

Sunny Day Stores, Inc.
Statement of Cash Flows

	2014	2013	2012
Cash flows from operating activities			
Net income (loss)	$(2,564,239)	$(1,042,297)	$ 613,423
Adjustments			
Depreciation and amortization	3,980,186	4,460,529	3,793,119
Deferred income taxes	(1,077,323)	(512,995)	577,235
Gain on sale of property	(532,570)	(174,657)	(100,322)
Decrease in unearned revenue	(67,798)	(83,804)	(84,235)
Changes in assets and liabilities			
(Increase) in accounts receivable	(280,064)	53,121	(358,982)
(Increase) in refundable income taxes	(264,169)	244,085	(113,675)
(Increase) in inventories	(1,737,379)	2,908,024	412,647
(Increase) in other assets	(263,981)	(141,910)	(241,347)
Increase in refundable deposits	(319,478)	(15,107)	(145,866)
Increase in accounts payable and other liabilities	4,409,596	(4,304,076)	3,807,200
Total adjustments	3,847,020	2,433,210	7,545,774
Net cash flow operations	1,282,781	1,390,913	8,159,197
Cash flows from investing activities			
Purchase of property and equipment, net	(2,390,832)	(2,871,399)	(9,593,270)
Sale of property and equipment	1,428,051	668,656	821,641
Collections of notes and loans receivables	10,318	(103,610)	7,775
Net cash used in investing activities	(952,463)	(2,306,353)	(8,763,854)
Cash flows from financing activities			
Issuance of long-term debt	82,515	2,633,454	4,528,915
Dividends	–0–	–0–	(204,198)
Payment of long-term debt	(1,932,602)	(3,108,251)	(1,588,391)
Net cash provided by financing activities	(1,850,087)	(474,797)	2,736,326
Net increase (decrease) in cash	$(1,519,769)	$(1,390,237)	$ 2,131,669

Sunny Day Stores, Inc.
Statement of Operations

	2014	2013	2012
Net revenue	$217,710,782	$202,393,136	$191,243,016
Cost and expenses			
Costs of goods sold	176,102,027	158,643,287	146,652,853
Selling, general, and administrative	44,631,749	43,687,704	41,805,330
Interest expense—net	1,551,138	1,728,650	1,658,732
Net gain from sale of property	(532,570)	(174,657)	(100,322)
	221,752,344	203,884,984	190,016,593
Income (loss) before taxes	(4,041,562)	(1,491,848)	1,226,423
Provision (benefit) for income taxes			
Current	(400,000)	63,444	50,000
Deferred	(1,077,323)	(512,995)	563,000
	(1,477,323)	(449,551)	613,000
Net income (loss)	$ (2,564,239)	$ (1,042,297)	$ 613,423
Earnings per common share	$(1.51)	$(0.61)	$0.36

Required:

It's late January 2015, and Prudential and First Florida have hired you to act on their behalf in negotiations with Sunny Day Stores. Both lenders want to restructure their loans to address the company's current financial problems, and the restructured loans may require covenant changes.

Prudential and First Florida seek your advice on the type and amount of collateral to be required, revised interest rates, and possible changes to the payment schedules. In addition, the lenders have asked you to suggest new minimum net worth, working capital, and interest coverage ratios for 2015 and 2016. Specifically:

1. What type and amount of collateral do you suggest be required?
2. Should a higher interest rate be charged? Why or why not?
3. What changes would you suggest be made to the payment schedule?
4. What new minimum net worth, working capital, and interest coverage limits would you suggest the lenders set?
5. Suppose the company asked permission to resume payment of its $0.12 per share dividend, which was suspended in 2013. What advice would you give Prudential and First Florida?

COLLABORATIVE LEARNING CASES

C6-3

Microsoft Corporation: Unearned revenues and earnings management **(LO 5)**

 **Collaborative**

Microsoft develops, manufactures, licenses, sells, and supports a wide range of software products for personal computers (PCs) and servers; business and consumer productivity applications; software development tools; and content such as MSN (the Microsoft Network online service).

The following excerpt is from an article that appeared in *The Wall Street Journal.*

MICROSOFT'S EARNINGS GROWTH SLOWED IN THE LATEST QUARTER

Microsoft Corp.'s growth juggernaut slowed in its fiscal fourth quarter, but the numbers masked a surprisingly potent performance by the software giant.

The Redmond, Wash., company's earnings barely topped Wall Street's consensus, breaking a pattern of dramatic upside surprises for the company. But the company's profit would have been considerably higher had it not salted away revenue in a special reserve account for use in future quarters. That account, dubbed "unearned revenues," continued to swell and underscore the returns Microsoft is reaping as a near-monopoly supplier of personal computer operating-software and key application

programs. The account represents revenues Microsoft has collected but hadn't yet reported. It was established because the company faces future costs to deliver upgrades and customer support for products that already have been paid for. The policy helps smooth out sharp swings in the company's quarterly results.

Microsoft reported net income of $1.06 billion, or 80 cents a share, for the quarter ended June 30, an increase of 89% from $559 million, or 43 cents a share, a year earlier. Analysts had expected per-share earnings of about 79 cents, according to First Call Corp. Quarterly revenue was $3.18 billion, up 41% from $2.26 billion a year earlier.

Source: "Microsoft's Earnings Growth Slowed in the Latest Quarter," *The Wall Street Journal,* July 18, 1997. Copyright © 1997 Dow Jones & Company, Inc. All rights reserved worldwide. Reprinted with permission.

Other Information:

1. Appearing in the accompanying tables are the comparative income statements for the fourth quarters of fiscal 1996 and 1997 and for the fiscal years 1996 and 1997. Also shown are portions of the balance sheets for fiscal 1996 and 1997.

2. The balance in the unearned revenues account on March 31, 1997 (the end of the third fiscal quarter of 1997) was $1,285 million.

3. The following description of Microsoft's unearned revenues account is taken from the company's SEC filings:

The portion of the Company's revenues that are earned later than billed is reflected in the unearned revenues account. Of the March 31, 1997, balance of $1,285 million, approximately $765 million represented the unearned portion of Windows desktop operating systems revenues and $150 million represented the unearned portion of Office 97 revenues. Unearned revenues associated with upgrade rights for Microsoft Office 97 were $190 million, and the balance of unearned revenues was primarily attributable to maintenance and other subscription contracts.

Microsoft Corporation Income Statements

($ in millions, except earnings per share)	Three Months Ended June 30,		Years Ended June 30,	
	1996	1997	1996	1997
Net revenues	$2,255	$3,175	$8,671	$11,358
Cost of revenues	241	242	1,188	1,085
Research and development	453	516	1,432	1,925
Sales and marketing	661	744	2,657	2,856
General and administrative	90	94	316	362
Total operating expenses	1,445	1,596	5,593	6,228
Operating income	810	1,579	3,078	5,130
Interest income	92	127	320	443
Other expenses	(42)	(80)	(19)	(259)
Income before income taxes	860	1,626	3,379	5,314
Provision for income taxes	301	569	1,184	1,860
Net income	559	1,057	2,195	3,454
Preferred stock dividends	–0–	7	–0–	15
Net income available for common shareholders	$ 559	$1,050	$2,195	$ 3,439
Earnings per share	$ 0.43	$ 0.80	$ 1.71	$ 2.63
Average shares outstanding	1,290	1,327	1,281	1,312

Balance Sheet (selected accounts)

($ in millions)	June 30, 1996	June 30, 1997
Liabilities and Stockholders' Equity		
Current liabilities		
Accounts payable	$ 808	$ 721
Accrued compensation	202	336
Income taxes payable	484	466
Unearned revenues	560	1,418
Other	371	669
Total current liabilities	$2,425	$3,610

Required:

1. Calculate Microsoft's net profit margin for the fourth quarter of 1996 and 1997 and for the fiscal years 1996 and 1997. Comment on the results.

2. Did Microsoft fall short of, meet, or exceed analysts' expectations for fourth-quarter 1997 EPS?

3. If no reductions were made from the Unearned revenues account during the fourth quarter of fiscal 1997, how much did Microsoft add to the account during that quarter?

4. Continuing requirement 3, how much higher or lower would Microsoft's fourth-quarter income before tax have been (on a per share basis) if this accrual adjustment had not been made?

5. Assume that Microsoft reduced its Unearned revenues account by $188.0 million during the first three quarters of fiscal 1997. How much did Microsoft add to the account during the fiscal year?

6. Continuing requirement 5, how much higher or lower would Microsoft's annual income before tax have been (on a per share basis) if this accrual adjustment had not been made?

7. How much income before tax (on a per share basis) does Microsoft have "stored" in the Unearned revenues account at the end of 1997?

8. How can the Unearned revenues account be used to manage EPS?

9. How can analysts monitor the extent to which the Unearned revenues account is being used to manage EPS?

10. Does the existence of the Unearned revenues account necessarily mean that Microsoft intends to manage its reported earnings? Explain.

.mhhe.com/revsine6e

**Remember to check the book's companion website
for additional study material.**

The Role of Financial | 7
Information in Contracting

"A verbal contract isn't worth the paper it's written on."

—Sam Goldwyn, film producer

LEARNING OBJECTIVES

After studying this chapter, you will understand:

1. What conflicts of interest arise between managers and shareholders, lenders, or regulators.

2. How and why accounting numbers are used in debt agreements, in compensation contracts, and for regulatory purposes.

3. How accounting-based contracts and regulations influence managerial incentives.

4. What role contracts and regulations play in shaping managers' accounting choices.

5. How and why managers cater to Wall Street using their accounting discretion.

A *contract* is a legally binding exchange of rights and obligations between parties. You enter into contracts every day, for example when you buy coffee or park your car in a public lot. In both of these cases, you exchange the obligation to pay money for the right to receive a good or a service. Like these contracts, most contracts are made orally and are relatively simple.

Some business contracts, however, are far more complicated. They might involve large sums of money and a complex set of rights and obligations that need to be specified precisely. United Airlines, for example, does not simply order an airplane. The purchase contract specifies the model of the plane, the number and types of engines and maybe even the engine manufacturer, the seat configurations, any special features United wants, and so on. It also specifies United's maintenance obligations and the manufacturer's warranty and repair obligations, as well as payment schedules and delivery dates, and penalties for missing them.

Complex contracts are made in writing in order to limit the possibilities for misunderstanding about the exact terms of the agreement. In many such contracts, the rights and obligations conferred by the contract will depend on data in financial statements that are issued *after the contract is executed*. For example, commercial lending agreements often require the borrower to maintain a minimum interest coverage ratio. This requirement protects the lender from a deterioration of the borrower's creditworthiness. Compliance with the requirement is assessed using data from financial statements issued by the borrower over the duration of the loan.

Why do contracts incorporate financial statement information and what financial reporting incentives does this phenomenon create? This chapter addresses the following questions:

• How do conflicts of interest arise?

• How are business contracts tailored to mitigate conflicts of interest?

• What role do accounting numbers play in contracts?

• What incentives do accounting-based contracts create for the parties involved?

Chapter

- How do these incentives help us to understand why managers make certain accounting choices?
- How do these incentives affect how contracts are written?
- How does regulation also create financial reporting incentives?
- How do financial reporting incentives influence when transactions are recorded?

CONFLICTS OF INTEREST IN BUSINESS RELATIONSHIPS

Conflicts of interest arise when one party to a business relationship can take actions for his or her own benefit that harm other parties in the relationship. Conflicts of interest permeate businesses. Will a manager always make decisions that are in the owner's best interest? Probably not, because some actions that benefit the owner might not benefit the manager, while other actions might benefit the manager at the owner's expense.

Here is a real, albeit extreme, example: In 2005, Dennis Kozlowski and Mark Swartz, Tyco International's CEO and CFO, respectively, were convicted of stealing more than $150 million from the company. Among other acts, Kozlowski threw a $2 million birthday party for his wife and charged half the cost to the company. But conflicts of interest do not have to manifest themselves in such extreme ways and generally do not involve any illegality. They arise any time one party makes a decision that affects another and the decision maker is prone to consider his or her own welfare above the other party's. Suppose Allen Ford, our By the Cup owner, hires a store manager and the manager's longtime friend arrives in town unexpectedly. The manager takes a long lunch to reminisce, even though it means closing the shop for several hours. Ford, not the manager, absorbs the cost (in terms of lost profits) of closing, while the manager receives the benefit of the long lunch.

The relationship between Ford and the manager is often called a **principal-agent** relationship, or simply an **agency** relationship. The agent is supposed to act on behalf of the principal, but because the principal generally cannot monitor the agent's every action, there is no assurance the agent will always act in the principal's best interests. The cost that arises because of this relationship is called an **agency cost,** and it is not necessarily borne by the principal alone. Without a way to commit never to act out of self-interest, the agent is likely to command a smaller salary in the marketplace than he or she could if such a commitment were possible. In that sense, the agent bears some of the agency costs that arise from the relationship.

Ford's loan illustrates another common conflict of interest. Once the loan is granted, Ford might be tempted to divert the loan proceeds toward other investment opportunities or even to personal use, which would increase the default risk. Aware of this possibility, the bank might refuse to make the loan or impose a higher interest rate to reflect the greater default risk, thus transferring some of the cost created by the conflict of interest back to Ford. Both parties could benefit if there were a way to reduce the conflict. Let's see how that might be accomplished.

DEBT COVENANTS IN LENDING AGREEMENTS

Most companies have some form of debt. When this is the case, debtholders and shareholders both have some of their wealth tied to the company's fortunes. The company's resources will be used to pay interest and principal to debtholders as well as to pay dividends to shareholders. However, the interests of these two groups often diverge. The conflict of interest between them creates incentives for shareholders (or managers acting on their behalf) to take actions that benefit shareholders to the detriment of bondholders.

Finalizing the By the Cup Loan

Here is an example that illustrates the conflicting incentives of creditors and borrowers. Allen Ford, our By the Cup owner, assembled the monthly cash flow projections and other materials requested by the loan officer. Ford's detailed financial projections revealed that, in addition to investing $50,000 of his own money, Ford would need a $75,000 loan, slightly more than he originally anticipated. Still, the business's prospects seemed bright.

Several days after Ford submitted the loan application, the loan officer phoned him to indicate preliminary approval of the loan. Ford was elated, but surprised by the interest rate. It seemed higher than what other local banks were charging for similar business loans.

Why was the interest rate so high? Once the loan is granted, a conflict of interests naturally arises between Ford and the bank. This conflict occurs because Ford, not the bank, will decide how the loan proceeds are spent. For example, after Ford obtained the loan, nothing would stop him from immediately declaring and paying a $75,000 dividend to himself, rather than buying inventory and equipment for the store. After all, he owns the business and therefore he can declare a dividend at any time. A $75,000 dividend payment would increase Ford's personal wealth but surely spell disaster for the By the Cup store because the cash needed to launch the business would no longer be available. The bank would have a $75,000 loan outstanding to a business whose only asset was $50,000 in cash. Ford would have transferred wealth from the bank to himself.

Creditors know that their interests often conflict with those of borrowers, and one way they protect themselves from these conflicts is to charge a higher rate of interest on the loan as compensation for the risky actions that owner–managers like Ford might take. ***Another approach is to reduce conflicts of interest between lenders and borrowers with contracts that restrict—explicitly or implicitly—the borrowers' ability to harm lenders.*** For instance, the bank could require Ford to guarantee the business loan personally. A personal guarantee would require Ford to repay the bank loan from his own funds if the coffee shop failed. This guarantee would certainly make the $75,000 dividend payment less attractive. Alternatively, the loan agreement might include covenants, such as a prohibition on dividend payments without the bank's approval, or a limitation on dividends to some fraction of net income. In fact, the loan officer suggested stricter debt covenants as a way to reduce the conflicts of interest so the bank could accept a lower interest rate.

Debt covenants serve three broad purposes:

1. *Preservation of repayment capacity:* Some covenants place strict limits on new borrowing, prohibit stock repurchases and dividends without prior lender approval, or ensure that cash generated both from ongoing operations and from asset sales will not be diverted away from servicing debt.

2. *Protection against credit-damaging events:* All lenders are concerned with the risk of a sudden deterioration in repayment ability that can result from a merger, acquisition, takeover, or recapitalization. Some covenants prevent these adverse events from happening unless the debt is first repaid, the interest rate is adjusted upward, or prior lender approval is obtained.

3. *Signals and triggers:* Many covenants are in place to ensure the steady flow of information from borrower to lender. This information flow can reveal declining sales and profits, diminished operating cash flows, or other facets of the business that signal increased repayment risk. When deterioration occurs, for example because an interest coverage ratio falls below the minimum level required, the lender obtains additional rights. These rights might include representation on the business's board of directors, the right to veto certain

transactions, such as dividends, or even the right to demand repayment. Triggers bring the borrower and lender to the negotiating table and place the lender in a position of strength because they enable the lender to decide whether it might modify or waive restrictions or assert its rights.

Debt covenants benefit both creditors and borrowers. Creditors benefit because the covenants reduce default risk. Borrowers benefit because the covenants provide a way to commit credibly to actions that keep default risk lower, which reduces the interest rates creditors demand.

Affirmative Covenants, Negative Covenants, and Default Provisions

Debt covenants require the borrower to maintain a certain financial status for the loan's duration, and they set minimum standards for the borrower's future conduct and performance. Covenants vary with the borrower's business characteristics, financial condition, and the length of the loan. Covenants are designed to reduce default risk and to provide early warning if the borrower's financial condition deteriorates.

Affirmative covenants stipulate actions the borrower *must* take. Generally, these include:

1. Using the loan for the agreed-upon purpose.
2. Providing periodic, audited financial statements.
3. Complying with financial covenants.
4. Complying with laws.
5. Allowing the lender to inspect business assets and business contracts.
6. Maintaining business records and business properties and carrying insurance on them.

For example, a loan agreement involving TCBY Enterprises, "The Country's Best Yogurt," as the borrower, requires the company to keep the lender informed about the company's financial and operating performance by providing annual, audited financial statements. Importantly, loan agreements often do not stipulate the accounting methods to be used when preparing financial statements, except that they must comply with generally accepted accounting principles (GAAP):

> [The company] will furnish . . . not later than one hundred twenty days (120) after the close of each fiscal year . . . consolidated balance sheets, income statements and statements of cash flow . . . and such other comments and financial details as are usually included in similar reports. . . . Such reports shall be prepared in accordance with GAAP and shall be audited by independent certified public accountants of recognized standing . . . and shall contain unqualified opinions. . . . (para. 5.1 of TCBY term loan agreement)

The financial covenants also define certain financial terms and ratios and provide restrictions on the values these ratios may have.

One of the affirmative covenants in TCBY's loan agreement requires it to maintain a **fixed-charge coverage** ratio greater than 1.0, where the ratio is defined as:

$$\text{Fixed-charge coverage} = \frac{\text{Net income} + \text{Noncash charges}}{\text{Current maturities} + \text{Dividends} + \text{Replacement CapEx}}$$

The fixed-charge coverage ratio requirement limits the company's ability to pay dividends. Suppose, for example, TCBY had net income of $50 million, noncash charges of $35 million, current loan maturities of $40 million, and replacement capital expenditures of $30 million. TCBY could pay a dividend of no more than $15 million because:

$$\text{Fixed-charge coverage} = \frac{\$50 + \$35}{\$40 + \text{Dividend} + \$30} = 1.0$$

$$= \frac{\$50 + \$35}{\$40 + \$15 + \$30} = 1.0$$

Dividends in excess of $15 million would put TCBY in violation of its fixed-charge coverage requirement.[1]

Negative covenants tend to be more significant and more intensely negotiated than affirmative covenants because they *restrict* the borrower's actions. Negative covenants include limits on total indebtedness, investment of funds, capital expenditures, leases, and corporate loans as well as restrictions on the payment of cash dividends, share repurchases, mergers, asset sales, voluntary prepayment of other indebtedness, and new business ventures. This example is from the TCBY loan agreement:

> [Borrower agrees that it will not] sell, lease, transfer, or otherwise dispose of any assets . . . except the sale of inventory in the ordinary course of business and disposition of obsolete or worn-out equipment upon the replacement thereof . . . [or to] repurchase the stock of TCBY using, directly or indirectly, the proceeds of any loan. (paras. 6.6 and 6.12 of TCBY term loan agreement)

Covenants restricting the use of funds for dividend payments, share repurchases, capital expenditures, and other business purposes assure the creditor that cash will be available to make interest and principal payments when due. By limiting the borrower's ability to sell, merge, or transfer operating assets, the creditor ensures the survival of the borrower's repayment potential.

Restrictions on total indebtedness limit the amount of additional debt the company may incur over the loan term. These restrictions can be stated as dollar amounts or as ratios (examples include total debt to assets, to working capital, or to tangible net worth). It is also common for a borrower to agree not to use any of its existing property as collateral on future loans without the lender's consent.

The **events of default** section of a loan agreement describes circumstances in which the creditor obtains additional rights. Situations commonly leading to default include the failure to pay interest or principal when due, inaccuracy in representations, failure to abide by a covenant, failure to pay other debts when due (known as *cross default*), impairment of collateral, change in management or ownership, and bankruptcy. Remedies for an event of default include renegotiating the debt contract terms such as an increase in the interest rate, seizing collateral, accelerating the maturity of the debt, or initiating bankruptcy proceedings.[2]

A common action creditors take in the event of default is to renegotiate the loan agreement. All aspects of the loan—payment schedule, interest rate, collateral, affirmative and negative covenants—may be renegotiated. When the circumstances of default are insignificant, the

> For example, TCBY would be in default if the company reported net income of $120 and had $100 in current maturities of long-term debt. These figures would equate to a profitability ratio (as defined in the loan agreement) of 1.2, which is less than the 1.5 required minimum.

---

[1] The obligation to comply with a financial covenant can be viewed as either an affirmative or a negative covenant. It is affirmative because it requires the company to comply with a restriction on a ratio value. It is negative in the sense that it restricts actions that would cause the covenant to be violated.

[2] Any covenant breach that existed at the date of the most recent balance sheet and that subsequently has not been cured (that is, remedied or corrected) should be disclosed in the notes to the financial statements (Financial Accounting Standards Board [FASB] Accounting Standards Codification [ASC] Section 235-10-S99: *Notes to Financial Statements—Overall—SEC Materials* also located in Rule 4–08[c] of Securities and Exchange Commission [SEC] Regulation S-X). When covenants are violated, the related debt must be reclassified as current if it is probable that the borrower will not be able to cure the default within the next 12 months. See FASB ASC 470-10-45-1: *Debt—Overall—Classification of Debt that Includes Covenants*.

creditor may waive the violation or give the borrower a period of time—a *grace period*—to correct the covenant breach. When the default is severe, the creditor may accelerate loan repayment (with interest) and terminate its relationship with the borrower. Although creditors rarely accelerate repayment, having this right substantially strengthens a lender's negotiating position with the borrower if problems arise.

RECAP

When it comes to a company's business decisions, what's best for managers and shareholders isn't always best for creditors. Debt covenants—including those based on accounting numbers—help reduce this conflict of interest. Creditors benefit because debt covenants reduce default risk, and shareholders benefit from the lowered cost of debt financing.

Mandated Accounting Changes May Trigger Debt Covenant Violation

When accounting standards setters such as the FASB or International Accounting Standards Board (IASB) issue new reporting standards, their goal is to improve the relevance and representational faithfulness of firms' financial statements. But new reporting standards often have unintended consequences. One of these unintended consequences is that adoption may trigger a debt covenant violation.

Electronic Data Systems Corporation (EDS) was one company with loan covenants potentially affected by what was then a proposed change in pension accounting. EDS had a loan covenant requiring a minimum amount of shareholders' equity (called *net worth* in the loan agreement), adjusted for net income and any money raised by selling new shares. A note in the 2005 annual report provides details about this covenant and two others with which EDS had to comply:

> Pension accounting rules are described in Chapter 14.

Following is a summary of the financial covenant requirements under our unsecured credit facilities and the calculated amount or ratios at December 31, 2005 (dollars in millions):

	As of and for the Year Ended December 31, 2005	
	Covenant	Actual
Minimum net worth	$6,420	$7,512
Leverage ratio	2.25	1.67
Fixed charge coverage ratio	1.15	2.37

The note shows that EDS was in compliance with all three covenants. Net worth, for example, was $7,512 million at the end of 2005, or 17% above the required minimum. Put another way, EDS had a net worth *safety margin* of $1,092 million (= $7,512 − $6,420), the dollar amount by which net worth could decline before triggering a covenant violation.

What would happen to this safety margin when EDS adopted the newly mandated pension accounting rules? According to one analyst, net worth was going to fall by as much as $1,060 million, eliminating virtually all of the safety margin, and placing EDS in a rather precarious position.

Borrowers and lenders recognize that covenant compliance can be jeopardized by mandated changes in accounting practices even though the real credit risk is unchanged. That is why many loan agreements have financial covenants that rely on *fixed GAAP*, that is, the accounting rules in place when the loan is first granted. This approach would allow EDS to continue to use old GAAP for covenant compliance tests even though new GAAP would be used in the company's audited financial statements. Loan covenants with fixed GAAP insulate the company from any adverse effects of mandatory accounting changes. However, fixed GAAP can be costly to implement, because it requires firms to operate multiple accounting systems. This problem can become even more difficult for a firm with several loan agreements entered into at different points in time, each calling for data based on a different version of GAAP.

How often is fixed GAAP used in loan agreements? One study found that roughly 75% of the loans examined included covenants tied to financial statement amounts. Roughly half of those used fixed GAAP and thus were insulated from mandatory accounting changes.[3]

When a loan agreement does not permit fixed GAAP, lenders still have the option to waive or renegotiate covenants that are distorted by an accounting standard update. That is what may have happened at EDS in 2006. The annual report that year indicated that EDS had renegotiated its unsecured credit facilities midyear, and the new loan no longer contained a minimum net worth covenant. Renegotiation thus alleviated the covenant violation problem caused when EDS began using the new pension accounting rule. Still, lenders are not required to renegotiate in such situations. So, if a borrower has become a less desirable credit risk over the years, a lender could use a covenant violation created by a mandated accounting change to force early repayment of a loan the lender would prefer not to hold any longer.

There may be more to the story, however. Elsewhere in the 2006 annual report, EDS revealed that when the new pension accounting rule took effect, it reduced net worth by only $0.566 billion, far less than the analyst had estimated. The covenant safety margin was reduced but a substantial margin remained intact. EDS may well have negotiated a new credit facility for other reasons such as to obtain a lower interest rate.

Managers' Responses to Potential Debt Covenant Violations

Violating a covenant is costly, so managers have strong incentives to make accounting choices that reduce the likelihood of technical default. Accounting choices include not only the selection of alternative accounting techniques (for example, LIFO versus FIFO inventory methods) but also accruals involving judgment (such as the bad debt provision) and decisions about when to initiate transactions that result in accounting gains or losses (for example, when assets are sold or the corporation is restructured). ***Readers of financial statements must be able to recognize and understand these incentives and their effects on managers' accounting choices.***

> A **technical default** occurs when the borrower violates one or more loan covenants but has made all interest and principal payments. A **payment default** occurs when the borrower is unable to make the scheduled interest or principal payment.

A number of studies have examined how debt-covenant-related incentives affect managers' accounting choices. One study looked at voluntary accounting changes made by 130 companies reporting covenant violations.[4] It found that net worth and working capital restrictions are the most frequently violated accounting-based covenants and that companies approaching default often make accounting choices that increase reported earnings. The most common techniques used at these companies to increase earnings are changes in pension cost assumptions (discussed in Chapter 14), the liquidation of LIFO layers, and the adoption of the FIFO inventory method (both discussed in Chapter 9).

Another study examined **discretionary accounting accruals,** noncash transactions that accrue revenues (as when Accounts receivable arising from credit sales are recognized) or expenses (as when Accrued warranties payable is increased by new warranty obligations).[5] This study looked at discretionary accruals by 94 companies reporting covenant violations

---

[3] M. B. Mohrman, "The Use of Fixed GAAP Provisions in Debt Contracts," *Accounting Horizons,* September 1996, pp. 78–91.

[4] A. P. Sweeney, "Debt-Covenant Violations and Managers' Accounting Responses," *Journal of Accounting and Economics,* May 1994, pp. 281–308.

[5] M. L. DeFond and J. Jiambalvo, "Debt Covenant Violation and Manipulation of Accruals," *Journal of Accounting and Economics,* January 1994, pp. 145–76.

Figure 7.1

HISTOGRAM OF NET WORTH COVENANT SLACK

Each column (bin) shows the frequency of loan/quarters (N = 2,339) when the borrowers' actual net worth falls below (negative slack) or above (positive slack) the minimum net worth level stipulated in each of 1,600 commercial loans.

Source: L. D. Dichev and D. J. Skinner, "Large-Sample Evidence on the Debt Covenant Hypothesis," *Journal of Accounting Research,* September 2002, pp. 1091–1124. Copyright © 2002. Used by permission of Wiley-Blackwell Publishing, Ltd.

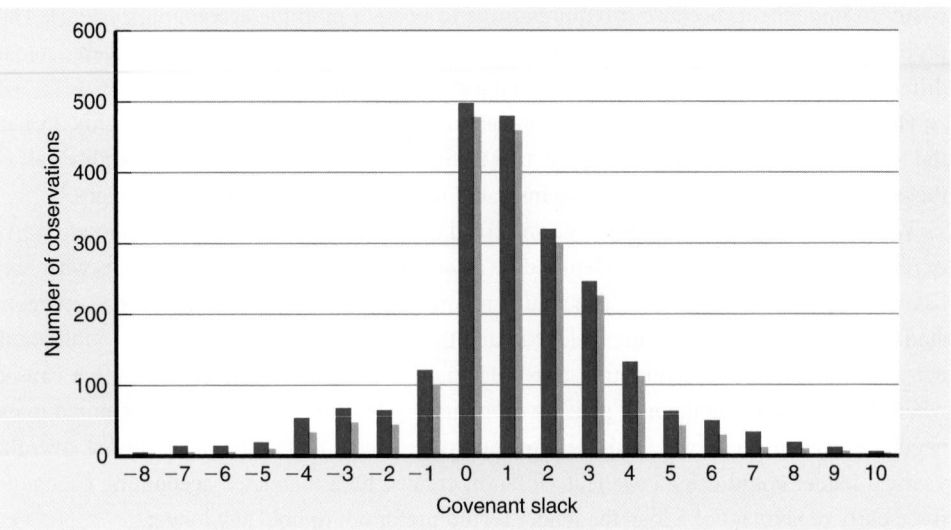

from 1985 to 1988. Accrual adjustments in the year prior to violation significantly increased reported earnings by accelerating revenue and postponing expenses. Moreover, these accrual adjustments also increased working capital in the year of the covenant violation.[6]

Yet another study provides compelling evidence that borrowers take actions to avoid debt covenant violations.[7] A detailed examination of roughly 1,600 commercial loans made to U.S. companies singled out two accounting-based covenants for analysis: a minimum net worth covenant and a minimum current ratio covenant. For each loan and covenant, the researchers calculated the amount of "slack" (or safety margin) available each quarter over the life of the loan. The data were then sorted into 19 bins based on the amount of slack available each quarter. If managers try to avoid covenant violations, we should see relatively few data points just below zero slack and relatively many data points just above zero.

Figure 7.1 depicts the results for minimum net worth covenants. As predicted, there are an unusually small number of loan/quarters where net worth falls just below the covenant minimum (i.e., slack is negative) and an unusually large number of loan/quarters with net worth just above the minimum (i.e., slack is zero or positive). A similar pattern was found for minimum current ratio covenants. Managers apparently take actions to avoid violating accounting-based covenants in commercial loans, but exactly how they sidestep a violation is less clear. As the researchers point out, borrowers can achieve the required covenant benchmark through their accounting choices, "real" actions such as issuing more stock to increase net worth, or other means.

Borrowers appear willing to pay substantially higher interest rates to retain accounting flexibility that may help them avoid covenant violations. One study of 206 bank loans found that interest rates are 75 basis points higher when the loan agreement allows "floating GAAP," meaning that accounting method changes can be used to increase covenant slack, rather than fixed GAAP.[8] Of course, these results could be because maintaining multiple sets of books, as would be the case under fixed GAAP, is more costly than the additional interest.

---

[6] Two early studies do not find support for the hypothesized influence of debt covenants on managers' accounting choices. See P. M. Healy and K. Palepu, "Effectiveness of Accounting-Based Dividend Covenants," *Journal of Accounting and Economics,* January 1990, pp. 97–133; and H. DeAngelo, L. DeAngelo, and D. J. Skinner, "Accounting Choice in Troubled Companies," *Journal of Accounting and Economics,* January 1994, pp. 113–43.

[7] L. D. Dichev and D. J. Skinner, "Large-Sample Evidence on the Debt Covenant Hypothesis," *Journal of Accounting Research,* September 2002, pp. 1091–1124.

[8] A. Beatty, K. Ramesh, and J. Weber, "The Importance of Accounting Changes in Debt Contracts: The Cost of Flexibility in Covenant Calculations," *Journal of Accounting and Economics,* June 2002, pp. 173–204.

These and other studies suggest that ***management tends to make accounting method changes and/or to manipulate discretionary accruals to avoid violating debt covenants.*** However, accounting maneuvers to avoid covenant violations are unlikely to be sustainable. Unsustainable earnings increases that boost net worth, for example, are unlikely to translate into permanent cash flow increases. Consequently, these "tenuous" earnings should be interpreted with caution.

Throughout the remainder of the book, we highlight how alternative accounting methods and accrual adjustments affect earnings, the balance sheet, and key financial ratios. We'll alert you to accounting choices that can have substantial implications for debt covenants. Keep them in mind as you go about interpreting and using accounting numbers for making economic decisions.

Although we have seen the important role covenants play in facilitating borrowing by reducing conflicts between lenders and borrowers, a number of so-called **covenant-lite** loans are made as well. These are loans that contain minimal covenants, providing the borrower with more freedom and the lender with less protection than an otherwise similar loan that is "covenant heavy." Covenant-lite loans became increasingly popular in 2006 and 2007 but lost popularity during the credit crisis. One study found that in 2007, covenant-lite loans accounted for over $140 billion, or about 20% of leveraged-loan[9] dollars. In 2008, that figure had dropped to about 3%. By 2011 it had grown again to about 18%. The study also found that covenant-lite loans are concentrated in high-risk borrowers (S&P ratings of BB and below), which is the opposite of what one might suspect at first. After all, when the borrower is a higher risk, the protection a covenant offers is likely to be seen as more valuable. Why have covenant-lite loans taken off and why are they concentrated in higher-risk companies? The study's authors argue that some institutional investors prefer the higher yields on covenant-lite loans to the lower yields they could get with covenant-heavy loans. That is, those investors value the extra yield more than they value the extra protection.[10]

MANAGEMENT COMPENSATION

Most modern corporations are not run by descendants of the founders but instead by professional managers. The resulting separation of ownership from control creates potential conflicts of interest between shareholders and managers.[11]

Consider a top executive whose job requires extensive travel and who, for reasons of "comfort and convenience," prefers the corporate jet to a commercial airline. Who receives the benefits of the comfort and convenience? And who pays the cost? If the comfort and convenience that comes from using the corporate jet leads to increased managerial productivity, both parties stand to gain. Shareholders lose, however, when the benefits of comfort and convenience accrue only to the executive and no productivity improvements result from it. That's because shareholders alone bear the added cost of corporate jet travel.

Potential conflicts of interest can be mitigated if managers are given incentives to behave as if they were owners. One way to do this is to provide a compensation package that links

> The corporate jet example illustrates one type of conflict between owners and managers: managers' tendency to "overconsume" company resources. But there are others. For example, managers who are near retirement age may have little incentive to adopt a long-term focus by investing in R&D because doing so reduces current earnings and thus earnings-based incentive pay.

[9] A leveraged loan is a loan made to a company that already is highly levered.

[10] See M. T. Billett, R. Elkamhi, L. Popov, and R. Pungaliya, "Bank Skin in the Game and Loan Contract Design: Evidence from Covenant-Lite Loans," Working Paper, August 2013. Their statistics are based on data from a proprietary database: S&P Leveraged Commentary and Data.

[11] To learn more about conflicts of interest between owners and managers see J. Boyd, R. Parrino, and G. Pritsch, "Stockholder-Manager Conflicts and Firm Value," *Financial Analysts Journal,* May/June 1998, pp. 14–30.

pay to improvements in firm value.[12] If a manager's compensation goes up as the organization's value increases, he or she has an incentive to take actions that lead to such an increase. As a result, both the manager and the owners will benefit.

Two ways to align managers' incentives with owners' interests are to link compensation to stock returns and/or to financial performance measures such as accounting earnings. Both approaches are widely used. Neither is perfect.

Consider stock returns. Managerial decisions clearly affect share prices in the long run. But in the short run, share prices could rise or fall due to factors that are beyond management's control, such as interest rate changes. And, for a division manager in a company with many divisions, most of the change in stock price is due to other managers' efforts and is not within that manager's control.

> Changes in interest rates affect stock prices for two reasons. To see why, consider the effect of a *decrease* in marketwide interest rates. First, notice that an interest rate decrease will reduce the company's cost of equity capital. As you know from Chapter 6, this will increase share price. Second, as interest rates decrease, the yields on fixed-rate bond investments fall, making them less attractive to investors. Both factors contribute to an increase in the demand for stocks and an increase in stock prices.

Similar problems cloud the linkage between compensation and financial performance measures such as earnings. On the positive side, earnings are probably less susceptible to the influence of temporary and external economic forces and, unlike stock returns, accounting-based financial performance measures can be tied to a manager's specific responsibilities, such as the profitability of a single product line, geographical region, or business unit. On the other hand, using accounting earnings as a performance measure is frequently criticized for its reliance on accruals, deferrals, allocations, and valuations that involve varying degrees of subjectivity and judgment. This is especially troublesome when the manager being evaluated can influence those judgments.

A good compensation plan must overcome the incentive alignment problems we have discussed and motivate managers to act like owners.[13]

How Executives Are Paid

Most compensation packages involve a base salary, an annual incentive, and a long-term incentive:

- **Base salary** is typically dictated by industry norms, the size of the company, and the executive's experience and specialized skills.

- **Annual incentives** set yearly financial performance goals that must be achieved if the executive is to earn various bonus awards. For example, a plan may specify that a bonus of 50% of annual salary is earned only if the after-tax return on assets for the company exceeds 12%. But a 100% bonus can be earned if the return on assets is 15% or more. Such plans link pay to performance; because compensation is "at risk," managers have an incentive to achieve plan goals.

- **Long-term incentives** motivate and reward executives for the company's long-term growth and prosperity (typically three to seven years). Long-term incentives are designed to counterbalance the inherently short-term orientation of other incentives.

---

[12] A more complete discussion of compensation incentives and owner-manager conflicts of interest is found in M. Jensen and W. Meckling, "Theory of the Firm: Managerial Behavior, Agency Costs and Ownership Structure," *Journal of Financial Economics,* October 1976, pp. 305–60; P. Milgrom and J. Roberts, *Economics, Organization, and Management* (Upper Saddle River, NJ: Prentice Hall, 1992); and R. Watts and J. Zimmerman, *Positive Accounting Theory* (Upper Saddle River, NJ: Prentice Hall, 1986). A summary of research on executive compensation is available in K. Murphy, "Executive Compensation," in O. Ashenfelter and D. Card (eds.), *Handbook of Labor Economics,* Vol. 3b (Elsevier Science North Holland, 1999), Chapter 38.

[13] Certain features of executive compensation packages are also designed to reduce the combined tax liability of the company and its managers. Tax considerations undoubtedly contribute to the popularity of certain pay practices and help explain their use by some companies but not others. See C. W. Smith and R. L. Watts, "Incentive and Tax Effects of Executive Compensation Plans," in R. Ball and C. W. Smith (eds.), *The Economics of Accounting Policy Choice* (New York: McGraw-Hill, 1992).

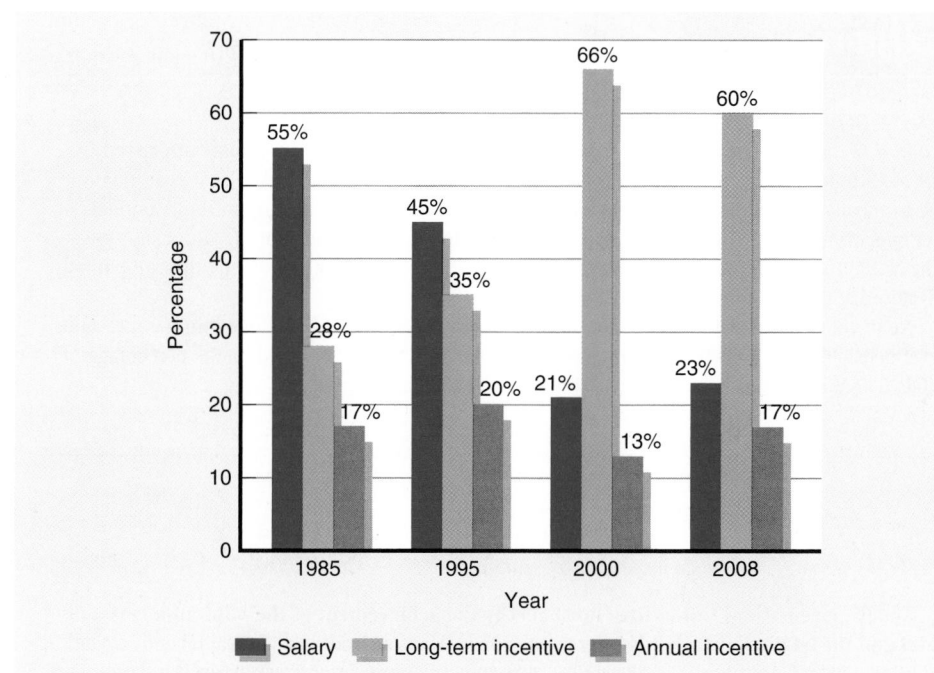

Figure 7.2

CEO COMPENSATION MIX

Annual incentive is a yearly performance-based bonus payment. Long-term incentive is a yearly award in cash, stock, or stock options for multi-year performance.

Source: The Conference Board, "Executive Annual Incentive Plans—1996" (New York: 1997); Hewitt Associates, "2008 Executive Compensation Pay Trends (2000–2008)" (Chicago, IL: November 2008).

Figure 7.2 shows the mix of compensation for chief executive officers in 1985, 1995, 2000, and 2008 based on annual surveys of pay practices at large U.S. companies. In 1985, base salary was 55% of the median total pay. Annual bonus payments and long-term incentive awards that year comprised 28% and 17%, respectively, of total pay.

Figure 7.2 shows that base salary has become a smaller component of total CEO compensation (55% in 1985 versus 23% in 2008), while long-term incentive awards have become a larger part of CEO pay (28% in 1985 versus 60% in 2008). This shift in compensation mix can be traced to the increased use of stock options and restricted stock in executive pay packages. As a result, $0.77 of each dollar of pay in 2008 came from annual incentives ($0.17) and long-term incentives ($0.60). This "at-risk" pay was substantially greater in 2008 than it was in 1985.

Within a given organization, the proportion of pay "at risk" falls off steeply for executives on lower rungs of the corporate ladder. One compensation survey found that corporate executives in large industrial companies had 71% of their pay at risk, midlevel managers had 20%, and nonmanagerial professionals had only 8%.[14]

> One of the earliest annual incentive plans was the General Motors Bonus Plan adopted in 1918. According to a former CEO of the company, "the interests of the corporation and its stockholders are best served by making key employees parties in the corporation's prosperity . . . each individual should be rewarded in proportion to his [sic] contribution to the profit of his [sic] own division and of the corporation as a whole."
>
> *Source:* Alfred P. Sloan, Jr., *My Years with General Motors* (New York: Doubleday & Company, 1964), p. 407.

Annual (Short-term) Incentives

The most common financial performance measure used in bonus plans is GAAP net income or some variation of it. For example, Exhibit 7.1 shows what Computer Associates International said about its 2003 annual incentive plan.

Notice that Computer Associates' shareholders approved the annual incentive plan (see ①). This means that the basic features of the plan—who participates, how performance is measured, the maximum payout as a percent of salary, and so on—were submitted to shareholders and approved by a formal vote at an annual meeting. Until recently, most companies did not

> Chapter 1 describes the accounting fraud uncovered in 2003 at Computer Associates—now CA Technologies. Case 7-5 tells you more.

---

[14] Hay Group, Inc., *1998 Hay Compensation Report* (1998).

EXHIBIT 7.1   **Computer Associates International**

Description of Annual Incentive Compensation Plan

Annual Incentives. [U]nder the Company's annual incentive plan ① **previously approved by the stockholders,** targeted payouts are determined at the beginning of each fiscal year based on the Company's ② achievement of (a) a minimum level of **revenue** and (b) threshold amounts of **net operating profit after taxes** (**NOPAT**), relative to the performance of the Company's peers. The NOPAT thresholds are derived from the financial forecasts of the Company that are publicly disclosed at the beginning of each fiscal year.

No payouts are made unless the minimum revenue level is achieved. If the minimum revenue level is reached, the **payout amount can range from 0% to 200%,** based on the percentage of NOPAT that is ③ achieved as compared to the threshold, as follows:

	% Target Payout
Below threshold	0%
At threshold	Up to 50%
Between threshold and target	Up to 100%
Between target and maximum	Up to 200%

The [Compensation] **Committee must certify the achievement of the minimum revenue level and the NOPAT thresholds** prior to each annual payout under the annual incentive plan. In addition, the ④ Committee has **discretion to reduce the amount of any payout** if it determines that, notwithstanding the achievement of the minimum amounts, a reduction is appropriate.

Source: Computer Associates International, 2003 Proxy Statement. (Emphasis and circled numbers added.)

request shareholder approval of their annual incentive plans, although a growing number began to do so because of shareholder pressure for pay transparency. Then, in 2010, Congress passed and President Obama signed the Dodd-Frank Wall Street Reform and Consumer Protection Act. Dodd-Frank mandated a nonbinding shareholder vote on executive compensation plans at least once every three years.

Computer Associates used two accounting-based performance measures, revenue and NOPAT, to determine managers' annual incentive pay (see ② and ③). The bonus formula had two components. First, the company must have achieved a minimum revenue goal each year before any bonus could be paid. Second, once the revenue goal was achieved, the amount of the bonus was determined by corporate profits (NOPAT) compared to a minimum and maximum profit threshold and a target profit amount.

Figure 7.3 illustrates how the NOPAT component of the bonus formula worked. Suppose revenue for the year exceeded the minimum required for bonus payments. The minimum NOPAT threshold for the year was set at $10 million, the target NOPAT at $20 million, and the maximum threshold at $30 million. To complete the illustration, assume the CEO's target bonus is $2 million, or a 10% share of the $20 million NOPAT.

As Figure 7.3 shows, no bonus would have been paid if NOPAT for the year were below the $10 million threshold. If NOPAT were to fall at the minimum threshold, the CEO would have received a bonus of $0.5 million (50% payout × 10% NOPAT bonus share × $10 million NOPAT). Between the minimum threshold and the target, the payout rate increases from 50% up to 100%. So, if the company reported NOPAT of $20 million, the CEO would have earned a bonus of $2 million (100% payout × 10% NOPAT bonus share × $20 million NOPAT).

Once NOPAT exceeded the $20 million target level, the payout rate would grow faster from 100% up to 200%. For example, the CEO would earn a bonus of $6 million if NOPAT reached $30 million ($6 million = 200% payout × 10% NOPAT bonus share × $30 million NOPAT). But there's a catch! The bonus formula put a cap on the *maximum* annual incentive

In the United States, top executive bonus opportunities typically range from 50% to 200% of salary as they did at Computer Associates. In the United Kingdom and other mature economies, maximum annual bonus levels have traditionally been lower. Short-term bonuses are also common in emerging economies.

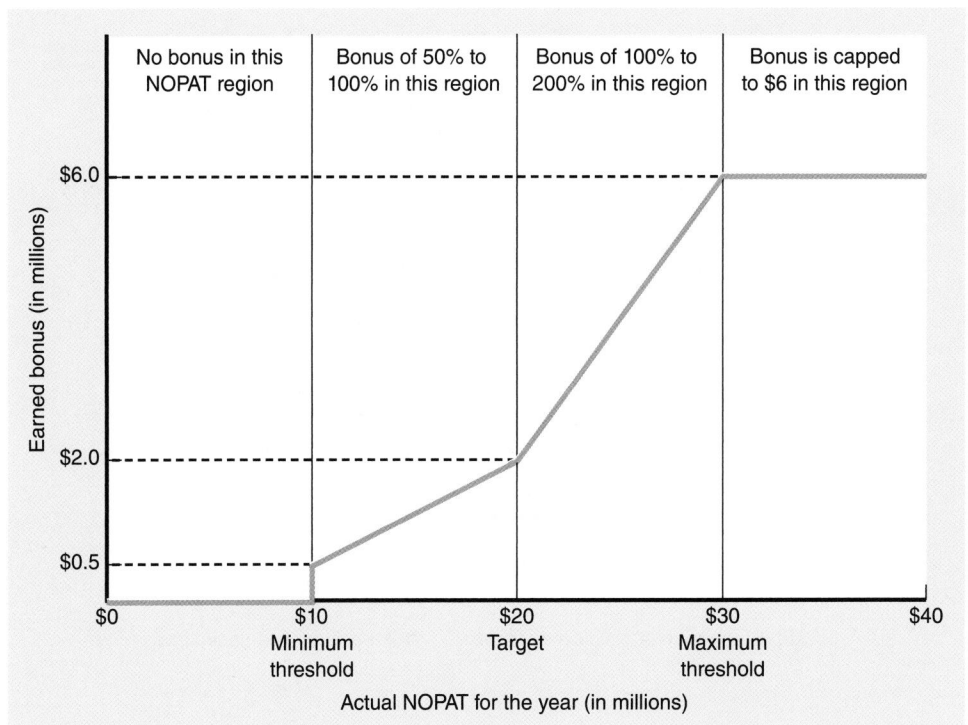

pay the CEO could earn. No matter how much above $30 million (the maximum threshold) NOPAT might be, the CEO's bonus would remain at $6 million that year.

At Computer Associates and most other companies, the compensation committee is responsible for implementing the executive pay plan (see ④). This committee selects the performance metrics to be used and sets the annual or multiyear performance goals for each executive. The committee can sometimes override the bonus formula when circumstances warrant. Computer Associates' compensation committee may reduce or eliminate the calculated award, but it may not increase the award. As we will see in a moment, compensation committees sometimes play an important role in reducing managers' incentives to meet the performance target using accounting "gimmickry."

Compensation committees are comprised of outside directors, ostensibly to eliminate the conflict of interest inherent in having executives set their own bonus targets. Still, it is never clear how independent outside directors really are from their internal peers on the board. Being an outside director can be lucrative, and even outside directors may not act entirely in the interests of shareholders if they fear that doing so could affect their ability to remain on the board.

> Notice how important one more profit dollar can be if it enables the company to report NOPAT of $10 million rather than $9,999,999. In our example, that one extra profit dollar causes the CEO's bonus to jump from $0 to $500,000. Top executive cash bonus awards at Computer Associates (now CA Technologies) are today still determined by a formula similar to the one depicted in Figure 7.3.

Long-Term Incentives　Long-term incentives constitute a large portion of total compensation for most CEOs, although many long-term plans are not tied directly to accounting numbers. Figure 7.4 shows the mix of long-term incentives by type.

> Stock options were not widely used by U.S. companies until the late 1980s. This form of long-term pay is less prevalent in other mature economies (e.g., the United Kingdom and Australia) and in emerging economies.

Stock options give the holder the right, but not the obligation, to buy company shares at a stated (exercise) price, typically the market price on the option grant date, for a period of years. If the stock price rises, the executive may trade in (or "exercise") each option plus pay the stated exercise price in exchange for a share of company stock. The option can only be

Figure 7.4

LONG-TERM
INCENTIVE MIX

SOURCE: Annual survey of 350 large U.S. companies conducted by Mercer Human Resource Consulting.

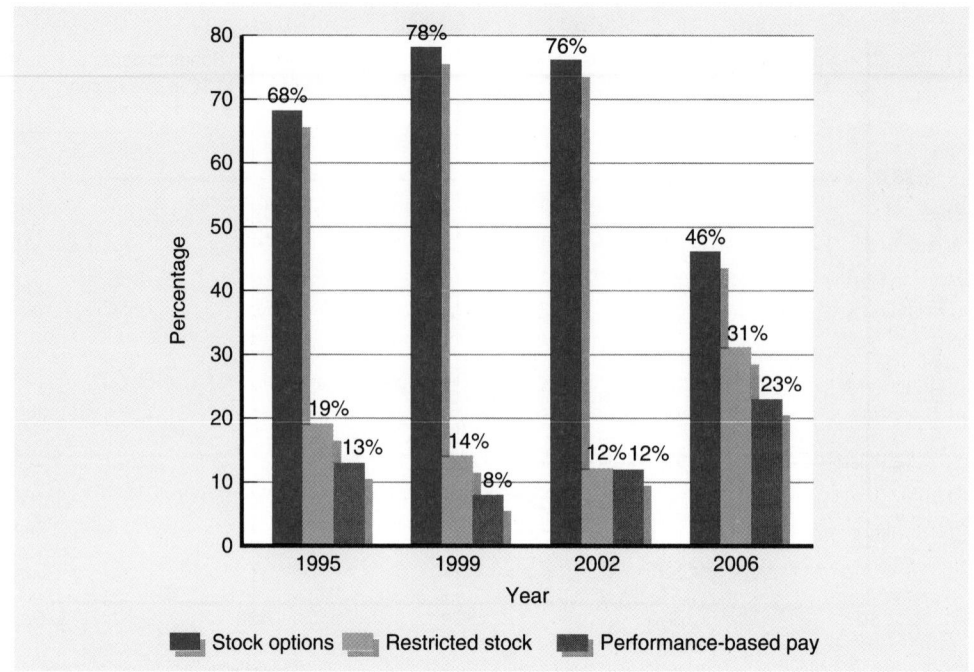

worth exercising if the market price of the underlying stock is above the exercise price. And, the option becomes more valuable as the stock price rises. So, the holder has an incentive to increase shareholder value as measured by stock price.

Stock grants give the executive outright ownership of company shares. **Restricted stock** is typically an award of stock that is nontransferable or subject to forfeiture for a period of years. The most prevalent restriction is one of continued employment, although performance-related conditions are sometimes applied. Dividends can be paid to the executive even when the stock is restricted, and some restricted stock awards carry immediate voting rights. Restricted stock grants provide a set of "golden handcuffs" for retaining executives, at least during the restriction period.

As Figure 7.4 shows, the use of restricted stock has grown substantially and the use of stock options has fallen since the FASB mandated the expensing of stock option costs in 2005. That rule change eliminated the financial reporting advantage stock options had over restricted stock.

Performance-based pay plans require the manager to achieve certain multiyear financial performance goals such as a three-year average return on equity (ROE) of at least 20%. The payout could be either cash or company shares. From a financial reporting perspective, these plans are important because performance goals are often tied to financial targets such as earnings per share growth or return-on-equity hurdles. Occasionally, the performance goals are strategic: increasing market share, reducing costs, or improving product quality. Performance goals are established at the beginning of the award period, which usually ranges from four to seven years, and may be stated in absolute terms or relative to the performance levels achieved by peer companies over the award period.

Performance plans have been a key element of long-term incentive compensation in many companies for a number of years. However, the Tax Reform Act of 1993 provided further impetus to link pay plans to specific performance goals. The Act limited to $1 million the federal income tax deduction that a public company may claim for nonperformance-based compensation paid to any of its top five executives. By linking top executive pay to specific performance goals, firms gain valuable tax benefits when compensation payouts exceed the $1 million threshold.

Proxy Statements and Executive Compensation

Information about a company's executive compensation practices can be found in the annual **proxy statement,** a notification of the annual shareholders meeting, filed each year with the SEC. Among other disclosures, this document describes both the compensation payments and awards made to the five highest paid executives of the company and any new executive compensation plans.

Although top executive compensation disclosures were mandated in 1933, a year before the SEC was created, the information provided was quite sparse. In the late 1980s, as top executive pay routinely began to exceed $1 million, major stockholders and the news media expressed outrage over the amounts paid, their questionable link to firm performance, and the inadequacy of required disclosures. This outrage was one reason the Tax Reform Act of 1993 included the $1 million cap on the corporate tax deduction for nonperformance-based top executive pay. The SEC also stepped into the fray in 1992 by dramatically expanding the required pay disclosures.

The stock option backdating scandal of 2006 led the SEC to expand the required disclosures for executive compensation even further.[15] By July of that year, the SEC was investigating more than 80 companies for reporting that options were granted at an earlier date than they in fact were. Invariably, the reported grant date coincided with a much lower stock price than the actual grant date, which allowed companies to set exercise prices below the stock price on the actual grant date without reporting any compensation expense under the accounting rules in effect at the time. More on this in Chapter 15.

Firms now provide a **compensation discussion and analysis (CD&A)** in the proxy statement. This disclosure requirement is similar in nature to the long-standing **management's discussion and analysis (MD&A)** for 10-K and 10-Q filings, which requires a report on the operations of the business "as seen through the eyes of management." Among other things, the CD&A must describe the specific items of corporate performance that are considered in making compensation decisions, how specific forms of compensation are structured and implemented to reflect performance, and the impact of accounting and tax treatments of the particular form of compensation.

> After the first batch of proxies arrived, the SEC told 350 companies they hadn't been specific enough. So, one of those companies—Applied Materials—expanded by 76% the word count of its proxy compensation section the next year. The expanded section was twice the length of the U.S. Constitution and its 27 amendments.
>
> *Source:* P. Drorak, "(New Math) × (SEC Rules) + Proxy = Confusion," *The Wall Street Journal,* March 21, 2008.

In addition to the CD&A, firms now provide detailed disclosure of three broad executive pay categories:

1. Compensation currently paid or deferred for the current fiscal year and the two preceding years, including stock options, restricted stock, and any other forms of compensation that are parts of the executive's pay plan.

2. Holdings of equity-related interests (stock options and restricted stock) that relate to current or prior period compensation.

3. Retirement and other postemployment compensation, including pensions, health care benefits, and benefits payable in the event of a change in control (so-called golden parachute payments).

---

[15] SEC Release 33-8765, *Executive Compensation Disclosure,* December 22, 2006; and Release 33-8732a, *Executive Compensation and Related Party Disclosure,* August 29, 2006. Release 33-8732a is 436 pages in length.

Whole Foods Market is one company that links incentive pay to economic value added, or EVA®, performance (see Case 7-3). EVA® is a performance metric popularized by the consulting firm Stern Stewart & Company. In its simplest form, EVA® is net operating profit after taxes (or NOPAT) minus a charge for the financial capital lenders and investors have put into the business (c* × Capital, where c* is the company's weighted average cost of capital). So, a company that earns $150 of NOPAT using $1,000 of capital with a c* of 10% will have generated $50 of EVA® ($150 − 0.10 × $1,000). Stern Stewart and most other economic value practitioners advocate making a variety of adjustments to GAAP income statements and balance sheets before performing the EVA® calculation. These adjustments are intended to eliminate certain accounting "distortions," many of which we describe in later chapters of this book.

This information must be disclosed for the chief executive officer and the chief financial officer regardless of their compensation and for the next three most highly paid executives serving as corporate officers if their total compensation is more than $100,000.

Incentives Tied to Accounting Numbers

Today, many companies use performance plans that rely on accounting information. Let's take a closer look at how annual bonus plans and long-term compensation are tied to accounting numbers.

The common performance measures used in annual and multiyear (long-term) incentive plans for senior corporate executives are shown in Figure 7.5. Most plans link incentive pay to one or more accounting-based performance measures, such as revenue, earnings per share, or return on equity. Economic value added (EVA®) is used in 12% of the plans, while operating cash flow is used in 10% of the plans.

In addition to accounting-based performance measures, the data in Figure 7.5 indicate that most plans also use nonfinancial performance measures to determine incentive pay. Financial metrics including last year's return on assets or earnings per share tell us about the past. However, nonfinancial metrics such as sales orders booked are lead indicators of future economic performance.[16] Many companies today combine nonfinancial performance metrics with accounting-based financial metrics (i.e., gross margin, operating income, and revenue) and market-based metrics (such as total shareholder return and stock price) to produce a "balanced scorecard" for evaluating managerial performance.[17] The balanced scorecard is intended to get managers to respond to the many facets of value creation and to recognize the tradeoffs to various actions, rather than to just maximize a single performance metric.

Figure 7.5

PERFORMANCE MEASURES USED IN ANNUAL AND MULTIYEAR CASH INCENTIVE PLANS

The individual percentages sum to more than 100% because many companies use multiple measures of performance. The results are based on a comprehensive survey of 2,700 U.S. companies.

Source: "Executive Annual Incentive Plans—1996." Copyright © 1996. Used with permission of The Conference Board. www.conference-board.org

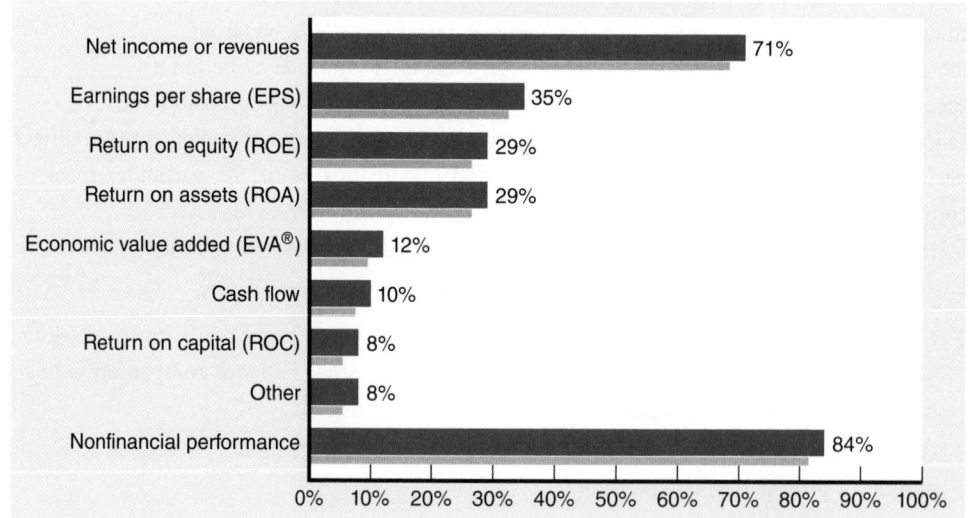

[16] To learn more about the use of nonfinancial performance measures in bonus plans, see C. D. Ittner, D. F. Larcker, and M. U. Rajan, "The Choice of Performance Measures in Annual Bonus Contracts," *The Accounting Review,* April 1997, pp. 231–55.

[17] See R. S. Kaplan and D. P. Norton, *The Balanced Scorecard* (Boston, MA: Harvard Business School Press, 1996).

The wide use of accounting-based incentives is controversial for at least four reasons:

First, sales and earnings growth does not automatically translate into increased shareholder value. Management can grow sales and earnings by expanding the size of the business through acquisitions or new investment. This strategy can produce substantial dollar increases in sales volume, operating earnings, and perhaps EPS. But these added profits don't necessarily increase shareholder value. For example, an acquisition at a price above the fair value of a target could increase sales and profits, but it will destroy value.

Second, the accrual accounting process itself can distort traditional measures of performance. Consider return on assets (ROA). Companies that show improving ROA often do so because of real profitability gains: higher revenues or lower expenses. However, some ROA improvements are due to the mechanics of depreciation accounting. To see this, consider a business that generates $150 of net income before depreciation each year and pays that same amount out as a dividend. The business opens on January 1, 2014, with total assets of $1,000 and no debt. Half of those assets ($500) are equipment. The annual depreciation charge for the equipment is $50, so net income is $100. The company's ROA for 2014 is 10% ($100 of net income divided by $1,000 of beginning assets). But next year ROA will increase to about 10.5%. And the year after that, ROA will be 11.1%. Why? Because depreciation accounting has reduced the book value of total assets.

As a stockholder in the company, you probably don't want to pay an ROA bonus for nothing more than depreciation accounting. It's better instead to reward management for real profitability improvement and to ignore the profit growth illusion created by depreciation accounting. That's why some companies prefer return on gross investment (ROGI, or net income divided by total *gross* assets) as a performance metric in their bonus plans.

> ROA for 2015 equals the $100 of net income, divided by net assets of $950 (after subtracting $50 of accumulated depreciation) or 10.5%. The 11.1% ROA calculation for 2016 is $100 of net income, divided by net assets of $900 (after subtracting $100 of accumulated depreciation).

Third, accounting-based incentive plans can encourage managers to adopt a short-term focus. Consider the typical bonus plan in Figure 7.6. The executive receives a bonus equal to 100% of base salary if annual EPS reaches the $3.50 target. The bonus award declines to 50% of base salary for EPS performance at the $3.00 level, and it escalates to 150% for EPS at the $4.00 level. If EPS falls below $3.00, no bonus is awarded; at EPS above $4.00, the bonus remains 150% of base salary.

To see how accounting-based incentives might contribute to a short-term focus, consider an executive who believes current business conditions will allow the company to earn only $2.80 EPS for the year. Despite these unfavorable (no bonus) conditions, the executive can

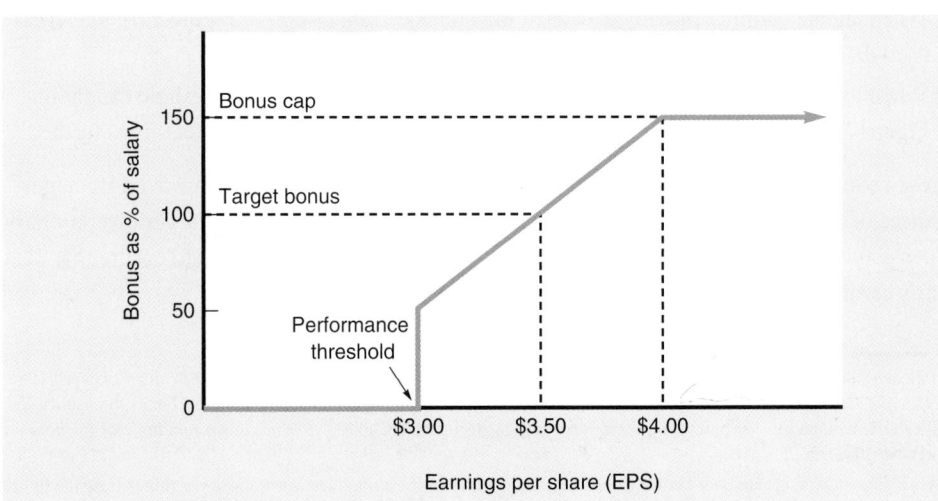

Figure 7.6

TYPICAL STRUCTURE OF
ANNUAL PERFORMANCE
BONUSES

still achieve the $3.00 EPS minimum required for a bonus by cutting back on critical research and development. Research expenses go down, reported earnings go up, and bonuses are paid! This short-term strategy can prove costly in the long term if a competitor introduces a new product based on the technology the company had been researching. Of course, the same unsustainable short-term earnings increase can be achieved by delaying essential maintenance and repairs or by postponing other key operating expenditures.

Executives also have an incentive to "manage down" reported earnings when the accounting benchmark (EPS in this example) is *above* the upper bonus limit. Suppose our executive believes that current business conditions will enable the company to earn $4.20 EPS this year. Here the executive has an incentive to reduce reported earnings to $4.00, deferring the excess to the future. After all, the same bonus is awarded no matter whether EPS is at the $4.00 or $4.20 level!

How can excess earnings be deferred? It's easy! Delay some fourth-quarter customer shipments until the beginning of next year. Current year's sales decline and earnings fall without affecting this year's bonus; the delayed sales and earnings count toward next year's bonus. You don't lose anything this year, and you increase the probability of earning the bonus next year.

Fourth, executives have some discretion over the company's accounting policies, and they can use that discretion to achieve bonus goals. For example, an executive falling short of the $3.00 EPS minimum might deliberately reduce fourth-quarter inventories, report a "LIFO liquidation" gain, and boost earnings to a level above the bonus threshold. (LIFO liquidations are discussed in Chapter 9.) Or, if earnings performance is so low that reaching the bonus threshold is impossible, the manager has an incentive to reduce earnings further. The objective of these deliberate earnings reductions, called *big baths,* is simple. Today's write-offs reduce future expenses because written-off assets will not be depreciated. The result is to increase future earnings—and future bonuses—with no reduction in current bonuses below the zero level they would be at anyway. Examples of big-bath write-offs include asset impairments and large restructuring charges as described in Chapter 3. Accounting discretion also allows managers who believe earnings will exceed the bonus ceiling to play bonus "games": reduce reported earnings down to the bonus ceiling and defer the excess.

Research Evidence   Do managers use accounting flexibility to achieve bonus goals? One study, which looked at annual bonus plans like the one in Figure 7.6, revealed two things:

1. When annual earnings already exceeded the bonus ceiling ($4.00 in Figure 7.6), managers used discretionary accounting options to *reduce* earnings.

2. When it was clearly evident that earnings would be below the bonus threshold ($3.00 in Figure 7.6), managers used their financial reporting flexibility to reduce earnings further.[18]

These reductions in earnings had no effect on that year's bonus but improved managers' chances of receiving bonuses the following year. That's because taking a larger discretionary expense this year often meant a smaller expense next year, and that helped to ensure that next year's earnings would meet or beat the bonus target.[19]

---

[18] P. Healy, "The Effect of Bonus Schemes on Accounting Decisions," *Journal of Accounting and Economics,* April 1985, pp. 85–108. Later studies find mixed evidence on managers' use of accounting discretion around bonus thresholds. See T. Fields, T. Lys, and L. Vincent, "Empirical Research on Accounting Choice," *Journal of Accounting and Economics,* September 2001, pp. 255–308.

[19] When current earnings are poor but future earnings are expected to be strong, managers borrow earnings from the future for use in the current period. See M. L. DeFond and C. W. Park, "Smoothing Income in Anticipation of Future Earnings," *Journal of Accounting and Economics,* July 1997, pp. 115–39.

Another study examined motivations for controversial debt extinguishment transactions called **insubstance defeasances.**[20] These transactions were widely believed to generate artificial profits, and the FASB subsequently forbade them in 1996.[21] The evidence is that some firms used these transactions to window-dress earnings and to avoid restrictions in bond covenants. Again, the research findings show that managers sometimes use accounting flexibility to evade contract constraints to gain bonus benefits.

Several studies show that incoming CEOs have an incentive to decrease earnings in the year of the executive change and increase earnings in the next year.[22] Doing so presumably allows the new CEO to take credit for the company's apparent improvement.

Another study confirmed that R&D expenditures tend to decline during the years immediately prior to a CEO's retirement.[23] Existing GAAP requires R&D expenditures to be expensed as incurred, thereby reducing income and bonuses.[24] By reducing R&D expenditures before they retired, CEOs were able to increase their final bonus payouts.

Protection Against Short-Term Focus   The abuses just described explain why compensation plans typically include long-term, equity-based incentive components that are specifically intended to mitigate the short-term focus of executives. Although early research findings were mixed, a recent and comprehensive study found no evidence indicating that CEO equity incentives contribute to accounting irregularities.[25] Stock options (and stock ownership) give managers a strong incentive to avoid shortsighted business decisions and instead operate the company in ways that create shareholder value. That's why today stock and stock option portfolios rather than cash compensation and other benefits are the major determinants of top executives' wealth.

Another factor that can reduce short-term focus is the fact that incentive compensation plans are administered by a compensation committee comprised of the company's outside (nonmanagement) directors. The committee can intervene when circumstances warrant modification of the scheduled incentive award. For example, intervention might arise when a mandatory change in an accounting principle occurs. In general, the compensation committee can adjust the incentive award whenever it believes that current earnings have been unduly influenced by special items or other possible accounting distortions.

For example, language of the following sort is typical in many compensation agreements:

> At any time prior to the payment of performance awards, the compensation committee may adjust previously established performance targets and other terms and conditions . . . to reflect major unforeseen events such as changes in laws, regulations, or accounting practices, mergers, acquisitions, divestitures, or extraordinary, unusual, or nonrecurring items or events.[26]

---

[20] J. R. M. Hand, P. J. Hughes, and S. E. Sefcik, "Insubstance Defeasances: Security Price Reactions and Motivations," *Journal of Accounting and Economics,* May 1990, pp. 47–89. The transaction allowed a company to account for a liability "as if extinguished" when cash or other assets were placed irrevocably in a trust that then made all remaining principal and interest payments on the debt.

[21] See FASB ASC Section 405-20-55-4: *Liabilities—Extinguishments of Liabilities—Implementation Guidance and Examples—In-Substance Defeasance Transactions.*

[22] J. Elliott and W. Shaw, "Write-offs as Accounting Procedures to Manage Perceptions," *Journal of Accounting Research,* Supplement 1988, pp. 91–119; J. Francis, D. Hanna, and L. Vincent, "Causes and Effects of Discretionary Accounting Write-offs," *Journal of Accounting Research,* Supplement 1996, pp. 117–34; S. Pourciau, "Earnings Management and Non-routine Executive Changes," *Journal of Accounting and Economics,* January–July 1993, pp. 317–36.

[23] P. M. Dechow and R. G. Sloan, "Executive Incentives and The Horizon Problem: An Empirical Investigation," *Journal of Accounting and Economics,* March 1991, pp. 51–89.

[24] FASB ASC 730-10-25: *Research and Development—Overall—Recognition.*

[25] C. Armstrong, A. Jagolinzer, and D. Larcker, "Chief Executive Officer Equity Incentives and Accounting Irregularities," *Journal of Accounting Research,* May 2010, pp. 225–88.

[26] J. D. England, "Executive Pay, Incentives and Performance," in D. E. Logue (ed.), *Handbook of Modern Finance* (Boston: Warren, Gorham & Lamont, 1996), p. E9–18.

Some companies have taken the added step of adopting formal "compensation recovery" policies. At Krispy Kreme Doughnuts, for example, top executives forfeit past annual and long-term incentive payments if it is later discovered that they engaged in financial reporting abuses, fraud, embezzlement, or other dishonest actions detrimental to the company.

Compensation committees *can* adjust incentive awards for unusual or nonrecurring items and events, but do they? One study looked at the pay practices of 376 large public companies and found that nonrecurring gains tend to flow through to compensation, but losses do not.[27] Compensation committees apparently shield top managers from bonus reductions when net income is decreased by nonrecurring losses, but top managers reap higher bonus awards when net income is increased by nonrecurring gains.

RECAP

Compensation plans should align managers' incentives with shareholders' objectives. Many compensation plans link incentive pay to accounting numbers. This linkage creates an effective management incentive because improved financial performance generally translates into greater shareholder wealth. Unfortunately, accounting numbers can be manipulated. Consequently, compensation plans tied to financial goals sometimes backfire because of the short-term, self-interest focus of executives. Multiyear incentive pay plans and compensation committee intervention can mitigate executives' short-term focus.

Catering to Wall Street

Many companies, at one time or another, massage their numbers using creative accounting techniques, and probably do it now more than ever. . . . The issue isn't so much whether many companies are committing fraud—that's likely confined to a small group of dishonest executives. For most companies, it isn't even a matter of stretching the rules to wildly inflate their results. It's more a question of how many companies, following standard accounting guidelines, use loopholes to tweak their earnings numbers here and there just to make the crucial number, earnings per share, look better.[28]

The prevalence of stock options in executive pay packages may actually contribute to, rather than moderate, managers' short-term focus. Penny differences in EPS matter a lot to investors; just watch what happens to a company's share price when quarterly EPS comes in one cent below analysts' expectations.[29] And when investors penalize firms that fail to meet analysts' EPS targets, the penalty—a lower stock price—makes executive stock options less valuable. In contrast, firms that report continuous growth in annual EPS are priced at a premium relative to other firms.[30] This price premium translates into more valuable executive stock options.

Critics argue that stock options thus encourage managers to cater to Wall Street's short-term earnings expectations. And managers appear to do so. As you may recall from Chapter 3, actual EPS numbers do not fall randomly around analysts' consensus EPS estimates. Instead, too many firms report EPS numbers that just meet or beat the estimate while too few report EPS that falls just short of the estimate (see Figure 3.2). As one commentator notes, "Managements try to give investors what they want, and companies whose earnings are predictable are prized on Wall Street, which does not like unhappy surprises."[31]

---

[27] J. J. Gaver and K. M. Gaver, "The Relation Between Nonrecurring Accounting Transactions and CEO Cash Compensation," *The Accounting Review,* April 1998, pp. 235–54.

[28] K. Brown, "Tweaking Results Is Hardly a Sometime Thing," *The Wall Street Journal,* February 6, 2002.

[29] In February 2001, Cisco Systems lost 13% of its market value over the two days after it announced earnings that fell one cent short of expectations. For large-sample evidence, see D. Skinner and R. Sloan, "Earnings Surprises, Growth Expectations, and Stock Returns or Don't Let an Earnings Torpedo Sink Your Portfolio," *Review of Accounting Studies,* June 2002, pp. 289–312.

[30] M. E. Barth, J. A. Elliott, and M. W. Finn, "Market Rewards Associated with Patterns of Increasing Earnings," *Journal of Accounting Research,* Autumn 1999, pp. 387–413.

[31] A. Berenson, "Tweaking Numbers to Meet Goals Comes Back to Haunt Executives," *The New York Times,* June 29, 2002.

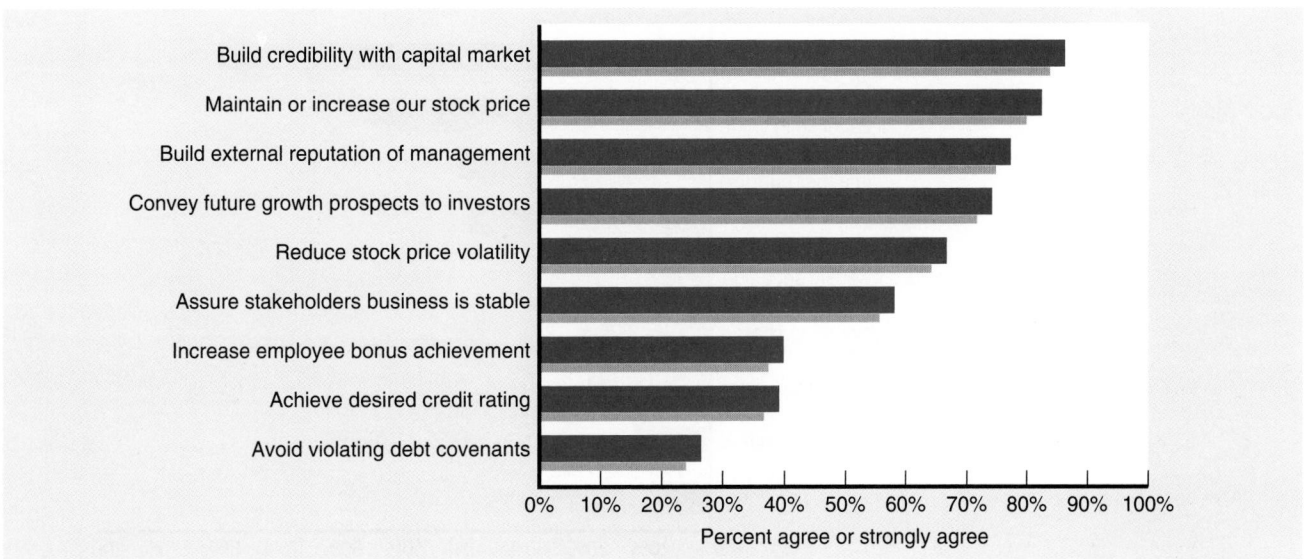

Figure 7.7 WHY MEET EARNINGS BENCHMARKS?

How 401 financial executives at U.S. companies responded to the question: "Meeting earnings benchmarks helps …"

Source: J. R. Graham, C. R. Harvey, and S. Rajgopal, "The Economic Implications of Corporate Financial Reporting," *Journal of Accounting and Economics,* December 2005, p. 27. Copyright © 2005 with permission from Elsevier Ltd.

A survey of more than 400 financial executives at U.S. companies paints a telling picture about why managers cater to Wall Street.[32] Figure 7.7 summarizes the findings. When asked why it is important to meet earnings benchmarks, an overwhelming 86% said it helps build credibility with the capital market. More than 80% agreed that meeting benchmarks helps maintain or increase the firm's stock price. They also believe that meeting earnings benchmarks enhances their external reputations, conveys favorable information about future growth prospects, and reduces stock price volatility. Compensation, credit ratings, and debt covenant violations are second-order concerns. Less than half of the financial executives said meeting earnings benchmarks helps employees achieve bonuses or the firm to achieve desired credit ratings. Fewer still (26%) said meeting earnings benchmarks helps to avoid debt covenant violations.

How do firms meet their earnings benchmarks? For many companies, the answer lies in operational excellence: providing customers highly-valued products and services, controlling costs, and attending to a myriad of business details. But what if it looks like the company will fall short of the desired earnings target? In this case, managers are tempted to take real actions to maintain accounting appearances, actions that are costly to shareholders. The evidence is in Figure 7.8.

Nearly 80% of the financial executives surveyed said they would decrease discretionary spending on items such as research, advertising, and maintenance to meet an earnings target. Some said they would put off or do only minimal maintenance to hit benchmarks even if it meant equipment would wear out more quickly. More than half reported they would postpone a new project even if it meant a sacrifice in long-term firm value.

The surveyed executives voiced little support for taking accounting actions to hit earnings targets. Less than half said they would borrow revenue from next quarter and use it to bolster

---

[32] J. R. Graham, C. R. Harvey, and S. Rajgopal, "The Economic Implications of Corporate Financial Reporting," *Journal of Accounting and Economics,* December 2005, pp. 3–73.

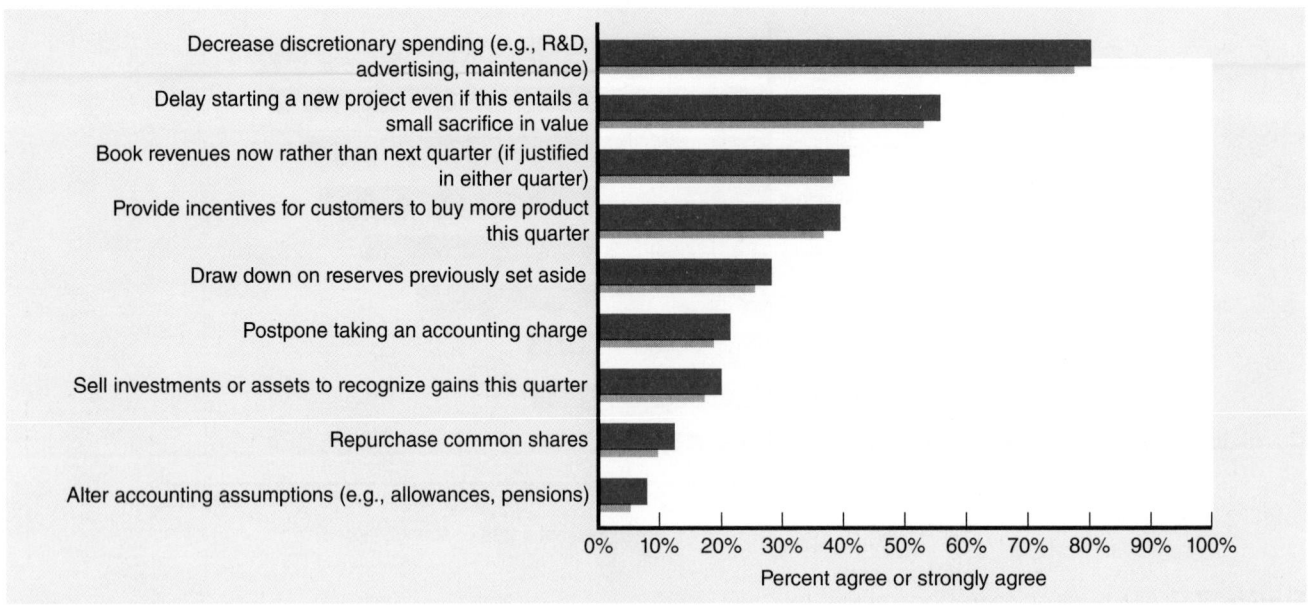

Figure 7.8 HOW EARNINGS BENCHMARKS ARE SOMETIMES MET

How 401 financial executives at U.S. companies responded to the question: "Near the end of the quarter, it looks like your company might come in below the desired earnings target. Within what is permitted by GAAP, which of the following choices might your company make?"

Source: J. R. Graham, C. R. Harvey, and S. Rajgopal, "The Economic Implications of Corporate Financial Reporting," *Journal of Accounting and Economics,* December 2005, p. 35. Copyright © 2005 with permission from Elsevier Ltd.

current period revenue. Fewer still said they would draw down accounting reserves (28%), postpone taking an accounting charge (21%), or alter accounting assumptions such as those relating to the allowance for doubtful accounts (8%). As one executive explained, auditors can second-guess the firm's accounting policies, but they can't readily challenge real economic actions to meet earnings targets that are taken in the ordinary course of business. What the executive failed to point out is that these accounting actions—drawing down a reserve, postponing a charge, and so on—violate GAAP and U.S. securities laws if the resulting financial statements misrepresent firm performance and condition.

Managers have strong incentives to achieve short-term earnings benchmarks. Some do so through operational excellence. For others, the path to beating benchmarks involves taking real actions that may harm shareholders in the long term or using accounting gimmicks that mask underlying firm performance.

REGULATORY AGENCIES

Financial statements used by creditors and shareholders are prepared under GAAP. But banks, insurance companies, public utilities, and many others must also provide financial statements to the government agencies that regulate them. Those statements are prepared under **regulatory accounting principles,** or **RAP,** to satisfy specific regulatory objectives.

RAP comprises the methods that must be followed in financial statements for the regulatory agency responsible for monitoring firm activities. Regulators may use RAP financial reports to set the prices customers may be charged, as a basis for supervisory action, as a source of statistical information, or as an early warning signal for monitoring a company's financial health. RAP often deviates from GAAP. Here's an example of a disclosure related to such a deviation:

> Under regulatory accounting, the company capitalizes both interest and equity costs during periods of construction. (SBC Communications, annual report)

GAAP allows the cost of debt (called *interest*) to be treated as just another construction project cost, but "equity costs" are not capitalized under GAAP (see Chapter 10). So, SBC Communications is telling annual report readers that its treatment of equity cost complies with RAP but deviates from GAAP. As a result, the company's completed construction projects— its telephone lines and related facilities—are shown at higher book values than would be the case if GAAP were used.

Why do shareholders, creditors, and other statement readers care about RAP if companies use it only when preparing financial reports for regulatory agencies? The answer is that ***RAP sometimes shows up in the company's GAAP financial statements too.*** Why? Because GAAP allows rate-regulated companies such as SBC Communications to account for and report assets and liabilities consistent with the way in which regulators establish rates as long as:

- the rates are designed to recover the costs of providing the regulated service, and
- the competitive environment makes it reasonable to assume that such rates can be charged and collected.[33]

So, SBC Communications not only capitalizes equity costs in its financial reports to industry regulators but also does so in its published financial statements for shareholders and creditors.

> *Knowing how a company accounts for its business transactions—whether it uses GAAP or RAP—is essential to gaining a clear understanding of its financial performance and condition.*

There's another reason why shareholders and creditors need to understand RAP as well as GAAP. Financial reports affect the regulatory process: a rate increase may be denied or a regulatory sanction may be imposed based on the reported numbers. This possibility can influence both management's GAAP accounting choices and when transactions are recorded.

To see how, let's take a look at banks, savings institutions, and credit unions.

> The published balance sheets of rate-regulated companies will also contain **regulatory assets and liabilities** that reflect anticipated future rate adjustments, deferred costs, and delayed obligations specific to the regulatory process.

Capital Requirements in the Banking Industry

Federal and state regulatory agencies require banks and other financial institutions to meet **minimum capital requirements.** The purpose of these requirements is to ensure the institution remains financially sound and can meet its obligations to depositors.

The test for capital adequacy involves the following question: Does the amount of investor capital (think of "adjusted" stockholders' equity) or the ratio of investor capital to gross assets—both defined by RAP—exceed the minimum level required? If so, the bank is considered to have adequate capital. If bank capital falls below the required level, regulatory intervention can be triggered.

Suppose that Hometown Bank & Trust has gross assets of $900 million and investor capital of $135 million, and suppose the bank's regulator sets a 10% minimum capital ratio.

---

[33] FASB ASC 980-10-15: *Regulated Operations—Overall—Scope and Scope Exceptions.*

Hometown is in compliance with the capital requirement because it has a **capital adequacy ratio** of 15%, calculated as:

> Because different types of financial assets have different credit risk profiles, banking regulators use a "risk-weighted" asset measure in the capital adequacy ratio. Bank capital requirements played an important role in the global financial meltdown of 2008 as you will soon learn from the discussion later in this chapter.

$$\text{Capital adequacy ratio} = \frac{\text{Invested capital (as defined by RAP)}}{\text{Gross assets (as defined by RAP)}}$$

$$= \frac{\$135 \text{ million}}{\$900 \text{ million}} = 15\%$$

which is above the 10% minimum benchmark.

Regulators have a powerful weapon to encourage compliance with minimum capital guidelines. They can impose costs on banks and financial institutions found to be in noncompliance. For example, a noncomplying bank:

- Is required to submit a comprehensive plan describing how and when its capital will be increased.
- Can be examined more frequently by the regulator.
- Can be denied a request to merge, open new branches, or expand services.
- Can be prohibited from paying any dividends.

> A bank's **loan loss provision** is the estimated bad debt expense associated with its loan receivables. Loan loss provisions are expenses that reduce bank net income but (under RAP) have no impact on invested capital. **Loan charge-offs** are loans the bank no longer expects to collect. Loan charge-offs decrease bank capital but have no impact on bank net income.

Because regulators can restrict bank operations, a bank with inadequate capital incurs greater regulatory costs than does a bank with adequate capital.

Bank managers can avoid the regulatory costs of failing to meet minimum capital requirements in several ways. The best approach is to operate profitably and invest wisely so the bank remains financially sound. Another way is to choose accounting policies that increase RAP invested capital or decrease RAP gross assets so the bank can pass its capital adequacy test. Let's examine this "artificial" approach to regulatory compliance.

The cash banks receive from depositors is used to make loans. These loans typically represent the bank's single largest asset. Uncollected loans are a significant cost in the banking industry. But bank managers have some discretion over estimates of uncollectibles and when those estimates are recorded. This discretion can be used to improve the bank's capital adequacy ratio. How? Understate the loan loss provision and loan charge-offs for the year. This improves the bank's capital adequacy ratio and simultaneously increases the net income figure reported to shareholders. But these improvements are just an illusion. In reality, the bank expects more uncollectibles than the financial reports show. Understating loan loss provisions and charge-offs may help avoid noncompliance with bank capital requirements, but this strategy hides the bank's true performance and condition from both regulators and shareholders. So, evading RAP guidelines can impede accurate financial analysis.[34]

Rate Regulation in the Electric Utilities Industry

Public utility commissions are governmental agencies that set prices utility companies may charge. Most commissions use accounting-determined costs and asset values in their rate formulas. A typical rate formula for an electric utility looks like this:

> Allowed revenue = Operating costs + Depreciation + Taxes + (ROA × Asset base)

---

[34] For more insights about the influence of capital adequacy regulation on banks' accounting choices, see A. Beatty, S. Chamberlain, and J. Magliolo, "Managing Financial Reports of Commercial Banks: The Influence of Taxes, Regulatory Capital, and Earnings," *Journal of Accounting Research,* Autumn 1995, pp. 231–261; and D. Skinner, "The Rise of Deferred Tax Assets in Japan: The Role of Deferred Tax Accounting in the Japanese Banking Crisis," *Journal of Accounting and Economics,* December 2008, pp. 218–39.

where allowed revenue determines the rates customers are charged and ROA is the return on assets allowed by the regulator. The rate formula sets total allowed revenue equal to an amount that covers the company's operating costs and provides a "fair" return on the capital invested in operating assets.

Suppose Midwest Power & Light has annual operating costs, depreciation, and taxes of $300 million, $500 million of capital is invested in operating assets, and the state public service commission sets the allowed ROA at 10%. The annual allowed revenue would be:

$$\text{Allowed revenue} = \$300 \text{ million} + (10\% \times \$500 \text{ million})$$
$$= \$300 \text{ million} + \$50 \text{ million} = \$350 \text{ million}$$

To arrive at a rate per kilowatt-hour of electricity, the $350 million of revenue allowed is divided by the company's *estimate* of total kilowatt-hours to be sold during the year.

Industry RAP governs what items are included in a regulated utility's operating costs and asset base. The definitions of what is included in operating costs and the asset base are important because included items are charged to customers, but disallowed items are charged to shareholders. Consider this example: Midwest Power & Light spends $10 million on customer safety advertising and $50 million on corporate "image" advertising. Customer safety advertising is an allowed operating cost, so it is included in the rate formula. Customers ultimately pay for the $10 million spent on safety advertising through higher electricity rates. Corporate image advertising is not an allowed cost in most states, so the $50 million Midwest Power & Light spent promoting itself cannot be passed on to customers in the form of higher electricity rates. Who pays the bill? Shareholders do. Regulators apparently see image advertising as unnecessary. Consequently, they do not require customers to pay for it through higher electricity rates.

Although industry RAP treats customer safety advertising and corporate image advertising differently, GAAP does not. Both types of advertising would be included in operating costs on the company's income statement. Other points of divergence between public utility RAP and GAAP are:

- **Deferring costs** that would otherwise be charged to expense by nonregulated companies: Utilities can postpone expensing storm damage costs, for example, as long as it is *probable* that those specific deferred costs are subject to recovery in future revenues,

- **Capitalizing equity costs** on construction projects whereas interest alone can be capitalized by nonregulated companies.

Rate regulation creates incentives for public utility managers to increase the reported asset base. Suppose Midwest Power & Light signs a $700,000, one-year rental agreement for service vehicles. If the rental payment is an allowed operating cost for rate-making purposes, customers would pay $700,000 in higher electricity rates. In contrast, if the rental is included in the company's regulatory asset base, customers would pay $770,000, or 10% more: $700,000 for depreciation (the full cost of the one-year asset) plus another $70,000 so that shareholders receive the allowed 10% return on the $700,000 asset.

Given the choice, utility company shareholders would prefer to have the rental payment treated as an asset for rate-making purposes. The company could then charge customers an extra $70,000. One way to make this happen is to design the rental contract so that it qualifies for RAP treatment as an asset. (We show you how in Chapter 12.) Another approach is to lobby regulators to relax the rules governing when a rental contract qualifies for asset treatment. ***Change the contract or change the accounting***

> In 2002, Duke Energy agreed to pay $25 million to its customers to settle allegations that the company had *underreported* its net income to avoid having to reduce its electricity rates. Profits were underreported by $123 million (pre-tax) because the company overstated RAP expenses. See Case 7-4.

rules. The result is the same. Adding more dollars to the asset base increases the allowed revenue stream for a rate-regulated company.

Taxation

Chapter 10 explains GAAP depreciation expense and the straight-line method; depreciation expense under tax law is described in Chapter 13.

The Internal Revenue Code (IRC), Internal Revenue Service (IRS) regulations, and court cases govern the determination of income for tax purposes. Tax accounting rules can be thought of as just another type of RAP. Many tax accounting rules are the same as GAAP rules. However, there are situations where tax rules differ from GAAP.

A case in point is depreciation expense. GAAP requires companies to spread the cost of assets like equipment and buildings over the period of intended use. The amount charged to depreciation each year can be computed using one of several methods. Tax rules, however, require companies to use a strict schedule called the Modified Accelerated Cost Recovery System to determine depreciation. The result is that GAAP depreciation expense will rarely (if ever) equal tax depreciation, which means that taxable income will almost always differ from GAAP pre-tax income.

LIFO means **"last-in, first-out,"** and here's how it works. Suppose a start-up bicycle retailer begins the year with no inventory. Ten bicycles are purchased for $150 each during the first week of operations and another five bicycles are purchased midmonth for $180 each: same brand and model, just a higher price from the manufacturer. Eight bicycles are sold during the month, leaving seven in inventory. Under LIFO, the retailer would calculate the cost of goods sold to be $1,350 (or five bicycles at $180 each plus three more at $150 each). Notice that this calculation presumes the *last* bicycles to come into the shop (those bought for $180 each) are the *first sold.* Notice also that with rising inventory costs, LIFO produces a larger cost of goods sold expense ($1,350 in our example) than does FIFO, or **"first-in, first-out"** (eight bicycles at $150 each, or $1,200). A higher cost of goods sold expense means a lower taxable income. Chapter 9 tells you more.

In general, U.S. firms are not required to use the same accounting methods for their financial statements and on their tax returns. Inventory accounting is the sole important exception. Companies that use LIFO for tax purposes must also use LIFO in their shareholder reports. When inventory costs are rising, companies prefer LIFO for tax purposes because it lowers taxable income. But, because of the "LIFO Conformity Rule," the tax benefits of LIFO can be obtained only when LIFO is also used in the GAAP financial statements. But doing so lowers GAAP net income when prices are rising. Because LIFO is widely used, many corporate managers must believe the tax benefits of LIFO outweigh its negative impact on GAAP net income.

Taxation and GAAP accounting are related in another way. Companies reporting large GAAP earnings sometimes attract the attention of politicians who threaten to impose "windfall profits" taxes. This has been true for big U.S. oil companies during periods of rapidly increasing oil prices and/or during oil shortages.

For example, during the 1970s, the federal government controlled the price of gasoline in an effort to reduce consumption and to dampen the inflationary impact of escalating oil prices. In 1979, the price of gasoline at the pump was decontrolled one week before big oil companies announced record third-quarter profits that were labeled by politicians as "obscene." After the earnings announcements, a windfall profits tax on oil company earnings was proposed, and politicians voted to reinstate gasoline price controls. These actions occurred even though part of the reported profit increase was due to an accounting change required by the FASB; most of the rest of the increase was due to overseas operations and inventory holding gains.[35]

[35] To learn more about the politics of oil and gas accounting in the 1970s (and 1990s), see J. Han and S. Wang, "Political Costs and Earnings Management of Oil Companies during the 1990 Persian Gulf Crisis," *The Accounting Review,* January 1998, pp. 103–18.

Sometimes it just doesn't pay to be seen as "too profitable." When that's the case, managers have incentives to make accounting choices that make the company look less profitable.

Government regulatory agencies can write their own accounting rules, and many do. The result is that some financial statements for shareholders and creditors contain special regulatory items or use regulatory accounting methods that deviate from normal GAAP. Accounting-based regulations and tax law also affect the choice of GAAP accounting methods for shareholder reports and when transactions are recorded.

FAIR VALUE ACCOUNTING AND THE FINANCIAL CRISIS

"The accountants let us down. That is one of the clear lessons of the financial crisis that drove the world into a deep recession."

—F. Norris, "Accountants Misled Us into Crisis,"
The New York Times (September 11, 2009)

Fair value accounting has been around in some form for two decades. It is the practice of continually revaluing an asset (or liability) to the price it would bring if sold (or the cost to settle) regardless of what was actually paid for the asset (or received for the liability). Banks and other financial services firms were content with the fair value rules when markets were going up. But those rules came under sharp criticism in late 2008 when the collapse of a global housing bubble triggered the failure of large financial institutions, the bailout of banks by national governments, and downturns in stock markets around the world.

As the crisis unfolded, banks in the United States and Europe were quick to blame the credit meltdown on FASB and IASB fair value accounting standards. Why? Because of the accounting-based minimum capital requirements that regulators impose on financial services firms. The fair value rules forced banks to disclose what their key assets were actually worth and revealed that regulatory capital was often woefully inadequate for the risks taken. Politicians were persuaded to intervene and force changes in the fair value rules. Here's what happened.

The Meltdown

A robust economy, low interest rates, and large inflows of foreign investment funds created a climate of easy credit in the United States beginning in the mid-1990s. Loans of all types— mortgages, home equity, credit cards, automobile—were simple to obtain, fueling a housing construction boom and encouraging debt-financed consumption. Between 1997 and 2006, the price of the typical American house increased by 124%.

The use of **mortgage-backed securities** (MBS) and **collateralized debt obligations** (CDO) greatly increased during the housing and credit booms. Mortgage originators—the banks and other financial services firms that loaned money directly to home buyers—turned to these financial instruments as a convenient and practical way to raise cash quickly. By packaging bundled mortgage loans as MBS and CDO securities for sale to third-party investors, originators could convert loans into immediate up-front cash rather than waiting for payments to flow in from borrowers. The cash could then be used to make new loans. (Chapter 8 tells you more.)

Investors around the world put money into the housing market by purchasing MBS and CDO securities. By about 2003, the supply of mortgages originated at traditional lending standards had been exhausted. Aggressive originators began to offer nontraditional loans to high-risk (or subprime) borrowers. Some loans offered low "teaser" interest rates that reset to higher market rates after a year or two. Other loans offered extraordinarily low monthly payments for the first several years, payments that failed even to cover loan interest. And then there were the so-called NINJA loans doled out to subprime borrowers with "No Income, No Job, and no Assets." These subprime loans were repackaged and sold to investors to meet continued strong demand for MBS and CDO securities.

The availability of these new forms of easy mortgage credit further increased housing demand and drove up home prices. Eventually, this speculative bubble proved unsustainable. Interest rates edged up in 2007, mortgage defaults rose, and home prices tumbled. Even some creditworthy borrowers had a financial incentive to halt loan payments and enter foreclosure when they discovered their homes were worth less than the mortgage balance. By year-end, nearly 12% of all U.S. mortgages were either delinquent or in foreclosure.

As housing prices declined and mortgage default rates escalated, major global financial institutions that had invested heavily in subprime MBS and CDO securities began reporting sizable investment losses. Although these big mark-to-market losses served to alert investors and analysts to the plummeting values of key investment assets, they also depleted regulatory capital and pushed several of the nation's largest financial services firms to the brink of failure. The tipping point occurred in September 2008, when:

- The U.S. government took control of the Federal National Mortgage Association (Fannie Mae) and the Federal Home Loan Mortgage Corporation (Freddie Mac), two financial institutions that owned or guaranteed about 57% of the $12 trillion U.S. mortgage market.
- The global financial services firm Lehman Brothers entered into the largest bankruptcy in U.S. history.
- The investment banking firm Merrill Lynch was rescued by Bank of America, and the two remaining U.S. investment banks—Goldman Sachs and Morgan Stanley—converted to bank holding companies.
- Washington Mutual, the nation's largest savings and loan, was seized by the Federal Deposit Insurance Corporation (FDIC), and the nation's fourth largest bank—Wachovia—agreed to be acquired by Citigroup.

Credit markets froze even though a vast majority of mortgage borrowers were still making loan payments. Banks could no longer raise the cash needed to sustain operations or to satisfy regulatory capital requirements. Those banks that lacked sufficient regulatory capital soon either ceased to exist or were acquired by healthy financial services firms. In 2008, financial services firms in the United States reported mortgage-related fair value accounting losses and loan write-downs totaling roughly $175 billion. Merrill Lynch ($22.4 billion) and Citigroup ($19.9 billion) topped the list.

The Controversy

When credit markets froze in the fall of 2008, they did so in part because investors no longer wanted to own MBS and CDO securities, especially those comprising subprime mortgages. The associated cash flows—mortgage interest and principal payments from borrowers—had become too unpredictable. On the rare occasions when MBS and CDO securities changed hands, they did so at distressed prices.

Financial services firms complained that fair value accounting rules turned a large problem into a humongous one. They argued that, by forcing firms to slash the reported values of their mortgage-related assets based on fire-sale prices from illiquid markets, fair value accounting contributed to a further depletion of regulatory capital. Fewer new loans could be granted, even by healthy institutions, and more banks were pushed toward insolvency. Financial services firms sought relief from the fair value rules, arguing that their own estimates of value were more realistic than what they—and others—were paying for those securities. Influential politicians echoed this sentiment and blamed the accounting rules for rising foreclosure rates, unemployment, and the unavailability of bank loans for businesses.

Securities regulators and accounting standards setters held a decidedly different view. They argued that the primary purpose of accounting is to report the financial condition and performance of a company, and that existing fair value rules were essential to achieving this goal for financial services firms. Regulatory accounting principles, on the other hand, serve a different purpose. As one observer noted, "If the banking regulators want to allow banks to use different rules in calculating capital—rules that would not require marking down assets, for example—then they can do so without depriving investors of important information."[36]

The battle lines were drawn: change the accounting rules to ease regulatory capital constraints or change the regulations themselves. Over the next several months, the politics of accounting standards became clearly evident:

- October 2008: The Emergency Economic Stabilization Act of 2008 (EESA)—introduced, deliberated, passed by the U.S. Congress, and signed into law by President Bush in just 10 days—contains provisions authorizing the SEC to suspend fair value accounting. It also required the SEC to study the effects of fair value accounting for financial services firms and to report its conclusions within 90 days. Later that month, the International Accounting Standards Board (IASB) bows to European political pressure by amending its mark-to-market rules so that banks reporting under IFRS can avoid using fair values for selected financial instruments.

- December 2008: The SEC issues its fair value accounting study and concludes that, while improvements are needed, existing fair value rules should not be suspended. Financial services firms and their trade groups, along with some politicians, continue to voice opposition to the fair value rules.

- January 2009: FASB amends some asset impairment guidelines, sheltering regulatory capital from the adverse impact of impairments in limited situations. FASB also reiterates its support for fair value accounting.

- February 2009: Thirty-one U.S. financial services firms and trade groups form the Fair Value Coalition and spend $27.6 million over the next two months lobbying. The Coalition's primary goal is to change fair value accounting rules to dampen their effect on regulatory capital.[37]

- March 2009: Congress introduces legislation to broaden oversight of the FASB beyond the SEC to four other federal agencies. Separately, in House Financial Services Subcommittee hearings, Representative Paul Kanjorski (Democrat—Pennsylvania) warns the

---

[36] F. Norris, "Accountants Misled Us into Crisis," *The New York Times* (September 11, 2009). Banking regulators in the United States are, however, prohibited by the Financial Institutions Reform, Recovery and Enforcement Act of 1989 and the Federal Deposit Insurance Corporation Improvement Act of 1991 from applying regulatory accounting principles that are any less rigorous than GAAP.

[37] To learn more about this lobbying effort, see S. Pulliam and T. McGinty, "Congress Helped Banks Defang Key Rule," *The Wall Street Journal* (June 3, 2009).

SEC and FASB that, "If the regulators and standards setters do not act now to improve the [fair value accounting] standards, then Congress will have no other option than to act itself."[38]

- March 2009: Under pressure from politicians, FASB issues a proposed change to the fair value rules that would have made it easier for firms to claim that quoted prices in inactive markets were from distressed transactions, thereby allowing them to ignore those market prices and instead use their own valuation models to estimate fair value.

- April 2009: After significant negative feedback from the accounting profession on the proposal, FASB revises the proposal and issues a rule that leaves intact most of the guidance relating to when firms may use their own valuation models in lieu of market prices to estimate fair value.

This view was not shared by all members of Congress. Fair value proponent Representative Alan Grayson (Democrat—Florida) likened changing the fair value rules to some rather outlandish ideas: changing the value of pi from 3.14 to 4 so that the crowded circular highway around Washington, D.C., would be larger and thus less congested; increasing the length of an inch so that passengers could be more comfortable on a plane; making 98 larger than 109, so that the loss the Washington Wizards pro basketball team had just suffered at the hands of the New Orleans Hornets would be recorded as a win.

Source: "Congress Members Fume at Fair Value," CFO.com, March, 17, 2009.

As the financial crisis ebbed in 2009, so, too, did political pressure to modify fair value accounting for financial services firms. Today, FASB and IASB continue to seek ways to improve the fair value rules. A recently completed FASB/IASB joint project aims to ensure that fair value has the same meaning in U.S. GAAP and IFRS, and that GAAP and IFRS guidance on fair value measurement is the same. A FASB proposal issued for comment in February 2013 would extend the scope of fair value accounting to an even broader set of financial assets and liabilities than existing rules now cover. Banks, for example, would have to report the fair value and amortized cost of all loans (as well as some other financial instruments) on their balance sheets under the proposed rules. It remains to be seen if this proposal sparks a new round of political intervention into the standards-setting process, although FASB has already received more than 100 comment letters suggesting the proposal is in need of changes.

RECAP

Fair value accounting did not cause the financial crisis, but the crisis may have been aggravated by the way in which fair value losses reduce regulatory capital. It is important to remember that financial statements are scrutinized by various groups and for different purposes. Investors and analysts use GAAP and IFRS statements to assess a firm's earnings and cash flow performance, and its financial health. Regulators of financial services firms use RAP statements to ensure that banks have sufficient capital to withstand losses on loans and other key assets. Politicians must recognize that there may be no single best accounting measurement rule for both purposes.[39]

ANALYTICAL INSIGHTS: INCENTIVES TO "MANAGE" EARNINGS

The message from this chapter is that managers often have powerful incentives to "manage" their companies' reported profitability and financial condition. These incentives arise from loan covenants, compensation contracts, regulatory agency oversight, tax avoidance efforts, and a desire to meet or beat analysts' quarterly earnings forecasts or to increase the company's stock price. Financial statement gimmicks are likely to be most prevalent when these accounting

---

[38] As quoted in "Congress Members Fume at Fair Value," *CFO.com* 3/17/2009.

[39] A comprehensive and insightful discussion of accounting and the financial crisis can be found in S. Ryan, "Accounting in and for the Subprime Crisis," *The Accounting Review,* November 2008, pp. 1605–38.

incentives are especially strong, for example, when the company is in danger of violating its debt covenants, when a large portion of top management pay comes from bonuses tied to earnings per share or sales growth, or when management has a lengthy record of beating "the Street's" earnings forecast by a penny. What's the penalty for failing to make the numbers? Loan default, lost bonuses, and an abrupt stock price decline.

So, now you know *when* to look for potential accounting distortions, but what exactly do you look *for* and *where* do you look? How do companies "manage" earnings? What accounting gimmicks are used? The remaining chapters of this book address these questions in detail.

SUMMARY

- Conflicts of interest among managers, shareholders, lenders, or regulators are natural features of business.

- Contracts and regulations help address these conflicts of interest in ways that are mutually beneficial to the parties involved.

- Accounting numbers often play an important role in contracts and regulations because they provide useful information about the company's performance and financial condition as well as about the management team's accomplishments.

- Accounting-based lending agreements, compensation contracts, and regulations shape managers' incentives; after all, that's why accounting numbers are included in contracts and regulations. They also help to explain the accounting choices managers make.

- Understanding why and how managers exercise their discretion in implementing GAAP can be extremely helpful to those who are analyzing and interpreting a company's financial statements.

EXERCISES

E 7-1

Understanding debt covenants **(LO 2)**

Required:
What is a debt covenant? Why do lenders include them in loan agreements? Why do borrowers agree to include covenants in loan agreements?

E 7-2

Tying contracts to accounting numbers **(LO 3)**

Required:
What are the advantages of loan agreements that contain covenants tied to accounting numbers? Are there any disadvantages? Explain.

E 7-3

Debt covenants and accounting methods **(LO 2)**

The debt covenants in TCBY's loan agreement do not mention explicitly the accounting methods the company must use when it prepares financial statements for submission to the lender.

Required:
Why don't lenders require the use of specific accounting methods rather than letting management pick from among GAAP alternatives?

E 7-4

Sunshine Groceries Inc.: Sales-based bonus plan **(LO 2)**

Sunshine Groceries operates a rapidly expanding chain of retail grocery stores in Europe. The company has grown from 10 stores in 2012 to 50 stores in 2014 and plans to add at least 10 stores each year for the next three years. Top executives at the company can earn annual cash bonuses of up to 200% of salary if board-approved sales growth goals are achieved.

Required:

Explain why it might make sense for this company to award bonuses based on sales growth. How might this approach encourage poor business decisions when compared to a bonus plan tied to earnings?

E7-5

McDonald's Corporation: Pay disclosure lawsuit   (LO 4)

McDonald's, the global fast-food restaurant giant, was sued in 2009 by a former employee who said she was dismissed because, as a senior director of executive compensation, she objected to a complex scheme to keep country club fees paid for a top executive out of the company's 2007 proxy statement. The fees amounted to roughly $2,940, a trifling amount when compared to the $3.5 million in total compensation paid to the executive that year.

Source: A. Barr, "McDonald's Suit Illustrates Pay Disclosure Dance," *The Wall Street Journal,* June 25, 2009.

Required:

Why might a company want to avoid disclosing in its proxy statements the amounts it pays for top executive benefits such as country club memberships?

E7-6

Regulatory costs   (LO 4)

Required:

What are regulatory costs, and why are they important for understanding a company's financial reporting choices?

E7-7

Regulatory accounting principles   (LO 3)

Some public service commissions let utilities include construction in progress—construction dollars spent for projects not yet completed—in their rate-making asset bases. Other states allow only completed projects to be included.

Required:

Which approach favors shareholders? Why?

E7-8

Equipment repairs and rate regulation   (LO 2)

Illinois Power & Heat just spent $5 million repairing one of its electrical generating stations that was damaged by a tornado. The loss was uninsured. Management has asked the public service commission for approval to treat the $5 million as an asset for rate-making purposes rather than as an allowed expense.

Required:

What difference will this make to customers and shareholders?

E7-9

Maintaining capital adequacy (LO 1)

Required:

Why do regulators require banks and insurance companies to maintain minimum levels of investor capital? What impact does this type of regulatory requirement have on the financial statements that banks and insurance companies prepare for shareholders?

E7-10

Identifying conflicts of interest and agency costs   (LO 1)

Suppose you and two friends each invested $100,000 in an oil and gas partnership. The general partner, Huge Gamble, Inc., invests no cash but makes all operating decisions for the partnership, including where and how deep to drill for oil. Drilling costs plus a management fee are charged against the $300,000 of cash you and your friends invested. If oil is found, you each get 15% of partnership net income with the remaining 55% going to Huge Gamble. But if the wells are dry, you get nothing except any cash that remains.

Required:

What is an agency relationship, and what are agency costs? How do these concepts apply to your investment in the oil and gas partnership?

PROBLEMS / DISCUSSION QUESTIONS

A brief description of Krispy Kreme's annual cash bonus plan for top executives follows.

P7-1

Krispy Kreme's bonus plan
(LO 3)

The Compensation Committee chose consolidated EBITDA [earnings before interest, taxes, depreciation and amortization] and revenue as the performance metrics for fiscal 2012, weighted at 80% and 20%, respectively. Consolidated EBITDA is defined the same way as it is defined in our secured credit facilities. The Compensation Committee assigned three levels of performance for consolidated EBITDA and for Revenue: threshold, target, and maximum.

Source: Krispy Kreme Doughnuts, Inc. 2012 Proxy, edited for brevity.

The disclosure further indicates that eligible recipients would receive 70%, 100%, or 140% of the portion of the target bonus for performance attributable to each performance metric for performance at the threshold, target, and maximum levels, respectively. The bonus for performance that falls between two of those levels would be prorated.

Required:

1. One way Krispy Kreme executives can achieve the revenue target is to open new stores as fast as possible. Explain why this might alarm shareholders.

2. Why might it be important for the bonus plan to use the same EBITDA definition used in Krispy Kreme's "secured credit facilities" (loan agreements)?

3. Describe how Krispy Kreme's executive bonus plan might lead to accounting abuses at the company.

An unusual feature of top executive pay at Krispy Kreme Doughnuts, Inc., is its compensation recovery policy. The policy allows Krispy Kreme to take back annual or long-term incentive compensation paid to executive officers and certain other management team members in the event they are later found to have engaged in conduct "detrimental" to the company. Three types of misconduct are specified: (a) financial accounting or reporting violations, whether from gross negligence or willful misconduct, that trigger a restatement of previously issued financial statements; (b) business actions that result in a material negative revision of a financial or operating measure that was the basis for incentive awards already paid; and (c) fraud, theft, and similar acts. What is the penalty for detrimental conduct? The executive may be required to reimburse the company for all, or a portion of, any incentive compensation (including equity-based awards) paid out during the previous 36 months as well as any profits realized from the sale of Krispy Kreme stock during that same period.

P7-2

Krispy Kreme's compensation recovery plan   **(LO 5)**

Source: Krispy Kreme Doughnuts, Inc. Compensation Recovery Policy, Effective April 6, 2009, as described in the 2012 Proxy.

Required:

1. Briefly explain how a typical annual and long-term management compensation plan tied to financial accounting numbers may contribute to agency problems within the firm.

2. Provide examples of the accounting abuses that Krispy Kreme's pay recovery policy is intended to discourage.

3. Explain why you do (or do not) believe the pay recovery policy will be effective in discouraging those accounting abuses.

P 7 - 3

Medical malprofits   **(LO 1)**

Required:

Explain the potential conflict of interest that arises when doctors own the hospitals in which they work. The following news article may help.

The executive who became the most visible symbol of profit-driven medical care stepped down yesterday as the top officer of the Columbia/HCA Healthcare Corporation amid a criminal investigation of whether the company's pursuit of profits has stretched beyond the legal limits. . . . [He] will be replaced by Thomas F. Frist, Jr., a surgeon by training, who has made his career in the hospital business. . . . Dr. Frist said he was ending Columbia's practice of selling ownership stakes in its hospitals to its doctors. That has been a critical piece of the strategy that helped propel Columbia's growth but led to great legal and ethical criticism that the company was compromising the medical independence of its doctors.

Source: The New York Times, July 26, 1997.

P 7 - 4

Foot Locker, Inc.: Anticipating covenant violation   **(LO 4)**

Foot Locker, Inc., reported an $18 million loss on sales of $1,283 million for the quarter ended August 4, 2007. The quarterly financial filing (10-Q) also contained this warning for investors and creditors.

Under the Company's revolving credit and term loan agreement, the Company is required to satisfy certain financial and operating covenants, including a minimum fixed charge coverage ratio. In addition, this agreement restricts the amount the Company may expend in any year for dividends to 50 percent of its prior year's net income. Based upon the Company's second quarter financial results and business uncertainties for the second half of the year, the Company may not continue to be in compliance with the fixed charge coverage ratio. In addition, the restricted payment provision may prohibit the Company from the payment of the dividend at the current rate in 2008.

Source: Foot Locker Inc. Form 10-Q for the quarter ended August 4, 2007.

Required:

1. What is a minimum fixed charge coverage ratio, and what purpose does it serve in the company's loan agreements?

2. Why would Foot Locker agree to restrict dividends to just 50% of its prior year's net income?

3. In general terms, explain how a company such as Foot Locker alters its accounting choices to avoid violating debt covenants tied to financial statement numbers.

4. What is likely to happen if Foot Locker does not satisfy one or more of the loan covenants at year-end?

FRISBY IN DEFAULT ON LOAN COVENANTS

Frisby Technologies has received a notice of default from two of its secured creditors. DAMAD Holdings AG and Bluwat AG have notified the company that it is in default of the tangible net worth covenant contained in its respective loan agreements with the lenders. The covenant requires the company to maintain a tangible net worth of not less than $1,250,000 as of the end of each fiscal quarter. A similar covenant is contained in the company loan agreements with its other secured lenders, MUSI Investments S.A. and Fin.part International S.A. As of September 30, 2002, the company's tangible net worth, calculated as provided in the respective loan agreements, was a negative $663,402.

Under the terms of the DAMAD and Bluwat loan agreements, the company has until December 18. . . . The company does not currently expect that it will be able to cure the default within the prescribed cure period.

If the default is not cured prior to the end of the cure period, then (i) the entire unpaid balance owed to the lenders, $1.25 million plus accrued interest, would become due and payable; (ii) the interest rate, to the extent permitted by law, could be increased by either or both lenders up to the maximum rate allowed by law; (iii) any accrued and unpaid interest, fees or charges could be deemed by either or both lenders to be a part of the principal balance, with interest to accrue on a daily compounded basis until the entire outstanding principal and accrued interest is paid in full; (iv) either or both lenders could foreclose on its security interest in substantially all of the company's assets; and (v) each lender would have all rights available to it at law or in equity.

In addition, repayment of the loans is secured by a limited guaranty by COB/CEO Gregory Frisby of up to one-third of the total amount outstanding under the loans.

The company has requested waiver of compliance of the tangible net worth covenant from each of the lenders, but no such waiver has been granted. The company will continue to pursue a waiver or otherwise to seek to negotiate a forbearance agreement or other satisfactory resolution with the lenders. If the company is unsuccessful, it may voluntarily seek protection from its creditors under federal bankruptcy laws, which would have a material adverse effect on the company's business, financial condition and prospects.

Source: R. Craver, "Default of Credit Agreement Adds to Frisby's Woes," *Winston-Salem Journal,* November 22, 2002. Copyright © 2002 Winston-Salem Journal. Used with permission.

Required:

1. What is a minimum tangible net worth covenant, and what purpose does it serve in the Frisby loan agreements?

2. Why might lenders be reluctant to waive Frisby's covenant violation?

3. Among the options available to Frisby's lenders is foreclosure: shuttering the company and selling off all assets. Why might lenders prefer to avoid this action?

John Brincat is the president and chief executive of Mercury Finance, an auto lender specializing in high credit-risk customers. The company's proxy statement contains the following description of Brincat's pay package.

Mr. Brincat is eligible for an annual incentive bonus equal to 1% of Net After-tax Earnings of the Company and is eligible for an additional bonus based upon annual increases in Net After-tax Earnings per share only after earnings exceed 20% over the prior year. The additional bonus is determined as follows:

- Earnings per share increases of 0% to 19.99%, no additional bonus is paid.
- Earnings per share increases of 20% to 29.99%, additional bonus will be equal to 2.5% of the amount of increase from the prior year.
- Earnings per share increases of 30% to 39.99%, additional bonus will be equal to 3.0% of the amount of increase from the prior year.
- Earnings per share increases of 40% or more, additional bonus will be equal to 3.5% of the amount of increase from the prior year.

In addition, at the time the employment contract was entered into, Mr. Brincat was issued a stock option grant . . . of 2,500,000 shares at a price of $17.375 per share, the fair market value on the date of the grant. The options vest equally during the next five years of the contract and are exercisable in increments of 500,000 shares annually only if earnings per share each year exceeds the prior year's earnings per share by 20%. If earnings per share do not increase by 20%, Mr. Brincat forfeits that year's options and has no further right or claim to that year's options.

Source: Mercury Finance 1995 proxy.

Required:

1. Suppose Mercury Finance had $50 million of net after-tax earnings for the year. How much of a bonus would Brincat receive if the EPS increase that year was only 10%?

2. How much of a bonus would Brincat receive if the EPS increase was 30%?

3. As a shareholder, how comfortable would you be if your company's managers had contracts with these types of bonus and stock option incentives? Why?

P7-7

Earnings quality and pay
(LO 4)

Following your retirement as senior vice president of finance for a large company, you joined the board of Cayman Grand Cruises, Inc. You serve on the compensation committee and help set the bonuses paid to the company's top five executives. According to the annual bonus plan, each executive can earn a bonus of 1% of annual net income.

No bonuses were paid in 2013 because the company reported a net loss of $6,588,000.

Shortly after the end of the year, the compensation committee received a letter signed by all five executives, indicating that they felt the company had performed well in 2013. The letter identified the following items from the 2013 income statement that the executives felt painted a less favorable view of performance than was actually the case:

Proposed Adjustments to 2013 Earnings	
($ in thousands)	
Loss on early retirement of debt	$131,474
Restructuring and other nonrecurring charges	63,000
Loss from discontinued operations	22,851

The letter asked the compensation committee to add these items back to the reported net loss and to then recalculate the bonus awards for 2013. The fiscal year 2013 income statement follows. Assume the tax rate is 30%.

Cayman Grand Cruises, Inc.

Consolidated Statement of Income

($ in thousands)	June 30, 2013
Net revenues	$1,024,467
Cost of sales	(535,178)
Gross margin	489,289
Selling, general, and administrative	(299,101)
Research, development, and engineering	(94,172)
Gain on sale of joint venture	33,000
Loss on early retirement of debt	(131,474)
Restructuring and other nonrecurring charges	(63,000)
Operating income (loss)	(65,458)
Gain on sale of investment	40,800
Interest expense	(7,145)
Interest income	2,382
Other income (expense)—net	(2,121)
Income before income taxes	(31,542)
Income tax benefit	9,462
Income from continuing operations	(22,080)
Income (loss) from discontinued operations (net of tax effect)	(22,851)
Gain on disposal of discontinued operations (net of tax effect)	38,343
Net income (loss)	$ (6,588)

Required:

1. As a member of the compensation committee, how would you respond to each suggested adjustment? Why?

2. What 2013 net income figure do you suggest be used to determine bonuses for the year?

Food Lion, Inc., operates a chain of retail supermarkets principally in the southeastern United States. The supermarket business is highly competitive, and it is characterized by low profit margins. Food Lion competes with national, regional, and local supermarket chains; discount food stores; single-unit stores; convenience stores; and warehouse clubs.

> **P 7-8**
>
> Avoiding debt covenant violations **(LO 4)**

Food Lion recently entered into a credit agreement with a group of banks. Excerpts taken from the loan agreement follow.

Section 5.19. Limitation on Incurrence of Funded Debt

The Borrower will not create, assume or incur or in any manner be or become liable in respect of any [additional] Funded Debt . . . [unless] the ratio of Income Available for Fixed Charges for the immediately preceding four Fiscal Quarters to Pro Forma Fixed Charges for such four Fiscal Quarters shall have been at least 2.00 to 1.00.

Section 5.20. Fixed Charges Coverage

At the end of each Fiscal Quarter . . . the ratio of Income Available for Fixed Charges for the immediately preceding four Fiscal Quarters then ended to Consolidated Fixed Charges for the immediately preceding four Fiscal Quarters then ended, shall not be less than . . . 1.75 to 1.0.

Section 5.21. Minimum Consolidated Tangible Net Worth

Consolidated Tangible Net Worth will at no time be less than (i) $706,575,475 plus (ii) 30.0% of the cumulative Consolidated Net Income of the Borrower during any period after [the new loan agreement is signed], calculated quarterly but excluding from such calculations of Consolidated Net Income for purposes of this clause (ii), any quarter in which the Consolidated Net Income of the Borrower and its Consolidated Subsidiaries is negative.

Source: Food Lion, Inc., loan agreement.

Required:

1. In two more weeks, the company's books will be closed for the quarter, and the *fixed charges coverage* might fall below the level required by the loan agreement. How can management avoid violating this covenant?

2. The company's *tangible net worth* may also fall below the amount specified in the loan agreement. How can management avoid violating this covenant?

3. Elsewhere in the loan agreement it says that the company's *ratio of consolidated debt to total capitalization* must be no more than 0.75 to 1.0. How can management avoid violating this covenant?

4. Suppose you were one of Food Lion's bankers, and you were thinking about making changes to the loan covenants. What management activities would you most want to limit? Why?

P7-9

Accounting in Regulated
Industries   **(LO 4)**

Duke Energy Corporation's 2012 annual report to shareholders contains the following note disclosure (edited for brevity):

> **Cost-based Regulation.** Duke Energy accounts for its regulated operations in accordance with applicable regulatory accounting guidance . . . Accordingly, Duke Energy records assets and liabilities that result from the regulated ratemaking process that would not be recorded under GAAP for non-regulated entities . . .
>
> **AFUDC and Interest Capitalized.** In accordance with applicable regulatory accounting guidance, Duke Energy records AFUDC, which represents the estimated debt and equity costs of capital funds necessary to finance the construction of new regulated facilities. The equity component of AFUDC is a non-cash amount . . . AFUDC is capitalized as a component of the cost of Property, Plant and Equipment.

Required:

1. Explain why Duke Energy alerts investors and other readers of its GAAP financial statements to the fact that it "records assets and liabilities that result from the regulated ratemaking process."

2. As you will learn in Chapter 10, GAAP does not allow firms to capitalize as a cost of construction the "equity costs" of funds needed to finance construction projects. GAAP does allow debt interest costs to be capitalized under certain circumstances. Explain why Duke Energy alerts investors and other readers of its GAAP financial statements to the "capitalization" of AFUDC.

3. Briefly describe the unique accounting-related conflicts of interest that arise in regulated electric utility companies such as Duke Energy.

P7-10

Understanding rate regulation
and accounting choices
(LO 4)

Alliant Energy just received regulatory approval for its 2014 electricity rate. The company has been authorized to charge customers $0.10 per kilowatt-hour (kwh), a rate lower than other utilities in the state charge. Details of the rate calculation follow:

Alliant Energy		
		2014 Rate Authorization
Allowed operating costs		$ 1,120 million
Assets in service	$3,200 million	
× Allowed rate of return	8.75% =	280 million
Revenue requirement		$ 1,400 million
÷ Estimated energy demand		14,000 million kwh
Rate allowed per kwh		$ 0.10

Shortly after the 2014 rate was set, the company's financial reporting staff circulated an internal memo recommending the following accounting changes:

1. Extend plant depreciation life by five years to reflect current utilization forecasts. This would add $175 million to the asset base and reduce annual depreciation (an operating cost) by $5 million.

2. Increase estimated bad debt expense from 1% to 1.5% of sales to reflect current forecasts of customer defaults. This would add $7 million to operating costs and reduce total assets by the same amount.

3. Amortize 2013 hostile takeover defense costs of $4.5 million over three years rather than take the entire expense in 2013. This would increase 2014 operating costs by $1.5 million and add $3 million to the asset base.

4. Write up fuel and materials inventories to their current replacement value. This would add $60 million to the asset base, but it would have no impact on 2014 operating costs.

Required:

1. Assess the impact of each proposed change on the company's 2014 revenue requirement and rate per kilowatt-hour, assuming that regulators will approve the accounting changes and adjust the allowed rate accordingly.

2. As a member of the state utility commission, comment on the merits of each proposed accounting change.

P7-11

Determining whether citizens should have a say in CEO pay: Practices in Europe **(LO 1)**

CEO LEADS SWISS BACKLASH OVER EXECUTIVE PAY

In Switzerland, long a haven for big money, a backlash is developing against outsized executive compensation.

The push is being spurred by an unlikely source: a CEO. Thomas Minder, a 47-year-old chief executive of small cosmetics manufacturer Trybol AG, is going to shareholder meetings at Swiss giants like Novartis SA to challenge their CEO pay packages.

Mr. Minder has been collecting signatures to call a national vote—as permitted under the Swiss constitution—to amend Swiss law to force more transparency and accountability on executive compensation. He says his goal is to create ways for shareholders to veto pay packages and create more "sensible" pay practices in Switzerland, a country where wealth has traditionally been welcomed, rather than frowned upon.

Across Europe, growing disenchantment with high executive pay is increasingly a political issue. In France, the losing candidate for the presidency, Ségolène Royal, called on Airbus to withdraw its proposed 10,000 job cuts after it disclosed that Noël Forgeard, former chief executive of Airbus and its parent, European Aeronautic Defence & Space Co., received €6.1 million

($8.2 million) in an exit pay package. The company said the package was provided for in his contract, but Ms. Royal called the payment a "scandal."

In Germany, Finance Minister Peer Steinbrück has said Europe's social model couldn't be sustained if the wages of low earners fall as company profits rise.

Switzerland is set to introduce greater disclosure of executive compensation for companies listed on the Swiss exchange. Starting next year, companies must disclose the salaries of the highest paid member of the management board. Previously, Swiss companies released only the total salaries of the combined board and the individual salary of the highest paid member of the supervisory board, which is akin to a U.S. board of directors. . . .

Current law allows Swiss companies to disclose less detail on executive pay than U.S. companies. They aren't required to disclose individual pay packages for chief executives and often don't have to mention benefits such as personal loans or housing allowances. . . .

Mr. Minder says he pays himself "far less" than 100,000 Swiss francs, or about $81,000, a year and took on his

(continued)

campaign because pay levels are so high that "executives don't suffer personal hardships even if their performance at the helm of the company is miserable." . . .

Among his 25 proposals: giving shareholders the right to block or approve pay packages; a complete ban on "golden parachutes" or pay packages given to executives upon leaving a company; and measures that would force institutional shareholders to disclose how they voted on issues such as approving bonuses. . . .

If Mr. Minder collects 100,000 signatures, his proposals will be put to the Swiss Parliament and federal councilors. They can

come up with a counter-proposal or allow a popular vote on Mr. Minder's proposals, thanks to the Swiss tradition of direct democracy. Mr. Minder has until May 2008 to hand in the signatures, and he says he is "very well on track," without being specific. A national vote may not follow for at least a year.

While the chances of success for a popular vote, known as a plebiscite, are very slim, the move to force a vote makes the issue part of the mainstream political agenda. . . .

Source: E. Taylor, "CEO Leads Swiss Backlash Over Executive Pay," *The Wall Street Journal*, May 26, 2007. Copyright © 2007 Dow Jones & Company, Inc. All rights reserved worldwide. Reprinted with permission.

Required:

1. Do shareholders vote on the compensation packages paid to top executives of U.S. companies?

2. One of Minder's proposals would ban the use of golden parachutes. How might this ban harm shareholders?

3. In the United States, the average big company CEO made $11.6 million in 2005, or 411 times the typical U.S. worker, according to the Institute for Policy Studies. That same year, average CEO compensation for companies with approximately $500 million in worldwide annual sales was $2.2 million in the United States, $1.4 million in Switzerland, and $1.2 million in France, the United Kingdom, and Germany. With these statistics as a backdrop, provide (a) three reasons in support of giving European shareholders the right to approve CEO pay packages and (b) three reasons why you are against doing so.

4. Should citizens have the right to approve CEO pay packages? Why or why not?

CASES

C7-1

Microsoft's "unearned revenue" account   **(LO 4)**

SOME SAVVY FANS COOL TO MICROSOFT

Some savvy investors, detecting fissures in Microsoft's armor, are pulling back from the world's most highly valued company.

The concern: the first-ever drop in an arcane but closely watched indicator of Microsoft's future results.

The balance in Microsoft's "unearned revenue" account, which declined to $4.13 billion on Sept. 30 from $4.24 billion

in June, has become a lightning rod for more general concerns about the price of the company's shares. . . . Managers of several large funds . . . are shedding part of their Microsoft holdings. The immediate trigger was the first quarter-to-quarter decline in Microsoft's unearned revenue account. . . .

In the software industry, Microsoft pioneered the practice of recording a portion of the revenue from some products as "unearned," starting with the release of Windows 95. The practice is common in some other fields: Many magazine publishers, for instance, record subscription revenues only when issues are shipped.

Similarly, Microsoft now holds back a portion of revenues from Windows 98, Windows NT and Office until it "earns" the revenue by delivering interim upgrades, bug fixes and other customer support. The account also includes the value of coupons that customers receive, which entitle them to free upgrades when they buy a Microsoft product before the next version is ready.

A delay in the shipment of Office 2000 earlier this year caused the company to add $400 million to the unearned revenue account in the March quarter to cover the coupons issued to buyers of Office 97. As copies of Office 2000 were shipped, half of that amount flowed into the June quarterly results; another $150 million was transferred in the fiscal quarter ended in September.

The effect was to bolster earned revenues in those quarters and lower unearned revenues. . . .

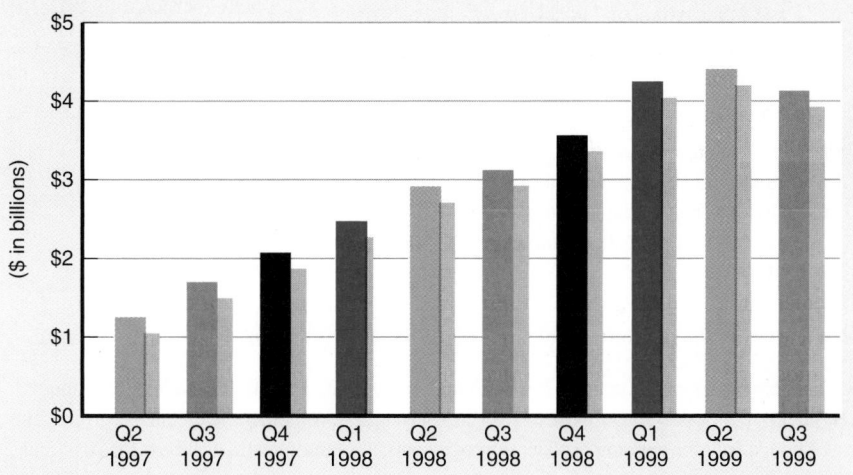

FUTURE OR FALLOUT?

Microsoft's unearned revenue account consists of revenues set aside from the sales of Windows 98, Windows NT and Office to pay for future improvements. It also includes the value of coupons that entitle users to upgrade to newer versions of Microsoft software.

Required:

1. Based on the revenue recognition principles discussed in Chapters 2 and 3, explain why a company such as Microsoft would set aside some software sales revenues as "unearned"?

2. How would you determine how much sales revenue to set aside each quarter? Is this number easy to calculate?

3. Suppose the Unearned revenue account is reduced by $100 million. Where do these dollars go? (The Unearned revenue account is reduced by a debit. What account receives the offsetting credit?)

4. Describe how contracting and regulatory incentives might influence how much revenue is set aside as unearned. How might these incentives influence when the Unearned revenue account is reduced and by how much?

5. Why do analysts and investors pay such close attention to changes in Microsoft's Unearned revenue account?

Margaret Magee has served both as an outside director to Maxcor Manufacturing since 2007 and as a member of the company's compensation committee since 2011. Margaret has been reviewing Maxcor's 2014 preliminary earnings statement in preparation for the February 2015 board and compensation committee meetings. She is uneasy about the company's definition and computation of operating profits for 2014, particularly because management bonuses at Maxcor are based on achieving specific operating profit goals.

C7-2

Maxcor Manufacturing: Compensation and earnings quality **(LO 4)**

Maxcor Manufacturing

Consolidated Results of Operations

($ in millions)	Years Ended December 31, 2014	Years Ended December 31, 2013
Sales	$98.4	$111.2
Operating costs		
Cost of goods sold	(81.5)	(92.2)
Selling, general, and administrative expenses	(12.5)	(12.9)
Operating profit	4.4	6.1
Research and development expenses (see note)	(5.7)	(2.4)
Provision for plant closings (see note)	(2.6)	–0–
Interest expense	(2.9)	(2.6)
Other income	0.7	1.2
Profit (loss) before taxes	(6.1)	2.3
Provision (credit) for income taxes	2.1	(0.8)
Profit (loss) of consolidated companies	(4.0)	1.5
Equity in profit of affiliated companies	0.2	0.3
Profit (loss)	$(3.8)	$ 1.8

The preliminary financial statements also contained the following notes:

Research and Engineering Expenses. Research and engineering expenses include both amounts charged to Research and development expenses for new product development and charges originally made to Cost of goods sold for ongoing product improvements. The amounts (in millions) for 2014 and 2013 were:

	2014	2013
Research and development expenses	$5.7	$2.4
Cost of goods sold	2.9	6.3
Research and engineering expense	$8.6	$8.7

Plant Closing Costs. In 2014, the Company recorded provisions for plant closing and staff consolidation costs totaling $2.62 million. Included in this total are charges related to the probable closing of the Company's York, Pennsylvania, facility ($1.75 million), the consolidation of the North American operations of the Building Construction Products Division ($0.63 million), and charges to reflect lower estimates of the market value of previously closed U.K. facilities ($0.24 million). These costs include the estimated costs of employee severance benefits, net losses on disposal of land, buildings, machinery and equipment, and other costs incidental to the closing and planned consolidation.

Maxcor Manufacturing is an established, privately held manufacturer that operates in two principal business segments: *Building construction products,* which involves the design, manufacturing, and marketing of construction and materials-handling machinery, and *Engines* for various off-highway applications. Before 2014, the company had experienced 15 years of steadily increasing sales and operating profits.

The company was founded in 1938 by Hugh Maxwell, a former Ford Motor Company engineer. Neither Maxwell nor any members of his family are currently company officers. Maxcor's common stock is held by the Maxwell Family Trust (35%), the Maxwell Employee Stock Ownership Plan (ESOP) Trust (50%), a venture capital firm (13%), and current management (2%). Magee also serves as an outside trustee for the Maxwell ESOP Trust.

Maxcor's senior management participates in an incentive bonus plan that was first adopted in 2004. The bonus formula for 2014 was approved by the compensation committee at its February 2014 meeting. According to the plan, each senior manager's 2014 bonus is to be determined as follows:

Bonus as Percentage of 2014 Salary	2014 Operating Profits ($ in millions)
0%	Below $4.0
100	At least $4.0
200	At least $6.0
300	At least $8.0

The compensation committee can award a lower amount than that indicated by the plan formula if circumstances warrant such action. No bonus reductions have occurred since the plan was adopted in 2004.

Required:

Why might Magee feel uneasy about Maxcor's computation of 2014 operating profits? Should she approve the 100% bonus payment for 2014 as specified by the plan formula? What changes (if any) would you recommend be made to the bonus formula for next year?

Whole Foods Market's Compensation Committee determines a portion of executive bonuses qualitatively. For the quantitative portion, the Committee selects from 13 performance metrics. For the fiscal year 2012, the Compensation Committee selected the following six quantitative performance criteria, formulas, and relative weightings:

C7-3

Whole Foods Market: EVA®-based compensation
(LO 2)

1. Comparable store sales growth — $5,000 is earned for every 10 basis points of improvement, and the total is multiplied by 20% to weight this portion of the quantitative bonus amount.

2. Year-over-year improvement in EBITANCE — For every dollar of results, $0.005 (or 0.50%) is earned, and the total is multiplied by 20% to weight this portion of the quantitative bonus amount.

3. NOPAT ROIC — $8,000 is earned for every 10 basis points of return, and the total is multiplied by 20% to weight this portion of the quantitative bonus amount.

4. Year-over-year improvement in EVA® — For every dollar of results, $0.0175 (or 1.75%) is earned, and the total is multiplied by 20% to weight this portion of the quantitative bonus amount.

5. Positive free cash flow — For every dollar of results, $0.0015 (or 0.15%) is earned, and the total is multiplied by 10% to weight this portion of the quantitative bonus amount.

6. Year-over-year improvement in average store development cost per square foot — $5,000 is earned for every 10 basis points of improvement, and the total is multiplied by 10% to weight this portion of the quantitative bonus amount.

Source: Whole Foods Market, Proxy Statement, January 25, 2013.

Comparable store sales growth represents growth in sales from stores open for the entirety of the current period and the comparison period. EBITANCE is earnings before interest, taxes, and non-cash expense. Noncash expense includes depreciation, amortization, fixed asset impairment charges, noncash share-based payment expense, deferred rent, and last-in, first-out ("LIFO") charge. NOPAT ROIC is net operating profit after tax divided by total invested capital. EVA® is economic value added, which is described in this chapter. Positive free cash flow is cash flow from operations minus capital expenditures.

Whole Foods does not use stock price performance as a factor in determining annual cash compensation. However, the company believes a relationship exists between stock price and team members' performance, so that its compensation plan is designed to reward team members for positive stock price performance.

Required:

1. Compared to GAAP earnings, what advantage does EVA® provide as a performance metric for incentive compensation purposes? Why might this advantage be particularly important for companies such as Whole Foods Market?

2. Explain why Whole Foods Market does not use stock price performance to determine annual compensation for its executives. What mechanisms other than annual compensation might the company use to encourage managers to create shareholder value?

3. What impact (if any) does EVA® use have on earnings management? In other words, will managers be more likely or less likely to use accounting tricks to achieve EVA® bonus targets than is the case for traditional GAAP earnings targets?

4. Explain how the EVA® pool works and why it might help overcome management's tendency to focus on the short term.

5. How does using a weighted-average of six performance metrics alter an executive's behavior relative to if he or she faced a single performance metric?

C7-4

Duke Energy Corp.: Rate regulation and earnings management **(LO 4)**

Regulated utilities such as Duke Energy are authorized to earn a specific rate of return on their capital investments. Energy regulators set a rate that the utility can charge its customers for the electricity. If the cost of fuel and other operations decreases and a utility earns more than its authorized rate of return, regulators may cut the rate a utility charges its customers.

DUKE ENERGY SETTLES WITH STATES ON CHARGES IT UNDERSTATED NET

Duke Energy Corp.'s regulated electric utility, Duke Power, agreed to pay $25 million to its customers to settle allegations the company had underreported profit in order to avoid having to reduce its electricity rates.

Energy regulators in North Carolina and South Carolina had ordered an audit of Duke Power's books. The inquiry, conducted by accounting firm Grant Thornton LLP, found the utility had failed to report about $123 million in pre-tax income from 1998 to 2000. . . .

"They manipulated their earnings in an effort to ensure that they didn't report numbers above the authorized rate of return," said Gary Walsh, executive director of the South Carolina [Public Service] commission.

Grant Thornton concluded that the $123 million in accounting entries were "inconsistent with applicable accounting principles, inconsistent with Duke Power's past practice and without proper justification." The report says there was a coordinated effort by the utility unit's top management to underreport net income by overreporting expenses, specifically insurance for its nuclear operations.

Duke Energy, in a written statement, said it had reached "different professional opinions" than Grant Thornton on the accounting issues but had agreed to change the way it accounts for certain items, specifically nuclear insurance, as part of the proposed settlement. Duke Energy, which hasn't admitted to any wrongdoing, said it would take a $19 million charge in the fourth quarter in connection with the settlement if it is approved. . . .

The utility's underreporting to regulators didn't affect Duke Energy's report of net income, the Grant Thornton report said. . . .

Duke Power's accounting problems started in late 1998 when a neighboring utility was ordered to cut rates to its customers after it had earned more than the amount allowed by state regulators. According to the audit of Duke Power's books, as well as Duke internal documents cited in the report, Duke executives at that point realized their utility risked a similar order and decided they had to change the handling of certain accounting items to avoid showing too high a rate of return.

Source: E. K. Kranhold, "Duke Energy Settles with States on Charges It Understated Net," *The Wall Street Journal,* October 23, 2002. Copyright © 2002 Dow Jones & Company, Inc. All rights reserved worldwide. Reprinted with permission.

Required:

1. Many earnings management devices are intended to accelerate revenue or delay expenses and thus increase current earnings. Explain how electricity rate regulation sometimes creates incentives for utility executives to *overstate* expenses and *understate* earnings.

2. Documents produced by Duke Energy in connection with this matter indicate that some personnel at the company characterized "above-the-line" expenses as those that Duke's electric customers paid—meaning they were accounted for and included in the electric rates paid by customers—while "below-the-line" expenses were characterized as "paid" by Duke's shareholders. Suppose Duke Energy spent $10 million hiring a consulting company to develop a new logo for the company. Explain why customers and shareholders care whether the cost of logo development is classified by the company as "above" or "below" the line.

3. According to the news article, "The utility's underreporting to regulators didn't affect Duke Energy's report of [GAAP] net income." Explain why.

C 7 - 5

Computer Associates
International: Compensation
and accounting irregularities
(LO 3)

CA'S EX-CEO PLEADS GUILTY TO SECURITIES FRAUD

Sanjay Kumar, the former chief executive of CA Inc., pleaded guilty to securities fraud and obstruction of justice charges stemming from a scheme that used backdated contracts to falsify the U.S. company's quarterly earnings reports.

The plea ends the career of a Sri Lankan immigrant who climbed to the top of the corporate ladder and made a fortune in the U.S. high-technology boom. Mr. Kumar now faces a maximum 90 years in prison if the eight counts to which he pleaded result in consecutive sentences. However, lighter sentencing of 10 to 30 years might be dictated under federal guidelines.

At the software company formerly known as Computer Associates, Mr. Kumar first gained note as the protégé of company founder Charles Wang. Together, the two built a fast-growing enterprise adept at taking over smaller companies specializing in software for corporate back offices.

But in 2000, when the company abruptly announced a change in auditors and accounting methodology, revenue started to plummet. The Securities and Exchange Commission began investigating in 2002 and eventually referred the case to the U.S. Justice Department, which has secured a number of guilty pleas of top CA Executives.

In September 2004, Mr. Kumar, 44 years old, was indicted with former sales chief Stephen Richards, 41, who also pleaded guilty yesterday. Mr. Kumar had left the company earlier in the year.

The defense decision to plead guilty followed the Friday arrest of Tommy Bennett, a former CA executive who recently has been working for Mr. Kumar. Mr. Bennett was charged with conspiracy to obstruct justice.

According to Mr. Bennett's arrest warrant, Mr. Bennett, who was senior vice president in change of business development

and who worked at CA from 1988 to 2004, became involved after prosecutors told the court they planned to introduce evidence that Mr. Kumar had erased the hard drive on his personal computer in 2003—after CA had advised employees to preserve all evidence. Mr. Bennett was arrested for approaching a former CA technician, who allegedly had helped Mr. Kumar erase the drive. . . .

Mr. Wang, 60, first spotted the younger Mr. Kumar when Mr. Kumar was a poor teenage immigrant. The two immigrants eventually became wealthy together, once sharing with another executive a $1 billion award of shares in the company. . . .

CA admitted in 2004 that it had improperly inflated quarterly revenue over several years. Four top officers and three financial officers of CA have pled guilty in connection with the case. CA itself was also charged, but it avoided an indictment by reaching a deferred prosecution agreement with the Justice Department. Under that agreement, CA has continued to cooperate with prosecutors, paid $225 million in restitution to shareholders and agreed to have a court-appointed independent examiner while restating some $2.2 billion in revenue, which was booked in the wrong periods. . . .

According to evidence presented by the government and described by CA in its restatements, much of the predictability of revenue was due to fraudulent accounting. According to the government, Mr. Kumar orchestrated "35-day months" at the end of each quarter, during which sales executives and Mr. Kumar himself frantically cut deals to persuade customers to sign needed contracts, which were then backdated to make it appear they had been signed in the previous quarter.

Required:

1. Refer to Exhibit 7.1, which describes the 2003 annual incentive compensation plan for top executives at Computer Associates International. (Details of the accounting abuses at Computer Associates are described in Chapter 1.) What features of this plan might have contributed to the illegal backdating of sales contracts?

2. Stock options and company shares comprised a substantial portion of Kumar's personal wealth. How might these equity-based incentives have contributed to the illegal backdating of sales contracts?

3. Why would Computer Associates' outside auditor have difficulty spotting the contract backdating?

.mhhe.com/revsine6e

**Remember to check the book's companion website
for additional study material.**

Receivables | 8

Receivables are amounts that outsiders owe to a business firm. In U.K. financial reports, receivables are called "debtors"—a term clearly connoting the legal obligation of outsiders to make payments to a firm. Most receivables arise from credit sales and are called **trade receivables** or **accounts receivable.** Receivables that result from other types of transactions and events (for example, insurance claims from casualty losses) are separately disclosed, if significant, on the balance sheet. This separate disclosure facilitates informed financial analysis.

ASSESSING THE NET REALIZABLE VALUE OF ACCOUNTS RECEIVABLE

Accounts receivable are generally[1] reflected in the balance sheet at **net realizable value.**[2] Two things must be estimated to determine the net realizable value of receivables:

1. The amount that will not be collected because customers are unable to pay—called **uncollectibles.**
2. The amount that will not be collected because customers return the merchandise for credit or are allowed a reduction in the amount owed—called **returns** and **allowances.**

The next sections discuss financial reporting issues relating to uncollectibles, returns, and allowances.

Estimating Uncollectibles

Receivables arising from some credit sales are never collected. These losses are an unavoidable cost of doing business. Companies could adopt such stringent credit standards that "bad debt" losses would be virtually zero. But if they sold only to customers with impeccable credit records, they would forgo many otherwise profitable sales opportunities.

Most companies establish credit policies by weighing the expected cost of credit sales—customer billing and collection costs plus potential bad debt losses—against the

---

[1] We say "generally" because firms may elect the fair value option for receivables. See FASB Accounting Standards Codification (ASC) Section 825-10-25: Financial Instruments—Overall—Recognition—Fair Value Option. Although all firms have this option, firms in the financial services industry would be the most likely firms to adopt it. We discuss briefly the fair value option as it applies to receivables later in the chapter. Chapters 6 and 11 discuss fair value measurement and the fair value option in more detail.

[2] *Net realizable value* refers to the selling price of an item minus reasonable further costs both to make the item ready to sell and to sell it. When applied to trade receivables, net realizable value refers to the amount of money the business can reasonably expect to collect from its credit customers.

Chapter

benefit of increased sales. Companies choose what they believe is a profit-maximizing balance. This trade-off between increased costs and additional profits from credit sales illustrates that bad debts are often unavoidable. Consequently, accrual accounting requires that some *estimate* of uncollectible accounts be offset against current period sales.

Traditionally, most firms have referred to losses from uncollectible accounts as *bad debt expense* and have treated them as operating expenses. Conceptually, losses associated with uncollectible accounts should be viewed as a reduction of revenue because the revenue should not have been recognized originally. The FASB takes this conceptual view in its recent Revenue Recognition exposure draft.[3] It states that revenues should be shown gross, and expected losses related to collectibility should be shown as reductions from the gross revenues. To be consistent with accounting theory, and to acknowledge the probable change in revenue recognition, we do not use *bad debt expense* in the remainder of the chapter. Instead, we use *bad debt provision* or *provision for doubtful accounts*. However, the reader should recognize that most firms will continue to treat these provisions as expenses until they adopt the new Revenue Recognition standard.

Suppose that Bristol Corporation estimates that, based on current industry trends and the company's experience, bad debt losses arising from first quarter 2014 sales are expected to be $30,000. The entry Bristol makes under GAAP is:

DR	Bad debt provision	$30,000
	CR Allowance for uncollectibles.	$30,000

The Allowance for uncollectibles (alternatively titled Allowance for doubtful accounts) is a contra-asset account that is subtracted from gross accounts receivable. If Bristol's Accounts receivable (gross) and Allowance for uncollectibles balance *before* recording this bad debt entry were $1,500,000 and $15,000, respectively, after recording bad debts, its balance sheet shows:

Accounts receivable (gross)	$1,500,000	
Less: Allowance for uncollectibles	(45,000)	$\begin{cases} (15,000) \text{ Initial balance} \\ (30,000) \text{ Addition} \end{cases}$
Accounts receivable (net)	$1,455,000	

> **A third approach, which is used only for tax reporting purposes, is the direct write-off method.** Under this approach, the bad debt provision is recorded at the time a specific account is written off, with an offsetting credit to Accounts receivable. No allowance account is used under this approach. Because tax reporting rules require the direct write-off method for recognizing uncollectible accounts while GAAP requires one of the two allowance methods described here, a temporary or timing difference between book income and taxable income is created (see Chapter 13 for further discussion).

Companies can use two alternative approaches to estimate uncollectible accounts. One multiplies a specific loss percentage by sales revenues; the other multiplies a (usually different) loss percentage by gross accounts receivable. Each approach is illustrated as follows.

1. *The sales revenue approach.* Assume that Bristol Corporation prepares quarterly financial statements and must estimate the bad debt provision at the end of each quarter. Analyzing past customer payment patterns, Bristol determined that bad debt losses average about 1% of sales. If first quarter sales in 2014 total $3,000,000, bad debt losses from those sales are expected to total $30,000. Bristol then makes the entry previously illustrated to record its estimate of bad debt losses arising from current quarter sales.

Sales Revenue Approach

Estimate the current period bad debt provision as a percentage of current period sales. For Bristol Corporation, the estimate is:

0.01 × $3,000,000 Sales for the quarter = $30,000 Bad debt provision

So, the entry is:

DR	Bad debt provision	$30,000
	CR Allowance for uncollectibles.	$30,000

---

[3] See FASB *Revenue Recognition (Topic 605)—Proposed Accounting Standards Update (Revised),* (Norwalk, CT: January 2012), paragraphs 68 and 69.

2. *The gross accounts receivable approach.* Suppose that instead of estimating bad debts as a percentage of sales, Bristol determined that at any given time, approximately 3% of gross accounts receivable eventually prove uncollectible. Gross receivables at March 31, 2014, total $1,500,000, which means that on that date the required allowance for uncollectibles is 3% of this amount, or $45,000. Because the allowance account balance is only $15,000, $30,000 must be added to the uncollectibles account at the end of the quarter. Doing this brings the allowance for uncollectibles balance up to $45,000.

Gross Receivables Approach

Estimate the required allowance account balance as a percentage of gross receivables and then adjust the allowance upward or downward to this figure. For Bristol Corporation, the required allowance account balance is:

　0.03 × $1,500,000 Outstanding receivables = $45,000 Allowance for uncollectibles

The allowance account currently has a $15,000 balance, so $30,000 is added:

DR	Bad debt provision	$30,000
	CR Allowance for uncollectibles.	$30,000

Writing Off Bad Debts

When a specific account receivable is known to be definitely uncollectible, the entire account must be removed from the books. For example, if Bristol determines that a $750 receivable from Ralph Company cannot be collected, it makes the following entry:

DR	Allowance for uncollectibles	$750
	CR Account receivable—Ralph Company	$750

Notice that this entry has no effect on income. A specific account receivable (Ralph Company) is eliminated from the books and the allowance contra-account is reduced, *but no bad debt provision is recorded.* This is consistent with the accrual accounting philosophy of recording estimated bad debts when the sale was made rather than at some later date when the nonpaying customer is identified. Of course, Bristol Corporation does not know at the time of each sale which particular customers will be unable to pay. That's why the offsetting credit for the bad debt provision was originally made to the contra-asset account, Allowance for uncollectibles. *Only when the seller knows which specific receivable is uncollectible can the individual account (Ralph Company) be written off.* This is what the preceding entry accomplishes.

"Backing into" the $30,000 with the use of a T-account is shown as follows:

Allowance for uncollectibles

$15,000	Current balance
(30,000)	Required adjustment
$45,000	Computed new balance

Assessing the Adequacy of the Allowance for Uncollectibles Account Balance

No matter which method—percentage of sales or percentage of gross receivables—is used to estimate bad debts, management must periodically assess the reasonableness of the allowance for uncollectibles balance. Given existing economic conditions and customer circumstances, is the balance in the Allowance for uncollectibles account adequate, excessive, or insufficient?

To make this judgment, management performs an **aging of accounts receivable.** As the name implies, an aging of receivables is simply a determination of how long each receivable has been on the books. Receivables that are long past due often exist because customers are experiencing financial difficulties and may ultimately be unable to pay. An aging is performed by subdividing total accounts receivable into several age categories (see Exhibit 8.1).

| EXHIBIT 8.1 | Bristol Corporation: Allowance for Uncollectibles Based on Aging of Receivables |

On December 31, 2014, Bristol Corporation's gross accounts receivable are $1,600,000, and the balance of the Allowance for uncollectibles is $39,000. Bristol's normal sales terms require payment within 30 days after the sale is made and the goods are received by the buyer. Bristol determines that the receivables have the following age distribution:

	Current	31–90 days old	91–180 days old	Over 180 days old	Total
Amount	$1,450,000	$125,000	$15,000	$10,000	$1,600,000

Once the receivables have been grouped by age category, a separate estimate of uncollectibles by category is developed. Based on past experience, Bristol determines the following estimate of expected bad debt losses by category:

| Estimated % of bad debt losses | 2.5% | 6% | 20% | 40% | |

The required balance in the Allowance for uncollectibles account would then be as follows:

	Current	31–90 days old	91–180 days old	Over 180 days old	Total
Amount	$1,450,000	$125,000	$15,000	$10,000	$1,600,000
× Estimated % of bad debt losses	2.5%	6%	20%	40%	
= Allowance for uncollectibles	$ 36,250	$ 7,500	$ 3,000	$ 4,000	$ 50,750

Because the balance of the Allowance for uncollectibles is only $39,000 on December 31, 2014, the account must be increased by $11,750. This is the difference between the $50,750 required balance (as computed) and the existing $39,000 balance. To bring the balance up to the $50,750 figure indicated by the aging, Bristol makes the following adjusting entry:

> **DR** Bad debt provision $11,750
>   **CR** Allowance for uncollectibles......................... $11,750

Obviously, considerable judgment goes into evaluating the adequacy of the Allowance for uncollectibles balance. Most companies carefully appraise this area because audit guidelines are well developed and auditors' scrutiny is intense.

Exhibit 8.2 contains selected financial information from 2007 to 2010 for Krispy Kreme Doughnuts, Inc. Accounts receivable arise primarily from franchise royalties, supply and equipment sales to franchisees, and off-premise sales by convenience and grocery stores. Part A

| EXHIBIT 8.2 | Krispy Kreme Doughnuts, Inc.: Analysis of Uncollectible Accounts Receivable |

($ in millions)	Jan. 31, 2010	Feb. 1, 2009	Feb. 3, 2008	Jan 28, 2007
A. Select Reported Amounts				
Revenues	$346.520	$385.522	$430.370	$461.195
Pre-tax income	0.418	(3.558)	(64.727)	(41.025)
Ending accounts receivables (gross)	18.714	22.086	27.741	29.514
B. Change in Allowance for doubtful accounts				
Balance at beginning of year	$ 2.857	$ 4.750	$ 2.745	$ 13.656
Provision for doubtful accounts	(0.651)	0.071	2.150	1.836
Chargeoffs	(0.863)	(2.064)	(0.145)	(12.632)
Other	—	0.100	—	(0.115)
Balance at end of year	$ 1.343	$ 2.857	$ 4.750	$ 2.745
C. Analysis				
Provision for doubtful accounts as a % of sales	−0.19%	0.02%	0.50%	0.40%
Provision for doubtful accounts as a % of ending receivables	−3.48%	0.32%	7.75%	6.22%
Allowance as a % of ending receivables	7.18%	12.94%	17.12%	9.30%

Source: Krispy Kreme Doughnuts, Inc. Form 10-Ks.

of Exhibit 8.2 shows that Krispy Kreme's revenue and accounts receivables declined over the four years. It incurred large losses in fiscal 2007 and 2008 and returned to profitability in 2010.

Part B shows how the allowance for doubtful accounts changed over the same period. The balance was $13.656 million at the beginning of fiscal 2007 but fell to $2.745 million by the end of the year. Krispy Kreme had increased its allowance in prior years because franchisees and other customers were having difficulties making scheduled payments. Note the large chargeoff of $12.632 million in 2007. These accounts were deemed as uncollectible in 2007 but had been charged against income in prior years. Expectations about future collections improved substantially after fiscal 2008, and Krispy Kreme actually **debited the allowance and credited the provision for doubtful accounts** for $0.651 million in fiscal 2010. **This is very unusual!** Even more unusual is that the credit to the provision is greater than Krispy Kreme's pre-tax income of 0.418 million.

Part C shows the provision as a percentage of sales and receivables. Note how the percentages decline over time as Krispy Kreme's collection experience improves. The allowance as a percentage of receivables in 2007 is 9.30% and rises to 17.12% in 2008. The rise indicates that Krispy Kreme was still expecting significant losses on its receivables. However, it began decreasing the percentage in fiscal 2009, and reduced the percentage to 7.18% in 2010, which is below the fiscal 2007 percentage. **This analysis shows that a firm must continually adjust its allowance as its collection experience changes.**

Determining whether the allowance for doubtful accounts is adequate requires judgment. Consequently, the temptation to "manage" earnings by using bad debt accruals can be strong. Research evidence suggests that companies reduce the bad debt provision when earnings are otherwise low and then increase the provision when earnings are high.[4] To evaluate whether the reduction in Krispy Kreme's ratio of Allowance for doubtful accounts to gross receivables is reasonable, the analyst should compare the ratio to other firms similar to Krispy Kreme, look for additional discussion in Krispy Kreme's 10-Ks, and listen to the analyst earnings briefings.

Estimating Sales Returns and Allowances

Sometimes a company ships the wrong goods to customers or the correct goods arrive damaged. In either case, the customer returns the item or requests a price reduction. When goods are returned or a price allowance granted, the customer's account receivable must be reduced and an income statement charge made. Assume that Bristol Corporation agrees to reduce by $8,000 the price of goods that arrived damaged at Bath Company. Bristol records this price adjustment as:

DR Sales returns and allowances	$8,000	
CR Accounts receivable—Bath Company		$8,000

Bath now owes $8,000 less than the amount it previously had been billed, as reflected by the reduction to Accounts receivable. The account that is debited here is an offset to sales revenues—termed a **contra-revenue account.** Sales revenues are not reduced directly; the contra-revenue account allows Bristol Corporation to keep a running record of the frequency

---

[4] See M. McNichols and G. P. Wilson, "Evidence of Earnings Management from the Provision for Bad Debts," *Journal of Accounting Research,* Supplement 1988, pp. 1–31; S. Moyer, "Capital Adequacy Ratio Regulations and Accounting Choices in Commercial Banks," *Journal of Accounting and Economics,* July 1990, pp. 123–54; M. Scholes, P. Wilson, and M. Wolfson, "Tax Planning, Regulatory Capital Planning and Financial Reporting Strategy for Commercial Banks," *Review of Financial Studies* 3, no. 4 (1990), pp. 625–50; J. Collins, D. Shackelford, and J. Wahlen, "Bank Differences in the Coordination of Regulatory Capital, Earnings, and Taxes," *Journal of Accounting Research,* Autumn 1995, pp. 263–91; and A. Beatty, S. Chamberlain, and J. Magliolo, "Managing Financial Reports of Commercial Banks: The Influence of Taxes, Regulatory Capital, and Earnings," *Journal of Accounting Research,* Autumn 1995, pp. 231–61. As the titles of these studies suggest, regulatory capital requirements in commercial banks and financial services companies also influence bad debt accruals.

and amount of returns and price reductions because these events represent potential breakdowns in customer relations.

At the end of the reporting period, companies estimate the expected amount of future returns and allowances arising from receivables currently on the books. If the estimated number is large in relation to the accounts receivable balance or to earnings, the adjusting entry is:

DR	Sales returns and allowances	XXX
	CR Allowance for sales returns and allowances	XXX

The debit is to a contra-revenue account that reduces net sales by the estimated amount of returns and allowances. Because it is not yet known which *specific* customer accounts will require future returns and allowances, the credit entry must be made to a contra-asset account that offsets gross accounts receivable. In practice, estimated sales returns and allowances are seldom material in relation to receivables. Consequently, no end-of-period accrual is typically made for these items.

Ordinary returns and allowances are seldom a major issue in financial reporting. On the other hand, companies occasionally adopt "aggressive" revenue recognition practices—meaning that they recognize revenue either prematurely or inappropriately. Examples include recognizing revenue on goods shipped on consignment or recognizing revenue when delivery is delayed, as discussed in Chapter 3. This revenue recognition aggressiveness generates significant returns in later periods. Aggressive revenue recognition overstates both accounts receivable and income. Consequently, analysts must understand that a sudden spurt in accounts receivable may be a danger signal, as we see next.

> Ignoring *estimated* future returns and allowances has a trivial effect on income when the amount of *actual* returns and allowances does not vary greatly from year to year.

Analytical Insight: Do Existing Receivables Represent Real Sales?

 **Analysis**

When a company's sales terms, customer creditworthiness, and accounting methods do not change from period to period, the growth rates in sales and in accounts receivable are roughly equal. If sales increase by 10%, accounts receivable should also increase by about 10%. Statement readers who understand this carefully monitor the relationship between sales growth and receivables growth. When receivables increase faster than sales, those statement readers see a potential "red flag." Receivables could increase at a higher rate than sales for several reasons. One reason is that the disparity in growth rates might reflect something positive such as a deliberate change in sales terms designed to attract new customers. Suppose that instead of requiring payment within 30 days of shipment, Hmong Company allows customers to pay in four months. Such changes broaden the potential market for the company's products and services by allowing slightly less creditworthy customers to buy the firm's products. In this case, receivables growth will far outpace sales growth. To illustrate, consider the following example:

> Assume that before introducing more lenient credit terms, Hmong Company had annual sales of $12 million and customers, on average, paid within 30 days. Outstanding accounts receivable, therefore, represent one month's sales, or $1 million. Under the new credit program, customer receivables would represent four months' sales, or $4 million; this represents a 300% increase in receivables even if total sales remain unchanged.

Another reason for receivables growth exceeding sales growth could be due to deteriorating creditworthiness among existing customers, which could represent an emerging problem.

If customers are unable to pay, receivables will not be collected when due and accounts receivable will increase at a faster rate than sales. However, the company's independent auditor would likely uncover this problem in the annual financial statements audit. Accordingly, when the cause for the unusual growth in receivables is due to an inability of customers to pay on time, GAAP financial statements would ordinarily show a large increase in estimated uncollectibles.

So, growth in accounts receivables can outstrip growth in sales revenues either because firms allow customers more time to pay or because customers are unable to pay due to their own cash flow problems.

Another reason why receivables growth could exceed sales growth is that the firm has changed its financial reporting procedures, which determine *when* sales are recognized. To illustrate this possibility, let's consider an automobile manufacturer that builds cars and ships them to a dealer who ultimately sells them to you and other individuals. Assume that the manufacturer in past years has recognized revenue from sales only when an automobile was sold to the final customer. But if the auto manufacturer in the current year suddenly decides to recognize automobile sales revenue when the cars are shipped to the dealer, *this represents a significant change in financial reporting principles.* To see how such a financial reporting change affects the relationship between receivables growth and sales growth, we discuss the classic case of Bausch & Lomb Inc. Exhibit 8.3 presents selected financial statement data for the years 1990–1993.

> Collectibility of receivables requires forecasts of future conditions. Forecasts are often inaccurate. However, existing auditing procedures for accounts receivable are very detailed and stringent, requiring auditors to send confirmations to randomly chosen customers verifying the legitimacy of the recorded receivables. Aging schedules to uncover payment problems are also required. Furthermore, auditors undertake credit checks on the company's largest customers to ascertain the probability of eventual collection. As a consequence of these procedures, while collectibility requires forecasts that could be wrong, extreme overstatement of net (collectible) receivables is rare. An exception to the general rule occurred in 2007 when the default rate on subprime loans was much higher than expected. See our discussion of subprime loans later in this chapter.

In Exhibit 8.3 net trade accounts receivable increased dramatically in both 1992 and 1993. This increase shows up in absolute dollar amounts (an increase of $72,076 in 1992 and $107,635 in 1993) as well as in relation to total balance sheet assets (11.8% in 1991 versus 14.8% in 1992 and 15.3% in 1993). What makes this growth seem "unusual," however, is the disparity in growth rates between sales and receivables. While sales grew 12.43% in 1992 and 9.54% in 1993, receivables jumped by 35.11% and 38.81% in those same years, respectively (highlighted areas in Exhibit 8.3). Clearly, something unusual was happening in both

EXHIBIT 8.3	**Bausch & Lomb, Inc.: Selected Financial Statement Data, 1990–1993**			
($000 omitted)	**1990**	**1991**	**1992**	**1993**
Net sales	$1,368,580	$1,520,104	$1,709,086	$1,872,184
Net trade accounts receivable	$202,967	$205,262	$277,338	$384,973
Days sales outstanding*	54 days*	49 days	59 days	75 days
Receivables as a % of total assets	12.1%	11.8%	14.8%	15.3%
Year-to-year growth in				
Net sales		$151,524	$188,982	$163,098
Net trade accounts receivable		$2,295	$72,076	$107,635
Net sales		11.07%	12.43%	9.54%
Net trade accounts receivable		1.13%	35.11%	38.81%

* *Days sales outstanding* is Net trade accounts receivables divided by Net sales per day. For example, the calculation for 1990 Days sales outstanding is $202,967 net trade receivables/($1,368,580 net sales/365 days) = 54 days

Source: Bausch & Lomb Inc. Annual Reports.

years. A partial explanation was provided one year later in the company's 1994 annual report, which stated:

> In the fourth quarter of 1993, the Company adopted a business strategy to shift responsibility for the sale and distribution of a portion of the U.S. traditional contact lens business to optical distributors. A 1993 fourth quarter marketing program to implement this strategy was developed, contributing one-time net income of approximately $10 million. Subsequently, this strategy proved unsuccessful.

Prior to this change in Bausch & Lomb's business strategy, revenues and associated receivables were recognized when sales were made to retailers or ultimate consumers. In the fourth quarter of 1993, however, shipments to distributors appear to have been treated as sales. This change in revenue recognition was in keeping with the shift in sales strategy, but the worry is that if distributors are unable to sell their inventory, they will return it to Bausch & Lomb for credit. This is exactly what happened, as described in the company's 1994 annual report:

> *In October 1994, the Company announced it had implemented a new pricing policy for traditional contact lenses and agreed on a one-time basis to accept returns from these distributors.* As a result, the Company recorded sales reserves and pricing adjustments which reduced operating earnings by approximately $20 million in the third quarter. The new pricing policy sought to enhance the Company's competitive position in a market segment where industry prices had declined since the business strategy was implemented. *The returns program allowed U.S. distributors to send back the excess portion of unsold traditional lenses and balance their overall contact lens inventories.* [Emphasis added.]

Authoritative accounting literature lists six criteria that must be satisfied before revenue is recognized when a sales agreement contains conditions that may allow the buyer to return the product.* The most important of these criteria for Bausch & Lomb are:

1. The return privilege has substantially expired because of performance by the seller, or other conditions.

2. The amount of future returns can be reasonably estimated.

These guidelines are imprecise and abuses of the rules have occurred, as discussed in Chapter 3.

* FASB ASC Section 605-15-25: Revenue Recognition—Products—Recognition.

So, we see that like our hypothetical automobile manufacturer, Bausch & Lomb began recognizing revenue when output was shipped to distributors rather than waiting until units were sold to final consumers.

Although the first 1994 annual report excerpt above suggests that the changes in sales strategy and revenue recognition began only in 1993, the data in Exhibit 8.3 reveal that a large disparity in sales and receivables growth rates occurred earlier. What explains this pre-1993 disparity?

A *BusinessWeek* article published six months after Bausch & Lomb released its 1994 annual report suggests several possible explanations.[5] The article asserts that top-down pressure to achieve sales and profit goals caused Bausch & Lomb managers to loosen revenue recognition standards in the early 1990s, an assertion that top Bausch & Lomb executives vehemently denied. Specifically, Bausch & Lomb sales representatives allegedly "gave customers extraordinarily long payment terms, knowingly fed gray markets, and threatened to cut off distributors unless they took on huge quantities of unwanted products. Some also shipped goods before customers ordered them and booked the shipments as sales. . . ."[6] The article further contends that this type of deal making "became frantic" from the last quarter of 1992 through early 1994 and that the U.S. contact lens division "had a habit of constantly rolling over unpaid bills so that customers wouldn't return unwanted goods for credit."[7] If *BusinessWeek*'s interpretations are correct, these practices would explain the unusual pre-1993 receivables growth.

See Figure 8.1 for the company's days sales outstanding (DSO) for receivables by quarter for March 1989 through the end of 1995. DSO receivables represent just the dollar amount of

---

[5] M. Maremont, "Blind Ambition," *BusinessWeek,* October 23, 1995, pp. 78–92.

[6] Ibid., pp. 79–80.

[7] Ibid., p. 86.

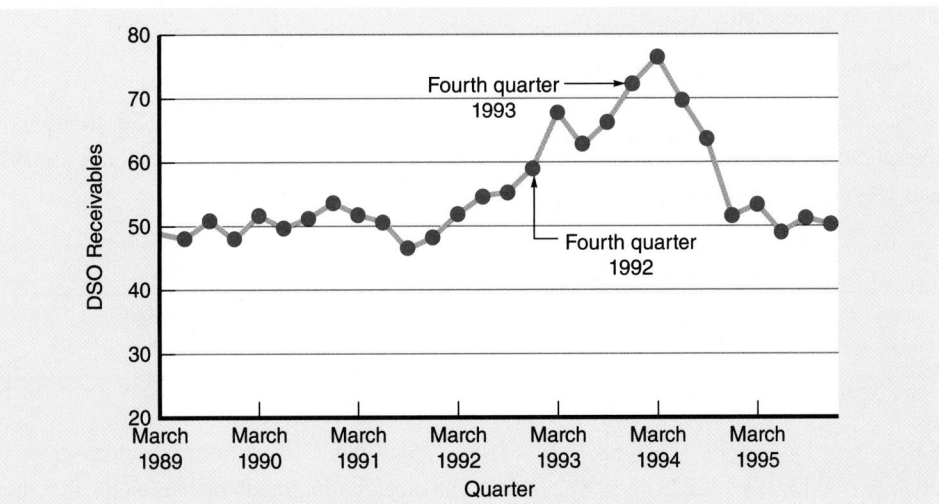

Figure 8.1

BAUSCH & LOMB, INC.

DSO Receivables* by Quarter

* DSO Receivables is Days sales outstanding for receivables and is defined as Net trade accounts receivable divided by Net sales per day.

outstanding receivables divided by average daily sales. From March 1989 to March 1992, Bausch & Lomb's DSO receivables averaged about 50 days and fluctuated little from quarter to quarter. By the end of 1992, however, DSO receivables had increased to 59 days, and by the fourth quarter of 1993, it stood at 72 days. This unusual pattern of increase in Bausch & Lomb's DSO receivables undoubtedly caused some financial statement readers to become skeptical about the company's revenue recognition practices.

One last point regarding Bausch & Lomb. The *BusinessWeek* article contends that the reported December 31, 1993, accounts receivable number of $385 million (see Exhibit 8.3) *understates* the real growth of outstanding customer credit. The understatement occurs, according to the article, because Bausch & Lomb sold some receivables to a third-party financing company for cash. Receivable sales of this sort are called **factoring:** Factoring transactions are discussed later in this chapter. Factored receivables are removed from the balance sheet. If the receivables had not been factored, the accounts receivable balance would have been higher and the disparity in sales and receivables growth rates for 1992 and 1993 would have been even larger!

Scrutiny of changes in accounts receivable balances is essential. Large increases in accounts receivable relative to sales frequently represent a danger signal. The two most likely causes are collection difficulties and sales contingencies or disputes that may lead to potential returns. Another possible explanation, however, as you just saw, is a change in revenue recognition methods.

Many revenue recognition "irregularities" can be discovered by tracking the relationship between changes in sales and changes in receivables. Sunbeam Corporation's 1997 annual report provides an example of how the evaluation of this relationship led to uncovering fraud.

Albert J. Dunlap joined Sunbeam Corporation as chairman and chief executive officer in July 1996. He had earned a reputation as a "turnaround" specialist because of his aggressiveness in restructuring and downsizing companies he had previously run, such as Scott Paper. By cutting costs and eliminating waste, Dunlap restored the companies to profitability. Sunbeam had mediocre performance in the years prior to Dunlap's arrival. But reported 1997 quarterly and annual financial results seemed to indicate considerable improvement.

At the start of his letter to shareholders in the 1997 annual report, Dunlap stated:

> We had an amazing year in 1997! During the past 12 months we set new records in almost every facet of the Company's operations. We experienced significant sales growth and concurrently increased margins and earnings.

The letter concluded:

Stay tuned, the best is yet to come!

Soon after the 1997 Sunbeam annual report appeared, some analysts raised questions about the quality of the reported earnings and the economic validity of the results.[8] Sales for 1997 and 1996 and year-end receivables were:

($000 omitted)	1997	1996
Net sales	$1,168,182	$984,236
Gross trade accounts receivable	313,013	229,455

Sales grew by 18.69% ([$1,168,182 − $984,236]/$984,236) while receivables grew by 36.42% ([$313,013 − $229,455]/$229,455). The disparity in growth rates is a clue that there may be a problem. Investigation is warranted because the following notes to the 1997 annual report in Exhibit 8.4 disclose "bill and hold sales" and disposal of receivables—events that affect both sales and receivables.

We first mentioned bill and hold sales in Chapter 3 in our discussion of revenue recognition abuses (see page 149). In a **bill and hold** sale, the company recognizes revenue and the associated account receivable but does not ship the product to the customer until later. One issue is whether these are real sales. The annual report note states that these bill and hold terms were at the customer's request and legal title to the inventory had passed. So, it's reasonable to conclude that the sales were legitimate even though the inventory hadn't been shipped. But the other issue is whether these are really sales of 1997 or instead 1998 sales that have been pulled into 1997 by the bill and hold terms. The amount in question isn't trivial—3% of Sunbeam's 1997 sales ($1,168,182,000) is $35,045,460. This represents 19.05% of the reported $183,946,000 sales increase between 1996 and 1997.

🔍 **Analysis**

Furthermore, the true growth in receivables is understated by the amount of receivables sold at the end of 1997. The $59 million cash received is the book value of the receivables minus a financing charge. So, $59 million roughly approximates the amount of receivables removed from the books.

EXHIBIT 8.4 Sunbeam Corporation Notes

Revenue Recognition

The Company recognizes revenues from product sales principally at the time of shipment to customers. In limited circumstances, at the customer's request the Company may sell seasonal product on a bill and hold basis provided that the goods are completed, packaged and ready for shipment, such goods are segregated, and the risks of ownership and legal title have passed to the customer. *The amount of such bill and hold sales at December 29, 1997, was approximately 3% of consolidated revenues.*

Credit Facilities

In December 1997, the Company entered into a revolving trade accounts receivable securitization program to sell without recourse, through a wholly-owned subsidiary, certain trade accounts receivable. The maximum amount of receivables that can be sold through this program is $70 million. *At December 28, 1997, the Company had received approximately $59 million from the sale of trade accounts receivable.*

Source: Sunbeam Corporation 1997 annual report. [Emphasis and highlighting added.]

---

[8] See Jonathan R. Laing, "Dangerous Games," *Barron's,* June 8, 1998.

Let's summarize the clues that were available to the auditor and/or analyst:

1. Receivables growth greatly exceeded sales growth.

2. Bill and hold sales raise the possibility that some of this disparity is because sales were booked too early, before delivery, thus generating receivables that won't be collected quickly. Worse yet, collection may never occur if delivery of "sold" items is ultimately refused.

3. Had Sunbeam not sold approximately $59 million of receivables, the "real" growth rate of receivables would have exceeded the reported rate of 36.42%, further increasing the disparity between sales and receivables growth rates. This even larger disparity increases the likelihood that Sunbeam may have engaged in "channel stuffing"—that is, recognizing revenue on shipped products that exceed customer needs and are likely to be returned.

> Sunbeam's board of directors fired Albert J. Dunlap on June 15, 1998. He personally paid $15 million as part of a $141 million settlement of a shareholder class action fraud lawsuit against Sunbeam. In addition, he later paid a $500,000 penalty to the SEC to settle civil allegations of accounting fraud. As part of the settlement, Dunlap agreed to a permanent ban on serving as an official of a public company.
>
> *Source:* Michael Schroeder, "Dunlap Settles Fraud Charges with the SEC," *The Wall Street Journal,* September 5, 2002.

These, as well as other issues unrelated to receivables, prompted a reaudit of Sunbeam's financial statements from the fourth quarter of 1996 through the first quarter of 1998. The reaudit disclosed that 1997 sales had been overstated by $95,092,000 (or 8.1%) with profits of $38,301,000 rather than $109,415,000, as reported.[9]

And it was careful scrutiny by informed analysts that led to inquiries that resulted in these corrections!

RECAP

Evaluating the net realizable value of accounts receivable requires analyzing the adequacy of estimated uncollectibles and provisions for returns and price adjustments. An increase in receivables growth exceeding sales growth could indicate aggressive revenue recognition policies. Statement readers who carefully examine receivables trends and levels can discern potential problems as they evolve.

IMPUTING INTEREST ON TRADE NOTES RECEIVABLE[10]

In certain industries, the seller sometimes extends long-term credit to the buyer, who then signs a note. If the note bears an interest rate that approximates prevailing borrowing and lending rates, the accounting is straightforward. Assume that Michele Corporation manufactures and sells a machine to Texas Products Company. The machine's cash selling price is $5 million. Michele accepts a three-year, $5 million interest-bearing note signed by Texas Products with 10% interest per annum to be paid in quarterly installments each year. Assume that 10% approximates prevailing borrowing rates for companies as creditworthy as Texas Products. Upon making the sale, Michele records:

DR Note receivable—Texas Products Company	$5,000,000	
CR Sales revenue		$5,000,000

Interest income accrues each quarter, and upon receipt of the cash payment, the accrued interest receivable is reduced. These are the entries:

DR Accrued interest receivable	$125,000	
CR Interest income		$125,000

To accrue three months' interest = [$5,000,000 × 0.10]/4.

---

[9] See Dana Canedy, "Sunbeam Restates Results, and 'Fix' Shows Significant Warts," *The New York Times,* October 21, 1998.

[10] This section assumes that you understand present value concepts. Please see the Appendix at the end of the book for a review of the time value of money.

DR Cash	$125,000	
CR Accrued interest receivable		$125,000

To record receipt of the interest payment.

Similar to accounts receivable, a firm would have to assess the collectibility of its notes and establish an appropriate allowance. Given that we have already discussed this issue with accounts receivable, we do not discuss it in this section.

A complication arises for a note that does not state an interest rate or when the stated rate is lower than prevailing rates for loans of similar risk. Suppose that Monson Corporation sells equipment it manufactured to Davenport Products in exchange for a $5 million noninterest-bearing note due in three years. The note bears no explicit interest. It says only that the entire $5 million is to be paid at the end of three years. Monson's published cash selling price for the equipment is $3,756,600, and the current borrowing rate for companies like Davenport is 10%.

The present value factor for a payment three years away at a 10% rate is 0.75132 (see book Appendix, Table 1). Therefore, the note's present value is $5 million times 0.75132, or $3,756,600—which exactly equals the equipment's cash selling price. Although the $5 million note itself does not contain any mention of interest, Monson will earn a return of 10% per year for financing Davenport's long-term credit purchase. This is demonstrated in Exhibit 8.5.

At the end of Year 3, Monson receives a $5 million payment, which consists of the cash sales price ($3,756,600) plus interest ($1,243,400 = $375,660 + $413,226 + $454,514).

Monson Corporation records the sale to Davenport Products as:

DR Note receivable—Davenport	$3,756,600	
CR Sales revenue		$3,756,600

Over the next three years, the note receivable is increased and interest income recognized. For example, at the end of Year 1, the entry is:[11]

DR Note receivable—Davenport	$375,660	
CR Interest income		$375,660

EXHIBIT 8.5	**Demonstration That Monson Earns 10% Interest for Three Years on Cash Sales Price of $3,756,600**

Present value of $5,000,000 payment in 3 years (cash sales price)	$3,756,600
Plus: Year 1 interest: 10% × $3,756,600	375,660
Equals: Present value of $5,000,000 payment due in 2 years	4,132,260
Plus: Year 2 interest: 10% × $4,132,260	413,226
Equals: Present value of $5,000,000 payment due in 1 year	4,545,486
Plus: Year 3 interest: 10% × $4,545,486	454,514*
Equals: Davenport payment at the end of Year 3	$5,000,000

* Rounded.

---

[11] For simplicity, we ignore the periodic recording of interest on a monthly or quarterly basis during the year. In reality, if quarterly financial statements were prepared, the first year interest income of $375,660 would be apportioned to each quarter.

Notice that after Monson records interest income of $413,226 in Year 2 and $454,514 in Year 3, the carrying amount of the note receivable is exactly $5 million, as shown in Exhibit 8.5. When Davenport makes the required payment at the note's maturity, Monson Corporation records:

DR	Cash	$5,000,000	
	CR Note receivable—Davenport		$5,000,000

This process of allocating the $5 million proceeds of the note between sales revenue and interest income is called **imputed interest.**

A complication also arises when the note receivable contains a stated interest rate ***but the stated rate is lower than prevailing borrowing rates at the time of the transaction.*** When this happens, interest must again be imputed. Assume that Quinones Corporation sells a machine to Linda Manufacturing in exchange for a $4 million, three-year, 2.5% note from Linda. There will be three annual payments at the stated 2.5% interest rate and a final payment of $4 million. However, at the time of the sale, the interest rate normally charged to companies with Linda's credit rating is 10%. Because the note's stated interest rate is far below Linda's normal borrowing rate, Quinones must determine the machine's implied sales price by computing the note's present value at the 10% rate. The computation of this implied sales price is shown in Exhibit 8.6.

This computation shows that the implied selling price of the machine is $3,253,966 because this amount equals the discounted present value of the note Quinones received in exchange for the machine. Quinones makes the following entry:

DR	Note receivable—Linda Mfg.	$3,253,966	
	CR Sales revenue		$3,253,966

Because payment is deferred, Quinones will earn 10% over the duration of the note on the amount of the credit sale ($3,253,966). The interest payments received consist of three $100,000 payments over each of the ensuing years and another imputed interest payment of $746,034 ($4,000,000 minus the $3,253,966 implied cash selling price) at maturity. Though interest will be collected at these times, the interest income will be recognized using the 10% rate. See Exhibit 8.7 for the composition of yearly interest income, and Figure 8.2 for the note receivable from the time of sale to maturity.

EXHIBIT 8.6	**Computation of Implied Sales Price in Conjunction with a Nominal Interest-Bearing Note**

Calculation of Present Value at 10% Effective Interest Rate

Present value of $4,000,000 principal repayment in three years at 10%:

	$4,000,000	×	0.75132	=	$3,005,280

Present value of three interest payments of $1,000,000 (that is, $4,000,000 × 0.025), each at 10%:

Year 1	$100,000	×	0.90909	=	90,909
Year 2	$100,000	×	0.82645	=	82,645
Year 3	$100,000	×	0.75132	=	75,132
Implied sales price of machine					$3,253,966

(*Note:* All present value factors are from the book Appendix, Table 1, 10% column.)

| | **EXHIBIT 8.7** | Quinones Corporation: Computation of Interest on Note Receivable | | |

	(a) Interest Income—10% of Column (d) Balance for Prior Year	**(b)** Cash Interest Received	**(c)** Increase in Present Value of Note (a) Minus (b)	**(d)** End-of-Year Present Value of Note
Inception	—	—	—	$3,253,966
Year 1	$ 325,397	$100,000	$225,397	3,479,363
Year 2	347,936	100,000	247,936	3,727,299
Year 3	372,701*	100,000	272,701	4,000,000
Total	$1,046,034			

* Rounded.

Figure 8.2

QUINONES
CORPORATION

Carrying Value of Note
Receivable

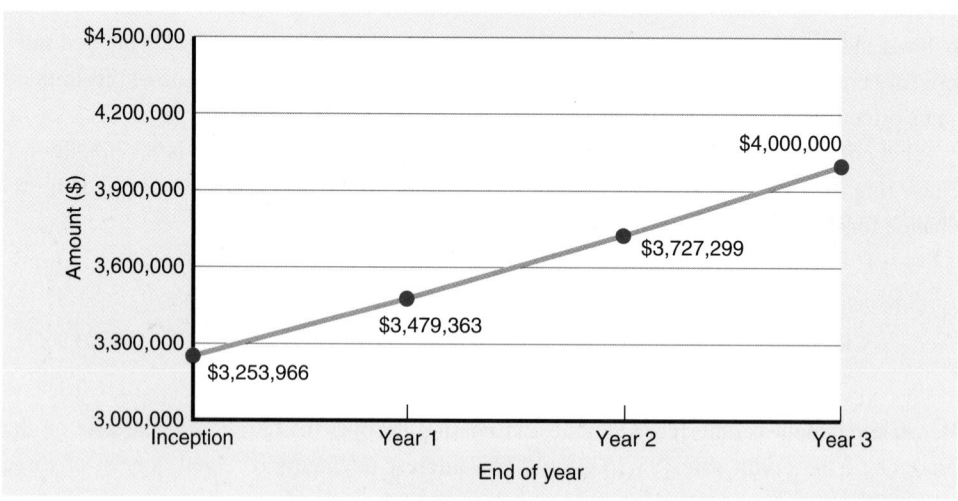

As shown in Exhibit 8.7 and Figure 8.2, the present value of the note, and thus its carrying value, increases each year (see column [d] of Exhibit 8.7). The increase in the carrying value of the note equals the difference between the annual 10% interest income earned—Column (a)—and the cash received—Column (b). For example, in Year 1, Quinones records:

DR	Note receivable—Linda Mfg.	$225,397	
DR	Cash	100,000	
	CR Interest income		$325,397

Similar entries are made in Years 2 and 3 using the amounts shown in Exhibit 8.7. At the end of Year 3, the note's carrying amount will be $4,000,000. When Linda pays the note on maturity, Quinones records the payment as:

DR	Cash	$4,000,000	
	CR Note receivable—Linda Mfg.		$4,000,000

For long-term credit sales transactions utilizing notes receivable:

- **Sales revenue is recorded at the known cash price (Monson Corporation) or at the implied cash price (Quinones Corporation) of the item sold. The implied cash price is determined by computing the note receivable's present value using the prevailing borrowing rate (that is, the effective market rate of interest).**

- **Interest income is recorded each period over the note's term to maturity using the prevailing borrowing rate.**

This approach achieves a clear separation between the two income sources—credit sales and interest earned. Income from the credit sale is recorded when the sale is made. Interest income from financing the customer's purchase, on the other hand, is recorded over time as it is earned. This separation of income sources makes it possible to assess the degree to which a company's overall earnings are due to profitable credit sales versus profitable customer financing—a potentially important distinction.

THE FAIR VALUE OPTION

Although most firms record accounts and notes receivable at net realizable value, they have the option to record them at fair value under FASB ASC Section 825-10-25.[12] Firms may choose the fair value option for a single financial instrument or a group of financial instruments. Generally, a financial institution would elect this option for a receivable if it expects the fair value of the receivable to move in the opposite direction of the fair value of another financial instrument that also is carried at fair value. The fair value option is discussed in detail in Chapter 11. However, we explain briefly how the fair value option would be different from the net realizable accounting discussed above.

We will first consider the Bristol Corporation accounts receivable example on page 418. Bristol Corporation reports a net realizable value of $1,455,000 (gross receivables of $1,500,000 minus allowance for uncollectibles of $45,000). As mentioned in Chapter 6 on page 314, fair value is "the price that would be received to sell an asset or paid to transfer a liability in an orderly transaction between market participants at the measurement date."[13] For Bristol Corporation, assume that there is an active market for these types of receivables and that the price is 95% of face value, or $1,425,000 (95% × $1,500,000). To adjust the receivable's carrying value to fair value, the difference between the fair value and the face amount of the receivable is recognized as an unrealized loss on the income statement as follows:

DR	Unrealized loss on receivables	$75,000	
	CR Fair value adjustment—Accounts receivable		$75,000

The Fair value adjustment—Accounts receivable account is an asset valuation account that would be adjusted upward or downward as fair values change and as the receivables are collected. In this example, the fair value is less than the net realizable value, but in other cases, the fair value could exceed or approximate net realizable value.

We will now consider the Quinones example from Exhibit 8.7. The carrying value of $3,479,363 at the end of year 1 is based on the interest rate in effect at the time of the original sale. If the fair value option is elected, the carrying value would reflect general changes in interest rates and changes in the creditworthiness of firms similar to Linda Mfg. Assume that there is an active

---

[12] FASB ASC Section 825-10-25: Financial Instruments—Overall—Recognition—Fair Value Option.
[13] FASB ASC Master Glossary: Fair Value.

market for these types of notes, and the fair value at the end of Year 1 is $3,542,631, resulting in a market yield of 9%.[14] To reflect the fair value on its balance sheet, Quinones would increase the carrying value by $63,268 (fair value of $3,542,631 minus the carrying value of $3,479,363) with the following entry:

DR	Fair value adjustment—note receivable	$63,268
	CR Unrealized gain on note receivable.	$63,268

The Fair value adjustment—note receivable account is a valuation account that increases the carrying value of the note in this case. It can carry a debit or credit balance depending on whether there is a cumulative gain or a cumulative loss. The Unrealized gain on note receivable is part of net income. Future interest income will be based on the new rate of 9% and will be recognized in net income. Subsequent changes to the fair value caused by changes in risk or interest rates will also be recorded in net income. See Chapter 7, page 393 for a discussion of how subsequent losses would affect bank capital requirements.

Exhibit 8.8 summarizes how the value of the note changes under the fair value option. We assume that fair values and interest rates are stable throughout Year 1. Consequently, the first Year 1 line is identical to the Year 1 line in Exhibit 8.7. The second Year 1 line contains the increase in fair value. The market interest rate of 9% is then used to compute interest income in subsequent periods. The rows for Year 2 and Year 3 assume that interest rates remain stable after Year 1. Note that the total income recognized over the three years is $1,046,034, the same amount that is shown in Exhibit 8.7. *The fair value option changes the pattern of income recognition but not the total amount recognized.*

When a firm does not adopt the fair value option, it still must disclose the fair value of its long-term notes receivable. The fair value of accounts receivable does not have to be reported if the reported value approximates fair value.

EXHIBIT 8.8	**Quinones Corporation: Note Receivable Recorded at Fair Value**			
	Interest Income or Unrealized Gain (loss)	**Cash Interest Received**	**Increase (Decrease) in Present Value of Note**	**End of Year Present Value of Note**
Inception	—	—	—	$3,253,966
Year 1	$ 325,397*	$100,000	$225,397	3,479,363
Year 1	63,268[†]		63,268	3,542,631
Year 2	318,837[‡]	100,000	218,837	3,761,468
Year 3	338,532	100,000	238,532	4,000,000
Total	$1,046,034			

* $3,253,966 × 10%

[†] Fair value of $3,542,631 minus $3,479,363 prior carrying value

[‡] $3,542,631 × 9%

---

[14] If the market yield is 9%, the fair value can be computed as follows:

Present value of $4,000,000 principal repayment in two years at 9%:

$4,000,000	×	0.84168	=	$3,366,720

Present value of two interest payments of $100,000 using an ordinary annuity of 9%:

$100,000	×	1.75911	=	175,911
				$3,542,631

ACCELERATING CASH COLLECTION: SALE OF RECEIVABLES AND COLLATERALIZED BORROWINGS

Companies collect cash from their credit customers according to the payment schedule called for in the note or trade receivable. Sometimes companies prefer not to wait until customer payments arrive in the normal course of business. Instead, they accelerate cash collection with the help of a bank or financing company.

There are two ways to accelerate cash collections as depicted in Figure 8.3, **factoring** and **collateralized borrowings.** In factoring, the company sells its receivables outright to a bank or factoring company in exchange for cash. Customer payments flow directly to the factor in most cases. Factoring can be **without recourse** (also called **nonrecourse**), meaning that the factor cannot turn to the company for payment in the event that some customer receivables prove uncollectible. Factoring can also be **with recourse,** meaning that the company must buy back any bad receivables from the factor.

> Credit card companies "buy" the receivables at a discount—they pay the restaurant, say, 97 cents for every dollar of receivables. The three-cent "discount" is the fee the credit card company charges for accelerating cash receipts.

The other way to accelerate cash collection is through a collateralized borrowing, where the receivables are the collateral. The company obtains cash from the bank or finance company and is responsible for repaying the loan.

Reasons why companies might accelerate cash collections include:

1. *Competitive conditions require credit sales but the company is unwilling to bear the cost of processing and collecting receivables.* Restaurants are an example of this. Customers of upscale restaurants expect to be able to charge meals rather than pay cash, yet most restaurants are reluctant to incur the costs of servicing receivables. Consequently, restaurants rely on third parties such as VISA, American Express, and Diners' Club, companies that, in effect, "buy" the customer receivable from the restaurant.

2. *There may be an imbalance between the credit terms of the company's suppliers and the time required to collect customer receivables.* Suppliers might extend credit on three-month terms to a company while inventory turnover (cost of goods sold/average inventory) plus receivables turnover (net credit sales/average accounts receivable) total six months. To pay suppliers within the due date, cash collection must be accelerated.

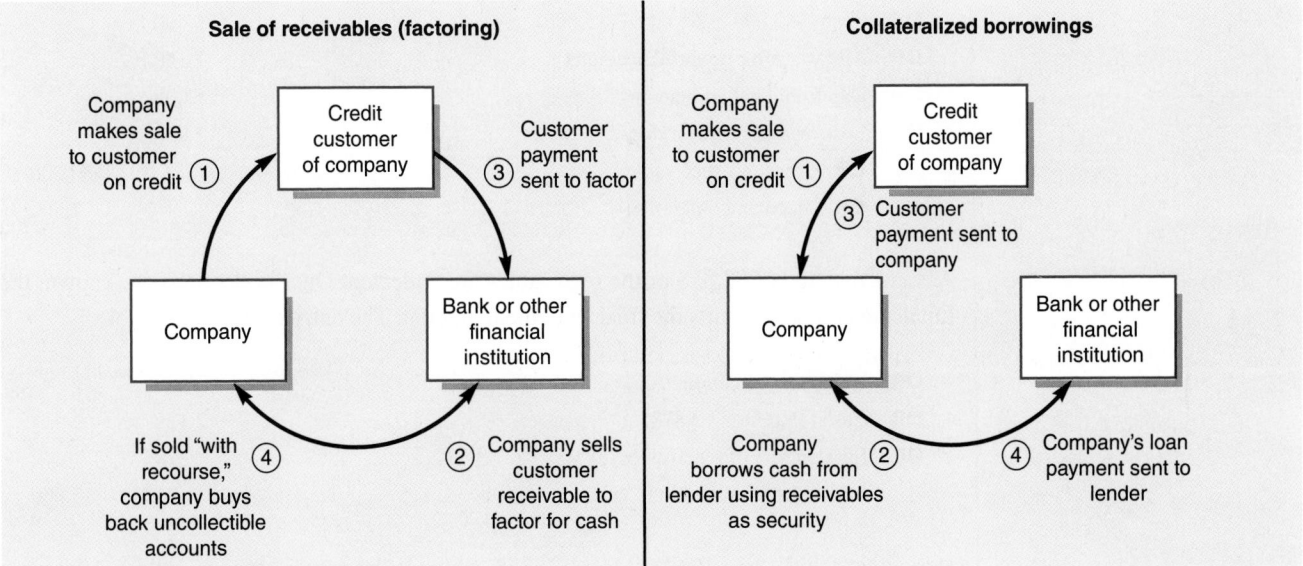

Figure 8.3 SALE OF RECEIVABLES AND COLLATERALIZED BORROWINGS

3. *The company may have an immediate need for cash but be short of it.* Selling receivables to a financial institution allows the company to raise cash quickly. Using receivables as collateral for a bank loan also represents a way to obtain quick cash (and perhaps low-cost financing).

Let's look at the accounting issues that arise when receivables are either sold or used in a collateralized borrowing.

Sale of Receivables (Factoring)

To illustrate a factoring transaction *without* recourse, suppose that Hervey Corporation sells to Leslie Financing gross receivables of $80,000 that have a related allowance for doubtful accounts of $2,150. The purchaser (Leslie Financing) is called the **factor.** Leslie charges a fee of 5% of gross receivables (0.05% × $80,000 = $4,000) for this service and pays Hervey $76,000. In a sale without recourse, if some of Hervey's customers fail to pay the amount owed, Leslie has no recourse against Hervey (hence, the term)—and thus, Leslie bears the loss. To record the factoring, Hervey would make the following journal entry:

DR	Cash	$76,000	
DR	Allowance for doubtful accounts	2,150	
DR	Loss on sale of receivables	1,850	
	CR Accounts receivable....................................		$80,000

The $1,850 is charged to a loss account because Hervey was willing to accept cash of $76,000 even though the net book value of the receivable was $77,850 ($80,000 gross amount less $2,150 allowance).

Next we illustrate the sale of accounts receivable *with* recourse. Again, assume that Hervey Corporation sells $80,000 of trade receivables to Leslie Financing. If any of the receivables are not paid, Hervey bears the loss up to a pre-established limit. Leslie's fee is reduced to 2% (0.02 × $80,000 = $1,600) with a recourse transaction rather than 5% because the risk to Leslie is lower. Assume that Hervey estimates that the fair value of the recourse obligation is $2,500. Leslie withholds $5,000 to cover possible late collections and noncollections. The entry on Hervey Corporation's books is:

DR	Cash ($80,000 − $1,600 − $5,000)........................	$73,400	
DR	Allowance for doubtful accounts	2,150	
DR	Due from Leslie Financing.................................	5,000	
DR	Loss on sale of receivables	1,950	
	CR Accounts receivable		$80,000
	CR Recourse obligation		2,500

Assume that all but $2,878 of the receivables are collected. Once collections are known, the financing company remits the final settlement amount. The entry on Hervey's books is:

DR	Recourse obligation.......................................	$2,500	
DR	Cash ($5,000 − $2,878)	2,122	
DR	Loss on sale of receivables	378	
	CR Due from Leslie Financing		$5,000

Hervey recognizes an additional loss of $378, which is the excess of the uncollected amounts of $2,878 over its Recourse obligation of $2,500.

Borrowing Using Receivables as Collateral

If the transaction between Hervey Corporation and Leslie Financing had been a **collateralized loan** rather than a sale of receivables, the Accounts receivable would not be removed from Hervey's books. Instead, Hervey would create a liability account to reflect the loan. Suppose that $80,000 of receivables was pledged as collateral for a loan; interest is 4% of $80,000. Then the entry is:

DR	Cash	$76,800	
	CR Loan payable—Leslie Financing		$76,800

The fact that the receivables have been pledged as collateral for this loan must be disclosed in the notes to the financial statements if material.[15] Once the loan is due, Hervey makes these entries:

DR	Loan payable—Leslie Financing...........................	$76,800	
DR	Interest expense	3,200	
	CR Cash		$80,000

Notes receivable can also be assigned or sold. Accelerating cash collection on notes in this way is called **discounting** because the financial institution advances cash to the company based on the *discounted* present value of the notes. For example, suppose Abbott Manufacturing received a $9,000, six-month, 8% per year interest-bearing note from Weaver Company, a customer. That same day, Abbott discounted the note at Second State Bank. If the bank discounts the note at 12%, Abbott receives only $8,798. The cash proceeds to Abbott are computed as follows:

Face amount of the note	$9,000
Interest to maturity ($9,000 $\times$ 0.08 $\times$ 6/12)	360
Maturity amount of the note	9,360
Interest charge by bank	
($9,360 $\times$ 0.12 $\times$ 6/12)	562
Cash proceeds	$8,798

Abbott makes the following entry when the note is discounted:

DR	Cash	$8,798	
DR	Loss on sale of notes receivable	202	
	CR Note receivable		$9,000

Accelerating cash collection generates a loss of $202, the difference between the note's book value and the cash proceeds.

At maturity, the bank will present the note to Weaver Company for payment. Notes can be discounted either with or without recourse. If discounted *with* recourse, Second State Bank would collect $9,360 ($9,000 principal + $360 interest) from Abbott if Weaver failed to pay the note at maturity. When a note is discounted with recourse, the selling firm removes the note from its books and records a recourse obligation, as shown in the receivables factoring example.

---

[15] FASB ASC 860-30-50-4: Transfers and Servicing—Secured borrowing and collateral—Disclosure—Public entities, Collateral.

Ambiguities Abound: Is It a Sale or a Borrowing?

Usually, the nature of a transaction involving receivables is clear. But in some situations, it is not obvious whether the receivables have been sold or are instead being used as collateral for a loan. The ambiguity arises when certain obligations, duties, or rights regarding the transferred receivables are retained by the firm undertaking the transfer (which is called the **transferor**).

The FASB has provided guidelines in the Accounting Standards Codification for distinguishing between sales and collateralized borrowings involving receivables.[16] The guidelines hinge on the issue of whether the transferor *surrenders control over the receivables.* If control is surrendered, the transaction is treated as a sale, and any gain or loss is recognized in earnings. However, if the criteria for a sale are not met because control has not been surrendered, the transaction is accounted for as a collateralized borrowing.

The issue of sale versus borrowing has assumed great importance with the growth of **financial asset securitization.** *Securitization occurs when receivables (such as mortgages and automobile loans) are bundled together and sold or transferred to another organization (securitization entity) that issues securities collateralized by the transferred receivables.* For example, the financing subsidiary of Honda Motor Co. (American Honda Finance Corporation) bundles large numbers of automobile loans together. It then uses these loans as collateral for interest-bearing notes that it sells to outside investors. The outside investors often earn a higher return than would otherwise be available to them because auto loans usually carry a relatively high rate of interest. By bundling large numbers of receivables, Honda creates value because the portfolio effect of the bundling itself reduces the risk of loss.

Home mortgages, car loans, and credit card debt are just a few of the receivables that have been securitized and sold to investors. New mortgage securitization issuances grew from under $25 billion (adjusted for inflation) in 1990 to more than $500 billion in 2006 before falling to almost zero during the height of the economic crisis in the fall of 2008.[17] As the securitization market grew, the FASB provided additional guidance on when to treat securitizations as sales and when to treat them as borrowings.

Ambiguities arise, for example, when a bank transfers a group of mortgages (which, to the bank, are receivables) to some other organization but retains the responsibility for servicing the mortgages. The bank often continues to collect the mortgage payments or to handle customer inquiries, or it even promises to buy back the mortgages at some future date if certain conditions occur.

The accounting treatment of these receivable transactions has important financial reporting implications. For example:

1. If the transaction is really a borrowing but is erroneously treated as a sale, both assets and liabilities are understated (that is, the loan liability does not appear on the company's balance sheet and neither do the receivables that were transferred). The understatements consequently distort ratios such as debt-to-equity and return-on-assets.

2. If the transaction is really a sale, a gain or loss on the transaction should be recognized. To erroneously treat such transactions as borrowings misrepresents the company's net assets.

> Authoritative accounting literature states that the transferor surrenders control over the receivables when *all* of the following conditions are met:*
>
> 1. The transferred assets have been isolated from the transferor and are beyond the transferor's creditors.
>
> 2. The transferee, or its investors in the case of a securitization entity, has the right to pledge or exchange the assets.
>
> 3. There is no agreement obligating the transferor to repurchase or redeem the transferred assets in the future, nor can the transferor unilaterally force the holder to return the assets.
>
> * FASB ASC Paragraph 860-10-40-5: Transfers and Servicing—Overall—Derecognition—Criteria for a Sale of Financial Assets.

Analysis

---

[16] FASB ASC Paragraph 860-10-40-3: Transfers and Servicing—Overall—Derecognition—General Principles.

[17] Government Accountability Office, "Troubled Asset Relief Program—One Year Later, Actions Are Needed to Address Remaining Transparency and Accountability Challenges," GAO-10-16 (Washington, D.C., October 2009, p. 43).

A Closer Look at Securitizations

Securitizations have been popular for two reasons:

1. During the 2004–2007 peak of the securitization activity, investors had a strong appetite for acquiring securitized assets.
2. Firms with large amounts of receivables have powerful incentives to engage in securitizations.

It can be a "win–win" situation for investors and firms; both parties benefit.

Investors benefit because they are able to obtain highly liquid financial instruments that diversify their risk. A simple example shows this. Suppose that the prevailing rate of return on debt instruments with "moderate" risk is 6% per year. The 6% yield is determined by the credit standing of large corporate and government issuers of bonds and other instruments. By contrast, people who take out home mortgages with banks do not have the same high credit standing as these bond issuers. Understandably, the rates people pay on their mortgages are higher—let's say 7% per year.

Assume that a bank forms a bundled portfolio of these home mortgages and is prepared to sell them at a price that yields the investor a return of 6%. The risk associated with the individual mortgages ranges from "low" to "moderately high" *but the risk of the bundled portfolio in the aggregate is moderate.* So, the investors have a new investment option that also provides a 6% per year yield at the same moderate risk level but responds differently than other debt instruments to changes in interest rates and other economic events. This diversifies risk, and that's attractive. Furthermore, the investors could not form a moderate-risk, 6% return mortgage portfolio themselves because the costs of identifying potential mortgagees and assessing credit are high and would lower their return below 6%. Even if they could construct their own portfolio, they'd have difficulty finding buyers for individual mortgages if investors later wanted to liquidate the investment. So, investors benefit from securitizations by gaining liquid portfolio diversification opportunities that they could not achieve on their own.

A bank may reduce risk further by paying an independent third party, a **guarantor,** to bear some of the default risk. For example, a guarantor may agree to pay security holders interest and principal payments for loans that default. Government-sponsored entities, such as Fannie Mae and Freddie Mac, are the primary guarantors for mortgage-backed securities. In its 2009 annual report, Fannie Mae states that it receives upfront fees and ongoing fees based on the amount and risk of the loans. In 2009, its effective fee rate was 0.25% of the amounts guaranteed.

Both the investors and the bank benefit from the reduction in risk. If the bank sells the 7% mortgages at a price that yields the purchasers a return of 6%, the selling price is higher than the carrying value of the mortgages on the bank's books. So, the bank records a gain on the sale of the receivables. ***This gain exists because the bank has created value.*** As you just saw, the individual investors would never consider lending directly to, say, two or three home purchasers. (It's too risky. Who knows how many will default?) But the large portfolio is less risky. Thus, investors who are unable to duplicate the bank's return on their own without assuming high risks (and costs) are very willing to accept the 6% return.

Banks and other firms that engage in securitization transactions do not transact directly with the investors. The process of securitization is somewhat convoluted for reasons we'll soon explain. See Figure 8.4 for how a typical securitization is structured.

The transferor forms what is called a **securitization entity (SE).**[18] The SE is usually a trust or corporation that is legally distinct from the transferor and is created solely for the purpose of undertaking the securitization transaction. The transferor then sells (transfers) the receivables

> When the expected interest and principal payments are discounted at a rate lower than the stated rate, the present value exceeds the face amount of the loans. The computational approach is similar to the one given in Exhibit 8.6 except that the discount rate is lower than the stated rate. Consequently, the present value is higher not lower than the note's face amount. Computational issues will be discussed in more detail in Chapter 11 in conjunction with bond payable premiums.

---

[18] We use the term **securitization entity,** which replaced **special purpose entity (SPE)** that had been used in prior accounting guidance. Company financial statements issued prior to 2010 used the SPE terminology.

Figure 8.4

STRUCTURE OF A
SECURITIZATION

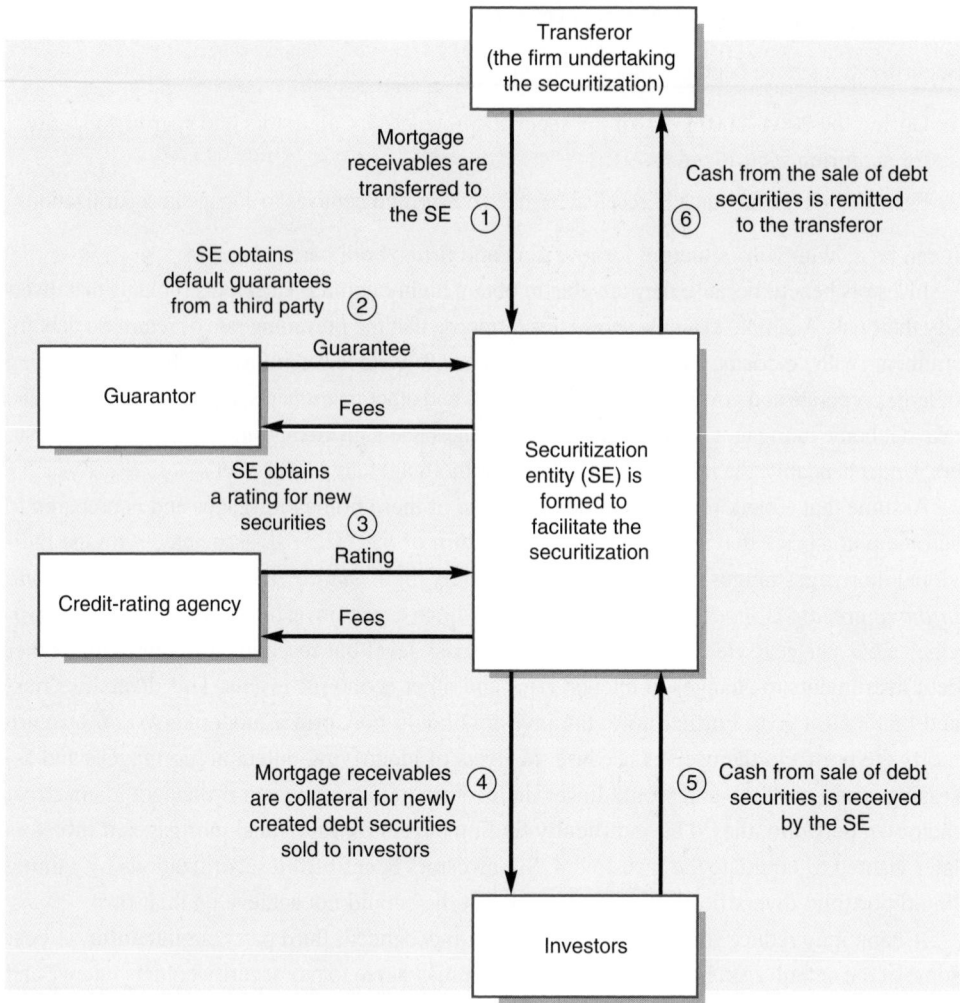

(mortgages in our example) to the SE (① in Figure 8.4). Because the receivables were sold to the SE, they are beyond the reach of the transferor and its creditors. *So, even if the transferor were to declare bankruptcy, the collateral underlying the notes is safe from seizure.* At the time of the transfer, the SE may also obtain guarantees from an outside entity (②). Before the SE markets the new debt securities, it usually obtains a credit rating for the new securities (③). Because the SE is legally separate from the transferor, the SE's credit rating depends on the quality of the transferred receivables and can differ from the rating of the transferor's general debt. The SE pays fees to the rating agency for its rating opinion.[19] The SE then creates and issues debt securities that it sells to outside investors (④ and ⑤). The cash that the SE receives from the investors is then remitted to the transferor (⑥). In many situations, the transferor continues to service the assets (that is, handle cash collections, recordkeeping, etc.), usually for a fee that the SE pays.

The cash flows from the mortgages themselves (that is, principal repayment and interest) are later used to make the periodic interest and principal repayments to the investors who bought the debt securities.

Prior to November 15, 2009, most of these structures were designed to meet the definition of a **qualifying special purpose entity (QSPE)** under pre-Codification *SFAS No. 140,* and the

---

[19] The largest credit-rating agencies are Fitch Ratings, Moody's Investor Service, and Standard & Poor's. For more information on institutional features related to ratings, see Chapter 6 and U.S. Securities and Exchange Commission, *Report on the Role and Function of Credit Rating Agencies in the Operation of the Securities Markets, As Required by Section 702(b) of the Sarbanes-Oxley Act of 2002* (Washington, DC, January, 2003).

transferor kept the debt and the assets of the SE off its balance sheet. The transferor received cash, removed the receivables, and did not record any of the SE's debt. QSPEs were supposed to be passive legal entities with "significantly limited and entirely specified" activities.[20] However, the FASB became concerned that SEs classified as QSPEs were involved in activities such as modifying loans, which was not consistent with the SE being a passive holder of securities. Consequently, the FASB removed the QSPE exception from the guidance contained in ASC Topic 860—Transfers and Servicing and ASC Topic 810—Consolidation.[21] Under the revised guidance, these SEs are treated as part of the transferor (consolidated) if the transferor directs the SE's activities and participates in the SE's gains and losses. In these cases, the transferor treats the securitization as a collateralized borrowing instead of a sale, thereby keeping the receivables on its balance sheet, recording the SE's debt, and not recognizing any gains on the receivable transfer to the SE.[22]

To illustrate the financial statement effects of treating the securitization as a sale versus a collateralized borrowing, consider the following example.

 **Analysis**

On December 31, 2014, Doyle securitized $1,000,000 of mortgages using a securitization entity (SE). The cash received from the SE was exactly $1,000,000, so it recognized no gain or loss on the transaction. If the transaction meets the criteria for *sale accounting*, it will make the following entry:

DR Cash. $1,000,000
    CR Mortgages receivable $1,000,000

The effects of this entry on Doyle's balance sheet are as follows:

	Balances Prior to Securitization	Change in Balances If Transaction Is Treated as a Sale	Balances After Securitization
Assets			
Mortgages receivable	$2,200,000	$(1,000,000)	$1,200,000
All other assets	800,000	1,000,000	1,800,000
Total assets	$3,000,000		$3,000,000
Liabilities and equity			
Liabilities	$2,700,000		$2,700,000
Equity	300,000		300,000
Total liabilities and equity	$3,000,000		$3,000,000

If the transaction does not meet the criteria for sale accounting, Doyle would treat the transaction as a *collateralized borrowing* and make the following entry:

DR Cash. $1,000,000
    CR Loan payable. $1,000,000

(continued)

---

[20] See FASB ASC Paragraph 810-10-05-8A: Consolidation—Overall—Overview and background—Variable interest entities—Consolidation of VIEs. The SE often represents a **variable interest entity** that must be consolidated by the **primary beneficiary,** in this case, the sponsor. See Chapter 16 for more detailed discussions of consolidations, variable interest entities, and primary beneficiaries.

[21] The largest credit-rating agencies are Fitch Ratings, Moody's Investor Service, and Standard & Poor's. For more information on institutional features related to ratings, see Chapter 6 and U.S. Securities and Exchange Commission, *Report on the Role and Function of Credit Rating Agencies in the Operation of the Securities Markets, As Required by Section 702(b) of the Sarbanes-Oxley Act of 2002* (Washington, DC, January 2003).

[22] Research suggests that the bond market did not reduce credit risk for securitized assets removed from the securitizing firms' balance sheets during the 2001 to 2006 time period. See M. Barth, G. Ormazabal, and D. Taylor, "Asset Securitizations and Credit Risk," *The Accounting Review*, vol. 87 (March 2012), pp. 423–48.

The effects of this entry on Doyle's balance sheet are as follows:

	Balances Prior to Securitization	Change in Balances If Transaction Is Treated as a Borrowing	Balances After Securitization
Assets			
Mortgages receivable	$2,200,000		$2,200,000
All other assets	800,000	$1,000,000	1,800,000
Total assets	$3,000,000		$4,000,000
Liabilities and equity			
Liabilities	$2,700,000	$1,000,000	$3,700,000
Equity	300,000		300,000
Total liabilities and equity	$3,000,000		$4,000,000

Doyle's net income for the year ended December 31, 2014, is $40,000.

Doyle National Bank's return-on-assets ratio and debt-to-equity ratio after completing this $1,000,000 transaction are computed in the following table. The left column reflects the ratio under sales treatment. The right column shows the ratio balances *that would have been reflected* if the transaction had been treated as a borrowing with the mortgages serving as collateral.

	Ratios under Sale Scenario	Ratios under Collateralized Borrowing Scenario
Return-on-assets ratio	$\dfrac{\$40,000}{\$3,000,000} = 0.013$	$\dfrac{\$40,000}{\$4,000,000} = 0.01$
Debt-to-equity ratio	$\dfrac{\$2,700,000}{\$300,000} = 9.000$	$\dfrac{\$3,700,000}{\$300,000} = 12.33$

So, you see that treating the transaction as a sale improves the return-on-assets ratio from 1% to 1.3%—a 30% increase. Similarly, the sale treatment improves (reduces) the debt-to-equity ratio from 12.33 to 9—a 27% reduction. If a gain had been recognized on the securitization, both ratios would have been improved even further.

A gain would arise if investors accept a rate that is lower than the face rate on the mortgages (e.g., the mortgages bear a 7% rate but investors accept a 6% rate).

The accounting guidance that became effective for fiscal years beginning after November 15, 2009, applied to both new and *existing* securitizations. As a result, firms often had to change retrospectively from sale accounting to collateralized borrowing accounting for many of its SEs. The differences between the sale scenario and the collateralized borrowing scenario in the Doyle National Bank example illustrate the financial statement impact of the accounting change. In moving from the sale scenario to the borrowing scenario, Doyle's return-on-asset ratio decreased by 23% (0.01/0.013 minus 1), and its debt-to-equity ratio increased by 37% (12.33/9 minus 1). In practice, the effect of the accounting change could be more dramatic. When the mortgage securitizer and guarantor, Fannie Mae, adopted the new accounting guidance at the beginning of 2010, its assets increased from $869.1 billion to $3,246.2 billion (a 274% increase), and its liabilities increased from $884.4 billion to $3,258.2 billion (a 268% increase).[23]

---

[23] See Federal National Mortgage Association (Fannie Mae) March 31, 2010, 10-Q, pages 116–20.

Securitization and the 2008 Financial Crisis

In its 2009 Form 10-*K* (p. 188), Fannie Mae defines a **subprime loan** as

> a mortgage loan made to a borrower with a weaker credit profile than that of a prime borrower. As a result of the weaker credit profile, subprime borrowers have a higher likelihood of default than prime borrowers. (p. 188)

Subprime loans can be securitized as part of a general portfolio of loans or can be put into a pool of subprime loans. Sometimes when loans are securitized, classes of securities with different levels of credit risk may be created. The senior securities receive payments first if there are defaults, and the junior securities receive payments last. Each class of security is then rated and sold. These senior securities could be rated AAA. The junior securities also could be bundled and resecuritized so that a senior class of junior loans could be created. This senior class of junior securities could also receive high credit ratings.[24]

Subprime lending increased substantially from 2004 to the first part of 2007. During these years, subprime lenders and borrowers counted on increasing home prices. However, home prices fell 8.4% in 2007, 18.3% in 2008, and 2.3% in 2009.[25] In addition, interest rates on adjustable-rate mortgages began to reset to higher rates in 2007. Default rates were much higher than expected, and originators, guarantors, and investors lost billions. For example, Fannie Mae's provision for credit losses on guarantees increased from ***$415 million in 2006 to $63.1 billion in 2009*** (2009 10-K, p. 94). In some instances, money market funds held these securities, and investors, who thought that they had highly rated (low-risk) investments, suddenly lost money.[26] In prior home price declines, the banks incurred most of the losses, but because of securitization, many small investors also suffered losses during 2007–2009. Defaults also resulted in firms such as AIG recognizing losses on credit default swaps.

How did everything go so wrong? Figure 8.4 can be used to illustrate where many of the problems occurred. First, originators had incentives to make as many loans as possible, and they were able to sell the loans. Consequently, many of them were not concerned about the underlying risk. Additionally, Fitch Ratings suggests that considerable mortgage application fraud took place.[27] Second, the originators and rating agencies underestimated substantially the risk associated with their guarantees. In addition, securitizers had incentives to "shop" for high ratings.[28] Third, when the borrowers began to default, some of the complex legal issues and structures related to the securitizations made it difficult for the SEs to modify loans. In some cases, the servicing firm had incentives to force the borrower into default.

Fourth, as the defaults began to occur, it was clear that the originators and guarantors had more loss exposure than was evident from their financial statements. Consequently, the FASB increased disclosure requirements and revised the criteria for treating a securitization as a sale. Fifth, the investors overrelied on the ratings agencies and underestimated the positive correlation of defaults across borrowers. This issue also affected firms that wrote credit default swaps. As the number of defaults increased in 2008, firms with large exposures to mortgage-backed securities (MBS), such as Bear Stearns, Lehman Brothers, and Fannie Mae, were

---

[24] See S. Ryan, "Accounting in and for the Subprime Crisis," *The Accounting Review,* vol. 83 (November, 2008), pp. 1615–1617; J. Tiemann, "A Pyramid of Little Golden Crumbs," Tiemann Investment Advisors, LLC (August 31, 2007), p. 7; and F. Norris, "Market Shock: AAA Rating May Be Junk," *The New York Times* (July 20, 2007).

[25] Author's calculation using the S&P/Case-Shiller Non-Seasonally-Adjusted U.S. National Home Price Indices.

[26] See D. Evans, "Subprime Infects $300 Billion of Money Market Funds, Hikes Risk," August 20, 2007, Bloomberg.com.

[27] See Fitch Ratings, The Impact of Poor Underwriting Practices and Fraud in Subprime RMBS Performance" (November 2007).

[28] See F. Sangiorgi, J. Sokobin, and C. Spatt, "Credit-Rating Shopping, Selection and the Equilibrium Structure of Ratings," unpublished working paper (Stockholm School of Economics, 2009) and A. Ashcraft, P. Goldsmith-Pinkham, and J. Vickery, "MBS Ratings and the Mortgage Credit Boom," Federal Reserve Bank of New York Staff Report 449, 2010.

acquired or declared bankruptcy. After Lehman Brothers declared bankruptcy, all securitization markets became inactive, and the world experienced a liquidity crisis. The inactive markets also called into question whether it was appropriate to use Level 1 (active market) information when determining fair values under ASC Topic 820: Fair Value Measurement.

Some Cautions for Financial Statement Readers

Factoring, assignment, and securitization of receivables raise some issues for those who analyze financial statements. Earlier in this chapter, you learned that one way to assess whether reported receivables arose from legitimate sales was to compare the growth rate of sales and the growth rate of receivables. This comparison in Exhibit 8.3 for Bausch & Lomb showed that receivables growth far outstripped sales growth between 1991 and 1993. Our conclusion—based on disclosures from the 1994 Bausch & Lomb annual report—was that the leap in receivables growth arose from "forcing" inventory on distributors and treating these shipments as sales. The way to recognize these potential trouble areas is to monitor receivables growth. *But when firms sell receivables, the receivables number reported in the ending balance sheet includes only the remaining receivables and thus understates the true growth in receivables over the period.*

Suppose that a company is "aggressively" booking sales to artificially raise current earnings. To avoid discovery, the company could factor some of its "good" receivables—those that don't arise from the questionable sales—and thus understate the true disparity in the growth rates of receivables and sales. So, the receivables remaining on the books are the "bad" ones and the factoring has disguised the deterioration in the *quality* of reported receivables. Consequently, statement readers must scrutinize notes and the financing activities section of the cash flow statement for evidence of dispositions of receivables that may be masking overly aggressive revenue recognition policies or bad receivables management.

The transferred receivables "disappear" from the balance sheet. Because receivables are lower, certain ratios such as return on assets and receivables turnover improve when compared to previous periods. But is the ratio improvement sustainable? Should the analyst "undo" the transfer and recompute the ratios with the receivables included? At a minimum, the analyst must be aware of the extent of the disruption in the year-to-year ratio pattern and its impact on financial forecasts. Other adjustments depend on the circumstances. Also, did the transferor "cherry-pick" the best receivables to make the transaction attractive to the purchasers? If it did, the analyst must scrutinize the quality of the remaining receivables as well as the adequacy of the allowance for uncollectibles.

For material transactions, ASC 860-10-50-3 requires firms to provide financial statement users with an understanding of all of the following:

1. A transferor's continuing involvement, if any, with transferred financial assets.
2. The nature of any restrictions on assets reported by an entity in its statement of financial position that relate to a transferred financial asset, including the carrying amounts of those assets.
3. How servicing assets and servicing liabilities are reported under ASC Subtopic 860-50.
4. For both of the following, how the transfer of financial assets affects an entity's financial position, financial performance, and cash flows:
   a. Transfers accounted for as sales, if a transferor has continuing involvement with the transferred financial assets.
   b. Transfers of financial assets accounted for as secured borrowings.

It is too early to tell whether the new disclosures make it easier for analysts to evaluate the effects of receivable sales.

TROUBLED DEBT RESTRUCTURING

What happens to a lender when a customer is financially unable to make the interest and principal payments required by an installment loan or other receivable? Rather than force the customer into bankruptcy, lenders frequently agree to **restructure** the loan receivable, thus allowing the customer to remain in business. The restructured loan can differ from the original loan in several ways:

- Scheduled interest and principal payments may be reduced or eliminated.
- The repayment schedule may be extended over a longer time period.
- The customer and lender can settle the loan for cash, other assets, or equity interests.

> To help you understand this financial instrument, we'll define each of the two words, in reverse order. **Debentures** are bonds that have no underlying collateral that could be seized if Bloom defaulted on the debt. It is an unsecured borrowing. **Subordinated** means that Bloom has other debt issues that "ranked ahead" of this debt in the event of liquidation—that is, investors in the other debt would be paid before investors in the subordinated debenture.

Lenders are willing to restructure a customer's loan to help the customer resolve present financial difficulties and stay in business. And lenders often receive more through restructuring than they would from foreclosure or bankruptcy.

Consider the hypothetical debt restructuring described in Exhibit 8.9. On December 31, 2014, Bloom Corporation owned and/or managed 47 hotel properties located primarily in the northeastern and southeastern United States. It financed these investments using long-term debt—a subordinated debenture. During 2014, the company suffered operating losses and cash flow difficulties that would not allow it to meet its current obligations. The subordinated debenture originally carried an interest rate of 7.5% per year and a maturity date of January 1, 2016. Because Bloom could not make the required loan payments, the lender (a mutual fund) canceled $4.5 million of the debt in exchange for the following:

- An acceleration of the maturity date by 8 1/2 months.
- An increase in the annual interest rate from 7.5% to 18.75%.

Obviously, the lender would have preferred that Bloom pay the original debt principal and interest on time. Faced with the company's inability to do so, it chose to restructure the debt rather than force the company into bankruptcy. The enormous leap in the interest rate from 7.5% to 18.75% reflects Bloom's precarious financial condition and the resulting risk of the restructured loan.

This example illustrates a key feature of **troubled debt restructurings** not present in ordinary debt refinancings. Authoritative accounting literature gives this definition:

> A restructuring of debt constitutes a troubled debt restructuring . . . if the creditor for economic or legal reasons related to the debtor's financial difficulties grants a concession to the debtor that it would not otherwise consider.[29]

EXHIBIT 8.9	**Bloom Corporation: Debt Restructuring**

In July 2014, the Company replaced its outstanding $7.5 million Subordinated Debenture to Oppenheimer Securities Fund with a new Subordinated Debenture bearing the following terms: principal balance of $3.0 million; interest rate of 18.75%; maturity date of April 15, 2015. As a result, the Company reported a gain from the debt restructuring, net of expenses, of approximately $4 million or $0.64 per common share—basic.

---

[29] FASB ASC Paragraph 310-40-15-5: Receivables—Troubled Debt Restructurings by Creditors—Scope and Scope Exceptions—Troubled Debt Restructuring.

In other words, for the restructuring to be **troubled,** the borrower (Bloom) must be unable to pay off the original debt and the lender (the mutual fund) must grant a **concession** to the borrower.

A lender must evaluate separately whether it has made a concession and whether the borrower is in financial difficulty to fall under troubled debt accounting.[30] FASB ASC 310-40-15-13 states that a creditor (lender) has granted a concession when it no longer expects to collect everything owed, including interest. The creditor would consider collateral in determining the amount expected to be collected. When assessing whether the debtor (borrower) is experiencing **financial difficulties,** the creditor should consider the following indicators:

1. The debtor is currently in default on any of its debt or default is probable,
2. The debtor is in the process of declaring bankruptcy,
3. The debtor is unlikely to remain a **going concern,**
4. The debtor has securities that are being delisted from an exchange,
5. The creditor forecasts that the debtor's cash flows are insufficient to pay interest and principal on its debt, and
6. Without the current modification, the debtor cannot obtain funds (other than from existing creditors) at nontroubled rates (FASB ASC 310-40-15-20).

Our Bloom example meets these guidelines. The company was unable to make its interest and principal payments because of financial difficulties. The lender then agreed to restructure the debt, and in so doing, granted the company a substantial economic concession—the $4.5 million of debt cancellation.

Troubled debt restructurings can be accomplished in two different ways:

- **Settlement,** which cancels the original loan by a transfer of cash, other assets, or equity interests (borrower's stock) to the lender.
- **Continuation with modification** of debt term by canceling the original loan and signing a new loan agreement.

Some troubled debt restructurings contain elements of both settlement and modification.

The accounting issues related to troubled debt restructuring encompass both the measurement of the new (modified) loan and the recognition of any gain or loss. The following example illustrates these issues.

Assume that Harper Companies purchased $75,000 of corn milling equipment from Farmers State Cooperative on January 1, 2011. Harper paid $25,000 cash and signed a five-year, 10% installment note for the remaining $50,000 of the purchase price. The note calls for annual payments of $10,000 plus interest on December 31 of each year. Harper made the first two installment payments on time but was unable to make the third annual payment on December 31, 2013. After much negotiation, Farmers State agreed to restructure the note receivable. At that time, Harper owed $30,000 in unpaid principal plus $3,000 in accrued interest. We assume that the restructuring was agreed to on January 1, 2014, and that both companies have already recorded interest up to that date.

---

[30] Troubled debt restructurings often involve complexities that are beyond the scope of our discussion here. See FASB ASC Subtopic 310-40: Receivables—Troubled Debt Restructuring by Creditors and FASB ASC Subtopic 470-60: Debt—Troubled Debt Restructuring by Debtors.

Settlement

Suppose Farmers State agrees to cancel the loan if Harper pays $5,000 cash and turns over a company car. The car was purchased 18 months ago for $21,000 cash, has a current fair value of $18,000, and is carried on Harper's books at $16,000 ($21,000 original cost minus $5,000 accumulated depreciation). Notice that the combined economic value of the cash ($5,000) and automobile ($18,000) is $23,000—or $10,000 less than the $33,000 Harper owes Farmers State.

The January 1, 2014, entries made to record settlement of the troubled debt are:

Harper Companies (Borrower)

DR	Automobile	$ 2,000	
	CR	Gain on disposal of asset		$ 2,000

To increase the net carrying amount of the automobile ($16,000) to its fair value ($18,000).

DR	Note payable	$30,000	
DR	Interest payable	3,000	
DR	Accumulated depreciation	5,000	
	CR	Cash		$ 5,000
	CR	Automobile		23,000
	CR	Gain on debt restructuring		10,000

To record the settlement.

Farmers State Cooperative (Lender)

DR	Cash	$ 5,000	
DR	Automobile	18,000	
DR	Loss on receivable restructuring	10,000	
	CR	Note receivable		$30,000
	CR	Interest receivable		3,000

To record the settlement.

What do these entries accomplish? The settlement creates two earnings gains for Harper:

- A gain on asset disposal of $2,000—the difference between the car's fair value ($18,000) and its book value ($16,000).
- A debt restructuring gain of $10,000—the difference between the note's book value plus accrued interest ($30,000 + $3,000) and the fair value of assets transferred ($5,000 cash plus $18,000 automobile).

> Farmers State's settlement loss would not be extraordinary but would instead be included in computating income from continuing operations. Because it's a lender, restructurings are a normal part of its business and are likely to recur. So, these transactions meet *neither* of the two criteria for extraordinary items—unusual nature and infrequency of occurrence—discussed in Chapter 2. Harper Companies' gain would be treated as extraordinary only if it met both of these criteria for extraordinary items.

Farmers State's has a debt restructuring loss for the same $10,000 figure. Both companies record all interest up to the restructuring date and then cancel the note and related interest receivable and payable.

Continuation with Modification of Debt Terms

Instead of reaching a negotiated settlement of the note receivable, Harper and Farmers State could have resolved the troubled debt by modifying the terms of the original loan. The possibilities are endless. For accounting purposes, what matters is whether the ***undiscounted sum*** *of future cash flows under the restructured note is more or less than the note's carrying value (including accrued interest) at the restructuring date.*

Sum of Restructured Flows Exceeds Carrying Value of Payable

Suppose that Farmers State agrees to postpone all principal and interest payments on the note receivable to maturity. Harper's final (and only) payment on December 31, 2015, would total $39,000 (the $30,000 principal plus $9,000 representing three years interest at 10%). Harper and Farmers State have already recorded $3,000 in accrued interest as of January 1, 2014. So, the book value of the note plus accrued interest is $33,000 at the restructuring date.

Because the sum of future cash flows on the restructured note ($39,000) is *greater* than the carrying value of the original payable ($33,000), Harper will not show a restructuring gain. Instead, Harper will compute a new (and lower) effective interest rate for the restructured note and accrue interest at that new rate until the loan is fully paid. The new effective interest rate is the rate that equates the present value of the restructured cash flows to the carrying value of the debt at the date of restructure.[31] The new effective interest rate for Harper Companies is 8.7% per year.

Farmers State will continue using the 10% interest rate on the original note.[32] To do so, it must value the restructured note payments using a 10% effective interest rate. Farmers State will then show a loss for the difference between the present value of the restructured note, which is $32,232, and the carrying value of the original note ($33,000). The entries made by both companies are:

To see this, notice that the restructured note calls for Harper to make a single payment of $39,000 on December 31, 2015—*two* years from the January 1, 2014, restructuring date. We need to find a discount rate that equates the present value of this $39,000 payment with the $33,000 carrying value of the note receivable. This means finding the rate r that solves the following equation:

$$\underbrace{\text{Carrying value}} = \underbrace{\text{Present value of future cash flows (in 2 years)}}$$

$$\$33,000 = \frac{\$39,000}{(1 + r)^2}$$

The value of r that satisfies this equation is 0.087. To verify this, go to our website—www.mhhe.com/revsine6e—and use the present value calculator to see that the present value factor for a single payment due in two periods at 8.7% is 0.84615, and $39,000 multiplied by this factor equals $33,000 (rounded).

The present value factor for a single payment due in two years at 10% is 0.82645. The value of the note is $39,000 × 0.82645, or $32,232 (rounded).

Harper Companies (Borrower)

DR	Note payable	$30,000	
DR	Interest payable	3,000	
	CR Restructured note payable		$33,000

To record the modified note (when sum of restructured cash flows is greater than note carrying value).

Farmers State Cooperative (Lender)

DR	Restructured note receivable	$32,232	
DR	Loss on receivable restructuring	768	
	CR Note receivable		$30,000
	CR Interest receivable		3,000

To record the modified note (when sum of restructured cash flows is greater than note carrying value).

---

[31] FASB ASC Paragraph 470-60-35-5: Debt—Troubled Debt Restructuring by Debtors—Subsequent Measurement—General.

[32] FASB ASC Paragraph 310-40-35-12: Receivables—Troubled Debt Restructuring by Creditors—Subsequent Measurement—Effective Interest Rate for a Restructured Loan.

Both companies accrue interest beginning on the debt restructuring date (January 1, 2014) and ending on the restructured note's maturity date (December 31, 2015). But they will *not* use the same interest rate, as you just saw. The borrower, Harper, will record annual interest at 8.7% of the note's carrying value at the beginning of each year, whereas Farmers State will use a 10% annual rate.

The FASB's choice of two different interest rates, one for the borrower and another for the lender, illustrates the role of conservatism in financial reporting. If the lender, Farmers State, used the 8.7% rate, it would continue to carry the note at $33,000 (see the present value calculation in the sidebar above) and recognize no loss although the cash inflows have been reduced. If the borrower, Harper, used the original 10% rate, this would cause it to reduce the note carrying value to $32,232 and recognize an up-front gain. So, to obtain conservative outcomes, the FASB required the parties to use different interest rates.

The entries for the next two years are:

Harper Companies (Borrower)

DR	Interest expense	$2,871	
	CR Restructured note payable		$2,871

($2,871 = $33,000 × 0.087)

To record interest on December 31, 2014.

DR	Interest expense	$3,121	
	CR Restructured note payable		$3,121

($3,121 = [$33,000 + $2,871] × 0.087)

To record interest on December 31, 2015.

Farmers State Cooperative (Lender)

DR	Restructured note receivable	$3,223	
	CR Interest income		$3,223

($3,223 = $32,232 × 0.10)

To record interest on December 31, 2014.

DR	Restructured note receivable	$3,546	
	CR Interest income		$3,546

($3,546 = [$32,232 + $3,223] × 0.10)

To record interest on December 31, 2015.

Over time, Harper Companies' note payable and Farmers State Cooperative's note receivable increase to the final balance of $39,000, the required payment at maturity (see Exhibit 8.10). The entry to record the payment is:

Harper Companies (Borrower)

DR	Restructured note payable	$39,000	
	CR Cash		$39,000

To record payment of balance on December 31, 2015.

Farmers State Cooperative (Lender)

DR	Cash	$39,000	
	CR Restructured note receivable		$39,000

To record receipt of balance on December 31, 2015.

	Harper Companies	Farmers State Cooperative
EXHIBIT 8.10 — Growth of Note Carrying Amount		
Restructured note, initial carrying amount	$33,000	$32,232
Accrued interest expense, Harper		
2014	2,871	
2015	3,121	
Accrued interest revenue, Farmers State		
2014		3,223
2015		3,546
Note carrying amount, December 31, 2015	$39,000*	$39,000*

* Rounded.

This example illustrates a restructured loan in which the total restructured cash flows are *greater* than the carrying value of the troubled debt. Next let's examine a situation in which the sum of the future cash flows is *less* than the carrying value of the troubled debt.

Sum of Restructured Flows Is Less Than Payable's Carrying Value

The $24,794 is just the present value of $30,000 received in two years at 10%, or $24,794 = $30,000 × 0.82645.

Suppose that Farmers State waives all interest payments (that is, the $3,000 unpaid accrued interest for 2013 as well as the 2014 and 2015 interest) and defers all principal payments until December 31, 2015. The restructured cash payments (now only $30,000) are *lower* than the receivable's carrying value ($33,000). Harper will show a gain on the debt restructuring and will treat the subsequent payment as a reduction of the restructured principal. Harper records no interest expense. But Farmers State follows the procedures outlined in the previous example. It values the restructured note at $24,794 (using the 10% effective interest rate from the original note), records a debt restructuring loss, and accrues interest income to maturity. The entries made at the restructuring date are:

Harper Companies (Borrower)

DR	Note payable	$30,000	
DR	Interest payable	3,000	
	CR Restructured note payable		$30,000
	CR Gain on debt restructuring		3,000

To record the modified note (when the sum of restructured cash flows is less than the note carrying value).

Farmers State Cooperative (Lender)

DR	Restructured note receivable	$24,794	
DR	Loss on receivable restructuring	8,206	
	CR Note receivable		$30,000
	CR Interest receivable		3,000

To record the modified note (when the sum of restructured cash flows is less than the note carrying value).

Harper would not record any interest over the life of the restructured note. The $30,000 cash payment on December 31, 2015, would reduce the outstanding balance of Harper's restructured note payable. Farmers State still records interest income over the life of the note. These entries would be:

Harper Companies (Borrower)

DR Restructured note payable $30,000

  CR Cash $30,000

(No entries are made until the cash payment at maturity.)

Farmers State Cooperative (Lender)

DR Restructured note receivable .... $ 2,479

  CR Interest income .... $ 2,479

($2,479 = $24,794 × 0.10)

To record interest on December 31, 2014.

DR Restructured note receivable .... $ 2,727

  CR Interest income .... $ 2,727

($2,727 = [$24,794 + $2,479] × 0.10)

To record interest on December 31, 2015.

The note receivable balance at Farmers State has now increased to $30,000 (that is, $24,794 + $2,479 + $2,727).

DR Cash $30,000

  CR Restructured note receivable $30,000

To record payment of receivable balance on December 31, 2015.

Evaluating Troubled Debt Restructuring Rules

The GAAP rules for troubled debt restructurings are subject to several criticisms.

First, an obvious (and uncomfortable) lack of symmetry exists in the financial reporting of the borrower and lender. Different measurement rules are used to value the borrower's restructured note payable and the lender's restructured receivable when there is continuation with modification of debt terms. Consequently, the initial book value that GAAP assigns to the payable is not the same as the initial book value assigned to the receivable. This also results in a difference between the borrower's restructuring gain and the lender's restructuring loss. We explained this as an instance of the FASB's opting for a conservative measurement method.

Second, the GAAP restructuring gains and losses do not always correspond to real economic gains and losses for the companies involved. For one thing, GAAP often assigns the gain or loss to the wrong time period. Although the accounting loss in the case of Farmers State Cooperative was shown in 2014, most of the economic loss occurred earlier when Harper became unable to make the loan payments.

Third, it's possible to question GAAP's use of the original loan's effective interest rate to value the restructured receivable and the lender's restructuring loss. Turning again to Farmers State, its original 10% loan to Harper used an interest rate that reflected the borrower's credit risk when the loan was first made. Over the ensuing three years, Harper's credit risk undoubtedly increased to the point where lenders would charge a higher rate of interest (say 15%) on new loans to the company. After all, Harper failed to meet its financial obligations in 2013. A higher effective interest rate on the restructured receivable will

EXHIBIT 8.11	Summary of Accounting Procedures for Troubled Debt Restructurings		

		Restructured Loan Cash Flows Are	
	Settlement Gain or Loss	Lower Than Current Carrying Value of Loan*	Higher Than Current Carrying Value of Loan*
Borrower			
New loan payable	—	Total of restructured cash flows	Current book value
Gain on debt restructuring	Ordinary†	Ordinary†	None
Gain (loss) on transfer of assets	Ordinary	—	—
Future interest expense	—	None, all payments applied to principal	Based on rate that equates current carrying value and restructured cash flows
Lender			
New loan receivable	—	Present value of new cash flows at original effective interest rate	Present value of new cash flows at original effective interest rate
Loss on debt restructuring	Ordinary	Ordinary	Ordinary
Future interest income	—	Based on original loan rate	Based on original loan rate

* Includes unpaid accrued interest.

† Unless it meets both criteria for extraordinary items.

produce a lower initial book value and a larger restructuring loss for the lender. The GAAP approach is a practical solution because it avoids the sometimes difficult task of estimating the borrower's real effective interest rate at the restructuring date. However, this approach also fails to fully reflect the economic realities of troubled debt restructurings and results in the conservatism discussed earlier.

Exhibit 8.11 summarizes, in general terms, the accounting illustrated in each of the Harper–Farmers State troubled debt restructurings.

GLOBAL VANTAGE POINT

Comparison of IFRS and GAAP Receivable Accounting

The general accounting for accounts and notes receivable under IFRS is similar to the accounting under U.S. GAAP.[33] The accounting is called *amortized cost,* which refers to the gross amount of the receivable. An allowance is still established for doubtful accounts. IFRS also allows a more limited version of the fair value option. Under IFRS, firms may elect the fair value option only in cases where it eliminates an accounting mismatch or because a group of assets are managed and evaluated using fair values (*IFRS 9,* para 4.1.5, B4.1.33). U.S. GAAP allows the fair value option for a broader set of transactions.

To help financial statement users understand better the value of certain financial instruments, *IFRS 7* requires firms to disclose the fair value of short-term trade receivables and loans in addition to long-term notes receivables, even when these are accounted for

---

[33] Current guidance is contained in "Financial Instruments," *IFRS 9* (London, 2009).

at amortized cost in the fundamental financial statements.[34] This disclosure provides the reader two different perspectives regarding the economic value of the financial instruments.

Guidance regarding sales of receivables is similar to the post-2009 U.S. accounting guidance. Under the prior U.S. guidance, QSPEs were off-balance-sheet. Most of these entities would now stay on the balance sheet under both IFRS and U.S. guidance.

Finally, IFRS for debt restructurings from the lender's perspective are similar to U.S. GAAP (see *IAS 39,* para. 63). No explicit international standards govern troubled debt restructuring from the borrower's perspective.

Expected FASB and IASB Actions

In February 2013, the FASB issued a proposed Accounting Standards Update on financial instruments.[35] Under the proposal, the accounting for short-term receivables would be measured at amortized cost, which is consistent with the current method in the United States. However, long-term receivables are likely to be accounted for at fair value (with changes through Other comprehensive income) if managers do not intend to hold these receivables until maturity. Long-term liabilities will likely stay at amortized cost.

In summary of this section, we do not expect the accounting for short-term receivables to change. However, the U.S. accounting for long-term receivables may move toward fair value reporting. The degree of convergence between U.S. GAAP and IFRS depends on whether these boards continue to work together to revise reporting standards for financial instruments.

SUMMARY

- GAAP requires that accounts receivable generally be shown at their net realizable value.
- Companies use one of two methods to estimate uncollectible accounts: (1) the sales revenue approach or (2) the gross accounts receivable approach. Under either approach, firms must periodically assess the reasonableness of the uncollectibles balance by performing an aging of accounts receivable.
- Analysts should scrutinize the allowance for uncollectibles balance over time. Significant increases in the allowance could indicate collection problems while significant decreases in the allowance could be a sign of earnings management.
- Receivables growth can exceed sales growth for several reasons, including a change in customer mix or credit terms. But a disparity in the growth rate of receivables and sales could also indicate that aggressive revenue recognition practices are being used.
- In certain long-term credit sales transactions, interest must be imputed by determining the note receivable's present value.
- Firms may elect the fair value option for accounts and notes receivable. Changes in fair value are recognized in net income.

---

[34] See "Financial Instruments: Disclosure," *IFRS 7* (London, amended through 2011).

[35] See Financial Instruments—Overall (Subtopic 825): Recognition and Measurement of Financial Assets and Financial Liabilities (Norwalk, CT: FASB, February 2013).

- Firms sometimes transfer or dispose of receivables before their due date to accelerate cash collection. Sales of receivables—also called *factoring*—can be with or without recourse.

- Receivables are also used as collateral for a loan.

- In analyzing receivables transactions, it is sometimes not obvious whether the transaction to accelerate cash collection represents a sale or a borrowing; however, authoritative accounting literature provides guidelines in *Topic 860 Transfers and Servicing of the FASB Accounting Standards Codification* for distinguishing between sales (when the transferor surrenders control over the receivables) and borrowings (when control is not surrendered). Sales of receivables change ratios such as receivables turnover as well as potentially masking the underlying real growth in receivables.

- Subprime loans and securitizations were at the heart of the 2008 economic crisis. Accounting and regulatory reforms are under way to address some of the problems identified during the crisis.

- Banks and other holders of receivables frequently restructure the terms of the receivable when a customer is unable to make required payments because of financial difficulties. These troubled debt restructurings can take one of two forms: (1) settlement or (2) continuation with modification of debt terms.

- When terms are modified, the precise accounting treatment depends on whether the sum of future cash flows under the restructured note is more or less than the note's carrying value at the restructuring date. The interest rate used in troubled debt restructurings may not reflect the real economic loss suffered by the lender.

- Both the FASB and IASB have projects on financial instruments and derecognition.

EXERCISES

E8-1

Analyzing accounts receivable
(LO 2)

AICPA
ADAPTED

For the month of December 2014, Ranger Corporation's records show the following information:

Cash received on accounts receivable	$35,000
Cash sales	30,000
Accounts receivable, December 1, 2014	80,000
Accounts receivable, December 31, 2014	74,000
Accounts receivable written off as uncollectible	1,000

Required:
Determine the gross sales for the month of December 2014.

E8-2

Analyzing accounts receivable
(LO 2)

AICPA
ADAPTED

At the close of its first year of operations on December 31, 2014, Clemens Company had accounts receivable of $300,000, which were *net* of the related allowance for doubtful accounts. During 2014, the company had charges to the provision for bad debts of $25,000 and wrote off accounts receivable of $15,000 that it deemed to be uncollectible.

Required:
What should Clemens Company report on its balance sheet at December 31, 2014, as accounts receivable *before* the allowance for doubtful accounts?

E8-3

Determining ratio effects of write-offs   **(LO 2)**

AICPA
ADAPTED

Echo Corporation had the following balances immediately prior to writing off a $100 uncollectible account:

Current assets	$30,000
Accounts receivable	3,300
Allowance for doubtful accounts	300
Current liabilities	10,000

Required:

Calculate the following amounts or ratios and determine the relationship between the amount or ratio before the write-off (*x*) with the amount or ratio after the write-off (*y*):

Amount or Ratio	Possibilities
1. Current ratio	a. *x* more than *y*
2. Net accounts receivable balance	b. *x* equals *y*
3. Gross accounts receivable balance	c. *x* less than *y*
	d. cannot be determined

The following information is available for Fess Company:

Credit sales during 2014	$150,000
Allowance for doubtful accounts at December 31, 2013	1,450
Accounts receivable deemed worthless and written off during 2014	1,800

During 2014, Fess estimated that its provision for bad debts should be 1% of all credit sales. As a result of a review and aging of accounts receivable in early January 2015, it has been determined that an allowance for doubtful accounts of $1,600 is needed at December 31, 2014.

Required:

1. What is the total amount that Fess should record as provision for bad debts for the year ended December 31, 2014?

2. Show the journal entries affecting the Allowance for doubtful accounts that Fess made during 2014.

E 8-4

Determining provision for bad debts **(LO 1)**

AICPA
ADAPTED

Lake Company sold some machinery to View Company on January 1, 2014, for which the cash selling price was $758,200. View entered into an installment sales contract with Lake at a 10% interest rate. The contract required payments of $200,000 a year over five years with the first payment due on December 31, 2014.

Required:

Prepare an amortization schedule that shows what portion of each $200,000 payment will be shown as interest income over the period 2014–2018.

E 8-5

Preparing an amortization schedule **(LO 4)**

AICPA
ADAPTED

Weaver, Inc., received a $60,000, six-month, 12% interest-bearing note from a customer. The note was discounted (sold) the same day to Third National Bank at 15%.

Required:

Compute the amount of cash Weaver received from the bank.

E 8-6

Discounting a note **(LO 6)**

AICPA
ADAPTED

On January 1, 2014, Wade Crimbring, Inc., a dealer in used manufacturing equipment, sold a CNC milling machine to Fletcher Bros., a new business that plans to fabricate utility trailers. To conserve cash, Fletcher paid for the machine by issuing a $200,000 note, payable in five years. Interest at 5% is payable annually with the first payment due on December 31, 2014. The going rate for loans of this type is 10%.

Required:

1. Record Crimbring's sale of the machine on January 1, 2014.

2. Prepare the entry that Crimbring would make on December 31, 2014, to record the receipt of the first interest payment.

3. What is the nature of the account that arises as a consequence of the difference between the 5% cash interest and the effective yield of 10%?

E 8-7

Recording note receivable carrying amount and fair value option **(LO 4, 5)**

AICPA
ADAPTED

4. Assume that Crimbring opted to carry this note at its fair value. What should be the value of the note on Crimbring's December 31, 2014, balance sheet if the market interest rate is then 12%? Assume that the December 31, 2014, payment has been made.

5. Prepare the entry that Crimbring would make on December 31, 2014, to record the note at its fair value.

E8-8

Aging accounts receivables
(LO 1)

AICPA
ADAPTED

On December 31, 2014, Vale Company had an unadjusted credit balance of $1,000 in its Allowance for uncollectible accounts. An analysis of Vale's trade accounts receivable at that date revealed the following:

Age	Amount	Estimated Uncollectible
0–30 days	$60,000	5%
31–60 days	4,000	10
Over 60 days	2,000	70

Required:

What amount should Vale report as Allowance for uncollectible accounts in its December 31, 2014, balance sheet?

E8-9

Analyzing accounts receivable
and fair value option **(LO 5)**

The following information relates to Zulu Company's accounts receivable for 2014:

Accounts receivable, 1/1/2014	$ 750,000
Credit sales for 2014	3,100,000
Accounts written off during 2014	45,000
Collections from customers during 2014	2,400,000
Estimated uncollectible accounts at 12/31/2014	95,000

A factor has recently offered to purchase all of Zulu's outstanding receivables without recourse for 94% of their face amount.

Required:

At what net amount should Zulu report its receivables assuming the company chooses to measure financial assets at fair value?

E8-10

Accounting for a
securitization **(LO 7)**

Kendall Corporation designs and manufactures sports cars. During the course of its business, Kendall generates substantial receivables from its customers. On July 1, 2014, to improve its cash flow, Kendall establishes a securitization entity (SE) and (1) transfers without recourse $20.5 million of its receivables to the SE and (2) surrenders control over these receivables. The SE then sells securities backed by the cash flows associated with Kendall's receivables. Because the SE is separate from Kendall, and the receivables are diversified across hundreds of customers, investors are willing to pay $24 million for the securities. The SE then transfers the $24 million to Kendall Corporation.

Required:

1. Prepare Kendall's entry to record the securitization as a sale.

2. Show how your answer to requirement 1 would change if control over the receivables is not surrendered at the time of the transfer (i.e., an agreement exists whereby Kendall would be forced to absorb significant losses associated with the SE's receivables).

Blue, Inc., sells playground equipment to schools and municipalities. It mails invoices at the end of each month for all goods shipped during that month; credit terms are net 30 days. Sales and accounts receivable data for 2014, 2015, and 2016 follow:

E 8-11

Determining whether it's a real sale   **(LO 3)**

	Years Ending December 31,		
	2014	**2015**	**2016**
Sales	$1,785,980	$1,839,559	$1,986,724
Accounts receivable at year-end	220,189	227,896	267,094

Required:

1. Calculate the rates of increase in sales and in receivables during 2015 and 2016.

2. Do your calculations indicate any potential problems with Blue's receivables?

3. If so, suggest a possible explanation for your findings and indicate what action, if any, would then be needed to bring Blue's financial statements into conformity with GAAP.

On December 31, 2014, Fenton Company sold equipment to Denver, Inc., accepting a $275,000 noninterest-bearing note receivable in full payment on December 31, 2017. Denver, Inc., normally pays 12% for its borrowed funds. The equipment is carried in Fenton's perpetual inventory records at 65% of its cash selling price.

E 8-12

Calculating imputed interest on noninterest-bearing note   **(LO 4)**

Required:

1. Prepare Fenton's journal entries to record the sale on December 31, 2014.

2. Prepare Fenton's journal entry on December 31, 2015, necessitated by this transaction. (*Hint:* Prepare an amortization schedule for the loan.)

3. Show Fenton's balance sheet presentation of Denver's note at December 31, 2015.

Binsford, Inc., sells $175,000 of its accounts receivable ($172,000 net of the allowance for doubtful accounts) to Upshaw Finance with recourse. Upshaw immediately remits cash equal to 90% of the gross receivable amount and retains the remaining 10% to cover its factoring fee (equal to 4% of the gross amount of factored receivables) and any bad debts under the agreement's recourse provisions. Binsford estimates the fair value of the recourse obligation to be $4,000.

E 8-13

Factoring receivables with recourse   **(LO 6)**

Required:

1. Prepare the journal entry Binsford would make to record the factoring.

2. Prepare Binsford's journal entry to record any subsequent cash received from Upshaw Finance if Upshaw collects all of the factored receivables except for $2,500 resulting from a bad debt.

Smithfield Farms purchased a combine from John Deere for $175,000 on January 2, 2014. Smithfield paid $25,000 in cash and signed an installment note calling for five annual payments of $39,569.58 beginning on December 31, 2014. Deere based the payments on a 10% rate of interest. Smithfield made the first payment, but a failed harvest in 2015 left it unable to make the upcoming payment. Deere agreed to repossess the combine, which had a market value of $132,000 on December 31, 2015, and cancel the note. Deere accrued interest on the loan for 2015 prior to canceling the note.

E 8-14

Recording troubled debt settlement   **(LO 8)**

Required:

Prepare the journal entry John Deere would make on December 31, 2015, to record the settlement.

E8-15	Central Valley Construction (CVC) purchased $80,000 of sheet metal fabricating equipment

E8-15

Recording troubled debt
restructuring   **(LO 8)**

Central Valley Construction (CVC) purchased $80,000 of sheet metal fabricating equipment from Buffalo Supply on January 1, 2014. CVC paid $15,000 cash and signed a five-year, 10% note for the remaining $65,000 of the purchase price. The note specifies that payments of $13,000 plus interest be made each year on the loan's anniversary date. CVC made the required January 1, 2015, payment but was unable to make the second payment on January 1, 2016, because of a downturn in the construction industry. At this time, CVC owed Buffalo Supply $52,000 plus $5,200 interest that had been accrued by both companies. Rather than write off the note and repossess the equipment, Buffalo Supply agreed to restructure the loan as one payment of $50,000 on January 1, 2018, to satisfy the restructured note.

Required:

Prepare the entries CVC and Buffalo Supply would make on January 1, 2016, to record the restructuring.

PROBLEMS / DISCUSSION QUESTIONS

P8-1

Determining balance sheet
presentation and preparing
journal entries for various
receivables transactions
(LO 1, 4, 6)

Aardvark, Inc., began 2014 with the following receivables-related account balances:

Accounts receivable	$575,000
Allowance for uncollectibles	43,250

Aardvark's transactions during 2014 include the following:

1. On April 1, 2014, Aardvark accepted an 8%, 12-month note from Smith Bros. in settlement of a $17,775 past due account.

2. Aardvark finally ceased all efforts to collect $23,200 from various customers and wrote off their accounts.

3. Total sales for the year (80% on credit) were $1,765,000. Cash receipts from customers as reported on Aardvark's cash flow statement were $1,925,000.

4. Sales for 2014 as reported included $100,000 of merchandise that Jensen, Inc., ordered from Aardvark. Unfortunately, a shipping department error resulted in items valued at $150,000 being shipped to Jensen. Because Jensen believed that it could eventually use the unordered items, it agreed to keep them in exchange for a 10% reduction in their price to cover storage costs. Neither the sales nor the receivable for the extra $50,000 of merchandise were recorded.

5. On February 1, 2014, Aardvark borrowed $65,000 from Sun Bank and pledged receivables in that amount as collateral for the loan. Interest of 5% was deducted from the cash proceeds. In June, Aardvark repaid the loan.

6. Aardvark estimates uncollectible accounts using the sales revenue approach. In past years, the bad debt provision was estimated at 1% of gross sales revenue, but a weaker economy in 2014 led management to increase the estimate to 1.5% of gross sales revenue.

7. On July 1, 2014, Aardvark sold equipment to Zebra Company and received a $100,000 noninterest-bearing note receivable due in three years. The equipment normally sells for $79,383. Assume that the appropriate rate of interest for this transaction is 8%.

Required:

1. Prepare journal entries for each of the preceding events. Also prepare any needed entries to accrue interest on the notes at December 31, 2014.

2. Show Aardvark's balance sheet presentation for accounts and notes receivable at December 31, 2014.

Baer Enterprises's balance sheet at October 31, 2014 (fiscal year-end) includes the following:

Accounts receivable	$379,000
Less: Allowance for uncollectible accounts	(33,000)
Accounts receivable (net)	$346,000

P 8-2

Determining balance sheet presentation and preparing journal entries for various receivables transactions **(LO 1, 4, 6)**

Transactions for fiscal year 2015 include the following:

1. Due to a product defect, previously sold merchandise totaling $10,500 was returned.

2. Customer accounts totaling $29,750 were written off during the year.

3. On November 1, 2014, Baer sold teleconferencing equipment and received a $75,000 noninterest-bearing note receivable due in three years. The normal cash selling price for the equipment is $56,349. Assume that the appropriate interest rate for this transaction is 10%.

4. Credit sales during the year were $395,000; collections totaled $355,000.

5. Baer sold Hartman, Inc., $45,000 of accounts receivable without recourse. Hartman's fee for factoring receivables is 9%.

6. Utilizing the gross receivables approach, Baer determined that the 2015 fiscal year-end Allowance for uncollectible accounts should be $35,000.

Required:

1. Prepare journal entries for each of these events. Also prepare the entry to accrue interest income on the note.

2. Show Baer's balance sheet presentation for accounts and notes receivable at October 31, 2015.

Avillion Corporation had a $45,000 debit balance in Accounts receivable and a $3,500 credit balance in Allowance for uncollectibles on December 31, 2014. The company prepared the following aging schedule to record the adjusting entry for bad debts on December 31, 2014.

P 8-3

Determining allowance for uncollectibles **(LO 1)**

Age of Receivables	Amount	Expected Bad Debts
0–30 days old	$30,000	5%
31–90 days old	10,000	11
Over 90 days old	5,000	30

1. On January 1, 2015, the company learned that one of its customers (Smith Corporation), which owed $2,000, had filed for bankruptcy and could be unable to pay the amount due.

2. On March 1, 2015, Smith Corporation's bankruptcy was finalized and the bankruptcy court notified all of its creditors (including Avillion Corporation) that Smith Corporation will pay 60 cents on the dollar for the amount owed to its creditors.

3. On May 7, 2015, Avillion Corporation received a check from Smith Corporation for the amount indicated by the court.

Required:

1. Provide journal entries to record the preceding transactions in Avillion's books. In addition, using the following table format, show the effects of each transaction on the following financial statement items. Clearly indicate the amount and the direction of the effects (use "+" for increase, "−" for decrease, and "NE" for no effect).

	Assets	Liabilities	Net Income	Cash Flow from Operations
Direction of effect				
Dollar amount of effect				

2. Assume that Avillion had instead prepared the following aging schedule on December 31, 2014:

Age of Receivables	Amount	Expected Bad Debts
0–30 days old	$30,000	3%
31–90 days old	10,000	8
Over 90 days old	5,000	22

Redo requirement (1) using the revised aging schedule.

P 8-4

Preparing journal entries, aging analysis, and balance sheet presentation **(LO 1)**

At December 31, 2013, Oettinger Corporation, a premium kitchen cabinetmaker for the home remodeling industry, reported the following accounts receivable information on its year-end balance sheet:

Gross accounts receivable	$850,000
Less: Allowance for uncollectibles	(25,000)
Accounts receivable (net)	$825,000

During 2014, the company had credit sales of $8,200,000 of which it collected $7,975,000. Oettinger employs the sales revenue approach to estimate its bad debt provisions and, continuing to use the same 1% used in previous years, made the normal adjustment at the end of 2014.

Although 2014 started off well, the industry experienced a slowdown in the last four months of the year, and cash collections consequently dropped off substantially. Moreover, a major customer, which owed Oettinger $85,000, unexpectedly filed for bankruptcy and went out of business during November, at which time its account was written off. Oettinger's controller is concerned that some customers are experiencing cash flow problems and that the company's allowance for uncollectible accounts is too low. As a result, she prepared the following schedule:

% of Accounts Receivable Balance	Number of Days Past Due	Estimated % Collectible
20%	0–30	98%
40	31–60	95
35	61–90	85
3	91–120	75
2	Over 120	50

Required:

1. Determine Oettinger's accounts receivable balance at December 31, 2014. Prepare a journal entry for each transaction affecting the accounts receivable balance for 2014.

2. Prepare an aging analysis to compute the required balance in the Allowance for uncollectible accounts at December 31, 2014.

3. Prepare any other required journal entries affecting the Allowance for uncollectible accounts for the year ended December 31, 2014. (Do not duplicate any entries from requirement 1.)

4. Show Oettinger's balance sheet presentation of accounts receivable at December 31, 2014.

On December 1, 2014, Eva Corporation, a mortgage bank, has the following amounts on its balance sheet (in millions):

Assets	
Cash	$ 10
Mortgage receivables	58
Investments	27
Other assets	13
Total	$108

Liabilities and Shareholders' Equity	
Notes payable	$ 50
Common stock	11
Retained earnings	47
Total	$108

Also on December 1, 2014, Eva transfers mortgage receivables with a book value of $20,000,000 to a securitization entity (SE). The average interest rate on the mortgages is 7%. Under the terms of the agreement, the SE is legally separate from Eva. After the transfer, Eva securitizes the mortgages and sells them to investors. Because the securities are considered to be less risky than the original mortgages, the investors are willing to receive a lower rate of return and consequently remit $20,750,000 to the SE. The SE then transfers the $20,750,000 to Eva Corporation. Eva does not direct the activities of the SE and will not participate in any of the SE's gains or losses.

Required:

1. Explain why this securitization qualifies for accounting treatment as a sale.

2. What entries should Eva make at the time of the securitization?

3. Show how the securitization will affect Eva's balance sheet at December 1, 2014, and compute the new debt/equity ratio.

4. Show the balance sheet effects and how the debt/equity ratio would be different if the securitization did not qualify for accounting treatment as a sale.

The following information pertains to the financial statements of Buffalo Supply Company, a provider of plumbing fixtures to contractors in central Pennsylvania.

	Fiscal Years Ended October 31,		
	2014	**2013**	**2012**
From Income Statements			
Revenues	$3,519,444	$3,877,135	$2,969,981
Provision for bad debts	45,753	50,403	38,610
From Balance Sheets			
Gross accounts receivable	$ 345,044	$ 362,349	$ 282,855
Less: Allowance for doubtful accounts	(54,654)	(74,365)	(47,612)
Net accounts receivable	$ 290,390	$ 287,984	$ 235,243

Required:

Reconstruct all journal entries pertaining to Gross accounts receivable and Allowance for doubtful accounts for the fiscal year ended October 31, 2014. Assume that all revenues are from credit sales. (*Hint:* Begin by doing a T-account analysis of both accounts, starting with the allowance account.)

P8-7		

Scheduling interest received
(LO 4)

mhhe.com/revsine6e

On December 31, 2008, Sea Containers Ltd., a company located in Hamilton, Bermuda, reported notes receivable of $63,930,000. This amount represents the present value of future cash flows (both principal and interest) discounted at a rate of 11.12% per annum. The schedule of collections of the receivables is provided next:

($ in thousands)	Year Ending December	Collections
	2009	$20,724
	2010	15,896
	2011	11,559
	2012	7,179
	2013	8,559
	2014	13
		$63,930

Assume that the interest due is paid along with the face value of the receivables at the end of each year.

Required:

Provide journal entries to record the interest received and the notes receivable collected in each year.

P8-8	

Imputing interest on a nominal interest-bearing note and fair value option   **(LO 4, 5)**

On January 2, 2014, Criswell Acres purchased from Mifflinburg Farm Supply a new tractor that had a cash selling price of $109,837. As payment, Criswell gave Mifflinburg Farm Supply $25,000 in cash and a $100,000, five-year note that provided for annual interest payments at 6%. At the time of the sale, the interest rate normally charged to farms with Criswell's credit rating is 10%.

Required:

1. Prepare Mifflinburg Farm Supply's journal entry to record the sale.

2. Prepare the journal entry to record the first interest payment Mifflinburg Farm Supply received on December 31, 2014.

3. Determine the note receivable balance that Mifflinburg Farm Supply will report on December 31, 2015.

4. Determine Mifflinburg Farm Supply's note receivable balance on December 31, 2015, assuming that the company reports notes receivable at fair value and the relevant rate of interest at that time has fallen to 8%. Assume that the December 31, 2015, interest payment has been made.

P8-9	

Recording cash discounts and sales returns   **(LO 1)**

On January 1, 2014, Hillock Brewing Company sold 50,000 bottles of beer to various customers for $45,000 using credit terms of 3/10, n/30. These credit terms mean that customers receive a cash discount of 3% of invoice price for payments made within 10 days of the sale (this is what the 3/10 signifies). If payment is not made within 10 days, the entire invoice price is due no later than the 30th day (this is what the n/30 signifies). At the time of sale, Hillock expects sales returns of 5%. On January 9, 2014, customers made payment on one-half of the total receivables. They returned goods with a selling price of $2,000 on January 15, 2014. They paid the balance due on January 28, 2014.

Required:

1. Provide journal entries to record the preceding transactions in Hillock's books; assume that Hillock records *expected sales* returns at the time of sales.

2. Redo requirement (1) assuming that customers returned goods with a selling price of $3,000 on January 15, 2014.

3. Provide journal entries to record the preceding transactions in Hillock's books; assume that Hillock records sales returns when customers *actually* return the goods.

4. Because the net sales revenue is the same under both methods—requirements 1 and 3— what is the advantage of recording anticipated sales returns rather than waiting to record them when the customers actually return the goods?

5. Assuming that the incremental annualized borrowing rate for a customer is 18%, are customers better off paying within 10 days to receive the discount or should they wait to pay until the 30th day?

Needham Corporation has a $200,000 balloon mortgage payment due in early August. To meet its obligation, it decided on August 1 to accelerate collection of accounts receivable by assigning $260,000 of specified accounts to a commercial lender as collateral for a loan. Under the agreement, Needham guarantees the accounts and will notify its customers to make their payments directly to the lender. In return, the lender advances to Needham 85% of the accounts assigned. The remaining 15% will be paid to Needham once the commercial lender has recovered its fees and related cash advances. The lender receives a fee of 5% of the total accounts assigned, which is immediately deducted from the initial cash advance. The lender also assesses a monthly finance charge of one-half of 1% on any uncollected balances. Finance charges are to be deducted from the first payment due Needham after the lender has recovered its cash advances. On August 31, Needham received a statement from the lender saying it had collected $160,000. On September 30, Needham received a check from the lender with a second statement saying it has collected an additional $80,000.

P8-10

Balance sheet effects of collateralized borrowing versus factoring   (**LO 6**)

Required:

1. Prepare all necessary journal entries made by Needham.

2. Show the balance sheet presentation of the assigned accounts receivable and any related liabilities at August 31.

3. Prepare all necessary journal entries made by Needham assuming these changes in the given scenario:

   a. The transaction qualifies under U.S. GAAP as a sale with recourse.

   b. The assessed monthly finance charge increases the Loss on sale of receivables account and is offset by a credit to Due from factor.

   c. Although Needham has guaranteed the transferred accounts, their high quality makes nonpayment unlikely.

Atherton Manufacturing Company sold $200,000 of accounts receivable to a factor. Pertinent facts about this transaction include the following:

P8-11

Factoring receivables
(**LO 6**)

1. The factored receivables had a corresponding $4,000 balance in Allowance for uncollectibles.

2. The receivables were factored on a without recourse basis with notification (that is, the customers were instructed to mail their checks directly to the factor).

3. Atherton remained responsible for sales returns, and the factor retained a 5% holdback for this purpose.

4. The factor charged 1% interest on the gross receivables factored plus a 6% factoring fee, both of which the factor deducted from the value of receivables.

5. Customers returned inventory with a $3,000 selling price. All remaining accounts were settled, and the factor paid the balance due. Assume that Atherton records sales returns only when goods are returned (that is, it does not record an allowance for sales returns).

6. The factor incurred actual bad debts of $7,500.

Required:

Provide journal entries to record:

1. The receipt of proceeds from the factor.

2. Treatment of sales returns.

3. Any other items related to the pertinent facts, including the final cash settlement from the factor.

P8-12

Reconstructing T-accounts
(LO 2)

The following information is taken from the financial statements of Ramsay Health Care Inc.:

	Excerpts from Balance Sheets **as of End of**	
	Year 3	**Year 2**
Gross accounts receivable	$26,944,000	$31,651,000
Allowance for doubtful accounts	(3,925,000)	(4,955,000)
Net accounts receivable	$23,019,000	$26,696,000

	Excerpts from Income Statements **for the Years Ended**		
	Year 3	**Year 2**	**Year 1**
Revenue	$137,002,000	$136,354,000	$136,946,000
Provision for doubtful accounts	5,846,000	8,148,000	8,628,000
Operating income before taxes	6,900,000	(1,048,000)	9,321,000

Required:

1. Reconstruct all journal entries relating to Gross accounts receivable and Allowance for doubtful accounts (that is, Allowance for uncollectibles) for the year ended December 31, Year 3. You may assume that all revenues are from credit sales.

2. Assume that the company computes its provision for doubtful accounts by multiplying sales revenues by some percentage (called the *sales revenue approach*). Recalculate the provision for doubtful accounts for Year 3; assume that Ramsay estimated the Year 3 bad debts at the same percentage of revenue as it did in Year 2. Based on the revised figure, show how to present Gross accounts receivable and Allowance for doubtful accounts as of the end of Year 3. Also calculate a revised operating income before taxes using the revised figure for the provision for doubtful accounts.

3. In answering this part, assume that the company is using the gross accounts receivable approach to estimate its provision for doubtful accounts (that is, assume that Allowance for doubtful accounts is fixed as a percentage of gross receivables). Recalculate the provision for doubtful accounts for Year 3 *and* the ending balance in Allowance for doubtful accounts at the end of Year 3; assume that Ramsay estimated the expected bad debts at the same percentage of receivables as it did in Year 2. Also, calculate the revised operating income before taxes using the revised figure for the provision for doubtful accounts.

4. Based on your answers to requirements 2 and 3, what inferences can be drawn about Ramsay's accounts receivables management and the adequacy of the Allowance for doubtful accounts?

Fish Spotters, Inc., purchased a single-engine aircraft from National Aviation on January 1, 2011. Fish Spotters paid $55,000 cash and signed a three-year, 8% note for the remaining $45,000. Terms of the note require Fish Spotters to pay accrued interest annually on December 31 with the remaining $45,000 balance due with the last interest payment on December 31, 2013. Fish Spotters made the first two interest payments but was unable to make the principal and interest payment due December 31, 2013. On January 1, 2014, National Aviation agreed to restructure the note receivable.

Required:

Provide the journal entries that National Aviation would record under each of the following independent scenarios.

1. It agrees to take the aircraft back in return for the outstanding note. Assume that the aircraft has a market value of $40,000.

2. It agrees to accept a $5,000 cash payment and a new $35,000 note receivable due in five years. The note stipulates payment of $4,200 annual interest each December 31. Prepare the note receivable amortization table through December 31, 2018, and all entries through December 31, 2016.

P 8 - 1 3

Restructuring a note receivable (**LO 8**)

mhhe.com/revsine6e

Mikeska Companies purchased equipment for $108,000 from Power-line Manufacturing on January 1, 2012. Mikeska paid $18,000 in cash and signed a five-year, 5% installment note for the remaining $90,000 of the purchase price. The note calls for annual payments of $18,000 plus interest on December 31 of each year. Mikeska made the first installment payment as scheduled, but was not able to make the installment due on December 31, 2013. On January 1, 2014, Power-line agreed to restructure the note receivable.

Required:

Provide journal entries in the books of both Mikeska Companies and Power-line Manufacturing for the period 2014–2016 under the following *independent* scenarios:

1. Power-line accepted $30,000 in cash and old equipment (fully depreciated on Mikeska's books) with a market value of $12,000 in exchange for the outstanding note.

2. Power-line Manufacturing agreed to receive a total of $86,400 ($72,000 plus $14,400, representing four years' interest at 5%) on December 31, 2016, in exchange for the outstanding note. (Interpolate for Mikeska's new effective interest rate.)

3. Power-line Manufacturing decides to waive all interest and defers all principle payments until December 31, 2016.

P 8 - 1 4

Restructuring a note receivable (**LO 8**)

The following notes are excerpted from the financial statements of three companies:

P 8 - 1 5

Accounting for transfer of receivables (**LO 6**)

Ricoh Company Ltd., March 31, Year 2

Note No. 7—Short-term Borrowings and Trade Notes Receivable Discounted with Banks

The Company and certain of its domestic subsidiaries regularly discount trade notes receivable on a full recourse basis with banks. These trade notes receivable discounted are contingent liabilities. The weighted average interest rates on these trade notes receivable discounted were 4.2% and 3.2% as of March 31, Year 1 and Year 2, respectively.

Crown Crafts Inc., March 31, Year 2

Note No. 4—Financing Arrangements

Factoring Agreement The Company assigns substantially all of its trade accounts receivable to a commercial factor. Under the terms of the factoring agreement, the factor remits invoiced amounts to the Company on the approximate due dates of the factored invoices. The Company does not borrow funds from its factor or take advances against its factored receivables balances. Accounts are factored without recourse as to credit losses but with recourse as to returns, allowances, disputes, and discounts. Factoring fees included in marketing and administrative expenses in the consolidated statements of earnings were $1,501,000 (Year 2), $1,223,000 (Year 1), and $1,077,000 (Year 0).

Foxmeyer Corporation, March 31, Year 2

Note C—Accounts Receivable Financing

On October 29, Year 1, the Corporation entered into a one-year agreement to sell a percentage ownership interest in a defined pool of the Corporation's trade accounts receivable with limited recourse. Proceeds of $125.0 million from the sale were used to reduce amounts outstanding under the Corporation's revolving credit facilities. Generally, an undivided interest in new accounts receivable will be sold daily as existing accounts receivable are collected to maintain the participation interest at $125.0 million. Such accounts receivable sold are not included in the accompanying consolidated balance sheet at March 31, Year 2. An allowance for doubtful accounts has been retained on the participation interest sold based on estimates of the Corporation's risk of credit loss from its obligation under the recourse provisions. The cost of the accounts receivable financing program is based on a 30-day commercial paper rate plus certain fees. The total cost of the program in Year 2 was $2.2 million and was charged against Other income in the accompanying consolidated statements of income. Under the agreement, the Corporation also acts as agent for the purchaser by performing recordkeeping and collection functions on the participation interest sold. The agreement contains certain covenants regarding the quality of the accounts receivable portfolio, as well as other covenants which are substantially identical to those contained in the Corporation's credit facilities.

Required:

How do the three companies record the transfer of their receivables—that is, as a sale or borrowing? Is their accounting treatment consistent with the economics of the transactions? Explain.

P 8-16

Determining whether existing receivables represent real sales **(LO 3)**

Moto-Lite Company is an original equipment manufacturer of high-quality aircraft engines that it traditionally has sold directly to aero clubs building their own aircraft. The engine's selling price depends on its size and horsepower; Moto-Lite's average gross profit per engine is 35%.

To expand its sales, Moto-Lite entered into an agreement with Macco Corporation, a British manufacturer of light aircraft, to be the sole supplier of its 80 horsepower, 2 stroke engines. Under the terms of the agreement, Moto-Lite will stock a minimum of 10 engines at Macco's production facility to service aircraft production requirements. Each engine has a firm selling price of $6,000. Title to the engines does not pass until Macco uses the engine in its production process.

During its quarter ending October 31, Moto-Lite shipped and billed 19 engines (DR Accounts receivable, CR Sales) to Macco Corporation. As of that date, Macco had used 9 engines in its production process. All but three of the engines used had been paid for prior to October 31. The remaining 10 engines will be used in November.

Required:

1. What type of agreement does this appear to be? Was Moto-Lite correct to record all 19 motors shipped as sales in the quarter ending October 31?

2. How should the transaction be accounted for and by how much, if at all, were Moto-Lite's sales, receivables, and gross profit overstated at October 31?

The following facts pertain to the year ended December 31, 2014, of Grosse Pointe Corporation, a manufacturer of power tools.

P8-17

Channel stuffing   **(LO 3)**

1. Based on year-to-date sales through early December, management projected 2014 sales to be 5% below their forecast target for the year.

2. The 2014 sales forecast included projected sales of a new string trimmer that it introduced late in the third quarter of 2014; unfortunately for Grosse Pointe, actual customer orders for the new product through early December had been disappointing.

3. Effective December 15, 2014, Grosse Pointe began providing the following incentives to boost sales of the new string trimmer: (a) normal 2/10, n/30 payment terms were extended to n/90 and (b) full right of return for 90 days was granted on all trimmers purchased during the last two weeks of December.

4. Grosse Pointe has never before been forced to offer such incentives and thus has no basis for estimating return rates or default rates on these sales.

5. Sales of the new trimmer for October 1 to December 15, 2014, were $1,265,000.

6. The marketing department began aggressively promoting the new trimmer by stressing the incentives' "no-risk" nature ("if you can't sell them, just return them") and generated sales for December 15 to 31, 2014, of $2,391,000. Management included all of this revenue to make the company's sales target for 2014. Grosse Pointe uses a perpetual inventory system and charged $1,650,000 to Cost of goods sold when these sales were made.

Required:

1. Is Grosse Pointe correct to recognize the incentive sales and related accounts receivable in 2014? Explain.

2. If Grosse Pointe's auditors do not concur with management's desired accounting treatment, what correcting entries are needed?

CASES

Appearing next is information pertaining to Garrels Company's Allowance for doubtful accounts. Examine this information and answer the following questions.

C8-1

Garrels Company: Analyzing allowances—Comprehensive **(LO 2)**

($ in thousands)	Years Ended December 31,		
	2014	**2013**	**2012**
Allowance for doubtful accounts			
Balance, beginning of year	?	?	$1,324
Provision charged to expense	?	502	1,349
Write-offs, less recoveries	1	622	?
Balance, end of year	1,453	?	1,302

Required:

1. Solve for the unknowns in the preceding schedule. (*Hint:* Use T-accounts.)

2. Make all entries related to the Allowance for doubtful accounts account for 2012–2014.

3. Make all entries for bad debts for 2012–2014 assuming that Garrels did not accrue for estimated bad debt losses but instead recorded its bad debt provisions once receivables were determined to be uncollectible. (This is called the *direct write-off method.*)

4. Why does GAAP require the allowance method over the direct write-off method?

5. Calculate the cumulative difference in reported pre-tax income under the allowance and direct write-off methods over the 2012–2014 period.

6. Assume that it is the end of 2015 and Garrels management is trying to decide on the amount of the bad debt provision for 2015. Based on an aging of accounts receivable, the accounting department feels that a $400,000 provision is appropriate. However, the company just learned that a customer with an outstanding accounts receivable of $300,000 may have to file for bankruptcy. The decision facing Garrels management is whether to increase the initial provision of $400,000 by $300,000, by some lesser amount, or by nothing at all. What is your recommendation?

7. Continuing the scenario from requirement 6 now consider the following additional information. Assume that you are a member of the company's compensation committee. Assume further that the company's chief financial officer (CFO) is solely responsible for deciding the amount of the bad debt provision to record and that the CFO has a cash bonus plan that is a function of reported earnings before income taxes. Specifically, assume that the CFO receives an annual cash bonus of zero if earnings before income taxes is below $17 million and 10.0% of the amount by which earnings before income taxes exceeds $17 million and up to a maximum bonus of $1 million (that is, when net income reaches $27 million, no further bonus is earned). What adjustment to the initial $400,000 bad debt provision might the CFO make in each of the following scenarios? Assume that the following earnings before income taxes include the initial $400,000 provision for bad debts.

    a. $11 million

    b. $18.2 million

    c. $38.25 million

    d. $27.15 million

8. What other scenarios can you identify in which managers might use the provision for bad debts to accomplish some contract-related strategy?

9. Identify other items in the financial statements (besides the bad debt provision) that managers have the ability to "manage."

C8-2

Citigroup, Inc.: Analyzing loan losses and securitizations
(LO 2, 7)

The following information was extracted from Citigroup, Inc.'s 2009 annual report.

From letter to shareholders:

Financial Strength

While Citi started the year as a TARP institution receiving "exceptional financial assistance," by the end of the year our capital and liquidity positions were among the strongest in the banking world. We repaid TARP and exited the loss-sharing agreement with the U.S. government. Tier 1 Common rose by nearly $82 billion to more than $104 billion, with a ratio of 9.6%, and we had a Tier 1 Capital Ratio[36] of 11.7%—one of the highest in the industry. Structural liquidity, at 73%, was in excellent shape. The allowance for loan loss reserves stood at $36 billion or 6.1% of loans. Worldwide, deposits grew by 8% to $836 billion. The other essential component of Citi's revived financial strength has been a large reduction in our risk exposure. By year end, we had reduced assets on our balance sheet by half a trillion dollars, or 21%, from peak levels in the third quarter of 2007. This includes a substantial decline in our riskiest assets over those years.

The actions we took restored Citi's financial strength and therefore were essential. I deeply regret that they also resulted in significant dilution for our shareholders. Citi remains committed to preserving our considerable financial strength and remaining one of the strongest banks in the world.

---

[36] *Tier 1 capital* is a term used to describe the capital adequacy of a bank and is the bank's equity capital and disclosed reserves. The tier 1 capital ratio is the ratio of a bank's core equity capital to its total assets. To be "well capitalized" under U.S. federal bank regulatory agency definitions, a bank holding company must have a Tier 1 capital ratio of at least 6%, a total capital ratio of at least 10%, and a leverage ratio of at least 3%, and not be subject to a Federal Reserve Board directive to maintain higher capital levels. As of December 31, 2009, Citigroup was "well capitalized," with a Tier 1 capital ratio of 11.7%, a total capital ratio of 15.2%, and a leverage ratio of 6.9%, as well as a Tier 1 common ratio of 9.6%.

From management's discussion and analysis:

Allowance for Loan Losses

Allowance for loan losses represents management's best estimate of probable losses inherent in the portfolio, as well as probable losses related to large individually evaluated impaired loans and troubled debt restructurings.

Citigroup increased its allowance for loan losses.

During 2009, Citi added a net build of $8.0 billion to its allowance for loan losses. The allowance for loan losses was $36 billion at December 31, 2009, or 6.1% of loans, compared to $29.6 billion, or 4.3% of loans, at year-end 2008. With the adoption of *SFAS 166* and *167* in the first quarter of 2010, loan loss reserves would have been $49.4 billion, or 6.6% of loans, each as of December 31, 2009, and based on current estimates.

Selected details of Citigroup's credit loss experience follow:

	2009	2008	2007	2006	2005
Allowance for loan losses at January 1	$29,616	$16,177	$ 8,940	$9,782	$11,269
Loans charged off	(32,784)	(20,760)	(11,864)	(8,640)	(9,168)
Recoveries on loans previously charged off	2,043	1,749	1,938	1,779	2,352
Net loans charged off	(30,741)	(19,011)	(9,926)	(6,861)	(6,816)
Other—Net*	(1,602)	(1,164)	271	(301)	(1,525)
Provision for loan losses	38,760	33,674	16,832	6,320	6,854
Balance at December 31	$36,033	$29,616	$16,117	$8,940	$ 9,782
Allowance for loan losses as a percentage of total loans	6.09%	4.27%	2.07%	1.32%	1.68%
Net consumer credit losses as a percentage of average consumer loans	5.44%	3.34%	1.87%	1.52%	1.76%
Net corporate credit losses as a percentage of average corporate loans	3.12%	0.84%	0.30%	0.05%	NM

* Other—net includes reductions to the loan loss reserve related to securitizations and the sale or transfers to held-for-sale of various loans.

In June 2009, the FASB issued *SFAS No. 166*, "Accounting for Transfers of Financial Assets, an amendment of *FASB Statement No. 140*," that will eliminate qualifying special purpose entities (QSPEs). This change will have a significant impact on Citigroup's Consolidated Financial Statements. Beginning January 1, 2010, the Company will lose sales treatment for certain future asset transfers that would have been considered sales under *SFAS 140*, and for certain transfers of portions of assets that do not meet the definition of participating interests. Simultaneously, the FASB issued *SFAS No. 167*, "Amendments to FASB Interpretation No. 46(R)," which details three key changes to the consolidation model. First, former QSPEs will now be included in the scope of *SFAS 167*. In addition, the FASB has changed the method of analyzing which party to a variable interest entity (VIE) should consolidate the VIE (known as the primary beneficiary) to a qualitative determination of which party to the VIE has "power" combined with potentially significant benefits or losses, instead of the current quantitative risks and rewards model.

As a result of implementing these new accounting standards, Citigroup will consolidate certain of the VIEs and former QSPEs with which it currently has involvement. The pro forma impact on certain of Citigroup's regulatory capital ratios of adopting these new accounting standards (based on financial information as of December 31, 2009), reflecting immediate implementation of the recently issued final risk-based capital rules regarding *SFAS 166* and *SFAS 167*, would be as follows:

	As of December 31, 2009	
	As Reported	**Pro Forma**
Tier 1 Capital	11.67%	10.26%
Total Capital	15.25%	13.82%

Required:

1. Examine the selected details of Citigroup's credit loss experience.

   a. How does the dollar amount of loans charged off in 2009 compare with that of 2008?

   b. How much was added to the Provision for loan losses in 2009?

   c. What is the trend in the allowance for loan losses as a percentage of total loans over the period 2005–2009?

2. As a consequence of your findings in requirement 1, how (if at all) does this new information affect your expectation regarding the future performance of Citigroup's existing loans? To answer this question, it will be helpful to read Citigroup's Management Discussion and Analysis (available at http://www.citi.com/citi/fin/data/ar09c_en.pdf.), particularly pages 10 and 11.

3. What is the effect of having to comply with *SFAS 166* and *SFAS 167* on Citigroup's capital ratios? Briefly explain why this effect occurs. Refer to the Doyle National Bank discussion on pages 439–440.

Remember to check the book's companion website for additional study material.

Inventories | 9

A wholesaler or retailer buys assets such as business suits or shoes that are immediately salable in their current form. Assets held for sale are called **inventories.** A typical wholesaler or retailer will have only one inventory account, called **Merchandise inventory,** on its balance sheet.

A manufacturing firm making a final product such as dishwashers uses inputs from many different suppliers. Consequently, manufacturers' balance sheets typically include three categories of inventory accounts:

1. **Raw materials inventory,** which consists of components such as steel that will eventually be used in the completed product.
2. **Work-in-process inventory,** which contains the aggregate cost of units that have been started but not completed as of the balance sheet date. Work-in-process inventory includes the cost of the raw materials, direct labor, and overhead that has been incurred in the manufacture of the partially completed units.[1]
3. **Finished goods inventory,** which represents the total costs incorporated in completed but unsold units.

For most firms, inventories are a significant asset, both in absolute size and in proportion to all of a company's other assets. Furthermore, selling inventories for a price more than their cost represents the main source of a firm's sustainable income. For these reasons, inventory accounting is exceedingly important.

AN OVERVIEW OF INVENTORY ACCOUNTING ISSUES

We will use an example of a retailer who sells refrigerators to illustrate the basic issues in inventory accounting. Assume that the retailer starts the year with a beginning inventory of one refrigerator it purchased for $300. During the year, the retailer's cost of identical refrigerators increases to $340, and the retailer purchases another refrigerator at this $340 cost. At the end of the year, the retailer sells one of the refrigerators to a consumer for $500. Assume also that it is not possible to ascertain which of the two refrigerators was actually sold.

LEARNING OBJECTIVES

After studying this chapter, you will understand:

1. The relationship between inventory valuation and cost of goods sold.
2. The two methods used to determine inventory quantities: the perpetual inventory system and the periodic inventory system.
3. What specific items and types of costs are included in inventory.
4. What absorption costing is and how it complicates financial analysis.
5. The difference between various inventory cost flow assumptions: weighted average, FIFO, and LIFO.
6. How to use the LIFO reserve disclosure to transform LIFO firms to a FIFO basis and improve analytical comparability.
7. How a LIFO liquidation distorts costs of goods sold.
8. How LIFO affects firms' income taxes.
9. How to eliminate realized holding gains from FIFO income.
10. What research tells us about the economic incentives guiding the choice of inventory accounting methods.
11. How to apply the lower of cost or market method.
12. The key differences between GAAP and IFRS requirements for inventory accounting.
13. How and why the dollar-value LIFO method is applied.

Chapter

---

[1] Manufacturing overhead includes items such as depreciation of production equipment and buildings, power, indirect labor, and so on.

It is easy to determine the total cost of the goods that were available for sale. This total cost is determined by adding the cost of the beginning inventory and the cost of any purchases during the period, that is:

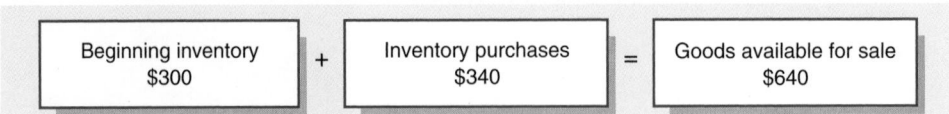

The total cost of the goods available for sale during the period was $640, a total that represents the aggregate *historical cost* of the two refrigerators.

The cost of the refrigerator that has been sold must be removed from the Inventory account and charged to Cost of goods sold, while the cost of the other refrigerator remains in inventory. In other words, the total cost of the goods available for sale ($640) must be allocated between ending inventory and cost of goods sold. This allocation process can be represented as follows:

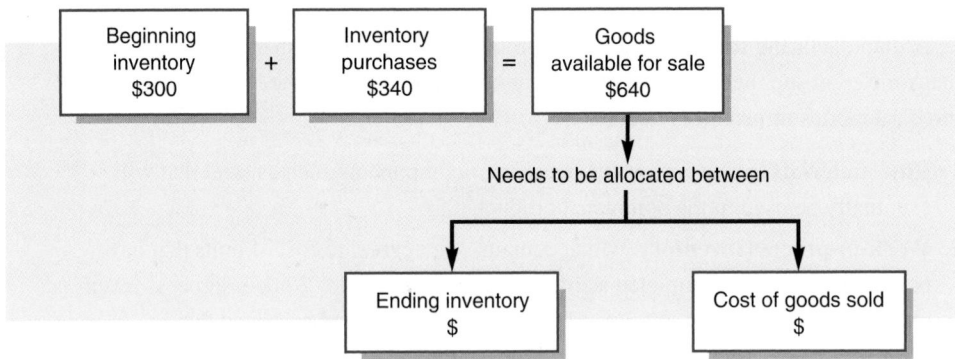

The choice of the method for making this allocation between ending inventory and cost of goods sold represents the major issue in inventory accounting.

Even in this simple case, the total for the goods available for sale ($640) can be allocated between ending inventory and cost of goods sold in at least three ways:

1. One way is to assume that the refrigerator that was sold should reflect the average of the cost of the two refrigerators ($640/2 = $320), which makes the allocation:

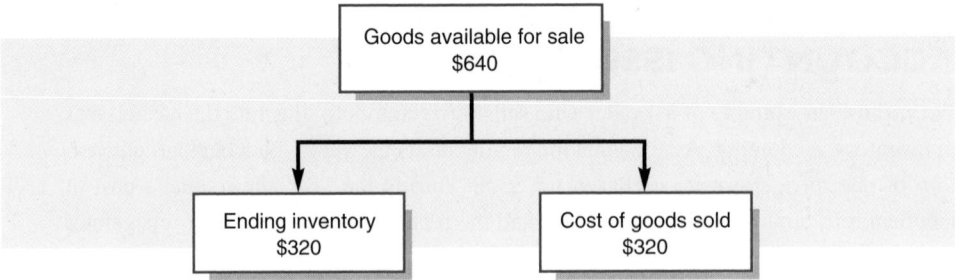

This is called the **weighted average** inventory costing method.

2. Another possibility is to assume that the refrigerator that was sold was the oldest refrigerator in stock, the $300 unit from the beginning inventory. This means the cost assigned to the refrigerator still on hand at the end of the year is the $340 cost of the most recently purchase unit. Here, the allocation is:

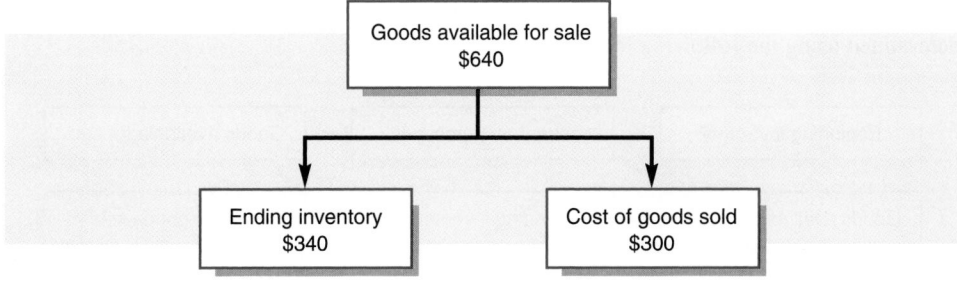

This method assumes that the first unit purchased is the first unit sold. Accountants call this **first-in, first-out (FIFO)**.

3. Another alternative is to assume that the refrigerator that was sold was the most recently purchased refrigerator, the one costing $340. This means the cost assigned to the refrigerator still on hand at the end of the year is the $300 cost of the oldest available unit that was in inventory at the start of the year, making the allocation:

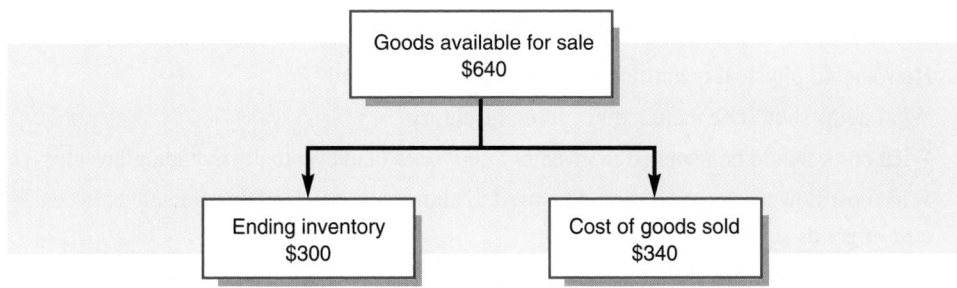

This method assumes the last unit purchased is the first unit sold. This is called **last-in, first-out (LIFO)**.

Each of these cost allocations assumes a different flow of inventory costs—average cost, FIFO, or LIFO—from goods available for sale to the ending Inventory account and to the Cost of goods sold expense account; this is why these methods are called *cost flow assumptions*. Generally accepted accounting principles (GAAP) do not require the *cost flow* assumption to correspond to the actual *physical flow* of inventory. ***If the cost of inventory never changed, all three cost flow assumptions would yield the same financial statement result.*** Also, under historical cost accounting, no matter what cost flow assumption is used, the total dollar amount allocated between cost of goods sold and ending inventory always equals the historical dollar cost of the goods available for sale ($640 in this case). This important point is shown in the following schedule:

> Although many firms use the LIFO cost flow accounting assumption, very few examples exist in which the real physical flow of units sold is also last-in, first-out. To see why, consider Kroger, a grocery store that uses LIFO. If it actually sold the most recently acquired items first—a LIFO flow—the unsold items that were received earlier would have spoiled!

Cost Flow Assumption	Total Historical Cost of Goods Available for Sale	=	Amount Allocated to Ending Inventory	+	Amount Allocated to Cost of Goods Sold
Weighted average	$640	=	$320	+	$320
FIFO	$640	=	$340	+	$300
LIFO	$640	=	$300	+	$340

Once an inventory cost flow assumption has been selected, the cost of goods sold can be determined using the following formula:

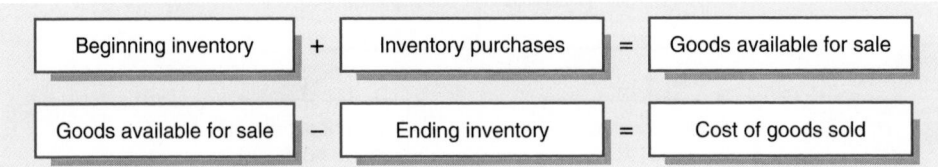

| Beginning inventory | + | Inventory purchases | = | Goods available for sale |
| Goods available for sale | − | Ending inventory | = | Cost of goods sold |

For example, assume that the FIFO cost flow assumption is selected, so ending inventory is $340. Then, cost of goods sold is calculated as:

Beginning inventory	$300
Inventory purchases	+340
Goods available for sale	640
Ending FIFO inventory	−340
Cost of goods sold	$300

This simple example illustrates basic inventory accounting relationships.[2] But actual business situations are more complex and encompass issues such as:

- How should physical quantities in inventory be determined?
- What items should be included in ending inventory?
- What costs should be included in inventory purchases (and eventually in ending inventory)?
- What cost flow assumption should be used to allocate goods available for sale between cost of goods sold and ending inventory?
- What if the fair value of the inventory declines?

We discuss each of these circumstances next.

DETERMINATION OF INVENTORY QUANTITIES

There are two different methods for determining inventory quantities, perpetual and periodic. A **perpetual inventory system** keeps a running (or "perpetual") record of the amount of inventory on hand. Purchases are debited to the Inventory account itself, and the cost of units sold is removed from the Inventory account as sales are made. Usually, these inventory records are maintained in both physical units and dollars. The physical amount of inventory on hand at any point in time should correspond to the unit balance in the Inventory account.

The Inventory T-account for a merchandising firm under a perpetual inventory system contains the following information at any point in time:

Inventory

Beginning inventory (units and $s)	
Plus:	Minus:
Cost of units purchased	Cost of units transferred to
(units and $s)	Cost of goods sold (units and $s)
Equals:	
Ending inventory	
on hand (units and $s)	

---

[2] We don't discuss the weighted average method in the cost flow assumptions section later in the chapter because it generates numbers that are between the LIFO and FIFO approaches, and it introduces no additional issues. However, we do illustrate weighted average in more detail in the self-study problem at the end of the chapter.

A **periodic inventory system** does not keep a running record of the dollar amount of inventory on hand. Purchases are accumulated in a separate income statement account, Inventory purchases (often called Purchases), and no entry is made at the time of sale to reflect cost of goods sold. The T-accounts for a periodic inventory system look like this:

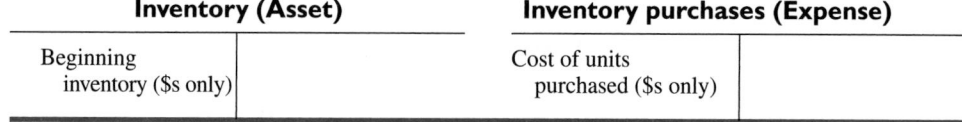

Inventory (Asset)		Inventory purchases (Expense)	
Beginning inventory ($s only)		Cost of units purchased ($s only)	

In a periodic inventory system, ending inventory and cost of goods must be determined by physically counting the goods on hand at the end of the period. The computation is:

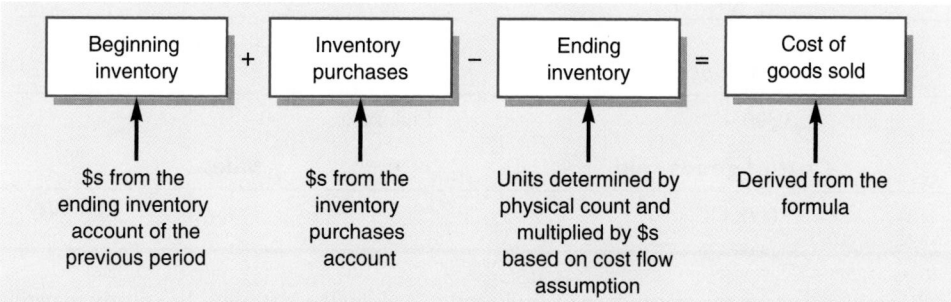

To illustrate the accounting entries under each system, assume the following data:

Sales	$10,000
Beginning inventory	1,400
Inventory purchases	9,100
Ending inventory	3,500

The following compares entries under the perpetual and periodic inventory systems.

Comparison of Entries—Perpetual versus Periodic Inventory System

Perpetual inventory system		Periodic inventory system	
Entry (1) To Record Purchases:			
DR Inventory.................... $ 9,100		**DR** Inventory purchases .... $ 9,100	
CR Accounts payable .... (or Cash)	$ 9,100	**CR** Accounts payable (or Cash)	$ 9,100
Entry (2) To Record Sales:			
DR Cash or Accounts receivable..... $10,000		**DR** Cash or Accounts receivable.... $10,000	
CR Sales revenues	$10,000	**CR** Sales revenues	$10,000
DR Cost of goods sold .... $ 7,000			
CR Inventory...............	$ 7,000	(NO ENTRY)	
Entry (3) To Close the Accounts:			
(NO ENTRY)		**DR** Inventory (ending) .... $ 3,500	
		DR Cost of goods sold 7,000*	
		CR Inventory (beginning)....	$ 1,400
		CR Inventory purchases	9,100

---

* Computed as Beginning inventory ($1,400) + Purchases ($9,100) − Ending inventory ($3,500) = Cost of goods sold ($7,000). Under a perpetual inventory system, cost of goods sold is just the per unit cost of each sold item and is recorded when the item is sold. Over the period in our example, the unit costs of sold items total $7,000.

The inventory-related accounts appear as follows under each method (entry numbers are indicated in parentheses):

PERPETUAL INVENTORY SYSTEM

Inventory				Cost of goods sold			
Beg. bal.	$1,400			(2)	$7,000		
(1)	9,100	(2)	$7,000				
				Sales			
End. bal.	$3,500					(2)	$10,000

PERIODIC INVENTORY SYSTEM

Inventory				Inventory purchases			
Beg. bal.	$1,400			(1)	$9,100	(3)	$9,100
(3)	3,500	(3)	$1,400				
End. bal.	$3,500			End. Bal.	–0–		

Cost of goods sold				Sales			
(3)	$7,000					(2)	$10,000

Periodic inventory systems reduce recordkeeping, making these systems less costly to maintain. However, this cost advantage is achieved at the expense of far less management control over inventory. For those firms that use a periodic inventory system, there is no running inventory record, and quantities on hand must be determined by physical count. Furthermore, the cost of goods sold number under the periodic system is a "plug" figure; that is, the computation assumes that goods not on hand when the physical count is taken were sold. But some of the goods not on hand may have been stolen or wasted. Under the periodic system, there is no way to determine the extent of these potential losses.

In March 2010, thieves broke into an Eli Lilly warehouse and stole $75 million worth of prescription drugs (e.g., Prozac and Cymbalta). Eli Lilly knew the amount stolen because it used a perpetual system. To account for the theft, Eli Lilly would have made the following entry:

DR   Loss from inventory shortage/theft
(or Cost of goods sold) . . . . $75 million
CR   Inventory . . . . $75 million

A perpetual inventory system is more complicated and usually more expensive. *It does not eliminate the need to take a physical inventory because the book inventory figures must be verified for accuracy at least annually.* But a perpetual system gives management greater control over inventories. For example, the running balance in inventory allows careful monitoring of stock levels. This is useful in avoiding stockouts, particularly in manufacturing where just-in-time inventory purchasing is practiced. Furthermore, the comparisons that must be made between book inventories and physical count figures reveal discrepancies that may be attributable to theft, employee carelessness, or natural shrinkage.

Choosing between the two systems depends on weighing their costs and benefits. Perpetual inventory systems are typically used where:

- *A small number of inventory units, each with a high unit value, exists.* An example is vehicles at an automobile dealership.
- *Continuous monitoring of inventory levels is essential.* An example is a production line where raw materials shortages would shut the operation down.

Periodic systems are used when inventory volumes are high and per unit costs are low. However, the widespread use of computerized optical scanning equipment has led to the adoption of perpetual systems in supermarkets and other high-volume settings where such systems were previously not cost effective. Walmart and Costco were among the first companies to utilize optical scanning and perpetual inventory systems. These firms share the information captured by their electronic inventory management systems with suppliers who are authorized to automatically ship new merchandise directly to these retailers' stores when their inventory levels fall below prescribed minimum levels. This approach shortens inventory restocking cycles at Walmart and Costco and reduces their need to warehouse inventories.

When a firm uses the *perpetual* method to manage its inventory, it also has the information needed to compute inventory and cost of goods sold under the *periodic* method. Why would a company use the periodic method for accounting purposes if it has real-time information? To get the most recent prices into costs of goods sold, a LIFO company uses the *periodic* method to compute its ending inventory and cost of goods sold. A firm may also use Dollar-value LIFO or other estimation techniques to convert perpetual FIFO or average cost inventory amounts to LIFO amounts. We discuss cost flow issues throughout the chapter and dollar-value LIFO in Appendix B.

Errors or intentional overstatements may occur under either type of system. Accounting for various types of inventory errors is discussed in detail in Appendix C.

ITEMS INCLUDED IN INVENTORY

All inventory items to which the firm has legal title should be included in the Inventory account. However, in day-to-day operations, most firms do not attempt to use the passage of legal title as the criterion for including items in their inventory records because this would be a time-consuming process. Instead, most firms record inventory only when they physically receive it.

This physical-receipt system creates no difficulties except when it comes time to prepare financial statements. At that time, the firm must determine whether all goods that were in fact legally owned have been included in the Inventory account. Goods in transit are the primary concern because legal title to such goods may transfer to the purchaser before the purchaser physically receives them. The purchaser determines the legal status of goods in transit by examining invoices pertaining to goods received during the first few days of the next accounting period and then uses this information to determine precisely when title passed.

Sometimes a firm may physically possess goods but does not legally own them. One example is goods shipped on **consignment.** Here the firm that holds the goods (the consignee) acts as an agent for the owner (the consignor) in selling the goods. The consignee receives a sales commission and forwards the net sales price (after deducting the commission and any selling expenses) to the consignor. Consignment goods should not be included in the consignee's inventory; but they must appear as part of the inventory of the consignor, the legal owner.

COSTS INCLUDED IN INVENTORY

The carrying cost of inventory should include all costs required to obtain physical possession of the merchandise and to make it salable. This includes the purchase cost, sales taxes and transportation costs paid by the purchaser, insurance costs, and storage costs. For a manufacturing firm, inventory costs also include those production costs, such as labor and overhead, that are incurred in making a finished salable product.[3]

In principle, inventory costs should also include the costs of the purchasing department and other general administrative costs associated with the acquisition and distribution of inventory. As a practical matter, however, such costs are extremely difficult to associate with

Analysis

> For example, in 2011, the Securities and Exchange Commission (SEC) charged DHB Industries, a body armor manufacturer, and its directors with overstating inventory (and consequently profits) and falsifying journal entries.
>
> *Source: SEC v. DHB Industries, Inc., n/k/a Point Blank Solutions, Inc.* February 28, 2011 (http://www.sec.gov/litigation/complaints/2011/comp21867-dhb.pdf)

> Consignment goods also raise potential revenue recognition issues for the consignor that analysts must consider. For example, manufacturers may ship products to their dealers on consignment and nevertheless try to treat such shipments as sales, thereby recognizing income prematurely. Consequently, if "sales" terms provide the "purchaser" the right to return unsold goods or if the cash payment terms are unusually long, it is possible that the manufacturer has inappropriately treated consignment shipments as sales, thereby overstating both sales revenues and net income and understating inventory (see Chapter 3).

---

[3] In certain cases, interest incurred during the time that inventory is being developed for sale can be capitalized, as described in Chapter 10. Examples include discrete projects such as shipbuilding or real estate development; that is, cases in which money is borrowed to finance construction over several reporting periods. See FASB Accounting Standards Codification (ASC) Paragraph 835-20-15-5: Interest—Capitalization of Interest—Scope and Scope Exceptions—Assets for Which Interest Shall be Capitalized.

To illustrate, assume that on February 9, 2014, Hernandez Company purchased inventory with a list price of $1,000 subject to a 2% cash discount if the invoice was paid within 10 days. Hernandez, like most companies, records the purchase at its net (after discount) cost of $980:

DR	Inventory...............................	$980	
	CR Accounts payable...................		$980

Due to an administrative oversight, the invoice is not paid until March 15, 2014. The entry Hernandez then makes is:

DR	Accounts payable	$980	
DR	Interest expense—purchase discount lost	20	
	CR Cash.............................		$1,000

So the cost associated with the lost discount is charged to Interest expense. The inventory carrying amount of these goods is $980.

individual purchases and would have to be allocated on some arbitrary basis. From a cost-benefit perspective, the effort expended in trying to assign these indirect inventory costs to unit purchases generally exceeds the benefits. That's why inventory costs shown in the accounting records are usually limited to *direct* acquisition and processing costs that can be objectively associated with specific goods. Costs that do not meet this criterion, such as purchasing department costs, are generally expensed in the period in which they arise. Furthermore, a cash purchase discount that is lost because of a late payment is recorded as interest expense rather than as a cost of acquiring inventory.

Manufacturing Costs

The inventory costs of a manufacturer include raw material, labor, and certain overhead items. Costs of this type are called **product costs;** they are assigned to inventory and treated as assets until the inventory is sold. When sold, the inventory carrying value is charged to cost of goods sold, and at that point all inventoried costs become an expense.

A manufacturer also incurs costs not considered to be closely associated with production. Examples include general administrative costs (such as the president's salary) and selling costs (say, the commissions earned by the firm's salespeople). These costs are not inventoried. Instead, they are treated as expenses of the period in which they are incurred and are called **period costs.**

The flow of product costs through the inventory accounts and, eventually, to the Cost of goods sold account is illustrated in Exhibit 9.1.

Absorption Costing versus Variable Costing

As indicated in Exhibit 9.1, manufacturing overhead costs comprise one element of product costs and are accordingly included in inventory. However, there are two views regarding the appropriate treatment of *fixed* manufacturing overhead costs. One view is called **variable costing** (or direct costing), while the other view is called **absorption costing** (or full costing).

Variable costing includes only the variable costs of production in inventory. **Variable costs** are those that change in proportion to the level of production. Examples include raw materials cost, direct labor, and certain overhead items such as electricity used in running production equipment. **Fixed costs** of production are costs that do not change as production levels change. Examples include rental of production facilities, depreciation of production equipment, and property taxes. ***When variable costing is used, these fixed production overhead costs are not included as part of inventory cost.*** Instead, fixed production overhead costs are treated as period costs and are expensed in the period in which they are incurred.

The logic underlying variable costing is that incurred costs are includable in inventory only if they provide future benefits to the firm. Proponents of variable costing argue that fixed production overhead costs are *not* assets because they expire in the period in which they are incurred and thus do not provide a future benefit to the firm. For example, factory insurance carried in June provides no benefit after June 30; for insurance protection in July, another month's premium must be paid. But future benefits *do* derive from variable costs such as materials used in production; once materials have been purchased and used in making an inventory

EXHIBIT 9.1   **Flow of Product Costs for Manufacturing Businesses**

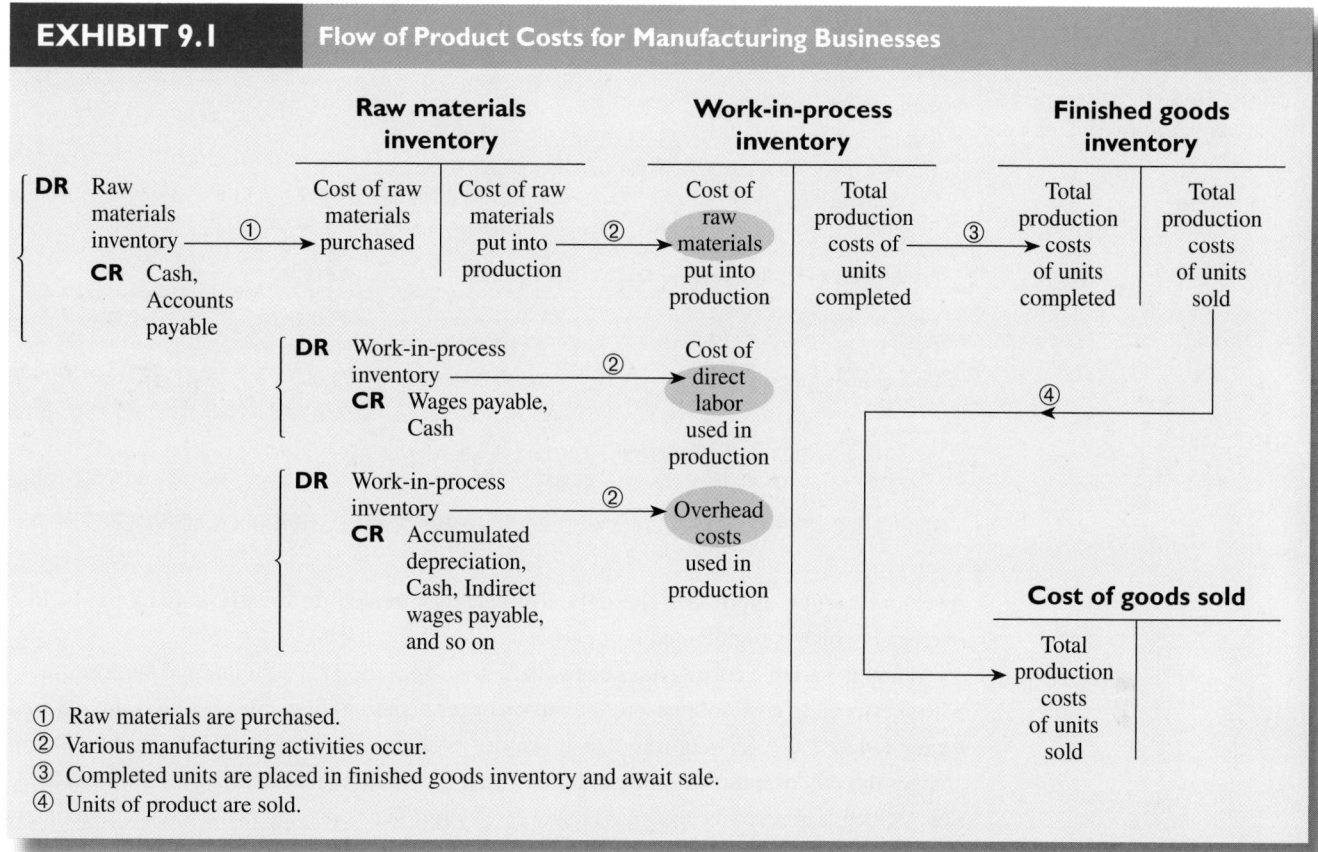

① Raw materials are purchased.
② Various manufacturing activities occur.
③ Completed units are placed in finished goods inventory and await sale.
④ Units of product are sold.

unit, that cost can be "stored" and will provide a future benefit when the inventory is eventually sold. These types of costs are includable in inventory under variable costing.

Under absorption costing, all production costs are inventoried. Fixed production overhead costs are not written off to expense as incurred. Instead they are treated as product costs and carried as assets in the appropriate inventory accounts. The rationale is that *both* variable and fixed production costs are assets because *both* are needed to produce a salable product. The exclusion of fixed costs would understate the carrying value of inventory on the balance sheet. In addition, absorption costing facilitates comparability when firms differ in the percentage of components that they buy versus manufacture themselves.

Both absorption costing and variable costing treat all selling, general, and administrative (SG&A) costs as period costs. These SG&A costs are *never* inventoried under *any* circumstances under either method. Exhibit 9.2 shows the treatment of costs by category under each

EXHIBIT 9.2   **Summary of Cost Treatment by Category under Variable and Absorption Costing**

Cost Category	Inventoried under Variable Costing?	Inventoried under Absorption Costing?
Production materials	Yes	Yes
Production labor	Yes	Yes
Variable production overhead	Yes	Yes
Fixed production overhead	No	Yes
Selling, general, and administrative	No	No

| EXHIBIT 9.3 | Absorption versus Variable Costing Illustration |

Selling price and cost data
Selling price = $8 per unit in both 2014 and 2015
Variable production costs = $3 per unit in both 2014 and 2015
Fixed production costs = $400,000 per year in both 2014 and 2015
Beginning inventory (FIFO basis), January 1, 2014 = 50,000 units @ $7

Production and Sales Volume Data	2014	2015
Units produced	100,000	125,000
Units sold	110,000	90,000
Ending inventory (in units)*	40,000	75,000

* Computations: 2014: 50,000 + 100,000 − 110,000 = 40,000 units
2015: 40,000 + 125,000 − 90,000 = 75,000 units

inventory costing approach. The only cost category treated differently is fixed production overhead, which is highlighted in the table.

Although variable costing has been widely used since the 1950s for internal purposes (e.g., when performing cost-volume-profit analysis or for planning), variable costing *is not allowed under GAAP.*[4] GAAP requires that inventory cost include "applicable expenditures and charges directly or indirectly incurred in bringing an article to its existing condition and location," which is absorption costing.[5] However, absorption costing can make it difficult to interpret year-to-year changes in reported income when inventory levels change significantly between one year and the next. We illustrate this issue in the example shown in Exhibit 9.3.

 **Valuation**

Over the two years in the example, selling price, variable production costs per unit, and total fixed production costs were constant. Units produced increased in 2015 (125,000 versus 100,000 in 2014), but units sold in 2015 dropped (90,000 versus 110,000 units in 2014).

Exhibit 9.4 shows that the reported GAAP gross margin under FIFO absorption costing increases from $110,000 in 2014 to $130,000 in 2015, an 18.2% increase. Income *increases* despite the fact that variable production cost and selling price per unit were constant, fixed costs did not change in total, and unit sales decreased.

Why do we get this strange result? The answer reveals a quirk of absorption cost financial statements. Production increased in 2015 to 125,000 units and exceeded sales, which totaled 90,000 units. Inventory therefore increased by 35,000 units (125,000 minus 90,000) to a year-end total of 75,000 units. When inventory increases under absorption costing, as in this illustration, the amount of fixed cost assigned to inventory increases. In Exhibit 9.4, the fixed costs in inventory at January 1, 2015, totaled $160,000 (that is, 40,000 units times $4 of fixed cost per *unit*). At December 31, 2015, fixed cost included in inventory had increased to $240,000

[4] Whether to use variable costing for external reporting was debated vigorously during the late 1950s and early 1960s. The issue arose as variable costing became more prevalent for internal purposes, and U.S. companies increased their investments in plant and equipment. Further, declining inventory levels caused by a recession in the late 1950s clearly demonstrated how absorption costing could distort net income. We discuss this issue in the next few paragraphs. For examples of the articles written on the variable costing versus absorption costing debate, see G. Sorter, "Reported Income and Inventory Change," *The Journal of Business* (January 1959), pp. 47–51; H. Bierman, Jr., "A Way of Using Direct Costing in Financial Reporting," *National Association of Accountants. NAA Bulletin* (November 1959), pp. 13–20; C. Horngren and G. Sorter, "Direct Costing for External Reporting," *The Accounting Review* (January 1961), pp. 84–93; J. Fremgen, "The Direct Costing Controversy—An Identification of the Issues," *The Accounting Review* (January 1964), pp. 43–51; and R. Schulte, "One More Time: Direct Costing Versus Absorption Costing," *Management Accounting* (November 1975), pp. 11–14.

[5] FASB ASC Paragraph 330-10-30-1: Inventory—Overall—Initial Measurement—Cost Basis.

EXHIBIT 9.4	Absorption versus Variable Costing Statements: Contrasting the Outcomes

Absorption Costing Income Statements (GAAP)

	2014			**2015**
Sales revenues (110,000 @ $8)	$880,000	Sales revenues (90,000 @ $8)		$720,000
Cost of goods sold		Cost of goods sold		
From beginning inventory		From beginning inventory		
(50,000 @ $7)	$350,000	(40,000 @ $7)	$280,000	
From 2014 production (60,000 @ $7*) 420,000		From 2015 production (50,000 @ $6.20†) 310,000		
	(770,000)			(590,000)
GAAP gross margin	$110,000	GAAP gross margin		$130,000
Gross margin %	12.50%	Gross margin %		18.06%
Ending inventory: 40,000 units @ $7*		Ending inventory: 75,000 units @ $6.20†		

* This cost is determined as follows:		† This cost is determined as follows:	
Variable productions costs (given)	$3.00/unit	Variable production costs (given)	$3.00/unit
Fixed production costs, unitized $400,000/100,000 =	4.00/unit	Fixed production costs, unitized $400,000/125,000 =	3.20/unit
Total production cost for 2014	$7.00/unit	Total production cost for 2015	$6.20/unit

Variable Costing Income Statements (Not GAAP)

	2014			**2015**
Sales revenues (110,000 @ $8)	$880,000	Sales revenues (90,000 @ $8)		$720,000
Variable cost of goods sold		Variable cost of goods sold		
From beginning inventory		From beginning inventory		
(50,000 @ $3)	$150,000	(40,000 @ $3)	$120,000	
From 2014 production (60,000 @ $3) 180,000		From 2015 production (50,000 @ $3) 150,000		
	(330,000)			(270,000)
Variable contribution margin	550,000	Variable contribution margin		$450,000
Less: Fixed production		Less: Fixed production		
costs treated as a period expense	(400,000)	costs treated as a period expense		(400,000)
Variable cost gross margin	$150,000	Variable cost gross margin		$ 50,000
Gross margin %	17.05%	Gross margin %		6.94%
Ending inventory: 40,000 units @ $3		Ending inventory: 75,000 units @ $3		

(that is, 75,000 units times $3.20 of fixed cost per unit). *As inventory absorbs more fixed cost, less fixed cost gets charged to the income statement and net income goes up.* Very large inventory increases produce a favorable absorption costing income effect that can offset an unfavorable income effect caused, say, by a sales decrease. This is what happened in Exhibit 9.4, and it is this effect that explains the jump in 2015 income. By contrast, variable costing income in Exhibit 9.4 falls from $150,000 in 2014 to $50,000 in 2015.

Generalizing from this example, the mechanics of absorption costing can lead to year-to-year income changes that may fool the unwary. *This can happen whenever production and sales are not parallel, that is, whenever physical inventory levels (in units) are either increasing or decreasing.* When the number of units in inventory is increasing, absorption cost gross margins tend to rise. This effect may be so large that it could obscure offsetting unfavorable effects (for example, sales decreases or deteriorating efficiency) that are taking place simultaneously. When physical

A research study found that firms in danger of producing zero earnings resort to (among other things) overproducing inventory to reduce cost of goods sold and thereby boost profits. So, the evidence suggests that absorption costing provides opportunities for firms to manipulate profits opportunistically.

Source: S. Roychowdhury, "Earnings Management through Real Activities Manipulation," *Journal of Accounting and Economics,* December 2006, pp. 335–70.

 **Analysis**

For example, in its 2010 first quarter 10-Q, P&F Industries, Inc. states:

> The reduction in gross margin [percentage], combined with the decrease in revenue, caused Hy-Tech's gross profit to decrease approximately $644,000. The decrease in gross margin reported this quarter at Hy-Tech is primarily due to lower overhead absorption which in turn was due to lower volume through the facility.

inventory levels decrease absorption cost income tends to fall because fixed overhead that was previously in inventory is charged against income as part of the cost of goods sold.

Here's an example of how an understanding of absorption costing can help careful analysts. In 2001 Intel Corporation's gross margin was 49.2%. According to a *New York Times* story, Intel management initially predicted that gross margins in the second quarter of 2002 would be 53%.[6] But one analyst warned his clients "that Intel's impressive margins were mostly a result of a buildup in inventory, not sales to end users, and that the margins were therefore unsustainable unless demand picked up."[7] Late in the second quarter, Intel reduced its profit margin forecast to 49% because of weak demand. "They continued to produce at high levels, which improved their gross margins, and then talked about efficiencies and productivity when it was only an inventory buildup," the analyst concluded.[8]

To reduce year-to-year fluctuations in fixed manufacturing overhead charged to inventory, as in Exhibit 9.4, GAAP specifies how production volume should be defined:

> However, the allocation of fixed production overheads to the costs of conversion is based on the normal capacity of the production facilities. Normal capacity refers to a range of production levels. Normal capacity is the production expected to be achieved over a number of periods or seasons under normal circumstances, taking into account the loss of capacity resulting from planned maintenance. Some variation in production levels from period to period is expected and establishes the range of normal capacity.
>
> The range of normal capacity will vary based on business- and industry-specific factors. Judgment is required to determine when a production level is abnormally low (that is, outside the range of expected variation in production).[9]

So, the basis for allocating fixed overhead should be normal capacity, but the authoritative accounting literature definition of normal capacity is very broad and subjective. In practice, this guidance might not affect the computation of fixed production overhead in inventory even when production volume does fluctuate from period to period. Thus, the potential time-series distortions generated by absorption costing will likely persist depending on an entity's accounting policy.

Vendor Allowances

It is common practice in certain industries such as retail sales for manufacturers of products (vendors) to provide cash payments and/or credits to their customers. These arrangements are called **vendor allowances.** A common type of vendor allowance is a **slotting fee,** which is described in the example below:

> Competition for shelf space in the supermarket soft drink section is intense. To gain access to space, Super Cola signs a contract with Plaid and Stripes, a national supermarket chain, to pay $50,000 per month for 20 lineal feet of prominent shelf space in each Plaid and Stripes store throughout the country.

---

[6] G. Morgenson, "Far from Wall Street, Intel's Bad News Was No Surprise," *The New York Times,* June 9, 2002.

[7] Ibid.

[8] Ibid.

[9] FASB ASC Paragraphs 330-10-30-3 and -4: Inventory—Overall—Initial Measurement—Cost Basis.

In this example, the $50,000 per month is a reduction in the cost of the Super Cola purchased by Plaid and Stripes.[10] So, the financial statement effect of the slotting fee should be to lower Super Cola's revenues. Equivalently, the $50,000 should be used to reduce Plaid and Stripes' inventory carrying value.

Managers at recipient firms have used some vendor arrangements to manage earnings. One example occurred at Kmart several years ago. In 2000, a vendor issued Kmart a $2 million allowance in exchange for Kmart's agreement to purchase an additional $15 million worth of goods in 2001 and beyond.

In an administrative proceeding, the Securities and Exchange Commission (SEC) stated:

> A significant number of allowances were recognized prematurely—or "pulled forward"—on the basis of incorrect information provided to Kmart's accounting department, while the correct terms of the payments were undisclosed. As a result of these accounting irregularities . . . Kmart's cost of goods sold was understated by $2 million in fiscal year 2000.[11]

So, although the $2 million vendor allowance was given to induce purchases in 2001 and beyond, they were recognized in income in 2000, according to the SEC. Other notable earnings management activities using vendor allowances occurred at Ahold, the Dutch supermarket operator; Saks Inc.; and CSK Auto Corporation, among others.

RECAP

To analyze comparative income statements, you must understand the mechanics of absorption costing and bear in mind that any imbalance between units produced and units sold may have a pronounced effect on reported income. For example, a sudden, unexpected sales jump, clearly a good news event, may cause an inventory depletion. With GAAP absorption costing, the inventory reduction forces an additional dose of fixed overhead through the income statement, thereby masking part of the income benefit arising from the sales jump. Additionally, consideration given by a vendor to a customer has specific income statement effects.

COST FLOW ASSUMPTIONS: THE CONCEPTS

For most publicly held firms, inventory is continuously purchased in large quantities. It is difficult to determine which purchase lots correspond to the units that have been sold, especially in firms whose manufacturing alters the form of the raw materials acquired. Consider an automobile manufacturer. It's not easy to know what specific steel purchase batch was used in the hood of a specific car.

In a few industries, however, it is possible to identify which particular units have been sold. In retail businesses such as jewelry stores and automobile dealerships, which sell a small number of high-value items, cost of goods sold can be measured by reference to the known cost of the actual units sold. This inventory accounting method is called **specific identification.** But this method suffers from a serious deficiency because it makes it relatively easy to manipulate income. Consider a large jewelry dealer with three identical watches in inventory that were acquired at three different purchase costs. Under the specific identification method, the reported profit on a sale can be raised (or lowered) by simply delivering the lowest (or highest) cost watch. An inventory method allowing such latitude is open to criticism.

---

[10] FASB ASC Section 605-50-45: Revenue Recognition—Customer Payments and Incentives—Other Presentation Matters.

[11] SEC, *Account and Auditing Enforcement Release No. 2300,* August 30, 2005, paras. 1 and 3.

Specific identification is usually not feasible for most businesses. Even when it is feasible, it has some serious drawbacks, as just illustrated. For these reasons, a **cost flow assumption** is usually required to allocate goods available for sale between ending inventory and cost of goods sold, that is,

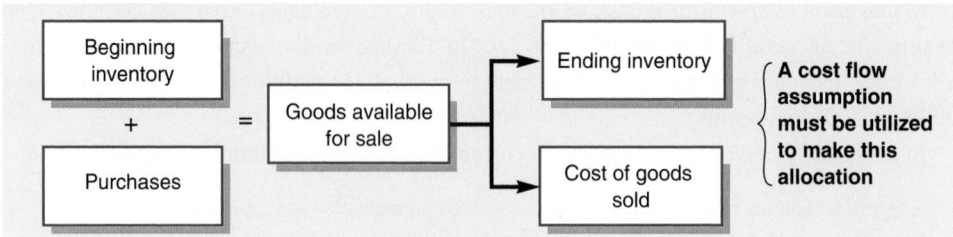

It is important to understand that GAAP does not require the cost flow assumption to conform to the actual physical flow of the goods.

The 2012 American Institute of Certified Public Accounting (AICPA) survey of U.S. company inventory cost flow assumptions indicates that approximately half of the firms with inventory use FIFO for all or part of their inventories.[12] LIFO is the next most popular (mentioned 24% of the time) and average cost (mentioned 20% of the time). Companies often use multiple methods for different types of inventory or inventory located in different countries. For example, of the 163 firms using LIFO in 2011, only four firms (2%) exclusively use LIFO for all inventories, largely because it is prohibited in most countries outside the United States. Thus, U.S.-domiciled multinational companies that use LIFO for domestic inventories would usually be required to use some other cost flow assumption for their foreign subsidiary inventories. *Forty-three percent of the 163 LIFO firms use LIFO for more than half of their inventories.*

When choosing specific cost flow assumptions, firms consider product type, inventory management strategy, taxes, and so on. We explore this choice in detail after we explain the mechanics of FIFO and LIFO more fully.

Let's revisit the refrigerator dealer to explore the underlying cost flow concepts. This simple example highlights key issues without cluttering the analysis with details that hinder comprehension. Recall the facts of the example.

> The retailer started the year with a beginning inventory of one refrigerator, which had an invoice cost of $300. During the year, the dealer cost of identical refrigerators increased to $340. Assume that the retailer purchases another refrigerator at this $340 cost. At the end of the year, one of the two refrigerators is sold for $500.

First-In, First-Out (FIFO) Cost Flow

The FIFO method assumes the oldest units available in inventory are the first units that are sold. This means that ending inventory on the FIFO basis always consists of the cost of the most recently acquired units. In the refrigerator example, the computations are:

Income statement		
Sales revenues	$500	
Cost of goods sold (FIFO)	300	(Cost of oldest unit)
Gross profit	$200	
Balance sheet		
Ending inventory (FIFO)	$340	(Cost of newest unit)

[12] See R. J. Petrino, D. J. Cohen, A. V. Patel, and K. A. Kraft (eds.), *Accounting Trends and Techniques* (New York: American Institute of Certified Public Accountants, Inc., 2012), pp. 192–93.

Figure 9.1

FIFO COST FLOW

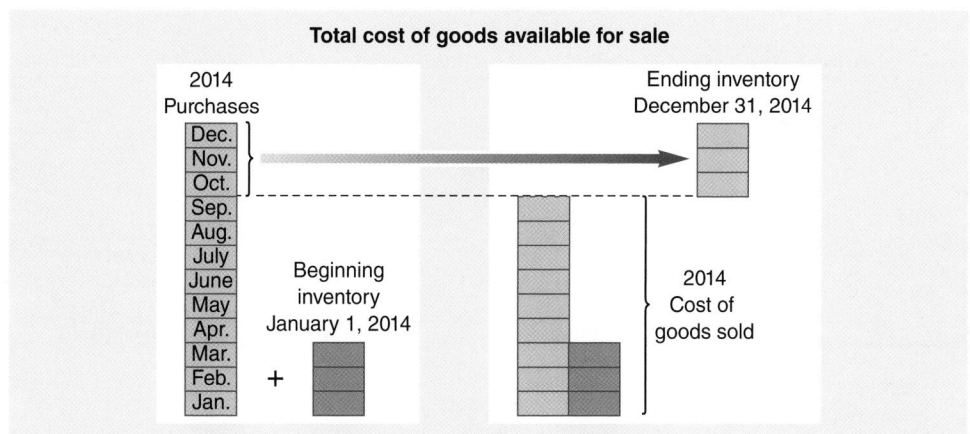

Figure 9.1 shows a more realistic FIFO cost flow case in which numerous purchases and sales are made throughout the year. The FIFO cost flow in this diagram illustrates that sales are presumed to have been made from the oldest available goods (in this case, from beginning inventory and the goods purchased in January through September) and that ending inventory consists of the most recently acquired goods (October through December).

FIFO charges the oldest costs against revenues on the income statement. This characteristic is often viewed as a *deficiency* of the FIFO method because the current cost of replacing the units sold is not being matched with current revenues. However, on the balance sheet, FIFO inventory represents the most recent purchases, and if inventory turnover is reasonably rapid, usually approximates current replacement cost.

Last-In, First-Out (LIFO) Cost Flow

The LIFO method presumes that sales were made from the most recently acquired units. In the refrigerator example, the computations are:

Income statement		
Sales revenues	$500	
Cost of goods sold (LIFO)	340	(Cost of newest unit)
Gross profit	$160	
Balance sheet		
Ending inventory (LIFO)	$300	(Cost of oldest unit)

This method seldom corresponds to the actual physical flow of goods, but remember that GAAP does not require conformity between the assumed cost flow and the physical flow of units.

LIFO matches the most recently incurred costs against revenues. When purchases and sales occur continuously, the most recently incurred costs are virtually identical to current replacement cost. So, LIFO provides a good match between current costs and current revenues. On the balance sheet, however, LIFO inventory consists of the oldest costs ($300 in the refrigerator example), which usually does not approximate the current replacement cost of inventory.

For firms that have used the LIFO method for many years, the LIFO inventory amount may reflect only a small fraction of what it would cost to replace this inventory at today's prices. A diagram of LIFO cost flow in Figure 9.2 shows how old **layers** can accumulate in ending inventory.

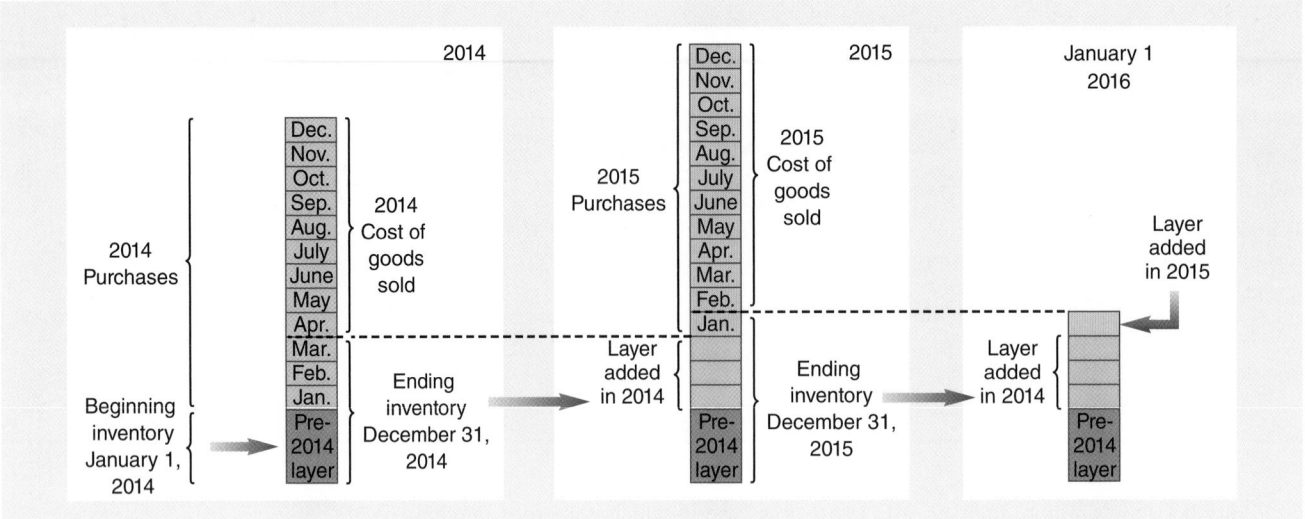

Figure 9.2 LIFO COST FLOW

As in Figure 9.2, when purchases exceed sales in any year, a new LIFO layer is formed. New inventory layers are valued using the *oldest* costs incurred during that year. For example, the LIFO layer added in 2014 comprises the inventory purchase costs expended from January through March 2014. Because sales under LIFO are always presumed to have been made from the most recent purchases (a periodic inventory method approach), the 2014 LIFO layer remains on the books at the end of 2015 as long as units sold in 2015 do not exceed units purchased in 2015. As in Figure 9.2, not only did the 2014 LIFO layer remain but also a small additional LIFO layer was added in 2015 because unit purchases again exceeded unit sales. A firm that has been on LIFO since, say 1964, could still be carrying a portion of its inventory at 1964 costs, a portion at 1965 costs, and so on. Some U.S. firms began using LIFO for financial reporting purposes right after the passage of the Revenue Act of 1939, which permitted LIFO for tax purposes.[13] So, it is not a stretch to think that a company, such as General Electric, could have a 1964 inventory layer in the inventory that it reports in 2014.

FIFO, LIFO, and Inventory Holding Gains

FIFO and LIFO give different financial statement results because each method treats inventory holding gains and losses in a different way. To understand the differences, we first need to understand inventory holding gains and losses.

Inventory holding gains and losses are the input cost changes that occur following the purchase of inventory. Let's go back to the refrigerator example. Assume that the replacement cost of each refrigerator at the end of the year was $340. However, both FIFO and LIFO are historical cost methods, and, therefore, goods available for sale reflect only the *historical cost* that was paid to acquire the two units on hand:

Beginning inventory (1 unit @ $300)	$300
Purchases (1 unit @ $340)	+340
Historical cost of goods available for sale	$640

---

[13] See R. Mock and A. Simon, "The LIFO, IFRS Conversion: An Explosive Concoction," *Tax Notes* (May 11, 2009), p. 741.

Notice that historical cost accounting ignores the $40 holding gain that arose on the unit of beginning inventory as its replacement cost increased from $300 to $340. Thus, goods available for sale are shown at their historical cost of $640 rather than at their current replacement cost of $680 (that is, to replace the two units would cost $340 each).

An accounting method called **current cost accounting** (also called **replacement cost accounting**) overcomes the above weakness and records holding gains on financial statements as they arise. ***Because of the large number of estimates needed to implement a current cost system, current cost accounting is not permitted in the basic financial statements under GAAP.*** However, the FASB does allow voluntary supplementary disclosure of current cost data in the annual report.[14]

In a current cost (non-GAAP) accounting system, the following entry is made at the time that inventory replacement cost increases:

DR	Inventory..	$40
CR	OCI—Unrealized holding gain on inventory	$40

> The holding gain takes place as the replacement cost of the inventory increases. But because the gain has not yet been included in net income, it is an **unrealized holding gain.** Once the gain is included in net income (as described in this section), it is a **realized holding gain.**

Whether these holding gains should be treated as a component of net income or included in other comprehensive income is a controversial issue. In this chapter, we ignore the controversy and treat holding gains as an element of other comprehensive income.

After the holding gains entry has been made, the current cost of goods available for sale is:

> You may wish to read Chapter 2, pages 81–87, to review other comprehensive income.

Beginning inventory (1 unit @ $300)	$300
Increase in the replacement cost of beginning inventory	+40
Purchases (1 unit @ $340)	+340
Current cost of goods available for sale (2 units @ $340)	$680

When the unit is sold for $500, the partial financial statements under current cost accounting are:

Income statement

Sales revenues	$500
Replacement cost of goods sold (1 unit @ $340)	340
Current cost operating profit	$160

Balance sheet

Ending inventory	$340

The current (or replacement) cost operating profit figure is the margin that results from matching current replacement cost against current revenues. It reflects the expected ongoing profitability of current operations at current levels of costs and selling prices.

Figure 9.3 contrasts the treatment of goods available for sale under (a) historical cost accounting and (b) current cost accounting. Notice that the total amount to be allocated between inventory and cost of goods sold is $40 higher under current costing ($680 versus $640). This

---

[14] FASB ASC Paragraph 255-10-50-11: Changing Prices—Overall—Disclosure—Additional Disclosures for the Current Year.

Figure 9.3

ALLOCATION OF GOODS
AVAILABLE FOR SALE:
HISTORICAL COSTING
VERSUS CURRENT
COSTING

(a) Historical Cost of Goods
Available for Sale = $640 and
(b) Current Cost of Goods
Available for Sale = $680.

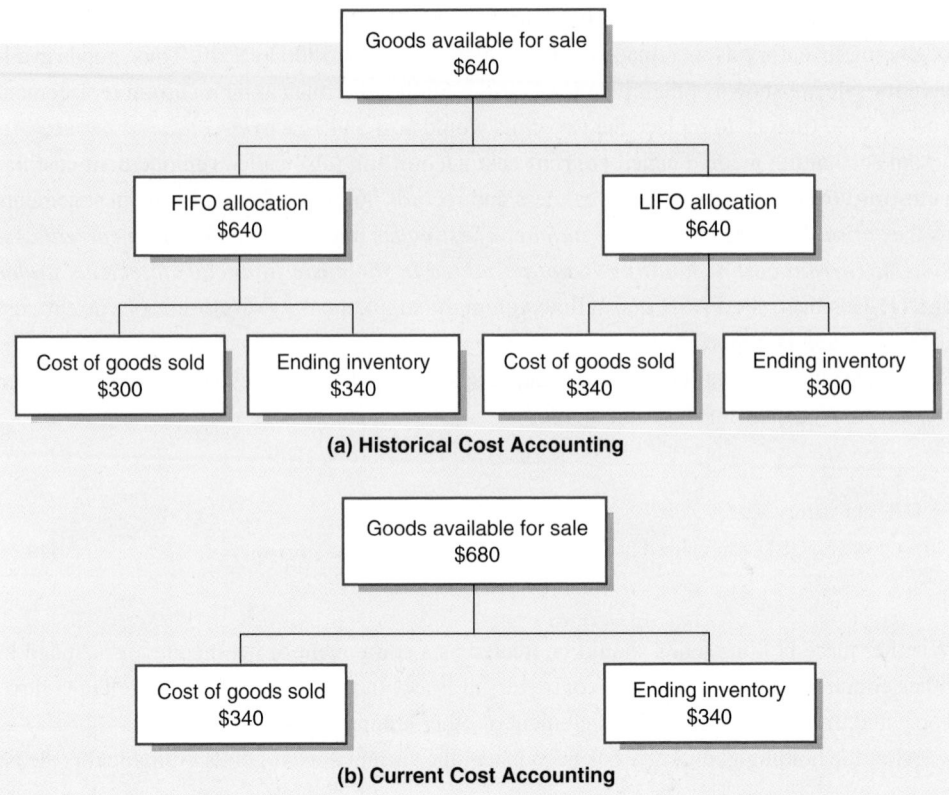

difference is attributable to the $40 holding gain that was added to goods available for sale under current costing (highlighted in the earlier table). With current costing, the total to be allocated is carried at current cost (two units at $340 each, for a total of $680). *This means that the balance sheet inventory number and the cost of goods sold number are both shown at current cost.*

By contrast, the historical cost figures for goods available for sale under both FIFO and LIFO ($640) are $40 less than the total current cost of the two units available ($680). This means that under either LIFO or FIFO it is impossible to simultaneously reflect both the balance sheet inventory *and* cost of goods sold at current cost: One can be shown at current cost, but the other must then be shown at historical cost. *The primary difference between FIFO and LIFO is that each method makes a different choice regarding which financial statement element is shown at the out-of-date cost.* FIFO shows inventory at approximately current cost but is then forced to reflect cost of goods sold at historical cost.[15] LIFO shows cost of goods sold at approximately current cost but is then forced to reflect inventory on the balance sheet at historical cost.

> Inventory quantity decreases—reductions in physical units in inventory—can produce a distortion known as a *LIFO liquidation,* discussed later in the chapter.

When input costs are rising, LIFO income is lower than FIFO income as long as inventory quantities remain constant or increase. In the refrigerator example, LIFO income is $160, whereas FIFO income is $200 (see pages 482–483). Income is *lower under LIFO because LIFO charges the new, higher cost units to cost of goods sold.*

---

[15] In our example, FIFO inventory is shown at *exactly* current cost because the purchase cost ($340) equals the end-of-year replacement cost. In more complicated situations that occur in real organizations, FIFO inventory amounts *approximate* current costs. The faster the inventory turnover (cost of goods sold divided by average inventory), the closer is the correspondence between inventory at FIFO cost and inventory at current (replacement) cost.

The income number under LIFO *usually* (but not always) closely approximates the income number under current costing:

LIFO Income		Current Cost Income	
Sales revenues	$500	Sales revenues	$500
Cost of goods sold	340	Replacement cost of goods sold	340
LIFO operating profit	$160	Current cost operating profit	$160

When purchases occur continuously, this near equivalence exists because LIFO charges the most recently acquired goods to cost of goods sold.

Now let's reexamine the FIFO income number. ***By charging the oldest costs to the income statement, FIFO automatically includes in income the holding gain on the unit that was sold.*** This result is seen by comparing the total income figures under FIFO and current costing:

FIFO Income		Current Cost Income	
Sales revenues	$500	Sales revenues	$500
Cost of goods sold	300	Replacement cost of goods sold	340
FIFO operating profit	$200	Current cost operating profit	$160

$40 difference

A comparison of the two income numbers shows that FIFO income is $40 higher. This $40 difference is, of course, the holding gain on the oldest refrigerator, which is the one that the FIFO assumption considers to have been sold. Another way to visualize this income difference is to decompose FIFO income into its component parts.

Components of FIFO Income	
Current (replacement) cost operating profit	$160
Holding gain on unit considered sold	40
FIFO operating profit	$200

This reformulation tells us that FIFO income consists of two components:

- Current (replacement) cost operating profit of $160

- A realized holding gain of $40 on the unit that was sold.

> Remember, "current cost operating profit" represents a matching against sales revenue of the then-current replacement cost of the inventory at the time of sale.

While these components are easy to extract in the simple refrigerator example, in actual financial statements, the components of FIFO profit are not disclosed and only the total figure is reported.

Some analysts argue that by merging current cost profit and realized holding gains, FIFO gives misleading signals about the company's sustainable operating profits. For example, operating profit is generally considered to be potentially sustainable if existing conditions continue. By contrast, holding gains depend on external prices increases, which may or may not be sustainable. But FIFO gives the impression that operating profit is $200, thus suggesting that $200, not $160, is sustainable. Because the higher FIFO income number includes potentially unsustainable gains, that $40 portion of FIFO income is considered to represent low-quality earnings.

In Chapter 1 we discussed political costs arising from reported profits in certain politically sensitive industries such as oil. All of us who fill our vehicle gas tanks are painfully aware of the steady rise in gasoline prices beginning in 2004. This made consumers unhappy, and human nature being what it is, many looked for a scapegoat. When multinational oil companies soon after began reporting record profits, they were an obvious target. Critics made charges (largely unsubstantiated) of price gouging. Some in the U.S. Congress proposed imposition of a "Windfall Profits" tax on oil companies.[16] Most U.S. oil firms use LIFO in an effort to better match revenues and expenses and thereby keep inventory holding gains out of income.[17]

Whereas most U.S. oil companies use LIFO for much of their inventory, companies using IFRS cannot use LIFO (see the Global Vantage Point section later in the chapter). This poses a serious political dilemma for a non-U.S. oil company such as BP. Its use of FIFO results in realized holding gains included in its net income. In an effort to reflect sustainable profits more clearly, BP provides in its annual report a supplemental disclosure of the amount of inventory holding gains included in FIFO historical cost income. Here is an excerpt:

> Profit attributable to BP shareholders for the year ended 31 December 2011, was $25,700 million and included *inventory holding gains, net of tax, of $1,800 million* and a net credit for non-operating items, after tax, of $2,195 million. [Emphasis added.]
>
> *Source:* BP 2011, Form 20-F, page 56.

If LIFO is eliminated under GAAP, U.S. firms may make similar disclosures.

The LIFO Reserve Disclosure

The previous section discussed income statement matching problems under FIFO. Remember, however, LIFO is also a historical cost accounting method with its own deficiencies. There is only $640 (rather than $680) to allocate between cost of goods sold and inventory in our refrigerator example. Because LIFO allocates the most recent cost of $340 to the income statement, that leaves only $300—the old historical cost—for allocation to the balance sheet.

Therefore, the LIFO balance sheet inventory number does not reflect current replacement cost. This leads to another set of issues that further cloud financial reporting. Let's examine them.

Because LIFO inventory costs on the balance sheet frequently include old inventory layers, the LIFO balance sheet amounts are much lower than FIFO inventory amounts. This can make it very difficult to compare LIFO versus FIFO firms meaningfully. To remedy this difficulty, the SEC requires LIFO firms to disclose the dollar magnitude of the difference between LIFO and FIFO (or current replacement cost) inventory costs. This disclosure, called the **LIFO reserve,** must be reported at each balance sheet date. Exhibit 9.5 illustrates a typical disclosure of this divergence between LIFO and FIFO inventory amounts for Aral Company.

Technically, the SEC rule requires firms to disclose "the excess of replacement cost or current cost over stated LIFO value . . ." [see FASB ASC 210-10-S99-1(6): Balance Sheet-Overall-SEC Materials-Balance Sheet (Inventories) (also located in Regulation S-X, Rule 5-02)]. In practice, most firms do measure the LIFO reserve as the difference between the LIFO inventory carrying amount and the replacement cost of the inventory. However, some firms compute the LIFO reserve by taking the difference between inventory book value at LIFO and inventory book value at FIFO. Presumably, this is justified if inventory turnover is reasonably rapid because FIFO inventory will then approximate replacement cost. Consequently, both of these alternative computations of the LIFO reserve will usually result in similar amounts and thus comply with the SEC directive.

---

[16] K. Phillips and J. Bosman, "Industry Thinks It Has a Message, but It Isn't Reaching Consumers," *The New York Times,* May 3, 2006.

[17] D. Reilly, "Big Oil's Accounting Methods Fuel Criticism—LIFO Leaves the Likes of Exxon with Big Balance-Sheet Reserves as Gas-Pump Prices Slam Drivers," *The Wall Street Journal,* August 8, 2006.

EXHIBIT 9.5	Aral Company: Inventory Note Disclosure	

	December 31,	
	2014	**2013**
Raw materials	$ 792,000	$ 510,000
Work-in-process	1,808,000	1,315,000
Finished goods	4,100,000	4,425,000
Inventory at FIFO cost	6,700,000	6,250,000
Less: LIFO reserve	1,720,000	2,375,000
Inventory at LIFO cost	$4,980,000	$3,875,000

The disclosure in Exhibit 9.5 provides statement readers an important tool. By adding the reported LIFO reserve amount at December 31, 2014, to the December 31, 2014, balance sheet LIFO inventory number, we can estimate the December 31, 2014, FIFO inventory. Specifically, the sum of the ending LIFO inventory ($4,980,000) and the year-end LIFO reserve ($1,720,000) totals $6,700,000. This sum represents an estimate of Aral Company's December 31, 2014, FIFO ending inventory. Notice that this result immediately follows from the definition of the LIFO reserve, which is the difference between FIFO inventory amounts and LIFO inventory amounts, that is,

$$\text{Inventory}_{\text{FIFO}} - \text{Inventory}_{\text{LIFO}} = \text{LIFO reserve}$$
$$\$6,700,000 - \$4,980,000 = \$1,720,000$$

Therefore, rearranging the equation yields the following:

$$\text{Inventory}_{\text{FIFO}} = \text{Inventory}_{\text{LIFO}} + \text{LIFO reserve}$$
$$\$6,700,000 = \$4,980,000 + \$1,720,000$$

Thus, we can think of the FIFO inventory cost as being composed of LIFO inventory cost plus a LIFO reserve adjustment that measures the difference between the current cost of inventory units and the historical cost of all LIFO layers. The LIFO reserve disclosure allows the analyst to convert reported LIFO inventory amounts to approximate FIFO amounts. This adjustment can be performed for all dates for which LIFO reserve amounts are disclosed. For example, using the beginning LIFO reserve disclosure in Exhibit 9.5, Aral's December 31, 2013, FIFO inventory can be estimated as:

$$\text{Inventory}_{\text{FIFO}} = \text{Inventory}_{\text{LIFO}} + \text{LIFO Reserve}$$
$$\$6,250,000 = \$3,875,000 + \$2,375,000$$

Remember that this conversion to FIFO is an approximation. As long as inventory turns fairly rapidly, the approximation is close.

FIFO inventory at December 31, 2013, equals $6,250,000. This number is also, of course, the FIFO beginning inventory for January 1, 2014.

Using the LIFO reserve disclosure in this way also makes it possible for analysts to convert LIFO cost of goods sold to a FIFO basis. This is most easily understood by looking at the

EXHIBIT 9.6			Adjusting Cost of Goods Sold from LIFO to FIFO		

(1)		(2)		(3)	
Beginning inventory$_{LIFO}$	+	Beginning LIFO reserve	=	Beginning inventory$_{FIFO}$	
Plus				Plus	
Purchases				Purchases	
Equals				Equals	
Goods available$_{LIFO}$				Goods available$_{FIFO}$	
Minus				Minus	
Ending inventory$_{LIFO}$	+	Ending LIFO reserve	=	Ending inventory$_{FIFO}$	
Equals				Equals	
	−	Increase in LIFO reserve			
Cost of goods sold$_{LIFO}$		or	=	Costs of goods sold$_{FIFO}$	
	+	Decrease in LIFO reserve			

basic cost of goods sold formula in column (1) of Exhibit 9.6. Notice that both the beginning and ending inventory *and* the cost of goods sold amounts in column (1) are measured at LIFO. (Inventory purchases represent the actual transactions and events of the period and do not require a cost flow assumption.) Column (2) shows the addition of the respective LIFO reserves to beginning and ending LIFO inventory. As we just saw, the sum that results from this addition yields FIFO inventory amounts shown in column (3). Using the basic cost of goods sold formula on the column (3) FIFO numbers plus actual purchases yields FIFO cost of goods sold. Thus, the LIFO reserve disclosures make it possible to convert LIFO cost of goods sold to a FIFO basis.

We apply this adjustment process to convert Aral Company's reported LIFO cost of goods sold number to a FIFO basis in Exhibit 9.7. Inventory purchases during 2014 are $22,165,000. FIFO cost of goods sold is $21,715,000. To make valid comparisons across firms that use different inventory accounting methods, you must make the adjustments like those in Exhibit 9.7. Because firms using IFRS cannot use LIFO, an analyst should *always* make these adjustments when comparing a LIFO firm to an international competitor using IFRS.

A shortcut procedure can be used to convert cost of goods sold from LIFO to FIFO. The shortcut focuses on the *change* in the LIFO reserve between the beginning and end of the year,

EXHIBIT 9.7			Aral Company: Adjusting from LIFO to FIFO Cost of Goods Sold		

($ in thousands)	As Reported in Financial Statements (LIFO)		LIFO Reserve		Adjusted to FIFO Basis
Beginning inventory, January 1, 2014	$ 3,875	+	$2,375	=	$ 6,250
Purchases	22,165				22,165
Goods available	26,040				28,415
Ending inventory, December 31, 2014	4,980	+	1,720	=	6,700
Cost of goods sold	$21,060	+	$ 655 decrease	=	$21,715

as reflected in the bracketed area at the bottom of column (2) in Exhibit 9.6. (This shortcut avoids the need to successively add the respective LIFO reserve amounts to beginning and ending inventory.) Applying this shortcut adjustment to the Aral Company data in Exhibit 9.7, we see that the change in the LIFO reserve was a *decrease* of $655,000 (that is, $2,375,000 at the start of the year versus $1,720,000 at the end of the year) and that FIFO cost of goods sold exceeds LIFO cost of goods sold by $655,000. So, when the LIFO reserve amount *decreases,* the shortcut conversion procedure is:

$$\text{Cost of goods sold}_{\text{LIFO}} \quad + \quad \text{Decrease in LIFO reserve} \quad = \quad \text{Cost of goods sold}_{\text{FIFO}}$$

When the LIFO reserve amount *increases,* the conversion is:

$$\text{Cost of goods sold}_{\text{LIFO}} \quad - \quad \text{Increase in LIFO reserve} \quad = \quad \text{Cost of goods sold}_{\text{FIFO}}$$

Aral uses LIFO for all of its inventory, but most public companies use a combination of inventory cost flow assumptions. The disclosures in Exhibit 9.8 illustrate this issue.

The LIFO-to-FIFO adjustment for a company such as Whole Foods Market, which uses LIFO for less than 100% of its inventory, is identical to the method used in Exhibit 9.7 for Aral Company. The beginning and ending LIFO reserves are added, respectively, to beginning and ending reported inventory amounts. It doesn't matter that LIFO was used for only 92.3% of the beginning inventory and 92.1% of the ending inventory. By adding the LIFO reserve to the reported inventory, *the LIFO portion is adjusted,* and what results is inventory on a 100% FIFO basis. In this case, Whole Foods reports inventory of $374.3 million on its September 30, 2012 balance sheet (not given in the note). So, its FIFO inventory would be $404.1 million ($374.3 million LIFO inventory + $29.8 million LIFO reserve).

There is no standardized GAAP format for disclosing the LIFO reserve. The format shown in Exhibit 9.5 for Aral Company is often seen. Other firms disclose the LIFO reserve amount in narrative form, as Whole Foods did. In Exhibit 9.8 Panel (a), we highlight Whole Foods Market's description, "excess of estimated current costs over LIFO carrying value, or LIFO reserve." Often companies do not provide the explanatory phrase "or LIFO reserve" and instead limit their description to the oblique phrase, "excess of estimated current costs over LIFO carrying value."

The second paragraph of Whole Foods' note provides additional details on how it calculates its inventory cost. It notes the importance of physical counts and estimates in its methods. Inventory cost based on a LIFO cost flow assumption often is estimated from the FIFO or average cost inventory values that may be used to manage the inventory. Dollar-value LIFO, a frequently used method, is illustrated in this chapter's Appendix B.

Exhibit 9.8 Panel (b) shows another disclosure format, this one from DuPont, a biotechnology, chemicals, and materials manufacturing company that uses LIFO for inventory reporting. Notice that DuPont, does not use the phrase "LIFO reserve" and instead uses the phrase "adjustment of inventories to a LIFO basis." The note also states that the *average cost* method (in contrast to *FIFO*) approximates current costs. In addition, similar to Whole Foods, DuPont does not use LIFO to value 100% of its inventory. In 2012, it used LIFO for 85% of its inventory. This percentage will decrease in 2013 as DuPont is changing to the average cost method for some of its inventory held in foreign locations (see the second paragraph in its note). The note explains that the change is being made to be consistent with how DuPont manages its inventory and to improve comparability.

EXHIBIT 9.8   Illustrative LIFO Reserve Disclosure Formats

Panel (a): Whole Foods Market, Inc. 2012 Disclosure

Inventories

The Company values inventories at the lower of cost or market. Cost was determined using the dollar value retail last-in, first-out ("LIFO") method for approximately 92.1% and 92.3% of inventories in fiscal years 2012 and 2011, respectively. Under the LIFO method, the cost assigned to items sold is based on the cost of the most recent items purchased. As a result, the costs of the first items purchased remain in inventory and are used to value ending inventory. The excess of estimated current costs over LIFO carrying value, or LIFO reserve, was approximately $29.8 million and $29.7 million at September 30, 2012 and September 25, 2011, respectively. Costs for remaining inventories are determined by the first-in, first-out ("FIFO") method.

Cost is determined using the item cost method and the retail method for inventories. The item cost method involves counting each item in inventory, assigning costs to each of these items based on the actual purchase cost (net of vendor allowances) of each item and recording the actual cost of items sold. The item cost method of accounting enables management to more precisely manage inventory and purchasing levels when compared to the retail method of accounting. Under the retail method, the valuation of inventories at cost and the resulting gross margins are determined by counting each item in inventory, then applying a cost-to-retail ratio for various groupings of similar items to the retail value of inventories. Inherent in the retail inventory method calculations are certain management judgments and estimates which could impact the ending inventory valuation at cost as well as the resulting gross margins.

Source: Whole Foods Market, Inc. September 30, 2012, Form 10-K.

Panel (b): DuPont (E.I. du Pont de Nemours and Company) 2012 Disclosure

9. INVENTORIES

December 31,	2012	2011
Finished products	$4,519	$4,541
Semifinished products	2,407	2,293
Raw materials, stores and supplies	1,332	1,262
	8,258	8,096
Adjustment of inventories to a LIFO basis	(836)	(901)
	$7,422	$7,195

Inventory values, before LIFO adjustment, are generally determined by the average cost method, which approximates current cost. Domestic and foreign inventories, excluding seeds, certain food-ingredients, enzymes, stores and supplies, valued under the LIFO method comprised 85 percent and 78 percent of consolidated inventories before LIFO adjustment as of December 31, 2012 and 2011, respectively. Seed, certain food-ingredient and enzyme inventories of $3,926 and $3,432 at December 31, 2012 and 2011, respectively, were valued under the FIFO method. Stores and supplies inventories of $263 and $258 at December 31, 2012 and 2011, respectively, were valued under the average cost method.

Effective January 1, 2013, the company changed its method of valuing inventory held at certain of its foreign and U.S. locations from the LIFO method to the average cost method. The company believes that the average cost method is preferable to the LIFO method as it more clearly aligns with how the company actually manages its inventory and will improve financial reporting by better matching revenues and expenses. In addition, the change from LIFO to average cost will enhance the comparability of our financial results with our peer companies. The impact of this change on income from continuing operations is $21, $(73), and $2 for 2012, 2011 and 2010, respectively. As described in the accounting guidance for accounting changes and error corrections, beginning with the first quarter 2013, the comparative Consolidated Financial Statements of prior periods will be adjusted to apply the new accounting method retrospectively.

Source: E. I. du Pont de Nemours and Company December 31, 2012, Form 10-K.

A self-study problem intended to solidify your understanding of the different inventory accounting methods appears at the end of the chapter. You may wish to refer to it now.

Under both FIFO and LIFO, the allocation of costs between ending inventory and cost of goods sold is limited to the *historical costs* incurred. As costs change, LIFO puts the "oldest" costs on the balance sheet while FIFO runs the "oldest" costs through the income statement. The LIFO reserve disclosure permits analysts to transform LIFO financial statements to a FIFO basis, thus making comparisons between firms more meaningful when one firm is using LIFO and the other FIFO. Because LIFO is not allowed under IFRS, analysts should adjust a LIFO firm's financial statements when comparing it to a competitor using IFRS.

INFLATION AND LIFO RESERVES

Figure 9.4 Panel (a) provides the average dollar value (in millions) of replacement cost inventory, balance sheet LIFO inventory, and LIFO reserve for a broad section of New York Stock Exchange firms that used LIFO for all or part of their inventories from 2004 to 2011. The sample size varies from a high of 307 firms in 2004 to a low of 229 firms in 2011. The decline in sample size is due to mergers, bankruptcies, and firms changing from LIFO. The replacement cost inventory (top line) is determined by summing the balance sheet inventory (middle line) and LIFO reserve (bottom line) amounts. Note that the average replacement cost inventory value climbs from approximately $1,223 million in 2004 to $1,830 million in 2011. The balance sheet LIFO inventory, which significantly understates the replacement cost, grew from $1,056 million in 2004 to $1,343 million. The average LIFO reserve grew from $168 million in 2004 to $487 million in 2011 after falling to $249 million in 2008.

So why did the LIFO reserve decrease in 2008? The LIFO reserve generally reflects changes in prices for the specific inventory accounted for under LIFO. As mentioned previously, most oil companies are on LIFO. Additionally, many steel, auto, and heavy equipment manufacturers also are on LIFO and are affected significantly by energy prices. Figure 9.4 Panel (b) shows that the CPI stayed flat during 2008. However, the price per barrel of Brent Crude fell significantly in 2008. At the end of 2004, the price of oil was $40.38 per barrel, but by the end of 2007, it was $93.68 before falling to $35.82 by the end of 2008. ***By 2011, the price of oil had risen to $108.09!*** Because the LIFO reserve is based on specific prices, it is understandable that the LIFO reserve pattern may be more consistent with the oil price pattern as opposed to the CPI.

Because of the downturn in the economy during 2008, some firms may have reduced inventory levels. Reductions in inventory levels (liquidations) also could have contributed to the decline in the average LIFO reserve in 2008. We address this issue in the next section.

LIFO LIQUIDATION

When a LIFO firm liquidates old LIFO layers, the net income number under LIFO can be seriously distorted. This is because the older (and usually lower) costs in the LIFO layers that are liquidated are "matched" against sales dollars that are stated at higher current prices. This results in an inflated or illusory profit margin. The following example illustrates the point.

Panel (a)

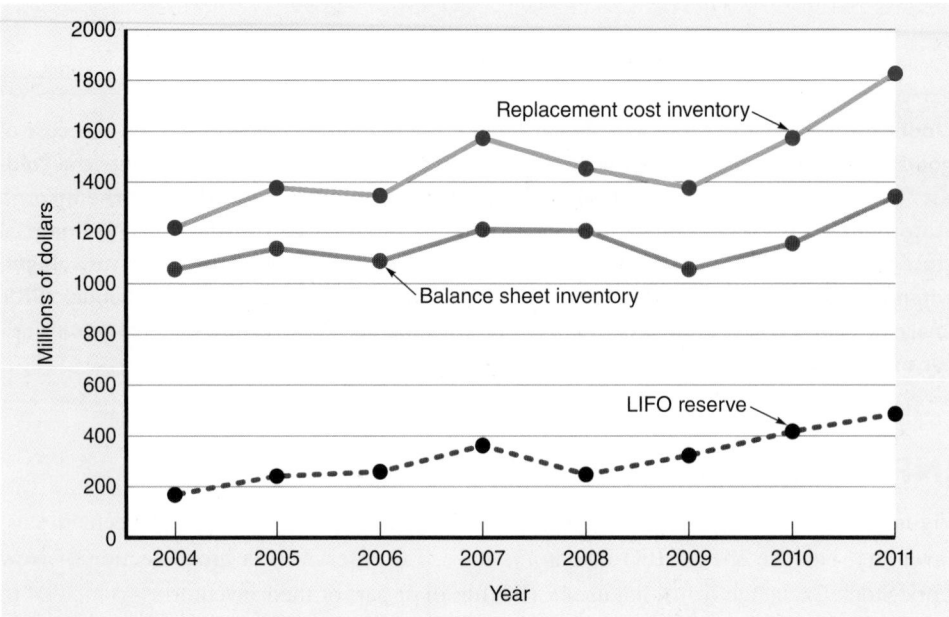

Panel (b)

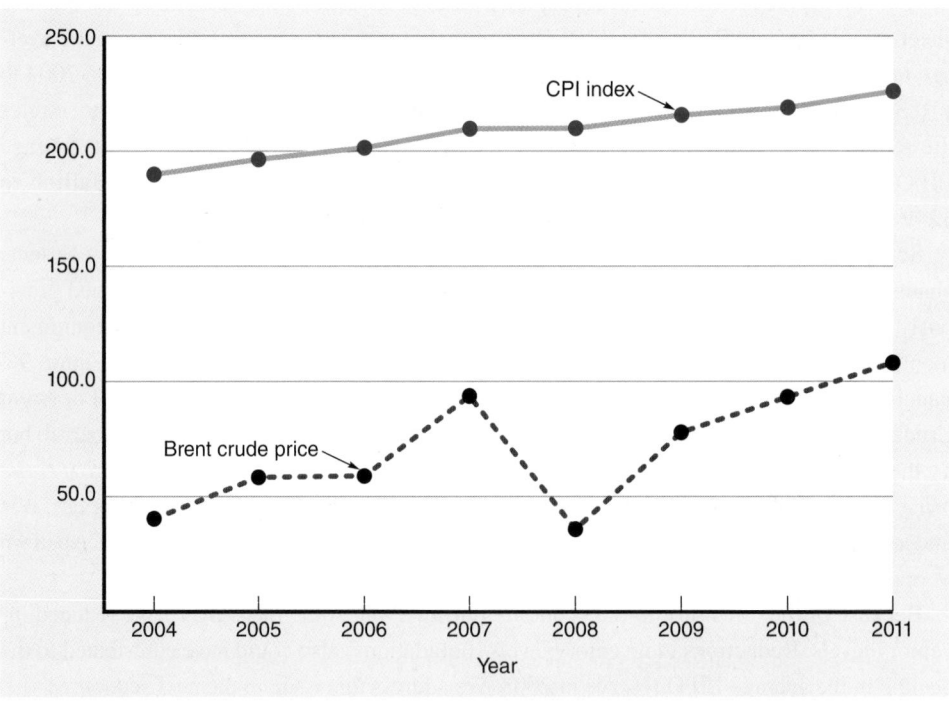

Figure 9.4 MAGNITUDE OF INVENTORY AND LIFO RESERVE RELATIVE
TO CPI AND OIL PRICES

(a) Average year-end replacement cost inventory, balance sheet Inventory at replacement cost
and LIFO reserve amounts and (b) December CPI Values and Brent Crude Oil Prices

Source: (a) Standard and Poor's Compustat® (b) U.S. Department of Labor (2013 series) and U.S. Department of Energy
(RBRTEd data series).

The Bernazard Company had the following layers in its LIFO inventory at January 1, 2014, at which time the replacement cost of the inventory was $600 per unit.

Year LIFO Layer Added	Units	Unit Cost	Total	LIFO Reserve as of 1/1/14
2011	10	$300	$ 3,000	($600 − $300) × 10 = $ 3,000
2012	20	400	8,000	($600 − $400) × 20 = 4,000
2013	30	500	15,000	($600 − $500) × 30 = 3,000
	60		$26,000	$10,000

Bernazard sets its selling price by adding a $400 per unit markup to replacement cost at the time of sale. As of January 1, 2014, the replacement cost was $600 per unit; this cost remained constant throughout 2014. During 2014 the company purchased 45 units at a cost of $600 per unit, and it sold 80 units at a price of $1,000 per unit. Pre-tax LIFO income for 2014 is:

Sales revenues, 80 @ $1,000		$80,000
Cost of goods sold		
2014 purchases, 45 @ $600	$27,000	
2013 purchases, 30 @ $500	15,000	
2012 purchases, 5 @ $400	2,000	
		44,000
LIFO gross margin		$36,000

Because the number of units sold (80) exceeded the number of units purchased in 2014 (45), Bernazard was forced to liquidate its entire 2013 LIFO layer (30 units) and 5 units from its 2012 LIFO layer. In such situations, LIFO's income statement matching advantages disappear. Indeed, a "mismatching" occurs because the reported LIFO margin per unit is only $36,000/80, or $450; this overstates the "real" current cost operating margin of $400 per unit. This $50 per unit overstatement of the margin occurs because some 2012 and 2013 purchase costs are being matched against 2014 revenues. If analysts use past margin numbers as a starting point in generating future profit or cash flow estimates, the LIFO income number is misleading when liquidation occurs. That is, the $450 *reported* LIFO unit margin overstates the current cost *real* margin of $400 used for pricing purposes and thus does not represent a sustainable future per unit margin number. LIFO earnings that include LIFO liquidation profits are considered to be lower quality earnings. The illusory profit elements would generally be assigned a lower earnings multiple for valuation purposes.

 **Valuation**

To understand better what happens when LIFO liquidations occur, let's examine the reported current cost operating margin for 2014:

Sales revenues (80 × $1,000)	$80,000
Replacement cost of goods sold (80 × $600)	48,000
Current cost operating margin (80 × $400)	$32,000

The 2014 LIFO gross margin of $36,000 in the example at the top of this page exceeds the 2014 current cost margin of $32,000. ***This "extra" LIFO income of $4,000 is the result of mismatching.*** In more technical terms, as LIFO layers are liquidated, some of the inventory holding gains of 2013 and 2012 that were ignored under historical cost LIFO in the years they occurred suddenly are recognized as income as the old, lower cost inventory layers are

EXHIBIT 9.9   Calculation of LIFO Liquidation Profits

LIFO Layer Liquidated

Year Added	Units Liquidated		Current Cost		Historical Cost		Effect on Earnings
2013	30	×	($600	–	$500)	=	$3,000
2012	5	×	($600	–	$400)	=	1,000
Total increase in pre-tax earnings due to LIFO liquidation							$4,000

matched against current selling prices. This can be seen by examining the December 31, 2014, LIFO inventory computation:

Year LIFO Layer Added	Remaining Units	Unit Cost	Ending Inventory 12/31/14 Total	LIFO Reserve as of 12/31/14
2011	10	$300	$3,000	($600 − $300) × 10 = $3,000
2012	15	400	6,000	($600 − $400) × 15 = 3,000
	25		$9,000	$6,000

The LIFO reserve was $10,000 at January 1, 2014 (see page 495). Notice that the LIFO liquidation has reduced the LIFO reserve to $6,000 at December 31, 2014. This $4,000 reduction in the LIFO reserve represents another way to visualize how LIFO liquidations create a mismatching on the income statement. Previously ignored unrealized holding gains are included in income as Bernazard liquidates the old LIFO layers. The $4,000 earnings "boost" equals the difference between the current cost to replace the liquidated layer of LIFO inventory (at date of sale) and the original cost of those units. This is demonstrated in Exhibit 9.9. When old LIFO layers are invaded, LIFO income jumps, but the increase is not sustainable.

When the income effect of a LIFO liquidation is material, the SEC requires that firms disclose the dollar impact of the liquidation on income. Most companies that provide the 10-Q or 10-K disclosure also disclose the dollar impact of the liquidation in the report. The statement user should be alert to the fact that the earnings effect of a LIFO liquidation can be reported on either a *before-tax* or *after-tax* basis. Exhibit 9.10 shows this disclosure (on both a before- and after-tax basis) from Aral Company's 2014 annual report.

The LIFO liquidation disclosure in Exhibit 9.10 indicates that 2014 earnings before income taxes increased by $2,600,000 as a consequence of matching old LIFO layer costs against 2014 revenues. This number represents the *pre-tax* effect of LIFO liquidation, indicating that the reported LIFO gross margin in 2014 overstated sustainable earnings by $2,600,000. Equivalently, the LIFO cost of goods sold number was lower than current cost of goods sold by $2,600,000.

EXHIBIT 9.10   Aral Company: Disclosure of LIFO Liquidation

During 2014, the Company liquidated certain LIFO inventories that were carried at lower costs prevailing in prior years. The effect of this liquidation was to increase earnings before income taxes by $2,600,000 ($1,690,000 increase in net earnings, or an increase of $.08 per share).

Reconciliation of Changes in LIFO Reserve

We are now able to explain more precisely what factors drive the LIFO–FIFO cost of goods sold difference computed for Aral in Exhibit 9.7. As we see in that exhibit, FIFO cost of goods sold exceeds LIFO cost of goods sold by $655,000, the dollar decrease in the LIFO reserve. LIFO liquidations reduce the LIFO reserve because old, lower cost LIFO layers are eliminated. But the LIFO reserve increases when input costs increase. So, to explain what causes the LIFO versus FIFO cost of goods sold difference, we need to explain what causes both upward and downward changes in the LIFO reserve. This is done in Exhibit 9.11.

We know the beginning and ending balance of the reserve as well as the decrease caused by the LIFO liquidation. To reconcile to the December 31, 2014, LIFO reserve amount, the reserve had to increase by $1,945,000 (the highlighted "plug" figure in Exhibit 9.11). This increase is attributable to rising input costs. So, the $655,000 difference between the LIFO and FIFO cost of goods sold numbers can be explained as:

1. Rising input costs *increased* LIFO cost of goods sold by	$1,945,000
2. The LIFO liquidation undercharged expense and thus *reduced* cost of goods sold by	(2,600,000)
3. Result: FIFO cost of goods sold exceeds LIFO cost of goods sold by	$ 655,000

Reconciling the LIFO reserve as in Exhibit 9.11 provides auditors and analysts information about the direction of input costs. When linked to other data, this cost information can be valuable. For example, if the auditor/analyst knows that input costs are rising but competition limits output price increases, it is likely that the firm's future margins will suffer. This will reduce future operating cash flows, adversely affecting the firm's value and perhaps even viability as a going concern.

Valuation

We explore the effects of cost increases and LIFO liquidations on the LIFO reserves and cost of goods sold in greater detail within the context of dollar-value LIFO in Appendix B.

Improved Trend Analysis

The LIFO to FIFO adjustment is also used in trend analysis as illustrated in Exhibit 9.12, where comparative gross profit data for Aral are shown for 2012 to 2014.

The Exhibit 9.12(a) data show that the gross profit percentage rose slightly in 2013 and more dramatically in 2014. But we have also seen (Exhibit 9.10) that in 2014 there was a LIFO liquidation, which increased the reported gross profit in 2014 over what it would have been without the liquidation. You might ask what the profit trend looks like after adjusting for

Analysis

EXHIBIT 9.11	Aral Company: Change in the LIFO Reserve

Beginning LIFO reserve, January 1, 2014	$2,375,000
Decrease in LIFO reserve due to LIFO liquidation (Exhibit 9.10)	(2,600,000)
Increase in LIFO reserve due to increases in input costs during the year (plug)	1,945,000
Ending LIFO reserve, December 31, 2014	$1,720,000

EXHIBIT 9.12   **Aral Company: Ratio Comparisons**

a. Comparative Gross Profit Data as Reported

	Years Ended December 31,		
($ in thousands)	**2014**	**2013**	**2013**
Net sales	$26,000	$25,000	$24,000
Cost of goods sold	21,060	21,000	20,400
Gross profit	$ 4,940	$ 4,000	$ 3,600
Gross profit as a percentage of sales	19.0%	16.0%	15.0%

b. Gross Profit Data Adjusted for LIFO Liquidation

	Years Ended December 31,		
($ in thousands)	**2014**	**2013**	**2013**
Gross profit as reported	$ 4,940	$ 4,000	$ 3,600
Pre-tax effect of LIFO liquidation on gross profit	2,600	—	—
Gross profit after eliminating LIFO liquidation effect	$ 2,340	$ 4,000	$ 3,600
Net sales (as reported)	$26,000	$25,000	$24,000
Adjusted gross profit percentage	9.0%	16.0%	15.0%
Exhibit 9.13(a) gross profit percentage	19.0%	16.0%	15.0%
Difference	−10%	N/A	N/A

The Aral disclosure revealed both the pre-tax *and* after-tax income effect of a LIFO liquidation. Some companies disclose only the increase in net (after-tax) earnings. In these instances, analysts can still easily convert the LIFO liquidation effect to a pre-tax basis and evaluate year-to-year changes in gross margin.

Here's how. Assume that a company discloses that a LIFO liquidation increased its (after-tax) net income by $1,690,000. Also assume that the income tax rate is 35%. Then:

$$\text{After-tax effect} = \text{Pre-tax effect} \times (1 - \text{Marginal tax rate})$$

or

$$\$1,690,000 = \text{Pre-tax effect} \times (1 - 0.35)$$

or

$$\frac{\$1,690,000}{0.65} = \text{Pre-tax effect of } \$2,600,000$$

The $2,600,000 pre-tax impact of the LIFO liquidation would then be used to undertake an analysis similar to Exhibit 9.12(b).

the LIFO liquidation. We can extend the previous analysis to address this question; see Exhibit 9.12(b).

The computations reveal that after removing the illusory income effect arising from the LIFO liquidation, the gross profit percentage for Aral shows a sharp decline in 2014. The adjusted gross profit percentage (highlighted in Exhibit 9.12[b]) fell from 15.0% in 2012 to 9.0% in 2014. This deterioration is not immediately evident in the *reported* gross margin figures. Analysis of trend data provides potentially important information regarding management's performance in adapting to new market conditions. Neglecting to adjust the year-to-year data for nonsustainable factors (such as the artificial margin improvement that results from a LIFO liquidation) could easily lead to erroneous conclusions.

Consider one final point regarding Exhibit 9.12(b). Many analysts believe that the most recent margin percentage provides the least biased estimate of the next year's margin percentage. (This belief is correct when margins follow a random-walk pattern. When they do, the best estimate of the next period's value is generated by simply extrapolating the most recently observed past value.) *After eliminating the effects of LIFO liquidations, the adjusted gross margin percentage provides a clearer picture of the underlying real sustainable gross margin in each year.* Analysts trying to estimate Aral Company's future performance must understand that it is the 9.0% adjusted margin percentage, not the 19.0% unadjusted figure, that represents the starting point for estimating the sustainable margin in subsequent periods.

To avoid being misled by transitory LIFO liquidation profits, statement users should carefully scrutinize the LIFO inventory note. The objective is to determine whether a LIFO liquidation occurred during the period and, if so, what impact it had on reported profits for the period. LIFO liquidations are more likely to occur during difficult operating conditions, as we saw during the 2008 to 2009 economic crisis.

Of course, LIFO liquidations don't occur only at the end of the year. When liquidations occur midyear, both the accounting treatment and accompanying 10-Q disclosure can differ slightly from the Aral Company example. The reason is that management must determine whether the midyear inventory reduction will persist to year-end or just be temporary.

Here's what one oil refining company said about its midyear LIFO liquidations (dollar amounts are in millions):

> During the second quarter of 2006, we incurred a **temporary** LIFO liquidation gain in our Refinery inventory in the amount of $178. This gain decreased by $19 during the third quarter and we expect it to be fully restored by the end of the year. The temporary LIFO liquidation gain has been deferred as a component of accrued expenses and other current liabilities in the accompanying September 30, 2006, condensed consolidated balance sheet.
>
> During the second quarter of 2006, we also incurred a **permanent** reduction in a LIFO layer resulting in a liquidation gain in our Refinery inventory in the amount of $1,026. In the third quarter, this gain decreased by $11. This liquidation gain, which represents a reduction of approximately 77,000 barrels, was recognized as a component of cost of goods sold in the nine month period ended September 30, 2006. [Emphasis added.]
>
> *Source:* Delek US Holdings, Inc. Form 10-Q filing for the period ended June 30, 2007.

As this example illustrates, midyear LIFO liquidation gains that are deemed to be permanent flow directly to cost of goods sold and thereby increase earnings in the quarter when they occur. However, temporary midyear LIFO liquidation gains don't flow to cost of goods sold in the quarter when they occur. These temporary gains are instead parked on the balance sheet. If inventory quantities increase to their former level by year-end, the temporary gain is reversed and eliminated. This accounting approach thus eliminates from quarterly earnings any volatility that would otherwise arise because of seasonal fluctuations in LIFO inventory levels. But what if inventory quantities remain low at year-end? In this case, the temporary LIFO liquidation gain is now deemed permanent and flows from the balance sheet to year-end cost of goods sold. Delayed recognition distorts fourth quarter net income, but that's the trade-off that results from an accounting approach that eliminates quarterly earnings volatility when inventory reductions are truly temporary.

LIFO liquidations occur frequently and often have a large impact on reported earnings. The earnings effect arises from a mismatching since LIFO layers carried at "old" costs are matched against current period revenues. Reported margins are distorted and so is the income trend.

ELIMINATING LIFO RATIO DISTORTIONS

LIFO inventory costing can lead to ratio distortions that can be corrected easily. For example, on its December 31, 2014, balance sheet, Aral Company reported total current assets of $14,460,000 and total current liabilities of $5,784,000. Utilizing these numbers, the current ratio at December 31, 2014, is:

$$\frac{\text{Current assets}}{\text{Current liabilities}} = \frac{\$14,460,000}{\$5,784,000} = 2.5$$

Analysis

However, Exhibit 9.5 disclosed that the LIFO inventory carrying amount understated FIFO (and replacement cost) inventory by $1,720,000. This amount is the LIFO reserve that we must add to the numerator to reflect the current ratio in truly *current* terms. The adjusted current ratio is ($000 omitted):

$$\frac{\$14,460 + \$1,720}{\$5,784} = 2.80$$

The current ratio improves after making the LIFO adjustment. Most other ratios deteriorate once the adjustments for LIFO effects have been included. To illustrate the general deterioration, consider the inventory turnover ratio:

$$\frac{\text{Cost of goods sold}}{\text{Average inventory}} = \text{Inventory turnover}$$

The inventory turnover ratio is designed to reflect the physical turnover of product, that is, how long the typical unit remains in inventory. Most firms have many inventory categories. This diversity renders unit measures of inventory turnover meaningless because unit turnover is difficult to interpret in a diversified firm. That's why dollar, rather than unit, inventory measures are used to compute the turnover ratio. For Aral, using the inventory amounts from Exhibit 9.5 and cost of goods sold from Exhibit 9.7, inventory turnover for 2014 is ($000 omitted):

$$\frac{\$21,060}{(\$3,875 + \$4,980)/2} = 4.76 \text{ times per year}$$

The typical unit turns over 4.76 times per year. Another way to understand what this means is to divide 4.76 into 365, the number of days in a year. The result $365/4.76 = 76.7$ shows that the typical unit remains in inventory for 76.7 days.

The inventory turnover ratio is structured to approximate *physical* unit flow. The numerator is the cumulative dollar cost of units that have been sold; the denominator is the average cost of units on hand during the year. Under "normal" circumstances, the quotient should reflect the physical unit turnover. Unfortunately, LIFO frequently distorts the representation of physical unit flow. To see why, consider the denominator of the Aral ratio; it does *not* reflect the then-current cost of the inventory at either the beginning or end of 2014 because there was a LIFO reserve at both times: $2,375,000 and $1,720,000, respectively. For a firm using LIFO:

- The numerator of the ratio—cost of goods sold—is predominantly current period costs, here, 2014, and
- The denominator—average inventory—consists of old LIFO costs.

The quotient will not capture physical unit turnover unless an adjustment is made to the denominator. Furthermore, an adjustment to the numerator is also required here because the pre-tax impact of the LIFO liquidation ($2,600,000) causes the cost of goods sold numerator to understate *current* cost of goods sold by this amount. To correctly gauge physical turnover, the analyst must *always* adjust the denominator of LIFO firms' turnover by adding the LIFO reserve amounts to beginning and ending inventory. In addition, the numerator must also be adjusted for LIFO liquidation profits whenever LIFO liquidations occur. The Aral 2014 inventory turnover ratio adjusting both the numerator and the denominator is ($000 omitted):

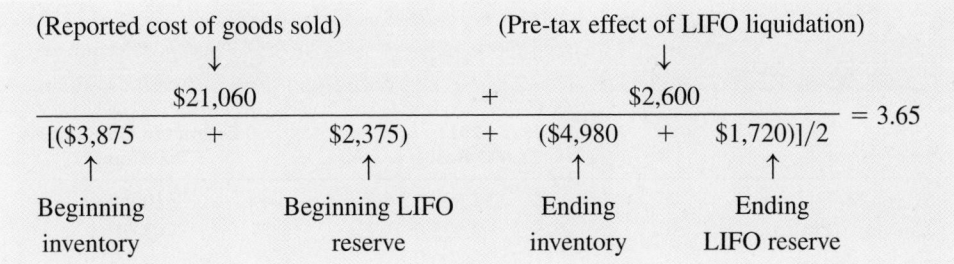

Dividing this LIFO–adjusted turnover (3.65) into 365 days reveals that the typical unit, in fact, remains in inventory for 100 days—considerably longer than the 76.7 days suggested by the unadjusted analysis.

TAX IMPLICATIONS OF LIFO

In the United States, the accounting principles that a firm uses in preparing its external financial statements need not be the same as the principles used in computing income taxes. A notable exception to this statement occurs under LIFO. U.S. tax rules specify that if LIFO is used for tax purposes, the external financial statements must also use LIFO. This is called the **LIFO conformity rule.**

The LIFO conformity rule partially explains the widespread use of LIFO for financial reporting purposes. To gain the tax advantage of LIFO, a firm must also use this method for recognizing Inventory on its balance sheet and Cost of goods sold in its income statement. LIFO's tax advantage is that it provides a lower income amount than FIFO during periods of rising prices and nondecreasing inventory quantities, thus lowering the immediate tax liability. However, this effect can be reversed if LIFO layers are liquidated or if future purchase costs fall.

The dollar amount of the tax saving provided by LIFO can easily be computed by reference to the LIFO reserve number. For example, in Exhibit 9.5 we saw that Aral's LIFO reserve at December 31, 2014, was $1,720,000. This number equals the cumulative excess of LIFO cost of goods sold over what the cost of goods sold would have been had FIFO been used. The $1,720,000 also represents the cumulative unrealized holding gain on the old LIFO layers. Under FIFO, the old, lower cost inventory would have been charged to cost of goods sold, thereby raising cumulative pretax income by this amount. Assuming an average tax rate over the past years of 40%. Aral has *postponed* approximately $688,000 in taxes (that is, $1,720,000 × 40%) since it began using LIFO.

> The marginal federal corporate tax rate immediately prior to 1986 was 46% and from 1986 to 1992 the rate was 34%. Since 1992 the rate has been 35%. With state and local taxes, the overall marginal tax rates obviously would be even higher. We use a flat 40% rate to simplify the calculations.

The amount of taxes that companies can postpone by using LIFO can be substantial; see Exhibit 9.13. This table lists the 20 firms with the largest LIFO reserves as of year-end 2011 with their estimated tax savings (based on using a 40% marginal tax rate). Note that oil companies dominate the list. Companies that produce or sell products with short shelf-lives, such as Kroger, Walgreen Co., and Altria Group, also appear on the list. The LIFO reserves for these companies have grown over decades, and old costs remain in inventory though the older physical units have been sold. This demonstrates that a cost flow assumption does not have to match the physical flow.

The LIFO tax benefit ranges from $10.2 billion for ExxonMobil to $240 million for Altria Group. The total amount of taxes postponed by these 20 firms was $29.7 billion in 2011. Clearly, these companies have received substantial cumulative cash flow benefits from using LIFO rather than FIFO. ***For the firms used in Figure 9.4 on page 494, the total tax deferral was $44.6 billion at the end of 2011.*** As Figure 9.4 shows, prices and LIFO reserves increased substantially between 2008 and 2011. Consequently, ExxonMobil's tax savings grew from

EXHIBIT 9.13	Estimated Tax Savings for Firms with the Largest LIFO Reserves

($ in millions)	2011 LIFO Reserve	Estimated Cumulative Tax Benefit*
Exxon Mobil Corp	$25,600.0	$10,240.0
Chevron Corp	9,025.0	3,610.0
ConocoPhillips	8,400.0	3,360.0
Valero Energy Corp	6,800.0	2,720.0
Marathon Petroleum Corp	5,015.0	2,006.0
Sunoco Inc.	2,920.0	1,168.0
Caterpillar Inc.	2,422.0	968.8
Tesoro Corp	1,700.0	680.0
Walgreen Co	1,587.0	634.8
Deere & Co	1,486.0	594.4
Hess Corp	1,276.0	510.4
Dow Chemical	1,105.0	442.0
United States Steel Corp	1,100.0	440.0
Kroger Co	1,043.0	417.2
Ford Motor Co	928.0	371.2
Du Pont (E I) De Nemours	901.0	360.4
Alcoa Inc.	801.0	320.4
Nucor Corp	763.2	305.3
Berkshire Hathaway	759.0	303.6
Altria Group Inc.	600.0	240.0
	$74,231.2	$29,692.5

* Based on average marginal tax rate of 40%.

Source: Compustat® as data source; methodology not verified or controlled by Standard & Poor's.

$4 billion in 2008 to $10.2 billion in 2011. In addition to the large public companies shown in the exhibit, thousands of small private companies also benefit from being on LIFO.

Although clear cash flow benefits result from using LIFO, critics argue that LIFO could induce undesirable managerial behavior. This could happen if a firm has depleted its inventory quantities toward the end of a year. If inventories are allowed to remain at the depleted level, the tax liability could increase considerably because the liquidation of old, low-cost LIFO layers increases income. However, a manager can avoid this increase in taxes by simply purchasing a large amount of inventory at the end of the year to bring the inventory back up to beginning-of-year levels. Doing this to avoid tax increases may cause unwise purchasing behavior: Excessive inventory levels could be carried, or year-end purchases could be made despite the fact that future purchase costs are expected to fall.[18]

ELIMINATING REALIZED HOLDING GAINS FOR FIFO FIRMS

LIFO puts realized holding gains into income when old LIFO layers are eliminated. In contrast, reported income for FIFO firms *always* includes some realized holding gains during periods of rising inventory costs because FIFO charges the *oldest* inventory to Cost of goods sold. Another way to say the same thing is that FIFO cost of goods sold is understated because

[18] Results consistent with the potential for tax-driven inventory management inefficiencies are reported in M. Frankel and R. Trezevant, "The Year-End LIFO Inventory Purchasing Decision: An Empirical Test," *The Accounting Review,* April 1994, pp. 382–98.

of the inventory holding gains that have occurred during the period. Because holding gains are potentially unsustainable, astute analysts try to remove them from reported FIFO income (or, equivalently, add them to FIFO costs of goods sold).

The size of divergence between FIFO cost of goods sold and replacement cost of goods sold depends on two factors:

1. *The severity of input cost changes:* All other factors being equal, the greater the amount of cost change, the larger the divergence between FIFO and replacement cost of goods sold.

2. *The rapidity of physical inventory turnover:* The slower inventory turnover, the larger the divergence.

We illustrate a simple procedure to convert cost of goods sold from FIFO to replacement cost and thereby eliminate realized holding gains from FIFO income.[19] The procedure requires estimating the inventory cost change and assumes rapid inventory turnover. Consider the following example.

Ray Department Store experienced the following inventory transactions during 2014.

Beginning inventory (FIFO basis)	$1,000,000
Merchandise purchases	+8,000,000
Goods available for sale	9,000,000
Ending inventory (FIFO basis)	−1,100,000
Cost of goods sold (FIFO basis)	$7,900,000

Assume that, on average, Ray's input costs for inventory increased by 10% during 2014. The adjustment procedure comprises three steps:

1. Determine FIFO cost of goods sold. In the example, this is $7,900,000. This amount is *not* adjusted.

2. Adjust the *beginning* inventory for one full year of specific price change. In the example, this is $1,000,000 times 10%, or $100,000.

3. Determine the replacement cost of goods sold, which is the sum of the amount in Step 1 ($7,900,000) and the amount in Step 2 ($100,000), that is, $8,000,000.

The difference between the computed replacement cost of goods sold ($8,000,000) and FIFO cost of goods sold ($7,900,000) equals the amount of realized holding gains included in the FIFO income figure ($100,000). This simple procedure gives results that accurately approximate tedious calculation approaches.

In Appendix A to this chapter, we provide an intuitive explanation for why this procedure for isolating realized holding gains for FIFO firms "works." We also discuss how analysts can use either price indices or competitors' data to estimate the rate of inventory cost change—10% in the Ray Department Store example.

ANALYTICAL INSIGHTS: LIFO DANGERS

LIFO makes it possible to manage earnings. To see how, consider a firm that has an executive bonus plan linked to earnings per share (see Figure 7.6). Assume that it is December 15, 2014, the firm reports on a calendar year basis, and the managers expect EPS for 2014 to be $4.40. (Because the year-end is only two weeks away, this estimate is likely to be very accurate.) As

---

[19] See A. Falkenstein and R. L. Weil, "Replacement Cost Accounting: What Will Income Statements Based on the SEC Disclosures Show?—Part II," *Financial Analysts Journal,* March–April 1977, pp. 48–57. We have altered the Falkenstein and Weil procedural description slightly to simplify the exposition.

described in Chapter 7, let's assume the bonus "tops out" at $4.00 per share. From the managers' perspective, 40¢ of expected earnings is wasted in the sense that it doesn't increase bonus payouts. So, the executives have an incentive to manage down reported earnings toward $4.00. LIFO makes this easy to do when input costs are rising. Here's why.

LIFO is applied using the periodic inventory method. Firms wait until the end of the year to compute cost of goods sold. So inventory purchased on December 31, 2014, is the "last in" and is considered to be the "first out" when LIFO cost of goods sold is computed. Similarly, inventory purchased on December 30 is considered to have been sold next, and so on. Because input costs are rising, if the managers buy unneeded, higher cost inventory during the last two weeks of 2014, this will raise cost of goods sold, lower income, and drive EPS down toward $4.00. Lowering earnings in this way doesn't decrease their bonus so long as they don't let EPS fall below $4.00. But this unneeded inventory *does* increase inventory carrying costs as well as the risk of loss from obsolescence and spoilage. So, managers don't suffer from the inventory buildup, but shareholders do.

But the story isn't over. In 2015, the firm has too much inventory; remember that the purchases at the end of 2014 were unneeded. So, in 2015, managers reduce inventory down to proper levels—a LIFO liquidation occurs. If input costs and output prices move together (that's the norm), then 2015 selling prices are higher than those in 2014. The LIFO liquidation in 2015 results in old, lower-cost, early 2014 purchases being matched against higher 2015 selling prices. This artificially raises 2015 income. So, it's a win-win situation for the managers! Playing this 2014 year-end LIFO game costs the managers no 2015 bonus and promises to increase 2015 income. At the end of 2014, they can't accurately forecast 2015 income. It might be below $3.00 per share, out of the bonus range. But the LIFO liquidation income could be enough to raise 2015 income above $3.00 per share, back into the bonus range. The effect of the income shift from 2014 into 2015 improves the likelihood that the managers will earn a bonus in 2015 as well.

To see the full range of earnings management "dangers" using LIFO, let's go to a totally new scenario. It's November 15, 2014. Again there's a bonus plan like the one in Figure 7.6 and input costs and output prices have been rising. But here, assume that forecasted EPS is only $2.60. At this earnings level, the managers won't qualify for a bonus. But if they deliberately stop normal purchases for the last six weeks of the year, LIFO layers will be depleted. Again a mismatching occurs as December sales revenues are matched against pre-November 15 costs. When this is done aggressively, EPS can be driven into the bonus area above $3.00 per share. Do managers engage in this type of deliberate removal of LIFO layers? Unfortunately, research evidence here is sparse. However, if bonus contracts do not subtract out LIFO liquidation "profits," there is an incentive to liquidate deliberately.

Using the perpetual method defeats the purpose of LIFO. Here's why. Suppose a calendar year firm makes a sale on January 4 and uses the perpetual method; under LIFO, the units sold are presumed to come from the most recent purchase, say January 3. But if the firm instead uses the periodic method and computes cost of goods sold on December 31, those early-in-the-year January purchases will be the *oldest* purchases and less likely to be considered sold. So, perpetual LIFO would not be used.

Remember that under LIFO, 2014 cost of goods sold assumed that December purchases were sold first, then November, and so on, working backward through the year. The new LIFO inventory layers added during the last two weeks of 2014 are costed out at cost levels in effect early in 2014, say, costs incurred in January and February.

EMPIRICAL EVIDENCE ON INVENTORY POLICY CHOICE

LIFO provides significant tax benefits when costs are rising. To obtain these tax benefits, Congress specified that companies must use LIFO not just for tax purposes but also for financial reporting. Despite this constraint, as reported earlier in the chapter, 24% of the inventory method choices are LIFO. Because costs have tended to rise consistently over most of the past 60 years, you may ask why more companies do *not* use LIFO. Are they squandering available tax benefits? Why many companies do not use LIFO has been the subject of numerous research studies.[20] Conjectures regarding the choice include the following:

1. The estimated tax savings from using LIFO are too small to justify the added complexity of the LIFO approach. There are two possible reasons for small tax savings:

   a. Inventory holding gains are trivial for non-LIFO firms.

   b. These non-LIFO firms have large tax loss carryforwards and are not currently paying taxes.

2. Firms in cyclical industries that are subject to extreme fluctuations in physical inventory levels would find LIFO unattractive because of the high probability of LIFO liquidations and consequent adverse tax effects.

3. Inventory obsolescence poses difficult issues under LIFO; consequently, firms subject to a high rate of inventory obsolescence may be reluctant to adopt LIFO.

> See the discussion of LIFO and the lower of cost or market rule in the next section.

4. During periods of generally rising prices, LIFO leads to lower profits. Managers may be reluctant to adopt LIFO under these conditions for either one or both of the following reasons:

   a. They believe that lower LIFO earnings will lead to lower stock price.

   b. They believe that the lower LIFO earnings will lead to lower compensation because management bonuses are often linked to reported earnings.

5. In a period of rising prices, LIFO causes certain ratios—such as the leverage ratio—used in loan agreements to deteriorate. Firms might be reluctant to adopt LIFO because adoption could result in loan covenant violations.

6. Smaller firms might not adopt LIFO because of the higher costs associated with maintaining the more complicated LIFO accounting records.

Research evidence is consistent with many (but not all) of these conjectures about why some firms don't use LIFO. Much of this work focused on the 1970s, a period of rapid and substantial price increases. Several studies found that the potential inventory holding gains are much higher for LIFO firms than for non-LIFO firms.[21] Accordingly, the tax saving for LIFO adopters is much higher than the potential savings for firms not using LIFO. Furthermore, non-LIFO firms generally have significantly larger tax loss carryforwards than LIFO firms, thereby obviating the need to adopt LIFO.[22] Research evidence is also generally consistent with the fact that LIFO adopters have lower levels of inventory fluctuations[23] and lower leverage in comparison with non-LIFO adopters.[24] In the aggregate, these studies suggest rational economic explanations for the decision by some firms to not adopt LIFO.

Researchers have also studied whether the stock market differentiates between LIFO earnings and FIFO earnings. In inflationary periods, LIFO firms would on average report lower profits than FIFO firms but would have higher after-tax cash flows. From an economic perspective, the LIFO firms are better off despite the lower reported earnings. Furthermore, the quality of reported LIFO earnings is presumably higher than FIFO earnings because LIFO

---

[20] See B. E. Cushing and M. J. LeClere, "Evidence on the Determinants of Inventory Accounting Policy Choice," *The Accounting Review,* April 1992, pp. 355–66.

[21] Two examples of such studies are Cushing and LeClere, ibid., and N. Dopuch and M. Pincus, "Evidence on the Choice of Inventory Accounting Methods: LIFO vs. FIFO," *Journal of Accounting Research,* Spring 1988, pp. 28–59.

[22] Cushing and LeClere, op. cit., and F. W. Lindahl, "Dynamic Analysis of Inventory Accounting Choice," *Journal of Accounting Research,* Autumn 1989, pp. 201–26.

[23] Examples include Dopuch and Pincus, op. cit., and C. J. Lee and D. A. Hsieh, "Choice of Inventory Accounting Methods: Comparative Analysis of Alternative Hypotheses," *Journal of Accounting Research,* Autumn 1985, pp. 468–85.

[24] Examples include Lindahl, op. cit., and Cushing and LeClere, op. cit.

earnings usually exclude inventory holding gains from net income; accordingly, LIFO earnings are presumably more sustainable than FIFO earnings during inflationary periods. Thus, the research question is whether investors differentiate between the quality of LIFO versus FIFO earnings or, instead, simply penalize LIFO firms for their lower reported earnings.

Valuation

Many of the studies of market reaction to LIFO versus FIFO examined instances in which firms switched from FIFO to LIFO as inflation accelerated. The research question frequently posed was:

> If the market simply reacts to bottom-line earnings, then stock prices of firms shifting to LIFO should, on average, fall. On the other hand, if the market considers earnings *quality,* then the relatively higher reported (and expected future) after-tax cash flows of new LIFO adopters should lead on average to stock price increases as the switch is announced.

Initial research studied the stock price reaction to announcements by firms that switched to LIFO as well as to the announcements of the new LIFO earnings numbers. These studies generated conflicting results, probably because of the failure to control for other factors influencing stock price behavior during the year of the inventory switch.

A later study that included such controls found consistent evidence that the market perceives LIFO earnings to be of higher quality than FIFO earnings.[25] This study produced the following findings:

1. When reported earnings included highly transitory inventory holding gains (either under FIFO or when LIFO liquidation occurs), the market perceives these earnings to be of lower quality. Thus, the share price increase is small relative to when high-quality (sustainable) earnings are reported.

2. The market response to earnings news is greater after LIFO adoption. This suggests that the market believes that LIFO produces a higher quality earnings signal.

3. Across all firms, there is a higher market response to a given dollar amount of earnings surprise under LIFO in comparison to FIFO. Again, this result is consistent with LIFO being perceived as the higher quality earnings number.

LOWER OF COST OR MARKET METHOD

This section covers a widely used method in inventory accounting, the lower of cost or market method. An asset represents a cost that has been incurred to create future service value for a firm. If subsequent events cause the future service value of an asset to drop below its cost, its carrying value must be reduced. In inventory accounting, this is called the **lower of cost or market method.**

It is more complicated than its name implies, although the reasoning underlying lower of cost or market is simple. Whenever the **replacement cost** of inventory declines below its original cost, the presumption is that the inventory's service value has been impaired and a write-down is warranted. If a unit of inventory originally cost $10 but its replacement cost falls to $8, a decrease in carrying value of $2 is required. *What's implied here is that inventory replacement cost and eventual selling price move together.* The decline in replacement cost is presumed to signal that the price at which the inventory can be sold—its future service value—has fallen. Thus, a loss has occurred that must be recognized in the accounts.

---

[25] T. Carroll, D. W. Collins, and W. B. Johnson, "The LIFO–FIFO Choice and the Quality of Earnings Signals," Working paper, University of Iowa, August 1997. Additional evidence on how the market values LIFO versus FIFO earnings can be found in R. Jennings, P. J. Simko, and R. B. Thompson, II, "Does LIFO Inventory Accounting Improve the Income Statement at the Expense of the Balance Sheet?" *Journal of Accounting Research,* Spring 1996, pp. 85–109.

In practice, the relationship between cost decreases and selling price decreases is unlikely to be perfect. For this reason, the market value used in applying lower of cost or market is subject to two constraints:

1. **Ceiling:** *Market* should not exceed the inventory's **net realizable value,** that is, the estimated selling price of the inventory in the ordinary course of business less the reasonably predictable costs of completing and selling it.

2. **Floor:** *Market* should not be less than the inventory's net realizable value reduced by an allowance for an approximately normal profit margin.[26]

The ceiling constraint (that market should not exceed net realizable value) is designed to avoid overstating obsolete goods. For example, assume that a motor originally costing $80 is now obsolete and has a net realizable value of only $50. Even if its replacement cost is $65, the inventory should be valued at its net realizable value of $50. To value the motor at its $65 replacement cost fails to recognize the full extent of the expected loss that has occurred.

The floor constraint covers situations in which declines in input replacement cost do not move perfectly with declines in selling price. To illustrate, assume the following:

	Original Cost	Replacement Cost	Net Realizable Value	Net Realizable Value Less Normal Profit of $11
Inventory item	$60	$46	$70	$59

This scenario assumes that the normal per unit profit margin is $11. An inventory write-down to $46 would lead to an abnormally high unit profit margin of $24 (net realizable value of $70 less the $46 replacement cost) when the inventory is sold in a later period. This $24 profit exceeds the $11 normal profit margin. A write-down to $59 would still afford the company a normal profit margin; any larger write-down would result in excess profits in future periods. The floor provides a lower bound for write-downs in situations when input replacement cost and selling price do not move together.

Together, these two constraints mean that *market* (the market value used in applying the lower of cost or market rule) is the *middle value* of (1) replacement cost, (2) net realizable value, and (3) net realizable value less a normal profit margin. This is depicted in Figure 9.5.

Applying the lower of cost or market rule is illustrated in Exhibit 9.14 using four scenarios. The inventory value used in each scenario is highlighted.

Scenario I   The inventory is valued at cost ($20). The reason is that $23 is the middle value of the three market values—$23 is between $21 and $27—and cost ($20) is lower than market ($23). This illustrates the straightforward lower of cost or market rule for inventory carrying values in historical cost accounting: Inventories are carried at original cost unless the item's future service value has been impaired. Of course, nothing here suggests impairment because the replacement cost of inventory ($23) exceeds the original cost ($20).

---

[26] FASB ASC Paragraphs 330-10-35-1 to -5: Inventory—Overall—Subsequent Measurement—Adjustments to Lower of Cost or Market.

Figure 9.5

LOWER OF COST OR
MARKET RULE FOR
INVENTORIES

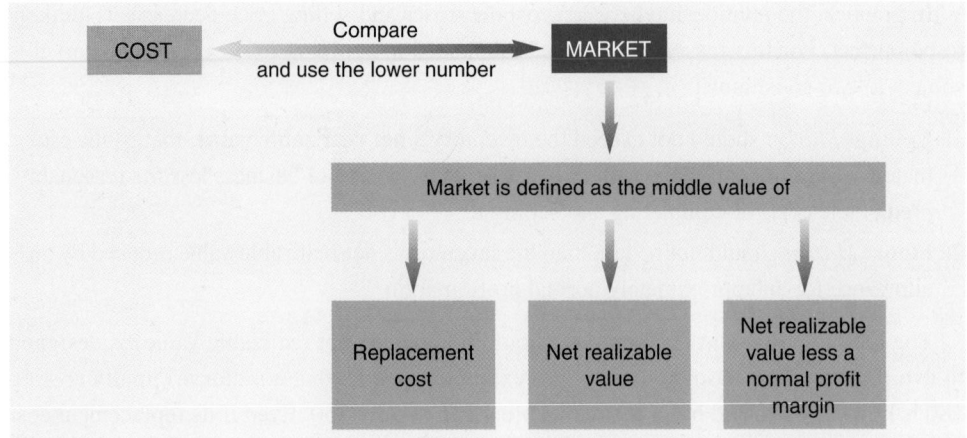

Scenario 2   The inventory is carried at replacement cost ($19). Market is again defined as the middle value of the three market value measures in Figure 9.5. The values are 18, 19, and 24; because 19 is between 18 and 24, it is market. Market is less than the original cost of $20 so it is presumed that a portion of the inventory's original service value has been impaired. Therefore, the inventory is written down from $20 to $19.

Scenario 3   The inventory is valued at net realizable value ($18) because net realizable value is the middle *market* value (that is, 18 is between 12 and 19) and is below cost. Here we see the operation of the ceiling. This rule is intended to avoid carrying obsolete goods at a cost in excess of the net value that will be realized on sale. If the rule were not invoked, inventory would be carried at $19 (its replacement cost), which is more than the $18 that it is expected to yield.

Scenario 4   The inventory is valued at net realizable value less a normal profit margin ($19) because this number is lower than original cost and is the middle value of the market price constraints. Scenario 4 illustrates the floor. If the rule were not invoked, inventory would be carried at $15 (its replacement cost). This would be an excessive write-down, because a $15 carrying cost would result in an above normal margin when the goods were later sold.

EXHIBIT 9.14	Application of Lower of Cost or Market				
		Market			
Scenario	Original Cost	Replacement Cost	Net Realizable Value	Net Realizable Value less a Normal Profit Margin	Middle of the Three Market Values	Inventory Value Used
1	$20	$23	$27	$21	$23	$20
2	20	19	24	18	19	19
3	20	19	18	12	18	18
4	20	15	25	19	19	19

When a perpetual inventory system is used and inventory is written down from a cost of, say, $1,000,000 to a market value of $970,000, the entry is:

> **DR** Loss from decline in market
> value of inventory... $30,000
> **CR** Inventory... $30,000

> If a periodic inventory system is used, this entry would not be made. Instead, the inventory's ending *market* value ($970,000) would be used as ending inventory in the cost of goods sold computation.

The lower of cost or market method can be applied to:

- Individual inventory items.
- Classes of inventory, say, fertilizers versus weed killers.
- The inventory as a whole.

Companies have discretion regarding how inventories are aggregated when applying the lower of cost or market rule (see Exhibit 9.15). Depending on whether the aggregation is by item of inventory, inventory class, or total inventory, the lower of cost or market value could be $27,000, $31,000, or $32,000.

Income tax regulations do not permit the use of the lower of cost or market rule in conjunction with LIFO. The reason for this prohibition is that LIFO provides tax advantages when prices are rising; if LIFO firms were permitted to use lower of cost or market, they would also gain tax advantages when prices are falling. Congress is unwilling to provide LIFO firms with tax savings that would occur regardless of the direction of input cost movements.

The Contracting Origins of the Lower of Cost or Market Method

The lower of cost or market method for inventories was widely practiced in the United States before the 1920s. Presumably, it evolved in the formative years of modern financial reporting to satisfy the information needs of what was then the most important external user group: commercial lenders. Banking in that era consisted mainly of securitized lending. Loans required collateral from the borrower, primarily in the form of inventory, accounts receivable, or fixed assets. Clearly, lenders wanted to avoid basing their decision on overstated asset values because they resulted in inadequate amounts of collateral. The conservatism inherent in lower of cost or market represented a mechanism for protecting the then-dominant user group from

 **Contracting**

EXHIBIT 9.15	**Aggregation Alternatives in Applying the Lower of Cost or Market Rule**				
				Lower of Cost or Market Aggregated by	
Inventory item	**Cost**	**Market**	**Item**	**Class**	**Total**
Class 1					
Item 1	$10,000	$ 6,000	$ 6,000		
Item 2	3,000	8,000	3,000		
	$13,000	$14,000		$13,000	
Class 2					
Item 3	20,000	18,000	18,000	18,000	
	$33,000	$32,000	$27,000	$31,000	$32,000

unpleasant surprise—lower than expected collateral values.[27] Thus, the lower of cost or market rule evolved because of the dominant form of lending contracts used years ago.

Evaluation of the Lower of Cost or Market Rule

Individual and institutional equity investors are now important users of financial statements. The conservative bias built into the lower of cost or market rule protects lenders, but it may sometimes harm these other statement users. Suppose you own stock in a company whose inventory is written down to market. If the write-down was unwarranted (for example, because the decline in replacement cost did not portend a decline in the inventory's eventual selling price), your financial position is worsened by lower of cost or market accounting. Why? Because the share price you could get if you sold your stock may be lower than the price you could sell the shares for if the accounting were less conservative. Clearly, conservative rules designed to systematically understate asset amounts favor lenders and equity purchasers over borrowers and equity sellers. This absence of neutrality that pervades lower of cost or market has troubled numerous financial reporting experts and has led to repeated criticisms of the approach.

In addition to its bias against those seeking loans and those selling equity securities, the lower of cost or market rule has another deficiency. It assumes that input costs and output prices generally move together. Therefore, a decline in input cost triggers a loss recognition because it is presumed that the cost decrease portends a selling price decrease. But there is little empirical evidence to corroborate this assumption. It is indeed possible that input costs and selling prices move together, but it is also possible that they do not. When input costs and selling prices do not move together, a loss may be recognized when, in fact, no loss has occurred. Consider, for example, the following illustration:

	Original Cost	Replacement Cost	Net Realizable Value	Net Realizable Value Less Normal Profit Margin
Cost relationships on January 1, 2014	$100	$100	$115	$90
Cost relationships on December 31, 2014	100	95	115	90

Strict application of the lower of cost or market rule at year-end would require a write-down of the inventory to $95 from its original cost of $100. However, the selling price of the inventory

---

[27] Evidence about the role that lenders played in the evolution of modern financial reporting and the lower of cost or market rule is contained in a proposal from the Federal Reserve Board that was designed to standardize financial reporting (*Federal Reserve Bulletin,* April 1, 1917, p. 270):

Because this matter was clearly of importance to banks and bankers, and especially to the Federal Reserve Banks which might be asked to rediscount commercial paper based on borrowers' statements, the Federal Reserve Board has taken an active interest in the consideration of the suggestions which have developed as a result of the Trade Commission's investigation, and now submits in the form of a tentative statement certain proposals in regard to suggested standard forms of statements for merchants and manufacturers. [Emphasis added.]

The problem naturally subdivides itself into two parts. (1) The improvement in standardization of the forms of statements; (2) the adoption of methods which will insure greater care in compiling the statements and the proper verification thereof.

The proposal (which was subsequently adopted) contained a specific reference to the importance of the lower of cost or market rule for inventories (p. 275):

. . . The auditor should satisfy himself that inventories are stated at cost or market prices, whichever are the lower at the date of the balance sheet. No inventory must be passed which has been marked up to market prices and a profit assumed that is not and may never be realized. . . . It may be found that inventories are valued at the average prices of raw materials and supplies on hand at the end of the period. *In such cases the averages should be compared with the latest invoices in order to verify the fact that they are not in excess of the latest prices.* . . . [Emphasis added.]

has not changed, since its net realizable value is still $115. Therefore, no loss exists but GAAP would require a $5 write-down!

In summary, the lower of cost or market rule reflects conservatism. But as financial statement users have become more diverse, the rule has been subjected to mounting criticism. First, conservatism is itself an elusive concept. While inventory write-downs may initially be conservative, the resulting higher margin in the period following the write-down provides opportunities for earnings management. Second, as the use of published financial statements has broadened over the years, conservatism strikes many observers as a violation of the neutrality posture that financial reporting rules are designed to achieve. For example, if downward changes in replacement cost are considered to be reliable evidence of a loss, logic suggests that upward changes in replacement cost should similarly be considered reliable evidence of a gain. Finally, the lower of cost or market rule relies on an implicit relationship between input costs and output prices that may not prevail. When the input/output relationship does not exist, inventory losses may be recognized even though no real loss has occurred. As a consequence of these limitations, the lower of cost or market approach constitutes GAAP but it does not hold a secure place in accounting theory.

GLOBAL VANTAGE POINT

Comparison of IFRS and GAAP Inventory Accounting

International Accounting Standard (IAS) 2, "Inventories," provides the guidance for inventory accounting under IFRS.[28] Much of the IFRS accounting guidelines for inventory are similar to those under U.S. GAAP. The IFRS definition of inventory is similar, absorption costing is required, there are cost flow assumptions, and inventory is carried at lower of cost or market. However, there are important nuances.

First, LIFO is not permitted under *IAS 2*. The IASB rationalizes the prohibition on LIFO by stating that this method "is generally not a reliable representation of actual inventory flows. . . . The use of LIFO in financial reporting is often tax-driven . . . (and) results in inventories being recognized in the balance sheet at amounts that bear little relationship to recent cost levels of inventories."[29] It permits the use of either the FIFO or weighted average cost flow assumption (para. 25). In special circumstances, the specific identification method can also be used (para. 23). Also related to cost flow, firms must use the same cost flow method for similar inventories (para. 25). Recall from our earlier discussion that U.S. firms use multiple methods for similar inventory items.

The inability to use LIFO presents a major conflict point that may affect the SEC's decision whether to eventually transition U.S. firms to IFRS. The SEC has been strongly considering this transition for several years and has solicited feedback from constituents regarding the potential transition. The SEC has received numerous comment letters from certain constituents articulating major concerns about potentially losing the LIFO method. The LIFO Coalition, a group of more than 120 businesses and trade associations that employ the LIFO method, wrote to the SEC in May 2011 that

> any requirement by the SEC that U.S. issuers adopt IFRS . . . means that issuers will be forced to violate the Conformity Requirement. Violation of the Conformity Requirement . . . may expose the taxpayer to serious adverse tax consequences immediately and in future years." (http://www.sec.gov/comments/4-600/4600-142.pdf)

[28] See *IAS 2* (revised 2009), "Inventories" (London: International Accounting Standards Board, 2009).
[29] See IAS 2, BC10-13.

EXHIBIT 9.16   **Danier Inventory Disclosures**

(j) Inventories:

Merchandise inventories are valued at the lower of cost, using the weighted average cost method, and net realizable value. For inventories manufactured by the Company, cost includes direct labour, raw materials, manufacturing and distribution centre costs related to inventories and transportation costs that are directly incurred to bring inventories to their present location and condition. For inventories purchased from third party vendors, cost includes the cost of purchase, duty and brokerage, quality assurance costs, distribution centre costs related to inventories and transportation costs that are directly incurred to bring inventories to their present location and condition. The Company estimates the net realizable value as the amount at which inventories are expected to be sold, taking into account fluctuations in retail prices due to seasonality, age, excess quantities, condition of the inventory, nature of the inventory and the estimated variable costs necessary to make the sale. Inventories are written down to net realizable value when the cost of inventories is not estimated to be recoverable due to obsolescence, damage or declining selling prices. When circumstances that previously caused inventories to be written down below cost no longer exist, the amount of the write-down previously recorded is reversed. Storage costs, administrative overheads and selling costs related to the inventories are expensed in the period the costs are incurred.

5. INVENTORIES:

	June 30, 2012	June 25, 2011	June 27, 2010
Raw-materials	$ 2,644	$ 2,655	$ 1,451
Work-in-process	183	265	105
Finished goods	22,064	26,044	24,983
	$24,891	$28,964	$26,539

	June 30, 2012	June 25, 2011
Cost of inventory recognized as an expense	$70,739	$70,439
Write-downs of inventory due to net realizable value being lower than cost	$ 1,746	$ 1,549
Write-downs recognized in previous periods that were reversed	$ 174	$ 5

Second, lower or cost of market is applied differently. Market is defined as *net realisable value* (para. 28). U.S. GAAP is more complicated in that market considers replacement cost, net realizable value, and net realizable value less normal markup. *IAS 2* also allows inventory reductions to be reversed if the market recovers, but the inventory carrying amount cannot exceed the original cost (para. 33). Under U.S. GAAP, once the carrying value of an item is reduced, it cannot be increased to its original cost. The amounts of inventory write-downs and recoveries must be disclosed in the financial statements.

Exhibit 9.16 reproduces a note by Canadian retailer Danier who files under IFRS. Note that Danier chooses to use "the lower of cost, using the weighted average cost method, and net realizable value." The "Cost of inventory recognized as an expense" is equivalent to cost of goods sold. Also note that Danier reports both write-downs of inventory and also reversals of write-downs recognized in previous periods. The latter is not allowed under U.S. GAAP.

Future Directions

Neither the FASB nor the IASB have projects related to inventory on their agendas. However, because of the **LIFO conformity rule,** firms would incur large tax liabilities if they eventually move to IFRS, which does not allow LIFO. The U.S. Congress could remove the conformity rule. However, given the budget deficits, Congress might be more likely to eliminate LIFO as an option and extend the period over which firms must pay the additional tax. Under the current tax law, the gain on the switch from LIFO could be spread over four years.[30] Also, as mentioned earlier in the chapter, most U.S. oil companies use LIFO. Consequently, a repeal of LIFO would be a way to increase taxes on oil companies, which could be popular politically.

SUMMARY

This chapter helps readers understand existing GAAP inventory methods and disclosures. It can also help readers compare and analyze profitability and net asset positions across firms that use different inventory methods. Here are the important messages from this chapter.

- Absorption costing is required by GAAP but may lead to potentially misleading period-to-period income changes when inventories increase or decrease sharply.

- Financial reporting rules allow firms latitude in selecting a cost flow assumption for determining the cost of goods sold reported on the income statement and the inventory values reported on the balance sheet. Firms use FIFO, LIFO, weighted average costing, or a combination of these methods.

- This diversity in practice can severely hinder interfirm comparisons when inventory purchase costs are changing over time, which is usually the case. Before comparing a LIFO firm to a FIFO firm, numbers for the LIFO firms should be transformed to the FIFO basis.

- Reported FIFO income merges sustainable operating profits and potentially unsustainable realized holding gains. Analysts must disentangle these elements when preparing earnings and cash flow forecasts.

- Similarly, LIFO liquidations distort reported margins because "old" costs are matched with current selling prices.

- To address inventory obsolescence, GAAP requires that inventory be carried at lower of cost or market.

- IFRS accounting for inventory is similar to the accounting under GAAP. However, LIFO is not allowed. In addition, when applying lower of cost or market, *market* is defined as *net realizable value* and write-downs may be reversed.

- The LIFO conformity rule requires firms to use LIFO for financial reporting if they use it for tax reporting. LIFO accounting gives firms significant tax deferrals. These deferrals may go away soon because of deficit pressures and conversions to IFRS, which does not allow LIFO.

- Most LIFO firms use some form of dollar-value LIFO. Dollar-value LIFO essentially converts FIFO inventory amounts to LIFO inventory amounts.

SELF-STUDY PROBLEM

MITSURU CORPORATION

Mitsuru Corporation began business operations on January 1, 2014, as a wholesaler of macadamia nuts. Its purchase and sales transactions for 2014 are listed in Exhibit 9.17. Mitsuru uses a periodic inventory system.

---

[30] R. Mock and A. Simon, "The LIFO, IFRS Conversion: An Explosive Concoction," *Tax Notes* (May 11, 2009), p. 746.

EXHIBIT 9.17   Mitsuru Corporation

Inventory Purchases and Sales

| Date | Purchases | | | Sales |
	Pounds	Dollars/Pound	Total Dollars	Pounds
January 1	1,000	$10.00	$ 10,000	
February 3	4,000	10.20	40,800	
February 9				3,600
April 1	4,000	10.30	41,200	
May 29				3,500
June 28	5,000	10.40	52,000	
July 20				4,100
September 14	5,000	10.50	52,500	
September 17				4,200
December 18	4,000	10.60	42,400	
December 22				3,600
	23,000		$238,900	19,000

1. **Compute 2014 ending inventory and cost of goods sold for Mitsuru Corporation using the weighted average cost flow assumption.**

   Ending inventory totals 4,000 pounds, that is, purchases of 23,000 pounds minus sales of 19,000 pounds. The average cost per pound (rounded) is:

$$\frac{\text{Total cost of goods available for sale} \rightarrow \$238,900}{\text{Total pounds available for sale} \quad \rightarrow \quad 23,000} = \$10.39/pound$$

   Ending inventory is 4,000 pounds times $10.39, or $41,560. Cost of goods sold is then determined as follows:

Total cost of goods available for sale	$238,900[31]
Less: Ending inventory just computed	(41,560)
Cost of goods sold (weighted average method)	$197,340

2. **Compute 2014 ending inventory and cost of goods sold for Mitsuru using the FIFO cost flow assumption.**

   Under the first-in, first-out (FIFO) cost flow assumption, the ending inventory consists of the 4,000 most recently purchased pounds of macadamia nuts. This ending inventory amount consists entirely of the December 18 purchase of 4,000 pounds for $42,400. Accordingly, FIFO cost of goods sold is:

Total cost of goods available for sale	$238,900
Less: Ending FIFO inventory	(42,400)
FIFO cost of goods sold	$196,500

---

[31] In subsequent years, the beginning inventory value also would be included in the goods available for sale amount.

3. **Compute 2014 ending inventory and cost of goods sold for Mitsuru using the LIFO cost flow assumption.**

Under last-in, first-out (LIFO), the ending inventory comprises the 4,000 pounds of oldest macadamia nut purchases. This 4,000 pounds would consist of two layers:

January 1	1,000 pounds	@	$10.00	=	$10,000
February 3	3,000 pounds	@	$10.20	=	30,600
	4,000 pounds				$40,600

Thus, LIFO cost of goods sold is:

Total cost of goods available for sale	$238,900
Less: Ending LIFO inventory	(40,600)
LIFO cost of goods sold	$198,300

4. **Assume that the December 31, 2014, macadamia nut replacement cost is $10.60 per pound. Compute Mitsuru's LIFO reserve and use the beginning and ending LIFO reserve amounts to reconcile between LIFO and FIFO cost of goods sold.**

The LIFO reserve at a given point in time is the difference between the LIFO inventory book value and its then-current replacement cost. At January 1, 2014, Mitsuru's LIFO reserve was $0 because the LIFO book value and replacement cost both equaled $10,000. At December 31, 2014, the LIFO reserve was $1,800, computed as follows:

December 31, 2014, inventory replacement cost; 4,000 pounds @ $10.60	$42,400
December 31, 2014, LIFO inventory	(40,600)
December 31, 2014, LIFO reserve	$ 1,800

Using the formula for converting cost of goods sold (COGS) from a LIFO to FIFO basis in conjunction with the answers to Parts 2 and 3 of this self-study problem yields:

$COGS_{LIFO}$	+	Beginning LIFO reserve	−	Ending LIFO reserve	=	$COGS_{FIFO}$
$198,300	+	0	−	$1,800	=	$196,500

Notice that $196,500 equals the FIFO cost of goods sold number computed in Part 2.

As the text discussed, the reconciliation procedure is an approximation. Adding the LIFO reserve to the LIFO inventory equals replacement cost. If the inventory turns quickly, then inventory replacement cost *approximates* FIFO inventory. In this self-study problem, ending FIFO inventory at $10.60 per pound exactly equals replacement cost. Hence, the adjustment is precise.

APPENDIX A

ELIMINATING REALIZED HOLDING GAINS FROM FIFO INCOME

In the chapter, we show a simple way to estimate the amount of realized holding gains included in the FIFO income figure. In this appendix, we provide a simple example to illustrate why this method works.

Consider a firm buying and selling inventory *in equal amounts* daily as you contemplate Figure 9.6. The *quantity* of inventory purchased during the year is the area denoted *P*.

Figure 9.6

FIFO TO LIFO COST
OF GOODS SOLD
APPROXIMATION
TECHNIQUE

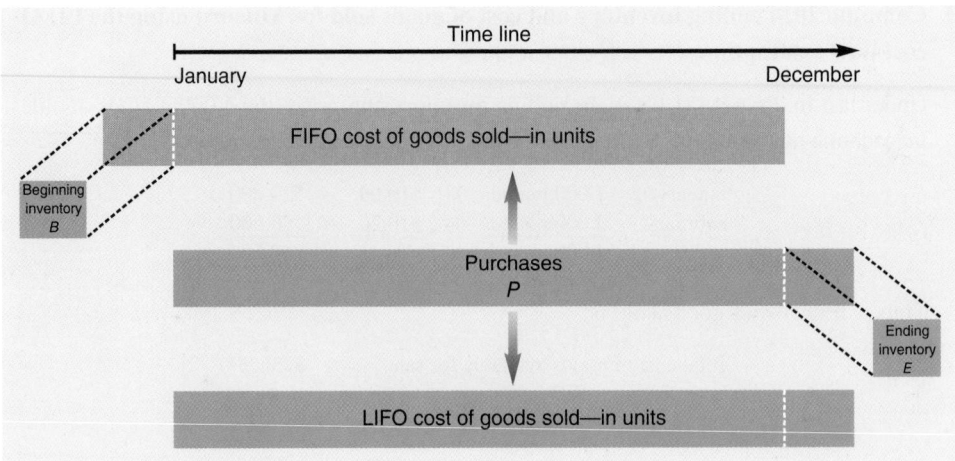

Beginning inventory *quantity* is the area denoted B, and ending inventory *quantity* is the area denoted E. Let's assume that B equals E; that is, the firm had exactly as many units in inventory at the year-end as it did at the start of the year. Under these conditions the *units* comprising FIFO cost of goods sold consists of the area $B + (P - E)$. In other words, under the FIFO cost flow assumption, cost of goods sold consists of the first, or oldest, units available, which is beginning inventory plus the earliest purchases. Under LIFO, cost of goods sold would comprise the area P, that is, the most *recently* purchased units. The difference between the units comprising the two cost of goods sold (COGS) measures is the area E minus B. Expressed in units:

$$\text{COGS}_{\text{LIFO}} = \text{COGS}_{\text{FIFO}} + E - B \tag{9.1}$$

Expressed in dollars:

$$\$\text{COGS}_{\text{LIFO}} = \$\text{COGS}_{\text{FIFO}} + \$E - \$B \tag{9.2}$$

Notice that if inventory costs do not change over the year, $\$E = \$B$ and $\$\text{COGS}_{\text{LIFO}} = \$\text{COGS}_{\text{FIFO}}$. In general, it's reasonable to expect inventory costs to change from the beginning to the end of the year. If we assume that inventory purchase costs changed over the year at the rate r, then $\$E$ will not equal $\$B$ although E units equal B units. Specifically, the dollar amount of ending inventory will equal $(1 + r)$ times the dollar amount of beginning inventory, that is,

$$\$E = \$B \times (1 + r) \tag{9.3}$$

Substituting the equation (9.3) value of $\$E$ into equation (9.2) yields:

$$\$\text{COGS}_{\text{LIFO}} = \$\text{COGS}_{\text{FIFO}} + \$B \times (1 + r) - \$B \tag{9.4}$$

or

$$\$\text{COGS}_{\text{LIFO}} = \$\text{COGS}_{\text{FIFO}} + \$B \times r \tag{9.5}$$

In this example, daily unit purchases and sales are equal. Under these conditions, LIFO cost of goods sold equals current cost of goods sold, so equation (9.5) can be rewritten:

$$\$\text{COGS}_{\text{CC}} = \$\text{COGS}_{\text{FIFO}} + \$B \times r \tag{9.6}$$

where $\$\text{COGS}_{\text{CC}}$ is current cost of goods sold. The difference between FIFO pretax income and current cost income (or, equivalently, FIFO cost of goods sold and current cost of goods sold) is the inventory holding gain or loss. Thus, the product $\$B \times r$ provides an estimate of the inventory holding gain (or loss) that is embedded in the FIFO earnings number.[32]

Notice that equation (9.6) is equivalent to the simple holding gain estimation procedure used in the chapter. This approximation works as long as the total number of inventory units on hand does not fluctuate much during the year and as long as inventory purchases and sales take place frequently. If these conditions aren't met for a specific firm, the conversion from FIFO cost of goods sold to current cost of goods sold will not be accurate.

To eliminate realized holding gains from FIFO income, we must estimate r, the percentage change in inventory purchase costs. One means for estimating this rate is to use some input cost price index, such as one of the various producer price indices (PPI) prepared by the U.S. Department of Labor, Bureau of Labor Statistics. Another approach is to select a competitor that is in the same industry as the FIFO firm being adjusted but that utilizes the LIFO inventory procedure. The rate r can then be estimated using the following ratio computed from the LIFO competitor's disclosures:

Rate of Inventory Input Cost Change (r)

$$= \frac{\text{Change in LIFO reserve}}{\text{Beginning inventory}_{\text{LIFO}} + \text{Beginning LIFO reserve}}$$

The denominator of the ratio is the initial current cost of the inventory, and the numerator is the change in current cost over the period. The quotient is an estimate of the desired rate, r. However, if the competitor liquidated LIFO layers over the period, the disclosed decrease in cost of goods sold because of the liquidation must be added back to the numerator. The reason is that LIFO liquidation reduces the LIFO reserve. Adding back the liquidation effect generates a more accurate measure of r. But, if the competitor's year-to-year inventory levels changed substantially, the derived rate will differ from the true rate of inventory cost increase.

APPENDIX B

DOLLAR-VALUE LIFO

The LIFO inventory method requires data on each separate product or inventory item, and it therefore has two drawbacks. First, item-by-item inventory records are *costly* to maintain; and second, when LIFO records are kept by individual item, the likelihood of *liquidating* a LIFO layer is greatly increased.

- *Cost:* Traditional LIFO systems kept by individual item require considerable clerical work. Detailed records for each separate product or item in beginning inventory must be kept both in terms of physical units and unit cost. Similar detail must be accumulated for all purchases during the period. Finally, ending inventory must also be costed individually by item. These data requirements quickly become unwieldy for firms with numerous inventory categories.

- *Liquidation:* One of the motivations for adopting LIFO is that it tends to keep inventory holding gains out of income and thereby lowers taxes. However, when old LIFO layers are liquidated, this objective is subverted and both income and income taxes rise. The

---

[32] Analysts generally perceive such inventory holding gains as low-quality earnings items because they cannot be sustained in the future unless inventory costs continue to increase. Consistent with this view, Carroll, Collins, and Johnson, op. cit., find that the market price adjustments associated with earnings surprises of firms whose earnings contain relatively large inventory holding gains are substantially smaller than those of firms with relatively smaller FIFO inventory holding gains.

possibility of liquidating a LIFO layer is very high when item-by-item LIFO is used. Consider the case of stores that sell televisions. As flat-panel televisions became prevalent, these stores reduced their inventories of old technology televisions. If LIFO always had to be kept on a per item basis, this decrease in the obsolete models would cause a liquidation of old LIFO layers and negate the benefits of LIFO.

To overcome both the clerical cost and liquidation problems associated with LIFO, the **dollar-value LIFO** method has been developed in which LIFO cost can be estimated for broad categories (pools) of inventory from simple inventory records that are kept in terms of end-of-period costs. Most firms on LIFO use some form of dollar-value LIFO.

Dollar-value LIFO avoids much of the detailed recordkeeping required under standard LIFO. Ending inventory is determined in terms of year-end prices, just as it is under FIFO. The ending inventory at year-end prices is then adjusted by a price index to estimate LIFO inventory.[33] Essentially, dollar-value LIFO converts FIFO inventory amounts to LIFO amounts. To illustrate the procedure in simplified form, let's assume that Gable Company first adopts LIFO on January 1, 2014, and elects to use dollar-value LIFO. The time of initial LIFO adoption is termed the **base period.** The facts of the example are:

Beginning inventory, LIFO, at base-period (1/1/14) costs	$100,000
Ending inventory at 12/31/14 costs	$140,000
Inventory price index at base period (1/1/14)	1.00
Inventory price index at 12/31/14	1.12

Under LIFO, a new LIFO layer is added only when the unit (or physical) quantity of inventory increases. In this example, we cannot compare the ending inventory dollars ($140,000) with the beginning inventory dollars ($100,000) to determine whether physical quantities increased. Why? Because the December 31 inventory is stated at year-end costs while the beginning inventory is stated at base-period costs.

---

[33] A *price index* is simply a ratio that compares prices during the current period with prices during some base period. Separate indices are computed for each period. If a price index for a given year is 1.12, this means that prices in that year are 12% higher than they were in the base period.

In applying dollar-value LIFO, the index used must reflect price changes for the specific inventory. General price indices are not permitted except in unusual situations. One method for computing the index is to determine the following ratio by reference to detailed purchase records:

$$\frac{\text{Cost of ending inventory at end-of-period prices}}{\text{Cost of ending inventory at base-period prices}} = \text{Index for Year}$$

However, this computation can be burdensome when the inventory consists of many different types of items. In such situations, an index can be computed based on a sample of representative purchases. One such approach is:

	Ending Inventory Units (1)	Base-Period Cost per Unit (2)	Current Period's Cost per Unit (3)	Total Base-Period Cost (1) × (2)	End-of-Period Cost (1) × (3)
Item A	20,000	$3	$ 4	$ 60,000	$ 80,000
Item B	5,000	7	8	35,000	40,000
Item C	11,000	9	10	99,000	110,000
				$194,000	$230,000

The resulting index is

$$\frac{\$230,000}{\$194,000} = 1.186$$

and measures the current cost of the purchase basket relative to the base-period cost of that same basket.

However, we can use the inventory price index to restate ending inventory (expressed in year-end costs) to base-period costs by dividing $140,000 by 1.12. The result, $125,000, is the December 31, 2014, inventory expressed in base-period (January 1, 2014) costs.

Once ending inventory is stated in base-period costs, it is possible to determine whether the physical quantity of inventory has increased during 2014:

Ending inventory expressed in base-period costs	
($140,000/1.12)	$125,000
Beginning inventory expressed in base-period costs	100,000
Inventory increase expressed in base-period costs	$ 25,000

Clearly, a new LIFO layer was added in 2014. However, the new LIFO layer must be recorded at the cost level that was in effect when the layer was added. Because the inventory increase expressed in terms of base-period costs was $25,000—and because costs increased 12% during 2014—the new LIFO layer would be computed as $25,000 × 1.12, or $28,000. Therefore, the December 31, 2014, ending inventory computed under the dollar-value LIFO method would consist of two layers:

	Base-Period Costs	Adjustment Factor	Dollar-Value LIFO Carrying Amount
Beginning inventory (1/1/14)	$100,000	1.00	$100,000
2014 layer	25,000	1.12	28,000
Ending inventory, dollar-value LIFO			$128,000

How does the LIFO reserve relate to this example? We will assume that the FIFO ending inventory value approximates replacement cost. FIFO inventory is $140,000, but we need to reflect $128,000 on the balance sheet. Therefore, we need a LIFO reserve of $12,000 ($140,000 − $128,000). To establish the reserve, Gable Company makes the following entry:

Cost of goods sold	$12,000	
LIFO reserve		$12,000

Gable's 2014 LIFO disclosures will appear as follows:

	2014
Inventory at FIFO	$140,000
Reserve needed to reduce inventory to LIFO	(12,000)
Inventory at LIFO	$128,000

As stated above, the balance sheet will reflect the $128,000.

To continue the example, let's assume that the December 31, 2015, inventory price index is 1.20 and that ending inventory at December 31, 2015, is $146,400 (expressed in year-end 2015 costs).

As before, it is necessary to determine whether a new LIFO layer was added in 2015. To do this, we must restate the December 31, 2015, inventory in terms of base-period costs and compare it to the January 1, 2015, inventory (expressed in base-period costs):

Ending inventory expressed in base-period costs ($146,400/1.20)		$122,000
Beginning inventory expressed in base-period costs		
Base-period layer	$100,000	
2014 layer ($28,000/1.12)	25,000	
		125,000
Inventory decrease expressed in base-period costs		$ (3,000)

Expressed in base-period costs, inventory decreased in 2015. Because the cost flow is LIFO, this decrease is assumed to have come from the 2014 layer. At base-period costs, the 2014 layer would be reduced to $22,000, that is, $25,000 minus the $3,000 inventory decrease. The December 31, 2015, dollar-value LIFO inventory would again consist of two layers:

	Base-Period Costs	Adjustment Factor	Dollar-Value LIFO Carrying Amount
Beginning inventory	$100,000	1.00	$100,000
2014 layer	22,000	1.12	24,640
Ending inventory, dollar-value LIFO			$124,640

Even though there was a LIFO liquidation, the LIFO reserve will increase because the difference between FIFO and the remaining LIFO layers has increased. Inventory at FIFO of $146,400 less LIFO inventory of $124,640 yields a LIFO reserve of $21,760. The entry to obtain this ending balance is:

Cost of goods sold	$9,760	
LIFO reserve		$9,760
($21,760 − $12,000)		

The effect of the LIFO liquidation on pre-tax income is $240 [($25,000 original 2014 layer minus $22,000 remaining 2014 layer) × (1.20 2012 index minus 1.12 2014 layer index)]. If not for the liquidation, the credit to the LIFO reserve would have been $240 higher. Gable's note would appear as follows:

In 2015, inventory levels declined resulting in old LIFO layers being partially removed. As a result, pretax income increased by $240. Inventory amounts are summarized as follows:

	2015	2014
Inventory at FIFO	$146,400	$140,000
Reserve needed to reduce inventory to LIFO	(21,760)	(12,000)
Inventory at LIFO	$124,640	$128,000

Note that the increase in the LIFO reserve indicates that prices increased. The entry to increase the reserve would have been larger if the LIFO liquidation had not occurred. The change in the reserve can be broken into the price change component and the liquidation component as was done for Aral Company on page 497.

1. Rising input costs *increased* LIFO cost of goods sold by
   [2015 beginning inventory at base year prices of $125,000 ×
   (ending price index of 1.2 less beginning price index of 1.12)] $10,000
2. The LIFO liquidation undercharged expense and thus *reduced* cost
   of goods sold by   (240)
3. Result: FIFO cost of goods sold exceeds LIFO cost of goods sold by $ 9,760

In the case of Aral Company, we had to back into the rising input component. However, in this example, where we have the underlying price indices, we can compute the effect directly. We hope that this analysis improves your understanding of the underlying economics represented by changes in the LIFO reserve.

Finally, assume that inventory at December 31, 2016, totals $170,100 at year-end costs and that the inventory price index at that date is 1.26. To determine whether a new LIFO layer was added in 2016, we must restate the December 31, 2016, inventory in terms of base-period costs:

Ending inventory expressed in base-period costs
($170,100/1.26) $135,000
Beginning inventory expressed in base-period costs
Base-period layer $100,000
2014 layer ($24,640/1.12)   22,000
                                                                                         122,000
Inventory increase expressed in base-period costs $ 13,000

The new 2016 LIFO layer must be added to LIFO inventory using the cost level in effect in 2016. To do this, we multiply the inventory increase expressed in base-period costs ($13,000) by the December 31, 2016, price index, which is 1.26. Thus, the December 31, 2016, dollar-value LIFO inventory would consist of three layers:

	Base-Period Costs	Adjustment Factor	Dollar-Value LIFO Carrying Amount
Beginning inventory	$100,000	1.00	$100,000
2014 layer	22,000	1.12	24,640
2016 layer	13,000	1.26	16,380
Ending inventory, dollar-value LIFO			$141,020

The LIFO reserve will increase because the difference between FIFO and LIFO has increased. Inventory at FIFO of $170,100 less LIFO inventory of $141,020 yields a LIFO reserve of $29,080. The entry to obtain this ending balance is:

Cost of goods sold $7,320
    LIFO reserve $7,320
    ($29,080 − $21,760)

Because there was not a liquidation in 2016, the $7,320 represents the effect of rising input prices. We compute the amount directly by multiplying the beginning 2016 base-year inventory of $122,000 by the change in the index for 2016 of 0.06 (1.26 minus 1.20).

The procedures for computing new dollar-value LIFO layers are technically inconsistent with a strict LIFO flow assumption. For example, notice that the 2016 layer added in the example is based on 1.26, a figure that represents 2016 *year-end* costs. Under traditional LIFO, new layers are added using beginning-of-year costs, not end-of-year costs. Because dollar-value LIFO is a computational convenience, this inconsistency in computing new layers is usually ignored to simplify the computations.

The steps required to compute dollar-value LIFO are summarized as follows:

1. Ending inventory is initially computed in terms of year-end costs (FIFO). This simplifies recordkeeping.

2. To determine whether a new LIFO layer had been added (or whether an existing layer has been liquidated), the ending inventory must be restated to base-period cost and compared to the beginning inventory at base-period cost. This eliminates the effect of input cost changes. After restatement, any difference between beginning and ending inventory is the inventory change expressed in base-period cost. It indicates whether inventory *quantities* have changed.

3. Any inventory change determined from Step 2 must be computed as follows:

   a. New LIFO layers are valued using costs of the year in which the layer was added.

   b. Decreases in old LIFO layers are removed using costs that were in effect when the layer was originally formed.

4. The LIFO reserve is computed as the difference between FIFO inventory and LIFO inventory. The change in the reserve represents the difference between FIFO and LIFO and cost of goods sold. When there are no liquidations, increases (decreases) in the LIFO reserve represent increases (decreases) in input prices.

APPENDIX C

INVENTORY ERRORS

Errors in computing inventory are rare and almost always accidental. For example, a computer programming mistake might assign the wrong costs to inventory items. But in occasional instances, companies deliberately (and fraudulently) misstate inventories to manipulate reported earnings. You must first understand how inventory errors affect reported results to understand why some managers use this misrepresentation technique.

To visualize the effect of inventory errors, let's assume that due to a miscount in the 2014 year-end physical inventory, Jones Corporation's ending inventory is *overstated* by $1 million. Also assume there are no other inventory errors. Using the cost of goods sold formula, we see that this error *understates* 2014 cost of goods sold by $1 million:

	Effect of 2014 Error on
Beginning inventory	No error
+ Purchases	No error
= Goods available	No error
− Ending inventory	Overstated by $1 million
= Cost of goods sold	Understated by $1 million

Because ending inventory is subtracted in the cost of goods sold computation, an overstatement of ending inventory leads to an understatement of cost of goods sold. Understating cost of goods sold by $1 million overstates pre-tax income by $1 million. Furthermore, if the error is not detected and corrected in 2014, it will also cause 2015 pre-tax income to be misstated. The reason that the error carries over into 2015 is that the December 31, 2014, ending inventory becomes the January 1, 2015, beginning inventory. So, the carryforward effect (assuming no other 2015 inventory errors) is:

Effect of 2014 Error on the 2015 COGS Computation	
Beginning inventory	Overstated by $1 million
+ Purchases	No error
= Goods available	Overstated by $1 million
− Ending inventory	No error
= Cost of goods sold	Overstated by $1 million

The 2015 cost of goods sold overstatement results in a $1 million understatement of 2015 pre-tax income. The carryforward effect in 2015 is equal in amount but in the opposite direction from the 2014 effect. Because the first year's income is overstated by $1 million and the second year's income is understated by the same amount, by December 31, 2015, the end of the two-year cycle, the Retained earnings account (which is cumulative, of course) will be correct.

If an inventory error is discovered during the reporting year, it is corrected immediately. However, if an error is not discovered until a subsequent year (say, 2015 in our example), then the Retained earnings balance as of the beginning of the discovery year (2015) is corrected. If the error has a material effect on the company's financial statements, it must be separately disclosed.

In recent years, the media have coined the phrase "accounting irregularities." Some of these irregularities simply relate to exuberant use of the flexibility within GAAP; others involve fraud. Accounting fraud is relatively rare, but it does happen. And some of the more spectacular frauds involve inventory misstatement. To offset an emerging profit shortfall, a company could overstate quarter-end inventory. As we just saw, overstating ending inventory decreases cost of goods sold, increases income, and masks the adverse real conditions facing a company. But as our numerical example illustrates, the phony earnings boost in the overstatement year reverses in the following year. So, if the economic adversity that motivated the deliberate initial inventory overstatement continues, the inventory overstatements have to continue as well.

If we assume that Jones Corporation's inventory error was discovered in January 2015 after the 2014 books were closed and that the income tax rate is 35%, the entry to correct the error is:

DR	Retained earnings	$650,000	
DR	Income tax payable	350,000	
	CR Inventory		$1,000,000

 **Analysis**

This is exactly what happened at Comptronix Corporation, an electronics manufacturer that lost an important customer in 1989.[34] After succumbing to the temptation to overstate profits by overstating inventory, the practice could not be abandoned without causing a reversal. So, the overstatement continued until late 1992.[35] The fraud was eventually discovered at both companies. Can auditors and other analysts be successful detectives and uncover these situations? For outsiders, fraud is difficult to detect, but sometimes there are clues.[36] For example, the reduction in cost of goods sold arising from inventory overstatement increases gross margins. ***So, an unexplained increase in gross margins during troubled economic times is suspicious and warrants investigation.***

---

[34] See C. Mulford and E. Comiskey, *Financial Warnings* (New York: John Wiley & Sons, Inc., 1996), pp. 228–33.

[35] For a comprehensive discussion of the accounting issues at Comptronix, see J. L. Boockholdt, "Comptronix, Inc.: An Audit Case Involving Fraud," *Issues in Accounting Education,* February 2000, pp. 105–28.

[36] For a discussion of these clues, see Mulford and Comiskey, op. cit.

EXERCISES

E 9 - 1

Computing inventory amount
from income statement
data   **(LO 1)**

AICPA
ADAPTED

On January 1, 2014, Manuel Company's merchandise inventory was $300,000. During 2014, Manuel purchased $1,900,000 of merchandise and recorded sales of $2,000,000. The gross profit margin on these sales was 20% of the selling price.

Required:

What is Manuel's merchandise inventory at December 31, 2014?

E 9 - 2

Distinguishing between
product and period
costs   **(LO 3)**

Sperry-New Holland manufactures farm machinery. During 2014, it incurred a variety of costs, several of which appear on the following list.

Nature of Incurred Cost

a. Comprehensive liability insurance premium on corporate headquarters

b. Depreciation on production equipment

c. Electricity consumed

d. Property and casualty insurance premiums

e. Raw material used

f. Royalties paid to the designer of one of the company's products

g. Salaries of corporate legal counsel

h. Travel expenses for sales force

i. Wages of plant maintenance personnel

j. Wages of production workers

k. Workers compensation insurance

Required:

Classify each listed cost as a product or period cost, or both. For costs that are probably allocable to both classifications, suggest a reasonable allocation approach.

E 9 - 3

Computing ending inventory
and cost of goods sold
under different cost flow
assumptions   **(LO 2, 5)**

AICPA
ADAPTED

Jessica's Office Supply, Inc., had 300 calculators on hand at January 1, 2014, costing $16 each. Purchases and sales of calculators during the month of January were as follows:

Date	Purchases	Sales
January 12		200 @ $25
14	150 @ $17	
29	100 @ $18	
30		150 @ $30

Jessica does not maintain perpetual inventory records. According to a physical count, 200 calculators were on hand at January 31, 2014.

Required:

1. What is the amount of ending inventory at January 31, 2014, and cost of goods sold for the month ended January 31, 2014, under the FIFO method?

2. What is the amount of ending inventory at January 31, 2014, and cost of goods sold for the month ended January 31, 2014, under the LIFO method?

3. What is the amount of ending inventory at January 31, 2014, and cost of goods sold for the month ended January 31, 2014, under the average cost method?

The following information is available for Day Company for 2014:

Cash disbursements for purchase of merchandise	$290,000
Increase in trade accounts payable	25,000
Decrease in merchandise inventory	10,000

Required:
What is the cost of goods sold for 2014?

E9-4

Computing cost of goods sold   (LO 1)

AICPA
ADAPTED

For the year 2014, Dumas Company's gross profit was $96,000; the cost of goods manufactured was $340,000; the beginning inventories of goods in process and finished goods were $28,000 and $45,000, respectively; and the ending inventories of goods in process and finished goods were $38,000 and $52,000, respectively.

Required:
What is the dollar amount of Dumas Company sales for 2014?

E9-5

Computing sales from inventory information   (LO 3, 4)

AICPA
ADAPTED

Hestor Company's records indicate the following information:

Merchandise inventory, January 1, 2014	$ 550,000
Purchases, January 1 through December 31, 2014	2,250,000
Sales, January 1 through December 31, 2014	3,000,000

On December 31, 2014, a physical inventory determined that ending inventory of $600,000 was in the warehouse. Hestor's gross profit on sales has remained constant at 30%. Hestor suspects some of the inventory may have been taken by some new employees.

Required:
At December 31, 2014, what is the estimated cost of missing inventory?

E9-6

Estimating missing inventory (LO 1)

AICPA
ADAPTED

On June 30, 2014, a tornado damaged Jensen Corporation's warehouse and factory, completely destroying the work-in-process inventory. Neither the raw materials nor finished goods inventories were damaged. A physical inventory taken after the tornado revealed the following valuations:

Raw materials	$ 87,000
Work-in-process	0
Finished goods	151,000
	$238,000

The inventory of January 1, 2014, consisted of the following:

Raw materials	$ 41,000
Work-in-process	128,000
Finished goods	173,000
	$342,000

A review of the books and records disclosed that the gross profit margin historically approximated 28% of sales. The sales total for the first six months of 2014 was $405,000. Raw material purchases totaled $150,000. Direct labor costs for this period were $112,000, and manufacturing overhead has historically been applied at 50% of direct labor.

E9-7

Computing work-in-process inventory from balance sheet and income statement information   (LO 1, 4)

AICPA
ADAPTED

Required:

Compute the value of the work-in-process inventory lost at June 30, 2014. Show supporting computations.

E9-8

Computing inventory and cost of goods sold under three flow assumptions
(LO 2, 5)

AICPA
ADAPTED

Frate Company was formed on January 1, 2014. The following information is available from Frate's inventory records for Product Ply:

	Units	Unit Cost
January 1, 2014		
Beginning inventory	800	$ 9.00
Purchases:		
January 5, 2014	1,500	10.00
May 25, 2014	1,200	10.50
July 16, 2014	600	11.00
November 26, 2014	900	11.50

A physical inventory on December 31, 2014, shows 1,600 units on hand.

Required:

Prepare schedules to compute the ending inventory at December 31, 2014, and cost of goods sold for the year ended December 31, 2014 under each of the following inventory methods:

1. FIFO

2. LIFO

3. Weighted average

Show supporting computations in good form.

E9-9

Computing ending inventory and cost of sales under direct and absorption costing
(LO 4)

AICPA
ADAPTED

Information from Jacob Perez Company's records is available as follows for the year ended December 31, 2014:

Net sales	$1,600,000
Cost of goods manufactured:	
Variable	$ 800,000
Fixed	352,000
Operating expenses:	
Variable	$ 78,000
Fixed	150,000
Units manufactured	80,000
Units sold	55,000
Finished goods inventory, 1/1/2014	None

No work-in-process inventories existed at the beginning or end of 2014.

Required:

1. What would be Perez's finished goods inventory and cost of goods sold under the variable (direct) costing method at December 31, 2014?

2. Under the absorption costing method, what would Perez's operating income be?

3. Calculate Jacob Perez Company's cost of goods sold and ending inventory under absorption costing.

Selected information concerning the operation of Kern Company for the year ended December 31, 2014, is available as follows:

Units produced	10,000
Units sold	9,000
Direct materials used	$40,000
Direct labor incurred	20,000
Fixed factory overhead	25,000
Variable factory overhead	12,000
Fixed selling and administrative expenses	30,000
Variable selling and administrative expenses	4,500
Finished goods inventory, January 1, 2014	None

No work-in-process inventories existed at the beginning or end of 2014.

Required:

1. What would be Kern's finished goods inventory cost under the variable (direct) costing method at December 31, 2014?

2. Which costing method—absorption or variable costing—would show a higher operating income for 2014, and by what amount?

E9-10

Computing ending inventory and cost of goods sold under absorption and variable costing **(LO 4)**

AICPA
ADAPTED

Blago Wholesale Company began operations on January 1, 2014, and uses the average cost method in costing its inventory. Management is contemplating a change to the FIFO method in 2015 and is interested in determining how such a change will affect net income. Accordingly, the following information has been developed:

	2014	2015
Final inventory:		
Average cost	$150,000	$255,000
FIFO	160,000	270,000

Condensed income statements for Blago Wholesale appear below:

	2014	2015
Sales	$1,000,000	$1,200,000
Cost of goods sold	600,000	720,000
Gross profit	400,000	480,000
Selling, general, and administrative	250,000	275,000
Net income	$ 150,000	$ 205,000

Required:

Based on this information, what would 2015 net income be after the change to the FIFO method? Ignore any income tax effects of this change in accounting method.

E9-11

Changing to FIFO method **(LO 5)**

AICPA
ADAPTED

KW Steel Corp. uses the LIFO method of inventory valuation. Waretown Steel, KW's major competitor, instead uses the FIFO method. The following are excerpts from each company's 2014 financial statements:

	KW Steel Corp.		Waretown Steel	
($ in millions)	2014	2013	2014	2013
Balance sheet inventories	$ 797.6	$ 692.7	$ 708.2	$ 688.6
LIFO reserve	378.0	334.9		
Sales	4,284.8	4,029.7	3,584.2	3,355.8
Cost of goods sold	3,427.8	3,226.5	2,724.0	2,617.5

E9-12

Converting LIFO to FIFO **(LO 6)**

Required:

1. Compute each company's 2014 gross margin percentage and inventory turnover using cost of goods sold as reported by each company. (Round answers to one decimal place.) For each ratio, how does KW Steel compare to Waretown Steel?

2. Restate KW's cost of goods sold and inventory balances to the FIFO basis. On the basis of its adjusted data, recompute KW's gross margin percentage and inventory turnover. Explain how the revised figures alter your earlier comparisons.

E9-13

Identifying effects of a LIFO liquidation   **(LO 7)**

Nathan's Grills, Inc., imports and sells premium-quality gas grills. The company had the following layers in its LIFO inventory at January 1, 2014, at which time the replacement cost of the inventory was $675 per unit.

Year LIFO Layer Added	Units	Unit Cost
2011	50	$450
2012	40	500
2013	60	600

The replacement cost of grills remained constant throughout 2014. Nathan's sold 275 units during 2014. The company established the selling price of each unit by doubling its replacement cost at the time of sale.

Required:

1. Determine gross margin and the gross margin percentage for 2014 assuming that Nathan's Grills purchased 280 units during the year.

2. Determine gross margin and the gross margin percentage for 2014 assuming that Nathan's Grills purchased 180 units during the year.

3. Explain why the assumed number of units purchased makes a difference in your answers.

E9-14

Eliminating FIFO holding gains   **(LO 1, 9)**

Watsontown Yacht Sales has been selling large power cruisers for 25 years. On January 1, 2014, the company had $5,950,000 in inventory (based on a FIFO valuation). While the number of yachts in Watsontown Yacht Sales' inventory remained fairly constant throughout 2014, by December 31, 2014, yacht prices were 7% higher than at the start of the year. The company reported cost of goods sold for 2014 of $23,800,000.

Required:

Calculate the amount of realized holding gains in Watsontown Yacht Sales' income for 2014.

E9-15

Correcting inventory errors   **(LO 1)**

AICPA
ADAPTED

The following inventory valuation errors have been discovered for Knox Corporation:

• The 2012 year-end inventory was overstated by $23,000.

• The 2013 year-end inventory was understated by $61,000.

• The 2014 year-end inventory was understated by $17,000.

The reported income before taxes for Knox was:

Year	Income before Taxes
2012	$138,000
2013	254,000
2014	168,000

Required:

Compute what income before taxes for 2012, 2013, and 2014 should have been after correcting for the errors.

Moore Corporation has two products in its ending inventory; each is accounted for at the lower of cost or market. A profit margin of 30% on selling price is considered normal for each product. Specific data with respect to each product follows:

E9-16

Applying lower of cost or market **(LO 11)**

AICPA
ADAPTED

	Product 1	Product 2
Historical cost	$17	$ 45
Replacement cost	15	46
Estimated cost to sell	5	26
Estimated selling price	30	100

Required:

In pricing its ending inventory using the lower of cost or market rule, what unit values should Moore use for products 1 and 2, respectively?

Acute Company manufactures a single product. On December 31, 2011, it adopted the dollar-value LIFO inventory method. The inventory on that date using the dollar-value LIFO inventory method was determined to be $300,000. Inventory data for succeeding years follow:

E9-17

Computing dollar-value LIFO **(LO 13)**

AICPA
ADAPTED

Year Ended December 31	Inventory at Respective Year-End Prices	Relevant Price Index (Base Year 2011)
2012	$363,000	1.10
2013	420,000	1.20
2014	430,000	1.25

Required:

Compute the inventory amounts at December 31, 2012, 2013, and 2014, using the dollar-value LIFO inventory method for each year.

On December 31, 2013, Fern Company adopted the dollar-value LIFO inventory method. All of Fern's inventories constitute a single pool. The inventory on December 31, 2013, using the dollar-value LIFO inventory method was $600,000. Inventory data for 2014 are as follows:

E9-18

Computing dollar-value LIFO **(LO 13)**

AICPA
ADAPTED

December 31, 2014, inventory at year-end prices	$780,000
Relevant price index at year-end (base year 2013)	1.20

Required:

Under the dollar-value LIFO inventory method, what would Fern's inventory be at December 31, 2014?

Cost for inventory purposes should be determined by the inventory cost flow method most clearly reflecting periodic income.

E9-19

Evaluating inventory costing concepts **(LO 5, 10, 11)**

AICPA
ADAPTED

Required:

1. Describe the fundamental cost flow assumptions for the average cost, FIFO, and LIFO inventory cost flow methods.

2. Discuss the reasons for using LIFO in an inflationary economy.

3. Where there is evidence that the utility of inventory will be less than cost, what is the proper accounting treatment, and under what concept is that treatment justified?

PROBLEMS / DISCUSSION QUESTIONS

P9-1

Calculating amounts and
ratios under FIFO and LIFO
(LO 2, 5)

Keefer, Inc., began business on January 1, 2013. Information on its inventory purchases and sales during 2013 and 2014 follow:

	Inventory Purchases		
Date	Units	Cost per Unit	Total
January 1, 2013	85	$25	$ 2,125
March 15, 2013	100	27	2,700
May 15, 2013	90	28	2,520
August 1, 2013	100	30	3,000
September 3, 2013	125	31	3,875
December 5, 2013	50	32	1,600
Total purchases—2013	550		$15,820
February 20, 2014	150	$31	$ 4,650
March 29, 2014	100	30	3,000
July 1, 2014	100	29	2,900
August 20, 2014	100	28	2,800
November 3, 2014	80	27	2,160
Total purchases—2014	530		$15,510

	Inventory Sales		
	Units	Price per Unit	Total
March 18, 2013	65	$50	$ 3,250
August 15, 2013	200	52	10,400
October 6, 2013	175	53	9,275
Total sales—2013	440		$22,925
February 12, 2014	100	$53	$ 5,300
June 2, 2014	200	52	10,400
September 30, 2014	210	50	10,500
Total sales—2014	510		$26,200

Required:

1. Calculate ending inventory, cost of goods sold, and gross margin for 2013 and 2014 under the periodic FIFO inventory valuation method.

2. Calculate ending inventory, cost of goods sold, and gross margin for 2013 and 2014 under the periodic LIFO inventory valuation method.

3. Discuss the difference in reported results under FIFO versus LIFO for each year.

P9-2

Determining income
statement amounts for a
manufacturer **(LO 1, 3, 4)**

The following information pertains to Yuji Corporation:

	January 1, 2014	December 31, 2014
Raw materials inventory	$ 34,000	$ 38,000
Work-in-process inventory	126,000	145,000
Finished goods inventory	76,000	68,000

Costs incurred during the year 2014 were as follows:

Raw material purchased	$116,000
Wages to factory workers	55,000
Salary to factory supervisors	25,000
Salary to selling and administrative staff	40,000
Depreciation on factory building and equipment	10,000
Depreciation on office building	12,000
Utilities for factory building	5,000
Utilities for office building	7,500

Required:

Sales revenue during 2014 was $300,000. The income tax rate is 40%. Compute the following:

1. Cost of raw materials used.

2. Cost of goods manufactured/completed.

3. Cost of goods sold.

4. Gross margin.

5. Net income.

Bravo Wholesalers, Inc., began its business on January 1, 2014. Information on its inventory purchases and sales during 2014 follows:

P9-3

Determining cost of sales under different flow assumptions—comprehensive **(LO 2, 5, 6)**

mhhe.com/revsine6e

	Inventory Purchases		
	Units	**Cost per Unit**	**Total**
January 1	8,000	$5.00	$ 40,000
March 10	10,000	5.10	51,000
April 15	12,000	5.30	63,600
September 11	10,000	5.55	55,500
November 12	6,000	5.75	34,500
December 1	7,500	5.85	43,875
December 29	6,500	6.10	39,650
Units available for sale	60,000		$328,125

	Inventory Sales		
	Units	**Price per Unit**	**Total**
March 3	6,000	$9.00	$ 54,000
September 2	24,000	9.50	228,000
December 5	10,000	10.00	100,000
Units sold	40,000		$382,000

Assume a tax rate of 40%.

Required:

1. Compute the cost of ending inventory and cost of goods sold under each of the following methods: (a) FIFO, (b) Weighted average cost, and (c) LIFO. Assume that Bravo uses the periodic inventory method.

2. Assume that Bravo uses the periodic LIFO method.

   a. Calculate the replacement cost of the ending inventory and the LIFO reserve as of year-end. You may assume that year-end purchase cost was still $6.10 per unit.

b. Estimate Bravo's cost of goods sold under the periodic FIFO method based only on the information that will be publicly available to Bravo's investors. Explain why your answer differs from FIFO cost of goods sold computed in requirement 1.

c. Bravo's purchasing manager was planning to acquire 10,000 units of inventory on January 5, 2015, at $6.10 per unit. Its accountant suggests that the company will be better off if it acquires the inventory instead on December 31, 2014. What are the pros and cons of the accountant's suggestion? Wherever possible, show supporting calculations.

3. Calculate the cost of goods sold assuming that Bravo uses (a) the perpetual FIFO method; (b) the perpetual weighted average method.

P9-4	
Determining the effects of absorption and variable costing **(LO 4)**	

Mastrolia Manufacturing produces pacifiers. The company uses absorption costing for external reporting, but management prefers variable costing for evaluating the profitability of each model. Bonuses, which make up a significant portion of each manager's annual compensation, are based on attaining certain minimum gross margin percentages. Selected data regarding production and sales of the company's popular "Little Eric" model follow:

	2014	2015	2016
Selling price per unit	$ 10.00	$ 10.00	$ 10.00
Variable production costs per unit	$ 4.00	$ 4.00	$ 4.00
Fixed production costs per year	$500,000	$500,000	$500,000
Beginning inventory 1/1/2014	30,000 units @$8.00		
(FIFO basis)	(variable cost = $4.00)		
Units produced	125,000	100,000	115,000
Units sold	100,000	85,000	140,000
Ending inventory (units)	55,000	70,000	45,000

Required:

1. Calculate Mastrolia's gross profit percentage each year under generally accepted accounting principles. Briefly explain the reasons for any variations in the annual gross profit percentage.

2. Calculate Mastrolia's gross profit percentage each year under variable costing. Briefly explain the reasons for any variations in the annual gross profit percentage.

3. If you were the manager of the "Little Eric" plant and your annual bonus was based on the plant achieving a gross profit percentage in excess of 15% each year, which method would you prefer and why? (Assume you can significantly influence annual production schedules.)

P9-5	
Determining items to be included in inventory **(LO 3)** **AICPA** ADAPTED	

Diana Gomez Corporation, a manufacturer of cowboy boots, provided the following information from its accounting records for the year ended December 31, 2014.

Inventory at December 31, 2014 (based on a physical count of goods on December 31, 2014)	$1,700,000
Accounts payable at December 31, 2014	1,150,000
Net sales (sales less returns and allowances)	9,500,000

Additional information is as follows:

a. Work-in-process inventory costing $30,000 was sent to an outside processor for hand-tooling on December 30, 2014, and was therefore not included in physical inventory.

b. Goods received from Smith, Inc., a vendor, on December 27, 2014, were included in the physical count; however, the invoice from Smith ($43,000) was not included in accounts payable at December 31, 2014, because the accounts payable department never received its copy of the receiving report.

c. Goods received from another vendor just before the plant closed on December 31, 2014, were reported on a receiving report dated January 2, 2015. The goods, invoiced to Gomez at $83,000, were not included in the physical count, but the invoice was included in the December 31, 2014, accounts payable balance.

d. Included in the physical count were boots billed to a customer f.o.b. shipping point (title transfers when goods are shipped) on December 31, 2014. These boots had a cost of $25,000 and were recorded as sales of $35,000. The shipment was on Gomez's loading dock waiting to be picked up by the trucking company.

e. Boots shipped to a customer f.o.b. destination (title transfers when goods are received) on December 28, 2014, were in transit at December 31, 2014, and had a cost of $40,000. Gomez issued a sales invoice for $58,000 on January 3, 2015, upon notification of receipt by the customer.

f. Boots returned by customers and held on December 31, 2014, in the returned goods area pending inspection were not included in the physical count. On January 5, 2015, after inspection, the boots were returned to inventory and credit memos were issued to the customers. The boots, costing $27,000, were originally invoiced for $39,000.

Required:

Using the following format, prepare a schedule of adjustments as of December 31, 2014, to the amounts Gomez initially reported in its accounting records. Show separately the effect, if any, of each of the six transactions on the December 31, 2014, amounts. Insert a –0– for any transactions that would not affect inventory, accounts payable, or net sales as originally reported.

	Inventory	Accounts Payable	Net Sales
Initial amounts	$1,700,000	$1,150,000	$9,500,000
Adjustments—increase (decrease)			
a.			
b.			
c.			
d.			
e.			
f.			
Total adjustments			
Adjusted amounts			

Jeanette Corporation's president is in a dilemma regarding which inventory method (LIFO or FIFO) to use. The controller provides the following list of factors that should be considered before making a choice.

P9-6

Choosing a cost flow assumption   **(LO 5, 8, 10)**

a. Jeanette has borrowed money during the current month and has entered into a debt contract. The covenants of this contract require Jeanette to achieve a certain amount of net income and maintain a certain amount of working capital.

b. The Jeanette's board of directors is contemplating a proposal to reward the top corporate management with an incentive bonus based on accounting net income.

c. The vice president of finance suggests using the LIFO method for tax purposes and the FIFO method for financial reporting purposes. With lower taxable income, Jeanette can save on the current tax it pays, and, at the same time, it can show higher income in the financial reports and "look good."

d. The controller cautions that while the LIFO method could reduce the current period tax liability, "it could hit us hard when things are not going so well." This potential problem with the LIFO method could be "avoided if we use FIFO in the first place."

e. However, the president would like to adopt the method that provides both a better application of the matching principle and a more current measure of inventory on the balance sheet.

f. The controller suggests that Jeanette adopt the FIFO method because higher accounting income means a higher stock price.

Required:

Jeanette's president has asked you to write a report evaluating the pros and cons of each of the issues raised. Given her busy schedule, she would like the report to be brief. In answering this question, assume that Jeanette Corporation expects an upward trend in inventory prices.

P9-7

Choosing a cost flow assumption   **(LO 5, 10)**

mhhe.com/revsine6e

Princess Retail Stores started doing business on January 1, 2014. The following data reflect its inventory purchases and sales during the year:

	Inventory Purchases		
	Units	Cost per Unit	Total
January 1	20,000	$ 7.00	$140,000
March 1	16,000	9.00	144,000
June 1	14,000	11.00	154,000
September 1	10,000	13.00	130,000
December 1	12,000	15.00	180,000
	72,000		$748,000

	Sales		
	Units	Price per Unit	Total
March 2	24,000	$14.00	$336,000
September 2	18,000	16.00	288,000
December 2	20,000	18.00	360,000
	62,000		$984,000

Required:

1. Compute gross margin and cost of ending inventory using the periodic FIFO cost flow assumption.

2. Compute gross margin and cost of ending inventory using the periodic LIFO cost flow assumption. Compute the dollar amount of the LIFO reserve. Using this additional disclosure, how might an analyst estimate Princess's cost of goods sold under the FIFO method based only on publicly available information? Show supporting calculations.

3. Under historical cost accounting, gross margin is calculated as current output price minus historical input price. For analytical convenience, we can break the gross margin into two components:

   a. Current cost operating margin = Current output price − Current input price.

   b. Inventory profits = Current input price − Historical input price.

   Provide an estimate of the Current cost operating margin for Princess Retail Stores.

4. The following are excerpts from a recent top management meeting at Princess Retail Stores. Your assignment is to clearly provide guidelines to the top management team on each issue raised in the meeting. Show calculations when necessary.

   a. "I am most concerned about appropriately matching revenues and expenses. I suggest that we look for an inventory accounting method that achieves this objective both during inflationary and deflationary times." (Frances Iyer, chairman)

b. "Frances, I think the choice is obvious. What other method can achieve better matching of revenues and expenses than the specific identification method? By choosing this method, we would send a clear signal to the stock market that we are not playing any earnings management games." (Sandra Kang, VP, Investor Relations)

c. "I would like to maximize our current profits. What inventory method might help us achieve this most important goal and why?" (Antonia Iyer, CEO)

d. "Antonia, I know you can't stop thinking about your earnings-based bonus. My primary objective is to minimize the present value of future income tax outflows." (Juanita Kang, CFO)

e. "I would like to have our cake and eat it too. Why don't we follow Juanita's suggestion for income tax accounting and follow Antonia's idea for external financial reporting?" (B. T. Kang, VP, Operations)

Packard, Inc., adopted the dollar-value LIFO inventory method on June 30, 2013, the end of its fiscal year. Packard's inventory records provide the following information:

Date	Year-End Current Cost	Relevant Cost Index
June 30, 2013	$345,000	1.00
June 30, 2014	340,000	0.96
June 30, 2015	385,000	1.04
June 30, 2016	398,000	1.09
June 30, 2017	410,000	1.10

P9-8

Computing dollar-value LIFO **(LO 13)**

AICPA
ADAPTED

Required:
Calculate the ending inventory for Packard, Inc., for 2014, 2015, 2016, and 2017 using the dollar-value LIFO method.

During your audit of Patti Company's ending inventory at December 31, 2014, you find the following inventory accounting errors:

a. Goods in Patti's warehouse on consignment from Valley, Inc., were included in Patti's ending inventory.

b. On December 31, 2014, Patti received $4,700 worth of inventory, which was included in the 2014 ending inventory. However, the invoice on this merchandise was not received by Patti until January 3, 2015, at which time the purchase was recorded. The purchase should have been recorded in 2014.

c. Patti purchased merchandise on account on December 30, 2014, but did not include these goods in inventory or record the purchase. These goods were shipped by the vendor f.o.b. shipping point (title transfers when goods are shipped) and were in transit on December 31, 2014.

d. Some of Patti's merchandise, shipped on consignment to Kaitlin Company in mid-December 2014, was excluded from the December 31, 2014, inventory.

e. On December 28, 2014, Patti shipped goods costing $10,000 to Likert, f.o.b. destination (title transfers when goods are received). Likert received the goods on January 4, 2015, and notified Patti of their arrival. The goods were not included in Patti's 2014 inventory balance.

P9-9

Correcting inventory errors **(LO 1)**

AICPA
ADAPTED

Required:

Assume that Patti uses the periodic inventory system. Indicate the effect (understate, overstate, or no effect) each of these errors would have on:

1. December 31, 2014, ending inventory
2. December 31, 2015, ending inventory
3. December 31, 2014, cost of goods sold
4. December 31, 2015, cost of goods sold
5. December 31, 2014, accounts payable
6. December 31, 2015, accounts payable

P9-10

Analyzing gross margins and cash flow sustainability
(LO 9)

Parque Corporation applied to Fairview Bank early in 2014 for a $400,000 five-year loan to finance plant modernization. The company proposes that the loan be unsecured and repaid from future operating cash flows. In support of the loan application, Parque submitted an income statement for 2013. Prepared using the FIFO inventory cost flow approach, this income statement reflected annual profit that was approximately 50% of the principal amount of the loan. It was offered as evidence that the loan could easily be repaid within the five-year term.

Parque is in the business of recycling yelpin, an industrial lubricant. The company buys used yelpin from large salvage companies and, after cleaning and reconditioning it, sells it to manufacturing companies. The recycling business is very competitive and has typically generated small gross margins. The salvage companies set yelpin prices on the first day of each quarter, and Parque purchases it at the established price for the entire quarter. Yelpin prices fluctuate with business conditions. Prices paid to salvage companies have risen in recent years but tend to fall during economic downturns.

Parque sells the recycled yelpin at $1 per pound above the currently prevailing price that it pays to acquire the used yelpin from salvage companies. December 31, 2012, inventory was 300,000 pounds at a cost of $7.00 per pound. Purchases and sales in 2013 were:

	Purchases	Sales
First quarter 2013	600,000 lbs. @ $7.20/lb.	700,000 lbs. @ $8.20/lb.
Second quarter 2013	700,000 lbs. @ $7.40/lb.	600,000 lbs. @ $8.40/lb.
Third quarter 2013	800,000 lbs. @ $7.80/lb.	700,000 lbs. @ $8.80/lb.
Fourth quarter 2013	600,000 lbs. @ $8.10/lb.	650,000 lbs. @ $9.10/lb.

Cash operating costs during 2013 totaled $2,800,000.

Required:

1. Compute 2013 income for Parque Corporation using the FIFO inventory flow assumption. Ignore income taxes.
2. Did Parque really earn a profit from its *operating* activities in 2013?
3. Given the circumstances described, what risks exist that could threaten ultimate repayment of the loan?

P9-11

Evaluating inventory cost flow changes **(LO 5)**

The following is an excerpt from the financial statements of Talbot Industries:

Effective September 30, 2013, the Company changed its method of accounting for inventories from the LIFO method principally to the Specific Identification method, because, in the opinion of management, there is a better matching of revenues and expenses, better correlation of accounting and financial information with the method by which the Company is managed, and better presentation of inventories at values that more fairly present the inventories' cost.

During 2014, Chaney Technologies changed its inventory cost flow assumption from LIFO to the average cost method. The following is an excerpt from Chaney Technologies financial statements.

The change to the average cost method will conform all inventories of the Company to the same method of valuation. The Company believes that the average cost method of inventory valuation provides a more meaningful presentation of the financial position of the Company since it reflects more recent costs in the balance sheet. Under the current economic environment of low inflation and an expected reduction in inventories and low production costs, the Company believes that the average cost method also results in a better matching of current costs with current revenues.

Required:

1. Evaluate each of the justifications provided by Talbot for changing its inventory cost flow assumption.

2. Evaluate each of the justifications provided by Chaney Technologies for changing its inventory cost flow assumption.

JKW Corporation has been selling plumbing supplies since 1981. In 2003, the company adopted the LIFO method of valuing its inventory. The company has grown steadily over the years and a layer has been added to its LIFO inventory in each of the years the method has been used. The company's inventory turnover ratio has averaged 4.5 in recent years. Management attempts to maintain a stable level of inventory at each store; the growth in inventory has been due to new stores being opened each year. In 2013, the board of directors approved an incentive program that pays managers a sizable bonus in each year that certain performance targets are met. For 2014, targeted earnings per share are $2.75. In an effort to track progress toward meeting this target, management produced the following income statement for the first nine months of 2014.

P9-12

Assessing managerial opportunism   **(LO 7, 10)**

JKW Corporation

Income Statement
January 1–September 30, 2014

Sales		$13,284,000
Cost of goods sold		7,970,400
Gross margin		5,313,600
Operating expenses		2,391,120
Income before taxes		2,922,480
Income tax expense		1,022,868
Net income		$ 1,899,612
Earnings per share (1,000,000 shares outstanding)		$ 1.90

Based on past history, management expects 30% of the company's annual sales to take place in the fourth quarter. Operating expenses and gross margin are expected to remain at 18% and 40% of sales, respectively, for the remainder of the year. The company's tax rate is 35%.

Required:

1. Assuming that management maintains a stable level of inventory, project earnings per share for 2014 based on the data provided.

2. Assume that you are JKW's independent auditor, and your analysis indicates that projected earnings per share will fall short of the bonus target. In the past, JKW's managers have used aggressive (and possibly unethical) behavior to achieve salary bonus targets. You suspect that the managers intend to deplete old LIFO layers deliberately in the fourth quarter. To help you detect such behavior, calculate the amount of the LIFO liquidation that would be needed in the fourth quarter to hit the EPS target in 2014.

P9-13

Computing LIFO and ratio
effects   **(LO 1, 6)**

Don Facundo Bacardy Maso founded the original Bacardi® rum business in Cuba in 1862. The following information is excerpted from Bacardi Corporation's annual report for the year ended December 31, Year 2. Bacardi's effective tax rate was 17% in Year 2.

The company follows the last-in, first-out (LIFO) method of determining inventory cost. The LIFO method is considered by management to be preferable because it more closely matches current costs with current revenues in periods of price level changes. Under this method, current costs are charged to costs of sales for the year.

In Year 2, LIFO liquidation was caused primarily by a substantial reduction during the year in [the inventory of] molasses (the major raw material). This LIFO liquidation, which resulted in cost of products sold being charged with higher inventory costs from prior years, caused a decrease in Year 2 net income of approximately $1,400,000 or $0.14 per share.

LIFO inventories at December 31, Year 2 and Year 1 were $51,892,000 and $53,812,000, respectively, which is approximately $700,000 and $20,800,000 less than replacement cost at those dates.

In accordance with generally recognized trade practices, inventories of distilled spirits in bonded aging warehouses have been included in current assets, although the normal aging period is usually from one to three years.

Ending inventories consist of the following:

($ in thousands)	Year 2	Year 1
Finished goods	$ 2,684	$ 2,420
Aging rum in bond	40,285	39,921
Raw materials and supplies	8,923	11,471
	$51,892	$53,812

Cost of goods sold and net income (after tax) during Year 2 were $65,374,000 and $45,568,000, respectively.

Required:

1. Compute the cost of goods manufactured (fully aged rum) during Year 2. Without using the LIFO reserve information, compute the finished goods inventory turnover (the number of days from inventory completion until its sale) and the work-in-process inventory turnover (the number of days the inventory is in the production cycle). Is the difference between the two inventory turnover ratios consistent with the nature of Bacardi's business? Explain.

2. On the basis of available information, estimate Bacardi's net income if the company had used FIFO during Year 2. By comparing the reported LIFO income with your estimate of FIFO income, what do you learn about the business conditions Bacardi faced during Year 2?

3. Using all available information, compute a total inventory turnover measure (expressed in number of days). Does your estimate of inventory turnover capture Bacardi's "true" physical turnover (based on what you know about the business)? Explain. If it does not capture the true physical turnover, provide possible reasons. Be specific.

P9-14

Determining LIFO
amounts—comprehensive
(LO 6, 7, 8)

Sirotka Retail Company began doing business in 2012. The following information pertains to its first three years of operation:

		Purchases		Sales	
Year	Operating Expenses	Units	Unit Cost	Units	Unit Price
2012	$60,000	15,000	$20.00	12,000	$35
2013	90,000	20,000	25.00	18,000	40
2014	65,000	5,000	30.00	10,000	40

Assume the following:

- The income tax rate is 40%.
- Purchase and sale prices change only at the beginning of the year.
- Sirotka uses the LIFO cost flow assumption.
- Operating expenses are primarily selling and administrative expenses.

Required:

1. Compute cost of goods sold and the cost of ending inventory for each of the three years. (Identify the number of units and the cost per unit for each LIFO layer in the ending inventory.)
2. Prepare income statements for each of the three years.
3. Compute the LIFO reserve at the end of 2012, 2013, and 2014.
4. Compute the effect of LIFO liquidation on the net income of the company for the years 2013 and 2014.
5. Compute the inventory turnover ratio for the years 2013 and 2014. Do not make adjustments for any potential biases in LIFO accounting. Comment on the direction of the bias (that is, understated/overstated) in the inventory turnover ratio under LIFO. Is the ratio in one year more biased than in the other? Explain.
6. How can the physical turnover of inventory (that is, true inventory turnover) best be approximated using *all* of the information available in a LIFO financial statement? Illustrate your approach by recomputing Sirotka's inventory turnover ratios for 2013 and 2014.
7. Compute the gross margin percentages for the years 2013 and 2014. Explain whether the difference in the gross margin percentages between 2013 and 2014 reflect the change in Sirotka's economic condition from 2013 and 2014.
8. Provide an *estimate* of the FIFO cost of goods sold for the years 2012, 2013, and 2014 using the information available in the financial statements.
9. Based on your answers to requirements 1 and 8, estimate Sirotka's tax savings for 2012, 2013, and 2014.
10. Assuming a discount rate of 10%, compute the January 1, 2012, present value of the tax savings over the period 2012–2014 (that is, discount the 2012 tax savings one period, and so on).

Caldwell Corporation operates an ice cream processing plant and uses the FIFO inventory cost flow assumption. A partial income statement for the year ended December 31, 2014, follows:

P9-15

Identifying FIFO holding gains **(LO 6, 9)**

Caldwell Corporation

Statement of Income
For the Year Ended December 31, 2014

Sales revenues	$680,000,000
Cost of goods sold	360,000,000
Gross margin	320,000,000
SG&A expenses	200,000,000
Income before taxes	$120,000,000

Caldwell's physical inventory levels were virtually constant throughout 2014. The FIFO dollar amount of inventory at January 1, 2014, was $60,000,000. During 2014, the Consumer

Price Index (an index of overall average purchasing power for typical urban-dwelling consumers) increased by 4%.

Caldwell Corporation's largest competitor, Cohen Confections, uses LIFO for inventory accounting. Excerpts from its December 31, 2014, inventory note were:

Cohen Confections

Inventory Note

Inventories are computed using the LIFO cost flow assumption. Comparative amounts were:

| | December 31, | |
	2014	2013
Raw materials	$ 8,100,000	$ 8,000,000
Finished goods	76,000,000	80,000,000
	$84,100,000	$88,000,000

The difference between the LIFO inventory amounts and the replacement cost of the inventory at December 31, 2014 and 2013, respectively, was $18,000,000 and $12,000,000. A LIFO liquidation occurred in 2014, which increased the reported gross margin by $1,000,000.

Required:

Using the preceding information, what is the *best* estimate of the amount of realized holding gains (or inventory profits) included in Caldwell Corporation's income before taxes?

P9-16

Applying lower of cost or market (LCM)   **(LO 11)**

Ramps by Jake, Inc., manufactures skateboard ramps. The company uses independent sales representatives to market its products and pays a commission of 8% on each sale. Data regarding the five styles of ramps in the company's inventory at December 31, 2014, follow. The normal profit margin on each style is expressed as a percentage of the item's selling price.

Inventory Item	Original Cost	Replacement Cost	Selling Price	Normal Profit Margin %
Style A	$150	$155	$210	35%
Style B	198	195	275	40
Style C	83	77	130	30
Style D	275	280	290	30
Style E	420	430	450	20

Required:

Determine the appropriate inventory value to use for each item in the company's December 31, 2014, inventory under U.S. GAAP.

P9-17

Applying lower of cost or market (LCM) under IFRS
(LO 11, 12)

Refer to the facts in Problem 9-16. Repeat the requirements using IFRS instead of U.S. GAAP.

Presented below are excerpts from the 2009 annual report of Daimler AG, a German company that manufactures luxury automobiles.

Inventories. Inventories are measured at the lower of cost and net realizable value. The net realizable value is the estimated selling price less any remaining costs to sell. The cost of inventories is based on the average cost principle and includes expenditures incurred in acquiring the inventories and bringing them to their existing location and condition. In the case of manufactured inventories and work in progress, cost also includes production overheads based on normal capacity.

16. Inventories

(in millions of €)	At December 31,	
	2009	**2008**
Raw materials and manufacturing supplies	1,517	1,725
Work-in-process	1,626	1,880
Finished goods, parts, and products held for resale	9,666	13,066
Advance payments to suppliers	36	134
	12,845	16,805

The amount of write-down of inventories to net realizable value recognized as expense in cost of sales was €299 million in 2009 (2008: €245 million; 2007: €111 million). The reversals of write-down on inventories were €7 million in 2009 (2008: €5 million; 2007: €12 million). At December 31, 2009, €1,482 million (2008: €1,894 million) of the total inventories were carried at net realizable value. Inventories that are expected to be turned over after more than 12 months amounted to €634 million at December 31, 2009 (2008: €583 million), and are primarily spare parts.

Based on the requirement to provide collateral for certain vested employee benefits in Germany, the value of company cars included in inventories at Daimler AG in an amount of €457 million (2008: €464 million) was pledged as collateral to the Daimler Pension Trust e.V.

The carrying amount of inventories recognized during the period by taking possession of collateral held as security amounted to €136 million in 2009 (2008: €102 million). The utilization of these assets occurs in the context of normal business cycle.

Required:

Using the Daimler note, identify the similarities and differrences between U.S. GAAP and IFRS regarding inventory accounting.

The following inventory note appears in General Electric's Year 3 annual report.

General Electric Company

Edited Inventory Note

($ in millions)	December 31	
	Year 3	**Year 2**
Raw materials and work in process	$4,894	$4,708
Finished goods	4,379	3,951
Unbilled shipments	372	312
	9,645	8,971
Less revaluation to LIFO	(606)	(676)
	$9,039	$8,295

LIFO revaluations decreased $70 million in Year 3, compared with decreases of $169 million in Year 2 and $82 million in Year 1. Included in these changes were decreases of $21 million, $8 million, and $6 million in Year 3, Year 2, and Year 1, respectively, that resulted from lower LIFO inventory levels. There were net cost decreases in each of the last three years.

GE's earnings before income taxes were $18.891 billion in Year 3. Assume a 35% marginal tax rate.

Required:

1. What are the total cumulative tax savings as of December 31, Year 3 that GE has realized as a result of using the LIFO inventory method?

2. What would GE's pre-tax earnings have been in Year 3 if it had been using FIFO?

3. What December 31, Year 3 balance sheet figures would be different—and by how much—if GE had used FIFO to account for its inventories?

4. What were the LIFO liquidation profits reported in Year 3 both pre-tax and after-tax?

5. Explain what factors cause the difference between the LIFO pre-tax income number and the FIFO pre-tax income number you estimated in requirement 2. (*Hint:* Reconcile the change in the LIFO reserve for Year 3.)

C9-3

ExxonMobil: Interpreting a
LIFO note   **(LO 6, 8)**

The following information related to ExxonMobil's inventories is taken from the company's 2009 annual report. You are to use this information in answering the questions that follow.

Inventories. Crude oil, products and merchandise inventories are carried at the lower of current market value or cost (generally determined under the last-in, first-out method—LIFO). Inventory costs include expenditures and other charges (including depreciation) directly and indirectly incurred in bringing the inventory to its existing condition and location. Selling expenses and general and administrative expenses are reported as period costs and excluded from inventory cost. Inventories of materials and supplies are valued at cost or less.

In 2009, 2008, and 2007, net income included gains of $207 million, $341 million, and $327 million, respectively, attributable to the combined effects of LIFO inventory accumulations and draw-downs. The aggregate replacement cost of inventories was estimated to exceed their LIFO carrying values by $17.1 billion and $10.0 billion at December 31, 2009 and 2008, respectively.

Crude oil, products and merchandise as of year-end 2009 and 2008 consist of the following:

(billions of dollars)	**2009**	**2008**
Petroleum products	$3.2	$3.7
Crude oil	3.2	3.1
Chemical products	2.0	2.2
Gas/other	0.3	0.3
Total	$8.7	$9.3

Required:

1. By how much would net income for 2009 have differed had ExxonMobil used FIFO to value those inventory items valued under LIFO? Assume a 35% marginal tax rate. Be sure to indicate whether FIFO income would be higher or lower than LIFO income.

2. What would the LIFO reserve have been on December 31, 2009, if no LIFO liquidation had occurred in 2009?

3. What was the net difference in 2009 income taxes that ExxonMobil experienced as a result of using LIFO rather than FIFO? Assume a 35% tax rate and indicate whether FIFO or LIFO would yield the higher tax and by how much.

4. What was the approximate rate of change in input costs in 2009 for ExxonMobil's inventory?

Baines Corporation manufactures fireplace tools and accessories. It has been prosperous since its incorporation in 1980, largely due to a small, exceptionally skilled, and highly motivated managerial staff. Baines has been able to attract and retain its excellent management team because of a very attractive managerial incentive plan. The plan allocates 23% of total pre-tax FIFO-absorption cost profits into a pool that is distributed to managers as a year-end bonus. The bonus pool is allocated to individual managers using a point system based on each manager's performance relative to a budgeted goal.

C9-4

Baines Corporation: Using absorption versus variable costing **(LO 4)**

mhhe.com/revsine6e

Data relating to 2013 operations follow:

Beginning inventory	1,500,000 units @ $2.95
Ending inventory	1,500,000 units @ $2.95
Production	4,000,000 units
Sales	4,000,000 units @ $3.50
Variable production costs	$1.45/unit
Fixed production costs	$6,000,000/year

Reported pre-tax profit for 2013 was:

Sales revenues	(4,000,000 @ $3.50)		$14,000,000
Costs of goods sold			
Variable production costs	(4,000,000 @ $1.45)	$5,800,000	
Fixed production costs	(4,000,000 @ $1.50)	6,000,000	
			11,800,000
Operating profit			2,200,000
Interest expense			200,000
Pre-tax profit			$ 2,000,000

Early in 2014, interest rates increased, and the company's president, Ross Eldred, was concerned about the rising cost of financing the inventory. After a careful study of the situation, he became convinced that inventory levels could be reduced considerably without adversely affecting sales or delivery performance provided certain changes in purchasing, production, and sales procedures were adopted. Accordingly, Eldred called a meeting of the management group in February 2014 and outlined his multifaceted plan for reducing inventories.

His basic strategy was immediately accepted, and several participants suggested various additional efficiencies and other inventory management improvements. The meeting adjourned with each manager resolving to do all that was possible to decrease inventory levels and thereby reduce interest expense.

As the year progressed, Eldred's proposals and the refinements suggested by the other managers were put into practice; as a result, inventory levels were significantly reduced by December 31, 2014. The managers were quite pleased with their successful implementation of the new strategy, and morale was quite high.

Basic facts concerning 2014 performance were as follows:

Beginning inventory	1,500,000 units @ $2.95
Ending inventory	700,000 units @ $3.325
Production	3,200,000 units
Sales	4,000,000 units @ $3.50
Variable production costs	$1.45/unit
Fixed production costs	$6,000,000/year
Interest expense	$100,000/year

Shortly after the final 2014 profit figures were reported early in 2015, a general management meeting was held. As he walked into the room, Eldred was somewhat surprised to see a rather sullen and dispirited group of managers confronting him. One was heard to mumble, "Well, I wonder what this year's double cross will be!"

Required:

1. What do you think caused the abrupt change in the mood of the management team at Baines Corporation? Cite figures to support your explanation.

2. How might this problem have been prevented? Cite figures to support your explanation.

C9-5

Consequences of IFRS adoption in the U.S.
(LO 5, 8, 12)

For several years, the Securities and Exchange Commission (SEC) has been considering whether to transition U.S. firms to International Financial Reporting Standards (IFRS) for filing public financial reports.

During 2011, Matthew J. Foehr, the vice president and comptroller for Chevron Corporation, sent comment letters to both the Securities and Exchange Commission (SEC) and the International Accounting Standards Board (IASB), stating, "Chevron would object to any plan to incorporate IFRS into U.S. GAAP if it would result in a significant income-tax penalty for our company."[37]

In its 2012 Annual Report, Chevron reports:

Inventories

Crude oil, petroleum products and chemicals inventories are generally stated at cost, using a last-in, first-out method. In the aggregate, these costs are below market. "Materials, supplies and other" inventories generally are stated at average cost.

Required:

1. Why might Mr. Foehr be concerned that IFRS would trigger a "significant income-tax penalty" for Chevron?

2. Comment letters and business press articles that discuss LIFO inventory method issues with IFRS transition suggest that these potential problems could be addressed or fixed by any of the following agencies: U.S. Congress, SEC, or the IASB. Explain what type of actions each of these bodies might take to remedy concerns like the one posed by Mr. Foehr.

www .mhhe.com/revsine6e

**Remember to check the book's companion website
for additional study material.**

---

[37] Matthew J. Foehr letter to the SEC, dated August 1, 2011 (http://www.sec.gov/comments/4-600/4600-123.pdf) and Matthew J. Foehr letter to the IASB, dated November 14, 2011 (http://www.ifrs.org/Current-Projects/IASB-Projects/IASB-agenda-consultation/agenda-consultation-2011/comment-letters/Documents/ChevronCorporatiionCommentLetterIASBWork PlanAgenda20122014.pdf).

Long-Lived Assets | 10

A n asset is something that generates future economic benefits and is under the exclusive control of a single entity. Assets can be tangible items such as inventories and buildings or intangible items such as patents and trademarks.

The previous two chapters—on receivables and inventories—examined current assets. Current assets represent a large part of total assets for many companies. Recall that a current asset is expected to be converted into cash within one year or within the operating cycle, whichever is longer.

This chapter concentrates on operating assets expected to yield their economic benefits (or service potential) over a period longer than one year. Such assets are called **long-lived assets.**

Long-lived assets represent a significant percentage of total assets in industries such as oil exploration and refining, automobile manufacturing, and steel. Exhibit 10.1 shows the asset portion of Exxon Mobil Corporation's balance sheet in both dollar and common-size terms at December 31, 2012. Notice that long-lived assets (Property, plant, and equipment) comprise 68.0% of total assets. Firms have latitude in how much detail they provide about separate long-lived asset components. ExxonMobil chose to provide a note breakdown of the total properties by industry segment (see Exhibit 10.2). Notice that the highlighted net properties total from Exhibit 10.1 ($226,949 million) appears again in Exhibit 10.2. Statement readers can then see the breakdown of gross and net property, plant, and equipment across industry segments.

> The *operating cycle* for a manufacturer begins with the receipt of raw materials inventory and ends when cash is received for the completed product that has been sold. If inventory turns over every 90 days and if the average receivables collection period is 50 days, then the operating cycle is 140 days (that is, 90 + 50).

Clearly, there's a high proportion of long-lived assets in some industries. However, there are many issues that complicate the accounting for long-lived assets, and we will see why next.

LEARNING OBJECTIVES

After studying this chapter, you will understand:

1. What measurement basis is used in accounting for long-lived assets and why this base is used.

2. What specific costs can be capitalized and how joint costs are allocated among assets.

3. How generally accepted accounting principles (GAAP) measurement rules can complicate both trend analysis and cross-company analysis and how to avoid misinterpretations.

4. Why balance sheet carrying amounts for internally developed intangibles usually differ from their real values.

5. When long-lived asset impairment exists and how it is recorded.

6. How to account for asset retirement obligations and assets held for sale.

7. How different depreciation methods are computed.

8. How analysts can adjust for different depreciation assumptions and improve interfirm comparisons.

9. How to account for exchanges of long-lived assets.

10. The key differences between GAAP and IFRS requirements for long-lived asset accounting.

EXHIBIT 10.1 — **Exxon Mobil Corporation: Partial Consolidated Statement of Financial Position—December 31, 2012**

($ in millions)		Percentage
Assets		
Cash and cash equivalents	$ 9,923	
Accounts and notes receivable, net	34,987	
Inventories	14,542	
Other current assets	5,008	
Total current assets	64,460	19.3%
Investments, advances, and long-term receivables	34,718	10.4
Property, plant, and equipment (net)	226,949	68.0
Other assets, including intangibles, net	7,668	2.3
Total	$333,795	100.0%

Source: Exxon Mobil Corporation 2012 annual report.

EXHIBIT 10.2 — **Exxon Mobil Corporation: Property, Plant, and Equipment Disclosure—December 31, 2012**

($ in millions)	Cost	Net
Upstream	$313,181	$181,795
Downstream	53,737	23,053
Chemical	29,437	14,085
Other	12,959	8,016
	$409,314	$226,949

Source: Exxon Mobil Corporation 2012 annual report.

MEASUREMENT OF THE CARRYING AMOUNT OF LONG-LIVED ASSETS

Long-lived assets could potentially be measured on balance sheets in two ways:

1. Assets could be measured at their estimated value in an *output* market—a market where assets are *sold.* We call measures that use output market numbers **expected benefit approaches.**

2. Assets could be measured at their estimated cost in an *input* market—a market where assets are *purchased.* Measures that use input market costs are called **economic sacrifice approaches.**

Expected benefit approaches recognize that assets are valuable because of the *future cash inflows* they are expected to generate. Consequently, these approaches measure various definitions of future cash inflows that are expected to be generated by the asset. One example of an expected benefit approach is **discounted present value.** Under it, the value of an item of manufacturing equipment is measured by estimating the discounted present value of the stream of future net operating cash inflows it's expected to generate over its operating life. Another example of an expected benefit approach is the cash inflow that the asset would bring if it were sold instead of being used in operations. Under this variant of the expected benefit approach, long-lived assets are reported at their **net realizable value**—the amount that would be received if the assets were sold in the used asset market. Under both approaches, the income statement effect is the change in the value of the asset.

Economic sacrifice approaches to asset measurement focus on the amount of resource expenditure necessary to acquire it. One example of an economic sacrifice approach is **historical cost** (the dominant GAAP measurement method)—that is, the historical amount spent to buy the asset constitutes the *past* sacrifice incurred to bring the asset into the firm. Another example of an economic sacrifice approach involves measuring the current (or replacement) cost of the asset. Under a **replacement cost** (sometimes called **current cost**) approach, assets are carried at their current purchase cost—the expenditure (sacrifice) needed *today* to buy the asset. Under both of these approaches, depreciation expense is recognized on the income statement. However, under replacement cost, a firm also recognizes in other comprehensive income holding gains (losses) for increases (decreases) in replacement costs. Depreciation expense is then based on the revised replacement cost amounts.[1]

The Approach Used by GAAP

Exhibit 10.3 shows a hypothetical range of long-lived asset carrying amounts as measured under each approach—expected benefit versus economic sacrifice. Assume that the fixed asset is a truck used by a freight hauler to transport heavy industrial equipment. Let's say the

EXHIBIT 10.3	**Hypothetical Long-Lived Asset Carrying Amounts (10-year life, 8 years remaining)**

Expected Benefit Approach Examples

1. Discounted present value:

   Expected net operating cash inflows = $16,275 per year (assumed) for eight remaining years, discounted at a 10% (assumed) rate

$$5.33493^* \times \$16,275 = \$86,826$$

2. Net realizable value:

   Current resale price from an over-the-road equipment listing (Purple Book) for the specific vehicle model

$$\$85,000 \text{ (assumed)}$$

Economic Sacrifice Approach Examples

3. Replacement cost:

   Replacement cost of a two-year-old vehicle in equivalent condition

$$\$130,000 \text{ (assumed)} - \left(\frac{\$130,000}{10 \text{ years}} \times 2 \text{ years} \right) = \$104,000$$

4. Historical cost less accumulated depreciation:

$$\$100,000 - \left(\frac{\$100,000}{10 \text{ years}} \times 2 \text{ years} \right) = \$80,000$$

---

* Discount factor for an ordinary annuity for eight years at 10%. See "Present Value of an Ordinary Annuity of $1" table in end-of-book appendix.

---

[1] This is analogous to the replacement cost discussion for inventory. We discuss replacement cost accounting in detail in the web appendix for this chapter. See **www.mhhe.com/revsine6e.**

truck originally cost $100,000, is two years old, has a remaining useful life of eight years, is being depreciated straight-line, and is expected to have no salvage value (fair value) at the end of its useful life.

U.S. GAAP uses historical cost—an economic sacrifice approach—to measure long-lived assets in most circumstances. The choice of historical cost is not an accident. It results from several pragmatic aspects of the existing financial reporting environment.

Contracting

As discussed in Chapter 1, financial reports play a critical role in resource allocation decisions such as equity investing and lending. Accounting numbers are widely used in contracts such as loan agreements, incentive compensation plans, and union contracts (see Chapter 7). Because of these uses, parties whose transactions are explicitly or implicitly tied to accounting numbers expect them to be **neutral (unbiased)** and **free from error** (accurate). Recall from Chapter 1 that these characteristics are ingredients of **faithful representation.**[2] If the numbers are easily manipulated or inaccurate, then cautious decision makers would be reluctant to enter into contracts using such "soft" numbers. The reason is that manipulation by one party could circumvent the contract terms. In addition, contracting parties desire timely and cost effective accounting so that contracts can be monitored and enforced.

Auditors also prefer that financial statement numbers have certain characteristics. One is that the numbers be verifiable. **Verifiability** means the numbers should arise from readily observable, corroborative facts rather than from subjective beliefs. Verifiable numbers are important to auditors because of the many lawsuits arising from audited financial statements. Auditors believe that verifiable data help provide a defense in court, reducing potential litigation losses.

As modern financial reporting evolved, neutrality, accuracy, verifiability, timeliness, and cost were used as guidelines for selecting acceptable long-lived asset measurement rules. Expected benefit approaches, such as discounted present value reporting, were not adopted because the resulting numbers were deemed subject to manipulation, inaccurate, and not verifiable. The present value computations require inherently subjective forecasts of future net cash flows as well as an assumed discount rate. This is illustrated in Exhibit 10.3 where alternative 1—the discounted present value/expected benefit approach—requires an estimate of expected net operating cash inflows ($16,275) and a choice of discount rate (10%). Most decision makers would not tie contracts to such numbers because the other party to the contract could easily evade accounting-based contract terms by simply altering the cash flow forecast amounts or the discount rate.

Another expected benefit approach—the net realizable value from selling the asset (alternative 2)—has also been rejected as a measurement base because of verifiability, accuracy, and cost concerns. Our example in Exhibit 10.3 assumes that the long-lived asset had a readily observable market price, as some do. However, many long-lived assets such as buildings are immobile, and others are highly specialized and therefore traded in thin markets. Consequently, selling prices are often not readily determinable. The current selling price for these long-lived assets needs to be estimated using past transaction prices or transactions involving similar (but not necessarily identical) assets. In addition, one would have to consider how to aggregate the assets. Should each asset be priced separately, or should synergies among assets be considered? Estimation procedures

Although U.S. GAAP does not allow present value accounting, Sheraton Corporation of America provided pro forma present value amounts for long-lived assets as early as 1967. Management believed that these values were more relevant and representationally faithful than the amounts provided under historical cost, in part, because of increased land values and rental and room rates.

See S. Zeff and T. Keller, *Financial Accounting Theory I: Issues and Controversies,* 2nd Ed. (New York: McGraw-Hill, 1973).

---

[2] For full explanations of the theoretical terms used in this discussion, see FASB Statement of Financial Accounting Concepts No. 8, Conceptual Framework for Financial Reporting, Chapter 1, *The Objective of General Purpose Financial Reporting* and Chapter 3, *Qualitative Characteristics of Useful Financial Information* (Norwalk, CT: FASB, 2010).

may be verifiable, but the amounts themselves may not be. Use of independent appraisals adds to the cost of financial reporting and reduces the timeliness of the information.

The economic sacrifice approach that uses replacement cost—that is, the estimated current cost of *replacing* the asset (alternative 3)—has also been disqualified on the basis of concerns similar to those expressed for net realizable values.

Because of the practical considerations discussed above, historical cost (less accumulated depreciation) has become the primary method for reporting long-lived assets in the United States. However, it also can have serious limitations. First, depreciation is an allocation of historical cost to time periods. Except by coincidence, the net book value amount at a point in time—original cost less accumulated depreciation—does not reflect the expected benefit of the asset. Long-lived assets typically last for many years, and the expected benefits might increase rather than decrease. U.S. GAAP prohibits upward adjustments to long-lived assets. Second, because the financial statements do not reflect replacement costs or present values, analysts may have difficulty making meaningful comparisons of old firms to new firms in the same industry or comparing firms across industries. This problem is exacerbated if a firm does not modernize and innovate. Under historical cost, the return-on-asset ratio increases as the book value of the asset declines from depreciation.

The analyst must monitor company capital expenditures and the average age of assets to determine whether the company is maintaining its productive capacity. We discuss these and other limitations throughout the chapter.

Although historical cost is the primary method of accounting for long-lived assets in the United States, we see the use of the expected benefits approaches in some situations. The most common setting is when management suspects that the expected benefits of an asset are below its book value. In such situations, because of **conservatism**, accountants are willing to accept the costs and limitations associated with the present value and net realizable value methods. We discuss impairment issues in detail later in the chapter.

> One would not have this issue with present value accounting. (Though, we would have the practical problems mentioned above.) Under present value accounting, the asset would decrease as the present value of the expected cash flows declines. In our example, the depreciation in Year 2 would have been $6,902, which is the difference between the present value at the end of Year 2 of $86,826 (item 1 in Exhibit 10.3) and the present value at the end of Year 1 of $93,728 ($16,275 × the present value of an ordinary annuity for 9 periods and 10%, or 5.75902). Note that this depreciation expense is lower than the $10,000 straight-line annual depreciation expense. *Consequently, the book value of the asset is higher than historical cost with straight-line depreciation.* Traditionally, accountants and regulators have sought conservative accounting, which may be another reason that historical cost was selected over the expected benefit approaches. P10-20 compares the effects of present value and straight-line depreciation in detail.

RECAP

Because long-lived assets are predominantly carried at depreciated historical cost, statement users should not expect balance sheet numbers for such assets to necessarily approximate their real economic worth. This is a limitation (with important implications for statement users) that we explore throughout the chapter.

LONG-LIVED ASSET MEASUREMENT RULES ILLUSTRATED

The initial balance sheet carrying amount of a long-lived asset is governed by two rules:

1. All costs necessary to acquire the asset and make it ready for use are included in the asset account. Costs included in the asset account are called **capitalized costs.** (Expenditures excluded from asset categories are "charged-off" to income—that is, expensed.)
2. **Joint costs** incurred in acquiring more than one asset are apportioned among the acquired assets on a relative fair value basis or some other rational basis.

Both rules are illustrated in the Canyon Corporation example that follows in Exhibit 10.4.

Capitalized land costs include many items in addition to the $6,000,000 cash payment. For example, the cost of demolishing (razing) the existing structure (net of salvaged materials) is added to the land account because the land had to be cleared before the new building could be

EXHIBIT 10.4	Canyon Corporation: Joint Cost Allocation, Fixed Asset Purchase

Canyon Corporation acquired a tract of land on June 1, 2014, by paying $6,000,000 and by assuming an existing mortgage of $1,000,000 on the land. Canyon demolished an empty structure on the property at a cost of $650,000. Bricks and other materials from the demolished building were sold for $10,000. Regrading and clearing the land cost $35,000. Canyon then began constructing a new factory on the site. Architectural fees were $800,000, and the payments to contractors for building the factory totaled $12,000,000. Canyon negotiated a bank loan to help ease the cash flow crunch during construction. Interest payments over the construction period totaled $715,000. Legal fees incurred in the transaction totaled $57,000, of which $17,000 was attributable to both examination of title covering the land purchase and legal issues linked to the assumption of the existing mortgage. The remaining $40,000 of legal fees related to contracts with the architect and the construction companies. The construction project was completed on December 31, 2014.

The amounts allocated to the land and building accounts, respectively, are:

Land

Cash payment		$ 6,000,000
Mortgage assumed		1,000,000
Demolition of existing structure	$650,000	
Less: Salvage value of material	(10,000)	
		640,000
Regrading and clearing land		35,000
Legal fees allocated		17,000
Capitalized land costs		**$ 7,692,000**

Building

Architectural fees	$ 800,000
Building costs	12,000,000
Interest capitalized	715,000
Legal fees allocated	40,000
Capitalized building costs	**$13,555,000**

erected. This illustrates initial carrying amount Rule 1—all costs necessary to prepare the asset for its intended use are capitalized—here as land costs. The legal fees illustrate Rule 2—joint costs are apportioned among assets to both the land and building in this case. It is important to distinguish the amounts allocated to the land from the amounts allocated to the building because land is not depreciated whereas a building is depreciated over its expected useful life.

The costs allocated to the building include the interest arising from the loan that Canyon negotiated to finance construction. GAAP requires capitalizing what are called **avoidable interest** payments. Authoritative accounting literature defines this as interest that "could have been avoided . . . if expenditures for the assets had not been made."[3] To qualify as avoidable interest, the interest doesn't have to arise from borrowing that is directly linked to a construction loan. So long as some debt was outstanding during the construction period, a portion of the interest was avoidable and qualifies for capitalization. Here's why. Building the asset required spending cash. *If the asset had not been built, that cash could have been used to retire debt, thereby lowering*

Apportionment is also necessary when more than one asset is acquired for a lump-sum price. Assume that two tracts of land are acquired for $1,000,000. For property tax purposes, the land tracts are assessed as follows:

	Assessment	Percentage
Tract 1	$240,000	40%
Tract 2	360,000	60%
Total	$600,000	100%

The $1,000,000 purchase price is then apportioned between the tracts in proportion to their assessed value—40% to Tract 1 and 60% to Tract 2.

---

[3] FASB Accounting Standards Codification (ASC) Paragraph 835-20-30-2: Interest—Capitalization of Interest—Initial Measurement—The Amount of Interest Cost to Be Capitalized.

interest costs. This is why the interest is *avoidable,* and this is why the capitalized interest doesn't have to arise from a dedicated construction loan. Capitalizing interest is another application of Rule 1—interest paid to lenders during the construction period is considered to be a cost necessary to prepare the asset for its intended use.

Interest can also be capitalized for borrowings that are outstanding when the assets are being constructed for others—that is, for inventory intended for sale or lease. To qualify for interest capitalization, the inventory being constructed must be an identifiable, discrete project (a three-year contract to construct two aircraft carriers for the Navy is an example).

Computing Avoidable Interest   Avoidable interest is the product of cumulative weighted average expenditures on the constructed asset times the interest rate. Let's first illustrate the computation of cumulative weighted average expenditures. The computation measures the timing of the dollar expenditures over the construction period. The earlier in the period the expenditure takes place, the more days that the expenditure needs to be financed—and the more interest is incurred. For example, assume that expenditures of $1,000,000 are incurred evenly over the 2014 year that construction took place. Here, cumulative weighted average expenditures are simply $1,000,000/2 = $500,000.

To illustrate the computation when construction expenditures do not take place evenly, assume the following timing of expenditures in Exhibit 10.4 on Canyon's construction project completed on December 31:

Date and Amount			Portion of Year		Cumulative Weighted Average Expenditures
June 1	$10,000,000	×	58.630%*	=	$5,863,000
August 22	3,558,788	×	36.164%†	=	1,287,000
					$7,150,000

---

* June 1 through December 31 = 214 days, and 214/365 = 58.630% of a year.

† August 22 through December 31 = 132 days, and 132/365 = 36.164% of a year (rounded).

Assuming a 10% interest rate on the outstanding debt, avoidable interest is $715,000 (10% × $7,150,000).[4]

DR	Construction in progress	$715,000	
	CR Interest expense		$715,000

If construction projects extend past one year, then the cumulative expenditures to date are assumed to have been made as of the beginning of the second reporting year. For example, if Canyon's project had not been completed by the end of the first year, the second year would have begun with cumulative expenditures of $14,273,788 ($10,000,000 + $3,558,788 + $715,000).

GAAP limits the amount of interest that can be capitalized to the *lower* of (1) interest actually incurred or (2) avoidable interest. If Canyon's interest actually incurred had been

---

[4] FASB ASC Paragraph 835-20-30: Interest—Capitalization of Interest—Initial measurement—The Amount of Interest to be Capitalized allows firms to use the interest rate on specific debt associated with the construction up to the amount of the specific debt. For additional accumulated expenditures, the company would use the average rate of its other debt, computed as interest expense on the other interest-bearing debt divided by the average other debt outstanding. A company may use a weighted average rate to compute all of its avoidable interest.

As discussed in Chapter 15, GAAP utilizes what is called the *proprietary view of the firm*. The proprietary view deems the firm and its owners to be indistinguishable. Consequently, funds contributed by owners do not come from "outsiders." *The firm can't charge itself interest on contributed ownership capital.*

$800,000, the capitalized amount would be limited to avoidable interest, $715,000. If interest actually incurred was only $600,000, then just $600,000 would be capitalized.

However, *capitalization is restricted to interest arising from actual borrowings from outsiders.* To see the financial statement effect of this restriction, let's assume that Canyon had not borrowed from a bank but had instead issued more common stock and used the proceeds to finance construction. Also assume that Canyon had absolutely no interest-bearing debt outstanding. Equity funds are not "free"—stockholders expect to earn a return and will replace management if it doesn't materialize! Despite this, GAAP does not allow Canyon to calculate an artificial interest charge on the equity financing and capitalize this "imputed interest" as a part of the cost of the building. *So, the way the construction is financed can alter the cost capitalized under GAAP when a company initially has no outstanding debt.*

Treating equity that is issued to finance construction as "free" (when there is no interest-bearing debt outstanding) is consistent with the traditional accounting model. That is, GAAP does not recognize the imputed cost associated with capital provided by stockholders. These funds are treated as if they are free. So, the cost of equity capital is ignored under GAAP in both income determination and asset costing.

 **Analysis**

Interest capitalization can complicate the analysis of firm performance over time. Because of interest capitalization, an increase in capital expenditures can temporarily decrease the amount of interest *expense* shown on the income statement and—all other factors being equal—increase income (or partially offset an income decrease). But this change in the income pattern does not result from increased sales, lower costs, or other operating efficiencies. Consequently, the year-to-year profit change is partially unrelated to operating activities and may not be sustainable. Exhibit 10.5 shows an excerpt from the Management's Discussion

---

EXHIBIT 10.5   **MGM Resorts International: Interest Capitalization**

The following table summarizes information related to interest on our long-term debt:

($ in thousands)	Year Ended December 31,		
	2009	**2008**	**2007**
Year Ended December 31,			
Total interest incurred	$ 997,897	$ 773,662	$ 930,138
Interest capitalized	(222,466)	(164,376)	(215,951)
Interest allocated to discontinued operations	—	—	(5,844)
	$ 775,431	$ 609,286	$ 708,343

In 2009, gross interest costs increased compared to 2008 mainly due to higher average debt balances during 2009, higher interest rates for borrowings under our senior credit facility in 2009, higher interest rates for newly issued fixed rate borrowings, as well as breakage fees for voluntary repayments of our revolving credit facility. In 2008, gross interest costs decreased compared to 2007 mainly due to lower interest rates on our variable rate.

Capitalized interest increased in 2009 due to higher CityCenter investment balances and higher weighted average cost of debt. Capitalized interest decreased in 2008 compared to 2007 due to less capitalized interest on CityCenter and cessation of capitalized interest related to our investment in MGM Grand Macau upon opening in December 2007. The amounts presented above exclude non-cash gross interest and corresponding capitalized interest related to our CityCenter delayed equity contribution.

Source: MGM MIRAGE 2009 annual report.

and Analysis section of the 2009 annual report of MGM Resorts International (formerly named MGM MIRAGE), which owns and operates casino resorts. This disclosure will help us see how interest capitalization can alter year-to-year profit assessments.

Exhibit 10.5 shows that capitalized interest increased from $164.4 million in 2008 to $222.5 in 2009, or 35%. The note also states that the amount of capitalized interest increased because of the higher cumulative construction costs associated with CityCenter (a new Las Vegas resort) and a higher weighted average interest rate. Given that the CityCenter project was finished in 2009 (stated elsewhere in the annual report), we would not expect as much capitalized interest in 2010, and in fact, there was zero interest capitalized in that year. Because MGM Resorts International will still have a similar amount of debt, we expect 2010 interest expense to increase and net income to decrease, which they did. By capitalizing interest, relevant costs are assigned to specific long-lived assets, but the practice makes year-to-year income changes in net income a function of changes in *both* operating performance and levels of capital expenditures. This complicates the analysis of earnings sustainability.

Tax versus Financial Reporting Incentives   The way incurred costs are allocated between land and building affects the amount of income that will be reported in future periods. Land is a permanent or nonwasting asset, so it's not depreciated. A factory building has a finite life and *is* depreciated over future years. For *financial reporting purposes,* the manner in which costs are allocated between, say, land and building, is guided by which one (land or building) generated the cost.

For *tax purposes,* the incentives for allocating costs between land and building asset categories are completely different because the objective of most firms is to minimize tax payments, not to "correctly" allocate costs. The higher the costs allocated to land for tax purposes, the *higher* the future taxable income becomes because land cannot be depreciated. Aggressive taxpayers seek to minimize the amount of joint expenditures allocated to nondepreciable assets such as land. Similarly, taxpayers would prefer not to capitalize interest payments for tax purposes because the benefits of the deduction would be spread over the depreciable life of the asset rather than being deductible immediately. However, U.S. income tax rules generally parallel financial reporting rules and *require* cost allocations between land and buildings that are similar to U.S. GAAP rules. The same is true for interest capitalization—U.S. tax rules closely parallel GAAP rules and therefore require avoidable interest to be capitalized for tax purposes.

Capitalization Criteria—An Extension   Businesses frequently upgrade their long-lived assets to increase their usefulness. For example, a trucking company might install new motors in its older vehicles. GAAP capitalizes such expenditures—that is, increases the carrying amount of a long-lived asset—when the expenditure causes *any* of the following conditions:

• The useful life of the asset is extended.
• The capacity of the asset is increased (that is, when attainable units of output increases).
• The efficiency of the asset is increased (that is, when fewer labor hours or raw material inputs are required).
• There is any other type of increase in the economic benefits (or future service potential) of the asset that results as a consequence of the expenditure.

EXHIBIT 10.6	**Winger Enterprises: Determination of Capitalized Costs**

On January 1, 2014, Winger Enterprises purchased a machine that will be used in operations. Its cash purchase price was $80,000. The freight cost to transport the machine to Winger's factory was $1,200. During the month of January 2014, Winger's employees spent considerable time calibrating the machine and making adjustments and test runs to get it ready for use. Costs incurred in doing this were:

Allocated portion of production manager's salary for coordinating machine adjustments	$2,200
Hourly wages of production workers engaged in test runs of the machine	3,600
Cost of raw materials that were used in test runs (the output was not salable)	1,500

Given these facts, on January 1, 2014, the capitalized amount of the machine would be the total of all of the costs ($80,000 + $1,200 + $2,200 + $3,600 + $1,500 = $88,500).

When the expenditure does not meet any of these conditions, it must be treated as a period expense and be charged to income. Routine equipment maintenance is one example.

To illustrate how these capitalization criteria work, consider the example in Exhibit 10.6. In it, total expenditures that are capitalized—that is, those that are included in the carrying amount of the machine—include *all* of the highlighted costs ($88,500) associated with getting the machine ready for production use, not just the invoice cost of $80,000.

To further illustrate the capitalization criteria, lets jump forward in time. Suppose that in January 2017, Winger spends an additional $8,000 on the machine. The total expenditure consisted of:

- $2,000 for ordinary repairs and maintenance, required every several years.

- $6,000 for the installation of a new component that allowed the machine to consume less raw material and operate more efficiently.

In this example, the $2,000 would be treated as a period expense while the $6,000 would be capitalized in 2017 and added to the carrying amount of the machine because it increases the asset's efficiency.

Executives of WorldCom, once the leading telecommunications company in the United States, were convicted of deliberately misapplying the asset capitalization rules to boost reported pre-tax income by approximately $3.8 billion over five quarters in 2001 and 2002.[5] WorldCom's method was simple. Normal operating costs of connecting to other firm's telecommunications lines—clearly period expenses—were instead capitalized. Because these items (called *line costs*) were debited to balance sheet asset accounts rather than charged to income statement expenses, income was overstated. The motive for this misrepresentation was to hide WorldCom's inherent unprofitability due to excess industry capacity. So, a failure to correctly apply the capitalization criteria resulted in an enormous income misstatement (see Figure 10.1).

---

[5] See J. Sandberg, D. Solomon, and R. Blumenstein, "Inside WorldCom's Unearthing of a Vast Accounting Scandal," *The Wall Street Journal,* June 27, 2002, and K. Eichenwald and S. Romero, "Inquiry Finds Effort at Delay at WorldCom," *The New York Times,* July 4, 2002.

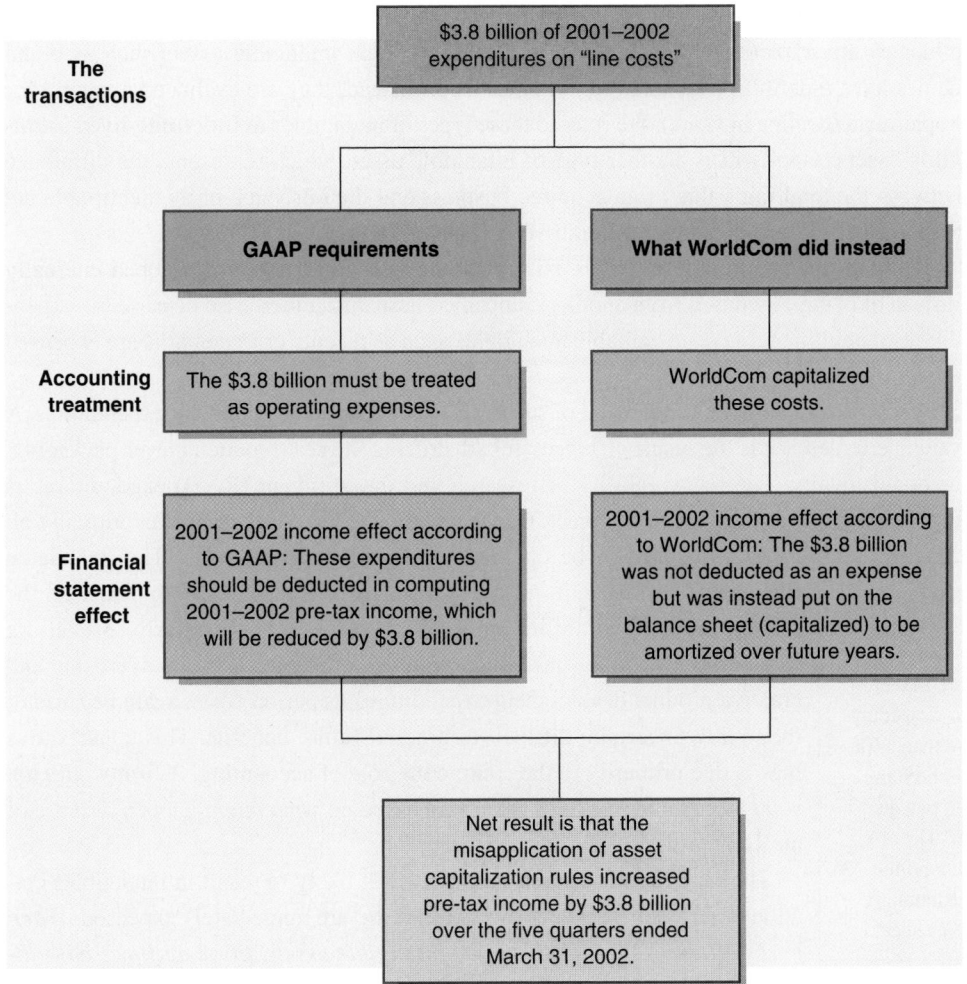

The transactions

$3.8 billion of 2001–2002 expenditures on "line costs"

GAAP requirements

What WorldCom did instead

Accounting treatment

The $3.8 billion must be treated as operating expenses.

WorldCom capitalized these costs.

Financial statement effect

2001–2002 income effect according to GAAP: These expenditures should be deducted in computing 2001–2002 pre-tax income, which will be reduced by $3.8 billion.

2001–2002 income effect according to WorldCom: The $3.8 billion was not deducted as an expense but was instead put on the balance sheet (capitalized) to be amortized over future years.

Net result is that the misapplication of asset capitalization rules increased pre-tax income by $3.8 billion over the five quarters ended March 31, 2002.

Figure 10.1

IMPACT OF WORLDCOM'S MISAPPLICATION OF ASSET CAPITALIZATION RULES

INTANGIBLE ASSETS

Intangible assets are long-lived assets that do not have physical substance. The category includes the following types of assets:

- Patents
- Copyrights
- Trademarks
- Brand names
- Customer lists
- Licenses
- Technology
- Franchises
- Employment contracts

When one firm purchases an intangible asset—for example, a valuable trademark—from another firm, few new accounting or reporting issues arise. The acquired intangible asset is recorded at the arm's-length transaction price. If the intangible asset is purchased with other assets, then the purchase price must be allocated among assets based on relative fair values as shown on pages 550–551. Most acquired intangible assets are amortized (depreciated) over their expected useful lives (discussed in more detail later in the chapter). We refer to these intangibles as **amortizable intangible assets.** However, some intangible assets such as brand names have indefinite lives and are not amortized. Instead, they are evaluated annually for impairment (decline in value). We refer to these types of intangibles as **indefinite-lived intangible assets. Goodwill** is another type of intangible asset, which represents the difference between the total fair value of an acquired business and the fair value of its identifiable net assets. We discuss accounting for goodwill in Chapter 16.

Difficult financial reporting issues exist when the intangible asset is developed internally instead of being purchased from another company. These difficulties arise because the expenditures that ultimately create valuable intangibles such as patents or trademarks are expensed as incurred.

A patent, for example, is the result of successful research and development expenditures. A valuable trademark is the result of successful advertising, a great product, clever packaging, or brand loyalty. The recoverability of research and development (R&D) expenditures is highly uncertain at the start of a project. Consequently, the GAAP requires that virtually all R&D expenditures be charged to expense immediately.[6] This mandated financial reporting uniformity is viewed as a practical way to deal with the risk of nonrecoverability of R&D expenditures. Similarly, prevailing accounting principles have long required companies to treat advertising and creative product development expenditures as period costs, again because of the highly uncertain, difficult-to-predict, future benefits. This conservative bias is due primarily to the contracting role of accounting. A firm would not want to pay bonuses to its managers based on what *might* happen because of an R&D project.

The major types of cash outflows most likely to result in intangibles creation (R&D, advertising costs, and so forth) are immediately expensed. *When past outflows successfully create intangible assets, these outflows have already been expensed and there are usually few remaining future outflows to capitalize!* Consequently, the balance sheet carrying amount for intangible assets is often far below the value of the property right.

> For example, TiVo's 2009 annual report indicated that "Purchased technology, capitalized software, and intangible assets, net" were valued at $9.6 million. However, a disclosure in that same annual report reveals that TiVo won court judgments in 2008 and 2009 of more than $400 million from lawsuits alleging that EchoStar Communications infringed on TiVo's patented "Multimedia Time Warping System." The size of the judgments indicated that the economic value of TiVo's patents exceeded substantially the book value recorded on the balance sheet.

As software development companies proliferated in the 1980s, authoritative accounting guidance was ultimately issued for software development costs.[7] This GAAP applies the previously described R&D rules to the particular circumstances faced by companies developing computer software products. Specifically, *prior to* establishing the **technological feasibility** of a computer software product, a company expenses *all* R&D costs incurred to develop it. After technological feasibility is established, additional costs incurred to ready the product for general release to customers are supposed to be capitalized. Capitalization of additional costs ceases when the final product is available for sale. The costs incurred before technological feasibility is established can be considerable; because feasibility may not be ensured until late in the expenditure cycle, there may be few costs left to capitalize. Accordingly, the intangible software asset may be recorded at an amount far lower than its value to the software development firm, just as in other (nonsoftware) R&D settings.

> Authoritative accounting literature states that technological feasibility is established "when the entity has completed all planning, designing, coding and testing activities that are necessary to establish that the product can be produced to meet its design specifications including functions, features, and technical performance requirements" (FASB ASC Paragraph 985-20-25-2: Software—Costs of Software to Be Sold, Leased, or Marketed—Research and Development Costs of Computer Software).

---

[6] FASB ASC Topic 730: Research and Development Costs. The only exception to immediate expensing is when the R&D expenditures will be reimbursed by some outside group (FASB ASC Paragraph 730-10-15-4: Research and Development—Overall—Scope and Scope Exceptions—Transactions).

[7] FASB ASC Subtopic 985-20: Software—Costs of Software to Be Sold, Leased, or Marketed.

The GAAP bias that leads to an understatement of internally developed intangible assets can fool analysts who are not acquainted with it. The issue has become more important as economic activity shifted in the 1980s from heavy manufacturing to high technology. In high-technology industries such as software development and biotechnology, research has contributed to large increases in the value of intellectual property rights such as patents and trademarks, yet most of it is not on the balance sheet if it has been developed internally.

In the pre-Codification document for research and development costs, the FASB justified expensing all R&D for three reasons:

1. The future benefits accruing from these expenditures are highly uncertain.
2. A causal relationship between current R&D and future revenue has not been demonstrated.
3. Whatever benefits may arise cannot be objectively measured.[8]

Even though the potential assets associated with R&D expenditures are not recognized under GAAP, research indicates that investors treat the expenditures as if they are assets. One study examined the relationship between R&D expenditures and both future earnings and share values.[9] The study found that a $1 increase in R&D expenditures results in a cumulative $2 profit increase over a seven-year period. Furthermore, a $1 increase in R&D expenditures leads to a $5 increase in the market value of a firm's shares, on average. So, R&D expenditures *are* related to future benefits, and logic suggests that a causal relationship exists. Another study developed statistically reliable estimates of unrecorded R&D asset costs.[10] These estimates were then used to adjust reported earnings and book values to reflect capitalization of R&D. The adjusted numbers that reflected R&D capitalization (and subsequent amortization) were strongly associated with stock prices and returns and, thus, were value-relevant to investors. So, investors' behavior suggests that the adjusted numbers are measuring R&D benefits. A recent study suggests that not all R&D is created equal. R&D appears to have the most impact on future earnings in industries where patents and other legal mechanisms are most effective in protecting R&D.[11] Given the above academic research, analysts should consider carefully R&D expenditures in their evaluations of companies though they are not on the balance sheet.

 **Valuation**

Some (often small) portion of total software development costs is capitalized once technological feasibility is established. But the proportion of total software development costs that is capitalized is subjectively determined and varies across firms. So, one question that arises is whether a GAAP standard that conveys such latitude also provides information that is relevant to investors. One study found that it does because the capitalization-related variables (annual amount capitalized, amount of the software asset, and annual amortization) were significantly associated with stock prices, returns, and future earnings.[12]

To summarize, research findings indicate that existing GAAP for both R&D and software development is conservative. The expenditures create assets that do not appear on balance sheets,

[8] Pre-Codification *SFAS No. 2*, paras. 39–46. The FASB considered this material to be nonessential for Codification and viewed it as background for the actual accounting principle. Material that the FASB views as nonessential is not found in the FASB Accounting Standards Codification but can be accessed at www.fasb.org under pre-Codification Standards.

[9] T. Sougiannis, "The Accounting Based Valuation of Corporate R&D," *The Accounting Review,* January 1994, pp. 44–68.

[10] B. Lev and T. Sougiannis, "The Capitalization, Amortization, and Value-Relevance of R&D," *Journal of Accounting and Economics,* February 1996, pp. 107–38.

[11] See N. Brown and M. Kimbrough, "Intangible Investment and the Importance of Firm-Specific Factors in the Determination of Earnings," *Review of Accounting Studies,* September 2011, pp. 539–73.

[12] D. Aboody and B. Lev, "The Value Relevance of Intangibles: The Case of Software Capitalization," *Journal of Accounting Research,* Supplement 1998, pp. 161–91.

and net income in the current and future years is misstated. Over time the amount of R&D expenditures in a given year may equal the amount of amortization for the year under a full capitalization approach, thereby reducing the misstatement of net income. However, the understatement of assets and shareholders' equity will continue as long as a firm invests in R&D. The cumulative understatement is similar to what we observed in Chapter 9 for firms on LIFO. Consequently, profitability and asset utilization ratios of R&D intensive firms will be higher than similar ratios of non-R&D intensive firms. Also, analysts have to watch for decreases in R&D expenditures, which could boost income at the expense of future new products and growth.

P10-13 illustrates this point.

Analysts can recast financial statements using required GAAP disclosures. For example, firms are required to disclose separately total expensed R&D costs.[13] Similarly, authoritative accounting literature requires disclosure of unamortized software assets, amortization and write-downs of the assets in each period, and all costs that are expensed prior to technological feasibility.[14] ***Analysts can use these disclosures to reconstruct what asset and amortization amounts would be if GAAP allowed full capitalization.*** (Analysts can create their own estimation procedures or use the methods in the article cited in footnote 10.) Unfortunately, disclosures of marketing and advertising expenditures are voluntary and therefore do not consistently permit a similar adjustment approach for trademarks or brands. So, it's harder to undo the limitations of GAAP for these unrecorded intangible assets.[15]

RECAP   **Balance sheet carrying amounts for internally developed intangible assets such as patents or trademarks are not dependable indicators of their value to the firm. Because the assets are understated, so too is income statement amortization in later years.**

ASSET IMPAIRMENT

Tangible and Amortizable Intangible Assets

Fair value is the price that would be received to sell an asset or paid to transfer a liability in an orderly transaction between market participants at the measurement date. See FASB ASC Master Glossary: Fair Value.

As mentioned early in this chapter, due to verifiability concerns, long-lived assets are carried at depreciated historical cost instead of net realizable value. However, the concept of **faithful representation** (see Chapter 1, page 18) outweighs verifiability concerns when there is evidence that the carrying value of long-lived asset exceeds the expected future economic benefits. When a long-lived asset is considered to be impaired, the carrying value is reduced to its **fair value,** and the new value is then depreciated over its remaining useful life.

Assets are often used in combination with other assets, not just singly. When applying the impairment guidelines to groups of assets, the unit of accounting should be "the lowest level for which identifiable cash flows are largely independent of the cash flows of other groups of assets and liabilities." FASB ASC 360-10-20: Property, Plant, and Equipment—Overall—Glossary: Asset Group.

The specific guidelines for addressing impairments are contained in various subtopics of FASB ASC Topic 360: Property, Plant, and Equipment.[16] We explain these guidelines step-by-step using the lettered stages in Figure 10.2.

Stage A. Authoritative accounting literature states that an impairment review should be made whenever external events raise the possibility that an asset's carrying amount (book value) may not be recoverable. Examples of such external events include a significant decrease in the asset's fair value, deterioration in the business climate, or forecasted future losses from using the asset.[17]

---

[13] FASB ASC Section 985-20-50: Software—Costs of Software to Be Sold, Leased, or Marketed—Disclosure.

[14] Ibid.

[15] Although most research to date supports a link between stock prices and R&D expenditures, the evidence is mixed for advertising.

[16] FASB ASC Topic 360: Property, Plant, and Equipment, and Subsections titled Impairment or Disposal of Long-Lived Assets.

[17] See FASB ASC Paragraph 360-10-35-21: Property, Plant, and Equipment—Overall—Subsequent Measurement—Impairment or Disposal of Long-Lived Assets—When to Test a Long-Lived Asset for Recoverability.

Figure 10.2

LONG-LIVED ASSET
IMPAIRMENT GUIDELINES

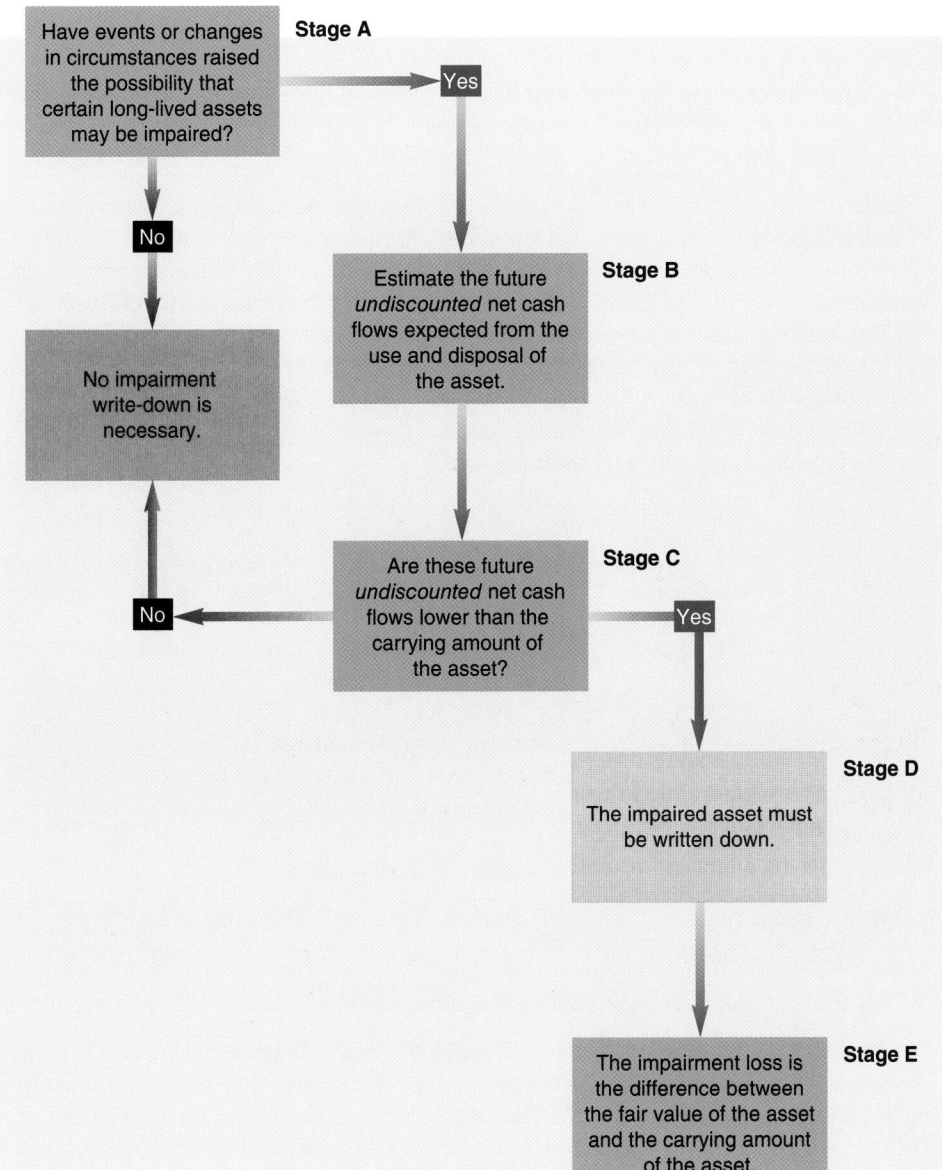

Stage B. *This stage defines the threshold loss level that triggers the write-down.*

Stage C. The threshold is triggered whenever the expected future *net* cash inflow—undiscounted total future inflows minus future outflows—is *lower* than the current carrying amount of the asset.

Stage D. When an impairment loss is recognized, the long-lived asset is written down. The income statement charge is included "above the line"—that is, as a component of income from continuing operations before income taxes.

Stage E. *This stage defines the amount of the write-down that must be recognized.* The write-down loss is measured as the difference between the fair value of the asset and the current carrying amount of the asset. Firms will often have to use an "expected present value technique" to estimate fair value.[18]

---

[18] See FASB ASC Paragraph 360-10-35-36.

Once an asset is written down, it cannot later be written back up to the original higher carrying amount if the fair value recovers.[19]

The following example illustrates how these impairment rules are applied.

Solomon Corporation manufactures a variety of computer products. The growing popularity of tablets is expected to reduce the demand for Solomon's notebook computers. The notebook computers are produced on an assembly line consisting of five special purpose assets with a carrying amount (cost of $5,300,000 less accumulated depreciation of $3,300,000) of $2,000,000. Solomon's management believes that this change in the business climate threatens the recoverability of these assets' carrying amount; accordingly, their answer to the question in **Stage A** of Figure 10.2 is yes. Consequently, to apply **Stage B,** they prepare the following estimate of future undiscounted cash flows over the expected three-year remaining life of the notebook computer assembly line:

Net operating cash flows	
2014	$ 800,000
2015	400,000
2016	200,000
Expected salvage value	100,000
Total undiscounted cash flows	$1,500,000

A comparison of the $2,000,000 carrying amount to the $1,500,000 undiscounted flows (**Stage C**) indicates that the asset must be written down (**Stage D**). By reference to used asset price lists, Solomon determines that the entire assembly line can be sold for $750,000. So, the amount of the impairment loss (**Stage E**) is $1,250,000 (that is, $2,000,000 − $750,000).

To record the loss, Solomon would make the following entry:

DR	Impairment loss......................................	$1,250,000	
	CR Equipment..................................		$1,250,000[20]

The impairment loss decreases both assets and net income.

The threshold for determining whether an impairment exists (**Stage B** in Figure 10.2) is the *undiscounted* future net cash flows the asset is expected to generate. When these undiscounted net cash flows are smaller than the asset's carrying amount, the GAAP guidance says the asset is impaired. By *not* discounting the future net cash flows, the threshold is higher than it would be if the flows were discounted. Obviously, the higher the threshold, the smaller is the likelihood that the impairment threshold will be triggered. So, the high threshold lessens the probability of recognizing an impairment when none exists.

---

[19] FASB ASC Paragraph 360-10-35-20: Property, Plant, and Equipment—Overall—Subsequent Measurement-Impairment or Disposal of Long-Lived Assets—Adjusted Carrying Amount Becomes New Cost Basis.

[20] GAAP is silent on which asset accounts to credit. Consequently, the same effect on book value could be accomplished by either of the following two entries:

Alternative 2

DR	Impairment loss	$1,250,000	
	CR Accumulated depreciation		$1,250,000

Alternative 3

DR	Impairment loss	$1,250,000	
DR	Accumulative depreciation	3,300,000	
	CR Equipment		$4,550,000

Alternative 2, credits Accumulated depreciation instead of Equipment. Alternative 3 reduces Equipment to the fair value of $750,000 and reduces Accumulated depreciation to zero. Under all three alternatives, the book value of the equipment is $750,000.

Indefinite-Lived Intangible Assets

The GAAP steps for evaluating indefinite-lived intangible assets for impairment are more straightforward than the steps discussed above.[21] Indefinite-lived intangible assets must be evaluated for impairment annually or more frequently if the firm observes events such as those discussed in Stage A for tangible assets. U.S. GAAP allows a two-step evaluation process where firms first assess *qualitative* factors to determine whether it is necessary to perform a *quantitative* impairment test. If based on this qualitative evaluation, management believes that it is **more likely than not** that an indefinite-lived intangible asset has been impaired, then it must go to the second step and perform a quantitative assessment by calculating the fair value of the intangible asset. If the book value of the asset exceeds the fair value, then the asset is considered impaired. The firm then reduces the book value of the asset to its estimated fair value and records a loss. As is the case with tangible assets and amortizable intangible assets, the book value of the asset cannot be increased later if the fair value recovers.

Case Study of Impairment Recognition and Disclosure—Krispy Kreme Doughnuts

We build on our prior discussions by analyzing the excerpts of Krispy Kreme Doughnuts' 2011 annual report provided in Exhibit 10.7. During the first part of the last decade, Krispy Kreme Doughnuts enjoyed rapid sales growth and expansion. However, subsequently, its profits declined, and some stores were no longer profitable.

The top schedule summarizes the impairment charges from 2009 to 2011. The schedule shows that Krispy Kreme recorded new impairment charges on its long-lived assets of $3,437 thousand for the year ended January 30, 2011. The paragraph below the schedule describes the company's impairment review and measurement process. Note that this process is consistent with our earlier discussion of the GAAP guidance for impairments.

Based on the disclosure in Exhibit 10.7 and other information provided in the annual report, Krispy Kreme made the following aggregate journal entry to record its new 2011 impairment losses (in thousands):

DR Impairment charges	$3,437	
CR Property and equipment		$3,437

Impairment charges is equivalent to the Impairment loss account that we used in the Solomon example. Also consistent with the Solomon example, Krispy Kreme reduced the asset cost when it recorded the impairment loss.

Management Judgments and Impairments

Contracting

Impairment write-downs present managers another set of potential earnings management opportunities. For example, in a very good earnings year, managers might be tempted to take an impairment write-down. Some research is consistent with this view.[22] The study found that

[21] This paragraph relies on FASB ASC Paras. 350-30-35-15 to 20: Intangibles—Goodwill and Other—General Intangibles Other than Goodwill—Subsequent Measurement—Recognition and Measurement of an Impairment Loss—Intangible Assets not Subject to Amortization.

[22] See E. J. Riedl, "An Examination of Long-Lived Asset Impairments," *The Accounting Review,* July 2004, pp. 823–52. This research was conducted when pre-Codification "Accounting for the Impairment of Long-Lived Assets and for Long-Lived Assets to Be Disposed of," *SFAS No. 121* (Norwalk, CT: FASB, 1995) constituted U.S. GAAP for impairment write-offs. The impairment guidelines under that now-superseded pronouncement are similar to the current guidelines.

EXHIBIT 10.7	Krispy Kreme Doughnuts, Inc.: Asset Impairment Charge

Note 12—Impairment Charges and Lease Termination Costs

The components of impairment charges and lease termination costs are as follows:

	Year Ended		
(in thousands)	January 30, 2011	January 31, 2010	February 1, 2009
Impairment charges:			
Impairment of long-lived assets-current period charges	$3,437	$3,108	$1,050
Impairment of long-lived assets-adjustment to previously recorded estimates	(173)	—	—
Impairment of reacquired franchise rights	40	40	—
Recovery from bankruptcy estate of former subsidiary	—	(482)	—
Total impairment charges	3,304	2,666	1,050
Lease termination costs:			
Provision for termination costs	1,449	4,195	316
Less—reversal of previously recorded accrued rent expense	(687)	(958)	(818)
Net provision	762	3,237	(502)
Total impairment charges and lease termination costs	$4,066	$5,903	$ 548

  The Company tests long-lived assets for impairment when events or changes in circumstances indicate that their carrying value may not be recoverable. These events and changes in circumstances include store closing and refranchising decisions, the effects of changing costs on current results of operations, observed trends in operating results, and evidence of changed circumstances observed as a part of periodic reforecasts of future of future operating results and as part of the Company's annual budgeting process. When the Company concludes that the carrying value of long-lived assets is not recoverable (based on future projected undiscounted cash flows), the Company records impairment charges to reduce the carrying value of those assets to their estimated fair values. Impairment charges related to Company Stores long-lived assets were approximately $3.4 million, $3.1 million and $900,000 in fiscal 2011, 2010 and 2009, respectively. Such charges relate to underperforming stores, including both stores closed or likely to be closed and stores which management believes will not generate sufficient future cash flows to enable the Company to recover the carrying value of the stores' assets, but which management has not yet decided to close. The impaired store assets include real properties, the fair values of which were estimated based on independent appraisals or, in the case of any properties which the Company is negotiating to sell, based on the Company's negotiations with unrelated third-party buyers; leasehold improvements, which are typically abandoned when the leased properties revert to the lessor; and doughnut-making and other equipment.

Source: Krispy Kreme Doughnuts, Inc., 2011 annual report.

impairment write-offs occurring after the issuance of *revised guidance* have a weaker association with economic factors that presumably drive impairments than was the case prior to *the guidance.* In other words, the relationship between write-offs and the firm's underlying economic condition was smaller. The author concluded that

> the results further indicate that managers are applying greater flexibility in the reporting decisions relating to write-offs after adoption of the standard, contrary to the intentions of the FASB. . . . Overall, the evidence suggests that the reporting of write-offs under SFAS No. 121 has decreased in quality relative to before the standard.[23]

This suggests that auditors and other financial statement analysts should be alert to the potential use of write-offs opportunistically by managers. The author cites "big bath" bunching of impairment write-off as an example.

---

[23] Ibid, p. 849.

OBLIGATIONS ARISING FROM RETIRING LONG-LIVED ASSETS

When an electric utility builds a nuclear plant or an oil company constructs an offshore drilling rig, regulatory authorities require public welfare and safety expenditures at the end of the asset's life. Nuclear plants must be decontaminated and drilling rigs must be disassembled. This costs money. And by law, these expenditures must take place. ***So, when certain types of assets are built, a liability simultaneously arises for future expenditures.*** Historically, there were not generally accepted accounting principles to guide the accounting for these required outflows at the end of an asset's life, so no liability appeared on firms' books. But current GAAP requires firms to record a liability when certain assets are placed into service.[24]

Here's how the rules work. Firms are required to estimate the expected present value of the outflows that will occur when assets are eventually retired. These outflows are discounted using a **credit-adjusted risk-free rate.** The liability's discounted present value is recorded along with an increase in the carrying amount of the related long-lived asset. Consider the following example.

> Sometimes the liability arises *after* the asset is placed into service. For example, suppose a new law is passed requiring removal of gasoline storage tanks at the end of their useful lives. For firms utilizing these tanks, the liability arises when the law is passed, not when the tank was first placed into service. Also, liabilities may arise over time as the asset is used. If a coal strip mine must be reclaimed, the liability arises proportionately as mining occurs.

> This is the risk-free rate of interest on U.S. Treasury instruments plus an adjustment for the credit standing of the firm. So, if the risk-free rate is 5% and the firm's credit standing allows it to borrow at 3% over the risk-free rate, the credit adjusted risk-free rate is 8%.

> Kalai Oil Corporation constructs on oil drilling rig off the Texas coast, which is placed into service on January 1, 2014. The rig cost $300 million to build. Texas law requires that the rig be removed at the end of its estimated useful life of five years. Kalai estimates that the cost of dismantling the rig will be $12 million and its credit-adjusted risk-free rate is 8%. The liability's discounted present value is $8,167,000. Assume that Kalai has already capitalized the $300 million cost of the rig in the account Drilling rig.

> The present value factor for a payment five years away at 8% is 0.68058. So rounded to the nearest thousand, the present value is $12 million × 0.68058 = $8,167,000.

When the asset is placed into service, Kalai records the asset retirement obligation (ARO) as:

DR	Drilling rig (asset retirement cost)	$8,167,000	
	CR ARO liability		$8,167,000

The $8,167,000 debit to the asset account is allocated to expense using some systematic method. Assuming straight-line depreciation over the expected useful life of five years, the entry is:

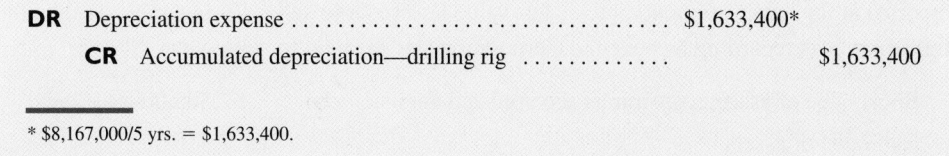

DR	Depreciation expense	$1,633,400*	
	CR Accumulated depreciation—drilling rig		$1,633,400

* $8,167,000/5 yrs. = $1,633,400.

The liability is initially recorded at its present value but increases over time as retirement nears. The liability's present value will increase by 8% per year, as the following schedule shows.

[24] FASB ASC Subtopic 410-20: Asset Retirement and Environmental Obligations—Asset Retirement Obligations.

	(a) Present Value of the Liability at Start of Year	(b) Accretion Expense [8% × Column (a) Amount]	(c) Present Value of the Liability at Year-End [Column (a) + Column (b)]
2014	$ 8,167,000	$653,360	$ 8,820,360
2015	8,820,360	705,629	9,525,989
2016	9,525,989	762,079	10,288,068
2017	10,288,068	823,045	11,111,113
2018	11,111,113	888,887*	12,000,000

* Rounded

The entry to record the increase in the liability in 2014 is:

DR	Accretion expense.	$653,360	
CR	ARO liability.		$653,36

Accretion expense is classified as an operating expense (above the line) in the income statement. It reflects the current period's increase, or *accretion,* of the liability.[25] Account titles other than Accretion expense can be used so long as the nature of the expense is clearly conveyed.

To complete the illustration, assume that an outside contractor dismantles the rig early in January 2019 at a cost of $11,750,000. The journal entry is:

DR	ARO liability	$12,000,000	
CR	Cash.		$11,750,000
CR	Gain on settlement of ARO liability.		250,000

ASSETS HELD FOR SALE

Firms constantly experience changing market conditions such as the emergence of new competing products or the development of more efficient distribution systems. In responding to these innovations, firms often seek to dispose of groups of assets that are no longer suited to the new environment they face. When firms actively try to sell some of the assets they currently own, these asset groups generally should be classified in the balance sheet as "held for sale" if they are expected to be sold within one year.[26] When assets are held for sale, they are reported at the lower of book value or fair value **less costs to sell.**[27] To illustrate, assume the following facts regarding Nebozenko Corporation's assets held for sale:

- Book value of assets (cost minus accumulated depreciation) $2,500,000
- Fair value of assets   2,350,000
- Expected legal fees associated with sale   46,000

---

[25] FASB ASC Paragraph 410-20-35-5: Asset Retirement and Environmental Obligations—Asset Retirement Obligations—Subsequent Measurement—Allocation of Asset Retirement Cost.

[26] FASB ASC Paragraphs 360-10-45-9 to -11: Property, Plant, and Equipment—Overall—Other Presentation Matters-Impairment or Disposal of Long-Lived Assets—Initial Criteria for Classification as Held for Sale.

[27] FASB ASC Paragraph 360-10-45-43: Property, Plant, and Equipment—Overall—Other Presentation Matters-Impairment or Disposal of Long-Lived Assets—Accounting While Held for Sale.

So, these assets would be shown on the balance sheet at \$2,304,000, that is, at fair value minus expected legal fees (\$2,350,000 − \$46,000). The operating results of asset components classified as "held for sale" are reported in the discontinued operations section of the income statement in the period(s) in which they occur even if the assets have not yet been sold as of the financial statement date.[28] Once the asset group has been sold, the assets are removed from the balance sheet and the income statement disclosure policies for discontinued operations discussed in Chapter 2 are applied. That is, the firm will separately disclose "below the line" the gain or loss (net of taxes) from utilizing these assets during the period covered as well as any gain or loss on disposal of the assets themselves.

Segregating the assets held for sale on the balance sheet and separately disclosing their operating results on the income statement are designed to help analysts better understand past firm performance and assess future prospects. For example, in evaluating the efficiency of past asset utilization using the return-on-assets ratio, assets that are destined for sale should be excluded from the rate-of-return denominator and their profit or loss contribution should be excluded from the numerator. This exclusion provides a better measure of expected *future* performance based on assets expected to remain in the firm. The disclosure rules provide guidance on when certain assets should be segregated on the balance sheet, which alerts analysts to items that should be omitted from rate-of-return calculations.[29] Similarly, income forecasts are enhanced insofar as the income or loss from the asset groups that have been or are about to be sold are isolated "below the line" and are no longer factored into the analysts' forecast.

> Assets that are eligible to be separately classified must comprise "operations and cash flows that can be clearly distinguished, operationally and for financial reporting purposes, from the rest of the entity" (FASB ASC Master Glossary: Component of an Entity). This is the same criterion that was used in Chapter 2 to identify elements that must be reflected in the discontinued operations section of the income statement.

 **Analysis**

DEPRECIATION

Productive assets such as buildings, equipment, and machinery eventually wear out. Assets including patents, which have a finite economic life, ultimately expire. Consequently, the cost of these assets must be apportioned to the periods in which they provide benefits. The systematic expensing and write-down of a tangible long-lived asset is called **depreciation.** For intangible assets, the allocation of costs to periods is referred to as **amortization.** For mineral deposits and other wasting assets, the assignment of expired costs to periods is called **depletion.** For simplicity, we refer collectively to any of these allocations of costs to periods as the **depreciation process.**

In financial reporting, the cost to be allocated to periods through the depreciation process is the asset's original historical cost minus its expected salvage value. The objective is to spread the original cost over the period of asset use; *depreciation is not intended to track the asset's declining market value.* Realistically, the asset's end-of-period book value (its original cost minus cumulative depreciation) would approximate its market value only by sheer coincidence. We stress this *absence of correspondence* between accounting measures of depreciation and value decrement because GAAP accounting depreciation, as we have said, is a process of cost allocation, *not* asset valuation.

Computing depreciation requires the reporting entity to estimate three things:

1. The expected useful life (in years or units) of the asset.
2. The depreciation pattern that will reflect the asset's declining service potential.
3. The expected salvage value that will exist at the time the asset is retired.

---

[28] FASB ASC Paragraph 205-20-45-3: Presentation of Financial Statements—Discontinued Operations—Other Presentation Matters—Reporting Discontinued Operations.

[29] FASB ASC Paragraph 205-20-45-10: Presentation of Financial Statements—Discontinued Operations—Other Presentation Matters—Disposal Group Classified as Held for Sale.

Each of these items requires estimates of future events, especially the pace of technological change and shifts in consumer tastes and preferences. Assets whose economic benefits expire evenly over time are depreciated on a straight-line basis while those that provide more valuable services in the early years are depreciated on an accelerated basis. The example in Exhibit 10.8 illustrates the procedures.

The **straight-line** (SL) depreciation method simply allocates cost minus salvage value evenly over the asset's expected useful life. The units-of-production (UP) depreciation method is similar to SL but allocates cost minus salvage over the expected units to be produced instead of the expected useful life. We compute a per unit rate instead of an annual rate of depreciation. To illustrate the method, we assume that 20,000 units are expected to be produced, and actual production follows the pattern given in Exhibit 10.8. Note that the amount of SL depreciation is constant, but UP depreciation does not follow a consistent pattern. In both cases, total depreciation expense equals $10,000 over the five-year period. The units-of-production method is often used in extractive industries. For example, the cost of exploring and drilling for oil would be capitalized and then depreciated on the basis of expected barrels of oil.

The depreciation rate for the **double-declining balance** (DDB) method is double the straight-line rate (in Exhibit 10.8, 20% per year for SL, 40% per year for DDB). Applying a constant DDB depreciation percentage to a declining balance will produce a book value at the end of the asset's economic life that is above or below the salvage value. To depreciate down to an asset's expected salvage value using DDB, two steps can be employed. First, apply the

---

EXHIBIT 10.8   **Depreciation Example**

Facts

Cost of the asset	$10,500
Expected salvage value	$ 500
Expected useful life	5 years
Expected units	20,000

Straight-Line Depreciation (SL)

$$(\text{Constant rate} \times \text{Constant base}) = \frac{1}{\text{Estimated life}} \times (\text{Cost} - \text{Salvage value})$$

$$\left(\frac{1}{5}\right) \times (\$10,500 - \$500) = \$2,000 \text{ per year for all 5 years}$$

Units-of-Production (UP)

$$(\text{Changing number of annual units} \times \text{Unit rate}) = \text{Annual units} \times \frac{(\text{Cost} - \text{Salvage value})}{\text{Expected units}}$$

Year	Unit Rate ($10,500 − $500) / 20,000	Units Produced (Assumed)	Depreciation
1	$0.50	4,200	$ 2,100
2	0.50	3,400	1,700
3	0.50	6,000	3,000
4	0.50	3,300	1,650
5	0.50	3,100	1,550
Total		20,000	$10,000

(continued)

EXHIBIT 10.8	Depreciation Example *(continued)*

Double-Declining Balance Depreciation (DDB)

(Constant rate × Changing base) = Double the straight-line rate × Book value at beginning of each period

Straight-line rate = 20% (that is, 5-year life)

Double straight-line rate = 20% × 2 = 40%

Year	Beginning-of-Year Book Value	Depreciation (40% of Beginning-of-Year Book Value)	Year-End Book Value
1	$10,500.00	$4,200.00	$6,300.00
2	6,300.00	2,520.00	3,780.00
3	3,780.00	1,093.33*	2,686.67
4	2,686.67	1,093.33	1,593.34
5	1,593.34	1,093.34	500.00

* Year 3: Switch to straight-line method (as explained in the text).
$3,780 − $500 = $3,280; $3,280/3 = $1,093.33

Sum-of-the-Years' Digits Depreciation (SYD)

$$\left(\begin{array}{c}\text{Changing} \\ \text{rate}\end{array} \times \begin{array}{c}\text{Constant} \\ \text{base}\end{array}\right) = \frac{\text{Years remaining in life}}{\text{Sum-of-the-years' digits}^\dagger} \times (\text{Cost} - \text{Salvage})$$

Sum-of-the-years' digits = 5 + 4 + 3 + 2 + 1 = 15

Year	Depreciable Basis ($10,500 − $500)	Applicable Fraction	Depreciation
1	$10,000	5/15	$ 3,333.33
2	10,000	4/15	2,666.67
3	10,000	3/15	2,000.00
4	10,000	2/15	1,333.33
5	10,000	1/15	666.67
Total		15/15	$10,000.00

† The formula for determining the sum-of-the-years' digits is $n(n + 1)/2$ where n equals the estimated life of the asset. In our example: $5(5 + 1)/2 = 15$. This, of course, is the answer we get by tediously summing the years' digits—that is, $5 + 4 + 3 + 2 + 1 = 15$.

40% rate to the book value of the assets *without subtracting the salvage value.* Second, once the DDB depreciation amount falls below what it would be with straight-line depreciation, as in Year 3 of the exhibit, a firm might use the straight-line method for the remaining years. In Year 3, DDB depreciation would have been $1,512 ($3,780 × 40%), which is less than the straight-line depreciation of $2,000. Therefore, straight-line depreciation could be used beginning in Year 3. The $1,093.33 SL amount is determined by taking the end of Year 2 remaining DDB book value of $3,780, subtracting the salvage value of $500, and dividing the result, $3,280, by 3. Companies may use alternative policies for the DDB method. They can shift from the double-declining rate to the straight-line method as described above, or may use the DDB method until they reach the salvage value or the end of the useful life. In this case, the last year of depreciation expense would be the difference between the salvage value and the beginning of the year book value.

Sum-of-the-years' digits (SYD) is another accelerated depreciation method. It depreciates an asset to precisely its salvage value.

Figure 10.3(a) shows the annual depreciation charges under the alternative depreciation methods; Figure 10.3(b) shows the resulting net book value at each year-end. Note that the methods with the higher depreciation in the early years also result in lower book values in the early years. However, all the methods yield the same total depreciation expense of $10,000 over the five years and the same book value of $500 at the end of five years. We raise this point here to help you understand better how different accounting approaches affect the income statement and balance sheet over time.

In preparing external financial reports, companies are free to select the depreciation method they believe best reflects both the pattern of an asset's use and the services it provides. Within

Figure 10.3

ALTERNATIVE DEPRECIA-
TION METHODS

(a) Annual Depreciation
Charges and (b) Net Book
Value

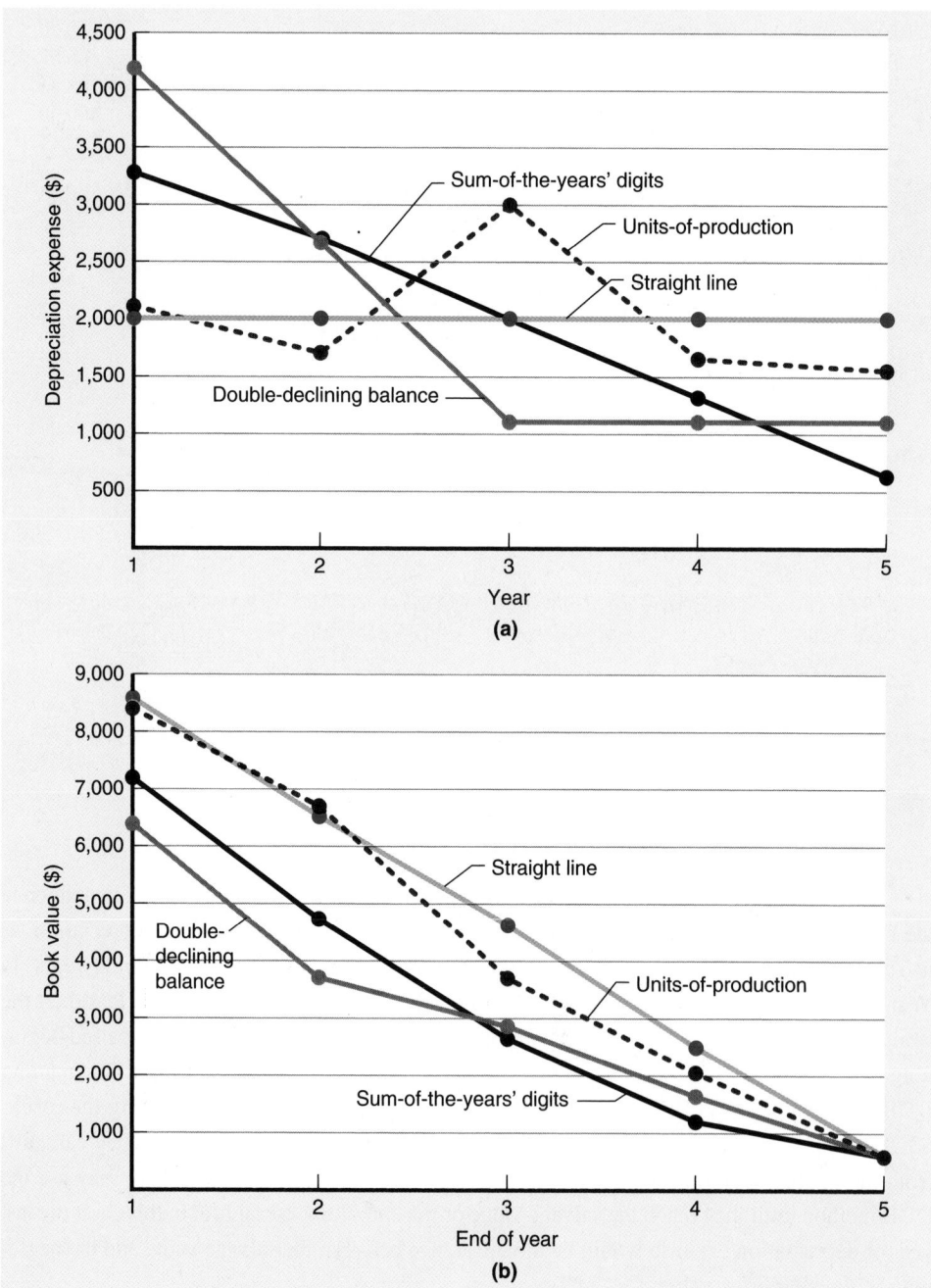

the same industry, different companies may use different methods. Even within the same company, different types of assets may be depreciated using different methods. For example, buildings might be depreciated using the SL method while trucks might be depreciated using the SYD method.

The 2012 AICPA survey of 2011 annual reports shows that the straight-line method is by far the favored method for financial reporting; 94% of the firms use the straight-line method for at least some of their long-lived assets.[30] The survey also reports that 4% of the firms use an accelerated depreciation method for some assets and 2% use the units-of-production method for some assets. Whereas most U.S. firms use the straight-line method for financial reporting purposes, they generally use MACRS (Modified Accelerated Cost Recovery System), an approach based on the DDB method, for tax purposes. We discuss how to handle different depreciation methods for financial reporting and tax purposes in Chapter 13.

Disposition of Long-Lived Assets

When individual long-lived assets are disposed of before their useful lives are completed, any difference between the net book value of the asset and the disposition proceeds is treated as a gain or loss. Assume that the asset in the Exhibit 10.8 example is being depreciated using the DDB method and is sold at the end of Year 2 for $5,000 when its book value is $3,780. The following entry is made:

DR	Cash	$5,000	
DR	Accumulated depreciation	6,720	
	CR Long-lived asset		$10,500
	CR Gain on sale of asset		1,220

Dispositions of individual assets occur frequently as firms respond to changing production and consumer-demand conditions. For this reason, gains and losses from asset sales do not satisfy the criteria for the extraordinary item treatment described in Chapter 2. Accordingly, such items are included in the income statement "above the line" as an element of pre-tax income from continuing operations.

> Gains or losses on sales of assets comprising a clearly distinguishable component of an entity, as described in the earlier section "Assets Held for Sale," are shown in the discontinued operations section.

Financial Analysis and Depreciation Differences

As noted previously, most U.S. firms use straight-line depreciation for financial reporting purposes. Nevertheless, making valid comparisons across firms is often hindered by other depreciation assumptions, especially differences in useful lives. Two firms in the same industry often depreciate their otherwise similar assets over different estimated lives. When this happens potentially significant income differences arise.

We now illustrate this issue and discuss ways to adjust depreciation to achieve greater comparability across firms. Exhibit 10.9 shows information extracted from the 2012 annual report of Whole Foods Market. Whole Foods depreciates its long-lived assets using the straight-line method. In Note (2), Whole Foods gives general information about the assumed lives of the

Analysis

[30] See R. Petrino, D. Cohen, A. Patel, and K. Kraft (eds.), *Accounting Trends and Techniques, U.S. GAAP Financial Statements* (New York: American Institute of Certified Public Accountants, Inc., 2012).

EXHIBIT 10.9   Whole Foods Market: Fixed Asset Information

(2) Summary of Significant Accounting Policies

Property and Equipment

Property and equipment is stated at cost, net of accumulated depreciation and amortization. The Company provides depreciation of equipment over the estimated useful lives (generally 3 to 15 years) using the straight-line method, and provides amortization of leasehold improvements and real estate assets under capital leases on a straight-line basis over the shorter of the estimated useful lives of the improvements or the expected terms of the related leases. The Company provides depreciation of buildings over the estimated useful lives (generally 20 to 50 years) using the straight-line method. Costs related to a projected site determined to be unsatisfactory and general site selection costs that cannot be identified with a specific store location are charged to operations currently. The Company recognizes a liability for the fair value of a conditional asset retirement obligation when the obligation is incurred. Repair and maintenance costs are expensed as incurred. Interest costs on significant projects constructed or developed for the Company's own use are capitalized as a separate component of the asset. Upon retirement or disposal of assets, the cost and related accumulated depreciation are removed from the balance sheet and any gain or loss is reflected in earnings.

(5) Property and Equipment

Balance of major classes of property and equipment are as follows (in thousands):

	2012	2011
Land	$ 76,592	$ 48,928
Buildings and leasehold improvements	2,219,763	1,958,612
Capitalized real estate leases	24,876	24,262
Fixtures and equipment	1,674,089	1,398,778
Construction in progress and equipment not yet in service	53,328	188,844
	4,048,648	3,619,424
Less accumulated depreciation and amortization	(1,855,965)	(1,622,212)
	$ 2,192,683	$ 1,997,212

Selected Income Statement Information

	Fiscal year	
($ in millions)	**2012**	**2011**
Depreciation	$296.8	$274.4
Income before incomes taxes	$752.0	$551.7

Source: Whole Foods Market 2012 annual report.

---

main categories of its assets (see highlighted statements). Although other firms may use straight-line depreciation, they may assume different age ranges or disclose different categories. Typically, the descriptive information is too general to know whether there are comparability issues. Despite this drawback, by making reasonable assumptions, we can estimate income effects arising from differences in assumed asset lives.

When a company uses straight-line depreciation, the ratio of average gross property, plant, and equipment divided by depreciation expense gives us a rough approximation of the estimated useful (depreciable) life of the average asset. Here's why. Straight-line depreciation expense (SL) is computed as:

$$SL = \frac{\text{Gross depreciable property, plant, and equipment}}{\text{Average useful life}} \qquad \textbf{(10.1)}$$

EXHIBIT 10.10	Computing Approximate Average Useful Life for Whole Foods Market

($ in millions)

Average gross property, plant, and equipment*
─────────────────────────────
Depreciation expense

$$\frac{(\$3,918.8 + \$3,381.7)/2}{\$296.8}$$

$$\frac{\$3,650.3}{\$296.8} = 12.3 \text{ years}$$

* Excludes Land and Construction in progress. For example, the 2012 numbers were computed as follows using Exhibit 10.9 data for Whole Foods (in millions): $2,219.8 for Buildings and leasehold improvements + $24.9 for Capitalized real estate leases + $1,674.1 for Fixtures and equipment = $3,918.8.

We omit salvage value from our analysis because companies usually do not disclose salvage values, and there is not a good way to estimate them. Rearranging terms:

$$SL \times (\text{Average useful life}) = \text{Gross depreciable property, plant, and equipment} \quad \textbf{(10.2)}$$

Further rearranging yields:

$$\text{Average useful life} = \frac{\text{Gross depreciable property, plant, and equipment}}{SL} \quad \textbf{(10.3)}$$

The computation of average useful life using the equation (10.3) approximation is shown in Exhibit 10.10. The company's end-of-year and start-of-year gross depreciable property are summed in Exhibit 10.10 and then divided by 2 to estimate its average gross depreciable property for 2012. Applying the equation (10.3) approach yields an average useful life of 12.3 years.[31]

To improve comparisons of profitability between Whole Foods and other firms in the industry or the industry average, an analyst could standardize the average useful life used to compute depreciation expense. If we assume an industry average of 15 years, we can adjust Whole Foods Market's depreciation expense to the industry average useful life by dividing the average gross depreciable property, plant, and equipment by the industry average depreciable life as follows:

$$\frac{\$3,650.3}{15.0 \text{ years}} = \$243.4$$

The quotient, $243.4 billion, is the approximate annual Whole Foods depreciation expense number that would result from using the industry's estimated useful life assumption. If these

---

[31] To understand why the Exhibit 10.10 answer is in years (that is, 12.3 years), let's express average gross depreciable property divided by depreciation expense in terms of the underlying measurement dimensions:

$$\frac{\text{Average gross depreciable property, plant, and equipment}}{\text{Depreciation expense}}$$

← The underlying measurement dimension is $s
← The underlying measurement dimension is $s per year

Expressing the computation in underlying measurement dimensions, the division in Exhibit 10.10 becomes:

$$\frac{\$s}{\$s/\text{Years}}$$

Following algebraic rules for division by fractions, we invert the denominator and multiply it by the numerator:

$$\$s \times \frac{\text{Years}}{\$s}$$

The $s cancel, and the answer is expressed dimensionally in years (for example, 12.3 years).

rough approximations are correct, Whole Foods' fiscal year 2012 depreciation would decline by $53.4 million—that is, the $243.4 million just computed minus the $296.8 million reported in Exhibit 10.9—and income before income taxes would increase by the same amount. This represents a pre-tax earnings increase of approximately 7.1% ($53.4 difference divided by $752.0 income before income taxes). The income effect could be larger or smaller depending on the company and the industry. Consequently, an analyst should take the time to make the calculations and evaluate whether there is a comparability issue. ***In addition, an analyst should watch for significant changes in the estimated depreciable life for the same firm over time.*** Changes could signal that management has changed depreciation assumptions or the rate at which it replaces equipment.

It is possible that the useful life differences reflect real economic differences rather than accounting choices. For example, Whole Foods' gross depreciable property, and equipment might be less durable and, on average, have shorter useful lives. If the useful lives differences are "real," then analysts' attempts to "undo" the differences may impede, rather than improve, profit comparisons.

This adjustment process relies on several assumptions. First, the adjustment assumes that the useful life differences are artificial and do not reflect real differences in expected asset longevity. Second, it assumes that the salvage value proportions are roughly equivalent for all firms in the industry, and third, the dollar breakdown within the asset categories (e.g., buildings versus leasehold improvements) are similar across the firms being compared. If these assumptions are incorrect, the average age computation for one firm cannot legitimately be applied to the other's asset base to estimate "adjusted" depreciation. However, if these assumptions hold, the adjusted numbers should make a comparison between Whole Foods and other firms in the industry more accurate.

In Chapter 13, we illustrate another adjustment approach for depreciation differences that uses data from the deferred income tax footnote.

EXCHANGES OF NONMONETARY ASSETS

Occasionally firms will exchange one nonmonetary asset such as inventory or equipment for another nonmonetary asset. Unless certain exceptions in the following discussion apply, the recorded cost of a nonmonetary asset acquired in exchange for some other nonmonetary asset is the fair value of the asset that was given up. Any resulting gain or loss on the transaction is recognized.[32] To illustrate how the cost of a nonmonetary asset acquired in an exchange is determined, consider the following example.

When the fair value of the asset *received* is more clearly evident than the fair value of the asset *given up*, the fair value of the asset received is used as the new cost base. See FASB ASC Paragraph 845-10-30-1: Nonmonetary Transactions—Overall—Initial Measurement—Basic Principle.

Rohan Department Store exchanges a delivery truck with a fair value of $70,000 for 10 checkout scanners from Electronic Giant Warehouse, Inc. The truck's book value is $60,000—original cost of $80,000 minus accumulated depreciation of $20,000. In addition to the truck, Rohan pays Electronic Giant $15,000.

The cost of the acquired assets (scanners) is the fair value of the assets (truck and cash) that were given in the exchange. So, in this example, the cost of the scanners is:

Fair value of the truck	$70,000
Cash payment	15,000
Cost of acquired assets	$85,000

---

[32] FASB ASC Paragraph 845-10-30-1: Nonmonetary Transactions—Overall—Initial Measurement—Basic Principle.

Rohan's entry is

DR	Store equipment		$85,000	
DR	Accumulated depreciation—delivery truck		20,000	
	CR	Delivery truck		$80,000
	CR	Cash		15,000
	CR	Gain on exchange		10,000

Notice that the amount in the Gain on exchange account is simply the difference between the truck's fair value ($70,000) and its book value ($60,000).

For many years, asset exchanges occurred infrequently, so the rule we just illustrated was seldom an important part of firms' financial statements. But that all changed during the boom years of the 1990s and beyond. Asset exchanges—or swaps—proliferated. One article stated:

> When the business history of the past decade is written, perhaps nothing will sum up the outrageous financial scheming of the era as well as the frenzied swapping that marked its final years. Internet companies . . . milked revenue from complex advertising exchanges with other dotcoms in ultimately worthless deals. In Houston, equal amounts of energy were pushed back and forth between companies. . . .
>
> But the swaps rage turned out to be no bargain for investors. The bad deals contributed to an epidemic of artificially inflated revenue. In many cases, swaps slipped through legal loopholes left in place by regulators who had failed to keep pace with the ever-changing deal-making of ever-changing industries. The unraveling of those back-scratching arrangements helped usher in the market collapse and led to the realization by investors that the highest-flying industries of the boom era—telecom, energy, the Internet—were built in part on a combustible mix of wishful thinking and deceit.[33]

Here's an example of the manipulation of these asset exchange rules to overstate revenues and income. Telecom companies would sign agreements with other telecom companies to exchange access to each other's fiber-optic network. These deals were termed "capacity swaps"[34] and were generally structured as leases. That is, Company One would agree to lease capacity to Asia on Company Two's network for 20 years and *simultaneously* Company Two would agree to lease capacity to Europe on Company One's network for 20 years. Each company would promise to pay the other $5 million per year under the two separate leases.

For a further discussion of this earnings management scheme, see Chapter 3.

Each company received cash, and the stage was therefore set for potentially recognizing revenues and income on these deals. These deals sometimes generated upfront income. Even if they didn't generate income, they did increase revenues—an important factor "since investors focused on revenue in new industries that often had little earnings to show for themselves."[35]

To prevent a repeat of these abuses, the FASB issued rules that now require companies to record certain exchanges of nonmonetary assets at the existing ***book value*** of the relinquished asset if any of the following conditions apply:[36]

1. The fair value of neither the asset(s) received nor the asset(s) relinquished is determinable within reasonable limits.

2. The transaction lacks commercial substance.

---

[33] D. K. Berman, J. Angwin, and C. Cummins, "As the Bubble Neared Its End, Bogus Swaps Padded the Books," *The Wall Street Journal,* December 23, 2002. Copyright © 2002 Dow Jones & Company, Inc. All rights reserved worldwide. Reprinted with permission.

[34] Ibid. Also see K. Brown, "Creative Accounting: How to Buff a Company," *The Wall Street Journal,* February 21, 2002.

[35] Op. cit.

[36] FASB ASC 845-10-30-3: Nonmonetary Transactions—Overall—Initial Measurement—Modifications of the Basic Principle.

3. The exchange transaction is made to facilitate sales to customers. Specifically, the transaction is an exchange of inventory or property held for sale in the ordinary course of business for other inventory or property to be sold in the same line of business.

In the next section, we illustrate these three circumstances under which exchanges of nonmonetary assets must be recorded at book value.

Exchanges Recorded at Book Value

Fair Value Not Determinable   To illustrate the accounting for exchanges of nonmonetary assets when the fair value of the exchanged assets cannot be determined, consider the following example.

> Denver Construction Corporation agrees to swap with Cody Company one type of crane in exchange for a slightly different model whose features are better suited for a highway bridge project it is currently engaged in. The old crane Denver is exchanging has a book value of $600,000 at the time of the transaction. Its original cost was $700,000, and accumulated depreciation is $100,000. Denver also pays Cody $40,000 to complete the transaction. It is not possible to measure the fair value of either crane within reasonable limits.

Because neither crane's fair value is known, the new crane is recorded at the sum of the *book value* of the old crane ($600,000) plus the cash given ($40,000). The entry is:

DR	Construction crane (new)	$640,000	
DR	Accumulated depreciation—construction crane (old)	100,000	
	CR Construction crane (old)		$700,000
	CR Cash		40,000

The Commercial Substance Criterion   Booking exchange transactions at fair value introduces the possibility of gains (or losses) on the transaction. To preclude firms from engaging in "sham" exchanges to generate artificial gains, GAAP requires that the transaction must possess **commercial substance.** An exchange transaction has commercial substance when the firm's future cash flows are expected to change significantly as a result of the exchange.

A significant cash flow change exists if either:

1. The configuration (risk, timing, and amount) of the future cash flows of the asset(s) received differs significantly from the configuration of the future cash flows of the asset(s) transferred.

2. The entity-specific value of the asset(s) received differs from the entity-specific value of the asset(s) transferred, and the difference is significant in relation to the fair values of the assets exchanged.[37]

If both conditions are *not* met, the transaction must be recorded using the book value of the asset(s) relinquished, using the procedure in the previous illustration. This precludes any gain recognition.

---

[37] FASB ASC 845-10-30-4: Nonmonetary Transactions—Overall—Initial Measurement—Commercial Substance.

Exchange Transaction to Facilitate Sales to Customers   Sometimes firms exchange assets with other firms—even competitors—to balance inventories, as in the following example.

> Lee Electronics faces a shortage of plasma television sets but has an excess of liquid crystal display (LCD) sets. It agrees to swap LCDs with a fair value of $50,000 and a book value of $40,000 for plasma sets with a fair value of $52,000 from Bonnie Enterprises.

Here, the assets being exchanged (plasma and LCD sets) are both stocked for sale to customers. The exchange does not culminate an earning process. One asset is merely traded for another that serves a similar purpose. For this reason, Lee Electronics does not report a gain but instead records the plasma sets at $40,000—the book value of the LCDs that were relinquished in the transaction. The entry is simply:

DR	Inventory—plasma sets	$40,000	
	CR Inventory—LCDs		$40,000

The apparent $12,000 gain on the swap ($52,000 fair value minus $40,000 book value) will be recognized only when the plasma sets are ultimately sold to customers.

This gain is determined as follows:	
Fair value of plasma	
television sets	$52,000
+ Cash received	5,778
Total consideration received	$57,778
− Book value of LCDs	
relinquished	(40,000)
Gain on transaction	$17,778

Cash Received—A Special Case   Let's continue the previous example with one difference. We still assume that the fair value of the plasma sets is $52,000, but we now assume that Lee Electronics also receives $5,778 from Bonnie Enterprises.

This transaction is more complicated because Lee received both cash and the plasma television sets. Indeed, cash represents 10% of the total proceeds:

$$\frac{\text{Cash received}}{\text{Total proceeds}} = \frac{\$5,778}{\$5,778 + \$52,000} = 0.10$$

Because 10% of the proceeds were received in cash, 10% of the LCD assets are considered to be sold, and that portion of the earning process is complete. So, 10% of the $17,778 gain on the transaction will be recognized.[38] The entry is:

DR	Cash	$ 5,778	
DR	Inventory—plasma sets	36,000	
	CR Inventory—LCDs		$40,000
	CR Recognized gain on exchange		1,778

The carrying amount of the inventory of plasma sets is computed as follows:		
Fair value of plasma sets		$52,000
Less: Portion of gain deferred:		
Total gain	$17,778	
Gain recognized	(1,778)	
Gain deferred		(16,000)
Inventory—plasma sets		$36,000

Notice that the $16,000 deferred gain will ultimately be recognized when the plasma sets are sold because the inventory carrying amount has been reduced by the amount of the deferred gain.

---

[38] FASB ASC 845-10-30-6: Nonmonetary Transactions—Overall—Initial Measurement—Commercial Substance.

GLOBAL VANTAGE POINT

Comparison of IFRS and GAAP Long-Lived Asset Accounting

Although there are many similarities between U.S. GAAP and IFRS, numerous important differences exist. IFRS allows more choice in valuation models and has different specific guidance for issues such as depreciation and impairments. Some of the key differences are discussed below.

Tangible Long-Lived Assets   The general accounting for tangible long-lived assets is contained in *International Accounting Standard (IAS) 16,* "Property, Plant, and Equipment."[39] *IAS 16* allows two different models for accounting for long-lived tangible assets:

1. **Cost method:** The asset is carried at cost less accumulated depreciation as under U.S. GAAP.
2. **Revaluation method:** The asset is carried at a revalued amount reflecting its fair value at the revaluation date. Subsequent depreciation should be based on the fair value, not original cost. The difference between depreciation based on the revalued carrying amount of the asset and depreciation based on the asset's original cost is transferred from the Revaluation surplus account to Retained earnings as the asset is depreciated.

For firms to use the revaluation method, they need reliable measurements, which often require the help of professional appraisers. When firms have reliable measurements and elect the revaluation method, the Accumulated depreciation account is typically removed and the revalued amount becomes the new book value.[40] If the asset is *originally written-up,* the amount of the write-up is credited to an owners' equity account called *Revaluation surplus* (equivalent to Accumulated other comprehensive income in U.S. GAAP). Subsequent write-downs are debited to this account until it is depleted. Any additional write-downs are debited as revaluation losses. If assets are *originally written-down,* the amount of the write-down is debited as a *revaluation loss.* Subsequent write-ups are credited as revaluation loss reversals through net income to the degree they reverse prior write-downs. Any additional write-ups are credited to Revaluation surplus.

Assume that a building that originally cost €20,000,000 and has an accumulated depreciation balance of €10,000,000 is appraised at €35,000,000 and accordingly written up, as permitted by *IAS 16.* The accounting entry is:

DR	Building	€15,000,000	
DR	Accumulated depreciation	10,000,000	
	CR Revaluation surplus		€25,000,000

The new net book value becomes €35,000,000 after this entry is made, as follows:

	Net Book Value prior to Revaluation	Revaluation		Net Book Value after Revaluation
Building	€20,000,000	**DR**	€15,000,000	€35,000,000
Less: Accumulated depreciation	(10,000,000)	**DR**	€10,000,000	—
Net book value	€10,000,000			€35,000,000

---

[39] "Property, Plant, and Equipment," *IAS 16* (London: IASB, 2008).

[40] *IAS 16,* paragraph 35 (a) alternatively allows firms to restate accumulated depreciation proportionately with the change in the gross carrying amount of the asset so that the carrying amount of the asset after revaluation equals its revalued amount.

Depreciation in subsequent periods is based on the revaluation net book value (€35,000,000). If the building has an expected remaining useful life of 20 years at the time of the revaluation, annual depreciation on the income statement will be €1,750,000 (that is, €35,000,000/20).

While revaluations are not mandatory, if a company does voluntarily revalue assets, all assets of a similar class (nature or function) must be revalued. Furthermore, once assets are revalued, regular reassessments are required to keep the valuations up to date.

Most firms do not choose the revaluation method for their tangible assets. This is not surprising given the cost of appraisals and estimating fair values. However, some firms use it for specific classes of assets with significant amounts of land. Given that firms can use the revaluation method for all, some, or none of its tangible assets, comparability across firms can be an issue.

> The amount in the owners' equity Revaluation surplus account would be transferred year-by-year to Retained earnings as the revalued asset is depreciated. For example, if we assume that the asset is not subsequently revalued over the ensuing 20 years, €1,250,000 (that is, €25,000,000/20) would be reclassified each year. The entry is:
>
> **DR** Revaluation surplus. €1,250,000
>   **CR** Retained earnings €1,250,000
>
> This reclassification entry is made to reduce the Revaluation surplus as the asset ages. If no entry were made, there would still be a Revaluation surplus amount on the books even after the asset is removed from service. The year-by-year transfer ultimately reduces the surplus to zero.

We use LVMH Group, a French company that specializes in luxury brands (e.g., Veuve Clicquot, Louis Vuitton, and TAG Heuer), to illustrate the revaluation method disclosure. Excerpts from its 2012 annual report appear in Exhibit 10.11.

The note states that Vineyard land is revalued, but all other Property, plant, and equipment is carried at amortized cost. The note also describes how the revaluations affect shareholders' equity. The second part of the exhibit highlights that Vineyard land was increased by €86 million. This increase also increased equity by €86 million (pretax). The gross value of Vineyard land and producing vineyards of €2,051 million represents 14% of LVMH's total Property, plant and equipment gross value. In addition, the Vineyard land and producing vineyards represent

---

EXHIBIT 10.11   **LVMH Group: Property, Plant and Equipment**

1.11. Property, plant and equipment
With the exception of vineyard land, the gross value of property, plant and equipment is stated at acquisition cost. Any borrowing costs incurred prior to the placed-in-service date or during the construction period of assets are capitalized.

Vineyard land is recognized at the market value at the balance sheet date. This valuation is based on official published data for recent transactions in the same region, or on independent appraisals. Any difference compared to historical cost is recognized within equity in "Revaluation reserves." If market value falls below acquisition cost the resulting impairment is charged to the income statement.

Note 6: Property, plant and equipment
Movements in property, plant and eqipment during 2012 break down as follows:

Gross Value (EUR millions)	Vineyard Land and Producing Vineyards
As of December 31, 2011	**1,965**
Acquisitions	14
Change in the market value of vineyard land	(86)
Disposals and retirements	(25)
Changes in the scope of consolidation	—
Translation adjustment	(5)
Other movements, including transfers	16
As of December 31, 2012	**2,051**

Source: LVMH Group 2012 annual report.

22% of net Property, plant, and equipment. These calculations show that the revaluation method could be used for a substantial portion of a firm's tangible assets.

As stated in prior paragraphs, under either the cost method or the revaluation method, assets with finite lives will be depreciated. The depreciation guidelines under IFRS also are different from U.S. GAAP guidelines. *IAS 16* requires companies to depreciate significant components of assets separately if they have different lives. Consider the example of a building. The lives may be different for the main structure, the windows, doors, and heating systems. Under IFRS, each of these items would be depreciated separately, whereas under U.S. GAAP, these items would be depreciated as one item. The same requirements apply to machines and equipment.

In addition, the cost of major required inspections (such as those associated with aircraft or ships) should be isolated from the total cost of the asset and depreciated from the purchase date to the inspection date. At the time of the inspection, companies would capitalize the cost of the inspection as part of the asset and depreciate this component over time until the next inspection.

To adopt the components approach, most U.S. companies would incur substantial costs to value the individual components, revise their depreciation policies, and modify their accounting systems.

Another area in which U.S. GAAP and IFRS rules for tangible long-lived assets potentially diverge is accounting for **investment property.**[41] Long-lived investment property consists of assets such as land, buildings, and equipment that are held to earn rentals, for capital appreciation, or for both. To understand how these differ from other long-lived assets under IFRS, investment properties are assets that are *not* used to produce or supply goods or services, nor are they held for sale in the ordinary course of business (as inventories are). They are distinct from the company's operating assets.[42]

When investment properties are initially acquired, they are measured at cost. Subsequently, however, *firms have the choice under IAS 40 to carry investment properties at either amortized historical cost or fair value.* The method selected must be applied to all investment properties. So, a firm would not be allowed to use the fair value method for investment land while simultaneously measuring buildings held for investment at cost.

However, comparability across firms will still be affected because firms have the choice of cost or fair value. Firms choosing the cost method still have to disclose fair values, and this disclosure would allow analysts to adjust historical cost method financial statements.

If the fair value method is chosen, any gain or loss arising from a change in fair value is recognized in net income in the period of the change. Notice that this differs from the treatment accorded revaluations of operating assets under *IAS 16,* as discussed earlier. Revaluations of operating long-lived assets are often debited or credited to Revaluation surplus and not included in net income. The reason for the different treatment is straightforward. Firms hold investment properties for the express purpose of generating market-driven gains. So, it is appropriate that these gains (or losses) be recognized in net income as they occur. In contrast, operating assets are held to generate future returns, not for short-term liquidation. Accordingly, revaluation increases or decreases typically go directly to the Revaluation surplus account.

Recall our Sheraton Corporation example early in the chapter. Hotel and real estate holding companies would be expected to classify a large portion of their assets as investment property. Unfortunately, the FASB has removed an investment property project from its active agenda.

Intangible Long-Lived Assets The accounting under *IAS 38,* "Intangible Assets," is very similar to the accounting under U.S. GAAP.[43] Generally, acquired assets are carried at amortized cost. A revaluation method is allowed, but an active market must be available for the intangible. There is a difference regarding internally developed intangibles. *IAS 38* distinguishes between research and development in determining when expenditures may be

---

[41] "Investment Property," *IAS 40* (London: IASB, 2008).

[42] For example, *IAS 40* treats assets held under capital leases by lessees and used exclusively for rental to others under operating leases as investment properties. See Chapter 12.

[43] "Intangible Assets," *IAS 38* (London: IASB, 2008).

capitalized. **Research** is defined as "original and planned investigation undertaken with the prospect of gaining new scientific or technical knowledge and understanding." **Development** is defined as "the application of research findings or other knowledge to a plan or design for the production of new or substantially improved materials, devices, products, processes, systems or services before the start of commercial production or use."[44]

Research must be expensed, but some development expenditures may be capitalized. To capitalize development expenditures, firms must demonstrate all of the following:

1. Technical feasibility.

2. Intention to complete and use or sell the asset.

3. Ability to use or sell the asset.

4. How the intangible asset will generate probable future economic benefits.

5. The technical and financial resources necessary to complete development.

6. Ability to measure reliably expenditures related to the intangible asset during development.[45]

This IFRS rule that allows firms to capitalize some development expenditures is similar to U.S. GAAP per ASC 985-20-25, which allows computer software development costs to be capitalized after firms establish the "technological feasibility". The difference, however, is that the U.S. GAAP rule applies only to software development while the IFRS rule applies more broadly and applies to firms in other industries.

Despite the broader application, many companies often have difficulty meeting the technological feasibility hurdle for most costs because of required regulatory approvals. For example, a pharmaceutical company may not be able to demonstrate technological feasibility until an agency such as the U.S. Food and Drug Administration has approved the proposed drug. An analyst must still be alert for material capitalized development costs when comparing a company on IFRS to a U.S. firm. To make the IFRS firm comparable, the analyst would remove the net book value of the capitalized costs from assets, add back the current year's after-tax amortization, and treat the current year's capitalized amount as an expense.

Impairments   *IAS 36,* "Impairment of Assets," provides the guidelines for impairments of long-lived tangible and intangible assets other than investment property measured at fair value.[46] For **tangible assets** and **amortizable intangible assets,** events that require an impairment review are similar to the U.S. GAAP events mentioned in Stage A on page 558. However, Stage C differs in that an impairment loss occurs if the carrying value exceeds the **recoverable amount,** defined as the higher of the asset's fair value (less costs to sell) and its **value in use,** which is the *discounted* net cash flows identified in Stage B. Because of the use of *discounted* instead of *undiscounted* net cash flows, IFRS guidelines could trigger an impairment loss that would not be triggered by GAAP. In addition, in the event of a write-down, IFRS guidance would reduce the carrying value to the higher of the discounted cash flows or fair value less selling costs, whereas GAAP would reduce the carrying value to fair value (see Stage E on page 559). *Consequently, we would expect to see more frequent, but smaller, impairments under IFRS than under GAAP.* IFRS rules also permit reversals of previously recognized impairment losses when there has been a change in the estimates that were previously used to measure the loss. The reversal increases net income.

---

[44] Ibid., para. 8.

[45] Ibid., para. 57.

[46] "Impairment of Assets," *IAS 36* (London: IASB, 2008).

To illustrate the differences between GAAP and IFRS, we use our prior example of Solomon Corporation from page 560 and add a discount rate assumption of 10%. The undiscounted and discounted cash flows appear below.

Year	Net Cash Flows	PV Factor	Present Value
2014	$ 800,000	0.90909	$ 727,272
2015	400,000	0.82645	330,580
2016	300,000	0.75131	225,393
Total	$1,500,000		$1,283,245

Note: The PV factor for 2014 is the present value of $1 discounted for 1 period, 10%. The 2015 and 2016 factors are based on two and three periods, respectively.

The net cash flow column is identical to the amounts presented on page 560 except that we have combined the 2016 cash flow with the expected salvage value given that both cash flows are occurring in 2016. Under GAAP, the threshold is $1,500,000, whereas the threshold for IFRS is $1,283,245 [the higher of value in use of $1,283,245 and fair value less selling costs (assumed to be $0) of $750,000]. Net book values below $1,500,000 and above $1,283,245 would not be considered impaired under GAAP but would be under IFRS.

In this case, the carrying value of $2,000,000 is above both thresholds. However, the loss to be recognized is different. Under GAAP, the loss is $1,250,000 ($2,000,000 carrying value less $750,000 fair value), but under IFRS, the loss is only $716,755 ($2,000,000 carrying value less $1,283,245 recoverable amount). In addition, under IFRS, if the recoverable amount increases in subsequent years, some of the impairment loss can be reversed. So, differences in impairment accounting can significantly affect comparisons of IFRS and GAAP firms.

IFRS accounting for **indefinite-lived intangible assets** is similar to GAAP. These intangibles should be reviewed at least annually for impairment. However, carrying values are compared to the **recoverable amount** instead of fair value to ascertain if a write-down is needed. Also, as is the case with tangible asset impairments under IFRS, impairment losses may be reversed if circumstances change.

Summary   In summary of this section, there are significant differences between GAAP and IFRS of which an analyst should be aware. The IASB appears to be more comfortable with using expected benefits approaches (present value and net realizable values) than is the FASB. IFRS allows extensive use of fair values and gains in addition to losses are recognized in net income or other comprehensive income. We have described some of the major differences that relate to revaluation, depreciation, investment property, capitalization of intangible development costs, and impairment losses.

SUMMARY

- U.S. GAAP for long-lived assets is far from perfect. The need for unbiased, accurate, cost-effective, and verifiable numbers causes these assets to be measured in terms of the economic sacrifice incurred to obtain them—their historical cost—rather than in terms of their current expected benefit—or economic worth—to the firm.

- Because it is uncertain whether future benefits result from research and brand development costs, these costs are generally expensed in the period incurred. Consequently, balance sheet carrying amounts for intangible assets often differ from their real value to the firm. Analysts must scrutinize disclosures of R&D expenses to undo the overly conservative accounting.

- Changes in the amount of capitalized interest from one period to the next can distort earnings trends. A thorough understanding of how the GAAP measurement rules are applied allows statement readers to avoid pitfalls in trend analysis when investment in new assets is sporadic.

- When comparing return on assets (ROA) ratios across firms, one must remember that historical cost leads to an upward drift in reported ROA as assets age. So, analysts must determine whether the average age of the long-lived assets for firms being analyzed is stable or rising. Inflation also injects an upward bias into reported ROA.

- Asset impairment write-downs depend on subjective forecasts and could be used to manage earnings.

- An understanding of differences in depreciation choices across firms permits better inter-firm comparisons. When making interfirm comparisons, analysts should use note disclo-sures to overcome differences in the long-lived asset useful lives chosen by each firm and, when possible, in their depreciation patterns.

- International practices for long-lived assets are sometimes very different from those in the United States. Statement users who make cross-country comparisons must exercise caution. IFRS allows much greater use of fair value than does U.S. GAAP.

- Some of the key differences between IFRS and U.S. GAAP relate to the revaluation of tangible assets, investment property, capitalization of intangible development costs, and impairment losses.

EXERCISES

Phoenix Co. acquired a large piece of specialized machinery used in its manufacturing process. The following costs were incurred in connection with the acquisition:

E10-1

Capitalizing costs   **(LO 2)**

Finder's fee	$ 2,000
List price	230,000
Transportation fee	4,000
Speeding ticket during transportation	65
Installation fee	2,500
Cost to repair a door damaged during installation	1,200

Required:
Which of the costs incurred by Phoenix Co. should be capitalized to the machinery account?

Union Company acquired machinery on January 2, 2014, for $315,000. The machinery's esti-mated useful life is 10 years, and the estimated residual value is $15,000. Union estimates that the machine will produce 15,000 units of product and that 20,000 direct labor hours will be utilized over the useful life of the machine. During 2014, Union produced 1,200 units of prod-uct and used 2,100 direct labor hours.

E10-2

Determining depreciation expense—multiple methods **(LO 7)**

Required:
Calculate depreciation expense for 2014 under each of the following methods:

1. Straight-line method.
2. Production method (units of output).
3. Use method (units of input—direct labor hours).
4. Sum-of-the-years' digits method.
5. Double-declining balance method.

E10-3

Capitalizing costs subsequent to acquisition **(LO 2)**

Gonzo Co. owns a building in Georgia. The building's historical cost is $970,000, and $440,000 of accumulated depreciation has been recorded to date. During 2014, Gonzo incurred the following expenses related to the building:

Repainted the building	$ 48,000
Major improvement to the plumbing	109,000
Replaced carpet in the plant's accounting offices	47,600
Added a 7,000-square-foot lobby	234,600
Repaired a broken water main	155,800

Required:

1. Which of the costs incurred by Gonzo Co. should be capitalized to the building account?

2. What is the subsequent carrying amount of the building prior to recording 2014 depreciation expense?

E10-4

Determining depreciation expense—multiple methods **(LO 7)**

On April 1, 2014, Mills Company acquired equipment for $125,000. The estimated useful life is six years, and the estimated residual value is $5,000. Mills estimates that the equipment can produce 25,000 units of product. During 2014 and 2015, respectively, 3,000 and 4,200 units were produced. Mills reports on a calendar year basis.

Required:

Calculate depreciation expense for 2014 and 2015 under each of the following methods (assume that Mills calculates depreciation to the nearest month in the year of acquisition):

1. Straight-line method.

2. Production method (units of output).

3. Double-declining balance method.

4. Sum-of-the-years' digits method.

E10-5

Determining depreciation base—straight-line depreciation **(LO 2, 7)**

AICPA
ADAPTED

Apex Company purchased a tooling machine on January 3, 2004, for $30,000. The machine was being depreciated on the straight-line method over an estimated useful life of 20 years, with no salvage value.

At the beginning of 2014, when the machine had been in use for 10 years, the company paid $5,000 to overhaul it. As a result of this improvement, the company estimated that the remaining useful life of the machine was now 15 years.

Required:
What should be the depreciation expense recorded for this machine in 2014?

E10-6

Accounting for asset exchanges **(LO 9)**

The Williamsport Crosscutters baseball team had a player contract with Clemens (a promising young catcher) that was recorded in its accounting records at $500,000. The Reading Phillies had a player contract with Ruiz (a veteran outfielder) that was recorded in its accounting records at $800,000. The Crosscutters traded Clemens to Reading for Ruiz by exchanging contracts. At the time of the trade, the estimated fair value of each contract was $1,000,000. Both teams were in the midst of pennant races and believed that the trade addressed weaknesses in their respective rosters.

Required:
Prepare the journal entries to record the player trade for both Williamsport and Reading.

E10-7

Determining asset cost and depreciation expense—straight-line **(LO 2, 7)**

AICPA
ADAPTED

Samson Manufacturing Company, a calendar year company, purchased a machine for $65,000 on January 1, 2012. At the date of purchase, Samson incurred the following additional costs:

Loss on sale of old machinery	$1,000
Freight-in	500
Installation cost	2,000
Testing costs prior to regular operation	300

The machine's estimated salvage value was $5,000, and Samson estimated it would have a useful life of 20 years with depreciation being computed on the straight-line method. In January 2014, accessories costing $3,600 were added to the machine to reduce its operating costs. These accessories neither prolonged the machine's life nor provided any additional salvage value.

Required:
What should Samson record as depreciation expense for 2014?

On January 1, 2014, Hardy, Inc., purchased certain plant assets under a deferred payment contract. The agreement called for making annual payments of $10,000 for five years. The first payment is due on January 1, 2014, and the remaining payments are due on January 1 of each of the next four years. Assume an imputed interest rate of 10%.

Required:
What entry should be made to record the purchase of these plant assets on January 1, 2014?

E10-8

Buying assets with a note
(LO 2)

For $20 million, Ross Adams Mining acquired a tract of land containing a large deposit of anthracite coal. Ross Adams believes the most economical way to extract the coal is to strip-mine the site. The company is required by environmental regulations to restore the land after it has extracted the coal to a condition suitable for recreational use and—given the intended mining method—estimates restoration costs to be $6 million. Ross Adams' mining engineers estimate that the site contains 4 million tons of recoverable coal and that it will take approximately four years to complete mining activities. Once restored, the estimated value of the land amounts to $1 million. Ross Adams Mining's credit-adjusted risk free interest rate is 7%.

Required:
What should be the depletion rate per ton of coal extracted from this mine?

E10-9

Determining retirement
obligation **(LO 6)**

AICPA
ADAPTED

Clay Company started construction on a new office building on January 1, 2014, and it moved into the finished building on July 1, 2015. Of the building's $2,500,000 total cost, $2,000,000 was incurred in 2014 evenly throughout the year. Clay's incremental borrowing rate was 12% throughout 2014, and the total amount of interest incurred by Clay during 2014 was $102,000.

Required:
What amount should Clay report as capitalized interest at December 31, 2014?

E10-10

Capitalizing interest **(LO 2)**

AICPA
ADAPTED

Kobe Company began constructing a building for its own use in February 2014. During 2014, Kobe incurred interest of $70,000 on specific construction debt and $15,000 on other borrowings. Interest computed on the weighted-average amount of accumulated expenditures for the building during 2014 was $60,000.

Required:
1. What amount of interest should Kobe capitalize? Prepare the journal entry to record payment of the interest.
2. If interest computed on the weighted-average amount of accumulated expenditures for the building during 2014 was instead $90,000, what amount of interest should Kobe capitalize?

E10-11

Capitalized interest **(LO 2)**

Weir Company uses straight-line depreciation for its property, plant, and equipment, which, stated at cost, consisted of the following:

	December 31,	
	2014	**2013**
Land	$ 25,000	$ 25,000
Buildings	195,000	195,000
Machinery and equipment	695,000	650,000
	915,000	870,000
Less accumulated depreciation	(400,000)	(370,000)
	$515,000	$500,000

E10-12

Analyzing changes in asset
account balances—straight
line **(LO 3, 7)**

AICPA
ADAPTED

Weir's depreciation expense for 2014 and 2013 was $55,000 and $50,000, respectively.

Required:

What amount was debited to accumulated depreciation during 2014 because of property, plant, and equipment retirements?

E10-13

Identifying depreciation expense patterns—SL, DDB, SYO   **(LO 7)**

AICPA
ADAPTED

The following graph depicts three depreciation expense patterns over time.

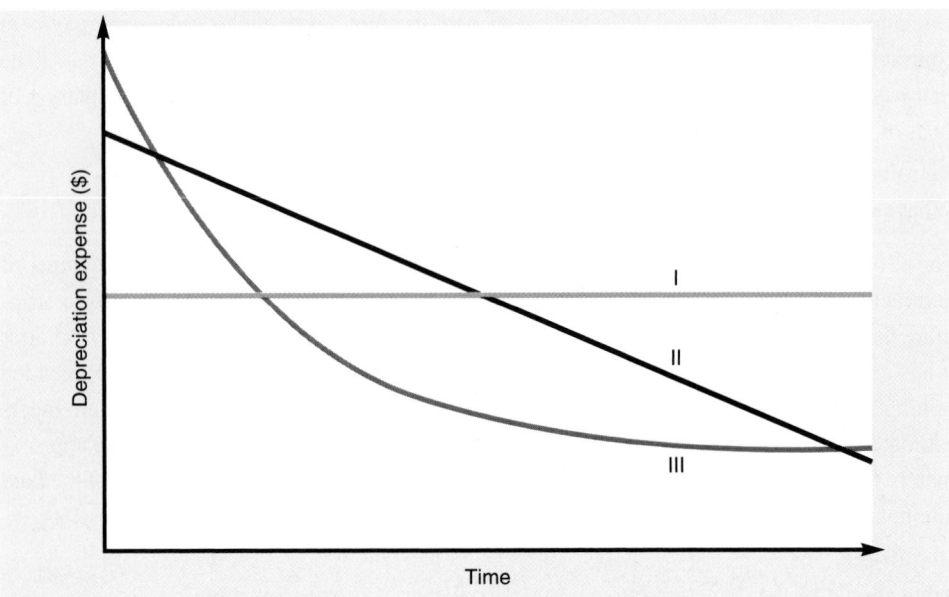

Required:

Pattern I, of course, is straight-line depreciation. Which depreciation expense pattern corresponds to the sum-of-the-years' digits method and which corresponds to the double-declining balance method? Explain why the shape of the Pattern II and Pattern III lines differs.

E10-14

Amortizing intangibles **(LO 4)**

AICPA
ADAPTED

On January 1, 2010, Vick Company purchased a trademark for $400,000, which had an estimated useful life of 16 years. In January 2014, Vick paid $60,000 for legal fees in a successful defense of the trademark.

Required:

How much should Vick record as trademark amortization expense for 2014?

E10-15

Determining amount of intangibles expensed **(LO 4)**

AICPA
ADAPTED

On January 2, 2011, Lava, Inc., purchased a patent for a new consumer product for $90,000. At the time of purchase, the patent was valid for 15 years; however, its useful life was estimated to be only 10 years due to the product's competitive nature. On December 31, 2014, the product was permanently withdrawn from sale under governmental order because of a potential health hazard in the product.

Required:

What should the total charge against income on this patent be in 2014?

E10-16

Accounting for R&D cost **(LO 4)**

AICPA
ADAPTED

During 2014, Orr Company incurred the following costs:

Research and development services performed by Key Corporation for Orr	$150,000
Design, construction, and testing of preproduction prototypes and models	200,000
Testing in search for new products or process alternatives	175,000

Required:

How much research and development expense should Orr report in 2014?

In 2014, Ball Labs incurred the following costs:

E10-17

Accounting for R&D cost
(LO 4)

AICPA
ADAPTED

Direct costs of doing contract research and development work for the government to be reimbursed by a governmental unit	$400,000

Research and development costs not included above were:

Depreciation	$300,000
Salaries	700,000
Indirect costs appropriately allocated	200,000
Materials	180,000

Required:
What was Ball's total research and development expense in 2014?

Pearl, Inc., develops and markets computer software. During 2013, one of Pearl's engineers began developing a new and very innovative software product. On July 1, 2014, a team of Pearl engineers determined that the software product was technologically feasible. Pearl engineers continued to ready the software for general release and in January 2015, the first product sales were made. Total costs incurred follow:

E10-18

Accounting for software
development costs **(LO 4)**

2013	$3,200,000
2014	$3,600,000 (evenly throughout the year)

Required:
1. How should Pearl account for the costs incurred during 2013, and what is the rationale for your answer?

2. How should Pearl account for the costs incurred during 2014? If your answer differs from your answer in requirement 1, explain why.

In January 2014, Vorst Company purchased a mineral mine for $2,640,000. Removable ore was estimated at 1,200,000 tons. After it has extracted all the ore, Vorst will be required by law to restore the land to its original condition. The expected present value of this obligation is $180,000. Vorst believes it will be able to sell the property after restoration for $300,000. During 2014, Vorst incurred $360,000 of development costs to prepare the mine for production, and it removed and sold 60,000 tons of ore.

E10-19

Determining depletion
expense with asset retirement obligation—units of
production **(LO 6, 7)**

AICPA
ADAPTED

Required:
In its 2014 income statement, what amount should Vorst report as depletion expense?

PROBLEMS / DISCUSSION QUESTIONS

On January 2, 2013, Half, Inc., purchased a manufacturing machine for $864,000. The machine has an eight-year estimated life and a $144,000 estimated salvage value. Half expects to manufacture 1,800,000 units over the machine's life. During 2014, Half manufactured 300,000 units.

P10-1

Computing depreciation
expense—SL, DDB, SYD,
and UP **(LO 7)**

AICPA
ADAPTED

Required:
For each item, calculate depreciation expense for 2014 (the second year of ownership) for the machine just described under each method listed below:

1. Straight-line

2. Double-declining balance

3. Sum-of-the-years' digits

4. Units-of-production

P10-2

Recording lump-sum purchases   (LO 2)

On June 30, 2014, Macrosoft Company acquired a 10-acre tract of land. On the tract was a warehouse that Macrosoft intended to use as a distribution center. At the time of purchase, the land had an assessed tax value of $6,300,000, and the building had an assessed tax value of $11,200,000. Macrosoft paid $15,000,000 for the land and building. After the purchase, the company paid $1,000,000 to have various modifications made to the building.

Required:

1. At what amount should Macrosoft record the land and building?

2. For financial reporting purposes, why might Macrosoft managers prefer to assign a larger portion of the $15,000,000 to the land rather than to the building?

P10-3

Determining asset cost when purchased with a note (LO 2)

Cayman Diving, Inc., needs to acquire a new dive boat. The seller will accept a noninterest-bearing note for $400,000 due in four years or $250,000 in cash. The company's incremental cost of borrowing is 10%.

Required:

Which option should Cayman Diving select? Would your answer change if Cayman's incremental borrowing rate was 13%? Why?

P10-4

Allocating acquisition costs among asset accounts and interest capitalization   (LO 2)

On April 23, 2014, Starlight Department Stores, Inc., acquired a 75-acre tract of land by paying $25,000,000 in cash and by issuing a six-month note payable for $5,000,000 and 1,000,000 shares of its common stock. On April 23, 2014, Starlight's common stock was selling for $80.00 a share and had a $2.50 par value. The land had two existing buildings, one that Starlight intended to renovate and use as a warehouse, and another that Starlight intended to demolish to make way for the construction of a new department store. At the time of the purchase, the assessed values for property tax purposes of the land and the building to be renovated were $105,000,000 and $20,000,000, respectively. To complete the purchase, Starlight incurred legal fees of $25,000. The cost of demolishing the unneeded building was $50,000. Starlight paid $250,000 to have the land graded so that the new store could be built. Starlight paid a total of $100,000,000 to have the new department store built and another $25,000,000 to renovate the old building. To fund the work on the renovation and the new store, Starlight obtained a loan from Gotham City Bank. During the construction period, Starlight incurred avoidable interest of $2,000,000 related to the warehouse renovation and $8,000,000 related to the new department store building. Because parking would be needed for both the new department store and the warehouse, Starlight had a portion of the land covered with asphalt at a cost of $450,000. Starlight also paid $200,000 to install lighting for the parking lots and $75,000 to install decorative fencing and a parking access gate. During 2014, Starlight paid $150,000 to new employees who will work at the new department store. The payments were made while the employees were being trained. All work was completed by December 31, 2014, and the new store and warehouse were placed in service on January 1, 2015.

Required:

Determine what costs should be assigned to the (1) land, (2) warehouse, (3) department store, and (4) land improvements asset accounts. (*Hint:* The allocation of the original purchase price between the land and warehouse should be made in proportion to the relative assessed values of the land and warehouse at the time of the purchase.)

P10-5

Exchanging assets   (LO 9)

Hoyle Company owns a manufacturing plant with a fair value of $4,600,000, a recorded cost of $8,500,000, and accumulated depreciation of $3,650,000. Patterson Company owns a warehouse with a fair value of $4,400,000, a recorded cost of $6,900,000, and accumulated depreciation of $2,800,000. Hoyle and Patterson exchange assets with Hoyle also receiving cash of $200,000 from Patterson. The exchange is considered to have commercial substance.

Required:

Record the exchange on the books of:

1. Hoyle

2. Patterson

Fly-by-Night is an international airline company. Its fleet includes Boeing 757s, 747s, 727s, Lockheed L-1011s, and McDonnell Douglas MD-83s, MD-80s, and DC-9s. Assume that Fly-by-Night made the following expenditures related to these aircraft in 2014:

1. New jet engines were installed on some of the MD-80s and MD-83s at a cost of $25.0 million.

2. The company paid $2.0 million to paint one-eighth of the fleet with the firm's new colors to create a new public image. It intends to paint the remainder of the fleet over the next seven years.

3. Routine maintenance and repairs on various aircraft cost $8.0 million.

4. Noise abatement equipment ("hush kits") was installed on the fleet of DC-9s to meet FAA maximum allowable noise levels on takeoff. Equipment and installation cost $7.5 million.

5. The avionics systems were replaced on the Lockheed L-1011s. This will allow the aircraft to be used four more years than originally expected.

6. The existing seats on all 747s were replaced with new, more comfortable seats at a cost of $0.5 million.

7. The jet engines on 50% of the Boeing 727s received a major overhaul at a cost of $5.0 million. As a result, the aircraft should be more fuel efficient.

Required:

1. Which of these expenditures should Fly-by-Night capitalize? Why?

2. How might Fly-by-Night use expenditures like these to manage its earnings?

Four years ago Omega Technology, Inc., acquired a machine to use in its computer chip manufacturing operations at a cost of $35,000,000. The firm expected the machine to have a seven-year useful life and a zero salvage value. The company has been using straight-line depreciation for the asset. Due to the rapid rate of technological change in the industry, at the end of Year 4, Omega estimates that the machine is capable of generating (undiscounted) future cash flows of $11,000,000. Based on the quoted market prices of similar assets, Omega estimates the machine to have a fair value of $9,500,000.

Required:

1. What is the machine's book value at the end of Year 4?

2. Should Omega recognize an impairment of this asset? Why or why not? If so, what amount of the impairment loss should be recognized?

3. At the end of Year 4, at what amount should the machine appear in Omega's balance sheet?

Yachting in Paradise, Inc., was founded late in 2007 by retired Admiral Andy Willits to provide executive retreats aboard a luxury yacht with ports of call scattered around the South Pacific. Yachting in Paradise is a U.S. firm and follows U.S. GAAP. On January 2, 2008, the company purchased the Sarah Mitcheltree, an Azimut 116 super yacht, for $15 million. Yachting in Paradise expects the Sarah Mitcheltree to have a life of 15 years and a $3 million residual value; the company uses straight-line depreciation. Charters, which can be arranged for periods lasting up to a month, are expected to generate annual net cash flows of $2.7 million. Business met expectations for the first few years, but by early 2014 the company faced a significant reduction in its future cash flows. The worldwide recession was depressing charters as client companies slashed discretionary spending, but what was really impacting Yachting in Paradise's prospects was a new—and rapidly gaining attention—phenomenon: Sick Yacht Syndrome. Norwalk Virus, bilge odors, flesh eating bacteria, mould, yeast, holding tank odors, VOC's, stale air, and diesel bacteria are all indoor air problems on a yacht. While Yachting in Paradise has yet to experience any of these symptoms on its yacht, a rash of highly publicized incidents on a larger competitor's fleet was having a ripple effect. Using probability-weighted cash flow forecasts, Yachting in Paradise now estimates that its annual net cash flows will be a disappointing $1.05 million for the next nine years and have $0 salvage value. Knowing that times were tough in the charter yacht business, a yacht broker that specializes in purchasing used luxury yachts recently offered the company $6 million for the Sarah Mitcheltree. Willits takes some comfort in knowing that at least the present value of the revised cash flows is $6.6 million, so the company will be better off by "sailing on."

Required:

1. What circumstances should prompt Yachting in Paradise, Inc., to perform an asset impairment test?

2. Is the Sarah Mitcheltree impaired? Why or why not? If the asset is impaired, how much loss should be recognized?

3. Prepare any journal entry necessary based on your answer in requirement 2.

4. If by early 2016 an economic recovery and a widely publicized cure for Sick Yacht Syndrome restore demand for executive yachting retreats, will this impact any entry made in requirement 3? Assume the recoverable amount at this time equals $8 million and that the original residual value remains unchanged.

5. Would your answer to requirement 4 be different if the recoverable amount equaled $10 million?

P10-9

Determining asset impairment under IFRS **(LO 5, 10)**

Required:

Refer to the facts in Problem 10-8. Repeat requirements 2 through 5 using the cost model (as opposed to the revaluation model) under IFRS.

P10-10

Accounting for computer software costs **(LO 4)**

In its Year 2 balance sheet, IBM reported the following account:

($ in millions)	Year 2	Year 1
Software, less accumulated amortization (Year 2: $11,276; Year 1: $10,793)	$2,419	$2,963

In the notes to its financial statements, IBM reported that it spent $2,997 million on computer software–related activities. Assume that these expenditures were related to projects in which technological feasibility has been proved.

Required:

1. How is IBM required to account for computer software–related expenditures?

2. As of the end of Year 2, how much has IBM spent on existing computer software–related activities in past years?

3. As of the end of Year 2, how much of its computer software–related expenditures has IBM capitalized?

4. Based on the information given, estimate IBM's amortization of computer software costs in Year 2.

5. Assume that IBM amortizes its capitalized software costs using the straight-line method. Estimate the average useful life of the software products developed as of the end of Year 2.

6. How might firms use the accounting for computer software costs to manage their earnings?

National Sweetener Company owns the patent to the artificial sweetener known as Super-sweet. Assume that National Sweetener acquired the patent on January 1, 2008, at a cost of $300 million dollars, expected the patent to have an economic useful life of 12 years, and has been amortizing the patent on a straight-line basis. Assume that when the patent was acquired, National Sweetener expected that the process would generate future net cash flows of $30 million the first year of its useful life and that the cash flows would increase at a 10% rate each year over the remainder of its useful life. By the year 2020, that is, after 12 years, National Sweetener expected that several other artificial sweeteners would be on the market and there-fore that it would sell the Supersweet patent then for about $60.0 million.

Year	Expected Future Cash Flows ($ in millions)	Year	Expected Future Cash Flows ($ in millions)
2008	$30.0	2015	$ 58.7
2009	33.0	2016	64.3
2010	36.3	2017	70.7
2011	39.9	2018	77.8
2012	43.9	2019	85.6
2013	48.3	Total	$641.6
2014	53.1		

On December 31, 2014, when the patent's book value was $160.0 million ($300.0 − $140.0), National Sweetener learned that one of its competitors had developed a revolutionary new sweetener that could be produced much more economically than Supersweet. National Sweet-ener expects that the introduction of this product on January 1, 2015, will substantially reduce the cash flows from its Supersweet patent process.

Consider the following two independent scenarios:

Scenario I: National Sweetener expects that the cash flows from Supersweet over the period 2015–2019 will be only 50% of those originally projected and that the sale of the Supersweet patent will bring only $25 million when sold. When discounted at a rate of 15% (which National Sweetener feels is appropriate), these amounts yield a present value of $129.0 million. National Sweetener estimates that the market value of the Supersweet patent on December 31, 2014, is $160.0 million.

Scenario II: National Sweetener expects that the cash flows from Supersweet over the period 2015–2019 will be only 25% of those originally projected and that the sale of the Supersweet patent will bring only $25 million when sold. When discounted at a rate of 15%, these amounts yield a present value of $70.7 million. National Sweetener estimates that the market value of the Supersweet patent on December 31, 2014, is $68.0 million.

Required:

1. Should National Sweetener recognize an impairment of its Supersweet patent in Scenario I? If so, what is the amount of the loss and at what amount should the patent be reported in National Sweetener's 2014 ending balance sheet?

2. Repeat requirement 1 for the second scenario.

To meet the increasing demand for its microprocessors, Intelligent Micro Devices began con-struction of a new manufacturing facility on January 1, 2014. Construction costs were incurred uniformly throughout 2014 and were recorded in the firm's Construction-in-progress account. The average balance in the Construction-in-progress account during 2014 was $150 million.

To facilitate the facility's construction, the firm arranged for an $80 million construction loan on January 1 at a rate of 13%. The firm also issued $40 million of common stock to help finance the project. Management estimates that the firm's cost of equity capital is 16%. On January 1, 2014, the firm also issued bonds in the amount of $200 million carrying a weighted-average interest rate of 11.5%. Earnings before interest and taxes for 2014 is $50 million.

Required:

1. What is the total amount of interest the firm incurred in 2014?

2. Assume that the firm bases the amount of capitalized interest on the average balance in the Construction-in-progress account. How much of the interest in requirement 1 should be capitalized?

3. How much of the amount in requirement 2 will be related to the firm's common stock issue? Why?

4. Where will the amount in requirement 2 appear in the firm's 2014 financial statements?

5. What amount of interest expense will appear in the firm's 2014 income statement?

6. Assume that the facility is completed on December 31, 2014, and that it is placed in service on January 1, 2015. How, if at all, will the amount in requirement 2 affect the future income of the firm?

7. Calculate the firm's interest coverage ratio (income before interest and taxes divided by interest expense) with and without the interest capitalization. Which coverage ratio would be more useful to a creditor in the evaluation of the firm's risk of insolvency?

P10-13

Accounting for internally developed patents versus purchased patents and making intercompany comparisons **(LO 3, 4)**

mhhe.com/revsine6e

Consider the following two scenarios:

Scenario I: Over the 2011–2015 period, Micro Systems, Inc., spends $10 million a year to develop patents on new computer hardware manufacturing technology. While some of its projects failed, the firm did develop several new patents each year during the period.

Scenario II: Over the 2011–2015 period, Macro Systems, Inc., a competitor of Micro Systems, Inc., paid $10 million each year to acquire patent rights from other firms. The firm assigned a five-year useful life to all of the patents.

1. Each firm had sales of $200 million, $242 million, $290 million, $350 million, and $400 million, respectively, over the 2011–2015 period.

2. Each firm's operating expenses (excluding the preceding patent-related information) were $140 million, $170 million, $205 million, $245 million, and $265 million, respectively, over the 2011–2015 period.

3. Assume that a 34% income tax rate applies to both firms.

Required:

1. How would the two firms account for their patent-related expenditure?

2. Calculate each firm's net income and net income as a percent of sales (that is, profit margin) for the 2011–2015 period. Contrast the reported profitability of the two firms.

3. Assume that the firms continue to spend $10 million per year in the way just described. How would the comparability of their income statements and balance sheets be affected?

P10-14

Determining earnings effects of changes in useful lives and salvage values—SL **(LO 7)**

Assume that Major Motors Corporation, a large automobile manufacturer, reported in a recent annual report to shareholders that its buildings had an original cost of $4,694,000,000.

1. Major Motors uses the straight-line depreciation method to depreciate the buildings over a useful life of 34 years.

2. Assume that the ratio of end-of-year accumulated depreciation on the buildings to their depreciable cost is 35.3%. This implies that the buildings, on average, are about 12 years old. Assume that Major Motors depreciates them to a salvage value of 5% of their original cost.

3. Assume that Major Motors' management is considering both extending the original useful lives of the buildings to 40 years from 34 years and increasing the salvage value to 10% of the buildings' original cost.

4. Assume a tax rate of 34%.

Required:

1. What is the book value of the buildings at the end of the current year (that is, before adjusting for any change in useful lives or salvage values)?

2. What would be the dollar amount and direction of the effect on Major Motors' net income if the proposed changes to the useful lives and salvage values were implemented at the start of the next fiscal year?

The 2013 income statement and other information for Mallard Corporation, which is about to purchase a new machine at a cost of $500 and a new computer system at a cost of $300, follows.

Sales	$1,000
Cost of goods sold	600
Gross profit	400
Operating expenses	150
Income before tax	250
Income taxes	85
Net income	$ 165

PI0-I5

Identifying straight-line versus accelerated depreciation ratio effects—SL and SYD
(LO 7, 8)

mhhe.com/revsine6e

Additional Information:

* The two new assets are expected to generate a 25% annual rate of growth in the firm's sales.

* The firm will include the machine's depreciation expense as part of cost of goods sold and the depreciation expense on the computer system as part of operating expenses.

* *Excluding* the new machine's depreciation, the firm's cost of goods sold is expected to increase at an annual rate of 7.5%.

* *Excluding* the new computer system's depreciation, the firm's operating expenses are expected to increase at an annual rate of 4.0%.

* The firm's gross total assets (net of asset retirements) are expected to increase at a rate of 20% per year. Average gross total assets in 2013 were $1,000. Assume that asset retirements generate no gains or losses.

* Both the machine and the computer system have a three-year useful life and a zero salvage value.

* Assume an income tax rate of 34%.

Required:

1. Assume that the assets are purchased on January 1, 2014. Prepare pro forma income statements for 2014 through 2016. Assume the firm elects to use the straight-line depreciation method for depreciating the new assets.

2. Repeat requirement 1 assuming instead that the firm elects to use the sum-of-the-years' digits method for depreciating the new assets.

3. For both requirements 1 and 2, calculate the firm's gross profit rate (gross profit divided by sales), NOPAT margin (net operating profit after tax divided by sales), and return on assets (NOPAT divided by average total assets). How does the use of the different depreciation methods affect the behavior of the ratios over the 2014–2016 period?

P10-16

Making asset age and
intercompany comparisons
(LO 3)

mhhe.com/revsine6e

Gardenia Co. and Lantana Co. both operate in the same industry. Gardenia began its operations in 2014 with a $20 million initial investment in plant and equipment with an expected life of 10 years. Lantana's net asset base is also $20 million, but its assets are, on average, 5 years old with 10-year expected useful lives on January 1, 2014. Lantana replaces 10% of its assets each year at year-end, while Gardenia, having just entered the industry, does not have immediate plans to replace any assets.

Per year pre-tax net operating cash flow generated $3 million for Gardenia, and $5 million for Lantana. Inflation is expected to be 2% per year, and each company expects to keep pace by increasing its pre-tax net operating cash flow by 2% per year. The cost of Lantana's planned asset replacements will also increase at 2% per year. (*Note:* For simplicity, assume that prior to 2014, the replacement cost of Lantana's assets remained constant.)

Required:

1. Compute return on assets for Gardenia Co. for 2014 through 2018.
2. Compute return on assets for Lantana Co. for 2014 through 2018.
3. Discuss the differences between your answers to requirement 1 and requirement 2.

P10-17

Accounting for asset
retirement obligations
(LO 6)

Coyote Co. is building a waste landfill in the desert between Arizona and California. Coyote estimates that this landfill will be in operation for five years, will cost $250 million to build, and will generate $800 million in revenues during its useful life. Federal law requires that Coyote decommission and decontaminate the site at the end of its useful life. A team of engineers has studied the decontamination procedure and has estimated that Coyote will have to spend $15 million on the decommissioning process when the landfill is shut down in five years. Coyote's credit-adjusted rate of interest is 10%.

Required:

1. In accordance with GAAP, how should Coyote Co. account for the costs associated with the decommissioning process? Prepare the journal entry required and prepare an amortization table.
2. How are the costs associated with the decommissioning process reflected on the income statement? Explain how this accounting treatment improves the matching process.

P10-18

Accounting for assets held
for sale   **(LO 6)**

Prescott Co. management has committed to a plan to dispose of a group of assets associated with the manufacture of railroad cars. This group of assets qualifies as a component of an entity for financial reporting purposes. As of December 31, 2014, management has located a likely purchaser and is in negotiations to complete the sale. It's expected that the component will be sold in late 2015 for $5,900,000 and that the following costs will be incurred in conjunction with the sale:

Brokers' fees	$360,000
Legal fees	246,000
Closing costs	67,000

The railroad manufacturing assets have a historical cost of $12,000,000 and accumulated depreciation of $5,500,000 computed using the straight-line method. These assets generated a net loss during 2014 of $475,000 on sales of $1,800,000 and are expected to generate a loss of $525,000 during 2015.

During 2014, Prescott had operating income, including the railroad component, of $7,400,000 and total productive assets, including the railroad component, of $94,500,000 (net of cumulative straight-line depreciation). Sales for the company as a whole for the year ended December 31, 2014, were $20,000,000.

Required:

1. Compute the carrying value at December 31, 2014, of the railroad assets held for sale. How are these assets reported on the December 31, 2014, balance sheet?

2. Prepare a partial income statement including the discontinued operations section for Prescott Co. for the year ended December 31, 2014. Ignore income taxes.

3. Ignoring income taxes, compute return on continuing operating assets and operating margin for Prescott Co. for 2014. Now, assuming that the asset group did **not** qualify for discontinued operations treatment, compute return on continuing operating assets and operating margin for Prescott for 2014. Contrast the two sets of ratios and comment on your results.

4. How will the group of railroad assets be accounted for during 2015?

Required:

1. Contrast the economic sacrifice and expected benefit approaches to long-lived asset valuation.

2. GAAP requires firms to use historical cost (in most cases) to report the value of long-lived assets. As a statement reader, do you think that firms should be encouraged to voluntarily report their asset values under alternative valuation approaches? Why or why not?

3. As the manager of a publicly held company, what costs and benefits do you see associated with the voluntary disclosure of asset values using approaches other than historical cost?

P10-19

Evaluating approaches to long-lived asset valuation **(LO 1)**

Zeff Company purchases a delivery van on January 1, Year 1, at a cost of $15,849. It has a useful life of four years and no estimated salvage value. When making the purchase decision, the company anticipated that the use of the van would generate a revenue (cash) inflow of $5,000 each year, assumed to occur at the end of the year. The discount rate that equates the purchase price to the expected cash inflows is 10%. Assume that depreciation is the company's only expense for the year.

P10-20

Weakness of the straight-line depreciation method **(LO 1, 7)**

Requirements:

1. Using straight-line depreciation, do the following for each of the four years:
   a. Compute accumulated depreciation and the net book value of the van.
   b. Prepare Zeff's income statement assuming that the $5,000 expected inflows occur.
   c. Compute the return on beginning net fixed assets.

2. Repeat requirements 1.a. through 1.c. using the discounted present value method of depreciation.

3. Which depreciation method provides the most useful information?

4. Why do you think that GAAP does not permit the discounted present value method of depreciation?

IceCap Hotels operates a series of northern European hotels and reports under IFRS. On June 30, 2013, IceCap purchased land for €3,000,000. IceCap reports land values on the balance sheet under Property, plant, and equipment. The appraisal value for the land (which you can assume is the same as the recoverable amount) was reported as:

P10-21

IFRS impairment and revaluation **(LO 10)**

Appraisal Date	Land Value
12/31/2013	€3,150,000
12/31/2014	€2,750,000
12/31/2015	€2,850,000

Required:

1. Prepare the journal entries at the end of 2013, 2014, and 2015 to record any changes in value to this land asset if IceCap chooses the IFRS cost model to value this property.

2. Prepare the journal entries at the end of 2013, 2014, and 2015 to record any changes in value to this land asset if IceCap chooses the IFRS revaluation model to value this property.

P10-22

IFRS impairment and
revaluation   **(LO 10)**

IceCap Hotels operates a series of northern European hotels and reports under IFRS. On June 30, 2013, IceCap purchased a hotel for €2,100,000. IceCap reports hotel values on the balance sheet under property, plant, and equipment. The estimated useful life of the hotel is 30 years from the date of purchase. The company uses straight-line depreciation for its hotels. The appraisal value for the hotel (which you can assume is the same as the recoverable amount) was reported as:

Appraisal Date	Hotel Value
12/31/2013	€2,200,000
12/31/2014	€1,400,000
12/31/2015	€1,700,000

Required:

1. Prepare the journal entries at the end of 2013, 2014, and 2015 to record any changes in value to this hotel asset if IceCap chooses the IFRS cost model to value this property.

2. Prepare the journal entries at the end of 2013, 2014, and 2015 to record any changes in value to this hotel asset if IceCap chooses the IFRS revaluation model to value this property.

CASES

C10-1

Target Corporation and
Wal-Mart Stores, Inc.:
Identifying depreciation
differences and performing
financial statement analysis
(LO 8)

Target Corporation operates as two reportable segments: Retail and Credit Card. The Retail Segment includes merchandising operations, including large-format general merchandise and food discount stores in the United States and a fully integrated online business. Target offers both everyday essentials and fashionable, differentiated merchandise at discounted prices. The Credit Card Segment offers credit to qualified guests through branded proprietary credit cards, the Target Visa and the Target Card.

Wal-Mart Stores, Inc., is engaged in the operations of retail stores located in all 50 states of the United States; has wholly owned subsidiaries in Argentina, Brazil, Canada, Japan, Puerto Rico, and the United Kingdom; majority-owned subsidiaries in Central America, Chile, and Mexico; and joint ventures in India and China. The company's merchandising operations serve its customers primarily through the operations of three segments: the Walmart Stores U.S. segment includes the company's mass merchant concept in the United States operating under the "Walmart" brand, as well as walmart.com; the International segment consists of the company's operations outside of the 50 United States; the Sam's Club segment includes the warehouse membership clubs in the United States, as well as samsclub.com.

Information taken from both firms' 2009 annual reports to shareholders follows.

Target Corporation

Property and Equipment

($ in millions)	January 30, 2010	January 31, 2009
Land	$ 5,793	$ 5,767
Buildings and improvements	22,152	20,430
Fixtures and equipment	4,743	4,270
Computer hardware and software	2,575	2,586
Construction in progress	502	1,763
Accumulated depreciation	(10,485)	(9,060)
Property and equipment—net	$25,280	$25,756

Property and equipment are recorded at cost, less accumulated depreciation. Depreciation is computed using the straight-line method over estimated useful lives. Accelerated depreciation methods are generally used for income tax purposes.

Estimated useful lives by major asset category are as follows:

Asset	Life (in Years)
Buildings and improvements	8–39
Fixtures and equipment	3–15
Computer hardware and software	4–7

Selected Income Statement Information

	Years Ended	
($ in millions)	January 30, 2010	January 31, 2009
Depreciation and amortization	$2,023	$1,826
Earnings before income taxes	3,872	3,536
Net earnings	2,488	2,214

Wal-Mart Stores, Inc.

Property and Equipment

($ in millions)	January 31, 2010	January 31, 2009
Land	$ 22,591	$19,852
Buildings and improvements	77,452	73,810
Fixtures and equipment	35,450	29,851
Transportation equipment	2,355	2,307
Property under capital lease	5,669	5,341
Less accumulated depreciation and amortization:		
Property owned	(38,304)	(32,964)
Property under capital leases	(2,906)	(2,544)
Total	$102,307	$95,653

Depreciation and amortization for financial statement purposes are provided on the straight-line method over the estimated useful lives of the various assets. For income tax purposes, accelerated methods are used with recognition of deferred income taxes for the resulting temporary differences.

Estimated useful lives for financial statement purposes are as follows:

Asset	Life (in Years)
Buildings and improvements	5–40
Fixtures and equipment	3–20
Transportation equipment	4–15

Selected Income Statement Information

	Years Ended	
($ in millions)	January 31, 2010	January 31, 2009
Depreciation and amortization	$ 7,157	$ 6,739
Income from continuing operations before income taxes	22,066	20,898
Net income	14,335	13,400

Required:

Assume a 35% tax rate.

1. Estimate the average useful life of each firm's long-lived assets.

2. Calculate a revised estimate of Walmart's 2009 depreciation expense using the estimated average useful life of Target's assets. Use this amount to recalculate Wal-Mart's income before taxes and net income.

3. Calculate a revised estimate of Target's 2009 depreciation expense using the estimated average useful life of Walmart's assets. Use this amount to recalculate Target's 2009 income before taxes and net income.

4. Why might a financial analyst want to make adjustments in requirements 2 and 3?

5. What factors will affect the reliability and accuracy of the adjustments performed in requirements 2 and 3?

C10-2

Granite Construction:
Analyzing financial statement effects of capitalized interest
(LO 2)

Granite Construction is one of the largest heavy civil construction contractors in the United States. Granite operates nationwide, serving both public and private sector clients. Within the public sector, the company primarily concentrates on infrastructure projects, including the construction of roads, highways, bridges, dams, tunnels, canals, mass transit facilities, and airport infrastructure.

The following information was taken from Granite's annual report to shareholders.

Granite Construction Incorporated

Consolidated Statement of Income

	Years Ended December 31,		
($ in millions)	2012	2011	2010
Interest expense	$10.6	$10.4	$ 9.7
Capitalized interest	(2.3)	(7.4)	(8.1)
Income before income taxes	81.0	89.4	(106.4)
Net income	$59.9	$66.1	$(62.4)

Consolidated Statement of Cash Flows

Cash paid during the year for interest	$11.5	$16.2	$ 15.7

Required:

1. What is the underlying rationale for the capitalization of interest?

2. Assume that none of the assets to which 2012 capitalized interest applies have been completed and placed into service. Calculate the firm's 2012 income before income taxes, assuming that no interest was capitalized in 2012. What is the percentage change from the reported amount?

3. Starting with net income of $59.9 million as reported in 2012, assume the same facts as in requirement 2 and recalculate Granite's *net* income.

4. Briefly discuss the impact of capitalized interest on a firm's future reported earnings.

C10-3

National Coal Corporation:
Analyzing financial statement effects of depreciation policy changes　**(LO 3, 7)**

National Coal Corporation mines, processes, and sells high-quality bituminous steam coal from mines located in Tennessee and southeastern Kentucky. The company owns the coal mineral rights to approximately 74,600 acres of land and leases the rights to approximately 40,900 additional acres. National Coal has expanded its operations considerably since commencing operations at a single surface mine in Tennessee in July 2003.

The following information is excerpted from National Coal Corporation's 2005 annual report to shareholders.

National Coal Corporation

Consolidated Statements of Operations

	Year Ended December 31,		Eleven Months Ended December 31,
	2005	2004	2003
Total revenues	$65,872,634	$ 16,998,912	$ 1,190,643
Expenses:			
Cost of sales	51,115,116	16,322,632	1,737,937
Depreciation, depletion, and amortization	10,107,723	2,473,369	617,155
General and administrative	7,213,346	5,242,437	1,871,414
Total operating expenses	68,436,185	24,038,438	4,226,506
Operating loss	(2,563,551)	(7,039,526)	(3,035,863)
Total other income (expense)	(4,227,620)	(3,389,604)	(297,022)
Net (loss)	$(6,791,171)	$(10,429,130)	$(3,332,885)

Property, Plant, Equipment and Mine Development

Property and equipment are stated at cost. Maintenance and repairs that do not improve efficiency or extend economic life are expensed as incurred. Plant and equipment are depreciated using the straight-line method over the estimated useful lives of assets which generally range from seven to thirty years for building and plant and one to five years for equipment. On sale or retirement, asset cost and re-lated accumulated depreciation are removed from the accounts and any related gain or loss is reflected in income.

The Company periodically reviews the estimated useful lives of its fixed assets. During the second quarter of 2005, this review indicated that the estimated useful lives for certain asset categories were gener-ally determined to be less than those employed in calculating depreciation expense. As a result, the Com-pany revised the estimated useful lives of mining equipment as of the beginning of the second quarter.

Depreciation, Depletion, Accretion and Amortization Expense

The increase in depreciation, depletion, accretion and amortization expense in the twelve-month period ended December 31, 2005, compared to the twelve-month period ended December 31, 2004, is primarily attributable to a 493.3% increase in depreciation. This change was due to the acquisition of $19.3 mil-lion of fixed assets, primarily mining equipment, and a change in the estimated useful lives of our min-ing equipment. On April 1, 2005, we changed our policy for the depreciable life of mining equipment to three to five years from seven years. Subsequently, most of our equipment was estimated to have a three-year useful life. This had the impact of increasing depreciation on mining equipment by approximately $3.6 million during 2005. This adjustment was treated as a change in accounting estimate and deprecia-tion expense was adjusted on a prospective basis.

Required:

1. Calculate the impact of the depreciation policy change on National Coal's 2005 net income (loss). Consider the effects of income taxes in your answer.
2. How will the change affect National Coal's reported earnings over the next few years?
3. How might a financial analyst determine whether the change National Coal made is reasonable in light of industry conditions?
4. How might firms use depreciation policy changes to manage their earnings? Is there anything to prevent rampant use of depreciation policy changes as a tool to manage reported earnings?
5. In light of contracting issues discussed in Chapter 7, speculate as to the possible reasons National Coal made the change in its depreciation policy.

C10-4

Royal Dutch Shell plc:
Identifying differences and
similarities between IFRS
and GAAP **(LO 10)**

Presented below are excerpts from the 2012 annual report of Royal Dutch Shell, a Dutch company that finds, extracts, processes, and sells oil and gas.

B—Depreciation, Depletion and Amortisation

Property, plant and equipment related to hydrocarbon production activities are depreciated on a unit-of-production basis over the proved developed reserves of the field concerned, except in the case of assets whose useful lives differ from the lifetime of the field, in which cases the straight-line method is applied. Rights and concessions in respect of proved properties are depleted on the unit-of-production basis over the total proved reserves of the relevant area. Where individually insignificant, unproved properties may be grouped and depreciated based on factors such as the average concession term and past experience of recognising proved reserves.

Other property, plant and equipment and intangible assets are depreciated and amortised on a straight-line basis over their estimated useful lives, except for goodwill, which is not amortised. They include major inspection costs, which are depreciated over the estimated period before the next planned major inspection (three to five years), and the following:

Asset type	Useful life
Upgraders	30 years
Refineries and chemical plants	20 years
Retail service stations	15 years
Property, plant and equipment held under finance leases	lease term
Software	5 years
Trademarks	40 years

Estimates of the useful lives and residual values of property, plant and equipment and intangible assets are reviewed annually and adjusted if appropriate.

C—Impairment

The carrying amount of goodwill is tested for impairment annually; in addition, assets other than unproved properties (see "Exploration costs") are tested for impairment whenever events or changes in circumstances indicate that the carrying amounts for those assets may not be recoverable. If assets are determined to be impaired, the carrying amounts of those assets are written down to their recoverable amount, which is the higher of fair value less costs to sell and value-in-use.

Value-in-use is determined as the amount of estimated risk-adjusted discounted future cash flows. For this purpose, assets are grouped into cash generating units based on separately identifiable and largely independent cash inflows. Estimates of future cash flows used in the evaluation of impairment of assets are made using management's forecasts of commodity prices, market supply and demand, product margins and, in the case of exploration and production assets, expected production volumes. The latter takes into account assessments of field and reservoir performance and includes expectations about both proved reserves and volumes that are expected to constitute proved reserves in the future (unproved volumes), which are risk-weighted utilising geological, production, recovery and economic projections. Cash flow estimates are risk-adjusted to reflect local conditions as appropriate and discounted at a rate based on Shell's marginal cost of debt.

Impairments, except those related to goodwill, are reversed as applicable to the extent that the events or circumstances that triggered the original impairment have changed.

Impairment charges and reversals are reported within depreciation, depletion and amortisation.

On reclassification as held for sale, the carrying amounts of intangible assets and property, plant and equipment are also reviewed and, where appropriate, written down to their fair value less costs to sell. No further provision for depreciation, depletion or amortisation is charged.

2012 $ million	Upstream	Downstream	Corporate	Total
Impairment losses	980	138	3	1,121
Impairment reversals	—	24	—	24

($ in millions)	2012	2011	2010
Impairment losses			
Exploration and production assets	940	317	1,620
Manufacturing and distribution	49	1,134	1,140
Other	93	36	33
Total	1,082	1,487	2,793
Impairment reversals			
Exploration and production assets	—	—	40
Manufacturing and distribution	23	4	7
Other	1	—	1
Total	24	4	48

Impairment losses and reversals have been recognised in the year in respect of a number of cash-generating units, although no single instance is individually significant. Impairment chares were driven generally by changes in development and production plans in Upstream and, in 2011 and 2010, by lower refining margins in Downstream. Information on the segments affected is presented in Note 4.

Required:
Using the Royal Dutch Shell excerpts, identify the similarities and differences between U.S. GAAP and IFRS regarding accounting for property, plant, and equipment.

Presented below are excerpts from the 2012 annual report of Marston's PLC, a UK-based company that operates pubs.

C10-5

Marston's PLC: Identifying differences and similarities between IFRS and GAAP **(LO 10)**

	Note	29 September 2012 £m	1 October 2011 £m
Shareholders' equity			
Equity share capital	27	44.3	44.3
Share premium account		332.8	332.6
Merger reserve	28	—	41.5
Revaluation reserve		560.4	411.4
Capital redemption reserve	28	6.8	6.8
Hedging reserve		(129.6)	(101.4)
Own shares	28	(130.9)	(130.9)
Retained earnings		78.2	213.3
Total equity		**762.0**	**817.6**

Property, plant and equipment

• Freehold and leasehold properties are initially stated at cost and subsequently at valuation. Plant and machinery and fixtures, fittings, tools and equipment are stated at cost.

• Depreciation is charged to the income statement on a straight-line basis to provide for the cost of the assets less residual value over their useful lives.

• Freehold and long leasehold buildings are depreciated to residual value over 50 years.

• Short leasehold properties are depreciated over the life of the lease.

• Plant and machinery and fixtures, fittings, tools and equipment are depreciated over periods ranging from 3 to 15 years.

• Own labour and interest costs directly attributable to capital projects are capitalised.

• Land is not depreciated.

   Residual values and useful lives are reviewed and adjusted if appropriate at each balance sheet date.

   Properties are revalued by qualified valuers on a sufficiently regular basis using open market value so that the carrying value of an asset does not differ significantly from its fair value at the balance sheet date. Substantially all of the Group's properties have been externally valued in accordance with the Royal institution of Chartered Surveyors' Red Book. These valuations are performed directly by reference to observable prices in an active market or recent market transactions on arm's length terms. Internal valuations are performed on the same basis.

The estate is reviewed for indication of impairment at each reporting date, using a process focusing on areas of risk and business performance throughout the portfolio to identify any exposure.

Impairment losses are charged to the revaluation reserve to the extent that a previous gain has been recorded, and thereafter to the income statement. Surpluses on revaluation are recognised in the revaluation reserve, except to the extent that they reverse previously charged impairment losses, in which case the reversal is recorded in the income statement.

Disposals of property, plant and equipment

Profit/loss on disposal of property, plant and equipment represents net sale proceeds less the carrying value of the assets. Any element of the revaluation reserve relating to the property disposed of is transferred to retained earnings at the date of sale.

Impairment

If there are indications of impairment or reversal of impairment, an assessment is made of the recoverable amount. An impairment loss is recognised where the recoverable amount is lower that the carrying value of assets, including goodwill. The recoverable amount is the higher of value in use and fair market value less costs to sell.

12. Property, Plant and Equipment

	Land and buildings £m	Plant and machinery £m	Fixtures, fittings. tools and equipment £m	Total £m
Cost or valuation				
At 2 October 2011	1,819.5	40.4	351.6	2,211.5
Additions	91.3	3.9	36.3	131.5
Net transfers to assets held for sale and disposals	(58.8)	(2.3)	(35.6)	(96.7)
Revaluation	(32.6)	—	—	(32.6)
At 29 September 2012	**1,819.4**	**42.0**	**352.3**	**2,213.7**
Depreciation				
At 2 October 2011	13.5	22.5	186.1	222.1
Charge for the period	2.0	3.2	34.5	39.7
Net transfers to assets held for sale and disposals	—	(2.3)	(28.4)	(30.7)
Revaluation/impairment	(15.2)	—	2.2	(13.0)
At 29 September 2012	**0.3**	**23.4**	**194.4**	**218.1**
Net book amount at 1 October 2011	1,806.0	17.9	165.5	1,989.4
Net book amount at 29 September 2012	**1,819.1**	**18.6**	**157.9**	**1,995.6**

Required:

Using the Marston's excerpts, identify the similarities and differences between U.S. GAAP and IFRS regarding accounting for property, plant, and equipment.

www .mhhe.com/revsine6e

Remember to check the book's companion website for additional study material.

Financial Instruments as Liabilities | 11

Lhe Financial Accounting Standards Board (FASB) says:

> Liabilities are probable future sacrifices of economic benefits arising from present obligations of a particular entity to transfer assets or to provide services to other entities in the future as a result of past transactions or events.[1]

Simply, this means that a financial statement liability is

1. An existing obligation arising from past events, which calls for
2. Payment of cash or provision of goods and services (say, delivery of a product for which a deposit has already been received) to some other entity at some future date.

Liabilities help businesses conduct their affairs by permitting delay—delay in payment or performance. But because "time is money," interest is a common feature of delayed payment liabilities. **Interest** is the price charged for delaying payment.

Most liabilities are **monetary liabilities** because they are payable in a future amount of cash. There are **nonmonetary liabilities** that are satisfied by the delivery of items other than cash, such as goods or services. An example of a nonmonetary liability is a product warranty. If the product fails during the warranty period, the warranty liability is satisfied by providing nonmonetary assets—labor and replacement parts from inventory or a new product—but not cash.

BALANCE SHEET PRESENTATION

Conceptually, monetary liabilities should be shown in the financial statements at the *discounted present value* of the future cash outflows required to satisfy the obligation. This discounted present value approach allows interest to accumulate over time through accounting entries that assign interest expense—the cost of delay—to the time period(s) over which payment is delayed. In practice, this is what is done with long-term monetary liabilities.

[1] "Elements of Financial Statements," *Statement of Financial Accounting Concepts No. 6* (Stamford, CT: FASB, 1985), para. 35.

Chapter

EXHIBIT 11.1 Oracle Corporation

Liabilities Section of Consolidated Balance Sheets

($ in millions)	2012	2011
Current liabilities:		
Notes payable, current and other current borrowings	$ 2,950	$ 1,150
Accounts payable	438	494
Accrued compensation and related benefits	2,002	2,320
Deferred revenues	7,035	6,802
Other current liabilities	2,963	3,426
Total current liabilities	$15,388	$14,192
Noncurrent liabilities:		
Notes payable and other noncurrent borrowings	13,524	14,772
Income taxes payable	3,759	3,169
Other noncurrent liabilities	1,569	1,157
Total noncurrent liabilities	$18,852	$19,098
Commitments and contingencies		

However, **current liabilities**—obligations due within a year or within the company's operating cycle, whichever is longer—are rarely discounted. Current liabilities are rarely discounted because their short maturity makes immaterial the difference between the amount due at maturity and the present value of that maturity amount. So, current liabilities are shown at the undiscounted amount due.[2] This treatment of current liabilities departs from the conceptual "ideal" solely on pragmatic grounds—the dollar difference between the maturity amount and present value amount is quite small.

Noncurrent monetary liabilities are initially recorded at their present value when incurred. There are occasional exceptions, which we discuss in Chapter 13, but the general rule is that noncurrent monetary liabilities are first recorded at their present value.

To help you visualize how these liability valuation concepts apply in practice, refer to Exhibit 11.1, which reproduces the liabilities section of Oracle Corporation's balance sheet. Oracle is one of the world's leading suppliers of software for information management.

Listed among the company's current liabilities you will find:

- Accounts payable that represent amounts owed to suppliers.

- Accrued compensation and related benefits that represent amounts owed to Oracle employees for services already rendered.

- Other current liabilities that represent amounts owed to various parties such as insurance providers, electric utility and telecommunication companies, and state and federal tax agencies.

Because these accounts are shown as current liabilities, you can be sure of two things:

1. The obligations are due within a year or within the company's operating cycle, whichever is longer—at Oracle, "current" means "due within one year."

2. These current liabilities are shown at the undiscounted amount due even though some may remain unpaid for a full year.

---

[2] An exception is the current portion of long-term debt.

Oracle's current liabilities also include deferred revenues that arise when customers pay for the company's software upgrades or consulting services in advance of actual delivery. Because Oracle is obligated to provide software products or consulting services—but not cash—in the future, this account is a nonmonetary liability and the amount shown represents a portion of the cash payments received from these customers. (Chapter 3 describes how the deferred revenue amount is determined.)

Oracle's long-term debt is shown in two places on the balance sheet:

- The amount due within one year is listed among current liabilities as Notes payable, current, and other current borrowings.

- Amounts due after one year are shown separately as Notes payable and other noncurrent borrowings.

> The deferred tax liabilities listed among noncurrent liabilities on Oracle's balance sheet are described in Chapter 13. Other long-term liabilities, which arise primarily from employee pension and health care benefits, are described in Chapter 14.

This classification helps analysts and investors spot any large debt payments that may come due next year—for Oracle, the amount of short-term borrowings and long-term debt due in 2013 (that is, the next year) is $2,950 million. Long-term debt is a noncurrent monetary liability and is shown at the discounted present value of the amount due.

GLOBAL VANTAGE POINT

 **International**

If you were to examine the liabilities section of a balance sheet prepared under international financial reporting rules, you would most likely find the format strikingly similar to the one shown in Exhibit 11.1 for Oracle, a U.S. company. That's because most foreign firms that use IFRS prepare classified balance sheets where current liabilities are listed first, long-term liabilities are listed second, and shareholders' equity accounts third. But there are exceptions.

Aixtron Aktiengesellschaft, the German semiconductor equipment manufacturer, presents its liabilities in reverse order. Those to be paid in the distant future (think long-term debt maturing in 30 years) are listed first whereas obligations to be paid near term (e.g., wages payable due in two weeks) are listed last. To further complicate the presentation format, Aixtron shows stockholders' equity accounts above (not below) its liabilities. Pick up a copy of Aixtron's balance sheet and you will find the accounts grouped in the following order: stockholders' equity, noncurrent liabilities, and finally current liabilities. This unusual presentation pattern is allowed under *International Accounting Standard 1,* "Presentation of Financial Statements" (International Accounting Standards Board, London, UK; revised January 2009).

DEBT OR EQUITY?

Suppose a start-up Internet company, Yellowbird.com, buys $100,000 of computers from a manufacturer, say Dell Inc. Instead of paying cash, Yellowbird promises to pay Dell $100,000 worth of Yellowbird stock when the company goes public (in about six months). Yellowbird is using its stock as "currency" for the transaction because it lacks cash. Should the promised payment be classified as a liability or as equity on Yellowbird's books?

Financial instruments with characteristics of both liabilities and equity are not easily assigned to either balance sheet category. In this example, the financial instrument is Yellowbird's payment promise. The promise does indeed constitute an *existing obligation* (to pay Dell $100,000) *arising from past events,* and these two characteristics meet the definition of an accounting liability as described earlier. However, cash is not the form of payment. Dell will instead receive shares of Yellowbird stock. This characteristic makes the transaction appear to be an equity investment by Dell. How then should Yellowbird classify its obligation to Dell?

GAAP guidance resolves the dilemma.[3] Notice that a fixed amount of value ($100,000), not a fixed number of Yellowbird shares, must be conveyed to Dell. GAAP says that this feature of the promise makes the relationship more like that of a debtor–creditor. Unlike an owner, Dell cannot benefit from increases or suffer from decreases in share value from the time of the promise to the time of payment because Yellowbird is obligated to deliver stock worth exactly $100,000. So, Yellowbird must record the payment obligation as a $100,000 liability.

Here is another financial instrument with characteristics of both debt and equity. Wilbourne Corporation issues $250,000 of 10% preferred stock to investors who pay cash for the shares. The "10%" means that investors can expect to receive a preferred dividend payment of $25,000 (or 10% of the $250,000 issue price) each year. Under normal circumstances, Wilbourne classifies the financial instrument (preferred stock) as equity on its balance sheet. But suppose the preferred shares are issued with a **mandatory redemption** feature that requires Wilbourne to buy back the stock in five years for $250,000. This unconditional obligation to repurchase makes the instrument much more like debt than equity. Notice that the preferred stock cash flow stream is identical to that for a five-year loan of $250,000 with annual interest payments set at 10% of the loan balance. So, even though the instrument's legal form is preferred stock, FASB Accounting Standards Codification™ (ASC) Topic 480 says Wilbourne must classify the payment obligation as a liability.

Financial instruments with both liability and equity characteristics are common today, and instruments with new characteristics are created every year. They pose significant challenges for accountants, who must determine the proper balance sheet classification for each instrument, and for analysts, who must unravel its implications for enterprise valuation and credit risk.

BONDS PAYABLE

> **Convertible bonds** give investors the opportunity—but not the obligation—to exchange a company's debt for common stock. Chapter 15 describes the accounting complexities that arise with convertible bonds.

Firms issue bonds to raise cash. A **bond** is a financial instrument that represents a formal promise to repay both the amount borrowed as well as the interest on the amount borrowed. **Debentures,** the most common type of corporate bond, are backed only by the company's general credit. **Mortgage bonds** use real estate as collateral for repayment of the loan. **Serial bonds** require periodic payment of interest and a portion of the principal (for example, an equal amount each year to maturity). Despite these and other differences, the accounting for these debt instruments follows the general approach described here.

The precise terms of the borrowing are specified in the **bond indenture agreement**—the contract between the bond's issuer (that is, the borrower) and the bond's investors (lenders). In this section, we look at how companies account for this debt instrument and how to interpret debt disclosures in financial statements.

Characteristics of Bond Cash Flows

Bond certificates are usually issued with a **principal amount** of $1,000. The principal amount—also called the **par value, maturity value,** or **face value**—represents the amount that will be repaid to the investor at the maturity date specified in the indenture agreement. The bond certificate also displays the **stated interest rate**—sometimes called the **nominal rate.**

---

[3] FASB ASC Topic 480: Distinguishing Liabilities from Equity. The FASB and its global counterpart, the International Accounting Standards Board (IASB), are working jointly to clarify and converge the reporting requirements for financial instruments with equity characteristics. The project timeline calls for some conclusions to be reached in 2014, so stay tuned in.

The annual cash interest payments on the bond are computed by multiplying the principal (face) amount by the stated interest rate. A bond with $1,000 principal and a 9% per year stated interest rate will have annual cash interest payments of $90. Typically, the total annual cash interest is paid in installments, either quarterly or semiannually.

While the face value is typically $1,000 per bond, the price at which it is issued can be equal to, less, or more than the face value.

> Investors must be careful to read the details of a bond's interest payment terms. For example, investors who own a bond that pays "9% interest annually" receive a single payment of $90 (per $1,000 of face value) each year. A bond that pays "9% interest semiannually" yields two payments of $45 each year (9%/2 = 4.5% each payment period). Although the total dollar interest payment is $90 per year in both cases, the semiannual bond is slightly more valuable because investors receive half of the cash earlier each year than in the case of the annual payment bond. Semiannual bonds are quite common, and the accounting for them is explored in Problems 11-2 and 11-3.

- When the issue price exactly equals the face value, the bond is sold at **par.**
- If the issue price is less than face value, the bond is sold at a **discount.**
- If the issue price is more than face value, the bond is sold at a **premium.**

Market conditions and the borrower's credit risk dictate the relationship between what investors are willing to pay—the issue price—and the bond's face value.

Bonds Issued at Par

A bond's issue price determines its **effective yield**—or true rate of return. When the bond's issue price equals its par value, the effective yield to investors exactly equals the stated (or nominal) rate. Consider this example:

> On January 1, 2014, Huff Corporation issued $1,000,000 face value of 10% per year bonds at par—that is, Huff obtained $1,000,000 cash from investors and promised to make interest and principal payments in the future. Because the cash interest payments on the bonds always equal the stated interest rate (10%) times the bond principal amount ($1,000,000), cash interest will total $100,000 per year. The bonds mature in 10 years (on December 31, 2023), and interest is paid annually on December 31 of each year.

The accounting entry to record issuance of these bonds on Huff's books is:

DR	Cash	$1,000,000	
	CR	Bonds payable	$1,000,000

The bonds are recorded at the issue price—the $1,000,000 cash Huff received.

To show that the effective yield equals 10% in this example, we list the cash payments and compute their present value as of the issue date—January 1, 2014—in Exhibit 11.2. The effective yield is precisely 10% because the present value of the 10 annual interest payments ($614,456) plus the present value of the principal repayment ($385,544) equals the issue proceeds received on January 1, 2014 ($1,000,000), when discounted at a 10% rate.

For bonds issued at par, the stated interest rate on the bond equals the effective yield earned by bond investors. Furthermore, recording the bonds at par on the issuer's books automatically records them at their discounted present value.

> The cash interest payments on the Huff bonds are an **annuity,** which means a series of payments in the same amount made at equally spaced time intervals. If the first payment is made at the start of Period 1, then it's an **annuity due.** Apartment leases often have this feature—the first month's payment is due when the lease is signed. The cash interest payments on Huff's bonds are an **ordinary annuity** (in arrears) because the first payment is due at the end of period 1 (December 31, 2014).

EXHIBIT 11.2	Huff Corporation

Demonstration that the Yield on Bonds Issued at Par Equals the Stated Interest Rate (here 10%)

Date of Payment	Type of Payment	Amount of Payment	10% Present Value Factor	Discounted Present Value
12/31/14	Interest	$ 100,000	0.90909	$ 90,909
12/31/15	Interest	100,000	0.82645	82,645
12/31/16	Interest	100,000	0.75131	75,131
12/31/17	Interest	100,000	0.68301	68,301
12/31/18	Interest	100,000	0.62092	62,092
12/31/19	Interest	100,000	0.56447	56,447
12/31/20	Interest	100,000	0.51316	51,316
12/31/21	Interest	100,000	0.46651	46,651
12/31/22	Interest	100,000	0.42410	42,410
12/31/23	Interest	100,000	0.38554	38,554
Total present value of interest payments				$ 614,456
12/31/23	Principal	$1,000,000	0.385544	385,544
Total issue price on January 1, 2014				$1,000,000

In the example, the amount received for the bonds ($1,000,000) exactly equals the present value of the future debt-related cash outflows (interest and principal payments) discounted at the 10% effective yield on the bonds.

Subsequent accounting for bonds issued at par is straightforward. Let's say that Huff prepares monthly financial statements; the *monthly* journal entry to record interest expense and Huff's liability for unpaid ("accrued") interest is:

DR	Interest expense	$8,333	
	CR Accrued interest payable		$8,333

This (rounded) amount represents $\frac{1}{12}$ of the $100,000 annual interest. At the end of the year, the accrued (unpaid) interest will be $100,000; upon Huff's payment of the interest, the entry is:

DR	Accrued interest payable	$100,000	
	CR Cash		$100,000

Bonds Issued at a Discount

Arranging for the sale of bonds can take considerable time. The terms of the indenture—the bond contract—must be drafted, the bond certificates themselves must be engraved and printed, and an investment banker must be found. Time is also consumed in waiting for the Securities and Exchange Commission (SEC) to review and accept the security-offering prospectus. Market interest rates may change during the time it takes to do this and before the bonds are ready to be issued.

Assume that the Huff bonds are printed during late 2013 and carry a 10% stated interest rate. The stated rate immediately establishes the yearly cash interest payout of $100,000 (10% multiplied by the $1,000,000 face amount of the bonds).

The issuing company seldom sells bonds directly to investors. Instead, the bonds are most often sold through a financial intermediary—an **investment bank.** In those cases, the investment bank purchases the bonds and resells them to institutional investors (for example, pension funds) at whatever price the market will bear. The investment bank's profit (or loss) is the difference between the price it pays to buy the bonds from the issuing company and the price it receives from investors, plus any fees paid by the company.

EXHIBIT 11.3	Huff Corporation

Determining the Issue Price for 10% Stated Interest Rate Bonds When the Market Rate Is 11%

Date of Payment	Type of Payment	Amount of Payment	11% Present Value Factor	Discounted Present Value
12/31/14	Interest	$ 100,000	0.90090	$ 90,090
12/31/15	Interest	100,000	0.81162	81,162
12/31/16	Interest	100,000	0.73119	73,119
12/31/17	Interest	100,000	0.65873	65,873
12/31/18	Interest	100,000	0.59345	59,345
12/31/19	Interest	100,000	0.53464	53,464
12/31/20	Interest	100,000	0.48166	48,166
12/31/21	Interest	100,000	0.43393	43,393
12/31/22	Interest	100,000	0.39093	39,093
12/31/23	Interest	100,000	0.35218	35,218
Total present value of interest payments			5.88923	$588,923
12/31/23	Principal	$1,000,000	0.352185	352,185
Total issue price on January 1, 2014				$941,108

Equivalently

December 31	2013	2014	2015	2016	2017	2018	2019	2020	2021	2022	2023
Cash interest payments		$100k	$100k	$100k	$100k	$100k	$100k	$100k	$100k	$100k	$100k
Cash principal payment		•	•	•	•	•	•	•	•	•	$1 m

Present value of single payment at 11%: $1 million × 0.352185 = $352,185

Present value of 10-period ordinary annuity at 11%: $100,000 × 5.88923 = $588,923

But let's say there's a sudden increase in the anticipated rate of inflation, causing investors to demand an 11% return on the Huff bonds as of the January 1, 2014, issue date. To provide the 11% return that investors now demand, Huff must sell the bonds at a *discount* relative to face value. Here's why. The annual cash interest and maturity payments are fixed by the indenture agreement at $100,000 and $1,000,000, respectively. If investors pay the full face amount ($1,000,000) for the bonds, they will just earn a 10% return on their investment. To attract investors who expect to earn an 11% return, Huff must be willing to issue the bonds at a price *lower* than the $1,000,000 face amount. How much lower than $1,000,000 must the issue price be? It must be reduced to a level that gives prospective investors exactly the 11% return they require. ***The bond's price is determined by discounting the contractual cash flows at 11%,*** as shown in Exhibit 11.3. Lowering the issue price gives investors the higher return they demand.

The price that yields the required 11% return, given the stipulated $100,000 annual contractual interest payments, is $941,108 (Exhibit 11.3). Investors seeking an 11% return will not be willing to pay more than $941,108 for 10-year bonds that have a $1,000,000 face value and a 10% stated interest rate. Why? Because if they pay more than $941,108, they will earn less than 11% on the bond's fixed cash flow stream. And Huff will not be willing to issue the bonds for less than $941,108 because to do so would mean paying more than 11% to investors. Market forces will thus set the issue price at $941,108.

Cumulative interest expense can also be thought of as follows. Investors will ultimately be paid total cash flows of $2,000,000 in principal plus cash interest; that is, $1,000,000 paid at maturity, and 10 annual payments of $100,000. Huff received only $941,108 when the bonds were issued. The difference between total cash payments and cash received at issuance ($2,000,000 − $941,108) is $1,058,892. This figure is the cumulative total interest expense over the life of the bond.

The accounting entry made on issuance of the 10% bonds at a price that yields an 11% return to investors is:

DR	Cash	$941,108	
DR	Bond discount	58,892	
	CR Bonds payable—par		$1,000,000

The Bond discount is a **liability valuation account** that is deducted from the Bonds payable account for financial reporting purposes. The net balance sheet (or carrying) value of the bonds when they are issued is $941,108 ($1,000,000 minus $58,892)—the amount of cash Huff received. This again illustrates the basic principle that newly issued bonds are recorded at the issue price, which exactly equals the present value of the contractual cash outflows for interest and principal repayment when those cash outflows are ***discounted at the effective yield on the bonds at the issuance date*** (here 11%).

When bonds are not sold at par, the calculation of annual interest expense and the accounting entry to record that expense are slightly more complicated. Consider the nature of the bond discount of $58,892. The discount amount is the difference between the cash Huff received from investors and the $1,000,000 principal amount Huff promised to repay them on December 31, 2023. This $58,892 is really just additional interest—over and above the contractual cash interest of $100,000 per year—that will be *earned* over the term of the loan, but it will not be *paid* until maturity. Cumulative interest expense over the 10 years will total $1,058,892—the stated interest of $1,000,000 paid out over the life of the bond plus the issue discount of $58,892 paid at maturity.

How should this "extra" interest of $58,892 be allocated across the 10 years? Generally accepted accounting principles (GAAP) recommend that the bond discount be allocated to interest expense on an **effective interest** basis. This requires the use of an amortization schedule, as shown in Exhibit 11.4. In Column (a), Huff received $941,108 on January 1, 2014, in exchange for issuing the bond certificates. Bondholders require an 11% return on the amount invested. Therefore, their interest income—and Huff's interest expense—in 2014 must be 11% of $941,108 or $103,522, as

But it's an unusual "recommendation" because GAAP allows other methods only if their results are not much different from the effective interest method.

EXHIBIT 11.4   Huff Corporation

Bond Discount Amortization Schedule

Year	(a) Bond Net Carrying Amount at Start of Year	(b) Interest Expense (Column [a] × 11%)	(c) Bond Discount Amortized (Column [b] − $100,000)	(d) Bond Discount Balance at End of Year	(e) Bond Net Carrying Amount at End of Year (Column [a] + Column [c])
2014	$941,108	$ 103,522	$ 3,522	$55,370	$ 944,630
2015	944,630	103,909	3,909	51,461	948,539
2016	948,539	104,339	4,339	47,122	952,878
2017	952,878	104,817	4,817	42,305	957,695
2018	957,695	105,346	5,346	36,959	963,041
2019	963,041	105,935	5,935	31,024	968,976
2020	968,976	106,587	6,587	24,437	975,563
2021	975,563	107,312	7,312	17,125	982,875
2022	982,875	108,116	8,116	9,009	990,991
2023	990,991	109,009	9,009	—	$1,000,000
		$1,058,892	$58,892		

Amounts rounded to nearest dollar.

EXHIBIT 11.5   Determining the Amortization Amount

$$
\text{Interest expense} \quad - \quad \text{Cash interest payment} \quad = \quad \frac{\text{Amortization}}{\text{amount}}
$$

$$
\begin{bmatrix} \text{Beginning-of-period} \\ \text{carrying amount} \\ \text{of bond} \end{bmatrix} \times \begin{matrix} \text{Effective} \\ \text{yield at} \\ \text{issuance} \end{matrix} \quad - \quad \begin{bmatrix} \text{Principal} \\ \text{amount of} \\ \text{bond} \end{bmatrix} \times \begin{matrix} \text{Stated} \\ \text{interest} \\ \text{rate} \end{matrix} \quad = \quad \frac{\text{Amortization}}{\text{amount}}
$$

shown in Column (b). The difference between Huff's $103,522 interest expense and the cash interest of $100,000 is the portion of "extra" interest allocated to 2014. This "extra" interest reduces the bond discount amount. If interest is recorded annually, the 2014 entry is:

DR	Interest expense	$103,522	
	CR	Accrued interest payable	$100,000
	CR	Bond discount	3,522

The process of "spreading" the discount on bonds to increase interest expense over the life of the bonds is called **discount amortization.** The yearly amortization amount is shown in Column (c) of Exhibit 11.4. After the amortization is recorded, the year-end balance in the Bond discount account—shown in Column (d)—will be $55,370 (the original discount of $58,892 minus the 2014 amortization of $3,522). Notice that the smaller the balance in the Bond discount account, shown in Column (d), the higher the **net carrying value** (book value) of the bond liability in Column (e). The balance sheet carrying value of the bonds increases toward the final maturity payment of $1 million as the discount is amortized.

The bond amortization schedule illustrates that annual interest expense, Column (b), always equals the effective interest rate (here 11%) multiplied by the start-of-the-year borrowing balance, Column (a). The difference between the accrual accounting interest expense, Column (b), and the $100,000 cash interest paid each year is the discount amortization, Column (c). This effective interest amortization process is represented in Exhibit 11.5.

Bonds Issued at a Premium

Recording bonds issued at a premium is similar to accounting for bonds issued at a discount. Assume that immediately after Huff Corporation bonds were printed late in 2013, interest rates *fell* to 9%. If these newly issued bonds were sold at par, Huff would be paying investors 10%—the stated interest rate as printed. But why should Huff pay 10% when investors are willing to accept 9% interest? Here's how Huff pays 9% instead of 10% despite the contractual 10% specified. Rather than selling the bonds at par, Huff will issue the bonds at a *premium*—that is, at an amount sufficiently higher than the $1,000,000 face value so that investors will receive only a 9% return. The exact amount is determined, as in the previous discount example, by taking the bond-related cash flows and discounting them at the effective yield rate (here 9%), as shown in Exhibit 11.6.

Market forces dictate that the bonds would be issued for $1,064,177—the present value of the contractual principal and interest payments at a discount rate of 9% as shown in Exhibit 11.6. Buying the bonds at this price will give investors a 9% effective yield.

The entry to record the bond issuance is:

DR	Cash	$1,064,177	
	CR	Bond premium	$ 64,177
	CR	Bonds payable—par.	1,000,000

EXHIBIT 11.6	Huff Corporation

Determining the Issue Price for 10% Stated Interest Rate Bonds When the Market Rate Is 9%

Date of Payment	Type of Payment	Amount of Payment	9% Present Value Factor	Discounted Present Value
12/31/14	Interest	$ 100,000	0.91743	$ 91,743
12/31/15	Interest	100,000	0.84168	84,168
12/31/16	Interest	100,000	0.77218	77,218
12/31/17	Interest	100,000	0.70843	70,843
12/31/18	Interest	100,000	0.64993	64,993
12/31/19	Interest	100,000	0.59627	59,627
12/31/20	Interest	100,000	0.54703	54,703
12/31/21	Interest	100,000	0.50187	50,187
12/31/22	Interest	100,000	0.46043	46,043
12/31/23	Interest	100,000	0.42241	42,241
Total present value of interest payments			6.41766	$ 641,766
12/31/23	Principal	$1,000,000	0.422411	422,411
Total issue price on January 1, 2014				$1,064,177

Equivalently

December 31	2013	2014	2015	2016	2017	2018	2019	2020	2021	2022	2023
Cash interest payments		$100k	$100k	$100k	$100k	$100k	$100k	$100k	$100k	$100k	$100k
Cash principal payment											$1 m

Present value of single payment at 9%: $1 million × 0.422411 = $422,411◄

Present value of 10-period ordinary annuity at 9%: $100 thousand × 6.41766 = $641,766◄

The Bond premium (like the Bond discount) is also a liability valuation account; the premium balance, $64,177 in this example, is added to the Bonds payable account to increase the balance sheet carrying value of the bonds. The Huff bonds will initially have a carrying value of $1,064,177. *When bonds are sold at a premium, interest expense will always be less than the cash interest payment.* The extra cash paid represents the amount of the premium being returned to bondholders. Exhibit 11.7 shows the amortization schedule. For example, the 2014 interest expense entry shows interest expense (from Column [b]) equal to $95,776, or the $100,000 cash interest payment minus the $4,224 premium amortization (from Column [c])— that is:

DR	Interest expense	$95,776
DR	Bond premium	4,224
CR	Cash	$100,000

Interest expense each year is less than the $100,000 annual cash interest payment. To see why, notice that Huff initially received more cash than it promised to pay back at the end of 10 years—that is, Huff received $1,064,177 but agreed to pay back $1,000,000. The difference— or premium—is returned to bondholders gradually over the entire period of the borrowing. For example, $4,224 of the premium is returned in 2014 (as shown in Column [c]), and a different amount ($4,604) is returned in 2015.

EXHIBIT 11.7	Huff Corporation

Bond Premium Amortization Schedule

Year	(a) Bond Net Carrying Amount at Start of Year	(b) Interest Expense (Column [a] × 9%)	(c) Bond Premium Amortized ($100,000 − Column [b])	(d) Bond Premium Balance at End of Year	(e) Bond Net Carrying Amount at End of Year (Column [a] − Column [c])
2014	$1,064,177	$ 95,776	$ 4,224	$59,953	$1,059,953
2015	1,059,953	95,396	4,604	55,349	1,055,349
2016	1,055,349	94,981	5,019	50,330	1,050,330
2017	1,050,330	94,530	5,470	44,860	1,044,860
2018	1,044,860	94,037	5,963	38,897	1,038,897
2019	1,038,897	93,501	6,499	32,398	1,032,398
2020	1,032,398	92,916	7,084	25,314	1,025,314
2021	1,025,314	92,278	7,722	17,592	1,017,592
2022	1,017,592	91,583	8,417	9,175	1,009,175
2023	1,009,175	90,825	9,175	—	1,000,000
		$935,823	$64,177		

Amounts rounded to nearest dollar.

Graphic Look at Bonds

The bar graphs in Figure 11.1 depict the components of issue price for Huff bonds when the interest rate is 10% (from Exhibit 11.2), 11% (from Exhibit 11.3), and 9% (from Exhibit 11.6). These bar graphs illustrate that *the issue price is determined by discounting the contractual principal and interest flows at the market yield rate.*

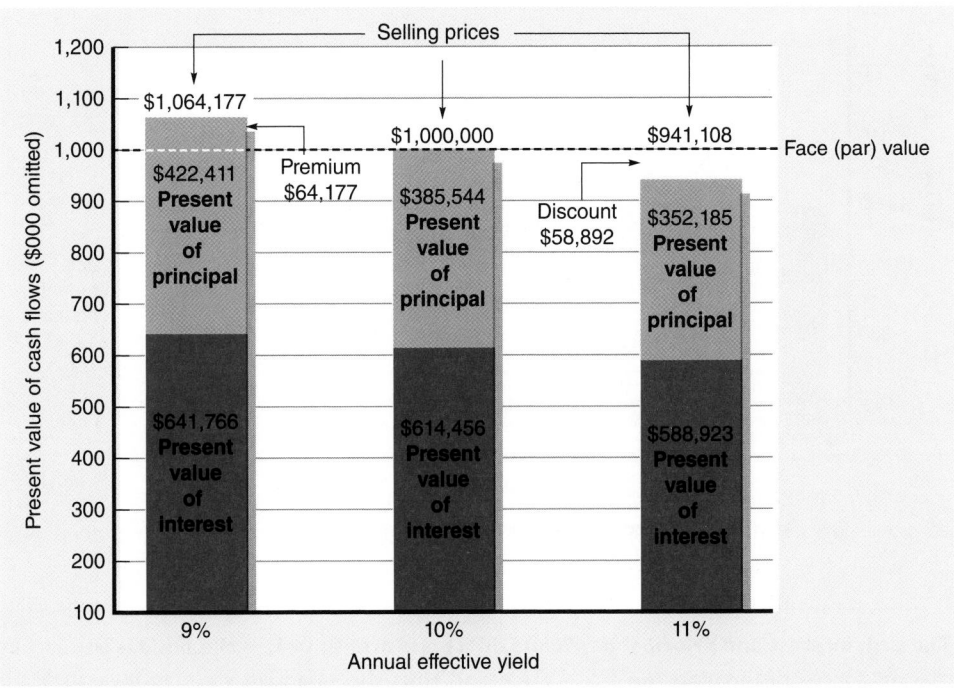

Figure 11.1

SELLING PRICES OF 10% STATED INTEREST RATE BONDS AT DIFFERENT MARKET (EFFECTIVE) YIELDS

Figure 11.2 is based on the amortization schedule numbers from Exhibit 11.4, where the Huff bonds sold at a discount because the market interest rate was 11%. Figure 11.2(a) shows the interest expense and cash interest payments for each year of the term of the bond, and the difference between the two amounts is the discount amortization. For example, the discount amortized in 2014 ($3,522) is the amount from Column (c) of Exhibit 11.4. The second chart (Figure 11.2 [b]) shows that the carrying value of the bonds increases as the discount is amortized each year, and the carrying value equals face value at the maturity date.

If the bond sells at a premium due to a 9% market interest rate, then interest expense each year is less than the coupon cash payment of $100,000, and the carrying value of the bond declines toward face value as the premium is amortized.

Figure 11.2(a)

CASH INTEREST PAYMENT
AND INTEREST EXPENSE

Market yield 11%

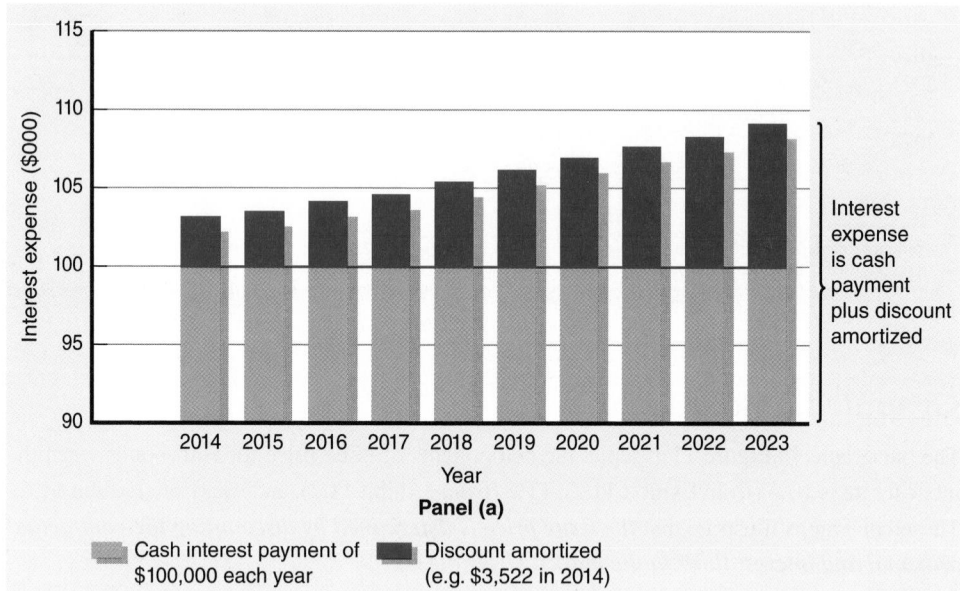

Panel (a)

Figure 11.2(b)

CARRYING VALUE FOR
10% STATED INTEREST
RATE BONDS SOLD AT
DISCOUNT

Market yield 11%

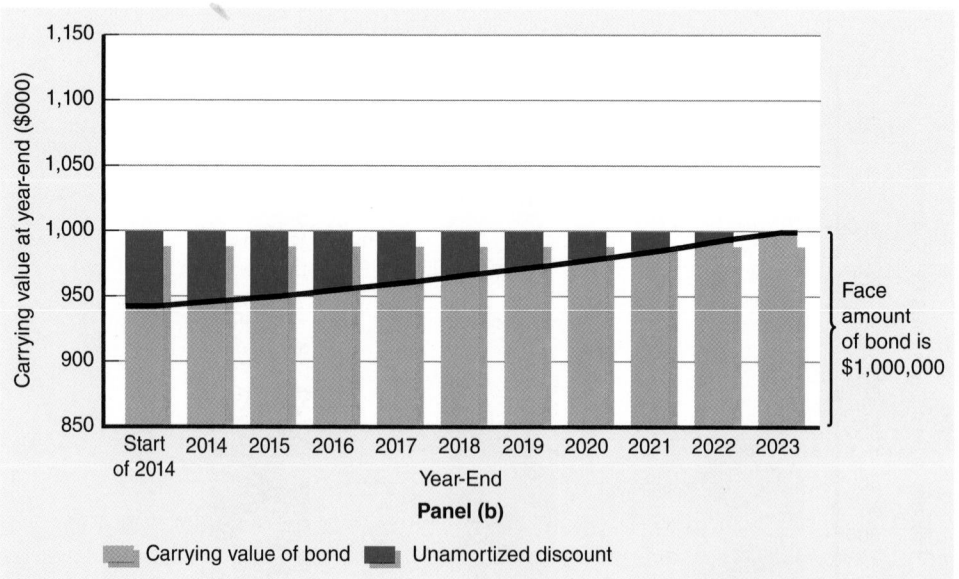

Panel (b)

   The cash interest and principal payments on a bond are set before the bond is issued, but market forces determine the issue price and thus the effective yield to investors. All bonds are first recorded on the borrower's books at the issue price. The issue price

exactly equals the present value of the cash payment obligation (interest payments plus principal payment) discounted at the effective interest rate. The effective interest rate is then used to compute interest expense and the carrying value of the bond in subsequent periods. When bonds are sold at a discount, the effective interest rate is higher than the stated interest rate. Amortization of the discount increases interest expense and adds to the bond's carrying value. When bonds are sold at a premium, the effective interest rate is lower than the stated interest rate. Amortizing the premium decreases interest expense and reduces the bond's carrying value. A liability valuation account is used to reflect the unamortized discount or premium.

Book Value versus Market Value after Issuance

Although bonds payable are recorded at their market value—meaning their present value—when first issued, their balance sheet carrying value will not necessarily equal their market value later. After issuance, the market value may not equal the balance sheet value when bonds payable are carried on the books at **amortized historical cost.** Because market interest rates often change, so do bond prices. *Thus, after issuance, the reported book value of bonds payable and their market value will likely differ.*

> Market interest rates change up or down almost on a daily basis and, thus, so do bond prices. Changes in a company's credit risk also influence bond prices. These changes are less frequent but no less important.

To see this, let's return to the Huff Corporation example with 10% stated interest rate bonds issued at par on January 1, 2014. Because the bonds were issued at par, there is no discount or premium to amortize. Hence, the amortized historical cost carrying (book) value of the bonds will always equal the principal amount of $1,000,000 each year the bonds are outstanding. Bonds payable would be shown on the balance sheet at $1,000,000 at December 31, 2014, one year after being issued.

Now it's January 1, 2015, one year after the bonds were first issued, and the market interest rate suddenly jumps to 11%. Remember that prevailing interest rates last year "set" the price at which the bonds were originally issued. It's no different after the bonds have been issued—prevailing interest rates still set the market price. So, the market price of Huff bonds after interest rates jump on January 1, 2015, equals the remaining cash interest and principal payments discounted at the new 11% effective yield that investors now require. The market price on January 1, 2015, would be $944,630 (see Exhibit 11.8). However, under GAAP, the bonds payable would still be shown on Huff's books at the original $1,000,000 amount. In general then, *reported book values after issuance will not necessarily equal the market value of the bonds because market interest rates fluctuate over time.*

> As we describe later in the chapter, firms now have the option to use fair value accounting rather than amortized historical cost accounting for bonds payable.

Floating-Rate Debt   Exhibit 11.8 illustrates that fluctuations in market interest rates change the value of financial instruments such as Huff's 10% stated interest rate bonds. In our example, a one percentage point increase in the market rate of interest (from 10% to 11%) at the beginning of 2015 would cause the value of Huff's bonds to fall by $55,370 (from $1,000,000 to $944,630). Investors who buy Huff bonds are exposed to market value losses because the stated interest rate is fixed at 10% per year for the term of the bonds. When market interest rates increase, Huff bonds continue to pay only the fixed rate of 10% even though investors could do better elsewhere.

Investors can protect themselves from such losses in several ways; the most common is investing in **floating-rate debt.** In contrast to Huff's fixed-rate bond, floating-rate debt has a stated interest rate that fluctuates in tandem with some interest rate benchmark such as the **London Interbank Offered Rate (LIBOR).** This widely used benchmark for floating-rate debt is the base interest rate paid on deposits between European banks.

Suppose that the contractual interest rate on Huff's bonds is "LIBOR plus 4%, reset annually" and that the bonds are issued on January 1, 2014, when the LIBOR is 6%. Investors will

EXHIBIT 11.8	Huff Corporation

Calculation of Bond Price after an Interest Rate Increase from 10% to 11%

Date of Payment	Type of Payment	Amount of Payment	11% Present Value Factor	Discounted Present Value
12/31/15	Interest	$ 100,000	0.90090	$ 90,090
12/31/16	Interest	100,000	0.81162	81,162
12/31/17	Interest	100,000	0.73119	73,119
12/31/18	Interest	100,000	0.65873	65,873
12/31/19	Interest	100,000	0.59345	59,345
12/31/20	Interest	100,000	0.53464	53,464
12/31/21	Interest	100,000	0.48166	48,166
12/31/22	Interest	100,000	0.43393	43,393
12/31/23	Interest	100,000	0.39093	39,093
Total present value of interest payments			5.53705	$553,705
12/31/23	Principal	$1,000,000	0.390925	390,925
Total market price on January 1, 2015				$944,630

receive a cash interest payment of $100,000 during 2014 because the contractual interest rate is 10% (LIBOR of 6% plus another 4%). If the LIBOR increases to 7% by January 1, 2015, investors will receive a cash interest payment of $110,000 (or 11%) that year because of the annual "reset" provision. The new rate equals the LIBOR of 7% plus 4% by contract. The additional $10,000 cash payment, if maintained over the bond's life, will exactly offset in present value terms the $55,370 value decline ($1,000,000 − $944,630) we computed in Exhibit 11.8. ***The market value of Huff's floating-rate debt would remain $1,000,000, and investors would be protected from losses such as those associated with Huff's fixed-rate debt.***

Floating-rate debt can also benefit the issuing company. If the LIBOR falls to 5%, Huff will be able to reduce its cash interest payments to $90,000 because the contractual interest rate would be reset to 9% (LIBOR of 5% plus another 4% by contract).

Investors benefit from floating-rate debt when market interest rates rise, and issuing corporations benefit when market rates fall. Floating-rate debt allows investors and issuing companies to share in the risks and rewards of changing market interest rates. Risk sharing lowers the company's overall borrowing costs, and this translates into floating-rate debt that has a lower (expected) interest rate than would be charged on comparable fixed-rate debt.

Because virtually all floating-rate debt is issued at par, the accounting entries required are simple. Interest expense and accrued interest payable are recorded using the contractual interest rate in effect during the period. Huff would make these entries if it had issued the "LIBOR plus 4%, reset annually" bonds on January 1, 2014:

1/1/14:	**DR**	Cash	$1,000,000	
		CR Bonds payable		$1,000,000
12/31/14:	**DR**	Interest expense............................	$100,000	
		CR Accrued interest payable................		$100,000
		2014 interest rate set at 10% (LIBOR of 6% plus 4%).		
12/31/15:	**DR**	Interest expense............................	$110,000	
		CR Accrued interest payable................		$110,000
		2015 interest rate reset to 11% (LIBOR of 7% plus 4%).		

The balance sheet would continue to show bonds payable at $1,000,000, which also equals the market value of the floating-rate debt.

Extinguishment of Debt

Interest rates constantly adjust to changes in levels of economic activity and changes in expected inflation rates among many other factors. When interest rates change, the market price of fixed-rate debt changes but in the opposite direction—as interest rates rise, the market price of debt falls; as interest rates fall, the market price of debt rises. However, as you just saw, most GAAP accounting for debt is at the original transaction price using the original effective interest rate. Subsequent market price changes are not recorded. Because market price changes of debt are not recorded, the balance sheet value of debt and its market value will differ (nearly always—unless the firm elects the fair value option described later). This divergence creates no accounting gain or loss for debt that is not retired before maturity—remember that book (carrying) value and debt market value are always equal on the maturity date.

> *Book value* equals *market value* on the maturity date because the principal payment is then due immediately and, consequently, is not discounted for time or risk.

However, when debt is retired before maturity, amortized historical cost book value and market value are not typically equal at the retirement date, generating an accounting gain or loss.

To see this, let's go back to Huff's $1,000,000 of 10% fixed-rate debt. On January 1, 2015, immediately after interest rates jump to 11%, Huff repurchases the 10% coupon bonds issued one year earlier. At the repurchase date, the bonds' market value is $944,630, as in Exhibit 11.8. The book value is $1,000,000 because the bonds were issued at par. The entry to record the repurchase (ignoring possible income taxes) is:

> When bonds are sold at a premium or discount, the initial carrying value equals the face value plus the premium or minus the discount. The premium or discount account must also be brought to zero when debt is retired. Remember that interest expense and accrued interest payable may need to be brought up to date before recording the extinguishment itself.

DR	Bonds payable....................................	$1,000,000	
CR	Cash		$944,630
CR	Gain on debt extinguishment		55,370

The accounting gain (or loss) at retirement—more commonly called **extinguishment**—is the difference between the cash paid to extinguish the debt and the debt's book value. Gains and losses from debt extinguishment are subject to the same criteria used to determine whether other gains and losses qualify for *extraordinary item* treatment.[4] From Chapter 2, remember that to qualify as an extraordinary item under GAAP, the event must be both *unusual* and *infrequent*. For many firms, debt extinguishment is neither unusual nor infrequent because early retirement is part of an ongoing interest rate risk management strategy.

One more thing! Where did Huff obtain the $944,630 cash needed to retire the old 10% fixed-rate bonds? The cash may have come from selling assets such as marketable securities, from operating cash flows, or a combination of the two, or Huff may have borrowed the money by issuing new nine-year, 10% fixed-rate bonds with a face value of $1,000,000. Per Exhibit 11.8, Huff would have received cash proceeds of $944,630 by issuing the new 10% bonds at a price that yields an 11% return to investors. The cash raised from selling the new

---

[4] FASB ASC Paragraph 470-50-45-1: Debt—Modifications and Extinguishments—Other Presentation Matters.

bonds could then be used to retire the old 10% fixed-rate debt. The entries to record this two-step process for retiring the 10% bonds are:

DR	Cash	$944,630	
	CR Bonds payable (new 10%)		$944,630

To record the issuance of nine-year, 10% fixed-rate bonds with a face value of $1,000,000.

DR	Bonds payable (old 10%)	$1,000,000	
	CR Cash		$944,630
	CR Gain on debt extinguishment		55,370

To record the retirement of the 10% fixed-rate bonds.

The two-step process removes a $1,000,000 liability from Huff's balance sheet but adds another $944,630 liability. Huff still reports a gain on debt retirement even though the company just replaced one debt instrument (the old 10% bonds) with another debt instrument (the new 10% bonds) of equal market value and the contractual cash flows for both bonds are the same. This is an odd accounting result—Huff records a GAAP extinguishment gain (and higher net income) yet its future cash flow obligation to bond investors is unchanged.

Option to Use Fair Value Accounting

Some U.S. firms have recognized as profit the falling value of their own debt without going through the effort and expense of an actual debt retirement. The reason why is that GAAP now allows firms to elect the **fair value option** for existing debt.[5]

Fair value option accounting works this way. Suppose that Elena Corporation issued $1,000,000 of bonds at par in 2004. By December 2007, the bonds had fallen in value to $950,000 because market interest rates had increased, Elena's creditworthiness had deteriorated, or both. Yet the bonds were carried on the balance sheet at $1,000,000 amortized historical cost. Under fair value option accounting (which became GAAP in 2007), Elena could elect in 2007 to use fair value rather than amortized historical cost as this liability's carrying value. Doing so would reduce the reported 2007 book value of Elena's balance sheet liability by $50,000, the difference between the bonds' fair value ($950,000) and the original carrying value ($1,000,000). The $50,000 difference would also appear on the 2007 income statement as a gain that boosts reported profits.

> What if the bonds had gained in value? In that case, the fair value option election would trigger an increase to Elena's reported balance sheet liabilities and an income statement loss.

Is this profit boost real or just illusory? Suppose that Elena was not planning to retire the bonds until they mature in 2013—10 years after they were first issued. As you already know from our previous discussion, the bonds will have a fair value of $1,000,000 at maturity. This means that any profit boost from temporary value declines in the early years will be offset by losses in later years when bond value recovers. In other words, Elena's $50,000 gain in 2007 is an illusion because fair value losses of $50,000 will eventually be booked in later periods as the bonds approach maturity.

This feature of the fair value option—that firms can record a profit when their own liabilities fall in value—is controversial. Critics claim it opens a new door for firms to dress up their balance sheets and massage earnings. Proponents, on the other hand, say that the fair value option eliminates accounting-induced volatility and improves financial statement transparency. Before we evaluate these opposing viewpoints, let's take a closer look at the fair value option guidelines.

---

[5] FASB ASC Topic 825: Financial Instruments, and Fair Value Subsections.

The Guidelines   Firms may choose to measure certain eligible financial instruments at fair value rather than historical cost. This option is available for most basic *financial assets*—accounts and notes receivable, investments in debt and equity securities—as well as most *financial liabilities* including accounts and notes payable plus long-term debt such as bonds payable.[6] In addition, firms may elect the fair value option on equity method investments (discussed in Chapter 16), debt and equity investments not traded in organized markets, and certain other obligations.

When must firms elect the fair value option? During the transition to this new GAAP, the choice for then existing financial instruments was made when the new accounting standard was first adopted in either 2007 or 2008. After transition, the election is made when a new financial asset or liability is first recognized on the company's books or later when some event (e.g., a business acquisition) triggers a new basis of accounting for that instrument. Once the choice has been made, it is irrevocable. If a firm elects the fair value option for a particular financial instrument, it must continue to use fair value measurement for that instrument until the asset is sold or liability extinguished. Similarly, once a firm elects to forgo the fair value option for an instrument, it may not later use fair value measurement on that specific instrument (unless a triggering event occurs). Special financial statement disclosures are required so that investors and analysts can understand:

- Management's rationale for electing the fair value option.
- The impact of changes in fair values on earnings for the period.
- The difference between fair values and contractual cash flows for certain items.

How the Fair Value Accounting Option Mutes Earnings Volatility

The chief benefit of the fair value option is that it reduces the volatility in reported earnings caused when certain financial instruments are measured using fair value while others are measured at cost. For some firms, this mismatch in measurement bases produces artificial earnings volatility. Before we illustrate how the fair value option dampens this artificial volatility, let's first take a look at how fair value accounting applies to financial assets.

> There are other benefits. It reduces the need for companies to comply with the complex and voluminous rules for hedge accounting described later in this chapter. It also contributes to the convergence of U.S. GAAP with international financial reporting standards by providing a fair value option that is similar, but not identical, to that found in *IAS No. 39*.[7]

Suppose Bluff bought for investment purposes some bonds issued by Apex Corp. The borrower (Apex) issued the bonds and the investor (Bluff) purchased them on January 1, 2014. Assume further that the bonds have a $1 million face value, pay 10% interest annually, and mature in 10 years on December 31, 2023. If the effective yield on the bonds at issuance is also 10%, Bluff pays Apex $1,000,000 and records the January 1, 2014, investment at cost:

DR	Investment in Apex bonds	$1,000,000	
	CR	Cash.		$1,000,000

Bluff elects to use fair value accounting for its Apex bonds investment.

---

[6] There are exceptions. The fair value option is not available for leasing assets and liabilities (Chapter 12), deferred income tax assets and liabilities (Chapter 13), pension assets and liabilities (Chapter 14), and items eliminated upon consolidation (Chapter 16). Nor does the fair value option apply to nonfinancial assets and liabilities such as inventory; property, plant, and equipment; intangible assets; warranty service obligations; and deferred revenues.

[7] "Financial Instruments: Recognition and Measurement," *International Accounting Standards (IAS) No. 39* [London: International Accounting Standards Board (IASB), 1998] as later revised.

At year-end, the market interest rate suddenly jumps to 11%, and the fair value of Apex bonds falls to $944,630. (The details are in Exhibit 11.8 because the Apex bonds are identical to those issued by Huff Corporation in our earlier example.) Bluff has a $55,370 **unrealized holding loss** on the investment. This unrealized loss is the difference between the initial fair value ($1,000,000) of the bonds and their fair value ($944,630) as of December 31, 2014. Having opted for fair value accounting, Bluff must recognize the unrealized loss and reduce the carrying value of its Apex investment:

DR Unrealized holding loss on Apex bonds	$55,370	
CR Fair value adjustment—Apex bonds		$55,370

The unrealized holding loss flows to the 2014 income statement. Bluff deducts the fair value adjustment (a credit amount) from the original $1,000,000 cost of the Apex bonds to arrive at the $944,630 fair value to be reported on the year-end balance sheet.

What if the investment's fair value changes again next year? In that case, Bluff would recognize an unrealized holding loss (if fair value declines in 2015) or gain (if fair value increases) equal to the fair value change that year. A corresponding dollar amount would be added to (if a loss) or subtracted from (if a gain) the Fair value adjustment account so that the year-end balance sheet would report Bluff's investment in Apex bonds at the new fair value.

> If Bluff does not elect to use the fair value accounting it would record no unrealized holding loss in 2014, and the year-end carrying value of the Apex investment would remain at $1,000,000 (historical cost).

Now that you understand how the fair value option works, let's see how it can reduce artificial earnings volatility. We need to make two important modifications to our example. First, suppose that existing GAAP rules already require Bluff to use fair value accounting for its Apex investment (described in Chapter 16).[8] Second, suppose that instead of using cash on hand, Bluff borrows the money it needs to buy Apex bonds by issuing at par $1,000,000 of 10-year, 10% bonds on January 1, 2014. Exhibit 11.9 illustrates the journal entries needed to record the borrowing and subsequent purchase of Apex bonds.

When the market interest rate suddenly jumps to 11% at year-end, the fair value of the Apex investments falls to $944,630. So does the fair value of the bonds payable liability. As proponents of the fair value accounting option are quick to point out, one fair value change offsets the other in real terms. But this is not what happens under prior GAAP! Without the fair value accounting option, Bluff must recognize the unrealized holding loss on the Apex investment as required but not the offsetting unrealized gain from its own bonds payable. Instead, bonds payable were carried on the books at amortized historical cost ($1,000,000 in this example). The resulting mismatch of measurement bases—fair value for the financial asset (Investment in Apex bonds) but amortized historical cost for the financial liability (Bonds payable)—induced artificial earnings volatility as shown in Panel (a) of Exhibit 11.9.

> To see this economic offset, notice that Bluff could unwind the investment by selling Apex bonds for $944,630 and then using the cash to extinguish its own bonds payable. The resulting realized loss ($55,370) on the sale of the Apex investment would then be offset by a corresponding realized gain (also $55,370) on early debt retirement.

The fair value accounting option can eliminate this artificial volatility. Panel (b) of Exhibit 11.9 illustrates how. In this case, Bluff elects to use fair value accounting for the bond liability and, therefore, must also record an unrealized holding gain at year-end. This gain just offsets the unrealized loss on the Apex investment. Earnings volatility is eliminated when fair value measurement is used for both the financial asset and its related financial liability.

---

[8] See FASB ASC Topic 320: Investments—Debt and Equity Securities.

EXHIBIT 11.9   **Bluff Corporation**

How the Fair Value Accounting Option Reduces Earnings Volatility

Panel (a) Without the Fair Value Accounting Option

January 1, 2014: To record Bluff's bond issuance and the purchase of Apex debt securities.

DR	Cash	$1,000,000	
	CR Bonds payable		$1,000,000
DR	Investment in Apex bonds	$1,000,000	
	CR Cash		$1,000,000

December 31, 2014: To record the year-end fair value adjustment required by GAAP.

DR	Unrealized holding loss—Apex investment . . .	$ 55,370	
	CR Fair value adjustment—Apex bonds . . .		$ 55,370

Panel (b) With the Fair Value Accounting Option

January 1, 2014: To record Bluff's bond issuance and the purchase of Apex debt securities. Bluff also elects to use the fair value accounting option for bonds payable

DR	Cash	$1,000,000	
	CR Bonds payable		$1,000,000
DR	Investment in Apex bonds	$1,000,000	
	CR Cash		$1,000,000

December 31, 2014: To record the year-end fair value adjustments required by GAAP.

DR	Unrealized holding loss—Apex investment . . .	$ 55,370	
	CR Fair value adjustment—Apex bonds . . .		$ 55,370
DR	Fair value adjustment—Bonds payable	$ 55,370	
	CR Unrealized holding gain—Bonds payable.		$ 55,370

Gain offsets the loss.

Opposing Views on the Fair Value Accounting Option   Companies are allowed to adopt fair value measurement selectively so that they can report financial assets and financial liabilities that are related to one another using the same measurement base. But GAAP does not limit the use of the fair value option to situations in which the financial assets and liabilities are related. For example, Bluff Corporation could use fair value accounting for its bonds payable liability—and boost 2014 earnings by $55,370—even though the cash received from issuing the bonds was used for general business purposes rather than to invest in Apex bonds. Critics assert that this creates the worrisome opportunity for companies to use fair value accounting to dress up their balance sheets and manage reported earnings.

It is easy to see why critics are concerned. Suppose that 2015 is an extremely difficult year for Bluff: Customers begin shopping elsewhere in large numbers, the company incurs a $200,000 operating loss, and its credit rating falls precipitously. The fair value of Bluff's debt goes down as well, say to $600,000, because creditors now fear that Bluff will be unable to make the bond interest and principal payments as required. Despite the company's obvious financial distress, Bluff would record a $344,630 ($944,630 − $600,000) unrealized holding gain that year and reduce its balance sheet debt by the same amount. An otherwise disastrous year is transformed into a seemingly profitable one—the unrealized holding gain more than offsets the operating loss—and less debt is reported on the balance sheet. The financial statement effects are counterintuitive and misleading. The earnings boost is not sustainable, and Bluff remains contractually obligated to repay the full amount borrowed ($1,000,000 plus interest), not just debt carrying value ($600,000).

Analysis

Analysts and investors must also rethink how they evaluate a company's debt-to-equity ratio. Conventional wisdom holds that firms in financial distress have higher debt-to-equity ratios than do healthy firms (recall the discussion in Chapter 5). But fair value accounting for debt can produce the opposite result. Bluff Corporation's debt-to-equity ratio might actually decline rather than increase as the company slides into financial distress. Under fair value accounting, Bluff's debt-to-equity ratio numerator (debt) is reduced by $344,630 and the denominator (equity) is increased by this same amount. The combined effect is a smaller, not larger, debt-to-equity ratio in 2015.

International

GLOBAL VANTAGE POINT

How does IFRS accounting for long-term debt differ from the U.S. GAAP guidelines we have described? When it comes to the most important elements of long-term debt accounting, IFRS and U.S. GAAP are quite similar in approach. For instance, fixed-rate bonds are initially recorded at the issue price (proceeds received) under both IFRS and U.S. GAAP rules. The subsequent balance sheet carrying value is amortized cost determined using the effective interest rate at the issue date. Periodic interest expense is computed using the issue date effective (not contractual) interest rate. Changes in interest rates occurring after the issue date do not alter the bond's carrying value unless fair value accounting is being used.

There are, however, several areas where U.S. GAAP and IFRS rules diverge. Here are two:

1. **Debt issue costs.** Under U.S. GAAP these costs—fees paid to underwriters, investment bankers, lawyers, and accountants who help with the bond documents and issuance transaction—are recorded separately as an asset and then amortized over the life of the bond. The IFRS approach is to reduce the recorded amount of the debt, thus treating issue costs as a reduction in the proceeds received. The result under IFRS is a slightly higher effective interest rate—fewer dollars are recorded as being received but the contractual repayment obligation is the same.

2. **Fair value option.** *IAS 39* permits companies to opt for fair value accounting for liabilities only under two specific circumstances: (1) the liabilities are actively managed on a fair value basis as part of the company's documented risk management or investment strategy; or (2) use of fair value accounting eliminates or significantly reduces the "mismatch" that arises when different measurement bases are used for related financial instruments. (This potential "mismatch" and its impact on earnings volatility is illustrated in Exhibit 11.9.). U.S. GAAP guidance is less restrictive in that it does not require that these two specific circumstances actually exist.

In May 2010, the FASB issued a controversial proposed accounting standards update that would, among other things, require nearly all financial instruments—including bonds and other forms of long-term debt—to be measured at fair value in the statement of financial position rather than at amortized cost.[9] Amortized cost information would be displayed

---

[9] Proposed Accounting Standards Update, "Accounting for Financial Instruments and Revisions to the Accounting for Derivative Instruments and Hedging Activities, Financial Instruments" (Topic 825) and "Derivatives and Hedging" (Topic 815) (Norwalk, CT: FASB, 2010).

on the balance sheet as supplemental data. This dual presentation presumably allows investors to

> . . . more easily incorporate either or both in their analyses of an entity. Fair value would provide users with the best available information about the market's assessment of an entity's expectation of its future cash flows . . . Amortized cost would provide users with information about the instrument's contractual cash flows. (Proposed ASU, p. 4)

The proposed Update was controversial for two reasons. First, many observers argued that liability fair values are of little relevance because the borrowing firm remains obligated to the contractual cash payments specified by the bond agreement regardless of market interest rates or the market's assessment of borrower cash-flow risk. According to those observers, amortized cost provides a more representative depiction of the borrowing firm's true financial condition under most circumstances. Second, the IASB had tentatively decided to retain existing guidance for financial liabilities such as bonds—meaning that it favored continued use of amortized cost accounting for long-term debt with a limited fair value option. For many observers, the FASB's proposal represented a troublesome departure from the path toward U.S. GAAP and IFRS convergence.

Responding to these and other concerns, the FASB has now altered its view in ways consistent with the IASB.[10]

When interest rates change after a bond has been issued, the bond's reported book value and market value are no longer the same. That's because GAAP requires bonds to be carried on the issuer's books at amortized historical cost (unless fair value accounting has been elected) using the effective yield to investors when the bonds were first issued. So, when interest rates have risen and bonds are retired before maturity, market value will be less than book value, generating an accounting gain. If interest rates have fallen, market value would be lower than book value, resulting in an accounting loss. Gains and losses from early debt retirement are sometimes treated as extraordinary items on the income statement if they qualify as such under GAAP.

GAAP allows firms to use fair value accounting for debt rather than amortized historical cost. This fair value accounting option can dampen artificial earnings volatility, but it may also open new doors for firms to dress up their balance sheets.

MANAGERIAL INCENTIVES AND FINANCIAL REPORTING FOR DEBT

In Chapters 1 and 7, we explained that accounting numbers are widely used to enforce contracts. One example involves debt covenants, which could motivate managers to manipulate accounting numbers to evade contract restrictions. Critics suggest that GAAP accounting for long-term debt makes it possible to "manage" accounting numbers to achieve this evasion.

Debt Carried at Amortized Historical Cost

Some analysts contend that reporting debt at amortized historical cost (the $1,000,000 bond shown on Huff Corporation's books)—rather than at current fair value (or $944,630 in the Huff example)—makes it easier to manipulate accounting numbers. **Debt-for-debt swaps** and **debt-for-equity swaps** illustrate the types of transactions that may be driven more by the financial statement effects they elicit than by any underlying economic benefits. In a debt-for-debt swap,

---

[10] Proposed Accounting Standards Update, "Financial Instruments—Overall" (Subtopic 825-10) (Norwalk, CT: FASB, 2013).

Figure 11.3

SHIFTY CORPORATION

Debt-for-Debt Swap

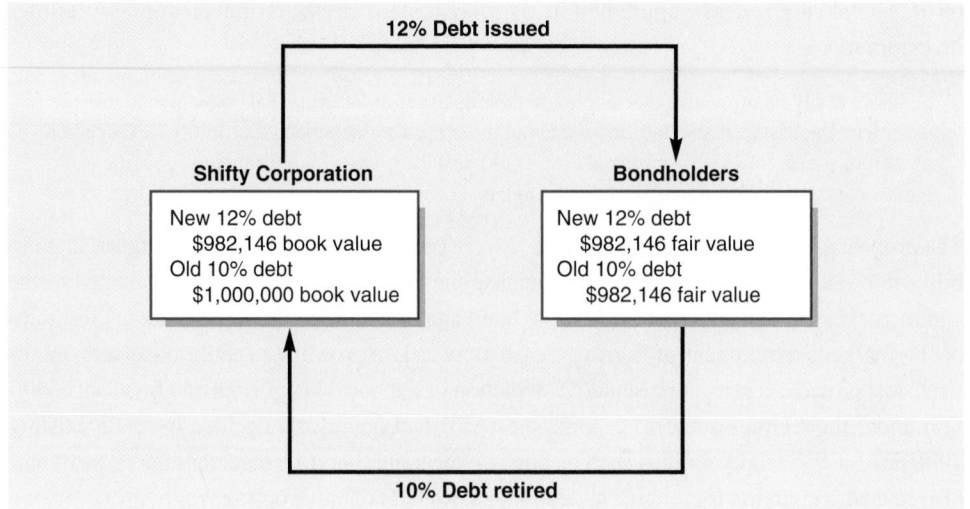

the company offers investors the opportunity to exchange existing (old) debt for new debt issued by the company. Debt-for-equity swaps give investors the opportunity to exchange old debt for the company's common stock.

To illustrate, suppose that Shifty Corporation has $1 million of outstanding 10% fixed-rate debt originally issued at par. This debt matures in exactly one year. Because the debt was sold at par, its book value is $1 million. Assume that the current market rate for bonds of similar risk is 12%, which means that Shifty's bonds have a fair value of $982,146. Shifty offers bondholders the opportunity to swap their old 10% bonds for new 12% bonds that also mature in exactly one year. Just to keep things simple, let's assume that bondholders are willing to swap as long as they receive 12% bonds worth $982,146, or the fair value of the old 10% bonds that will be given back to the company. If the market interest rate is 12%, the new 12% bonds will be issued at par, and the face value will be $982,146. This debt-for-debt swap is illustrated in Figure 11.3.

Bondholders will be presumably indifferent between the old 10% bonds and the new 12% bonds because the fair values are identical. (To induce real-world bondholders to exchange the 10% bonds for 12% bonds, some "sweetener"—a slightly higher interest rate or a slightly higher face value—would need to be included.) The fair values are identical precisely because the present values of the two cash flow streams are identical when discounted at the prevailing 12% market interest rate:

> This $982,146 fair value corresponds exactly to the present value of the principal payment ($1,000,000/1.12 = $892,860 rounded) plus the present value of the final interest payment ($100,000/1.12 = $89,286 rounded), both discounted at the market rate of 12%.

Old 10% Bonds at 12% Market Interest Rate		New 12% Bonds at 12% Market Interest Rate	
Principal Repayment		**Principal Repayment**	
$1,000,000 × 0.89286 = $892,860		$ 982,146 × 0.89286 = $876,919*	
Interest Payment		**Interest Payment**	
$ 100,000 × 0.89286 = 89,286		$ 117,854* × 0.89286 = 105,227*	
$1,100,000 $982,146		$1,100,000 $982,146	
Interest Computation		**Interest Computation**	
$1,000,000 × 10% = $100,000		$ 982,146 × 12% = $117,858*	

Note: The present value of $1 due in one year at 12% is 0.89286.

* Rounded.

As the computation reveals, even the *undiscounted* cash flows are identical because the principal payment plus interest payment is $1,100,000 in both cases. A debt-for-debt swap such as this has no real economic benefit to Shifty (there may be income tax effects). However, if the swap was consummated, the entry on Shifty's books would be:

DR	Bonds payable (old 10%)	$1,000,000	
	CR	Bonds payable (new 12%)	$982,146
	CR	Gain on debt extinguishment	17,854

Despite the absence of real economic substance, an accounting "gain" would still be reported.[11] The gain really arose in earlier periods as unanticipated inflation or other factors caused the market interest rate on the bonds to rise above the stated interest rate. Because Shifty was paying interest at 10% when prevailing rates were higher, a year-by-year wealth transfer from the pockets of the original bondholders into the pockets of Shifty's shareholders was taking place. Historical cost accounting ignores this wealth transfer until the "artificial" swap transaction triggers recognition of the gain.

> This same financial statement result would occur if Shifty first issued the new 12% bonds for cash and then used the cash proceeds to retire old 10% bonds. (See the Huff Corporation two-step debt retirement mentioned earlier in the chapter.) Income tax considerations and transaction costs may favor a debt-for-debt swap rather than a two-step debt extinguishment.

This example demonstrates the potential incentive for managerial opportunism that historical cost accounting for debt introduces.[12] Critics of historical cost accounting raise the possibility that managers whose bonuses are tied to reported earnings might use swap gains to boost their firm's earnings (and thus their bonuses) in years of poor operating performance. Also, a reduction in the book value of debt (from $1,000,000 to $982,146 in our example) would improve the debt-to-equity ratio—thus providing "opportunistic" motivations for companies in danger of violating covenant restrictions tied to this ratio.

> The wealth transfer gain from bondholders to stockholders is reflected obliquely in historical cost statements because historical cost interest expense is lower than interest expense would be at current market rates. Accordingly, *net income is higher than it would have been at current interest rates.*

Now that you can visualize the problem, let's make the example more realistic.

To induce bondholders to swap, they must be offered some sweeteners to do so. One inducement is to offer a higher principal amount of new bonds—say, $990,000. *This change makes the net present value of the swap negative for Shifty because it is retiring debt with a market value of $982,146 by giving bondholders something worth $990,000.* Despite this real economic loss to Shifty, if the swap went through on these altered terms, Shifty would still report an accounting *gain* of $10,000—the difference between the $1 million book value of the old bonds and the $990,000 market value of the new bonds. Extinguishment gains are generally taxable, and fees must be paid to investment bankers who orchestrate the transaction. These added costs further increase the potential disparity between the reported accounting gain and the economic effects of the swap.

---

[11] FASB ASC Topic 470-50-40 *Debt—Modifications and Extinguishments—Derecognition* says that any difference between the price paid to reacquire (and thus retire) debt and the net carrying amount of the extinguished debt is to be recognized currently in income as a loss or gain and identified as a separate item. This means it doesn't matter whether Shifty uses cash or the new bonds to retire the old bonds. In either case, GAAP requires Shifty to record an accounting gain on the debt extinguishment.

[12] Shifty's debt-for-debt swap would not produce an accounting gain under IFRS. Why? Because *IAS 39* says an exchange of financial instruments—as when Shifty's new 12% bonds are exchanged for the old 10% bonds—qualifies as an extinguishment of debt only if the terms of the instruments are *substantially* different. They are not different in the Shifty example, so the swap would instead be treated as a modification of the original bond terms (*IAS 39* describes the details). No IFRS extinguishment, and thus no IFRS accounting gain on extinguishment for Shifty.

Figure 11.4

THE SEQUENCE OF
EVENTS IN A DEBT-FOR-
EQUITY SWAP

Source: From J. R. M. Hand, "Did Firms
Undertake Debt–Equity Swaps for an
Accounting Paper Profit or True Financial
Gain?" *The Accounting Review,* October
1989, pp. 587–623. Reprinted with
permission.

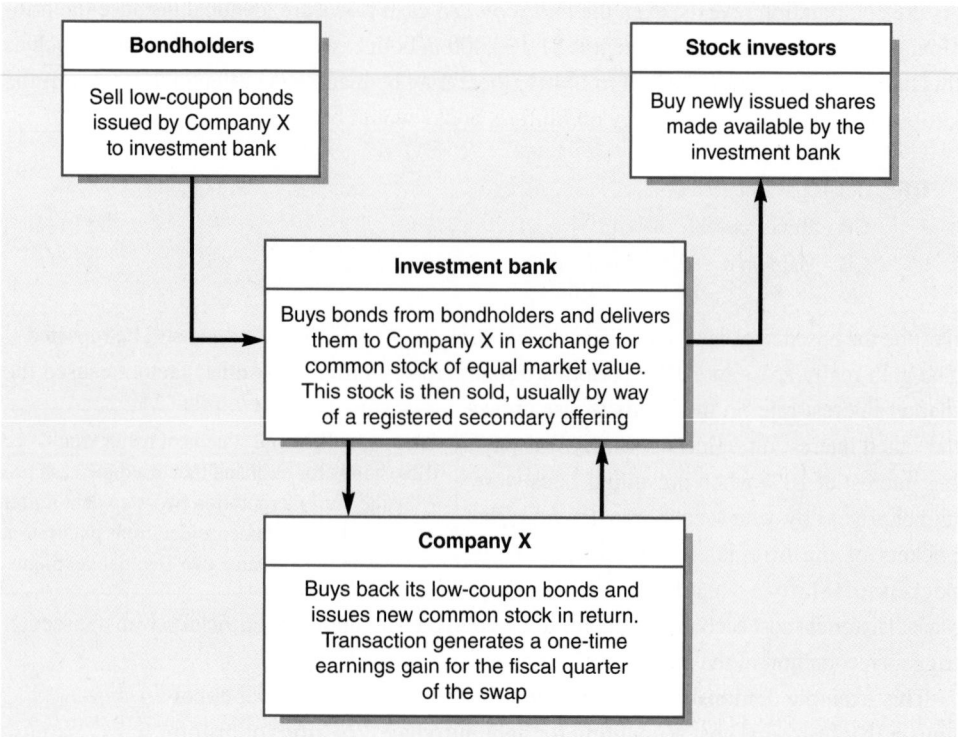

On the other hand, sometimes real economic benefits are associated with debt-for-debt exchanges. In the real world, debt-for-debt swaps are rarely designed to be a "wash" in which debt instruments with identical maturities and market values are exchanged. Typical swaps are structured to extend debt maturity, postpone cash outflows by altering the mix of interest and principal payments, or take advantage of expiring operating loss carryforwards, thus making the swap tax free. On balance, therefore, it is entirely possible that some debt-for-debt exchanges generate real economic benefits even after factoring in transaction costs.

Differences between book profits and real profits have aroused curiosity about the motives underlying another—somewhat similar—debt extinguishment transaction: debt-for-equity swaps.

The conditions for a debt-for-equity swap exist when a company has low stated interest rate (say, 4½%) debt outstanding and market rates are much higher (say, 12%). ***The market value of that debt is much lower than its book value.*** As Figure 11.4 shows, Company X retires its low stated-rate debt by issuing common stock of equal market value. The difference between the book value of the debt and the market value of the stock that is issued is recorded as an accounting gain. The convoluted nature of the transaction, as well as the investment bank's involvement, is required to make the gain on debt extinguishment tax free.

The accounting entry on the books of Company X is:

DR Bonds payable (and discount or premium)	$ Book value	
CR Common stock		$ Market value
CR Gain on debt extinguishment		$ Difference

Debt book value is higher than the market value of stock issued because the debt has a low stated interest rate but the market interest rate is high.

Debt-for-equity swaps alter the company's capital structure and undoubtedly precipitate real economic effects. However, companies also can use debt-for-equity swaps to smooth otherwise unexpected and transitory decreases in quarterly earnings per share or to relax otherwise binding covenant constraints.[13]

Debt-for-debt swaps, debt-for-equity swaps, and other similar transactions may serve valid economic purposes in certain instances. Nevertheless, some analysts still believe that the dominant motivation for these transactions is to increase reported income. But no matter what motivates management to swap old debt, the result is the same: an earnings boost that may not reflect economic reality but instead represents the difference between the book value and market value of the liabilities.

> As you will discover in Chapter 15, no gain (or loss) is recognized when debtholders simply exercise a traditional conversion option and exchange their bonds for shares of common stock in the company.

In response to this and other criticisms of accounting for liabilities, the FASB requires note disclosure of the fair value of all financial instruments—both financial liabilities and assets.[14] However, disclosure alone is unlikely to eliminate "accounting-driven" liability transactions. While the fair value disclosures appear in a note to the financial statements, the carrying amount of liabilities on the balance sheet itself is not altered. Consequently, the swap transactions described here still generate income statement gains and favorable financial ratio effects. Managers can still use these transactions as mechanisms for influencing bonus payouts as well as for evading loan covenant restrictions or other contracting effects when the contracts are tied to the financial numbers reported in the body of the statement.

GAAP for long-term debt creates opportunities for managing reported earnings and balance sheet numbers using debt-for-debt or debt-for-equity swaps. So, statement readers must be alert to the possibility that reported swap gains (and losses) are just window dressing. How can you tell? Look behind the accounting numbers and see whether the swap offers real economic benefits.

RECAP

IMPUTED INTEREST ON NOTES PAYABLE

Salton, Inc. (known today as Russell Hobbs, a division of Spectrum Brands), designs and markets a variety of popular household appliances including the George Foreman Grill, the BreadMan bread machine, and Toastmaster toaster ovens. At one time, the company paid Foreman a royalty equal to 60% of the gross profit on sales of George Foreman Grills. (It's a hefty sum, but then Foreman—a past heavyweight boxing champion—is undoubtedly a tough negotiator.) At the beginning of 2000, the company purchased the rights to use the George Foreman name in perpetuity in exchange for shares of Salton stock valued at $23.750 million and a $113.750 million note payable in five annual installments of $22.750 million each. Foreman received a check for the first installment the

---

[13] J.R.M. Hand, "Did Firms Undertake Debt–Equity Swaps for an Accounting Paper Profit or True Financial Gain?" *The Accounting Review,* October 1989, pp. 587–623.

[14] FASB ASC Section 820-10-50: Financial Instruments—Overall—Disclosure.

same day the deal was inked. Here is how Salton recorded its purchase of the George Foreman name (amounts in millions):

DR	Intangible asset (George Foreman name)	$121.020	
	CR Common stock		$23.750
	CR Note payable		$97.270

To record the purchase of the rights to use the George Foreman name in perpetuity.

DR	Note payable	$ 22.750	
	CR Cash		$22.750

To record the immediate payment to Mr. Foreman of the first installment on the note.

And here's what Salton had to say about the transaction in its 2000 financial statements: "The effect of the acquisition of the George Foreman name related to fiscal 2000 was the elimination of royalty payments partially offset by amortization of $8.1 million and **imputed interest** of $6.3 million."

Several aspects of this accounting treatment may at first seem perplexing. For example, why did Salton record the $113.750 million note payable at a value of only $97.270 million? What is "imputed interest," how is it calculated, and when is it recorded? The answers to these questions illustrate once again that noncurrent monetary liabilities are recorded initially at their present value.

> Salton amortizes the intangible asset over 15 years, so the $8.1 million of amortization is computed as $121.020/15 with slight rounding. Imputed interest on notes receivable is discussed in Chapter 8.

Let's start with the value assigned to the note itself and assume that both Salton and Foreman agree that the note is worth $97.270 million at the signing date. Why isn't the note worth the full $113.750 million contractual payment amount? Because the installment payments are spread over five years, and the extra $16.480 million is interest that Foreman will receive as compensation for delayed payment.

What is the rate of interest on the note payable? To answer that question, we need to find an interest rate that makes the value of the note ($97.270 million) equal to the present value of the installment payments. The actual calculation can be cumbersome, although a financial calculator or computer spreadsheet can make the solution easy. The following diagram illustrates how to find a note's imputed rate of interest.

		Payment in Millions at the Beginning of the Year				
	2000	**2001**	**2002**	**2003**	**2004**	**Total payments**
	$22.750	$22.750	$22.750	$22.750	$22.750	$113.750
Present value of 2001 payment	20.968 ◄───── 0.92166					
Present value of 2002 payment	19.325 ◄──────────── 0.84946					
Present value of 2003 payment	17.811 ◄───────────────────── 0.78291					
Present value of 2004 payment	16.416 ◄──────────────────────────────── 0.72157 = Present value factor for 4 years at 8.5%					
Present value of note	$97.270					
Imputed rate of interest	8.50%					

Notice that all installment payments occur at the beginning of the year. As a result, the present value of the first $22.750 million installment payment is exactly $22.750 million. However, the present value of the second installment payment—which occurs at the beginning of 2001—is smaller than $22.750 million. How much smaller depends on the interest rate. Let's take a guess that the correct imputed interest rate is 8.50%. (In a moment, we will show you why 8.50% is a reasonable "guestimate" for the imputed interest rate.) In this case, the second installment payment needs to be discounted for one year at 8.50% and the discount factor is 0.92166 [or $1/(1 + 0.085)$]. The present value of the 2001 payment is $20.968 million, which equals the $22.750 million cash payment multiplied by the 0.92166 discount factor. A similar process is used to compute the present value for each remaining installment payment. When all five present value amounts are summed, they total $97.270 million. And that's the key step: 8.50% is the imputed rate of interest on the note precisely because it is the interest rate that makes the value of the note ($97.270) equal to the present value of the installment payments (also $97.270 million).

Was our 8.50% interest rate estimate just a lucky guess? Not exactly. Salton's financial statement indicates that interest expense on the note payable was $6.3 million in 2000. Because interest is a charge for delayed payment and the first installment payment was made immediately, the $6.3 million in interest must represent a charge for the $74.520 million unpaid balance of the note ($74.520 = $97.270 initial note value − $22.750 first payment). We can now derive an estimate of the note's true imputed interest rate using the ratio of interest expense to the unpaid balance of the note. The result is ($6.3/$74.520) = 0.08454, or 8.45%. Why doesn't this process yield the correct 8.50% imputed interest rate? Because the $6.3 million interest expense figure Salton mentions is rounded slightly. The actual interest expense on the note that year was $6.3342 million (or $74.520 × 8.50%).

If Salton records interest expense only once a year, it makes the following entry at the end of 2000 (dollars in millions):

DR Interest expense	$6.3342	
CR Note payable		$6.3342

To record interest expense on the unpaid balance of the Foreman note payable.

The unpaid interest is added to the note payable balance. This means that the note payable, a noncurrent monetary liability, will be shown on the 2000 year-end balance sheet at an amount ($80.8542) that corresponds to its present value (using the 8.5% imputed interest rate) as of the balance sheet date. We leave the task of verifying this fact to you.

Noncurrent monetary liabilities are initially recorded at their present value when incurred. This is true even for installment notes that make no mention of an interest rate. In such cases, an interest rate must be imputed.

ANALYTICAL INSIGHTS: FUTURE CASH FLOW EFFECTS OF DEBT

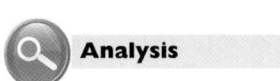

See Exhibit 11.10 for excerpts from Dentsply International's 2009 financial statement note for long-term debt. Dentsply develops, manufactures, and markets medical instruments and supplies for the global dental market. This example illustrates the type of information about a company's long-term debt that is available in corporate annual reports. Problem 11-22 gives you an opportunity to apply the analytical tools illustrated in this example to the company's 2012 financial statement note for long-term debt.

Among the company's long-term debt items, notice the 57 million Swiss francs-denominated revolving credit agreement shown next to ①. The U.S. dollar-equivalent amount of this loan was $53.507 million at the end of 2008 but zero at the end of 2009. Where did Dentsply

EXHIBIT 11.10 Dentsply International

Long-Term Debt

($ in millions)	December 31, 2009	December 31, 2008
Multicurrency revolving credit agreement expiring May 2010:		
Swiss francs 65 million at 0.60%	$ 62,844	$ 60,809
Swiss francs 57 million	—	53,507 ①
Private placement notes:		
U.S. dollar denominated expiring March 2010 at 0.55%	150,000	150,000
Term loan agreement:		
Japanese yen denominated expiring March 2012 at 1.00%	134,775	138,247
U.S. dollar commercial paper:		
Facility rated A/2-P/2 U.S. dollar borrowings at 0.30%	85,200	—
Other borrowings various currencies and rates	20,911	25,095
	$453,731	$427,659
Less: Current portion (included in notes payable and current portion of long-term debt)	66,580	3,980 ③
Long-term portion	$387,151	$423,679

The Company has a $500 million revolving credit agreement with participation from thirteen ② banks, which expires in May 2010. The revolving credit agreements contain a number of covenants and two financial ratios that the Company is required to satisfy. The most restrictive of these covenants pertain to asset dispositions and prescribed ratios of indebtedness to total capital and operating income plus depreciation and amortization to interest expense. Any breach of any such covenant would result in a default . . . [and] permit the lenders to declare all borrowings . . . immediately due and payable and, through cross-default provisions, would entitle the Company's other lenders to accelerate their loans. At December 31, 2009, the Company was in compliance with these covenants.

The table below reflects the contractual maturity dates of the various borrowings at December 31, 2009. The borrowings under the U.S. Private Placement Note and the commercial paper program are considered contractually due in 2014 and 2015 and beyond.

(in thousands)	
2010	$ 66,580 ④
2011	5,299
2012	139,470
2013	1,215
2014	75,682
2015 and beyond	165,485
	$453,731

Source: Dentsply International 2009 Annual Report.

Commercial paper refers to debt obligations with maturities ranging from 2 to 270 days issued by banks, corporations (for example, Dentsply), and other borrowers to investors. Why does Dentsply report its commercial paper borrowing as part of long-term (rather than short-term) debt? Even though the contractual maturity of commercial paper is less than one year, Dentsply intends to refinance the paper as it becomes due thus extending the effective maturity date of the loan to beyond one year. In such circumstances, firms alert financial statement readers to the intended refinancing by presenting the otherwise short-term debt as a long-term liability.

get the cash needed to pay off this debt? By comparing the amounts in the table for each major class of long-term debt, we can see that Dentsply raised $85.200 million that year by issuing commercial paper. It is reasonable to presume that the cash from this new source was used to pay off the revolving credit loan.

Dentsply provides details about interest rates and maturity dates for each major class of long-term debt. However, the company provides only general information about the covenants contained in its various borrowing agreements (see the paragraph next to ②). This nondisclosure is typical and imposes a burden on the financial analyst who must search through the lending agreements themselves to discover covenant details.

Dentsply's note provides a wealth of information useful for determining the future cash-flow implications of the company's long-term debt. For example, the table reveals current maturities (that is, the "Current portion" of long-term debt) of $66.580 million at the end of 2009 (see highlighted figure next to ③). This is the debt principal amount that Dentsply must repay in 2010.

Like all U.S. companies today, Dentsply is required to disclose scheduled debt payments for each of the five years after the balance sheet date. From the table adjacent to ④, we can see that these repayments are particularly large in 2012 ($139.470 million). Analysts studying the company will want to estimate whether Dentsply's operating cash flows that year will be sufficient when combined with cash on hand to meet this scheduled debt principal payment. Any anticipated shortfall could necessitate asset sales or additional financing.

Elsewhere in the annual report, we learn that Dentsply paid $23.231 million in interest during 2009. (Interest expense that year was $21.896 million, but this figure excludes some interest capitalized as part of plant assets.) The cash amount represents interest Dentsply paid on the long-term debt shown in Exhibit 11.10 plus any short-term interest-bearing debt reported elsewhere on the company's balance sheet. Dividing this cash interest payment by the average book value of outstanding long-term debt—or ($453.731 + $427.659)/2 = $440.695—plus the average short-term debt from the balance sheet—or ($15.600 + $21.800)/2 = $18.700 not shown in Exhibit 11.10—suggests that the company's "cash" interest rate for 2009 was about 4.8%, or $21.896/($440.695 + $18.700). Using this imputed interest rate as the basis for forecasting 2010 interest payments, we discover that Dentsply will likely spend about $22.528 million (4.8% × $469.331 million of interest-bearing debt outstanding) for interest that year. This forecasted cash outflow is in addition to the $65.580 million principal repayment scheduled for 2010. Cash flow forecasts of this type can be constructed for each year from 2010 through 2014.

> Elsewhere in the note on debt, Dentsply provides a forecast of 2010 interest payments ($19.181 million). The $469.331 outstanding amount comprises $453.731 in long-term debt (Exhibit 10.11) plus $15.600 million in short-term debt.

Will Dentsply have the cash needed to make the forecasted $88.108 interest and principal payments in 2010? The company's cash flow statement reveals operating cash flows in excess of $300 million in each of the past two years, coupled with minimal capital expenditures. It seems safe to presume that Dentsply will generate a similar level of operating cash flow in 2010. But even if 2010 operating cash flows fall short of this projected amount, the company has over $450 million in cash (and cash equivalents) on hand at the end of 2009. The availability of ample cash from these two sources—operations and existing cash balances—means that Dentsply should have little difficulty meeting its interest and principal repayment obligations in 2010.

Here is what Dentsply tells us about the fair value of its long-term debt in a separate annual report note:

> The fair value of financial instruments is determined by reference to various market data and other valuation techniques as appropriate . . . The Company estimates the fair value and carrying value of its total long-term debt, including current portion of long-term debt, was $453.7 million and $427.7 million as of December 31, 2009 and 2008, respectively. The fair value of the Company's long-term debt equaled its carrying value [because] the Company's debt is variable rate and reflects current market rates.

The fair value of Dentsply's long-term debt equals its balance sheet carrying value. Why? As the company points out, most of Dentsply's debt has variable (floating not fixed) interest rates that approximate current market rates. As we have already discussed, this loan feature insulates debt fair values from changes in market interest rates, and so it is not at all surprising to learn that debt fair value and carrying value are the same.

The situation is quite different at Blockbuster Inc., the movie and video game rental company that at the time had customers in over 17 countries. According to the company's

Fair Value of Financial Instruments

At April 4, 2010, our carrying value of financial instruments approximated fair value except for our $300.0 million aggregate principal amount of 9% senior subordinated notes due 2012 (the "Senior Subordinated Notes") and our 11.75% Senior Secured Notes due 2014. The estimated fair values of our Senior Subordinated Notes and Senior Secured Notes at April 4, 2010, and January 3, 2010, are based on trading activity.

A summary of the carrying values and the fair values of our Senior Secured Notes and our Senior Subordinated Notes is as follows:

	April 4, 2010			January 3, 2010		
	Principal Amount	**Carrying Value**	**Fair Value**	**Principal Amount**	**Carrying Value**	**Fair Value**
Senior Secured Notes	$630.0	$595.4	$459.9	$675.0	$637.6	$641.3
Senior Subordinated Notes	300.0	300.0	60.8	300.0	300.0	168.0

Source: Blockbuster Inc. 10-Q filing for the quarter ended April 4, 2010.

quarterly financial statement note (Exhibit 11.11), the fair value of Blockbuster's fixed-rate long-term debt is less than the balance sheet carrying value (amortized historical cost) of the debt. There are two reasons this might happen:

1. Blockbuster is a worse credit risk in 2010 than it was several years earlier when the notes were first issued. As a company's creditworthiness deteriorates, the fair value of its debt decreases even though the carrying value of the debt is unchanged.

2. Interest rates have increased since the notes were first issued for reasons unrelated to the company itself (for example, higher expected inflation or a weakening economy). From our earlier discussion, you know that an interest rate increase—whether due to company-specific factors or to macroeconomic forces—will cause the fair value of fixed-rate debt to decrease. Of course, amortized historical cost accounting for long-term debt relies only on the effective interest rate prevailing when the fixed-rate debt is first issued. Subsequent interest rate changes do not alter the carrying value of fixed-rate debt.

Which of these two explanations is the most plausible in Blockbuster's case? Notice that the notes carry relatively hefty fixed interest rates (9% and 11.75%) at a time when overall market rates in the United States were historically low. Notice also that the note fair values fell substantially between January and April 2010, a period when market rates were stable. Macroeconomic forces are thus an unlikely explanation for why the fair value of Blockbuster's debt is less than the balance sheet carrying value.

So, the answer must lie in Blockbuster's worsening credit risk. In April 2010, the company was struggling to address a variety of thorny operational issues that limited its ability to generate the cash needed for scheduled debt payments. Investors priced those cash flow concerns into their assessment of debt fair value, and the price discount was steep! Notice that investors were saying they anticipate receiving only 20 cents of each $1 borrowed under the senior subordinated notes because the debt fair value ($60.8 million) is just 20.2% of the principal amount ($300 million). Blockbuster filed for bankruptcy in September 2010 and in April 2011 was bought by satellite television provider Dish Network for $233 million and the assumption of $87 million in liabilities and other obligations. Dish Network was unable to revive the company and all Blockbuster stores owned by Dish were closed in 2014.

INCENTIVES FOR OFF-BALANCE-SHEET LIABILITIES

In Chapters 1 and 7, we described business contracts linked to (among other things) the amount of liabilities on a company's balance sheet. Examples include loan covenants and bond indentures. These contracts usually contain terms and conditions designed to protect the lender against loss. The protection is in the form of contract terms (covenant triggers) tied to the borrower's debt-to-equity ratio, debt-to-tangible-asset ratio, or some other financial ratio that includes reported liabilities. Accounting-related covenants typically contain language such as "the debt-to-equity ratio may not exceed 1.7 in any quarter." The intent of such covenants is to provide an early warning signal regarding deteriorating creditworthiness. In principle, the early warning allows the lender to require repayment of the loan before the borrower's condition worsens further.

 **Contracting**

Such loan contract terms create incentives for managers of borrowing companies to minimize *reported* financial statement liabilities. Reducing the total amount of reportable liabilities in the contractual ratio makes covenant violations less likely.

Consider one example of the way these incentives influence business behavior: **Unconsolidated subsidiaries** are sometimes established to finance specialized projects or **joint ventures.** Critics say these separately incorporated entities have sometimes been used to evade loan covenants linked to reported liabilities and to misrepresent the firm's total liabilities. This strategy exploits a loophole in the rules governing when subsidiaries need to be consolidated.

> As explained in Chapter 16, **consolidation** essentially means that the separate financial statements of the parent and subsidiary are added together line-by-line to form a single combined ("consolidated") set of financial statements. For example, the consolidated balance sheet would report as Cash the sum of the parent's cash plus the subsidiary's cash. Similarly, total consolidated liabilities would consist of the sum of the parent's liabilities plus those of the subsidiary. Chapter 16 provides the details and describes the accounting rules for unconsolidated subsidiaries.

When one company owns *more* than 50% of the stock of another affiliated company, the owner (parent) is deemed to "control" the other company (subsidiary). The financial statements of subsidiaries that are under the control of a parent must be consolidated with those of the parent. But when one company owns 50% or *less* of another company's stock, consolidation is not required except under special circumstances described in Chapter 16. Instead, the owner's *net investment* in the subsidiary is reported as an asset in the owner's balance sheet using what is called the **equity method** of accounting.

The equity method is described in Chapter 16. Here's an example illustrating all you need to know about it now.

Assume that Blue Company and Black Company both use an identically manufactured input, T-spanners, in their respective production processes. Manufacturing T-spanners requires a large investment in plant and equipment that must be financed by borrowing. Both Blue Company and Black Company wish to avoid adding more debt to their balance sheets, so they agree to form a separate jointly owned venture called Gray Company.

> In real-world joint ventures, the debt is often guaranteed by the parent companies because the joint venture (Gray Company) is usually thinly capitalized and lenders accordingly look to the parents (Blue Company and Black Company) for added assurance that the loan will be repaid.

Each venture partner contributes $25 million cash to establish Gray Company and receives common stock representing a 50% ownership interest in it. A bank then loans Gray $300 million to purchase the plant and equipment needed to produce T-spanners. This loan is collateralized by Gray's factory and guaranteed by both Blue Company and Black Company. Immediately after these transactions take place, Gray Company's balance sheet would appear as shown in Figure 11.5.

The balance sheets of Blue Company and Black Company would each show that company's $25 million investment in the asset account Investment in joint venture. Under the equity method, this account balance would increase if further investments were made in the joint venture or if Gray earned a profit. Because Blue and Black own Gray equally,

Figure 11.5

JOINT VENTURE
FINANCING

($ in millions)

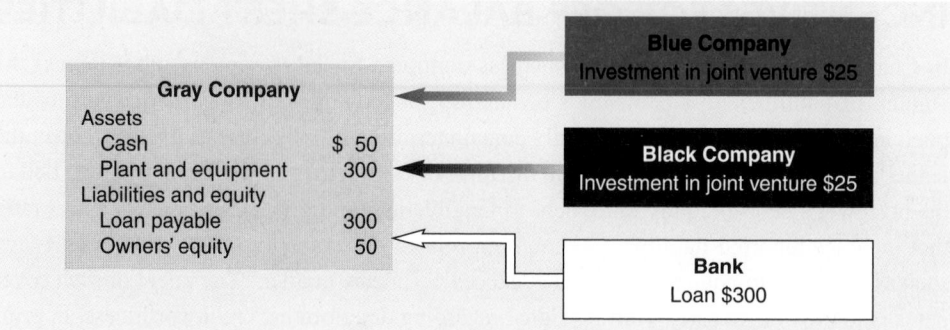

each would add 50% of Gray's profit to the balance in its Investment in joint venture account.

The partners' balance sheets do not report any of the joint venture's $300 million bank loan! Neither Blue nor Black owns more than 50% of Gray, so neither needs to consolidate it. Consequently, the borrowing necessary to fund the venture appears on neither partner's financial statements under the equity method. The Investment in joint venture account on each company's books would continue to show $25 million, yet Blue and Black have effectively each borrowed $150 million "off balance sheet"![15] Proportionate consolidation, the benchmark accounting treatment under IFRS and required by Canadian GAAP, would solve this problem (see Chapter 16).

> The Investment in joint venture account is unchanged because each partner's investment in the net assets (that is, assets minus liabilities) of the joint venture is unchanged by the borrowing. Gray Company's assets increased by $300 million but so did its liabilities. Consequently. Gray's *net* assets remained at $50 million after the borrowing.

So-called **special purpose entities** (SPEs) represent a variation of the simple joint venture arrangement between Blue Company and Black Company. One common type of SPE involves assets with more or less predictable cash flows such as credit card receivables. Without going into all of the details, suppose a retailer such as Neiman Marcus (the luxury department store chain) needs to borrow money and wants to do so at the best available interest rate. Instead of obtaining a traditional bank loan, Neiman Marcus decides to create an SPE (called NM Receivables Trust) and then transfers a portion of its customer credit card receivables to the new entity. The trust next obtains a low-interest loan to be repaid from the future cash flows associated with the credit card receivables, sending the borrowed money to Neiman Marcus as payment for the transferred receivables. Although the transaction may seem unduly complex, the structure allows Neiman Marcus to isolate assets with predictable cash flows (in this case, the credit card receivables) from its other assets with less predictable cash flows. Isolating the credit card receivables in this way reduces the lender's credit risk, which in turn reduces the interest rate that Neiman Marcus must pay on the loan. Entities of this type were often not required to be consolidated on the financial statements of the parent company (that is, Neiman Marcus), so the loan was another example of "off-balance-sheet" debt.

Special purpose entities became notorious following the collapse of Enron. In November 2001, Enron announced that it would restate earnings for 1997 through 2001 downward by

---

[15] Prior to the issuance of pre-Codification "Consolidation of All Majority-Owned Subsidiaries," *SFAS No. 94* (Stamford, CT: FASB, 1987), incorporated in FASB ASC Topic 810, even 100% wholly owned subsidiaries were accounted for in many cases under the equity method. This kept the subsidiaries' debt off the balance sheet in much the same manner as joint-venture debt. Here's how: In many industries, companies help customers finance the purchase of their products. One example is the automobile industry. If no financing subsidiary were to be formed, the cash necessary to finance the credit extended to dealers and consumers would come from bank loans or other borrowing by the parent. As a consequence, the parent's debt-to-equity ratio would be worsened. However, if a separate finance subsidiary were to be formed and this subsidiary borrowed the funds directly in its own name, the borrowing would be effectively kept off the parent's balance sheet. The trick here was accomplished by using equity method accounting for subsidiaries, as will be discussed in Chapter 16. This is no longer permitted.

$1.2 billion because the company and its auditors had determined that three unconsolidated SPEs should have been consolidated. As part of the restatement, Enron increased its balance sheet debt by $628 million in 2000. Over the course of the next several months, investors and creditors learned that Enron's off-balance-sheet SPEs were used to hide the company's mounting losses and cash flow problems. Several former Enron senior officials were later charged with violating the antifraud provisions of the federal securities laws.

The FASB has tightened the rules governing the consolidation of special purpose entities, which are now called **variable interest entities** (VIEs), in an effort to avoid future Enron debacles. Chapter 16 tells you more.

> **RE**CAP
>
> **The motivation for off-balance-sheet financing transactions is strong. Managers continue to develop innovative strategies to understate reported liabilities and to ensure that certain items remain "off the balance sheet." Financial analysts and auditors must remember the motivations behind off-balance-sheet financing, know how to identify peculiar and contorted borrowing arrangements, and adjust the reported financial statement numbers to better reflect economic reality.**

HEDGES

Businesses are exposed to **market risks** from many sources—changes in interest rates, foreign currency exchange rates, and commodity prices.[16] Suppose a bank makes numerous five-year term loans at an annual interest rate of 8%. The earnings from those loans generate the cash needed to pay interest to "money market" account depositors. The loans expose the bank to interest rate risk: If money market interest rates rise, the 8% fixed return from the loans may not be adequate to pay the new higher rates promised to depositors.

> Commodities are bulk goods such as wheat, corn, lumber, jet fuel, and copper.

Similar risks confront manufacturers. Consider Ridge Development, a real estate company that simultaneously constructs many single-family homes. Buyers make a down payment and agree to a fixed contract price to be paid when the home is completed. The typical home is completed in four months or less, and lumber comprises the bulk of construction costs. Because lumber prices are volatile, the developer is at risk that profits could erode (or disappear entirely) if lumber prices were to soar during the four-month construction cycle.

Or consider Southwest Airlines. It sells airline transportation services to passengers, many of whom pay a month or more in advance of the actual flight. Fuel is a major cost component in the airline industry, and fuel prices fluctuate on almost a daily basis. Because the passenger ticket price is set prior to the flight, Southwest Airlines is at risk that escalating fuel prices could turn an otherwise profitable flight into a loss.

> Businesses are also exposed to **operating risks** from severe weather conditions, industrial accidents, raw material shortages, labor strikes, and so on. Insurance contracts, financial guarantees, and other business arrangements are used to hedge operating risks—but these risks (and arrangements) do not qualify for the special hedge accounting rules described later in this section. Only certain financial risks qualify for hedge accounting.

Managing market risk is essential to the overall business strategies of most companies today. This trend has been driven by the need to reduce cash flow volatility that arises from factors beyond management's control—the exchange rate of U.S. dollars to Japanese yen, the LIBOR interest rate (the benchmark interbank interest rate for European banks), or the price of natural gas to run a factory. In response to these and other market risks, many companies today engage in **hedging**—business transactions designed to insulate them from commodity price, interest rate, or exchange rate risk. **Derivative securities,** which we explain next, are often used to accomplish this insulation.

---

[16] We gratefully acknowledge the substantial contribution of Professor Thomas Linsmeier, now serving as an FASB member, to the material in this section.

Typical Derivative Instruments and the Benefits of Hedging

Derivative instruments are so named because they are securities that have no inherent value but instead represent a claim against some other asset—their value is *derived* from the value of the asset underlying that claim.[17]

A **forward contract** is one example of a derivative instrument. In a forward contract, two parties agree to the sale of some asset on some *future* date—called the *settlement date*—at a price specified today. You have been dealing with forward contracts for much of your life, perhaps without knowing it. Suppose you walk into a bookstore on October 5 to buy the best-selling *Seven Unbeatable Strategies for Social Media Marketing.* The book is sold out, but the clerk offers to reorder it for you and call you when it arrives. The clerk says that the book should arrive in about 15 days and will cost $39.95. If you agree on October 5 to pick up and pay for the book when called, you and the clerk have agreed to a forward contract. Three elements of this contract are key: the agreed upon price ($39.95) to be paid in the future; the delivery date ("in about 15 days"); and that you will "take delivery" by paying for the book and picking it up when notified. The clerk has "sold" you a forward contract for the best seller.

> What happens if you pay for the book on October 5? Then it's a simple cash sales transaction (with a promised future delivery date). As long as *both parties are obligated* to perform at some future date under the agreement, it's a forward contract. Here this means the clerk is required to obtain a copy of the best seller and deliver it to you within the specified time. And you are required to pay the agreed upon price and to take delivery if and when the book arrives.

Futures Contracts A variation of a forward contract takes place on financial exchanges such as the New York Mercantile Exchange (NYMEX) where **futures contracts** are traded daily in a market with many buyers and sellers. Futures contracts exist for commodities such as corn, wheat, live hogs and cattle, cotton, copper, crude oil, lumber, and even electricity. Here is how they work.

Suppose on October 5 you "write" (meaning sell) a futures contract for 10 million pounds of February copper at 95 cents per pound—we'll show why you might want to do so in just a moment. By selling the contract, you are obligated to deliver the copper at the agreed-upon price in February. The buyer (or contract counterparty) is obliged to pay the fixed price per pound and take delivery of the copper. So far this looks like a forward contract because both parties have an obligation to perform in the future (February).

But there's more! Futures contracts do not have a predetermined settlement date—you (the seller) can choose to deliver the copper on any day during the delivery month (February). This gives sellers additional flexibility in settling the contract. When you decide to deliver the copper, you notify the exchange clearinghouse, which then notifies an individual—let's call her Anne Smythe—who bought February copper contracts. (The clearinghouse selected Smythe at random from among all individuals who hold February copper contracts.) Smythe is then told to be ready to accept delivery within the next several days.

But wait a moment! Suppose she bought the contract as a speculative investment, has no real use for the copper, and doesn't want delivery? Futures contracts have an added advantage over forward contracts because futures are actively traded on an exchange. This means Smythe can avoid delivery by immediately selling a February copper contract for 10 million pounds, thus creating a zero net position. The first contract obligates Smythe to accept delivery of 10 million pounds of copper, but the second contract obligates her to turn over 10 million pounds to someone else. One contract cancels the other, and Smythe avoids the embarrassment of having all of that copper dumped on her garage floor.

> How can you (the seller) avoid having to deliver the copper? Form a zero net position of your own by *purchasing* a February copper contract from someone else—perhaps even from Anne Smythe.

---

[17] For an overview of the characteristics and uses of derivative securities, see S. A. Ross, R. W. Westerfield, and B. D. Jordan, *Fundamentals of Corporate Finance,* 8th ed. (New York: McGraw-Hill, 2008); S. Ryan, *Financial Instruments and Institutions* (Hoboken, NJ: Wiley & Sons, 2007); and C. W. Smithson, C. W. Smith, and D. S. Wilford, *Managing Financial Risk* (Homewood, IL; Irwin, 1995).

Now that you understand how futures contracts work, let's see how they can be used to hedge financial risk.

Consider the opportunities confronting Rombaurer Metals, a copper mining company. On October 1, 2014, Rombaurer has 10 million pounds of copper inventory on hand at an average cost of 65 cents per pound. The "spot" (current delivery) price for copper on October 1 is 90 cents a pound. Rombaurer could receive $9 million (10 million pounds × $0.90 per pound) by selling its entire copper inventory today. This would yield a $2.5 million gross profit ($0.90 selling price − $0.65 average cost per pound × 10 million pounds). However, Rombaurer has decided to hold on to its copper until February 2015 when management believes the price will return to a normal level of 95 cents a pound. The commodities market seems to agree because February copper futures are priced as though copper will sell for 95 cents in February. The decision not to sell copper in October exposes Rombaurer to **commodity price risk** from a possible future decline in copper prices.

Figure 11.6(a) illustrates the company's commodity price risk exposure. If copper prices increase to 95 cents by February as expected, Rombaurer will receive $9.5 million for its copper and earn $3 million ($0.95 selling price − $0.65 average cost per pound × 10 million pounds). That's $0.5 million more than Rombaurer would earn by selling the copper on October 1. But what if the February price of copper falls to 85 cents? The cash received from selling copper would then be only $8.5 million, and the gross profit would be only $2 million. Each 10-cent decline in the February copper price lowers the company's cash flows and expected gross profits by $1 million. At 65 cents per pound, Rombaurer just breaks even (zero gross profit) and, at any price below 65 cents, the company has a loss. These potential cash flow and gross profit declines represent the *downside risk* associated with the uncertain February price of copper.

There is *upside potential* as well. Each 10-cent increase in the February copper price will produce a $1 million increase in the company's cash flow and gross profit.

One way Rombaurer can protect itself from a decline in the price of copper is to hedge its position with futures contracts. Suppose that Rombaurer sells 400 copper contracts—each contract is for 25,000 pounds—at 95 cents a pound for February delivery. The delivery month is chosen to coincide with the company's expected physical sale of the copper. The ultimate value of these contracts depends on the February price of copper as shown in Figure 11.6(b).

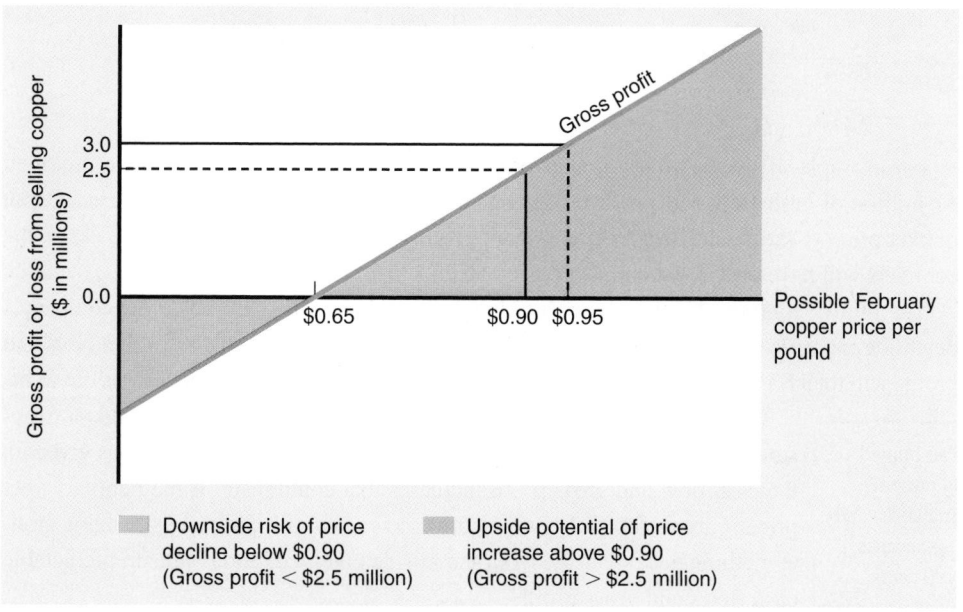

Figure 11.6(a)

ROMBAURER METALS

Using Futures Contracts to Hedge Copper Inventory: Before the Hedge

Potential gross profit or loss from the sale of copper in February

Figure 11.6(b)

ROMBAURER METALS

Using Futures Contracts to
Hedge Copper Inventory:
The Hedging Instrument

*Potential value of futures contract for
February copper*

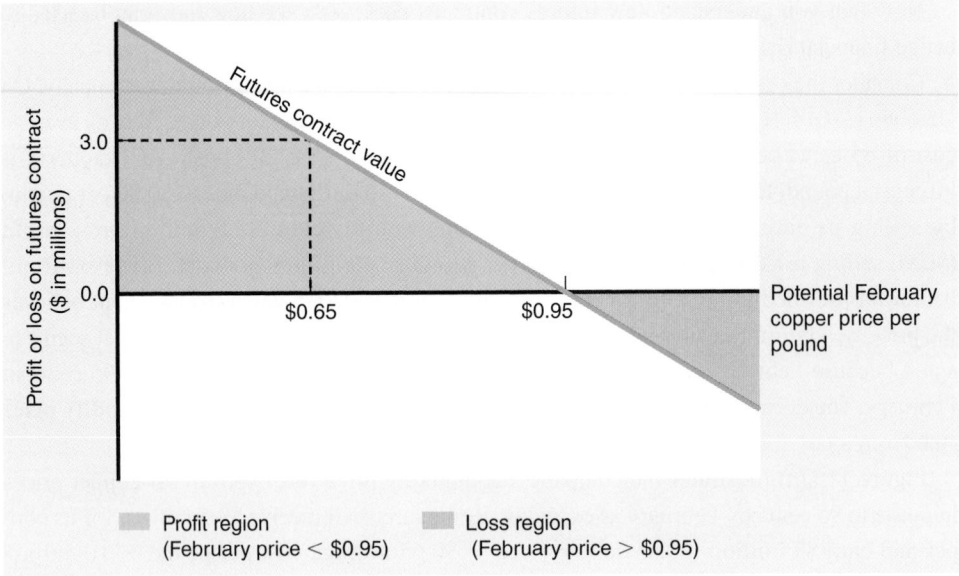

Figure 11.6(c)

ROMBAURER METALS

Using Futures Contracts to
Hedge Copper Inventory:
After the Hedge

*Gross profit from hedged position:
Combination of unhedged copper inventory
and futures contract*

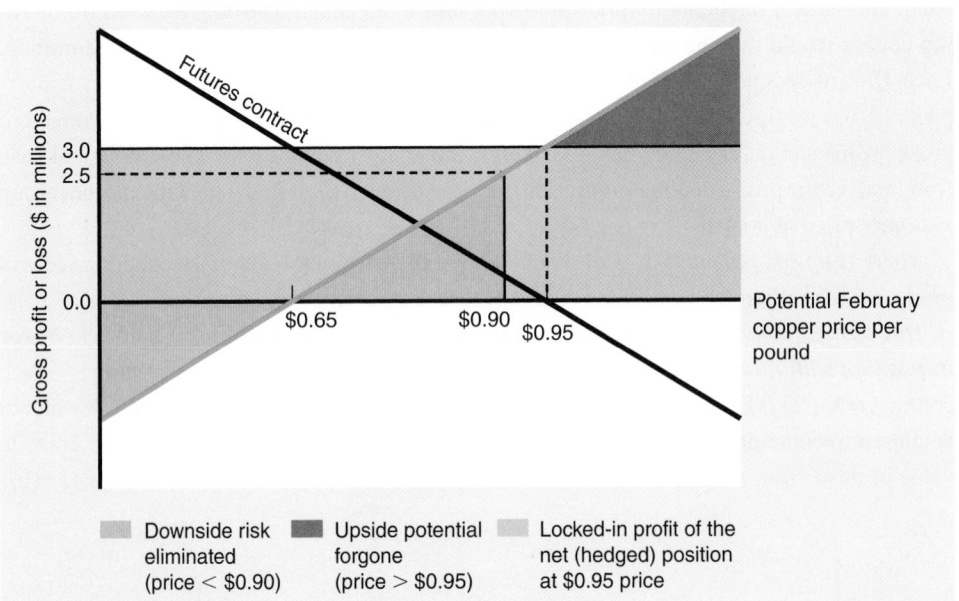

For example, if the February copper price is 85 cents, the contracts will have provided $1 million of cash flow and profit protection ($0.95 contract price − $0.85 February spot market price × the 10 million pounds of copper). If the February spot price is 65 cents, the contracts will have provided $3 million of protection.

The futures contracts "lock in" a February price of 95 cents and eliminate the company's downside exposure to a decline in copper prices. February cash receipts will be $9.5 million, and profits will total $3.0 million, no matter what the February spot price for copper turns out to be.

Of course, there is another side to the story. By hedging its original exposure to commodity price risk with futures contracts, Rombaurer has given up the cash flow and gross profit increases that could result if the February spot price is above $0.95. Figure 11.6(c) shows how the company's hedging strategy eliminates downside risk (and upside potential) and results in predictable cash flows and gross profits.

Indeed, the futures contracts provide an immediate 5 cent per pound benefit (ignoring present value considerations, inventory holding costs, and fees and commissions of the contracts) because the October 1 price of copper is only 90 cents.

Swap Contracts   Another common derivative instrument is a **swap contract.** This contract is a popular way to hedge interest rate or foreign currency exchange rate risk. Let's say that Kistler Manufacturing has issued $100 million of long-term 8% fixed-rate debt and wants to protect itself against a *decline* in market interest rates. The company could reduce its exposure in several ways. We mentioned one approach earlier in this chapter, using a debt-for-debt exchange offer to replace fixed-rate debt with a floating-rate loan. A second and perhaps less costly way that Kistler can reduce its interest rate risk exposure is to create *synthetic* floating-rate debt using an **interest rate swap.**

This form of hedging is accomplished with a "swap dealer." Swap dealers are typically banks that locate another company—called a *counterparty*—who is willing to make fixed-rate interest *payments* in exchange for floating-rate interest *receipts.* (Recall that Kistler wants to make floating-rate interest payments.) The swap transaction in Figure 11.7 includes Kistler with fixed-rate debt outstanding, the swap dealer, and the swap counterparty—a company with floating-rate debt and interest payments linked to the one-year LIBOR benchmark interest rate. This is exactly the type of interest payment Kistler seeks.

Kistler and the counterparty agree to swap interest payments on $100 million of debt for the next three years with settlement every year. At each settlement date, the counterparty gives Kistler the fixed-rate payment of $8 million, which is then passed on to Kistler's lender. At the same time, Kistler gives the counterparty cash equal to the counterparty's payment (say $7 million based on a LIBOR-linked rate of 7%), and this too is passed on to the counterparty's lender. In reality, only the $1 million difference in interest payments would be exchanged between Kistler and the swap counterparty.

The swap transforms Kistler's fixed-rate debt into floating rate because the money Kistler receives from the counterparty offsets the fixed payment Kistler is obligated to make to the lender. Figure 11.8 shows how the swap transaction eliminates Kistler's downside exposure to interest rate risk. If the LIBOR rate falls to 7%, Kistler will receive a net cash inflow of $1 million from the swap counterparty; that is, the difference between Kistler's $8 million fixed-rate payment and the counterparty's $7 million floating-rate payment. Kistler then pays its lender $8 million as required with $1 million of the payment coming from the swap counterparty.

> One reason protection might be needed is that Kistler's operating cash flows are positively correlated with interest rates. A decline in market rates would then be accompanied by a decrease in operating cash flows, and the company might lack the cash flow needed to meet its fixed-rate payment.

> What does the counterparty gain? By replacing floating-rate interest payments with synthetic fixed-rate payments, the counterparty has reduced its exposure to cash flow volatility from interest rate changes.

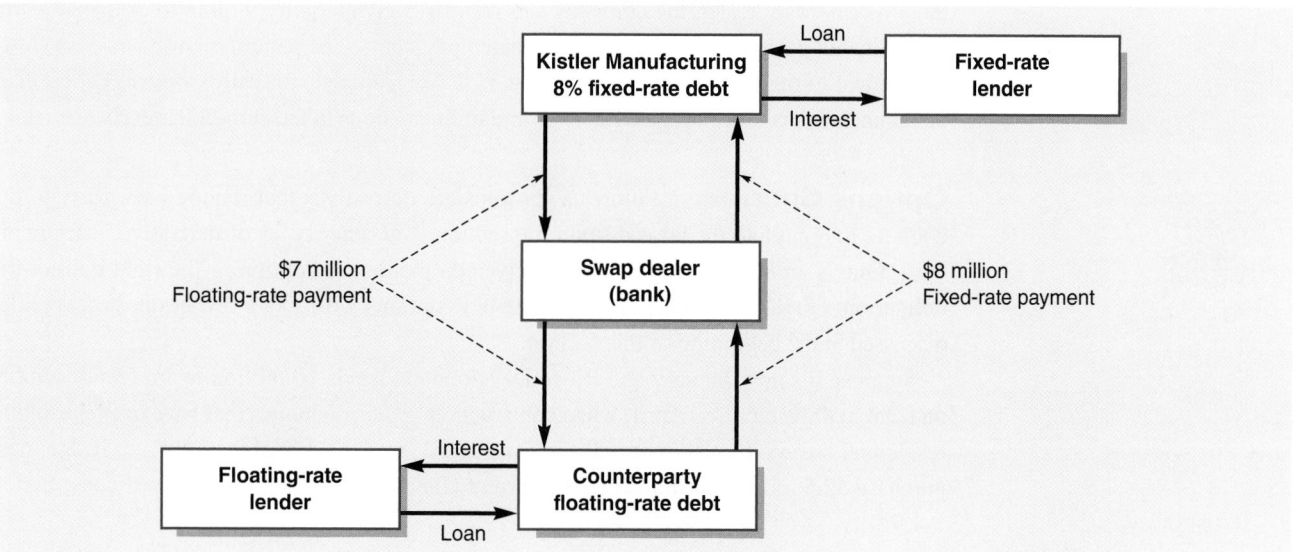

Figure 11.7 KISTLER MANUFACTURING

An Interest Rate Swap That Creates Synthetic Floating-Rate Debt

Figure 11.8

KISTLER MANUFACTURING

Using a Swap to Hedge
Interest Rate Risk

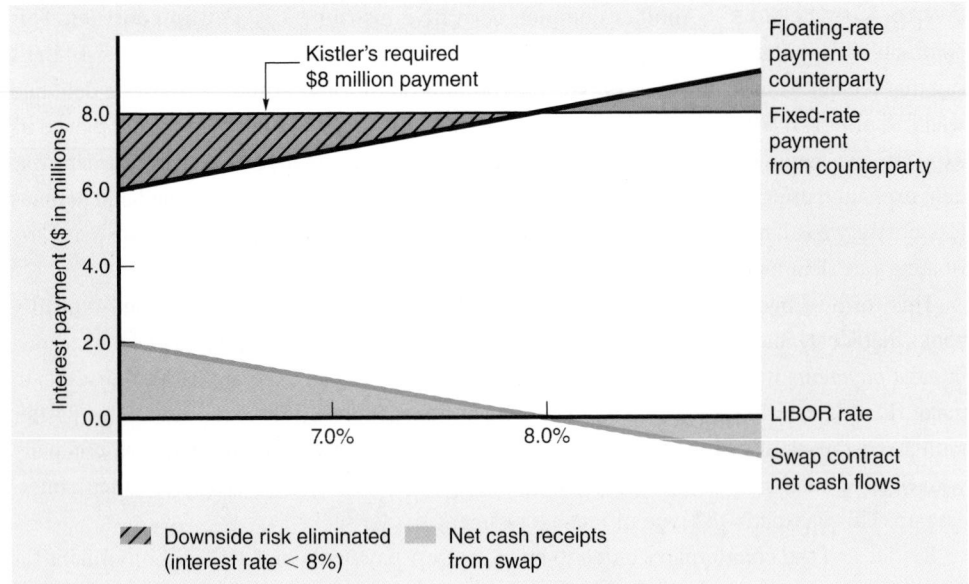

Kistler's out-of-pocket interest cost is just $7 million, the amount it would have been required to pay if it had issued floating-rate debt in the first place.[18]

Kistler ends up with floating-rate debt that it could perhaps not otherwise obtain at attractive rates. The result is that the counterparty has fixed interest payments, and the bank earns a fee for arranging the swap transaction. Everybody wins—as long as all parties fulfill their payment obligations.

A **foreign exchange (currency) swap** has the same structural features as those outlined in Exhibits 11.7 and 11.8 except that the loans are denominated in different currencies. Suppose that St. Jean Inc. manufactures products in France but sells them exclusively in the United States. The company borrows euros to finance construction of a manufacturing plant in France, and it wants to hedge its foreign exchange exposure on the loan. The company's exposure arises because its operating cash flows are in U.S. dollars but its loan payments are in euros. With the aid of a swap dealer, the company can identify a counterparty willing to exchange euro-denominated payments for dollar-denominated payments. The pattern of swapped cash flows is identical to the flows depicted in Figure 11.7. St. Jean ends up with *synthetic* U.S. dollar-denominated debt and eliminates its exposure to fluctuations in the euro-dollar exchange rate.

Options Contract   Futures and swaps are derivatives that require each party to the contract to complete the agreed-upon transaction. But other types of derivative instruments exist. One is an *option contract,* which gives the holder an "option"—the right but not the obligation—to do something. To illustrate how options work, let's revisit our homebuilder discussed at the beginning of this section.

Suppose it's now January and Ridge Development needs 10 million board feet of lumber on hand in three months (April) when construction begins on homes that have been presold to residential buyers. Lumber currently sells for $250 per 1,000 board feet (kbf), so Ridge must purchase $2.5 million of lumber at the current (January) price to meet its April construction

---

[18] An **interest rate "collar"** may be part of the swap agreement as well—for example, the two parties could agree that the swap remains in force as long as the LIBOR-linked rate is less than 8.5% and more than 6%. What if the LIBOR rises to 9%? Kistler then pays $8 million to its lender and another $1 million to the swap counterparty. The swap benefits Kistler when LIBOR rates fall but not when LIBOR rises.

commitment. But Ridge has no place to store the lumber, and lumber prices are expected to increase over the next few months. How can the company eliminate its commodity price risk from its *anticipated* lumber purchase three months from now?

One approach is to buy a futures contract for April lumber. Ridge can "lock in" the profit margin on unbuilt homes it has sold by agreeing to pay a set price now (in January) for lumber to be delivered in April. But if lumber prices fall over the next three months, the builder—now locked into higher lumber prices by the futures contract—would forgo the increased profits from lower lumber prices.

By using options instead of futures, Ridge can protect against lumber cost increases without sacrificing potential gains if lumber prices decline. This can be accomplished by purchasing a call option on lumber—an option to buy lumber at a specified price over the option period. The call option protects the builder against lumber cost increases. But because it is an *option,* Ridge is not obligated to exercise the option should lumber prices fall. Options enable Ridge to hedge unfavorable price movements and still participate in the upside possibility of increased profit margins if lumber prices fall. Figure 11.9 shows how.

Without hedging its anticipated lumber purchase, Ridge is exposed to commodity price risk if lumber prices rise above the current $250 level over the next three months. To eliminate this exposure, Ridge buys a call option for 10 million board feet of April lumber at $250 per 1,000 board feet. If the April price of lumber is more than $250 per 1,000 board feet, Ridge will exercise the option and pay just the $250 contract price. But if the April price is, say, $200, Ridge will let the option expire and instead buy lumber in the open market—saving $500,000 in lumber costs ($50 per 1,000 board feet). The net result of the option hedge is a "hockey stick" shape (see Figure 11.9)—the *downside risk* of a lumber price increase is eliminated but the *upside potential* of a lumber price decrease is retained.

When options are used in this way, they do not necessarily "lock in" a specified profit margin or price. Instead, they provide a hedge that resembles insurance. Options allow companies to hedge against downside risk—value losses—while retaining the opportunity to benefit from favorable price movements. Insurance does the same thing. It provides protection against losses.

> Some option contracts give the holder the right to *buy* a specific underlying asset at a specified price during a specified time. These are known as **call options.** Other option contracts give the holder the option to *sell* an asset at a specified price during a specified time period. These are **put options.**

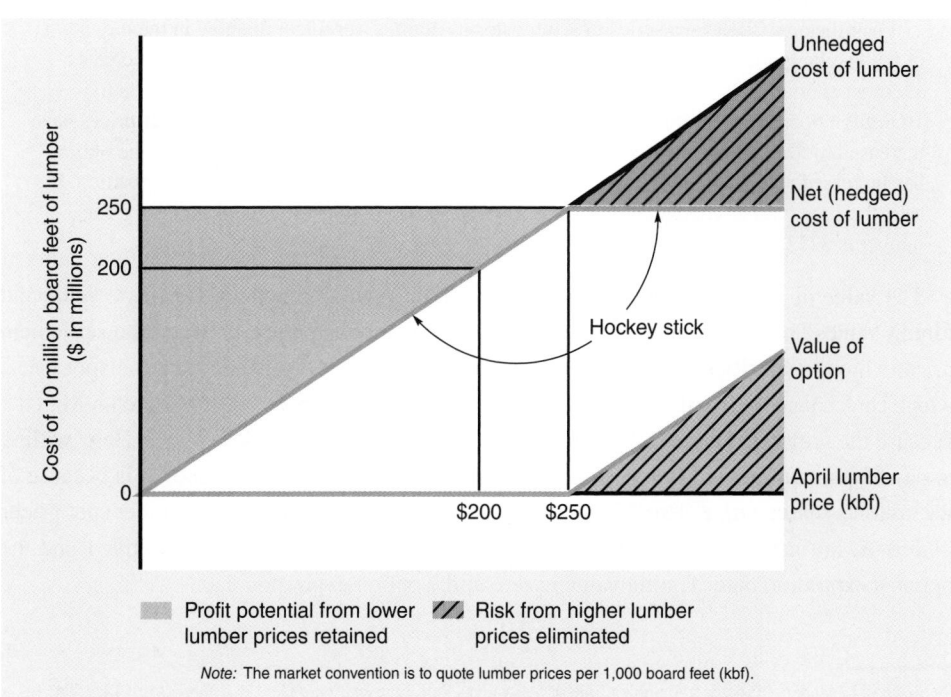

Figure 11.9

RIDGE DEVELOPMENT COMPANY

Using an Option to Hedge Commodity Price Risk

Legend (from figure):
Profit potential from lower lumber prices retained
Risk from higher lumber prices eliminated

Note: The market convention is to quote lumber prices per 1,000 board feet (kbf).

Derivative instruments are extremely useful tools for managing financial risk. New and more complicated hedging instruments and transactions are created each year, and they sometimes have unintended consequences. That is what the soap company Procter & Gamble learned in 1994 when it had to liquidate two contracts for interest rate swaps. The lesson cost the company $157 million, one of the largest derivative losses suffered by a U.S. company at the time. William J. McDonough, president of the Federal Reserve Bank of New York, said at the time, "People of my generation who are not astrophysicists have to strain to understand these products [hedging instruments and transactions]. To put it simply and directly, if the bosses do not or cannot understand both the risks and the rewards in their products, their firm should not be in the business."[19]

Financial Reporting for Derivative Instruments

Before we turn our attention to hedge accounting, let's consider how GAAP treats stand-alone derivatives in the absence of a hedging transaction. Here's a quick synopsis:

- All derivatives must be carried on the balance sheet at fair value—no exceptions. Fair value is the derivative's market price at the balance sheet date (except when other levels of the fair value measurement hierarchy apply).

- Generally, changes in the fair value of derivatives must be recognized in income when they occur. The only GAAP exception is for derivatives that qualify as hedges (explained later).

This example illustrates the basic accounting treatment for derivatives that do *not* qualify for special hedge accounting rules:

> On March 1, 2014, Heitz Metals buys call options (that is, options to purchase) for 10 million board feet of June lumber. Each call option gives Heitz the opportunity to purchase 1,000 board feet of lumber, so the firm bought a total of 10,000 option contracts (10 million board feet divided by 1,000 per contract). Heitz has no use for the lumber, nor is the company hedging a financial risk. ***Instead, Heitz is just speculating that lumber prices will increase during the next several months.*** The settlement price is $240 per 1,000 board feet, the current spot price is $240, and Heitz pays $50,000 for the contracts.
>
> Over the next 30 days, a series of winter storms dump several feet of snow in the mountains of the Pacific Northwest. This late snowfall delays the timber-harvesting season and creates a lumber shortage. By March 31, the spot price for lumber is $245, and June contracts for 10 million board feet are trading for $75,000 at the commodities exchange. Lumber prices have increased to $245, but Heitz owns an option to buy lumber at $240, so the value of the option has increased along with lumber prices. On April 15, Heitz decides to liquidate its position. It sells the June lumber contracts for $13 each (or $130,000 in total) when the spot price for lumber is $252.

The value of an option contract can be broken into two components: intrinsic value and timing value. The option contract's *intrinsic value* is the difference between the settlement price, which is specified in the contract and does not change over time, and the spot price, which can change on a daily basis. The Heitz option has an intrinsic value of zero on March 1 because the settlement price ($240) equals the spot price ($240) that day. Why is Heitz willing to pay $5 per contract on March 1 for an option that has zero intrinsic value? It is because of the option's *timing value*. This $5 timing value reflects the possibility that lumber spot prices (and thus, intrinsic value) may rise above the current $240 level between March 1 and the option's expiration date. Timing value is zero at the option expiration date.

---

[19] Quoted in L. Malkin, "Procter & Gamble's Tale of Derivatives Woe," *International Herald Tribune*, April 14, 1994.

The accounting entry to record Heitz Metals' *speculative* purchase—remember that Heitz has no real use for lumber—of June lumber contracts is:

DR	Marketable securities—lumber options	$50,000	
	CR Cash		$50,000

The derivative contracts (call options) are recorded as an asset at fair value—the purchase price paid. At the end of March, the call option price has increased to $7.50 per contract. Heitz records the derivative's *change* in fair value for the month ($75,000 fair value at the end of March − $50,000 fair value at the start of March, or $25,000):

DR	Market adjustment—lumber options	$25,000	
	CR Unrealized holding gain on lumber options (to income)		$25,000

The $25,000 Market adjustment is added to the $50,000 balance in Marketable securities. The contracts are now carried on the balance sheet at $75,000—which is their fair value as of the end of March—and a $25,000 unrealized gain has been recorded in March income. (If the options had declined in value, Heitz would have recorded an unrealized holding loss along with a downward adjustment in the carrying value of the options.) Heitz then liquidates the options contracts on April 15:

> The unrealized gain (or loss) would be included in Income from continuing operations on the Heitz income statement.

DR	Cash	$130,000	
	CR Marketable securities—lumber options		$50,000
	CR Market adjustment—lumber options		25,000
	CR Realized holding gain on lumber options (to income)		55,000

These accounting entries are used for all types of derivatives—forwards, futures, swaps, and options—unless the special hedge accounting rules described next should apply. Three key points about derivatives that do not qualify for special hedge accounting treatment should be remembered:

1. Derivative contracts represent balance sheet assets and liabilities.
2. The carrying value of the derivative is adjusted to fair value at each balance sheet date.
3. The amount of the adjustment—the change in fair value—flows to the income statement as a holding gain (or loss).

As a result of these GAAP rules, speculative investments in derivative contracts can increase the volatility of reported earnings. But the earnings volatility that results from this accounting treatment perfectly reflects the derivative's inherent economic risk.

Hedge Accounting

When a company successfully hedges its exposure to market risk, any economic loss on the hedged item (for example, copper inventory) will be offset by an economic gain on the derivative (for example, copper futures contracts). *To accurately reflect the underlying economics of the hedge, the company should match the loss on the hedged item with the derivative's offsetting gain in the income statement of the same period.* This matching is what the GAAP rules governing hedge accounting try to accomplish.[20] The special hedge accounting rules eliminate or reduce the earnings volatility that would otherwise result from reporting the change in the derivative's fair value in income each period.

> The matching process works like this. If an economic gain (or loss) on the *hedged item* flows to accounting income in the current period, so does the offsetting loss (or gain) on the derivative. But if the hedged item's economic gain (or loss) flows to accounting income some time later, then income statement recognition of the derivative's offsetting loss (or gain) is also postponed to that later period.

---

[20] FASB ASC Topic 815: Derivatives and Hedging. To learn more about hedge accounting, see S. Ryan, *Financial Instruments and Institutions* (Hoboken, NJ: Wiley & Sons, 2007) and M. Trombley, *Accounting for Derivatives and Hedging* (New York: McGraw-Hill, 2003).

The type of special hedge accounting to be applied varies depending on the nature of the exposure being hedged. In some cases, changes in the derivative's fair value are reported in income as they occur, but the earnings impact is then offset by a corresponding charge (or credit) from adjusting the carrying value of the asset or liability being hedged. In other cases, earnings volatility is avoided by recording changes in the fair value of the derivative directly in Other comprehensive income.

When can hedge accounting be used? The answer depends on four considerations:

- Hedged item
- Hedging instrument
- Risk being hedged
- Effectiveness of hedge

> You may want to review Chapter 2 for a discussion of **other comprehensive income** and the income statement.

Stringent GAAP criteria must be met to qualify for hedge accounting. To fulfill the criteria, management must do three things: designate the derivative as a hedging instrument; describe the hedging strategy; and document its effectiveness in eliminating a specific market risk for a specific hedged item. The details are voluminous and complex, so we cannot possibly cover all bases here. What we can do is provide an overview of the most common hedging situations and how hedge accounting works. The basics are outlined in Figure 11.10.

The **hedged item** can be either (1) an existing asset or liability on the company's books, (2) a firm commitment, or (3) an anticipated (forecasted) future transaction. Inventories of commodities such as copper and lumber, receivables and loans, and debt obligations are examples of *existing assets and liabilities* that qualify as hedged items. If Hess Company agrees in June to buy network storage equipment from another company at a specific price with delivery in the future (say, August), that's a *firm commitment*. If, on the other hand, Hess just knows in June that it must buy the equipment by August but has signed no purchase agreement, it's an *anticipated transaction*.

The **hedging instrument** is commonly a derivative instrument, although not all derivatives meet the strict GAAP rules and some qualifying hedges (for example, the call provision of a callable bond) do not involve derivatives as the term is commonly used. Qualifying hedging instruments include options to purchase or sell an exchange-traded security, futures and forward contracts, and interest rate and currency swaps. *Insurance contracts, options to purchase real estate, traditional equity and debt securities, and financial guarantee contracts do not qualify as hedging instruments.*

> Derivatives that fail to meet the GAAP rules for hedge accounting—because either the hedged item, the derivative itself, or the hedged risk doesn't qualify—are treated as though they were speculative investments.

The **risk being hedged** must meet certain GAAP criteria. The eligible market risks are limited to risks arising from overall changes in the fair value or cash flow of the hedged item or risks from changes in benchmark interest rates (for example, LIBOR), commodity prices (such as copper), foreign currency exchange rates (for example, Japanese yen to U.S. dollar), and the creditworthiness of the party (a company, institution, or government agency) that issued a financial security. Other financial and operating risks (such as risks from weather conditions, industrial accidents, or labor strikes) do not qualify for hedge accounting. (We discuss hedge effectiveness later.)

GAAP groups the risks being hedged into three categories:

1. **A fair value hedge** is a hedge of the exposure to changes in the *fair value* of an *existing* asset or liability, or a *firm commitment*. Common examples of a fair value hedge include:
   - An interest rate swap that synthetically converts fixed-rate debt into floating-rate debt (interest rate risk exposure of an existing liability).
   - A gold futures contract that "unlocks" a gold mining company's contractual agreement to sell refined gold to a jewelry manufacturer next year at a fixed price (commodity price risk exposure of a firm commitment).

2. **A cash flow hedge** is a hedge of the exposure to changes in *cash flows* of an *existing* asset or liability, or an *anticipated transaction.* Common examples of a cash flow hedge include:

- An interest rate swap that synthetically converts floating-rate debt into fixed-rate debt (interest rate risk exposure of an existing liability).
- A lumber futures contract that "locks in" the price a building contractor will pay in two months for lumber (commodity price risk exposure for an anticipated transaction).

3. **A foreign currency exposure hedge** is a hedge of the exposure to changes in currency exchange rates of an existing asset or liability, a firm commitment, a forecasted transaction, or a multinational company's net investment in a foreign operation. Here, GAAP applies the fair value and cash flow hedge accounting rules to foreign currency exchange exposure. The unique element of this exposure is a net investment in foreign operations. In Chapter 16, we describe the accounting and reporting issues unique to foreign subsidiaries.

> How can an interest rate swap qualify as both a fair value hedge and a cash flow hedge? The answer lies in understanding how interest rate changes affect the market values and cash flows of debt obligations. For fixed-rate debt, interest rate changes produce market value changes in the opposite direction but debt cash flows are "fixed" (meaning unchanged). So, an interest rate swap that converts fixed-rate debt into floating-rate debt eliminates fluctuations in market values and thus is a fair value hedge. For floating-rate debt, interest rate changes produce changes in debt cash flows—if rates increase, the borrower must make additional cash interest payments—but debt market value is unaffected. So, an interest rate swap that converts floating-rate debt into fixed-rate debt eliminates fluctuations in cash flows and thus is a cash flow hedge.

Figure 11.10 describes the accounting procedures for (Panel [a]) derivatives that qualify for hedge accounting and (Panel [b]) derivatives that do not qualify for hedge accounting. GAAP requires all derivative instruments—whether held for trading and speculation or as financial hedges—to be **marked-to-market,** meaning that they are carried at fair value on the balance sheet as assets or liabilities. The offsetting debit or credit that results from marked-to-market accounting then flows either to current income (for fair value hedges, certain foreign currency hedges, and derivatives that do not qualify for hedge accounting) or to Other comprehensive income (for cash flow hedges and most other foreign currency hedges).

Fair Value Hedge Accounting

Hedge accounting makes it possible for companies engaged in financial risk management to recognize the gain (or loss) on the hedged item in the same period as the offsetting loss (or gain) on the derivative. To see how this is done, let's return to Rombaurer Metals and its copper inventory hedge:

On October 1, 2014, Rombaurer has 10 million pounds of copper inventory on hand at an average cost of $0.65 a pound. The spot price for copper is $0.90 a pound. Instead of selling copper now, Rombaurer decides to hold the inventory until February 2015 when management believes the price will return to a normal level of $0.95 a pound. To hedge its position, Rombaurer sells futures contracts for 10 million pounds at $0.95 for February delivery. The margin deposit on the contracts is $280,000—the amount the commodities broker requires as a good-faith cash deposit on the contracts. The market's spot and futures prices over the next several months are:

	NYMEX Copper Prices	
	Spot Price	**February 2015 Futures Price**
October 1, 2014	$0.90	$0.95
December 31, 2014	0.85	0.91
February 26, 2015	0.94	0.94

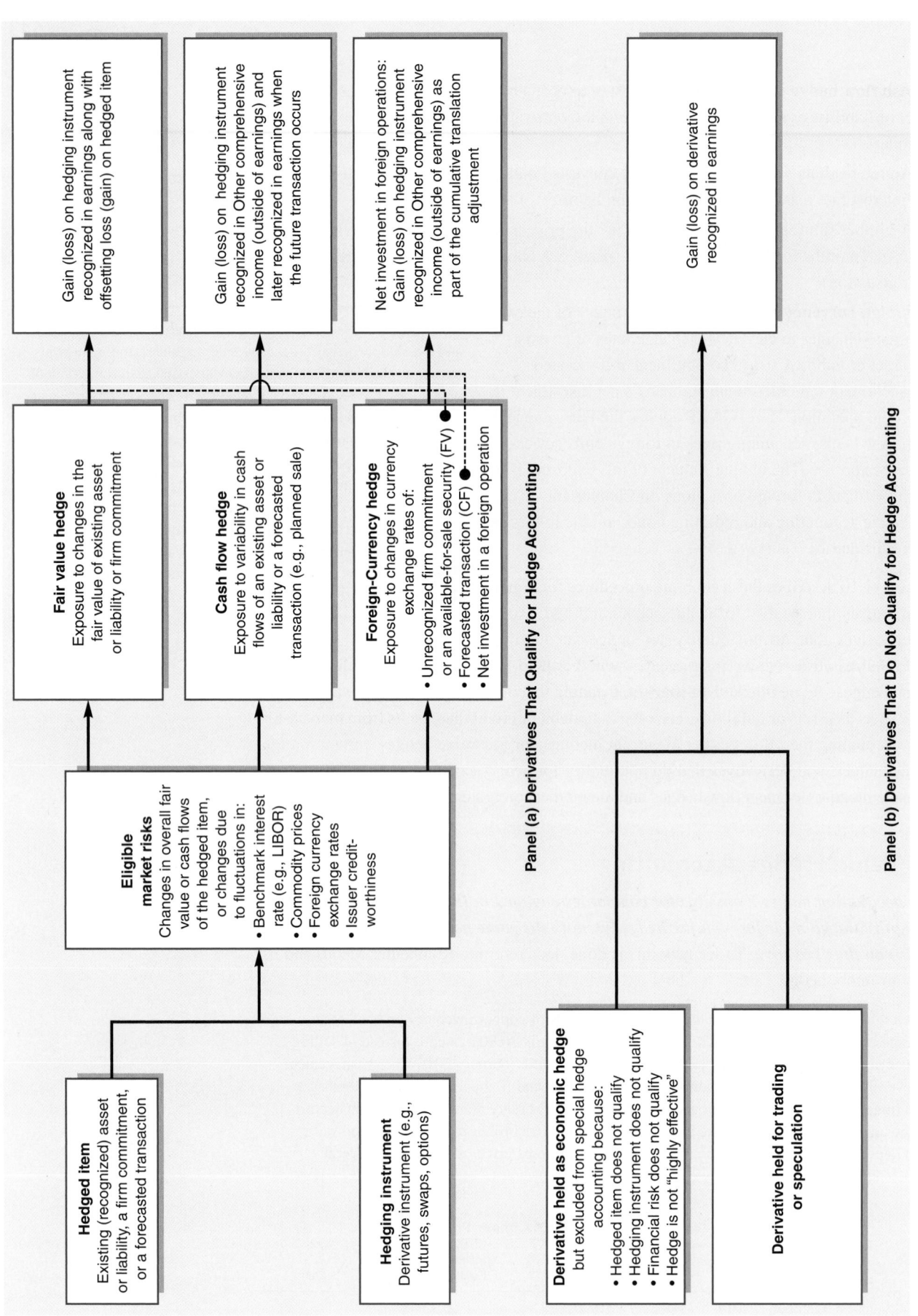

Figure 11.10 FINANCIAL REPORTING FOR DERIVATIVE INSTRUMENTS

Rombaurer has successfully hedged its exposure to commodity price risk—and the fair value of its existing copper inventory—by selling futures contracts. Rombaurer then designates the futures contracts (the hedging instrument) as a **fair value hedge** of its exposure to February 2015 market price fluctuations (the hedged risk) for existing copper inventory (the hedged item). As long as the futures contracts pass the GAAP test for hedge effectiveness—and they do, as you will later see—Rombaurer can use the special **fair value hedge accounting** rules. Here are the accounting entries.

On October 1, 2014, Rombaurer records the initial margin deposit on its fair value hedge:

DR Amount due from broker (a receivable)	$280,000	
CR Cash		$280,000

No entry is made that day for the futures contracts themselves because they have zero value at inception—the February contract price ($0.95) equals the current $0.95 market price of February copper (and we are ignoring any timing value).

The spot price and the February futures price of copper both decline over the next several months. Rombaurer makes two journal entries at year-end, December 31. The first entry records the fair value increase for the hedging instrument:

DR Amount due from broker	$400,000	
CR Gain on hedge activity (to income)		$400,000

The futures contracts are worth $400,000 on December 31, 2014. This amount is the difference between the copper price guaranteed by the contracts ($0.95) and the current futures price of February copper ($0.91) multiplied by the 10 million pounds of copper being hedged. Copper prices have fallen, but the hedge has provided $400,000 of commodity price protection. Notice too that the broker receivable now has a balance of $680,000 representing the initial margin deposit ($280,000) *plus* the fair value of the futures contracts ($400,000).

The second year-end entry adjusts the carrying value of the hedged item—copper inventory—for the change in fair value ($0.91 − $0.95, a $0.04 loss, × 10 million pounds):

DR Loss on hedge activity (to income)	$400,000	
CR Copper inventory		$400,000

The carrying value of the copper inventory is now $6.1 million; that's the inventory's $6.5 million historical cost minus the $400,000 decline in the February fair value since October 1, 2014. (Note that GAAP measures this fair value decline using the October 1 $0.95 *futures* contract price as the benchmark. The October 1 *spot* price of $0.90 does not enter into the GAAP calculation of the fair value decline.)

In the first December 31 entry, the derivative is marked-to-market and Rombaurer records a gain on the hedging instrument to income. But the gain from the futures contracts is fully offset by the loss on copper inventory in the second entry. (In practice, only one Gain or loss on hedge activity account is used to record the gain and the loss.) These offsetting gains and losses eliminate earnings volatility.

On February 26, 2015, Rombaurer sells the copper on the spot market for $0.94 a pound and cancels the futures contracts. It makes three journal entries at this time.

The first entry records the fair value change for the hedging instrument ($0.91 − $0.94, a $0.03 loss, × 10 million pounds), the cash returned by the broker, and eliminates the broker receivable:

DR Cash	$380,000	
DR Loss on hedge activity (to income)	300,000	
CR Amount due from broker		$680,000

February copper prices have increased $0.03 a pound since December, and the futures contracts are now worth only $100,000 ($0.95 − $0.94 × 10 million pounds), so Rombaurer records a $300,000 loss. This $300,000 loss is the fair value change in the futures contracts since December 31. Rombaurer also receives $380,000 from the broker. This amount is the sum of the returned margin deposit ($280,000) and the settlement value of the contracts ($100,000).

The second entry adjusts the carrying value of the hedged copper inventory for the fair value change ($0.94 − $0.91 × 10 million pounds):

DR	Copper inventory	$300,000	
CR	Gain on hedge activity (to income)		$300,000

In this case, the loss from the futures contracts (the first entry) is offset by a gain on copper inventory (the second entry).

The third and final entry records the credit sale of copper inventory at the spot market price:

DR	Accounts receivable	$9,400,000	
DR	Cost of goods sold	6,400,000	
CR	Sales revenue		$9,400,000
CR	Copper inventory		6,400,000

Rombaurer's gross profit from selling copper is $3 million (the $9.4 million selling price − the $6.4 million adjusted carrying value of the inventory sold). This is exactly the gross profit Rombaurer would have reported if it had sold the inventory—originally carried on the books at $6.5 million—at the anticipated February price of $0.95 a pound, or $9.5 million. By selling futures contracts, Rombaurer "locked in" the February price of $0.95 a pound and eliminated its exposure to commodity price risk.

That's the economics behind Rombaurer's hedging activities, and that's what the accounting statements report.

What if Rombaurer did not (or could not) use hedge accounting rules for the copper futures contracts? In that case, GAAP still requires the derivative to be marked-to-market. So, Rombaurer would record a $400,000 gain on December 31, 2014, followed by a $300,000 loss on February 26, 2015—the change in fair value of the futures contracts. But GAAP would not allow an offsetting loss (on December 31, 2014) or gain (on February 26, 2015) to be recorded on the copper inventory itself. Instead, the inventory would continue to be carried at its historical cost of $6,500,000 until sold. The net result is increased earnings volatility: Net income for 2014 would include a $400,000 gain, while net income for 2015 would include a $300,000 loss and a $100,000 gross margin reduction due to the higher carrying value of inventory ($0.65 per pound original cost rather than $0.64 per pound adjusted carrying value).

> The $6.4 million adjusted carrying value ($0.64 per pound) is determined as:
>
> | | | |
> |---|---|---|
> | 10/1/14 | cost at $0.65 per pound | $6.5 million |
> | 12/31/14 | adjustment for $0.04 decline | (0.4) million |
> | 2/26/15 | adjustment for $0.03 increase | 0.3 million |
> | 2/26/15 | adjusted carrying value | $6.4 million |

> You may recall Dentsply's floating-rate Swiss francs-denominated debt shown in Exhibit 11.10. Dentsply uses interest rate swaps to eliminate its exposure to cash flow volatility from interest rate changes by agreeing to pay fixed-rate interest to the swap counterparty. Dentsply uses cash flow hedge accounting for the interest rate swaps.

Cash Flow Hedge Accounting

Exhibit 11.12 illustrates the accounting for a **cash flow hedge.** Chalk Hill Inc. issues a $10 million, three-year floating-rate note with interest equal to the LIBOR rate, reset annually. To hedge its exposure to cash flow variability from changes in the LIBOR, Chalk Hill enters into an interest rate swap with a bank. The bank agrees to make the required floating-rate interest payments, and Chalk Hill agrees to pay the bank 7.5% fixed-rate interest annually for the entire three years. The interest rate swap allows Chalk Hill to "lock in" the 7.5% fixed-rate cash payment for interest even though the actual interest rate charged on the note will rise or fall with changes in the LIBOR rate.

EXHIBIT 11.12 Chalk Hill's Cash Flow Hedge

Using an Interest Rate Swap to Hedge Variable Rate Debt

On January 1, 2014, Chalk Hill borrows $10 million by signing a three-year note with interest equal to the LIBOR (currently at 7.5%), reset annually on December 31. To hedge its exposure to the variability in cash flows associated with the floating-rate note, Chalk Hill enters into a three-year interest rate swap with Beringer Bank. Under the swap contract, Chalk Hill pays interest to the bank at the fixed 7.5% rate and receives interest payments from the bank at a variable rate equal to the LIBOR, based on a notional amount of $10 million. Both the note and swap require that payments be made or received annually on December 31 of each year.

Chalk Hill designates the swap (hedging instrument) as a ***cash flow hedge*** of its exposure to variability in the cash flows of the floating-rate note (hedged item) with the specific risk being changes in cash flows due to changes in the LIBOR rate. This hedge is fully effective because the key terms of the note and swap are identical. The LIBOR rates, cash payments made and received, and the fair value of the swap contract (based on dealer quotes) are:

	LIBOR Rate	Gross Cash Flow To Beringer Bank	From Beringer Bank	Net Cash Flow	Swap Fair Value Asset (Liability) from Dealer Quotes
January 1, 2014	7.50%	$750,000	$750,000	—	—
December 31, 2014	8.50	750,000	850,000	$100,000	$323,000
December 31, 2015	7.00	750,000	700,000	(50,000)	(55,000)

Interest rate swap contracts are not traded in an organized exchange (such as the NYMEX where copper futures contracts are traded), so contract fair values can be difficult to determine. Chalk Hill's fair value estimates ("quotes") are from knowledgeable "dealers" (usually investment banks) who are actively involved in structuring swap transactions.*

Chalk Hill makes the following entries over the life of the swap contract and note (OCI denotes Other comprehensive income):

January 1, 2014

| **DR** Cash | $10,000,000 | |
| **CR** Note payable | | $10,000,000 |

To record the company's initial borrowing. There is no entry for the swap contract because it has no initial value—the "pay" and "receive" rates for both parties are the same, 7.5% times $10 million.

December 31, 2014

| **DR** Interest expense | $750,000 | |
| **CR** Interest payable | | $750,000 |

To accrue annual interest at a 7.5% variable rate—the LIBOR rate on January 1, 2014.

| **DR** Interest payable | $750,000 | |
| **CR** Cash | | $750,000 |

To record the annual interest payment on the note. There is no entry for the swap settlement this year because the "pay" and "receive" amounts are the same, $750,000.

| **DR** Swap contract | $323,000 | |
| **CR** OCI—Unrealized gain on swap contract | | $323,000 |

To record the change in fair value of the swap based on dealer quotes.

December 31, 2015

| **DR** Interest expense | $850,000 | |
| **CR** Interest payable | | $850,000 |

To accrue annual interest at an 8.5% variable rate—the LIBOR rate on December 31, 2015.

| **DR** Interest payable | $850,000 | |
| **CR** Cash | | $850,000 |

To record the annual interest payment on the note.

(continued)

* To learn more about how practitioners value swaps and other derivatives, see C. W. Smithson, *Managing Financial Risk* (Homewood, IL: Irwin, 1998).

EXHIBIT 11.12	Chalk Hill's Cash Flow Hedge (*continued*)

DR Cash $100,000

    CR Interest expense $100,000

To record the swap settlement net receipt from Beringer Bank.

DR OCI—Unrealized loss on swap contract $378,000

    CR Swap contract $378,000

To record the change in fair value of the swap based on dealer quotes. The Swap contract account now has a $55,000 credit balance.

December 31, 2016

DR Interest expense $700,000

    CR Interest payable $700,000

To accrue annual interest at a 7.0% variable rate—the LIBOR rate on December 31, 2016.

DR Interest payable $700,000

    CR Cash $700,000

To record the annual interest payment on the note.

DR Interest expense $50,000

    CR Cash $50,000

To record the swap settlement net payment to Beringer Bank.

DR Swap contract $55,000

    CR OCI—Unrealized gain on swap contract $55,000

To record the change in fair value of the swap. The swap agreement has now been concluded, and the contract has no further value to either party. (You should confirm that the swap contract account now has a zero balance.)

DR Note payable $10,000,000

    CR Cash $10,000,000

To record payment of the note principal.

As you work through the journal entries in Exhibit 11.12, notice that the hedging instrument (swap contract) shows up as a balance sheet asset or liability. (If the account has a debit balance, it's an asset; if the balance is a credit, it's a liability.) The swap's carrying value is its fair value at each balance sheet date. This means that changes in the swap's fair value are recorded when they occur—**but they do not flow directly to the income statement.** Instead, swap contract gains and losses flow to Other comprehensive income and shareholders' equity as in Figure 11.10. What's the reason for this accounting treatment? Changes in the LIBOR rate do not affect the underlying economic value of the floating-rate note—as interest rates on a floating-rate liability change, the liability's market price remains constant. So, we are unable to offset fair value changes in the hedging instrument with changes in the hedged item's fair value. The only way earnings volatility can be avoided is to keep swap gains and losses off the income statement by allowing them to flow to Other comprehensive income.

You need to observe one more feature of the Chalk Hill example. Interest expense is $750,000 each year, or the 7.5% fixed-rate of interest multiplied by the $10 million note principal amount. This may at first seem surprising because Chalk Hill makes a floating-rate interest payment each year, and the amount paid varies from $700,000 to $850,000 over the three years. But the interest rate swap insulates Chalk Hill from this cash flow volatility. For example, in 2015, Chalk Hill pays $850,000 in interest on the note but receives $100,000 from the swap counterparty. Chalk Hill's net cash payment for interest that year is $750,000, which is also the amount of interest expense reported.

Problem 11-9 illustrates the accounting for Chalk Hill's swap when it does not qualify for hedge accounting.

Hedge Accounting for a Forecasted Transaction

Now let's see how hedge accounting for a **forecasted transaction** works. In this example, Vintage Construction uses lumber options contracts as a *cash flow* hedge for its projected lumber needs during the year:

> Vintage Construction Corporation builds residential homes in the far northern United States from April through November. It builds no homes on speculation. Building begins only after the home buyer and Vintage sign a firm contract. Construction takes about four months. Because contract prices with home purchasers are fixed, Vintage is vulnerable to lumber price increases during construction. To protect its margins, Vintage buys 20 lumber futures contracts on April 1, 2014. The expiration dates on these contracts are staggered over the April–November building season to approximate the monthly level of construction activity.
>
> Lumber prices rise during the 2014 season. These unanticipated higher costs reduce gross profits from home construction by $600,000. However, Vintage realized a $580,000 gain on the futures contracts due to the lumber price increase. How did the company's financial statements reflect this gain?

Vintage designates the lumber contracts as a ***cash flow hedge*** of forecasted lumber purchases with commodity price volatility being the source of market risk. At inception, it records the futures contracts as an asset at the purchase price. At each monthly balance sheet date, the contracts are marked-to-market with the change in fair value flowing to Other comprehensive income and then shareholders' equity. As homes are completed each month, Vintage records the revenues and expenses from the construction business. At the same time, the cumulative gain and loss on the lumber contracts for completed homes is transferred out of Other comprehensive income to the income statement.

Because Vintage doesn't yet own the lumber, the futures contracts cannot qualify as a fair value hedge of an *existing* asset.

This accounting treatment offsets changes in the gross profit from construction due to lumber price fluctuations (the hedged item) with realized gains and losses from lumber futures contracts (the hedging instrument). Earnings volatility is avoided by allowing the futures contracts gains and losses to initially flow to shareholders' equity. These gains and losses eventually flow to earnings, but only when the forecasted transaction is completed. For Vintage Construction, that means when the homes are finished and the buyer takes possession—not earlier when lumber is purchased.

Because all of the futures contracts were realized in 2014, the $580,000 gain is included in income and largely offsets the $600,000 gross margin reduction reflected in income that same period. This income statement result corresponds to the almost perfect hedging strategy followed by Vintage Construction. A "perfect" hedge would have exactly offset the $600,000 margin shortfall.

Hedge Effectiveness

Few hedges are perfect. When they are not—as here—notice that reported income corresponds to the underlying economics. That is, while Vintage insulated itself from most of the lumber price increase, it did experience a $20,000 earnings reduction. This is precisely the reported income statement effect (that is, a $580,000 futures contracts gain and a $600,000 gross margin reduction).

Hedge effectiveness—the derivative's ability to generate offsetting changes in the fair value or cash flows of the hedged item—is a key qualifying criterion for hedge accounting. If

For interest rate swaps such as the one described in Exhibit 11.12, the critical terms include the notional (that is, principal) amount, contract term and loan maturity date, "pay" and "receive" rates on the benchmark interest rate, and the interest rate reset dates.

critical terms of the hedging instrument and hedged item are the same, changes in the derivative's fair value or cash flow (for example, a $1 gain) completely offset changes in the fair value or cash flow of the hedged item (a $1 loss). In this case, the hedge is "fully effective." Except for Vintage Construction, all of our examples have involved fully effective hedges.

But what if the hedge is not fully effective? Does that disqualify the derivative from special hedge accounting rules? It does not necessarily because GAAP requires only that the hedge be "highly effective"—as defined by GAAP—in offsetting changes in those fair values or cash flows that are due to the hedged risk. This requirement must be met both at the inception of the hedge and on an ongoing basis. GAAP provides general guidelines but does not say exactly how effectiveness should be determined.

How effective is "highly effective"? The hedging instrument should offset somewhere between 80% and 125% of the hedged item's fair value or cash flow changes attributable to the hedged risk. For Vintage Construction, this means that the company must purchase enough staggered lumber futures contracts to hedge at least 80% of its exposure to lumber price fluctuations. Purchase less than this amount and the futures contracts are an "ineffective" hedge according to GAAP. On the other hand, if Vintage buys too many contracts, the hedge is also considered ineffective. That's because the futures contracts are excessive and more like a speculative investment than a true hedge of underlying market risk.

The guidelines in ASC Topic 815: Derivatives and Hedging do not provide a bright line that defines "highly effective," so interpretation of this phrase is a matter of professional judgment. The range of 80% to 125% is becoming an accepted threshold for high effectiveness, but the FASB has not sanctioned it. You should know about one more feature of hedge effectiveness. Vintage Construction can instead purchase 10 lumber futures contracts and still have a "highly effective" hedge if (1) it designates the contracts as a "partial hedge" of its risk exposure (for example, 50% of its lumber purchases) and (2) the contracts are "highly effective" in hedging that partial exposure.

The GAAP distinction between *highly effective* and *ineffective* hedges determines when gains and losses on the hedging instrument flow to current income.[21] A highly effective hedge qualifies for special hedge accounting treatment; an ineffective hedge does not. Even if the highly effective test is met, some ineffectiveness may occur. And when it does, the ineffective portion of the hedge must flow directly to income. So, if Vintage Construction buys futures contracts that hedge just 50% of its full exposure, all of the gains and losses from this *ineffective* hedge flow directly to current income. That's because the contracts are ineffective and do not qualify for hedge accounting. And if the company buys futures contracts to hedge 110% of its exposure, the gains and losses on the *ineffective* portion of the hedge (the portion over 100% coverage) also flow directly to current income. Gains and losses on the remaining effective portion (equal to 100% coverage) of the hedge flow to Other comprehensive income because the contracts qualify as a "highly effective" hedge and hedge accounting rules apply.

In a letter to the FASB, Al Wargo of Eastman Chemical said that hedge accounting could cause his company's quarterly earnings per share (EPS) to fluctuate by roughly 100% in either direction—from a $0.12 loss to a $2.24 profit based on Eastman's $1.12 EPS for the second quarter of 2000. The only way Eastman can eliminate this EPS volatility is to change how it hedges financial risk. But this means replacing a sound economic hedging transaction with a less effective hedge. EPS would then be less volatile, but the company may be more exposed to financial risks.

Source: P. A. McKay and J. Niedzielski, "New Accounting Standard Gets Mixed Reviews," *The Wall Street Journal,* October 23, 2000.

Critics of hedge accounting claim that additional income statement and balance sheet volatility is created when the gains and losses on the hedging instrument exceed the losses and gains on the hedged item. ***This added volatility may force managers to choose between achieving sound economic results—meaning hedges that effectively address real financial risks—or minimizing accounting volatility using risk management approaches that are less efficient or simply not prudent.***

---

[21] In 2010 the FASB proposed changes to the way in which hedge effectiveness is assessed, with an emphasis on qualitative rather than quantitative considerations and a relaxation of the threshold from "highly effective" to "reasonably effective." As before, no bright line definition of "reasonably effective" is contained in the proposed ASU. See Proposed Accounting Standards Update, "Accounting for Financial Instruments and Revisions to the Accounting for Derivative Instruments and Hedging Activities," Financial Instruments (Topic 825) and Hedging (Topic 815) (Norwalk, CT: FASB, 2010). As this book goes to press, the FASB has yet to resume deliberations on this proposal.

GLOBAL VANTAGE POINT

As you no doubt now realize, the U.S. GAAP rules for derivatives and hedge accounting are quite complex. The same can be said for IFRS guidance (*IAS 39*). Despite some important differences in the details, there are striking similarities between IFRS and U.S. GAAP for derivatives and hedge accounting.

When it comes to *freestanding* derivative contracts—those that do not qualify for special hedge accounting treatment—IFRS and U.S. GAAP are in agreement. A derivative contract represents a balance sheet asset or liability; the carrying value of the derivative is adjusted to fair value at each balance sheet date; and the amount of the adjustment—the *change* in fair value—flows to the income statement as an unrealized gain (or loss).

IFRS and U.S. GAAP guidelines are also in agreement on most key elements of the approaches used for derivative contracts that qualify for special hedge accounting treatment. Like U.S. GAAP, IFRS recognizes two broad types of hedging relationships: a fair value hedge and a cash flow hedge. Also like U.S. GAAP, IFRS require that derivatives—the hedging instrument or hedged item—be marked-to-market at each balance sheet date with the fair value change flowing either to current earnings (for fair value hedges) or to Other comprehensive income (for cash flow hedges). Arrangements that hedge foreign currency exposure risk also fall into one of these two hedge accounting buckets—fair value hedge or cash flow hedge.

In late 2013 the IASB published an amendment to IFRS 9 "Financial Instruments" intended to improve and simplify its hedge accounting requirements.[22] The amendment contains two key provisions. One major change is the elimination of the requirement that a hedging transaction must be "highly effective"—a bright line threshold for 80 to 125 percent. Under the IASB's new approach, hedge accounting will be permitted where there is an "economic relationship" between the hedging instrument and the hedged item such that the values of the two items *generally* move in opposite directions. This change will likely expand the range of transactions and instruments that qualify for special hedge accounting treatment under IFRS. The amendment also will allow companies to designate a specified portion of an nonfinancial item as the hedged risk as long as that risk is separately identifiable and measurable.

As this book goes to press, the IASB has yet to establish a mandatory adoption date for these new hedge accounting rules but voluntary adoption is encouraged.

> There are subtle differences between IFRS and U.S. GAAP guidance as to the particular characteristics a derivative contract must possess, but these (and other) differences are unimportant for our broad-brush discussion.

RECAP

Derivatives, when used properly, allow companies to stabilize their operating cash flows by eliminating specific sources of volatility such as fluctuations in interest rates, exchange rates, and commodity prices. The GAAP rules for derivatives are detailed and complex, but the essential points are simple. Derivative contracts represent balance sheet assets and liabilities that must be marked-to-market at each balance sheet date. The resulting mark-to-market adjustment—the change in fair value—then flows either to current earnings (for fair value hedges, certain foreign currency hedges, and derivatives held for trading and speculation) or to Other comprehensive income (for cash flow hedges and most other foreign currency hedges). Other aspects of hedge accounting then match gains (or losses) on the derivative with offsetting losses (or gains) on the hedged item. This allows the financial statements to reflect accurately the underlying economics of the hedge.

---

[22] See International Financial Reporting Standards, IFRS 9 *Financial Instruments*—Hedge Accounting and amendments to IFRS 9, IFRS 7, and IAS 39 (IASB: November 2013).

CONTINGENT LIABILITIES

Contingent liabilities differ in one important way from the liabilities described elsewhere in this chapter—contingent liabilities are shrouded in uncertainty as to whether or not an obligation actually exists. And the uncertainty will be resolved only at some future date when an event does or does not occur. For example, suppose that Whiffle Toy is being sued for $10 million in alleged damages related to its Whamo lawn dart game. If the court rules against Whiffle, an obligation exists because the company then owes plaintiffs the $10 million in damages. But if the court rules for Whiffle, no obligation exists. Loss contingencies of this type arise from factors such as litigation, industrial accidents, debt guarantees, and product warranties. For financial reporting purposes, two questions about contingent liabilities must be resolved: (1) When do loss contingencies need to be measured and recognized in the financial statements? (2) Under what circumstances do these contingencies need to be disclosed in notes, even when no liability is recorded on the balance sheet itself?

Measuring and Recognizing Loss Contingencies

The rules for measuring and recognizing loss contingencies in the financial statements are similar to the rules governing revenue recognition. GAAP states that a loss contingency shall be accrued by a charge to income if *both* of the following conditions exist:

1. Information available before the financial statements are issued indicates that it is *probable* that an asset has been impaired or a liability has been incurred at the date of the financial statements.
2. The amount of loss can be *reasonably estimated.*[23]

Here's an example of an accrued loss contingency disclosure taken from the financial statements of Stanley Inc., the hardware and tool manufacturer:

> The Company's policy is to accrue environmental investigatory and remediation costs for identified sites when it is probable that a liability has been incurred and the amount of loss can be reasonably estimated.... As of January 2, 2010, the Company had reserves of $30 million for remediation activities associated with Company-owned properties, as well as for Superfund sites, for losses that are probable and estimable.
>
> *Source:* Stanley Inc., 2009 annual report.

Stanley has recorded a $30 million loss contingency for environmental cleanup at some of its current and former manufacturing sites. A corresponding $30 million contingent liability is shown on the company's balance sheet. Stanley also explains why it has already accrued the loss: The company believes that it is probable that an obligation to clean up these sites exists, and the amounts involved can be reasonably estimated. Under these circumstances, GAAP requires that a contingent loss and corresponding liability be recorded.

Loss contingency disclosures are also sometimes made even when no loss has been recognized in the income statement itself. For example, if the loss probability is only "reasonably possible" or "remote" (refer to Figure 11.11), then no loss accrual needs to be made in the financial statements. ***Nevertheless, note disclosure of loss contingencies is necessary when the loss is both reasonably possible and can be estimated.*** Furthermore, even contingencies arising from remote possibilities must be disclosed in certain circumstances, such as when one company guarantees another company's debt—that is, it agrees to repay a loan if the borrower cannot.

Here's an example of a loss contingency disclosure when no loss has been recognized on the income statement. An individual named Avraham Wellman has sued Hansen Natural

When companies accrue a loss contingency, they also usually disclose other information regarding the loss separately in notes to the financial statements. GAAP requires this disclosure when a failure to provide additional supplemental data could lead to misleading inferences. To learn more about contingent environmental liabilities and why the true cost of cleanup may be understated, see M. Leone and T. Reason, "Dirty Secrets," *CFO Magazine,* September 2009, pp. 50–57.

---

[23] FASB ASC Paragraph 450-20-25-2: Contingencies—Loss Contingencies—Recognition—General Rule.

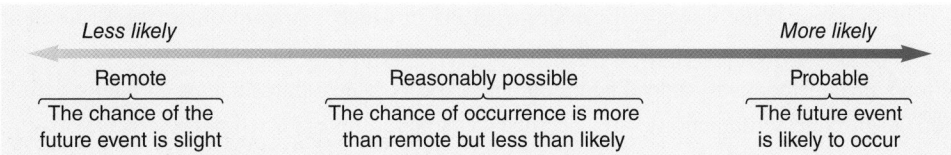

Figure 11.11

FASB ASC TOPIC 450 LOSS
PROBABILITY CONTINUUM

Corporation, the beverage company known for its Monster Energy drink, for reasons described in the company's financial statement note:

> In May 2009, Avraham Wellman, purporting to act on behalf of himself and a class of consumers in Canada, filed a putative class action in the Ontario Superior Court of Justice, in the City of Toronto, Ontario, Canada, against the Company and its former Canadian distributor, Pepsi-Cola Canada Ltd., as defendants. The plaintiff alleges that the defendants misleadingly packaged and labeled Monster Energy® products in Canada by not including sufficiently specific statements with respect to contra-indications and/ or adverse reactions associated with the consumption of the energy drink products. The plaintiff's claims against the defendants are for negligence, unjust enrichment, and making misleading/false representations in violation of the Competition Act (Canada), the Food and Drugs Act (Canada) and the Consumer Protection Act, 2002 (Ontario). The plaintiff claims general damages on behalf of the putative class in the amount of CDN$20 million, together with punitive damages of CDN$5 million, plus legal costs and interest . . . The Company believes that the plaintiff's complaint is without merit and plans a vigorous defense.

Source: Hansen Natural Corporation 2009 annual report.

Hansen Natural mentions the specific dollar amount of damages sought by the plaintiff (Wellman) but does not reveal its internal assessment of the probability that the court will find in favor of the plaintiff. The language Hansen Natural uses—"complaint is without merit" and "vigorous defense"—suggests management believes the court will decide the matter in Hansen's favor. Accordingly, the company has not yet accrued a contingent loss for the ongoing litigation.

FASB ASC Topic 450 *Contingencies* establishes a range representing the likelihood of losses occurring, which is depicted in Figure 11.11, where "probable" indicates the highest likelihood. GAAP requires contingent loss recognition if the future event is *probable* and the amount of the loss can be *reasonably estimated.*[24] Notice that the two loss contingency recognition conditions correspond to the two income recognition conditions—"critical event" and "measurability"—discussed in Chapter 2. Specifically, the critical event for loss recognition is that it is probable that a loss has occurred or will occur; similarly, the measurability criterion corresponds closely to how well the loss can be estimated. In this sense, the criteria that trigger income and loss recognition are roughly parallel.

For certain categories of events, applying the loss contingency rules has become routine. One example of a routine loss contingency is the expense for **estimated uncollectible receivables** described in Chapter 8. Uncollectibles represent a normal cost of business when companies sell goods or services on credit, but the amount of the uncollectible loss is unknown at the time of sale. Because some loss is probable and the amount can be estimated, an expense (estimated uncollectible loss) is recorded in the same period that the sale occurs.

In other situations, the issue of whether to recognize a loss contingency is highly subjective and complicated by the fact that recognizing and disclosing the loss could itself cause further harm. Consider a company that is being sued for actions that allegedly harmed others.

> Wren Corporation manufactures a wide range of chemical food additives sold to numerous food processors throughout the country. Due to a serious production error, Wren produced and sold a highly toxic batch of a flavor enhancer in October 2014. Thousands of consumers were made seriously ill; some died. A class action lawsuit seeking $10 billion in damages has been filed.

---

[24] FASB ASC Topic 450 defines "probable" as "likely to occur"; "remote" as a "slight" chance of occurring; and "reasonably possible" as being "more than slight but less than likely."

The fictitious Wren scenario illustrates a setting in which a straightforward application of the loss contingency recognition rules could prove harmful to the company. Let's say that Wren's management was indeed negligent and expects to negotiate an approximately $2 billion out-of-court settlement. If Wren accrued a charge for this expected payout, its negotiating position could be seriously weakened by a disclosure to the plaintiffs that it is prepared to pay at least $2 billion. Because the plaintiffs might be willing to settle for less than $2 billion, candid disclosure of the minimum estimated loss by Wren could raise the ultimate loss payout. Companies like Wren have strong incentives to either:

1. Accrue a loss that is significantly *smaller* than the real estimated loss.
2. Disclose that while a loss may have occurred, its amount is not yet measurable.

Consequently, the GAAP guidelines for loss contingencies arising from litigation are difficult to enforce. ***Statement readers must be aware of the potential understatement of litigation losses and liabilities.***

Recording Gain Contingencies

When they are recorded, the gain flows to income, and a corresponding contingent receivable is shown on the balance sheet.

While the defendant in a lawsuit (for example, Hansen Natural) faces a contingent loss, the other side—the plaintiff—has a contingent gain reflecting the possibility that the court will decide that monetary damages must be paid to the plaintiff. As you now know, loss contingencies are accrued when the event confirming the obligation is probable and the amount can be reasonably estimated. **Gain contingencies,** on the other hand, are not recorded until the event actually occurs and the payment obligation is confirmed. This differing treatment of loss contingencies and gain contingencies illustrates **accounting conservatism**—the notion that it's desirable to anticipate losses, but recognizing gains should wait until their confirmation and realization.

Loan Guarantees

Companies sometimes provide loan guarantees that require them to make payments to a lender on behalf of a borrower based on some future event. Krispy Kreme Doughnuts, for example, sells its famous Original Glazed doughnuts and coffee in 748 company-owned and franchised stores located in 22 countries around the world. When a franchise store in which Krispy Kreme has a partial ownership interest borrows money from a local bank, Krispy Kreme may agree to repay the loan if and when the franchisee fails to do so. By providing this guaranty, Krispy Kreme helps the franchisee borrow money at a lower rate of interest than would otherwise be the case.

Here is what Krispy Kreme says about its loan guarantees:

> The Company has guaranteed a portion of certain loan obligations of certain franchisees in which the Company owns an interest. The Company assesses the likelihood of making any payments under the guarantees and records estimated liabilities for anticipated payments when the Company believes that an obligation to perform under the guarantees is probable and the amount can be reasonably estimated. No liabilities for the guarantees were recorded at the time they were issued because the Company believed the value of the guarantees was immaterial. As of February 3, 2013, the Company has recorded liabilities of approximately $1.6 million related to such loan guarantees. The aggregate outstanding principal balance that was guaranteed by the Company was approximately $2.1 million at that date. (*Source:* Krispy Kreme Doughnuts, Inc. Form 10-K filing for the fiscal year ended February 3, 2013)

FASB ASC Topic 460 *Guarantees* views this sort of arrangement as having two components that may affect the financial statements of Krispy Kreme (the guarantor): (1) a *certain* "stand ready obligation" to meet the terms of the guarantee, and (2) the *uncertain* contingent obligation to make future payments depending on future events (e.g., the failure of the franchisee to repay the bank loan in full). The "stand ready obligation" is recorded initially at fair value, while the contingent obligation is handled as an ordinary contingent loss as provided by FASB ASC Topic 450.

To illustrate the guarantor's accounting issues, suppose Mason Mechanical Toys agrees to guarantee a $2,000,000 loan made by Continental Bank to Mia Fabrications, an unrelated party that supplies essential subcomponents used by Mason. Mia will use the borrowed funds to expand its production line so that it can more efficiently provide the higher volume of sub-components that Mason requires each month. Mia also agrees to pay a $50,000 fee to Mason for providing the loan guarantee.

Should Mason recognize a liability for the guarantee at inception of the Mia Fabrications loan? The answer according to FASB ASC Topic 460 is "Yes." The standard allows Mason to use the fee amount as a practical expedient for the fair value of the guarantee. The journal entry to record Mason's "stand ready obligation" at loan inception is:

DR Accounts receivable (or Cash)	$50,000	
CR Guarantee liability		$50,000

The Guarantee liability account represents deferred revenue associated with the "stand ready" fee. This revenue is earned (and the Guarantee liability account decreased) over the life of the loan as Mason is released from the risk of repaying Mia's loan.

No entry is made by Mason at loan inception for its contingent obligation to pay Continental Bank unless it is deemed probable that payments under the guarantee will be required and the amount of those payments can be reasonably estimated. These are recognition criteria used in ASC 450.

Krispy Kreme says it did not record a "stand ready obligation" at the time the bank loans were issued to franchisees because the fair value of the guarantees was deemed immaterial by management. However, a $1.6 million contingent obligation for the loan guarantees was recorded sometime later as a contingent loss:

DR Guarantee loss	$1,600,000	
CR Guarantee liability		$1,600,000

When this entry was made, Krispy Kreme management had determined that partial repayment of the franchisee bank loans was now probable. Notice that the amount of the contingent loss is less than the total $2.1 million owed by franchisees.

GLOBAL VANTAGE POINT

IFRS guidance on accounting for contingencies is found in *IAS 37*.[25] It is quite similar to the U.S. GAAP approach just outlined except that IFRS guidance is built around a balance sheet perspective where contingent liability and asset recognition takes the center stage. U.S. GAAP relies on an income statement perspective (contingent loss and gain recognition). Like U.S. GAAP, IFRS requires recognition of a contingent liability, called a *provision*—and the associated contingent loss—when it is both probable and can be reasonably estimated. However, *probable* is interpreted under IFRS to mean "more likely than not" and thus represents a lower recognition threshold than is the case for U.S. GAAP (see Figure 11.11). Contingent assets and their associated gains are not recognized.

---

[25] *IAS 37,* "Provisions, Contingent Liabilities and Contingent Assets" (London UK: IFRS, July 1999 as revised).

U.S. GAAP and IFRS also differ when it comes to determining the dollar amount of contingent loss to be recognized. Suppose the probable loss is estimated by management to range between $450,000 and $650,000. Management further believes that no amount within this range is a better estimate than any other amount. What dollar amount should be recorded? U.S. GAAP solves this problem by using the low end of the estimated range ($450,000) whereas IFRS uses the midpoint of the range ($550,000).

There is one other point that can be a source of confusion. The IFRS phrase *contingent liability* refers to *possible* (but unrecognized) contingent obligations perhaps disclosed in the financial statement notes. U.S. GAAP uses this same term to refer to both recognized and unrecognized contingent loss obligations.

SUMMARY

- An astounding variety of financial instruments and nontraditional financing arrangements is now used to fund corporate activities and to manage risk. Statement readers face a daunting task when trying to grasp the economic implications of some financial innovations.

- Off-balance-sheet obligations and loss contingencies are difficult to evaluate because the information needed for that evaluation is often not disclosed.

- Derivatives—whether used for hedging or speculation—pose special problems because of both their complexity and the involved details of hedge accounting.

- For many companies, the most important long-term obligation is still traditional debt financing. IFRS and U.S. GAAP guidance in this area is quite clear. Noncurrent monetary liabilities are initially recorded at the discounted present value of the contractual cash flows—that is, the amount borrowed. The effective interest method is then used to compute interest expense and net carrying value in each period. Interest rate changes occurring after the debt has been issued are ignored. Of course, firms may instead opt for fair value accounting for their long-term debt.

- Long-term debt accounting makes it possible to "manage" reported income statement and balance sheet numbers when debt is retired before maturity. The opportunity to "manage" those numbers comes from the difference between debt book value and market value when interest rates have changed.

- The incentives for "managing" income statement and balance sheet numbers may be related to debt covenants, compensation, regulation, or just the desire to paint a favorable picture of the company's performance and health.

- Extinguishment gains and losses from early debt retirement and swaps require careful scrutiny. Statement readers need to know whether real economic benefits for the company and its shareholders are produced—or if the gains or losses are just window dressing.

SELF-STUDY PROBLEM

MALLARD CORPORATION

Mallard Corporation constructs and operates private waterfowl hunting facilities throughout the western United States. On July 1, 2014, the company issued $5 million of par value, 10-year bonds to finance construction of a guest lodge at its newest site in Klamath, Oregon. The bonds pay interest semiannually (on December 31 and June 30) at an annual rate of 8% and are callable by Mallard at 102% of par value. The bonds were issued at a price that yields 10% annually to maturity.

1. **Compute the issue price of the bonds.** The bond cash flows include a semiannual interest payment of $200,000 (or $5 million at 4%) plus the principal payment of $5 million at maturity. With an effective (market) interest rate of 5% for each six-month interval, the present value factors are:

> 20-period ordinary annuity at 5% = 12.46221
>
> 20-period single payment = 0.37689

Multiplying each factor by the corresponding cash flow gives the issue price as:

$$\begin{array}{r} \$200{,}000 \times 12.46221 = \$2{,}492{,}442 \\ + 5{,}000{,}000 \times \ \ 0.37689 = \underline{\ \ 1{,}884{,}450} \\ \$4{,}376{,}892 \end{array}$$

The bonds were thus issued at a discount of $623,108 (or $5,000,000 − $4,376,892).

2. **Compute the amount of interest expense on the bonds for 2014. Mallard Corporation uses the effective interest method for amortizing bond discounts and premiums.** Because the bonds were issued on July 1, 2014, only six months of interest need be recorded for the year. Interest expense is computed at the effective interest rate of 5%. This rate is multiplied by the amount borrowed (beginning book value) to find interest expense:

> $4,376,892 × 5% = $218,845 (rounded)

Computed interest expense is more than the required $200,000 cash payment. The $18,845 difference represents amortization of the bond discount—that is, an increase to the bond's book value. Mallard Corporation's year-end financial statements would show the bond at $4,395,737 ($4,376,892 + $18,845).

3. **Mallard uses the indirect method of computing cash flows from operations on its cash flow statement. Indicate how much will be added to (or subtracted from) the 2014 accrual-basis net income figure that is related to the bonds to obtain cash flows from operations.** The accrual income figure contains interest expense of $218,845, but the cash interest payment is only $200,000. The additional $18,845 interest expense does not represent an operating cash outflow for the year, and so it is added back to net income to arrive at cash flows from operations. Notice that this amount equals the discount amortization for the year.

4. **Assume that the market yield on the bonds had fallen to 9% by July 1, 2016, and that Mallard decided to retire the debt on that date either by purchasing the bonds on the open market or by exercising its 102% call option. Which method of debt retirement is the least expensive for Mallard?** Under the terms of the call option, Mallard can retire the debt by paying bond holders 102% of par value, or:

> $5,000,000 × 1.02 = $5,100,000

However, the bonds' current market value at an annual yield of 9% is:

$$\begin{array}{r} \$200{,}000 \times 11.23402 = \$2{,}246{,}804 \\ + 5{,}000{,}000 \times \ \ 0.49447 = \underline{\ \ 2{,}472{,}350} \\ \$4{,}719{,}154 \end{array}$$

The open-market purchase is the least expensive way for Mallard to retire its debt. (Notice that the present value factors used to compute the current market price are based on a 4.5% semiannual yield and 16 six-month periods to July 1, 2024.)

5. **Prepare the journal entry that Mallard Corporation recorded on July 1, 2016, when it retired the bonds through an open market purchase.** Assume that all interest expense and cash interest payments have been recorded. Then the bonds' book value on July 1, 2016, is $4,458,115, as shown in the amortization table.

Date	Period (six-month interval)	Liability at Start of Period	Effective Interest: 5% per Period	Stated Rate: 4% of Par	Increase in Recorded Book Value	Liability at End of Period
7/1/14	0					$4,376,892
1/1/15	1	$4,376,892	$218,845	$200,000	$18,845	4,395,737
7/1/15	2	4,395,737	219,787	200,000	19,787	4,415,524
1/1/16	3	4,415,523	220,776	200,000	20,776	4,436,300
7/1/16	4	4,436,300	221,815	200,000	21,815	4,458,115

Based on our previous calculation, we find that Mallard would pay $4,719,154 to retire the bonds on that date, so the entry is:

DR	Bonds payable	$5,000,000	
DR	Loss on debt retirement	261,039	
CR	Discount on bonds		$ 541,885
CR	Cash		4,719,154

where $541,885 represents the remaining (unamortized) balance of the original issue discount ($5,000,000 face value − $4,458,115 book value).

SELF-STUDY PROBLEM

SNAP-ON, INC.

Exhibit 11.13 is taken from the 2012 Shareholder Report of Snap-On, Inc., a manufacturer and marketer of high-quality professional automotive and industrial tools. The exhibit typifies the required disclosures for long-term debt, although Snap-On also devotes a portion of this footnote to a discussion of its short-term debt. The exhibit also identifies the various debt categories and describes the major debt instruments' key characteristics—such as covenants tied to financial statement ratios. An enumeration of scheduled principal repayments over the ensuing five years is also provided. The intent of the disclosure is to provide data on future cash outflows and credit risk; these data help analysts and others generate cash flow forecasts.

1. **The financial statement note contains a table indicating that $970.4 million in short-term and long-term debt was outstanding at the end of 2012. What are the individual components that make up this total debt amount?** The company's short-term and long-term debt at 2012 year-end consists of several fixed-rate unsecured notes ($950 million) and unspecified "other" debt ($25.6 million). The company classifies $5.2 million of notes payable as short-term debt.

2. **Since 2009 Snap-On has issued only one several new fixed-rate unsecured note: the $250 million of unsecured notes due in 2018. What can you learn about the company's credit risk from the interest rate on these recently issued notes?** The company's older unsecured notes carry interest rates that range from 5.50% to 6.70%. The rate of interest charged on the new notes would be lower (higher) than this if the company was now

EXHIBIT 11.13   Snap-On, Inc.

Note 9: Short-term and Long-term Debt

Short-term and long-term debt as of 2012 and 2011 year-end consisted of the following:

(Amounts in millions)	2012	2011
5.85% unsecured notes due March 2014	$100.0	$100.0
5.50% unsecured notes due 2017	150.0	150.0
4.25% unsecured notes due 2018	250.0	250.0
6.70% unsecured notes due 2019	200.0	200.0
6.125% unsecured notes due 2021	250.0	250.0
Other debt*	25.6	34.1
	975.6	984.1
Less: Short-term notes payable	(5.2)	(16.2)
Total long-term debt	$970.4	$967.9

*Includes fair value adjustments related to interest rate swaps.

The annual maturities of Snap-On's long-term debt and notes payable over the next five years are $5.2 million in 2013, $100.0 million in 2014, no maturities in 2015 or 2016, and $150.0 million in 2017.

Average notes payable outstanding were $14.1 million in 2012 and $15.8 million in 2011. The weighted-average interest rate on notes payable was 6.34% in 2012 and 6.14% in 2011. As of 2012 and 2011 year-end, the weighted-average interest rate on outstanding notes payable was 6.36% and 6.57%, respectively. No commercial paper was outstanding as of 2012 or 2011 year-end.

Snap-On has a five-year, $500 million multi-currency revolving credit facility that terminates on December 8, 2016; as of 2012 year-end, no amounts were outstanding under this facility. Borrowings under the $500 million revolving credit facility bear interest at varying rates based on Snap-On's then-current, long-term debt ratings. The $500 million revolving credit facility's financial covenant requires that Snap-On maintain, as of each fiscal quarter end, either (i) a ratio of total debt to the sum of total debt plus equity (including noncontrolling interests) of not greater than 0.60 to 1.00; or (ii) a ratio of total debt to the sum of net income plus interest expense, income taxes, depreciation, amortization, and other non-cash or extraordinary charges for the preceding four fiscal quarters then ended of not greater than 3.50 to 1.00. As of 2012 year-end the company's actual ratios of 0.35 and 1.55, respectively, were both within the permitted ranges set forth in this financial covenant.

Snap-On also has a 364-day loan and servicing agreement that allows Snap-On to borrow up to $200 million (subject to borrowing base requirements) through the pledging of finance receivables under an asset-backed commercial paper conduit facility; the loan and servicing agreement expires on September 27, 2013 (unless earlier terminated or subsequently extended pursuant to the terms of the agreement). As of 2012 year-end, no amounts were outstanding under the loan and servicing agreement.

In addition to the financial covenant required by the $500 million multi-currency revolving credit facility discussed above, Snap-On's debt agreements and credit facilities, including the $200 million loan and servicing agreement, also contain certain usual and customary borrowing, affirmative, negative, and maintenance covenants. As of 2012 year-end, Snap-On was in compliance with all covenants of its debt agreements and credit facilities.

viewed as a lesser (greater) credit risk than when the older notes were first issued. The recently issued unsecured notes have a 4.25% interest rate, a decrease from the older notes. This decrease may reflect an improvement in the company's credit risk. Alternatively, 2009 may have been a period when low interest rates prevailed throughout the U.S. economy because of general macroeconomic forces.

3. **How much cash did the company receive when it issued the 6.70% unsecured notes due in 2019?** Notice from the table that the carrying value of the notes is $200 million in both 2012 and 2011, and that there is no mention of either a note discount or an effective interest rate that is different from the contractual fixed-rate of 6.70%. Apparently, Snap-On issued the notes at face value (or par) and thus received $200 million of cash. Had the notes been issued at a discount (premium) from face value, the carrying value of the notes would have increased (decreased) from 2011 to 2012.

4. **How much interest expense will be recorded in 2012 on the 6.70% unsecured notes due in 2019?** Interest expense will be $13.4 million; that is, the 0.067 effective (and contractual) interest rate multiplied by the $200 million borrowed.

5. **Does the company face any near-term cash flow problems as a consequence of its current borrowings?** Snap-On faces debt principal payments of just $5.2 million in 2013. As indicated in the first paragraph of the note, another $100 million comes due in 2014 (the 5.85% unsecured notes) but no principal payments are required in 2015 or 2016.

6. **Does Snap-On have any untapped access to cash that could be used to help meet the 2014 debt payment?** The company has a $500 million multi-currency revolving credit facility, and none of this potential borrowing capacity has been tapped at 2012 year-end. In addition, Snap-On has another $200 million in unused debt capacity under a renewable loan and servicing commitment. In short, the company has substantial financial flexibility to address any cash flow shortages over the next two years.

7. **Is Snap-On close to violating any debt covenants?** Apparently not. The third paragraph of the financial statement note outlines a financial covenant contained in the revolving credit facility that specifies a maximum debt-to-capital (debt plus shareholders' equity) ratio and a maximum debt-to-adjusted net income ratio. The company's actual ratios were below the allowed maximums and thus within the permitted range of values. There is little mention of covenants for the company's other debt instruments—and there surely are some—but they may be less restrictive than are those of its revolving credit line. Snap-On does say that it was in compliance at 2012 year-end with all covenants of its debt agreements and credit facilities.

EXERCISES

E11-1

Finding the issue price
(LO 2)

AICPA
ADAPTED

mhhe.com/revsine6e

Akers Company sold bonds on July 1, 2014, with a face value of $100,000. These bonds are due in 10 years. The stated annual interest rate is 6% per year, payable semiannually on June 30 and December 31. These bonds were sold to yield 8%.

Required:
How much did these bonds sell for on July 1, 2014?

E11-2

Determining market price following a change in interest rates **(LO 2)**

mhhe.com/revsine6e

By July 1, 2015, the market yield on the Akers Company bonds described in E11–1 had risen to 10%.

Required:
What was the bonds' market price on July 1, 2015?

E11-3

Finding the discount at issuance **(LO 2)**

AICPA
ADAPTED

On January 1, 2014, when the market interest rate was 14%, Luba Corporation issued bonds in the face amount of $500,000 with interest at 12% payable semiannually. The bonds mature on December 31, 2023.

Required:
Calculate the bond discount at issuance. How much of the discount should be amortized by the effective interest method on July 1, 2014?

On January 2, 2014, West Company issued 9% bonds in the amount of $500,000 that mature on December 31, 2023. The bonds were issued for $469,500 to yield 10%. Interest is payable annually on December 31. West uses the effective interest method of amortizing bond discounts.

Required:

In its June 30, 2014, balance sheet, what net amount should West report as bonds payable?

E11-4

Determining a bond's balance sheet value **(LO 2)**

AICPA
ADAPTED

On February 1, 2012, Davis Corporation issued 12%, $1,000,000 par, 10-year bonds for $1,117,000. Davis reacquired all of these bonds at 102% of par, plus accrued interest, on May 1, 2015, and retired them. The unamortized bond premium on that date was $78,000.

Required:

Before income taxes, what was Davis's gain or loss on the bond extinguishment?

E11-5

Calculating gain or loss at early retirement **(LO 4)**

AICPA
ADAPTED

Webb Company has outstanding a 7% annual, 10-year, $100,000 face value bond that it had issued several years ago. It originally sold the bond to yield 6% annual interest. Webb uses the effective interest rate method to amortize the bond premium. On June 30, 2014, the outstanding bond's carrying amount was $105,000.

Required:

What amount of unamortized premium on the bond should Webb report in its June 30, 2015, balance sheet?

E11-6

Amortizing a premium **(LO 2)**

AICPA
ADAPTED

Brower Corporation owns a manufacturing plant in the country of Oust. On December 31, 2014, the plant had a book value of $5,000,000 and an estimated fair value of $8,000,000. Oust's government has clearly indicated that it will expropriate the plant during the coming year and will reimburse Brower for only 40% of the plant's estimated fair value.

Required:

What journal entry (if any) should Brower make on December 31, 2014, to record the intended expropriation?

E11-7

Recording loss contingencies **(LO 7)**

AICPA
ADAPTED

Zero coupon bonds pay no interest—the only cash investors receive is the lump-sum principal payment at maturity. On January 1, 2014, The Ledge Inc. issued $250 million of zero coupon bonds at a market yield rate of 12%. The bonds mature in 20 years.

Required:

1. What was the January 1, 2014, issue price of these zero coupon bonds?
2. How much interest expense will The Ledge record on the bonds in 2014?
3. How much interest expense will The Ledge record on the bonds in 2015?

E11-8

Zero coupon bonds **(LO 2)**

eXcel

mhhe.com/revsine6e

On January 1, 2014, 3Way Energy issued $200 million of 15-year, floating-rate debentures at par value. The debentures pay interest on June 30 and December 31 of each year. The floating interest rate is set equal to "LIBOR plus 6%" on January 1 of each year. The LIBOR was 6% when the bonds were issued and 8% on January 1, 2015.

Required:

1. How much cash interest did 3Way Energy pay on the debentures in 2014? How much will it pay in 2015?
2. How much interest expense did the company record on the debentures in 2014? How much will it record in 2015?

E11-9

Floating-rate debt **(LO 3)**

E11-10 Identifying incentives for early debt retirement **(LO 4)**  mhhe.com/revsine6e	On January 1, 2013, Roland Inc. issued $125 million of 8% bonds at par. The bonds pay interest semiannually on June 30 and December 31 of each year, and they mature in 15 years. On December 31, 2014 (one day before the next interest payment is to be made), the bonds are trading at a market yield of 12% plus accrued interest. **Required:** 1. Suppose that Roland repurchased the entire $125 million bonds for cash at the market price on December 31, 2014. Using a 40% corporate tax rate, how much gain or loss would the company record on this transaction? 2. Why might the company want to retire the debt early?
E11-11 Off-balance-sheet debt **(LO 7)**	Wood Company and Willie Inc. form a joint venture—Woodlie Partners—to manufacture and distribute agricultural pesticides. Wood and Willie each contribute $20 million cash and receive 50% of Woodlie's common stock. Woodlie then borrows $200 million from a consortium of banks and uses the money to build its manufacturing and distribution facilities. The loan is made on December 31, 2014, and is fully guaranteed by both Wood and Willie. **Required:** How much of the $200 million debt shows up on the December 31, 2014, balance sheet of Wood Company? Why? Would the same be true for Willie Inc.? Why or why not?
E11-12 Noninterest-bearing loan **(LO 3)**	McClelland Corporation agreed to purchase some landscaping equipment from Agri-Products for a cash price of $500,000. Before accepting delivery of the equipment, McClelland learned that the same equipment could be purchased from another dealer for $460,000. To avoid losing the sale, Agri-Products has offered McClelland a "no interest" payment plan—McClelland would pay $100,000 at delivery, $200,000 one year later, and the final $200,000 in two years. **Required:** 1. McClelland would usually pay 9% annual interest on a loan of this type. What is the present value of the Agri-Products loan at the delivery date? 2. What journal entry would McClelland make if it accepts the deal and buys from Agri-Products? 3. What should McClelland do?

E11-13
 	
Understanding GAAP hedges **(LO 9)**
	Required:
	
	1. Which of the following qualifies as a hedged item?
	   a. A company's work-in-process inventory of unfinished washers, dryers, and refrigerators.
	   b. Credit card receivables at JCPenney.
	   c. Bushels of corn owned by the Farmers' Cooperative.
	   d. Salaries payable to employees of Ford Motor Company.
	   e. A three-year note issued by General Motors and payable in U.S. dollars.
	   f. A three-year note issued by Chrysler and payable in euros.
	
	2. Which of the following qualifies as a hedging instrument?
	   a. An electricity futures contract purchased by Alliant Energy, an electrical power company.
	   b. A crop insurance contract purchased by Farmers' Cooperative that pays the co-op for crop losses from drought or flood.
	   c. An option to buy shares of common stock in Ford Motor Company.
	   d. An option to sell shares of common stock in General Motors.
	   e. A four-year lease for office space in downtown Toronto.

3. Which of the following qualifies as an eligible risk for hedge accounting?

   a. Alliant Energy's risk that summer demand for electricity may exceed the company's power-generating capacity.

   b. Ford Motor Company's risk that not enough steel will be available in six months when the company must purchase steel to produce a new sports utility vehicle.

   c. The risk to American Express that its members won't pay their credit card bills.

   d. The risk to Farmers' Cooperative that corn mold will destroy its inventory of corn held in silos for sale next year.

   e. The possibility of changes in the exchange rate of U.S. dollars for Mexican pesos for Coca-Cola Company, which has a major foreign investment in Mexico.

PROBLEMS / DISCUSSION QUESTIONS

Greg Miller wants to buy a new automobile. The dealer has the exact car Miller wants and has given him two payment options: pay (1) the full cash price of $19,326 today or (2) only $2,000 down today and then make four more annual payments of $5,000 beginning one year from to-day. Miller doesn't have the cash needed to pay the car's full price, but he does have enough for the down payment. He can also obtain an automobile loan from his bank at 5% interest per year.

P11-1

Imputing interest **(LO 3)**

Required:

1. Verify that the imputed interest rate on the dealer's loan is 6%. That is, show that the present value of Miller's payments equal $19,326 (rounded to the nearest dollar) when discounted at 6%.

2. Which payment option should Miller accept?

On July 1, 2014, McVay Corporation issued $15 million of 10-year bonds with an 8% stated interest rate. The bonds pay interest semiannually on June 30 and December 31 of each year. The market rate of interest on July 1, 2014, for bonds of this type was 10%. McVay closes its books on December 31.

P11-2

Reporting bonds issued at a discount **(LO 2)**

mhhe.com/revsine6e

Required:

1. At what price were the bonds issued?

2. Using the effective interest method, prepare an amortization schedule showing interest expense, discount or premium amortization, and bond carrying value for each of the first four semiannual interest payment periods.

3. Prepare journal entries to record the first four semiannual interest payments.

4. How should the bonds be shown on McVay's December 31, 2014, balance sheet and on its December 31, 2015, balance sheet?

On January 1, 2014, Fleetwood Inc. issued bonds with a face amount of $25 million and a stated interest rate of 8%. The bonds mature in 10 years and pay interest semiannually on June 30 and December 31 of each year. The market rate of interest on January 1, 2014, for bonds of this type was 6%. Fleetwood closes its books on December 31.

P11-3

Reporting bonds issued at a premium **(LO 2)**

mhhe.com/revsine6e

Required:

1. At what price were the bonds issued?

2. Using the effective interest method, prepare an amortization schedule showing interest expense, amortization, and bond carrying value for each of the first four semiannual interest payment periods.

(Continued on next page.)

3. Prepare journal entries to record the first four semiannual interest payments.

4. How would the bonds be shown on Fleetwood's December 31, 2014, balance sheet and on its December 31, 2015, balance sheet?

P11-4

Analyzing installment note and imputed interest
(LO 3)

On January 1, 2014, Newell Manufacturing purchased a new drill press that had a cash purchase price of $6,340. Newell decided instead to pay on an installment basis. The installment contract calls for four annual payments of $2,000 each beginning in one year. Newell was not required to make an initial down payment for the drill press.

Required:

1. Verify that the imputed interest rate on the installment loan is 10%. That is, show that the present value of the payments Newell must make is $6,340 (rounded to the nearest dollar) when discounted at a 10% rate of interest.

2. What journal entry would Newell make on January 1, 2014, to record the drill press purchase?

3. How much interest expense would Newell record in 2014 for the installment loan? What would the loan balance be on January 1, 2015, after Newell made the first loan payment?

4. How much interest expense would Newell record in 2015 for the installment loan? What would the loan balance be on December 31, 2015—one day before Newell makes the second loan payment?

P11-5

Understanding the fair value option **(LO 5)**

On January 1, 2014, Mason Manufacturing borrows $500,000 and uses the money to purchase corporate bonds for investment purposes. Interest rates were quite volatile that year and so were the fair values of Mason's bond investment (an asset) and loan (a liability):

	Fair Value	
2014	**Bond Investment**	**Loan**
January 1	$500,000	$500,000
March 31	450,000	465,000
June 30	480,000	493,000
September 30	510,000	504,000
December 31	485,000	495,000

Required:

1. Mason is required to use fair value accounting for the bond investment. Prepare the journal entry to record the investment purchase on January 1, 2014, and the fair value adjustments required at the end of each quarter: March 31, June 30, September 30, and December 31.

2. Suppose that Mason uses conventional amortized cost accounting for the loan. The loan principal is due in five years. Ignore interest on the loan to simplify the problem. What will be the loan's carrying value at the end of each quarter?

3. Suppose that instead Mason elects to use the GAAP fair value option permitted by FASB ASC Topic 825 for the loan. What dollar impact will this change have on reported profits each quarter?

4. Which accounting approach—amortized cost or fair value—do you believe Mason should use for the loan? Why?

P11-6

Call options as investments
(LO 8)

On July 1, 2014, Stan Getz, Inc., bought call option contracts for 500 shares of Selmer Manufacturing common stock. The contracts cost $200, expire on September 15, and have an exercise price of $40 per share. The market price of Selmer's stock that day was also $40 a share. On July 31, 2014, Selmer stock was trading at $38 a share, and the option contracts' fair value was $125—that is, Getz could buy the identical $40 strike price contracts on July 31 for $125.

On August 31, 2014, the market price of Selmer stock was $44 a share, and the fair value of the options contracts was $2,075.

Required:

1. Prepare the journal entry to record Getz's purchase of call option contracts on July 1, 2014.

2. Prepare the journal entry to record the change in fair value of the option contracts on July 31, 2014.

3. Prepare the journal entry to record the change in fair value of the option contracts on August 31, 2014.

4. Why are the option contracts worth so much more on August 31 ($2,075) than they were worth on July 31 ($125)?

5. What entry would Getz make to record exercising the options on September 15, 2014, when Selmer's shares were trading at $46?

6. Suppose instead that Getz allowed the option contracts to expire on September 15, 2014, without exercising them. What entry would Getz then make?

On January 1, 2014, Tango-In-The-Night, Inc., issued $75 million of bonds with a 9% coupon interest rate. The bonds mature in 10 years and pay interest semiannually on June 30 and December 31 of each year. The market rate of interest on January 1, 2014, for bonds of this type was 11%. The company closes its books on December 31.

P11-7

Retiring debt early **(LO 4)**

mhhe.com/revsine6e

Required:

1. At what price were the bonds issued?

2. What is the book value of the bonds on January 1, 2016?

3. On January 1, 2016, the market interest rate for bonds of this type is 10%. What is the market value of the bonds on this date?

4. Suppose that the bonds were repurchased for cash on January 1, 2016, at the market price. If you ignore taxes, what journal entry would the company make to record the debt retirement?

P11-8

Sharp Pencil Lets Citigroup Declare a Profit **(LO 4)**

After more than a year of crippling losses and three bailouts from Washington, Citigroup, a troubled giant of American banking, said Friday that it had done something extraordinary: it made money.

But the headline number—a net profit of $1.6 billion for the first quarter—was not quite what it seemed. Behind that figure was some fuzzy math.

Like several other banks that reported surprisingly strong results this week, Citigroup used some creative accounting, all of it legal, to bolster its bottom line at a pivotal moment . . .

Citigroup posted its first profitable quarter in 18 months, in part because of unusually strong results from its trading operations. It also made progress in reducing expenses and improving its profit margins.

But the long-struggling company also employed several common accounting tactics—gimmicks, critics call them—to increase its reported earnings.

One of the maneuvers, widely used since the financial crisis erupted last spring, involves the way Citigroup accounted for the decline in the value of its own debt . . . This strategy added $2.7 billion to the company's bottom line during the quarter, a figure that dwarfed Citigroup's reported net income . . .

Source: Excerpt from E. Dash, "Sharp Pencil Lets Citigroup Declare a Profit," *The New York Times,* April 18, 2009.

Required:

1. Suppose Citigroup had issued at par on January 1, 2005, $500 million of 10-year bonds with a fixed annual interest rate of 6% reflecting the company's financial soundness at the time. Calculate the proceeds received by Citigroup, the interest expense recorded in 2005, and the bond carrying value on January 1, 2009. Assume cash interest payments are made on December 31 of each year.

2. Suppose the market interest rate had increased to 12% by January 1, 2009. Compute the market value of the bonds on that date.

3. At the time the news article above was published, Citigroup's debt had lost value in the bond market because of investors' concerns about the company's ability to meet the required debt payments when due. Explain how this perceived increase in Citigroup's credit risk translates into a decline in the market value of its bonds.

4. How did Citigroup account for the $2.7 billion decline in the value of its own debt?

5. Explain why the accounting treatment used by Citigroup and other banks was so controversial.

P11-9

Chalk Hill: Using an interest rate swap as a speculative investment **(LO 9)**

Exhibit 11.12 describes Chalk Hill's use of an interest rate swap to hedge its cash flow exposure to interest rate risk from variable rate debt. The journal entries in the exhibit illustrate how special "hedge accounting" rules apply to the swap. Suppose instead that the swap *did not qualify* for special hedge accounting—but that all other aspects of the transaction remain as described in the exhibit.

Required:

Prepare the journal entries needed to account for the variable rate debt and swap transaction for January 1, 2014, through December 31, 2016.

P11-10

Hedging raw material price swings **(LO 8)**

SMALL FIRMS LOOK TO DERIVATIVES TRADING TO MANAGE COSTS

Karl Fowler isn't a traditional publisher. His books, which chronicle major sporting events and teams, can weigh more than 90 pounds and go for as much as $4,000. So to control the costs of the raw materials Mr. Fowler needs to produce these hefty tomes, the entrepreneur is using an equally untraditional approach for small businesses: derivatives trading.

These sophisticated financial instruments—which allow investors to hedge risks and bet on fluctuations in anything from the weather to orange-juice prices—might not seem relevant to a small book publisher. But Mr. Fowler cut his teeth as a derivatives trader. So when he left the finance world in 2002 for book publishing, it was only natural for him to apply his specialty to help insulate his British firm, Kraken Group, from rising prices for raw materials like paper, ink, and silk. . . .

Required:

1. One strategy used by Kraken Group is to buy pulp-paper futures on commodities exchanges. Paper prices can go up and down by more than 10% in a short period. When paper prices increase, Kraken's operating profits fall. Explain how pulp-paper futures can be used to protect Kraken's profits from harmful paper price increases.

2. How will the pulp-paper futures affect profits if paper prices instead decline?

3. Ink prices tend to be even more volatile than paper prices but cannot be hedged by exchange-traded futures. So, Mr. Fowler asked an ink supplier to set up a forward contract for about half of the amount purchased each year. Explain how a forward contract can be used to protect Kraken's profits from harmful ink price increases.

4. How will the forward contract affect profits if ink prices instead decline?

The following information appeared in the 2011 annual report of Rumours, Inc.:

P11-11

Discount and premium amortization **(LO 2)**

Long-Term Debt

[Rumours, Inc. issued] $10 million, 10% coupon bonds on January 1, 2008, due on December 31, 2012. The prevailing market interest rate on January 1, 2008, was 12%, and the bonds pay interest on June 30 and December 31 of each year.

On January 1, 2009, [Rumours issued] $10 million, 10% coupon bonds due on December 31, 2013. The prevailing market interest rate on January 1, 2009, was 8%, and the bonds pay interest on June 30 and December 31 of each year.

Required:

1. See the following (incomplete) table for each bond's carrying value. Calculate the missing values.

	Carrying Value	
	December 31, 2010	**December 31, 2011**
10% bonds due in 2012	$9,653,550	?
10% bonds due in 2013	?	$10,362,950

2. How much interest expense did Rumours record in 2011 on the bonds due in 2012?

3. How much interest expense did Rumours record in 2011 on the bonds due in 2013?

Information taken from a Sears, Roebuck and Company annual report follows.

P11-12

Sears: Reading the financials **(LO 1)**

	December 31	
Long-Term Debt ($ in millions)	**Year 2**	**Year 1**
7% debentures, $300 million face value, due Year 11, effective rate $14.6%	$ 188.6	$ 182.7
Zero coupon bonds, $500 million face value, due Year 8, effective rate 12.0%	267.9	239.2
Participating mortgages, $850 million face value, due Year 5, effective rate 8.7%, collateralized by Sears Tower and related properties	834.5	833.9
Various other long-term debt	12,444.2	16,329.2
Total long-term debt	$13,735.2	$17,585.0

Required:

1. How much interest expense did the company record during Year 2 on the 7% debentures? How much of the original issue discount was amortized during Year 2?

2. How much interest expense did the company record during Year 2 on the zero coupon bonds?

3. Suppose that interest payments on the participating mortgages are made on December 31 of each year. What journal entry did the company make in Year 2 to recognize interest expense on this debt?

4. How much cash interest did the company pay out during Year 2 on the 7% debentures and the zero coupon bonds?

P11-13

Hedging **(LO 8)**

There following excerpts are from the financial statement note on Derivative Instruments and Hedging Activities in Molson Coors Brewing Company's 2009 annual report:

Cross Currency Swaps

Simultaneous with the September 22, 2005, U.S. private debt placement, we entered into a cross currency swap transaction for the entire USD $300 million issue amount and for the same maturity of September 2010. In this transaction we exchanged our USD $300 million for a CAD $355.5 million obligation with a third party. The swaps also call for an exchange of fixed CAD interest payments for fixed USD interest receipts. We have designated this transaction as a hedge of the variability of the cash flows associated with the payment of interest and principal on the USD securities. Changes in the value of the transaction due to foreign exchange are recorded in earnings and are offset by a revaluation of the associated debt instrument. Changes in the value of the transaction due to interest rates are recorded to OCI.

Commodity Swaps

As of period end, we had financial commodity swap contracts in place to hedge certain future expected purchases of natural gas. Essentially, these contracts allow us to swap our floating exposure to natural gas prices for a fixed rate. These contracts have been designated as cash flow hedges of forecasted natural gas purchases. . . . These swaps [are used] to hedge forecasted purchases up to twenty-four months in advance.

MillerCoor's LLC, a wholly-owned subsidiary of Molson Coors Brewing Company, said this about its derivative instruments and hedging activities:

The Company's objective in managing its exposure to fluctuations in commodity prices is to reduce the volatility in its cash flows and earnings caused by unexpected adverse fluctuations in the commodity markets. To achieve this objective, the Company enters into futures contracts, swaps and purchased option collars. In general, maturity dates of the contracts coincide with market purchases of the commodity. As of December 31, 2009, the Company had financial commodity swap and futures contracts in place to hedge certain future expected purchases of aluminum can sheet, aluminum cans, natural gas, and electricity. The Company also hedges the diesel fuel surcharge exposure that it subsidizes for its distributors. These contracts are either marked-to-market, with changes in fair value recognized in cost of goods sold, or have been designated as cash flow hedges of forecasted purchases, and recognized in other comprehensive income (loss).

Required:

1. What did Molson Coors accomplish by swapping its $300 million U.S. dollar-denominated debt for a $355.5 million Canadian-dollar obligation?

2. Why was the cross-currency swap designated as a cash flow hedge rather than a fair value hedge?

3. Why do some cross-currency swap's fair value changes flow to earnings (through Cost of goods sold) while other fair value changes bypass earnings and flow to Other comprehensive income?

4. What did the company accomplish with its financial commodity swap contract for natural gas?

5. Why was the natural gas commodity swap designated as a cash flow hedge rather than a fair value hedge?

6. What did the company accomplish with its commodity swaps and futures contracts for aluminum, natural gas, electricity, and diesel fuel surcharges?

7. Why do some fair value changes associated with these commodity swaps and futures contracts flow to earnings (through Cost of goods sold) while other fair value changes bypass earnings and flow to Other comprehensive income?

P11-14

Contingent losses and debt covenants **(LO 7)**

TROUBLE LOOMS FOR CHECKPOINT SYSTEMS

Shares of Checkpoint Systems, which makes electronic anti-theft tags used by retailers, have dropped from 18 in April to 12.50 lately, in part because of an unseasonably warm winter, which dampened apparel sales. But don't expect the stock to rebound soon, say some pros: The stock may well keep tumbling because of an antitrust lawsuit that Checkpoint lost. . . .

In late May, a U.S. District Court in Pennsylvania assessed damages of $26 million. . . . The verdict could put Checkpoint in violation of bank covenants on 1999 bank loans. Even if Checkpoint appeals and puts off paying damages, accountants may require it to acknowledge the potential damages in its financial statement. Therein lies the problem: It had borrowed $273.9 million from banks. Those loans have covenants that might be violated by putting new debt on its balance sheet. The covenants also require Checkpoint to have a net worth of $200 million. Its current net worth is $240 million, and the damages it will have to pay will bring it below required levels.

Source: "Trouble Looms for Checkpoint Systems," *BusinessWeek,* June 17, 2002.

Required:

1. When must U.S. firms record contingent losses and the related balance sheet liability?

2. What does IFRS say about when firms must record contingent provisions?

3. Here is what Checkpoint Systems said about its litigation loss contingency in a note to the 2001 financial statements released on March 28, 2002:

The Company is involved in certain legal and regulatory actions, all of which have arisen in the ordinary course of business. . . . Management does not believe that the ultimate resolution of such matters will have a material adverse effect on its consolidated results of operations or financial condition.

The Company is a defendant in a Civil Action No. 99-CV-577, served February 10,1999, in the United States District Court for the Eastern District of Pennsylvania filed by Plaintiff, ID Security Systems Canada Inc. The suit alleges a variety of antitrust claims; claims related to unfair competition, interference with a contract, and related matters. Plaintiff seeks damages of up to $90 million, before trebling, if an antitrust violation were to be determined. This matter is scheduled for a jury trial commencing April 22, 2002. Management is of the opinion that the claims are baseless both in fact and in law, and intends to vigorously defend the suit. If, however, the final outcome of this litigation results in certain of the Plaintiff's claims being upheld, the potential damages could be material to the Company's consolidated results of operations or financial condition.

Based on the information provided in this note, does it appear as though Checkpoint Systems has already recognized a loss contingency related to this lawsuit? Why or why not?

4. How does the district court decision influence whether Checkpoint's litigation contingency must be recorded?

5. Explain how recognition of the contingent liability will cause Checkpoint to violate its net worth covenant.

6. Is it likely that the banks will just waive the covenant violation if it occurs? (*Hint:* You may want to review the covenant violation discussion in Chapter 7.)

PI1-15

Working backward from an amortization table **(LO 2)**

Clovis Company recently issued $500,000 (face value) bonds to finance a new construction project. The company's chief accountant prepared the following bond amortization schedule:

Date	Interest Expense	Semiannual Payment	Premium Amortization	Net Liability
7/1/14				$540,554
12/31/14	$21,622	$25,000	$(3,378)	537,176
6/30/15	21,487	25,000	(3,513)	533,663
12/31/15	21,347	25,000	(3,653)	530,010
6/30/16	21,200	25,000	(3,800)	526,210
12/31/16	21,048	25,000	(3,952)	522,258
6/30/17	20,890	25,000	(4,110)	518,148
12/31/17	20,726	25,000	(4,274)	513,874
6/30/18	20,555	25,000	(4,445)	509,429
12/31/18	20,377	25,000	(4,623)	504,806
6/30/19	20,194	25,000	(4,806)	500,000

Required:

1. Compute the discount or premium on the sale of the bonds, the semiannual coupon interest rate, and the semiannual effective interest rate.

2. The company's vice president of finance wants any discount (or premium) at issuance of the bonds to be recorded immediately as a loss (or gain) at the issue date. Do you agree with this approach? Why or why not?

3. On December 31, 2016, the bonds' net carrying value is $522,258. In present value terms, what does this amount represent?

4. Suppose that market interest rates were 6% semiannually on January 1, 2017, or 12.36% annually. [This 12.36% annual rate of interest is equal to the 6% semiannual rate, compounded: $0.1236 = (1.06 \times 1.06) - 1.00$.] What is the bond's market price on that date? Is the company better or worse off because of the interest rate change? Explain.

PI1-16

Recording floating-rate debt **(LO 3)**

On January 1, 2014, Nicks Corporation issued $250 million of floating-rate debt. The debt carries a contractual interest rate of "LIBOR plus 5.5%," which is reset annually on January 1 of each year. The LIBOR rates on January 1, 2014, 2015, and 2016, were 6.5%, 7.0%, and 5.5%, respectively.

Required:

1. Prepare a journal entry to record the issuance of the bonds on January 1, 2014, at par. What was the effective (or market) interest rate when the bonds were issued?

2. Prepare a journal entry to record interest expense for 2014, 2015, and 2016. Assume that interest is paid annually on December 31.

3. What is the market value of the debt at December 31, 2016, assuming Nicks Corporation's credit risk has not changed.

The following information appeared in the 2002 annual report of Lyondell Petrochemical Company, a manufacturer of petrochemicals and refined petroleum products such as gasoline, heating oil, jet fuel, aromatics, and lubricants:

PII-17

Unconditional purchase obligations **(LO 7)**

The Company is party to various unconditional purchase obligation contracts as a purchaser for products and services, principally for steam and power. At December 31, 2002, future minimum payments under these contracts with noncancelable contract terms in excess of one year and fixed minimum payments were as follows ($ in millions):

2003	$ 164
2004	168
2005	169
2006	157
2007	151
Thereafter	1,749
Total minimum payments	$2,558

Required:

1. Suppose that the company is obligated to purchase $349.8 million per year in 2008 and each of the next four years for a total of $1,749. If Lyondell's normal rate of interest for a 10-year loan is 8%, what is the present value of the company's purchase commitments?

2. The company's 2002 balance sheet shows long-term debt of $3,926 million and shareholders' equity of $1,179 million. The unconditional purchase obligation is not shown on the balance sheet. What impact would including the present value of unconditional purchase obligations as part of long-term debt have on the company's 2002 ratio of long-term debt to shareholders' equity?

3. Why are unconditional purchase obligations an off-balance-sheet liability? Why might some companies prefer to keep the purchase commitment off the balance sheet?

The following information appeared in the annual reports of Borden, Inc., Exxon Corporation, and Visa Inc.

PII-18

Loss contingencies **(LO 7)**

Borden, Inc.

Accruals for environmental matters are recorded when it is probable that a liability has been incurred and the amount of the liability can be reasonably estimated. Environmental accruals are routinely reviewed on an interim basis as events and developments warrant and are subjected to a comprehensive review annually during the fiscal fourth quarter. The Company and the Combined Companies have each accrued approximately $26 million (including those costs related to legal proceedings) at December 31, 2000 and 1999, for probable environmental remediation and restoration liabilities. This is management's best estimate of these liabilities. Based on currently available information and analysis, the Company believes that it is reasonably possible that costs associated with such liabilities may exceed current reserves by amounts that may prove insignificant, or by amounts, in the aggregate, of up to approximately $16 million. [Excerpt from the company's 2000 annual report.]

Exxon Corporation

A number of lawsuits, including class actions, have been brought in various courts against Exxon Corporation and certain of its subsidiaries relating to the release of crude oil from the tanker *Exxon Valdez* in 1989. Most of these lawsuits seek unspecified compensatory and punitive damages; several lawsuits seek damages in varying specified amounts. Certain of the lawsuits seek injunctive relief. The claims of many individuals have been dismissed or settled. Most of the remaining actions are scheduled for trial in federal court commencing May 2, 1994. Other actions will likely be tried in state court later in 1994. The cost to the corporation from these lawsuits is not possible to predict; however, it is believed that the final outcome will not have a materially adverse effect upon the corporation's operations or financial condition. [Excerpt from the company's 1993 annual report.]

Visa Inc.

Accrued litigation. The Company evaluates the likelihood of an unfavorable outcome in legal or regulatory proceedings to which it is a party and records a loss contingency when it is probable that a liability has been incurred and the amount of the loss can be reasonably estimated. These judgments are subjective, based on the status of such legal or regulatory proceedings, the merits of the Company's defenses and consultation with corporate and external legal counsel. Actual outcomes of these legal and regulatory proceedings may differ materially from the Company's estimates. Litigation accruals associated with settled obligations to be paid over periods longer than one year are recorded at the present value of future payment obligations. The obligation is accreted to its full payment value with the corresponding accretion charge included in interest expense on the consolidated statements of operations. The Company expenses legal costs as incurred in professional fees.

The Company recorded litigation provisions of $4.1 billion and $7 million in fiscal 2012 and 2011, respectively. The litigation accrual is an estimate and is based on management's understanding of its litigation profile, the specifics of each case, advice of counsel to the extent appropriate and management's best estimate of incurred loss at the balance sheet date.

The following table summarizes the activity related to accrued litigation for the years ended September 30, 2012 and 2011:

(in millions)	2012	2011
Balance at October 1	$ 425	$ 697
Provision for unsettled legal matters	4,100	—
Provision for settled legal matters	—	7
Reclassification of settled matters[1]	—	12
Interest accretion on settled matters	1	11
Payments on settled matters	(140)	(302)
Balance at September 30	**$4,386**	**$ 425**

[1] Reclassification of amount previously recorded in accrued liabilities.

For the quarter ended June 30, 2012, the Company recorded a litigation provision of $4.1 billion, which increased its total reserve for the covered litigation from $285 million to $4.4 billion, to reflect the class plaintiffs' Settlement Agreement and the resolution of the Individual Plaintiffs' claims. [Excerpt from the company's 2012 annual report. Author Note: The Court granted preliminary approval of the Settlement Agreement on November 9, 2012.]

Required:

1. What is a loss contingency, and why is it disclosed in financial statements? Which of the preceding examples represents a recognized loss contingency?

2. Borden has a $26 million liability on its 2000 balance sheet for "probable environmental remediation and restoration." But the company says actual remediation and restoration

costs could be up to $16 million more than this amount. Why doesn't Borden's balance sheet liability include the additional $16 million?

3. Why doesn't Exxon report a dollar amount for its litigation cases? Does the lack of a specific dollar amount in Exxon's cases mean that stock analysts will just ignore the litigation when valuing the company? Why or why not?

4. In its 2002 annual report, Exxon (now ExxonMobil) had more to say about the *Exxon Valdez* incident:

> [O]n September 24, 1996, the United States District Court for the District of Alaska entered a judgment in the amount of $5.058 billion. The District Court awarded approximately $19.6 million in compensatory damages to plaintiffs, $38 million in prejudgment interest on the compensatory damages, and $5 billion in punitive damages. . . . The District Court stayed execution on the judgment pending appeal. . . . ExxonMobil appealed the judgment. On November 7, 2001, the United States Court of Appeals for the Ninth Circuit vacated the punitive damage award as being excessive under the Constitution and remanded the case to the District Court for it to determine the amount of the punitive damage award. . . . On December 6, 2002, the District Court reduced the punitive damages from $5 billion to $4 billion. . . .

   Based on the information provided, when did Exxon first report a balance sheet liability for the *Exxon Valdez* litigation? What was the amount of that liability?

5. In October 2007, the U.S. Supreme Court agreed to decide whether Exxon should be required to pay $2.5 billion in punitive damages to oil spill victims. Explain how the Court's willingness to hear the Exxon appeal affects the company's accounting for this contingent liability.

6. Why does Visa Inc. sometimes record litigation accruals (loss contingency provisions) at the present value rather than the full amount to be paid? Explain the accounting purpose behind the $11 million item labeled "Interest accretion on settled matters" recorded in 2011.

7. Explain why Visa Inc. increased its accrued litigation liability $425 million to $4,386 million in 2012.

On January 1, 2004, Chain Corporation issued $5 million of 7% coupon bonds at par. The bonds mature in 20 years and pay interest semiannually on June 30 and December 31 of each year. On December 31, 2014, the market interest rate for bonds of similar risk was 14%, and the market value of Chain Corporation bonds (after the December 31 interest payment) was $3,146,052.

Although the company's books are not yet closed for the year, a preliminary estimate shows net income to be $500,000. This amount is substantially below the $3 million management had expected the company to earn. The company has long-term debt totaling $7.5 million (including the $5 million bond issue) and shareholders' equity of $12.5 million (including the $500,000 of estimated net income). This means the company's long-term debt-to-equity ratio is 60%.

Unfortunately, a covenant in one of the company's loan agreements requires a long-term debt-to-equity ratio of 55% or less. Violating this covenant gives lenders the right to demand immediate repayment of the loan principal. Worse yet, a "cross default" provision in the $5 million bond makes it immediately due and payable if the company violates any of its lending agreements.

Because the company does not have the cash needed to repurchase the bonds, management is considering a debt-for-debt exchange in which the outstanding 7% bonds would be replaced by new 14% bonds with a face amount of $3.2 million. The interest rate on the new bonds is equal to the market interest rate.

P11-19

Debt-for-debt swaps
(LO 10)

Required:

1. Prepare a journal entry to record the swap on December 31, 2014. (Any gain or loss to the company would be taxed at 35%, and the tax should be included in your entry.)
2. What would the company's debt-to-equity ratio be after the swap?
3. What impact would the transaction have on net income for the year?
4. How else could management have avoided violation of the loan covenant?
5. IFRS guidance on the recognition of extinguishment gains in debt-for-debt swap transactions is more restrictive than U.S. GAAP. What additional factors must be considered in determining if Chain Corporation should recognize the swap gain under IFRS?

P11-20

Zero coupon bonds **(LO 2)**

The following information was taken from the financial statements of ALZA Corporation.

Note 6: Borrowings

On July 28, 2000, ALZA completed a private offering of the 3% Zero Coupon Convertible Subordinated Debentures, which were issued at a price of $551.26 per $1,000 principal amount at maturity. At December 29, 2002, the outstanding 3% Debentures had a total principal amount at maturity of $1.0 billion with a yield to maturity of 3% per annum, computed on a semiannual bond equivalent basis. . . . At December 29, 2002, the fair value based on quoted market value of the 3% Debentures was $813 million. . . .

Required:

1. ALZA issued zero coupon debentures with a total maturity value of $1.0 billion at a price of $551.26 per $1,000 principal amount at maturity. How much cash did the company receive when it issued these debentures?
2. The debentures mature in 20 years from the date of issuance, but no interest payments are made until maturity. Show that the issue price of $551.26 gives investors a 3% yield to maturity.
3. Suppose that the debentures were issued on January 1, 2000, instead of July 28, 2000. Reproduce the journal entries ALZA would record in 2000 for the debentures. For each *cash entry,* indicate whether the cash increase or decrease represents an operating, investing, or financing activity.
4. Explain why the debentures have a market value of $813 million at the end of 2002, almost $300 million more than the 2000 issue price.

P11-21

Comprehensive problem on bond premium **(LO 2)**

mhhe.com/revsine6e

On July 1, 2014, LekTech Corporation issued $20 million of 12%, 20-year bonds. Interest on the bonds is paid semiannually on December 31 and June 30 of each year, and the bonds were issued at a market interest rate of 8%.

Required:

1. Compute the bonds' issue price on July 1, 2014.
2. Prepare an amortization schedule that shows interest expense, premium or discount amortization, bond carrying value, and cash interest payment for each interest payment period through June 30, 2019.
3. Prepare the journal entries to record all interest expense and all cash interest payments for 2015.
4. A new employee in the accounting group at LekTech has asked you to explain why interest expense on the bonds changes each year. Write a two-paragraph memo that helps the employee understand interest recognition for these bonds.

5. LekTech used the bonds' proceeds to construct a new manufacturing facility near Waterloo, Iowa. The company will make taillight lenses for tractors manufactured by Deere & Company at its Waterloo plant. In fact, Deere has signed a letter guaranteeing payment of the LekTech bonds. How is the guarantee shown in Deere's financial statements?

6. On July 1, 2019, the company exercised a call provision in the debenture agreement and redeemed 40% of the bonds at 105% of par. What journal entry did the company make to record this partial redemption?

7. The market yield for the bonds on July 1, 2019, was 10%. How much less did the company pay to retire bonds using the call provision than it would have paid using an open market purchase?

The following information was taken from the 2012 financial statements of Dentsply International, a company that develops, manufactures, and markets medical equipment and supplies for the global dental market.

PII-22

Comprehensive problem on long-term debt disclosures **(LO I)**

Long-Term Debt

Long-term debt consisted of the following

	December 31,			
	2012		**2011**	
(in thousands)	**Principal Balance**	**Interest Rate**	**Principal Balance**	**Interest Rate**
Floating rate senior notes $250 million due August 2013	$ 250,000	1.8%	$ 250,000	2.0%
Term loan Japanese yen denominated expiring September 2014	144,681	1.1%	162,956	1.1%
Private placement notes $250 million expiring March 2016	254,560	4.1%	254,512	4.1%
Fixed rate senior notes $300 million due August 2016	299,689	2.8%	299,603	2.8%
Term loan Swiss francs denominated expiring September 2016	71,027	1.2%	69,197	1.2%
Fixed rate senior notes $450 million due August 2021	448,653	4.1%	448,497	4.1%
Other borrowings, various currencies and rates	4,303		6,654	
	$1,472,913		$1,491,419	
Less: Current portion (included in notes payable and current portion of long-term debt)	250,878		1,409	
Long-term portion	$1,222,035		$1,490,010	

The Company has a $500.0 million five-year revolving credit agreement with participation from 16 banks, which expires in July 2016. The revolving credit agreement contains a number of covenants and two financial ratios, which the Company is required to satisfy. The most restrictive of these covenants pertain to asset dispositions and prescribed ratios of indebtedness to total capital and operating income excluding depreciation and amortization to interest expense. Any breach of any such covenants or restrictions would result in a default under the existing borrowing documentation that would permit the lenders to declare all borrowings under such documentation to be immediately due and payable and, through cross default provisions, would entitle the Company's other lenders to accelerate their loans. At December 31, 2012, the Company was in compliance with these covenants.

The term loans and private placement notes ("PPN") contain certain affirmative and negative covenants relating to the Company's operations and financial condition. At December 31, 2012, the Company was in compliance with all debt covenants.

At December 31, 2012, the Company had total unused lines of credit, including lines available under its short-term arrangements and revolving credit agreement, of $527.4 million.

The table below reflects the contractual maturity dates of the various borrowings at December 31, 2012 (in thousands):

2013	$ 250,878
2014	221,865
2015	102,230
2016	448,440
2017	442
2018 and Beyond	449,058
	$1,472,913

Required:

1. Exhibit 11.10 in this chapter reproduces excerpts from Dentsply's 2009 financial statement note for long-term debt. How has the amount and composition of the company's long-term borrowing changed between 2009 and 2012?

2. How have the interest rates charged on Dentsply's long-term debt changed between 2009 and 2012? Explain why (or why not) these changes are indicative of Dentsply's *decreased* credit risk.

3. Comment on the future cash flow implications of the change between 2009 and 2012 in the contractual maturity dates of Dentsply's various borrowings.

4. Calculate the weighted-average rate of interest on the company's long-term debt as of December 31, 2012. You should ignore "Other borrowings, various currencies and rates."

5. Based on your answer to requirement 4, estimate the amount of interest expense Dentsply will record in 2013.

6. How much cash will the company pay out to debt holders in 2013?

P11-23

Hedging a purchase commitment **(LO 9)**

Silverado Inc. buys titanium from a supplier that requires a six-month firm commitment on all purchases. On January 1, 2014, Silverado signs a contract with the supplier to purchase 10,000 pounds of titanium at the current forward rate of $310 per pound with settlement on June 30, 2014. However, Silverado wants to actually pay the June 30 market price for titanium. To achieve this goal, the company enters into a forward contract to sell 10,000 pounds of titanium at the current forward price of $310 per unit. The firm commitment contract and the forward contract both have zero value at inception. Titanium spot prices and the contract fair values are:

		Forward	Contract Fair Value	
	Spot Price	Price (June 30)	Forward	Firm Commitment
January 1, 2014	$300	$310	–0–	–0–
March 31, 2014	292	297	$128,079	($128,079)
June 30, 2014	285	N.A.	250,000	(250,000)

Required:

1. Why did Silverado hedge its firm commitment with the supplier? After the fact, was it a good idea to do so?

2. What journal entries were made when the two contracts are signed on January 1, 2014?

3. Silverado designated the forward contract as a fair value hedge of its future titanium purchase. What journal entries were made on March 31, 2014?

4. What journal entries were made on June 30, 2014, when the contracts are settled and Silverado pays for the titanium?

Newton Grains plans to sell 100,000 bushels of corn from its current inventory in March 2015. The company paid $1 million for the corn during the fall 2014 harvest season. On October 1, 2014, Newton writes a forward contract to sell 100,000 bushels of corn on March 15, 2015, for $1,100,000. The forward contract has zero value at inception. On December 31, 2014, the March forward price for corn is $1,050,000 and the forward contract has a fair value of $95,000. On March 15, 2015, Newton sells the corn for $1,075,000 and settles the forward contract (now valued at $25,000).

PI1-24

Hedging a planned sale
(LO 9)

Required:

1. Why did Newton hedge its planned sale of corn? Was it a good idea to do so?

2. Newton designated the forward contract as a cash flow hedge of its exposure to corn price fluctuations. What journal entries were made when the forward contract was signed on October 1, 2014?

3. What journal entries were made on December 31, 2014?

4. What journal entries were made on March 15, 2015, when the forward contract was settled and Newton sold the corn?

5. How would your original journal entries change if the forward contract covered only 50,000 bushels of corn? (Contract fair values would then have been $47,500 on December 31, 2014, and $12,500 on March 15, 2015.)

Basie Business Forms borrowed $5 million on July 1, 2014, from First Kansas City Bank. The loan required annual interest payments at the LIBOR rate, reset annually each June 30. The loan principal is due in five years. The LIBOR rate for the first year is 6.0%.

Basie decided to swap its variable interest payments for fixed interest payments of 6.0%. Basie will pay 6.0% interest to the swap counterparty—Quincy Bank & Trust—and receive LIBOR payments based on a $5 million notional amount for the entire five-year term of the original loan. The swap has no value at its inception on July 1, 2014.

Basie designates the swap as a hedge of its cash flow exposure to interest rate risk on its variable rate debt. The hedge is fully effective because the key terms of the loan and swap are identical. The variable rate was reset to 6.25% on June 30, 2015, and to 5.75% on June 30, 2016. Basie uses a June 30 fiscal year-end and records interest expense annually.

PI1-25

Using interest rate swap as a cash flow hedge **(LO 9)**

Required:

1. How much net cash settlement will Basie pay to (or receive from) Quincy Bank & Trust on July 1, 2015? On July 1, 2016?

2. How much cash will Basie pay to First Kansas City Bank on July 1, 2015? On July 1, 2016?

3. On June 30, 2015, the swap has a fair value of $40,000 based on dealer quotes. Prepare journal entries to record Basie's cash interest payments and receipts as well as interest expense for the year ended June 30, 2015.

4. On June 30, 2016, the swap has a fair value of $(28,000), a negative amount. Prepare journal entries to record Basie's cash interest payments and receipts as well as interest expense for the year ended June 30, 2016.

Using interest rate swap as a
fair value hedge   **(LO 9)**

On January 1, 2014, Four Brothers Manufacturing borrowed $10 million from Guiffrie Bank by signing a three-year, 8.0% fixed-rate note. The note calls for interest to be paid annually on December 31. The company then entered into an interest rate swap agreement with Herman Bank. The agreement is that Four Brothers will receive from Herman a fixed-rate interest payment of 8.0% based on a $10 million notional amount each December 31 for three years. Four Brothers will pay Herman a variable LIBOR rate reset every December 31. The LIBOR rate for the first year is 8.0%.

Four Brothers designates the swap as a hedge of its fair value exposure to interest rate risk on its fixed-rate note. The hedge is fully effective because the key terms of the note and swap are identical. The variable rate was reset to 8.25% on December 31, 2014, and to 7.75% on December 31, 2015. Four Brothers uses a December 31 year-end and records interest expense annually.

Required:

1. How much net cash settlement will Four Brothers pay to (or receive from) Herman Bank on December 31, 2014? On December 31, 2015?

2. How much cash will Four Brothers pay to Guiffrie Bank on December 31, 2014? On December 31, 2015?

3. On December 31, 2014, the swap has a fair value of $(45,000), a negative amount, and the fair value of the $10 million note was $9,955,000. Prepare journal entries to record Four Brothers' cash interest payments and receipts as well as interest expense for the year ended December 31, 2014.

4. On December 31, 2015, the swap has a fair value of $23,000, and the fair value of the $10 million note was $10,023,000. Prepare journal entries to record Four Brothers' cash interest payments and receipts as well as interest expense for the year ended December 31, 2015.

Determining hedge
effectiveness   **(LO 9)**

Recall the Rombaurer Metals example in the chapter: On October 5, 2014, Rombaurer has 10 million pounds of copper inventory on hand at an average cost of $0.65 a pound. The spot price for copper is $0.90 a pound. Instead of selling copper now, Rombaurer decides to hold the inventory until February 2015 when management believes the price will return to a normal level of $0.95 a pound. To hedge its position, Rombaurer sells futures contracts at $0.95 for February delivery. Spot and futures prices over the next several months are as follows:

	NYMEX Copper Prices	
	Spot Price	**February 2012 Futures Price**
October 5, 2014	$0.90	$0.95
December 31, 2014	0.85	0.91
February 26, 2015	0.94	0.94

On February 26, 2015, Rombaurer sells its copper on the spot market for $0.94 a pound and cancels the futures contracts.

The chapter described how "hedge accounting" rules are used when Rombaurer hedges its entire 10 million pounds of copper inventory.

Required:

1. Suppose that Rombaurer sells futures contracts for only 5 million pounds of copper. (Management had decided that it is prudent to hedge only half of the company's economic exposure.) The margin requirement on these contracts is $140,000. Because the futures contracts are now "ineffective" in hedging the company's entire fair value exposure to copper price fluctuations, Rombaurer cannot use hedge accounting. Prepare all journal entries needed to account for the futures contracts and sale of copper from October 5, 2014, through February 26, 2015.

2. Now assume that Rombaurer designates these futures contracts as a "fully effective" hedge of its risk exposure for 5 million pounds of copper inventory. (The remaining 5 million pounds of inventory is not being hedged.) Rombaurer can now use hedge accounting for the futures contracts. Prepare all journal entries needed to account for the futures contracts and sale of copper from October 5, 2014, through February 26, 2015.

3. What impact does changing the definition of the hedged item (10 million pounds of copper inventory versus 5 million pounds) have on the company's financial statements for 2014 and 2015?

CASES

As a senior partner at one of the nation's largest public accounting firms, you serve as chairperson of the firm's financial reporting policy committee. You are also the firm's chief spokesperson on financial reporting matters that come before the FASB and the Securities and Exchange Commission. The year is 1997.

> **C11-1**
>
> Century and beyond bonds
> **(LO 1, 2)**

Two new debt securities have caught the attention of your committee, the FASB, the SEC, and the Treasury Department. Dresser Industries recently completed a $200 million offering of so-called **century bonds** that mature in 2096, or in 100 years. Safra Republic Holdings announced that in October it will issue $250 million of **millennium bonds** that mature in 2997, or in 1,000 years. Neither company is a client of your firm.

SAFRA REPUBLIC $250 MILLION 1000-YEAR SUBORDINATED DEBENTURES RATED 'AA-' BY FITCH

Safra Republic Holdings S.A.'s (SRH) $250 million issue of 7.125% subordinated debentures, due October 15, 2997, is rated 'AA-' by Fitch. The rating reflects superior risk-based capital ratios, indicative of the modest amount of assets represented by loans; sizable liquidity; comfortable funding from a growing client base; and a management organization seasoned in relationships with high net worth clients in over 80 countries. SRH's 49% ownership by the Republic National Bank of New York provides important support by a risk averse U.S.

banking institution, whose fundamentals garner a 'AA+' senior debt rating.

SRH is a Luxembourg-based holding company, operated through six wholly owned banking subsidiaries. These units provide international private banking, asset management and other related investment services to over 22,000 high net worth individuals, partnerships and closely held corporations. Client assets at SRH, both on- and off-balance sheet, stood at $29 billion at the end of September, compared to $20.8 billion at the like date in 1996.

Source: "Safra Republic $250 Million 1000-Year Subordinated Debentures Rated 'AA–' by Fitch," *PR Newswire,* October 16, 1997.

FIRM TO ISSUE $200 MILLION IN BONDS AS 100-YEAR PAPER

Dresser Industries Inc. said it will join the ranks of the small number of companies that have century bonds with the sale of $200 million of debentures due 2096. The oil-field services company said the sale, with Salomon Brothers Inc. as lead underwriter, is expected to occur this week. Proceeds will be used for general corporate purposes, including repayment of commercial paper outstanding and share repurchases.

The issue hasn't been priced, but analysts expect the rate to be about 7.5%. Only nine companies have issued 100-year paper since 1993, when Walt Disney Co. began the modern trend; no such bonds had been sold for more than 20 years. Earlier this year, the U.S. Treasury Department proposed that companies be prohibited from deducting interest on bonds with a maturity of more than 40 years, but Congress hasn't voted on the matter.

Source: "Firm to Issue $200 Million in Bonds as 100-Year Paper," *The Wall Street Journal,* August 7, 1996. Copyright ©1996 Dow Jones & Company, Inc. All rights reserved worldwide. Reprinted with permission.

Required:

1. Suppose that Dresser Industries issued its $200 million century bonds on January 1, 1996, at a market yield of 7.5%, the same as the stated interest rate. To keep things easy, also assume that the bonds pay interest just once a year, on December 31. Compute the bonds' issue price. How much of that price comes from the present value of the interest payments, and how much comes from the promised principal payment?

2. In present value terms, how much of a tax savings does the company obtain from its century bond? (Use a 40% effective tax rate.) How much of a tax savings would be lost if only the first 40 years of interest deductions were allowed?

3. Suppose that Dresser Industries' century bonds were issued with a stated rate of 7.5% when the market yield rate was 8.5%. What would the issue price be? How about if the market yield were 6.5%?

4. In October 2011, The Ohio State University sold $500 million worth of 100-year bonds, becoming the first public university to issue a so-called "century" bond. The bonds were priced to yield 4.849% which was 1.70 percentage points over 30-year Treasury rates. Ohio State was established in 1870, has 64,077 enrolled students, and a campus of more than 1,700 acres with 457 buildings. Two private universities, Massachusetts Institute of Technology (MIT) and the University of Southern California, had issued century bonds earlier that year. Typically, universities such as Ohio State issue 30-year tax-free bonds with fixed or floating interest rates. Public and private universities are tax-exempt institutions but the income from century bonds is taxable to the buyer. What are the likely economic advantages to Ohio State of issuing century bonds?

5. Suppose that Safra Republic issued its $250 million of millennium bonds on January 1, 1998, at a market yield of 7.125%, the same as the stated interest rate. Assume that the bonds pay interest just once a year, on December 31. What is the issue price of these bonds, and how much of that price comes from the present value of interest payments?

6. Suppose that Safra Republic were a U.S. company paying taxes at a 40% rate. In present value terms, how much of a tax savings does the company receive from its millennium bonds? How much of a tax savings would be lost if only the first 40 years of interest deductions were allowed?

7. Suppose that the millennium bonds were issued with a 7.125% stated interest rate when the market yield rate was 8.125%. What would the issue price be? How about if the market yield were 6.125%?

8. In early 1997, the U.S. Treasury Department proposed eliminating the corporate tax deduction for interest paid on the last 60 years of century bonds (see "Is the Party Over for
100-Year Bonds?" *The Wall Street Journal,* February 4, 1997). The Treasury argued that
100-year debt should be treated the same as equity because the bonds are more like permanent capital. Since stock dividend payments can't be deducted from taxable corporate
earnings, the Treasury said, interest payments on the last 60 years of 100-year debt
shouldn't be deducted either. Why would the Treasury department be opposed to unlimited interest deductions on century and millennium bonds? According to U.S. GAAP, are
these securities debt or equity?

Tuesday Morning Corporation operates a chain of discount retail stores. The company purchases closeout merchandise at prices generally ranging from 10% to 50% of the normal
wholesale price and sells the merchandise at prices that are 50% to 80% lower than retail
prices generally charged by department and specialty stores.

The following is information taken from a recent Tuesday Morning annual report.

CII-2

Tuesday Morning Corpora-
tion: Interpreting long-term
debt disclosures   **(LO 6)**

Note 5: Mortgages on Property, Plant, and Equipment

($ in thousands)	Year 2	Year 1
Industrial development bond, payable in quarterly installments of $108 plus interest at 91.656% of prime (not to exceed 15%), maturing March 31, Year 6	$1,401	$1,834
Payable to bank, payable in quarterly installments of $104 plus interest at LIBOR plus 2.50%, maturing September 30, Year 5, with remaining principal due at that time	4,504	4,920
Payable to bank, payable in quarterly installments of $112 plus interest at LIBOR plus 2.50% through October 15, Year 2, with the remaining principal and interest due April 30, Year 3	1,794	2,243

In connection with these mortgages, the Company is required to maintain minimum net worth and comply with other financial covenants, including a restriction limiting loans to officers to less than
$2,000,000. At December 31, Year 2, the Company is in compliance with these covenants.

The $1,794,000 note payable to bank due on April 30, Year 3, is classified as a current liability at
December 31, Year 2. The aggregate maturities of mortgages are as follows ($ in thousands):

Year	Amount
Year 3	$2,747
Year 4	849
Year 5	4,003
Year 6	100

Consolidated Balance Sheet

($ in thousands)	Year 2	Year 1
Current liabilities:		
Current installments on mortgages	$ 2,747	$ 1,402
Current installments on capital lease obligation	607	–0–
Accounts payable	12,916	15,859
Accrued sales tax	1,574	1,760
Other accrued expenses	1,945	3,118
Deferred income taxes	303	146
Due to officer	–0–	599
Income taxes payable	988	–0–
Total current liabilities	$21,080	$22,884

Consolidated Statement of Cash Flows

($ in thousands)	Year 2	Year 1
Cash flows from financing activities:		
Net increase (decrease) in notes payable	$ –0–	$ (3,500)
Principal payments on mortgages	(1,298)	(1,194)
Principal payments under capital lease obligation	(214)	–0–
Proceeds from common stock offering	–0–	–0–
Proceeds from exercise of common stock options	255	145
Repurchase of common stock	–0–	(3,383)
Net cash provided by (used in) financing activities	$ (1,257)	$ (7,932)

Required:

1. What was the *current portion* of Tuesday Morning's mortgage payable at the end of Year 1?

2. How much did Tuesday Morning pay in cash to reduce its mortgage payable during Year 2?

3. Explain the difference between your answer to requirement 1 and your answer to requirement 2.

4. What are the components of the current portion of the mortgage payable as of the end of Year 2?

5. Assume that the next quarterly installment on the industrial development bond is due on March 31, Year 3. Prepare a journal entry to record the installment payment and any interest. Assume that the effective interest rate for the bond is 14% per year.

6. The company has a mortgage note payable for $1,794,000 that comes due on April 30, Year 3. Suppose that this note is paid by the signing of a new 14% note for the amount due. Prepare the April 30, Year 3, journal entry to record this refinancing of the old note.

7. Instead of refinancing the note, suppose the company pays the principal along with any remaining interest on April 30, Year 3. Prepare a journal entry to record this cash payment.

CI1-3

Groupe Casino: Determining whether it is debt or equity
(LO 10)

Groupe Casino is a French multinational company that operates more than 9,000 multiformat retail stores—hypermarkets, supermarkets, discount stores, convenience stores, and restaurants—throughout the world. In January 2005, Casino issued €600 million of undated deeply subordinated fixed-to-CMS-floating-rate notes at a price of 101. The offering circular described certain aspects of the notes as follows:

Deeply Subordinated Obligations

The Notes are deeply subordinated obligations of the Issuer and are the most junior debt instruments of the Issuer, subordinated to and ranking behind the claims of all other unsubordinated and subordinated creditors of the Issuer.

Undated Securities

The Notes are undated securities, with no specified maturity date. The Issuer is under no obligation to redeem the Notes at any time. The Noteholders have no right to require redemption of the Notes, except if a judgment is issued for the judicial liquidation (*liquidation judiciaire*) of the Issuer or, following an order of *redressement judiciaire,* the sale of the whole of the business (*cession totale de l'enterprise*) of the Issuer, or in the event of the voluntary dissolution of the Issuer or if the Issuer is liquidated for any other reason.

Interest Interruption

The Issuer has the option to decide not to pay interest on the Notes on any Interest Payment Date if, during the 12-months period preceding such Interest Payment Date, it has not paid or declared any dividend on its Equity Securities and provided it has not made, during any such period, any payments on (including *inter alia* by way of redemption, purchase or redemption of) any Equity Securities. The interest payment provisions of the Notes are non-cumulative. Accordingly, any interest not paid on the Notes as a result of the valid exercise by the Issuer of such option will be forfeited and accordingly will no longer be due and payable by the Issuer.

No Voting Rights
The Notes are nonvoting.

No Prior Market for the Notes; Resale Restrictions
There is no existing market for the Notes, and there can be no assurance that any market will develop for the Notes or that holders of the Notes will be able to sell their Notes in the secondary market.

Interest Rate
The coupon on the Notes for each Floating Rate Interest Period is linked to the 10-year Constant Maturity Swap (CMS 10), the annual rate for euro interest rate swap transactions with a maturity of 10 years. The CMS 10 is a variable rate and as such is not pre-defined for the lifespan of the Notes; conversely it allows investors to follow market changes with an instrument reflecting changes in the levels of yields. Higher rates mean a higher coupon and lower rates mean a lower coupon.

In summary, the floating-rate notes:

- Are Casino's undated perpetual obligations in that they have no maturity date and the lender (investor) cannot force redemption.
- Pay interest at fixed and floating rates, but Casino may "interrupt" interest payments at any time and for any reason and the lender has no claim to interrupted interest payments.
- Do not confer voting rights to the investor, nor are they convertible into shares of common or preferred stock of Casino or any other company.

Required:
1. Casino management intends to treat the notes as equity instruments for financial reporting purposes in accordance with International Financial Reporting Standards (IFRS). What specific IFRS guidance helps accountants and auditors distinguish between liabilities and equities?
2. Do you concur with management's decision to treat the notes as equity instruments? Why?
3. Suppose the notes are issued on January 1, 2005, that the first year's interest rate is 5%, and that interest is paid on December 31 of each year. Prepare the journal entries Casino would use to record (a) issuance of the notes on January 1, 2005, (b) interest expense for the year, and (c) the cash interest payment on December 31, 2005. Income tax considerations may be ignored. Use an 8% interest rate for these journal entries.
4. The notes were issued at a price of 101, which is a slight premium over the face value. What "red flags" does this issue price raise?

The cereal division of Kellogg Company intends to test market next year an organic corn-based cereal to be called NutriFlakes^TR. The business plan calls for production to begin in late May 2015, with retail store delivery starting in early June. Annie Gleason, the marketing brand manager with overall responsibility for the product, has identified 15 metropolitan areas in the upper Midwest of the United States where organic foods already capture a large share of the consumer wallet.

NutriFlakes^TR will be manufactured and distributed using existing technologies and facilities. Kellogg's has entered into long-term contracts for organic corn with producers located in close proximity to these manufacturing sites. The contracts specify the amount (in bushels) of organic corn to be delivered at each site monthly from May through December 2015, when the market test ends. The price to be paid by Kellogg's is not contractually specified, but will instead be determined by market conditions at the time of delivery.

C11-4

Kellogg Company's organic corn hedge **(LO 9)**

Kellogg's is not the first company to offer consumers an organic corn-based breakfast cereal. Organic corn flake cereals available currently in the designated test markets sell at the retail level for between $10 and $14 per 11 oz. box. The NutriFlakes^TR business plan calls for the retailer to pay Kellogg's $9 for each 11 oz. box. The retailer then adds a $5 markup and the consumer pays $14 per box. Gleason believes that Kellogg's strong brand awareness and reputation for high-quality, nutritional breakfast products justifies the high-end price point for NutriFlakes^TR. Gleason's business plan calls for the wholesale price to remain constant for the duration of the test market.

Two features of the NutriFlakes^TR business plan expose Kellogg's to the financial risk that organic corn prices might increase substantially during the test market production run: (1) Kellogg's will receive a fixed dollar amount ($9) for each box of NutriFlakes^TR sold, but (2) must pay the corn grower a price that is only determined upon delivery. There is no organized market for organic corn—buyers such as Kellogg's must negotiate price and other contract terms directly with each local grower. There is, however, an active market for traditional (nonorganic) corn at the Chicago Board of Trade (CBT) where standardized futures contracts for common corn are traded on a daily basis. Briefly, each corn futures contract entails:

- The right to take delivery of 5,000 bushels ($\approx$127 metric tons) of common corn at a pre-designated location. To put this amount in perspective, a typical railroad grain car can hold between 3,200 and 3,500 U.S. bushels depending on the kernel size and weight.

- Delivery occurs on the second business day following the last trading day of the delivery month. This means that the buyer of a December 2014 contract either must accept delivery of the 5,000 bushels on Thursday, January 3, 2015, or sell (cancel) the contract before the close of trading on December 31, 2014.

- Costs of transporting the corn from the designated delivery location to the buyer's facilities are not included in the quoted CBT contract price and are the responsibility of the buyer.

- The price of a contract is quoted in cents per bushel; e.g., a price of say "743" is understood to mean $7.43 per bushel or $37,150 per contract.

Large fluctuations in common corn production can occur from one year to the next. Consequently, corn futures contract prices on the CBT tend to be quite volatile during the growing and harvesting season, which for the upper Midwest is May through October. One important factor contributing to this volatility is the unpredictability of weather during the growing and harvesting season and its impact on corn production.

The corporate finance group at Kellogg's has decided to hedge its exposure to fluctuations in the price of organic corn needed for NutriFlakes^TR by purchasing several common corn futures contracts on the CBT. These futures contracts are "matched" in bushel amount and delivery month to the amount and timing of organic corn required for the NutriFlakes^TR test market production run. The following table provides information about several transactions related to the company's purchase of organic corn and to this hedge:

Date	Description	Dollar amount
3/31/2015	"Matched" contracts purchased on CBT exchange	$3,200,000
4/30/2015	Fair value of "matched" contracts	$3,500,000
5/31/2015	Accepted delivery of 50,000 bushels of organic corn at the prevailing (negotiated) market price	$ 445,000
	Sold the May 2015 delivery futures contract*	$ 420,000
	Fair value of remaining "matched" contracts	$3,800,000

---

*The May 2015 contract was purchased on March 31 for $371,500. The contract's fair value on April 30 was $420,000.

Required:

1. Explain why Kellogg's corn price hedge is only partially effective?

2. Explain why the Kellogg hedge qualifies for special GAAP "hedge accounting" treatment by describing the eligible market risk being hedged, the required accounting approach (fair value hedge, cash flow hedge, or foreign-currency hedge), and why that accounting treatment is appropriate. You should assume that the hedge is sufficiently effective to qualify for GAAP hedge accounting treatment.

3. Prepare general journal entries to reflect the purchase of the "matched" CBT corn futures contracts on March 31, 2015, and the fair value of those contracts on April 30.

4. Prepare general journal entries to reflect the May 31 transactions and events.

5. Explain in words and numbers the economic benefit (if any) of the hedge to Kellogg over the period from March 31 through May 31.

6. Suppose corn futures prices (and thus the hedge fair value) had moved in the direction opposite to that shown in the table. Explain in words the economic cost (if any) of the hedge to Kellogg over the same period.

The following article raises questions about Cardinal Health's accounting for an expected legal settlement. Management responded to the accusations by sending a letter to all shareholders and to analysts who covered the firm.

C11-5

Cardinal Health: Contingent receivables **(LO 7)**

CARDINAL HEALTH'S ACCOUNTING RAISES SOME QUESTIONS

It's a cardinal rule of accounting: Don't count your chickens before they hatch. Yet new disclosures in Cardinal Health Inc.'s latest annual report suggest that is what the drug wholesaler has done not just once, but twice, independent accounting specialists say.

As the disclosures show, Cardinal recorded $22 million of an expected legal settlement with certain vitamin manufacturers that it had accused of overcharging for products—in advance of an actual settlement. Specifically, Cardinal recorded a $10 million pre-tax gain, as well as a corresponding receivable on its balance sheet, during its December 2000 quarter. It recorded a further $12 million gain during the quarter ended Sept. 30, 2001, after concluding that its minimum future recovery would be that much bigger.

Cardinal, which says it has done nothing improper, did reach a $35.3 million settlement in the vitamin antitrust litigation last spring. The company recorded the remaining $13.3 million during the final quarter of its past fiscal year, ended June 30.

To those unfamiliar with accounting rules, the posting of the two initial sums might not raise obvious questions. Yet even first-year accounting students are taught this: Under generally accepted accounting principles, companies aren't supposed to record expected gains as current income until they

are certain the gains will be realized. When it comes to litigation settlements, that means waiting until an actual settlement agreement has been reached with a party that is able to pay, independent accounting specialists say.

Now consider this twist: Had Cardinal not recorded the two initial gains when it did, it would have fallen short of Wall Street analysts' earnings targets by two cents a share for both the December 2000 and September 2001 quarters; Cardinal's earnings met analysts' targets for each of the quarters. Cardinal didn't disclose the size of the gains until September 2002, when it filed its latest annual report.

"That's abracadabra accounting," says Walter Schuetze, a former chief accountant for the Securities and Exchange Commission. "Cardinal should not have recognized a receivable and a gain until June 2002." Before then, "it was all a matter of speculation," he says, adding, "Cardinal's actions explain what is meant by the term earnings management. This is diddling the numbers." . . .

"Cardinal Health is absolutely confident in our accounting and report practices and our adherence to high ethical standards," Mr. Miller [Cardinal's chief financial officer] says. "With regard to GAAP and SEC regulations, we are in full compliance in all material respects." . . .

CARDINAL HEALTH

A Note from Steve Fischbach, VP Investor Relations

I wanted to make sure all of our investors and analysts received some information that responds to today's *Wall Street Journal* Heard on the Street article titled "Cardinal Health's Accounting Raises a Number of Questions." . . .

Here are the facts:

As we have explained to the reporter, this item was not a recording of a contingent gain under *SFAS 5*. The recoveries that Cardinal Health recorded related to vendor overcharges in our vitamin business were based on the virtual certainty of the recovery as supported by numerous external factors.

The reporter questioned the timing of two items recorded by the company ($10 million in the second quarter of fiscal year 2001 and $12 million in the first quarter of fiscal year 2002) related to the vitamin overcharge situation. This event was the recognition of an asset related to recoveries for vendor overcharges, based on the following five factors:

1. Vendors had admitted overcharging and plead guilty in a criminal proceeding. In prior periods Cardinal Health was in fact overcharged by those vendors and those charges were reflected in prior periods as higher cost of sales.

2. Vendors had settled with a number of plaintiffs, based on their admission of guilt.

3. Vendors were all major pharmaceutical companies with a clear ability to pay.

4. Issue was not "if" we would recover, but "how much."

5. Quantification of the amount of recovery that was virtually certain was supported by written legal opinions from independent outside legal counsel that served as substantial audit evidence.

As it turned out, Cardinal Health received over $120 million from the defendants in the case which exceeded what was actually recorded by over $100 million. That is a very important point because it demonstrates the conservatism with which Cardinal Health dealt with the issue. . . .

Source: Cardinal Health Letter to Shareholders (April 2, 2003).

Required:

1. Are the GAAP rules for recognizing contingent gains (and a corresponding receivable) the same or different from those for recognizing contingent losses (and a corresponding liability)? Consult FASB ASC Topic 450 Contingencies.

2. In view of the details outlined in Cardinal Health's letter to analysts and investors, do you believe the company fully complied with FASB ASC Topic 450 as it pertains to recognizing contingent gains? Why or why not?

3. If asked, how might management respond to questions about the timing of the gain recognition in 2001 and 2002?

4. Suppose that management was intent on informing analysts and investors about an expected litigation settlement amount. How might this be done in situations where GAAP precludes recognizing the gain on the financial statements?

.mhhe.com/revsine6e

Remember to check the book's companion website for additional study material.

Financial Reporting for Leases | 12

> "Humans have three basic needs: food, shelter, and . . . keeping debt off the balance sheet."
>
> —Author unknown

A *lease* is a contract in which the owner of an asset—the **lessor**—conveys to another party—the **lessee**—the right to use that asset. This right is granted in exchange for a fee—the **lease payment**—that is usually paid in installments. The lessor typically retains legal title to the asset, which reverts to the lessor at the end of the lease term. The asset's expected fair value at the end of the lease is the **residual value.** The duration of a lease may be short, such as a one-week car rental agreement, or long, such as a 20-year lease for retail space in a shopping center.

At its inception, a lease is a **mutually unperformed contract.** This means that neither party to the lease arrangement has yet performed all of the duties called for in the contract. For example, the lessor has an obligation to provide the lessee with the right to use the asset for the entire duration of the lease; in exchange, the lessee has an obligation to pay the stipulated periodic fee to the lessor during the lease term. When the lease contract is first signed, the right to use the asset has not been provided, nor have the required periodic contract payments been made. As you will see, the accounting for these unperformed contracts is controversial.

EVOLUTION OF LEASE ACCOUNTING

Before the issuance of pre-Codification *Statement of Financial Accounting Standards (SFAS) No. 13,* virtually all leases were accounted for using the **operating lease** approach.[1]

The following example illustrates the operating lease approach.

> Crest Company owns a building with a $200,000 book value. It leases this building to Iris Company under a five-year lease for a monthly rental of $2,000, which is to be paid at the end of each month.

[1] "Accounting for Leases," *SFAS No. 13* (Stamford, CT: Financial Accounting Standards Board [FASB], 1976). This standard as amended by subsequent literature is contained under the FASB Accounting Standards Codification (ASC) Topic 840.

LEARNING OBJECTIVES

After studying this chapter, you will understand:

1. The structure of a lease.
2. Lessees' incentives to keep leases off the balance sheet.
3. The criteria used to classify leases on the lessee's books.
4. The financial statement effects of executory costs, residual values, purchase options, and other aspects of lease contracts.
5. The effects of capital lease versus operating lease treatment on lessees' financial statements.
6. That lessors also classify leases either as capital leases or as operating leases, but that their reporting incentives are very different from those of lessees.
7. The difference among sales-type, direct financing, and operating lease treatment by lessors and the criteria for choosing the accounting treatment.
8. How the different lessor accounting treatments can affect income and net asset balances.
9. Sale/leaseback arrangements and other special leasing considerations.
10. The key differences between current GAAP and IFRS requirements for lease accounting and the changes proposed by the FASB and the IASB.
11. How to use financial statement disclosures to estimate the financial statement effects of treating operating leases as capital leases.

Upon signing the lease, Iris Company, the lessee, makes no entry on its books. The accounting here conforms to the legal structure of lease arrangements. Because lease contracts typically do not convey title, the asset remains on the lessor's books and no asset is reflected on the lessee's books. Furthermore, under the operating lease approach, the lessee does not immediately record as a liability the stream of future payments specified in the contract. No liability is recorded because the lessee is not legally obligated to make the payments until the lessor performs the duties specified in the contract. Because these are mutually unperformed contracts—sometimes called **executory** contracts—accounting entries are made over time in piecemeal fashion only as partial performance under the contract takes place. *As each party performs its respective duties, that portion of the contract that has been performed is no longer considered executory and is accordingly recognized in the financial records.*

Each month, as Crest performs its part of the agreement by making the premises available to Iris Company, Iris accrues a liability for that portion of the contract that has been performed:

DR	Rent expense	$2,000	
	CR Lease liability		$2,000

Upon payment of the stipulated rental fee at month-end, Iris makes the following entry:

DR	Lease liability	$2,000	
	CR Cash		$2,000

> In practice, the accrual for the lease liability is seldom made. Instead, only one entry is made at the time of cash payment:
>
> | | | | |
> |---|---|---|---|
> | **DR** | Rent expense | $2,000 | |
> | | **CR** Cash | | $2,000 |

Iris records no liability on its books for *future* rental payments—neither at the signing of the lease nor afterward. The reason is that these future rental payments are contingent upon future performance by Crest, the lessor. The stipulated payments do not become a liability to Iris under the operating lease approach until time passes and performance takes place.

Similarly, Crest, the lessor, would make no entry on its books at the time this operating lease was signed. However, as piecemeal performance takes place month-by-month and it receives payment, Crest makes the following entry on its books:

DR	Cash	$2,000	
	CR Rental revenue		$2,000

Because the building remains an asset on Crest's books, periodic depreciation is also recorded:

DR	Depreciation expense—leased building	$XXX	
	CR Accumulated depreciation—leased building		$XXX

 RECAP

The operating lease approach conforms to the legal structure of lease arrangements. Journal entries are made piecemeal over time as partial performance takes place.

Why Lessees Like the Operating Lease Method

Lessees prefer the operating lease approach for lease accounting. One obvious reason is that this method doesn't reflect the cumulative liability for all future lease payments on the lessee's balance sheet. Instead, only a portion of the obligation gets accrued piecemeal as partial performance takes place under the lease. The phrase **off-balance sheet financing** is used to reflect the fact that the lessee has financed the acquisition of asset services without recognizing a liability on the financial statement.

As we will show you, GAAP requires *note* disclosure of the lessee's future cash outflows arising from operating leases. And because reasonably informed financial decision makers do read financial statement disclosures, the liability isn't really "hidden." Nevertheless, it is easy to envision circumstances in which lessees would be better off by using the operating lease method. To see how they are made better off, recall that many contracts are linked to financial statement numbers. One example is bank lending agreements that contain **covenants**—safety measures to protect banks against the borrower's financial deterioration. Because most covenants are based on financial statement numbers—not on note numbers—keeping liabilities off the balance sheet may convey benefits to borrowers even if the liabilities aren't hidden in a real sense. For example, the numerator of the lessee's debt-to-equity ratio is unaffected at the inception of an operating lease because no liability is recorded on signing. Keeping the liability off the balance sheet strengthens the debt-to-equity ratio. The off-balance-sheet liability reduces the likelihood that the lessee-borrower will violate a debt-to-equity loan covenant.

 **Contracting**

Furthermore, some lessees believe that omitting the lease liability improves their ability to obtain *future* credit. Keeping the lease liability off the books lowers reported leverage. Lenders use leverage ratios as a rule of thumb in assessing borrowing capacity—that means the amount that can safely be borrowed. Supposedly, the lower the firm's reported leverage, the greater is that firm's perceived borrowing capacity.

Lessees also like the operating lease accounting method because it keeps the leased *asset* off the balance sheet. Certain long-term leases give lessees the *exclusive* right to use assets for most of their economic life. Nevertheless, despite the "ownershiplike" property rights conveyed to the lessee, there is no balance sheet asset recorded with operating leases.

Keeping leased assets off the books produces a favorable impact on the lessee's financial statements that is just as substantial as the benefit that arises from omitting lease liabilities. Consider an airline that leases a portion of its aircraft fleet and accounts for the leases using the operating lease method. The leased aircraft generate gross revenues and net profits just as the owned aircraft do. However, not reporting the leased aircraft as assets under the operating lease approach understates assets in some profitability and turnover ratios. Sales generated by the leased assets will appear in the numerator of the total asset turnover ratio, but the leased assets will not appear in the denominator. The net effect increases the ratio.

 **Analysis**

Investors and others use asset-based ratios to evaluate a firm's performance. The operating lease method makes the leverage and turnover ratios for companies that lease a significant portion of their assets *appear* to be more favorable than the corresponding ratios for companies that own their assets outright. (See the example illustrated in the appendix to this chapter.)

The Securities and Exchange Commission's Initiative

Throughout the 1960s, leasing became an important financing vehicle for three reasons. First, leasing provided firms the opportunity to use assets without expending the entire cash purchase price. Second, if the leased asset became technologically obsolete, the lessee could simply lease a newer model. Third, leasing allowed the lessor and lessee to optimize tax incentives and subsidies for capital investments.[2] But the virtually exclusive use of the operating lease approach was criticized, especially by the Securities and Exchange Commission (SEC) because it believed that this accounting approach did not portray the economics of many leasing transactions.

The SEC issued *Accounting Series Release (ASR) No. 147* in 1973 to improve financial reporting for leases.[3] The SEC took what is called a **property rights** approach to lease accounting. This approach views leases as conveying property rights in the asset to the lessee and the payment stream as representing the lessee's liability. Following this accounting method, the lessee records both an asset and a liability on its books equal to the present value of future lease payments when a lease is signed:

DR	Leased asset (to reflect the property right the lessee now has in the asset)	$XXX
	CR Lease obligation (to reflect the liability arising from the future lease payments)	$XXX

This is called the **capital lease** approach because the lessee capitalizes the lease (i.e., puts it on the balance sheet). However, *ASR No. 147* emphasized disclosure and thus stopped short of requiring balance sheet recognition of leases that conveyed property rights. The FASB soon extended and embellished the SEC property rights approach, as we discuss next.

Figure 12.1 provides an overview of the two different lease accounting approaches.

LESSEE ACCOUNTING

Under FASB Accounting Standards Codification Topic 840 (ASC 840), leases that transfer **substantially all** of the benefits and risks of ownership *must* be treated as capital leases. Consequently, a lease asset and a lease liability appear on the lessee's balance sheet. ASC 840 provides specific criteria for assessing "substantially all." Leases not meeting the criteria *cannot* be capitalized. Noncapitalized leases are called **operating leases** and are accounted for using the procedures we described earlier.

FASB ASC 840 Criteria for Capital Lease Treatment

If, at its inception, a lease satisfies *any one or more* of the following criteria, it must be treated as a capital lease on the lessee's books.

1. The lease transfers ownership of the asset to the lessee by the end of the lease term.
2. The lease contains a bargain purchase option.
3. The noncancelable lease term is 75% or more of the estimated economic life of the leased asset.
4. The present value of the minimum lease payments equals or exceeds 90% of the current fair value of the leased asset.

Each criterion represents a situation under which property rights in the leased asset have been transferred to the lessee. The transfer of property rights is easily seen in criterion (1). If a

---

[2] See M. H. Miller and C. W. Upton, "Leasing, Buying, and the Cost of Capital Services," *The Journal of Finance,* June 1976, pp. 761–86.

[3] "Notice of Adoption of Amendments to Regulations S-X Requiring Improved Disclosure of Leases," *ASR No. 147* (Washington, DC: SEC, 1973).

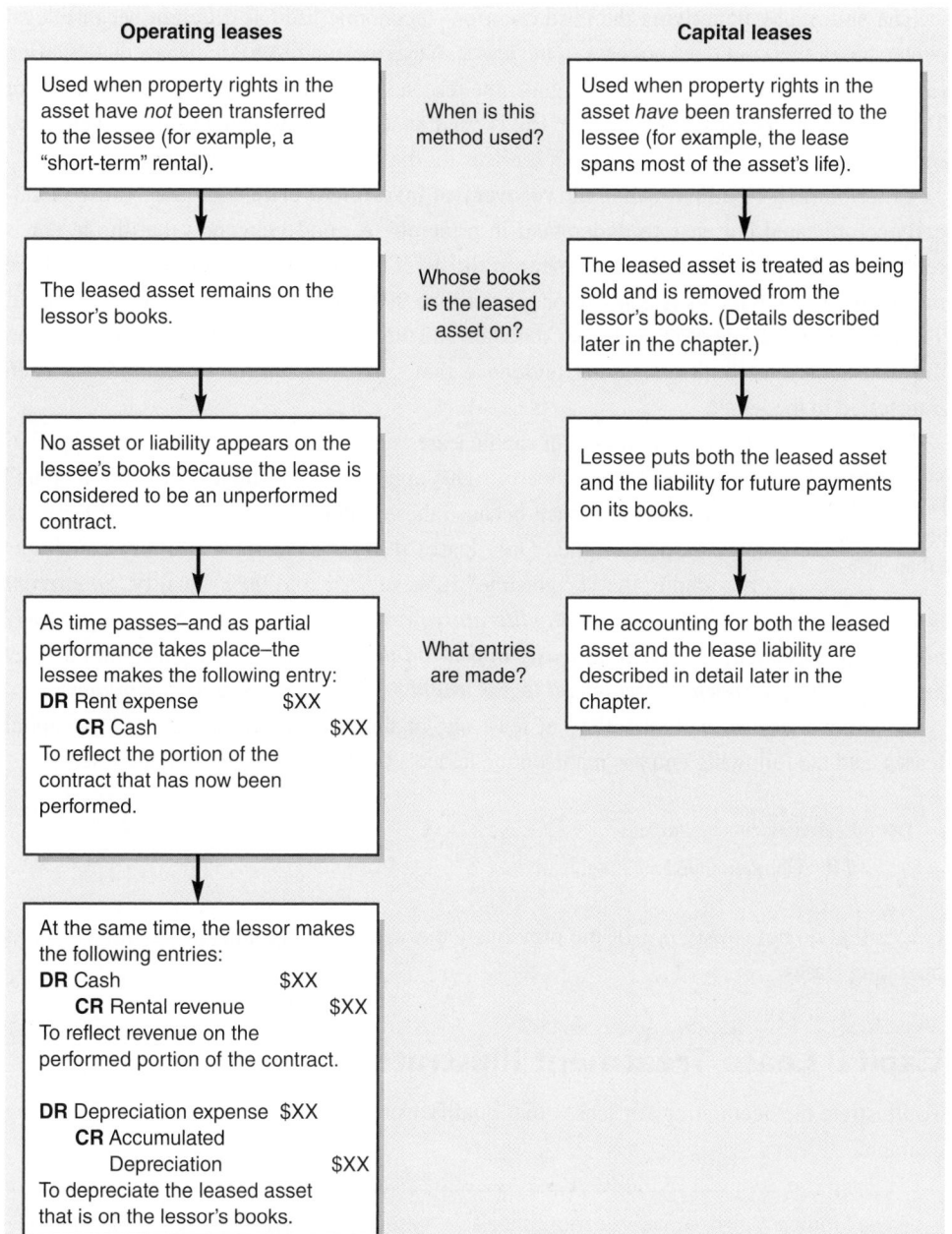

Figure 12.1

DIFFERENCES BETWEEN OPERATING AND CAPITAL LEASES

lease transfers ownership, title to the asset will eventually pass to the lessee, and the FASB requires that the accounting method conform to the substance of the transaction—an install-ment purchase—rather than to its legal form—a long-term rental agreement. Similarly, in lease arrangements in which a **bargain purchase option**[4] exists—criterion (2)—there is a strong probability the lessee will exercise the option and obtain ownership. These two criteria represent instances in which ownership will likely transfer, thus conveying significant prop-erty rights in the leased asset. This is the reason GAAP requires that such leases be treated as capital leases.

---

[4] FASB ASC 840-10-20 (Glossary, **Bargain Purchase Option**) defines *bargain* as a price that is low enough that the purchase is "reasonably assured." For example, the lessee may have a purchase option of $1,000 for an asset that is expected to be worth $10,000 at the end of the lease term. The lessor and the lessee determine whether a purchase option is a bargain at the beginning of the lease. Subsequent price changes do not change the initial determination.

The philosophy underlying the third criterion—economic life—is different because legal ownership of the asset does not pass to the lessee. Nevertheless, GAAP indicates that criterion (3) also conveys significant property rights. The reason is that the *right to use* a leased asset for 75% or more of its expected economic life is *itself* an asset—a valuable property right representing an exclusive claim to the asset's services for the preponderance of its benefit period.

Criterion (4), sometimes called the **recovery of investment criterion,** is the most technically complicated but easy to understand in principle. A good indication that the lessor is recovering virtually all of the investment in the asset occurs when the present value of the minimum lease payments is equal to or greater than 90% of the fair value of the asset itself. The relative magnitude of the payment schedule and the willingness of the lessee to engage in the transaction are both considered evidence that substantial property rights have been transferred to the lessee.

> For example, criterion (4) is triggered if a lessee leases an asset with a fair value of $100,000 and agrees to a payment stream whose present value is $93,000 because $93,000 is more than 90% of $100,000.

These four criteria for capital leases suggest that the FASB has moved part of the way toward the property rights approach. Nevertheless, it is not a "pure" property rights approach because these criteria do not consider *all* leases to convey property rights. Only leases that satisfy certain arbitrary conditions (for example, the "bright-line" rules of 75% and 90%) qualify. *So current authoritative accounting literature presents a compromise between the operating lease approach, for which no leases appear on the lessee's balance sheet, and a strict property rights approach, for which all leases would be shown as assets and liabilities.*

To summarize, leases that satisfy at least one of the four criteria are treated as capital leases, and the following entry is made on the lessee's books at the inception of the lease:

DR	Leased asset—capital lease	$XXX
CR	Obligation under capital lease	$XXX

Leases that do not satisfy *any* of the previously discussed criteria must be accounted for as operating leases.

Capital Lease Treatment Illustrated

To illustrate the accounting for leases that qualify as capital leases, consider the following example.

> Lessee Company signs a five-year noncancelable lease with Lessor Company on January 1, 2014, when the lease begins. Several other facts pertain to the lease:
>
> 1. The lease calls for five payments of $79,139.18 to be made at the end of each year.[5]
> 2. The leased asset has a fair value of $315,041.60 on January 1, 2014.
> 3. The lease has no renewal option, and possession of the asset reverts to the lessor on January 1, 2019.
> 4. Lessee Company regularly uses the straight-line method to depreciate assets of this type that it owns.
> 5. The leased asset has an expected economic life of six years.

---

[5] Lessees often make **monthly** rental payments at the *beginning* of the period instead of annually at the end of the period as is the case in this example. We use end of period annual payments in many of our examples to build on discussions of amortization schedules contained in Chapters 8 and 11 and to facilitate discussions of financial statement effects by year. In a later section, we discuss how to modify amortization tables for beginning of period payments. The end of chapter materials use both beginning of period and end of period payments.

Because the five-year lease term covers more than 75% of the asset's six-year expected economic life (5/6 = 83.3%), this lease must be treated as a capital lease, following criterion (3). Thus, Lessee Company must recognize both an asset and a liability on its books.

But what is the asset and liability dollar amount that should be recorded? ASC 840 requires that the dollar amount be equal to the discounted present value of the **minimum lease payments** specified in the lease. Contingent rentals are ignored. The discount rate used to determine the present value is the *lower* of the lessee's incremental borrowing rate[6] or the lessor's rate of return implicit in the lease.[7] If the lessee can't determine the lessor's rate of return, the lessee uses the incremental borrowing rate.

Assume that Lessee Company's incremental borrowing rate is 10% and the lessee can't determine the lessor's implicit rate of return on the lease. The discount rate is accordingly 10%, and the present value of the minimum lease payments in our example is:

> *Minimum lease payments* are defined as the noncontingent, fixed payments specified in the lease agreement. For example, if the payment schedule called for a fixed fee of $79,139.18 per year plus an additional fee of five cents per unit for each unit manufactured using the leased asset, only the $79,139.18 would be included in the computation of minimum lease payments. The five cents per unit for each unit manufactured is *a contingent rental that is ignored in the calculation.* In more complicated leases, the minimum lease payments also include:
>
> 1. The amount of any **residual value guarantee** by the lessee (as discussed later).
> 2. Any penalties that must be paid if the lessee chooses not to renew the lease.
> 3. The amount of any bargain purchase option payment if the lease contains a bargain purchase option.

Present value of minimum lease payments		Minimum lease payment	×	Present value factor for an ordinary annuity for five years at 10%
$300,000	=	$79,139.18	×	3.79079 (from this book's Appendix, Present Value Tables, Table 2)

On January 1, 2014, at the inception of the lease, Lessee Company makes the following entry:

DR Leased asset—capital lease $300,000
    CR Obligation under capital lease $300,000

It is important to understand that the amount shown for the asset and the amount shown for the related liability ($300,000) are equal only at the inception of the lease. Thereafter, as the term of the lease progresses, the amount in the asset account will equal the amount in the liability account only by sheer coincidence. The reason that the two amounts will differ subsequently is that the asset account will be reduced in accordance with Lessee Company's depreciation schedule for assets of this type, whereas the liability account is reduced in accordance with the payment schedule contained in the lease. The asset account and liability account are reduced at independent—and usually different—rates over the life of the lease. (A later section illustrates the effect of these different reduction rates on the carrying value of the lease asset and liability.)

Each lease payment of $79,139.18 consists of two elements. One represents interest on the present value of the obligation that was outstanding during the year. The other represents a

> The lease also meets criterion (4) because 90% of the asset's $315,041.60 fair value equals $283,537, and the present value of the minimum lease payments ($300,000) is greater than $283,537.

---

[6] FASB ASC 840-10-20 (Glossary) defines the lessee's **incremental borrowing rate** as the rate that the lessee "would have incurred to borrow over a similar term the funds necessary to purchase the leased asset."

[7] The **interest rate implicit in the lease** is the pre-tax internal yield on the lease contract (that is, the rate that equates the fair value of the asset and the present value of the payments). See FASB ASC 840-20-10 (Glossary, Interest rate implicit in the lease).

EXHIBIT 12.1	Lessee Company: Amortization Schedule—Effective Interest Method

Date	(a) Total Payment	(b) Interest Expense*	(c) Principal Reduction†	(d) Lease Obligation Balance	(e) Depreciation of Asset	(f) Total Annual Capital Lease Expense (Col. [b] + Col. [e])
1/1/14				$300,000.00		
12/31/14	$ 79,139.18	$30,000.00	$ 49,139.18	250,860.82	$ 60,000.00	$ 90,000.00
12/31/15	79,139.18	25,086.08	54,053.10	196,807.72	60,000.00	85,086.08
12/31/16	79,139.18	19,680.77	59,458.41	137,349.31	60,000.00	79,680.77
12/31/17	79,139.18	13,734.93	65,404.25	71,945.06	60,000.00	73,734.93
12/31/18	79,139.18	7,194.12‡	71,945.06	—	60,000.00	67,194.12
	$395,695.90	$95,695.90	$300,000.00	$ –0–	$300,000.00	$395,695.90

* Column (d) for preceding year times 10%.
† Column (a) minus Column (b).
‡ Rounded.

repayment of a portion of the principal amount of the obligation. FASB ASC 840 requires that the interest and principal repayment portions of each $79,139.18 outflow be measured using the **effective interest method.** The amortization schedule in Exhibit 12.1 shows this break-down in Column (b), Interest Expense, and Column (c), Principal Reduction. For example, the $79,139.18 payment made on December 31, 2014, consists of a $30,000 interest component and a $49,139.18 principal payment component. The schedule is similar to the ones used for notes receivable (Chapter 8) and bonds (Chapter 11).

On December 31, 2014, Lessee Company records both the $79,139.18 cash payment (Column [a]) and the depreciation of the capitalized leased asset (Column [e]). Based on the figures in Exhibit 12.1, the entries are:

DR	Obligation under capital lease	$49,139.18
DR	Interest expense	30,000.00
CR	Cash	$79,139.18
DR	Depreciation expense—capital lease	$60,000.00
CR	Accumulated depreciation—capital lease	$60,000.00

If a lease meets either the first or second capital lease criterion, the leased asset is depreciated over the *asset's* life because the asset's legal title ultimately passes to the lessee. If the lease is a capital lease because it meets either the third or fourth criterion but not the first or second criterion, it is depreciated over the *lease's* life because the asset reverts to the lessor at lease-end. In Exhibit 12.1, the asset is depreciated over five years because it qualified under both the third and fourth criteria but not the first or second criterion.

The amount of interest expense recognized each year equals 10% (the discount rate) times the present value of the obligation outstanding at the start of the year. Because the present value of the lease obligation at the start of the lease on January 1, 2014, was $300,000 (Column [d]), the interest expense for 2014 is $300,000 times 10%, or $30,000. The difference between the $79,139.18 cash payment and the $30,000 interest expense represents repayment of principal. This 2014 difference—$49,139.18 (Column [c])—reduces the remaining principal balance of the lease at December 31, 2014, to $250,860.82 ($300,000 − $49,139.18) as shown in Column (d). The $49,139.18 would be classified as a current liability at

January 1, 2014, because it is due within one year. Interest expense for 2015 would then be $250,860.82 times 10%, or $25,086.08. The 2015 journal entry for the cash payment is:

DR	Obligation under capital lease	$54,053.10	
DR	Interest expense	25,086.08	
	CR Cash		$79,139.18

The 2015 $54,053.10 decrease in lease obligation is classified as a current liability at **December 31, 2014,** because it is due within one year.

The depreciation expense is based on the $300,000 capitalized amount, not the $315,041.60 fair value. Notice that the entry to record depreciation expense is the same in all years of the lease because Lessee Company uses the straight-line depreciation method.

Figure 12.2 summarizes lessees' accounting for capital leases.

Executory Costs

Executory costs represent costs of *using* assets, such as maintenance, taxes, and insurance. Often the lessee pays these costs directly. Sometimes the lessor pays them and passes them along to the lessee as an additional lease payment. For example, if executory costs paid by Lessor Company total $2,000 per year, Lessor would include an added yearly charge of $2,000 in the lease in addition to the basic $79,139.18 rental fee.

Because executory costs represent a cost of using assets—rather than a cost of the assets themselves—these costs are omitted when determining minimum lease payments, and thus they are not a component of the capitalized amount shown in the Leased asset—capital lease

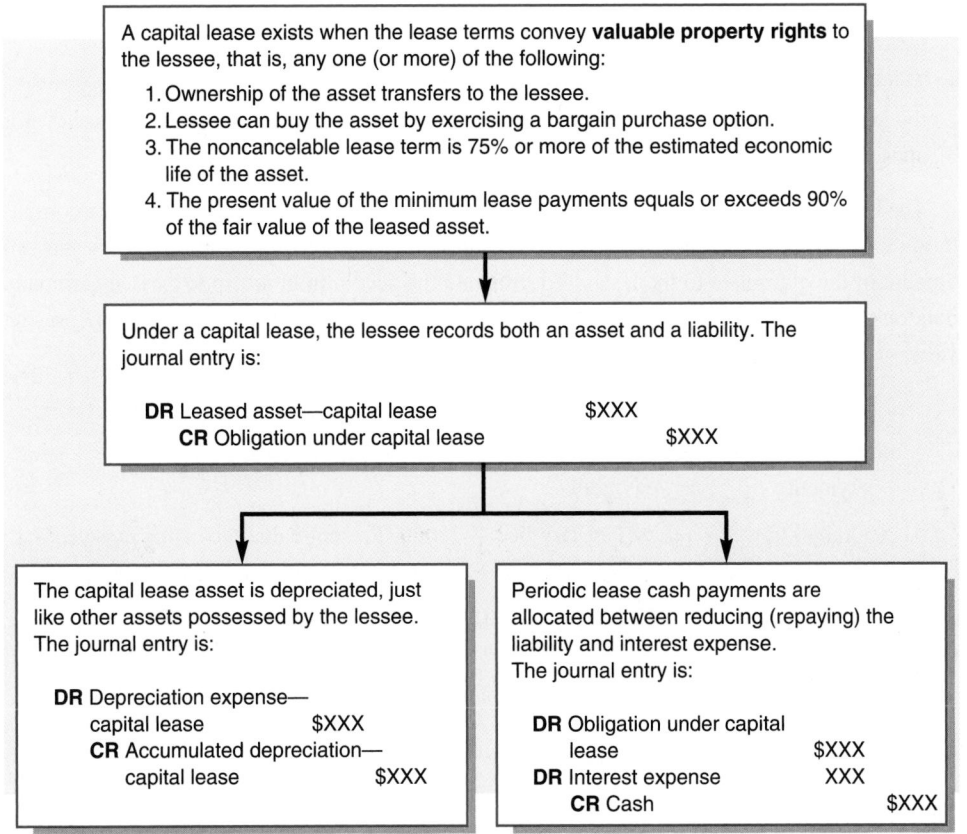

Figure 12.2

LESSEES' ACCOUNTING FOR CAPITAL LEASES

account. Consider this extension of the previous example. If Lessee Company's annual rental fee totals $81,139.18, which includes a $2,000 per year maintenance contract with the lessor, the minimum lease payments to be capitalized would be $79,139.18 (that is, $81,139.18 − $2,000). Under this assumption, the capitalized amount would still total $300,000 and the amortization schedule would be identical to that in Exhibit 12.1. Lessee Company would treat the $2,000 of executory costs from the maintenance contract as a period cost and charge it to expense when paid. For example, the $81,139.18 payment on December 31, 2014, would trigger this entry:

DR	Obligation under capital lease	$49,139.18
DR	Interest expense	30,000.00
DR	Maintenance expense	2,000.00
CR	Cash	$81,139.18

Residual Value Guarantees

Lease contracts sometimes contain a provision under which the lessee guarantees that the leased asset will have a certain value at the end of the lease. If the actual fair value of the asset is less than this **residual value guarantee,** the lessee must pay the difference to the lessor. Continuing the previous example, assume that the lease required Lessee Company to guarantee that the asset's residual value would be no lower than $20,000 when the lease ends on January 1, 2019. If the asset's fair value on that date is $20,000 or higher, Lessee would simply return it to the lessor because the residual value guarantee is satisfied. But if the fair value is only $15,000 on January 1, 2019, Lessee would return the asset and pay Lessor Company $5,000 cash.

Leased assets often revert to the lessor at the end of the lease term. Residual value guarantees protect the lessor against two types of losses:

- Unforeseen technological or marketplace changes erode residual value; the residual value guarantee insulates the lessor from these unanticipated changes.
- The lessor is vulnerable to losses if the lessee does not take proper care of the asset over the lease period; the residual value guarantee gives lessors protection against lessees who abuse leased assets.

The lessee must include the amount specified as the residual value guarantee in the computation of minimum lease payments. The reason is that the lessee potentially owes the full amount of the guarantee to the lessor. To illustrate the accounting, return to Lessee Company data on page 692 and now assume there is a $20,000 residual value guarantee. The present value of the minimum lease payments is:

Present value of minimum lease payments		Minimum lease payment	×	Present value factor at 10%
$300,000.00	=	$79,139.18	×	3.79079 (Present value factor for five-year ordinary annuity)
12,418.40	=	$20,000.00	×	0.62092 (Present value factor for $1 due in five years, from this book's Appendix, Table 1)
$312,418.40				

The $312,418.40 is less than the $315,041.60 fair value. The difference in the two values implies that the lessor is using a different discount rate or the lessee is not guaranteeing 100% of

EXHIBIT 12.2	Lessee Company: Amortization Schedule—Effective Interest Method with Guaranteed Residual Value

Date	(a) Total Cash Payment	(b) Interest Expense*	(c) Principal Reduction†	(d) Lease Obligation Balance	(e) Depreciation of Asset; Residual Value Return	(f) Lease Asset Balance	(g) Total Annual Capital Lease Expense (b) + (e)
1/1/14	—	—	—	$312,418.40	—	$312,418.40	—
12/31/14	$ 79,139.18	$ 31,241.84	$ 47,897.34	264,521.06	$ 58,483.68‡	253,934.72	$ 89,725.52
12/31/15	79,139.18	26,452.11	52,687.07	211,833.99	58,483.68	195,451.04	84,935.79
12/31/16	79,139.18	21,183.40	57,955.78	153,878.21	58,483.68	136,967.36	79,667.08
12/31/17	79,139.18	15,387.82	63,751.36	90,126.85	58,483.68	78,483.68	73,871.50
12/31/18	79,139.18	9,012.33§	70,126.85	20,000.00	58,483.68	20,000.00	67,496.01
1/1/19#	—	—	20,000.00	—	20,000.00	—	—
	$395,695.90	$103,277.50	$312,418.40	$ –0–	$312,418.40	$ –0–	$395,695.90

---

* Column (d) for preceding year times 10%.

† Column (a) minus Column (b).

‡ ($312,418.40 − $20,000) ÷ 5.

§ Rounded.

\# Asset returned.

the expected residual value. With the residual value guarantee, Lessee makes the following entry on January 1, 2014, at the inception of the lease:

DR	Leased asset—capital lease	$312,418.40	
	CR Obligation under capital lease		$312,418.40

Exhibit 12.2 shows the amortization schedule that Lessee uses when this residual value guarantee is included in the lease. Lessee treats the guaranteed residual as the salvage value and computes the annual depreciation of $58,483.68 ([$312,418.40 present value less $20,000 guaranteed residual]/5 years). After making the December 31, 2018, cash payment of $79,139.18, the lease obligation balance (Column [d]) and the lease asset balance (Column [f]) both are $20,000 (see the highlighted numbers). We're assuming that the asset's value at the end of the lease on January 1, 2019, equals or exceeds $20,000—the amount of the residual value guarantee. When Lessee returns the asset on that date, it satisfies its obligation to Lessor Company, and the following entry results:

Columns (a) through (d) would be similar for a lease with a bargain purchase option. However, a bargain purchase would have required the lessee to depreciate the asset over the economic life of six years, resulting in annual depreciation expense of $52,069.73 ($312,418.40/6), thereby making columns (e) through (g) different.

DR	Obligation under capital lease	$20,000.00	
	CR Leased asset—capital lease		$20,000.00

Now let's alter the example and assume that the asset has a fair value of only $15,000 at December 31, 2018. Lessee Company would have to pay $5,000 in addition to relinquishing the asset. The entry is:

DR	Obligation under capital lease	$20,000.00	
DR	Loss on residual value guarantee	5,000.00	
	CR Leased asset—capital lease		$20,000.00
	CR Cash		5,000.00

Payments in Advance

When lease payments are due at the *start* of each lease period, the journal entries and amortization tables differ slightly. We'll use the original Lessee Company example on page 692 to illustrate this. Assume that the annual payment is due at the start of each year and, because the payments are received earlier, the lessor lowers the required annual payment to $71,945. Under these slightly altered conditions, the present value of the minimum lease payments is:

Present value of minimum lease payments	=	Minimum lease payment	×	Present value factor for an annuity in advance for five years at 10%
$300,000	=	$71,945	×	4.16987 (from this book's Appendix, Table 3)

Exhibit 12.3 shows the amortization schedule for this lease with up-front payments. The form of the schedule is identical to the form used in Exhibit 12.1. However, we have added the shaded second row to reflect that the entire first payment reduces the lease obligation. The remainder of the schedule functions the same as Exhibit 12.1. The interest expense associated with the January 1, 2015, payment is computed by multiplying the prior balance of $228,055 by 10%. The January 1, 2015, lease obligation balance is reduced by $49,139.50, the difference between the lease payment of $71,945 and the interest expense of $22,805.50.

Lessee records the following two entries on January 1, 2014, upon signing the lease and making the required lease payment:

DR	Leased asset—capital lease	$300,000	
	CR Obligation under capital lease		$300,000
DR	Obligation under capital lease	$ 71,945	
	CR Cash		$ 71,945

Notice in both the second journal entry and Exhibit 12.3 that no portion of the January 1, 2014, payment represents interest expense; instead, all of the $71,945 payment reduces the principal balance. The reason is that interest expense ensues only as time passes, not at the lease's inception.

EXHIBIT 12.3	**Lessee Company: Amortization Schedule—Effective Interest Method with Payments at the Start of Each Period**

Payment Date	(a) Total Payment	(b) Interest Expense*	(c) Principal Reduction†	(d) Lease Obligation Balance	(e) Depreciation of Asset	(f) Total Annual Capital Lease Expense (b) + (e)
1/1/2014				$300,000.00		
1/1/2014	$ 71,945.00		$ 71,945.00	228,055.00		
1/1/2015	71,945.00	$22,805.50	49,139.50	178,915.50	$ 60,000.00	$ 82,805.50
1/1/2016	71,945.00	17,891.55	54,053.45	124,862.05	60,000.00	77,891.55
1/1/2017	71,945.00	12,486.21	59,458.79	65,403.26	60,000.00	72,486.21
1/1/2018	71,945.00	6,541.74‡	65,403.26	—	60,000.00	66,541.74
1/1/2019	—	—	—	—	60,000.00	60,000.00
	$359,725.00	$59,725.00	$300,000.00	—	$300,000.00	$359,725.00

* Column (d) for preceding year times 10%.

† Column (a) minus Column (b).

‡ Rounded.

In the case of Exhibit 12.1, the payments are made at the end of the calendar years ended December 31, and interest expense for each year is recorded at the time of payment. However, in this case, (Exhibit 12.3), the second and all future payments are made after the end of the calendar reporting year and, therefore interest expense must be accrued at the end of each year. Accordingly, we would make the following entry at December 31, 2014:

DR	Interest expense	$22,805.50	
	CR Obligation under capital lease		$22,805.50

With this entry, the total lease obligation balance grows to $250,860.50 ($228,055.00 + $22,805.50). Both the interest accrual of $22,805.50 and the January 1, 2015, principal reduction of $49,139.50 would be reclassified as a current liability with the following entry:

DR	Obligation under capital lease	$71,945.00	
	CR Obligation under capital lease—current		$71,945.00

On January 1, 2015, when the payment is made, we make the following entry:

DR	Obligation under capital lease—current	$71,945.00	
	CR Cash		$71,945.00

This entry removes the increase in the obligation from the interest accrual and reduces the lease obligation balance to $178,915.50, the amount shown in the amortization schedule. Depreciation expense also must be assigned to the appropriate year. In this case, the $60,000 depreciation expense associated with the January 1, 2015, payment would be recognized in 2014 net income. *These types of entries have to be made any time that the date of the payments do not align with the end of the accounting year.* For example, a lease could begin on October 1, and one-quarter year's interest and depreciation would have to be accrued at December 31. We have illustrated this issue with payments made at the beginning of the period, but the issue also occurs with end of period payments.

Before we leave this example, note the end of the Exhibit 12.3 amortization schedule. The last lease payment is made on January 1, 2018, but the lessee still has use of the asset for all of 2018. During 2018, the lessee will still have depreciation expense, but it will not have interest expense. As we saw in Exhibit 12.1, total lease expense of $359,725.00 is the sum of total interest expense and total depreciation expense and equals total cash outflows. The large difference between the 2018 interest expense of $7,194.12 in Exhibit 12.1 and the 2018 interest expense of $0 in Exhibit 12.3 occurs primarily because the final payment is one year apart (January 1, 2018, versus December 31, 2018). In a lease contract with monthly payments, annual interest expense would be similar whether the payment is made at the beginning or the end of the month.

Financial Statement Effects of Treating a Lease as a Capital Lease versus Treating It as an Operating Lease

To understand the financial statement effects of lease capitalization, we need to compare the amounts that result from the capital lease approach with the amounts that would have resulted had the operating lease method been used instead.

As you read this section, keep in mind that in a bankruptcy there is no distinction between a capital and operating lease. The lessor has rights similar to a creditor with a loan secured by an asset. The creditor can renegotiate the lease terms or take control of the asset. For example, in the American Airlines (AMR) Chapter 11 proceedings, lessors took back some aircraft and renegotiated leases for other aircraft.[8]

To make that comparison, return to the beginning of the Lessee Company example (page 692) in which we assumed that lease payments were due at year-end, executory costs were zero, and there was no residual value guarantee. If that lease had been accounted for as an operating lease, the following journal entry would have been made in each of the five years of the lease:

> Assuming zero executory costs is equivalent to assuming that the executory costs are paid directly by the lessee and are not included in the payments due to the lessor.

DR Rent expense......................................	$79,139.18	
CR Cash		$79,139.18

Under the operating lease method, the total lease expense over the life of the lease equals the total cash outflow. This total expense number under the operating lease method is $395,695.90 and is shown at the bottom of Column (a) of Exhibit 12.1.

Under the capital lease method, the total lease expense over the life of the lease comprises both (1) the interest payments and (2) the amortization of the capitalized asset amount. The sum of these two elements is shown at the bottom of Column (f) of the amortization schedule in Exhibit 12.1. This total is also $395,695.90.

A comparison of the Exhibit 12.1 Column (a) total (lifetime expense under the operating lease method) and the Column (f) total (lifetime expense under the capital lease method) demonstrates that *the two methods give rise to identical cumulative total lifetime charges to expense.* Over the life of a lease, total expense is unaffected by the choice of lease accounting method. However, a comparison of the year-by-year amounts in Columns (a) and (f) demonstrates that the *timing* of the expense charge for the two methods differs. The capital lease approach leads to higher expense in the earlier years of the lease and lower lease expense in the later years, as shown in Figure 12.3. You can see in the graphical representation that in the early lease years, expenses under the capital lease approach exceed lease expenses that would be recognized under the operating lease approach. Ultimately, capital lease expense drops below operating lease expense.

Note in Figure 12.3 that the operating lease expense and capital lease expense are almost equal in year 2016, halfway through the life of the lease. Exhibit 12.1 indicates that operating lease expense in 2016 is $79,139.18 while capital lease expense is $79,680.77—virtually the same. The intuition behind the intersecting operating lease and capital lease lines in Figure 12.3 extends to comparisons of real companies. For mature firms, the *net income* effect of capital lease versus operating lease treatment is often not significantly different. However, the split between operating expense and interest expense is different. Refer to the 2016 expense amounts in Exhibit 12.1 once again. Under operating lease treatment, the rent expense of $79,139.18 is classified as an operating expense. In contrast, under capital lease treatment, only the depreciation expense of $60,000 is deducted in determining operating income. The interest expense of $19,680.77 is classified as a financing (other) expense, which is below operating income. The distinction in classification affects ratios based on operating income such as return on assets. This issue is discussed in more detail in the constructive capitalization example contained in this chapter's appendix.

This accelerated recognition of lease expenses under the capital lease approach provides another reason why many lessees prefer the operating lease method. Consider the incentives of a manager whose performance evaluations and bonuses are tied to financial numbers. Because the capital lease accounting method loads the lease expenses at the front end of the

 **Contracting**

---

[8] See American Airlines, Inc., Form 10-K, December 31, 2012, p. 69 for a detailed discussion.

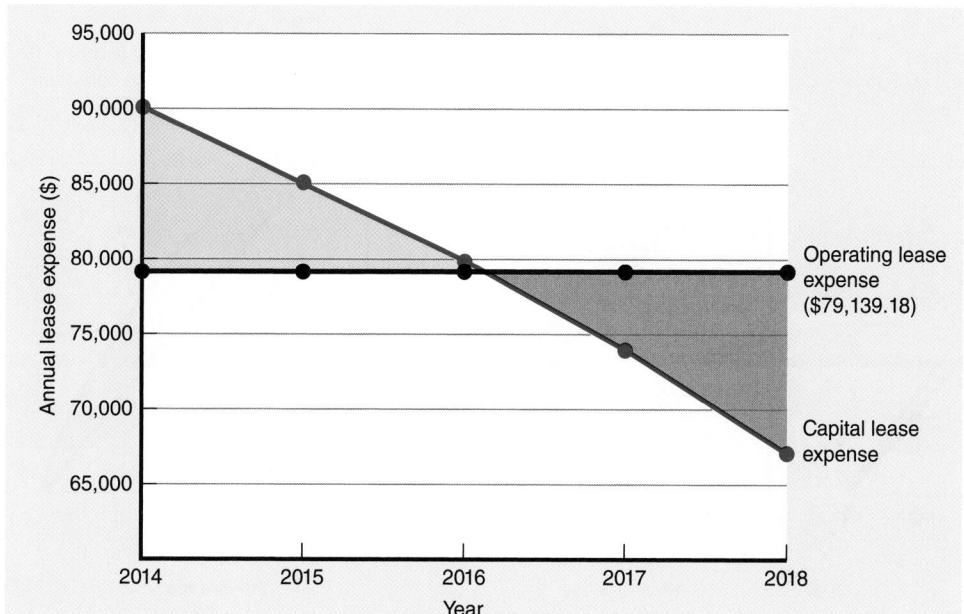

Figure 12.3

LESSEE COMPANY
PATTERN OF EXPENSE
RECOGNITION: CAPITAL
VERSUS OPERATING LEASE
METHOD

lease term, it lowers income during that front-end period and thus reduces the discounted present value of expected bonuses. Worse yet, if managers' accomplishments are evaluated "strictly by the numbers," the higher expenses and lower profitability could jeopardize their continuing employment and advancement. So, managers have a strong incentive to structure lease contracts in ways that circumvent the capitalization rules.

The higher initial expense under the capital lease method also results in a weaker balance sheet. ***The capital lease method requires the lessee to record additional liabilities, and the amount of these liabilities often exceeds the net asset value.*** This is the case in our initial example. Exhibit 12.1 indicates that the liability at December 31, 2014, is $250,860.82. However, the book value of the Leased asset—capital lease is $240,000 ($300,000 asset less accumulated depreciation of $60,000). The lease obligation exceeds the leased asset by $10,860.82.

Figure 12.4(a) graphically represents data from the Lessee Company illustration in Exhibit 12.1. The year-end book value of the capitalized asset (the black line in the graph) starts at $300,000 and declines yearly by $60,000—the straight-line depreciation amount from Column (e) in Exhibit 12.1—until it reaches zero at the end of 2018. The blue curved line depicts the year-end lease obligation balance from Column (d) in Exhibit 12.1. While the two balances are obviously equal at the beginning and end of the lease, for all intermediate periods, the asset amount is lower than the liability. This relationship holds in general because the reduction in the lease obligation in the beginning part of the lease term is less than the reduction in the carrying value of the leased asset caused by depreciation (for example, compare Columns [c] and [e] of Exhibit 12.1 for December 31, 2014). Notice that Figure 12.4(a) includes the percentage relationship between the capitalized asset and liability balances for all intermediate lease years. For example, at December 31, 2014, the asset balance is 95.7% of the obligation balance for the five-year lease.

Parts (b) and (c) in the figure show the relationship between the lease asset and lease liability balances for the same basic facts as in (a), but in (b) and (c), the lease period is for 10 years and 20 years, respectively. The *difference* between the asset and liability balances *increases* the longer the life of the lease. The reason is that the lease liability balance decreases at a lower rate when lease payments are spread over longer periods—that is, a larger portion of each early lease payment is for interest, and a correspondingly smaller portion goes toward reducing the lease obligation the longer the term of the lease.

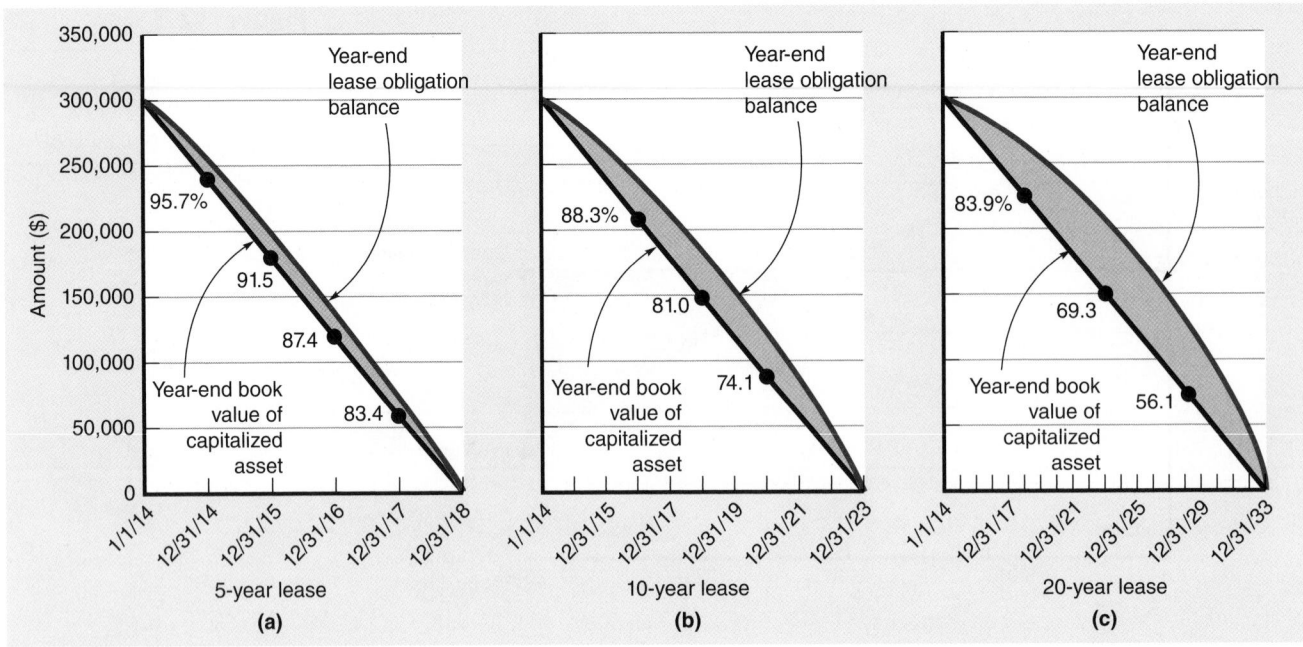

Figure 12.4 LESSEE COMPANY

General Relationship between Capital Lease Asset and Liability When Payments Are at *End* of Period (a) 5-Year Lease, (b) 10-Year Lease, and (c) 20-Year Lease

The specific relation between the lease asset and the lease liability depends on the depreciation method, interest rate, timing and frequency of payments, and life of the lease. For example, if *annual* payments are made at the *beginning* of the year, then the obligation could be lower than the depreciated asset for all or part of the life of the lease. However, if beginning of the period payments are made *monthly,* the lease obligation is usually greater than the book value of the lease asset within the first year of the lease. For mature firms using straight-line depreciation, a general rule-of-thumb is that the depreciated asset is 70% of the obligation.[9]

Analysis

The capital lease approach invariably worsens certain key ratios on the lessee's balance sheet—thus providing another explanation for lessees' resistance to lease capitalization. One ratio that deteriorates under capital lease accounting is the current ratio. Using numbers in the Lessee Company example from Exhibit 12.1, *we will demonstrate that the current ratio over the lease term will be lower under the capital lease approach than it would be under the operating lease approach.* To see this, assume that Lessee is preparing a balance sheet on January 1, 2014, immediately after signing the lease. Under the operating lease approach, the first cash payment of $79,139.18 due on December 31, 2014, is not considered to be a liability; it will accrue as a liability only as time passes and as the lessor performs its duties under the lease. Because no part of the year-end 2014 payment of $79,139.18 is recognized as a liability at January 1, 2014, under the operating lease approach, the current ratio would be unaffected on signing if Lessee were somehow able to avoid capitalization and were allowed to treat this as an operating lease.

By contrast, at the inception of the lease, the capital lease approach *does* recognize a liability—called Obligation under capital lease. As shown in Exhibit 12.1, the balance in this liability account at January 1, 2014, is $300,000.00. Furthermore, GAAP requires that a portion

---

[9] See E. A. Imhoff Jr., R. C. Lipe, and D. W. Wright, "Operating Leases: Impact of Constructive Capitalization," *Accounting Horizons,* March 1991, pp. 51–63. The 70% is derived from an analysis (based on end-of-year payments) of asset-to-liability ratios for leases of various duration and interest rates.

of this $300,000.00 balance be classified as a current liability. As mentioned on page 694, the current portion of the Obligation under capital lease is the reduction in the principal balance that will take place over the ensuing 12 months of 2014. Exhibit 12.1 shows the current portion to be $49,139.18, the expected 2014 reduction in the principal balance. Thus, treating the lease as a capital lease rather than as an operating lease will increase Lessee's current liabilities by $49,139.18 and thereby lower its January 1, 2014, current ratio. Exhibit 12.1 illustrates that this negative effect on the current ratio *increases* as the lease ages because the portion of each $79,139.18 cash outflow that represents principal reduction increases over time.

> When lease payments must be paid in *advance,* there is also a current ratio *numerator* effect under the capital lease approach. The advance payment reduces cash as well as the liability account Obligation under capital lease, as shown in the journal entry on page 698. The net effect is to lower the numerator of the current ratio. By contrast, if the same lease were treated as an operating lease, when cash is credited, the offsetting debit is to Prepaid expense—a current asset account. Accordingly, the current ratio numerator is unchanged.

To protect the lender, many loan agreements require borrowers to maintain a certain prespecified current ratio level. It is not surprising, therefore, that lessees resist lease capitalization. As the preceding discussion illustrates, treating a lease as a capital lease lowers the current ratio; therefore, capitalization could push financially struggling lessees into technical violation of their existing loan agreements by lowering their current ratio below the prespecified limit.

 **Contracting**

Two far more obvious cases of ratio deterioration under capital lease accounting relate to the leverage ratio and the asset turnover ratio. These effects were discussed at the beginning the chapter and will not be repeated here.

Lease treatment also has cash flow statement implications. To see this, refer back to Exhibit 12.1, which shows the amortization schedule for a capital lease. On the cash flow statement, the interest expense component—Column (b)—of each yearly payment would be classified as an *operating* cash flow while the principal reduction component—Column (c)—would be classified as a *financing* cash flow. Depreciation expense would be an addition in an *indirect* method presentation of operating activities and would not be shown at all in a *direct* method presentation. In contrast, if the lease had been treated as an operating lease, the entire $79,139.18 annual payment would be classified as an operating cash flow. So, when lessees successfully keep leases off the balance sheet,

> As an example, several telecom firms artificially increased reported revenues by simultaneously leasing line capacity *to* a competitor (thereby generating revenue) while at the same time leasing an equivalent amount of capacity *from* that same competitor. The cash inflows from one lease were exactly equal to the cash outflows on the other. These transactions were designed to overstate not just revenues but *operating* cash flows too. Here's how it worked. The lease of line capacity *to* the competitor was treated as an operating lease. So, these cash inflows were classified as operating cash inflows on the cash flow statement. But the lease of line capacity *from* the competitor was treated as a capital lease. As you just saw, the principal payment component of the cash outflow is a *financing flow* on the cash flow statement. So, from a cash flow statement perspective, this "round-trip" pair of leases with equal cash inflows and outflows nevertheless increased reported operating cash inflows.
>
> *Source:* K. Brown, "Creative Accounting: How to Buff a Company," *The Wall Street Journal,* February 21, 2002.

reported cash flow from operations is *lower* than it would be under the capital lease approach.

Exhibit 12.4 shows the total amount of scheduled capital lease payments versus operating lease payments for five of the largest firms in each of five industries that use leases extensively. Notice that the dollar amount of the minimum lease payments arising from operating leases is, on average, 42 times more than the capital lease payments for supermarkets and 33 times more for airlines. This demonstrates that capital leases arise infrequently even in industries that utilize leasing heavily.

One possible explanation for the preponderance of operating leases in Exhibit 12.4 is that the criteria for capitalizing lease commitments in FASB ASC 840 can be readily circumvented. For example, a lessee can simply refuse to sign a lease contract that transfers legal title or contains a bargain purchase option. This avoids triggering the first and second capitalization criteria. Criterion (3)—the 75% rule—can also be circumvented by bargaining with the lessor to shorten the lease term until it is less than 75% of the asset's expected economic life. However, criterion (4)—

EXHIBIT 12.4	Comparison of Undiscounted Dollar Magnitudes of Capital and Operating Lease Payments

2012 Fiscal Year

| ($ in millions) | Total Scheduled Minimum Lease Payments | | Ratio of Operating to Capital Lease Payments |
	Operating Leases	Capital Leases	
Department/Variety Stores			
Wal-Mart	$16,803	$6,213	2.7
Target	4,029	4,997	0.8
Costco Wholesale	2,747	328	8.4
Sears	4,535	643	7.1
Macy's	2,714	67	40.5
Average			11.9
Supermarkets			
Kroger	5,003	449	11.1
Safeway	4,084	739	5.5
Supervalu	638	451	1.4
Publix Super Markets	4,274	—	*
Whole Foods	6,775	45	150.6
Average			42.2
Railroads			
Union Pacific Corporation	4,241	2,441	1.7
BNSF Railway	5,119	1,275	4.0
CSX Corp	689	—	*
Norfolk Southern Corporation	749	8	93.6
Kansas City Southern	716	26	27.7
Average			31.8
Airlines			
AMR	9,011	682	13.2
UAL	17,214	1,454	11.8
Delta Airlines	13,846	914	15.1
Southwest Airlines	5,086	46	110.6
Jet Blue Airways	1,492	96	15.5
Average			33.3
Communications			
Verizon Communications Inc.	11,841	407	29.1
AT&T Inc.	24,065	—	*
Sprint Nextel Corporation	15,666	1,603	9.8
Comcast	3,217	113	28.5
Qwest Communications	1,221	244	5.0
Average			18.1

* Ratio cannot be computed due to immaterial capital leases.

Source: Company SEC filings and annual reports

the 90% rule (or recovery of investment criterion)—is the most difficult to circumvent and undoubtedly accounts for many capital leases that ultimately appear on financial statements.

We can only infer why companies in these five industries that extensively use leases have so few capital leases. A reasonable conjecture is that they have chosen to keep these leases "off the balance sheet" to improve ratios such as debt to equity and asset turnover.

Lessees' Financial Statement Disclosures

The ratio of operating lease payments to capital lease payments in Exhibit 12.4 is typical of other industries as well. Operating leases predominate by a wide margin. However, capital leases *do* exist, and their frequency differs across companies even within the same industry. For this reason, analysts try to adjust financial statements to include the effects of off-balance-sheet operating leases to enhance comparisons between firms in an industry. The note disclosures required by ASC 840 make these adjustments possible. Exhibit 12.5 shows portions of the lease disclosure from the 2012 annual report of Whole Foods Market, Inc., one of North America's largest supermarket chains.

Exhibit 12.5 contains the disclosures required of all lessees. Notice that a schedule of future minimum lease payments must be reported both for capital leases and for operating leases. (We used these schedules to develop the data in Exhibit 12.4.) Payments for each of the ensuing five years must be separately disclosed, as Whole Foods has done for 2013 through 2017. Minimum lease payments for all later years may be aggregated (for example, $30.7 million for capital leases and $4,922.8 million for operating leases). U.S. GAAP requires the disclosure of the present value of the minimum lease payments **only for capital leases.**[10] However, the scheduled payments on operating leases make it possible for analysts to estimate the discounted present value of the off-balance-sheet leases. In the appendix to this chapter, we use the Whole Foods disclosures to illustrate this computation step-by-step. Once the present value of the off-balance-sheet leases is determined, the computed dollar amount can be added to both the asset account (Leased asset—capital lease) and the liability account (Obligation under capital lease). This adjustment allows analysts to compensate for distortions that can arise from off-balance-sheet leases when making interfirm comparisons.

> Some lenders and analysts will use a short-cut approach to estimate the operating lease liability by multiplying the annual rent expense by an industry multiple, e.g., eight. The resulting liability can be included in ratios used for analysis or debt covenants. For example, Whole Foods Market multiplies its rent expense by eight and adds the amount to its invested capital when computing return on invested capital (see Whole Foods Market, Inc., September 30, 2012, Form 10-K, p. 24).

EXHIBIT 12.5 Whole Foods Market, Inc. Lessee Disclosure

Excerpts from Lease Disclosure, September 30, 2012

Rental expense charged to operations under operating leases for fiscal years 2012, 2011, and 2010 totaled approximately $353.4 million, $321.6 million and $303.5 million, respectively. Minimum rental commitments and sublease rental income required by all noncancelable leases are approximately as follows (in thousands):

	Capital	Operating
Fiscal year 2013	$ 2,967	$ 309,058
Fiscal year 2014	2,743	364,330
Fiscal year 2015	2,817	385,540
Fiscal year 2016	2,644	396,112
Fiscal year 2017	2,697	396,976
Future fiscal years	30,722	4,922,823
	44,590	$6,774,839
Less amounts representing interest	20,468	
Net present value of capital lease obligations	24,122	
Less current installments	1,012	
Long-term capital lease obligation, less current installments	$23,110	

The present values of future minimum obligations for capital leases shown above are calculated based on interest rates determined at the inception of the lease, or upon acquisition of the original lease.

---

[10] *ASR No. 147* required the disclosure of the present value of lease payments under long-term leases by property type from 1973 to 1982. Preparers had previously lobbied the Accounting Principles Board against disclosing present values of off-balance sheet leases by asserting that the disclosure would be admitting that the leases should be on the balance sheet. See S. Zeff, "Lobbying on lessee accounting in 1972–73, and the role of the SEC," *World Accounting Report,* August 2, 2012, www.worldaccountingreport.com.

Our discussion for operating leases so far has assumed that payments are constant. Under this scenario, the entire operating lease obligation is generally off-balance-sheet. However, FASB ASC 840-20-25 requires that rent expense be recognized on a straight-line basis even if payments are not the same over time. For example, to make a lease more attractive, the lessor may offer a "rent holiday" by suspending rent payments for the first year. Under FASB ASC 840, firms must determine total rent to be paid over the life of the lease and accrue it evenly over the lease term. The form of the accrual and payment entry is:

DR	Rent expense	$XXX	
	CR Accrued rent expense		$XXX
	CR Cash		XXX

As a result of this entry, the balance sheet has a liability. This liability is reduced as the rental payment amounts increase during the lease term. For example, on its September 30, 2012, balance sheet, Whole Foods Market had a liability of $440.8 million for expected increases. The liability of $440.8 million represents only 6.5% of the off-balance sheet undiscounted operating lease liabilities of $6,774.8 million. Between 2004 and 2006, more than 250 firms had to restate their financial statements because of this and other issues related to operating lease accounting.[11]

 **RECAP** **We have shown that lease capitalization affects financial statement ratios and that the FASB ASC 840 capitalization criteria can be circumvented. Because different firms can conceivably treat virtually identical leases dissimilarly, financial statements may not be immediately comparable across firms. To make comparisons, statement users need to adjust for these differences. The appendix to this chapter outlines procedures for using financial statement disclosures to capitalize operating leases, thereby increasing interfirm statement comparability.**

LESSOR ACCOUNTING

In addition to outlining rules for lessees, ASC 840 specifies the treatment of leases on lessors' books. While lessees have been reluctant to treat leases as capital leases, lessors have not. Treating a lease as a capital lease on the lessor's books accelerates the timing of the recognition of leasing income—thus creating favorable financial statement effects for the lessor, as we'll show in the following sections.

Sales-Type and Direct Financing Leases

From the perspective of the lessor, if a lease arrangement

1. Transfers property rights in the leased asset to the lessee *and*
2. Allows reasonably accurate estimates regarding the amount and collectibility of the eventual net cash flows to the lessor,

the lessor treats the lease as a capital lease. In a lessor's capital lease, the leased asset is considered to be "sold" and is removed from the lessor's books. Lessors use two types of capital leases:

1. A **sales-type lease,** which exists when the lessor is a manufacturer or dealer.
2. A **direct financing lease,** which exists when the lessor is a financial institution (for example, an insurance firm, bank, or financing company).

---

[11] For more information on the restatements, see A. A. Acito, J. J. Burks, and W. B. Johnson, "Materiality Decisions and the Correction of Accounting Errors," *The Accounting Review,* May 2009, pp. 659–688.

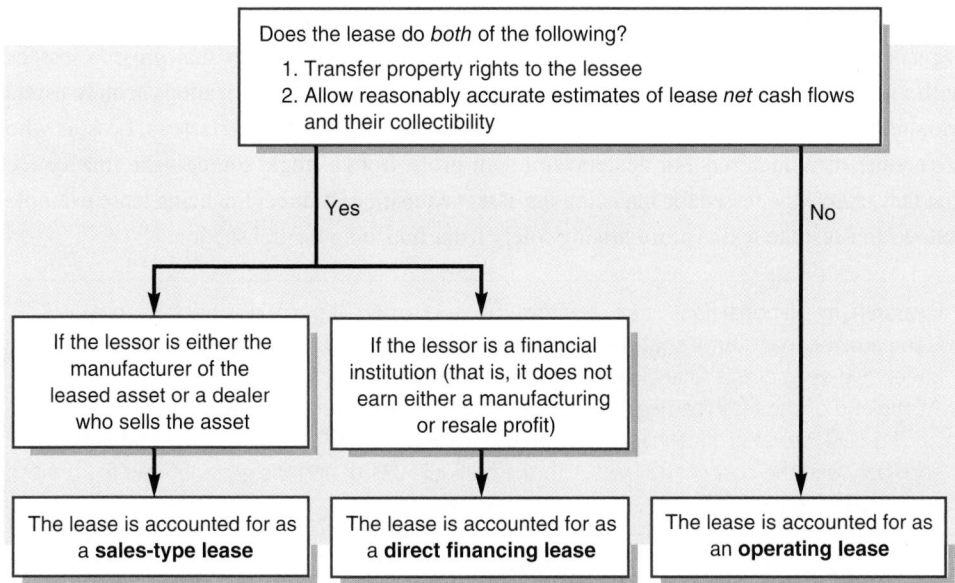

Figure 12.5

DECISION TREE FOR
LESSOR'S TREATMENT
OF LEASES

When both conditions—the transfer of property rights *and* reasonably accurate estimates of net cash flows—are *not simultaneously* met, the lease must be treated as an operating lease.

Figure 12.5 diagrams the various possibilities for lessor accounting, which we are about to explain in detail.

Sales-Type Leases   For manufacturers or dealers, leases can serve as a marketing vehicle because leasing arrangements generate "sales" from potential customers who are unwilling or unable to buy the assets outright for cash. For example, Deere & Company manufactures farm equipment for sale and leases farm equipment through its wholly owned subsidiary, John Deere Credit. A lessor who uses leasing as a means for marketing products earns a profit from two sources:

1. One component of the total return on the lease is the **manufacturer's or dealer's profit**—the difference between the fair value (*cash* sales price) of the asset and its cost to the manufacturer or dealer.

2. Another component of the lessor's return is **financing profit**—the difference between the total (undiscounted) minimum lease payments plus unguaranteed residual value and the fair value of the leased asset.

The following sales-type lease example illustrates these components.

ABC Company manufactures tractors. Each tractor has a total production cost of $36,000 and a cash sales price of $50,000. ABC Company "sells" some of these tractors under five-year sales-type leases, which call for annual lease payments of $15,000. At the end of the fifth year, legal ownership of the tractor transfers to the lessee.

ABC Company's total profit over the five years of the lease is $39,000—that is, the lessee's payments of $75,000 ($15,000 per year times five years) minus the production cost of $36,000. This total profit comprises two components:

Manufacturer's profit: Cash sales price of $50,000 minus production cost of $36,000	$14,000
Financing profit: The difference between the cash sales price of the tractor ($50,000) and the gross inflows from the lessee ($15,000 × 5 years = $75,000)	25,000
Total profit	$39,000

Direct Financing Leases Some lessors are not manufacturers or dealers; they are organizations such as banks, insurance firms, or financing companies that provide lessees with a means to finance asset acquisitions. These banks and other organizations acquire assets from manufacturers by paying the fair value and then leasing the asset to lessees. Lessors who are neither manufacturers nor dealers earn their profit from a single source—the finance fee that they charge the lessee for financing the asset acquisition. A direct financing lease example follows to illustrate lessor profit arising solely from financing the transaction.

> Pleasant City National Bank leases tractors to local farmers. It purchases tractors from ABC Company, the manufacturer, at their fair value of $50,000. The Bank then leases the tractors under five-year direct financing leases, which call for annual lease payments of $15,000. At the end of the fifth year, legal ownership of the tractor transfers to the lessee.
>
> The Bank's total profit (finance fee) on this lease is $25,000, which represents the difference between the cost of the tractor to the bank ($50,000) and the gross inflows from the lessee ($75,000).

Lessors' Operating Leases

Some lease arrangements do not transfer property rights in the asset to the lessee, or if they do transfer property rights, there may be great uncertainty about the ultimate profit or its collectibility. In either case, the leased asset is not considered to be "sold" and *remains on the lessor's books.* Such leases are called *operating leases.*

Distinction between Capital and Operating Leases

FASB ASC 840 identifies two types of characteristics that must be met for a lease to be treated as a capital lease—either a sales-type lease or a direct financing lease—on the lessor's books. For ease of reference, these will be called Type I and Type II characteristics. A lease meeting *at least one* of the Type I characteristics and *both* of the Type II characteristics is a capital lease. The Type I characteristics are identical to the lessee's criteria for capital lease treatment.

Type I Characteristics
1. The lease transfers ownership of the asset to the lessee by the end of the lease term.
2. The lease contains a bargain purchase option.
3. The noncancelable lease term is 75% or more of the estimated economic life of the leased asset.
4. The present value of the minimum lease payments equals or exceeds 90% of the leased asset's fair value.

Type II Characteristics
1. The collectibility of the minimum lease payments is reasonably predictable.
2. No important uncertainties surround the amount of unreimbursable costs yet to be incurred by the lessor under the lease.

The purpose of these Type I and Type II characteristics is to establish the appropriate time for recognizing revenue and income on the lessor's books. We already know from Chapter 2 that revenue should be recognized when both of the following conditions exist:

1. The "critical event" in the process of earning the revenue has taken place.
2. The amount of the revenue that has been earned is measurable with a reasonable degree of assurance.

Accounting rules for the lessor are directly linked to these two revenue recognition criteria. The Type I characteristics dealing with transfer of property rights identify the critical event in determining whether a lease is in substance a "sale of assets." That is, if any one of the four Type I characteristics is met, valuable property rights have been transferred to the lessee. This transfer of property rights constitutes the "critical event." The Type II characteristics relate to the predictability and risk of cash flows and thus to the measurability of revenue.

When at least one of the Type I characteristics and both of the Type II characteristics are satisfied by a lease, the criteria for revenue recognition are met. This means that manufacturers or dealers can immediately recognize the sale, match costs, and reflect manufacturer's or dealer's profit. (By contrast, under the operating lease treatment, this profit recognition occurs over the life of the lease as each party performs its duties.) Furthermore, lessors can begin to recognize financing profit using an effective interest approach when the Type I and Type II characteristics exist in a lease.

> Under the operating lease treatment, the recognition of financing profit is related to performance (that is, passage of time). As we will see, the recognition of financing profit is accelerated when it is recognized using an effective interest approach rather than as a function of performance.

When a lease does not meet *any* of the Type I characteristics, or when it meets at least one of the Type I characteristics but not *both* of the Type II characteristics, that lease must be accounted for on the lessor's books as an operating lease. Under the operating lease approach, the lessor's recognition of income takes place piecemeal as contractual performance progresses, as we illustrate later.

Figure 12.6 summarizes the rules for how to classify and record leases on the lessor's books. This figure is a more detailed expansion of Figure 12.5.

FASB ASC 840 tries to establish symmetry in the accounting for leases by lessors and lessees. If a lease qualifies as a "sale" from the lessor's perspective, the property rights inherent in the lease require asset recognition by the lessee. Of course, this symmetry is not perfect because a particular lease may meet at least one of the Type I characteristics but not both of the Type II characteristics. In such cases, the asset appears on *both* the lessor's and the lessee's books. Another factor that inhibits symmetry is that the discount rate used by the lessor and the lessee could differ. ***The lessor is required to use the rate of return that is implicit in the lease.*** If this rate is *higher* than the lessee's incremental borrowing rate, the lessor and the lessee use different discount rates when accounting for the lease.

Direct Financing Lease Treatment Illustrated

To illustrate the accounting for leases that qualify as direct financing leases, we use a variation of our earlier Lessee Company scenario on page 692.

> Assume that Lessee Company signs a noncancelable five-year lease on January 1, 2014, with Lessor Company. The lease begins on January 1, 2014, and has the following terms:
>
> 1. It calls for five payments of $79,139.18 to be made at the end of each year.
> 2. The leased asset has a cost and fair value of $315,041.60 on January 1, 2014.
> 3. The lease has no renewal option, and possession of the asset reverts to Lessor Company on January 1, 2019.
> 4. The leased asset has an expected economic life of six years.
> 5. The collectibility of the lease payments is reasonably predictable.
> 6. No important uncertainties regarding unreimbursable costs yet to be incurred by Lessor Company exist.
> 7. The lease contract requires the lessee to guarantee a residual value of $38,000 at the end of the fifth year of the lease.
> 8. The implicit rate in the lease is 11%.

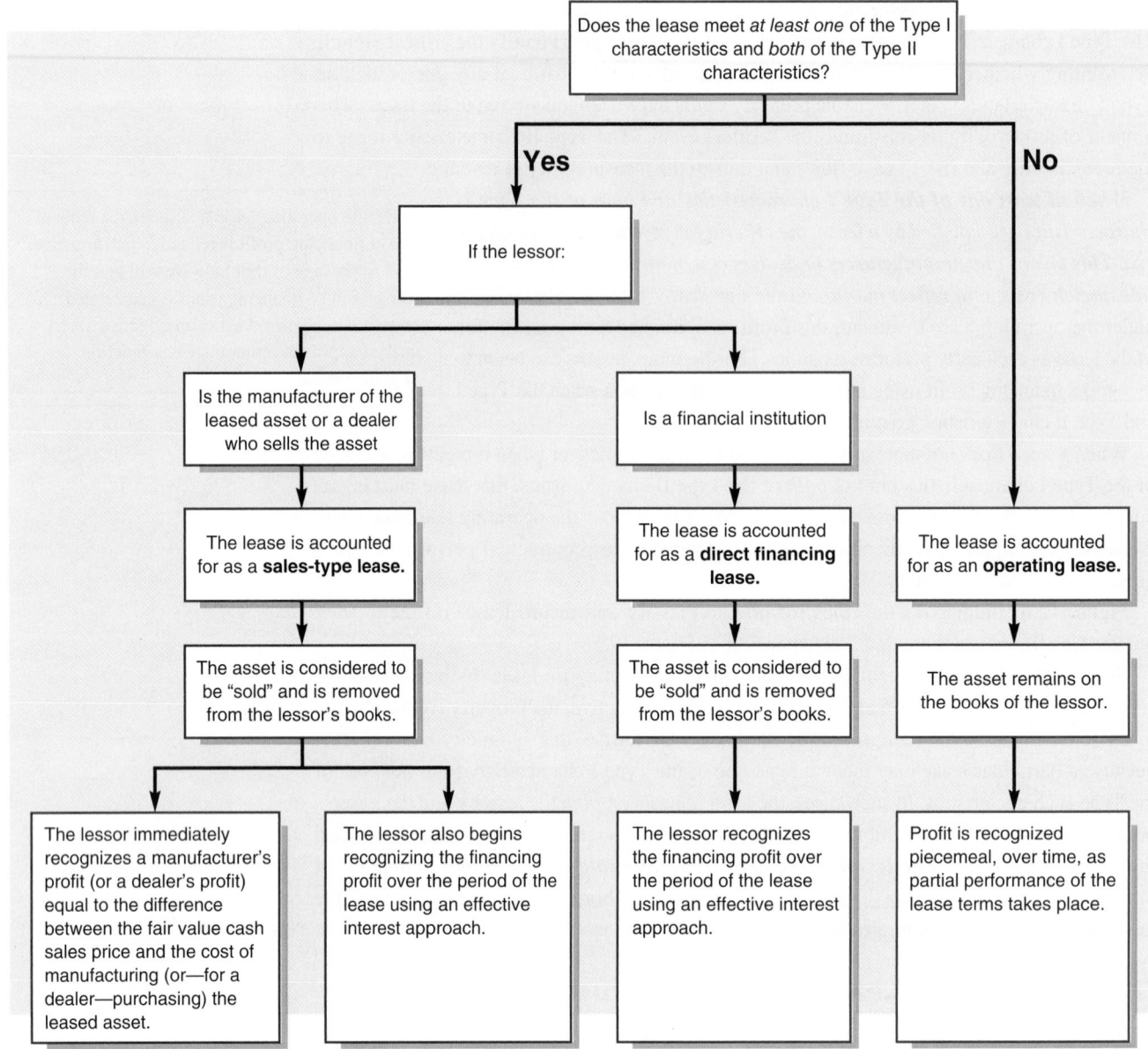

Figure 12.6 DETAILED EXPANSION OF FIGURE 12.5—DECISION TREE FOR LESSOR'S TREATMENT OF LEASES

Note that differences from the prior Lessee Company example relate to items 7 and 8. In the original example, Lessee Company did know the implicit interest rate and did not guarantee a residual value of $38,000.

Exhibit 12.6 shows how the 11% rate is used to compute the lease payment. The lessor begins with the fair value of $315,041.60 and subtracts the $22,551.10 present value of the $38,000 guaranteed residual. (The lessor would deduct the present value of a bargain purchase option or an unguaranteed residual in the same way that the present value of the guaranteed residual is deducted in Exhibit 12.6.) The amount to be recovered through lease payments of $292,490.50 is divided by 3.69590 (the present value factor for a five-year ordinary annuity at 11%) to obtain the annual rent payment of $79,139.18. The bottom of Exhibit 12.6 diagrams how the sum of the present value of the rent payments and the present value of the guaranteed residual value equals the fair value of $315,041.60.

EXHIBIT 12.6	Lessor Company: Computation of Lease Payment

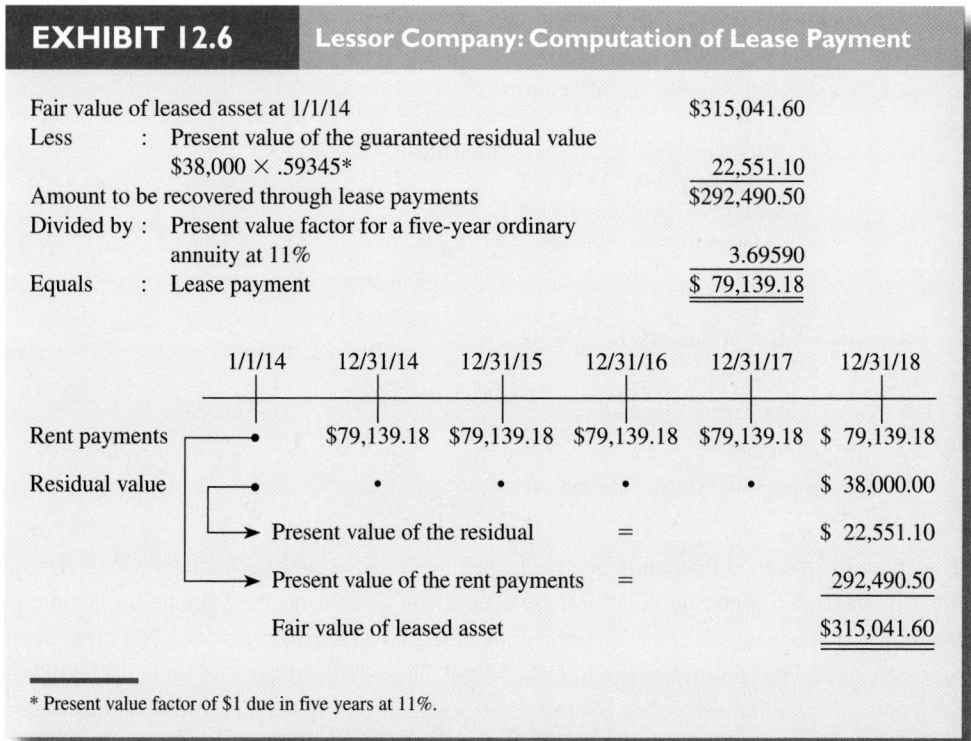

Fair value of leased asset at 1/1/14 $315,041.60
Less   :   Present value of the guaranteed residual value
                    $38,000 × .59345*   22,551.10
Amount to be recovered through lease payments $292,490.50
Divided by :   Present value factor for a five-year ordinary
                    annuity at 11%   3.69590
Equals   :   Lease payment $ 79,139.18

	1/1/14	12/31/14	12/31/15	12/31/16	12/31/17	12/31/18
Rent payments		$79,139.18	$79,139.18	$79,139.18	$79,139.18	$ 79,139.18
Residual value		•	•	•	•	$ 38,000.00

Present value of the residual   = $ 22,551.10
Present value of the rent payments   =   292,490.50
Fair value of leased asset $315,041.60

* Present value factor of $1 due in five years at 11%.

The lease terms satisfy both the third and the fourth Type I characteristics. We will assume that the lease also satisfies both Type II characteristics. Therefore, this is a capital lease. Assume that Lessor Company is not a manufacturer or dealer, so this lease is a direct financing capital lease.

Lessor Company's amortization schedule for this lease is shown in Exhibit 12.7. Notice that the initial amount in Column (d), Remaining Principal Amount, equals the asset's fair value. The lessor's table always begins with the fair value and uses the implicit rate. The beginning balance of $315,041.60 also represents the present value of the rental payments and the expected residual value (see Exhibit 12.6).

EXHIBIT 12.7	Lessor Company: Amortization Schedule—Effective Interest Method

Date	(a) Total Receipts	(b) Interest (Financing) Income*	(c) Principal Reduction†	(d) Remaining Principal Amount
01/01/14				$315,041.60
12/31/14	$79,139.18	$34,654.58	$44,484.60	270,557.00
12/31/15	79,139.18	29,761.27	49,377.91	221,179.09
12/31/16	79,139.18	24,329.70	54,809.48	166,369.61
12/31/17	79,139.18	18,300.66	60,838.52	105,531.09
12/31/18	79,139.18	11,608.09‡	67,531.09	38,000.00
	$395,695.90	$118,654.30	$277,041.60	

* Column (d) for preceding year times 11%.
† Column (a) minus Column (b).
‡ Rounded.

At the lease's inception, Lessor records in a receivable account, Gross investment in leased asset, the undiscounted sum of the minimum rental payments plus the guaranteed residual value of the asset at the end of the lease term.

Minimum rental payments over the life of the lease ($79,139.18 × 5)	$395,695.90
Guaranteed residual value at 12/31/18	38,000.00
Gross investment in leased asset	$433,695.90

The journal entry on January 1, 2014, is:

DR	Gross investment in leased asset	$433,695.90	
CR	Equipment		$315,041.60
CR	Unearned financing income—leases		118,654.30

The credit to Unearned financing income—leases is the difference between the Gross investment in leased asset and the $315,041.60 cost of the asset. Unearned financing income—leases, a contra-account to Gross investment in leased asset, is used to arrive at Net investment in leased asset. The Net investment in leased asset also equals the present value of the future payments and residual value (see Exhibits 12.6 and 12.7). Only the Net investment in leased asset appears on the balance sheet, but the lessor's note disclosure for leases shows:

Gross investment in leased asset	$433,695.90
Less: Unearned financing income—leases	(118,654.30)
Net investment in leased asset	$315,041.60

This entry removes the asset account representing the equipment being leased and replaces it with two accounts that together reflect the net investment in the lease. The dollar amount for the equipment removed ($315,041.60) equals the dollar amount for the net investment in leased asset ($433,695.90 − $118,654.30).

At December 31, 2014, when the first cash payment is received from the lessee, Lessor Company makes the following journal entries:

DR	Cash	$79,139.18	
CR	Gross investment in leased asset		$79,139.18
DR	Unearned financing income—leases	$34,654.58	
CR	Financing income—leases		$34,654.58

The amount of financing income recognized in each year equals the amounts shown in Column (b) of Exhibit 12.7, Lessor's amortization schedule. For example, the $34,654.58 is the product of the January 1, 2014, net investment in leased asset ($315,041.60 from Column [d]) multiplied by 11%, Lessor's rate of return on the lease. Lessor records no depreciation because the equipment itself was removed from its books (see the preceding January 1, 2014, journal entry).

After the last payment is received at the end of the lease term on December 31, 2018, the balance in the Gross investment in leased asset account will be $38,000 (Column [d] of the amortization schedule). This amount represents the guaranteed residual value of the asset on the date that possession of the asset reverts to Lessor Company. Assume that the asset's fair value equals or exceeds $38,000; then the following entry will be made on December 31, 2018, to reflect the end of the lease and physical repossession of the asset.

DR	Equipment—residual value	$38,000.00	
	CR Gross investment in leased asset		$38,000.00

If the equipment's residual value is less than $38,000, the lessee must remit the deficiency in cash when it returns the asset to Lessor Company. So, if the asset's residual value is only $33,000 on December 31, 2018, the entry is:

DR	Cash	$ 5,000	
DR	Equipment—residual value.	33,000	
	CR Gross investment in leased asset.		$38,000

Guaranteed versus Unguaranteed Residual Values

Lease contracts do not usually require the lessee to guarantee that the residual value will exceed a certain dollar amount. When no such contract clause exists, the residual value is **unguaranteed.**

If the asset reverts to the lessor at the end of the lease term, the initial entry to record the lease is identical regardless of whether the residual value is guaranteed or unguaranteed. To see why, return to the example in Exhibit 12.6. It assumed that the residual value would be $38,000 and that the lessee would make up any deficiency if the December 31, 2018, value were less than $38,000. So, the discounted present value at 11% of the $38,000 residual value ($22,551.10) belongs to the lessor and is subtracted from the fair value of $315,041.60. If we alter the example and assume that the expected asset residual value of $38,000 is *un*guaranteed, the asset still reverts to the lessor at December 31, 2018, and the expected (but now unguaranteed) net present value of the residual value ($22,551.10) still belongs to the lessor. So, the $22,551.10 is still subtracted from the fair value just as it would be if it were guaranteed.

Because the lessor includes unguaranteed residual values in its Net investment in leased asset and bears the risk associated with declines in values, it must review the estimated residual values annually. If the declines are viewed to be other than temporary, the lessor must reduce its Net investment in leased asset and record a loss for that period.[12] For example, in 2010, Toyota recalled millions of its cars because of accelerator pedal issues. If a lessor held capital leases with unguaranteed residuals on some of these cars, then it would have recorded losses for declines in the residual values if the lessors viewed the declines to be permanent.

From the lessee's perspective, the initial entry to record the lease *is* different if the residual value is unguaranteed. Only *guaranteed* residual values are obligations to the lessee and thereby included in the computation of minimum lease payments, as discussed on page 696.

Financial Statement Effects of Direct Financing versus Operating Leases

Comparing the financial statement effects of direct financing versus operating lease treatment allows a more complete understanding of lessor accounting.

Had Lessor Company accounted for the previous lease as an operating lease, it would make the following journal entry each year:

DR	Cash	$79,139.18	
	CR Rental revenue		$79,139.18

---

[12] See FASB ASC 840-30-35-25.

EXHIBIT 12.8

Lessor Company: Operating Lease Method versus Direct Financing Method Income and Asset Balance Comparison

	Operating Lease Method			(d) Direct Financing Method Income†	(e) Income Difference between Methods	Net Asset Balance at End of Year		(h) Asset Balance Difference between Methods
Year	(a) Lease Payment Received	(b) Depreciation	(c) Operating Lease Method Income*			(f) Operating Method‡	(g) Direct Financing Method§	
2014	$ 79,139.18	$ 55,408.32	$ 23,730.86	$ 34,654.58	$10,923.72	$259,633.28	$270,557.00	$10,923.72
2015	79,139.18	55,408.32	23,730.86	29,761.27	6,030.41	204,224.96	221,179.09	16,954.13
2016	79,139.18	55,408.32	23,730.86	24,329.70	598.84	148,816.64	166,369.61	17,552.97
2017	79,139.18	55,408.32	23,730.86	18,300.66	(5,430.20)	93,408.32	105,531.09	12,122.77
2018	79,139.18	55,408.32	23,730.86	11,608.09	(12,122.77)	38,000.00	38,000.00	$ 0.00
	$395,695.90	$277,041.60	$118,654.30	$118,654.30	$ 0.00			

* Column (a) minus Column (b).

† From Column (b) of Exhibit 12.7.

‡ $315,041.60 minus the period-to-date cumulative depreciation amount from Column (b).

§ From Column (d) of Exhibit 12.7.

Because the leased asset remains on the lessor's books under the operating lease method, annual depreciation must be recognized. Assume that the asset is depreciated down to a $38,000 residual value on a straight-line basis; then the annual depreciation expense is $55,408.32 ([$315,041.60 − $38,000.00]/5), and the entry each year is:

> **DR** Depreciation expense $55,408.32
> 　　**CR** Accumulated depreciation . . . . 　　　　　$55,408.32

Exhibit 12.8 shows operating lease method amounts in Columns (a), (b), (c), and (f) and contrasts these numbers with direct financing amounts in Columns (d) and (g). Income for the operating lease method totals $118,654.30 over the life of the lease, as shown in Column (c). This total is identical to the income recognized under the direct financing method, as the total in Column (d) reflects. *So, income over the life of the lease is unaffected by which accounting method—the operating lease method or the direct financing method—is used. However, the timing of income does differ for the two methods,* as indicated in the highlighted Column (e) of Exhibit 12.8. The direct financing method recognizes income sooner. Notice that the income timing difference would widen if an accelerated depreciation method were used in conjunction with the operating method as opposed to the straight-line method employed in the example.

 **Contracting**

The "front loading" of income under the direct financing method may explain why lessors—unlike lessees—have never seriously opposed the capital lease approach to lease accounting. Furthermore, the direct financing method results in other favorable financial statement effects. For example, the lessor's rate of return on assets ratio usually improves under the direct financing method in the early years of a lease. Highlighted Columns (e) and (h) in Exhibit 12.8 illustrate this effect. Income and the end-of-year asset balance are both $10,923.72 more under the direct financing method in 2014. An equal dollar increase in the numerator and denominator of a ratio increases the ratio value as long as the ratio of initial value is less than 100%. Because reported rates of return on assets are almost always far less than 100%, the adoption of the direct financing method almost always increases the lessor's reported rate of return in the lease's early years.

Of course, Exhibit 12.8 also illustrates that this effect reverses as the lease ages. In 2018, for example, income is $12,122.77 less under the direct financing method while the end-of-year asset value equals what it would have been under the operating lease treatment. This would make the 2018 return on the direct financing method less than the return that would have been reported on the operating lease approach.[13]

The current ratio of a lessor that uses the direct financing method will also be improved. Consider the current ratio at December 31, 2014. Under the operating lease method, the December 31, 2015, expected lease cash receipt of $79,139.18 would not be shown as an asset on Lessor's books on December 31, 2014, because performance under the lease contract has not yet taken place and will not take place until 2015. Under the direct financing method, however, the 2015 lease payment would be included as a component of the Net investment in leased assets account. Returning to Exhibit 12.7, look at the December 31, 2014, balance in this account (Column [d]), which is $270,557.00; of this amount, $49,377.91 (the principal reduction in the next 12 months) is classified as a current asset. This amount shown in Column (c) of Exhibit 12.7 represents the difference between the gross December 31, 2015, cash receipt of $79,139.18 from the lessee and the interest income of $29,761.27 that will be recognized in 2015. Thus, current assets on the direct financing basis would be higher than they would have been under the operating lease approach—and the current ratio is accordingly improved.

Sales-Type Lease Treatment Illustrated

Accounting for sales-type leases is a simple extension of the direct financing method. A sales-type lease includes a manufacturer's or dealer's profit *in addition to* financing profit; a direct financing lease has only the financing profit component.

To illustrate the accounting for sales-type leases, we now assume that Lessor Company *manufactures* the leased equipment. Prior to the start of the lease on January 1, 2014, the equipment was carried on Lessor's books at its manufactured cost of $240,000. All other facts in the original lessor example (page 709) remain unchanged.

Lessor records the transaction on January 1, 2014, as:

This entry assumes that the residual value is guaranteed. If it is not, the discounted present value of the residual value—which at 11% is 0.59345 × $38,000 = $22,551.10—is deducted from both sales revenue and cost of goods sold. The reason $22,551.10 is deducted is that if the residual value is unguaranteed, the "critical event" in recognizing revenue on the residual value has not yet occurred. There is no assurance that the residual value will ultimately be realized. Only a portion of the asset has been "sold." So, both Sales revenue and Cost of goods sold are reduced by $22,551.10. The entries with an unguaranteed residual value are:

DR	Gross investment in leased asset	$433,695.90
DR	Cost of goods sold	217,448.90*
CR	Sales revenue	$292,490.50[†]
CR	Unearned financing income—leases	118,654.30
CR	Inventory	240,000.00

Notice that the amount of Gross investment in leased asset is $433,695.90 regardless of whether the residual value is unguaranteed or guaranteed. Similarly, the amount of manufacturing profit is $75,041.60 (that is, $292,490.50 − $217,448.90), the same net amount when the residual value is guaranteed (that is, $315,041.60 − $240,000.00 = $75,041.60).

* $240,000 − $22,551.10
[†] $315,041.60 − $22,551.10 = $292,490.50

DR	Gross investment in leased asset	$433,695.90
DR	Cost of goods sold	240,000.00
CR	Sales revenue	$315,041.60
CR	Unearned financing income—leases	118,654.30
CR	Inventory	240,000.00

---

[13] The ratio effect described here holds for each lease in isolation. However, most lessors have many leases of various ages outstanding. In these situations, the number of leases outstanding over time determines the effect on the return ratio. Assume that Lessor Company's total number of leases is constant over time. Initially, when Lessor uses the direct financing method for new leases, its reported rate of return will increase. However, with a constant volume of leases, the average age of the leases accounted for on the direct financing method will eventually stabilize. When this happens, the return on assets ratio under the direct financing method will essentially equal what it would have been under the operating approach. If Lessor's leasing business expands over time, there will be a constant infusion of new leases, and the average age of the leases in place will be falling. When this situation exists, the rate of return on assets will be higher under the direct financing method.

The net effect of this entry is to recognize $75,041.60 of manufacturing profit ($315,041.60 − $240,000.00) immediately. The $118,654.30 of financing profit will be recognized over the life of the lease, as shown in Column (b) of the amortization schedule in Exhibit 12.7. The entries for recording this financing profit over the life of the lease are identical to the entries for the direct financing method on page 712.

Let's extend the example by assuming that Lessor also promises to provide maintenance services on the leased asset for an additional annual fee of $2,000. So, Lessee Company's annual payments now total $81,139.18—that is, the $79,139.18 basic fee plus the $2,000 executory maintenance costs. But the amount recorded by Lessor as Gross investment in leased asset is still $433,695.90; that is:

Annual total payments	$ 81,139.18
Less: Executory cost	(2,000.00)
Payments net of executory cost	79,139.18
Number of years	× 5
	$395,695.90
Plus: Residual value	38,000.00
Gross investment in leased assets	$433,695.90

Notice that the executory costs are subtracted in computing the capitalized amount.

At December 31, 2014, when the first cash payment is received from Lessee Company, Lessor Company makes the following journal entries:

DR	Cash		$81,139.18	
	CR	Gross investment in leased asset		$79,139.18
	CR	Maintenance revenue		2,000.00
DR	Unearned financing income—leases		$34,654.58	
	CR	Financing income—leases		$34,654.58

The costs incurred over the year in fulfilling the maintenance contract (not shown) will be expensed and deducted from the Maintenance revenue of $2,000.

RECAP

The capital lease versus operating lease dichotomy also exists for lessors. The criteria for classifying these leases include the same four criteria that apply to lessees plus two additional criteria. Lessors' incentives regarding how to classify leases are different from lessees' incentives because capital lease treatment accelerates the timing of income recognition for lessors. In addition, capital lease treatment improves many ratios for lessors in comparison to the level of these ratios under the operating lease approach.

ADDITIONAL LEASING ASPECTS

Sale and Leaseback

A sale and leaseback occurs when one company sells an asset to another company and immediately leases it back. This is done as a way to finance asset acquisition and/or for tax reasons. For example:

> First Company sells a manufacturing plant (excluding land) with a book value of $800,000 to Second Company for $1,000,000. First Company immediately leases the plant from Second Company for 20 years at an annual rental of $120,000.

First Company (the seller-lessee) can treat the entire annual rental of $120,000 as a deductible expense for tax purposes; if it had continued to own the asset, it could deduct depreciation only for the building itself but not for the land on which the building is located. Thus, total tax deductions could be higher under sale and leaseback arrangements. Also, the cash infusion of $1,000,000 could help meet cash flow needs.

No new *lease* accounting issues arise in sale and leaseback transactions. If the lease satisfies any of the four lessees' criteria on page 690, First Company must account for the lease as a capital lease; if none of the criteria is met, it must be treated as an operating lease. If the lease satisfies at least one of the lessor's Type I characteristics and both of the Type II characteristics (page 708), Second Company (the buyer-lessor) treats the lease as a direct financing lease; otherwise, it is an operating lease on Second Company's books.

The only complication in sale and leaseback arrangements is the treatment of the difference between the $1,000,000 sale price and the $800,000 carrying value of the manufacturing plant on First Company's books. Typically, when the assets are sold, this $200,000 will be recognized immediately on First Company's books as a gain on sale.

But this is not the way gains are treated in sale and leaseback transactions. Instead, First Company must record the $200,000 as a balance sheet credit, called a **deferred gain.** If the lease is a capital lease to First Company, this gain is then amortized into income using the same rate and life used to amortize the asset itself. If the lease is an operating lease to First Company, the gain is amortized in proportion to rental expense.

Assume that the lease qualifies as a capital lease; then First Company's entries are initially:

DR	Cash (or receivable)	$1,000,000	
	CR Property		$800,000
	CR Deferred gain		200,000
DR	Leased asset—capital lease	$1,000,000	
	CR Obligation under capital lease		$1,000,000

[This assumes that the discounted present value of the minimum lease payments equals $1,000,000.]

The rationale for deferring the gain is simple. Notice that at the time of "sale," the $1,000,000 sales price and the $120,000 annual lease payment schedule are simultaneously set, and the transaction will continue for 20 years. It may be that the property is "worth" only $800,000 and that Second Company is effectively loaning $200,000 to First Company, which will be recovered over time through the $120,000 annual payments on the lease. Recognizing a gain in such circumstances allows First Company to initially overstate its income by $200,000; this will be offset in later years by overstating its expenses by an identical amount. Thus, the GAAP requirement of deferring the gain protects against income manipulation possibilities such as creating artificial "gains on sale" by overstating the asset's "sale" price. However, the conservatism inherent to GAAP requires that losses in sale and leaseback transactions be recognized immediately on the seller's books.

Notice that if the sale and leaseback terms do not trigger any of the four lessees' criteria, the transaction is an operating lease to First Company (the lessee). So, carefully structured transactions allow firms to:

 **Analysis**

1. Remove *existing* assets from their books using sale and leaseback accounting.
2. Keep the asset and associated liability from reappearing by treating the lease as an operating lease.

In the past, the continuing involvement rule was sometimes circumvented through the use of a **special purpose entity** (SPE) that technically received the residual value. But the FASB has tried to close such loopholes by requiring that these SPEs be consolidated in many circumstances. If the SPE is consolidated, the off-balance-sheet treatment of the sale and leaseback is reversed. See FASB ASC Topic 810 Subsections for Variable Interest Entities.

Sale and leaseback accounting cannot be used when the seller-lessee (First Company in our example) retains some of the risks and rewards of ownership, such as the right to participate in any future appreciation in the value of the leased property. Such **continuing involvement** with ownershiplike characteristics is inconsistent with a "sale." That's why the existence of any such features disqualifies a transaction from sale and leaseback treatment.[14]

Other Special Lease Accounting Rules

ASC 840 also covers a number of highly specialized leasing situations and outlines in detail the rules for handling these situations. A real estate lease is an example of a situation requiring specialized rules in ASC 840.[15] A leveraged lease represents another example. In a **leveraged lease,** the lessor obtains nonrecourse financing for the leased asset from a third party, such as a bank. The lease is "leveraged" because the lessor borrows to finance the transaction. A leveraged lease does not affect the lessee's accounting. For these leases, lessees use the standard lease classification procedures outlined earlier. However, the lessor must account for leveraged leases using the direct financing approach, and special details—outlined at length in ASC 840—apply.

Financial Reporting versus Tax Accounting for Leases

The U.S. income tax rules also distinguish between operating leases and capital leases. However, the tax criteria for differentiating between them are not the same as the GAAP criteria. Further, the lessor's and the lessee's incentives are reversed for tax purposes. *Lessees* prefer the capital lease approach because it accelerates recognition of expenses and thereby lowers the discounted present value of their tax liability. *Lessors* prefer the operating lease approach on the tax return because it delays recognition of revenue and lowers the present value of the tax liability. So, book-versus-tax differences are frequent for both lessors and lessees.

The divergence between book accounting and tax accounting for lessees widened in recent years with the creation of **synthetic leases.** Synthetic leases result from complicated arrangements that include a lender, outside investors, a SPE, and the lessee. We'll skip the gory details of the legal arrangement and give you the punchline. A synthetic lease was structured to achieve the best of both worlds from the lessee's perspective: operating lease treatment on the books and capital lease treatment on the tax return. The lease contract carefully avoided triggering any of the four ASC 840 criteria, so it was an operating lease for financial reporting purposes. But for tax purposes, the lessee is considered the asset's owner because the contractual arrangement gives the lessee the proceeds of any appreciation in the asset's value at the end of the lease term.

The SPE played a crucial role in keeping the asset and liability off the lessee's books. However, after the Enron and subprime market collapses, the FASB tightened the rules for consolidating SPEs. Under these new rules, when the lessee is the potential beneficiary of the appreciation rights, the SPE must be consolidated. This effectively puts the lease asset and liability on the lessee's books, thereby negating the off-balance-sheet treatment of synthetic leases.

Lessors' Disclosures

Exhibit 12.9 is taken from the notes to the December 31, 2012, financial statements of Boeing Corporation, the aircraft manufacturer. The exhibit illustrates ASC 840 disclosure requirements for lessors. Capital and operating leases must be disclosed separately, and lessors must

---

[14] FASB ASC 840-40: Leases—Sale—Leaseback Transactions.
[15] FASB ASC Section 840-10-25: Leases—Overall—Recognition.

EXHIBIT 12.9 — Boeing Corporation: Illustration of Lessor's Financial Statement Note Disclosures

Customer financing at December 31 consisted of the following:

(amounts in millions)	2012	2011
Investment in sales-type/finance leases	$1,850	$2,037
Operating lease equipment, at cost, less accumulated depreciation of $628 and $765	2,038	1,991
Gross customer financing	$3,888	$4,028

Scheduled receipts on customer financing are as follows:

Year	2013	2014	2015	2016	2017	Beyond 2017	Total
Sales-type/finance lease payments receivable	290	231	230	226	207	803	1,987
Operating lease equipment payments receivable	474	172	162	97	55	104	1,064

The components of investment in sales-type/financing leases at December 31 were as follows:

	2012	2011
Minimum lease payments receivable	$1,987	$2,272
Estimated residual value of leased assets	544	541
Unearned income	(681)	(776)
Total	$1,850	$2,037

Authors' note: This financial statement note has been edited and a portion of the disclosure format has been modified slightly. The unedited note also includes notes receivable from customers.

provide a minimum lease payment schedule—just as lessees must do. Furthermore, the components of the net investment in capital leases (minimum lease payments, estimated residual values, etc.) are delineated, as are the cost and accumulated depreciation of assets under operating leases. The proportion of operating leases to capital leases for lessors is frequently less than 1—a stark contrast with lessees. The ratio for Boeing in Exhibit 12.9 is $1,064 ÷ $1,987 (see highlighted numbers), which equals 0.54. If we contrast this value with those in Exhibit 12.4 (page 704), we see that—unlike the ratio values for lessees—it is below 1.00. This is consistent with the fact that lessors like capital lease treatment because it accelerates income recognition and improves certain financial statement ratios in comparison to the operating lease approach.

GLOBAL VANTAGE POINT

 **International**

Comparison of IFRS and GAAP Lease Accounting

Accounting requirements under *International Accounting Standard (IAS) 17—Leases* are similar to those under FASB ASC 840.[16] IFRS differentiate between the concepts of operating leases and capital leases (called **finance leases** in IFRS) and generally follows the approach described in the chapter for GAAP. The subsequent paragraphs identify some of the key differences.

---

[16] "Leases," *IAS 17* (Revised 2003) (London: International Accounting Standards Board [IASB], 2009).

First, the classification criteria for both the lessee and the lessor are different from the FASB ASC 840 criteria. Classification is based on which party has the risks and rewards of ownership. Criteria that are similar to the four FASB ASC 840 criteria are cited as examples of situations in which lease should be classified as a finance lease. The specific criteria of *IAS 17* are:

Whether a lease is a finance lease or an operating lease depends on the substance of the transaction rather than the form of the contract. Examples of situations that individually or in combination would normally lead to a lease being classified as a finance lease are:

a. the lease transfers ownership of the asset to the lessee by the end of the lease term;

b. the lessee has the option to purchase the asset at a price that is expected to be sufficiently lower than the fair value at the date the option becomes exercisable for it to be reasonably certain, at the inception of the lease, that the option will be exercised;

c. the lease term is for the major part of the economic life of the asset even if title is not transferred;

d. at the inception of the lease the present value of the minimum lease payments amounts to at least substantially all of the fair value of the leased asset; and

e. the leased assets are of such a specialised nature that only the lessee can use them without major modifications (para. 10).

Indicators of situations that individually or in combination could also lead to a lease being classified as a finance lease are:

a. if the lessee can cancel the lease, the lessor's losses associated with the cancellation are borne by the lessee;

b. gains or losses from the fluctuation in the fair value of the residual accrue to the lessee (for example, in the form of a rent rebate equalling most of the sales proceeds at the end of the lease); and

c. the lessee has the ability to continue the lease for a secondary period at a rent that is substantially lower than market rent (para. 11).

Instead of using the ASC 840 bright-line of 75% of the economic life, *IAS 17* states "major part," and instead of 90% of fair value, *IAS 17* states "substantially all." When computing the present value of minimum lease payments, the lessee should use the **implicit interest rate** if known, whereas under FASB ASC 840, the lessee should use the *lower of* the implicit or the **incremental borrowing rate.** In addition, IFRS identifies other potential indicators for capitalization. For example, finance lease treatment could be required if the leased asset is so specialized that significant modifications would be needed for another party to use it. Finance lease treatment may also be warranted if the lessee bears the risk associated with changes in residual value fair values or the lease contains bargain renewals. These additional criteria could increase the probability of classifying a lease as a finance lease. Under *IAS 17,* the classification criteria for the lessor and lessee are the same; the two additional lessor criteria provided under FASB ASC 840 are absent.

A second difference relates to the ability for lessees to classify some assets held under leases as **investment property.**[17] Recall that investment property is defined as long-lived assets that are held to earn rentals or for capital appreciation. These assets may be accounted for using historical cost or fair value. Lessors would also have the choice between fair value and historical cost for *investment property* provided to lessees under operating leases.

The lessee and lessor disclosure requirements are similar to the requirements under GAAP. However, the lessee future minimum lease payment disclosures are for the periods: within one year, within years two through five, and after five years.[18] For finance leases, the standard also requires that the present value of minimum lease payments be given for each of the three intervals. In contrast, GAAP requires that "within years two through five" disclosure be given for each individual year, and only the present value in total must be disclosed. *IAS 17* lessor

---

[17] "Investment Property" (Revised 2003) (London: IASB, 2009). See Chapter 10, page 578.

[18] *IAS 17,* paras. 31 and 35.

disclosures also are similar to FASB ASC 840 requirements but combine the payments for years two through five, as is done for lessees.

Exhibit 12.10 provides selected lessee disclosures from the December 31, 2012, annual report of British Airways. The top schedule presents future payments and present values for finance leases and **hire purchase contracts.** These disclosures differ from GAAP in that they use the

IAS 17 defines hire purchase contracts as "contracts for the hire of an asset that contain a provision giving the hirer an option to acquire title to the asset upon the fulfillment of agreed conditions." IAS 17 treats these types of contracts as leases. See IAS 17, para. 6.

EXHIBIT 12.10	**British Airways: Edited Excerpts from Lessee Note Disclosures, December 31, 2012**

Long-Term Borrowings

Obligations under finance leases and hire purchase contracts

The Group uses finance leases and hire purchase contracts principally to acquire aircraft. These leases have both renewal options and purchase options. These are at the option of the Group. Future minimum lease payments under finance leases and hire purchase contracts are as follows:

	Group	
(£ million)	**2012**	**2011**
Future minimum payments due:		
Within one year	335	259
After more than one year but within five years	1,146	1,111
In five years or more	1,086	1,174
	2,567	2,544
Less: Finance charges	247	317
Present value of minimum lease payments	2,320	2,227
The present value of minimum lease payments is analysed as follows:		
Within one year	281	193
After more than one year but within five years	1,005	927
In five years or more	1,034	1,107
At 31 December	2,320	2,227

Operating Lease Commitments

The Group has entered into commercial leases on certain properties, equipment and aircraft. These leases have durations ranging from five years for aircraft to 150 years for ground leases. Certain leases contain options for renewal.

Fleet

The aggregate payments, for which there are commitments under operating leases fall due as follows:

	Group	
(£ million)	**2012**	**2011**
Within one year	111	63
Between one and five years	205	144
Over five years	86	109
At March 31	402	316

Property and equipment

The aggregate payments, for which there are commitments under operating leases fall due as follows:

	Group	
(£ million)	**2012**	**2011**
Within one year	87	84
Between one and five years	274	251
Over five years, ranging up to the year 2145	1,689	1,692
At 31 December	2,050	2,027

"after more than one year but within 5 years" category and provide a schedule of present values for each time interval. The bottom schedule provides a similar breakdown of future payments for operating leases but does not provide present values.

The schedules show total future minimum lease payments of £2,567 million for finance leases and hire purchase contracts and £2,452 (£402 for Fleet + £2,050 for Property and equipment) for operating leases. These amounts result in a ratio of operating lease payments to finance lease payments of .96 (£2,452/£2,567). This ratio is significantly lower than the Airlines average of 33.3 under GAAP found in Exhibit 12.4. One explanation is that the additional "specialized" indicator under *IAS 17* may lead to capitalizing most of the plane leases.

FASB and IASB Joint Exposure Draft

Lease accounting has been criticized for years because it allowed significant off-balance-sheet financing and lowered comparability by treating economically similar leases differently in financial statements (capital versus operating). Because of these and other criticisms, the FASB and the IASB have been working together to improve lease accounting. Based on this work, in May 2013, the FASB and the IASB issued a jointly developed leasing exposure draft.[19]

The FASB and IASB take a property rights approach and would require lessees to record a "right-of-use" asset and the associated liability. In essence, all leases would be classified as capital leases. To obtain the initial present values of the leased asset and the lease obligation, lessees will use the implicit rate. If the implicit rate cannot be determined then the lessee will use the incremental borrowing rate. Lease terms will include renewal options where the lessee has significant economic incentives to renew. In addition, lessees also will include variable rental payments tied to an index, such as the Consumer Price Index, in their present value calculations. Recall that Exhibit 12.4 shows for several companies the magnitude of undiscounted minimum lease payments under operating leases. Under the FASB's proposal, firms would discount these payments and place the resulting present values on their balance sheets as capital leases.[20] The constructive capitalization approach described in the appendix to this chapter can be used to estimate the initial balance sheet effects of the exposure draft.

Although the initial balance sheet effect is the same for all long-term leases, subsequent changes to the balance sheet depend on whether the leased asset is equipment or property (i.e., land and buildings). Equipment leases are defined as **Type A leases,** and property leases are defined as **Type B leases.** Lessee accounting for a *Type A lease* is essentially the same as the current accounting for a capital lease. The right-of-use asset is normally depreciated using the straight-line method, and the lease liability is amortized using the effective interest method. Exhibit 12.1 illustrates the depreciation expense and interest expense calculations and shows that total expense declines over time as interest expense declines. For the year ended December 31, 2014, Lessee Company reports Interest expense of $30,000 and Depreciation expense of $60,000.

In contrast, for a *Type B lease,* depreciation on the asset would equal the difference between the lease payment and interest expense for the period. Again, looking at Exhibit 12.1 for the year ended December 31, 2014, Depreciation expense would equal $49,139.18 (Total

---

[19] See "Leases (Topic 840)," Proposed Accounting Standards Update (Revised) (Norwalk CT: FASB, 2013) and "Leases," Exposure Draft (London: IASB, 2013). The 2013 exposure drafts reflect revisions made after the FASB and IASB considered comments on their 2010 exposure drafts.

[20] The exposure draft allows operating lease treatment when the maximum lease term, including renewal options, is less than 12 months.

payment of $79,139.18 less Interest expense of $30,000). Consequently, total expense (Interest expense of $30,000 + Depreciation expense of $49,139.18) for the year equals the amount of the lease payment ($79,139.18). In addition, the net lease asset would equal the lease liability. Specifically, the net lease asset equals $250,860.82 (Gross asset of $300,000 less Accumulated depreciation of $49,139.18) and the Lease obligation equals $250,860.82 (Initial obligation of $300,000 less the Principal reduction of $49,139.18). This depreciation method is called **interest-based (or, present value) amortization** and is not allowed under U.S. GAAP for other types of nonfinancial assets (see Chapter 10 discussion on page 549). Whereas Type A leases have separate amounts for depreciation expense and interest expense on the income statement, Type B leases report total lease expense as a single line item. In addition, the lease expense is shown only in the operating section of the statement of cash flows. In summary, the Type B lease is similar to a capital lease on the balance sheet and similar to an operating lease on the income statement and statement of cash flows.

Introducing the concept of a Type B lease is controversial from theoretical, complexity, and cost-benefit viewpoints. In fact, three of the seven FASB board members have provided alternative lease accounting models, largely because of the Type B leases found in the exposure draft.

The exposure draft *lessor* accounting also distinguishes between Type A and Type B leases based on whether the lease is equipment or property. Accounting for a *Type A lease* is similar to the accounting for direct financing and sales-type leases. However, the lease payments and the residual asset must be accounted for separately. Lessor accounting for a Type B lease is essentially operating lease accounting. The underlying asset remains on the lessor's balance sheet, and no receivable is established. Rental income equals total cash expected to be received and is spread evenly over the lease term.

The IASB exposure draft is nearly identical to the FASB's proposal. However, differences arise because both lessees and lessors have the ability to classify some types of assets as investment property (see the discussion in Chapter 10).

At the time of this writing, we do not know when or if the most recent exposure draft will be passed. Practitioners suggest that a new lease standard may not be effective until 2017.[21]

SUMMARY

- The treatment of leases under *FASB* ASC 840 represents a compromise between the unperformed-contracts and property-rights approaches.

- *FASB ASC 840* adopts a middle-of-the-road position that neither capitalizes all leases nor prohibits capitalization.

- GAAP contains criteria for determining the circumstances under which leases are capitalized.

- The lease capitalization criteria rely on bright-line rules such as 75% of economic life and 90% of fair value. Because lease capitalization adversely affects lessees' financial statements, many lessees structure agreements to avoid lease capitalization.

- The proportion of operating lease commitments to capital lease commitments can vary greatly even between firms in the same industry. This complicates financial analysis

---

[21] See KPMG, "FASB and IASB Issue Revised Exposure Drafts on Lease Accounting," *Defining Issues*, May 2013, No. 13-24.

because keeping leases off the balance sheet improves various ratios (e.g., turnover, debt-to-equity, and the current ratio). Consequently, analysts must constructively capitalize operating leases to make valid comparisons between firms with different proportions of capitalized leases.

- Lessors' use of the capital lease approach accelerates income recognition in contrast to the timing of income recognition under the operating lease approach. Lessors' financial statement ratios are also improved. It is perhaps not surprising, therefore, that capital leases appear frequently on lessors' financial statements.

- IFRS also distinguishes between operating and capital (finance) leases. Although the rules are similar to the GAAP rules, there are important differences. Key differences relate to classification criteria, investment property, and disclosure.

- The FASB and IASB have issued a jointly developed exposure draft on lease accounting. The proposed accounting adopts a "right-of-use" approach and would require lessees to treat most leases as capital leases on the balance sheet. However, the exposure draft introduces a controversial second method of accounting for real estate leases that is essentially capital lease accounting on the balance sheet and operating lease accounting on the income statement and statement of cash flows. Lessors also have a different model of accounting for real estate leases.

APPENDIX

MAKING FINANCIAL STATEMENT DATA COMPARABLE BY ADJUSTING FOR OFF-BALANCE-SHEET LEASES

Analysis

To make their debt burden appear lower, some lessees carefully design their lease contracts to evade capital lease criteria, thereby keeping most of their leases off the balance sheet. Other companies structure their leases and apply the lease accounting rules less aggressively and have a higher proportion of capital leases. This complicates comparisons between companies because each may have similar lease contract terms but very dissimilar lease balance sheet numbers. Despite this complication, comparisons can still be made.

The most straightforward method for making lessees' balance sheet data comparable is to treat *all* leases as if they were capital leases. That is, analysts should use the disclosed minimum *operating* lease payment schedule as a basis for approximating what the balance sheet numbers would have been had those operating leases been treated instead as capital leases. This is **constructive capitalization.** We use the Whole Foods Market, Inc., 2012 data from Exhibit 12.5 to illustrate how this is done. For convenience, these numbers for Whole Foods are reproduced in the following table.

The liability that would appear on the balance sheet if these operating leases were instead treated as capital leases is the *discounted present value* of the stream of minimum operating lease payments. This payment stream (undiscounted) totals $6,774.8 million. Two items must be estimated to compute this present value. First, an appropriate discount rate must be determined. Second, each year's payments beyond 2017 must be estimated because lease payments for all years after 2017 are aggregated under the caption "Future fiscal years," often called "thereafter."

Whole Foods Market, Inc.

Operating Lease Payments from Lease Note, 2012 Annual Report

($ in millions)	Minimum Operating Lease Payments
Fiscal year 2013	$ 309.1
Fiscal year 2014	364.3
Fiscal year 2015	385.5
Fiscal year 2016	396.1
Fiscal year 2017	397.0
Future fiscal years	4,922.8
	$6,774.8

Determining the Discount Rate   Two alternatives for determining the discount rate for computing the present value of operating lease payments exist:

- The weighted average discount rate implicit in capital leases.
- The weighted average discount rate on interest-bearing long-term debt (including capital lease commitments).

In some cases, a company discloses the weighted average discount rate used for capital leases in its lease footnote. If this rate is not disclosed, it can be estimated provided the current portion of capital leases (that is, that portion that represents a current liability) is disclosed. This information is often provided either on the balance sheet or in the lease footnote.

We now turn to how the calculation is made. Recall from the discussion in the chapter that each periodic lease payment comprises two elements: (1) interest based on the present value of the lease obligation at the beginning of the period and (2) the principal payment on the unpaid lease obligation. The current portion of the capital lease obligation represents the second component—that is, the amount of next year's lease payment that reduces the principal balance of the lease obligation. Therefore, subtracting this principal reduction amount from the total scheduled lease payment for the coming year leaves the interest expense component. Dividing the interest expense *component* by the present value of the capital lease obligation shown in the lease note on the current balance sheet date (which is also the present value of the lease obligation at the beginning of the next fiscal year) yields the average implicit interest rate for capital leases. To summarize:

$$\frac{\text{Interest expense on}}{\text{capital leases}} = \frac{\text{Implicit interest rate}}{\text{in capital lease contracts}} \times \frac{\text{Present value of lease obligation}}{\text{at beginning of year}}$$

Rearranging we get:

$$\frac{\text{Interest expense on capital lease}}{\begin{array}{c}\text{Present value of lease obligation}\\\text{at beginning of year}\end{array}} = \frac{\text{Implicit interest rate in}}{\text{capital lease contracts}}$$

> The schedule of lease payments found in the lease note always provides the amount of next year's lease payment. The current portion may be found in the lease note, the debt note, or the balance sheet.

Whole Foods' lease note in Exhibit 12.5 reveals that the current portion of capital leases is $1.012 million. Subtracting this from the $2.967 million scheduled capital lease payment in 2013 leaves $1.955 million as the interest expense component of the 2013 lease payment. Dividing this number by the September 30, 2012, capital lease obligation of $24.122 million, yields an average implicit interest rate of 8.10%. This rate can then be used to compute the present value of the scheduled operating lease payments.

A second estimate of the discount rate can be derived from the lessee's financial statement note for long-term debt. This note discloses the interest rate on each debt issue. The weighted average rate on long-term debt provides an alternative rate for discounting the operating lease payments. Another, and somewhat easier, way to approximate the weighted average interest rate on long-term debt is to compute the ratio of total interest expense (often shown on the income statement or in statement notes) by the average of beginning and end-of-year interest bearing long-term debt outstanding (including the long-term portion of capital leases). We cannot use this approach for Whole Foods because it does not have any long-term interest-bearing debt in 2012.

Estimating Payments beyond Five Years Procedures for estimating annual operating lease payments for periods after 2017 can also be developed. One approach is as follows. Notice from the prior page that the annual increase in minimum operating lease payments between 2015 and 2016 is $10.6 million (that is, $396.1 million − $385.5 million); between 2016 and 2017, the decrease is $0.9 million (that is, $397.0 million − $396.1 million). So, the average annual increase over the three-year period is $5.8 million (that is [$10.6 million + $0.9 million]/2). This suggests that the undisclosed minimum operating lease payment for 2018 is probably in the vicinity of $402.8 million—the $397.0 million 2017 payment plus $5.8 million of estimated yearly increase. The simplest approach for estimating a schedule of annual payments for 2018 and beyond is to assume that all subsequent payments are also somewhere near $402.8 million per year. Dividing the future fiscal years minimum operating lease payments of $4,922.8 million by $402.8 million yields an *initial* estimate of how many years beyond 2017 the existing operating leases run. The computation is:

> Because the payments after 2017 are assumed to be spread evenly over a 12-year period, we adjust our estimated yearly lease payment to be $410.2 million ($4,922.8 million/12 years) in Exhibit 12.11.

$$\frac{\text{Minimum operating lease payments for years after 2017}}{\substack{\text{Estimated yearly lease payment (assumed to be the same for all years)}}} = \frac{\$4,922.8 \text{ million}}{\$402.8 \text{ million per year}} = 12.2 \text{ years}$$

The initial estimate is 12.2 years, which we round to 12 years. Based on this estimate, the net minimum lease payments will be discounted over a 17-year period—that is, 2013 through 2017 (5 years) plus the estimated 12 years we just computed.

Our estimate of the amount of additional liability on Whole Foods Market's balance sheet at September 30, 2012, if all operating leases were capitalized is the highlighted amount of $3,569.7 million shown in Exhibit 12.11.[22] A small portion ($23.5 million) would be a current liability and $3,546.2 million (total obligation of $3,569.7 million less current obligation of $23.5 million) would be a long-term liability.

> The $23.5 million current liability is determined as follows. Interest expense in 2013 on these capitalized operating leases would be $3,569.7 million × 8%, or approximately $285.6 million. The 2013 minimum operating lease payment is $309.1 million in Exhibit 12.11. Because interest is a liability that accrues over time, only the difference between the total 2013 payment of $309.1 million and the as yet unaccrued interest of $285.6 million is a current liability as of September 30, 2012.

[22] The Exhibit 12.11 present value calculations assume that all lease payments are made at year-end. Typically payments are made throughout the year, so a more realistic assumption would be that payments are made halfway through the year. We can adjust the present value of $3,569.7 million to reflect the midyear assumption by multiplying $3,569.7 by 1.04 (1 + 0.08/2) to obtain $3,712.5. Subsequent calculations could be done using this amount instead of the $3,569.7. However, given that we probably have some measurement error in the timing of the amounts after 2017 and the choice of discount rate, analysts may not want to take the time to make the additional adjustment. The ratios computed in Exhibit 12.12 are nearly identical under either approach.

EXHIBIT 12.11	Whole Foods Market, Inc.: Estimate of Capitalized Operating Lease Liability as of September 30, 2012

($ in millions) Fiscal Year	Minimum Operating Lease Payment	Present Value Factor* at 8%	Discounted Present Value
2013	$309.1	0.92593	$ 286.2
2014	364.3	0.85734	312.3
2015	385.5	0.79383	306.0
2016	396.1	0.73503	291.1
2017	397.0	0.68058	270.2
2018⎫ 2029⎭	410.2	5.12893†	2,103.9
Total			$3,569.7

* Present value factors for interest rates not included in this book's Appendix can be found at the text website: www.mhhe.com/revsine6e.

† Present value of an ordinary annuity for 17 years at 8% minus present value of an ordinary annuity for five years at 8%, or 9.12164 minus 3.99271.

When the capitalized operating lease liability has been estimated, the next task is to estimate the capitalized operating lease asset amount. Recall from pages 701 and 702 that the lease asset book value is often less than the lease obligation. That discussion also notes that a common rule of thumb is that the asset is 70% of the obligation. To refine this estimate, one can often use the capital lease asset disclosure the company makes for capital leases. One would divide a firm's net capital lease assets by its capital lease obligations to estimate the ratio. It may be reasonable to use this same percentage to estimate the operating lease asset to be capitalized. Though Whole Foods discloses its total capital lease assets and capital lease obligations, it does not disclose separately accumulated depreciation for the capital lease assets. Therefore, we must use the rule of thumb of 70% to estimate the net asset associated with the constructively capitalized operating leases. Multiplying 70% by the estimated operating lease liability of $3,569.7 million yields an estimated operating lease asset of $2,498.8 million. Note that the lease liability is 10 times the 2012 rent expense of $353.4 shown in Exhibit 12.5, and the asset is seven times the rent expense amount. Consequently, the multiple of eight that Whole Foods uses in its return on investment calculations is reasonable but not as accurate as is the present value approach. In addition, given that the amount of rent expense changes each year and lease terms change over time, the short-cut multiple approach could be less accurate in subsequent years unless the multiplier is updated.

Exhibit 12.12 illustrates the estimated ratio effects for 2012 that result from capitalizing operating leases for Whole Foods. Exhibit 12.12(a) Column (a) shows financial statement amounts as reported in Whole Foods' fiscal year-end September 30, 2012 financial statements. Column (b) shows the adjustments for operating lease capitalization. Notice, in addition to the capital lease asset and liability adjustments, there is a decrease to liabilities for $440.8 million due to "Deferred lease liabilities." These liabilities represent accruals associated with rent holidays under operating leases (see discussion on page 706). These *operating* lease liabilities must be removed when we shift to *capital* lease accounting and record the $3,569.7 million present value of lease payments. In addition, there is a "net debit to balance" of $630.1 million determined as follows:

Lease asset	$2,498.8
Less: Lease liability	(3,569.7)
Plus: Removed operating lease liability	440.8
	$ (630.1)

EXHIBIT 12.12   Whole Foods Market, Inc.—Constructive Capitalization of Operating Leases

Panel (a): Financial Statement Data

($ in millions) Statement Item	(a) September 30, 2012 Financial Statements	(b) Adjustments for Constructive Capitalization		(c) Total after Constructive Capitalization
Total assets	$5,294.2	Capital lease asset	+ $2,498.8	$ 7,793.0
Current portion of lease obligation	1.0	Current portion lease obligation	+ 23.5	24.5
Total long-term obligations	514.5	Long-term lease obligation Deferred lease liabilities	+ 3,546.2 − 440.8	3,619.9
Shareholders' equity	3,802.4	Net debit to balance	− 630.1	3,172.3
NOPAT*	465.7	After-tax income effect of capitalizing operating leases	+ 128.0	593.7
Sales	11,698.8		+ –0–	11,698.8

Panel (b): Adjusted Ratios after Capitalization

Ratio	As Reported in 09/30/2012 Financial Statements	Ratio after Constructive Capitalization of Operating Leases
Total long-term obligations to equity ratio	0.14	1.14[†]
ROA	8.8%	7.62[‡]
Total asset turnover (Sales/total assets)	2.21	1.50[§]

---

* NOPAT refers to the company's net operating profit after taxes. To compute NOPAT, you (1) eliminate nonoperating or nonrecurring items from reported income and (2) add back after-tax interest expense. (See Panel [b].)

[†] Computed by dividing the adjusted Total long-term obligations amount of $3,619.9 million by the adjusted Shareholders' equity of $3,172.3 million. This ignores the unknown deferred tax effect and distorts the adjusted ratio slightly.

[‡] Computed by dividing the adjusted NOPAT of $593.7 million by the adjusted Total assets of $7,793.0. This ignores the unknown deferred tax effect and distorts the adjusted ratio slightly. The ending balance of adjusted total assets was used to compute ROA as follows. The tax rate was assumed to be 38%.

$$ROA = \frac{NOPAT}{Total\ assets} = \frac{Net\ income + [Charges\ and\ gains \times (1 - Tax\ rate)] + [Interest \times (1 - Tax\ rate)]}{Total\ assets}$$

[§] Computed by dividing the reported Sales of $11,698.8 million by the adjusted Total assets of $7,793.0 million.

The $630.1 million debit comprises two items: (1) a debit to a deferred tax asset and (2) a debit to Retained earnings. A deferred tax asset arises because capitalization accelerates expense recognition. Accordingly, constructively capitalizing these leases means that expenses are recognized earlier on the books than on the tax return, which creates a deferred tax asset. The amount of the deferred tax asset can be approximated by multiplying the "net debit to balance" of $630.1 by Whole Foods' effective tax rate of 38% (computed in the next paragraph) to obtain $239.4 million. Whether this amount is added to assets or deducted from liabilities depends on the amounts of Whole Foods' other deferred tax assets and liabilities. One needs to understand concepts from Chapter 12 to address this issue fully. Therefore, to reduce the complexity of the example, we place the entire $630.1 million debit into Retained earnings and do not allocate an amount to a deferred tax asset or deferred tax liability.

> This paragraph assumes that you are comfortable with deferred tax concepts. If you are not, you can safely skip this paragraph and return to Exhibit 12.12 after reading Chapter 13.

To compute a revised return on asset (ROA), we must adjust the numerator of the ratio, net operating income after taxes (NOPAT). Although, we capitalized the lease asset at 70% of the lease liability, we still need to depreciate the remaining balance over the assumed 17-year remaining lease period. Depreciation expense on a straight-line basis for the lease asset is

$147.0 million (lease asset of $2,498.8 million ÷ 17-year life). To adjust pretax NOPAT, we subtract the $147.0 million depreciation expense and add back the 2012 rent expense of $353.4 million shown in Exhibit 12.5 for a net pretax addition of $206.4 million. No adjustment is made for interest expense because it is not deducted when computing NOPAT. We approximate Whole Foods' effective tax rate by dividing its reported income tax expense of $286.5 million by its pre-tax income of $752.0 million to obtain 38%. We then obtain the after-tax NOPAT effect of $128.0 million by multiplying the pretax NOPAT effect of $206.4 million by 1 minus the 38% tax rate.

The adjusted ratios after capitalization are shown in Exhibit 12.12(b). Notice that the adjustments from capitalizing operating leases alter Whole Foods' ratios. The total long-term obligations to equity ratio increases from 0.14 to 1.14, an increase of approximately 714%! Return on assets (ROA) decreases from 8.80% to 7.62%, a decrease of 13.4%. Although we added a significant amount of assets to the denominator, we also increased the numerator for the after-tax difference between the prior operating lease rent expense and depreciation expense on the new lease assets. Because both the numerator and denominator increase, the specific effects will vary by firm. For the total asset turnover ratio, only the denominator increases. Consequently, the turnover ratio decreased from 2.21 to 1.50, a 32.1% decline.

> Exhibit 12.4 shows that the other firms in the supermarkets industry have lower ratios of operating to capital lease payments than Whole Foods. This difference underscores the importance of making adjustments to Whole Foods' competitors before undertaking financial comparisons.

It is important to make such adjustments when making financial comparisons *across* firms. While the effect on Whole Foods is significant, some of its competitors could be more or less aggressive in keeping leases off the balance sheet. So, interfirm comparisons may be misleading unless adjustments are also made to the competitors' statements. The underlying real economic differences are revealed only by comparing the adjusted statements for all firms. The easiest way to overcome these capitalization differences between firms is to treat all leases that convey significant property rights as though they were capital leases.

Constructively capitalizing operating leases also gives us a preview of how the FASB/IASB 2013 proposals will affect lessee financial statements. The above calculations are consistent with *Type A* lease accounting. However, if Whole Foods' classifies most of its leases as *Type B* leases, the numerator in the return on assets ratio will remain at $465.7 million, but assets will increase to $7,793.0 million. ***The resulting ratio of 5.98% is even lower than the 7.62% shown in Exhibit 12.12.***

EXERCISES

Monk Company, a dealer in machinery and equipment, leased equipment with a 10-year life to Leland Inc. on July 1, 2014. The lease is appropriately accounted for as a sale by Monk and as a purchase by Leland. The lease is for an eight-year period, expiring June 30, 2022. The first of eight equal payments of $300,000 is due on June 30, 2015. Leland has an option to purchase the equipment on June 30, 2022, for $100,000 even though the expected residual value at that time is $600,000. Leland's incremental borrowing rate is 7%, and it uses straight-line depreciation. The equipment is expected to have a salvage value of zero at June 30, 2024.

E12-1

Accounting for lessee with purchase option
(LO 3, 4, 5)

AICPA
ADAPTED

Required:

1. At what amount should Leland record the leased equipment on July 1, 2014?

2. Prepare Leland's amortization table for the leased equipment.

3. What is the amount of depreciation and interest expense that Leland should record for the year ended December 31, 2014, and for the year ended December 31, 2015?

E12-2	

Accounting for lessee with purchase option
(LO 3, 4, 5)

Use the information in E12-1, except that the payments are made at the beginning of the period (July 1, 2014) instead of the end of the rental period (June 30, 2015).

Required:

Repeat the requirements of E12–1.

E12-3	

Accounting for lessee:
Purchase option
(LO 3, 4, 5)

AICPA
ADAPTED

East Company leased a new machine from North Company on May 1, 2014, under a lease with the following information:

Lease term	10 years
Annual rental payable at beginning of each lease year	$40,000
Useful life of machine	12 years
Implicit interest rate	15%

East has the option to purchase the machine on May 1, 2024, by paying $50,000, which approximates the expected fair value of the machine on the option exercise date.

Required:

What is the amount of the capitalized leased asset on May 1, 2014?

E12-4	

Accounting and reporting for lessee **(LO 5)**

AICPA
ADAPTED

On December 31, 2014, Ball Company leased a machine from Cook for a 10-year period, expiring December 30, 2024. Annual payments of $100,000 are due on December 31. The first payment was made on December 31, 2014, and the second payment was made on December 31, 2015. The present value at the inception of the lease for the 10 lease payments discounted at 10% was $676,000. The lease is appropriately accounted for as a capital lease by Ball.

Required:

1. Compute the December 31, 2015, amount that Ball should report as a lease liability after the first payment has been made.

2. What portion of this total liability should be classified as a current liability?

E12-5	

Accounting for lessor
(LO 4, 6, 7, 8)

AICPA
ADAPTED

Beard Company purchased a machine on January 1, 2014, for $620,000. The machine is expected to have a 10-year life, no residual value, and will be depreciated by the straight-line method. On January 1, 2014, it leased the machine to Child Company for a three-year period at an annual rental of $125,000. Beard could have sold the machine for $817,298 instead of leasing it. Beard incurred maintenance and other executory costs of $5,000 in 2014 under the terms of the lease.

Required:

1. What amount should Beard report as operating profit on this leased asset for the year ended December 31, 2014?

2. Assume that the lease term is eight years instead of three years. What amount should Beard report as operating profit on this leased asset for the year ended December 31, 2014?

E12-6	

Accounting for a sales-type lease **(LO 7, 8)**

AICPA
ADAPTED

Benedict Company leased equipment to Mark Inc. on January 1, 2014. The lease is for an eight-year period, expiring December 31, 2021. The first of eight equal annual payments of $600,000 was made on January 1, 2014. Benedict had purchased the equipment on December 29, 2013, for $3,200,000. The lease is appropriately accounted for as a sales-type lease by Benedict. Assume that at January 1, 2014, the present value of all rental payments over the lease term discounted at a 10% interest rate was $3,520,000.

Required:

What amount of interest income should Benedict record in 2015 (the second year of the lease period) as a result of the lease?

Glade Company leases computer equipment to customers under direct financing leases. The equipment has no residual value at the end of the lease term, and the leases do not contain bargain purchase options. Glade wishes to earn 8% interest on a five-year lease of equipment with a fair value of $323,400.

Required:

Compute the total amount of interest revenue that Glade will earn over the life of the lease.

E12-7

Accounting for a direct financing lease (**LO 1, 7, 8**)

AICPA
ADAPTED

Below are three independent lease scenarios. Payments are made at the **end of each year.**

	Case 1	Case 2	Case 3
Cost of equipment to lessor	$50,000	$64,000	$100,000
Fair value of equipment	$70,000	$80,000	$100,000
Guaranteed residual value	$10,000		
Unguaranteed residual value		$ 8,000	
Bargain purchase option			$ 4,500
Life of lease	10 years	15 years	8 years
Economic life of asset	12 years	16 years	10 years
Rate of return required	12%	9%	7%

E12-8

Determining lease payment and depreciation amounts (**LO 1, 3, 4, 5**)

Required:

1. Calculate the lease payments for the above three cases.
2. Based on the relation between the lease life and economic life, the lessees will classify the leases as capital leases. For each lease, compute the lessee's depreciation expense for the first year of the lease. Assume the use of the straight-line method and no salvage value at the end of the economic life.

On December 31, 2014, Day Company leased a new machine from Parr with the following pertinent information:

Lease term	6 years
Annual rental payable at beginning of each year	$50,000
Useful life of machine	8 years
Day's incremental borrowing rate	15%
Implicit interest rate in lease (known by Day)	12%

E12-9

Using the appropriate discount rate (**LO 3, 5**)

AICPA
ADAPTED

The lease is not renewable, and the machine reverts to Parr at the termination of the lease. The cost of the machine on Parr's accounting records is $375,500.

Required:

Compute the amount of Day's lease liability at the beginning of the lease term.

On October 1, 2014, Vaughn, Inc., leased a machine from Fell Leasing Company. The lease qualifies as a capital lease and requires nine annual payments of $10,000 beginning September 30, 2015. The lease specifies a purchase option of $10,000 at September 30, 2023, even though the machine's estimated value on that date is $30,000. Vaughn's incremental borrowing rate is 11% and has a calendar year-end for reporting purposes. The machine has a 12-year economic life with zero salvage value.

E12-10

Accounting for lessee's accruals and purchase option (**LO 3, 4, 5**)

AICPA
ADAPTED

Required:

1. At what amount should Vaughn record the leased equipment on October 1, 2014?
2. What is the amount of depreciation and interest expense that Vaughn should record for the year ended December 31, 2014, and for the year ended December 31, 2015?
3. How much of the lease liability should be classified as current on December 31, 2014, and December 31, 2015?

E12-11

Accounting for lessee guaranteed residual
(LO 4, 5)

AICPA
ADAPTED

On January 1, 2014, Babson, Inc., leased two automobiles for executive use. The lease requires Babson to make five annual payments of $13,000, beginning January 1, 2014. At the end of the lease term on December 31, 2018, Babson guarantees that the residual value of the automobiles will total $10,000. The lease qualifies as a capital lease. The interest rate implicit in the lease is 9%.

Required:

Compute Babson's recorded capital lease liability immediately after the first required payment.

E12-12

Accounting for executory costs (LO 4, 5)

AICPA
ADAPTED

On December 31, 2014, Roe Company leased a machine from Colt for a five-year period. Equal annual payments under the lease are $105,000 (including $5,000 annual executory costs) and are due on December 31 of each year. The first payment was made on December 31, 2014, and the second payment was made on December 31, 2015. The five lease payments are discounted at 10% over the lease term. The present value of minimum lease payments at the inception of the lease and before the first annual payment was $417,000. Roe appropriately accounts for the lease as a capital lease.

Required:

What is the lease liability that Roe should report in its December 31, 2015, balance sheet?

E12-13

Accounting for sale and leaseback (LO 3, 9)

AICPA
ADAPTED

On December 31, 2014, Lane, Inc., sold equipment to Noll and simultaneously leased it back for 12 years. Pertinent information at this date is as follows:

Sales price	$480,000
Carrying amount	$360,000
Estimated remaining economic life	15 years

Required:

1. At December 31, 2014, should Lane report a gain from the sale of the equipment?

2. If not, how should it account for the sale and leaseback?

E12-14

Determining cash flow statement effects of capital versus operating leases (LO 5)

Mickelson reports on a calendar year basis. On January 1, 2014, Mickelson Corporation enters into a three-year lease with annual payments of $30,000. The first payment will be due on December 31, 2014. The present value of the payments at 8% is $77,313. If the lease is classified as a capital lease, the following amortization table would be used to record interest expense:

Payment Date	Payment	Interest Expense	Principal Reduction	Lease Obligation Balance
01/01/14				$77,313
12/31/14	$30,000	$6,185	$23,815	53,498
12/31/15	30,000	4,280	25,720	27,778
12/31/16	30,000	2,222	27,778	—

Required:

1. If the lease were classified as an operating lease, show for each year the effects on the operating, investing, and financing activities sections of the statement of cash flows (direct method).

2. If the lease were classified as a capital lease, show for each year the effects on the operating, investing, and financing activities sections of the statement of cash flows (direct method). Assume that the leased asset is depreciated over three years.

3. If the lease were classified as a Type B lease under the FASB's 2013 Exposure Draft, show for each year the effects on the operating, investing, and financing activities sections of the statement of cash flows (direct method). Assume that the leased asset is depreciated over three years.

Sandra Company and Nova Inc. each signed lease agreements on January 1, 2014. Nova's lease qualified for capital lease treatment, but Sandra's lease did not. All other information for both companies is identical. Payments on each lease were due at the end of each year. The following information is from each company's December 31, 2013, financial statements:

	Sandra	Nova
Current assets	$ 2,000	$ 2,000
Total assets	5,000	5,000
Current liabilities	2,000	2,000
Total liabilities	2,500	2,500
Sales	10,500	10,500

Required:

1. Based on this information, what will be the impact of the lease transaction on Nova's current ratio and debt-to-equity ratio on January 1, 2014, immediately after signing the lease?

2. What will be the impact on the total asset turnover ratio for 2014?

3. How would Sandra's ratio effects differ from Nova's? (*Hint:* Compute Nova's ratios before and after the capital lease transaction and assume that the lease liability and asset were recorded at $1,000.)

On January 1, 2014, Draper Inc. signed a five-year noncancelable lease with Thornhill Company for custom-made equipment. The lease calls for five payments of $161,364.70 to be made at the beginning of each year. The leased asset has a fair value of $900,000 on January 1, 2014. There is no bargain purchase option, and ownership of the leased asset reverts to Thornhill at the lease end. The leased asset has an expected useful life of six years, and Draper uses straight-line depreciation for financial reporting purposes. Its incremental borrowing rate is 8%. Draper uses a calendar year for financial reporting purposes.

Required:

1. Under U.S. GAAP, would Draper classify this lease as a capital lease or as an operating lease? Explain.

2. Under IFRS, would Draper classify this lease as a capital lease or as an operating lease? Explain.

On January 1, 2014, Walker, Inc., signs a 5-year lease for two floors of a 20-floor building. The building has an expected remaining life of 20 years. The space is available immediately, and Walker agrees to make annual payments $325,000 on December 31 of each year. The lease contains no renewal or purchase options. The implicit rate in the lease is 7%.

Required:

1. What journal entry would Walker prepare on January 1, 2014, under U.S. GAAP existing in 2014?

2. What journal entry would Walker prepare on January 1, 2014, under the FASB's 2013 lease exposure draft?

3. Compute and label the amounts that would be shown on Walker's income statement, balance sheet, and statement of cash flows for the year ended December 31, 2014, assuming that it uses the FASB's 2013 lease exposure draft.

PROBLEMS / DISCUSSION QUESTIONS

P12-1

Making computations and journal entries for lessee
(LO 3, 4, 5)

Bunker Company negotiated a lease with Gilbreth Company that begins on January 1, 2014. The lease term is three years, and the asset's economic life is four years. The annual lease payments are $7,500, payable at the end of the year. The cost and fair value of the asset are $23,000. The lessee's cost of borrowing is 9%.

Required:

1. Determine whether Bunker must treat this lease as an operating lease or a capital lease.

2. Prepare an amortization table for the lease.

3. Prepare Bunker's journal entries for the first two years of the lease.

4. Assume that all facts remain the same except that the asset's useful life is six years. Is this an operating lease or a capital lease? Prepare journal entries for the first two years of the lease.

5. Compare the financial statement effects of the lease treatment you selected in requirement 3 with the financial statement effects of the treatment you selected in requirement 4. Specifically, compare the effects on assets, liabilities, and equity under the two alternative sets of assumptions as of December 31, 2014, immediately *after* the first lease payment is made.

P12-2

Making computations for lessee and lessor
(LO 1, 4, 5, 8)

Lessor Company has a machine with a cost and fair value of $100,000 that it leases for a 10-year period to Lessee Company. The machine has a 12-year expected economic life. Payments are received at the beginning of each year. The machine is expected to have a $10,000 residual value at the end of the lease term. (Lessee is not guaranteeing the residual value.)

Required:

1. What would the lease payments be if Lessor wants to earn a 10% return on its net investment?

2. What lease obligation would Lessee report when the lease is signed?

3. What would be the interest revenue reported by Lessor and the interest expense reported by Lessee in the first year, assuming they both use the 10% discount rate?

4. How would the answers to requirements 2 and 3 change for Lessee if it guaranteed the residual value?

P12-3

Accounting for lessees' capital leases   **(LO 3, 4, 5)**

mhhe.com/revsine6e

On January 1, 2014, Seven Wonders Inc. signed a five-year noncancelable lease with Moss Company. The lease calls for five payments of $277,409.44 to be made at the end of each year. The leased asset has a fair value of $1,200,000 on January 1, 2014. Seven Wonders cannot renew the lease, there is no bargain purchase option, and ownership of the leased asset reverts to Moss at the lease end. The leased asset has an expected useful life of six years, and Seven Wonders uses straight-line depreciation for financial reporting purposes. Its incremental borrowing rate is 12%. Moss's implicit rate of return on the lease is unknown. Seven Wonders uses a calendar year for financial reporting purposes.

Required:

1. Why must Seven Wonders account for the lease as a capital lease?

2. Prepare an amortization schedule for the lease liability. Round the amount of the initial lease liability at January 1, 2014, to the nearest dollar. Round all amounts in the amortization table to the nearest cent.

3. Prepare the journal entry to record (a) the lease as a capital lease on January 1, 2014; (b) the lease payments on December 31, 2014 and 2015; and (c) the leased asset's depreciation in 2014 and 2015.

Continued on next page

4. What is the total amount of expense reported on Seven Wonders' 2014 income statement from the lease? Is this amount the same as, more than, or less than the amount that would have been reported if the lease had been classified as an operating lease? Why?

Required:

1. Repeat requirement 2 of P12–3. Assume that the lease payments are due at the beginning rather than at the end of the year. In this case, the first $277,409.44 payment would be made on January 1, 2014. Round the amount of the initial lease liability at January 1, 2014, to the nearest dollar. Round all amounts in the amortization table to the nearest cent.

2. Prepare the journal entry to record the lease as a capital lease on January 1, 2014. Also prepare the lessee's adjusting entries for December 31, 2014 and 2015, as well as the entries to record the lease payments on January 1, 2015 and 2016, and the leased asset's depreciation in 2014 and 2015.

P12-4

Accounting for lessees' capital leases **(LO 3, 4, 5)**

mhhe.com/revsine6e

On January 1, 2014, Bare Trees Company signed a three-year noncancelable lease with Dreams Inc. The lease calls for three payments of $62,258.09 to be made at each year-end. The lease payments include $3,000 of executory costs. The lease is nonrenewable and has no bargain purchase option. Ownership of the leased asset reverts to Dreams at the end of the lease period, at which time Bare Trees has guaranteed that the leased asset will be worth at least $15,000. The leased asset has an expected useful life of four years, and Bare Trees uses straight-line depreciation for financial reporting purposes. Bare Trees' incremental borrowing rate is 9%, which is less than Dreams' implicit rate of return on the lease.

P12-5

Accounting for lessees' capital leases including executory costs and residual value guarantee **(LO 3, 4, 5)**

Required:

1. Prepare an amortization schedule for the lease liability. Round the amount of the initial lease liability at January 1, 2014, to the nearest dollar. Round all amounts in the amortization table to the nearest cent.

2. Make the journal entry to record (a) the lease on January 1, 2014; (b) the lease payments on December 31, 2014 and 2015; and (c) the leased asset's depreciation in 2014 and 2015.

3. Assume that at the end of the lease term, the leased asset will be worth $16,000. Make the journal entry to account for the residual value guarantee.

4. Repeat requirement 3, but assume that the leased asset will be worth only $12,000 at the end of the lease term.

On January 1, 2014, Task Co. signs an agreement to lease office equipment from Coleman Inc. for three years with payments of $193,357 beginning December 31, 2014. The equipment's fair value is $500,000 with an expected useful life of four years. At the end of three years, the equipment is expected to have a $50,000 residual value, which Task does not guarantee. Both Task and Coleman use a 12% rate of return in evaluating this transaction. Task uses straight-line depreciation.

P12-6

Assessing guaranteed and unguaranteed residual values for the lessee **(LO 3, 4, 5)**

Required:

1. What type of a lease is this for Task and why?

2. Prepare a schedule to amortize the lease liability. Round the amount of the initial lease liability to the nearest dollar and all amounts in the schedule to the nearest cent.

3. Prepare the journal entries required on Task's books for 2014 and 2016.

4. Assume now that Task guarantees the residual value. Prepare an amortization table and the journal entries necessary on Task's books for 2014 and 2016. Further assume that the equipment's residual value on December 31, 2016, is $40,000.

P12-7

Assessing guaranteed and unguaranteed residual values for the lessor
(LO 3, 4, 5, 8)

Required:

Using the data in P12–6, prepare the journal entries required by Coleman Inc. on January 1, 2014, assuming that (a) Task does not guarantee the residual value and (b) Task does guarantee it. Coleman paid $500,000 to acquire the office equipment several weeks prior to the leasing transaction.

P12-8

Evaluating effects of lease accounting on ratios and income   **(LO 2, 5)**

On December 31, 2014, Thomas Henley, financial vice president of Kingston Corporation, signed a noncancelable three-year lease for an item of manufacturing equipment. The lease called for annual payments of $41,635 per year due at the *end* of each of the next three years. The leased equipment's expected economic life was four years. No cash changed hands because the first payment wasn't due until December 31, 2015.

Henley was talking with his auditor that afternoon and was surprised to learn that the lease qualified as a capital lease and would have to be put on the balance sheet. Although his intuition told him that capitalization adversely affected certain ratios, the size of these adverse effects was unclear to him. Because similar leases on other equipment were up for renewal in 2015, he wanted a precise measure of the ratio deterioration. "If these effects are excessive," he said, "I'll try to get similar leases on the other machinery to qualify as operating leases when they come up for renewal next year."

Assume that the appropriate rate for discounting the minimum lease payments is 12%. Also assume that the asset Leased equipment under capital leases will be depreciated on a straight-line basis.

Required:

1. Prepare an amortization schedule for the lease.

2. The effect of lease capitalization on the current ratio worried Henley. *Before factoring in the capital lease signed on December 31, 2014,* Kingston Corporation's current ratio at December 31, 2014, was:

$$\frac{\text{Current assets } \$500,000}{\text{Current liabilities } \$294,118} = 1.7$$

   Once this lease is capitalized on December 31, 2014, what is the adjusted December 31, 2014, current ratio?

3. Henley was also concerned about the effect that lease capitalization would have on net income. He estimated that if the lease previously described were treated as an *operating* lease, 2015 pre-tax income would be $225,000. Determine the 2015 pre-tax income on a capital lease basis if this lease were treated as a capital lease and if the leased equipment were depreciated on a straight-line basis over the life of the lease.

P12-9

Recording capital lease for lessee and comparing to operating lease treatment
(LO 2, 3, 4, 5)

mhhe.com/revsine6e

On July 1, 2014, Burgundy Studios leases camera equipment from Corningstone Corporation. The lease covers eight years and requires lease payments of $42,000, beginning on July 1, 2014. The unguaranteed residual value is $90,000. On July 1, 2014, the equipment has a fair value of $278,966 and an estimated life of 10 years. The implicit rate in the lease is 11%. Burgundy's fiscal year ends on June 30, and the company depreciates its other equipment on a straight-line basis.

Required:

Part A

1. Show why this is a capital lease for Burgundy Studios.

2. Prepare an amortization table for the lease.

3. Prepare Burgundy's journal entries from the inception of the lease through June 30, 2015. Be sure to make any necessary reclassifications to current liabilities at the end of each reporting period.

Part B

Assume that Burgundy's reporting year ends on December 31 instead of June 30.

1. Prepare the entries to be made on December 31, 2014, July 1, 2015, and December 31, 2015.

2. Compute and label the amounts to be shown on the balance sheet and income statement for the years ended December 31, 2014, and December 31, 2015.

3. Show how the income statement and balance sheet would differ for 2014 and 2015 if the lease were treated as an operating lease.

On January 1, 2014, Railcar Leasing Inc. (the lessor) purchased 10 used boxcars from Railroad Equipment Consolidators at a price of $8,345,640. Railcar leased the boxcars to the Reading Railroad Company (the lessee) on the same date. The lease calls for eight annual payments of $1,500,000 to be made at the beginning of each year (that is, the first payment is due at the inception of the lease on January 1, 2014). The boxcars have an eight-year remaining useful life, the lease contains no renewal or bargain purchase option, and possession of the boxcars reverts to the lessor at the lease's end. The lease does not require the lessee to guarantee any residual value for the boxcars. The payment's collectibility is reasonably certain with no important uncertainties regarding unreimbursable costs to be incurred by the lessor. The lessor has structured the lease to earn a rate of return of 12.0%.

P12-10

Recording lessors' direct financing lease **(LO 7, 8)**

mhhe.com/revsine6e

Required:

1. What method must Railcar Leasing Inc. use to account for the lease?

2. Prepare an amortization schedule for the lease for Railcar. (Round all amounts to the nearest cent.)

3. Prepare all journal entries for Railcar for 2014 and 2015. Assume that it reports on a calendar-year basis.

Refer to the information in P12–10. Assume that collectibility of the payments is *not* reasonably certain and that the lessor uses the straight-line depreciation method.

Required:

1. Prepare the necessary journal entries for Railcar for 2014 and 2015 under the lease.

2. How much total income before tax does the firm expect to recognize over the life of the lease in these altered circumstances?

3. Is the amount in requirement 2 the same as, more than, or less than the total amount of income before tax that is recognized in P12–10?

P12-11

Recording lessors' direct financing lease **(LO 6, 7, 8)**

Moore Company sells and leases its computers. Moore's cost and sales price per machine are $1,200 and $3,000, respectively. At the end of three years, the expected residual value is $400, which is guaranteed by the lessee. Moore leases 20 of these machines to Mitchum Co. on September 1, 2014. Moore has no additional costs to complete, and Mitchum is creditworthy. Both Moore and Mitchum use straight-line depreciation. The economic life of each computer is four years. Be sure to use a spreadsheet program for this problem.

P12-12

Accounting for monthly rental payments **(LO 1, 4, 5, 8)**

mhhe.com/revsine6e

1. Compute the monthly rental payment for a three-year lease, assuming that Moore wishes to earn 1% per month. Payments are to be made at the beginning of each month.

2. What type of lease is this for Moore? Explain.

Continued on next page

3. What entry(ies) does Moore make at September 1, 2014, related to the lease?

4. Prepare an amortization table using a spreadsheet package for the life of the lease.

5. Show how Moore's income statement for the year ended December 31, 2014, will be affected.

6. What accounts and amounts are on Moore's balance sheet at December 31, 2014? Be sure to address reclassifications between current and noncurrent.

7. Repeat requirements 2 through 6 for Mitchum.

P12-13

Comparing financial statement effects of capital and operating leases
(LO 2, 3, 5)

mhhe.com/revsine6e

Assume that on January 1, 2014, Trans Global Airlines leases two used Boeing 737s from Aircraft Lessors Inc. The eight-year lease calls for payments of $10,000,000 at each year-end. On January 1, 2014, the Boeing 737s have a total fair value of $60,000,000 and a remaining useful life of 11 years. Assume that Trans Global's incremental borrowing rate is 9% and that it uses straight-line depreciation for financial reporting purposes. The lease is noncancelable, and Trans Global cannot renew it. In addition, there is no bargain purchase option, and ownership of the leased asset reverts to Aircraft Lessors at the end of the lease. Aircraft Lessors' implicit rate of return on the lease is unknown.

Required:

1. Should Trans Global account for the lease as a capital or an operating lease? Why?

2. Based on your answer to requirement 1, make all journal entries that Trans Global would make related to the lease for 2014, 2015, 2016, and 2017. Round all amounts to the nearest dollar.

3. Assume that Trans Global accounts for the lease using whichever method (capital or operating) that you did not select in requirement 1. Make all journal entries related to the lease for 2014, 2015, 2016, and 2017.

4. Prepare a schedule of the year-to-year and total (before-tax) income differences that would result from accounting for the lease as a capital lease versus an operating lease. Round all amounts to the nearest dollar.

5. Why might Trans Global's managers prefer the lease to be accounted for as an operating lease rather than as a capital lease?

P12-14

Comparing financial statement effects of direct financing and operating leases (LO 7, 8)

mhhe.com/revsine6e

On January 1, 2014, Overseas Leasing Inc. (the lessor) purchased five used oil tankers from Seven Seas Shipping Company at a price of $99,817,750. Overseas immediately leased the oil tankers to Pacific Ocean Oil Company (the lessee) on the same date. The lease calls for five annual payments of $25,000,000 to be made at each year-end. The tankers have a remaining useful life of five years with no salvage value, and the lease does not require the lessee to guarantee any residual value for the tankers. The lessor has structured the lease to earn a rate of return of 8.0%.

Required:

Prepare a schedule like the one appearing in Exhibit 12.8 of the text. This schedule should contain the year-to-year income statement and balance sheet differences that would arise depending on whether this lease is accounted for as a direct financing lease or as an operating lease.

P12-15

Constructively capitalizing operating leases
(LO 2, 10, 11)

As a loan officer for First Bank, you're evaluating Newton Co.'s financial statements. Your evaluation reveals that Newton has no capital leases recorded on its financial statements while most other companies in its industry do have such leases. To effectively evaluate Newton's financial position and compare it to industry standards, you've decided to constructively capitalize Newton's operating leases. The following information is available from Newton's financial statements for the year ended December 31, 2014:

Operating Lease Payments

Year	Minimum Operating Lease Payments
2015	$ 500
2016	450
2017	410
2018	380
2019	350
After 2019	2,880
Total	$4,970

Required:

1. Assuming that Newton's long-term debt rate is 8%, estimate its constructively capitalized operating lease liability.

2. How might you estimate the capitalized operating lease asset amount?

3. How will constructive capitalization affect Newton Co.'s debt-to-equity ratio?

On January 1, 2014, Merchant Co. sold a tractor to Swanson Inc. and simultaneously leased it back for five years. The tractor's fair value is $250,000, but its carrying value on Merchant's books prior to the transaction was $200,000. The tractor has a six-year remaining estimated useful life, and Merchant and Swanson both used 8% interest in evaluating the transaction. Merchant has agreed to make five payments of $57,976 beginning January 1, 2014.

P12-16

Evaluating sale and leaseback **(LO 3, 9)**

Required:

1. What type of a lease is this for Merchant and why?

2. Compute the amount of Merchant's gain on the transaction and explain how Merchant will account for it.

3. Prepare the January 1, 2014, entries on Merchant's books to account for the sale and leaseback.

4. Assume that the tractor's carrying value on Merchant's books was $260,000. Explain how Merchant would account for the loss.

This problem is designed to allow you to see how different lease durations and interest rates affect the relationship between the capitalized lease asset and lease liability. Of course, these same asset–liability relationships apply if you wish to constructively capitalize a lease that the lessee has treated as an operating lease.

Assume that Cambria Corporation signs a noncancelable lease that obliges it to make annual payments of $10,000. This amount excludes all executory costs, and the lease term includes no residual value guarantee. The lease will be treated as a capital lease. Cambria uses straight-line depreciation for the leased asset.

P12-17

Visualizing the asset–liability relationship over time for a capital lease **(LO 1, 5)**

mhhe.com/revsine6e

Required:

1. Assume that the lease payments are made at the *beginning* of each period.

   a. If the discount rate is 8% and the lease runs for 20 years, approximately when—if at all—does the capitalized lease liability first exceed the depreciated net carrying value of the leased asset?

   b. Repeat this calculation using a 12% discount rate for 20 years.

   c. Repeat this calculation using a 12% discount rate for 12 years.

2. Assume that the lease payments are made at the *end* of each period.

   a. If the discount rate is 8% and the lease runs for 20 years, does the depreciated carrying value of the leased asset ever exceed the capitalized lease liability?

   b. Will this result change if you raise the interest rate and/or shorten the duration of the lease?

P12-18

Analyzing U.S. GAAP and IFRS operating lease disclosures   **(LO 10, 11)**

In its 2012 Annual Report, Singapore Airlines, which primarily complies with IFRS, reported the following expected future minimum lease payments (in $ million).

35 Capital and Other Commitments (in $ million)
   (b) Operating lease commitments
   As lessee
   Aircraft
   Future minimum lease payments under non-cancellable operating leases are as follows:

Not later than one year	561.5
Later than one year but not later than five years	1,968.1
Later than five years	927.0
	3,456.6

In its 2012 Annual Report filed under U.S. GAAP, United Continental Holdings, which owns United Airlines, reported the following expected future minimum lease payments as of December 31, 2012 (in billions):

	2013	2014	2015	2016	2017	After 2017	Total
Aircraft operating lease obligations	1.5	1.5	1.2	1.0	0.9	1.4	7.5

Required:

1. Assume you were interested in estimating the value of each firms' liability if these operating leases for aircraft were capitalized. Which of these notes provides more useful information and why?

2. Describe some techniques an analyst could use to determine the annual cash flows for Singapore Airlines that comprise "Later than one year but not later than five years." Why do the analyst's assumptions matter for this?

CASES

C12-1

AMR Corporation: Constructively capitalizing operating leases   **(LO 2, 5, 10, 11)**

mhhe.com/revsine6e

AMR Corporation is the parent of American Airlines, one of the largest airline companies in the world. Excerpts from its 2009 annual report follow.

	December 31,	
($ in millions)	2009	2008
Assets		
Equipment and property under capital leases		
Flight equipment	$ 651	$ 561
Other equipment and property	215	215
	866	776
Less accumulated amortization	571	536
	$ 295	$ 240
Total assets	$25,438	$25,175

(continued)

Liabilities
  Current liabilities

Current obligation under capital leases	$ 90	$ 107
Obligations under capital leases, less current obligations	$ 599	$ 582
Total liabilities	$28,927	$28,110

Note 5. Leases

AMR's subsidiaries lease various types of equipment and property, primarily aircraft and airport fa-cilities. The future minimum lease payments required under capital leases, together with the present value of such payments, and future minimum lease payments required under operating leases that have initial or remaining noncancelable lease terms in excess of one year as of December 31, 2009, were (in millions):

Year Ending December 31	Capital Leases	Operating Leases
2010	$181	$1,057
2011	184	1,032
2012	134	848
2013	119	755
2014	98	614
2015 and thereafter	436	5,021 (1)
	A	$9,327
Less amount representing interest	B	
Present value of net minimum lease payments	C	

---

(1) As of December 31, 2009, included in Accrued liabilities and Other liabilities and deferred credits on the accompanying consolidated balance sheet is approximately $1.2 billion relating to rent expense being recorded in advance of future oper-ating lease payments.

At December 31, 2009, the Company was operating 181 jet aircraft and 39 turboprop aircraft under operating leases and 80 jet aircraft under capital leases. The aircraft leases can gener-ally be renewed at rates based on fair market value at the end of the lease term for one to five years. Some aircraft leases have purchase options at or near the end of the lease term at fair market value, but generally not to exceed a stated percentage of the defined lessor's cost of the aircraft or a predetermined fixed amount.

Required:
All questions relate to 2009 unless stated otherwise.

1. Solve for the unknowns (A, B, and C).
2. What is the net amount of capital lease assets on the balance sheet?
3. Why is the net amount of capital lease assets on the balance sheet different from the total amount of liabilities recorded on the balance sheet?
4. Compute AMR's Total debt to Total assets.
5. What entry would AMR make in 2010 to record the effects of capital leases existing at December 31, 2009? You may omit the depreciation entry.
6. What is the amount of operating lease obligation on the balance sheet?
7. What is the present value of operating lease payments? Assume a 13% discount rate.
8. What entry would be made to constructively capitalize the leases. Assume the net asset to liability ratio observed for the capital leases and ignore the effects of taxes.
9. Recompute the Total debt to Total assets ratio after making the entry in requirement 8. What is the percentage change from the ratio computed in requirement 4?

C12-2 IFRS and FASB/IASB Exposure Draft **(LO 10, 11)**	Refer to the AMR Corporation financial statement information contained in C12-1. **Required:** 1. Explain how the financial statements and disclosures would change if AMR were using *IAS 17* instead of FASB ASC 840. Be as specific as possible. 2. Explain how the financial statements and disclosures would change if AMR were using the FASB proposed accounting standards update for leases instead of FASB ASC 840. Be as specific as possible.

C12-3 Guaraldi Bank, Inc.: Determining lease classification and the times-interest-earned ratio **(LO 2, 3, 5)**	The following information is based on an actual annual report. In a recent lending agreement (dated March 3, 2014), Guaraldi Bank, Inc., included the following definitions for terms used in its loan covenants with a borrower: Fixed Charges means the sum of, for Borrower and its Subsidiaries, determined in accordance with GAAP on a consolidated basis, (a) interest expense (including interest expense pursuant to Capital Leases), plus (b) lease expense payable for Operating Leases, determined for the four fiscal quarters preceding the date of calculation. Net Earning Available for Fixed Charges means, for Borrower and its Subsidiaries, determined in accordance with GAAP on a consolidated basis, (a) Net Income before Taxes, plus (b) extraordinary noncash charges, plus (c) interest expense (including interest expense pursuant to Capital Leases), plus (d) lease expense pursuant to Operating Leases, determined for the fiscal quarter preceding the date of calculation. Fixed Charges Coverage Ratio means the ratio of Net Earnings Available for Fixed Charges to Fixed Charges. Borrower shall not permit the Fixed Charges Coverage Ratio to be less than the following ratios for the fiscal quarters ending as follows:

December 31, 2013	0.70 to 1.00
March 31, 2014	1.00 to 1.00
June 30, 2014	1.20 to 1.00
September 30, 2014	1.50 to 1.00
December 31, 2014	1.75 to 1.00

Notice that the definitions of Fixed charges and Net earnings available for fixed charges *both* add back lease expenses under operating leases. The objective of this case is to allow you to see why astute lenders carefully design covenants to protect themselves against borrowers who might use the latitude in GAAP lease accounting rules to circumvent covenant restrictions.

Assume the following initial conditions for the borrower on June 30, 2014:

Income before interest and taxes	$120,000
Interest on capital lease	$ 60,000
Interest on other borrowings	40,000
Fixed charges	$100,000
Fixed charges coverage ratio	1.20

Notice that the fixed charges coverage ratio equals the covenant constraint at June 30, 2014; even minor adversity might cause a covenant violation in the next quarter. In addition, the borrower is required to increase the ratio to 1.50 by September 30, 2014.

Required:
1. Assume that the borrower "somehow" restructures the existing lease to have it qualify as an operating lease. What effect will this change in lease classification have on the times-interest-earned ratio as typically defined? (See Chapter 5.) What effect will this change have on the fixed charges coverage ratio as defined in the lending agreement? What does your answer to this part tell you about the vigilance that credit analysts must exert in designing and monitoring financial contractual restrictions?

2. Now assume that the initial times-interest-earned ratio was less than 1.00 to 1.00. Would changing the capital lease to an operating lease benefit the borrower's compliance with lending covenants?

(*Note:* In answering both parts, make assumptions when sufficient information is not available.)

C I 2 - 4

Walgreens: Lessee reporting and constructively capitalizing operating leases
(LO 2, 5, I I)

mhhe.com/revsine6e

Walgreen Co. (Walgreens) is based in Illinois and was originally incorporated in 1909. As of August 31, 2009, it operated 7,496 locations in 50 states, the District of Columbia, Puerto Rico, and Guam. Walgreens' 2009 net income was $2,006 million, and its interest expense was $91 million. The company faced a 37% effective tax rate. At August 31, 2009, the balance sheet showed $25,142 million of assets and liabilities of $10,766 million. Excerpts from the 2009 annual report that relate to leases are reported below:

(3) Leases

The company owns 20.7% of its operating locations; the remaining locations are leased premises. Initial terms are typically 20 to 25 years, followed by additional terms containing cancellation options at five-year intervals, and may include rent escalation clauses. The commencement date of all lease terms is the earlier of the date the company becomes legally obligated to make rent payments or the date the company has the right to control the property. Additionally, the company recognizes rent expense on a straight-line basis over the term of the lease. In addition to minimum fixed rentals, most leases provide for contingent rentals based upon a portion of sales.

Minimum rental commitments at August 31, 2009, under all leases having an initial or remaining non-cancelable term of more than one year are shown below (in millions):

	Capital Lease	Operating Lease
2010	$ 5	$ 2,024
2011	4	2,101
2012	3	2,085
2013	4	2,044
2014	4	2,002
Later	45	24,696
Total minimum lease payments	$65	$34,952

The capital lease amount includes $25 million of executory costs and imputed interest. Total minimum lease payments have not been reduced by minimum sublease rentals of approximately $33 million on leases due in the future under non-cancelable subleases.

The company remains secondarily liable on 20 assigned leases. The maximum potential of undiscounted future payments is $11 million as of August 31, 2009. Lease option dates vary, with some extending to 2014.

Rental expense was as follows (in millions):

	2009	2008	2007
Minimum rentals	$1,973	$1,784	$1,614
Contingent rentals	11	13	16
Less: Sublease rental income	(9)	(10)	(11)
	$1,975	$1,787	$1,619

Required:
All questions relate to 2009 unless stated otherwise.

1. Compute Walgreens' debt-to-equity ratio and return-on-assets ratio using reported numbers for fiscal 2009.

2. Assume that the amount of Walgreens' operating lease payment due each year after 2014 is equal and is paid at the end of each fiscal year. Assume that all of these leases terminate

at the end of fiscal 2027. Using an interest rate of 7%, calculate the present value of the operating lease payments at August 31, 2009.

3. Make the journal entry that would be necessary at August 31, 2009, to put the operating leases on the balance sheet. Ignore income taxes and assume that the amount of the capitalized asset equals the capitalized liability.

4. Based on your answer to requirement 2, make the necessary journal entries related to the income statement for the fiscal year ended August 31, 2010, assuming operating leases are accounted for as capital leases. Assume an 18-year useful life, zero salvage value, and straight-line depreciation for the capitalized leased assets.

5. Calculate Walgreens' total debt to shareholders' equity ratio after treating its operating leases as capital leases.

6. Calculate Walgreens' return on assets. Use the income information that you computed for requirement 4.

7. Comment on the differences between the unadjusted ratios in requirement 1 and the adjusted ratios in requirements 5 and 6.

.mhhe.com/revsine6e

**Remember to check the book's companion website
for additional study material.**

Income Tax Reporting | 13

*"I'm proud to be paying taxes to the United States. The only thing is . . .
I could be just as proud for half the money."*

—Arthur Godfrey, television host
1940s–1970s

I
n the United States and many other industrialized countries, the rules for determining income for financial reporting purposes—known as **book income**—do not correspond to the rules for determining income for taxation purposes—referred to as
taxable income. This divergence arises because of the different objectives underlying
book income and taxable income.[1] Book income is intended to reflect increases in a
firm's "well-offness"; it includes all changes in net assets except those due to transactions with owners (e.g., stock issuances, stock repurchases, and dividends) and those
recognized in other comprehensive income. ***Book income includes all earned inflows
of net assets, even inflows not immediately convertible into cash, and it reflects expenses as they accrue, not just when they are paid.***

In contrast, taxable income is not determined solely by changes in well-offness. Instead, taxable income is governed by the "constructive receipt/ability to pay" doctrine.
Under this doctrine, when liquid assets enter the firm, they are frequently taxed because
it is easiest to collect money from the taxpayer at that time. For example, rent received
in advance is taxed when received even though it is not yet earned from an accounting
standpoint. Similarly, tax deductions generally are allowed only when expenditures are
made or when a loss is realized. In addition, Congress may enact tax laws to encourage
particular activities, rather than in an attempt to measure income. For example, state and
municipal bond interest income is generally exempt from federal income tax, not because anyone believes it is not income, but rather to make such bonds more attractive to
investors and thus lower the borrowing costs of state and local governments. ***Because of
different underlying objectives, the rules for determining book income diverge from
the rules for determining taxable income. This divergence complicates the way income taxes are reflected in financial reports.***

This chapter describes the major differences between U.S. book income and taxable
income and how these differences affect the reporting of income tax expense and

LEARNING OBJECTIVES

**After studying this chapter, you
will understand:**

1. The different objectives underlying
   income determination for financial
   reporting (book) purposes versus
   tax purposes.

2. The distinction between temporary
   (timing) and permanent book/tax
   differences, the items that cause
   these differences, and how they
   affect book income versus taxable
   income.

3. The distortions created when the
   deferred tax effects of temporary
   differences are ignored.

4. How income tax expense is determined with interperiod tax allocation and the relations among taxes
   payable, changes in deferred taxes,
   and tax expense.

5. The reporting rules for net operating
   loss carrybacks and carryforwards.

6. Measuring and reporting valuation
   allowances for deferred tax assets.

7. How tax rate changes affect reported income tax expense.

8. How to read and interpret tax note
   disclosures.

9. How financial statement disclosures
   reveal information about firms'
   uncertain tax positions.

10. How tax note disclosures can be
    used to improve financial statement
    analysis.

11. Key differences between IFRS and
    U.S. GAAP rules for reporting of
    income taxes.

---

[1] Countries in which the rules for determining accounting (book) income and taxable income are essentially the same
include Germany, Japan, and Switzerland.

tax obligations. First we outline the major categories of differences between book income and taxable income, and we illustrate the distortions that would result in GAAP income statements if income tax expense were set equal to the amount of income taxes owed. Next we explain and illustrate the GAAP solution for avoiding these distortions—referred to as **deferred income tax accounting** or **interperiod tax allocation.** We also discuss the accounting for special tax laws that apply to unprofitable firms, and we explore what happens when taxing authorities change income tax rates.

Interperiod tax allocation refers to the allocation of income tax expense *across periods* when book and tax income differ. **Intraperiod tax allocation,** introduced in Chapter 2, refers to the allocation of the tax cost (benefit) across various components of book income *within a given period.* For example, the current tax provision (expense) is related to (pre-tax) income from continuing operations while gains and losses from discontinued operations and extraordinary items are reported *net of tax* on the income statement.

The chapter also guides you through an analysis of typical income tax note disclosures. Our purpose is to explain the wealth of information that can be extracted from these disclosures. We demonstrate how analysts can use tax note disclosures to glean information not provided elsewhere in the financial statements to better understand a firm's performance and future prospects.

UNDERSTANDING INCOME TAX REPORTING

Temporary and Permanent Differences between Book Income and Taxable Income

The differences between pre-tax income as reported in external financial statements and taxable income fall into two broad categories:

1. **Temporary (timing) differences**
2. **Permanent differences**

Most accountants use the terms *temporary difference* and *timing difference* interchangeably. *Timing difference* is a term used in an early pre-Codification standard issued by the Accounting Principles Board and this term is still used conversationally. Current authoritative accounting literature uses the term *temporary difference.*

A temporary difference results when a revenue (gain) or expense (loss) enters into the determination of book income in one period but affects taxable income in a different (earlier or later) period. A brief summary of common temporary differences is provided in Exhibit 13.1. Temporary differences are so named because they eventually reverse. That is, a revenue (or expense) item that causes book income to be more (less) than taxable income when it is initially recorded—called an *originating* **temporary difference**—will eventually reverse. These reversals cause book income to be less (more) than taxable income in future periods and are called *reversing* **temporary differences.**

In contrast to a temporary difference, a **permanent difference** does not reverse. A permanent difference is caused by items that (1) enter into the determination of accounting income but *never* affect taxable income, or (2) enter into the determination of taxable income but *never* affect accounting income. Exhibit 13.2 provides examples of permanent differences.

RECAP

A temporary difference occurs when a revenue (gain) or expense (loss) enters into the determination of book (GAAP) income and taxable income in different periods. Permanent differences are revenue or expense items that are recognized as part of book income but are *never* recognized as part of taxable income, or vice versa.

EXHIBIT 13.1	Examples of Temporary Differences between Book Income and Taxable Income

Depreciation Expense

Accelerated depreciation is used for taxable income but straight-line is typically used for book income. **Modified Accelerated Cost Recovery System** (MACRS) useful lives are employed for taxable income whereas useful economic lives are employed for book income. Both of these items result in larger depreciation deductions for tax purposes than for book purposes in the early years of an asset's life, and the opposite effect occurs in later years.

Bad Debts Expense

Bad debts are accrued and recognized under the allowance method for book purposes, but tax rules follow the direct write-off method, allowing a deduction only when a particular account is deemed to be uncollectible and written off.

Warranty Expense

Warranty expenses are accrued and recorded in the year the product is sold for book purposes, but for tax purposes, the deduction is allowed when the actual warranty expenditures are made to correct the defect.

Prepaid Expenses

Some business expenses, such as insurance premiums and rent, are paid in advance. For book purposes, these expenditures are initially recorded as assets—Prepaid insurance or Prepaid rent—but later are expensed over the periods when the benefits are received. Tax rules allow a current deduction in the period the payment is made, as long as the payment covers a reasonable period.

Pension and Other Post-Retirement Benefits (OPEB) Expenses

For book purposes, the expense is based on the amount of pension or OPEB expense accrued. For pensions, a tax deduction is allowed for the amounts funded (that is, contributed to the pension fund) each period, and for OPEB costs, a deduction is allowed for benefit payments made during the period.

Acquired Goodwill

Although the Revenue Reconciliation Act of 1993 allows firms a deduction for goodwill amortization on a 15-year straight-line basis under certain special conditions, in most situations goodwill is *not* deductible. For book purposes, acquired goodwill is subject to periodic impairment tests (see Chapter 16). If impaired, goodwill is written down to fair value with an offsetting charge to earnings.

A great deal of confusion surrounds the tax deductibility of goodwill. The financial press and even financial analysts often assume that recorded goodwill is deductible for tax purposes, but in most cases, it is not.

When is goodwill tax deductible? Goodwill is tax deductible when the *tax basis* of the acquired firm's assets are stepped-up (that is, recorded at fair value at date of acquisition). Whether goodwill is deductible for tax purposes hinges on whether the acquiring entity is buying the assets of another entity directly (for example, ABC Company buys a division of XYZ Company) or whether the acquiring entity gains control over the assets of another entity by buying the voting stock of that entity (for example, ABC Company acquires 80% of the common stock of XYZ Company). Goodwill that arises from direct asset purchases may be amortized for tax purposes, giving rise to a tax deduction, while it may not be amortized for the indirect stock purchase. Because most goodwill on consolidated balance sheets arises from stock transactions rather than outright asset purchases, it is generally not deductible for tax purposes.

See M. Scholes, M. Wolfson, M. Erickson, E. Maydew, and T. Shevlin, *Taxes and Business Strategy: A Planning Approach*, 4th ed. (Upper Saddle River, NJ: Pearson Education, 2009).

Installment Sales

Sales are generally recognized for book purposes when the goods are delivered to the customer regardless of when collections are made. If collections are made over an extended period, tax law calls for the sales revenue to be recognized as payments are received.

Long-Term Construction Contracts

For long-term construction contracts (Chapter 3), firms may generally use either the percentage-of-completion method or the completed-contract method of revenue recognition for book purposes. In general, taxpayers may only use the percentage-of-completion method to account for long-term contracts entered into after July 11, 1989.

Revenues Received in Advance

Revenues received in advance (for example, rent revenue or subscription revenue) are initially recorded as a liability for book purposes and are transferred to income as those revenues are "earned." For tax purposes, these amounts are taxed when received.

Equity in Undistributed Earnings of Investees

If a company (Investor) owns 20% or more of the outstanding voting stock of another corporation (Investee), the equity method of accounting is generally used for book purposes (Chapter 16). Under the equity method, the Investor records as income its share of Investee profits for the period. For tax purposes, income is recognized when Investee dividends are received, but this recognition is subject to special dividends-received deduction rules discussed next under permanent differences.

| EXHIBIT 13.2 | Examples of Permanent Differences between Book Income and Taxable Income |

Items Recognized for Book Purposes but *Not* for Tax Purposes

- Interest received on state and municipal bonds is not subject to federal tax but it is included in book income.
- If a company pays fines or expenses resulting from violations of the law (for example, environmental damages), these payments are not tax deductible but would be an expense in determining book income.
- Goodwill write-offs generally are not deductible for tax purposes unless they meet certain special conditions.[*] A goodwill write-down as a result of impairment is a loss in determining book income (see Chapter 16).
- Premiums for life insurance on executives paid for by a company that is the designated beneficiary are not deductible for tax purposes. Similarly, any benefits collected are not taxed. For book purposes, both the premiums paid and benefits received are used in determining pre-tax income.
- Compensation expense associated with qualified employee stock options, also known as Incentive Stock Options, is not tax deductible but is an expense in determining book income.
- GAAP allows U.S. parent companies to treat undistributed earnings of a foreign subsidiary or foreign joint venture as a permanent difference if the parent company plans to permanently reinvest the earnings abroad (i.e., remittance of those earnings back to the U.S. parent is postponed indefinitely).
- U.S. tax law allows a deduction from taxable income for 9% of the profit derived from domestic production activities. The effect is to exclude a portion of income from taxation, resulting in a permanent difference.

> Unless otherwise specified, you should assume for purposes of working problems in this chapter that a goodwill write-off is treated as a permanent difference item— that is, it is *not* deductible for tax purposes.

Items Recognized for Tax Purposes but *Not* for Book Purposes

- Tax laws allow a statutory depletion deduction on certain natural resources that may be in excess of the cost-based depletion recorded for book purposes. This excess statutory depletion is a permanent difference between book and taxable income.
- U.S. corporations that own stock in other U.S. companies are allowed to deduct a portion of the dividends received from these investees, effectively excluding that portion from taxable income, according to the following schedule:

Ownership Portion	Deductible Portion of Dividends
Less than 20%	70%
Equal to or greater than 20%, but less than 80%	80
Equal to or greater than 80%	100

* See P. McConnell, "Goodwill: The Facts," *Accounting Issues* (New York: Bear Stearns & Co., August 26, 1994); and Sections 1060 and 338 of the Internal Revenue Code.

Problems Caused by Temporary Differences

To illustrate the issues related to interperiod tax allocation, consider the most common temporary book/tax difference: depreciation expense. For tax purposes, value-maximizing firms try to *minimize* the discounted present value of their future tax payments. Assuming tax rates do not change, each dollar of tax deduction today is more valuable than a dollar of tax deduction in the future. This time-value-of-money principle is why most firms use accelerated depreciation for tax purposes. But many of these same firms use straight-line depreciation for financial reporting purposes. This creates a temporary difference between book income and taxable income.

> Technically, firms are required to use MACRS depreciation schedules for tax purposes, and these differ by type of asset and useful life. We use SYD here to simplify the illustration of depreciation-induced temporary differences.

Consider this illustration. Assume Mitchell Corporation buys new equipment for $10,000 on January 1, 2014. The asset has a five-year life and no salvage value. It will be depreciated using the straight-line method for book purposes, but the sum-of-the-years'-digits (SYD) method will be used for tax purposes. Refer to Exhibit 13.3 and Figure 13.1(a) for the two depreciation schedules.

Let's assume depreciation constitutes Mitchell Corporation's only book-versus-tax difference. Income before depreciation and taxes is expected to be $22,000 each year over the

EXHIBIT 13.3 — Mitchell Corporation

Book-versus-Tax Depreciation

Year	(a) Book Depreciation	(b) Tax Depreciation	(c) Excess of Tax Depreciation over Book Depreciation	
2014	$ 2,000	$ 3,333	$ 1,333 ⎱	Originating temporary
2015	2,000	2,667	667 ⎰	differences
2016	2,000	2,000	—	
2017	2,000	1,333	(667) ⎱	Reversing temporary
2018	2,000	667	(1,333) ⎰	differences
	$10,000	$10,000	–0–	

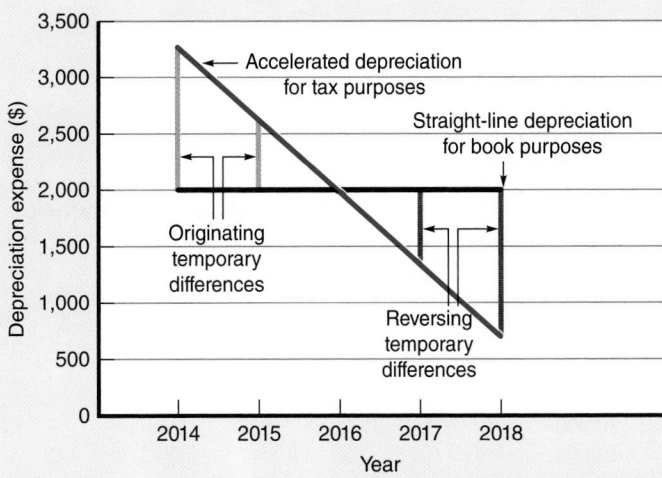

Figure 13.1(a)

MITCHELL CORPORATION

Comparison of Book-versus-Tax Depreciation Expense

next five years and the statutory tax rate is 35%. Exhibit 13.4 shows pre-tax book income, taxable income per Mitchell's tax return, and taxes payable for the years 2014–2018. Figure 13.1(b) displays graphically the relation between taxable income and pre-tax book income over the five-year period.

> The **statutory tax rate** for corporations is the rate set by law—in this case, 35%.

EXHIBIT 13.4 — Mitchell Corporation

Income and Income Tax Payable

Year	(a) Pre-Tax Book Income ($22,000 – Book Depreciation)	(b) Taxable Income per Tax Return ($22,000 – Tax Depreciation)	(c) Income Tax Payable (Col. [b] × 35%)
2014	$ 20,000	$ 18,667*	$ 6,533
2015	20,000	19,333	6,767
2016	20,000	20,000	7,000
2017	20,000	20,667	7,233
2018	20,000	21,333	7,467
Total	$100,000	$100,000	$35,000

* For example, in 2014, $22,000 − $3,333 (Exhibit 13.3, column [b]) = $18,667.

Figure 13.1(b)

MITCHELL CORPORATION

Pre-tax Book Income and
Taxable Income

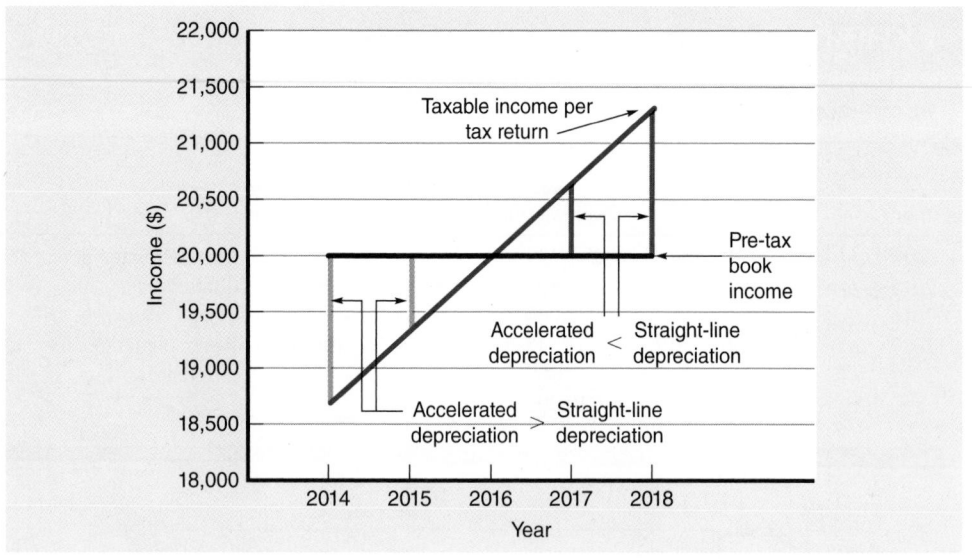

<table>
<tr><td colspan="2">**EXHIBIT 13.5**</td><td colspan="3">**Mitchell Corporation**</td></tr>
<tr><td colspan="5"></td></tr>
<tr><td colspan="5">**Result from Treating Actual Taxes Paid as Income Tax Expense**</td></tr>
</table>

Year	(a) Pre-Tax Book Income	(b) Tax Expense = Income Tax Payable	(c) Effective Tax Rate (b/a)	(d) After-Tax Book Income
2014	$20,000	$6,533	32.7%	$13,467
2015	20,000	6,767	33.8	13,233
2016	20,000	7,000	35.0	13,000
2017	20,000	7,233	36.2	12,767
2018	20,000	7,467	37.3	12,533

The **effective tax rate** is the tax expense divided by pre-tax income as reported in the GAAP income statement.

The easiest way to record income tax expense here would be to treat the taxes payable each year (Column [c] of Exhibit 13.4) as the reported *book* income tax expense. Exhibit 13.5 and Figure 13.2 show what would happen if this were done.

As you can readily see in the exhibit and figure, this approach causes the effective tax rate to increase from 32.7% in 2014 to 37.3% in 2018, while after-tax earnings would decline from $13,467 in 2014 to $12,533 in 2018 (Column [d] of Exhibit 13.5). This occurs even though pre-tax book income ($20,000) and the statutory tax rate (35%) are stable over the five-year period.

The changing effective tax rate that would result if tax payments were used to measure income tax expense is due to a mismatching of income tax expense and book pre-tax income. Recall from Chapter 2 that a general accounting principle is that costs should be recognized as expenses in the same period as the related revenue is recognized. When we apply this principle to income tax accounting, it suggests that income tax expense should include the tax consequences of amounts recognized in current period pre-tax income, regardless of when those tax consequences are realized in cash. In other words, it is not the payment of taxes that triggers income tax expense, but rather the recognition of pre-tax income that *ever* has an associated tax payment.

Besides the income statement mismatch, treating actual cash taxes paid as income tax expense introduces a reporting distortion on the balance sheet. This distortion occurs because total tax depreciation deductions on an asset cannot exceed the asset's cost minus its salvage value. Accordingly, "extra" tax depreciation in early years will be offset by lower allowable

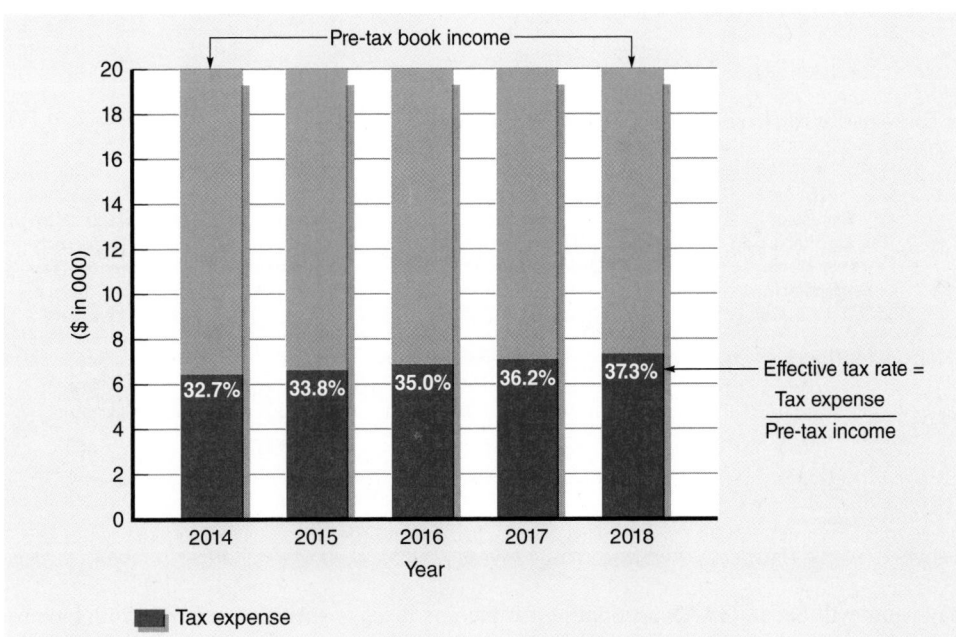

Figure 13.2

MITCHELL CORPORATION

Tax Expense *without* Interperiod Tax Allocation

tax depreciation in later years. As shown in Column (c) of Exhibit 13.3, during 2014 tax depreciation exceeds book depreciation by $1,333. So, future years' *tax* depreciation must be $1,333 lower than future years' *book* depreciation. Thus, the extra tax depreciation taken in 2014 generates a "liability" for future taxes of $1,333 times 35%, or $467, but this "liability" goes unrecorded when the tax expense is set equal to actual cash taxes paid or payable.

There is another way to visualize how the extra tax depreciation creates a liability for future taxes. GAAP assumes "the reported amounts of assets . . . will be recovered. . . . Based on that assumption, a difference between the tax basis of an asset . . . and its reported amount . . . will result in taxable . . . amounts . . . when the reported amounts . . . are settled. . . ."[2] In our example, at the end of 2014, the reported (book) amount of the asset is $8,000 (that is, $10,000 − $2,000 book depreciation), while the tax basis is $6,667 (that is, $10,000 − $3,333 tax depreciation). Notice that if the asset were sold for its $8,000 GAAP net book value, a taxable gain of $1,333 would ensue, measured as the difference between the $8,000 cash received and the asset's $6,667 *tax* basis. Thus, given the GAAP assumption that reported amounts of assets will be recovered, the extra depreciation in 2014 would generate a liability for future taxes of $1,333 times 35%, or $467.

Setting tax expense equal to current taxes payable (as in Column [b] of Exhibit 13.5) ignores the future tax liability that results from temporary differences between book and taxable income, and it results in a mismatching of tax expense with the related revenue and expense items reported on the GAAP income statement.

Deferred Income Tax Accounting: Interperiod Tax Allocation

To avoid the drawbacks just illustrated, accounting for income taxes does not simply equate income tax expense with current taxes paid (or payable). Instead, income tax expense reflects all tax payments related to current period pre-tax income, regardless of when those tax

---

[2] FASB Accounting Standards Codification (ASC) Paragraph 740-10-25-20: Income Taxes—Overall—Recognition—Temporary Differences.

| EXHIBIT 13.6 | Mitchell Corporation |

Computation of Income Tax Expense with Interperiod Tax Allocation

Year	(a) Income Tax Payable (Exhibit 13.4, Col. [c])	(b) Excess of Tax Depreciation over Book Depreciation (Exhibit 13.3, Col. [c])	(c) Increase (Decrease) in Deferred Income Tax Liability (Col. [b] × 35%)	(d) Total Income Tax Expense (Col. [a] + Col. [c])	(e) Balance in Deferred Income Tax Liability at Year-End
2014	$ 6,533	$1,333	$467	$ 7,000	$467
2015	6,767	667	233	7,000	700
2016	7,000	–0–	–0–	7,000	700
2017	7,233	(667)	(233)	7,000	467
2018	7,467	(1,333)	(467)	7,000	–0–
	$35,000	–0–	–0–	$35,000	

payments will occur. GAAP accounting for income taxes is specified in Topic 740: Income Taxes.[3] It calls for recognizing deferred tax liabilities, which reflect future tax payments related to amounts previously recognized as pre-tax income, and deferred tax assets to reflect reductions to future tax payments related to amounts previously recognized in pre-tax income. To illustrate these rules, we continue with the Mitchell Corporation example in Exhibit 13.6.

Deferred Tax Liabilities

Columns (a) and (b) of Exhibit 13.6 repeat information from earlier exhibits. Column (a) shows the amount of tax that must be paid each year and column (b) shows the difference between book depreciation and tax depreciation each year. Now consider what happens in 2014. Mitchell must pay $6,533 in taxes, which was determined as taxable income of $18,667 times the 35% tax rate. But book pre-tax income was $20,000 (Exhibit 13.4). The $1,333 difference between taxable income and book pre-tax income was because of the different depreciation methods used in the books and in the tax return. So now we ask the question, will there *ever* be a tax payment on the additional $1,333 of book pre-tax income recognized in 2014? The answer is yes because tax depreciation will be less than book depreciation in the later years of the asset's life, causing taxable income to exceed pre-tax book income when that happens. So, in 2014 there is an increase in a deferred tax liability to reflect the future tax payment on future taxable income corresponding to 2014 pre-tax book income. This increase in the deferred tax liability increases 2014 income tax expense accordingly.

Column (c) shows that for 2014, the *change* in the liability for future taxes is an increase of $467 ($1,333 depreciation temporary difference × 35% tax rate). Under GAAP, income tax expense equals the sum of the current taxes owed (that is, income taxes payable) and the *change* in the deferred tax liability. This sum represents the income taxes that will *ever* be paid related to current period pre-tax income. The computation is:

Computation of Income Tax Expense for 2014	
Current income tax payable ($18,667 × 35%)	$6,533
Increase in liability for future taxes arising during the year ($1,333 × 35%)	467
Income tax expense for 2014	**$7,000**

[3] Ibid.

The accounting entries for 2014 income taxes are:

DR	Income tax expense..	$6,533	
	CR	Income tax payable...................................		$6,533
DR	Income tax expense..	$467	
	CR	Deferred tax liability.................................		$467

These entries can be combined into a single entry, which we will do for the remainder of the chapter.

DR	Income tax expense..	$7,000	
	CR	Income tax payable		$6,533
	CR	Deferred tax liability		467

As this entry illustrates, the debit to income tax expense represents the combination of current taxes payable and any *change* in the deferred tax liability balance during the year. When the deferred tax liability increases, the increase is *added* to current income tax payable to arrive at income tax expense. When the deferred tax liability decreases, the decrease is *subtracted* from current income tax payable to determine income tax expense. Figure 13.3 summarizes these important relationships.

The 2014 accounting entry we just described records an originating book/tax temporary difference for depreciation expense that results in an increase in the deferred tax liability. A similar entry would be made in 2015. Tax expense in that year would be $7,000, or the current tax payable amount ($6,767) plus the increase in the deferred tax liability ($233) shown in Exhibit 13.6.

> Temporary differences that result in deferred tax liabilities are called future taxable amounts because **future taxable income** will be greater that future book income.

To see what happens when book-versus-tax temporary differences reverse, let's consider the income tax entry in 2017. From Figure 13.3, we see that income tax expense in 2017 is equal to current income tax payable minus the decrease in deferred tax liability during the year. Because book depreciation exceeds tax depreciation by $667 in 2017, the deferred tax liability *decreases* by $667 times 35%, or $233. Therefore, tax expense for 2017 is:

Computation of Income Tax Expense for 2017

Current income tax payable ($20,667 × 35%)	$7,233
Decrease in liability for future taxes ($667 × 35%)	(233)
Income tax expense for 2017	**$7,000**

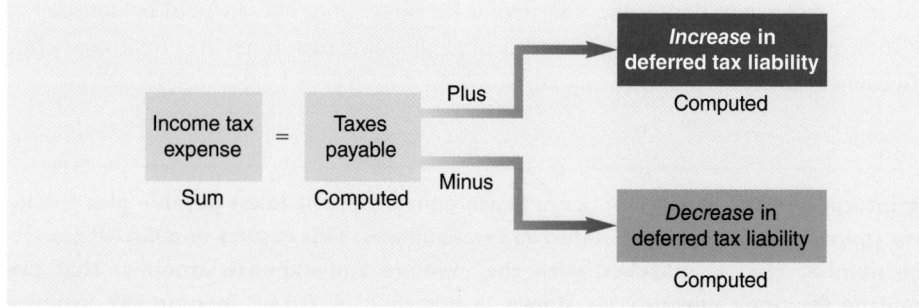

Figure 13.3

RELATIONS AMONG INCOME TAX EXPENSE, TAXES PAYABLE, AND CHANGES IN DEFERRED TAX LIABILITIES

The journal entry for 2017 income taxes is:

DR	Income tax expense	$7,000	
DR	Deferred tax liability	233	
	CR Income tax payable		$7,233

Return to Mitchell Corporation's computation of income tax expense for each year using interperiod tax allocation in Exhibit 13.6. Notice that in 2014 and 2015, the deferred tax liability *increases* and these increases are *added* to taxes payable to arrive at the tax expense reported on the income statement for those years. In 2017 and 2018, the depreciation temporary differences reverse, resulting in *decreases* in the deferred tax liability (because the additional taxes are now being paid), and these decreases are *subtracted* from taxes payable to arrive at tax expense for those years. By the end of 2018, the depreciation book-versus-tax temporary differences have totally reversed, and the balance in the deferred tax liability account is zero. With constant tax rates of 35% over the entire period, income tax expense (Column [d] in Exhibit 13.6) is always 35% times pre-tax book income of $20,000, and the pattern of tax expense matches the pattern of pre-tax book income.

When tax rates do not change from year to year, the tax entries we have seen simultaneously overcome both of the drawbacks that would exist if we measured income tax expense as cash taxes paid—the liability for future taxes is explicitly recognized, and the reported tax expense (in the Mitchell case) is exactly 35% of pre-tax book income of $20,000 ($7,000/$20,000 = 35%). Thus, tax expense is also "matched" with book income.

> In any year that tax rates change, this matching disappears. The reason is that GAAP focuses on the liability for future taxes, which changes as tax rates change. More on this later in the chapter.

This constant effective tax rate at exactly the 35% statutory tax rate resulted from a combination of factors. First, we applied interperiod tax allocation, or deferred tax accounting, rather than basing income tax expense on the amount of taxes to be paid in a given year. Second, we assumed the statutory tax rate itself was constant at 35%. (We have already mentioned that if the tax rate changes, the effective tax rate will be affected, and we will illustrate how that happens later in the chapter.) Third, we assumed there were no permanent differences. Permanent differences cause the effective tax rate to deviate from the statutory tax rate because they affect book pre-tax income without a corresponding effect on income tax expense or vice versa. In either case, when there are permanent differences and we divide income tax expense by book pre-tax income, we no longer get 35%. For example, suppose that in any year we examined, Mitchell also had $5,000 of municipal bond interest. This interest is *never* subject to tax, so there should be no income tax expense associated with it. Because the income is not subject to tax, currently payable taxes are unaffected. And because the municipal bond interest does not create a temporary difference, there is no change in any deferred tax asset or liability. So there is no effect on income tax expense as a result of this income. However, pre-tax book income would be $5,000 higher, so the effective tax rate would be $7,000/($20,000 + $5,000) = 28%. If this level of municipal bond interest were constant across years, the effective tax rate would still be constant due to the interperiod tax allocation, but it would be constant at 28%. If the level of municipal bond interest were changing over time, the effective tax rate would change as well.

 RECAP

With interperiod tax allocation, tax expense equals current taxes payable plus the increase (minus the decrease) in deferred tax liabilities. This results in a GAAP tax expense number that is matched with the revenue and expense amounts that are recognized for book purposes as shown in Figure 13.4. GAAP income tax expense

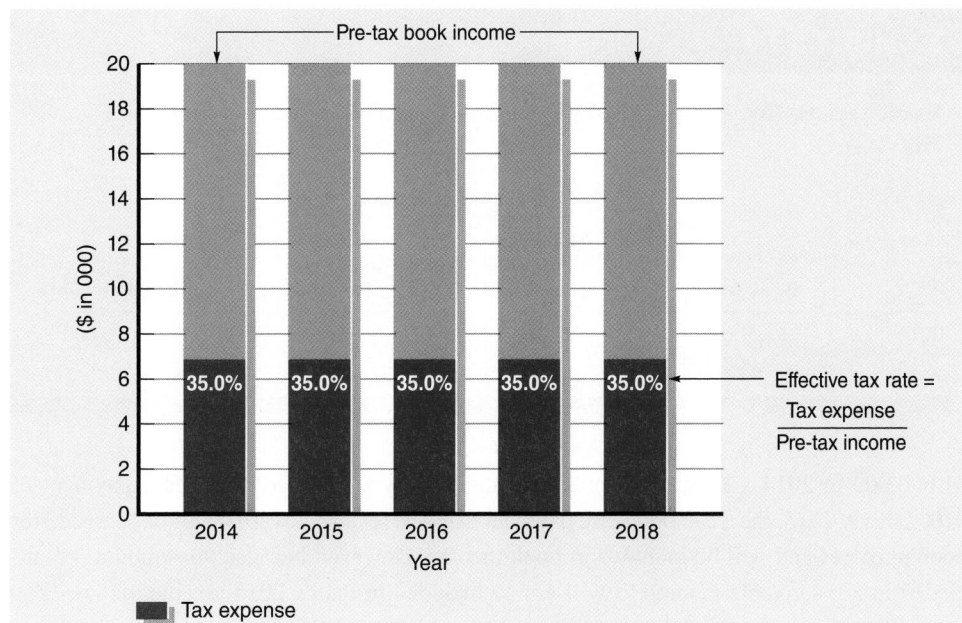

properly includes no amounts related to book revenues that are never subject to tax (e.g., municipal bond interest) or book expenses that are never tax deductible (e.g., certain fines and penalties).

Deferred Tax Assets

The Mitchell Corporation example illustrates a situation in which pre-tax book income initially exceeds taxable income, creating a deferred tax liability. But temporary differences can go in the opposite direction as well. In many circumstances, taxable income initially exceeds pre-tax book income, thereby giving rise to deferred tax assets. ————————

> Temporary differences that result in deferred tax assets are called **future deductible amounts** because future taxable income—all other factors being equal—will be lower than future book income.

To illustrate how a deferred tax asset arises, let's assume that in December 2014 Paul Corporation leases an office building it owns to another company for $100,000. The lease covers all of 2015 and specifies that the tenant pay the $100,000 to Paul Corporation immediately on signing the lease in 2014. On an accrual basis, rental income will be earned entirely in 2015, the period covered by the lease. Accordingly, Paul Corporation makes the following entry on receiving the lease payment:

DR Cash	$100,000	
CR Unearned rental income		$100,000

The account Unearned rental income is a liability. For GAAP reporting purposes this liability will be reduced monthly by $8,333 (with an offsetting credit to a revenue account) in 2015 as Paul provides the tenant with the use of the facility and earns the lease revenue. For tax purposes, the entire $100,000 rent prepayment is included in Paul Corporation's 2014 taxable income, consistent with the "constructive receipt/ability to pay" doctrine.

Assume the lease receipt represents the only book/tax temporary difference for Paul and that 2014 pre-tax book income totals $1,500,000. Accordingly, taxable income will total

EXHIBIT 13.7 Paul Corporation

Book-versus-Tax Temporary Differences That Give Rise to a Deferred Tax Asset

| | Book Income | 2014 Lease Receipt of $100,000 | | Taxable Income |
		Included in Book Income?	Included in Taxable Income?	
2014	$1,500,000	No	Yes	$1,600,000
2015	2,000,000	Yes	No	1,900,000

$1,600,000 in 2014—$1,500,000 plus the immediately taxable advance lease payment of $100,000. In 2015, the $100,000 lease payment that was received in 2014 will be "earned" for book purposes and will be included in book income. However, because this amount was included in 2014 taxable income, it will *not* be included in Paul's 2015 taxable income. The temporary difference that originated in 2014 reverses in 2015. Suppose book income is $2,000,000 in 2015. Taxable income will be $100,000 lower, or $1,900,000, because it will exclude the rental income, and the temporary difference will reverse. These relationships are summarized in Exhibit 13.7.

When the rent is earned in 2015 for book purposes, accounting income will exceed taxable income by $100,000—but no tax will be due on this difference because the tax was already paid in 2014. Thus, the temporary difference ($100,000) that originates in 2014 because of book/tax differences in lease revenue represents a deferred tax asset at the end of 2014. If we assume the income tax rate is 35%, 2014 income tax expense is composed of the current taxes payable *minus* the deferred tax asset increase, as shown in Exhibit 13.8.

Paul Corporation makes the following 2014 entry for income taxes:

DR	Income tax expense	$525,000	
DR	Deferred tax asset	35,000	
	CR Income tax payable		$560,000

Book pre-tax income is $2,000,000 in 2015, including the $100,000 of rental income *earned* that year, whereas taxable income is $1,900,000. The $100,000 temporary difference that originated in 2014 reverses, and the related deferred tax asset of $35,000 created in 2014 (Exhibit 13.8, Column [e]) is eliminated. As shown in Column (f), the $35,000 decrease in deferred tax assets is added to the taxes payable of $665,000 to arrive at income tax expense of $700,000. Paul makes the following income tax expense entry in 2015 when the temporary difference reverses:

DR	Income tax expense	$700,000	
	CR Deferred tax asset		$ 35,000
	CR Income tax payable		665,000

EXHIBIT 13.8	Paul Corporation

Computation of Tax Expense *with* Interperiod Tax Allocation

Year	(a) Taxable Income	(b) Book Income	(c) Excess of Tax Lease Revenue over Book Lease Revenue	(d) Taxes Payable (Col. [a] × 35%)	(e) Increase (Decrease) in Deferred Tax Asset (Col. [c] × 35%)	(f) Total Income Tax Expense (Col. [d] − Col. [e])
2014	$1,600,000	$1,500,000	$100,000	$560,000	$35,000	$525,000
2015	1,900,000	2,000,000	(100,000)	665,000	(35,000)	700,000

Figure 13.5 depicts the relationships for computing income tax expense under interperiod tax allocation by adjusting taxes payable for changes in deferred tax assets and liabilities.[4]

Net Operating Losses: Carrybacks and Carryforwards

Because firms pay taxes during profitable years, denying them some form of tax relief in unprofitable years would be inequitable. That is why the U.S. Internal Revenue Code (as well as the tax laws of many other countries) provides an opportunity for firms reporting net operating losses to offset those losses against either past or future taxable income. When deductible expenses exceed taxable revenues, a net operating loss occurs and firms will:

1. Carry back the incurred loss and carry forward any remaining unused loss, or
2. Elect to forego the carryback and carry forward the incurred loss.

Assume Unfortunato Corporation had a $1,000,000 net operating loss in 2014. Under the U.S. Internal Revenue Code, Unfortunato will carry back the net operating loss and

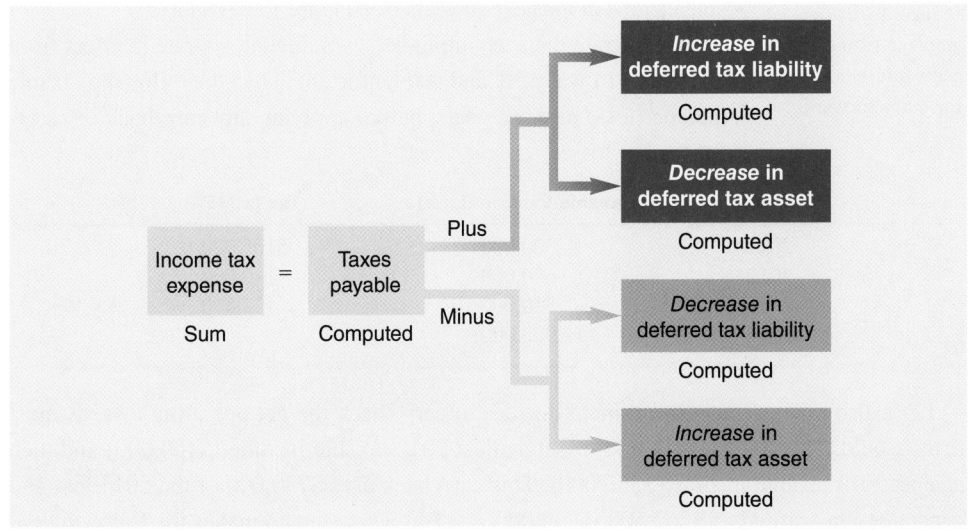

Figure 13.5

RELATIONS AMONG INCOME TAX EXPENSE, TAXES PAYABLE, AND CHANGES IN DEFERRED TAX ASSETS AND LIABILITIES

[4] Later in the chapter, we describe how changes in a tax contingency reserve for uncertain tax positions can also affect the determination of tax expense reported on a firm's income statement.

Figure 13.6

UNFORTUNATO
CORPORATION

Panel (a): Illustration of Tax
Loss Carryback/Carryforward
Provision

Panel (b): Illustration of Tax
Loss Carryforward

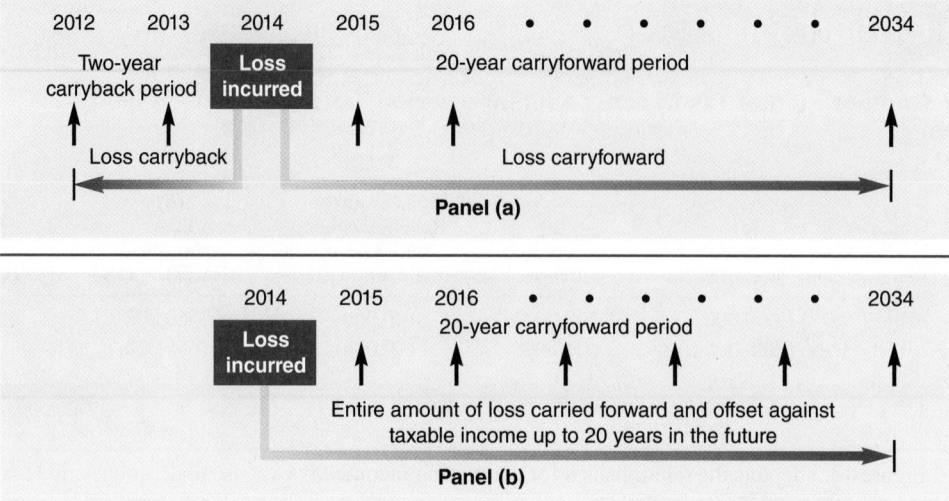

The Worker, Homeownership, and Business Assistance Act of 2009 allowed a temporary five-year carryback period for losses arising in 2008 or 2009 (but not both). Congress occasionally extends temporarily the carryback period, as it did with this act, generally during difficult economic times under the theory that providing additional cash to struggling companies will assist them.

offset it against taxable income in the previous two years, 2012 and 2013. The loss must be offset against the earlier year first—in this case, 2012. If the loss exceeds the total taxable income for the 2012–2013 period, the remaining portion of the loss can be carried forward and offset against *future* taxable income in the ensuing 20 years—2015 through 2034—as shown in Figure 13.6, Panel (a).

When a firm carries losses back, it receives a refund of taxes previously paid. In effect, the firm amends its tax return(s) for the year(s) to which losses are carried back, as if those losses had occurred in those year(s). The government then refunds the overpayment.

Most companies carry back first because that strategy usually maximizes the discounted present value of the benefit. Why would firms ever elect to carry forward only, thereby foregoing an immediate income tax refund? In unusual situations—for example, a firm expects to be profitable in the future and expects future tax rates to be much higher than past rates—the carry forward-only option may be preferred.

Unfortunato has another option. Rather than first carrying the loss back and then carrying forward any unused amounts, Unfortunato could elect not to carry the loss back and *only* carry the loss forward to reduce taxable income in the next 20 years (see Figure 13.6, Panel [b]).

To illustrate the accounting, let's assume the tax rate in effect from 2011 to 2014 was 35% and that Unfortunato had the following taxable income (loss) in those years, before applying any carryback or carryforward of losses.

Year	Taxable Income (Loss)	Tax (at 35%)
2011	$ 300,000	$105,000
2012	400,000	140,000
2013	350,000	122,500
2014	(1,000,000)	—

Let's also assume that Unfortunato decides to carry back the net operating loss, as most firms would. The 2014 loss is first offset against 2012 taxable income ($400,000) and then against 2013 taxable income ($350,000). This carryback uses $750,000 of the 2014 loss and generates a tax refund of $262,500 ($750,000 × 35%). Unfortunato makes the following entry in 2014 to reflect the refund due:

DR	Income tax refund receivable	$262,500	
	CR Income tax expense (*carryback* benefit)		$262,500

The unused loss ($1,000,000 − $400,000 − $350,000 = $250,000) will result in future tax benefits—if Unfortunato becomes profitable again before 2034. If we assume that future tax rates will remain at 35%, these future benefits would total $87,500 ($250,000 × 35%). Unfortunato makes an additional entry in 2014:

DR	Deferred tax asset	$87,500	
	CR Income tax expense (*carryforward* benefit)		$87,500

The Income tax refund receivable account would be shown among current assets on the balance sheet, and the deferred tax asset would be apportioned between current and noncurrent categories in accordance with the expected timing of the future income. If we assume that the pre-tax book loss equaled the taxable loss, the credits would be reflected in the accompanying income statement for 2014 as:

Income (loss) before tax	$(1,000,000)
Income tax benefit ($262,500 due to operating loss *carryback* and $87,500 due to operating loss *carryforward*)	350,000
Net income (loss)	$ (650,000)

Although it is an uncommon practice, Unfortunato could have elected only to carry forward its loss. In that case, it would not have received a refund and it would have created a deferred tax asset of $1 million × 35% = $350,000. The entry to record income taxes for 2014 would be:

DR	Deferred tax asset	$350,000	
	CR Income tax expense (carryforward benefit)		$350,000

Unfortunato would report the same income tax benefit of $350,000 and the same net loss of $650,000. However, it would not actually realize any benefit as a reduced income tax payment until it became profitable again and was able to avoid paying taxes that would otherwise be due.

RECAP

U.S. tax law allows firms to offset operating losses against taxable income. Firms can elect to carry back losses up to two years with any unused loss carried forward up to 20 years; or they can elect only to carry forward the loss up to 20 years. The tax benefit associated with the loss carryback or carryforward is recorded as an adjustment to income tax expense in the year of the loss. Many other countries have similar laws.

Deferred Tax Asset Valuation Allowances

There is no guarantee a firm will be profitable in the future. And, if a firm does not generate any taxable income, it may not be able to realize the tax benefits represented by the deferred tax assets it recorded. That is, those benefits can only be realized through reduced tax payments if there are tax payments to be reduced. For this reason, GAAP requires firms to assess the likelihood that deferred tax assets may not be fully realized in future periods.

If management believes the probability of future taxable income being sufficient to realize fully its deferred tax assets is more than 50%, then deferred tax assets can be recognized in their entirety. However, if management's assessment indicates that *it is more likely than not* that some portion of the benefit will *not* be realized, then a **deferred tax asset valuation allowance** is required. GAAP states that this valuation allowance *"shall be sufficient to reduce the deferred tax asset to the amount that is more likely than not to be realized."*[5]

To illustrate the procedure for establishing a deferred tax asset valuation allowance, let's assume that (1) for book purposes, Norman Corporation reported pre-tax book income of $600,000 in 2014, its first year of operations, after accruing $900,000 of estimated warranty expenses associated with product sales in 2014 and (2) the actual warranty parts and services from these sales are provided in 2015 and beyond. Because the U.S. Internal Revenue Code allows companies to deduct warranty expense only when the warranty services are provided, there is a temporary difference that gives rise to a deferred tax asset of $315,000 ($900,000 × 35%) which would be recorded in 2014. The 2014 income tax expense entry is:

DR Income tax expense	$210,000	
DR Deferred tax asset ($900,000 × 0.35)	315,000	
CR Income tax payable ($1,500,000 × 0.35)		$525,000

Now suppose that prior to completing its 2014 financial statements Norman determines it is unlikely to earn enough taxable income in future years to realize more than $200,000 of the deferred tax asset. The additional entry made for 2014 is:

DR Income tax expense ($315,000 − $200,000)	$115,000	
CR Allowance to reduce deferred tax asset to expected realizable value		$115,000

The allowance is a contra-account that reduces the net carrying amount of the deferred tax asset from $315,000 to $200,000—its estimated realizable value. Income tax expense is increased in the year during which it is determined that a portion of the deferred tax asset is unlikely to be realized. If Norman Corporation's future prospects improve and if in a subsequent year it determines that an allowance account is no longer needed, then the allowance account would be reduced to zero and there would be a *credit* to Income tax expense.

Now that we have seen how valuation allowances are recorded, let's return to the two examples we considered earlier that involved deferred tax assets—Paul Corporation with its leasing income and Unfortunato, which had an operating loss carryforward. Paul recorded a $35,000 deferred tax asset after it included the $100,000 lease payment it received in 2014 in that year's taxable income, even though it was not considered income under GAAP until 2015. In our original example, Paul had $1,900,000 of taxable income in 2015, certainly enough to ensure realization of the deferred tax asset. But suppose instead Paul was expected to run a loss in 2015 and the loss would be $1,000,000 for tax purposes and therefore $900,000 under GAAP. (The 2015 GAAP loss is $100,000 lower than the taxable loss because of the recognition of lease income in 2015 under GAAP, whereas the lease income was already recognized in 2014 for tax purposes.) Will Paul realize the deferred tax asset? The answer is yes because Paul will carry back the 2015 loss to 2014. Therefore, Paul would not record a valuation allowance at December 31, 2014.

The entry to record taxes in 2015 (when the loss is incurred) would be:

DR Income tax receivable	$350,000	
CR Deferred tax asset		$35,000
CR Income tax expense (benefit)		315,000

---

[5] FASB ASC Paragraph 740-10-30-5e: Income Taxes—Overall—Initial Measurement—Deferred Tax Expense (or Benefit). Operationally, "more likely than not" means the probability of occurrence is more than 50%.

Paul records a receivable for the $350,000 due from the government as a result of carrying back its $1,000,000 tax loss to earlier periods. The deferred tax asset is eliminated with the reversal of the temporary difference related to the lease and a credit to income tax expense of $315,000 is recorded. This income tax benefit is 35% of the $900,000 pre-tax book loss incurred in 2015.

What about Unfortunato (using the more common situation where Unfortunato carries back losses as they are incurred to the extent possible)? It recorded a deferred tax asset of $87,500 to reflect the $250,000 net operating loss carryforward it had. Unfortunato already used its carryback, so whether the company will realize the tax benefit from the carryforward depends entirely on its ability to generate taxable income in the future. Suppose there is substantial doubt about the company's future viability and the company's management cannot assert it is more likely than not that the company will have any future taxable income. Unfortunato would record a valuation allowance for the entire deferred tax asset of $87,500. It would establish a contra-account, bringing the net value of the deferred tax asset to be reported in the balance sheet to zero. It would increase its 2014 income tax expense (reduce the income tax benefit) by $87,500, thereby reporting an income tax benefit of only $262,500, the known, expected tax refund. So, Unfortunato would record the following entries in 2014. (The first two entries are the ones we showed in the original example. The third entry is the additional entry the company makes to establish the valuation allowance.)

DR Income tax refund receivable	$262,500	
CR Income tax expense (carryback benefit)		$262,500
DR Deferred tax asset	$87,500	
CR Income tax expense (carryback benefit)		$87,500
DR Income tax expense	$87,500	
CR Allowance to reduce deferred tax asset to expected realizable value		$87,500

The third entry, establishing the valuation allowance, effectively negates the second entry, where Unforunato recorded the deferred tax asset in the balance sheet and the corresponding income tax benefit in the income statement. The income tax benefit will therefore be reported as just $262,500 (from the first entry, reflecting the carryback) and the deferred tax asset will be reported in the balance sheet net of the valuation allowance, for a balance of zero.

Assessing the Need for a Valuation Allowance When There Is No History of Profitability The guidance on how to assess whether a valuation allowance is necessary requires firms to consider all available information, both positive and negative. The guidance notes, however, that for start-up companies, the full assortment of information normally examined is likely not to be available. In particular, there may not be a history of profitable operations to suggest the firm will be profitable in the future. The guidance goes on to say that forming a conclusion that a valuation allowance is not necessary would be difficult when there is negative evidence, such as losses in recent periods, particularly if there was no taxable income in any prior years to which those losses could be carried back.

For this reason, it is quite common for start-up companies to record valuation allowances for a large portion, if not all, of the company's deferred tax assets. The result of this approach is that no tax benefit is recognized in the income statement in those firms' early

EXHIBIT 13.9	Amazon.Com		
(Dollars in thousands)	**2004**	**2003**	**2002**
Net sales	$6,921,124	$5,263,699	$3,932,936
Cost of sales	5,319,127	4,006,531	2,940,318
Gross profit	1,601,997	1,257,168	992,618
Operating expenses	1,161,572	986,573	928,494
Income from operations	440,425	270,595	64,124
Non-operating expenses	84,555	231,607	214,757
Income (loss) before income taxes	355,870	38,988	(150,633)
Provision (benefit) for income taxes	(232,581)	3,706	(700)
Income (loss) before change in accounting principle	588,451	35,282	(149,933)
Cumulative effect of change in accounting principle			801
Net income (loss)	$ 588,451	$ 35,282	$ (149,132)

years, and the net loss is equal to the pre-tax loss. However, once a firm becomes profitable and is expected to remain so, the valuation allowance may be eliminated, giving an enormous boost to reported net income in the year(s) the allowance is reversed. In fact, the reversal is often so large that a firm with *positive* pre-tax income reports *negative* income tax expense, resulting in net income that exceeds pre-tax income! The resulting effective tax rate can be negative and in some cases it can even exceed (in magnitude) *minus* 100%. Exhibit 13.9 presents Amazon.com's condensed income statements for the three years 2002–2004. Amazon lost about $150 million in 2002 and, as it did in prior periods, reported income tax expense (benefit) close to zero. The company was building up net operating loss carryforwards, but without any history of profitability, there was not sufficient evidence to assert that a valuation allowance was not necessary, so it also built up a valuation allowance, resulting in virtually no income tax benefit reported in its income statements. In 2003 Amazon was close to breakeven and reported a small income tax expense. Then, in 2004, Amazon reported pre-tax income of $355.9 million and it became clear Amazon would be profitable in the future. The company reversed more than $600 million in valuation allowances that year alone, which reduced income tax expense to the *negative* $232.6 million amount it reported. Amazon's effective tax rate in 2004 was −65.4% (−$232,581/$355,870).

Valuation Allowances at Profitable Companies
It is not unusual to see a valuation allowance at a profitable company, although this might seem counterintuitive. If a firm has deferred tax assets in a particular tax jurisdiction, it will have to generate taxable income in *that* jurisdiction to realize the value of the deferred tax assets. So if, for example, a company has a European subsidiary that has no history of profits, it might need a valuation allowance even if the U.S. parent is profitable overall.

Subjectivity of Valuation Allowances
The decisions to establish a deferred tax asset valuation allowance and, if so, what amount to record are subjective assessments. Readily observable criteria do not exist, and the dollar amounts involved can be very large, so the potential for abuse is clear. For an example of how large a valuation allowance can be relative to the rest of the financial statements, we consider Ford Motor Company's 2011 valuation

---

EXHIBIT 13.10	**Ford Motor Company**		

Consolidated Income Statement—Abridged

(Dollars in millions)	2012	2011	2010
Income before income taxes	$7,720	$ 8,681	$7,149
Provision for (benefit from) income taxes	2,056	(11,541)	592
Net income	$5,664	$20,222	$6,557

---

allowance reversal. In January 2012, Ford issued a press release disclosing its earnings results for 2011. Two key bullets in the press release were:

- Full year pre-tax operating profit was $8.8 billion, or $1.51 per share, an increase of $463 million from a year ago
- Full year net income was $20.2 billion, or $4.94 per share, an increase of $13.7 billion, or $3.28 per share, from a year ago. Net income includes a favorable one-time, non-cash special item of $12.4 billion from release of almost all of the valuation allowance against net deferred tax assets in the fourth quarter

Exhibit 13.10 is an abridged version of Ford's 2012 income statement, showing results for 2010, 2011, and 2012. The press release and the income statement illustrate the potential magnitude of a valuation allowance reversal. Valuation allowances built up over many years can be released all at once, possibly even resulting in a negative tax provision in a year when the company reports positive pre-tax income. In 2011, Ford reported about $8.7 billion in pre-tax income. It reported a tax *benefit* (negative income tax expense) that year, due to elimination of $12.4 billion of valuation allowance, effectively reinstating the related deferred tax assets that had been de-recognized over the years through the application of the valuation allowance. The result was net income substantially in excess of pre-tax income and an effective tax rate of −132.9% (−$11,541/$8,681) in 2011. In 2012, Ford's effective tax rate returned to a more normal 26.6% ($2,056/$7,720).

Although we are not suggesting Ford's actions were inappropriate or constituted any sort of accounting abuse, there was certainly some amount of subjectivity in the company's decision to release the valuation allowance. It cannot know, with objective certainty, the probability of attaining a particular level of income in the future. The inherent subjectivity of the valuation allowance means that a company that is so inclined could use the valuation allowance to "manage" earnings. For example, management might decide to establish an allowance account in a "good" earnings year when the offsetting charge to earnings is relatively small. Once the allowance is established, it can be diminished or even eliminated in subsequent "bad" earnings years. Doing so decreases tax expense, thereby partially offsetting the lower earnings. The result is that income fluctuations are smoothed across years.

 **Analysis**

Two notable studies investigate whether managers use the valuation allowance to manage earnings. One study finds that bank managers appear to use the valuation allowance to manage earnings toward consensus analysts' forecasts and toward average historical earnings.[6] Another study using a broader sample of manufacturing firms finds that managers use the valuation

---

[6] C. Schrand and F. Wong, "Earnings Management Using the Valuation Allowance for Deferred Tax Assets under *SFAS No. 109*," *Contemporary Accounting Research,* Fall 2003, pp. 579–611.

allowance to manage earnings up (down) when analysts' earnings forecasts are above (below) the premanaged earnings number.[7] Taken together, these two studies provide compelling evidence that managers take advantage of the discretion associated with setting the deferred tax asset valuation allowance to manage earnings in both a positive and a negative direction.

RECAP

When circumstances indicate that it is "more likely than not" that some portion of the future tax benefit from a deferred tax asset will not be realized, a deferred tax asset valuation allowance must be established to reduce the deferred tax asset book value to the amount expected to be realized. Because the determination of "more likely than not" is subjective, the valuation account can be used to manage earnings up or down.

Classification of Deferred Tax Assets and Deferred Tax Liabilities

In general, U.S. GAAP requires firms to classify deferred tax assets or deferred tax liabilities as current or noncurrent according to how the asset or liability giving rise to the temporary difference is classified. For example, a deferred tax asset related to doubtful accounts on accounts receivable (a current asset) would be classified as current, whereas a deferred tax liability for temporary differences on depreciation of fixed assets would be classified as noncurrent. A temporary difference is related to an asset or liability if reduction of that asset or liability causes the temporary difference to reverse. The term *reduction* includes amortization, sale, or other realization of an asset and amortization, payment, or other satisfaction of a liability. If a deferred tax asset or liability is not related to an asset or liability (e.g., a deferred tax asset related to a net operating loss carryforward), it is classified according to the expected reversal date of the temporary difference. In the case of Unfortunato's $87,500 deferred tax asset related to its net operating loss carryforward, the portion expected to be realized in the coming year would be classified as current and the remainder would be classified as noncurrent.

For tax-paying components of an entity (e.g., subsidiaries) that are within a common tax jurisdiction, all current deferred tax assets and liabilities can be netted and presented as a single amount and all noncurrent deferred tax assets and liabilities can be netted and presented as a single amount. However, firms are not allowed to net deferred tax liabilities and assets attributable to different tax-paying components or to different tax jurisdictions.

Deferred Income Tax Accounting When Tax Rates Change

Taxing authorities change tax rates periodically. When this happens, the expected tax effects of existing deferred tax assets and liabilities change as well. GAAP uses the so-called **liability approach,** whereby deferred tax assets and deferred tax liabilities are always valued at the enacted tax rate expected to be in effect when the related temporary differences reverse. *In any year that current or future tax rates change, the income tax expense number absorbs the full effect of the change, and the usual relationship between that year's income tax expense and book income is destroyed.*

Returning to the Mitchell Corporation example in Exhibit 13.6, assume that on December 31, 2016, a new income tax law is enacted that raises the income tax rate from 35% to 38% beginning January 1, 2017. Just prior to the tax law change on December 31, 2016, the amount

---

[7] S. Rego and M. Frank, "Do Managers Use the Valuation Allowance Account to Manage Earnings Around Certain Earnings Targets?" *Journal of the American Taxation Association*, vol. 28, 2006, pp. 43–65.

of deferred tax liability for Mitchell was $700 (Column [e] of Exhibit 13.6). That number represents the cumulative excess of tax depreciation over book depreciation in 2014–2016 (the dollar amount of temporary depreciation differences = $1,333 + $667 + $0 or $2,000) times the original tax rate of 35%. But because future tax rates have increased, the liability for future taxes is actually more than the $700 amount currently reported. At the new, higher income tax rate that will be in effect in 2017 and 2018, the liability for future taxes becomes $760, not $700. This future liability represents the cumulative excess of tax depreciation over book depreciation ($2,000) multiplied by the new 38% tax rate that will be in effect beginning January 1, 2017.

HEALTH CARE REFORM AND DEFERRED TAX ASSETS

On March 23, 2010, President Obama signed the Patient Protection and Affordable Care Act, which had passed the House two days earlier and the Senate the previous December. In addition to altering the structure of medical care in the United States, the act affected the amounts many firms reported as deferred tax assets and affected their income tax provisions in the year the act was passed. Here is how that effect arose.

Prior to the act, the federal government had put in place a subsidy to encourage employers to provide prescription drug benefits to retirees. The subsidy partially offset the cost of providing prescription benefits that exceeded that available from Medicare Part D. The subsidy was not taxable and also did not reduce the amount a firm could deduct for providing the benefits. That is, even though the cost was partially subsidized by the government, the full amount of benefits provided could be deducted.

Under the accounting rules for other postemployment benefit (OPEB) plans (Chapter 14), firms with OPEB plans accrue the cost of providing retiree health benefits over employees' working years. However, these firms do not receive a tax deduction until they actually provide the benefits to retirees. These disparate treatments—GAAP recognition over the employment life; tax deduction during retirement—create a temporary difference. As a result, firms record a reduction in income tax expense over the employment life to reflect the future deductions that will be available during retirement, creating a deferred tax asset.

Because the subsidy did not reduce the amount that could be deducted, when firms recorded on their balance sheets the deferred tax assets related to the future tax deductions they would receive upon providing the benefits, they did not reduce the amounts of the deferred tax assets because of the subsidy. After all, those tax deductions were going to be available even after the subsidy was received.

Although the act did not repeal the subsidy, it did repeal its tax-free nature. Tax deductions for providing the benefit must be reduced by the amount of the subsidy received. As a result, many firms were required to de-recognize deferred tax assets to the extent their deductions would be reduced by the change in the law, resulting in an immediate charge against income via the income tax provision. Boeing, for example, announced on March 31, 2010, that it would take a $150 million charge as a result of the act. For the year, Boeing's income tax provision was $1,296 million and the charge increased its effective tax rate by 3.3 percentage points.

There was extensive publicity about this issue as firms announced their expected charges due to the act. Predictably, those who opposed the act seized upon the charges as evidence of the costs the act would impose on corporate America. Just as predictably, those who supported the act argued that the charges against income were not meaningful numbers—just bookkeeping entries. As is the case with most highly politicized topics, the truth lies somewhere between the partisan spins. The act does make providing drug benefits more costly for firms by eliminating the tax-free nature of the subsidy. Some might argue that there was no reason for the subsidy to be tax-free in the first place and that the act corrected an inequity in the law. On the other hand, the government made the subsidy tax-free in order to encourage firms to provide the benefit, and firms made decisions about what benefits to provide given the incentives the government had put in place through the tax code. They later found themselves facing a different set of rules than they thought would be in place when they made their decisions.

Although some of the charges were quite large, it was not always apparent to those reading articles in the popular press that these charges would not be recurring. Boeing's $150 million charge, for example, eliminated the deferred tax assets it had built up over many years to the extent they would not be realized under the new law. There would, of course, be no such charge the following year. Anyone interpreting Boeing's charge as a $150 million increase in annual tax costs would be wrong.

For more information on this topic, see Financial Reporting Alert 10-3, Deloitte, and "Don't Believe the Writedown Hype" by Secretary of Commerce Gary Locke in the *The Wall Street Journal*, April 1, 2010.

Under the liability approach of Topic 740: Income Taxes, the full change in the amount of future liability for income taxes (in this case, $60) is recognized as an increase or decrease in income tax expense in the year the tax rate change is enacted. Accordingly, income tax expense for 2016 is computed as:

Current 2016 income tax payable (35% × $20,000 [see Exhibit 13.4])	$7,000
Increase in the liability for future taxes arising during 2016	
($1,333 + $667 + $0) × (0.38 − 0.35)	60
Income tax expense for 2016	**$7,060**

The accounting entry for 2016 income taxes is:

DR	Income tax expense	$7,060	
	CR Income tax payable		$7,000
	CR Deferred tax liability		60

After this entry is made, the balance in Deferred tax liability will total $760, which is the liability for future taxes at the new 38% rate. Also, because tax rates for future years were changed in 2016, the debit to Income tax expense does not equal the $20,000 pre-tax book income times the 2016 tax rate of 35%.

Exhibit 13.11 shows the revised computation of income tax expense and deferred tax liability for Mitchell Corporation for 2016 through 2018 after reflecting the income tax rate increase. The journal entry for income taxes in 2017 is:

DR	Income tax expense	$7,600	
DR	Deferred tax liability	253	
	CR Income tax payable		$7,853

Similarly, the 2018 entry is:

DR	Income tax expense	$7,600	
DR	Deferred tax liability.	507	
	CR Income tax payable.		$8,107

As shown in Column (f) of Exhibit 13.11, the balance in the Deferred tax liability account will be zero after the year 2018 entry is made.

EXHIBIT 13.11   **Mitchell Corporation**

Revised Computation of Income Tax Expense

Year	(a) Taxable Income (Exhibit 13.4, Col. [b])	(b) Current Income Tax Payable = Col. (a) × 38%	(c) Excess of Tax Depreciation over Book Depreciation (Exhibit 13.3, Col. [c])	(d) Increase (Decrease) in Deferred Tax Liability = Col. (c) × 38%	(e) Income Tax Expense = Col. (b) + Col. (d)	(f) Balance in Deferred Tax Liability at Year-End
2016	$20,000	$7,000*	—	$ 60†	$7,060	$760
2017	20,667	7,853	$ (667)	(253)	7,600	507
2018	21,333	8,107	(1,333)	(507)	7,600	–0–

---

* Tax rate is still 35% in 2016 so this is $20,000 × 35%.

† This is the increase that arose in 2016 when the rate went from 35% to 38% (that is, 3% × $2,000 cumulative depreciation differences in Column [b] of Exhibit 13.6).

Because the effects of income tax rate changes are recognized through an adjustment to income tax expense, analysts must be alert to recognize how tax rate changes can inject one-time (transitory) shocks to earnings in the year a taxing authority adopts new tax rates. Moreover, it is important to recognize that the effect of a tax rate change on bottom-line earnings can vary considerably across companies depending on three factors:

Analysis

A change in tax rates of this magnitude is not uncommon. For example, the 1986 Tax Reform Act lowered the marginal corporate tax rate for large firms from 46% to 34%.

1. Whether the tax rate increased or decreased.
2. Whether the firm has net deferred tax assets or net deferred tax liabilities.
3. The magnitude of the net deferred tax position.

Consider how differently a tax rate change can affect firms' bottom-line earnings: Suppose Congress enacts a new tax law in 2014 that raises the statutory corporate tax rate from 35% to 45% effective in 2015. Also assume that Companies A, B, and C have the following net deferred tax asset (liability) balances on their books when the new tax law is passed:

($ in millions)	Company A	Company B	Company C
Net deferred tax asset (liability) balance at end of 2014	$100	$0	($100)

The effect of the change in tax rate on the after-tax earnings of these three companies in 2014—the year the new tax rate is passed—is shown in Exhibit 13.12. We first divide the net deferred tax asset (liability) balance by the old marginal tax rate to get the dollar magnitude of the cumulative temporary differences that gave rise to these account balances. Recall that the deferred tax asset (liability) account balances equal the cumulative temporary differences giving rise to future deductible (taxable) amounts times the marginal corporate tax rate. Therefore, to derive the cumulative temporary differences, we divide the deferred tax asset and liability balances by 0.35.[8]

In Exhibit 13.12, Company A has $285.71 ($100/0.35) million of future *deductible* amounts, Company C has $285.71 of future *taxable* amounts, and Company B has neither future deductible nor taxable amounts. These cumulative temporary differences are multiplied by the *difference* between the new tax rate and the old tax rate (that is, 10%) to obtain the increase in the deferred tax asset (liability) balance and the corresponding increase (decrease) in reported after-tax earnings. (Equivalently, we could multiply the cumulative temporary

---

EXHIBIT 13.12   **Computation of How Change in Tax Rate Affects Earnings in Year That Rate Change Is Enacted**

($ in millions)	Company A	Company B	Company C
Net deferred tax asset (liability) balance at end of 2014	$ 100	$ 0	$ (100)
Divide by old marginal tax rate	÷35%	÷35%	÷35%
Dollar amount of cumulative temporary difference	$ 285.71 ◄— Future deductible amount	$ 0	$ (285.71) ◄— Future taxable amount
Multiply by difference between old and new tax rates (45% − 35%)	×10%	×10%	×10%
Increase (decrease) to after-tax earnings in year of rate change	$ 28.571	$ 0	$ (28.571)

---

[8] We use the old tax rate of 35% here because we are inferring the amount of the cumulative temporary difference from the deferred tax asset or liability that was determined using the old tax rate.

difference by the new tax rate to determine the new deferred tax asset or deferred tax liability amount. The increase or decrease would be the difference between this amount and the original deferred tax asset or deferred tax liability.)

As shown, Company A's 2014 earnings will *increase* by $28.571 million. This is because each dollar of future deductible amounts will yield an additional $0.10 in tax savings under the newly enacted tax rates (that is, when these temporary differences reverse). Company C, on the other hand, will report a $28.571 million *decrease* to its after-tax earnings number because each dollar of future taxable amounts will generate $0.10 of additional taxes as these temporary differences reverse in future years (when the tax rates will be higher). Company B's 2014 after-tax earnings are unaffected by the tax rate change because no cumulative temporary differences exist.

If the tax rates had been reduced from 35% to 25%, the earnings effects reported for Companies A and C would have been reversed. As this example demonstrates, tax rate changes can have very different effects on firms' reported earnings depending on their deferred tax status and the direction of the tax rate change.

Company A's situation illustrates the counterintuitive result that occurs when a firm is in a net deferred tax asset position. In that case, an increase in tax rates increases the value attributed to the net deferred tax assets, resulting in a reduction in income tax expense and an increase in net income. When the tax rate decreases, the opposite happens and a firm in a net deferred tax asset position reports lower net income. The result is counterintuitive because a reduced tax rate, which is surely a good thing for a company, causes reported net income to be lower, while a higher tax rate results in greater income in the year of the tax rate change.

The reason for this counterintuitive result is that deferred tax accounting brings onto the balance sheet, as deferred tax assets, the firm's future tax benefits that arose from prior transactions, such as past losses. The firm will realize these benefits through lower tax payments in the future. As the tax rate increases (decreases), the firm will save more (less) in future tax payments.

Consider a company with a $100 million net operating loss carryforward and, as a result, a $35 million deferred tax asset (based on a 35% tax rate). The company expects to have $50 million of taxable income per year for the foreseeable future. The value of the deferred tax asset represents the future taxes the firm will avoid by applying the net operating loss carryforward to the next two years of taxable income. If the tax rate were to increase to 36%, the net operating loss carryforward would allow the firm to avoid $36 million in tax payments that would otherwise be due, so the deferred tax asset is more valuable. But the firm is still worse off because, beginning three years hence, its tax payments will be $18 million per year ($50 million × 36%) instead of $17.5 million.[9] The effect is analogous to a motorist holding a coupon for a free tank of gas. If the price of gas goes up, the coupon is worth more, but the motorist, who will have to pay for his or her gas after the next fill-up, would hardly be happy about the situation.

Although the U.S. federal corporate income tax rate has not changed that often—most recently in 1993—a change in the tax rate in any jurisdiction in which a company operates could affect the value of the company's deferred tax assets and liabilities. For example, deferred tax assets and liabilities related to a foreign subsidiary will be revalued if the income tax rate in the country in which that subsidiary operates were to change. Similarly, a change in a state income tax rate would affect the values of deferred tax assets and liabilities related to items in that state. So, income tax rate changes and their corresponding effects on income tax expense are not unusual events.

To illustrate the potential magnitude of a tax rate change and how it is reported, we examine General Motors' income statement for 1993, which is provided in Exhibit 13.13. The federal corporate income tax rate increased that year from 34% to 35%. GM had a net deferred tax asset

[9] For a discussion of this effect, see D. Reilly, "Banks' Unlikely Hit from Tax Cuts," *The Wall Street Journal,* July 27, 2010; and M. Rapoport, "Tax Twist: At Some Firms, Cutting Corporate Rates May Cost Billions," *The Wall Street Journal,* November 8, 2012.

| **EXHIBIT 13.13** | **General Motors Corporation** | | |

Statement of Consolidated Operations (Edited for Brevity)	1993	1992	1991
($ in millions)			
Total net sales and revenues	$138,219.5	$132,242.2	$123,108.8
Total costs and expenses	135,644.2	135,575.3	129,001.1
Income (loss) before income taxes	2,575.3	(3,333.1)	(5,892.3)
Income tax expense (benefit)	109.5	(712.5)	(900.3)
Income (loss) before cumulative effect of accounting change	2,465.8	(2,620.6)	(4,992.0)
Cumualtive effect of accounting changes		(20,877.7)	539.2
Net income	$ 2,465.8	($23,498.3)	($4,452.8)

position of about $16.4 billion at the time the tax rate changed. That net position would equate to roughly $48.2 billion in cumulative temporary differences ($16.4/0.34), which would have been revalued to $48.2 billion $\times$ 35% = $16.9 billion. The increase in the value of the deferred tax assets—about a half billion dollars—reduced GM's income tax expense in 1993 and accounted for much of the reason its effective tax rate in that year was only about 4% ($109.5/$2,575.3). That reduction in income tax expense alone was 19.4% ($500 million/$2,575.3 million) of pre-tax income, so it reduced the effective tax rate in 1993 by nearly 20%.

In general, deferred tax assets and liabilities are classified as current or noncurrent based on the classification of the related asset or liability giving rise to the temporary difference. Under GAAP, when tax rates change, the additional tax benefits or costs are recognized as an adjustment to tax expense in the year that the tax rate changes are *enacted*, not when they *become effective*. These one-time earnings shocks can be difficult to detect because they are reported as part of the tax expense line on the income statement. However, a careful reading of the tax note, which includes a reconciliation of the book-effective tax rate with the statutory tax rate (described in detail later in this chapter), can reveal the magnitude of earnings increases or decreases due to tax rate changes.

Permanent Differences

We have not said much about permanent differences yet, other than to define them. Permanent differences are items (either revenue/gain or expense/loss) that are included in book pre-tax income but not taxable income, or vice versa. It is not just a difference in when the item is reported, but whether it is reported at all, ever. For example, municipal bond interest income is never included in taxable income but it is part of pre-tax book income, so it represents a permanent difference.

The reason we have not said much about permanent differences yet is because our approach to determining income tax expense implicitly deals with permanent differences. Income tax expense should include the income tax consequences of any amounts included in pre-tax book income, regardless of when those tax consequences are realized in cash through higher or lower tax payments. An item included in pre-tax book income that will never be included in taxable income has no tax consequences ever and so it should not affect income tax expense. By summing the income tax currently payable and the change in deferred tax assets and liabilities, we properly incorporate the fact that there are no tax consequences for items included in pre-tax income but not taxable income.

Recall that earlier we showed how Mitchell Corporation's income tax expense was unaffected by the addition of municipal bond interest, which reduced the company's effective tax rate. Similarly, our approach to determining income tax expense works for an item included in taxable income or otherwise affecting the amount of tax paid, but not affecting pre-tax book income. For example, suppose Mitchell Corporation had been entitled to a $1,000 tax credit for operating in an "enterprise zone." Its currently payable tax would have been $6,000 instead of $7,000. There would again be no change in any deferred tax items. So, the decrease in income tax expense would be properly reflected when we sum currently payable tax ($1,000 lower) with the same change in deferred tax liability as in the original example.

UNDERSTANDING INCOME TAX NOTE DISCLOSURES

Income tax note disclosures provide financial statement users with a wealth of information. If you understand these disclosures, you'll be able to extract useful insights about a firm's past performance, future prospects, and tax planning strategies. To illustrate, let's look at the income tax note from the annual report of Deere & Company for the year ended October 31, 2012, shown in Exhibit 13.14. To make the discussion easier to follow, we divided the note into Panels (a) through (d) and numbered key lines or sections in these panels.

Current versus Deferred Portion of Current Period's Tax Provision

GAAP requires firms to disclose separately the current and deferred portions of the current period's income tax provision. The components of Deere's income tax provision are shown in Panel (a) of Exhibit 13.14. Notice how Deere differentiates between the portion of tax expense that is currently payable (denoted Item ①) and the portion that is deferred (Item ②). Within each category, separate amounts for U.S. federal, state, and foreign taxes are disclosed. In the aggregate, the 2012 entry for taxes was ($ in millions):

DR	Income tax expense (Item ③)	$1,659	
DR	Deferred tax assets and liabilities (Item ②)	92	
	CR Income tax payable (Item ①)		$1,751

The $92 million debit to deferred tax assets and liabilities arises because of temporary differences between pre-tax income reported in Deere's 2012 GAAP income statement and what appeared in its 2012 tax return. In the aggregate, these temporary differences caused book income to be less than taxable income in 2012. The result was either an increase in deferred tax assets or a decrease in deferred tax liabilities (both debits), or some combination of the two.

Reconciliation of Statutory and Effective Tax Rates

The reconciliation in Exhibit 13.14(b) is required under GAAP.[10] It shows why the debit to income tax expense in the 2010–2012 period was different from the U.S. federal statutory corporate tax rate of 35% times pre-tax book income. For example, the $1,659 million debit to income tax expense in the previous entry is not equal to 35% of Deere's reported 2012 pre-tax income of $4,734.4 million × 35% = $1,657.0 million, although in this particular year the difference is quite small. The reconciliation [Item ④ in Exhibit 13.14(b)] explains what caused the divergence.

The reconciliation is useful to analysts because it provides information about the firm's tax planning and policies. It is also useful to assess the quality of earnings and for forecasting future income tax expense. A large year-to-year decrease in effective tax rates translates into an increase

---

[10] FASB ASC Section 740-10-50: Income Taxes—Overall—Disclosure.

EXHIBIT 13.14	Deere & Company: Excerpts from 2012 10-K Note on Income Taxes

Panel (a):

The provision for income taxes by taxing jurisdiction and by significant component consisted of the following in millions of dollars:

	2012	2011	2010
Current:			
U.S.:			
Federal	$1,277	$928	$574
State	119	144	50
Foreign	355	520	363
Total current	1,751	1,592	987
Deferred:			
U.S.:			
Federal	(76)	(135)	156
State	(7)	(28)	11
Foreign	(9)	(5)	8
Total deferred	(92)	(168)	175
Provision for income taxes ◄——————③——————►	$1,659	$1,424	$1,162

① — bracket grouping Federal, State, Foreign, Total current
② — bracket grouping Federal, State, Foreign, Total deferred

Panel (b):

A comparison of the statutory and effective income tax provision and reasons for related differences in millions of dollars follow:

	2012	2011	2010
U.S. federal income tax provision at a statutory rate of 35%	$1,657	$1,478	$1,059
Increase (decrease) resulting from:			
Valuation allowance on foreign deferred taxes	200	18	5
State and local income taxes, net of federal income tax benefit	73	75	40
Nondeductible health care claims*			123
Nondeductible goodwill impairment charge	6		7
Nontaxable foreign partnership earnings	(172)		
Tax rates on foreign earnings	(69)	(70)	(59)
Research and development tax credits	(10)	(38)	(5)
Wind energy production tax credits			(30)
Other-net	(26)	(39)	22
Provision for income taxes	$1,659	$1,424	$1,162

④ — bracket grouping the reconciling items
⑤ — dotted arrow from $1,657 to $1,659

At October 31, 2012, accumulated earnings in certain subsidiaries outside the U.S. totaled $3,209 million for which no provision for U.S. income taxes or foreign withholding taxes has been made, because it is expected that such earnings will be reinvested outside the U.S. indefinitely. Determination of the amount of unrecognized deferred tax liability on these unremitted earnings is not practical. At October 31, 2012, the amount of cash and cash equivalents and marketable securities held by these foreign subsidiaries was $628 million.

---

* Cumulative adjustment from change in law. Effect included in state taxes was $7 million.

(continued)

EXHIBIT 13.14 Deere & Company: Excerpts from 2012 10-K Note on Income Taxes (*continued*)

Panel (c):

Deferred income taxes arise because there are certain items that are treated differently for financial accounting than for income tax reporting purposes. An analysis of the deferred income tax assets and liabilities at October 31 in millions of dollars follows:

	2012		2011	
	Deferred Tax Assets	Deferred Tax Liabilities	Deferred Tax Assets	Deferred Tax Liabilities
Other postretirement benefit liabilities	$2,136		$1,944	
Tax over book depreciation		$ 606		$ 492
Accrual for sales allowances	546		438	
Pension liabilities—net	457		279	
Lease transactions		317		309
Accrual for employee benefits	249		189	
Tax loss and tax credit carryforwards	249		121	
Share-based compensation	133		113	
Inventory	131		152	
Goodwill and other intangible assets		110		123
Allowance for credit losses	92		115	
Deferred gains on distributed foreign earnings	84		83	
Deferred compensation	40		37	
Undistributed foreign earnings		11		19
Other items	443	115	348	112
Less valuation allowances ⟵⟶⑧	(285)		(74)	
Deferred income tax assets and liabilities ⟵⟶⑨	**$4,275**	**$1,159**	**$3,745**	**$1,055**

⑥ ⑦

Panel (d):

At October 31, 2012, certain tax loss and tax credit carryforwards for $249 million were available with $127 million expiring from 2013 through 2032 and $122 million with an indefinite carryforward period.

――――――
* Deere's 2012 pre-tax income was $3,582 million. So its effective tax rate for 2012 was $1,659/$4,734 = 35.04%.

in bottom-line earnings that may not be sustainable. The divergence between the **statutory tax rate** (the 35% tax rate set forth in U.S. federal tax laws) and the **effective tax rate** (measured by book tax expense divided by book pre-tax income) arises from a number of sources.

1. Permanent difference items that are not taxed or are not tax deductible but are included in book income.

2. State and local taxes.

3. Changes in the valuation allowance.

4. Differential tax rates in foreign jurisdictions in which the firm operates.

5. Various tax credits offered by the federal government.

Permanent Differences A frequent cause of differences between statutory and effective tax rates are the permanent differences that arise when tax law treats a GAAP revenue item as nontaxable or a GAAP expense as nondeductible. Permanent difference items that cause book income to be *higher* but are not taxed (such as interest on municipal bonds) cause the effective tax rate to be *lower* than the statutory tax rate. Conversely, permanent differences that cause book income to be *lower* but that are not deductible for tax purposes cause the effective tax rate to be *higher* than the statutory rate. The $6 million add-back in Deere's reconciliation schedule for the nondeductible goodwill impairment charge is an example.

State and Local Taxes   Another common source of difference between the federal statutory tax rate and the firm's effective tax rate is state and local income taxes. The $73 million addition shown in the reconciliation schedule causes Deere's effective tax rate to be higher than the federal statutory rate of 35%. Note that the caption on this item indicates it is "net of federal income tax benefit." State and local taxes are deductible for federal tax purposes. As a result, the net effect of $1 in state and local taxes is to increase the overall income tax expense by $0.65, $1 minus the $0.35 of federal taxes saved. Exhibit 13.14(a) showed the state tax provision was $112 million (119–7). Sixty-five percent of that amount is $73 million, the amount shown in the reconciliation in Exhibit 13.14(b).

Changes in Valuation Allowance   Recall from our earlier discussion of valuation allowances that a change in the valuation allowance is reflected immediately in income tax expense, even though there is no corresponding amount in pre-tax book income. Therefore, changes in the valuation allowance cause the effective tax rate to deviate from the 35% statutory tax rate and create a reconciling item in the tax rate reconciliation. Deere's income tax rate reconciliation in Exhibit 13.14(b) shows the company's income tax expense was $200 million higher in 2012 than it otherwise would have been because of a change in the valuation allowance. This amount is approximately equal to the $211 million difference between the valuation allowance reported at October 31, 2012, and October 31, 2011 (285 − 74, from Exhibit 13.4(c), item ⑧). The fact that these two amounts are not identical could be explained by changes in exchange rates used to translate valuation allowances related to foreign operations.

Differential Foreign Tax Rates   Tax rates differ across countries. When foreign income is taxed at a lower rate than the U.S. tax rate, it causes the effective tax rate to deviate from the statutory federal tax rate and creates a reconciling item. In 2012, Deere's income tax expense was $69 million lower than it would have been if its foreign income had been taxed at the U.S. tax rate. The United States has one of the highest corporate income tax rates in the world, so most often the tax rates in other countries in which U.S. firms operate are lower. So, as was the case with Deere, the reconciling item is usually negative.

The United States imposes tax on worldwide income of U.S. companies, meaning it taxes all of a U.S. company's earnings, regardless of where they are earned. However, foreign earnings are not subject to the tax until the earnings are repatriated (i.e., returned to the United States), at which time the earnings are subject to the 35% tax, but the firm receives a credit for foreign income taxes paid. The net result is that the combined U.S. and foreign taxes are 35% of the foreign earnings in the typical situation where the foreign rate is less than 35%. That raises the question of why there is a reconciling item. If the foreign earnings are eventually taxed at 35%, then the tax provision should be at 35% of the pre-tax amount, resulting in no item in the tax rate reconciliation.

For example, suppose Mavrogenes Corporation, a U.S. company, has a Greek subsidiary. Greece's corporate income tax rate is 20%. Suppose further the Greek subsidiary earns $100 million. The entry to reflect the income tax expense related to the Greek subsidiary would be:

DR	Income tax expense	$35,000,000	
	CR Income tax payable		$20,000,000
	CR Deferred tax liability		15,000,000

The subsidiary would owe the Greek government $20 million and it would incur a deferred tax liability of $15 million, which will only become payable when the Greek earnings are repatriated to the U.S. parent. The effective tax rate on this income would be 35% and there would in fact be no item in the tax rate reconciliation. Upon repatriation, the United States would tax the earnings at 35% but allow a $20 million foreign tax credit, resulting in a U.S. tax liability of $15 million. An income tax payable would be recognized and the deferred tax liability would be eliminated.

Of course, delaying repatriation delays the obligation to pay U.S. taxes, so firms have a financial incentive to do just that. And, if a firm deems its foreign earnings to be "permanently reinvested" overseas, the deferred tax liability need not be recorded. After all, if the earnings are never going to be repatriated, they will never be taxed in the United States, so it would not be appropriate to recognize an income tax expense related to U.S. taxes on the foreign income. In that case, only the $20 million of currently payable tax is recognized in income tax expense, no deferred tax liability is recognized, and an item *does* appear in the tax rate reconciliation because the tax provision deviates from 35% of pre-tax earnings. So in Deere's case, income tax expense was $69 million lower in 2012 due to the lower tax rates of its foreign operations whose earnings are deemed to be permanently reinvested.[11] So, in addition to the tax incentive to delay repatriation, there is a financial reporting incentive as well. Having a policy of indefinitely reinvesting foreign earnings reduces current period income tax expense.

Research confirms that the tax and financial reporting incentives have the expected effect and cause firms to delay repatriation.[12] A recent study finds that this behavior creates agency costs. That is, in an effort to avoid repatriation, firms enter into suboptimal transactions, namely acquisitions of foreign companies that are value-destroying transactions.[13]

Tax Credits   Finally, federal tax laws provide tax credits (dollar for dollar credit against tax burden otherwise owed) for certain types of expenditures. By reducing income tax expense without altering pre-tax book income, these tax credits reduce the effective tax rate below the statutory rate. Deere's reconciliation shows adjustments for two tax credits. The company received a tax credit for wind energy production in 2010 ($30 million). It also received research and development tax credits in all three years presented. The amount of the credits totaled $10 million in 2012.

> In the next section, we consider disclosures required under GAAP for uncertain tax positions taken by companies for which the taxing authorities may disallow a deduction (or income exclusion) in whole or in part.

The reconciliation between effective and statutory tax rates, such as that shown in Exhibit 13.14(b) (Item ④), can reflect important elements of a firm's tax policy decisions. Effective tax rates that are far lower than statutory tax rates might indicate aggressive tax postures. This could benefit shareholders. But aggressive tax positions might also generate future tax audits and additional tax assessments.[14] In addition, the tax rate reconciliation is useful for forecasting subsequent year's income tax expense amounts and effective tax rates. Because income taxes are such a large part of any company's cost structure, being able to forecast income tax

---

[11] For an expanded discussion of tax planning with foreign operations, see M. Scholes, M. Wolfson, M. Erickson, E. Maydew, and T. Shevlin, *Tax and Corporate Financial Strategy: A Global Planning Approach* (Upper Saddle River, NJ: Prentice Hall, 2009).

[12] See, for example, J. Graham, M. Hanlon, and T. Shevlin, "Real Effects of Accounting Rules: Evidence from Multinational Firms' Investment Location and Profit Repatriation Decisions," *Journal of Accounting Research,* March 2011, pp. 137–85; J. Blouin, L. Krull, and L. Robinson, "Where In the World Are 'Permanently Reinvested' Foreign Earnings?" University of Pennsylvania, University of Oregon, and Dartmouth College working paper; J. Blouin, L. Krull, and L. Robinson, "Is U.S. Multinational Intra-Firm Dividend Policy Influenced by Capital Market Incentives?" *The Accounting Review,* September 2012, pp. 1463–92; and F. Foley, J. Hartzell, S. Titman, and G. Twite, "Why Do Firms Hold So Much Cash? A Tax-Based Explanation," *Journal of Financial Economics,* December 2007, pp. 579–607.

[13] A. Edwards, T. Kravet, and R. Wilson, "Trapped Cash and the Profitability of Foreign Acquisitions" University of Toronto, University of Texas at Dallas, and University of Iowa working paper, June 27, 2012.

[14] For an analysis of tax note disclosures from the perspective of tax aggressiveness and future tax audit risk, see R. Weber and J. Wheeler, "Using Income Tax Disclosures to Explore Significant Economic Transactions," *Accounting Horizons,* September 1992, pp. 14–29.

expense reliably is essential to a good earnings forecast. For example, seeing that Deere's income tax expense was $200 million higher because of the change in its valuation allowance and given that this change is unlikely to recur, an analyst might estimate the 2013 effective tax rate to be ($1,659 − $200)/$4,734 = 30.8%.

Details on the Sources of Deferred Tax Assets and Liabilities

Items ⑥ and ⑦ of Exhibit 13.14(c) show year-end balances in deferred tax asset and deferred tax liability accounts and the sources of those amounts. The amount shown for each of the individual line items in this schedule is obtained by multiplying the difference between the book basis and tax basis of the related asset or liability by the tax rate related to the item (e.g., the 35% federal statutory rate plus a state tax effect for most items). After deducting the valuation allowance of $285 million on deferred tax assets (Item ⑧), Deere had a *net* deferred tax asset balance at October 31, 2012, of $3,116 million, or $4,275 million of deferred tax assets minus $1,159 million of deferred tax liabilities (Item ⑨). One year earlier, Deere had a *net* deferred tax asset balance (after allowance) of $2,690 million ($3,745 − $1,055). Thus, the year-to-year change in *net* deferred tax assets was an increase of $426 million.

Notice that the $426 million increase in Deere's net deferred tax assets (net debits to these accounts) in Exhibit 13.14(c) does not equal the $92 million debit to Deferred tax assets and liabilities shown in the journal entry on page 770 to record Deere's 2012 tax expense, taxes payable, and deferred taxes. The discrepancy is partially explained by **intraperiod income tax allocation,** discussed briefly in Chapter 2. Recall that all income statement items shown below Income from continuing operations and any direct charges or credits to stockholders' equity are shown *net of any related income tax effects.* Accordingly, tax effects (including deferred tax effects) that arise from discontinued operations, extraordinary items, direct charges or credits to stockholders' equity for prior period adjustments, or other comprehensive income items are not included in Deere's tax journal entry on page 770. This journal entry is limited to income tax effects that relate to income from continuing operations. Deere reported no discontinued operations and no extraordinary items in 2012. However, Deere's Statement of Changes in Stockholders' Equity (not shown) reveals four items of Other comprehensive income— retirement benefits adjustment, cumulative translation adjustment, unrealized loss on derivatives, and unrealized gain on investments. Generally, all of these items except for the translation adjustment would be shown net of deferred tax effect. Deere reported an increase in accumulated other comprehensive loss of $623.8 million in fiscal 2012 related to the three items that are shown net of deferred tax effect. We can estimate the pre-tax amount related to these items as $623.8 million/(1 − 0.35) = $959.7 million and the tax effect to be $959.7 million × 0.35 = $335.9 million. This tax effect would increase the deferred tax asset during the year. So, it explains essentially the entire $334 million difference between the $426 million that net deferred tax assets increased and the $92 million increase in net deferred tax assets that is explained by the deferred tax provision. The deferred tax asset also would have been affected by any revaluation of foreign deferred tax assets and liabilities for changes in exchange rates, although we do not have sufficient information to determine those amounts.

Another common source of changes in deferred tax assets and liabilities that are not seen in the deferred tax provision is acquisitions, although Deere did not have any in 2012. When an acquired company holds assets having tax bases that differ from their respective book values, changes occur in deferred tax accounts on the consolidated balance sheet. This situation further complicates any attempt to reconcile the change in deferred tax assets and liabilities with the deferred tax provision.

Exhibit 13.14(c) also shows the specific items that collectively constitute the deferred tax asset (Item ⑥) and deferred tax liability (Item ⑦) balances at October 31, 2012. The major items giving rise to deferred tax assets are other postretirement benefit liabilities and pension liabilities (discussed more fully in Chapter 14), accrual for sales allowances and employee benefits, and tax loss and tax credit carryforwards. Major items giving rise to deferred tax liabilities are tax versus book depreciation differences and lease transactions.

GAAP rules require that the amounts and expiration dates of net operating loss and tax credit carryforwards for which tax benefits have *not* been recognized be disclosed in the income tax note. Panel (d) of Exhibit 13.14 illustrates Deere's compliance with this disclosure requirement.

Why Don't a Company's Deferred Tax Assets and Liabilities Seem to Reverse?

We have seen that deferred tax assets and liabilities reverse eventually. However, we almost never see a deferred tax asset or liability balance of zero in a balance sheet. Why? Because even though *individual* deferred tax assets and liabilities reverse, as they do, they are replaced by new deferred tax assets and liabilities that arise. Whether a company's *overall* deferred tax position is growing or shrinking is likely to be related to whether the company itself is growing or shrinking.

Consider once again the Mitchell Company example from earlier in the chapter. Mitchell acquired a machine and depreciated it over a five-year period using straight-line depreciation for financial reporting and sum-of-the-years-digits for tax purposes. Suppose Mitchell bought one of these machines every year and its profits reflected the expanding production capacity as Mitchell went from one machine to two to three and so on. But as soon as a machine reached five years old, it was no longer usable and Mitchell disposed of it. So, after five years, Mitchell would be in a "steady state" with five machines operating. Each year it would acquire a new machine but dispose of an old one. After some years, suppose Mitchell stopped replacing machines so that the company would shrink in size.

Exhibit 13.15 builds up book and tax depreciation by calendar year, given asset purchases in 2014 through 2020. For example, the assets acquired in 2014 generate $2,000 of book depreciation per year in 2014 through 2018, as shown in the first line of the book depreciation section of Exhibit 13.15. That same asset purchase generates $3,333 of tax depreciation in 2014, $2,667 in 2015, and so on, as shown in the first line of the tax depreciation section. Assets acquired in each subsequent year create depreciation in the acquisition year and the next four.

In the calendar years when Mitchell is growing (2014–2017), its total company tax depreciation exceeds its total company book depreciation. It is creating additional temporary differences and its deferred tax liability position grows. Once Mitchell is in steady state (2018–2020), tax and book depreciation are equal, even though they are based on different depreciation methods. There is no net change in the cumulative temporary difference. Originating temporary differences exactly offset reversing temporary differences. The deferred tax liability remains constant at $6,666 × 35% = $2,333. As Mitchell starts to shrink, book depreciation exceeds tax depreciation and the company has net reversals of its deferred tax liabilities (2021–2024).

For young companies that are growing, you should expect to see deferred tax positions growing. Companies in a net deferred tax liability position, which most are, will see their deferred tax liabilities increasing each year as production capacity grows and originating temporary differences outpace reversing temporary differences. Mature companies (e.g., Mitchell in steady state) will have only small changes in their deferred tax positions and, as a result, taxes paid will be close to income tax expense. Once companies start to shrink, their deferred tax positions reverse. For companies with deferred tax liabilities, that means tax payments will begin to exceed income tax expense.

| **EXHIBIT 13.15** | Mitchell Company Deferred Taxes assuming Annual Machine Purchase 2014–2020 | | | | | | | | | |

Book Depreciation	2014	2015	2016	2017	2018	2019	2020	2021	2022	2023	2024
Asset Acquisition Year											
2014	$2,000	$2,000	$2,000	$2,000	$2,000						
2015		2,000	2,000	2,000	2,000	$2,000					
2016			2,000	2,000	2,000	2,000	$2,000				
2017				2,000	2,000	2,000	2,000	$2,000			
2018					2,000	2,000	2,000	2,000	$2,000		
2019						2,000	2,000	2,000	2,000	$2,000	
2020							2,000	2,000	2,000	2,000	$2,000
Total	$2,000	$4,000	$6,000	$8,000	$10,000	$10,000	$10,000	$8,000	$6,000	$4,000	$2,000

Tax Depreciation	2014	2015	2016	2017	2018	2019	2020	2021	2022	2023	2024
Asset Acquisition Year											
2014	$3,333	$2,667	$2,000	$1,333	$ 667						
2015		3,333	2,667	2,000	1,333	$ 667					
2016			3,333	2,667	2,000	1,333	$ 667				
2017				3,333	2,667	2,000	1,333	$ 667			
2018					3,333	2,667	2,000	1,333	$ 667		
2019						3,333	2,667	2,000	1,333	$ 667	
2020							3,333	2,667	2,000	1,333	$ 667
Total	$3,333	$6,000	$8,000	$9,333	$10,000	$10,000	$10,000	$6,667	$4,000	$2,000	$ 667

	2014	2015	2016	2017	2018	2019	2020	2021	2022	2023	2024
Temporary Differece Originating (Reversing)	$1,333	$2,000	$2,000	$1,333	$ 0	$ 0	$ 0	($1,333)	($2,000)	($2,000)	($1,333)
Cumulative Temporary Difference	$1,333	$3,333	$5,333	$6,666	$ 6,666	$ 6,666	$6,666	$5,333	$3,333	$1,333	$ 0
Deferred Tax Liability at Year-End	$ 467	$1,167	$1,867	$2,333	$ 2,333	$ 2,333	$ 2,333	$1,867	$1,167	$ 467	$ 0

Deferred Taxes and Cash Flow

It is often said that generating deferred tax liabilities increases cash flow. This statement is not actually true. Using tax accounting methods that accelerate deductions or delay income recognition increases cash flow, at least in the early years. This strategy may or may not also create deferred tax liabilities, but it is the tax strategy, not whether a deferred tax liability is created, that affects cash flow.

Let's return to the Mitchell Corporation example yet again. In 2014, Mitchell would have reported the income statement and cash flow statement shown in the first column of Exhibit 13.16. Note that in the cash flow statement depreciation and the deferred portion of the income tax provision are both added back to net income to derive cash flow from operating activities. Both of these items are noncash components of net income and therefore must be reversed in the operating activities section of the cash flow statement.

Now, suppose Mitchell had instead used sum-of-the-years digits depreciation for financial reporting, in addition to using it for tax purposes. Its tax payments would remain unchanged so its cash flow would be the same as in the original example. But, because net income has changed, there must be different addbacks in the cash flow statement. The second column of Exhibit 13.16 shows that using sum-of-the-years digits for financial reporting would have reduced pre-tax

EXHIBIT 13.16	Mitchell Company Cash Flow Statement—2014	
	Original Example	**Using SYD for Books**
Pre-tax income before depreciation	$22,000	$22,000
Depreciation expense	(2,000)	(3,333)
Pre-tax income	20,000	18,667
Income tax expense	(7,000)	(6,533)
Net income	$13,000	$12,134
Net income	$13,000	$12,134
Depreciation	2,000	3,333
Deferred taxes	467	
Cash flow from operating activities	15,467	15,467
Cash flow from investing activities	0	0
Cash flow from financing activities	0	0
Net change in cash	$15,467	$15,467

income to $18,667 in 2014. Net income would have been 65% of that amount, or $12,134. The depreciation addback would now be $3,333. And, because the book and tax depreciation methods now match, there would be no deferred taxes to add back in the cash flow statement. The result is the same $15,467 cash flow from operating activities as in the original example. The key insight here is that tax choices, not financial reporting choices, affect a firm's cash flow. A financial reporting choice might affect the cash flow statement because it affects net income and therefore other items in the statement as well, but it does not affect the amount of cash flow.

MEASURING AND REPORTING UNCERTAIN TAX POSITIONS[15]

A **tax position** is "a position in a previously filed tax return or a position expected to be taken in a future tax return that is reflected in measuring current (taxes payable) or deferred income tax assets and liabilities for interim or annual periods. . . . The term tax position also encompasses, but is not limited to:

a. A decision not to file a tax return
b. An allocation or a shift of income between jurisdictions
c. The characterization of income or a decision to exclude reporting taxable income in a tax return
d. A decision to classify a transaction, entity, or other position in a tax return as tax exempt
e. An entity's status, including its status as a pass-through entity or a tax-exempt not-for-profit entity."[16]

This definition is a broad one that includes virtually any decision affecting the amount or timing of tax payments a firm will ultimately make. A tax position can result in a permanent reduction of income taxes payable, a deferral of income taxes otherwise currently payable to future years (creating a temporary difference), or a change in the expected realizability of a deferred tax asset.

Uncertainty abounds in tax law, and whether a tax position will ultimately be upheld often is unclear because of ambiguity in the law or conflicting court decisions. An **uncertain tax position** is a tax position that may, as a result of such ambiguity, be challenged by taxing

---

[15] The authors thank Amy Dunbar, John Phillips, and Ryan Wilson for their comments and suggestions on this section.
[16] FASB ASC Master Glossary: Tax Position.

authorities. If the firm is not successful in defending its position either in discussions with the taxing authority or in court, the amount and timing of the firm's tax payments ultimately will differ from what the firm envisioned. For example, since 2005, firms have been permitted to deduct a portion of their profits from certain domestic production activities. (That portion currently stands at 9%.) Gibson & Associates, an engineering and construction firm, took the deduction, claiming that some of its activities fell within the law's definition of production activities. The IRS disagreed and challenged. The parties went to tax court. From the time Gibson first claimed the deduction until the case was resolved, the company had an uncertain tax position because it would not know with certainty what the amount and timing of its tax payments would be until the court ruled or the parties settled.[17]

In the pre-Codification period, the FASB issued an interpretation (often referred to as *FIN48*) of then-existing GAAP literature on income taxes because it observed inconsistencies in how firms recognized, de-recognized, and measured benefits related to uncertain tax positions. These guidelines are currently in the FASB Accounting Standards Codification under Topic 740, Income Taxes, which sets forth the measurement and reporting of uncertain tax positions in firms' financial statements.

GAAP sets out a two-step process to determine how much benefit may be recognized from an uncertain tax position and correspondingly how much a firm should report in its tax contingency reserve as a liability for unrecognized tax benefits. Step 1 involves a recognition threshold. A firm must determine whether the uncertain tax position meets the threshold of "more likely than not" that it will be able to sustain its position based solely on technical merits.[18] The term "more likely than not" means a likelihood of more than 50%. The more-likely-than-not recognition threshold is a positive assertion by management of the belief that the firm is entitled to the economic benefits associated with the tax position (e.g., the firm is entitled to a deduction taken on its tax return).

Once a tax benefit meets the recognition threshold, the firm moves to Step 2 and measures the tax benefit as the largest amount of benefit that is cumulatively greater than 50 percent likely of being realized. The difference between the tax benefit as shown on the tax return and the tax benefit as determined using the two-step recognition/measurement process is recorded as a Tax contingency reserve account, sometimes referred to as Liability for unrecognized tax benefits.

GAAP specifically forbids the use of a valuation allowance in place of a contingency reserve. Valuation allowances are used when it is uncertain the firm will be sufficiently profitable to realize tax benefits, but it is not appropriate when the firm's tax positions may not be sustained.

Assessing Uncertain Tax Position Related to a Permanent Difference

> This is an example of a permanent difference uncertain tax position because the tax rules are unclear as to whether this expense will ever be deductible.

Doyle Company reports pre-tax book income of $10,000 that includes a $1,000 expense that is also deducted on the company's tax return. The tax law is unclear as to whether the deduction is permitted now or at any point in the future, so taking the deduction leads to an uncertain tax position. Assuming Doyle has no other uncertain tax positions, no book-tax differences, and a tax rate of 40%, this deduction results in a $400 uncertain tax benefit. Management's assessment is that it is 65% likely the deduction will be sustained based on

---

[17] In February 2011 the tax court ruled in favor of Gibson. For a discussion of the case, see "Highway Repairs Are Domestic Production Property," *The Journal of Accountancy,* June 2011.

[18] Factors to be considered in assessing the more-likely-than-not criterion include (1) a presumption that the tax position will be examined by the relevant taxing authority that has full knowledge of all relevant information, (2) technical merits of the tax position are to be based on relevant tax law (legislation, statutes, regulations, tax rulings, and case law), and (3) each tax position must be evaluated without consideration of the possibility of offset or aggregation with other positions. See FASB ASC Paragraph 740-10-25-7: Income Taxes—Overall—Recognition—Basic Recognition Threshold.

the technical merits. Assume the amounts and related individual probabilities of estimated outcomes are as follows:

Possible Estimated Outcome ($ amount of benefit)	Individual Probability of Estimated Outcomes	Cumulative Probability of Estimated Outcomes
$400	10%	10%
300	30	40
250	20	60
–0–	40	100

Because Doyle's management assesses the likelihood of this uncertain tax position being sustained on its merits to be 65%, the more-likely-than-not recognition condition is satisfied. Doyle next moves to the measurement step. The largest amount of benefit that is cumulatively greater than 50 percent likely of being realized is $250 (see shaded items in the table above). So, Doyle may recognize $250 of the tax benefit in its financial statements in the current period. The difference between the tax benefit that would be recorded as part of the normal tax entry due to this deduction ($400) and the $250 determined from the two-step process represents the amount that Doyle must record as a tax contingency reserve. Accordingly, the entry Doyle makes to record tax expense, taxes payable, and the tax contingency for the unrecognized tax benefit associated with this uncertain tax position would be as follows:

DR	Income tax expense	$4,150[a]	
	CR Income taxes payable		$4,000[b]
	CR Tax contingency reserve		150[c]

[a] $10,000 × 40% + ($400 − $250)
[b] $10,000 × 40%
[c] $400 − $250

To see how this entry records a $250 uncertain tax benefit, first consider the $4,000 in taxes Doyle will pay currently. That amount is computed assuming the item in question is fully deductible. The $4,000 amount would also be the income tax provision for the year if it were certain Doyle's tax position would be sustained. In contrast, if the deduction were known to be impermissible, Doyle's income tax expense would have been $11,000 × 40% = $4,400. So, any tax provision between $4,000 and $4,400 must be recording a portion of the uncertain tax benefit.

By recording a Tax contingency reserve of $150, along with the $4,000 of income tax payable, Doyle records income tax expense of $4,150. The result is that income tax expense is $4,400 − $4,150 = $250 lower than in the nondeductible scenario, so a $250 uncertain tax benefit has been recorded.

Recording Uncertain Tax Position Related to Timing of Deductibility

Uncertain tax positions can sometimes arise because of uncertainty about the timing of the deductibility of an expense under the tax code. Assume now that Doyle Company's $1,000 deduction fails to meet the more-likely-than-not condition. That is, the full deduction taken in the current period's tax return is unlikely to be sustained upon review. However, it is certain based on current tax law that this expenditure would be amortizable (deductible) for tax purposes over a five-year period. In other words, Doyle is certain it will eventually get to deduct $1,000, but it believes it is unlikely to sustain its position that the entire deduction may be taken immediately.

Under GAAP, Doyle subtracts only $200 of the expenditure ($1,000/5) when it computes the taxable income amount to be used to determine the current portion of its income tax expense. That is because only $200 is sufficiently certain to be deductible in the current year that it may enter into Doyle's computation of the current portion of income tax expense. So, the current portion of Doyle's income tax expense is ($11,000 − $200) × 40% = $4,320.

Doyle also has a deferred tax asset arising for the future tax deduction it is certain to be entitled to if it must ultimately amortize the $1,000 cost for tax purposes rather than deduct it immediately. The deferred tax asset is recorded at $800 × 40% = $320. Income tax expense is the current portion of income tax expense minus the increase in the deferred tax asset, or $4,000. This should make intuitive sense because regardless of the outcome of the uncertain tax position, $1,000 is eventually tax deductible, so Doyle's pre-tax income of $10,000 will have tax consequences, eventually, of exactly $10,000 × 40% = $4,000.

With a $4,000 debit to Income tax expense and a $320 debit to Deferred tax asset, we would normally complete the entry with a $4,320 credit to Income taxes payable. And this is the amount that will in fact be due if, as Doyle expects, it does not sustain its tax position. However, Doyle does not plan to pay $4,320 now. It will, instead, file a tax return claiming the full $1,000 deduction and make a payment of only $4,000. So the credit to Income taxes payable is for only $4,000. The remaining credit of $320 is to the Tax contingency reserve, representing the additional amount that will be due if Doyle is unable to sustain its tax position. The full entry is:

DR Income tax expense	$4,000	
DR Deferred tax asset	320	
CR Income tax payable		$4,000
CR Tax contingency reserve		320

Doyle records a reclassification entry in each of the subsequent years in which the tax position remains uncertain as a ratable portion ($200) of the original $1,000 expenditure becomes deductible with certainty under current tax law. Note that this entry reverses the Deferred tax asset and Tax contingency reserve accounts over the remaining four-year amortization period of the capitalized expenditure.

DR Tax contingency reserve	$80	
CR Deferred tax asset		$80

Making Changes or Resolving Uncertain Tax Positions

If the original assessed probabilities of outcomes for uncertain tax positions later change or if the uncertain tax position is settled with the taxing authority, appropriate adjustments are made to the Tax contingency reserve account with offsetting adjustments to the Tax expense or Cash account. To illustrate these adjustments, we return to the first example in which Doyle recorded $150 in the Tax contingency reserve account on the $1,000 deduction taken in Year 1. Recall that a $250 tax benefit associated with this uncertain tax position was recognized as a reduction of Tax expense in Year 1.

Assume that in Year 2 management is more optimistic about the uncertain tax position. Management now believes the largest benefit amount that is cumulatively greater than 50 percent likely to be realized is $300. As the amount of the tax benefit likely to be realized increases, the tax contingency for unrecognized tax benefits is reduced with a corresponding reduction in Tax expense (thereby recognizing a portion of the uncertain benefit). To reflect this change, the Tax contingency reserve is debited with an offsetting adjustment to Tax expense in Year 2 for $300 − $250 = $50.

DR Tax contingency reserve	$50	
CR Income tax expense		$50

EXHIBIT 13.17 Deere & Company 2012 Disclosures on Uncertain Tax Positions

A reconciliation of the total amounts of unrecognized tax benefits at October 31 is as follows:

($ in millions)	2012	2011	2010
Beginning of year balance	$199	$218	$260
Increases to tax positions taken during the current year	46	23	36
Increases to tax positions taken during prior years	54	13	83
Decreases to tax positions taken during prior years	(14)	(42)	(133)
Decreases due to lapse of statute of limitations	(9)	(13)	(2)
Settlements		(1)	(19)
Foreign exchange	(11)	1	(7)
End of year balance	$265	$199	$218

If in Year 3 Doyle settles the issue with the taxing authority and pays $130, the entry to close out the Tax contingency reserve account and to pay the settlement is:

DR Tax contingency reserve	$100	
DR Income tax expense	30	
CR Cash		$130

Income tax expense is debited for $30 in this final entry because the settlement with the taxing authority is $30 more than the $100 contingency reserve that previously existed for this uncertain tax position.

Assessing Disclosures on Uncertain Tax Positions

Exhibit 13.17 provides Deere & Company's 2012 note disclosure for uncertain tax positions. This note explains how Deere's tax contingency reserve changed in each of the last three years.

In 2012, Deere took uncertain tax positions that resulted in a $46 million increase in the tax contingency reserve. In addition, the tax reserve related to tax positions previously taken increased by $31 million, consisting of $54 million in increases and $23 million in decreases, $9 million of which was because the statute of limitations expired, meaning the taxing authorities could no longer challenge those positions. The foreign exchange amount arises because the tax contingency reserves from foreign subsidiaries are denominated in other currencies. When the exchange rate with the U.S. dollar changes, these reserves, in U.S. dollar terms, are revalued to reflect the current exchange rate.

 RECAP

GAAP requires a two-step process to determine how much benefit a firm can recognize from an uncertain tax position and correspondingly how much a firm should report in its tax contingency reserve for unrecognized tax benefits. The recognition threshold requires management to assess whether the uncertain tax position is "more likely than not" (greater than 50 percent) to be sustained based on the technical merits of the position. If the recognition threshold is met, the firm then measures the amount of the tax benefit to recognize as the largest amount of benefit that is cumulatively greater than 50 percent likely of being realized. The difference between the tax benefit reported on the tax return and the tax benefit recognized using the two-step recognition/measurement process for measuring uncertain tax positions is recorded as an increase in the Tax contingency reserve, sometimes referred to as Liability for unrecognized tax benefits.

EXTRACTING ANALYTICAL INSIGHTS FROM NOTE DISCLOSURES

Tax notes provide useful information beyond taxes. Information about deferred tax assets and liabilities, in particular, can help assess earnings quality and enhance interfirm comparisons. This is because, generally, all firms will select tax policies that minimize the present value of their tax payments, even though their financial reporting choices might differ substantially. As a result, firms' tax choices are likely to be more similar to each other than their financial reporting choices, providing a useful benchmark for assessing quality and comparing firms.

Using Deferred Tax Notes to Assess Earnings Quality

Companies must disclose details about individual temporary differences that give rise to the deferred tax asset and deferred tax liability balances on the balance sheet. Scrutiny of the details comprising deferred taxes can reveal important analytical insights about the actions management has taken to boost short-term earnings. To illustrate, refer to Exhibit 13.18, which contains excerpts from the Year 2 income tax note for ChipPAC Inc. This excerpt identifies major elements of the deferred tax asset and liability balances. Notice that the deferred income taxes attributable to book-versus-tax depreciation differences (highlighted area) went from a $92 thousand *debit* balance (asset) in Year 1 to a $10.870 million *credit* balance (liability) in Year 2, an increase of $10.962 million. Some portion of this increase is likely due to acquisitions of new property, plant, and equipment during the year that were depreciated at a faster rate for tax purposes than for book purposes. (ChipPAC's cash flow statement reveals that $93.174 million was spent in Year 2 for acquisition of property and equipment.) However, fixed asset growth explains only a small part of the increase. What else might explain the rather large increase in this component of deferred tax liabilities? In another note in its Year 2 annual report, ChipPAC states:

> Effective January 1, Year 2, the Company re-evaluated the estimated useful lives of equipment. Based on an independent appraisal to evaluate the useful lives of such equipment and the Company's internal assessment, the Company changed the estimated useful lives of assembly and test product equipment and furniture and fixtures from five to eight years. Previously, such equipment was depreciated on a straight-line basis over an estimated useful life of five years.

Analysis

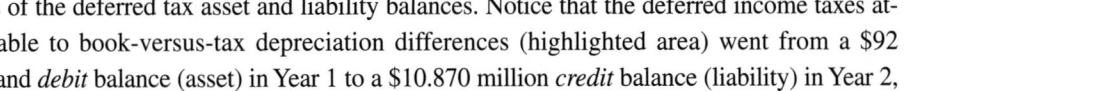

EXHIBIT 13.18   ChipPAC Inc.

Excerpt from Year 2 Annual Report Income Tax Note

The tax effects of temporary differences that give rise to significant portions of the deferred tax assets and deferred liabilities at December 31, Year 2 and December 31, Year 1 follow:

($ in thousands)	Year 2	Year 1
Deferred tax assets:		
Income recognized for tax but not for books	$ 7,598	—
Tax credits	2,663	—
NOL carryforward	3,490	—
Other	3,381	$6,270
Total gross deferred assets	17,132	6,270
Less: Valuation allowance	(6,122)	
Net deferred tax assets	11,010	6,270
Deferred tax liabilities:		
Depreciation	(10,870)	92
Reserves deducted for tax and not for books	(570)	(621)
Total deferred tax liabilities	(11,440)	(529)
Net deferred tax liabilities	$ (430)	$5,741

The net book values of assembly and test product equipment and furniture and fixtures, as of January 1, Year 2, are now being depreciated over the remaining useful life, based on eight years from the date such assets were originally placed into service. This change resulted in a decrease in depreciation expense for the year ended December 31, Year 2 being $29.0 million lower than would have been recorded using five years.

By extending the useful lives of fixed assets, ChipPAC lowered book depreciation and widened the excess of Year 2 pre-tax book income over taxable income. This increased the deferred tax liability related to depreciation temporary differences by $0.35 \times \$29$ million = $10.15 million, or about 93% of the $10.962 million total increase from the prior year. Interestingly, ChipPAC reported a pre-tax *profit* of $18 million in Year 2. Without the $29 million pre-tax earnings boost from lengthening the useful lives, ChipPAC would have reported an $11 million ($18 − $29) pre-tax *loss*.

> This calculation assumes the statutory tax rate of 35% was used to calculate the change in deferred taxes.

A financial statement reader can glean important information from changes in deferred tax balances, as demonstrated in Exhibit 13.18. It was possible to infer that depreciable lives were extended because of the relatively large increase in deferred taxes arising from book-versus-tax depreciation differences. As we saw, ChipPAC clearly disclosed this change in estimated useful lives. GAAP requires disclosure of a change in an accounting estimate only if the impact of the change is material.[19]

Unfortunately, widely accepted guidelines for assessing materiality do not exist. Consequently, firms that are not as candid as ChipPAC could conceivably decide to extend asset lives and not disclose the change. Their motive could be to manipulate or smooth income, and they would justify nondisclosure by contending that the impact of the change is immaterial. Because materiality guidelines are subjective, careful scrutiny of the income tax note provides analysts a way to detect subtle changes in accounting estimates that affect bottom-line earnings but are not separately disclosed. This avenue is especially useful to auditors. A detailed examination of deferred income tax balances provides auditors evidence for evaluating management's candor.[20]

RECAP

Increases in deferred tax liability balances result from a widening excess of book income over taxable income. These increases represent a potential danger signal that should be investigated because an increase in a deferred tax liability might indicate deteriorating earnings quality. One way to uncover such subtle deterioration in earnings quality is to investigate all large, sudden changes in deferred tax balances. The analyst should try to understand *why* the deferred tax liability balance increased.

Sudden decreases in deferred tax assets are also a potential sign of deteriorating earnings quality. Using warranty expense as an example, we next explain why a sudden decrease in a deferred tax asset may be a danger signal.

Analysis

We saw earlier that accruals for product warranties generate deferred tax assets. The reason is that GAAP requires warranty expenses to be matched against the revenues of the products to which the warranties apply. But income tax rules do not allow deductions for warranty expenses until the costs of providing the warranty services are actually incurred, which generally occurs in a later period than when the revenues were recognized. Because GAAP warranty expenses are recognized sooner than warranty expenses for tax purposes, a deferred tax asset results.

Assume that on January 1, 2014, Carson Company begins offering a one-year warranty on all sales. Its 2014 sales were $20,000,000, and Carson estimates that warranty expenses will be

---

[19] FASB ASC Paragraph 250-10-50-4: Accounting Changes and Error Corrections—Overall—Disclosure—Change in Accounting Estimate.

[20] For readers who are neither auditors nor studying to be auditors, some elaboration is necessary. At the start of an audit, the auditor discusses significant issues with the client's managers to identify potential problem areas. When managers do not voluntarily disclose things such as income-increasing changes in accounting estimates, auditors consider this to be a potential danger signal that warrants an expansion in the scope of the audit. Scrutiny of the tax note provides auditors another tool for identifying problem areas.

EXHIBIT 13.19   **Carson Company**

Illustration of Decline in Deferred Tax Assets

Panel (a) Warranty Percentage Unchanged

	2015	2014
Sales revenues	$20,000,000	$20,000,000
Estimated warranty cost percentage	0.01	0.01
Warranty expense per books	200,000	200,000
Warranty expense per tax return		
Attributable to 2014 sales	200,000	—
Attributable to 2015 sales	—	—
Excess of book over tax expense		
Arising from 2014 sales	—	200,000
Arising from 2015 sales	200,000	—
Tax rate	0.35	0.35
December 31 deferred tax asset balance	$ 70,000	$ 70,000

2015 Reversal (arrow from 2014 "Excess of book over tax expense Arising from 2014 sales, 200,000" to 2015 "Warranty expense per tax return Attributable to 2014 sales, 200,000")

Panel (b) Warranty Percentage Lowered in 2015

	2015	2014
Sales revenues	$20,000,000	$20,000,000
Estimated warranty cost percentage	0.005	0.01
Warranty expense per books	100,000	200,000
Warranty expense per tax return		
Attributable to 2014 sales	200,000	—
Attributable to 2015 sales	—	—
Excess of book over tax expense		
Arising from 2014 sales	—	200,000
Arising from 2015 sales	100,000	—
Tax rate	0.35	0.35
December 31 deferred tax asset balance	$ 35,000	$ 70,000

2015 Reversal (arrow from 2014 "Excess of book over tax expense Arising from 2014 sales, 200,000" to 2015 "Warranty expense per tax return Attributable to 2014 sales, 200,000")

1% of sales; so, $200,000 of warranty expense is charged against Carson's pre-tax book income in 2014.

Assume no warranty repairs were made in 2014, so the tax deductions for warranties are zero. If the tax rate is 35%, Carson will have a deferred tax asset of $70,000 for warranties at December 31, 2014—the $200,000 book-versus-tax warranty difference times 35%. If *actual* warranty costs incurred in 2015 but associated with 2014 sales are precisely $200,000, then it would mean Carson's 2014 warranty estimate was accurate and should be maintained in 2015.

Panel (a) of Exhibit 13.19 shows what will happen if Carson Company uses the same warranty expense estimate of 1% of sales in 2015. It is assumed that sales in 2015 again will be $20,000,000 and that actual warranty costs on 2015 sales will not be incurred until 2016. Given these assumptions, Carson's December 31, 2015, deferred tax asset balance will still be $70,000. That is, the 2014 temporary difference reversed in 2015 (see arrow in Exhibit 13.19[a]), but a new $200,000 temporary difference on warranties associated with 2015 sales originated. ***The example in Exhibit 13.19(a) demonstrates that the deferred tax asset balance will remain stable if the warranty estimate is accurate and sales volume is unchanged.***

Let's now assume that instead of maintaining the warranty expense estimate at 1% of sales, Carson lowers the estimate to 0.5% of sales in 2015. Carson does this because management wishes to increase 2015 income despite the fact that the 1% number reflects actual warranty experience. Notice that because the 1% estimate accurately reflects estimated warranty costs in 2014, this change of an accounting estimate in 2015 represents a deterioration in earnings quality.

Panel (b) of Exhibit 13.19 shows that the deferred tax asset balance will decrease from $70,000 to $35,000 under the new assumptions. The reason for the decrease in the deferred tax asset balance is that the book-versus-tax difference narrowed from $200,000 in 2014 to $100,000 in 2015 as a consequence of the reduction in estimated warranty expense from 1% to 0.5% of sales.

RECAP

This example demonstrates why shrinkage in a deferred tax asset balance should be investigated. Year-to-year changes in warranty expense estimates are just like other changes in accounting estimates in that they need to be disclosed only if they are material. Because materiality guidelines are subjective, companies can conceivably use undisclosed estimate changes as a way to artificially increase earnings. Decreases in deferred tax asset balances can provide clues about such possibilities to statement readers.

Using Tax Notes to Improve Interfirm Comparability

Analysis

SIC is a system maintained by the Office of Federal Statistical Policy and Standards in the Department of Commerce to classify firms by the nature of their operations.

The deferred tax portion of the income tax note can be used to undo differences in financial reporting choices across firms and thus to improve interfirm comparisons. Here's a specific illustration. Cubic Corporation and Nanometrics are both classified in Standard Industrial Classification (SIC) code 3829—Measuring and Controlling Devices. But the two companies use different depreciation methods.

Cubic Corporation's 10-K for the year ended September 30, 2012 states:

Property, Plant and Equipment: We carry property, plant and equipment at cost. We provide depreciation in amounts sufficient to amortize the cost of the depreciable assets over their estimated useful lives. Generally, we use straight-line methods for depreciable real property over estimated useful lives or the term of the underlying lease for leasehold improvements. We use accelerated methods (declining balance and sum-of-the-years-digits) for machinery and equipment over their estimated useful lives.

So, for financial reporting purposes, Cubic uses accelerated depreciation for its machinery and equipment, which accounts for about 57% of its property, plant, and equipment in terms of gross cost (before accumulated depreciation).

In contrast, Nanometrics' Form 10-K for the year ended December 29, 2012, says:

Property, Plant and Equipment—Property, plant and equipment are stated at cost. Depreciation is computed using the straight-line method over the following estimated useful lives of the assets:

Building and improvements	5–40 years
Machinery and equipment	3–10 years
Furniture and fixtures	3–10 years

It's possible that the two firms' different depreciation choices conform perfectly to differences in the service potential of each their respective assets. But what if they don't? How can an analyst adjust the numbers to improve interfirm comparisons?

Exhibit 13.20 contains several key financial statement figures from each company's 10-K, along with the deferred tax amounts related to property, plant, and equipment reported in their income tax notes. Let's begin by looking at Panel (a), which relates to Cubic Corporation. It shows the company had a $471,000 deferred tax *asset* related to property, plant, and equipment at the end of fiscal 2012. It is unusual for companies to have deferred tax assets related to property, plant, and equipment, but given the company uses accelerated methods for a large portion of its assets, it is possible to have a small deferred tax asset. The deferred tax asset is in fact small, indicating that cumulatively, book depreciation has exceeded tax depreciation by only a small amount.

EXHIBIT 13.20	Selected Financial Statement Disclosures from Recent 10-K Reports of Cubic Corporation and Nanometrics Incorporated	

Panel (a): Cubic Corporation	9/30/12	9/30/11
($ in thousands)		
Book depreciation	$ 8,000	$ 7,700
Income before income taxes	130,287	116,277
Property, plant and equipment, net of accumulated depreciation (at year-end)	55,327	48,467
Included in Deferred Tax Assets:		
Book over tax depreciation	471	709

	Year Ended	
Panel (b): Nanometrics	12/29/12	12/31/11
($ in thousands)		
Book depreciation	$ 4,800	$ 3,300
Income before income taxes	4,619	44,584
Property, plant and equipment, net of accumulated depreciation (at year-end)	43,213	35,521
Included in Deferred Tax Liabilities:		
Depreciation and amortization	5,797	6,229

Cubic's deferred tax asset related to property, plant, and equipment declined by $238,000 during fiscal 2012, from $709,000 to $471,000. An increase in a deferred tax liability or a decrease in a deferred tax asset would occur in a period when tax depreciation exceeds book depreciation. So, using the statutory rate of 35%:

$$\$238,000 = (\text{Tax depreciation} - \text{Book depreciation}) \times 0.35$$

Dividing both sides by 0.35 yields:

$$\$680,000 = \text{Tax depreciation} - \text{Book depreciation}$$

Because Panel (a) of Exhibit 13.20 shows that Cubic's book depreciation was $8.0 million, tax depreciation must have been $8.7 million (rounded to the nearest $0.1 million).

We can now perform the same analysis on Nanometrics to determine what its tax depreciation was in 2012. Panel (b) of Exhibit 13.20 shows that Nanometrics' depreciation-related deferred tax liability was $5,797,000 at the end of fiscal 2012—a decrease of $432,000 from a year earlier. Repeating the analytical approach we used for Cubic (and noting that a decrease in deferred tax liability occurs when book depreciation exceeds tax depreciation):

$$\$432,000 = (\text{Book depreciation} - \text{Tax depreciation}) \times 0.35$$

Therefore:

$$\$1,234,000 = \text{Book depreciation} - \text{Tax depreciation}$$

Nanometrics' book depreciation was $4,800,000 (Exhibit 13.20 [b]) in fiscal 2012, so tax depreciation must have been $3,566,000 million.

We have now approximated the depreciation taken by each firm for tax purposes and established a "common denominator" for interfirm analysis. While we do not have enough information to put Cubic on Nanometrics' book depreciation basis, we do have enough information to put the two firms on an identical tax depreciation basis. This approach facilitates interfirm comparisons because it is likely the two companies' tax depreciation methods are more comparable—because they are essentially set by law so that similar assets use similar depreciation methods and lives—than are their financial reporting depreciation choices.

Adjusting each firm's financial reporting to the same depreciation methods and useful lives reduces Cubic's pre-tax income by 680,000, or 0.5% ($680,000/$130,287,000). Nanometrics' pre-tax income increases by $1,234,000, or 26.7% ($1,234,000/$4,619,000). In various circumstances, the difference may—or may not—be significant. But making interfirm comparisons using comparable data is better than basing the analysis on diverse financial reporting choices.

It is important to note that the preceding analysis is appropriate only in situations where firms have not had substantial asset disposals during the year. When depreciable assets are sold, the deferred tax amounts for these assets are eliminated from the Deferred tax liability account. Moreover, the amount eliminated due to asset sales is rarely disclosed. So, the year-to-year change in the deferred tax liability balance for depreciation no longer reflects only current period book-versus-tax depreciation differences. We can determine whether the firm sold assets during the period by looking in the Investing Activity section of the cash flow statement to see whether cash was generated from asset sales. In this particular case, neither Cubic nor Nanometrics reported substantial asset sales their fiscal 2012 cash flow statements.

 **International**

GLOBAL VANTAGE POINT

Although IFRS and U.S. GAAP accounting for income taxes largely overlap, there are important, but subtle, differences. This section highlights key differences between IFRS and U.S. GAAP accounting for income taxes in five areas: (1) the approach for recognizing deferred tax assets; (2) reconciliation of statutory and effective tax rates; (3) reporting of deferred taxes on the balance sheet; (4) disclosure of income tax amounts recognized directly in equity; and (5) uncertain tax positions. We also briefly discuss a 2009 Exposure Draft issued by the IASB that was intended to bring IFRS accounting for income taxes closer to U.S. GAAP. The Exposure Draft was tabled recently because the IASB now plans to undertake "a fundamental review of accounting for income taxes at some time in the future." However, the Exposure Draft still illustrates some initiatives the IASB is considering to help converge standards.

Approach for Recognizing Deferred Tax Assets

IFRS rules for measuring and reporting income taxes are set forth in *IAS 12,* "Income Taxes."[21] IFRS rules, like GAAP, take an asset–liability approach to accounting for income taxes, which is intended to recognize, in the balance sheet, the future tax consequences of events or transactions that are recognized on the financial statements and tax return in different periods (temporary difference). A temporary difference is the difference between the book basis and the tax basis of an asset or liability multiplied by the appropriate tax rate. For U.S. GAAP, the applicable tax rate is the **enacted tax rate** based on legislation already passed by Congress (currently 35%). IFRS requires firms to use the enacted or **substantively enacted** tax rates. The interpretation of "substantively enacted" varies from country to country. The IASB has published guidelines that address the point in time when a tax law change is substantively enacted in many jurisdictions that apply IFRS.

Both U.S. GAAP and IFRS record a deferred tax liability if the book basis of the underlying asset (liability) is greater (less) than the tax basis of the underlying asset (liability). Such

---

[21] "Income Taxes," *International Accounting Standards (IAS) 12* [London: International Accounting Standards Board (IASB), revised 2001].

differences result in future taxable amounts that cause future taxable income to be greater than book income resulting in the need to report a deferred tax liability on the balance sheet.

Similar to U.S. GAAP, *IAS 12* requires firms to recognize a deferred tax asset if the book basis of the underlying asset (liability) is less (greater) than the tax basis of the underlying asset (liability), which results in future deductible amounts. This will cause taxable income to be lower than book income in the future. U.S. GAAP requires a two-step approach for determining the amount of deferred tax assets recorded on a firm's balance sheet. First, deferred tax assets are recognized for the full amount of future deductible amounts multiplied by the tax rate. Second, if it is deemed more likely than not (greater than 50% likelihood) that the deferred tax asset will not be realized because of uncertainty about whether the firm will have future taxable income to utilize fully the future deductible amount when it reverses, an adjustment is made to deferred tax assets through the use of a valuation allowance account.

No valuation allowance account is used for deferred tax assets under IFRS rules. Instead, IFRS requires a one-step approach that provides for recognition of deferred tax assets only to the extent it is deemed probable that they will be realized.[22] Firms are required to review the carrying value of deferred tax assets at the end of each reporting period and to reduce their carrying value to the extent it is estimated that future taxable income will not be available against which to use the asset. This reduction can be reversed in the future if taxable income becomes available. Although there is no valuation allowance account used under IFRS, there should be no substantive differences in the net deferred tax assets that are recognized on the balance sheet under U.S. GAAP versus IFRS. The adjustments made to deferred tax assets are just less visible under IFRS.

Reconciliation of Statutory and Effective Tax Rates

Both IFRS and U.S. GAAP require a numerical reconciliation that explains the differences between statutory and effective tax rates. However, there are differences regarding the particular tax rates to be used in preparing this reconciliation. U.S. GAAP requires that the domestic federal statutory rate be used as the starting point (currently 35% in the United States). Although IFRS allows firms to use this approach, it also allows firms to use a statutory rate that aggregates domestic rates in various jurisdictions. An example of this alternative approach is provided in Exhibit 13.21, which provides the 2012 reconciliation schedule for Allianz Group, a large international insurance and asset management company headquartered in Germany with subsidiaries operating throughout the world. Germany's statutory federal tax rate (including surtaxes) is approximately 30%. But the expected (statutory) rate that Allianz uses in its reconciliation schedule differs from this rate as explained in the shaded portion of the note that accompanies this schedule. Note that Allianz uses individual company reconciliations that are based on the respective country-specific tax rates and that the statutory rate includes corporate, trade, and solidarity surcharge taxes.

Reporting Deferred Taxes in the Balance Sheet

U.S. GAAP calls for firms to classify deferred tax assets and liabilities as current or noncurrent depending on the classification of the asset or liability giving rise to the temporary difference. For example, a deferred tax asset due to rent received in advance (an unearned revenue

---

[22] "Probable" is not defined in *IAS 12,* but in *IAS 37* on contingent liabilities and assets, probable is defined as a likelihood greater than 50%.

EXHIBIT 13.21	Allianz Group 2012 Annual Report Excerpts from Income Tax Note

The recognized income taxes for the year ended 31 December 2012 are €591 MN above (2011: €644 MN above; 2010; €135 MN below) the expected income taxes. The following table shows the reconciliation from the expected income taxes of the Allianz Group to the effectively recognized taxes. The Allianz Group's reconciliation is a summary of the individual company-related reconciliations, which are based on the respective country-specific tax rates after taking into consideration consolidation effects with an impact on the Group result. The expected tax rate for domestic Allianz Group companies applied in the reconciliation includes corporate tax, trade tax and the solidarity surcharge, and amounts to 31.0% (2011: 31.0%; 2010: 31.0%).

The effective tax rate is determined on the basis of the effective income tax expenses on income before income taxes.

EFFECTIVE TAX RATE

€MN	2012	2011	2010
Income before income taxes			
Germany	963	(711)	651
Other countries	7,668	5,557	6,522
Total	8,631	4,846	7,173
Expected income tax rate	29.5%	28.8%	29.3%
Expected income taxes	2,548	1,398	2,099
Trade tax and similar taxes	237	201	176
Net tax exempt income	(189)	(40)	(571)
Effects of tax losses	2	178	279
Other effects	542	305	(19)
Income taxes	3,140	2,042	1,964
Effective tax rate	36.4%	42.1%	27.4%

account that most likely would be classified among current liabilities) would be considered current, while a deferred tax liability due to temporary differences related to depreciation on property, plant, and equipment should be classified as noncurrent. Under IFRS rules, no consideration is given to the classification of the underlying asset or liability to which the deferred tax item relates. Rather, deferred tax assets and deferred tax liabilities are reported as *noncurrent* in a classified balance sheet. U.S. GAAP requires the netting of deferred tax assets and liabilities (both for current and noncurrent amounts) on the face of the balance sheet when they relate to the same tax-paying component of an entity and the same tax authority. IFRS rules are more stringent and require offsetting (netting) of deferred tax assets and deferred tax liabilities if, and only if, both of the following conditions exist:[23]

1. The entity has a legally enforceable right to set off current tax assets against current tax liabilities.

2. The deferred tax assets and deferred tax liabilities relate to income taxes levied by the same taxing authority on either of the following:

   a. The same taxable entity.

   b. Different taxable entities which intend either to settle current tax liabilities and assets on a net basis, or to realize the assets and settle the liabilities simultaneously in each future period in which significant amounts of deferred tax liabilities or assets are expected to be settled or recovered.

---

[23] *IAS 12*, para. 74.

EXHIBIT 13.22	ArcelorMittal: Excerpts from Income Tax Note

Income Tax Recorded Directly in Equity

Income tax recognized in equity for the years ended December 31, 2011 and 2012 is as follows:

	2011	2012
Recognized in other comprehensive income on:		
Current tax expense (benefit)		
Foreign currency translation adjustments	12	(3)
	12	(3)
Deferred tax expense (benefit)		
Unrealized gain (loss) on available-for-sale securities	(1)	—
Unrealized gain (loss) on derivative financial instruments	(88)	(210)
Call options on ArcelorMittal shares	—	—
Foreign currency translation adjustments	9	79
	(80)	(131)
	(68)	(134)

As a practical matter, these stringent requirements for netting result in deferred tax asset and deferred tax liabilities being reported separately on the face of the balance sheet for most firms that follow IFRS reporting rules.

Disclosure of Income Tax Amounts Recognized Directly in Equity (Other Comprehensive Income)

IFRS rules require firms to disclose the aggregate amount of current and deferred income tax expense on income relating to items charged or credited directly to equity through Other comprehensive income.[24] Such a disclosure is not currently required under U.S. GAAP. Given that the amount and frequency of items reported as Other comprehensive income is becoming increasingly important, we believe that this is important information that is lacking under current GAAP. Exhibit 13.22 shows an example of this disclosure requirement taken from the 2012 annual report of ArcelorMittal Corporation, a large international steel company headquartered in Luxembourg.

Uncertain Tax Positions

As discussed earlier in this chapter, ASC 740-10 provides extensive guidance on recognition and measurement of liabilities related to firms' uncertain tax positions. There is currently no specific guidance in *IAS 12* with respect to uncertain tax positions. Rather, *IAS 12* calls for tax assets and liabilities to be measured at the *amount expected to be paid*. In practice, this frequently results in the recognition principles in *IAS 37* that relates to the recognition and measurement of contingent liabilities being applied.[25] *IAS 37* requires that a contingent liability be recognized when: (1) an entity has a present obligation as a result of a past event; and (2) it is probable that an outflow of resources will be required to settle

---

[24] *IAS 12,* para. 81.

[25] "Provisions, Contingent Liabilities, and Contingent Assets," *International Accounting Standards (IAS) 37* [London: International Accounting Standards Board (IASB), revised 2001].

the obligation and a reliable estimate can be made of the amount. This general guidance has resulted in mixed practice with respect to recognition and measurement of contingent obligations related to uncertain tax positions for firms following IFRS accounting.

IASB Exposure Draft on Income Taxes

In March 2009, the IASB issued an exposure draft that would have eliminated many of the differences between IFRS and U.S. GAAP with respect to income tax reporting.[26] Four of the more important of the proposed changes were as follows:

1. Similar to provisions under U.S. GAAP, firms would be required to recognize a valuation allowance against deferred tax assets. The net amount of deferred tax assets would equal the highest amount that is more likely than not to be realizable against taxable profit.

2. Firms would be required to recognize income tax expense (or benefit) arising at the time of the transactions and other events in the same component of comprehensive income (i.e., continuing operations, discontinued operations, or items in other comprehensive income) in which they recognize the related transaction or event. Currently, there is no explicit requirement for intraperiod tax allocation under *IAS 12* as exists under U.S. GAAP.

3. In a classified balance sheet (statement of financial position), firms would be required to disaggregate deferred tax liabilities and deferred tax assets into a current amount and a noncurrent amount on the basis of the classification of the related asset or liability. The valuation allowance on deferred tax assets would be required to be allocated pro rata between current and noncurrent deferred tax assets by tax jurisdiction.

4. *IAS 12* is silent on how to account for uncertainty over whether the taxing authority will accept the amounts reported to it. The exposure draft proposes that current and deferred tax assets and liabilities should be measured at the probability-weighted average of all possible outcomes, assuming that the taxing authority examines the amounts reported to it and has full knowledge of all relevant facts. Thus, the approach for measuring uncertain tax positions is somewhat different from the two-step approach in ASC 740-10.

The IASB is planning a fundamental review of accounting for income taxes. Based on the now-tabled 2009 Exposure Draft, one might expect future changes to narrow the differences between IFRS and U.S. GAAP for income tax reporting.

IFRS and U.S. GAAP rules for income tax reporting largely overlap but differ in several subtle, but important, ways. Differences exist in: (1) the approach for determining the net amount of deferred tax assets; (2) what statutory rate is used in the schedule that reconciles statutory and effective tax rates; (3) where deferred tax assets and liabilities are reported in a classified balance sheet (statement of financial position); (4) disclosure of income tax amounts (both current and deferred) recognized directly in shareholders' equity (Other comprehensive income); and (5) recognition and measurement of uncertain tax positions.

---

[26] "Income Tax," Exposure Draft, IASB, 2009.

- The rules for determining income for financial reporting purposes—book income—differ from the rules for determining income for tax purposes.

- The differences between book income and taxable income are caused by both permanent and temporary differences in the revenue and expense items reported on a company's books versus its tax return.

- A temporary difference gives rise to either a deferred tax asset or a deferred tax liability.

- Deferred tax accounting generally requires firms to report tax costs or benefits on the income statement in the period in which the related revenue and expense items are recognized for book purposes regardless of when these amounts are reported on the tax return.

- The income tax note provides useful information for understanding how much of the current period's tax provision (expense) is actually payable to federal, state, and foreign governments, and how much is deferred. Tax notes also allow users to understand why firms' effective tax rates differ from the statutory rate.

- GAAP disclosures are useful in assessing a firm's uncertain tax positions and whether the firm is aggressive or conservative in recognizing the benefits associated with these positions.

- Tax notes provide a wealth of information that can be exploited to improve interfirm comparability and evaluate firms' earnings quality.

- There are a number of difference between IFRS and U.S. GAAP rules for accounting for income taxes that you should be aware of as you analyze financial statements across countries.

APPENDIX

COMPREHENSIVE INTERPERIOD TAX ALLOCATION PROBLEM

The following example for Hawkeye Corporation combines the various aspects of accounting for income taxes discussed in this chapter to demonstrate the interrelation between pre-tax accounting income, taxable income, taxes payable, deferred taxes, and tax expense. Working through this example will demonstrate the following points:

1. How to convert a pre-tax accounting income number to a taxable income number.
2. How to determine taxes payable.
3. How to determine the change in deferred tax assets and deferred tax liabilities.
4. How to determine tax expense.
5. How to reconcile the total tax costs (benefits) reported in the income statement with the total taxes payable according to the tax return for the period.
6. How various tax items are represented in the tax note.

Figure 13.7 provides a road map for understanding how the various book and taxable income numbers and tax amounts relate to one another. Before working through each set of computations in the Hawkeye Corporation example, we will refer to this road map to help visualize the role of each computation.

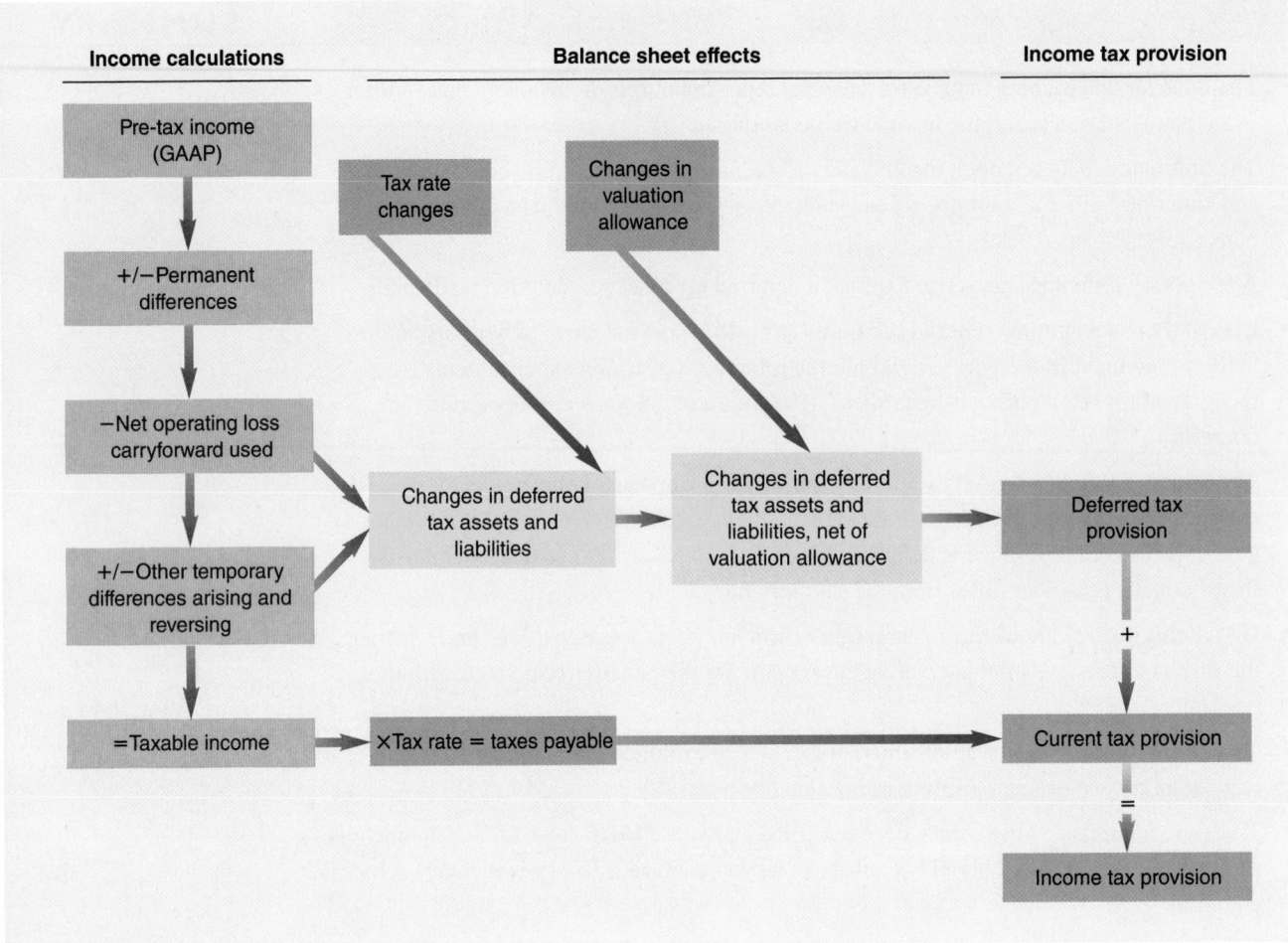

Figure 13.7 OVERVIEW OF INTERPERIOD TAX ALLOCATION

EXAMPLE: INTERPERIOD TAX ALLOCATION

Hawkeye Corporation starts the current year, 2014, with a deferred tax asset balance of $32,000 and a deferred tax liability balance of $42,000. The deferred tax assets at the beginning of the year are from the following items: net operating loss carryforward ($14,000), warranties ($10,000), and bad debts ($8,000). The deferred tax liabilities are from the following items: depreciation ($37,000) and installment sale profit ($5,000). The statutory tax rate is 40% and it is projected to be in effect when all temporary differences reverse. Reported pre-tax accounting income is $500,000 in 2014.

Analyze the following items to determine taxable income, the *change* in deferred tax assets and liabilities (future taxable and deductible amounts), and the tax expense to be reported in the income statement for 2014. Assume there is no need for a valuation allowance.

ITEM DESCRIPTIONS

① Book pre-tax income includes $12,000 of interest income from municipal bonds.

② Straight-line depreciation for book purposes is $100,000 in the current year, and $140,000 is deductible for tax purposes under the Modified Accelerated Cost Recovery System (MACRS).

(continued)

③ Hawkeye collected $60,000 of rent on a warehouse it leases to a local manufacturer. Of this amount, $40,000 will not be recognized under GAAP until 2015 when it is earned.

④ Hawkeye accrued $50,000 for estimated future warranty costs in 2014 and paid $35,000 in warranty expenses in the current period.

⑤ Bad debts written off in the current period totaled $20,000, and the provision for bad debts under the allowance method amounted to $15,000. Hawkeye uses the direct write-off method for tax purposes and the allowance method for book purposes.

⑥ Book income includes an $18,000 expense for premiums paid on executive life insurance under which the company is the named beneficiary.

⑦ In 2014, Hawkeye collected $15,000 on an installment land sale made several years earlier. The profit on the sale, all of which was recorded at the time of sale for book purposes, amounted to 30% of the selling price. The installment method of recognizing profit is being used for tax purposes. Ignore any imputed interest on the deferred payments.

⑧ Hawkeye has a $35,000 net operating loss carryforward at the beginning of 2014.

Computation of Taxable Income

Reading from top to bottom down the left side of Figure 13.7, we see three categories of items that cause differences between pre-tax book income and taxable income:

1. Permanent differences.

2. Net operating loss carryforwards used.

3. Temporary differences.

The first category of reconciling items is permanent differences. These are revenue or expense items that the tax rules treat differently—on a permanent basis—than the GAAP (book) rules treat them for income determination purposes.

Schedule 13.1 shows that Hawkeye Corporation has two permanent difference items—Item ①, Interest income on municipal bonds and Item ⑥, Premium on executive life insurance.

As part of the reconciliation from pre-tax income to taxable income, the municipal bond interest must be *subtracted* from the reported pre-tax book income number because it is not taxable even though it has been included in pre-tax book income. In addition, the executive life insurance premiums that were subtracted in arriving at pre-tax book income must be *added back* because they are not tax deductible when the company is the named beneficiary.

The second general category of reconciling items is net operating loss carryforwards used. As shown in Item ⑧, Hawkeye has a $35,000 net operating loss carryforward available at the beginning of 2014. This amount represents losses reported on previous years' tax returns (that is, tax-deductible expenses and losses exceeded taxable income and gains) that can be offset against 2014 taxable income. Because Hawkeye's taxable income before applying the net operating loss carryforward exceeds the amount of the carryforward available, the entire $35,000 is subtracted from pre-tax book income to arrive at taxable income in 2014.

The final category of reconciling items involves temporary differences. These are revenue and expense items that enter into the determination of book income in one period and taxable income in a different period. Hawkeye has several temporary differences:

- Item ②: *Depreciation expense.* Hawkeye's pre-tax book income includes $100,000 of straight-line depreciation expense. But for tax purposes, Hawkeye uses an accelerated depreciation method, which produces a $140,000 deduction in the current period. To arrive at taxable income, this $40,000 originating temporary difference must be subtracted from

SCHEDULE 13.1	Hawkeye Corporation

Calculation of Taxable Income and Taxes Payable

Computation of taxable income

Pre-tax accounting income (given)	$500,000
Adjustments for permanent differences	
−Interest on municipal bonds (Item ①)	(12,000)
+Premium on executive life insurance (Item ⑥)	18,000
Income before adjustments for temporary differences	$506,000
Adjustment for use of net operating loss carryforward (Item ⑧)	(35,000)
Adjustments for temporary differences	
−Excess of accelerated over straight-line depreciation (Item ②)	
($140,000 − $100,000)	(40,000)
+Rent received in excess of rent earned (Item ③)	
($60,000 − $20,000)	40,000
+Excess of accrued warranty costs over actual costs incurred	
on warranties (Item ④)	
($50,000 − $35,000)	15,000
−Excess of accounts written off over current provision	
for bad debts (Item ⑤)	
($20,000 − $15,000)	(5,000)
+Installment profit recognized for tax purposes in 2014 but	
recognized in earlier periods for book purposes (Item ⑦)	
(30% × $15,000)	4,500
Taxable income	$485,500
Tax rate	× 40%
Taxes payable for 2014	$194,200

pre-tax book income because it represents an additional amount that is deductible on the 2014 tax return over the expense recorded in pre-tax book income.

- Item ③: *Rent collections.* In 2014, Hawkeye collects $60,000 of rent, all of which is taxable when received. However, only $20,000 of rental income is included in pre-tax book income. Therefore, a $40,000 originating temporary difference must be added to pre-tax income to arrive at 2014 taxable income.

- Item ④: *Warranty expenses.* Hawkeye accrues $50,000 for estimated warranty costs that were subtracted in arriving at the pre-tax book income number. For tax purposes, Hawkeye may deduct only the $35,000 of warranty costs that were actually paid. The $15,000 difference represents an originating temporary difference that must be added back to the pre-tax book income number to yield taxable income.

- Item ⑤: *Bad debt provisions.* For book purposes, Hawkeye uses the allowance method (described in Chapter 8) to determine the $15,000 bad debt expense in 2014. For tax purposes, Hawkeye is allowed to take a deduction only when accounts are actually written off; this is the direct write-off method. As shown, Hawkeye writes off $20,000 of accounts receivable in 2014. Note that all or a portion of the accounts written off in 2014 would have been expensed under GAAP in prior accounting periods. Accordingly, the additional $5,000 deductible for tax purposes, an amount that represents a reversing temporary difference, must be subtracted from pre-tax book income to arrive at taxable income for 2014.

- Item ⑦: *Profit on installment sale.* Hawkeye uses the installment method (Chapter 3) for tax purposes to record profit on a land sale made in a previous period. All of this profit was recorded in a previous period's book income number. Thus, the gross profit on the amounts collected in 2014 (30% × $15,000 collected = $4,500) represents a reversing temporary difference that must be added to the pre-tax book income number to arrive at taxable income.

After adjustments for the net operating loss carryforward used and the temporary difference items, Hawkeye's 2014 taxable income is determined to be $485,500 (see Schedule 13.1).

Calculation of Taxes Payable

Our road map in Figure 13.7 shows that taxes payable are determined by multiplying taxable income by the applicable tax rate. For simplicity, we have assumed that a flat tax rate of 40% applies to all components of taxable income. Schedule 13.1 shows that Hawkeye's taxes payable in 2014 are $194,200. As Figure 13.7 indicates, this amount is also called the current tax provision.

Calculation of Change in Deferred Tax Asset and Liability Accounts

The next step in determining the tax provision (expense) to report in Hawkeye's 2014 GAAP (book) income statement is to determine the *change* in the deferred tax asset and deferred tax liability accounts. These calculations are represented in the center of Figure 13.7. It shows that the change in deferred tax assets and deferred tax liabilities depend on the amount of temporary differences originating and reversing (including from the use of net operating loss carryforwards) and any changes in tax rates. The latter cause of changes in deferred tax assets and liabilities arises because deferred tax assets and liabilities are always valued at the enacted tax rate expected to be in effect when the temporary differences reverse. The Hawkeye example does not involve a tax rate change, so only changes in temporary difference amounts will cause changes in the deferred tax assets and liabilities.

Schedule 13.2 provides the detailed calculations of the changes in deferred tax assets and liabilities. For each temporary difference (including net operating loss carryforwards used), we must determine three things:

1. Whether an item is an originating or reversing temporary difference.
2. Whether it affects a deferred tax asset or a deferred tax liability balance.
3. What the applicable tax rate is for determining the tax effect of the temporary difference.

Originating temporary differences are "new" differences between book and taxable income that cause *increases* in either a deferred tax asset or a deferred tax liability. Reversing temporary differences are realizations or reversals of "old" temporary differences that gave rise to deferred tax assets or liabilities in previous accounting periods. Because they represent reversals of previously recorded temporary differences, reversing temporary differences are *decreases* in either a deferred tax asset or a deferred tax liability.

Determining whether a particular temporary difference affects a deferred tax asset or liability balance hinges on whether the item causes taxable income to be higher or lower than book income in the current period and whether it is an originating or reversing temporary difference.

Hawkeye has one originating temporary difference that causes taxable income to be *lower* than book income in the *current* period (creating future taxable amounts):

- Item ②. Accelerated depreciation deductions for tax purposes ($140,000) exceed straight-line depreciation expense for book purposes ($100,000). This temporary difference gives

SCHEDULE 13.2 · Hawkeye Corporation

Calculation of Changes in Deferred Tax Accounts

	Deferred Tax Asset	Deferred Tax Liability
Originating Temporary Differences:		
Future taxable amounts:		
Depreciation (Item ②)		$16,000 **CR**
Future deductible amounts:		
Rent received in advance (Item ③)	$16,000 **DR**	
Excess of accrued warranty expense over warranty costs paid (Item ④)	6,000 **DR**	
New bad debt provisions (Item ⑤)	6,000 **DR**	
Reversing Temporary Differences:		
Realization of future taxable amounts:		
Installment method profit recognized for tax purposes (Item ⑦)		1,800 **DR**
Realization of future deductible amounts:		
Net operating loss carryforward used (Item ⑧)	14,000 **CR**	
Bad debts written off (Item ⑤)	8,000 **CR**	
Change in Deferred Tax Assets and Liabilities	6,000 **DR**	14,200 **CR**
Beginning balance	32,000 **DR**	42,000 **CR**
Ending balance	$38,000 **DR**	$56,200 **CR**

rise to a future taxable amount—that is, taxable income will be *higher* than book income in future periods when this temporary difference reverses. Therefore, this temporary difference causes an increase (credit) in deferred tax liabilities of $16,000, as shown in Schedule 13.2.

Hawkeye has three originating temporary differences that cause taxable income to be *higher* than book income in the *current* period (creating future deductible amounts):

- Item ③. Rent received ($60,000) is in excess of rent earned for book purposes ($20,000).
- Item ④. Accrued warranty expenses for book purposes ($50,000) is in excess of warranty expenditures for tax purposes ($35,000).
- Item ⑤. Bad debt expense of $15,000 that is accrued under the allowance method for book purposes will not be deductible for tax purposes until specific accounts are written off in future periods.

Each of these items gives rise to a future deductible amount and accordingly causes increases (debits) to the Deferred tax asset account of 40% times the respective temporary difference that arose, as shown in Schedule 13.2.

Hawkeye has one temporary difference that is a reversal of a deferred tax liability due to the realization of a future taxable amount.

- Item ⑦. This $4,500 amount represents a reversing temporary difference that causes taxable income to be higher than book income in 2014. Because a deferred tax liability would have been set up in a previous period (when the land was sold and the entire profit was recognized for book purposes), the Deferred tax liability account is being reduced (debited) now by $1,800 ($4,500 × 40%) because the tax will be paid in the current period.

Hawkeye has two reversing temporary differences that cause taxable income to be *lower* than book income in the *current* period (realization of future deductible amounts):

- Item ⑧. The $35,000 net operating loss carryforward is used, resulting in a reversal of the corresponding $14,000 deferred tax asset.
- Item ⑤. The bad debts write-off is $20,000, resulting in an $8,000 reversal of an existing deferred tax asset.

Both of these items represent realizations of future deductible amounts and result in a decrease (credit) to the deferred tax asset account, as we see in Schedule 13.2.

The assumed marginal corporate tax rate of 40% is applied to all temporary differences to determine the dollar amount of the change in the Deferred tax asset or liability account. This is appropriate when no enacted changes in the tax rates are scheduled to go into effect in future periods. Using the 40% rate, the net effect of the temporary differences for Hawkeye is to increase deferred tax assets by $6,000 and increase deferred tax liabilities by $14,200 as shown in Schedule 13.2.

Calculation of Income Tax Expense

The right side of Figure 13.7 shows that income tax expense is the amount of taxes currently payable plus or minus changes to the deferred tax asset and liability accounts. A more detailed presentation of the calculation of income tax expense Hawkeye will report in its 2014 GAAP income statement (assuming a 40% tax rate for all periods) follows the formulas presented in Figure 13.5 and is reproduced in Figure 13.8. The numbers appearing below the appropriate boxes are taken from Schedules 13.1 and 13.2.

When tax rates are *not* scheduled to change in the future, the tax expense reported for book purposes can be computed directly by multiplying the pre-tax book income number, after adjusting for permanent difference items, by the current tax rate. The pre-tax book income number of Hawkeye adjusted for permanent differences is $506,000 (Schedule 13.1); and the current tax rate is 40%, thus yielding income tax expense of $202,400, which is the same number determined under the indirect approach in Figure 13.8. When tax rates are scheduled to change, income tax expense must be determined using the indirect approach, which incorporates the effect of tax rate changes on deferred tax assets and liabilities in the determination of income tax expense.

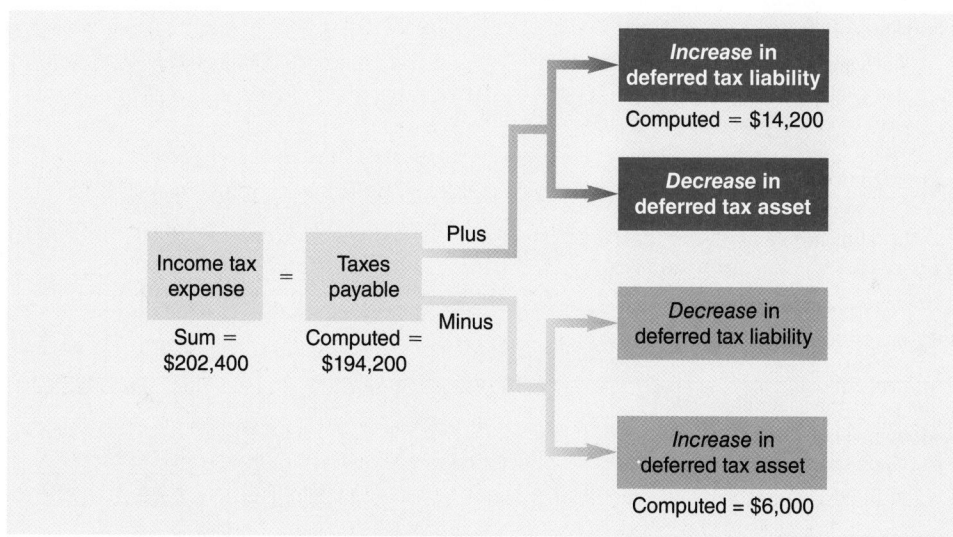

Figure 13.8

CALCULATION OF
INCOME TAX EXPENSE:
INDIRECT APPROACH

Hawkeye's Tax Note

We now examine how Hawkeye's income tax situation appears in its 2014 income tax note. There are three main schedules in the tax note we will consider: the summary of income tax provision, the summary of deferred tax assets and liabilities, and the tax rate reconciliation.

Exhibit 13.23 presents these three schedules from Hawkeye's tax note. Panel (a) contains the summary of the tax provision. It shows that the $202,400 income tax expense that would be found in Hawkeye's income statement consists of a current provision of $194,200 and a deferred provision of $8,200. We have not considered the role of state and foreign taxes in this example. If we had, the current and deferred provisions each would have been further detailed as federal, state, and foreign. Note that because this schedule provides detail about an income statement amount, it shows three years of data, just as the income statement does.

Panel (b) of Exhibit 13.23 presents the summary of deferred tax assets and liabilities. This schedule provides two years of data because it represents detail about balance sheet amounts. Note that the change in each deferred tax asset or liability amount agrees with the change we used to compute the deferred tax provision. For example, we used a $16,000 ($40,000 × 40%) increase in deferred tax liability related to depreciation in Schedule 13.2 and the deferred tax liability related to depreciation in Panel (b) of Exhibit 13.23 increased from $37,000 at December 31, 2013, to $53,000 at December 31, 2014.

Panel (c) of Exhibit 13.23 presents the tax rate reconciliation. It shows the reasons why the tax provision differs from the amount it would have been if every component of pre-tax income had a corresponding tax provision at the statutory rate of (in this example) 40%.

EXHIBIT 13.23 Hawkeye Corporation Income Tax Note

Panel (a): Summary of income tax provision:	2014	2013	2012
Current tax provision	$194,200	XXX	XXX
Deferred tax provision	8,200	XXX	XXX
Total income tax provision	$202,400	XXX	XXX

Panel (b): Summary of deferred tax assets and liabilities:	December 31,	
	2014	2013
Deferred tax assets:		
Net operating loss carryforward	$ —	$ 14,000
Warranties	16,000	10,000
Bad debts	6,000	8,000
Rent received in advance	16,000	—
	38,000	32,000
Deferred tax liabilities:		
Depreciation	53,000	37,000
Installment sale profit	3,200	5,000
	56,200	42,000
Net deferred tax liabilities	$ (18,200)	$(10,000)

Panel (c): Income tax rate reconciliation:	2014	2013	2012
Tax provision at statutory rate (40%)	$200,000	XXX	XXX
Municipal bond interest	(4,800)	XXX	XXX
Premium on executive life insurance	7,200	XXX	XXX
	$202,400	XXX	XXX

Because the two permanent differences in this example resulted in amounts recognized under GAAP but not for tax purposes, those differences caused the income tax provision to be different from 40% of pre-tax book income. For example, because the $12,000 of municipal bond interest income is never taxed, no tax provision is recorded related to that income, even though it is included in pre-tax book income. As a result, the tax provision is lower than it would have been if such a tax provision had been recorded by 40% × $12,000 = $4,800.

EXERCISES

On January 2, 2013, Allen Company purchased a machine for $70,000. This machine has a five-year useful life, a residual value of $10,000, and it is depreciated using the straight-line method for financial statement purposes. For tax purposes, depreciation expense was $25,000 in 2013 and $20,000 in 2014. Allen's 2014 book income, before income taxes and depreciation expense, was $100,000, and its tax rate was 30%. Allen has no book-tax differences other than due to the machine.

E13-1
Determining current taxes payable **(LO 2, 4)**
AICPA
ADAPTED

Required:
If Allen had made *no* estimated tax payments during 2014, what amount of current income tax liability would it report in its December 31, 2014, balance sheet?

In its 2014 income statement, Tow Inc., reported proceeds from an officer's life insurance policy of $90,000 and depreciation of $250,000. Tow was the owner and beneficiary of the life insurance on its officer. Tow deducted depreciation of $370,000 in its 2014 income tax return when the tax rate was 30%. Data related to the reversal of the excess tax deduction for depreciation follow:

E13-2
Determining deferred tax liability **(LO 2, 4)**
AICPA
ADAPTED

Year	Reversal of Excess Tax Deduction for Depreciation	Enacted Tax Rates
2015	$50,000	35%
2016	40,000	35
2017	20,000	25
2018	10,000	25

Tow has no other temporary differences.

Required:
In its December 31, 2014, balance sheet, what amount should Tow report as a deferred tax liability?

Mill Company began operations on January 1, 2014, and recognized income from construction-type contracts under the percentage-of-completion method for tax purposes and the completed-contract method for financial reporting purposes. Information concerning income recognition under each method is as follows:

E13-3
Determining deferred tax effects on long-term contracts **(LO 2, 4)**
AICPA
ADAPTED

Year	Percentage of Completion (Tax Purposes)	Completed Contract (Book Purposes)
2014	$400,000	$ –0–
2015	625,000	375,000
2016	750,000	850,000

Required:
Assume the income tax rate is 40% in all years and that Mill has no other temporary differences. In its December 31, 2016, balance sheet, Mill should report deferred income taxes of how much? Indicate whether the amount is an asset or a liability.

E13-4

Determining current portion
of tax expense   **(LO 2, 4)**

AICPA
ADAPTED

For the year ended December 31, 2014, Tyre Company reported pre-tax financial statement income of $750,000. Its taxable income was $650,000. The difference was due to the use of accelerated depreciation for income tax purposes and straight-line for financial reporting. Tyre's income tax rate is 30%, and it made estimated tax payments of $90,000 during 2014.

Required:

1. What amount should Tyre report as the current portion of income tax expense for 2014?

2. What amount should Tyre report as the deferred portion of income tax expense for 2014?

3. Give the journal entry Tyre would make to record 2014 taxes.

E13-5

Determining current taxes
payable   **(LO 2, 4)**

AICPA
ADAPTED

Dunn Company's 2014 income statement reported $90,000 income before provision for income taxes. To aid in the computation of the provision for federal income taxes, the following 2014 data are provided:

Rent received in advance	$16,000
Income from tax-exempt municipal bonds	20,000
Depreciation deducted for income tax purposes in excess of depreciation reported for financial statement purposes	10,000
Enacted corporate income tax rate	35%

Required:

What amount of current federal income tax liability should Dunn report in its December 31, 2014, balance sheet?

E13-6

Determining deferred tax
liability and current portion
of tax expense   **(LO 2, 4)**

AICPA
ADAPTED

Kent Inc.'s reconciliation between financial statement and taxable income for 2014 follows:

Pre-tax financial income	$150,000
Permanent difference	(12,000)
	138,000
Temporary difference—depreciation	(9,000)
Taxable income	$129,000

Additional Information:

	At December 31,	
	2013	**2014**
Cumulative temporary difference (future taxable amounts)	$11,000	$20,000

The enacted tax rate was 35% for 2013 and 40% for 2014 and years thereafter.

Required:

1. In its December 31, 2014, balance sheet, what amount should Kent report as its deferred tax liability?

2. In its 2014 income statement, what amount should Kent report as the current portion of income tax expense?

E13-7

Determining deferred tax
asset amounts   **(LO 2, 4)**

AICPA
ADAPTED

West Corporation leased a building and received the $36,000 annual rental payment on June 15, 2014. The beginning of the lease period was July 1, 2014. Rental income is taxable when received. West's tax rates are 30% for 2014 and 40% thereafter. West had no other permanent or temporary differences. It determined that no valuation allowance was needed.

Required:

What amount of deferred tax asset should West report in its December 31, 2014, balance sheet?

Black Company, organized on January 2, 2014, had pre-tax accounting income of $500,000 and taxable income of $800,000 for the year ended December 31, 2014. The only temporary difference is accrued product warranty costs, which are expected to be paid as follows:

2015	$100,000
2016	50,000
2017	50,000
2018	100,000

E13-8

Determining deferred tax asset amounts **(LO 2, 4)**

AICPA
ADAPTED

Circumstances indicate that it is highly likely that Black will have taxable income in the future. It had no temporary differences in prior years. The enacted income tax rates are 35% for 2014, 30% for 2015 through 2017, and 25% for 2018.

Required:
In Black's December 31, 2014, balance sheet, how much should the deferred tax asset be?

Quinn Company reported a net deferred tax asset of $9,000 in its December 31, 2014, balance sheet. For 2015 Quinn reported pre-tax financial statement income of $300,000. Temporary differences of $100,000 resulted in taxable income of $200,000 for 2015. At December 31, 2015, Quinn had cumulative taxable differences of $70,000. The income tax rate is 30%.

E13-9

Reporting deferred portion of tax expense **(LO 2, 4)**

AICPA
ADAPTED

Required:
In its December 31, 2015, income statement, what should Quinn report as the deferred portion of income tax expense?

(*Note:* Students may want to review the material on the equity method of accounting in Chapter 16 before beginning work on this exercise.) Tara Corporation uses the equity method of accounting for its 40% investment in Flax's common stock. During 2014, Flax reported earnings of $750,000 and paid dividends of $250,000. Assume that:

E13-10

Assessing temporary and permanent differences **(LO 2, 4)**

AICPA
ADAPTED

- All undistributed earnings of Flax will be distributed as dividends in future periods.
- The dividends received from Flax are eligible for the 80% dividends received deduction.
- No other temporary differences exist.
- Tara's 2014 income tax rate is 30%.
- Enacted income tax rates after 2014 are 25%.

Required:
What would be the increase in the deferred tax liability during 2014 from the preceding transactions?

Dix Company reported operating income/loss before income tax in its first three years of operations as follows:

2013	$ 100,000
2014	(200,000)
2015	400,000

E13-11

Determining tax effects of loss carryback and carryforward **(LO 4, 5)**

AICPA
ADAPTED

Dix had no permanent or temporary differences between book income and taxable income in these years. Dix elected to carry the 2014 loss back to the extent possible. Assume a 40% tax rate for all years.

Required:
1. What amount should Dix report as a tax benefit on its 2014 income statement?
2. What amount of deferred tax asset should Dix report on its December 31, 2014, balance sheet?
3. What amount should Dix report as current taxes payable on December 31, 2015 (the year after the loss)?

E13-12 Accounting for loss carryforwards **(LO 4, 5)** AICPA ADAPTED	As of December 31, 2014, Colt Corporation has a loss carryforward of $180,000 available to offset future taxable income. At December 31, 2014, the company believes that realization of the tax benefit related to the loss carryforward is probable. The tax rate is 30%. **Required:** 1. What amount of the tax benefit should be reported in Colt's 2014 income statement assuming (a) the loss carryforward arose in 2014 and (b) the loss carryforward arose prior to 2014? 2. What additional account(s) would be affected when the loss carryforward is recognized?

E13-13 IFRS vs. U.S. GAAP tax entries **(LO 11)** AICPA ADAPTED	Melissa Corporation is domiciled in Germany and is listed on both the Frankfurt and New York Stock Exchanges. Melissa has chosen to prepare consolidated financial statements in accordance with U.S. GAAP for filing with the U.S. Securities and Exchange Commission but must also prepare consolidated financial statements in accordance with IFRS in accordance with European Union regulations. On December 31, 2014, Melissa Corporation purchased a small office building for $1,380,000. For tax and financial reporting purposes, Melissa estimates that the building has a useful life of 40 years with an estimated residual value of $100,000. Melissa uses straight-line depreciation for financial reporting. Assume that, for tax purposes, Melissa is permitted to deduct 5% of an asset's depreciable base in the first year. This is the only building that Melissa owns.

At the end of 2015, Melissa had the building appraised by a qualified real estate appraiser who estimated the fair value of the building was $1,172,500. Melissa intends to occupy the building itself, and therefore, the building is classified as property, plant, and equipment under both U.S. GAAP and IFRS. After being revalued under IFRS, the Building account has a balance of $1,172,500 and the Accumulated depreciation account has a balance of zero. Assume Melissa will have sufficient income in the future to recover any deferred tax assets that might be recognized.

	U.S. GAAP	IFRS
Model used for subsequent measurement	Cost	Revalued at fair value
Income before temporary differences	$500,000	$500,000
Enacted tax rate*	35%	35%

* We are assuming, for simplicity, that the relevant tax rate is 35% for all jurisdictions where Melissa is required to pay income tax. No new tax laws are substantively enacted at December 31, 2014.

Required:
Answer the following questions for each of the following scenarios:

1. Melissa prepares its consolidated financial statements under U.S. GAAP.
   a. Calculate taxable income in 2015.
   b. Prepare the journal entry to record tax expense, deferred taxes, and taxes payable.
   c. What is the effective tax rate?
2. Melissa prepares its consolidated financial statements in accordance with IFRS.
   a. Calculate taxable income in 2015.
   b. Prepare the journal entry to record tax expense, deferred taxes, and taxes payable.
   c. What is the effective tax rate?

E13-14 Computing deferred tax asset and valuation allowance **(LO 2, 6)** AICPA ADAPTED	In Figland Company's first year of operations (2014), the company had pre-tax book income of $500,000 and taxable income of $800,000 at the December year-end. Figland's only temporary difference is for accrued product warranty costs, which are expected to be paid as follows: 2015 $100,000 2016 $200,000

The enacted income tax rate for these years is 30%. Figland believes there is a high likelihood that one-third of the tax benefit associated with this future deductible amount will not be realized.

Required:

Compute the amount of deferred tax asset and related valuation allowance that would be reported in Figland's 2014 tax note.

(*Note:* Students may want to review the material on the equity method of accounting in Chapter 16 before beginning work on this exercise.) Taft Corporation uses the equity method to account for its 25% investment in Flame, Inc., which it made on January 1, 2014. During 2014, Taft received dividends of $30,000 from Flame and recorded $180,000 as its equity in Flame's earnings. Additional information follows:

- All Flame's undistributed earnings will be distributed as dividends in future periods.
- The dividends received from Flame are eligible for the 80% dividends received deduction.
- Flame has no other temporary differences.
- Enacted income tax rates are 30% for 2014 and thereafter.

Required:

In its December 31, 2014, balance sheet, what amount should Taft report for deferred income tax liability related to its investment in Flame?

E13-15
Determining deferred tax liability for equity method earnings **(LO 2, 6)**

AICPA
ADAPTED

On January 1, 2015, Toms River Rafting, Inc. (TRR), has a deferred tax asset representing $250,000 in net operating loss carryforwards on its balance sheet. When it recognized this asset, TRR expected to have sufficient earnings to utilize these loss carryforwards. However, TRR's business has been very slow because of a severe drought and it determines at December 31, 2015, that it is likely the company will only be able to recover half of the net operating loss carryforward available at this date. TRR reported pre-tax book income of $100,000 and taxable income of $97,700 in 2015.

The difference between pre-tax book income and taxable income relates to one temporary difference for depreciation of property, plant, and equipment that originated in 2015.

The enacted tax rate is 35%. The substantively enacted tax rate is 40%.

Required:

Prepare the journal entries to record tax expense in 2015 under both U.S. GAAP and IFRS.

E13-16
IFRS vs. U.S. GAAP tax entries **(LO 11)**

CMA
ADAPTED

Millie Co. completed its first year of operations on December 31, 2014, with pre-tax financial income of $400,000. Millie accrued a contingent liability of $900,000 for financial reporting purposes; however, the $900,000 will be paid and therefore is deductible for tax purposes in 2015. Millie also has gross profit from installment sales of $800,000 recognized currently for financial reporting purposes but that will be taxable in 2015 and 2016 when the cash is received ($400,000 each year). Millie's pre-tax financial income includes $38,000 interest earned on its holdings of the bonds of the State of Montana. The tax rate is 30% for all years.

Required:

1. Determine Millie's taxable income and taxes payable for 2014.
2. Determine the changes in Millie's deferred tax amounts for 2014.
3. Calculate tax expense for Millie for 2014.

E13-17
Computing tax payable, deferred taxes, and tax expense **(LO 2, 4)**

	E13-18
Determining tax benefit for uncertain tax position **(LO 9)**	

Collins Company incurs a $1,000 book expense that it deducts on its tax return. The tax law is unclear whether this expense is deductible, so the deduction leads to an uncertain tax position. Assuming a 35% tax rate, the deduction results in a $350 tax benefit.

Required:

For each of the following independent cases, determine how much of the tax benefit associated with the uncertain tax position Collins can recognize and how much of a tax contingency reserve for uncertain tax benefits Collins needs to record.

	Case I	Case 2	Case 3
Management's assessment of the likelihood of the uncertain tax position being sustained based on technical merits	65%	40%	80%
Likelihood of realizing $350	10	5	55
Likelihood of realizing $250	30	5	25
Likelihood of realizing $100	20	35	15
Likelihood of realizing $0	40	55	5

PROBLEMS / DISCUSSION QUESTIONS

	P13-1
Calculating deferred tax amounts with different tax rates **(LO 2, 4)** **AICPA** ADAPTED	

Moss Inc. uses the accrual method of accounting for financial reporting purposes and appropriately uses the installment method of accounting for income tax purposes. It will collect $250,000 of installment income in the following years when the enacted tax rates are as indicated.

	Collection of Income	Enacted Tax Rates
2013	$ 25,000	35%
2014	50,000	30
2015	75,000	30
2016	100,000	25

The installment income is the firm's only temporary difference.

Required:

What amount should be included as the deferred tax liability in Moss's December 31, 2013, balance sheet?

	P13-2
Calculating the amount of temporary and permanent differences and tax entry **(LO 2, 4)**	

The following information pertains to Ramesh Company for the current year:

Book income before income taxes	$106,000
Income tax expense	52,000
Income taxes payable for this year	32,000
Statutory income tax rate	40%

The company has one permanent difference and one temporary difference between book and taxable income.

Required:

1. Calculate the amount of temporary difference for the year and indicate whether it causes book income to be more or less than taxable income.

2. Calculate the amount of permanent difference for the year and indicate whether it causes book income to be more or less than taxable income.

3. Provide the journal entry to record income tax expense for the year.

4. Compute the effective tax rate (that is, income tax expense divided by book income before taxes). Explain why this rate is different from the statutory tax rate of 40%.

For financial statement reporting, Lexington Corporation recognizes royalty income in the period earned. However, royalties are taxed when collected. At December 31, 2013, unearned royalties of $400,000 were included in Lexington's balance sheet. All of these royalties had been collected in 2013. During 2014, royalties of $600,000 were collected. Unearned royalties in Lexington's December 31, 2014, balance sheet amounted to $350,000. Assume that the income tax rate was 40%.

P13-3

Reporting deferred tax amount on income statement (LO 2, 4)

AICPA
ADAPTED

Required:

What amount should be reported as the deferred portion of the provision for income taxes in Lexington's income statement for the year ended December 31, 2014?

Nelson Inc. purchased machinery at the beginning of 2014 for $90,000. Management used the straight-line method to depreciate the cost for financial reporting purposes and the sum-of-the-years-digits method to depreciate the cost for tax purposes. The life of the machinery was estimated to be three years, and the salvage value was estimated at zero. Revenues less expenses other than depreciation expense and goodwill impairment equaled $500,000 for 2014, 2015, and 2016. Nelson pays income tax at the rate of 20% of taxable income. The goodwill impairment equaled $50,000 for 2014 and 2015. There was no impairment in 2016.

P13-4

Computing tax expense and making deferred tax calculations (LO 2, 4)

Required:

1. Compute Nelson's taxable income and financial reporting income (before tax) for all three years.

2. What are permanent and temporary differences? Give an example of each for Nelson.

3. For 2014, 2015, and 2016, determine Nelson's income tax payable at December 31, income tax expense for the year, and deferred tax asset or liability at December 31. For the last item, be sure to specify whether the item is a deferred tax asset or liability.

4. Assume the federal government changes the tax rate to 30% at the beginning of 2015. Compute the following:

> Income tax payable for 2015
> Income tax expense for 2015

Metge Corporation's worksheet for calculating taxable income for 2014 follows:

P13-5

Determining current and deferred portion of tax expense and reconciling statutory and effective tax rates (LO 2, 4, 8)

($ in thousands)	2014
Pre-tax income	$1,000
Permanent differences	
Goodwill impairment	400
Interest on municipal bonds	(200)
Temporary differences	
Depreciation	(800)
Warranty costs	400
Rent received in advance	600
Taxable income	$1,400

The enacted tax rate for 2014 is 35%, but it is scheduled to increase to 40% in 2015 and subsequent years. All temporary differences are originating differences.

Required:

1. Determine Metge's 2014 taxes payable.

2. What is the change in deferred tax assets (liabilities) for 2014?

3. Determine tax expense for 2014.

4. Provide a schedule that reconciles Metge's statutory and effective tax rates (in both percentages and dollar amounts).

P13-6

Recording entries for loss carrybacks and carryforwards (**LO 2, 4, 5**)

Smith Corporation started doing business in 2013. The following table summarizes the company's taxable income (loss) over the 2013–2025 period and the statutory tax rate effective in each year:

Year	Taxable Income (Loss)	Enacted Tax Rate
2013	$ 100,000	40%
2014	200,000	40
2015	250,000	35
2016	400,000	32
2017	(350,000)	30
2018	(275,000)	30
2019	125,000	30
2020	175,000	30
2021	275,000	30
2022	300,000	35
2023	(800,000)	35
2024	(250,000)	35
2025	150,000	35

Because Smith had no permanent or temporary differences during this period, its pre-tax financial reporting income was identical to its taxable income in each year. During the 2022–2025 period, Smith expected the current and future tax rates to be 35%. When possible, the company took advantage of the loss carryback provision of the tax law. When recording the tax benefits of the loss carryforward provision, management believed it was more likely than not that the tax benefits would be fully realized.

Required:

1. Provide journal entries to record income tax expense for the years 2017, 2018, 2023, 2024, and 2025.

2. In answering this requirement, make the following assumptions. At December 31, 2023 and 2024, Smith management believed it was more likely than not that only 40% of the tax benefits would be realized through a loss carryforward. However, at December 31, 2025, the company revised its expectation, believing that it was more likely than not that 100% of the tax benefits would be fully realized through a loss carryforward. Provide journal entries to record income tax expense for the years 2023, 2024, and 2025. Also show how to report the deferred tax asset as of the end of 2023, 2024, and 2025.

P13-7

Tax effects of differences between IFRS and U.S. GAAP related to impairment charges (**LO 11**)

On January 1, 2008, the Dolan Company purchased a new office building in Las Vegas, for $6,100,000, which it holds for rentals and capital appreciation. Dolan estimated the building would have a useful life of 25 years and a residual value of $1,100,000. Dolan uses straight-line depreciation for financial reporting and double-declining balance for tax purposes. There are no other permanent or temporary differences between taxable income and book income.

During 2014 and continuing into 2015, the building remains only partially occupied. Rental revenue in 2014 totaled $500,000. Dolan had plans to hold the building for 10 years and then sell it. Dolan estimates that the occupancy level will remain below its original estimates but will increase slightly (2% per year) from 2016–2025. Maintenance and other expenses are expected to remain steady at 80% of estimated rents.

At December 31, 2015, the fair value of the building based on an independent appraisal is $4,300,000. Estimated costs to sell the building are $200,000. The sum of the estimated net cash flows from the building is $4,598,000. The present value of the net cash flows at 8% is $4,258,000.

Any impairment charge that Dolan records in 2015 is not tax deductible and would only reverse when the asset is sold. If Dolan does not recognize an impairment loss on the building, book income before depreciation and taxes is $8,200,000.

The enacted tax rate is 30%.

Required:

Before attempting this problem, review the discussion in Chapter 10 regarding the differences between IFRS and U.S. GAAP requirements for testing for and recognizing impairment losses on noncurrent, tangible assets.

1. Determine the book and tax bases of the building on December 31, 2015.

2. Determine the amount by which the deferred tax liability increased in 2015.

3. Determine the impairment loss (if any) Dolan would recognize under U.S. GAAP and prepare the resulting 2015 tax expense journal entry, assuming Dolan expects to have sufficient future income to fully utilize any deferred tax assets.

4. Determine the impairment loss (if any) Dolan would recognize under IFRS and prepare the resulting 2015 tax expense journal entry, assuming Dolan expects to have sufficient future income to fully utilize any deferred tax assets.

Bryan Trucking Corporation began business on January 1, 2014, and consists of the parent entity, domiciled and operating in Country X, and a subsidiary operating in Country Y. Bryan is required, as a listed company in Country X, to prepare IFRS financial statements.

P13-8

Tax rate reconciliation schedules for IFRS vs. U.S. GAAP **(LO 11)**

Bryan is also listed on the New York Stock Exchange (NYSE). Therefore, Bryan is registered as a "foreign private issuer" with the U.S. Securities and Exchange Commission and must file financial statements with the SEC in accordance with SEC regulations for foreign private issuers. These regulations permit Bryan to file its IFRS financial statements with the SEC, but it has decided to prepare U.S. GAAP financial statements as well for the convenience of its U.S. shareholders.

With respect to the reconciliation of the statutory tax rate to the effective tax rate in the income tax note disclosure, SEC regulations for foreign private issuers permit them to reconcile to either the relevant statutory income tax rate in their country of domicile or to another applicable tax rate. Reconciling to the statutory income tax rate in its country of domicile would be comparable to a U.S. company reconciling to the U.S. federal tax rate.

Bryan carefully selected its accounting policies under IFRS and U.S. GAAP so that, in 2014, it reported the same pre-tax book income in both the U.S. GAAP and IFRS financial statements. Therefore, the only difference in the tax rate reconciliation results from use of either a country-specific statutory tax rate (statutory tax rate in Country X) or a weighted-average statutory tax rate (another applicable tax rate) when reconciling to the effective tax rate.

The table below presents Bryan's pre-tax book income and the applicable statutory tax rates in each country and permanent differences between taxable and book income in the two countries in which it operates. Bryan has no temporary differences in 2014.

	Country X	Country Y	Total
Pre-tax book income	$1,250,000	$1,100,000	$2,350,000
Permanent differences:			
Tax exempt income	$40,000	$60,000	$100,000
Nondeductible expense	$25,000	$35,000	$ 60,000
Applicable statutory tax rates in 2014	28%	35%	

Both Country X and Country Y tax only profits earned within the country.

Required:

Prepare the portion of the income tax note that details the reconciliation of the statutory or other applicable tax rate to the effective tax rate as follows:

1. Assume Bryan uses the statutory tax rate in Country X for the tax rate reconciliation in its U.S. GAAP financial statements.

2. Assume Bryan uses a weighted-average statutory rate for the tax rate reconciliation in its IFRS financial statements.

P13-9

Differences in revenue recognition and tax reporting under IFRS vs. U.S. GAAP **(LO 11)**

mhhe.com/revsine6e

The Lance Construction Company, which began business on January 1, 2014, builds custom homes on the buyer's land. Lance's income and job costs from construction contracts that were started and completed during the same fiscal year are as follows:

	Contracts Started and Completed in		
	2014	2015	2016
Total contract revenues	$ 550,000	$ 605,000	$ 665,500
Total construction costs	(325,000)	(363,000)	(399,300)
Total general and administrative costs*	(55,000)	(60,000)	(65,000)
Income before taxes	$ 170,000	$ 182,000	$ 201,200

* Total costs for the year not allocated to construction contracts.

Some contracts were started in the last quarter of one fiscal year and completed in the first quarter of the next. Total estimated revenues and costs equaled actual total revenues and costs for each contract. The following table shows the total contract revenues and costs for these contracts. Fifty percent (50%) of the work on these contracts was completed in the year that construction began. For example, for those contracts begun in 2014 and completed in 2015, 50% of total costs were incurred in 2014 and 50% were incurred in 2015.

	Contracts Started and Completed in Different Years		
Construction started in 4th quarter of year:	2014	2015	2016
Construction completed in 1st quarter of year:	2015	2016	2017
Total contract revenues	$600,000	$800,000	$900,000
Total construction costs	(400,000)	(520,000)	(585,000)
Gross profit	$200,000	$280,000	$315,000

Domiciled in the United States, Lance prepares consolidated financial statements in accordance with U.S. GAAP and pays taxes under U.S. tax law. However, Lance is trying to increase its appeal to European investors and, therefore, decided to prepare an additional set of financial statements in accordance with International Financial Reporting Standards (IFRS).

Because all of its construction contracts are completed in less than six (6) months, Lance concludes that the completed-contract method is more appropriate for financial reporting in the United States. Lance also qualifies for and will use the **completed-contract method for U.S. tax reporting.**

The completed-contract method is not permitted under IFRS and Lance is required to use the percentage-of-completion method as long as it can make reliable estimates of total contract costs, revenues, and stage of completion of the project.

Lance invoices customers promptly as work is completed. Cash collections are not affected by its choice of accounting policy for financial reporting purposes.

The enacted tax rate is 35%. No change in the tax law has been proposed.

Note to students: Before completing the requirements of this problem you should review the Global Vantage Point section of Chapter 3.

Required:

Determine the following amounts under U.S. GAAP and IFRS and explain the classification of any deferred tax assets or liabilities on the balance sheet.

	U.S. GAAP			IFRS		
	2014	2015	2016	2014	2015	2016
Revenue						
Construction costs						
Gross profit						
General and administrative costs						
Income before tax						
Tax expense						
Net income						
Taxable income						
Tax payable						
Deferred tax asset (if any)						
Deferred tax liability (if any)						

P13-10

Converting book income to taxable income and computation of taxes payable **(LO 2, 4)**

(*Note:* Students may want to review the material on accounting for trading securities in Chapter 16 before beginning this problem.)

Over the past two years, Madison Corporation has accumulated operating loss carryforwards of $66,000. This year, 2014, Madison's pre-tax book income is $101,500. The company is subject to a 40% corporate tax rate. The following items are relevant to Madison's deferred tax computations for 2014.

1. Equipment purchased in 2011 is depreciated on a straight-line basis for financial reporting purposes and using an accelerated method for tax purposes as follows:

Year	Book	Tax
2011	$100,000	$200,000
2012	100,000	150,000
2013	100,000	100,000
2014	100,000	50,000
2015	100,000	–0–

2. Madison's trading securities portfolio generated a $13,000 unrealized gain that is not recognized for tax purposes until the securities are sold.

3. Madison has not yet paid its rent for November and December of 2014, a total of $25,000. The expense was accrued for book purposes and is included in pre-tax book income, but it is not tax deductible until paid.

4. During 2014, Madison paid a $6,500 fine to its state corporation commission for allegedly violating state security laws. Madison neither denied nor admitted guilt related to the charges. The payment is not deductible for tax purposes but has been included in computing pre-tax book income.

Required:
1. Determine Madison Corporation's taxable income for 2014.
2. Calculate the amount of tax payable for Madison Corporation for 2014.

P13-11

Calculating taxes payable, deferred taxes, and tax expense **(LO 2, 4)**

(*Note:* Students may want to review the material on accounting for trading securities in Chapter 16 before beginning this problem.)

At the end of its third year of operations, December 31, 2014, Delilah Corp. is reporting pre-tax book income of $223,000. The following items are relevant to Delilah's deferred tax computations:

1. A $55,000 unrealized holding gain on its trading securities that is not recognized for tax purposes until it sells the securities.

2. Bad debt expense of $24,000 was recorded on its accounts receivable, although during 2014 no actual write-offs took place.

3. During 2014, Delilah received $19,000 cash from one of its customers. The payment received relates to a product that will be completed and delivered to the customer in late January 2015, at which time it will be taxable.

Delilah is subject to a 40% corporate tax rate.

Required:
1. Determine Delilah Corp.'s taxable income and taxes payable for 2014.
2. Determine the changes in Delilah Corp.'s deferred tax amounts for 2014.
3. Calculate tax expense for Delilah Corp. for 2014.

P13-12

Converting from taxable income to book income **(LO 2, 4)**

Mozart Inc.'s $98,000 taxable income for 2014 will be taxed at the 40% corporate tax rate. For tax purposes, its depreciation expense exceeded the depreciation used for financial reporting purposes by $27,000. Mozart has $45,000 of purchased goodwill on its books; during 2014, the company determined that the goodwill had suffered a $3,000 impairment of value for financial reporting purposes. None of the goodwill impairment is deductible for tax purposes. Mozart purchased a three-year corporate liability insurance policy on July 1, 2014, for $36,000 cash. The entire premium was deducted for tax purposes in 2014.

Required:
1. Determine Mozart's pre-tax book income for 2014.
2. Determine the changes in Mozart's deferred tax amounts for 2014.
3. Calculate tax expense for Mozart Inc. for 2014.

P13-13

Making entries for uncertain tax positions **(LO 9)**

In Year 1, Phillips Company reported $10,000 of pre-tax book income and also had $10,000 of taxable income. It incurred a $1,000 book expense that it deducted on its tax return. Assuming a 35% tax rate, this deduction results in a $350 tax benefit. The tax law was unclear at that time whether this expense was deductible, so it led to an uncertain tax position.

In Year 1, this uncertain tax position had a 60% likelihood of being sustained based on technical merits, $150 of the benefit was recognized, and a tax contingency reserve of $200 was created for this position.

A court decision in Year 2 lowered the likelihood that this uncertain tax position could be sustained on technical merits to 40% and led to the following amounts and related individual probabilities of possible outcomes:

10% likelihood of realizing $350

15% likelihood of realizing $250

30% likelihood of realizing $50

45% likelihood of realizing $0

Required:

1. Based on these facts, provide the journal entry that Phillips would make in Year 1 to record tax expense, taxes payable, and the tax contingency for unrecognized tax benefits.

2. Provide the entry Phillips would make in Year 2 to record any change in the status of the tax contingency reserve.

In Year 1, MB Inc. is subject to a 40% tax rate. For book purposes, it expenses $1,500 of expenditures. MB intends to deduct these expenditures on its Year 1 tax return despite tax law precedent that makes it less than 50% probable that the deduction will be sustained on its technical merits. Instead, the best estimate is that the IRS will allow these expenses to be amortized straight line over a 15-year period. In Year 1 and each of the subsequent 14 years, $100 of amortization would be allowed.

P13-14

Making entries for uncertain tax positions **(LO 9)**

Required:

1. In Year 1, determine which accounts MB would debit and credit and for how much in properly accounting for this uncertain tax position.

2. Prepare the journal entries that MB would make in Year 2 related to this uncertain tax position.

Flower Company started doing business on January 1, 2013. For the year ended December 31, 2014, it reported $450,000 pre-tax book income on its income statement. Flower is subject to a 40% corporate tax rate for this year and the foreseeable future. Additionally, it has the following issues that impact its tax situation:

P13-15

Comprehensive tax allocation problem **(LO 2, 4)**

1. At the beginning of 2014, Flower acquired $600,000 of specialized productive machinery that it depreciates using the straight-line method over five years with no salvage value for accounting purposes. For tax purposes, this specialized equipment is being depreciated $200,000 per year for the first three years of its productive life.

2. During 2014, the federal government fined Flower $100,000 for violating environmental laws. The amount was paid on November 15, 2014, and was expensed in determining 2014's book income. The fine is not tax deductible.

3. Flower received $40,000 of interest income as a result of its investment in the bonds issued by the State of Arizona.

4. On January 2, 2014, Flower leased warehouse space for $2,000 per month for a three-year period. On January 2, 2014, as a condition of the lease, Flower paid $30,000 to the lessor to cover the first 15 months of rent. Because Flower leased space in excess of its needs, it immediately (January 2, 2014) subleased part of the warehouse to a small, local company. The sublease was also for a period of three years and required the tenant to make $800 monthly rent payments to Flower. During 2014, Flower received $8,800 in monthly rental payments from the sublessee. Pre-tax book income includes an accrual for rent revenue earned but not yet received in cash.

5. During 2014, Flower's CEO was killed in an automobile accident. The company had a $200,000 life insurance policy on the CEO and collected the proceeds of the policy during October 2014.

6. During 2014, Flower sold a parcel of land held for speculative purposes. The historical cost of the land was $320,000, and it was sold for $680,000. The cash will be collected from the purchaser in 10 monthly installments of $68,000 each. During 2014, Flower collected five of these $68,000 payments; the remaining payments are assumed to be fully collectible during 2015.

7. During 2013, Flower accumulated a $22,000 net operating loss carryforward it can use to offset 2014 taxable income.

8. At the beginning of 2014, the balance in the Deferred tax asset account was $8,800 and there was no balance in the Deferred tax liability account.

Required:

1. Beginning with pre-tax accounting income, compute taxable income and taxes payable for 2014. Clearly label all amounts used in arriving at taxable income.

2. Using the following schedule, compute the change in the Deferred tax asset and Deferred tax liability accounts for 2014. The depreciation temporary difference has been completed as an example.

Temporary Difference	Deferred Tax Asset	Deferred Tax Liability
Depreciation ($200,000 − $120,000) × 40%		$32,000 **CR**

3. Determine income tax expense for 2014.

P13-16

Determining taxes payable, deferred taxes, and tax expense   **(LO 2, 4)**

mhhe.com/revsine6e

(*Note:* Students may want to review the material on the equity method of accounting in Chapter 16 before beginning work on this problem.)

In the current year, 2014, Reality Corporation reported $200,000 of pre-tax earnings on its income statement. The corporate tax rate is 40% in the current year and next year, and it is scheduled to remain at this level for the foreseeable future. Additional information relevant to figuring taxes is as follows:

1. Reality acquired $500,000 of machinery in 2013. The machinery is being depreciated on a straight-line basis over five years (zero salvage) for accounting purposes and MACRS

for tax purposes. A comparison of depreciation charges under these two methods is as follows:

	2013	2014	2015	2016	2017
Straight line	$100,000	$100,000	$100,000	$100,000	$100,000
MACRS	165,000	225,000	75,000	35,000	–0–

2. Investment income from a 30% ownership of an investee company carried under the equity method is shown on the income statement as $80,000. The investee paid $30,000 in dividends to Reality in the current year. The remaining undistributed earnings total for 2014 is expected to be received in equal amounts over the next two years in the form of dividends. All dividends are subject to the 80% dividend exclusion rule.

3. During the year, Reality recognized $4,000 of rental income that had been collected and taxed in 2013. In addition, $10,000 of rent revenue was received in advance in the current year. This amount was deferred for accounting purposes and will be recognized as income in 2015.

4. Reality received $5,000 of interest on State of North Carolina bonds in the current year that is included in pre-tax income.

5. Reality sold land in the current year for $50,000 that had a $20,000 book value and tax basis. The entire gain (not considered extraordinary) was recognized for accounting purposes in 2014. However, because collections are to be received in three equal installments, Reality elected to use the installment sales method for tax purposes and picked up one-third of the gain on its tax return in 2014. The remaining amount of the gain will be recognized equally in 2015 and 2016.

6. Reality provided for future product warranty costs in the amount of $50,000 in the current year for book purposes. For tax purposes, such costs are deductible when paid. Actual warranty costs paid in 2014 were $15,000. It is expected that the remainder of the accrued warranty costs will be paid in 2015.

7. Included in pre-tax accounting income is an expense for $3,000 for insurance premiums paid on Mr. Reality's life.

8. Reality made charges to bad debts expense in the current year of $15,000. The beginning balance in the Allowance for bad debts account was $12,000, and $6,000 of accounts was written off in the current year. It is expected that the 2014 year-end balance in the allowance account will be written off in 2015.

9. Reality has a $10,000 net operating loss carryforward that can be used to offset the current period's taxable income.

10. The balance in the deferred tax asset (liability) account was $40,000 ($50,000) at the beginning of 2014.

11. It is estimated to be more likely than not that 20% of the deferred tax asset at the end of 2014 will not be realized.

Required:

1. Starting with pre-tax accounting income, compute taxable income and taxes payable for 2014. Clearly label all amounts used in arriving at taxable income.

2. Using the following schedule, compute the change in the deferred tax asset (liability) account for 2014. The depreciation temporary difference has been completed as an example.

Temporary Difference Item	Deferred Tax Asset	Deferred Tax Liability
Depreciation ($225,000 − $100,000) × 40%		$50,000 **CR**

3. Determine Reality's income tax expense for 2014.

CASES

C13-1

Pepsico: Analyzing the tax note   (LO 2, 4, 8)

The following tables were excerpted from Pepsico's 2012 Form 10-K. All amounts are in millions of dollars and the deferred tax asset and liability amounts are as of December 31 of the respective year.

	2012	2011	2010
Provision for income taxes			
Current: U.S. Federal	$ 911	$ 611	$ 932
Foreign	940	882	728
State	153	124	137
	2,004	1,617	1,797
Deferred: U.S. Federal	154	789	78
Foreign	(95)	(88)	18
State	27	54	1
	86	755	97
	$2,090	$2,372	$1,894
Deferred tax liabilities			
Investments in noncontrolled affiliates	$ 48	$ 41	
Property, plant and equipment	2,424	2,466	
Intangible assets other than nondeductible goodwill	4,388	4,297	
Other	1,088	1,012	
Gross deferred tax liabilities	7,948	7,816	
Deferred tax assets			
Net carryforwards	1,378	1,373	
Stock-based compensation	378	429	
Retiree medical benefits	411	504	
Other employee-related benefits	672	695	
Pension benefits	647	545	
Other	1,372	1,384	
Gross deferred tax assets	4,858	4,930	
Valuation allowances	(1,233)	(1,264)	
Deferred tax assets, net	3,625	3,666	
Net deferred tax liabiliities	$4,323	$4,150	

Required:

1. Provide journal entries to record the income tax expense for 2010 through 2012. You may indicate the sum of the changes in the various deferred tax assets/liabilities by a single debit or credit to the Net deferred tax asset/liability account.

2. Refer to the deferred tax asset and liability items reported by Pepsico at December 31, 2012 and 2011. For each item (except Other), determine whether the balance changed because of a net originating or net reversing temporary difference. Provide a likely explanation for each of the temporary differences and clearly discuss whether it indicates a higher or lower financial reporting revenue or expense relative to the amount reported in the 2012 tax return.

3. Pepsico's reported deferred tax expense in 2012 ($86 million) does not equal the reported increase in net deferred tax liability ($4,323 − $4,150 = $173 million) over the course of 2012. What is the likely source of this discrepancy?

Edited excerpts from Google Inc.'s 2012 tax note follow:

Excerpts from Tax Note

CI3-2

Google Inc.: Analyzing tax notes   **(LO 2, 4, 8)**

($ in millions)	2010	2011	2012
Expected provision at federal statutory rate (35%)	$3,779	$4,314	$4,685
State taxes, net of federal benefit	322	122	99
Stock-based compensation expense	79	105	52
Change in valuation allowance	(34)	27	1,921
Foreign rate differential	(1,769)	(2,001)	(2,200)
Federal research credit	(84)	(140)	0
Tax exempt interest	(12)	(10)	(7)
Non-deductible legal settlement	0	175	0
Basis difference in investment in Home business	0	0	(1,960)
Other permanent differences	10	(3)	8
Provision for income taxes	$2,291	$2,589	$2,598
Current:			
Federal	$1,657	$1,724	2342
State	458	274	171
Foreign	167	248	358
Total	2,282	2,246	2,871
Deferred:			
Federal	(25)	452	(328)
State	47	(109)	(19)
Foreign	(13)	0	74
Total	9	343	(273)
Provision for income taxes	$2,291	$2,589	$2,598
Deferred tax assets:			
Stock-based compensation expense		$288	$311
State taxes		138	184
Capital loss carryforward		285	236
Settlement with the Authors Guild and AAP		35	28
Vacation accruals		52	67
Deferred rent		43	50
Accruals and reserves not currently deductible		268	688
Acquired net operating losses		156	505
Tax credit		55	274
Basis difference in investment in Home business		0	2,043
Other		11	128
Total deferred tax assets		1,331	4,514
Valuation allowance		(333)	(2,629)
Total deferred tax assets net of valuation allowance		998	1,885
Deferred tax liabilities:			
Depreciation and amortization		(479)	(761)
Identified intangibles		(398)	(1,496)
Unrealized gains on investments and other		(90)	(105)
Other prepaids		(70)	(118)
Other		(33)	(133)
Total deferred tax liabilities		(1,070)	(2,613)
Net deferred tax liabilities		($72)	($728)

Required:

1. Prepare the book journal entry for income tax expense for 2012 (combine U.S., foreign, and state income taxes). Clearly indicate both the account title and whether the account is being debited or credited.

2. Using information given in the tax rate reconciliation, estimate Google's pre-tax book income for 2012. Show your work.

3. What was Google's 2012 effective tax rate? Show your work.

4. Estimate Google's taxable income. (*Note:* You do not have enough information to do this by category; therefore, combine U.S., foreign, and state taxes.) Show and clearly label all work.

5. Using information found in the tax note, determine whether depreciation and amortization expense was higher for book or tax purposes in 2012 and by how much.

6. Based on information in the tax note, are the tax rates in foreign countries in which Google operates greater than or less than the U.S. tax rate?

7. Explain why federal research credits appear in the tax rate reconciliation.

C13-3

Motorola vs. Intel: Adjusting for depreciation differences (LO 2, 4, 8)

Motorola and Intel are both in the semiconductor industry and compete in many of the same product sectors. But each uses a different depreciation method. Motorola's Year 2 10-K states the following:

Depreciation is recorded principally using the declining-balance method based on the estimated useful lives of the assets (buildings and building equipment, 5–50 years; machinery and equipment, 2–12 years).

So, Motorola is using accelerated depreciation for most of its assets. By contrast, Intel's Year 2 report says:

Depreciation is computed for financial reporting purposes principally by use of the straight-line method over the following estimated useful lives: machinery and equipment, 2 to 4 years; land and buildings, 4 to 45 years.

The following table gives several key financial statement figures for each company from its respective Year 2 10-K and excerpts from its income tax footnote:

From the Year 2 10-Ks of Motorola and Intel

Selected, Edited Financial Statement Disclosures

Motorola

($ in millions)	Year 2	Year 1
Book depreciation	$2,308	$1,919
Income before income taxes	1,775	3,225
Property, plant and equipment, net of accumulated depreciation (at year-end)	9,768	9,356

	December 31	
Significant Deferred Tax Assets (Liabilities)	**Year 2**	**Year 1**
Inventory reserves	$440	$345
Contract accounting methods	231	157
Employee benefits	291	286
Capitalized items	138	89
Tax basis differences on investments	(199)	(176)
Depreciation	(213)	(197)
Deferred taxes on non-U.S. earnings	(545)	(382)
Other deferred income taxes	329	132
Net deferred tax asset	$472	$254

(continued)

Intel

($ in millions)	Year 2	Year 1
Book depreciation	$1,888	$1,371
Income before income taxes	7,934	5,638
Property, plant and equipment, less		
accumulated depreciation (at year-end)	8,487	7,471

	December 31	
Significant Deferred Tax Assets (Liabilities)	**Year 2**	**Year 1**
Deferred tax assets		
Accrued compensation and benefits	$ 71	$ 61
Deferred income	147	127
Inventory valuation and related reserves	187	104
Interest and taxes	54	61
Other, net	111	55
	$ 570	$ 408
Deferred tax liabilities		
Depreciation	(573)	(475)
Unremitted earnings of certain subsidiaries	(359)	(116)
Other, net	(65)	(29)
	$(997)	$(620)

Assume a statutory tax rate of 35% for all years.

Required:

1. Using the information provided and the analytical techniques illustrated in the chapter, determine the tax depreciation for Motorola and Intel for Year 2.

2. Adjust each firm's pre-tax income to reflect the same depreciation method and useful lives used for tax purposes.

3. Explain why the adjusted numbers provide a better basis for comparing the operating performance of the two companies.

ABC Inc. is in the business of airframe maintenance, modification and retrofit services, avionics and aircraft interior installations, the overhaul and repair of aircraft engines, and other related services.

The following are excerpted from its income statement for the year ended December 31, 2014.

($ in thousands)	2014
Earnings (loss) before income taxes	$10,891
Income tax benefit (provision)	(3,267)
Net earnings (loss)	$ 7,624

C13-4

ABC Inc.: Interpreting tax notes and reconciling statutory and effective rates (LO 2, 4, 6, 8)

The details for the income tax expense or provision follow.

Income Tax Expense	2014
Current	$1,756
Deferred	1,511
Income tax expense	$3,267

Because a goodwill impairment charge taken under GAAP may not be deducted for tax purposes, the company's tax expense was higher by $1,076 than would be expected based on the statutory tax rate of 35%. State taxes added another $927 to the tax expense. However, the reduction in the valuation allowance decreased the accounting income tax expense. In addition, several other items caused the tax expense to deviate from the tax liability. Because these items by themselves are immaterial, no separate breakdowns are available.

The following breakdowns are available for the balance sheet values of deferred tax assets and liabilities:

	December 31,	
($ in thousands)	2014	2013
Deferred Tax Assets		
Accounts receivable	$ 977	$ 1,070
Inventories, principally due to additional costs inventoried for tax purposes and financial statement allowances	3,523	1,679
Employee benefits, principally due to accrual for financial reporting purposes	9,814	13,510
Accrual for costs of restructuring	5,392	8,750
Accrual for disposal of discontinued operations	4,312	5,020
Others	23,634	19,257
Gross deferred tax assets	47,652	49,286
Less: Valuation allowance	(13,588)	(15,710)
Total deferred tax asset	34,064	33,576
Deferred Tax Liability		
Plant and equipment	(7,770)	(8,993)
Others	(5,187)	(1,964)
Total deferred tax liability	(12,957)	(10,957)
Net deferred tax asset	$21,107	$22,619

The book value of the company's inventories increased from $91,130 at the end of 2013 to $127,777 at the end of 2014.

Required:

1. Prepare a schedule reconciling the statutory and effective tax rates of ABC Inc. for the year ended 2014.

2. Provide the journal entry to record the income tax expense for 2014, showing separately the effects on deferred tax asset, valuation allowance, and deferred tax liability.

3. For each component of deferred tax asset/liability, provide possible reasons for the change in its value from 2013 to 2014.

C13-5

Understanding tax note disclosures **(LO 2, 4, 8)**

Excerpts from Starbucks Corporation's tax note from the company's Form 10-K for the year ended September 30, 2012, follow.

($ in millions) Fiscal Year Ended	Sep. 30, 2012	Oct. 2, 2011	Oct. 3, 2010
Current taxes:			
Federal	$466.0	$344.7	$457.5
State	79.9	61.2	79.6
Foreign	76.8	37.3	38.3
Total current taxes	622.7	443.2	575.4
Deferred taxes:			
Federal	49.2	111.6	(76.0)
State	(0.7)	8.3	(9.3)
Foreign	3.2	0.0	(1.4)
Total deferred taxes	51.7	119.9	(86.7)
Total provision for income taxes	$674.4	$563.1	$488.7

(continued)

Fiscal Year Ended	Sep. 30, 2012	Oct. 2, 2011	Oct. 3, 2010
Statutory rate	35.0%	35.0%	35.0%
State income taxes, net of federal income tax benefit	2.5%	2.5%	2.5%
Benefits and taxes related to foreign operations	(3.3)%	(3.1)%	(2.5)%
Domestic production activity deduction	(0.7)%	(0.8)%	(0.9)%
Other, net	(0.7)%	(2.5)%	(0.1)%
Effective tax rate	32.8%	31.1%	34.0%

	Sep. 30, 2012	Oct. 2, 2011
Deferred tax assets:		
Property, plant and equipment	$62.7	$46.4
Accrued occupancy costs	72.0	55.9
Accrued compensation and related costs	66.9	69.6
Other accrued liabilities	15.7	27.8
Asset retirement obligation asset	20.1	19.0
Deferred revenue	43.7	47.8
Asset impairments	38.5	60.0
Tax credits	14.6	23.0
Stock based compensation	131.8	128.8
Net operating losses	99.2	85.5
Other	80.9	58.6
Total	646.1	622.4
Valuation allowance	(154.2)	(137.4)
Total deferred tax asset, net of valuation allowance	491.9	485.0
Deferred tax liabilities:		
Property, plant and equipment	(89.0)	(66.4)
Intangible assets and goodwill	(34.0)	(25.2)
Other	(44.8)	(18.1)
Total	(167.8)	(109.7)
Net deferred tax asset	$324.1	$375.3
Reported as:		
Current deferred income tax assets	$238.7	$230.4
Long-term deferred income tax assets		
(included in Other assets)	97.3	156.3
Current deferred income tax liabilities		
(included in Accrued liabilities)	(1.3)	(4.9)
Long-term deferrred income tax liabilities		
(included in Other long-term liabilities)	(10.6)	(6.5)
Net deferred tax asset	$324.1	$375.3

Required:

1. Provide a journal entry to record the aggregate income tax expense for the year ended September 30, 2012.

2. What amount of Starbucks' income tax expense for the year ended September 30, 2012, was deferred? Did this deferral result in an increase in deferred tax liabilities or a decrease in deferred tax assets?

3. Estimate Starbucks' earnings before taxes in the year ended September 30, 2012.

4. What tax policy or operating decision accounts for the majority of the divergence between Starbucks' statutory tax rate and effective tax rate?

5. Estimate the amount by which Starbucks' tax provision was lower in the year ended September 30, 2012, as a result of the domestic production activity deduction.

C13-6

Using tax note disclosures to forecast next year's tax provision   **(LO 10)**

The following partial income statement and income tax note excerpts were taken from Sirius XM Inc.'s 2012 Form 10-K.

SIRIUS XM RADIO INC. AND SUBSIDIARIES
CONSOLIDATED STATEMENTS OF INCOME

(Condensed from original)

	For the Years Ended December 31,		
(in thousands, except per share data)	2012	2011	2010
Total revenue	$3,402,040	$3,014,524	$2,816,992
Total operating expenses	2,530,015	2,338,407	2,351,578
Income from operations	872,025	676,117	465,414
Total other expense	(397,557)	(234,922)	(417,739)
Income before income taxes	474,468	441,195	47,675
Income tax benefit (expense)	2,998,234	(14,234)	(4,620)
Net income	$3,472,702	$ 426,961	$ 43,055

SIRIUS XM RADIO INC. AND SUBSIDIARIES
NOTES TO CONSOLIDATED FINANCIAL STATEMENTS

(Dollar amounts in thousands, unless otherwise stated)

(16) Income Taxes (Excerpt)

The following table indicates the significant elements contributing to the difference between the federal tax (benefit) expense at the statutory rate and at our effective rate:

	For the Years Ended December 31,		
	2012	2011	2010
Federal tax expense, at statutory rate	$ 166,064	$ 154,418	$ 16,678
State income tax expense, net of federal benefit	16,606	15,751	1,620
State income rate changes	2,251	3,851	(2,252)
Non-deductible expenses	477	457	4,130
Change in valuation allowance	(3,195,651)	(166,452)	(21,749)
Other, net	12,019	6,209	6,193
Income tax (benefit) expense	$(2,998,234)	$ 14,234	$ 4,620

During 2012, Sirius XM eliminated most of the valuation allowance it had built up, reducing it to $9.8 million at December 31, 2012.

You are forecasting Sirius XM's earnings for 2013. Your best estimate is that income before income taxes will be up 5% relative to 2012. You believe there will be no tax law changes in 2013. You also believe that in 2013 Sirius XM will eliminate the remainder of its valuation allowance and that its effective income tax rate will be unchanged except for the effects of the valuation allowance reversals in 2012 and 2013.

Required:

1. Forecast Sirius XM's 2013 income before income taxes.

2. What was Sirius XM's effective tax rate in 2012?

3. What would Sirius XM's effective tax rate have been in 2012 if not for the valuation allowance reversal?

4. Assume you expect Sirius XM's 2013 *adjusted* effective income tax rate to equal its 2012 *adjusted* effective tax rate where the *adjusted* effective income tax rate is the effective income tax rate excluding the impact of changes in the valuation allowance on the income tax provision. Forecast Sirius XM's 2013 income tax expense, assuming it eliminates the remainder of its valuation allowance in that year.

5. Forecast Sirius XM's 2013 net income.

COLLABORATIVE LEARNING CASES

Under Armour, a maker of athletic sportswear, had a tax provision of about $75 million in 2012. Following is the 2012 note disclosure for Under Armour's uncertain tax positions. All amounts are in thousands of dollars.

C13-7

Interpreting uncertain tax
position disclosures **(LO 9)**

Collaborative

Provision for Income Taxes (Excerpt)

As of December 31, 2012 and 2011, the total liability for unrecognized tax benefits, including related interest and penalties, was approximately $17.1 million and $11.2 million, respectively. The following table represents a reconciliation of the Company's total unrecognized tax benefits balances, excluding interest and penalties, for the years ended December 31, 2012, 2011, and 2010:

($ in thousands)	2012	2011	2010
Beginning of year	$ 9,783	$5,165	$2,598
Increases as a result of tax positions taken in a prior period	0	0	0
Decreases as a result of tax positions taken in a prior period	0	0	0
Increases as a result of tax positions taken in the current prior period	5,702	4,959	2,632
Decreases as a result of tax positions taken in the current prior period	0	0	0
Decreases as a result of settlements during the current period	0	0	0
Reductions as a result of a lapse of statute of limitations during the current period	(188)	(341)	(65)
End of year	$15,297	$9,783	$5,165

As of December 31, 2012, $14.1 million of unrecognized tax benefits, excluding interest and penalties, would impact the Company's effective tax rate if recognized.

As of December 31, 2012, 2011, and 2010, the liability for unrecognized tax benefits included $1.8 million, $1.4 million, and $1.3 million, respectively, for the accrual of interest and penalties. For each of the years ended December 31, 2012, 2011, and 2010, the Company recorded $0.7 million, $0.4 million, and $0.3 million, respectively, for the accrual of interest and penalties in its consolidated statements of income.

The Company files income tax returns in the U.S. federal jurisdiction and various state and foreign jurisdictions. The majority of the Company's returns for years before 2009 are no longer subject to U.S. federal, state and local, or foreign income tax examinations by tax authorities. The Company does not expect any material changes to the total unrecognized tax benefits within the next twelve months.

Required:

1. Prepare the journal entry that Under Armour made for 2012 related to its uncertain tax positions.
2. What was the total amount in the Tax contingency reserve account for Under Armour on December 31, 2012?
3. Of the total Tax contingency reserve account on December 31, 2012, what amount represents interest and penalties?

Lufthansa Group operates an international airline based in Germany. Lufthansa files its annual reports under International Financial Reporting Standards (IFRS). In its 2012 Annual Report to shareholders, Lufthansa presented the following information in a note to the financial statements:

C13-8

Tax note under IFRS **LO11**

International

Deferred tax items

In accordance with IAS 12, deferred taxes are recognised for all temporary differences between the balance sheets for tax purposes of individual companies and the consolidated financial statements. Tax loss carry-forwards are recognised to the extent that the deferred tax assets are likely to be used in the future. Company earnings forecasts and specific, realisable tax strategies are used to determine whether deferred tax assets from tax losses carried forward are usable or not, i.e. whether they have a value that can be realised.

The total amount of deferred tax assets that could not be capitalised as of 31 December 2012 was EUR 498m (previous year: EUR 633m).

Required:

1. Does Lufthansa report a valuation allowance relating to its deferred tax assets? If so, how much is it? If not, why not?

2. Why was Lufthansa not able to capitalize €498 million of deferred tax assets as of December 31, 2012?

3. In its 2012 Annual Report, AMR Corp., which operates American Airlines and reports under U.S. GAAP, reported an increase in its deferred tax valuation allowance of $282 million (approximately €212 million as of December 31, 2012).

   a. Did Lufthansa experience a similar increase?

   b. What does this likely indicate about Lufthansa's ability to recover its deferred tax assets relative to AMR Corp.?

Remember to check the book's companion website for additional study material.

Pensions and Postretirement Benefits | 14

Employer-provided pension and retiree health benefits represent valuable income security to the elderly during retirement. These benefits can also represent substantial liabilities and cash outflows for employers. Because the workers earn the benefits over their work lives and receive the benefits during retirement, employer accounting for some types of plans must use numerous assumptions regarding return on plan assets, life expectancy, salary at retirement, and so on. Actual experience can deviate substantially from these assumptions. Most of the accounting challenges revolve around these estimation issues.

RIGHTS AND OBLIGATIONS IN PENSION CONTRACTS

A **pension plan** is an agreement by an organization (**sponsor**) to provide payments—called a **pension**—to employees when they retire, either in a series of payments (an **annuity**) or as a one-time "lump-sum" distribution. In the United States, the plan sponsor makes contributions to a **pension trust**—a legal entity that invests and holds the assets for the employee's benefit—over the employee's career. The retiree then receives pension payments from the trust during retirement. In most instances, these company pension payments supplement payments from government-sponsored pension plans—such as Social Security in the United States. A pension plan represents a valuable benefit to employees. Employers create these plans as a way to attract and retain a qualified workforce. Because pensions benefit firms in the form of higher productivity from employees, the cost of a worker's pension plan is treated as an expense over that worker's period of employment.

Pension plans can be divided into two categories—*defined contribution plans* and *defined benefit plans*—based on the nature of the plan promise.

Defined contribution plans specify the amount of cash that the employer puts *into* the plan trust. No explicit promise is made about the size of the periodic benefits the employee will receive during retirement. Rather, the promise is the amount of contributions the employer will make periodically. The employee exchanges service for this promise. The employee is generally given a variety of alternative investment funds (broad stock funds, growth stock funds, bond funds, etc.), and the ultimate size of the payments the employee will receive depends on the success of these investments. The employer receives a tax deduction for amounts contributed to the pension plan trust, and subsequent investment returns do not generate tax for the employer or

LEARNING OBJECTIVES

After studying this chapter, you will understand:

1. The rights and obligations in defined contribution and defined benefit pension contracts.

2. The legal form, regulatory environment, and terminology associated with pension plan arrangements.

3. The components of pension expense and their relation to pension assets and pension liabilities.

4. How GAAP smooths the volatility inherent in pension estimates and forecasts.

5. The determinants of pension funding.

6. How to analyze and use the retirement benefit disclosures.

7. Other postretirement benefit plan concepts and financial reporting rules.

8. What research tells us about the usefulness of the detailed pension and other postretirement benefits disclosures.

9. The key differences in defined benefit plan reporting between current U.S. GAAP and current IFRS requirements.

Chapter

the employee until the employee retires. The retiree is taxed on the amount of annual withdrawals at ordinary income tax rates. The amount that will ultimately be paid to the employee is determined by the accumulated value at retirement of the amounts contributed to the plan over the period of employment. In defined contribution plans, the *employee* bears the risk that the ultimate pension payments will be large enough to sustain a comfortable retirement income.

The common types of defined contribution plans are money purchase, profit sharing, and 401(k). In a **money purchase plan,** the employer contributes a fixed percentage of an employee's salary to the pension plan. The employer must make this contribution whether it is having a good year or a bad year. In a **profit-sharing plan,** the employer contributes to the plan only when profits exceed a predetermined threshold. The contribution may then be allocated to participants on the basis of salary or seniority. In a **401(k) plan,** the employer makes a contribution only if the employee voluntarily contributes to a pension plan. The terms of the plan specify the matching percentage (often 50%) and the maximum annual employer contribution or the maximum percentage of salary eligible for matching. Some 401(k) plans have very generous terms; others are somewhat miserly. Because of the fixed commitments associated with money purchase plans, they consistently result in cash outflows for the firm whereas the cash outflows for the other types of defined contribution plans vary from year to year.

> The employer's contributing of assets to the plan trust is termed **funding.** Employees may also be required to contribute to the plan. For example, a plan might specify that the employer is to contribute 10% of the employee's salary to the plan and that the employee is to contribute 5%, for a total of 15%. The employees' 5% contributions are typically deducted from their paychecks and directly transferred to the plan trust.

A **defined benefit plan** is quite different. These agreements specify the formula that determines the annual benefit amount (lifetime annuity) to be *paid out* to the employee during retirement rather than the annual amount that will be *contributed* to the plan. The annual pension benefit typically depends on each employee's years of service and salary. For example, a defined benefit plan may specify that an employee will receive an annual pension equal to 3% (called a *generosity factor*) of his or her salary at retirement for each year of service. An employee with 25 years of service and an annual salary at retirement of $60,000 would receive an annual pension benefit of $45,000 (25 years of service × 3% for each year × the ending salary of $60,000). Because the pension payout formula is specified in advance in a defined benefit plan, the *employer* bears the investment risk instead of the *employee*.[1] However, the employee bears the risk that the firm will go bankrupt and default on unfunded pension liabilities. Determining how much cash must be contributed to the fund to provide the annual pension benefit of $45,000 is complex and may be expensive to compute. These amounts must be computed using assumptions and procedures described later in the chapter.[2] The tax treatment for defined benefit plans is similar to that for defined contribution plans. The employer receives tax deductions for amounts contributed to the pension trust, and the employee does not pay tax until pension

---

[1] **Cash balance plans** also are defined benefit plans. This type of plan requires employers to contribute a fixed amount per year (say, 5% of annual pay) to the account of individual employees. The employer also guarantees a minimum rate of return on the pension assets (e.g., the rate on long-term U.S. Treasury bonds). This guarantee makes them defined benefit plans "because the employer [still ultimately] bears the investment risks and rewards and the mortality risk if the employee elects to receive benefits in the form of an annuity." See A. T. Arcady and F. Mellors, "Cash Balance Conversions," *Journal of Accountancy,* February 2000, pp. 22–28. IBM and many other employers have switched from final pay formulas to this type of formula to mimic the pension accumulations in a defined contribution plan.

[2] **Actuaries** use statistical methods to estimate the defined benefit plan obligation and annual funding. Assumptions must be made about length of service, return on assets, life expectancy, and salaries at retirement. These assumptions are called **actuarial assumptions.** When actual experience is different from assumptions, **actuarial gains or losses** arise.

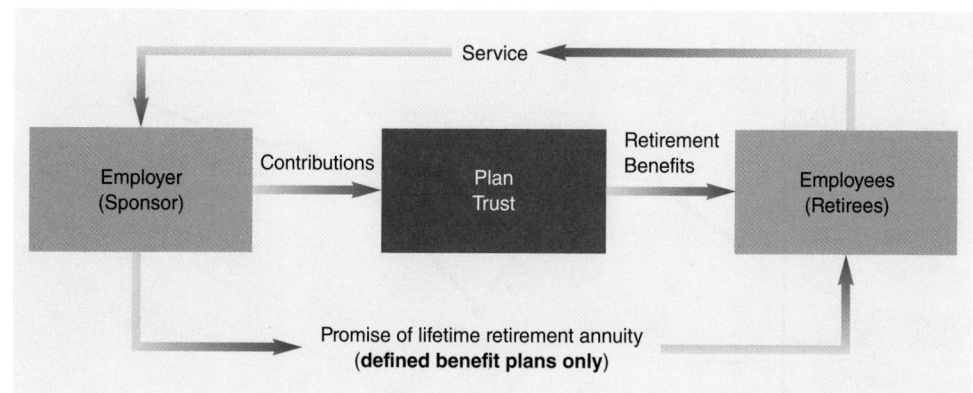

Figure 14.1

PENSION PLAN ENTITIES
AND RELATIONSHIPS

payments are received during retirement. Also, the parties involved in a defined benefit plan are the same as those in a defined contribution plan. However, under a defined benefit plan, employees receive in exchange for service the promise of a lifetime annuity instead of the promise of contributions to a trust.

> A plan is **fully funded** if its assets equal its liabilities. If assets exceed liabilities, the plan is said to be **overfunded;** if liabilities exceed assets, it is said to be **underfunded.**

The relationships among the employer (plan sponsor), the plan trust, and the employees (the eventual retirees) for both types of plans are summarized in Figure 14.1. In a *defined contribution* plan, the employee exchanges service for contributions, determined according to the plan formula, and returns on the invested contributions. However, under a *defined benefit* plan, the employee exchanges service for the promise of the lifetime annuity. The employer then determines the contribution necessary to fulfill this promise. This promise of an annuity leads to complex calculations and accounting. In both types of plans, the employer makes contributions to a separate legal trust, and the trust makes payments to the retirees.

Figure 14.2 shows the total nominal dollar amount of assets in each of the two types of pension plans over the years from 2005 to 2012. The proportion of assets in defined contribution plans as a percent of total pension assets continues to grow. Defined benefit plans, which have been in existence since the late 19th century, grew rapidly in the manufacturing, telecommunication, airline, and utility industries in the first half of the 20th century. These plans still exist, but young firms tend to have defined contribution plans because they are less costly to manage, less risky for the employer, improve job mobility for the employee, and may not be at risk if the employer declares bankruptcy.[3] In the 1980s, the value of defined contribution plan assets in the United States was less than the value of defined benefit plan assets. However, by the end of 2012, the value of defined contribution plan assets was 61% higher than the value of defined benefit plan assets. The figure also reveals that both types of plans experienced severe asset value declines in 2008 when the stock market was weak. At the end of 2012, defined contribution plan assets were significantly higher than pre-2008 levels, and defined benefit plan assets were near the pre-2008 levels. Despite the trend toward defined contribution plans, data in Figure 14.2 show that defined benefit plans held $2.5 trillion in assets at the end of 2012. In addition, the majority of S&P 500 firms sponsor defined benefit pension plans.

---

[3] A defined contribution plan may be an **employee stock ownership plan (ESOP)** whose primary asset is employer stock. For example, Procter & Gamble Co. sponsors a profit-sharing plan that also is an ESOP. If an employee has invested 100% of his or her account in employer stock, the pension is essentially worthless in the event of employer bankruptcy, which is what occurred with Enron in 2001.

Figure 14.2

ASSETS BY PLAN TYPE

Source: Board of Governors of the Federal Reserve System, Washington, D.C., www.federalreserve.gov, *Flow of Funds Accounts of the United States, Z.1.,* L.116 Private Pension Funds, June 7, 2012 and June 6, 2013.

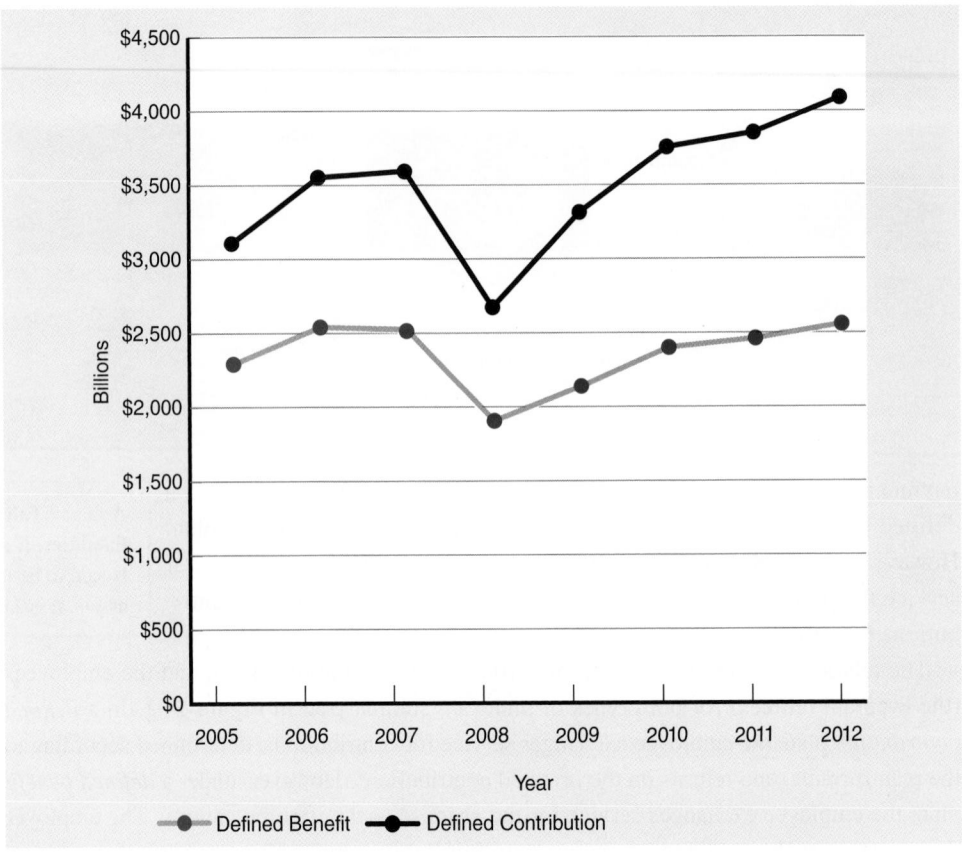

ACCOUNTING ISSUES RELATED TO DEFINED BENEFIT PENSION PLANS

The employer accounting for defined contribution plans is straightforward, as the following example shows.

Assume that a defined contribution pension plan agreement requires ***the company to make an annual contribution equal to 10% of each employee's salary into a fund whose accumulated proceeds will be paid to the employee at retirement.*** Employees' salaries in 2014 total $10 million. Accordingly, the company records pension expense equal to the amount of cash contributed to the plan ($10,000,000 × 10%) as follows:

DR	Pension expense	$1,000,000	
	CR Cash		$1,000,000

Upon retirement, individual employees receive their share of the accumulated balance from the investments.

Unfortunately, the accounting for defined benefit pension plans is not this easy. Therefore, we use much of the remainder of this chapter to explain it. The accounting complications arise because the employer must estimate the current financial statement effects of the lifetime annuities promised to employees. These estimates rely heavily on the present value techniques discussed in the appendix to this book on page 1093. To determine the financial statement effects, an employer must consider the following factors:

1. What proportion of the workforce will remain with the company long enough to qualify for benefits under the plan? Qualifying for benefits is called **vesting.** For example,

an employee may have to stay with a firm for at least one year to become part of a plan and may not fully participate for five years. A forecast of the length of employee service requires assumptions regarding personnel turnover, mortality rates, and disability.

2. At what rate will salaries rise over the period until eventual retirement?

3. What is the life expectancy of covered employees after retirement—that is, over what length of time will the pension benefits be paid?[4]

4. What is the appropriate discount rate in computing the present value of the future benefits earned by employees in the current period?

5. What do firms do when actual experience differs from expectations? It's impossible to predict exactly how long someone will work for a company, what she or he will be earning at retirement, and how long she or he will live after retiring. Consequently, the accounting must address the differences between actual and expected experience.

The accounting problem is further complicated by the presence of the pension trust assets. In a defined contribution plan the *employee* bears the risk associated with pension investments. However, in a defined benefit plan the *employer* bears the risk. Just as pension liabilities can change over time because actual experience differs from expectations, pension asset returns can vary greatly from year to year. Consequently, the accounting must incorporate asset returns and expected fluctuations in returns.

In December 1985, the Financial Accounting Standards Board (FASB) issued specified measurement and disclosure requirements for defined benefit pension plans.[5] The disclosure aspects of these GAAP rules were amended in 1998 and again in 2003.[6] In 2006, the FASB further revised both recognition and disclosure requirements.[7] The current authoritative accounting literature for pension measurement and reporting requirements is found in the FASB ASC Topic 715, Compensation–Retirement Benefits.

Pension expense measurement for financial reporting includes several smoothing features to make annual pension expense less volatile. These smoothing features were included to respond to corporate lobbying and to acknowledge that short-term gains and losses on pension assets and obligations may not result in cash inflows or outflows. These gains and losses are omitted from pension expense. From 1986 to 2006, they also were excluded from the balance sheet and were merely disclosed in notes. Since 2006, these temporary gains and losses have been recognized in **accumulated other comprehensive income (AOCI)**[8] with a corresponding offset to a balance sheet pension asset or liability account. Despite the numerous changes to pension accounting since 1985, the FASB still views the existing GAAP as an interim measure and continues to study pension presentation and measurement issues.

---

[4] Upon a retired worker's death, plans often pay pension benefits (at a reduced amount) to a surviving spouse. Consequently, actuaries must estimate for these plans the life of the spouse in addition to that of the employee.

[5] Pre-Codification, entitled "Employers' Accounting for Pensions," *SFAS No. 87* replaced both *Accounting Principles Board (APB) Opinion No. 8,* "Accounting for the Cost of Pension Plans," 1966, and *SFAS No. 36,* "Disclosure of Pension Information," 1980, which previously governed pension accounting and disclosure.

[6] Pre-Codification "Employers' Disclosures about Pensions and Other Postretirement Benefits," *SFAS No. 132* (Norwalk, CT: FASB, 1998), and *SFAS No. 132* (revised 2003). The pre-Codification revised version of *SFAS No. 132* has the same title as the 1998 version. For simplicity, citations throughout the chapter simply refer to pre-Codification *SFAS 87,* pre-Codification *SFAS No. 132,* and pre-Codification *SFAS 132(R).*

[7] Pre-Codification "Employers' Accounting for Defined Benefit Pension and Other Postretirement Plans," *SFAS No. 158* (Norwalk, CT: FASB, 2006).

[8] This chapter assumes a thorough knowledge of **other comprehensive income (OCI)** and AOCI. Please review Chapter 2 if you have questions on these concepts.

The smoothing techniques and recognition rules that govern pension accounting can make it very difficult for accountants, analysts, and other external users to understand how pensions affect financial statements. We try to clarify the topic by providing an intuitive overview of the financial reporting rules for defined benefit pension plans.

> **Market-related value** of pension plan assets is a technical term. It can be either (1) the fair value of the assets or (2) a smoothed value that recognizes gains and losses more slowly (over not more than five years).

FINANCIAL REPORTING FOR DEFINED BENEFIT PENSION PLANS

Under current GAAP, pension expense comprises five separate components[9] (a + indicates increase in expense, and a − indicates decrease in expense):

1. Service cost (+).
2. Interest cost (+).
3. Expected return on the market-related value of pension plan assets (−).
4. Recognized gains or losses (− or +).
5. Recognized prior service cost (− or +).

We use a simple example to illustrate how to compute pension expense Components 1 through 3. The example assumes an environment characterized by *complete certainty*. This assumption simplifies the setting and clarifies the relationship between the various pension expense components. Under a complete certainty assumption, Components 4 and 5 would not be needed. We also use the example to introduce institutional features of defined benefit plans and employer balance sheet recognition. In subsequent examples, we show how Components 4 and 5 come into play in a world of *uncertainty* in which expectations are often not realized and changes in assumptions occur frequently.

> Usually, pension plans provide survivor benefits and pay benefits monthly. To make calculations easier to follow, we exclude survivor benefits and use annual pension payments in our hypothetical examples.

A Simple Example: A World of Complete Certainty

Consider the following example of a hypothetical company with a defined benefit retirement plan:

> On January 1, 2014, Robie Corporation hires Francie Stevens and also begins a defined benefit pension plan. Annual pension benefits are based on the formula: *n* (years of service) times 0.05 (generosity factor) times the highest salary before retirement (salary base). Francie will receive payments once per year on December 31. Robie can predict with certainty Francie's life expectancy, the duration of her employment service, and her salary before retirement. Francie will retire on December 31, 2015, and live until January 1, 2019. Francie will receive an annual salary of $182,000 and $200,000 for 2014 and 2015, respectively. To compute the present value of pension benefits, Robie uses a 7% **discount rate,** which represents the average rate for annuities that could be purchased with similar payment schedules.[10] In this example, the **expected long-term rate of return,** the average rate of earnings expected for the pension plan assets, and the actual return on plan assets also equal 7%.[11] At the end of each year, Robie contributes to the pension plan trust amounts equal to the present value of new benefits earned for the year. Robie's accounting year ends on December 31.

---

[9] If a company either (1) curtails a plan or (2) settles a plan's liabilities by purchasing an annuity contract and generates a gain or loss from either event, that gain or loss would also be included in pension expense as another element. Measuring the gain or loss on plan settlements or curtailments is included in various sections of FASB ASC Topic 715, Compensation–Retirement Benefits.

[10] See FASB ASC 715-30-35-43: Compensation–Retirement Benefits—Defined Benefit Plans–Pension—Subsequent Measurement—Discount Rates.

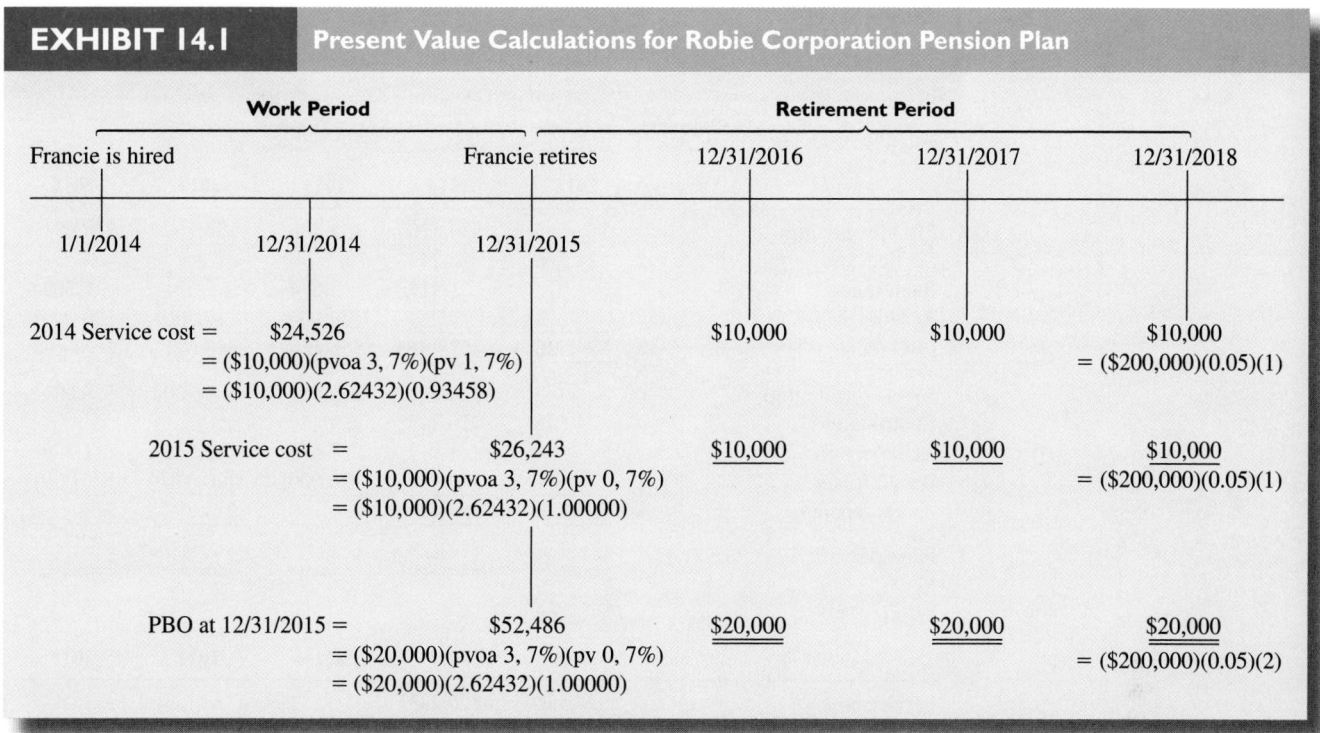

EXHIBIT 14.1   Present Value Calculations for Robie Corporation Pension Plan

We now show how to compute Components 1 through 3 for this simple example.

Component 1—Service Cost

In a typical defined benefit pension plan, the pension payout increases for each additional year of service. The present value of this increase is **service cost.** Stated more rigorously, ***service cost is the increase in the discounted present value of the pension benefits ultimately payable that is attributable to an additional year's employment.***

Exhibit 14.1 diagrams Francie's work life and retirement period and shows the service cost calculations for 2014 and 2015. By working in 2014, Francie earns one year of pension benefits. Although the pension is being earned when Francie's salary is $182,000 per year, the pension payment will be based on the highest annual salary at retirement, $200,000. To accrue the appropriate amount of pension liability, Robie computes the expected pension benefit per retirement year based on the $200,000. Under the formula, Francie will receive $10,000 (1 year × 0.05 generosity × $200,000 highest salary) each year during retirement because of her work in 2014. Based on her life expectancy, she will receive three payments. To obtain the present value of these payments, we use a present value of an ordinary annuity (pvoa) factor to discount the payments to the retirement date and a present value of an amount (pv) factor to further discount the one year from the retirement date of December 31, 2015, to December 31, 2014, the balance sheet date. December 31, 2014 (as opposed to January 1, 2014), is used here because Francie does not earn a pension benefit until she has worked an entire year. The service cost for 2014 is $24,526 ($10,000 × *pvoa* 3, 7% of 2.62432 × *pv* 1, 7% of 0.93458). Because no obligation existed at the beginning of 2014,

---

[11] See FASB ASC 715-30-35-47: Compensation–Retirement Benefits—Defined Benefit Plans—Pension—Subsequent Measurement—Expected Long-Term Rate of Return.

	EXHIBIT 14.2	**Robie Corporation Pension Plan Assets and Liabilities and Pension Expense**

Panel (a) Reconciliation of Robie Corporation PBO and Pension Plan Assets

	2014	2015	2016	2017	2018
PBO (beginning)	$ —	$24,526	$52,486	$36,160	$18,691
Service cost	24,526	26,243			
Interest cost		1,717	3,674	2,531	1,309*
Benefits paid			(20,000)	(20,000)	(20,000)
PBO (ending)	$24,526	$52,486	$36,160	$18,691	$ —
Assets (beginning)	$ —	$24,526	$52,486	$36,160	$18,691
Contributions	24,526	26,243			
Actual return		1,717	3,674	2,531	1,309*
Benefits paid			(20,000)	(20,000)	(20,000)
Assets (ending)	$24,526	$52,486	$36,160	$18,691	$ —
Funded status: Asset (liability)	$ —	$ —	$ —	$ —	$ —

Panel (b) Robie Corporation Pension Expense

	2014	2015	2016	2017	2018
Service cost	$24,526	$26,243			
Interest cost		1,717	3,674	2,531	1,309*
Expected return on plan assets		(1,717)	(3,674)	(2,531)	(1,309)*
Pension expense	$24,526	$26,243	—	—	—

* Rounded.

this amount also is the cumulative pension liability at the end of 2014. The $24,526 present value of pension benefits earned to date is called the **projected benefit obligation (PBO).** Note that the PBO calculation is based on service to date and *future salaries.* The change in PBO due to service cost also is reflected in the reconciliation of the Robie Corporation Pension Plan PBO given in Exhibit 14.2 Panel (a).

Exhibit 14.2 Panel (a) shows what happens to the plan over the five-year period. *The gross assets and PBO of the pension plan do not appear on Robie's balance sheet.* Instead, Robie recognizes the **funded status,** the net difference between the fair value of plan assets and the PBO, through its pension expense and plan contribution (funding) journal entries. To record its pension expense, which includes only service cost in 2014 [see Exhibit 14.2 Panel (b)], Robie makes the following entry:

DR	Pension expense	$24,526	
	CR Pension liability		$24,526

In this example, Robie contributes to the plan trust $24,526, the new benefits earned (i.e., service cost), and makes the following entry:

DR	Pension liability	$24,526	
	CR Cash		$24,526

The above entries result in Pension expense of $24,526, a reduction in Cash of $24,526, and a Pension liability of $0. Exhibit 14.2 Panel (b) shows that the contribution from Robie Corporation increases the plan assets of the Robie Corporation Pension Plan. It is important to remember that Robie Corporation and Robie Corporation Pension Plan are separate legal entities. After the contribution, the plan assets equal the PBO, and the funded status equals $0. Recall that the Pension liability on Robie's balance sheet also is $0.

Exhibit 14.1 shows that in 2015, Francie earns another $10,000 per year of pension benefits, but the present value of those benefits is now $26,243 because she is one year nearer to her retirement date (in this case she is at her retirement date). The pvoa factor is identical to the one used for 2014, but the pv factor is one year less than the one used for 2014. In addition to service cost, the 2015 *total* pension expense for Robie Corporation includes two other items—interest cost and return on plan assets.

Component 2—Interest Cost

A plan incurs interest on PBO until it is paid. Therefore, in 2015 in addition to service cost, **interest cost** arises from the passage of time and increases both PBO and pension expense. ***The Interest cost of $1,717 is computed by taking the PBO at the beginning of the period (here $24,526) and multiplying it by the discount rate (here 7%).*** We did not have interest cost in 2014 because the liability did not arise until December 31, 2014, when Francie completed a year of service. Exhibit 14.2 Panel (a) shows that the beginning PBO of $24,526 is increased by service cost of $26,243 and interest cost of $1,717 to obtain an ending balance of $52,486. Because both service cost and interest cost increase PBO, they also increase pension expense for Robie Corporation [see Exhibit 14.2 Panel (b)].

For this simple example, we can compute the PBO amount directly. Refer to Exhibit 14.1 again. After working two years, Francie has earned a total of $20,000 per year in pension benefits. When we discount the three $20,000 payments using the same present factors used to compute 2015 service cost, we obtain the $52,486 PBO balance shown in Exhibit 14.2 Panel (a). We illustrate the calculation of service cost and PBO in Exhibit 14.1 to help you understand the concepts of service cost and PBO. For most situations, actuaries must calculate the PBO and service cost, and analysts and accountants must focus on the reconciliation contained in Exhibit 14.2 (a).

Component 3—Expected Return on Plan Assets

Plan assets are invested in stocks and bonds that pay dividends and interest. Furthermore, the stocks and bonds could appreciate in value. The dividends, interest, and appreciation constitute the **actual return** on plan assets. At December 31, 2014, the pension plan assets (held by the trust) had a balance of $24,526. The 2015 **expected return** of $1,717 is computed by multiplying the beginning plan assets of $24,526 by the expected long-term rate of return assumption of 7%. ***For this simplified example, recall that we assume that the actual return equals the expected return (see page 830).*** We did not have a return in 2014 because the plan did not have assets until the December 31, 2014, contribution. The actual return *increases* plan assets, and the expected return *decreases* pension expense for Robie Corporation. Conceptually, the expected return on plan assets offsets increases to PBO created by the service cost and interest cost components. In this specific case of certainty, the expected return offsets exactly the interest cost com ponent. Exhibit 14.2 Panel (a) shows the effect of actual return on plan assets, and Exhibit 14.2 Panel (b) shows the effect of expected return on pension expense.

> In this example, Robie makes contributions at year-end, and the pension trust pays benefits at year-end. In practice, interest cost reflects the timing of benefit payments made throughout the year. Similarly, the expected return reflects the timing of both the employer contributions and benefit payments. For example, if Robie had not funded its 2014 pension cost until April 1, 2015, the expected return would have been $1,288 ($24,526 × 0.07 × 9/12) instead of $611.

To record its 2015 pension expense, Robie makes the following entry:

DR	Pension expense	$26,243	
CR	Pension liability		$26,243

The amount equals the 2015 service cost because the expected return on plan assets offsets the interest cost. Robie contributes $26,243, equal to the new benefits earned in 2015, to the plan trust and makes the following entry:

DR	Pension liability	$26,243	
CR	Cash		$26,243

The above entries result in Pension expense of $26,343, a reduction in Cash of $26,243, and a Pension liability of $0. Exhibit 14.2 Panel (a) shows that after the 2015 contribution is made to the plan, pension plan assets equal the PBO, and consequently, the funded status is $0, the same as the Pension liability on Robie's balance sheet.

Exhibit 14.2 shows how the plan assets and the PBO change during the retirement period. Interest costs increase the PBO, but they are offset by the actual return on plan assets. Similarly, payments to Francie reduce the PBO *and* the plan assets, thereby keeping the funded status at zero. There is no longer any service cost because Francie has retired. And, the expected return offsets interest cost, so pension expense is zero from 2016 to 2018 [see Panel (b)]. Also, because the plan is fully funded at this point, Robie does not have to make any more contributions to the plan. Given that Robie does not have pension expense or contributions from 2016 to 2018, it does not make any journal entries related to the plan. So in a world with perfect certainty, all of the sponsor's accounting is finished when the employee retires.

We use perfect certainty in this example to help you see the relationship among the components constituting pension expense. Of course, no perfect certainty exists in the real pension world. On the contrary, unforeseen pension events arise continually. Examples include the following:

1. Employee turnover may be higher or lower than anticipated.
2. Preretirement mortality may be unusually high or low (vis-à-vis actuarial estimates).
3. The actual return earned on pension plan assets could differ significantly from expectations.
4. Interest rates change, thereby causing changes in discount rate assumptions.
5. Changes in social and economic conditions may prompt companies to retroactively alter the level of benefits.

All of these factors explain why, in the real world, no simple equality exists between pension plan assets and pension plan liabilities and why pension expense does not equal service cost. Depending on the age distribution of the workforce, interest cost instead of service cost could be the dominant part of pension expense.

RECAP   **Pension expense is determined by changes in pension plan assets and liabilities. If the future were known with certainty, pension expense for defined benefit plans would always equal service cost, and pension plan assets would always equal pension plan liabilities. Starting with this simple setting will help you understand the complications that uncertainty introduces.**

The Real World: Uncertainty Introduces Gains and Losses

Uncertainty requires assumptions for discount rates, expected return on plan assets, and numerous other future events such as employee turnover and mortality. GAAP requires that the same interest rate be used for computing both the service cost *and* the interest cost components of pension expense. However, companies are free to choose some other rate for computing the *expected* rate of return on pension plan assets, and most do so.

A firm could temporarily lower its pension expense by assuming a higher than justified discount rate (which reduces the service cost component) or a higher than justified expected rate of return (which increases the expected return component that is deducted). A higher discount rate assumption also reduces PBO, thereby increasing funded status. To avoid such manipulation, GAAP provides guidelines for the assumptions.

GAAP provides explicit criteria for estimating discount rates. It states that "assumed discount rates shall reflect the rates at which the pension benefits could be effectively settled" (FASB ASC 715-30-35-43: Compensation–Retirement Benefits—Defined Benefit Plans–Pension—Subsequent Measurement—Discount Rates). It also suggests that employers look to prevailing rates of return on high-quality debt instruments with maturities that match expected payouts to retirees. Because average time to retirement and average life expectancy can differ across firms, assumed discount rates also can differ. The GAAP guidance reduces managers' ability to manipulate its pension expense and its projected benefit obligation but does not eliminate it.

See Figure 14.3 for a graphic comparison of discount rates and rate of return assumptions for plan assets used by a sample of Compustat firms from 2005 to 2012.[12] The sample for Figure 14.3 includes all U.S. NYSE firms with available data for expected long-run rate of return, discount rate, pension assets, and PBO. The sample size ranges from a low of 798 firms in 2012 to a high of 932 firms in 2005. The top and bottom lines in each graph represent the rates in the 90th and 10th percentiles, respectively. The middle line is the median. The highest median discount rate of approximately 6.3% occurred in 2008. From 2008 to 2012, discount rates fell significantly to a low of 4.0%. As interest rates change, companies must recompute their PBOs using the new rates. When interest rates decline, the resulting increase (decrease) in PBO is called an **actuarial loss (gain)**. *The recent decline in rates coupled with low asset returns have led to significant underfunding in both private and government pension plans.* In 2013, severely underfunded pensions were key factors in Chicago's and Illinois' bond rating downgrades and Detroit's bankruptcy. We discuss private pension funding levels later in the chapter.

Note that there is little variability in the discount rate assumed by firms. For example, the discount rate at the 10% percentile is only 1% lower than the assumption at the 90th percentile. One reason for the narrow range of assumptions is SEC scrutiny of pension accounting practices. A second reason is that Citigroup provides a discount rate yield curve that allows a sponsor to select a discount rate appropriate for the average age of its pension plan participants.[13] Most of the variation across firms should be due to differences in participant demographics.

---

[12] Compustat® is a computerized financial database for more than 10,000 active firms listed on the New York Stock Exchange (NYSE) and National Association of Securities Dealers Automated Quotations (NASDAQ) exchanges that is developed and distributed by Standard & Poor's Corporation. The samples for Figure 14.3 and subsequent figures exclude non-U.S. corporations (corporations with American depositary receipts [ADRs] or incorporated outside the United States).

[13] This yield curve was originally developed by Salomon Brothers in 1994 when the SEC issued new guidance regarding choice of discount rates for pension and retiree health care benefits. Citigroup continues to estimate this yield curve, and the Society of Actuaries maintains a website that provides current Citigroup estimates and the history of the pension rate yield curve. See www.soa.org/professional-interests/pension/resources/pen-resources-pension.aspx. I thank James Boatsman for making me aware of this resource.

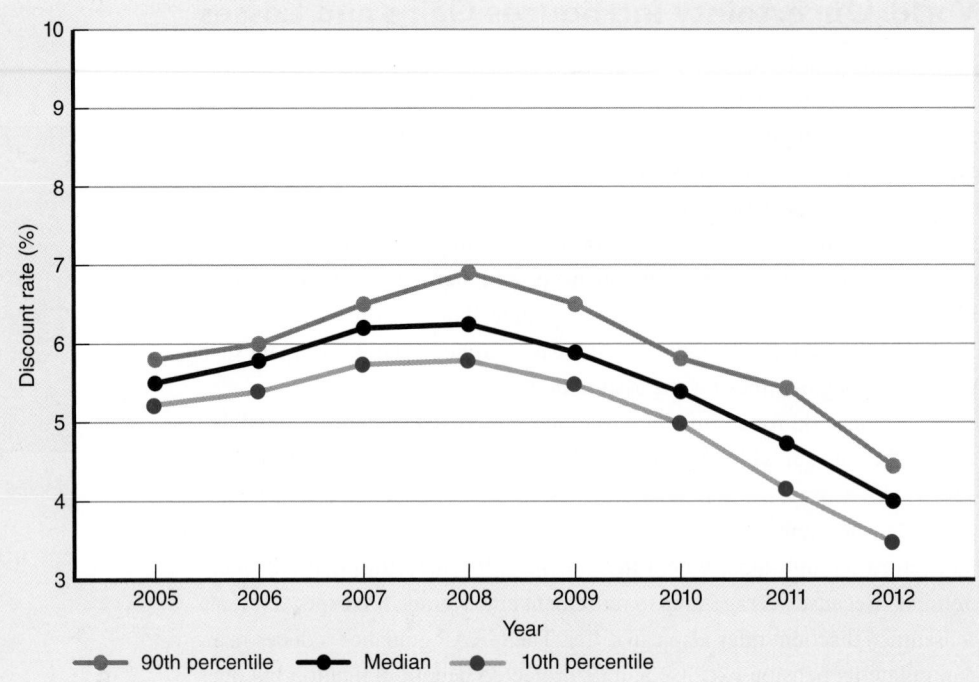

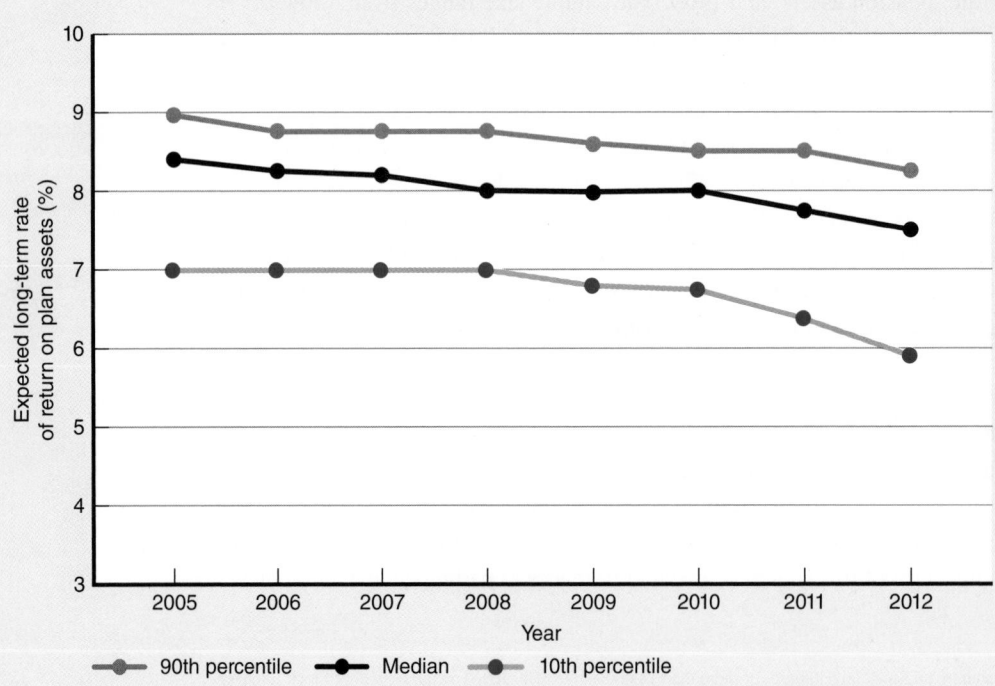

Figure 14.3 PENSION DISCOUNT RATE AND EXPECTED LONG-TERM RATE OF RETURN ON PLAN ASSETS 2005–2012

Sample consists of all U.S. NYSE firms with defined benefit plans and necessary data.

Source: Standard & Poor's Compustat® as data source; methodology not verified or controlled by Standard & Poor's.

The expected rates of return on plan assets are higher than the discount rates. In addition, the expected rates did not decline as much as the discount rates. The median rate of return was 8.5% in 2005 and declined to 7.5% in 2012. We observe more variation across firms in the choice of the rate of return assumption than we saw with discount rate assumptions. However, most of the variation is at the low end. The 90th percentile rate is generally within 0.5% of the median rate of return of assumption. Again, this may be the result of SEC scrutiny of high expected rates. In addition, firms are now required to disclose the target percentages for the classes (i.e., investment types) of plan assets and the actual asset allocations to help analysts assess the reasonableness of the assumptions.[14]

Uncertainty not only complicates the measurement of service cost and interest cost but also means that actual outcomes will likely differ from expectations. For example, the **actual return** (the interest, dividends, and appreciation obtained during the year) on pension plan assets differs from the expected return, and actual turnover and pay increases differ from actuarial assumptions. As we are about to show, *these deviations between expected and actual events if recognized immediately—would inject volatility into the periodic measure of pension expense.* Managers abhor earnings volatility because of its potential negative effects on stock valuations and accounting-based contracts (see Chapters 6 and 7) and, not surprisingly, strong sentiments for reducing this volatility emerged early in the exposure draft stage of pre-Codification *SFAS No. 87*. Components 4 and 5 of the annual pension expense calculation are designed to smooth this volatility. Our discussion now turns to each of these smoothing components of pension expense.

Component 4—Recognized Gains or Losses

In a real-world environment that contains uncertainty, the actual return on pension plan assets can differ considerably from the expected return in any year. Without some smoothing mechanism, volatility in asset returns would translate directly into net income volatility because the return on plan assets reduces pension expense. As mentioned above, changes in assumptions underlying the PBO calculations can also give rise to losses (gains). We focus on plan asset losses (gains) in the illustration that follows. We discuss PBO actuarial gains and losses later in this section and throughout the remainder of the chapter.

To illustrate this volatility, let's assume that at the beginning of 2014, Roger Corporation's pension plan assets and PBO equal $200,000. There are no deferred gains or losses, and the balance sheet asset (liability) equals zero. Roger assumes a 5% discount rate. Also assume that it does not make contributions or pay benefits in 2014 or 2015. Its service cost and actual return are as follows:

	2014	2015
Service cost	$ 7,000	$7,500
Actual return	22,000	9,760

Interest cost is $10,000 (PBO of $200,000 × discount rate of 5%) in 2014 and $10,850 (PBO of $217,000 [beginning 2014 PBO of $200,000 + 2014 service cost of $7,000 + 2014 interest

---

[14] See FASB ASC Section 715-20-50: Compensation–Retirement Benefits—Defined Benefit Plans–General—Disclosure.

cost of \$10,000] × discount rate of 5%) in 2015. Using these amounts, the resulting plan assets, PBO, and funded status for 2014 and 2015, respectively follow:

	2014	**2015**
Fair value of plan assets		
Balance at 1/1	\$200,000	\$222,000
Actual return	22,000	9,760
Balance at 12/31	\$222,000	\$231,760
Projected benefit obligation		
Balance at 1/1	\$200,000	\$217,000
Service cost	7,000	7,500
Interest cost	10,000	10,850
Balance at 12/31	\$217,000	\$235,350
Funded status: Asset (liability)	\$ 5,000	\$ (3,590)

If no smoothing were permitted, Roger's pension expense in the two years would be:

	2014	**2015**
Service cost	\$ 7,000	\$ 7,500
Interest cost	10,000	10,850
Less: Actual return on plan assets	(22,000)	(9,760)
Pension expense (income)	\$ (5,000)	\$ 8,590

This accounting would result in recognition of the funded status on Roger's balance sheet. In 2014, to offset the pension income, a pension asset equal to \$5,000 would be created. In 2015, this asset would be reduced by the pension expense of \$8,590, resulting in a pension liability of \$3,590.

Although the funded status would be on the balance sheet, the extreme change in year-to-year pension expense (income)—\$5,000 income versus \$8,590 expense—would cause year-to-year volatility in the firm's operating income. GAAP guidance makes it possible to avert this volatility in pension expense by allowing firms to reduce pension expense by the *expected* return on plan assets rather than by the *actual* return. This result is accomplished in two steps:

> Recall from Chapter 2 that AOCI is the cumulative gain and that **OCI** is the change in AOCI for the year. OCI is the net of new gains and losses and reclassifications of prior gains and losses into net income.

- First, firms make an assumption about the expected long-term rate of return on plan assets (**rate of return assumption**). This rate should reflect the average long-term returns on the types of investments held in the pension trust. For example, long-term returns for stock investments would be expected to be higher than long-term returns for U.S. Treasury bonds. The dollar a mount of the expected return is computed by multiplying this rate by the market-related value of plan assets.

- Second, any difference between the dollar amount of the expected return and the actual return that is earned in a given year is recognized in OCI instead of pension expense.

If the cumulative balance of these gains (losses) becomes large relative to the pension plan assets and liabilities, some of the cumulative amount is shifted from AOCI to pension expense. The specific details of this shifting process are discussed in a later example.

To show how the initial smoothing works, assume that Roger expects to earn an 8% return. Under the GAAP smoothing approach, Roger's pension expense would be reduced by the *expected* return in each year—\$16,000 in 2014 (plan assets of \$200,000 × 8%) and \$17,760 in 2015 ([beginning 2014 plan assets of \$200,000 + 2014 actual return of 22,000] × 8%).

This expected return is pension expense Component 3 discussed earlier. The difference between the expected and actual return in each year is deferred using AOCI. Specifically:

	2014		2015	
Service cost		$ 7,000		$ 7,500
Interest cost		10,000		10,850
Less:				
Actual return on plan assets	$(22,000)		$(9,760)	
Gain (loss) excluded from pension expense	6,000		(8,000)	
Expected return on plan assets		(16,000)		(17,760)
Pension expense		$ 1,000		$ 590

In years such as 2014 when the actual return ($22,000) exceeds the expected return ($16,000),
an unrecognized gain of $6,000 (see highlight) occurs. ***Although the $6,000 is not recognized
in pension expense, it is recognized in OCI.*** In 2015, the expected return of $17,760 exceeds
the actual return of $9,760 by $8,000. The $17,760 is included in pension expense, and the
$8,000 difference between expected return and actual return represents a loss within OCI. By
using the ***expected*** return to compute pension expense, the year-to-year *decrease* in Roger
Corporation's pension expense was only $410 (2015 pension expense of $590 less the 2014
pension expense of $1,000). In contrast, if ***actual*** return had been used to compute pension
expense, the year-to-year change in pension expense would have been an *increase* of $13,590
([2015 pension expense of $590 plus 2015 unrecognized loss of $8,000] minus [2014 pension
expense of $1,000 minus 2014 unrecognized gain of $6,000]).

The pre-tax effects on OCI and AOCI follow:

	2014	2015
AOCI (loss) – 1/1	$ 0	$ 6,000
OCI (loss)	6,000	(8,000)
AOCI (loss) – 12/31	$6,000	$(2,000)

From these effects, we can see that OCI reflects the volatility removed from pension expense.
By recognizing the gain and loss in OCI, Roger will still recognize a balance sheet pension
asset (liability) equal to the funded status—just as it would have if actual return had been used
to compute pension expense. The details of the journal entries to obtain the asset (liability)
amount are discussed later in the chapter.

See Figure 14.4 for a graphic presentation of how much actual returns can differ from
expected returns. The data in Figure 14.4 come from the pension notes for General Electric
Company (GE) for the years 2006–2012, excerpts of which are given in Exhibit 14.3. The data
highlighted in the last row of Exhibit 14.3, Panel (a) represent the deferred portion of each
year's actual return. This is the amount of the gain or loss excluded from pension expense, and
it is represented by the vertical distance between the actual return line and expected return line
in Figure 14.4. Note that in four of the years (2006, 2007, 2010, and 2012), this deferral increases (debits) pension expense. In three years (2008, 2009, and 2011), the deferral reduces
(credits) pension expense. The deferred gains and losses were off-balance-sheet prior to 2006.
Upon adoption of pre-Codification *SFAS No. 158,* the cumulative gains and losses became
part of AOCI. So, in 2008, the $20.867 billion loss for the difference between actual return
and expected return was ***excluded*** from pension expense but was ***included*** in OCI. We discuss
GE's journal entries for 2012 in detail later in the chapter.

Figure 14.4

GENERAL ELECTRIC
COMPANY

Comparison of Actual and
Expected Return on Pension
Plan Assets (2006–2012)

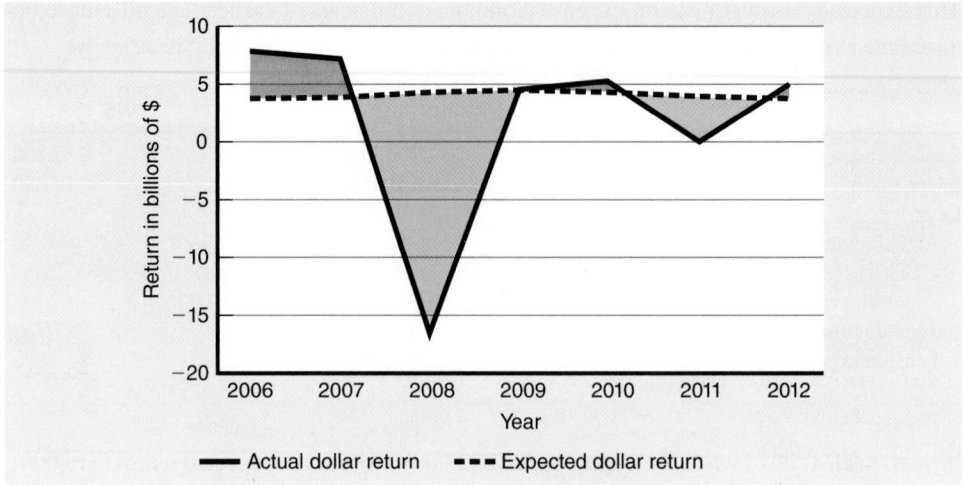

Exhibit 14.3, Panel (b) shows that GE's expected return as a percentage of beginning plan assets remained relatively stable during the period, while the actual rate of return ranged from a high of 16.0% in 2006 to a low of negative 27.8% in 2008. For the years 2007 to 2008, the actual dollar return on GE's plan assets went from *positive* $7.188 billion to *negative* $16.569 billion. GE's earnings before income taxes were $27.528 billion and $19.782 billion for 2007 and 2008, respectively. Clearly, without some mechanism to smooth out the big swings in the yearly actual returns on pension assets, considerable volatility would be introduced into GE's pension expense and net income.

How Component 4 Is Measured   Because pension accounting requires numerous assumptions about future events, differences between forecasted amounts and subsequent

EXHIBIT 14.3	**Excerpts from General Electric Company Notes Underlying Figure 14.4 Data**						
($ in billions)	**2006**	**2007**	**2008**	**2009**	**2010**	**2011**	**2012**
Panel (a)—Difference between actual and expected return							
Actual dollar return	$ 7.851	$ 7.188	($16.569)	$ 3.859	$ 5.280	$ 0.088	$ 4.854
Less: Expected dollar return	$ 3.811	$ 3.950	$ 4.298	$ 4.505	$ 4.344	$ 3.940	$ 3.768
Difference [gain (loss) excluded from pension expense]	$ 4.040	$ 3.238	($20.867)	($ 0.646)	$ 0.936	($ 3.852)	$ 1.086
Panel (b)—Expected return and actual return as a % of beginning plan assets							
Fair value of plan assets[†]	$49.096	$54.758	$59.700	$40.730	$42.097	$44.801	$42.137
Expected return as a % of beginning plan assets	7.8%	7.2%	7.2%	11.1%	10.3%	8.8%	8.9%
Actual return as a % of beginning plan assets	16.0%	13.1%	−27.8%	9.5%	12.5%	0.2%	11.5%

[†] This is the value of the plan assets at the *start* of each year.

Source: General Electric Company annual reports, 2006–2012.

occurrences should be expected. Cumulative deferred net gains or losses can arise from three causes:

1. Cumulative differences between actual and expected returns on pension plan assets as illustrated in Exhibit 14.3 and Figure 14.4.
2. Cumulative differences between actuarial assumptions and actual experience (e.g., employee turnover, pay increases, and longevity beyond retirement).
3. Changes in assumptions (e.g., a change in the discount rate used for computing service cost and interest cost).

Authoritative accounting literature does not require each year's pension expense to reflect actual returns on plan assets or observed actuarial outcomes. Instead, the deferred loss (gain) is recognized in OCI with a corresponding increase (decrease) to the balance sheet pension liability. However, if the gains and losses do not offset one another over time, the periodic differences will ultimately accumulate and exceed a materiality threshold, called the **corridor** (discussed in detail below). Some of the excess gains or losses should be recognized as a component of pension expense once the corridor has been exceeded. This is the role of Component 4—recognized gains or losses.

The approach described below is the ***minimum*** amortization required by authoritative accounting literature.[15] First, the corridor is computed. It is defined as 10% of the *higher* of the following two numbers:

1. The PBO.
2. The market-related value (MRV) of the pension plan assets.

Second, the corridor is compared to the beginning balance of net actuarial loss (gain) in AOCI to determine whether it exceeds the corridor. If it does, then, third, the excess AOCI loss (gain) above the 10% corridor is amortized straight-line over the estimated **average remaining service period** (*an actuarial computation of the average number of years over which existing employees are expected to continue on the job*). We now walk through an example to illustrate the corridor method step-by-step.

On January 1, 2014, Dore Corporation has ($1,600,000) in AOCI−actuarial (gain) loss. The MRV of pension plan assets on that date is $10,000,000, and the PBO is $8,500,000. The estimated average remaining service period of active employees is 15 years.

Figure 14.5 shows the steps in computing Component 4—recognized gains or losses. The 10% corridor is computed by first comparing the size of the MRV ($10,000,000) with the PBO ($8,500,000) and choosing the higher—the $10,000,000 MRV in this instance. This $10,000,000 is then multiplied by 10% to arrive at the corridor of $1,000,000 (see Step 1 in Figure 14.5). Because the gain of $(1,600,000) is more than the $1,000,000 corridor, the recognition mechanism is triggered (see Step 2). ***This means that component 4—recognized gains or losses—will be included in computing pension expense for the year.*** The $(600,000) amount in excess of the threshold will be amortized over 15 years. This amortization means that pension expense component 4 will be *reduced* for $40,000 ($[600,000]/15), thereby *reducing* pension expense (see Step 3). AOCI—actuarial (gain) loss also will be reduced by $40,000, thereby decreasing it to $(1,560,000).

If there were no future actuarial gains or losses and the MRV remained constant, the $560,000 unamortized excess ($600,000 − $40,000) would be fully amortized into income over the ensuing

---

[15] A systematic method consistently applied to both gains and losses that results in a larger amount is permissible [FASB ASC Paragraphs 715-30-35-24 and -25: Compensation–Retirement Benefits—Defined Benefit Plans–Pension—Subsequent Measurement—Gains and Losses]. This approach is discussed further at the end of this section.

Figure 14.5

COMPUTING COMPONENT
4—RECOGNIZED GAINS
OR LOSSES

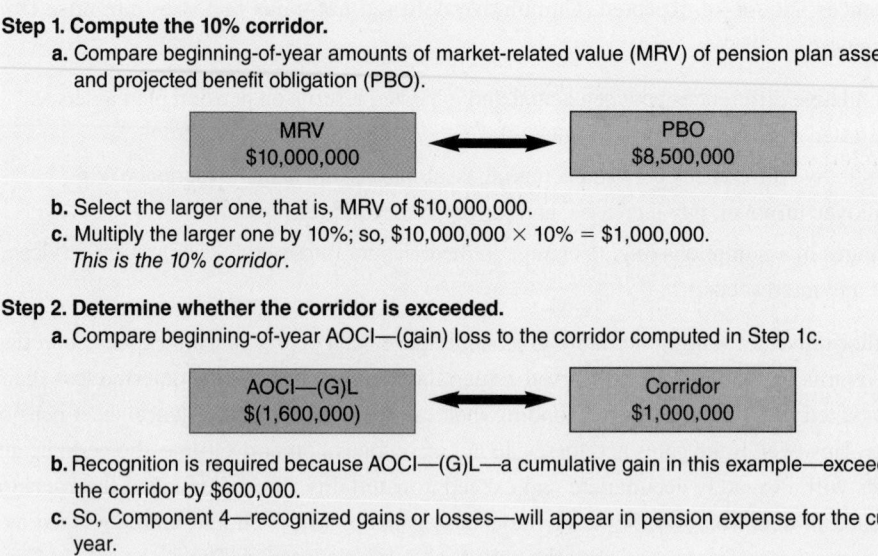

Step 1. Compute the 10% corridor.
  a. Compare beginning-of-year amounts of market-related value (MRV) of pension plan assets and projected benefit obligation (PBO).

MRV		PBO
$10,000,000	⟷	$8,500,000

  b. Select the larger one, that is, MRV of $10,000,000.
  c. Multiply the larger one by 10%; so, $10,000,000 × 10% = $1,000,000.
  This is the 10% corridor.

Step 2. Determine whether the corridor is exceeded.
  a. Compare beginning-of-year AOCI—(gain) loss to the corridor computed in Step 1c.

AOCI—(G)L		Corridor
$(1,600,000)	⟷	$1,000,000

  b. Recognition is required because AOCI—(G)L—a cumulative gain in this example—exceeds the corridor by $600,000.
  c. So, Component 4—recognized gains or losses—will appear in pension expense for the current year.

Step 3. Compute the current year's Component 4 amortization.
  a. Obtain the average remaining service period (ARSP) figure from the actuary. Here, ARSP equals 15 years.
  b. Divide the amount by which AOCI—(G)L exceeds the corridor (Step 2.b) by ARSP.

AOCI—(G)L – Corridor		ARSP
$(600,000)	÷	15 years

  c. *The quotient from Step 3b, $(40,000) (that is, $[600,000]/15) is the Component 4 amount for the current year. Pension expense will be reduced by $40,000 in the current year.*

14 years. Realistically, however, pension accounting requires many assumptions about uncertain future events, and uncertainty means that further adjustments are likely. Consequently, **GAAP *requires that the computation illustrated in the example be recalculated at the start of each subsequent year to determine that year's pension expense Component 4.*** Nonetheless, just because Component 4 was required in 2014 doesn't necessarily mean it will be required again in 2015.

To illustrate, let's assume that one year later—on January 1, 2015—Dore Corporation's AOCI—actuarial (gain) loss has fallen to $(250,000), plan assets are $11,000,000, and the PBO is $9,000,000. The 10% corridor is now $1,100,000 (that is, $11,000,000 × 0.10). This is higher (in terms of absolute value) than the $(250,000). Thus, the corridor is not exceeded, and no amortization would be required in 2015.

Why does GAAP use the PBO and the MRV of pension plan assets as the two benchmarks that potentially trigger the Component 4 amortization? Measures of projected benefit obligations and plan assets constitute the "critical 10% corridor" because the factors giving rise to the cumulative gain or loss represent misestimates of the "real" pension plan obligations and assets. In other words, gains and losses occur because the expected return on plan assets included in pension expense understated or overstated the actual return on pension assets. Similarly, gains or losses related to service cost and interest cost included in pension expense understated or overstated the actual increase in pension obligations. Thus, obligations and assets constitute the appropriate benchmarks for assessing when the cumulative error is "excessive." The 10% corridor is simply an arbitrary measure of this "excessiveness."

Immediate Recognition of Losses (Gains)   In 2010 and 2011, a number of companies with significant pension/other postretirement benefit exposure changed from the corridor method to the immediate recognition method for recognizing actuarial losses (gains).[16] As mentioned earlier, U.S. GAAP allows faster amortization methods as long as the methods are systematic. AT&T was one the first companies to make the change. The effect of the change was to transfer $17.0 billion of losses held in AOCI to Retained earnings.[17] Examination of prior years' financial statements shows that most of these losses came from poor asset returns in 2008.

By making the change, AT&T kept these losses from being amortized to pension/other postretirement expense in future years. However, the change exposed the company to future volatility in pension expense (see the prior Roger example). Because of the severe interest rate declines in 2011 and 2012 (see Figure 14.3), AT&T suffered large actuarial losses that had to be recognized in pension expense immediately. ***AT&T recognized pre-tax net actuarial losses of $9.4 billion and $6.2 in 2012 and 2011, respectively.*** To put these amounts in perspective, service cost was $1.5 billion in 2012. Other companies that followed AT&T's approach experienced similar fates.

Component 5—Recognized Prior Service Cost

Pension plans may be amended to increase or decrease benefits to employees. Firms may enhance—or "sweeten"—pension plans for various reasons. One is to generate employee goodwill and loyalty to the organization, thereby retaining a quality workforce. Another reason for pension enhancement—particularly retroactive enhancement—is a result of union demands in labor negotiations. However, if a company suffers financial difficulties, as have many airlines in recent years, it may amend the plan to *reduce* benefits. When a firm *retroactively* enhances (reduces) the benefits provided by its pension plan, past pension expense and pension funding—which were both based on the "old" pension plan terms—were too low (high). This also means that when a firm enhances (reduces) its pension plan benefits, it immediately increases (decreases) its projected benefit obligation under the plan. The dollar amount of the increase (decrease) in the projected benefit obligation due to plan enhancements (reductions) is called **prior service cost.** Component 5 adjusts pension expense for prior service cost. Here's an example that illustrates how prior service cost arises:

Schiller Corporation's pension plan contract grants employees a pension of 2% of ending salary at retirement for each year of service to a maximum of 30 years. Therefore, an employee with 30 years of service at Schiller could retire with a pension equal to 60% of her or his salary at retirement.

Schiller's management now believes that the 60% pension maximum is inadequate given existing general economic conditions. The pension plan is retroactively changed on January 1, 2014. Under the revised plan, employees qualify for a pension of 2.25% of ending salary at retirement for each year of service, again to a maximum of 30 years. Under the revised plan, the maximum pension is 67.5% of the employee's salary at retirement (2.25% × 30 years).

Based on Schiller's employee demographics and expected salaries, the plan enhancement increases the projected benefit obligation by $14,000,000. The average remaining service period of employees expected to receive benefits under the plan is 10 years.

Although the plan enhancements are computed on the basis of services rendered in prior periods, the benefits to the firm will be realized in future periods. The firm realizes the benefits of retroactive plan enhancements in future periods because of decreased employee turnover or better labor relations. Accordingly, authoritative accounting literature allows this

[16] See B. Burr, *Pensions & Investments,* February 21, 2011, www.pionline.com.
[17] See AT&T Inc. Form 8-K, January 13, 2011.

$14,000,000 amount of prior service costs to be amortized into pension expense on a straight-line basis over the expected remaining 10-year service lives of employees who are expected to receive benefits under the plan. So, $1,400,000 would be added to pension expense over each of the next 10 years (that is, $14,000,000/10). This is the role of Component 5.

Similar to net actuarial losses, *new* prior service costs credit (increase) the balance sheet liability and debit (decrease) OCI and AOCI. In the Schiller example, as the prior service cost is amortized, pension expense is debited for $1,400,000, and OCI—Prior service cost is credited for the same amount. The amortization effectively transfers debits held in AOCI to pension expense (and consequently, net income and retained earnings). We discuss the balance sheet effects of Components 4 and 5 in detail in the Adess Corporation example below.

RE CAP

Assumptions pervade pension accounting. When reality is different from assumptions or assumptions change, the resulting change in estimate could be recognized immediately as part of pension expense. Doing this would make pension expense volatile from year to year. GAAP allows the gains and losses to be initially recognized in OCI. If the cumulative net gains or losses exceed a materiality threshold called the *corridor*, a portion of the excess is recognized as Component 4 of pension expense. Firms may amend pension plan agreements to improve or reduce pension benefits as market conditions change. When an amendment is made, the effect on PBO is initially recognized in OCI and amortized from AOCI to Component 5 of pension expense over future years.

Journal Entries for Changes in Funded Status

To illustrate the journal entries for pension expense, let's assume that Adess Corporation discloses the following components in its pension note at December 31, 2014:

Service cost (Component 1)	$23,000
Interest cost (Component 2)	42,500
Expected return on plan assets (Component 3)	(38,250)
Amortization of actuarial loss (Component 4)	10,000
Amortization of prior service cost (Component 5)	12,750
2014 Pension expense	$50,000

> In the journal entries involving AOCI and OCI, we make entries to OCI. New gains or losses and reclassifications included in OCI for the year must be closed to AOCI and disclosed in the notes related to comprehensive income or the statement of shareholders' equity. We discuss this issue in more depth at the end of the General Electric pension example.

Service cost (Component 1) and interest cost (Component 2) increase PBO, and expected return (Component 3) increases plan assets. Because the sum of service cost and interest cost exceeds expected return by $27,250 ($23,000 + $42,500 − $38,250), funded status declines by $27,250. To reflect this decline in funded status, Adess makes the following journal entry:

Journal Entry 1: Pension expense Components 1–3

DR	Pension expense	....	$27,250	
	CR	Pension asset (liability)	....		$27,250

If the net balance in the Pension asset (liability) is a debit, it would be classified as an *asset*. If the net balance is a credit, it would appear on the balance sheet as a *liability*. Components 4 and 5 are transfers from AOCI and do not affect funded status. Consequently, we make the following entry to record their effects on pension expense:

Journal Entry 2: Pension expense Components 4 and 5

DR	Pension expense	....	$22,750	
	CR	OCI—net actuarial loss	....		$10,000
	CR	OCI—prior service cost	....		12,750

These two entries may be combined into one entry, but we use two entries to make it easier to trace the effects.

   In addition to service cost and interest cost, plan amendments also can change PBO. If the amendment increases pension benefits, the PBO increases, thereby decreasing funded status at the time of the amendment. Decreases in benefits would have the opposite effects on PBO and funded status. Amendments are recognized in the Pension asset (liability) account, but the offset is recorded in OCI—prior service cost instead of Pension expense. To illustrate, assume that Adess adopted an amendment, the total of which increased PBO by $27,700. To record the effect of the amendment, Adess makes the following entry:

Journal Entry 3: Plan amendment

DR	OCI—prior service cost	$27,700	
	CR Pension asset (liability)		$27,700

The net effect of entries 2 and 3 is a debit to OCI—prior service cost of $14,950 ($27,700 from journal entry 3 less $12,750 from journal entry 2).

   We now turn to events that affect plan assets. Entry 1 was based on expected return. If the actual return differs from expected return, then an additional entry must be made to reflect funded status on the balance sheet. As stated earlier, the difference between actual and expected return must be recognized in OCI with the offsetting debit or credit to the Pension asset (liability) account. To illustrate, assume that Adess Corporation's expected return exceeds its actual return by $5,000. To record this difference, Adess makes the following entry:

Journal Entry 4: Difference between actual and expected return

DR	OCI—net actuarial loss	$5,000	
	CR Pension asset (liability)		$5,000

The net effect of entries 2 and 4 is a credit to OCI—net actuarial loss of $5,000 ($10,000 from journal entry 2 less $5,000 from journal entry 3).

   An entry identical to Entry 4 would be made for increases or decreases to PBO caused by changes in assumptions or experience losses or gains.

   A firm typically funds an amount different than pension expense. (Factors that affect firms' funding policies are discussed in the next section.) Also, the timing of pension plan contributions does not usually match the timing of expense recognition. As contributions increase plan assets, the Pension asset (liability) account is *debited* for the amount of the contribution. Assuming that Adess Corporation chooses to fund $53,000 in 2014, the entry is:

Journal Entry 5: Plan contribution

DR	Pension asset (liability)	$53,000	
	CR Cash..		$53,000

   After making these entries, Adess Corporation's balance sheet Pension asset (liability) account will equal its funded status. Consistent with the prior Robie example, we did not make an entry for benefits paid to retirees. Because both plan assets and PBO are typically reduced by the same amount for benefits paid to retirees, there is no effect on funded status, and consequently, no journal entry is required.

Determinants of Pension Funding

Labor law, income tax rules, and varying cash flow needs strongly impact a firm's pension plan funding. Let's first consider the role of labor law.

   The U.S. Congress enacted legislation to regulate private U.S. *defined benefit* pension plans in 1974. The **Employees Retirement Income Security Act (ERISA)** was designed to protect workers covered by company- or industry-sponsored pension plans. This law was deemed necessary because some companies with underfunded pension plans went out of business and defaulted on their obligations to pay benefits to employees. When Studebaker Corporation—once a major automobile manufacturer headquartered in South Bend, Indiana—experienced severe economic hardship and declared bankruptcy in 1964, its pension liabilities greatly exceeded its plan assets. Studebaker retirees were unprotected and consequently lost most of their promised pensions. Such hardships ultimately motivated legislation designed to prevent recurrences.

ERISA introduced minimum funding requirements, limited investments in employer stock to 10% of plan assets, and created the **Pension Benefit Guaranty Corporation (PBGC)** to assume pension obligations when sponsors are bankrupt and plan assets are inadequate.[18] The PBGC receives its funds from defined benefit plan sponsors.[19] In 2000, the PBGC had a surplus of $9.7 billion. However, low stock returns and low discount rates led to a $23.3 billion deficit by the end of 2004.[20] The bankruptcies of large airlines and manufacturers with billions of unfunded pension liabilities worsened the deficit.

To provide additional protection to plan participants and to improve PBGC's health, **The Pension Protection Act of 2006 (PL 109-280)** [hereafter, PPA] amended ERISA. Its provisions were implemented in phases from 2008 to 2011. The law required firms to reduce the amount of underfunding more quickly than they would have under prior law. Additionally, the law created an "at-risk" category for severely underfunded plans and required them to reduce the underfunding faster. The PPA included guidelines for determining whether a plan is overfunded or underfunded, and the PBGC issued additional interpretive regulations.[21] These guidelines and regulations differ from those in authoritative accounting literature as to how liabilities are defined and what assumptions are to be used.

As of September 30, 2008, the deficit had fallen to $10.7 billion. However, *within one year, at September 30, 2009, this deficit approximately doubled to $21.1 billion* due to low interest rates and the assumption of pension obligations of bankrupt companies, such as Lehman Brothers, Delphi Corporation, IndyMac Bank, Circuit City, and Nortel.[22] Despite the PPA, in 2012, the PBGC's deficit of $29.14 billion was larger than the deficit that prompted the PPA. To reduce the PBGC deficits, the U.S. Congress has now indexed for inflation the flat and variable premiums. In addition, the PBGC works with companies and manages its assets to mitigate its losses.

The U.S. income tax law also influences pension plan funding. Because plan contributions are tax deductible and plan earnings are nontaxable to the plan sponsor, there is a tax incentive to overfund pension plans. Because of this incentive, the tax law limits the deductibility of contributions to already overfunded pension plans. Consequently, a firm with an overfunded plan limits its funding to an amount that is deductible for tax purposes.

Finally, firms with pension plans have a wide range of other uses for cash flows generated by operating activities. Examples include plant expansion, corporate acquisitions, debt retirement, and dividend increases. So, firms sometimes reduce or even forgo funding of the current period's pension expense—provided minimum ERISA funding guidelines are satisfied—to meet competing investment or financing cash needs.

---

[18] The PBGC only partially guarantees benefits. The maximum annual pension benefit it guaranteed in 2012 was $55,840.92. This amount is adjusted for changes to the Social Security wage base. See Pension Benefit Guaranty Corporation, 2012 Annual Report, p. 30. This limitation affects high-wage employees, such as pilots, autoworkers, and investment managers.

[19] The payment formula has been amended several times since 1974. In 2013, sponsors paid a $42 flat fee per participant plus a variable premium of $13 per $1,000 of underfunding. See Pension Benefit Guaranty Corporation, 2012 Annual Report, p. 28.

[20] See J. VanDerhei, "Retirement Income Adequacy after PPA and FAS 158: Part One—Plan Sponsors' Reactions," *EBRI Issue Brief no. 307,* n.d., www.ebri.org, July 2007, p. 4.

[21] See Pension Benefit Guaranty Corporation, *Federal Register* 72, no. 104 (May 31, 2007).

[22] See Pension Benefit Guaranty Corporation, 2009 Annual Report, pp. 3 and 79.

The long term pension funding strategy that a firm chooses to follow is determined not only by its internal cash flow needs but also by many complex economic forces. Two studies sought to explain firms' funding strategies by examining the relationship between **funding ratios**—plan assets divided by pension obligations—and a variety of variables that represent the economic incentives (and costs) associated with pension funding.[23] These economic incentives can be broadly classified as (1) tax incentives, (2) finance incentives, (3) labor incentives, and (4) contracting/political cost incentives.

The findings of this research follow:

- Firms with high marginal tax rates tend to have higher funding ratios—higher marginal tax rates provide an incentive to overfund.

- Firms with less stringent capital constraints and larger union membership tend to have higher funding ratios.

- Firms with more "precarious" debt/equity ratios (that is, firms close to violating debt covenant restrictions) tend to fund a lower proportion of their pension obligations.

In general, variables designed to measure political costs were not found to be significant determinants of pension funding ratios.

Tax and labor laws govern pension funding. While economic incentives appear to influence long-term corporate pension funding strategies, our understanding of this multidimensional decision is far from complete.

RECAP

CASE STUDY OF PENSION RECOGNITION AND DISCLOSURE—GENERAL ELECTRIC

To understand how pension plan assets and liabilities change during the year and how these changes affect the financial statements, analysts must understand the pension note disclosures required under FASB ASC 715. We build on prior examples by analyzing excerpts of General Electric's 2012 pension note (see Exhibit 14.4). We have numbered the schedules to make it easier to follow our explanations.

> The total is called "cost," not "expense," because some of the pension costs go into inventory before they are expensed in cost of sales.

Schedule 1 shows the components of pension cost. Note that they mirror the components described in prior examples. Expected return, service cost, and interest cost are relatively stable for the three-year period. Service cost is less in absolute magnitude than expected return and interest cost, which is typical of mature plans. Service cost is 56% of interest cost and 37% of expected return. In younger plans, service cost would be a higher percentage. GE's service cost will decrease in future years because it has ended defined benefit coverage for new workers (see plan description above Schedule 1). GE reports an increasing amount of prior service cost amortization due to a 2011 plan amendment. The amount of net actuarial loss recognition increased from $1,336 million in 2010 to $3,421 million in 2012. The increase in amortization comes from the large asset and PBO losses incurred in prior years. The note under Schedule 6 states that GE expects to amortize $3,650 million of actuarial losses in 2013.

Schedule 2 provides the actuarial and accounting assumptions. The 4.21% discount rate for 2011 is used to compute the PBO at December 31, 2011, and the service cost and interest cost for 2012. The 3.75% assumed compensation increases is also used to compute the December 31,

---

[23] See J. R. Francis and S. A. Reiter, "Determinants of Corporate Pension Funding Strategy," *Journal of Accounting and Economics,* April 1987, pp. 35–60; and J. K. Thomas, "Corporate Taxes and Defined Benefit Pension Plans," *Journal of Accounting and Economics,* July 1988, pp. 199–238.

EXHIBIT 14.4	General Electric Company: Edited, Condensed 2012 Pension Benefits Note

PRINCIPAL PENSION PLANS are the GE Pension Plan and the GE Supplementary Pension Plan.[*]

The GE Pension Plan provides benefits to certain U.S. employees based on the greater of a formula recognizing career earnings or a formula recognizing length of service and final average earnings. Certain benefit provisions are subject to collective bargaining. Salaried employees who commence service on or after January 1, 2011 and any employee who commences service on or after January 1, 2012 will not be eligible to participate in the GE Pension Plan, but will participate in a defined contribution retirement program.

The GE Supplementary Pension Plan is an unfunded plan providing supplementary retirement benefits primarily to higher-level, longer-service U.S. employees. . . .

Schedule 1: Cost of Pension Plans

($ in millions)		2012	2011	2010
Expected return on plan assets	①	$(3,768)	$(3,940)	$(4,344)
Service cost for benefits earned	②	1,387	1,195	1,149
Interest cost on benefit obligation	③	2,479	2,662	2,693
Prior service cost amortization	④	279	194	238
Net actuarial loss amortization	⑤	3,421	2,335	1,336
Pension plans cost		$3,798	$2,446	$1,072

Schedule 2: Actuarial Assumptions

The actuarial assumptions at December 31 are used to measure the year-end benefit obligations and the pension costs for the subsequent year.

	December 31,			
	2012	2011	2010	2009
Discount rate	3.96%	4.21%	5.28%	5.78%
Compensation increases	3.90	3.75	4.25	4.20
Expected return on assets	8.00	8.00	8.00	8.50

Schedule 3: Accumulated Benefit Obligation

	December 31,	
($ in millions)	2012	2011
GE Pension Plan	$55,664	$53,040
GE Supplementary Pension Plan	4,114	3,643

Schedule 4: Projected Benefit Obligation

($ in millions)		2012	2011
Balance at January 1		$60,510	$51,999
Service cost for benefits earned		1,387	1,195
Interest cost on benefit obligations		2,479	2,662
Plan amendments	⑥	—	804
Participant contributions		157	167
Actuarial loss[(a)]	⑦	2,021	6,803
Benefits paid		(3,052)	(3,120)
Balance at December 31[(b)]		$63,502	$60,510

[(a)] Principally associated with discount rate changes.

[(b)] The PBO for the GE Supplementary Pension Plan, which is an unfunded plan, was $5,494 million and $5,203 million at year-end 2012 and 2011, respectively.

(continued)

EXHIBIT 14.4   **General Electric Company: Edited, Condensed 2012 Pension Benefits Note *(continued)***

Schedule 5: Fair Value of Plan Assets

($ in millions)		2012	2011
Balance at January 1		$42,137	$44,801
Actual gain on plan assets	⑧	4,854	88
Employer contributions	⑨	642	201
Participant contributions	⑩	157	167
Benefits paid	⑪	(3,052)	(3,120)
Balance at December 31		$44,738	$42,137

Schedule 6: Pension Asset (Liability)

	December 31,	
($ in millions)	2012	2011
Funded status[c]	$(18,764)	$(18,373)
Pension asset (liability) recorded in the Statement of Financial Position		
Pension asset	$ —	$ —
Pension liabilities		
Due within one year[d]	(159)	(148)
Due after one year	(18,605)	(18,225)
Net amount recognized	$(18,764)	$(18,373)
Amounts recorded in shareowners' equity (unamortized)		
Prior service cost	$ 1,406	$ 1,685
Net actuarial loss	24,437	26,923
Total	$25,843	$28,608

[c] Fair value of assets less PBO, as shown in the preceding tables.

[d] For principal pension plans, represents the GE Supplementary Pension Plan liability.

In 2013, we estimate that we will amortize $245 million of prior service cost and $3,650 million of net actuarial loss for the principal pension plans from shareowners' equity into pension cost. Comparable amortized amounts in 2012, respectively, were $279 million and $3,421 million for the principal pension plans. . . .

Schedule 7: Estimated Future Benefit Payments

($ in millions)	2013	2014	2015	2016	2017	2018–2022
Principal pension plans	$3,040	$3,100	$3,170	$3,230	$3,275	$17,680

FUNDING POLICY for the GE Pension Plan is to contribute amounts sufficient to meet minimum funding requirements as set forth in employee benefit and tax laws plus such additional amounts as we may determine to be appropriate. We contributed $433 million to the GE Pension Plan in 2012. The ERISA minimum funding requirements do not require a contribution in 2013. In addition, we expect to pay approximately $230 million for benefit payments under our GE Supplementary Pension Plan and administrative expenses of our principal pension plans. . . .

* *Author note:* The 2012 GE note includes additional sets of columns for other pension plans. These columns have been omitted to facilitate our discussion. We also have numbered the schedules and reordered some descriptions to make it easier for the reader to follow our discussions.

2011, PBO and the 2012 service cost. This rate is compounded annually to estimate the average salary at retirement. The 8.0% expected-return on assets assumption is used for accounting purposes to compute the expected return component of pension cost.[24] Changes in various pension rate assumptions affect reported pension amounts. An increase in the discount rate lowers service cost and PBO. If the assumed rate of compensation increases used in determining the PBO is lowered, service cost is reduced too. Also, an increase (decrease) in the *spread* between the discount rate and the assumed rate of compensation increase lowers (raises) service cost. Finally, an increase (decrease) in the expected return on plan assets decreases (increases) pension cost.

Schedule 3 provides an alternative measure of the pension liability, the **accumulated benefit obligation** (**ABO**). The ABO differs from the PBO in that the ABO does not include projected salary increases between the statement date and the employee's expected retirement date. Note that GE's reported ABO in Schedule 3 is less than its reported PBO in Schedule 4. If GE terminated its pension plan (i.e., prevented employees from earning additional pension benefits) as of December 31, 2012, it would have to pay only the ABO of $59,778 million ($55,664 million + $4,114 million) instead of the PBO of $63,502 million. This difference also represents the losses workers would suffer if they leave GE prior to retirement. Note that ***U.S. GAAP uses PBO for balance sheet and income statement recognition.***

Analysis

Schedule 6 provides the funded status of GE's pension plans. GE's funded status of $(18,764) million for 2012 is computed as the difference between the fair value of plan assets of $44,738 million (Schedule 5) and the PBO of $63,502 million (Schedule 4). As mentioned earlier in the chapter, when the fair value of pension assets exceeds plan liabilities, a plan is **overfunded.** If pension liabilities exceed the fair value of plan assets, a plan is **underfunded.** This funded status disclosure is important to statement readers because the plan sponsor—the reporting entity—is ultimately responsible for underfunded pension plans. Moreover, sometimes the reporting entity can reclaim a portion of the excess in overfunded plans. So, information about the funded status helps analysts assess the sponsor's financial condition.

Figure 14.6 summarizes the causes for increases and decreases in plan assets in a T-account format.[25] We use GE's fair value of plan assets disclosures in Exhibit 14.4, Schedule 5 to explain each element in the figure.

- Item A represents the beginning-of-period fair value of the pension plan assets. For GE, the January 1, 2012 (from December 31, 2011) amount totaled $42,137 million.

- Item B, the actual return on plan assets, increased the dollar value of plan assets. Generally, the amount is positive, but in very bad investment years, Item B can be negative as it was in 2008 [see Exhibit 14.3, Panel (a)]. GE's 2012 actual return on plan assets was a positive $4,854 million.

- Item C, the amount that the plan sponsor funds during the period, further increases plan assets. GE's 2012 contribution was $642 million.

- Item D, contributions by plan participants, also increases plan assets. During 2012, contributions by GE plan participants totaled $157 million.

---

[24] FASB ASC Section 715-30-50: Compensation–Retirement Benefits—Defined Benefit Plans–Pension–Disclosure requires firms to describe their approach to establishing the assumption, the target and actual asset allocation, and investment guidelines. Firms also must disclose investment categories, concentration of risk, fair value measurement methods, and the effects of using unobservable inputs (Level 3) on changes in asset values. These disclosures have been omitted from the GE excerpts to facilitate discussion.

[25] In addition to the items shown in Figure 14.6, FASB ASC Section 715-30-50: Compensation–Retirement Benefits—Defined Benefit Plans—Disclosure requires, if applicable, disclosure of (1) changes in plan assets arising from exchange rate changes for pension plans of certain foreign subsidiaries and (2) changes in plan assets arising from business combinations, divestitures, and plan settlements.

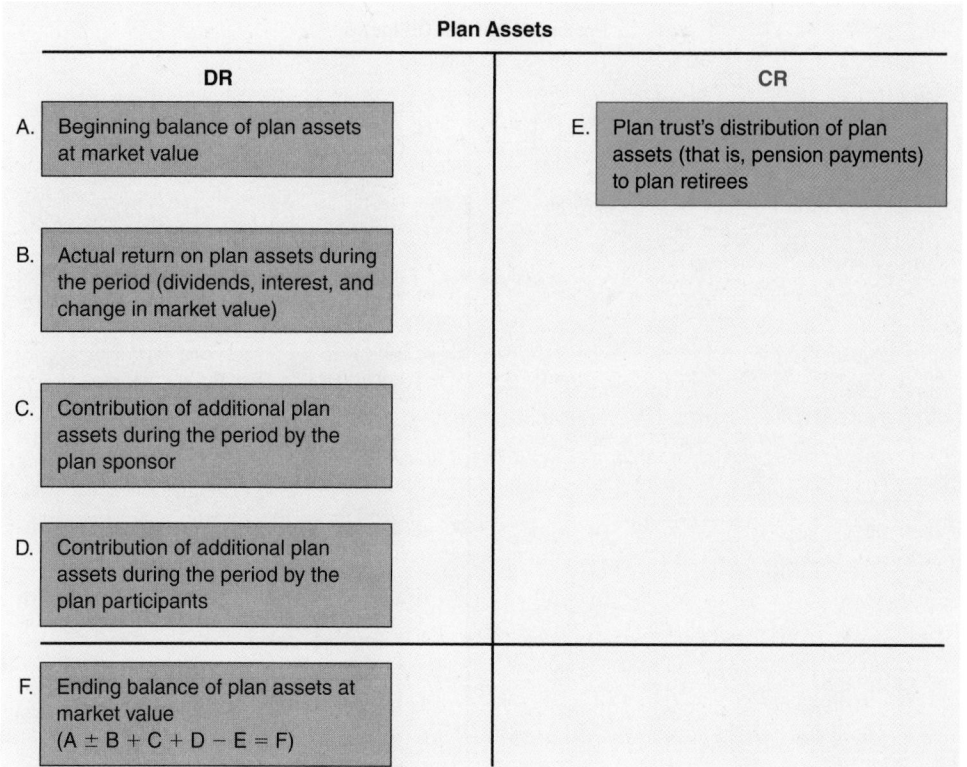

Plan Assets

DR	CR
A. Beginning balance of plan assets at market value	E. Plan trust's distribution of plan assets (that is, pension payments) to plan retirees
B. Actual return on plan assets during the period (dividends, interest, and change in market value)	
C. Contribution of additional plan assets during the period by the plan sponsor	
D. Contribution of additional plan assets during the period by the plan participants	
F. Ending balance of plan assets at market value $(A \pm B + C + D - E = F)$	

Figure 14.6

CAUSES OF INCREASES AND DECREASES IN PLAN ASSETS

Compare with Schedule 5 of Exhibit 14.4

- Retirees receive benefits during the period; these benefits are disbursed by the plan trust and reduce plan assets, as indicated by Item E. Benefits paid to participants by the plan trust in 2012 were $3,052 million.

- The end-of-period fair value of plan assets is Item F. This amount totaled $44,738 million for the GE plans.

Figure 14.7 summarizes the general reasons for increases and decreases to the PBO.[26] We use GE's projected benefit obligation disclosures in Exhibit 14.4, Schedule 4 to explain each element in Figure 14.7.

- Item G is the start-of-period present value of expected future benefits that will ultimately be paid both to active and already retired employees. The 2012 GE beginning amount is $60,510 million (also the December 31, 2011 amount).

- Item H represents the increase in benefits that active employees continue to earn from additional years of work. This increase in the PBO is service cost. GE's service cost in 2012 was $1,387 million.

- As time passes, interest accrues on the PBO (as shown in Item I). GE's 2012 interest cost was $2,479 million.

- Changes in economic and other social conditions cause firms to adjust promised benefits, as Item J indicates. These amendments either increase the PBO (when the plan is sweetened) or

---

[26] In addition to the items shown in Figure 14.7, FASB ASC Section 715-30-50: Compensation–Retirement Benefits—Defined Benefit Plans–Pension—Disclosure requires, if applicable, disclosure of (1) changes in the PBO arising from exchange rate changes for pension plans of certain foreign subsidiaries and (2) changes in the PBO arising from business combinations, divestitures, curtailments, plan settlements, and special termination benefits.

Figure 14.7

CAUSES OF INCREASES
AND DECREASES IN PBO

Compare with Schedule 4 of
Exhibit 14.4

Projected Benefit Obligation

DR	CR
M. Plan trust's distribution of plan assets (that is, pension payments) to plan retirees	G. Beginning balance. Start-of-period discounted present value of expected pension benefits that will ultimately be paid
	H. Service cost during the period
	I. Interest cost during the period
	J. Change in promised benefits arising from plan amendments or curtailments during the period
	K. Contribution of additional plan assets during the period by plan participants
	L. Actuarial gains or losses during the period from changes in assumptions (for example, mortality and turnover rates, interest rates)
	N. Ending balance. End-of-period discounted present value of expected pension benefits $(G + H + I \pm J + K \pm L - M = N)$

decrease it (when benefits are reduced). GE did not increase benefits for these plans in 2012. However, in 2011, a plan amendment increased PBO by $804 million (see item ⑥ in Schedule 4)

- Item K, contributions by plan participants, also increases the PBO. During 2012, such contributions totaled $157 million, which matches the employer contribution in the plan assets analysis (Schedule 5).

- The assumptions used in estimating the pension liability lead to gains or losses due to changing medical, lifestyle, and economic conditions. Denoted by Item L, these increases (or decreases) in the PBO can also arise from revised interest rate assumptions. Recall from earlier discussions that a *decrease* in the discount rate assumption results in an *increase* to the PBO. In 2012, GE decreased its discount rate assumption from 4.21% to 3.96%, which is consistent with the $2,021 million increase to PBO in 2012. If the changed assumptions produced gains, the PBO would have been reduced.

- Item M represents the payout of retirement benefits to participants. This is the offsetting debit to the Item E credit in Figure 14.6. GE's 2012 amount was $3,052 million.

- Finally, the ending PBO balance (Item N) is the net result of each of the preceding items. This amount totaled $63,502 million for the GE plans.

Often Exhibit 14.4 Schedules 4 (PBO) and 5 (plan assets) are shown in the same schedule, and the ending balances are netted to obtain the funded status (see the funded status schedule in the earlier Roger example). In GE's case, funded status is shown in Schedule 6—Pension Asset (Liability). The 2012 reported $(18,764 million) funded status is obtained by subtracting the ending PBO of $63,502 million (Schedule 4) from the ending plan assets of $44,738 million (Schedule 5). *The low asset returns and low discount interest rates occurring between 2008 and 2012 moved GE from an overfunded position of $16,753 million at the end of 2007 to the underfunded position of $(18,764 million) we observe in Schedule 6.*

Schedule 6 also shows how the funded status is recognized on the balance sheet. In 2012, the $(18,764) million in net pension liabilities is recognized across three accounts: Pension asset of $0, Pension liabilities—due within one year of $(159 million), and Pension liabilities—due after one year of $(18,605 million). In the previous examples, each firm had only one pension plan. However, it is common for large public companies such as GE to have multiple pension plans. Companies may wish to have different plan formulas for salaried versus nonsalaried workers or union versus nonunion workers. In addition, firms may have obtained a variety of plans by acquiring other companies. ASC paragraph 715-20-45-3 requires firms to group plans according to whether they are overfunded or underfunded. For underfunded plans, the portion of the PBO due in the next 12 months that exceeds plan assets must be classified as a current liability. For GE, the current liability relates to the GE Supplementary Pension Plan because it is unfunded (see note (d) below Schedule 6). There are no pension assets on the balance sheet because GE did not have any overfunded plans at the end of 2012.

Schedule 6 also shows the portion of the balance sheet pension assets and liabilities that have not yet been recognized in pension expense. As mentioned previously, these amounts are in AOCI. In GE's case, at the end of 2012, AOCI includes reductions for prior service cost of $1,406 million and net actuarial losses of $24,437 million. We show how AOCI changed during 2012 in conjunction with the journal entry discussion below.

To understand how pension accounting affected GE's 2012 financial statements, we use Schedules 1, 4, 5, and 6 to reconstruct the journal entries. In discussing them, we follow the order of the GE schedules and use the circled numbers. The entries are very similar to the ones we made in the Adess example earlier in the chapter. Some of these entries could be combined, but we try to make it easier to link the amounts in the note with the amounts in the journal entries.

We begin with the first three components of pension cost (Schedule 1, items ①, ②, and ③). The service cost and interest cost components of pension cost decrease funded status and increase the pension liability on the balance sheet. The *expected* return increases funded status and decreases the balance sheet pension liability.[27] To record these components of pension cost, we make the following journal entry:

Journal Entry 1	
	($ in millions)
DR Pension plans cost	$98
CR Pension liabilities—Due after one year	①+②+③ $98

The prior service cost (Schedule 1, item ④) and actuarial loss amortization (Schedule 1, item ⑤) components of pension cost do not affect funded status. Instead they represent

---

[27] Journal Entry 5 increases the balance sheet liability for the difference between actual return and expected return that is recognized in OCI.

transfers from AOCI. Consequently, the credits for these items go to OCI, not to Pension liabilities—Due after one year. Therefore, we make the following entry:

Journal Entry 2

			($ in millions)
DR	Pension plans cost		$3,700
	CR	OCI—Prior service cost	④ $ 279
	CR	OCI—Net actuarial loss	⑤ 3,421

The net effect of these two entries on pension cost is $3,798 million ($3,700 million from Journal Entry 2 plus $98 million from Journal Entry 1), the total pension cost shown in Schedule 1.

We now turn to the PBO reconciliation (Schedule 4). We have already made a journal entry for service cost and interest cost. The next row in the reconciliation shows that GE had plan amendments of $0 million. Although GE did not have amendments in 2012, we show how they would be handled to give a comprehensive explanation of how the PBO elements affect firm financial statements. These amendments normally increase PBO, and consequently decrease funded status and increase the pension liability. Under GAAP, the amendment affects OCI, not pension expense. Consequently, we make the following entry:

Journal Entry 3

			(in millions)
DR	OCI—Prior service cost		⑥ $0
	CR	Pension liabilities—Due after one year	$0

The next row in the reconciliation is participant contributions. We do not make an entry for this row because it is offset by an increase in plan assets (see Schedule 5, item ⑩). We use a similar rationale for benefits paid. The decrease of $3,120 million in the PBO reconciliation (Schedule 4) is offset in the plan assets reconciliation (Schedule 5, item ⑪).

The remaining row in the PBO reconciliation is an actuarial loss of $2,021 million (Schedule 4, item ⑦). In the Adess Corporation example, the only new actuarial gain was caused by the difference between the expected and the actual return on plan assets. In most cases, we also see gains or losses for changes in estimates of PBO. As mentioned in conjunction with Figure 14.7, these losses are consistent with the decrease in the discount rate assumption from 4.21% in 2011 to 3.96% in 2012 shown in Schedule 2. These losses increase PBO, and consequently, decrease the funded status and increase pension liabilities. We increase the net actuarial loss in AOCI at the beginning of the year with the following entry:

Journal Entry 4

			(in millions)
DR	OCI—Net actuarial loss (gain)		$2,021
	CR	Pension liabilities—Due after one year	⑦ $2,021

We now turn to the reconciliation of plan assets (Schedule 5). Journal entry 1 decreased Pension liabilities—Due after one year for *expected* return, but plan assets and consequently the funded status and the Pension liabilities—Due after one year must reflect *actual* return. Therefore, we must adjust the Pension liabilities—Due after one year for the difference between the actual return of $4,854 (Schedule 5, item ⑧) and the expected return of $3,768

(Schedule 1, item ①). In this case, the actual return exceeds the expected return by $1,086, so we credit decrease AOCI—Net actuarial loss with the following entry:

Journal Entry 5

		(in millions)
DR	Pension liabilities—Due after one year	$1,086
CR	OCI—Net actuarial loss (gain)	⑧+① $1,086

The next row in Schedule 5 is the employer contribution of $642 million item ⑨, which increases funded status and decreases the balance sheet pension liability. Consequently, we make the sixth journal entry:

Journal Entry 6

		(in millions)
DR	Pension liabilities—Due after one year	$642
CR	Cash..	⑨ $642

As mentioned in our earlier discussion of Schedule 6, the pension liabilities must be *reclassified* between long-term and current accounts. To obtain this entry, we compute the difference between the beginning and ending pension liability accounts shown in Schedule 6. The difference for the pension liabilities—Due within one year account is $11 million (the ending balance of $159 million less the beginning balance of $148 million). To accomplish the reclassification, we make the following entry:

Journal Entry 7

		(in millions)
DR	Pension liabilities—Due after one year	$11
CR	Pension liabilities—Due within one year	$11

Often when a firm has multiple plans, it may also have to reclassify some of the Pension liabilities—Due after one year to a Prepaid pension asset.

Figure 14.8 shows the cumulative effects of the journal entries on the Pension liabilities and OCI accounts. Note that the Pension liabilities—Due within one year and Pension

Journal Entry		(in millions) Pension liabilities— Due after one year	
	January 1, 2012		$18,225
1	Pension cost		98
3	Plan amendment		–
4	PBO actuarial loss		2,021
5	Actual return less expected return	$1,086	
6	Employer contribution	642	
			$18,616
7	Reclassification	11	
	December 31, 2012		$18,605

		Pension liabilities— Due within one year
	January 1, 2012	$148
7	Reclassification	11
	December 31, 2012	$159

Journal Entry		(in millions) OCI— Prior service cost	
2	Amortization		$279
3	Plan amendment	$ –	
			$279

		OCI— Net actuarial loss (gain)	
2	Amortization		$3,421
4	PBO actuarial loss	$2,021	
5	Actual return less expected return		1,086
			$2,486

Figure 14.8 ANALYSIS OF BALANCE SHEET LIABILITY AND OCI ACCOUNTS

liabilities—Due after one year accounts have ending balances of $(18,605 million) and $(159 million), respectively, which sum to the funded status of $(18,764 million) given in Exhibit 14.4, Schedule 6. Each OCI account also represents the change in AOCI balances given in Exhibit 14.4, Schedule 6. For example, AOCI—Net actuarial loss at December 31, 2012, of $24,437 million less the balance at December 31, 2011, of $26,923 million equals the Figure 14.8 OCI—Net actuarial loss (gain) of $2,486 million.

Accumulated Other Comprehensive Income Disclosure and Deferred Income Taxes

Thus far, we have ignored the effects of income taxes. As you learned in Chapter 2, all AOCI items must be shown net of tax. Additionally, the OCI components related to new plan amendments or new actuarial (gains) losses must be distinguished from the components related to amortization. The reason for distinguishing the sources of (gain) loss is so that investors can separate new changes in firm wealth from transfers of prior (gains) losses to pension expense and net income. See Exhibit 14.5 for the required disclosure for the GE pension plan. This type of disclosure is usually found in the statement of shareholders' equity or a note related to the statement.

The beginning and ending pre-tax AOCI amounts come from Exhibit 14.4, Schedule 6 and represent the total of the AOCI—Prior service cost and AOCI—Net actuarial loss. It is common to aggregate the separate beginning and ending AOCI balances. In fact, the beginning and ending balances often include gains and losses related to available-for-sale securities, derivatives, and foreign currency. The remaining pre-tax amounts can be traced directly to the OCI T-accounts in Figure 14.8. The New actuarial loss (gain) arising during period of $935 million equals the PBO actuarial loss of $2,021 million less the difference between the actual return and expected return of $1,086 million. The shaded pre-tax OCI amount of $(2,765 million) is the sum of the Figure 14.8 OCI T-account balances of $(279 million) and $(2,486 million).

The Tax Effect column in Exhibit 14.5 gives the tax effect for the pre-tax amounts. We obtain the tax effects by multiplying the assumed tax rate of 39% by the pre-tax amount. This rate is based on information in Note 15—Shareholder's Equity in GE's 2012 Annual Report.

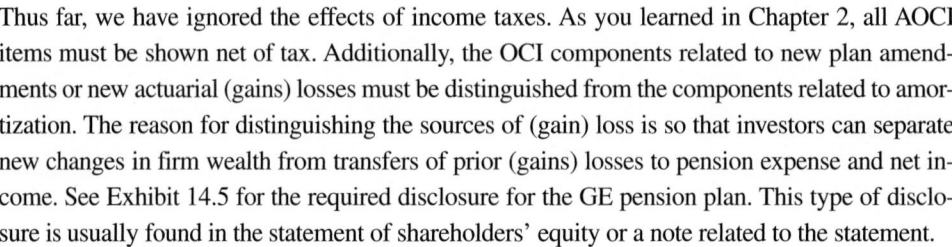

EXHIBIT 14.5	General Electric Company: AOCI Effects

Impact of Pensions on 2012 OCI and AOCI (Author Calculations)

	Pre-Tax	Tax Effect	After-Tax
AOCI—January 1, 2012	$28,608*	$11,157†	$17,451‡
Prior service cost from plan amendment	—		
Less: Amortization of prior service cost	(279)	(109)	(170)
Net prior service cost arising during period	(279)	(109)	(170)
New actuarial loss (gain) arising during period	935§	365	570
Less: Amortization of net actuarial loss	(3,421)	(1,334)	(2,087)
Net actuarial loss (gain) arising during period	(2,486)	(969)	(1,517)
OCI	(2,765)	(1,078)	(1,687)
AOCI—December 31, 2012	$25,843	$10,079	$15,764

* December 31, 2011 AOCI—Prior service cost of $1,685 million + December 31, 2011 AOCI—Net actuarial loss of $26,923 million (Exhibit 14.4, Schedule 6).

† The assumed tax rate is 39% for all rows. This rate is based on information contained in Note 15—Shareholders' Equity of GE's annual report. The tax effect amount is obtained by multiplying the tax rate by the pre-tax amount.

‡ The after-tax amount equals the difference between the pre-tax and the tax effect amounts.

§ PBO actuarial loss of $2,021 million less the difference between the actual return and expected return of $1,086 million.

Recall from our earlier discussions that GE receives a tax deduction when contributions are made and does not obtain tax deductions for pension expense or OCI losses recognized for GAAP purposes. Therefore, the tax effects result in a deferred tax asset instead of reductions in income tax payable. At January 1, 2012, GE has OCI tax-effect contra-accounts to offset the pre-tax shareholders' equity in the Figure 14.8 T-accounts. The AOCI—Prior service cost tax effect and AOCI—Net actuarial loss tax effect credit balances are $657 million ($1,685 million × 39%) and $10,500 million ($26,923 million × 39%), respectively. These balances sum to the $11,157 tax effect shown for the AOCI—January 1, 2012, row in Exhibit 14.5. The offsetting debit is to a Deferred tax asset account. To update the tax accounts for 2012 activity, GE makes the following entry:

		($ in millions)	
DR	OCI—Prior service cost **tax effect**	$109	
DR	OCI—Net actuarial loss (gain) **tax effect**	969	
	CR Deferred tax asset		$1,078

We debit the tax effect for OCI—Prior service cost because the amortization reduced the loss in AOCI. We also debit the tax effect for OCI—Net actuarial loss (gain) because there is a net credit to the pre-tax OCI account. The sum of these two entries reduces the Deferred income tax asset account discussed above.

The After-Tax column in Exhibit 14.5 represents the actual effects on AOCI income and OCI. Recall from Chapter 2 that OCI is added to net income to obtain comprehensive income. Because pension notes usually show before tax amounts and shareholders' equity notes show aggregate after-tax amounts, it is often difficult for the financial statement reader to link the two notes. We hope that this detailed analysis helps you understand better the ultimate after-tax effects of pensions on AOCI and OCI.

Additional Issues in Computing Expected Return

The GE example illustrates other complications that arise in calculating the expected return component of pension expense. Refer to Exhibit 14.4, Schedule 1. If we divide the 2012 $3,768 million expected return by the assumed rate of return of 8.0%, we obtain $47,100 million. Why doesn't this amount equal the beginning $42,137 million fair value of plan assets? Two factors contribute to the difference. First, recall from our initial discussion of expected return calculations that firms may define the MRV as fair value at a point in time or a smoothed fair value measured over several years. GE uses a smoothed fair value. Some of the asset losses arising from the low returns in 2008 and 2011 (see Figure 14.4) have not been included in the smoothed asset value.

Second, the expected return is to be computed using the beginning fair value of plan assets *after* adjusting for the timing of contributions and benefit payments made during the year. If GE had used the fair value of plan assets (as opposed to a smoothed value), the approximate value used to compute the expected return would have been $41,010.5 million, computed as $42,137 million Beginning fair value + (0.5 × [Employer contributions of $642 million, item ⑨ + Participant contributions of $157.0 million, item ⑩ − Benefits paid of $3,052.0 million, item ⑪]). Multiplying the payments and contributions by 0.5 assumes that they were made evenly throughout the year. In the prior examples, we did not have to make this adjustment because contributions were made at the end of each year, thereby receiving zero weight in the expected return calculation. Note that the $41,010.5 million is lower than the beginning fair value of plan assets and considerably lower than the asset value obtained by dividing the expected return by 8.0%.

The use of smoothed values also affects the amount of actuarial losses (gains) to be amortized. FASB ASC paragraph 715-30-35-24 states that the minimum amortization method should exclude gains and losses not yet included in the MRV. Furthermore, as mentioned earlier, the corridor is based on the higher of the MRV or the PBO.

The effects of these rules on GE's 2012 amortization calculations can be shown as follows:

($ in millions)

Net actuarial loss at January 1	$26,923.0
Difference between MRV and fair value	
($41,010.5 fair value less $47,100.0 MRV)	(6,089.5)
Amount subject to amortization	$20,833.5
Corridor − 10% of January 1 PBO (10% × $60,510)	6,051.0
Amount outside corridor	$14,782.5

As the MRV is decreased for prior asset losses, GE's amortization will increase because additional losses will increase the loss subject to amortization. The note below Schedule 6 states that GE will amortize $3,650 million of net actuarial losses in 2013, which is slightly higher than the 2012 amount of $3,421 million. In 2012, PBO was used to compute the corridor because it exceeded the MRV. When the MRV exceeds PBO, use of the MRV affects both the amount subject to amortization *and* the corridor.

Analysis

Unfortunately, the use of smoothed values is not clearly disclosed in financial statement notes. Most firms do not disclose their use of a smoothed MRV to compute expected return, and firms that do disclose the use of smoothed values generally do not describe their smoothing techniques. Firms may average gains and losses for both investment in equity and fixed income securities or limit smoothing to gains and losses on equity investments only. Furthermore, some firms may smooth gains and losses over three years while other firms smooth them over five years. A study of approximately 200 U.S. firms with large pension plans suggests that two-thirds of them were using some form of smoothing.[28] During the bull market of the late 1990s, fair values exceeded smoothed values by 15% to 20% for firms using the most extreme forms of smoothing. When interpreting financial statements, readers must assume that the expected return has been computed correctly. Because of the use of smoothed values, financial statement readers are not usually able to verify the expected return dollar amount by multiplying the stated rate of return by the beginning fair value of plan assets (adjusted for contributions and benefits). Estimating the next year's amortization component also is difficult. This problem is mitigated by the requirement to disclose the actuarial (gain) loss to be amortized to pension expense in the subsequent year (as we saw with GE).

Extraction of Additional Analytic Insights from Note Disclosures

By scrutinizing the causes for increases and decreases in plan assets in the pension note (see Figure 14.6), analysts can often make more refined estimates of future cash flows. For example, let's assume that the plan assets disclosure shows that a firm did not contribute additional funding during the reporting period. Also assume that the note shows that the fair value of plan assets barely exceeds the PBO at year-end. Because the plan was overfunded, the firm could *temporarily* suspend funding. But can it continue not to fund? Depending on the extent of the overfunding

---

[28] See P. Davis-Friday, J. Miller, and H. F. Mittelstaedt, "Market-Related Values and Pension Accounting," Working Paper, Mendoza College of Business, University of Notre Dame, 2007. The authors determine the extent of smoothing using an approach similar to the one used here in the analysis of General Electric's expected return calculation.

and future asset returns, the answer may be no. ***If its funded status were to change in future periods, the firm would be compelled to fund the plan in future years, thereby decreasing future net operating cash flows.*** Lenders and others who forecast future cash flows to estimate "safety cushions" must consider these factors when preparing their forecasts. Merely extrapolating the most recent net operating cash flow into future years would overlook the possibly unsustainable "boost" provided by the absence of current pension funding. Thus, while companies with greatly overfunded plans can suspend funding for long periods and use the cash for other operating purposes, underfunded plans may reflect past and continuing cash flow difficulties. Recall from earlier discussions that severely underfunded plans will be put into an at-risk category and be required to increase cash contributions. GAAP requires firms to provide their best estimate of the amount of funding expected to be paid into the plan in the ensuing year. This disclosure will help analysts forecast firms' future funding requirements. GE states that it expects to contribute $230 million to its Supplementary Pension Plan but it will not make a contribution to the GE Pension Plan. Despite the fact that GE's pension plan is underfunded for GAAP purposes, it will not be required to make contributions under tax and labor laws (see the discussion below Schedule 7 in Exhibit 14.4).

To help analysts determine whether fund assets are large enough to satisfy currently anticipated pension benefit payouts, FASB ASC Topic 715 requires firms to provide a table that lists the dollar benefits expected to be paid in each of the ensuing five years and in the aggregate for the five years thereafter. GE's information is shown in Schedule 7. For the next five years, annual payments increase from $3,040 million in 2013 to $3,275 million in 2017. The total amount expected to be paid from 2013 to 2022 is $33,495 million, or approximately 75% of the fair value of plan assets. Consequently, we would conclude that GE's pension plans could be a drain on long-term cash flow if plan assets do not recover.

As stated earlier in the chapter, the PBGC will take over an underfunded plan when a firm sponsor is in bankruptcy. But the PBGC tries to recover the pension payments from the pension plan sponsor. The PBGC claim ranks on an equal footing with those of unsecured creditors; accordingly, the funded status reconciliation could serve as an early warning device for signaling other cash demands on the firm.

Because pension funding status is important for assessing a firm's current and future cash flows, it is important to understand how sensitive the asset and liability measures are to changes in interest rates. For firms with a young workforce whose pension commitments will be paid 20 to 30 years in the future, small changes in discount rate assumptions can cause large increases in the present value of these estimated obligations. This large multiplier effect is due to the impact of duration—the further into the future the cash flows are to be paid out, the greater the impact of a change in interest rates on the present value of those cash flows. A common rule of thumb is that a 1% decrease in discount rate would *increase* PBO by 17.0% whereas a 1% increase would *decrease* it by 14.5%.[30] Again, the specific effect depends on the workforce demographics.

The effect of a 1% change in interest rates on the asset side is typically much smaller because fixed income investments generally represent only 30% to 40% of the pension asset

> As part of its bankruptcy reorganization in 2006, Delta Air Lines, Inc., terminated its pilots' pension plan and reached an agreement with the PBGC to assume responsibility of the plan in exchange for unsecured notes and claims totaling $2.425 billion. At the time of the agreement, the estimated underfunding in the pension plan was $3 billion. When Delta emerged from bankruptcy in April 2007, the PBGC converted $800 million of the claims into Delta common stock and continued to attempt to collect its remaining claims.[29]

---

[29] See R. Grantham, "Delta Air Lines: Pensions Fatter for Some Pilots: Guarantor Cites Stock, Assets," *The Atlanta Journal-Constitution,* August 21, 2007, p. C1; and "Business Brief—Delta Air Lines Inc.: Deal Is Reached with PBGC to End Pilots' Pension Plan," *The Wall Street Journal,* December 5, 2006, p. B10.

[30] See H. E. Winklevoss, *Pension Mathematics with Numerical Illustrations,* 2nd ed. (Philadelphia: University of Pennsylvania Press, 1993), pp. 213–14. The specific rule of thumb is that for each 0.25% change in discount rate, the liability will be altered by 4%. For a 1% change, there are four 0.25% changes. Using the Winklevoss method, we compute the effect of a 1% decrease as $1.04^4 - 1 = 17.0\%$ and the effect of a 1% increase as $1.04^{-4} - 1 = -14.5\%$.

Figure 14.9

FUNDING RATIOS AND
PERCENT OF FIRMS
OVERFUNDED (2005–2012)

Source: Standard & Poor's Compustat® as
data source; methodology not verified or
controlled by Standard & Poor's.

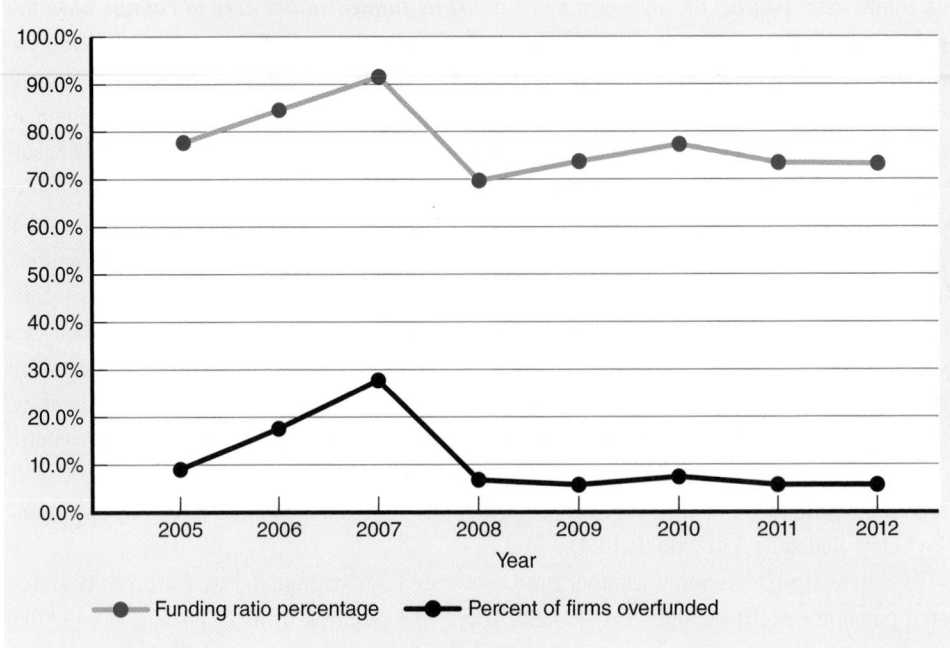

portfolio and the maturity of those investments is often shorter than the duration of the pension liability. ***Therefore, even modest declines in interest rates can easily shift the funded
status of pension plans from year to year.***

Figure 14.9 provides the median funding ratio—fair value of plan assets (FVPA) divided
by PBO and the percentage of firms that are overfunded (funding ratio > 1) for the 2005–2012
period.[31] During the eight-year period, the median *funding ratio* fell from a high of 91% in
2007 to a low of 70% in 2008. The *percentage of overfunded firms* follows a similar pattern.
In 2005, 28% of the firms were overfunded, but by 2008, only 7% of them were overfunded.
The plunge in the proportion of firms with overfunded plans resulted from two factors: (1) the
sharp drop in equity market prices (see GE's actual returns during this period in Figure 14.4)
and (2) the decline in discount rate assumptions (see Figure 14.3). As the data show, the actual
return performance of pension assets from year to year and changes in discount rates can
quickly—and materially—alter funded status. Because of low assumed discount rates, most
pension plans have remained underfunded with funding ratios near 70% since 2008.

The preceding analysis shows how both equity returns and interest rates can have dramatic
effects on a firm's funded status. Analysts suggest that this uncertainty makes pension debt
riskier than traditional debt.[32] Consequently, analysts have developed metrics to assess short-
term and long-term pension risk. Short-term risks include liquidity problems, debt downgrades, union negotiations, and possibility of bankruptcy.[33] Long-term risks address the
possibility that declines in interest rates or equity values could force firms to make additional
cash outflows. Specifically, the two pension-related risk ratios are defined as follows:

$$\text{Short-term pension risk ratio} = \frac{\text{PBO} - \text{Pension assets}}{\text{Market value of common stock}}$$

$$\text{Long-term pension risk ratio} = \frac{\text{PBO}}{\text{Market value of common stock}}$$

---

[31] The sample for Figure 14.9 is the same sample used for Figure 14.3.

[32] Bear Stearns & Co. Inc., "Pension Tension: When the Benefits Tail Wags the Dog Quantifying Pension and Other Postretirement Benefit Risk," *Accounting Issues,* New York, NY, June 2007. Bear Stearns is now part of JP Morgan Chase.

[33] Ibid., p. 8.

To illustrate the calculations, we again use GE's disclosures. On December 31, 2012, the market value of GE's outstanding common stock was approximately $218,422 million ($20.99 price × 10,406 million outstanding shares). From Exhibit 14.4, we see that the PBO is $63,502 million and the fair value of plan assets is $44,738 million. The resulting short-term and long-term ratios (in millions) are:

$$\text{Short-term pension risk ratio} = \frac{\$63,502 - \$44,738}{\$218,422} = 0.086$$

$$\text{Long-term pension risk ratio} = \frac{\$63,502}{\$218,422} = 0.291$$

To put these ratios in perspective, Bear Stearns reports that most short-term ratios fell between −0.03 and 0.06 and most long-term ratios were between 0 and 0.25 in 2006.[34] Firms with the highest short-term ratios include Delta Air Lines, 0.67; Ford, 0.49; and Goodyear Tire & Rubber, 0.34. Firms with the highest long-term ratios include General Motors, 5.56; Ford, 4.74; and AMR, 1.8. Interestingly, Delta Air, General Motors, and AMR have declared bankruptcy since the time of the Bear Stearns report. Based on these statistics, it appears that GE has both high short-term pension risk and high long-term pension risk. It is trying to reduce this risk by ending defined benefit pension coverage for new employees (see Exhibit 14.4, paragraphs above Schedule 1).

As mentioned early in the chapter, most young firms avoid these risks and the potential drain on cash flows by offering defined contribution plans. However, it can be difficult for employers to replace or modify existing defined benefit plans because of collectively bargained contracts or concerns about the effect of the replacement plan on employee productivity.

RECAP

A company's pension disclosures provide information about the current economic status of its pension plans. This provides insights regarding expected future pension-related cash flows and their potential effect on firm cash flows. The funded status and the PBO can be used to assess defined benefit pension risk for the firm. Underfunded pension plans represent a potential drain on future cash flows and should be viewed as unsecured debt.

POSTRETIREMENT BENEFITS OTHER THAN PENSIONS

Many companies promise to provide health care and life insurance to employees and their spouses during retirement. The intent of these benefits is to attract and retain a highly qualified workforce just as pensions are intended to do. Also, the employment contract and accounting issues are similar to those encountered for pensions. We discuss the similarities and point out important differences in these benefits.

Under accrual accounting, an expense and liability should be recognized over the period of employment as employees qualify for these **other postretirement benefits (OPEB).** Historically, however, few companies with postretirement benefit plans made expense accruals. Instead, "pay-as-you-go" accounting was employed—that is, as cash payments were made to provide the health care benefit coverage to retired employees, the amount of the cash outflow was charged to expense. No liability appeared on the books. Additionally, few

---

[34] Ibid., p. 20.

companies funded these OPEB plans as benefits were earned. Two reasons for this lack of funding were:

- First, in contrast to pension plans, no ERISA rules required that the benefits be funded.
- Second, even if firms did consider voluntarily funding their plans, the payments would not have been deductible for U.S. income tax purposes, thus creating a disincentive to fund.[35]

Contracting

As a result of both of these circumstances, enormous unrecorded (off-balance sheet) liabilities for postretirement benefits existed by the mid-1980s, but neither periodic debits to expense nor credits to a liability account were made to reflect the continued growth of these obligations. To correct for the lack of transparency with respect to OPEB benefits, the FASB issued pre-Codification *SFAS No. 106* in December 1990.[36] To give some idea of the size of these previously unrecorded postretirement benefit liabilities, when General Motors (GM) adopted pre-Codification *SFAS No. 106* in 1992, its liability totaled $33.1 billion, and its after-tax charge to the income statement was $20.8 billion. In 1992, GM's pre-tax loss *before* this accounting change was $3.3 billion.

Near the time that the FASB issued pre-Codification *SFAS No. 106,* many firms reduced retiree health benefit coverage by limiting which employees could qualify for benefits, shifting costs to retirees, or in some cases, ending benefits entirely. One study suggests that firms with high OPEB liabilities and high debt-to-asset ratios prior to the adoption of pre-Codification *SFAS No. 106* were more likely to reduce retiree benefits.[37] The authors argue that potential debt covenant violations may have motivated the firms to reduce plan benefits and that employment contracts would have been written differently if current OPEB GAAP had always been in effect.

The accounting recognition and disclosure requirements are nearly identical to the ones that we discussed for pensions earlier in this chapter. See Exhibit 14.6 for excerpts from the postretirement benefit plans note in General Electric Company's 2012 annual report.

EXHIBIT 14.6 | General Electric Company: Edited, Condensed 2012 Retiree Health and Life Benefits Note

We sponsor a number of retiree health and life insurance benefit plans (retiree benefit plans). Principal retiree benefit plans are discussed below; other such plans are not significant individually or in the aggregate. We use a December 31 measurement date for our plans.

PRINCIPAL RETIREE BENEFIT PLANS provide health and life insurance benefits to certain eligible participants and these participants share in the cost of healthcare benefits. In 2012, we amended our principal retiree benefit plans such that, effective January 1, 2015, our post-65 retiree medical plans will be closed to salaried and retired salaried employees who are not enrolled in the plans as of that date, and we will no longer offer company-provided life insurance in retirement for certain salaried employees who retire after that date. These plans cover approximately 205,000 retirees and dependents.

Schedule 1: Cost of Principal Retiree Benefit Plans

($ in millions)	2012	2011	2010
Expected return on plan assets	$ (73)	$ (97)	$ (116)
Service cost for benefits earned	219	216	241
Interest cost on benefit obligation	491	604	699
Prior service cost	518	647	631
Net actuarial loss (gain) amortization	32	(110)	(22)
Net curtailment/settlement gain	(101)	—	—
Retiree benefit plans cost[(a)]	$1,086	$1,260	$1,433

(continued)

---

[35] Employers can achieve limited tax benefits by making contributions to a **Voluntary Employees Beneficiary Association (VEBA) trust.**

[36] FASB ASC Subtopic 715-60: Compensation–Retirement Benefits—Defined Benefit Plans–Other Postretirement (pre-Codification "Employers' Accounting for Postretirement Benefits Other Than Pensions," *SFAS No. 106* (Norwalk, CT: FASB, 1990).

[37] See H. F. Mittelstaedt, W. Nichols, and P. Regier, "SFAS No. 106 and Benefit Reductions in Employer-Sponsored Retiree Health Care Plans," *The Accounting Review,* October 1995, pp. 535–56.

EXHIBIT 14.6	General Electric Company: Edited, Condensed 2012 Retiree Health and Life Benefits Note *(continued)*

Schedule 2: Actuarial Assumptions

The actuarial assumptions at December 31 are used to measure the year-end benefit obligations and the retiree benefit plan costs for the subsequent year.

	December 31,			
	2012	**2011**	**2010**	**2009**
Discount rate	3.74%	4.09%[b]	5.15%	5.67%
Compensation increases	3.90	3.75	4.25	4.20
Expected return on assets	7.00	7.00	8.00	8.50
Initial healthcare trend rate[a]	6.50	7.00	7.00	7.40

[a] For 2012, ultimately declining to 5% for 2030 and thereafter.

[b] Weighted average discount rate of 3.94% was used for determination of costs in 2012.

Schedule 3: Accumulated Postretirement Benefit Obligation (APBO)

($ in millions)	**2012**	**2011**
Balance at January 1	$13,056	$12,010
Service cost for benefits earned	219	216
Interest cost on benefit obligation	491	604
Participant contributions	54	55
Plan amendments	(832)	25
Actuarial loss (gain)	(60)	911[c]
Benefits paid	(758)	765
Net curtailment settlement	(366)	—
Balance at December 31[d]	$11,804	$13,056

[c] Primarily associated with discount rate change.

[d] The APBO for the retiree health plans was $ 9,218 million and $ 10,286 million at year-end 2012 and 2011, respectively.

A one percentage point change in the assumed healthcare cost trend rate would have the following effects.

($ in millions)	1% increase	1% decrease
APBO at December 31, 2012	$1,017	$(860)
Service and interest cost in 2012	76	(63)

Schedule 4: Fair Value of Plan Assets

($ in millions)	**2012**	**2011**
Balance at January 1	$1,004	$1,125
Actual gain on plan assets	98	15
Employer contributions	548	574
Participant contributions	54	55
Benefits paid	(758)	(765)
Balance at December 31	$ 946	$1,004

(continued)

EXHIBIT 14.6 General Electric Company: Edited, Condensed 2012 Retiree Health and Life Benefits Note (continued)

Schedule 5: Retiree Benefit Asset (Liability)

($ in millions)	December 31, 2012	December 31, 2011
Funded status[e]	$(10,858)	$(12,052)
Liability recorded in the Statement of Financial Position		
Retiree health plans		
Due within one year	$ (589)	$ (602)
Due after one year	(8,629)	(9,684)
Retiree life plans	(1,640)	(1,766)
Net liability recognized	$(10,858)	$(12,052)
Amounts recorded in shareowners' equity (unamortized)		
Prior service cost	$ 1,356	$ 2,901
Net actuarial loss	182	401
Total	$ 1,538	$ 3,302

[e] Fair value of assets less APBO, as shown in the preceding tables.

In 2013, we estimate that we will amortize $395 million of prior service cost and $15 million of net actuarial loss from shareowners' equity into retiree benefit plans cost. Comparable amortized amounts in 2012 were $518 million of prior service cost and $32 million of net actuarial loss.

Schedule 6: Estimated Future Benefit Payments

($ in millions)	2013	2014	2015	2016	2017	2018–2022
	$780	$785	$785	$785	$785	$3,800

FUNDING POLICY. We fund retiree health benefits on a pay-as-you-go basis. We expect to contribute approximately $600 million in 2013 to fund such benefits. We fund retiree life insurance benefits at our discretion.

Author note: We have numbered the schedules and reordered some information to make it easier for the reader.

The computations for postretirement benefits expense and measures of the liability generally parallel the format for pension expense and liability. Notice in Exhibit 14.6 that GE maintains both retiree health and life insurance benefit plans. Similar to the pension components of the pension cost discussed earlier, the net postretirement benefit cost of $1,086 million for 2012 (as shown in Exhibit 14.6, Schedule 1) includes expected return, service cost, interest cost, prior service cost, and recognized actuarial loss (gain) components.

Retiree benefit plans cost also is reduced for a Net curtailment/settlement gain of $(101 million). The gain is a direct result of ending post-65 retiree health care and life insurance benefits for a significant portion of GE's employees (see the paragraph above Schedule 1 in Exhibit 14.6). Reductions in *earned* benefits reduce the Accumulated postretirement benefit obligation (APBO) and AOCI—Prior service cost as a **negative plan amendment.** However, **curtailment** losses (gains) also may be recognized for amendments that prevent employees from earning benefits tied to *future* service. For example, GE's accruals for retiree life insurance may have been based on future salary levels. Consequently, GE would recognize a gain. A loss related to faster recognition of prior service cost could also occur. **Settlement** losses (gains) also may be recognized when a company relieves itself of primary responsibility or significant risks associated with the plan. Accounting for curtailments and settlements is complex, and we cannot determine how GE calculated the amounts allocated to the Net curtailment/settlement gain, OCI—Prior service cost, OCI—Net actuarial loss, or losses (gains) outside of pension accounts.[38] As we will see in subsequent schedules, most of the change is viewed as a negative plan amendment, thereby reducing AOCI—Prior service cost.

Further scrutiny of this section shows that OPEB accounting guidance also incorporates smoothing devices that are virtually identical to Components 4 and 5 in pension accounting. Specifically, when OPEB plans are funded and thus have plan assets, postretirement benefit expense is reduced by the *expected* return on plan assets. To accomplish this smoothing, asset gains or losses are excluded from pension expense but recognized as a component of OCI. Similarly, these gains and losses are accumulated and amortized as Component 4 if they exceed a 10% corridor. OPEB Component 5—amortization of prior service cost—exists as well in instances in which firms enhance or reduce the level of postretirement benefits.

GE's other OPEB schedules are similar to its pension schedules. Schedule 2 gives the assumptions for its OPEB plans. Note that instead of a salary growth assumption, the schedule contains an assumption for health care cost trend rates. The cost trend includes projected costs related to physician care, hospital care, prescription drugs, medical equipment, and so on. Health care liabilities are rarely tied to salary at retirement. The typical postretirement benefit plan promises employees full coverage (for example, comprehensive postretirement health insurance) after a certain period of employment—say, 10 years. In such circumstances, the actuarially determined service cost of the plan is accrued over the first 10 years of the employee's service. The liability attributed to service to date is the **accumulated postretirement benefit obligation (APBO)**. The health care cost trend rate can have a dramatic effect on the estimated APBO. Consequently, firms are required to make sensitivity disclosures regarding the effect of a 1% increase or decrease in the health care trend rate assumption. In the disclosure following Schedule 3, GE states that a 1% increase (decrease) could increase (decrease) it's APBO by $1,017 million or 8.6% ($860 million or 7.3%).

Schedules 3 and 4 relate to the APBO and plan assets, respectively, and are nearly identical in form to the ones presented for pensions. Note that the change in postretirement benefits reduces the APBO significantly. Plan amendments reduce it by $832 million and the Net curtailment/settlement reduces it by $366 million. Together, they reduce the January 1 obligation by 9.2% [(Plan amendments of $832 million + Net curtailment/settlement of $366 million)/ January 1 APBO of $13,056 million]. The Plan amendments reduce the AOCI—Prior service, and the reduction from Net curtailment/settlement is spread among Retiree benefits plan cost, AOCI—Prior service cost, and AOCI—Net actuarial loss.

Schedule 5, the funded status and balance sheet accounts, is also very similar except that the balance sheet titles differ. Note that the ending 2012 amounts for both the Net liability recognized and the costs/losses recorded in shareowners' equity are significantly lower than observed in 2011. Again, most of this reduction results from the cut in retiree health care and life insurance benefits mentioned earlier. The journal entries could be reconstructed in the same manner as we reconstructed the pension journal entries. ——————

| Case 14-1 requires the reconstruction of GE's OPEB journal entries. |

Schedule 6 gives the estimated future payments.

---

[38] For a detailed discussion of these issues, see FASB ASC Section 715-60-35-150 to 176: Compensation—Retirement Benefits—Defined Benefit Plans—Other Postretirement—Subsequent Measurement—Settlements, Curtailments, and Certain Termination Benefits.

Analytical Insights: Assessing OPEB Liability

Similar to pensions, the OPEB liability is riskier than many traditional forms of debt. To assess the magnitude of this risk, analysts have developed risk measures for OPEBs similar to the ones discussed earlier for pensions. The specific ratios are defined as follows:

$$\text{Short-term OPEB risk ratio (quick version)} = \frac{\text{APBO} - \text{Plan assets}^{39}}{\text{Market value of common stock}}$$

$$\text{Short-term OPEB risk ratio (extended version)} = \frac{5 \text{ years of expected benifit payment} - \text{Plan assets}}{\text{Market value of common stock}}$$

$$\text{Long-term OPEB risk ratio} = \frac{\text{APBO}}{\text{Market value of common stock}}$$

To illustrate the calculations, we again use GE's disclosures. On December 31, 2012, the market value of GE's outstanding common stock was approximately $218,422 million ($20.99 price × 10,406 million outstanding shares). From Exhibit 14.6, we see that the APBO is $11,804 million (Schedule 3) and the fair value of plan assets is $946 million (Schedule 4). The sum of the net estimated future benefit payments for the next 5 years is $3,920 million (Schedule 6). The resulting short-term and long-term ratios ($ in millions) are:

$$\text{Short-term OPEB risk ratio (quick version)} = \frac{\$11,804 - \$946}{\$218,422} = 0.050$$

$$\text{Short-term OPEB risk ratio (extented version)} = \frac{\$3,920 - \$946}{\$218,422} = 0.014$$

$$\text{Long-term OPEB risk ratio} = \frac{\$11,804}{\$218.422} = 0.054$$

To put these ratios in perspective, Bear Stearns reported that most short-term quick version ratios fell between 0.00 and 0.03[40] and most long-term ratios were between 0 and 0.04 in 2006. Firms with some of the highest short-term quick version ratios included GM, 2.63; Ford, 1.56; and AMR Corp., 0.50. Firms with the highest long-term ratios included GM, 3.50; Ford, 1.85; and Delta Air Lines Inc., 0.76. As we saw with the pension risk ratios, most of the companies with the highest OPEB risk ratios declared bankruptcy. GE's is ratios are far below the ratios of the extreme firms but they are higher than most firms.

 RECAP

The accounting and disclosures for postretirement benefit plans are similar to pension accounting and disclosures. However, most postretirement benefit plans are not well-funded. Additionally, firm sponsors bear the risk of future medical inflation unless they have capped their share of the expected cost. Consequently, financial statement readers must be mindful that the future cash outflows associated with these plans could be much different than the current cash outflows.

---

[39] If VEBA trust assets are not included in plan assets (i.e., they are included elsewhere on the balance sheet), then they would also be deducted in the numerator in both short-term OPEB risk ratios.

[40] Bear Stearns, op. cit., p. 25.

Evaluation of Pension and Postretirement Benefit Financial Reporting

Although the FASB issued pre-Codification *SFAS No. 87* more than 25 years ago, many of its sections remain controversial. Calculations are extremely complex, and net income does not reflect immediately actual asset returns or PBO actuarial (gains) losses as they arise. However, current GAAP requires the funded status of pension and postretirement plans to be recognized as a liability or an asset on a firm's balance sheet. Management has discretion in choosing the rate of return assumption and the measurement method for the market-related value. Allowing actual return to come through net income instead of showing the unexpected portion in OCI would eliminate the discretionary expected rate of return, but it would make net income more volatile. Most managers and many accountants argue that such a move could reduce the predictive power and faithful representation of net income.

In addition, some analysts and financial writers argue that deducting pension expense or adding pension income in the operating section of the income statement misstates operating income. They maintain that only service cost is a true current period operating item because service cost represents the present value of the increased pension payout arising from current services. They believe interest cost (Component 2 of pension expense) is a financing cost, not an element of operating income. Similarly, these critics believe that the expected return on plan assets (Component 3) should be shown in Other income just like the return on investment securities firms may hold.[41]

Despite concerns about prior accounting, studies provide evidence that pension and OPEB expense components found in notes are priced by the market.[42] Additionally, other studies suggest a positive relationship between stock prices and the funded status of pension and OPEB plans disclosed in the notes (and not recognized on the balance sheet prior to 2006). These studies also show that the perceived reliability of the pension and OPEB amounts affects their relation with stock prices.[43] Although the studies suggest that the market finds the pension and OPEB information useful, the results are not always consistent across years, and some results suggest that investors may not *fully* price the impact of the pension disclosures.[44] Regulators, analysts, preparers, and researchers will continue to debate the appropriate recognition, disclosure, and valuation techniques for pensions and OPEBs.

---

[41] For example, see R. McGough and E. E. Schultz, "How Pension Surpluses Lift Profits," *The Wall Street Journal,* September 20, 1999; G. Morgenson, "What's Hiding in Big Blue's Small Print," *The New York Times,* June 4, 2000; and Bear Stearns, "Retirement Benefits Impact Operating Income," *Accounting Issues* (New York: Bear Stearns & Co. Inc., September 17, 1999).

[42] See, for example, M. E. Barth, W. H. Beaver, and W. R. Landsman, "The Market Valuation Implications of Net Periodic Pension Cost Components," *Journal of Accounting and Economics,* March 1992, pp. 27–62; and E. Amir, "The Effect of Accounting Aggregation on the Value-Relevance of Financial Disclosures: The Case of SFAS No. 106," *The Accounting Review,* October 1996, pp. 573–90.

[43] See M. E. Barth, "Relative Measurement Errors among Alternative Pension Asset and Liability Measures," *The Accounting Review,* July 1991, pp. 443–63; B. Choi, D. Collins, and W. Johnson, "Valuation of Reliability Differences: The Case of Nonpension Postretirement Obligations," *The Accounting Review,* July 1997, pp. 351–83; P. Y. Davis-Friday, L. B. Folami, C. Liu, and H. F. Mittelstaedt, "The Value Relevance of Financial Statement Recognition versus Disclosure: Evidence from SFAS No. 106," *The Accounting Review,* October 1999, pp. 403–23; and P. Y. Davis-Friday, C. Liu, and H. F. Mittelstaedt, "Recognition and Disclosure Reliability: Evidence from SFAS No. 106," *Contemporary Accounting Research,* Summer 2004, pp. 399–427.

[44] See, for example, M. Picconi, "The Perils of Pensions: Does Pension Accounting Lead Investors and Analysts Astray?" *The Accounting Review,* July 2006, pp. 925–55.

GLOBAL VANTAGE POINT

Comparison of IFRS and GAAP Retirement Benefit Accounting

International Financial Reporting Standards (IFRS) for pensions are specified by *International Accounting Standard (IAS) 19*—"Employee Benefits."[45] Many of the concepts and accounting requirements parallel the provisions in FASB ASC Subtopic 715-30: Compensation–Retirement Benefits—Defined Benefit Plans–Pension. However, there are some important differences, which we describe in the subsequent paragraphs.

The first difference relates to prior service costs, called past service costs under IFRS. Under *IAS 19,* past service cost is recognized immediately as part of pension expense. In contrast, GAAP requires firms to recognize new prior service costs as part of OCI and recycles them to pension expense over the shorter of the average remaining work life or the period covered under a collective bargaining agreement.

The second difference relates to the computation and treatment of actuarial gains and losses and comprises one of the major fundamental differences between current U.S. GAAP and IFRS. *IAS 19* (revised June 2011, effective January 1, 2013) now requires that the **discount rate** be used to compute the expected return on plan assets. Consequently, the finance component of pension expense can be computed by multiplying the funded status (adjusted for contributions and benefit payments) by the discount rate. Actuarial gains and losses on the PBO and the actual return (less the expected return on plan assets) are recognized in OCI **without subsequent amortization** to pension expense. As a result, periodic pension expense computed under IFRS generally consists only of current service cost, past service cost, and net interest on the net defined benefit liability or asset (i.e., funded status).

One final difference relates to placement on the statement of comprehensive income. Service cost is part of operating activities, the finance component is part of finance costs within profit and loss, and actuarial gains and losses (remeasurement component) is part of OCI.

Prior to 2013, IFRS alternatives had more similarities to current or prior U.S. GAAP. For example, firms could use a rate of return assumption that was higher than the discount rate, use the corridor method for amortizing actuarial losses (gains), and elect to keep actuarial losses (gains) off the balance sheet (similar to U.S. accounting prior to 2006). In addition, firms could amortize some prior service costs over several years. As this edition goes to press, firms under IFRS are reporting significant effects from the retrospective change in accounting. For example, upon adoption, Volvo Group reduced its Shareholders' equity by 10%. Its restated 2012 income statement amounts indicate that the accounting change decreased 2012 comprehensive income by 24%. *In its 2012 annual report, Lufthansa Group reported that the change in accounting would decrease its Shareholders' equity by €3.5 billion (42%)!*

Because the FASB has not yet changed U.S. GAAP with respect to pensions, pension expense is likely more volatile under U.S. GAAP in that it requires firms to amortize actuarial gains and losses. Also, U.S. GAAP pension expense is likely lower because it allows the expected rate of return to exceed the discount rate.[46]

---

[45] "Employee Benefits," *IAS 19,* International Accounting Standards Board (London, UK, 1998, amended through June 2011).

[46] See PricewaterhouseCoopers, "Pension and OPEB Accounting: A study of the IASB's proposal" (New York, 2010).

SUMMARY

- Pension plan contracts allow employees to exchange current service for payments to be received during retirement.

- Defined contribution pension plans specify amounts to be invested for the employee during the employee's career, and the employee's pension will be based on the value of those investments at retirement.

- In the United States, most new pension plans are defined contribution plans. Consequently, defined contribution pension plans now hold 30% more assets than do defined benefit plans. Still, U.S. defined benefit pension plans hold approximately $2 trillion in assets.

- The accounting for defined contribution plans is straightforward. Defined benefit pension plans specify amounts to be received during retirement, thereby complicating the underlying economics of the exchange and the accounting.

- Under ASC Topic 715, pension expense for defined benefit pension plans consists of service cost, interest cost, expected return on plan assets, and two other "smoothing" components.

- The two smoothing mechanisms avoid year-to-year volatility in pension expense but make pension accounting exceedingly complex because many pension-related items are presented in AOCI.

- Under pre-Codification *SFAS No. 87,* the balance sheet asset (liability) on the balance sheet differed from the plan's actual funded status. Current GAAP requires that the balance sheet asset (liability) equal the plan's funded status.

- Employer funding of defined benefit pension plans is influenced by tax law, labor law, union membership, and the employer's financial needs.

- The reporting rules for other postretirement benefits (OPEB) closely parallel the pension accounting rules.

- GAAP requires information about expected future cash flows, future amortization amounts, and major classes of investments so that investors can make cash flow projections, assess risk, and evaluate rate of return assumptions.

- Academic research suggests that stock prices reflect pension and OPEB disclosures but their impact may not be fully valued.

- Statement readers should view the following circumstances as potential warning signals or indicators of earnings management:

  - A significant disagreement between any of the various pension and OPEB rates selected by a firm (that is, the discount rate, the expected rate of return on plan assets, or the rate of increase in future compensation levels or health care costs) and the rates chosen by other firms in its industry.

  - A very large difference between the chosen expected rate of return on plan assets and the discount rate used.

  - An increase in the year-to-year expected rate of return on plan assets that seems unrelated to changes in market conditions.

  - A decrease in the assumed rate of increase in future compensation levels (or, for OPEB, future health cost trends) that cannot be explained by changing industry or labor market conditions.

  - Rate of return assumptions that are inconsistent with prior investment experience or mix of equity and debt investments.

- *IAS 19* (revised 2011) offers guidance that is markedly different from U.S. GAAP. Among other things, it requires that the discount rate be used to measure both the expected return on assets and the interest cost on PBO to obtain a net financing component. Additionally, actuarial losses (gains) recognized in OCI are not subsequently amortized into pension expense. It also requires new past service cost to be recognized immediately as a component of pension expense.

EXERCISES

E14-1

Determining projected benefit obligation **(LO 3)**

AICPA
ADAPTED

The following information pertains to Seda Company's pension plan:

Actuarial estimate of projected benefit obligation at 1/1/14	$72,000
Service cost for 2014	18,000
Pension benefits paid on 12/31/14	15,000
Assumed discount rate	10%

Required:
If no change in actuarial estimates occurred during 2014, how much would Seda's projected benefit obligation be at December 31, 2014?

E14-2

Determining balance sheet pension asset (liability) **(LO 2, 3)**

AICPA
ADAPTED

At December 31, 2014, Kerr Corporation's pension plan administrator provided the following information:

Fair value of plan assets	$3,450,000
Accumulated benefit obligation	4,300,000
Projected benefit obligation	5,700,000

Required: '
What amount of the pension liability should be shown on Kerr's December 31, 2014, balance sheet?

E14-3

Determining balance sheet pension asset (liability) **(LO 3)**

AICPA
ADAPTED

On January 2, 2014, Loch Company established a defined benefit plan covering all employees and contributed $1,000,000 to the plan. At December 31, 2014, Loch determined that the 2014 service and interest costs totaled $620,000. The expected and the actual rate of return on plan assets for 2014 was 10%. Loch's pension expense has no other components.

Required:
What amount should Loch report in its December 31, 2014, balance sheet as a pension asset (liability)?

E14-4

Determining PBO and ABO **(LO 1, 2, 3)**

AICPA
ADAPTED

Mary Abbott is a long-time employee of Love Enterprises, a manufacturer and distributor of farm implements. Abbott plans to retire on her 65th birthday (January 1, 2019) five years from today. Her current salary is $48,000 per year, and her projected salary for her last year of employment is $60,000.

Love Enterprises sponsors a defined benefit pension plan. It provides for an annual pension benefit equal to 60% of the employee's annual salary at retirement. Payments commence on the employee's 66th birthday or one year after the anniversary date of his or her retirement. The discount and earnings rate on plan assets is 8%. The average life expectancy for male and female employees is 76 and 80, respectively.

Required:
1. Compute the PBO related to Abbott's pension benefits as of January 1, 2014.
2. Compute the ABO for the year ended December 31, 2014.

Use the facts given in E14-4. Repeat the requirements assuming that the discount and earnings rate is 11% instead of 8%.

E14-5

Determining PBO and ABO
(LO 1, 2, 3)

AICPA
ADAPTED

The following information pertains to Gali Company's defined benefit pension plan for 2014:

Fair value of plan assets, beginning of year	$350,000
Fair value of plan assets, end of year	525,000
Employer contributions	110,000
Benefits paid	85,000

Required:

What was the dollar amount of actual return on Gali Company's plan assets in 2014?

E14-6

Determining actual return on
plan assets   (LO 2, 3)

AICPA
ADAPTED

The following information pertains to Kane Company's defined benefit pension plan:

Balance sheet asset, 1/1/14	$ 2,000
AOCI—prior service cost, 1/1/14	24,000
Service cost	19,000
Interest cost	38,000
Expected return on plan assets	22,000
Prior service cost amortization	6,000
Employer contributions	40,000

Kane has no net actuarial gains or losses in AOCI.

Required:

In its December 31, 2014, balance sheet, what amount should Kane report as a pension asset (liability)?

E14-7

Determining balance sheet
pension asset (liability)
(LO 3, 4)

AICPA
ADAPTED

Dell Company adopted a defined benefit pension plan on January 1, 2014. Dell amortizes the initial prior service cost of $1,334,400 over 16 years. It assumes a 7% discount rate and an 8% expected rate of return. The following additional data are available for 2014:

Service cost for 2014	$320,000
Prior service cost amortization	83,400
Employer contribution made at 12/31/14	335,000

Required:

Compute the pension asset (liability) to be reported on Dell's December 31, 2014, balance sheet.

E14-8

Determining balance sheet
pension asset (liability)
(LO 3, 4)

AICPA
ADAPTED

On January 1, 2014, East Corporation adopted a defined benefit pension plan. At plan inception, the prior service cost was $60,000. In 2014, East incurred service cost of $150,000 and amortized $12,000 of prior service cost. On December 31, 2014, East contributed $160,000 to the pension plan. East assumes a 6% discount rate and 5% expected rate of return.

Required:

At December 31, 2014, what amounts should East report as a pension asset (liability) and AOCI on its balance sheet?

E14-9

Determining balance sheet
pension asset (liability)
(LO 3, 4)

AICPA
ADAPTED

E14-10

Adjusting balance sheet pension asset (liability) **(LO 3)**

AICPA
ADAPTED

Nome Company sponsors a defined benefit plan covering all employees. Benefits are based on years of service and compensation levels at the time of retirement. Nome has a September 30 fiscal year-end. It determined that as of September 30, 2014, its ABO was $320,000, its PBO was $380,000, and its plan assets had a $290,000 fair value. Nome's September 30, 2014, trial balance showed a balance sheet asset of $20,000.

Required:

What adjustment should Nome make to report the appropriate pension asset (liability) on its September 30, 2014, balance sheet?

E14-11

Determining postretirement expense **(LO 7)**

AICPA
ADAPTED

Hukle Company has provided the following information pertaining to its postretirement plan for 2014:

Service cost	$240,000
Benefit payment made at 12/31/14	110,000
Interest on accumulated postretirement benefit obligation	40,000
Prior service cost amortization	10,000

Required:

Calculate Hukle Company's 2014 net postretirement benefit cost.

E14-12

Determining pension expense **(LO 3)**

AICPA
ADAPTED

The following information pertains to Lee Corporation's defined benefit pension plan for 2014:

Service cost	$160,000
Actual and expected return on plan assets	35,000
Amortization of prior service costs	5,000
Interest on pension obligation	50,000

Required:

Determine the pension expense that Lee Corporation would include in its 2014 net income.

E14-13

Determining pension expense, fair value of plan assets, and deferred return on plan assets **(LO 3, 4)**

Bostonian Company provided the following information related to its defined benefit pension plan for 2014:

PBO on 1/1/14	$2,500,000
Fair value of plan assets on 1/1/14	2,000,000
Service cost	120,000
Actual return on plan assets	320,000
Payments made to retirees on 12/31/14	100,000
Amortization of prior service cost	40,000
Recognized actuarial losses	50,000
Contributions made to plan during 2014	80,000
Interest rate for discounting pension obligations	6%
Expected return on plan assets	8%

Required:

1. What amount of pension expense should Bostonian report for 2014?

2. What is the fair value of plan assets at December 31, 2014?

3. What dollar amount of return on plan assets was deferred in 2014?

Cummings Inc. had the following reconciliation at December 31, 2014:

Fair value of plan assets	$5,000
PBO	4,200
Funded status	$ 800
AOCI—prior service cost	$ 300
AOCI—net actuarial (gain) loss	700
Total	$1,000

E 14-14

Determining pension expense and AOCI balances
(LO 3, 4)

The following assumptions are being used for the pension plan in 2015:

Discount rate	5%
Expected rate of return on assets	8%
Average remaining worklife	10 years
Remaining amortization period for prior service costs	6 years

Additional 2015 Information:

Service cost	$442
Cash contributed to the plan (year-end)	250
Pension benefits paid by the plan (year-end)	465
Actual return on plan assets	650
New actuarial (gain) loss on the PBO	64

Required:

1. Compute pension expense for 2015.

2. Compute the fair value of plan assets at December 31, 2015.

3. Compute the PBO at December 31, 2015.

4. Compute AOCI—net actuarial (gain) loss as of December 31, 2015.

Jones Company has a postretirement benefit (health care) plan for its employees. On January 1, 2014, the balance in the Accumulated postretirement benefit obligation account was $300 million. The assumed discount rate—for purposes of determining postretirement obligations and expenses—is 8%. Jones does not prefund postretirement benefits, so there are no plan assets. It created a $45 million prior service cost *credit* at the end of 2013 when the company modified the health care plan to reduce the maximum benefits paid to each employee. This amount is being amortized over 15 years. The service cost component of postretirement benefits for 2014 is $35 million.

E 14-15

Determining postretirement (health care) benefits expense and obligation   **(LO 7)**

Required:

1. Determine the amount of postretirement benefits cost for 2014.

2. If benefits paid to retirees totaled $64 million in 2014, determine the balance in the Accumulated postretirement benefit obligation account on December 31, 2014.

Zeff Manufacturing provides the following information about its postretirement health care plan for 2014:

E 14-16

Determining postretirement health care expenses and plan assets and liabilities balances
(LO 7)

Accumulated postretirement benefit obligation on 1/1/14	$300,000
Fair value of plan assets on 1/1/14	30,000
Benefits paid to retirees at 12/31/14	6,500
Service cost for 2014	20,000
Recognized prior service cost	10,000
Recognized actuarial loss	7,000
Actual return on plan assets	4,500
Contributions to the plan at 12/31/14	12,000
Discount rate	8%
Expected long-run rate of return on plan assets	10%

Required:

1. Determine Zeff's postretirement health care expense in 2014.

2. Determine the fair value of plan assets at December 31, 2014.

3. Determine the APBO amount at December 31, 2014.

E14-17

Determining plan assets, PBO, and AOCI **(LO 3, 4)**

Bonny Corp. has a defined benefit pension plan for its employees who have an average remaining service life of 10 years. The following information is available for 2013 and 2014 related to the pension plan:

	2014	2013
Projected benefit obligation, 1/1	?	$750,000
Service cost	$ 70,000	60,000
Actual return on plan assets	66,400	72,000
Bonny Corp. contributions for year ended 12/31	74,000	68,000
Benefits paid during year	67,000	60,000
Fair value of plan assets, 1/1	?	600,000
Actuarial (gain) loss on PBO during year	(13,000)	4,400
Expected return on plan assets	7%	7%
Discount rate	6%	6%

Bonny Corp. had no beginning balance in its AOCI—net actuarial (gain) loss on January 1, 2013. The actuarial (gains) losses on PBO arose due to changes in assumptions made by the actuaries regarding salary increases (2013) and mortality estimates (2014).

Required:

1. Compute Bonny's PBO at December 31, 2013, and December 31, 2014.

2. Compute the fair value of plan assets at December 31, 2013, and December 31, 2014.

3. Compute the year-end balance in AOCI—net actuarial loss (gain) for Bonny Corp. for 2013 and 2014.

4. Compute OCI for the years ended December 31, 2013, and December 31, 2014.

E14-18

Determining amount of recognized net gain or loss using the corridor approach **(LO 3, 4)**

At January 1, 2014, Milo Co.'s projected benefit obligation is $300,000, and the fair value of its pension plan assets is $340,000. The average remaining service period of Milo's employees is 10 years. The following additional information is available for Milo's net actuarial gains and losses:

	2014	2015	2016
AOCI—net actuarial (gain) loss at 1/1	$ 40,000	$ 28,000	$ 53,000
PBO at 12/31	341,000	402,000	416,000
Fair value of plan assets at 12/31	323,000	419,000	438,000

Required:

Compute the amount of recognized gain or loss to be included in pension expense for each year, 2014 through 2016. Indicate whether the recognized amount increases or decreases pension expense.

At January 1, 2014, Archer Co.'s PBO is $500,000 and the fair value of its pension plan assets is $630,000. The average remaining service period of Archer's employees is 12 years. The AOCI—net actuarial loss (gain) at January 1, 2014, is $(70,000). The following additional information is available related to Archer's actuarial gains and losses:

E14-19

Determining amount of recognized net gain or loss using the corridor approach **(LO 3, 4)**

	2014	2015	2016
New actuarial loss (gain) on PBO	$(30,000)	$ 65,000	$(63,000)
New deferred loss (gain) on plan assets	60,000	55,000	(32,000)
PBO at 12/31	560,000	675,000	628,000
Fair value of plan assets at 12/31	575,000	530,000	650,000

Required:

For each year, 2014 through 2016, compute

1. The amount of recognized loss (gain) to be included in pension expense. Be sure to indicate whether the recognized amount increases or decreases pension expense.

2. The ending balance of AOCI—net actuarial (gain) loss.

3. OCI—net actuarial (gain) loss.

George Corporation has a defined benefit pension plan for its employees. The following information is available for 2014:

E14-20

Determining pension elements **(LO 3, 4)**

PBO at 1/1	$930,000
Payments made to retirees at 12/31/14	204,000
Service cost	196,000
Actual return on plan assets	30,000
Plan contributions at 12/31/14	130,000
Fair value of plan assets at 12/31/14	880,000
Amortization of prior service cost	76,000
Discount rate	10%
Expected rate of return on plan assets	6%

Required:

1. What was the January 1, 2014, fair value of the plan assets?

2. What is the expected dollar return on plan assets for 2014?

3. What amount of pension expense should George report for the year ended December 31, 2014?

4. What was the dollar amount of return (loss) on plan assets that was deferred during 2014?

5. Prepare the journal entries to record pension expense, the contribution, and the deferred return (loss).

On January 1, 2014, Cello Co. established a defined benefit pension plan for its employees. At January 1, 2014, Cello estimated the service cost for 2014 to be $45,000. At January 1, 2015, it estimated 2015 service cost to be $49,000. On the plan inception date, prior service credit was granted to employees for five years, the period of time between the company's formation and plan inception. The prior service cost was estimated to be $650,000 at January 1, 2014. Cello uses a 10% discount rate and assumes a return on plan assets of 9%. The average remaining service life of employees is 20 years, and the

E14-21

Determining pension elements **(LO 3, 4, 6)**

company will fund at the end of each year an amount equal to service cost plus interest cost for 2014 and 2015.

	December 31,	
	2015	**2014**
PBO	?	?
Benefits paid at 12/31	2,000	–0–
Fair value of plan assets	?	–0–
Contributions at 12/31	?	?
Actual return on plan assets	3,200	–0–

Required:

1. Compute the amount of prior service cost to be included as a component of pension expense for 2014.

2. Compute pension expense for 2014.

3. Compute the fair value of plan assets at December 31, 2014.

4. Compute the PBO balance at December 31, 2014.

5. Prepare the company's required journal entries to record the effects of its pension plan in 2014.

6. Repeat requirements 1 through 5 for 2015.

7. Prepare T-accounts for Pension asset (liability), OCI—prior service cost, and OCI—net actuarial (gain) loss to show the effects of the entries made in requirements 5 and 6. Label the effects.

PROBLEMS / DISCUSSION QUESTIONS

P14-1

Determining components of pension expense
(LO 3, 4, 6)

The following information pertains to Sparta Company's defined benefit pension plan:

Discount rate	8%
Expected rate of return on plan assets	10%
Average service life	12 years
At 1/1/14	
PBO	$600,000
Fair value of pension plan assets	720,000
AOCI—prior service cost	240,000
AOCI—net actuarial (gain) loss	(96,000)
At 12/31/14	
PBO	910,000
Fair value of pension plan assets	825,000

Service cost for 2014 was $90,000. No contributions were made or benefits paid during the year. Sparta's Accrued pension liability was $8,000 at January 1, 2014. Sparta uses the straight-line method of amortization over the maximum period permitted.

Required:

Determine the amount for each of the following items:

1. Interest cost.

2. Expected dollar return on plan assets.

3. Actual return on plan assets.

4. Recognized actuarial gain (minimum amortization).

5. Recognized prior service costs.

6. Balance in the AOCI—net actuarial (gain) loss account on December 31, 2014.

Turner Inc. provides a defined benefit pension plan to its employees. The company has 150 employees. The average remaining service life of employees is 10 years. The AOCI—net actuarial (gain) loss was zero at December 31, 2013. Turner uses a market-related (smoothed) value to compute expected return.

Additional Information:

P14-2

Determining expense and balance sheet amounts (journal entries)
(LO 3, 4, 6)

	December 31,	
Description	**2014**	**2013**
PBO	$1,450,000	$1,377,000
ABO	1,425,000	1,350,000
Fair value of plan assets	1,395,000	1,085,000
Market-related value of plan assets	1,369,000	1,085,000
AOCI—prior service cost	?	292,000
Balance sheet pension asset (liability)	?	(292,000)
Service cost	117,400	
Contribution	169,000	
PBO actuarial gain	182,100	
Benefit payments made	None	None
Discount rate	10%	10%
Expected rate of return	10%	10%

Required:
Round all amounts to the nearest dollar:

1. Compute the amount of prior service cost that would be amortized as a component of pension expense for 2014 and 2015.

2. Compute the actual return on plan assets for 2014.

3. Compute the unexpected net gain or loss on plan assets for 2014.

4. Compute pension expense for 2014.

5. Prepare the company's required pension journal entries for 2014.

6. Compute the 2014 increase/decrease in AOCI—net actuarial (gain) loss and the amount to be amortized in 2014 and 2015.

7. Confirm that the pension asset (liability) on the balance sheet equals the funded status as of December 31, 2014.

Puhlman Inc. provides a defined benefit pension plan to its employees. It uses a market-related (smoothed) value to compute its expected return. Additional information follows:

P14-3

Determining expense and balance sheet amounts (journal entries)
(LO 3, 4, 6)

	December 31,	
Description	**2014**	**2013**
PBO	?	$2,500,000
ABO	$2,335,000	2,150,000
Fair value of plan assets	?	2,100,000
Market-related value of plan assets	2,342,800	2,100,000
Benefit payments made	272,000	231,000
AOCI—net actuarial (gain) loss	114,000	–0–
AOCI—prior service cost	?	400,000
Balance sheet pension asset (liability)	?	(400,000)
Service cost	214,000	
Contribution	321,000	
Actual return	129,000	
Discount rate for PBO	9%	10%
Expected rate of return	10%	10%
Average remaining service life of employees	15 years	15 years

During 2014, the PBO increased by $33,000 due to a decrease in the discount rate from the previous year. The 2013 discount rate assumption was used to compute 2014 service cost and interest cost.

Required:

Round all amounts to the nearest dollar:

1. Compute the fair value of plan assets at December 31, 2014.
2. Compute the prior service cost that would be amortized as a component of pension expense for 2014 and 2015.
3. Compute the PBO at December 31, 2014.
4. Compute pension expense for 2014.
5. Prepare the company's required pension journal entries for 2014.
6. Compute the 2014 increase/decrease in AOCI—net actuarial (gains) or losses and the amount to be amortized in 2014 and 2015.
7. Confirm that the pension asset (liability) on the balance sheet equals the funded status as of December 31, 2014.

P14-4

Relating pension concepts to pension accounting
(LO 1, 2, 3)

You have the following information related to Chalmers Corporation's pension plan:

1. Defined benefit, noncontributory pension plan.
2. Plan initiation, January 1, 2014 (no credit given for prior service).
3. Retirement benefits paid at year-end with the first payment one year after retirement.
4. Assumed discount rate of 7%.
5. Assumed expected rate of return on plan assets of 9%.
6. Annual retirement benefit equals years of credited service × 0.02 × highest salary.

You have the following information for Frank Bullitt, the firm's only employee:

Start date	January 1, 2011
Expected retirement date	December 31, 2028
Expected number of payments during retirement	20

Selected actual and expected salary levels:

Date	Salary Level
January 1, 2011	$22,000
January 1, 2014	27,000
January 1, 2015	30,000
January 1, 2028	75,000

Required:

1. Calculate the service cost and the interest cost components of pension cost for 2014 and 2015.
2. Calculate the PBO at the end of 2014 and 2015.
3. Compute the fair value of plan assets for 2014 and 2015, assuming that $1,200 in contributions is made to the pension fund at the end of each year. There were no actuarial gains or losses during 2014 or 2015.
4. Calculate pension expense for 2014 and 2015.

(problem continued on next page)

5. Prepare the required journal entries for 2014 and 2015.

6. Show how your answer for 2014 would change if the plan had granted credit for prior service.

Assume that the pension benefit formula of ABC Corporation calls for paying a pension benefit of $250 per year for each year of service with the company plus 50% of the projected last year's salary at retirement. Payments begin one year after the employee attains the age of 65 and are paid annually thereafter. The average life expectancy of employees is 76.

The pension plan is adopted on January 1, 2014. One of the company's employees, I.M. Workaholic, is granted credit for 10 years of prior service. He is 50 years old at the date the plan is adopted. His current annual salary is $20,000, but his salary level when he retires in 15 years is expected to be $30,000.

Assume a 10% rate of interest for both the discount rate and the expected rate of return on plan assets.

P14-5

Calculating PBO, ABO, and pension expense
(LO 1, 2, 3)

Required:

1. Determine the PBO and ABO related to Workaholic's pension benefits as of January 1, 2014.

2. What would the projected benefit obligation be on December 31, 2014?

3. How much pension expense should ABC Corporation recognize in 2014 for Workaholic? Show the components of pension expense.

Assume the same facts for ABC Corporation as in P14-5 with the following exceptions:

• Assume both that ABC fully funds the estimated PBO on January 1, 2014, and that invested funds earn an actual return of 12% in 2014.

• Suppose that in addition to funding the estimated PBO on January 1, 2014, ABC follows a policy of contributing to the pension fund (at the end of each year) an amount equal to the estimated pension expense less the prior service cost component, which was prefunded. On January 1, 2015, the discount rate drops from 10% to 9% while the expected return on plan assets remains at 10% for 2015.

P14-6

Determining PBO, ABO, and pension expense
(LO 1, 2, 3)

Required:

1. How much pension expense should ABC recognize in 2014? Show the components of pension expense. Explain how this differs from your answer in requirement 3 of P14-5.

2. Compute the pension expense and amount funded in 2015. (Assume that the actual return on plan assets was 10% in 2015.) Compare the funded status of the plans at the end of 2015 and 2014. Explain the change.

On January 1, 2014, Magee Corporation started doing business by hiring R. Walker as an employee at an annual salary of $50,000, with an annual salary increment of $10,000. Based on his current age and the company's retirement program, Walker is required to retire at the end of the year in 2017. However, at his option, he could retire any time after completing one full year of service. Regardless of when he retires, the company will pay a lump-sum pension at the end of 2018. The lump-sum payment is calculated to be 25% of the cumulative lifetime salary Walker earned. Magee's annual discount rate is 10%. Assume that Walker retires at the end of 2017.

P14-7

Identifying effect of funding and discount rate assumption on pension expense
(LO 2, 3, 5)

mhhe.com/revsine6e

Required:

1. Assuming that Magee Corporation does not fund its pension expense, calculate this expense for 2014–2017. Clearly identify the service and interest cost components. Based on your calculations, provide journal entries to record the effects of pensions during 2011–2018.

2. Assume that Magee fully funds its pension cost as soon as it vests and that the contributions to the pension fund earn exactly a 10% rate of return annually. Based on these revised assumptions, redo requirement 1.

3. Explain why the total pension expense in requirement 1 and in requirement 2 differ.

4. Assume that Magee does not fund its pension expense. Discuss how different assumptions regarding the discount rate affect the pension expense. Compare the pension expense with discount rates of 5%, 10%, and 15%.

P14-8

Determining effect of discount rate assumption on pension expense and PBO **(LO 2, 3, 5)**

mhhe.com/revsine6e

Use the same set of facts as in P14-7. In addition, assume that based on ERISA rules, Magee Corporation must contribute the following amounts to the pension fund:

	2014	2015	2016	2017
Contributions	$8,475	$11,000	$15,000	$18,000

Magee intends to fund the pension plan only to the extent required by ERISA rules. Assume that the contributions to the pension fund earn exactly a 10% rate of return annually.

Required:

1. The CEO of the company, Reece Magee, is considering three possible discount rates (8%, 10%, and 12%) for calculating the annual pension expense. Provide schedules showing how much pension expense will be reported under each of the three scenarios during the 2011–2018 period.

2. Provide schedules showing the funded status of the pension plan during the 2014–2017 period.

3. Magee is wondering which of the three discount rate assumptions would be considered the most and least conservative for the purposes of determining net income. Prepare a schedule that shows how total pension expense compares across the three discount rate assumptions. Explain your results.

P14-9

Interpreting OPEB disclosures and making journal entries **(LO 3, 6, 7)**

The following information is based on an actual annual report. Different names and years are being used.

Bond and some of its subsidiaries provide certain postretirement medical, dental, and vision care and life insurance for retirees and their dependents and for the surviving dependents of eligible employees and retirees. Generally, the employees become eligible for postretirement benefits if they retire no earlier than age 55 with 10 years of service. The liability for postretirement benefits is funded through trust funds based on actuarially determined contributions that consider the amount deductible for income tax purposes. The health care plans are contributory, funded jointly by the companies and the participating retirees. The December 31, 2015 and 2014, postretirement benefit liabilities and related data were determined using the January 1, 2015, actuarial valuations.

Information related to the accumulated postretirement benefit obligation plan for the years 2015 and 2014 follows:

($ in thousands)	Years Ended December 31,	
	2015	**2014**
Change in benefit obligation		
Benefit obligation at beginning of period	$1,236,000	$1,139,000
Service cost	41,000	38,000
Interest cost	82,000	78,000
Plan participants' contributions	4,000	3,000
Actuarial loss (gain)	(188,000)	25,000
Benefits paid	(51,000)	(47,000)
Special termination benefits	27,000	—
Benefit obligation at end of period	1,151,000	1,236,000
Change in plan assets		
Fair value of plan assets at beginning of period	865,000	767,000
Actual return on plan assets	105,000	122,000
Employer contributions	24,000	20,000
Plan participants' contributions	4,000	3,000
Benefits paid	(51,000)	(47,000)
Fair value of plan assets at period-end	947,000	865,000
Plan assets less than benefit obligations	(204,000)	(371,000)
AOCI—net actuarial (gain) loss	(555,000)	(352,000)
AOCI—prior service cost	41,000	48,000

The assumed discount rates used to determine the benefit obligation as of December 31, 2015 and 2014, were 7.75% and 6.75%, respectively. The fair value of plan assets excludes $9 million and $7 million held in a grantor trust as of December 31, 2015 and 2014, respectively, for the payment of postretirement medical benefits.

The components of other postretirement benefit costs, portions of which were recorded as components of construction costs for the years 2015, 2014, and 2013 follow:

($ in thousands)	2015	2014	2013
Service cost	$?	$?	$ 34,000
Interest cost on APBO	?	?	76,000
Expected return on plan assets	?	?	(61,000)
Amortization of prior service costs	4,000	4,000	4,000
Recognized gain	(14,000)	(14,000)	(13,000)
Curtailment loss	30,000	–0–	–0–
Net periodic benefit cost	$?	$?	$ 40,000

The other postretirement benefit curtailment losses in December 2015 represent the recognition of $3,000 of additional prior service costs and a $27,000 increase in the benefit obligations resulting from special termination benefits.

The health care cost trend rates used to measure the expected cost of the postretirement medical benefits are assumed to be 8.0% for pre-Medicare recipients and 6.0% for Medicare recipients for 2015. Those rates are assumed to decrease in 0.5% annual increments to 5% for the years 2021 and 2017, respectively, and to remain level thereafter. The health care cost trend rates, used to measure the expected cost of postretirement dental and vision benefits, are a level 3.5% and 2.0% per year, respectively. Assumed health care cost trend rates have a significant effect on the amounts reported for the health care plans. A percentage change of one point in the assumed health care cost trend rates would have the following effects:

($ in thousands)	I Percentage Point	
	Increase	**Decrease**
Effect on total 2015 service and interest cost components	$ 26,000	$ (20,000)
Effect on APBO as of 12/31/2015	190,000	151,000

Required:

1. Assuming an expected rate of return on plan assets for 2015 and 2014 of 8.8% and 9%, respectively, compute the missing amounts in the first table and determine the Net periodic benefit cost for years 2015 and 2014. (Round amounts to nearest million.)

2. Assuming that the employer submitted the $4,000,000 of participant contributions directly to the trust, show the journal entry that Bond would make to record its 2015 company (employer) contribution, Net periodic benefit cost, and AOCI effects.

3. Show that the 2015 journal entries result in a balance sheet pension asset (liability) equal to the funded status. Assume that the beginning 2015 balance equals the ending 2014 funded status.

P14-10

Amortizing actuarial (gains) losses **(LO 3, 4)**

mhhe.com/revsine6e

The following information pertains to the pension plan of Beatty Business Group:

		Beginning of the Year		
Year (1)	PBO (2)	Fair Value of Pension Plan Assets (3)	(Gain) Loss for the Year (4)
---	---	---	---
2011	$ 400,000	$ 390,000	
2012	450,000	410,000	$ (60,000)
2013	570,000	500,000	(120,000)
2014	840,000	800,000	120,000
2015	1,000,000	1,100,000	175,000
2016	1,200,000	1,280,000	250,000
2017	1,450,000	1,310,000	80,000

Note that the information in Columns (2) and (3) are as of the beginning of the year, whereas the information in Column (4) is measured *over* the year.

The AOCI—net actuarial (gain) loss at the end of 2011 was $(70,000). The Gain (loss) for the year account represents the excess of the realized return on pension plan assets over the expected return for the specific year. When a (gain) loss was reported, the realized return was (higher) lower than the expected return during that year. The estimated remaining service period of active employees is five years for each of the calendar years.

Required:

Provide a schedule showing how the (gain) loss is amortized over the 2012–2017 period. Clearly indicate whether the amortization increases or decreases the pension expense in each year.

P14-11

Interpreting pension disclosures **(LO 2, 3, 4, 6)**

Selected pension information extracted from the retirement benefits note that appeared in Green's 2014 annual report follows. (These numbers have been modified but are based on the activities of a real company whose name has been disguised.)

All employees of Green and employees of certain other subsidiaries are eligible to participate in the company's pension plans. The defined benefit plans provide benefits for participating employees based on years of service and average compensation for a specified period of time before retirement.

The following table provides a reconciliation of the changes in the plans' benefit obligations and fair value of assets for the years ended December 31, 2014 and 2013:

Reconciliation of Projected Benefit Obligation

($ in millions)	2014	2013
Obligation at January 1	$6,117	$5,666
Service cost	236	213
Interest cost	433	418
Actuarial loss (gain)	?	300
Plan amendments	?	–0–
Benefit payments	?	(480)
Obligation at December 31	$5,624	$6,117

Reconciliation of Fair Value of Plan Assets

($ in millions)	2014	2013
Fair value of plan assets at January 1	$5,564	$5,127
Actual return on plan assets	7	847
Employer contributions	100	70
Benefit payments	?	(480)
Fair value of plan assets at December 31	?	$5,564

The following table provides a statement of funded status of the plans as of December 31, 2014 and 2013:

Funded Status

($ in millions)	2014	2013
Projected benefit obligation	$(5,624)	$(6,117)
Fair value of assets	?	5,564
Funded status at December 31:	$ (341)	$ (553)
AOCI—Actuarial (gain) loss	$ 288	$ 651
AOCI—Prior service costs	138	68
Total	$ 426	$ 719

The following table provides the components of net periodic pension cost for the years ended December 31, 2014, 2013, and 2012:

Components of Net Periodic Pension Cost

($ in millions)	2014	2013	2012
Defined benefit plans:			
Service cost	$236	$213	$179
Interest cost	433	418	393
Expected return on assets	(514)	(472)	(421)
Amortization of:			
Prior service cost	5	4	4
Actuarial (gain) loss	21	22	26
Net periodic benefit cost	$181	$185	$181

The following assumptions were used by the Company in the measurement of the benefit obligation as of December 31:

Weighted-Average Assumptions	2014	2013
Discount rate	8.25%	7.00%
Salary growth rate	4.26	4.26
Expected return on plan assets	9.48	9.59

Required:
Show supporting computations with clear labels for all calculations.

1. What is the fair value of plan assets as of December 31, 2014?
2. What was the amount of benefit payments distributed to retirees in 2014?
3. Determine the amount of increase (decrease) in the projected benefit obligation (PBO) as a result of amendments to the plan during 2014 and reconcile it to AOCI—prior service costs.
4. Determine the amount of the actuarial loss (gain) on the PBO in 2014.
5. What was the effect of increasing the discount rate from 7.00% in 2013 to 8.25% in 2014?
6. Give the journal entries that Green would have made to record the effects of its pension plan for 2014.
7. Verify that the journal entries result in a balance sheet pension asset (liability) that is equal to the December 31, 2014, funded status.

P14-12

Evaluating the effects of unreasonable rate of return assumptions **(LO 3, 4, 6, 9)**

Berle Corp. has a defined benefit pension plan that features the following data:

Jan 1, 2013 (beginning of fiscal year):

Fair value of plan assets	$4,000
Projected benefit obligation	$6,200
Accumulated benefit obligation	$5,900
AOCI balance relating to actuarial estimates	$900 (debit/loss)

The following assumptions are used for the pension plan in 2013:

Discount rate	7.5%
Average remaining employee service life	25 years

Additional information relating to 2013:

New service cost	$300
Cash contributions to the plan assets (end of 2013)	$150
Pension benefits paid by the plan (end of 2013)	$350
Actual return on plan assets	$360
Actuarial estimate adjustment to the PBO	$50 (debit/loss)

The CFO of Berle Corp. devises a plan to inflate artificially net income by using an estimate for expected return on plan assets of 25% (the traditional estimate for return on plan assets is 10%). Under U.S. GAAP, the CFO chooses to amortize only the portion of any beginning AOCI balance outside the corridor into pension expense/income.

Required (ignore potential deferred tax effects):

1. Compute the 2013 pension expense/income under U.S. GAAP. What was the effect of the CFO's plans on 2013 pension expense/income?
2. Compute the 2013 pension expense/income under IFRS. What was the effect of the CFO's plan on 2013 pension expense/income?

(problem continued on next page)

3. Compute the effect of the CFO's plan on 2014 pension expense/income under U.S. GAAP. In other words, what is the effect of the plan on future period amortization of the AOCI balance?

4. Compute the effect of the CFO's plan on 2014 pension expense/income under IFRS. In other words, what is the effect of the plan on future period amortization of the AOCI balance?

CASES

Refer to the 2012 General Electric Retiree Health and Life Benefits disclosure appearing in Exhibit 14.6.

C14-1

Interpreting OPEB disclosures **(LO 6, 7)**

Required:

1. Reconstruct the journal entries that GE would have made in 2012 to record the effects of its retiree health and life benefits plans.

2. Explain how GE's health and life benefits plans affected its OCI account for 2012.

Hint on Curtailment/settlement: Follow the first six journal entries made for the GE pension example before addressing the curtailment/settlement. The curtailment entry includes the following:

DR	Curtailment loss (outside of Retiree benefit plans cost)	$32	
	CR OCI—Prior service cost		$195
	CR OCI—Net actuarial loss (gain)		102

You should be able to reconstruct the rest of the curtailment entry from information in the Retiree Health and Life Benefits disclosure.

Novartis, which files under IFRS, reported the following information in its first quarter report for 2013:

C14-2

Novartis: Interpreting IFRS pension accounting **(LO 3, 6, 9)**

Impact of introducing revised accounting standard on Employee Benefits in 2013
The Group introduced the revised IFRS accounting standard IAS 19 (R) "*Employee Benefits*," on January 1, 2013. The principal impact of this is that the return on pension plan assets and the interest calculated on the defined benefit obligations now use the same interest rate reflecting the current market yield of high-quality corporate bonds. Previously the return on plan assets was calculated based on the higher long-term expected return on assets, so the adoption of the new accounting standard increases the annual cost of post-employment benefits included in Corporate Other Expense. It has also been required to restate for the amortization of previously unrecognized past service credits. As required by the new standard, the Group's 2012 Consolidated Financial Statements have been retrospectively restated to reflect these changes. For the full year 2012, the impact of these restatements is an additional expense of USD 318 million before tax (USD 235 million after tax) and in the first quarter of 2012 an additional expense of USD 79 million before tax (USD 58 million after tax), offset by a corresponding adjustment of the actuarial losses recognized in comprehensive income.

Required:

1. Did the adoption of the revised *IAS 19* increase or decrease Novartis' annual pension expense? Why?

(case continued on next page)

2. Why did Novartis have to adjust its 2012 (prior year's) financial reporting for its pensions?

3. Are there any cash flow implications of these changes for Novartis?

C14-3

Union Pacific Corporation: Interpreting pension and OPEB note disclosures (LO 3, 6, 7)

Presented below are excerpts from the 2008 annual report of Union Pacific.

At December 31, 2008, Union Pacific had a stock price of $47.80 and 503.2 million shares outstanding. Its balance sheet at December 31, 2008, shows total assets of $39.7 billion and total liabilities of $24.3 billion. Its income statement for the year ended December 31, 2008, shows net income of $2.3 billion and interest expense of 0.5 billion.

4. Retirement Plans
Pension and Other Postretirement Benefits

Pension Plans—We provide defined benefit retirement income to eligible non-union employees through qualified and non-qualified (supplemental) pension plans. Qualified and non-qualified pension benefits are based on years of service and the highest compensation during the latest years of employment, with specific reductions made for early retirements.

Other Postretirement Benefits (OPEB)—We provide defined contribution medical and life insurance benefits for eligible retirees. These benefits are funded as medical claims and life insurance premiums are paid.

Changes in our PBO and plan assets are as follows for the years ended December 31:

Funded Status	Pension		OPEB	
(Millions of Dollars)	**2008**	**2007**	**2008**	**2007**
Projected Benefit Obligation				
Projected benefit obligation at beginning of year	$2,112	$2,113	$ 326	$ 374
Service cost	34	34	3	3
Interest cost	137	124	24	20
Plan amendments	—	—	(9)	(10)
Actuarial loss (gain)	132	(33)	101	(34)
Gross benefits paid	(143)	(126)	(27)	(27)
Projected benefit obligation at end of year	$2,272	$2,112	$ 418	$ 326
Plan Assets				
Fair value of plan assets at beginning of year	$2,058	$1,989	$ —	$ —
Actual return on plan assets	(592)	183	—	—
Voluntary funded pension plan contributions	200	—	—	—
Other funded pension plan contributions	8	—	—	—
Non-qualified plan benefit contributions	12	12	27	27
Gross benefits paid	(143)	(126)	(27)	(27)
Fair value of plan assets at end of year	$1,543	$2,058	$ —	$ —
Funded status at end of year	$ (729)	$ (54)	$(418)	$(326)

Components of pension expense for **2008** include the following:

	Pension	OPEB
Service cost	$ 34	$ 3
Interest cost	137	24
Expected return on plan assets	(152)	—
Amortization of prior service cost/(credit)	6	(34)
Amortization of actuarial loss	10	13
	35	6

Pre-tax amounts recognized in accumulated other comprehensive income/(loss) as of **December 31, 2007,** consist of:

(Millions of Dollars)	Pension	OPEB
Prior service cost/(credit)	$ 18	$(137)
Net actuarial loss	158	85
Total	$176	$ (52)

Assumptions—The weighted-average actuarial assumptions used to determine **benefit obligations** at December 31:

Percentages	2008	2007
Discount rate	6.25%	6.50%
Expected return on plan assets	8.00%	8.00%
Salary increase	3.50%	3.50%

Assumptions—The weighted-average actuarial assumptions used to determine **expense** were as follows for the years ended December 31:

Percentages	2008	2007	2006
Discount rate	6.50%	6.00%	5.75%
Expected return on plan assets	8.00%	8.00%	8.00%
Salary increase	3.50%	3.00%	2.75%

For 2008, the discount rate was based on a Mercer yield curve of high quality corporate bonds with cash flows matching our plans' expected benefit payments. For 2007 and 2006, the discount rate was based on a hypothetical portfolio of high quality corporate bonds with cash flows matching our plans' expected benefit payments. The expected return on plan assets is based on our asset allocation mix and our historical return, taking into account current and expected market conditions. The actual return (loss) on pension plan assets, net of fees, was approximately (30)% in 2008, 9% in 2007, and 14% in 2006.

Required:

1. What is the amount of assets or liabilities recognized on Union Pacific's balance sheet for its U.S. pension benefits at December 31, 2008?

2. Compute the ending balance of Accumulated Other Comprehensive Income—Actuarial (Gains) Losses for the **Pension Plans.** The amounts are **before taxes.** Be sure to label your items and show your computations.

**Accumulated Other Comprehensive Income—
Actuarial (Gains) Losses (Pension Plans)**

Beginning	$158	
Ending		

3. Based on information in the pension note, would you expect the pension expense to be higher or lower than its 2008 amount? Explain.

(case continued on next page)

4. Compute the short-term pension risk ratio and the short-term OPEB risk ratio (extended version) as of December 31, 2008.

5. Compute the long-term pension risk ratio and the long-term OPEB risk ratio as of December 31, 2008.

6. Based on your answers to requirements 4 and 5, explain whether Union Pacific has significant pension and OPEB risk.

C14-4

Union Pacific Corporation: Comparing U.S. GAAP and IFRS pension and OPEB accounting **(LO 9)**

Refer to the Union Pacific information in Case 14-3.

Required:

Explain how pension expense and OCI would change if Union Pacific were using *IAS 19*.

 .mhhe.com/revsine6e

Remember to check the book's companion website for additional study material.

Financial Reporting for Owners' Equity | 15

S tatement readers must understand the accounting procedures and reporting conventions for owners' equity for these reasons:

1. *Appropriate income measurement.* Differentiating between owners' equity changes that increase income or decrease income and changes that don't increase or decrease income will help answer these questions: Why are bond interest payments an expense that reduces net income while dividend payments on common and preferred stock are not an expense that reduces net income? Why do certain financing transactions—such as early debt retirements—generate accounting gains and losses while others—such as stock repurchases and debt conversions—do not generate accounting gains and losses?

2. *Compliance with contract terms and restrictions.* Many "exotic" securities having characteristics of both debt and equity have been developed over the years by investment bankers. How should these hybrid securities be classified for monitoring compliance with contractual restrictions such as maximum allowable debt-to-equity ratios?

3. *Legality of corporate distributions to owners.* Owners' equity is generally regarded as a financial "cushion" protecting corporate creditors. Cash distributions to shareholders—dividends and stock repurchases—reduce this cushion. How much of this cushion can legally be distributed as dividends? When a company liquidates, in what order of priority can cash payouts be made to its various claimants?

4. *Linkage to equity valuation.* Analyzing the true worth of equity shares requires an understanding of the amount of earnings that accrue to each share. Equity valuation thus depends on how a company's options, warrants, and convertible securities affect its earnings per share.

After discussing each of these issues, we describe how earnings per share (EPS) is calculated and then look at the controversy surrounding GAAP for employee stock options. The chapter concludes with a discussion of accounting for hybrid securities—convertible debt and others—that contain both debt-like and equitylike features.

LEARNING OBJECTIVES

After studying this chapter, you will understand:

1. Why some financing transactions— such as debt redemptions—produce reported gains and losses while others—such as stock repurchases— do not.

2. Why companies buy back their stock, and how they do it.

3. Why some preferred stock resembles debt, and how preferred stock is reported on financial statements.

4. How and when retained earnings limits a company's distributions to common stockholders.

5. How to interpret the balance sheet items that constitute shareholders' equity.

6. How to calculate basic earnings per share (EPS) and diluted EPS, and whether EPS is a meaningful number.

7. What generally accepted accounting principles (GAAP) says about employee stock options, and why the accounting treatment has been controversial.

8. How and why GAAP understates the true cost of most convertible debt, and how IFRS guidelines avoid this understatement.

APPROPRIATE INCOME MEASUREMENT

Some increases (decreases) in owners' equity are considered to be income (loss), while other increases (decreases) are not income (loss). To know why, you must understand the modern GAAP definition of the "firm."

Chapter

What Constitutes the "Firm"?

Although GAAP is intended to address the information needs of both lenders and investors, when it comes to measuring net income GAAP adopts a decidedly "ownership" perspective.[1] To see why and how consider the basic accounting principle that income can be earned (or expenses incurred) *only* through transactions between the firm and "outsiders." But who is "inside" the firm, and who are the outsiders? *Under the GAAP view, the firm* is the net capital deployed:

$$\underbrace{\text{Assets} \;-\; \text{Liabilities}}_{\text{Net capital deployed}} \;=\; \underbrace{\text{Owners' equity}}_{\text{Owners' capital}}$$

Owners are the "insiders" who provide that net capital. Consequently, no income or loss can arise from transactions between the firm and its owners because owners are *not* outsiders. This perspective explains why interest payments to banks or bondholders are expenses that reduce net income while dividend payments to common and preferred shareholders are *not* expenses that reduce net income.

- Banks and bondholders are outsiders—hence, interest costs are expenses.
- Shareholders are not outsiders—thus, dividends are a *distribution of earnings* to owners, not an expense of the company.

This "ownership" perspective of GAAP income measurement helps us understand why certain financing transactions generate income or losses while other transactions do not.

One way corporations raise capital is by selling equity shares to investors. Called **common stock,** equity shares provide the opportunity for purchasers to participate in the company's future profitability.[2] In addition to conveying ownership rights, common stock has **limited liability.** As long as each share is initially sold for more than the per share dollar amount—called **par value**—printed on each stock certificate the shareholder's potential loss is limited to the original purchase price of the common share. Limited liability makes investing in common stock attractive because although potential gains from ownership are unlimited, the risk of loss is limited to the share purchase price.

> The term *par value* refers to the **nominal** value or **face value** of a security—a dollar amount printed on the face of each stock certificate. With common stock, par value is set by the company issuing the stock. At one time, par value represented the original investment in cash, goods, or services behind each share of stock. Today, par value is an assigned amount (such as $1 per share) used to compute the dollar accounting value of the common shares on the company's balance sheet. *Par value has no relation to market value.*

To see how the accounting for common stock works, assume that at its formation, Nahigian Corporation issues (meaning "sells to investors") 5,000 shares of common stock at $50 per share and that the shares have a par value of $1 each. Nahigian records the stock issuance as:

DR	Cash	$250,000	
CR	Common stock—$1 par value		$ 5,000
CR	Paid-in capital in excess of par		245,000

---

[1] According to the Financial Accounting Standards Board (FASB) "[t]he objective of general purpose financial reporting is to provide financial information about the reporting entity that is useful to existing and potential investors, lenders, and other creditors in making decisions about providing resources to the entity. Those decisions involve buying, selling, or holding equity and debt instruments and providing or settling loans and other forms of credit." See *Statement of Financial Accounting Concepts No. 8* "Conceptual Framework for Financial Reporting, Chapter 1: The Objective of General Purpose Financial Reporting" (Norwalk, CT: FASB, 2010). Accounting Standards Codification (ASC) Topic 480: *Distinguishing Liabilities from Equities* provides guidance useful for determining which particular providers of capital qualify as "owners" for GAAP income measurement purposes.

[2] Investors who buy **preferred stock** (discussed later in the chapter) also participate in the company's future profitability. However, investors who buy debt instruments do not participate in the company's future profitability. Instead, debtholders gain only a specified (fixed or variable) rate of return—for example, "7% interest per annum," or in the case of variable rate debt, "LIBOR plus 1/2%."

The $1 par value per share bears no necessary relationship to the *market value* of each share at issuance ($50) or later. (Remember that par value is just the dollar amount printed on each stock certificate.) The difference between the $50 issue price and the $1 par value is credited to the separate owners' equity account Paid-in capital in excess of par—sometimes called Additional paid-in capital.

Suppose that several years later, Nahigian Corporation reacquires 200 of these shares at a cost of $48 each. When a corporation buys back its own shares, the repurchased shares are called **treasury stock** if the shares are to be held in the corporate treasury for later use. The accounting entry is:

DR Treasury stock	$9,600	
CR Cash		$9,600

Notice that no gain or loss is recorded for the difference between the $50 per share price at which the shares were first issued and the $48 repurchase price. ***The reason stock repurchases do not involve accounting gains and losses is that they are transactions between the company and its owners.***

When treasury stock is acquired, it is not considered a corporate asset. Instead, treasury stock is treated as a reduction in owners' equity. Treasury stock is debited, as shown above, and it then appears on the balance sheet as a **contra-equity** account. Here's how the owners' equity section of Nahigian's balance sheet looks after the company repurchased 200 shares of common stock for $9,600:

Nahigian Corporation

Owners' Equity

Common stock, $1 par value, 5,000 shares issued	$ 5,000
Paid-in capital in excess of par	245,000
Retained earnings (assumed for illustration)	700,000
Total paid-in capital and retained earnings	$950,000
Less: Treasury stock (at cost)	(9,600)
Total owners' equity	$940,400

Now assume that Nahigian decides several months later to raise more equity capital by reselling all 200 treasury shares at $53 per share. The entry would be:

DR Cash	$10,600	
CR Treasury stock		$9,600
CR Paid-in capital in excess of par		1,000

This entry eliminates the contra-equity account Treasury stock. The $53 per share selling price is $5 per share higher than the $48 paid to reacquire the shares. Despite this "excess," *no income is recognized on this transaction between the firm and its owners.* Instead, the difference of $1,000 (or 200 shares × [$53 − $48]) is added to the Paid-in capital in excess of par account.

What if rather than being held in treasury for later use, Nahigian permanently retires the repurchased shares by cancelling the stock certificates. When shares are repurchased and retired, the Common

> But if Nahigian had reacquired outstanding *debt* at a price lower than its book value, an extinguishment gain *would* be recorded, as described in Chapter 11. Debt redemptions generate accounting gains (and losses) while stock repurchases do not.

stock account is reduced for the par value of shares retired ($200 in our example) and the Paid-in capital account is reduced for the "excess" purchase price ($9,600 − $200 = $9,400) as:

DR	Common stock—$1 par value	$ 200	
DR	Paid-in capital in excess of par	9,400	
CR	Cash		$9,600

The share certificates are then canceled, thus reducing the total number of shares issued.

A further complication arises when repurchased shares are to be retired and the excess purchase price ($9,400 in our example) exceeds the available Paid-in capital balance. To illustrate this complication, suppose the Paid-in capital account balance just prior to the share buyback is only $5,000. Nahigian would then record the share repurchase and retirement as:

DR	Common stock—$1 par value	$ 200	
DR	Paid-in capital in excess of par	5,000	
DR	Retained earnings	4,400	
CR	Cash		$9,600

Notice that (1) $5,000 of the excess purchase price is used to reduce the Paid-in capital account to zero, and (2) the remaining excess purchase price ($9,400 − $5,000 = $4,400) is then recorded as a reduction to Retained earnings.

RE**CAP**

The "ownership" perspective of GAAP income measurement explains why financing transactions with banks or bondholders generate income or losses while transactions with shareholders do not. This same intuition explains why treasury stock gains and losses are not recognized. Because treasury stock transactions are between the company and its shareholders (owners) and not outsiders, no income is recognized—even when the successive stock transactions are favorable such as those in the Nahigian Corporation illustration.

Why Companies Repurchase Their Stock

Firms reacquire their own common stock for many reasons. Sometimes a company needs shares for employee stock option redemptions. Sometimes management may conclude that the company's shares are undervalued at the prevailing market price and that the best use of corporate funds is to invest in those shares by buying some of them back from stockholders. At other times, perhaps management just wants to distribute surplus cash to shareholders rather than to keep it inside the company.

A company's *surplus* cash—the amount over and above the cash needed for day-to-day operating activities—can be a problem for management and for shareholders. Management worries that another company or investor group might launch a hostile takeover of the business, using the company's own cash surplus to partially finance the takeover. If a hostile takeover is successful, some managers will inevitably lose their jobs. Shareholders, on the other hand, worry that management might spend the company's surplus cash on unprofitable—negative net present value— projects and on lavish "perks" such as corporate speedboats or race cars. So, its better to give the money to shareholders—after all, it is money to which they are entitled.

> Suppose that Raider Company intends to acquire Target Company for $150 million in cash. Raider already has $30 million cash set aside for the takeover and has lined up another $100 million from a bank loan. But that still leaves Raider $20 million short. Where can it find the money it needs to complete the takeover? One possibility is to tap into Target's surplus cash. In other words, the more surplus cash that Target has, the easier it becomes for Raider to use the money to help pay for the takeover.

Stock repurchases have one other advantage: Shareholders who take the stock repurchase cash are taxed at capital gain rates. If instead the cash is paid out as dividends, shareholders would be taxed at ordinary income rates, which are often higher than capital gain tax rates.

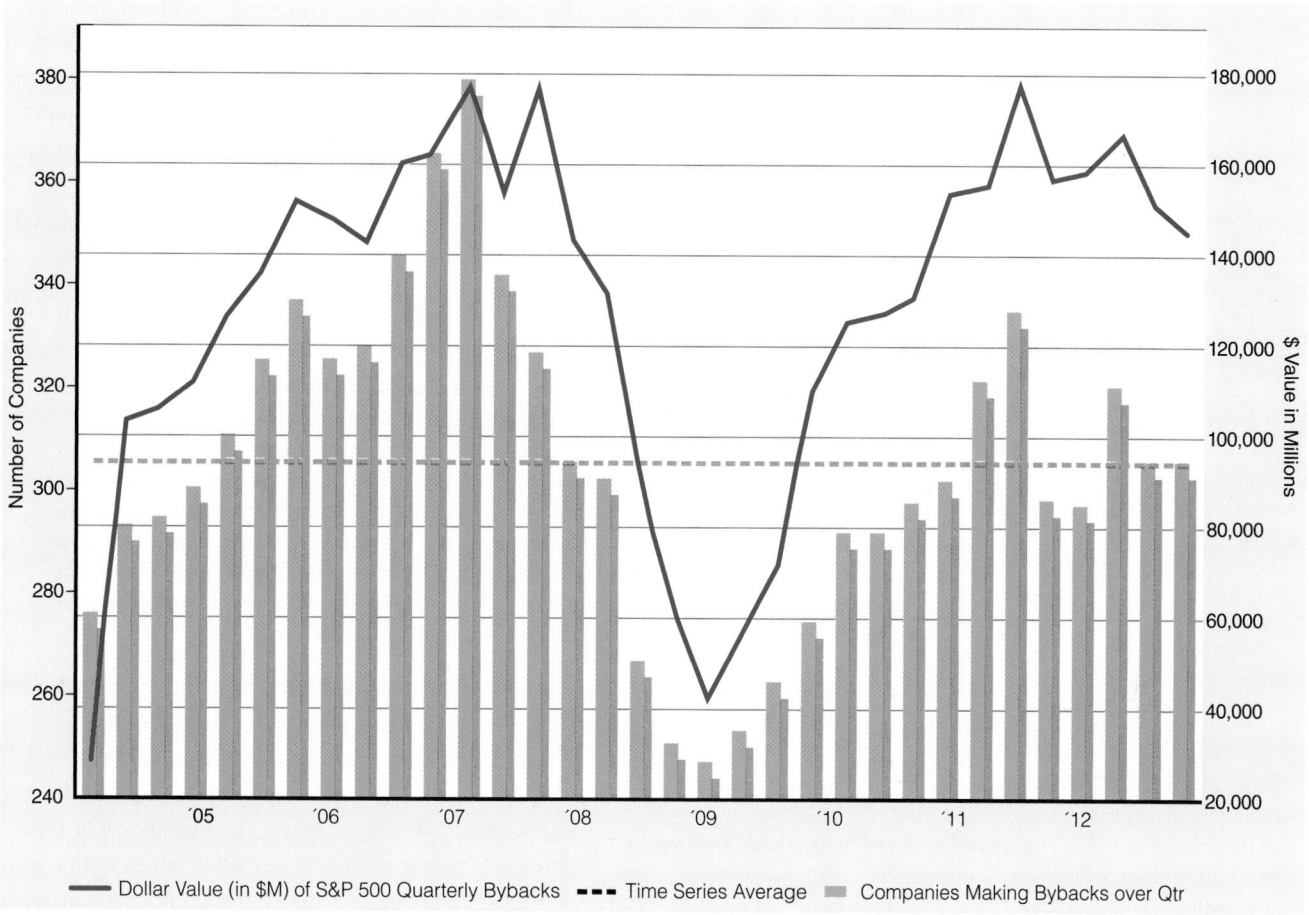

Figure 15.1 THE DOLLAR VALUE OF STOCK REPURCHASED EACH QUARTER 2005–2012 BY U.S. COMPANIES IN THE STANDARD & POOR'S 500 INDEX (IN $ MILLIONS)

Source: "Buyback Quarterly," FactSet Research Systems Inc., April 2, 2013. The Standard & Poor's 500 Index (S&P 500) is one of the most commonly used benchmarks for the overall U.S. stock market. A team of analysts and economists at Standard & Poor's chooses 500 stocks for the index based on market size, liquidity, and industry grouping, among other factors.

The popularity of stock repurchases has varied over time as a result of changes in the economic climate, stock market price levels, and the availability of surplus corporate cash. Only 87 U.S. companies announced stock buyback plans in 1980, with the dollar value totaling $1.4 billion. In 1998, 1,570 U.S. companies announced stock repurchases that totaled $222.0 billion.[3] Figure 15.1 shows the total dollar value of the buybacks for each quarter from 2005 through 2012 for Standard & Poor's 500 companies. These large U.S. firms repurchased more than $384 billion worth of their shares during the four quarters of 2012, an amount that represents roughly 80% of the free cash flows the companies produced that year.

The typical share repurchase is at a price about 23% more than the stock's market value just before the repurchase offer is announced.[4] Those shareholders who sell their stock back to the company capture this price premium. But what about the shareholders who don't sell? According to perhaps the best-known study on the subject, the stock of the average corporation that repurchases its shares outperforms the rest of the market by 12% over the four years

---

[3] G. Grullon and D. Ikenberry, "What Do We Know about Stock Repurchases?" *Journal of Applied Corporate Finance,* Spring 2000, pp. 31–51.

[4] D. Ikenberry, J. Lakonishok, and T. Vermaelen, "Market Underreaction to Open Market Share Repurchases," *Journal of Financial Economics,* October 1995, pp. 181–208.

following the announcement of the repurchase program. Even better, high book-to-market price stocks that are repurchased beat the market by 45% over the next four years.[5] So, it seems that everybody wins when shares are repurchased. Those who sell shares back to the company capture a price premium for doing so, and those who don't sell but instead continue to own the shares capture an above-market return on their investment over the next four years.

But not all buybacks are created equal.[6] While share repurchases as a whole help to boost investor returns, not all companies use repurchases to demonstrate that their stock is undervalued or to distribute excess cash to shareholders, skeptics say. Instead, share repurchases are sometimes used for other purposes. For example, here's what Microsoft said in 1997 about its stock repurchase program:

 **Analysis**

> Management believes existing cash and short-term investments together with funds generated from operations will be sufficient to meet operating requirements for the next twelve months. Microsoft's cash and short-term investments are available for strategic investments, mergers and acquisitions, other potential large-scale cash needs that may arise, and to fund an increased stock buyback program over historical levels to reduce the dilutive impact of the Company's employee stock option and purchase programs. *Despite recent increases in stock repurchases, the buyback program has not kept pace with employee stock option grants or exercises.* Beginning in fiscal 1990, Microsoft has repurchased 134 million common shares for $4.2 billion while 336 million shares were issued under the Company's employee stock option and purchase plans.[7] [Emphasis added.]

Microsoft's buyback program partially offsets **share dilution**[8] caused by the company's stock option and repurchase plans. But what does a company gain from buying back its shares with one hand while issuing shares through options with the other hand? Some analysts answer not much. While an employee usually buys shares for less than the market price under stock option programs, the company pays the market price to buy them back. In dollar terms, the number of shares outstanding may seem to be shrinking because the company has spent more to buy back shares than employees have spent to acquire them. But in fact, the number of shares could remain unchanged or even increase.

Another concern for analysts is that many companies borrow to finance their stock repurchase programs. While such moves might have tax or other advantages, these companies simply replace equity with debt. Shareholders get the buyback's benefits only at the expense of owning a more leveraged company—one with more debt and less equity than before the repurchase. Also, these companies face the risk that an economic downturn could make it more difficult to service debt.

Intel's experience highlights the issue. Every year since 1992, this semiconductor manufacturer bought back stock. But in 1999, for example, while it issued only $543 million of stock and bought back a whopping $4.6 billion of stock under its share repurchase plan, its common shares outstanding actually increased to 3,334 million from 3,315 million. What is the reason for this growth in the number of shares? The company paid $64.95 a share for the stock it repurchased—but it received only $9.70 for each share issued when employees exercised their stock options. More shares were issued than were repurchased.

Microsoft terminated its stock buyback program in 2000. Before doing so, the company sold "put" warrants for 157 million shares. The warrants entitled holders to sell shares of Microsoft back to the company at a price of about $74 per share. If Microsoft shares are trading at $54 when the warrants are later exercised and the average purchase price is $74, the company then must come up with $20 a share—or $3.14 billion—to settle the warrants. That's a lot of cash!

---

[5] Ibid.

[6] G. Morgenson, "Why Buybacks Aren't Always Good News," *The Wall Street Journal,* November 12, 2006.

[7] Microsoft Corporation, Quarterly Report to Shareholders (10-Q filing), March 31, 1997.

[8] Share dilution is akin to taking an apple pie that is already cut into six large pieces and then slicing each piece in half again so that the pie ends up divided into 12 much smaller pieces. Consider a simplified example of share dilution. Suppose that a company is worth $60 million, and 6 million shares of stock are in the hands of investors. Each share is then worth $10. Next suppose that management gives stock options for 6 million shares to employees, who then exercise their options and receive the new shares. If the company's value is unchanged, each outstanding share is now worth only $5 because the same $60 million pie (that is, the company) is now divided into twice as many slices (the 12 million shares outstanding). That's share dilution in a nutshell.

Even more worrisome is that ***some stock buybacks are motivated solely by a desire to boost EPS.*** Consider Rocket Software, which completed a successful third quarter with earnings of $220,000 and EPS of $1.00. This was the ninth consecutive quarter that Rocket Software's EPS increased by 10% or more. But it appears that this string of EPS increases is about to be broken—fourth quarter earnings were projected to be only $220,000, unchanged from the third quarter.

How can the company keep its EPS record intact? Management could increase earnings (as well as EPS) by finding ways to grow sales revenues or reduce expenses. Or Rocket Software could buy back some of its common stock:

	Without Buyback	With Buyback
Projected fourth quarter earnings	$220,000	$220,000
Common shares outstanding	220,000	200,000
Projected EPS	$ 1.00	$ 1.10

If the buyback should reduce total shares outstanding from 220,000 to 200,000, fourth quarter EPS will be $1.10, and the company can claim another quarter of 10% EPS growth.

Sounds simple? It's not! There is a hidden assumption. Stock buybacks consume cash. Where did Rocket Software get the cash needed for its buyback? Suppose that the company had to borrow the cash. Then the (after-tax) interest expense on the loan—let's say it's $5,500—would have reduced projected fourth quarter earnings to $214,500. The company would then have to buy back 25,000 shares—or 5,000 more than originally anticipated—to reach its $1.10 EPS goal ($1.10 EPS = $214,500/195,000 shares outstanding after the expanded buyback). Instead of borrowing the cash, Rocket Software could sell some of its marketable securities, investments, or other productive assets. But asset sales may also have a dampening effect on future earnings.

As long as earnings fall by less (in percentage terms) than the buyback percentage reduction in shares outstanding, EPS will indeed go up! But this EPS increase may actually mask deteriorating business fundamentals. Here's an example. In July 2003, AutoNation reported record second quarter EPS of $0.37, a 16% increase from its quarterly EPS one year earlier. But the company's second quarter net income was up only a paltry 2.4% from the previous year's figure. AutoNation achieved the added jump in EPS by repurchasing 47.8 million of its shares over the year—shrinking its outstanding shares by nearly 14%, thus boosting its EPS.

By artificially inflating a company's reported EPS, stock buybacks can be used to camouflage business slowdowns. Research evidence confirms that firms sometimes use stock buybacks to boost EPS and thereby meet (or beat) the quarterly earnings targets set by Wall Street analysts.[9] Buybacks can also wind up bolstering top executives' pay when short-term or long-term incentive compensation is tied to EPS performance.

When it comes to stock buybacks and EPS growth, it pays to look behind the numbers. That is why it has become increasingly important for prudent investors and analysts to sort through firms' share repurchase plans and to determine the reasons behind each buyback. Only then can investors and analysts figure out whether a repurchase plan is a sign to buy—or not to buy—the stock.

---

[9] P. Hribar, N. Thorne-Jenkins, and W. B. Johnson, "Stock Repurchases as an Earnings Management Device," *Journal of Accounting and Economics,* April 2006, pp. 3–28.

COMPLIANCE WITH CONTRACT TERMS

Owners' equity is one of the accounting numbers used in many contracts with lenders, suppliers, and others (Chapter 7). For example, lending agreements usually include covenants that restrict maximum allowable debt-to-equity levels, where equity refers to the book value amount disclosed on the company's balance sheet. Firms have incentives to use their financial reporting latitude to circumvent these contractual restrictions. Consequently, financial statement analysts must understand how owners' equity is reported to determine whether a company they are evaluating is in compliance with its contract terms.

For example, the 2012 annual report of National Beverage Corporation contained the following statement:

Contracting

> [A] subsidiary of the Company maintains unsecured revolving credit facilities with banks aggregating $75 million (the "Credit Facility"). . . . The Credit Facility requires the subsidiary to maintain certain financial ratios, principally debt to net worth and debt to EBITDA (as defined in the loan agreements) and contains other restrictions, none of which are expected to have a material effect on our operations or financial position. At April 28, 2012, we were in compliance with all loan covenants and approximately $1.2 million of **retained earnings** was restricted from distribution.

In this case, lending banks are using several financial statement items—debt, net worth (think "owners' equity"), and a variation of accounting net income called EBITDA—to restrict National Beverage's ability to distribute cash to stockholders. This restriction is intended to ensure that National Beverage maintains a cash cushion for repayment of the bank loans. Monitoring compliance with the form and substance of this contractual restriction requires an understanding of accounting for owners' equity.

Some financial experts suggest that certain equity instruments, such as **preferred stock,** are popular because they can be used to avoid various contractual restrictions. Preferred stock gets its name because relative to common stock, it confers on investors certain *preferences* as to dividend payments and

> Preferred stock does not ordinarily carry voting rights. *Participating* preferred stock entitles its holders to share in profits above the declared dividend along with common shareholders. Most preferred stock is *nonparticipating,* meaning that holders are entitled to receive only the stipulated dividends.

the distribution of corporate assets. Preferred shareholders must be paid their dividends in full before *any* cash distribution can be made to common shareholders; if the company is liquidated, preferred stockholders must receive cash or other assets at least equal to the **stated (par) value** of their shares before any assets are distributed to common shareholders.

The stated value of preferred stock is typically $25 per share. The dividend is often expressed as a percentage of the stated value. A typical 8% preferred issue would promise a dividend of $2 per share ($25 stated value × 8%). Unlike bond interest expense,

> An alternative to the 8% fixed-rate preferred stock is an **adjustable-rate preferred,** which pays a dividend that is adjusted, usually quarterly, based on changes in the Treasury bill rate or other money market rates.

however, preferred stock dividends are not contractual obligations that, if unpaid, could precipitate steps toward bankruptcy. Instead, the company's board of directors must declare each quarterly preferred dividend and can omit them even in profitable years. Bank loans do not provide the flexibility to omit payments when cash flows are tight.

However, preferred shares are usually *cumulative.* This means that if for any reason a particular quarter's preferred dividend is not declared, no dividends on common shares can be paid until all unpaid past and current preferred dividends are paid. This feature protects purchasers of preferred shares from excessive cash distributions to common stockholders.

Also because it's okay to occasionally "skip" a preferred dividend, preferred shares are less risky to issuing corporations than is debt.

Companies' widespread use of preferred stock is a curious phenomenon. Preferred dividends—unlike bond interest expense—are not a deductible corporate expense for tax purposes. Why do companies choose to raise capital through preferred stock rather than through debt where tax-deductible interest payments reduce financing costs relative to preferred stock?

One reason preferred stock is attractive to *corporate investors* is that 70% to 80% of the dividends that corporations receive from their stock investments can be tax free (Chapter 13) whereas the interest income corporations receive from debt investments is fully taxable. So, preferred shares offer tax advantages to corporate investors but what about the companies that issue preferred stock?

Corporations that *issue* preferred stock do so because:

1. Preferred stock is less risky than debt because missing a preferred dividend payment, unlike missing an interest payment, will not trigger bankruptcy. This feature of preferred stock appeals to financially weak companies.

2. Companies with a history of operating losses usually don't pay income taxes because of their operating loss carryforwards. For these companies, debt no longer has a tax advantage, and thus preferred stock becomes more attractive as a source of new money.

3. Preferred stock is treated as equity rather than debt on financial statements. Companies precluded from issuing more debt because of covenant restrictions can sometimes issue preferred stock instead and sidestep these restrictions.

The distinction between preferred stock and debt can be murky because preferred stock (like debt) usually does not grant its holders voting rights so preferred shareholders often have no direct control over the company's affairs.

The distinction between debt and preferred stock has been further blurred as companies began issuing **mandatorily redeemable preferred stock.** Although called preferred *stock,* mandatorily redeemable preferred stock *requires* the issuing company to retire it (as with debt) at some future date—usually in 5 or 10 years. This type of preferred stock represents what many consider to be debt "disguised" as equity.

Redeemable preferred stock—where the issuing company has the option, but not the obligation, to redeem—has been around since the 1940s, but its use increased substantially during the late 1970s and 1980s. At first, the accounting approach used for this new form of preferred stock was identical to that for traditional (nonredeemable) preferred shares; namely, the proceeds obtained from issuing the stock were shown as part of owners' equity and any periodic cash distributions to preferred shareholders were recorded as dividends. Things changed in 1979 when the Securities and Exchange Commission (SEC) prohibited firms issuing such securities from including them under the balance sheet caption Owners' Equity.[10] This prohibition meant that amounts for redeemable preferred stock could no longer be combined with true owners' equity items such as traditional (nonredeemable) preferred stock and common stock in financial statements filed with the SEC. Redeemable preferred stock was instead to be shown on a separate line *between* liabilities and shareholders' equity—the so-called *mezzanine* section to the balance sheet.

Then in May 2003, the Financial Accounting Standards Board (FASB) went one step further by requiring "liability" treatment for most *mandatorily* redeemable preferred stock.[11] The

---

[10] *Accounting Series Release No. 268* "Presentation in Financial Statements of Redeemable Preferred Stocks" (Washington, DC: Securities and Exchange Commission [SEC], July 1979).

[11] FASB Accounting Standards Codification (ASC) Topic 480: Distinguishing Liabilities from Equity.

FASB concluded at the time that, even though the securities are called "preferred stock," they meet the definition of a balance sheet liability and should be classified as such. In other words, if it walks like a duck and quacks like a duck, it must indeed be a duck!

What did this mean for firms with mandatorily redeemable preferred stock? Beginning in 2003, these securities could no longer be shown on the balance sheet in the "mezzanine" between liabilities and shareholders' equity. Instead, mandatorily redeemable preferred stock would be shown as a balance sheet liability and included alongside long-term debt. The FASB's "liability" treatment for mandatorily redeemable preferred stock also requires companies to record as interest expense any dividends on the preferred stock.[12] For example:

> Class A Preferred Stock is mandatorily redeemable on March 31, 2028, and has been classified as debt in the accompanying consolidated balance sheet . . . The dividends on the mandatorily redeemable Class A Preferred stock are recorded as interest expense in the accompanying consolidated statements of operations.
>
> *Source:* The Hillman Companies, Inc. 2009 annual report.

> Later in this chapter, we describe the issues that arise when *conversion* is mandatory.

The SEC and the FASB exclude mandatorily redeemable preferred stock from the owners' equity section of the balance sheet. However, this classification exclusion may not capture the real economic characteristics of these securities because many companies have issued mandatorily redeemable preferred shares that are convertible—at the option of the investor—into common stock. It's possible that the company may never redeem preferred shares with this convertibility feature for cash. If instead it retires the preferred shares by converting them into common shares, then they truly represent equity, not debt—and thus their presentation status as nonequity may be arguable.[13]

 **Valuation**

Investors seem to be aware of the possibility that some redeemable preferred shares are a lot like debt while other redeemable preferred shares are a lot like equity. One study confirmed that the stock price behavior of companies whose redeemable preferred shares had clear debtlike characteristics was different from the behavior of companies whose shares had equitylike characteristics.[14] Investors apparently use disclosures about redeemable preferred shares to assess whether a particular issue should be regarded as debt or equity for valuation purposes.

A new form of mandatorily redeemable preferred stock, called a **trust preferred security,** has become popular. The company first creates a special purpose entity—the trust—that then sells redeemable preferred stock to outside investors. The company then borrows money from the trust with repayment terms identical to those of the preferred stock issued by the trust. Outside investors own "trust preferred" stock, but the company itself has issued debt—not preferred stock—and thus gains the tax advantages associated with debt.

---

[12] Buried in the details of GAAP is an exception to the required liability treatment. Suppose that the preferred shares can be converted into common stock. The conversion option makes the preferred stock **conditionally** (not mandatorily) redeemable in the FASB's eyes—the stock must be redeemed only if stockholders do not exercise their option to convert the preferred into common shares. Because the company's ultimate obligation to redeem the preferred shares is uncertain, GAAP does not require immediate "liability" treatment for conditionally redeemable preferred stock. This means that a company can continue to classify its redeemable preferred stock in the balance sheet mezzanine between liabilities and owners' equity and that preferred dividends need not be reflected as interest expense. "Liability" treatment at fair value is required, however, once the conversion privilege expires and the preferred stock becomes mandatorily redeemable.

[13] See P. Kimmel and T. D. Warfield, "Variation in Attributes of Redeemable Preferred Stock: Implications for Accounting Standards," *Accounting Horizons,* June 1993, pp. 30–40. These authors report that almost 69% of the mandatorily redeemable preferred stock issued in 1989 and included in their sample was convertible into common stock.

[14] P. Kimmel and T. D. Warfield, "The Usefulness of Hybrid Security Classifications: Evidence from Redeemable Preferred Stock," *The Accounting Review,* January 1995, pp. 151–67.

Here's what Motorola said about its trust preferred securities:

> In February, Motorola Capital Trust I, a . . . wholly-owned subsidiary of Motorola, sold 20 million Trust Originated Preferred Securities ("TOPrS") to the public at an aggregate offering price of $500 million. The Trust used the proceeds from this sale . . . to buy . . . Subordinated Debentures from Motorola with the same payment terms as the TOPrS. Motorola, in turn, used the $484 million of net proceeds from the sale of the Subordinated Debentures to reduce short-term indebtedness.

Motorola formed a wholly owned subsidiary—Motorola Capital Trust—that sold $500 million of trust preferred stock to the public. Motorola then borrowed $484 million of cash ($500 million of proceeds minus $16 million in investment banking fees and other transaction costs) from the Trust in exchange for Motorola's subordinated debentures. Motorola has the cash and debt, its wholly owned subsidiary has the debentures receivable, and outside investors have trust preferred stock. This transaction structure sounds complicated, but it's really quite simple to create. And here's the final piece of the puzzle: The interest and principal payments on the loan are matched to the dividend and mandatory redemption payments on the preferred stock. So, when Motorola makes an interest (or principal) payment to the trust, the trust then makes a dividend (or redemption) payment to outside investors.[15]

The benefit to Motorola should now be clear—interest expense is tax deductible but preferred dividends are not. By issuing trust preferred securities instead of traditional preferred stock, Motorola transformed what would otherwise have been a nondeductible preferred dividend payment into an interest expense tax deduction.

How are trust preferred securities shown on the balance sheet? Despite having the characteristics of debt—a required payment each period (called a *dividend* instead of *interest*) and a final payment at the end (called a *mandatory redemption payment* instead of a *principal payment*)—these hybrid securities have *not* always been classified as debt on the balance sheet. Before 2003, they were often listed in the "mezzanine" section of the balance sheet between debt and equity along with all other mandatorily redeemable preferred stock. However, most trust preferred securities—as well as most mandatorily redeemable preferred stock—are now shown as balance sheet liabilities.[16]

> Motorola's debt held by the wholly owned trust is eliminated when the company prepares its consolidated financial statements (Chapter 16 tells you why this occurs). That leaves only the redeemable preferred stock sold to outside investors on the consolidated balance sheet.

SEC rules require companies to differentiate clearly between common stock and any type of preferred stock, whether redeemable or not. This means that preferred stock must always be shown separately from common stock on the balance sheet. Finally, GAAP requires companies to disclose the dollar amount of preferred stock redemption requirements for each of the five years following the balance sheet date.[17] Accordingly, future cash flow commitments for redeemable preferred stock are clearly highlighted for statement users.

Here's what Samsonite Corporation said in 2003 about its preferred stock redemption schedule:

> The Company is required to redeem all of the Senior Redeemable preferred Stock outstanding on June 15, 2010, at a redemption price equal to 100% of the liquidation preference thereof, plus, without duplication, all accumulated and unpaid dividends to the redemption date. The Senior Redeemable Preferred Stock is redeemable at the option of the Company in whole or in

---

[15] The key features of trust preferred securities are described in P. J. Frischmann, P. D. Kimmel, and T. D. Warfield, "Innovation in Preferred Stock: Current Developments and Implications for Financial Reporting," *Accounting Horizons,* September 1999, pp. 201–18.

[16] FASB ASC Paragraphs 480-10-55-6 to -8: Distinguishing Liabilities from Equity—Overall—Implementation Guidance and Illustrations—Trust Preferred Securities.

[17] FASB ASC Paragraph 505-10-50-11: Equity—Overall—Disclosure—Redeemable Securities.

part, at any time and from time to time on or after June 15, 2001, at redemption prices ranging from 110% of the liquidation preference to 100% of the liquidation preference depending on the redemption date.[18]

Samsonite had about $286 million of mandatorily redeemable preferred stock outstanding. The redemption provision required Samsonite to redeem all of the outstanding shares on June 15, 2010, at 100% of the liquidation preference ($286 million). Samsonite had the option to redeem shares as early as 2001, but it will then have pay a higher price for the shares (up to 110%).

RE CAP

Equity or debt? When it comes to redeemable preferred stock, the answer isn't obvious. That's why the FASB now requires redeemable preferred stock to be classified as a balance sheet liability as long as the obligation to redeem is unconditional. When redemption is conditional—for example, because the preferred can be converted into common shares—liability treatment is not required until changing circumstance makes redemption inevitable.

LEGALITY OF CORPORATE DIVIDEND DISTRIBUTIONS

> Remember, managers have incentives to borrow money and then pay all of the cash to shareholders, leaving the company insolvent and the bank with a loan receivable that will never be repaid!

State laws govern corporate dividend distributions to shareholders, and these laws vary from state to state. The intent of these laws is to prohibit companies from distributing "excessive" assets to owners and thereby making themselves insolvent—that is, incapable of paying creditor claims. Some states limit dividend distributions to owners to the amount of retained earnings; in other states, the limit is retained earnings plus paid-in capital in excess of par. These laws protect creditors by ensuring that only solvent companies distribute cash to owners. (Stock repurchases, another way companies can distribute cash to owners, are not subject to these dividend distribution limitations.)

Assume that the Owners' Equity section on Delores Corporation's balance sheet appears on December 31, 2014, as:

Common stock, $1 par value	$20,000,000
Paid-in capital in excess of par	35,000,000
Retained earnings	43,000,000
Owners' equity	$98,000,000

> If the distribution involves inventory, equipment, or land, it's called a **property dividend.**

In some states, Delores Corporation could distribute only up to $43,000,000 of assets—the retained earnings amount—as dividends to owners. The dividend distribution could be in the form of cash or other assets such as inventory, equipment, or even land. In other states, the maximum might be $78,000,000—retained earnings ($43,000,000) plus paid-in capital ($35,000,000). Many states would require corporations to give public notice if their dividends were "paid" from paid-in capital.

Existing GAAP disclosures focus on the *source* of owners' equity—*contributed* capital (par plus capital in excess of par) versus *earned* capital (retained earnings, from which GAAP deducts dividends)—under the often erroneous presumption that this distinction informs analysts about legally permitted asset distributions. But many states have adopted the **1984 Revised Model Business Corporation Act** as a guide to the legality of dividend distributions. This act redefined solvency. Under this act, as long as the *fair value of assets* exceeds the *fair value of liabilities* after the distribution, the company is considered to be solvent. In

---

[18] Samsonite Corporation 2003 annual report.

extreme cases, this means that an asset distribution would be legal even if the *book value* of net assets is *negative* after the distribution. If Delores Corporation's fair value of assets minus fair value of liabilities totaled $200 million, then $200 million (rather than $43 million or $78 million) would be the maximum legal asset distribution. Notice that a $200 million distribution would result in negative owners' equity of $102 million. ***The point is that the book value of owners' equity may not give an accurate picture of potentially legal distributions in states that have adopted the 1984 Act.***[19]

To ascertain the amount of potential cash distributions, statement analysts need to know two things: (1) the distribution law in the state where the firm is incorporated and (2) fair value information if state law permits distributions based on the excess fair value of net assets. Unfortunately, this fair value information may be difficult to obtain because GAAP does not yet require that information to be disclosed except for marketable securities and certain investments (Chapter 16) and limited other items.

> More than 500 public companies in the United States paid cash dividends in 2012 despite having negative retained earnings.

Certain limited disclosures regarding potential distributions are required by GAAP. When mandatorily redeemable preferred stock has been issued, the dollar amount of the redemption requirement for each of the ensuing five years after the balance sheet date must be disclosed. Similarly, preferred stock dividend and liquidation preferences must be disclosed along with significant differences between the liquidation amount and the par or stated value of the underlying shares.[20] Nevertheless, these disclosures still do not allow interested readers to compute the *total* potential distribution to owners.

What happens when companies distribute stock instead of cash? Under current U.S. GAAP, stock *dividends* reduce retained earnings, but stock *splits* may not. Small stock distributions (less than 25% of shares outstanding) are required to be recorded as stock dividends: The market value of the distributed shares is transferred from retained earnings to the par value and paid-in capital accounts. Distributions that equal or exceed 25% of shares outstanding—commonly called *stock splits*—can be treated in either of two ways: (1) like a true split, which reduces the per share par value and increases the number of shares proportionately or (2) like a stock dividend. Consequently, stock dividends—and stock splits recorded as stock dividends—reduce the company's future cash dividend-paying ability in states where cash dividends are limited by retained earnings. Peterson, Millar, and Rimbey (1996) report that 83% of the 285 "stock split" companies in their study actually accounted for the distribution as stock dividends.[21] They also found that the stock market does indeed recognize that retained earnings reductions may restrict future dividends in some states but *not* in others.

The United States is the only country that records stock dividends at market value. All other countries record the "dividend"—a distribution in name only—at a nominal amount, either par value or book value.

GAAP reporting rules may not be sufficient to allow analysts to ascertain the maximum legal dividend distribution available to common stockholders. Analysts must be aware that other data may have to be gathered to ascertain the dollar amount that can be distributed.

RECAP

---

[19] See M. L. Roberts, W. D. Samson, and M. T. Dugan, "The Stockholders' Equity Section: Form without Substance?" *Accounting Horizons,* December 1990, pp. 36–37.

[20] FASB ASC 505-10-50: Equity—Overall—Disclosure.

[21] C. A. Peterson, J. A. Millar, and J. N. Rimbey, "The Economic Consequences of Accounting for Stock Splits and Large Stock Dividends," *The Accounting Review,* April 1996, pp. 241–53.

SHAREHOLDERS' EQUITY: FINANCIAL STATEMENT PRESENTATION

The shareholders' equity section from a recent balance sheet of Whole Foods Markets is shown in Exhibit 15.1. Most companies report as separate capital contribution amounts a figure for Common stock—par value and another figure for Paid-in capital in excess of par. Because Whole Foods' common stock has no par value, the company's balance sheet displays a single Common stock figure ($1,283,028) that represents the total capital contributed to the company by common stock investors. The balance sheet indicates that none of Whole Foods' common shares are held in treasury. So, shares repurchased (if any) must have been retired rather than held for later distribution.

As you may recall from Chapter 7, loan agreements and regulatory agency rules sometimes restrict the amount of dividends a company can distribute to shareholders. Because of such restrictions, the entire balance of retained earnings may not be available for dividend distribution. Cortland Bancorp, for example, is regulated by the Ohio Division of Financial Institutions which restricts Cortland's dividends to (undistributed) statutory earnings of the current and prior two years. To alert financial statement readers to these dividend restrictions, some companies disclose **restricted retained earnings** separately from unrestricted retained earnings amounts on their balance sheets. Others disclose their dividend restrictions only in financial statement notes. What about Whole Foods Markets? No dividend restriction is mentioned in the notes and none is indicated on the balance sheet (Exhibit 15.1).

An unusual feature of the Whole Foods' balance sheet is that the company's $413 million of redeemable preferred stock is shown in the mezzanine between total liabilities and shareholders' equity. Here's what the company said about the preferred stock:

> On December 2, 2008, the Company issued 425,000 shares of Series A 8% Redeemable, Convertible, Exchangeable, Participating Preferred Stock . . . for approximately $413.1 million . . . The Series A Preferred Stock is classified as temporary shareholders' equity since the shares are (i) redeemable at the option of the holder and (ii) have conditions which are not solely within the control of the Company.

The preferred stock is convertible into common shares at any time holders so desire. The stock can also be exchanged for other securities—in this case, convertible notes—or redeemed for

EXHIBIT 15.1	Whole Foods' Markets, Inc. Balance Sheet Excerpts		
($ in thousands)		**2009**	**2008**
Liabilities and Shareholders' Equity			
Total liabilities		$1,742,460	$1,874,712
Series A redeemable preferred stock, $0.01 par value, 425,000 and no shares authorized, issued and outstanding in 2009 and 2008, respectively		413,052	—
Shareholders' equity:			
Common stock, no par value, 300,000 shares authorized; 140,542 and 140,286 shares issued and outstanding in 2009 and 2008, respectively		1,283,028	1,266,141
Accumulated other comprehensive income (loss)		(13,367)	422
Retained earnings		358,215	239,461
Total shareholders' equity		1,627,876	1,506,024
Commitments and contingencies			
Total liabilities and shareholders' equity		$3,783,388	$3,380,736

EXHIBIT 15.2   **Whole Foods' Markets, Inc.**
Statement of Shareholders' Equity Excerpts

($ and share amounts in thousands)	Shares Outstanding	Common Stock	Common Stock in Treasury	Accumulated Other Comprehensive Income (Loss)	Retained Earnings	Total Shareholders' Equity
Balances at September 28, 2008	$140,286	$1,266,141	—	$ 422	$239,461	$1,506,024
Net income	—	—	—	—	146,804	146,804
Foreign currency translation adjustments	—	—	—	(8,748)	—	(8,748)
Reclassification adjustments for amounts included in income, net of income taxes	—	—	—	8,440	—	8,440
Change in unrealized loss on cash flow hedge instruments, net of income taxes	—	—	—	(13,481)	—	(13,481)
Comprehensive income						133,015
Redeemable preferred stock dividends	—	—	—	—	(28,050)	(28,050)
Issuance of common stock pursuant to team member stock plans	256	4,286	—	—	—	4,286
Excess tax benefit related to exercise of team member stock options	—	54	—	—	—	54
Share-based payment expense	—	12,795	—	—	—	12,795
Other	—	(248)	—	—	—	(248)
Balances at September 27, 2009	$140,542	$1,283,028	—	$(13,367)	$358,215	$1,627,876

Note: Statement details for the 2007 and 2008 are required disclosures but have been omitted from this exhibit for brevity.

cash. However, redemption is not mandatory. These features make it unclear whether the preferred stock is best viewed as equity or debt, so Whole Foods has opted for a mezzanine presentation intended to convey the temporary equity nature of the preferred stock.

A balance sheet only reports the end-of-period amount of each shareholders' equity account. Analysts and investors turn to the statement of shareholders' equity to learn about the detailed changes in each account, as illustrated in Exhibit 15.2. These disclosures reveal that Whole Foods:

> Shortly after the 2009 year-end, Whole Foods' announced its intention to redeem the preferred stock. Investors had a simple choice: take the cash value offered by the company or convert the preferred stock into shares of Whole Foods' common stock. Investors chose the more valuable alternative, converting all outstanding preferred shares into about 29.7 million shares of common stock.

- Declared preferred stock dividends during the year but did not declare dividends on common stock.

- Issued 256,000 shares of common stock to employees and incurred $12.8 million in share-based pay expense, but no shares of common stock were repurchased and retired.

- Experienced $13.7 million in (net) unrealized losses charged to other comprehensive income (recall our discussion of comprehensive income in Chapter 2).

Look to the statement of shareholders' equity if you want to fully understand how and why the individual shareholders' equity accounts changed during the period.

RECAP

GLOBAL VANTAGE POINT

International

The balance sheet presentation of shareholders' equity under IFRS closely mirrors that used by U.S. GAAP firms, although the terminology may at first seem odd. Exhibit 15.3 shows the shareholders' equity accounts of Vodafone Group Plc, the global mobile telecommunications company based in the United Kingdom. Several of the account titles

EXHIBIT 15.3	Vodafone Group Plc Equity Section of Balance Sheet		

(£ in millions)	2013	2012
Equity		
Called up share capital	3,866	3,866
Additional paid-in capital	154,279	154,123
Treasury shares	(9,029)	(7,841)
Retained losses	(88,785)	(84,184)
Accumulated other comprehensive income	11,146	10,971
Total equity shareholders' funds	71,477	76,935

should seem familiar. Additional paid-in capital, Treasury shares, and Accumulated other comprehensive income are items found on most U.S. company balance sheets and their meaning is unchanged. Retained losses is the term Vodafone uses to denote its retained earnings deficit (negative balance). That just leaves the Called up share capital account which, as you've probably guessed, is somewhat akin to the Capital stock-par value account sometimes found on U.S. company balance sheets. Suppose Vodafone's issues shares with a nominal £10 value per share but investors pay less than this amount (say only £8 per share) to the company. Vodafone can, at a later date, ask for payment of the remaining £2 by "calling up" the shares. A financial statement note reveals that all of Vodafone's shares are fully paid, so the Called up share capital account balance just reflects the nominal value of shares issued.

There are several other aspects of IFRS for shareholders' equity that you should know:

- As Chapter 2 mentions, an IFRS balance sheet often presents shareholders' equity before liabilities.

- A statement of changes in shareholders' equity is required, and the format closely mirrors that required by U.S. GAAP as illustrated in Exhibit 15.2.

- Most redeemable preferred stock is reported as debt even when redemption is not mandatory, as is some preferred stock that is not redeemable. The reason why can be found in *IAS No. 32,* which says that preferred stock ("preference shares") is classified as debt if the issuer is or can be required to deliver cash (or another financial instrument) to the holder.[22] So, don't be surprised to see preferred stock listed as an IFRS balance sheet liability and, when it is, the dividends on those preference shares will be treated as interest expense.

EARNINGS PER SHARE

The amount of future income and cash flow that a company is expected to generate is a major determinant of that company's value (Chapter 6). Valuing the firm *as a whole* is crucial during merger negotiations, corporate takeovers, and buyouts—relatively rare events in the ongoing life of a firm. For day-to-day valuations, many analysts prefer to focus on the value of *individual* common shares. For this purpose, knowing how much of

---

[22] *International Accounting Standard No. 32,* "Financial Instruments: Presentation" (IASC 1995), as amended effective January 1, 2009.

the company's total earnings accrue to each share is helpful. This is why **earnings per share (EPS)** is computed and required to be shown on the income statement.

Computing EPS is straightforward when the company has a simple capital structure. We first describe the procedures for computing EPS for a simple capital structure and then extend those procedures to situations involving more complicated capital structures.

Simple Capital Structure

A simple capital structure exists when a company has no convertible securities (neither convertible debt nor convertible preferred stock) and no stock options or warrants outstanding. In these circumstances, a straightforward formula is used to compute **basic earnings per common share:**[23]

$$\text{Basic EPS} = \frac{\text{Net income} - \text{Preferred dividends}}{\text{Weighted average number of common shares outstanding}}$$

To illustrate, assume that Solomon Corporation had the following capital structure in 2014:

	January 1	December 31
Preferred stock, $100 par value, 7%,		
10,000 shares issued and outstanding	$ 1,000,000	$ 1,000,000
Common stock, $1 par value		
160,000 shares issued and outstanding	160,000	
200,000 shares issued and outstanding		200,000
Paid-in capital in excess of par	12,000,000	16,000,000
Retained earnings	1,100,000	1,800,000
Total stockholders' equity	$14,260,000	$19,000,000

The 40,000 additional common shares were issued on September 1 and thus were outstanding for the last third of the year. The change in Retained earnings during 2014 is:

Retained earnings, January 1	$1,100,000
Net income for the year	1,257,331
Preferred stock dividends	(70,000)
Common stock dividends	(487,331)
Retained earnings, December 31	$1,800,000

The denominator of the basic EPS formula uses the **weighted average** number of common shares outstanding. Because additional shares were issued in September, this weighted average number of outstanding shares is computed as follows:

Time Span	(a) Shares Outstanding	(b) Portion of Year	(c) Weighted Shares ([a] × [b])
January 1–August 31	160,000	$2/3$	106,667
September 1–December 31	200,000	$1/3$	66,667
			173,334

---

[23] The guidance for computing EPS is contained in FASB ASC Topic 260: Earnings per Share.

Solomon Corporation's basic EPS for the year 2014 is:

$$\text{Basic EPS} = \frac{\text{Net income} - \text{Preferred dividends}}{\text{Weighted average number of common shares outstanding}}$$

$$= \frac{\$1,257,331 - \$70,000}{173,334 \text{ shares}} = \$6.85 \text{ per share}$$

You should know about a wrinkle in the computation of basic EPS. Sometimes companies issue securities—most commonly it's preferred stock—that *must* be converted into common shares. The FASB and the International Accounting Standards Board (IASB) at one time agreed that these **mandatorily convertible securities** should also be included in the computation of basic EPS as soon as conversion becomes obligatory.[24] The rationale for doing so is that mandatorily convertible securities will eventually be included in the basic EPS computation anyway once they are converted into common stock. But why wait until the conversion actually occurs because conversion is mandatory and thus inevitable? It makes more sense to include them in the weighted average common shares outstanding as if they had already been converted.

To see how mandatorily convertible securities alter the computation of basic EPS, suppose that Solomon Corporation's 10,000 shares of preferred stock mandatorily convert into 20,000 shares of common stock on January 1, 2018. (Notice that preferred stockholders have no say in the matter—the preferred shares will automatically convert into common stock on the designated date.) Two adjustments to our basic EPS computation are required to accommodate the mandatorily convertible preferred:

> Mylan Inc., a global pharmaceutical company, issued about 2.2 million shares of such preferred stock in 2007. Each preferred share automatically converted into common shares on November 15, 2011.

1. Increase the weighted average common shares outstanding by 20,000 shares to reflect the "as if" conversion of preferred into common as of the first day of the reporting period (here, January 1, 2014) because the preferred shares were outstanding for the entire period.
2. Eliminate the preferred dividend adjustment to net income because preferred stockholders are now viewed as though they are common stockholders.

Solomon Corporation's basic EPS for the year 2014 now becomes:

$$\text{Basic EPS} = \frac{\text{Net income} - \text{Preferred dividends}}{\text{Weighted average number of common shares outstanding}}$$

$$= \frac{\$1,257,331 - \$0}{173,334 \text{ shares} + 20,000 \text{ "as if" shares}} = \$6.50 \text{ per share}$$

> **Convertibles** are corporate securities—usually preferred shares or bonds—that are exchangeable for a set number of other securities—usually common shares—at a prestated price and at the option of the security holder. Convertibility "sweetens" the marketability of the bond or preferred stock. A **call option** gives the holder the right to buy shares (typically 100) of the underlying stock at a fixed price before a specified date in the future—usually three, six, or nine months. **Employee stock options** are often of three to five years in duration. If the stock option is not exercised, the right to buy common shares expires. A **subscription warrant** is a security usually issued with a bond or preferred stock that entitles the holder to buy a proportionate amount of common stock at a specified price—usually higher than market price at the time of issuance—for a period of years or in perpetuity.

Complex Capital Structure

A firm has a **complex capital structure** when its financing includes either securities that are convertible into common stock or options and warrants that entitle holders to obtain common stock under specified conditions. These financial instruments increase the likelihood that additional common shares will be issued in the future. This possible increase in the number of shares is called **potential dilution** because,

---

[24] As this book goes to press, the FASB and IASB have yet to formally ratify this proposed change to the computation of basic EPS. See FASB ASC Paragraph 260-10-45-60: Earnings per Share—Overall—Other Presentation Matters—Participating Securities and the Two Class Method and "Short-Term International Convergence," *Project Updates* (Norwalk, CT: FASB, 2010). As you are about to discover, convertible securities have always been considered in the computation of diluted EPS.

once the additional common shares are issued, current shareholders—those who did not receive any of the new shares—will then own a smaller slice of the company.

To illustrate the EPS calculation for a complex capital structure, suppose that Jackson Products has 20,000 shares of common stock outstanding and $100,000 of convertible debentures—that is bonds that can be converted into common stock at a specified price (say, $5 per share of common stock) at anytime at the bondholder's option. According to the terms of the debenture agreement, each $1,000 face value bond can be exchanged for 200 shares of common stock (200 shares = $1,000 bond/$5 per share conversion price). If all debentures were exchanged, bondholders would receive 20,000 new shares of common stock. The effect on current common shareholders would be to *dilute* their claim to earnings from 100% (when they own all of the common shares outstanding) to 50% (when they own only half of the common shares outstanding).

Computed basic EPS overlooks this potential dilution of current shareholders' ownership interest in the company. To recognize the increase in outstanding shares that would ensue from conversion or options exercise, GAAP requires companies with complex capital structures to compute another measure called **diluted EPS.**

The diluted EPS figure is a conservative measure of the earnings flow to each share of stock. It's conservative because the diluted EPS measure presumes the *maximum* possible new share creation—and thus the *minimum* earnings flow to each share. The computation of diluted EPS also requires that certain reasonable assumptions be made. For example, consider the potential conversion of convertible debentures into common shares. Once the bonds are converted to common stock, the company no longer needs to make further debt principal and interest payments. Consequently, the diluted EPS computation recognizes that:

1. New shares are issued upon conversion (a denominator effect).
2. After-tax net income increases when the debt interest payments are eliminated after conversion (a numerator effect).

Assumptions must also be made for employee stock options or warrants when computing diluted EPS. When holders of options or warrants exercise them, they receive common shares; but at the same time, the company receives cash in an amount representing the exercise price of the options or warrants. In the computation of diluted EPS, this cash is assumed to be used to acquire already outstanding common shares in the market. Because of adjustments for assumptions such as these, the diluted EPS formula is slightly more complicated:

$$\text{Diluted EPS} = \frac{\text{Net income} - \text{Preferred dividends} + \begin{array}{c}\text{Income adjustments due to}\\\text{dilutive financial instruments}\end{array}}{\begin{array}{c}\text{Weighted average number of}\\\text{common shares outstanding}\end{array} + \begin{array}{c}\text{Newly issuable shares due to}\\\text{dilutive financial instruments}\end{array}}$$

To illustrate how the diluted EPS computation works, we extend the Solomon Corporation example. Assume that as of January 1, 2014, Solomon also had the following financial instruments outstanding:

- $1,000,000 of 5% convertible debenture bonds due in 15 years, which were sold at par ($1,000 per bond). Each $1,000 bond pays interest of $50 per year and is convertible into 10 shares of common stock.

- Options to buy 20,000 shares of common stock at $100 per share. These options were issued on February 9, 2012, and expire on February 9, 2015.

Assume that the tax rate is 35% and Solomon stock sold for an average $114 market price during 2014. Each of these two financial instruments is potentially dilutive and must be incorporated into the diluted EPS computation as shown in the following equations. (To keep things simple, assume also that Solomon's preferred stock does not have a mandatory conversion feature so that basic EPS is still $6.85.)

The convertible debentures are included in diluted EPS by assuming conversion on the first day of the reporting period (here, January 1, 2014). The after-tax effect of interest payments on the debt is *added back* in the EPS numerator, and the additional shares that would be issued on conversion are added to the denominator. This is called the **"if-converted" method.** We now illustrate the computation of diluted EPS in the presence of convertible debt.

> There are 1,000 bond certificates outstanding ($1,000,000/$1,000 par value = 1,000 certificates), each convertible into 10 shares of common stock. Conversion of all bond certificates results in 10,000 new shares (or 1,000 certificates × 10 shares per certificate).

The convertible debentures are presumed to have been converted into 10,000 additional shares of stock at the beginning of the year (January 1, 2014). Accordingly, 10,000 new common shares are added to the diluted EPS denominator. Under the if-converted method, no interest would have been paid on the debentures this year because all bonds are assumed to be converted as of January 1. This means that interest of $50,000 would not have been paid on the presumptively converted bonds. With a 35% tax rate, net income would increase by $32,500 ($50,000 × [1 − 0.35]), and this amount is added to the diluted EPS numerator.

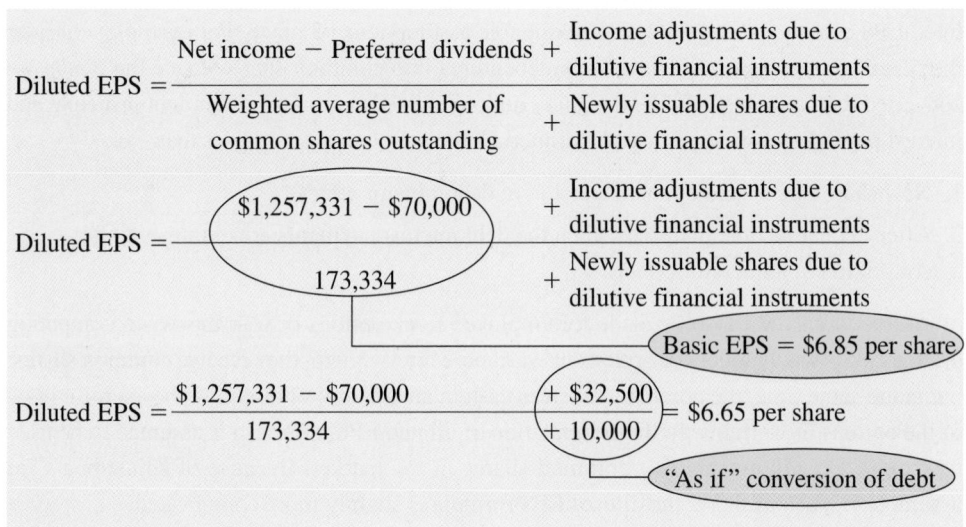

The outstanding stock options in our example will affect only the denominator of the diluted EPS computation. This denominator adjustment reflects the difference between the option *exercise price* ($100 per common share) and the **average market price** ($114 per common share) during the period. GAAP guidance assumes that any proceeds received on exercise of the options ($100 per share) are used to buy back already outstanding common shares at the average market price for the period. This is called the **treasury stock method.**

> In-the-money options are said to be dilutive because the number of shares that can be repurchased with the proceeds from the options is smaller than the number of new shares issued on exercise of the options. To see this dilution, suppose that employees exercise options for 1,000 shares of common stock at a $10 per share exercise price when the stock is trading at $20 per share. The company will receive proceeds of $10,000 cash from employees ($10 per share exercise price × 1,000 options) and issue 1,000 new shares of stock. The company can then use the cash proceeds to buy back at most 500 shares ($10,000/$20 market price per share) from other investors. The net result is dilution because 500 additional shares of common stock are now outstanding.

We next illustrate the adjustment to compute diluted EPS under the treasury stock method.

Stock options are dilutive when they are "in the money"—that is, when the average market price (here, $114) exceeds the option exercise price ($100). Using the treasury stock method, we assume that the $2,000,000 proceeds to the company from presumptive exercise of the options (that is, 20,000 shares at $100 per share) are used to repurchase previously issued common shares at the $114 average market price. The cash from the options is sufficient to acquire 17,544 shares (that is, $2,000,000/$114 per share = 17,544 shares). Because 20,000 shares are presumed issued and 17,544 are presumed acquired, the difference (2,456 net new common shares) is added to the diluted EPS denominator:

$$\text{Diluted EPS} = \frac{\$1,257,331 - \$70,000 + \$32,500}{173,334 + 10,000 + \underbrace{2,456}} = \$6.57 \text{ per share}$$

Treasury stock
conversion of options

> ***Antidilutive securities*** are those where conversion or exercise ***increases*** EPS. Such securities are ignored when calculating basic or diluted EPS.

Notice that diluted EPS equals $6.57, which is lower than the basic EPS number $6.85. This potential decrease in the computed earnings flow to each common share motivates the diluted EPS computation. Diluted EPS allows current shareholders to see how small their slice of earnings will be when the potential dilution from convertible securities, options, and warrants is considered.

Analytical Insights

Now that you understand how GAAP computes diluted EPS, let's revisit our earlier claim that the diluted EPS figure is a conservative measure of the potential dilution from convertible securities. To see why this is so, consider how the if-converted method is applied in computing diluted EPS for Jackson Products. Recall that the company issued its convertible bonds with a conversion price of $100 per share of common stock, meaning that the bondholder can exchange each $1,000 bond certificate for 10 shares of common stock at any time. Remember too that the if-converted method assumes that all of the bonds are exchanged for common shares at the beginning of the reporting period (January 1, 2014).

But what if Jackson Products' common stock is worth only $75 per share on January 1, 2014? Are bondholders willing to exchange their certificates for common shares under these conditions?

Probably not. If bondholders surrender their certificates, they will receive 10 shares of stock for each certificate. Each share of stock is worth only $75, so the total value of shares received is just $750 per certificate. That's what bondholders get when they elect to convert a certificate into common shares, but what do they give up? By surrendering the certificate, bondholders forgo the right to collect $1,000 in cash later when the bonds mature. Unless the risk of nonpayment is extremely high, bondholders will hold on to their certificates rather than exchange them for common shares.

The message here is that conversion—and thus EPS dilution—is unlikely when a company's stock price ($75 in our example) is substantially below the conversion price ($100). Conversion becomes much more attractive to bondholders once the underlying stock price rises above the conversion price. For example, if Jackson Products' common stock was trading at $150 per share, bondholders would then receive $1,500 worth of stock for each $1,000 bond certificate surrendered rather than just $1,000 when the bond matures (plus, of course, some interest paid along the way).

The if-converted method for computing EPS dilution ignores the fact that bondholders are unwilling to convert their debt certificates into shares of common stock when the share price is below the conversion price. Instead, the if-converted method presumes that all convertible debt certificates are exchanged for common shares at the beginning of the reporting period regardless of the prevailing share price. This approach yields a diluted EPS figure that is conservative because it reflects the maximum potential new common shares from conversion. The resulting EPS figure overstates earnings dilution—and understates diluted earnings per share—when a company's share price is substantially below the conversion price of the debt.

The treasury stock method suffers from the opposite problem. The treasury stock method tends to understate potential earnings dilution—and overstate diluted EPS—from employee stock options in some situations. To see why, recall from the Solomon Corporation example that the treasury stock method for computing diluted EPS involves a denominator adjustment that reflects the difference between the option exercise price ($100 per common share) and the average market price ($114 per common share) during the period. Any proceeds received on exercise of the options ($100 per share) are presumed to be used to buy back already outstanding common shares at the average market price for the period.

But what if the average market price of Solomon shares is slightly *below* the exercise price, say $99.95 per share? According to the treasury stock method, employee stock options are no longer dilutive when the average share price during the period falls below the exercise price. So, no adjustment at all is made to the denominator in computing diluted EPS. This approach ignores the possibility that Solomon's share price may rise above the exercise price ($100) sometime in the near future. As a result, the treasury stock method understates potential earnings dilution—and overstates diluted EPS—from employee stock options when the average share price for the period is slightly below the exercise price.[25]

Is Earnings per Share a Meaningful Number?

Analysis

EPS data are reported in the financial news and are prominent in corporate financial reports even though EPS can be a misleading financial performance measure. One reason for this is that managers can use their accounting discretion to distort reported earnings, the EPS numerator. These potential threats to earnings quality are described throughout this book. A second reason is that stock repurchases can be used to distort the EPS denominator, as previously mentioned in this chapter. But there is still another reason that EPS can be a misleading financial performance measure.

EPS ignores the amount of *capital* required to generate the reported earnings. This is easy to show. Consider the 2014 financial performance of two companies:

	Company A	Company B
Net income available to common shareholders	$ 1,000,000	$ 1,000,000
Weighted average common shares outstanding	100,000	100,000
Basic earnings per share	$10	$10
Gross assets	$20,000,000	$30,000,000
Liabilities	10,000,000	10,000,000
Equity capital (Assets − Liabilities)	10,000,000	20,000,000
Return on equity (ROE)	10%	5%

Company A and Company B report identical basic EPS of $10, but Company B needed twice as much equity capital and 50% more gross assets to attain the $1,000,000 net income. Even though both A and B report the same *level* of net income and EPS, B has a return on equity of only 5%, while A's figure is 10%. Company A generates more earnings from existing resources—that is, from its equity capital.

Because EPS ignores capital commitments, problems can arise when trying to interpret EPS. The narrow focus of the EPS ratio clouds comparisons between companies as well as

---

[25] One study confirms that GAAP systematically underestimates the economic dilution from stock options. See J. Core, W. Guay, and S. P. Kothari, "The Economic Dilution of Employee Stock Options: Diluted EPS for Valuation and Financial Reporting," *The Accounting Review,* July 2002, pp. 627–52.

year-to-year EPS changes for a single company. For example, even if year-to-year earnings' levels are the same, a company can "improve" its reported EPS by simply repurchasing some outstanding common shares.

GLOBAL VANTAGE POINT

Although the GAAP guidance on earnings per share has much in common with IFRS requirements, a few differences remain. These include differences in the application of the treasury stock method, the way contingently issuable shares are treated, and in the details that pertain to contracts that can be settled in cash or shares.

EPS is a popular and useful summary measure of a company's profit performance. It tells you how much profit (or loss) each share of common stock has earned after adjustments for potential dilution from employee stock options, warrants, and convertible securities are factored in to the calculation. But as discussed, EPS has its limitations.

ACCOUNTING FOR SHARE-BASED COMPENSATION

Many U.S. companies compensate managers and other salaried employees with a combination of cash and stock options—that is, options to purchase equity shares in the company. A typical employee stock option gives the employee the right to purchase a specified number of common shares at a specified price within some specified time period. The specified price—called the **exercise price**—usually equals or is higher than the market price of the company's shares at the time the options are issued. But not always. An option to buy 100 shares at $50 per share at any time within the next five years might be granted (issued) to employees when the shares themselves are selling for $30. When the exercise price exceeds the current share price, as it does in this example, the stock option is "out of the money." Nevertheless, an option to purchase common shares at $50 is valuable even though the shares are currently selling for only $30 because there's a chance the stock price will climb above $50 sometime during the ensuing five years.

The number of U.S. employees holding stock options rose dramatically beginning in the late 1970s. Only about 250,000 employees held stock options in 1975. Five years later, stock options were an important part of the compensation paid to roughly 3.1 million employees, and by 2002, this number had increased to 9.3 million employees. According to one estimate, companies in the Standard & Poor's 500 stock index awarded $126 billion in employee stock options in 2002 alone, more than the 2002 gross domestic product of Ireland.[26] Senior executives in these companies are not the only ones who receive part of their pay in the form of stock options. Almost all of Amazon.com's 7,700 full- and part-time employees and a "very large percentage" of Microsoft's 50,500 employees had been granted stock options by 2002. According to one 2010 estimate, 36% of the employees that worked for U.S. companies with stock owned shares of the company through some kind of formal benefit plan (e.g., direct stock grant, 401(k) plan, and so on), and 24% held stock options.[27]

> The popularity of stock options has fallen for reasons you will soon discover. A little more than 75% of companies in the S&P 1500, which tracks the stocks of small and mid-cap firms along with those of larger S&P 500 firms, relied on stock options in 2009 to pay their CEOs. In 2005, the figure stood at 93%.

---

[26] L. Lavelle, A. Borrus, R. D. Hof, and J. Weber, "Options Grow Onerous," *BusinessWeek*, December 1, 2003.

[27] "Data Show Widespread Employee Ownership in U.S.," The National Center for Employee Ownership.

Companies use stock options to augment cash compensation for several reasons:

- Options help align employees' interests with the interests of owners (stockholders). Employees with stock options have an incentive to make decisions that ultimately cause the share price to exceed the option exercise price.

- Many "start-up" high-growth companies are "cash starved" and cannot afford to pay competitive cash salaries. Stock options provide a way for them to attract talented employees while conserving cash.

- As long as the exercise price is equal to or more than the market price of the underlying stock when the option is issued, this compensation is not taxable to the employee until the option is exercised. This is an attractive feature because it allows employees to accumulate wealth while postponing taxes.

> Granting employee stock options with an exercise price *less than* the current market price of the firm's common stock—for instance, an exercise price of $10 per share when the grant date market price is $15 per share—imposes a tax cost on employees. This is because the excess of market price over exercise price ($5 in our example) must be included in employees' taxable income when the options are granted.

The GAAP that governs financial reporting for employee stock options granted as compensation have evolved over time as options-based pay gained in popularity. The controversy over stock options reporting that raged during this evolution was unprecedented in the history of U.S. accounting standards setting. Companies that issued employee stock options, their auditors, the SEC, and ultimately, the U.S. Senate lobbied the FASB to influence the final reporting rules. The intense debate over stock options presents an opportunity to discuss financial reporting incentives (Chapters 1 and 7) in a concrete setting and to illustrate how politics often enters the standards-setting process.[28]

Historical Perspective

Suppose an employee agrees to work this year in exchange for a small current salary and the promise of additional cash compensation to be paid in five years. No one disputes the notion that the employee's salary should be recorded on the company's books as an expense of the current year. But what about promised compensation? Should it be recorded as a current year's expense, or should expense recognition be postponed five years until the employee actually receives the cash? This question is at the heart of the employee stock options debate.

Before 1995, accounting for stock-based compensation was governed by *Accounting Principles Board (APB) Opinion No. 25.*[29] It was issued in 1972, one year prior to publication of what is now the universally accepted approach for valuing traded stock options: the Black–Scholes method.[30] Because *APB Opinion No. 25* preceded modern option pricing theory, it offered no mechanism for establishing the value of stock options granted as compensation to employees. Options issued with an exercise price equal to or more than the market price of the underlying common shares **were assumed to have no intrinsic value** for compensation expense purposes because their value could not be established with reasonable objectivity. Under this approach, if on June 28, 1972, Ramos Corporation issued 10-year options to employees that entitled each to buy 100 shares at $10 per share when the existing share price was also $10, **no compensation expense would be recognized because the value of these options could not be established reliably.**

---

[28] For a blow-by-blow account of the stock option controversy in the 1990s, see S. Zeff and B. Dharan, *Readings and Notes on Financial Accounting* (New York: McGraw-Hill, 1987), pp. 507–17.

[29] Pre-Codification "Accounting for Stock Issued to Employees," *APB Opinion No. 25* (New York: American Institute of Certified Public Accountants [AICPA], 1972). This pronouncement was superseded by *SFAS No. 123.*

[30] F. Black and M. Scholes, "The Pricing of Options and Corporate Liabilities," *Journal of Political Economy,* May–June, 1973, pp. 637–54. Corporate finance books explore the derivation of the Black–Scholes method and other option valuation techniques in detail; for example, see R. A. Brealey, S. C. Myers, and F. Allen, *Principles of Corporate Finance,* 8th ed. (New York: McGraw-Hill, 2005).

Obviously, options with terms such as those in the Ramos Corporation example are valuable: the price of the company's common stock could easily rise above the $10 exercise price sometime during the option's 10-year life. Over the 1970s and early 1980s, option pricing *theory* evolved into option pricing *practice* using the Black–Scholes model as the standard for valuing traded options. Despite this post-*APB Opinion No. 25* breakthrough, options issued as compensation were generally treated as being valueless at the grant date for accounting purposes. Compensation expense *was* recognized in rare instances.

> An expense would be recorded under the intrinsic value approach if the option exercise price is *below* the market price of the shares at the grant date. For example, Ramos would record $200 of compensation expense (and a corresponding increase to owners' equity) if the option exercise price was $8 per share and the grant-date market price was $10 per share. This pattern of exercise price and market price rarely occurred, so most companies did not record an expense.

During the 1980s, U.S. companies increasingly adopted employee compensation packages designed to link employee pay to company performance. Stock option plans proliferated as an element of employee compensation. Many auditors and other financial experts considered the then-existing GAAP presumption that options were valueless to be simply incorrect. Because these beliefs were widespread, the FASB began reconsidering the accounting for stock options in 1984.

Strong and widespread opposition to the FASB's stock options initiative surfaced quickly as it became clear to the business community that the new proposal would result in expenses being recognized on the income statement when stock options were granted. Those opposed to the FASB's proposal raised arguments against expense recognition that roughly parallel the four themes of this chapter:

1. Appropriate income measurement.
2. Compliance with contract terms and restrictions.
3. Legality of corporate distributions to owners.
4. Linkage to equity valuation.

Objections to the FASB's stock option approach reflected each of these themes. Next, we survey those objections.

Opposition to the FASB

Some opponents of the FASB's proposal questioned whether providing stock options to employees constituted an accounting expense. These opponents said that treating stock options as an expense would violate ***appropriate income measurement*** because stock options do not involve a cash outflow. On the contrary, they argued, when—and if—the options were eventually exercised, cash would flow *into* the company, not *out*.[31] FASB supporters counterargued that cash was not the issue. Expenses often arise independently of cash outflows. One prominent advocate of this position was Warren Buffett, chairman of Berkshire Hathaway, Inc., who said:

> [Some contend] that options should not be viewed as a cost because they "aren't dollars out of a company's coffers." I see this line of reasoning as offering exciting possibilities to American corporations for instantly improving their reported profits. For example, they could eliminate the cost of insurance by paying for it with options. So if you're a CEO and subscribe to this "no cash–no cost" theory of accounting, I'll make you an offer you can't refuse: Give us a call at Berkshire and we will happily sell you insurance in exchange for a bundle of long-term options on your company's stock.

---

[31] To illustrate the point, there is no cash outflow or inflow to the company when Ramos Corporation first grants 100 options with a $10 exercise price to an employee. But there may be a cash inflow to Ramos at some later date if (and when) the employee exercises the options. At the exercise date, Ramos will receive $1,000 cash ($10 per option × 100 options) from each employee if all of the options are exercised.

Shareholders should understand that companies incur costs when they deliver something of value to another party and not just when cash changes hands.[32]

Buffett's position that expenses arise when stock options are issued is consistent with how we account for issued stock. When stock is issued, shareholders give up something of value—a portion of their ownership interest—in exchange for something else of value, usually cash from new investors. Both the value given up and the value received are recorded. Buffett argued that the same accounting rules should apply for employee stock options. Shareholders are giving up a portion of their ownership interest by having the company issue additional stock—or options for stock—to employees. In exchange, shareholders receive valuable services from the employees that are paid for in stock options rather than in cash. From this perspective, issuing stock options to employees represents an expense to the company.

 **Contracting**

Another argument raised by opponents was that treating employee stock options as an expense could jeopardize **compliance with contract terms and conditions.** Companies with large employee stock option awards might, under the FASB's approach, violate loan covenants tied to reported earnings. For example, the times-interest-earned ratio would deteriorate if option grants were expensed because the recorded expense would reduce the earnings number used in this ratio.

Impartial observers who understand contracting incentives can see why companies with significant employee options would raise this objection. Their interests would be harmed, and economic intuition tells us that companies would resist such initiatives. But you can appreciate the FASB's mission to "do the right thing"—to draft rules that closely mirror underlying economic circumstances. If a particular accounting approach correctly captures these economic effects, it presumably should be used even though some companies may be harmed. Furthermore, some of the most vocal opponents were companies whose employee stock options—if expensed—would have decreased earnings by a trivial amount. Because the potential impact of the FASB proposal on these firms' covenants was insignificant, what was really motivating their opposition? Perhaps the answer lies in how (and how much) corporate executives are paid.

The compensation paid to top corporate executives was under intense scrutiny in the early 1990s. Corporate restructurings and layoffs were widespread, a recession was in progress, and many companies demonstrated lackluster financial performance. In this climate, some critics questioned whether top corporate executives should continue to enjoy increasingly large salaries and bonuses while their employees were experiencing financial hardship. The issue quickly became political.

In 1993, the U.S. Congress limited the tax deductibility of executive compensation to $1,000,000 per employee—any excess over that amount could not be claimed as a deduction on the corporate tax return except when compensation was tied to the achievement of explicit and preset performance goals. The passage of this law clearly illustrates public sentiment on this issue. Corporate leaders, sensitive to the increasing scrutiny of executive compensation levels, may have felt that the FASB's plan to expense stock options would draw unwanted attention to executive pay.

The **legality of corporate distributions to owners** was never at issue regarding executive compensation. Political considerations aside, companies are free under the law to pay corporate executives whatever amounts their boards of directors deem appropriate. However, an issue of whether large executive salaries were *proper* did arise. Some companies were

---

[32] Warren Buffett, Letter to Shareholders, Berkshire Hathaway, Inc., 1992 annual report.

perceived to oppose the FASB's stock options expense proposal because it would add the value of options to cash compensation and thus make it easier for critics of "excessive" pay to spotlight certain companies and executives.

Opponents also invoked an argument based on ***equity valuation.*** They believed that a simple "price–earnings multiple" relationship exists between reported earnings and common stock values. Under the FASB's plan, they argued, employee stock option grants would increase compensation expense and lower earnings—and thus lower stock price. (Our discussion of equity valuation in Chapter 6 suggests that the relationship between earnings and share price is more complicated than this.) Opponents argued that as stock prices fell, small companies who were heavy users of stock options would have difficulty raising new equity capital. This position was voiced by Senator Dianne Feinstein (Democrat, California) when she introduced legislation designed to block the FASB's stock option expensing initiative. She said:

> [The Bill] will also require the Financial Accounting Standards Board (FASB) to reexamine [its] recent decision to impose huge new accounting charges on the use of employee stock options. I am seriously concerned that if FASB's rule is adopted, tens of thousands of desperately needed jobs in California and the Nation will never be created.[33]

Senator Feinstein believed that the proposed stock options expense rule would make it more difficult for high-technology companies to raise new equity capital, thereby inhibiting expansion and job creation. Senator Feinstein may also have thought that cash-starved start-ups in Silicon Valley would have to let employees go if the companies had to pay workers in cash rather than stock options.

Despite growing business opposition, the FASB persisted and continued to move toward expense treatment of stock-based compensation. In response to intense business lobbying, Congress later initiated legislation which would have eliminated the FASB's independence by requiring the SEC to approve all new accounting standards.[34] Faced with this threat, the FASB was compelled to abandon its proposal and implement a compromise treatment.

The Initial Compromise—*SFAS No. 123*

The widespread, powerful opposition to recognizing stock-based compensation as an expense caused the FASB to allow a choice of accounting methods:

1. Companies could choose to continue using the intrinsic value approach under which compensation expense was rarely recognized.

2. Alternatively, companies could measure the **fair value** of the stock option at the grant date and charge this amount to expense.[35]

A stock option's fair value is measured using standard option-pricing models with adjustments for factors unique to employee stock options. The FASB encouraged companies to adopt the fair value approach rather than to continue using the intrinsic value approach because it considered the fair value approach to be preferable. Companies that chose to continue using intrinsic value accounting were also required to disclose in a financial statement note what net income would have been

> Suppose that Ramos Corporation used the fair value approach for its employee stock options. Recall that Ramos granted 100 options with a $10 exercise price to an employee. Let's assume that these options vest immediately—meaning the employees can exercise them at any time after the grant date—and have a fair value of $1.50 each (or $150 in total), as determined by an appropriate options-pricing model. Under the fair value approach, Ramos would record $150 of compensation expense on the date the options were granted. Ramos would also record a corresponding increase to owners' equity.

---

[33] Congressional Record—Senate, June 29, 1993, S8252.

[34] Called the *Accounting Standards Reform Act of 1994,* this bill was introduced by Senator Joe Lieberman (Democrat, Connecticut). Congressional Record—Senate, October 6, 1994, S14510.

[35] Pre-Codification "Accounting for Stock-Based Compensation," *SFAS No. 123* (Norwalk, CT: FASB, 1995) para. 11. In December 2004, the FASB ended the favorable accounting treatment employee stock options received under *SFAS No. 123.* This pronouncement was accordingly excluded from the FASB Accounting Standards Codification and it is not part of GAAP.

Figure 15.2

EMPLOYEE STOCK OPTION
REPORTING ALTERNATIVES
UNDER *SFAS NO. 123*

SFAS No. 123 was revised in June 2005 to prohibit continued use of the intrinsic value approach (Method 1). Now firms must use the fair value approach (Method 2).

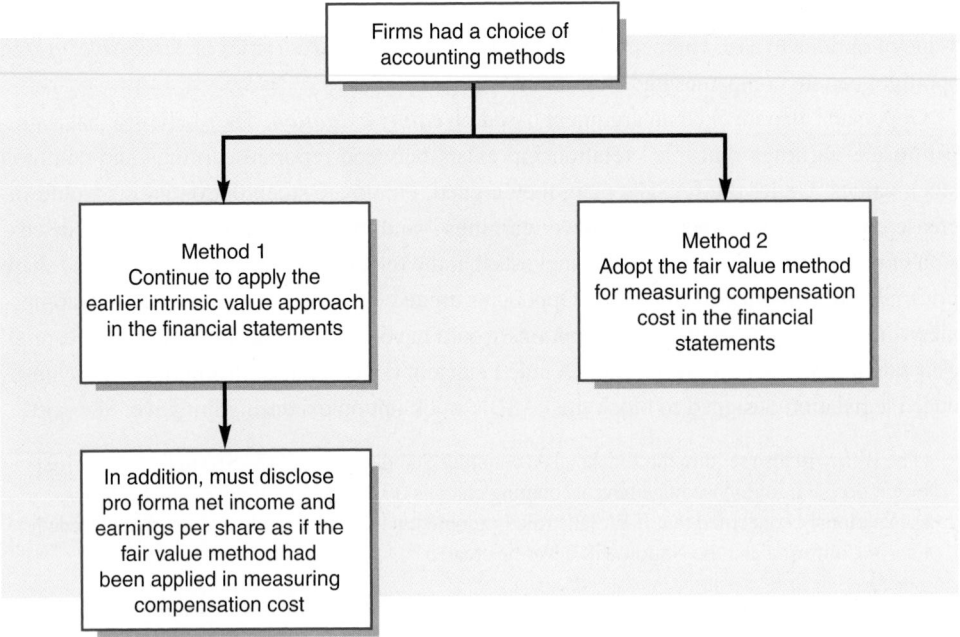

had compensation expense been recognized under the fair value approach. See Figure 15.2 for a diagram of the stock option reporting alternatives.

SFAS No. 123 was a political compromise. FASB members were unanimous in the belief that companies incur expenses when they grant stock options to employees as part of a compensation package, yet *SFAS No. 123* allowed companies to avoid doing so by continuing their use of the intrinsic value method. Most companies opted to account for employee stock options as they had in the past. This meant that they recorded no compensation expense except in those rare cases where the option exercise price was below the stock price on the grant date.

Because two methods were allowed, companies not using the fair value approach were required to provide **pro forma**—"as-if"—disclosures of net income and EPS calculated with a charge to compensation expense for options granted.

The dollar impact of stock compensation expense for some companies was staggering. Cisco Systems' net income for 2002 was $1.893 billion or $0.26 per share, but this figure did not include compensation expense for employee stock options because the company still used the intrinsic value method allowed by *SFAS No. 123*. If it had included compensation expense, Cisco Systems' 2002 EPS would have been reduced from $0.26 to just $0.05, a decrease of $0.21 per share. This 81% decline represents $1.520 billion of the company's 2002 earnings. Of course, for many companies, the dollar impact was much smaller.

Stock Options Debate Rekindled

"It's going to happen, and quite appropriately so."

> Federal Reserve Chairman—Alan Greenspan, referring to the
> growing momentum for counting stock options as an expense, in
> testimony before the Senate Banking Committee July 16, 2002

In October 2002, the FASB and IASB signed a memorandum of understanding (called the Norwalk Agreement) which, among other things, committed both organizations to work toward mutual convergence of their accounting standards. In November 2002, the IASB issued an exposure draft that called for mandatory expensing of the fair value of employee stock options. The FASB, which had hoped to avoid revisiting this accounting issue, was obliged by the Norwalk Agreement to do so and to converge with the IASB's exposure draft position.

In early March 2003, the FASB renewed its deliberation of stock-option compensation accounting. It reached a tentative decision in April 2003 to require all companies to expense the fair value of employee stock options at the grant date. For most U.S. companies, this meant that they would have to abandon the intrinsic value method and begin using the fair value method. The dollar impact of this required accounting change would be substantial. For example, the composite 2001 earnings per share of firms in the Standard & Poor's 500 Index would have been reduced by 24.5% (representing about $45 billion in composite earnings) if the fair value of options granted that year had been expensed.

Congress reacted swiftly to forestall the move. In late March 2003, Representatives David Dreier (Republican, California) and Anna Eshoo (Democrat, California) introduced legislation entitled the "Broad-Based Stock Option Plan Transparency Act of 2003" (H.R. 1372). If enacted, the bill would direct the SEC to require enhanced reporting disclosures for employee stock options. It would also prevent the SEC from recognizing any new stock option accounting standard until the SEC submitted a report to Congress on the effectiveness of the new disclosures *following a three-year period of study.*

The IASB opposed the bill and expressed concern about the impact it could have on accounting standards in general: "If the U.S. Congress or political authorities in other countries seek to override the decisions of the competent professional standards setters . . . accounting standards will inevitably lose consistency, coherence, and credibility."[36] In testimony before a house committee, FASB chairman Robert Herz warned in June 2003 that the bill to delay new rules on stock options would set a "dangerous precedent" of congressional interference in accounting standards setting.[37]

What sparked renewed debate over stock option accounting? Two factors brought the issue back into the political and regulatory arena:

1. The explosive increase in stock option grants during the late 1990s.
2. Public outrage over the accounting abuses uncovered subsequently at many companies.

Stock option "overload" was widely regarded as one—perhaps the most important—factor contributing to the accounting fiascoes at companies such as Enron and WorldCom. The prevailing view was that managers who were eager to cash in their options resorted to questionable accounting practices designed to inflate revenues and earnings, and boost share prices. Rather than align the interests of shareholders and managers, options were thought to have done the opposite: transferring vast amounts of wealth to executives even as outside shareholders suffered. These concerns spawned a reform movement aimed at curbing the use of options by forcing companies to count them as an expense.

---

[36] Paul A. Volcker, former Federal Reserve Board chairman and chairman of the foundation that oversees the IASB, in written testimony to Congress, as quoted in C. Schneider, "Who Rules Accounting," *CFO Magazine,* August 2003.

[37] A companion bill was introduced in the Senate in May 2003. A third bill, introduced in November 2003 by Senator Michael Enzi (Republican, Wyoming) would limit expensing to options granted to a company's five highest paid executives. In response to this proposal, one financial commentator quipped: "While Congress is at it, why not make only the salaries of the top dogs expenses, while the lower rungs of employees get to be free for a company. Think how many employees a company could hire if it didn't cost them anything. Why, if Congress could outlaw all expenses, the economy would really boom." See J. Eisinger, "Microsoft Can Count, Intel Can't," *The Wall Street Journal,* July 21, 2004.

But not everyone agreed! The battle between those who favored and those who opposed stock options expensing involved familiar arguments:

NEWS CLIP

WHY CRITICS SAID OPTIONS SHOULD BE EXPENSED

- Some 75% to 80% of executive pay now comes in the form of options. Because all other forms of compensation must be deducted from earnings, options should be treated the same.
- Deducting the cost of options will yield more accurate earnings numbers, which should help restore investor confidence.
- Because options are now all but free to companies, excessive grants to top execs have been encouraged. But options do have costs: They dilute shareholders' stakes and deprive companies of the funds they would otherwise get by selling those shares in the open market. Such costs should be reflected in earnings.
- Bringing more discipline to options grants will also reduce the incentives top execs now have to pump their stocks through short-term earnings maneuvers in the hope of cashing in big option gains.

WHY OPTIONS EXPENSING DEFENDERS DISAGREED

- Unlike salaries or other perks, granting options requires no cash outlay from companies. Because there is no real (cash) cost to the company to deduct, doing so will unjustly penalize earnings.
- There are no universal standards for expensing options; all valuation methods require big assumptions and estimates. So, expensing them will reduce the accuracy of income statements and leave them open to manipulation.
- Deducting the cost of options will reduce earnings, which is likely to drive down share prices.
- Rather than take the hit to earnings, companies can issue far fewer options. That would hurt morale, limit a key tool used to lure talent, and inhibit companies from aligning employee and shareholder interests.
- Tech firms argue that generous option grants have spurred the risk taking and entrepreneurship so crucial to innovation. Expensing options risks damaging that benefit.

Source: A. Borrus, P. Dwyer, D. Foust, and L. Lavelle, "To Expense or Not to Expense," *BusinessWeek,* July 29, 2002.

"It's an accounting issue that shouldn't be resolved by our yelling, that shouldn't be political, that shouldn't be settled in op-ed columns—it should [be] settled by [the] FASB going away on a deserted island and thinking about it. A lot of emotion has blocked this rational accounting issue. A lot of what people are pissed about is executive compensation. The distinction between executive compensation and option expensing kind of gets lost."

Source: Andy Grove, CEO of Intel Corporation, as quoted in *Fortune,* September 16, 2002.

As the options reform movement gained steam in 2003, nearly 500 U.S. companies—including Amazon.com, Bank One, Coca-Cola, Computer Associates, and Procter & Gamble—said that they would soon begin expensing stock options voluntarily using the *SFAS No. 123* fair value alternative. (Boeing and Winn Dixie had been doing so already for several years.) Other companies such as General Electric and Microsoft curtailed their employee stock options programs in favor of outright stock grants.[38] Still others, most notably Intel and Sun Microsystems, remained steadfast in their opposition to counting stock options as an expense.

By February 2004, Canadian accounting regulators and the IASB had issued new standards mandating the use of fair value approaches to employee stock option accounting.[39] Then in December 2004, the FASB released a revised version of *SFAS No. 123* (known as *SFAS No. 123R* "Share-Based Payment") which is now codified and which affirms its earlier tentative decision to prohibit the use of the intrinsic value method of stock option compensation accounting.[40] Share-based payment GAAP thus required all U.S. firms to use the fair value method. In

---

[38] Under a stock grant program, employees receive shares of common stock as part of their compensation packages. The employer (say, Microsoft) must record as compensation expense the fair value of the shares granted.

[39] "Share-Based Payment," *International Financial Reporting Standard [IFRS] No. 2* (London: IASB, 2004).

[40] FASB ASC Topics 505: Equity and 718: Compensation—Stock Compensation. Although it focuses primarily on stock option compensation and other equity payments for employee services, it also establishes guidance for a much broader class of transactions in which a company either (1) exchanges equity instruments for any goods or services or (2) incurs a liability in exchange for goods and services, and that liability's settlement amount is linked to the fair value of the company's equity instruments.

February 2005, the European Commission endorsed the new IASB stock option accounting rules for required use in the European Union. By then, more than 800 U.S. firms had announced their intent to voluntarily adopt the fair value method. Companies that expensed their employee stock options voluntarily tended to experience a positive or neutral share price reaction when the decision to expense was announced.[41]

Current GAAP Requirements

The key provisions of the current authoritative guidance are:

1. Companies must record the cost of employee services received in exchange for a stock option award (limited exceptions exist).
2. This compensation cost is determined by the award's grant-date fair value measured using option-pricing models adjusted for the unique characteristics of employee stock options (unless observable market prices are available).[42]
3. This grant-date compensation cost is recognized as an expense on a straight-line basis over the vesting period.
4. Incremental compensation cost arising from modifications to the original award terms is also recognized during the vesting period; however, changes in the fair value of the original options award itself are not recognized.

Implementing the fair value approach is not difficult but firms' option compensation practices are widely varied and so are the detailed GAAP rules for measuring compensation expense.[43] We describe these procedures tersely using a "big-picture" approach—that's all you need to grasp the overall impact of the fair value approach on financial numbers.

Assume that Guyton Corporation grants 100 common stock options to each of its top 300 managers on January 1, 2014. At that date, both the exercise price of the options and the market price of Guyton's stock is $30. To provide managers an incentive to remain at Guyton, the options cannot be exercised before January 1, 2017. This time span between the grant date and the first available exercise date is called the **vesting period.** Guyton's options do not expire until January 1, 2024, giving the options a 10-year legal life. But GAAP requires that we estimate the **expected life of the options**—meaning we must forecast when employees are likely to exercise the options. Factors to consider in estimating the expected life include the average length of time similar grants have remained outstanding in the past and the expected volatility of the company's common stock price. Let's assume that Guyton's options have an expected life of five years.

> For most companies today, the expected life of employee stock options is somewhere between three and five years.

The fair value of stock options is measured at the **grant date**—the date when both the grant's terms are set and the stock options are awarded to individual employees. Here's how the fair value of a stock option should be determined:

> The fair value of an equity share option . . . shall be measured based on the observable market price of an option with the same or similar terms and conditions, if one is available . . . [If an

---

[41] See D. Aboody, M. Barth, and D. Kasnik, "Firms' Voluntary Recognition of Stock-Based Compensation Expense," *Journal of Accounting Research,* May 2004, pp. 123–50; and F. Elayan, K. Pukthuanthong, and R. Roll, "Investors Like Firms That Expense Employee Stock Options and They Dislike Firms That Fail to Expense," *Journal of Investment Management,* 2005.

[42] For a detailed comparison of the option prices obtained by using different valuation models, see M. Amman and R. Seiz, "Valuing Employee Stock Options: Does the Model Matter?" *Financial Analysts Journal,* September/October 2004, pp. 21–37. Research on the use of the modified Black–Scholes–Merton model for valuing employee options includes J. Carpenter, "The Exercise and Valuation of Executive Stock Options," *Journal of Financial Economics,* May 1998, pp. 127–58; C. Marquardt, "The Cost of Employee Stock Option Grants: An Empirical Analysis," *Journal of Accounting Research,* September 2002, pp. 1191–1217; and C. Bettis, J. Bizjak, and M. Lemmon, "Exercise Behavior, Valuation, and the Incentive Effects of Employee Stock Options," *Journal of Financial Economics,* May 2005, pp. 445–70.

[43] FASB ASC Topic 718: Compensation—Stock Compensation.

observable market price is not available, the equity share option fair value] shall be estimated using a valuation technique such as an option pricing model . . . that takes into account, at a minimum, all of the following: the exercise price of the option; the expected term of the option . . . ; the current price of the underlying share; the expected volatility of the price of the underlying share for the expected term of the option . . . ; the expected dividends on the underlying share . . . ; [and] the risk-free interest rate(s) for the expected term of the option.[44]

GAAP says that an *observable market price* is the starting point for determining the fair value of employee stock options. Of course, the problem is that a market price is rarely (if ever) available because employee stock options are not traded on an organized exchange. When a market price is not available, GAAP says that fair value is to be determined using an options pricing mode but it does not specify which particular model—the Black-Scholes model or some other theoretically sound approach—is to be used.

Volatility in option pricing models is measured using a benchmark of 1 standard deviation of a stock's return over a specified time period. Assume that Guyton stock has experienced an average annual historical return of 10%, higher in some years and lower in others. Because 1 standard deviation is roughly 66% of a normal distribution, the 20% expected volatility means there is a 66% probability that the return on Guyton's stock will be 10% ± 20% in any one year—that is, there is a two-thirds chance that the return in any one year will range between a low of −10% and a high of +30%.

It is not necessary to understand the theory behind option pricing models to understand the financial reporting for employee stock options. As the preceding excerpt indicates, measuring fair value requires estimating several other variables that we have not yet specified in the Guyton example. We will assume that the risk-free interest rate is 6.75%, no dividends are forecasted for the company's common stock, and the expected volatility of Guyton's common stock is 20%. See Exhibit 15.4 for a summary of these facts.

Firms are required by GAAP to estimate what proportion of the options originally granted will never vest due to employee turnover. Compensation expense includes only those options that are not forfeited. For example, if Guyton Corporation estimates that only 29,000 options would ultimately vest, total compensation cost would be $291,450 (that is, $10.05 × 29,000) rather than $301,500.

Inserting the numbers from the top at Exhibit 15.4 into the Black–Scholes option pricing model indicates that each option has a fair value of $10.05 at the grant date.[45] The total compensation cost of all employee stock option awards is $301,500 ($10.05 × 30,000 options).

Let's assume that all 300 managers will meet the vesting requirements and ultimately exercise all 30,000 options.

EXHIBIT 15.4   **Guyton Corporation**

Variables Used to Estimate the Value of Employee Stock Options

Options granted (100 shares × 300 employees)	30,000
Exercise price	$30
Stock price at grant date	$30
Expected life of options	5 years
Risk-free interest rate	6.75%
Expected volatility of common stock	20%
Expected dividends on common stock	–0–

Using the Black–Scholes Option Valuation formula, the fair value of each Guyton option is estimated to be $10.05 at the grant date.

---

[44] FASB ASC Topic 718, various paragraphs.

[45] Designed for valuing options traded in open stock exchanges, the standard Black–Scholes formula doesn't consider the added restrictions of employee options, such as vesting and lack of transferability. Those limits make employee options worth much less than exchange-traded options. So, companies that strictly follow the standard Black–Scholes formula to determine options expense would take a much larger charge to earnings than is necessary. Another way to calculate option expense is called the *binomial* (or *lattice*) *model*. This approach uses a different mathematical formula and requires more assumptions including those that explicitly address vesting and other features unique to employee stock options. A key advantage of the binomial model is that it considers the possibility that changes in the stock price may influence the timing of when employees exercise options.

Stock-based compensation is intended to increase the employees' stake in the firm, creating an incentive for them to work in the best interests of all owners. The vesting requirements provide an extra incentive to stay with the company long enough to benefit from the anticipated value of the options. For these reasons, GAAP assigns total compensation cost of $301,500 to expense on a ***straight-line basis over the vesting period.*** Guyton Corporation would recognize $100,500 ($301,500/3 years) as compensation expense in each of the years 2014 through 2016:

> For income tax purposes, employers can deduct from taxable income the *tax cost* of options—calculated as the difference between the exercise price and the stock price on the day the employee exercises the options. The deduction is available only in the period when the options are exercised.

DR	Compensation expense	$100,500	
	CR Paid-in capital—stock options		$100,500

This same entry is made each year although the market value of the company's stock—and therefore the fair value of outstanding employee stock options—will undoubtedly change over time. ***GAAP specifies that compensation cost—option fair value—is measured only once, at the grant date.***

Let's say that Guyton's share price rises above the $30 exercise price after the vesting period and managers exercise all 30,000 options on the same day. The entry to record the exercise of employee stock options (assuming $20 par value stock) is:

DR	Cash (30,000 × $30)	$900,000	
DR	Paid-in capital—stock options ($100,500 × 3 years)	301,500	
	CR Common stock—par ($20 × 30,000)		$600,000
	CR Paid-in capital in excess of par		601,500

Notice that (1) compensation expense is recognized in the same amount each year over the vesting period and (2) if the options are exercised, the total amount added to the common stock and capital in excess of par is $1,201,500—the sum of the cash received when the options are exercised plus the calculated fair value of the options at the grant date.

If we assume that Guyton's share price never rises above the exercise price, the options will never be exercised. No cash will flow in. The offset to cumulative three-year compensation expense ($301,500) will remain in the Paid-in capital—stock options account. This dollar figure represents the estimated value of employee productivity (measured at the option grant date) that in effect was "donated" to the company without any corresponding ownership claim being given up to Guyton's employees.

There's one more wrinkle you should understand. As share prices tumbled during the 2008 global recession, a number of companies "repriced" their employee stock options. Why? Because options no longer provide a meaningful pay incentive when they are "underwater" in the sense that the share price (say $15) is below the exercise price (say $30). Employees perceive underwater options to be worthless when there is only a remote chance that the share price will rise above the exercise price at sometime in the future. Option repricing is a way to solve this incentive problem. In Guyton's case, repricing might entail reducing the original $30 exercise price to just $15, the share price prevailing when the options are repriced.

Here's what CounterPath Corporation, a Canadian software design company, said about its repriced options:

> On March 12, 2009, the company reduced the exercise price of 1,282,711 employee incentive stock options to $0.47 (CDN $0.60) per common share for all of its employees and contractors holding stock options, other than for its officers and directors. In accordance with ASC 718 the Company measured the new fair value of the repriced options and also revalued the original

options as of the date of modification. The excess fair value of the repriced options over the re-measured value of the original options represents incremental compensation cost. The total incremental cost of the repriced options is approximately $191,425 of which $139,281 has been recognized to the statement of operations on the transaction date with $52,144 to recognize over the remaining service period of the repriced options.

 Analysis

CounterPath uses stock options to pay, in part, employee wages and contractor fees. The company's share price fell from $2.35 per share in November 2007 to just $0.25 per share in February 2009. As a result of this steep share price decline, the options went underwater. CounterPath then repriced its options by lowering the exercise price. The added compensation cost associated with the repriced options is $191,425, determined according to FASB ASC 718. A portion of this cost ($139,281) is recognized immediately as compensation expense, while the remaining cost ($52,144) is recognized gradually over the service period because some options are not yet fully vested.

Accounting for stock-based pay has also changed the way companies must report on their cash flow statements the tax benefits they obtain from employee stock option compensation. The income tax and accounting details are somewhat complex, but we can use the Guyton Corporation example to illustrate the major points. Recall that Guyton issued options for 30,000 shares with an exercise price of $30 per share. Suppose the stock's market value is $50 per share when the options are later exercised. Under current U.S. tax law, Guyton is allowed a tax deduction for the intrinsic value of the options ($50 share price − the $30 option exercise price, or $20 per share) in the exercise year. (Employees who exercise stock options must pay ordinary income taxes that same year on the $20 per share intrinsic value.) Guyton's tax deduction ($600,000, assuming that all 30,000 options are exercised) exceeds the total compensation expense ($301,500) the company has recorded. Because Guyton pays out less cash in taxes, this $104,475 excess tax benefit—or ($600,000 − $301,500) × 0.35 if Guyton's marginal income tax rate equals 35%—is recognized on the cash flow statement.

Prior to current GAAP, most firms listed their excess tax benefits as part of operating cash flow, which is where tax-related items typically are shown. Analysts and investors closely watch operating cash flow. They see it as perhaps the purest measure of company performance because it is immune to accrual accounting gimmicks that can distort reported earnings. Firms now must shift the excess tax benefit to financing cash flow, a less important part of the cash flow statement that measures cash flowing in and out of the company for things such as stock and debt offerings, dividend payments, and share repurchases (see Chapter 17). The classification shift required by GAAP slashed millions of dollars off operating cash flow at

The accounting for restricted stock awards is simple enough. Suppose that Guyton grants 10,000 shares of restricted stock to its employees when the stock is trading at $30 per share. Employees can't sell any shares for three years (the vesting period). The shares' value at the grant date ($300,000) increases owners' equity, and an equal amount representing deferred compensation is recorded as an offsetting contra-equity account. The net effect on owners' equity at the grant date is zero. Guyton then recognizes one-third of the grant-date fair value (or $100,000) as compensation expense each year during the service (vesting) period and records a corresponding reduction to the deferred compensation contra-equity account.

some companies—$260 million at Cisco Systems and $77.3 million at Google—but left total company cash flow unchanged.

Fewer companies today than in the past use employee stock options as a form of compensation. One popular alternative to stock options is **restricted stock,** which are shares issued to employees that can be sold only in the future (say three years) after the stock vests. Employees forfeit their shares if they leave the company during the vesting period. Other companies have abandoned stock options in favor of larger annual performance-based cash bonuses. Among companies that still use stock options, many have cut back the size of their awards, shortened the exercise life, or reduced the number of employees covered by the options plan.

Options Backdating Scandal

On a summer day in 2002, shares of Affiliated Computer Services Inc. sank to their lowest level in a year. Oddly, that was good news for Chief Executive Jeffrey Rich. His annual grant of stock options was dated that day, entitling him to buy stock at that price for years. Had they been dated a week later, when the stock was 27% higher, they'd have been far less rewarding. It was the same through much of Mr. Rich's tenure: In a striking pattern, all six of his stock-option grants from 1995 to 2002 were dated just before a rise in the stock price, often at the bottom of a steep drop.[46]

In March 2006, *Wall Street Journal* reporters Charles Forelle and James Bandler published a story alleging that top executives at six companies repeatedly received stock option grants on days when share prices hit lows. Was this pattern just blind luck? In Jeffrey Rich's case, the likelihood is extraordinarily remote according to the reporters: "around one in 300 billion. The odds of winning the multistate Powerball lottery with a $1 ticket are one in 146 million."[47] If not just luck, then why were such favorable grant dates chosen? One possibility is that the effective dates on some options were deliberately and improperly changed—a practice known as **backdating**—thus conferring extra pay to executives regardless of company stock performance.

> The exercise (or "strike") price on employee stock options typically equals whatever the market price of the stock happens to be on the day the options are granted. The lower the strike price, the better the employee's chance for future profit when later exercising the options. For example, an options grant made on August 4 when the stock is trading at $30 per share becomes more valuable to the employee if it is backdated to July 8 when the market price of the stock was only $22.

Forelle and Bandler's *Wall Street Journal* article was the tipping point in the options backdating scandal. One week after the allegations first surfaced, federal or state officials were investigating more than 20 companies for backdating options grants, and 10 executives or directors at those companies had resigned. Over the next 12 months, more than 260 companies launched internal reviews of their options grants. More than 50 top executives and directors lost their jobs. Criminal investigations by the Department of Justice were under way at 54 companies, and many others were targets of SEC inquiries. Shareholders at 158 companies brought suit against officers and directors seeking monetary damages.

How did the two *Wall Street Journal* reporters spot questionable options timing? They enlisted the help of Erik Lie, a University of Iowa finance professor, whose results of a 2005 study of nearly 6,000 option grants between 1992 and 2002 strongly suggested that some option awards had grant dates retroactively set to an earlier date when the stock price was lower.[48] Backdating can be detected by carefully analyzing stock prices before and after the grant date. While companies can (and do) time their option awards to coincide with stock price downturns, they cannot predict with certainty when prices will rebound upward. Thus, it would be highly unlikely for option grants to routinely be awarded on dates just ahead of sharp stock price gains. Statistical procedures estimate just how unlikely are the option grant dates. Utilizing Lie's data, the two *Wall Street Journal* reporters identified a number of suspicious option grants including those at Affiliated Computer Services (Figure 15.3).

Backdating stock option awards can violate accounting rules and SEC disclosure regulations and, depending on how it is done, may constitute fraud. The practice also can violate federal income tax rules. To understand how the accounting and tax rules are violated, let's first consider an award that is not backdated. Suppose that Streit Corporation grants stock options to employees on August 4 when the stock is trading at $30 per share but the strike price is set at only $22. (Firms are free to set strike prices at whatever level they deem appropriate.) Using the intrinsic value method, as did most firms at the time, Streit immediately recognizes compensation expense equal to the $8 per share difference between the grant date share price ($30) and the strike price ($22). Employees who receive the option awards also have to pay ordinary

> Of course, firms using the fair value method immediately recognized an even larger compensation expense.

---

[46] C. Forelle and J. Bandler, "The Perfect Payday," *The Wall Street Journal*, March 18, 2006.

[47] Ibid.

[48] E. Lie, "On the Timing of CEO Stock Option Awards," *Management Science*, May 2005, pp. 802–12.

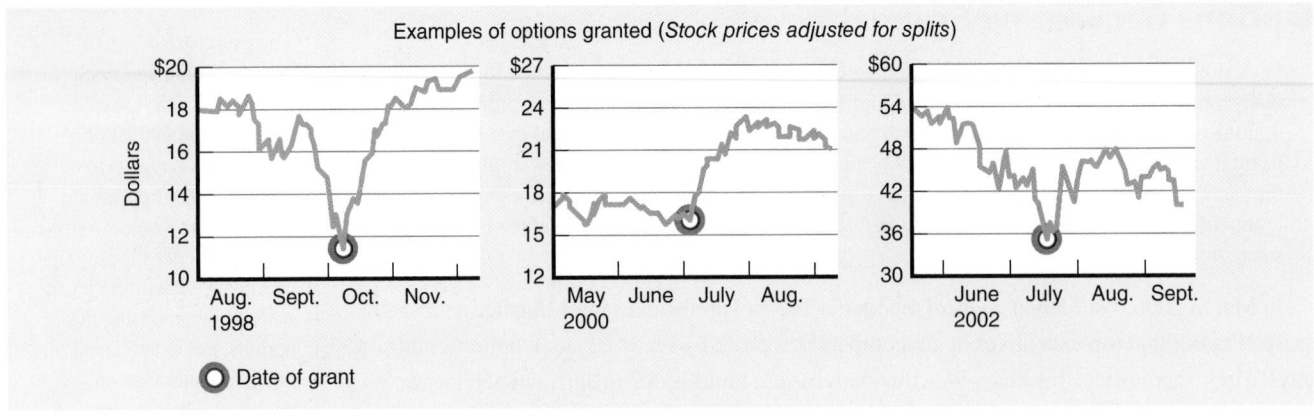

Figure 15.3 SUSPICIOUS STOCK OPTION AWARD GRANT DATES

Three especially favorable stock grants to Jeffrey Rich, former CEO at Affiliated Computer Services, and what the stock price did two months before and after each grant date.

SOURCE: Graph from C. Forelle and J. Bandler, "Perfect Payday: Options Scorecard," *The Wall Street Journal*, March 18, 2006. Copyright © 2006 Dow Jones & Company, Inc. All rights reserved worldwide. Reprinted with permission.

income taxes that year on the $8 per share. Backdating the award to, say, July 8 when the stock's market price was also $22 meant that Streit and unscrupulous managers at other firms could claim that the grant date intrinsic value was zero for both accounting and tax purposes. This result misstates GAAP compensation expense and employees' taxable income.

To rectify the GAAP violation, backdating firms must restate previously issued financial reports. That's what happened at Affiliated Computer Services. An internal investigation unearthed a handwritten note in which the company's chairman discussed the practice of always picking the lowest price "so far" in the quarter to award stock options.[49] The company later acknowledged that it had issued backdated stock options to top executives, including former CEO Jeffrey Rich. Compensation expense in earlier years was understated and pre-tax income overstated by $51 million. Several top executives resigned in the wake of the scandal.

The Wall Street Journal won a Pulitzer Prize, journalism's highest honor, for exposing the widespread practice of backdating stock option awards, and *Time* magazine recognized Erik Lie as among the 100 most influential people in the world.

 RE CAP

Stock options are an important part of employee pay at many corporations today and for good reason. They save cash and motivate employees, and companies previously could avoid recording compensation expense for options grants. Now firms must record as compensation expense the grant-date fair value of any option awards.

CONVERTIBLE DEBT

Several years ago, Smithfield Foods offered investors the opportunity to purchase up to $400 million of convertible notes. These notes paid a stated interest rate of 4% annually, matured in five years, and could be exchanged at any time for Smithfield Food stock at a conversion price of $22.68 per common share. Because the notes were issued in units of $1,000 face value, the

---

[49] J. Bandler and C. Forelle, "Note Raises Pressure on ACS," *The Wall Street Journal*, March 22, 2007. Prior to enactment of the Sarbanes-Oxley Act in August 2002, firms reported their stock option grants to the SEC on a monthly basis with a window of 10 days after the close of each calendar month—conceivably, a 40-day window. Now companies have only 2 days after the grant date to report awards.

conversion price meant investors could exchange each note for slightly more than 44 shares of stock ($1,000 face value/$22.68 per share conversion price = 40.082 shares). Investors snapped up the entire $400 million of the convertible note.

What price do you suppose Smithfield Foods received for each $1,000 face value note?

To put this question in context, the average yield to maturity—that's the effective interest rate—on newly issued high-grade industrial debt was about 8% per year at that time. Smithfields' nonconvertible debt borrowing rate was estimated to be over 10% per year. Given the economic climate of the time, it may surprise you to learn that the company was able to sell its 4% notes at par, receiving $1,000 in cash for each $1,000 face value issued. By contrast, the promised cash flows associated with each note—$40 each year plus another $1,000 at maturity in the year 2013—had a discounted present value at 10% of only $772.55. *Investors were willing to pay $227.45 more than the present value of each Smithfield note because of the conversion feature attached to the debt.*

We now explain the financial reporting for convertible debt and its implications for those who use financial statements.

Background

Convertible notes and bonds give investors the opportunity—but not the obligation—to exchange a company's debt for common stock in accordance with terms in the bond indenture. The **conversion price**—the dollar value at which the debt can be converted into common stock—is typically higher than the prevailing market price of the company's common shares when the debt is issued. The option to convert is solely at the investor's discretion and it will be exercised only when and if the investor finds the exchange financially desirable. Shares of Smithfield Foods were trading around $20 at the time the convertible notes were issued—or about $2.68 less than the conversion price. Investors had little incentive to exchange their notes for stock immediately. The conversion feature's real value to investors was the possibility that the stock price might climb higher than $22.68 sometime over the next five years.

Convertible notes and bonds are also usually **callable,** or redeemable, by the issuer at a specified price before maturity. When convertible debt is called, investors must either convert or have the debt redeemed for a cash price that is generally less than the value of the common stock into which the debt can be converted. Call provisions protect the company against extreme price increases by forcing investor action. Otherwise, investors would simply continue holding the debt in anticipation of further share price increases.

Convertible debt is a common form of borrowing. In the third quarter of 2012, for example, 186 companies worldwide issued convertible debt totaling nearly $20.7 billion. This compares to the roughly $55 billion raised by over 220 companies during the second quarter of 2007, just prior to the onset of the global financial crisis of 2007–2008 and the Great Recession of 2009.[50] Convertible debt offerings increase during periods of rising stock prices or turmoil in debt markets. The opportunity to share in future stock price increases is more attractive to potential debt investors during a period of bullish market expectations for common stocks or when debt markets are illiquid and there is little investor interest in traditional debt securities. This sentiment is what enables companies to issue convertibles on favorable terms.

> To illustrate, suppose that Smithfield Foods' stock price reached $25 per share several years after the notes were first issued. Each $1,000 par value convertible note would then represent a claim to $1,100 in common stock (44 shares × $25 per share). Suppose that Smithfield's notes were callable at a redemption price of $1,027.50 each. Smithfield could force conversion by "calling" the debt and investors would then take the more valuable common stock ($1,100) rather than the less valuable redemption cash payment ($1,027.50).

[50] "Credit Trends: Convertible Bond New Issuance Picks Up in Second-Half of 2012," *RatingsDirect,* Standard & Poor's Ratings Services (December 3, 2012).

Financial Reporting Issues

Convertible debt poses this financial reporting dilemma: Should a value be assigned to the debt's conversion feature? Clearly, conversion features are valuable to both the issuing company and investors. The conversion option enabled Smithfield Foods to borrow $100 million at 4% annual interest when other companies were paying 8% annual interest. Moreover, the availability of Black–Scholes and other option pricing models means that we now have well-established methods for assigning values to option features such as the Smithfield conversion privilege. However, GAAP for convertible debt predates the development of modern option pricing theory.[51]

GAAP specifies that convertible bonds must be recorded as *debt only,* with no value assigned to the conversion privilege. (There is an exception—described later in the chapter—if conversion can be settled by cash payment rather than by delivery of stock.) Two reasons for not assigning a value to the conversion privilege are cited:

1. The inseparability of the conversion feature from the debt component of the convertible security.

2. The practical problems of determining separate values for the debt and the conversion option in the absence of separability.

Given the lack of option pricing models at the time, standards setters concluded:

In the absence of separate transferability, values are not established in the marketplace, and accordingly, the value assigned to each feature is necessarily subjective. A determination of the value of the conversion feature poses problems because of the uncertain duration of the right to obtain the stock and the uncertainty as to the future value of the stock obtainable upon conversion. Furthermore, issuers often claim that a subjective valuation of a debt security without the conversion option but with identical other terms . . . is difficult because such a security could not be sold at a price which the issuer would regard as producing an acceptable cost of financing.[52]

Given modern option pricing methods, it is unlikely that accounting standards setters would reach the same conclusion today. Nevertheless, GAAP for most convertible debt continues to reflect the "debt only" approach.

Here's how Smithfield Foods records the issuance of all $400 million of its convertible notes at par value:

DR Cash	$400,000,000	
CR Convertible subordinated debentures		$400,000,000

This entry assigns the entire $400 million to the convertible debt liability. One year later, Smithfield records interest expense of $16,000,000 (or 0.04 × $400 million) and the cash interest payment, which also occurs that day:

DR Interest expense	$16,000,000	
CR Cash		$16,000,000

(This entry ignores the real-world complication that arises when companies accrue interest throughout the year.)

---

[51] FASB ASC Subtopic 470-20: Debt—Debt with Conversion and Other Options, which builds on the much earlier pre-Codification *APB Opinion No. 14*.

[52] Pre-Codification *APB Opinion No. 14* para. 8. This paragraph is considered nonessential for Codification purposes and therefore does not appear in the FASB ASC.

Thus far, the accounting for convertible debt parallels the accounting for the straight-debt securities described in Chapter 11. Smithfield Foods will continue to record interest expense at the rate of 4% annually—the effective borrowing rate if the conversion option is ignored—until the debt is retired or converted. Let's move several years forward to see what happens at conversion.

> At the stated conversion price, investors will receive about 4,400,000 common shares for their $100 million of notes ($100 million conversion price per share). Because each share has a $22.68 market value, investors receive stock worth about $110 million.

Suppose that some (but not all) investors have now chosen to exercise their conversion privilege by exchanging $100 million of the notes. Furthermore, the company's stock has a current market value of $25 per share, which is above the $22.68 conversion price. This means that investors will surrender notes with a face value (and book value) of $100 million in exchange for common stock with a market value of about $110 million. GAAP permits companies to record debt conversion in either of two ways:

1. The **book value method** records the newly issued stock at the book value of debt retired.

DR	Convertible subordinated debentures	$100,000,000	
	CR Common stock ($1 par)		$ 4,400,000
	CR Paid-in capital in excess of par		95,600,000

2. The **market value method** records the newly issued shares at their current market value. Any difference between that $25 market value and the $22.68 conversion price is recognized as a loss (or gain) on conversion.

DR	Convertible subordinated debentures	$100,000,000	
DR	Loss on debt conversion	10,000,000	
	CR Common stock ($1 par)		$ 4,400,000
	CR Paid-in capital in excess of par		105,600,000

The conversion loss is not classified as an extraordinary item because it is neither *unusual in nature* nor *infrequent in occurrence*.[53] Of course, Smithfield Foods would continue to record interest expense on the remaining $300 million of convertible notes outstanding.

The book value approach recognizes no accounting gain or loss at retirement because the debt book value is just transferred to the common stock accounts. The market value approach, however, credits common stock at full market value *as if* the shares issued were sold for cash on the conversion date. It's easy to see why the book value method is more popular. Almost all debt conversions occur when the company's stock price is above the conversion price, and this situation triggers recognition of an accounting loss under the market value method. Managers can avoid recording this loss by instead selecting the book value approach.

Analytical Insights

This discussion of convertible debt has two messages for financial statement readers.

One message: ***Estimating the future cash flow implications of convertible debt is difficult.*** This is because it is necessary to consider both the scheduled interest and principal payments for the debt as well as the likelihood of conversion prior to maturity. Option pricing methods can be used to evaluate the probability of conversion over long time intervals. For near-term

---

[53] From Chapter 2, remember that to qualify as an extraordinary item under GAAP, the event must be both unusual *and* infrequent.

projections, however, a simple comparison of the conversion price with the current market price of common stock can prove informative. If the options are "underwater" (meaning that the exercise price is more than the current share price) and close to expiration, they are unlikely to be exercised. The debt agreement should also be examined for call provision details.

The other message: ***Recorded interest expense may seriously understate the true cost of debt financing for companies that issue convertible bonds or notes.*** Few people would argue that Smithfield Foods is as creditworthy as the U.S. government. Yet the company borrowed money at 4% annually when investors were charging the federal government 3.5% annual interest for loans of similar duration. By ignoring the value of conversion features, current GAAP understates interest expense.

The appearance of "zero-coupon, zero-yield" convertible debt issued by U.S. companies has served only to underscore the inherent deficiencies of GAAP when it comes to interest expense.[54] To see why, consider this example. In April 2014, Skagit Inc. sells $750 million of "zero-coupon" convertible notes and received proceeds equal to the notes' $750 million face value. The notes mature in 2019 and can be converted into shares of Skagit common stock at the noteholder's option.

Recall from Chapter 11 that "zero-coupon" notes do not require the borrower (in this case, Skagit) to make periodic interest payments over the life of the loan. And, because the Skagit notes were issued at par—meaning that Skagit received cash equal to the $750 million face value—there is no discount to amortize over the life of the loan. No periodic coupon interest and no discount amortization together mean no interest expense gets recorded. In short, Skagit will not recognize any interest expense on the loan even though the notes may never be converted into shares of common stock.

The lesson for corporate managers is clear: Current GAAP allows you to avoid interest expense as long as you issue zero-coupon convertible debt and structure the conversion features so that the debt sells for par (face) value. The lesson for analysts is equally clear: Interest expense sometimes can seriously understate a company's true cost of debt.

Convertible Debt That May Be Settled in Cash

The FASB has on occasion revisited the question of how best to account for convertible debt, but U.S. GAAP continues to specify that traditional convertible debt must be recorded as debt only and with no value assigned to the conversion privilege.[55] There is a GAAP exception for convertible debt where the borrower has the right, upon conversion, to pay some or all of the conversion value in cash rather in shares of stock.[56] In this special case, GAAP requires separate recognition of the debt and equity components.

To illustrate this required accounting treatment, suppose Lebeda Corporation issues on January 1, 2014, convertible notes with an aggregate face value of $100 million and a 2% nominal (stated) interest rate. The notes mature in 10 years and interest payments occur annually on December 31. In other words, the notes specify promised cash flow payments to investors of $2 million in December of each year plus the $100 million principal in December of

[54] Because the debt pays no interest ("zero coupon") and is issued at no discount ("zero yield"), it's known as *no-no* debt.

[55] During its deliberation of pre-codification *SFAS No. 150* "Accounting for Certain Financial Instruments with Characteristics of both Liabilities and Equity," the FASB proposed separate recognition of the debt and equity components of a convertible debt instrument. However, the final version of *SFAS No. 150,* issued in May 2003 (and incorporated in the Codification as FASB ASC Topic 480: Distinguishing Liabilities from Equity), did not address so-called compound financial instruments such as convertible debt.

[56] FASB Staff Position No. APB 14-1, "Accounting for Convertible Debt Instruments That May Be Settled in Cash upon Conversion (Including Partial Cash Settlement)," issued in May 2008 and incorporated in the Codification as part of FASB ASC Subtopic 470—20: Debt—Debt with Conversion and Other Options.

2023. The notes are convertible into 1 million shares and, if exercised, Lebeda can either deliver shares or pay cash equal to the settlement-date market value of the shares. So, if investors were to exercise the conversion feature at a time when Lebeda's share price was $115, management would either hand over the 1 million shares or pay $115 million in cash. Finally, the notes are assumed to be issued at par, meaning that Lebeda received $100 million cash from investors. Without the conversion feature, investors would have priced the notes to yield an 8% effective return that properly reflects Lebeda's credit risk and the company would have raised only $59,739,512 at issuance.

> You should verify that the present value of the note cash flows is $59,739,512 when discounted at an 8% effective interest rate.

Because the convertible debt may be cash-settled at conversion, GAAP requires Lebeda to recognize the convertible debt as part debt and part equity. The initial carrying value of the debt component is measured as the fair value of a similar liability that does not possess the conversion feature. The carrying value of the equity component is measured by deducting this liability fair value from the proceeds received when the convertible debt was issued. Here is the journal entry Lebeda would record on January 1, 2014, when the convertible debt is issued:

DR	Cash	$100,000,000	
	CR Convertible notes payable		$59,739,512
	CR Shareholders' equity—Conversion option		$40,260,488

Because the notes have a fair value of $59,739,512 in the absence of the conversion feature, the remaining portion of the convertible debt proceeds ($40,260,488 = $100,000,000 − $59,739,512) is assigned to the conversion (equity) component.

In subsequent years, accounting for the convertible notes adheres to the effective interest method described in Chapter 11. For example, Lebeda will make the following December 31, 2014, journal entry to record interest expense for the year and the $2 million cash interest payment:

DR	Interest expense	$4,779,161	
	CR Interest payable		$2,000,000
	CR Convertible notes payable		$2,779,161

To record interest expense for 2014 using the effective interest method ($4,779,161 = $59,739,512 × 0.08)

DR	Interest payable	$2,000,000	
	CR Cash		$2,000,000

To record the cash interest payment for 2014.

As you may recall, Lebeda's interest expense in 2015 (next year) will be $5,001,494 (= [$59,739,512 + $2,779,161] × 0.08) under the effective interest method even though the cash interest payment that year is still just $2,000,000.

Let's jump ahead several years and suppose investors exercise the conversion feature on January 1, 2019, when the market price of Lebeda's common stock is $140 per share. The cash settlement amount to be paid by Lebeda is $140 million but GAAP requires that we split—accounting professionals use the term "bifurcate"—this amount into two components: one amount paid to repurchase the debt component of Lebeda's convertible note and a second amount paid for the equity component. Bifurcation is accomplished using the same approach employed when the notes were issued. Lebeda management first measures the debt repurchase amount as the fair value of a similar liability that does not possess the conversion feature. The equity settlement amount is then measured by deducting this liability fair value from the cash settlement amount. For example, if Lebeda's borrowing cost for five-year debt is 7.5% on the conversion date, the debt repurchase fair value would be $77,747,633. (You should verify that the January 1, 2019, present value of remaining note interest and principal payments is $77,747,633 when discounted at 7.5%!) The equity settlement amount then is $62,252,367 (= $140,000,000 − $77,747,633). Given this fact pattern, Lebeda would record the following journal entry to reflect cash settlement of the conversion option:

DR Convertible notes payable	$76,043,740	
DR Loss on debt settlement	$1,703,893	
DR Shareholders' equity—Conversion option	$40,260,488	
DR Paid-in capital in excess of par..................	$21,991,879	
CR Cash		$140,000,000

To record cash settlement of the convertible notes payable. The Loss on debt settlement amount ($1,703,893) is measured as the bifurcation-determined debt repurchase amount ($77,747,633) minus the January 1, 2019, carrying value of the convertible notes payable liability ($76,043,740). The Paid-in capital in excess of par reduction ($21,991,879) is the bifurcation-determined equity settlement amount ($62,252,367) minus the conversion option carrying value ($40,260,488).

Although the accounting treatment illustrated by this example may seem overly complex, the key point to remember is quite simple. When a convertible debt instrument contains this sort of cash settlement provision, GAAP requires more interest expense to be recognized than would otherwise be the case. Without the cash settlement provision, Lebeda will record only $2 million of interest expense each year the convertible notes are outstanding, based on a 2% nominal interest rate. Because of the cash settlement provision, Lebeda must bifurcate the convertible notes and recognize 2014 interest expense of $4,779,161 based on an 8% effective interest rate that reflects the company's actual credit risk.

 **International**

GLOBAL VANTAGE POINT

In 2006, the French telecommunications company Alcatel merged with Lucent Technologies, a U.S. counterpart, to form Alcatel-Lucent. The combined French company has operations in more than 130 countries. Here is what Alcatel-Lucent says about its convertible debt:

It's a bit more complicated for convertible debt issued by historical Lucent Technologies. The financial liability component is a present value computed as of the business combination date. The amount assigned to equity equals the difference between the convertible's fair value at that date and the financial liability component amount.

> Certain financial instruments contain both a liability and an equity component, including bonds that can be converted into or exchanged for new or existing shares and notes mandatorily redeemable for new or existing shares. The different components of compound financial instruments are accounted for in equity and in bonds and notes issued according to their classification, as defined in *IAS 32* "Financial Instruments: Disclosure and Presentation."
>
> For instruments issued by historical Alcatel, the financial liability component was valued on the issuance date at the present value (taking into account the credit risk at issuance date) of the future cash flows (including interest and repayment of the nominal value) of a bond with the same characteristics (maturity, cash flows) but without any equity component. The portion included in equity is equal to the difference between the debt issue amount and the financial liability component.

Unlike U.S. GAAP, the IFRS guidance for convertible debt require the liability and equity components to be separated.[57] This approach recognizes that when a company such as Alcatel-Lucent issues convertible debt it is really issuing two distinct types of securities—

---

[57] IFRS has required the separation of convertible securities into debt and equity components since 1996. See "Financial Instruments: Disclosure and Presentation," *International Accounting Standard No. 32* (London: International Accounting Standards Committee, 1996). International Accounting Standards are now known as *International Financial Reporting Standards,* and the International Accounting Standards Committee (IASC) is now the IASB.

(1) debt that may be in the form of a bond or note and (2) an option to convert that debt into shares of stock—even though investors pay just one price for the combined financial instrument. The debt represents a balance sheet liability and the option is shareholders' equity.

To illustrate how this separation of liability and equity components is achieved, suppose Alcatel-Lucent issues €500 million of 10-year convertible notes that pay interest at 5% annually. Investors pay €500 million for the notes even though the company's credit risk at the time implies a 10% interest rate for traditional debt of similar duration. To record the convertible note issuance, Alcatel-Lucent must first determine the present value of the financial liability component using the 10% interest rate. The figure turns out to be €346.4 million, an amount you should confirm. Alcatel-Lucent then makes the following entry:

DR	Cash	€500.0 million	
	CR Convertible notes payable		€346.4 million
	CR Shareholders' equity—Conversion option		€153.6 million

When Alcatel-Lucent records interest expense later in the year, it will do so using the effective 10% rate of interest rather than the nominal 5% interest rate stated in the note. As illustrated in Chapter 11, this effective interest rate approach results in the following entry for annual interest expense in the first year:

DR	Interest expense	€34.64 million	
	CR Cash (interest payment)		€25.00 million
	CR Convertible notes payable		€9.64 million

The cash interest payment of €25 million is determined by the nominal rate of interest (5%) and the face amount of the notes (€500 million), but interest expense is determined by the effective borrowing rate (10%) and the amount borrowed (€364.4 million). The difference between these two figures is recorded as an increase to the note payable. Over time, the convertible note payable balance will grow to equal €500 million at maturity.

Canadian GAAP has required the use of this components approach to convertible debt accounting for quite some years. It was also part of U.S. GAAP, but only briefly. In 1966, the Accounting Principles Board (APB)—the U.S. GAAP standards setter at the time—issued guidance that required explicit recognition of the conversion option value derived in a manner similar to our Alcatel-Lucent example. This U.S. GAAP guidance was "suspended temporarily" in 1967 and then rescinded two years later. Why? Some observers claim that the APB bowed to pressure from the investment banking community, which had argued that the discounted present value approach was too subjective for their clients. Investment bankers may also have been concerned about the possible loss of business. As illustrated in our Alcatel-Lucent example, the component approach results in higher interest expense (€34.64 million rather than €25.00 million) and thus lower reported profits. Investment bankers may have feared that required use of the components approach would dampen client demand for convertible debt securities and thus reduce the fees they earned from helping clients issue those securities. In either case, the APB rescinded the component approach requirement in 1969.

> Of course, this components approach is required by U.S. GAAP when the convertible debt permits full or partial settlement in cash upon conversion.

RECAP

Convertible debt gives investors the upside potential of common stock and the safety net of debt. That's why the effective interest rate on convertible debt seems so low—the option value of the conversion feature compensates for the lower interest paid to investors. Because GAAP ignores the conversion option except when cash settlement is a possibility, interest expense may be understated and cash flow forecasting may be impeded.

SUMMARY

- Many aspects of financial reporting for owners' equity transactions are built on technical rules and procedures that have evolved over time.

- Other aspects of owners' equity accounting have not changed despite changing economic and legal environments.

- Still other aspects of owners' equity accounting involve complicated pronouncements that reflect political compromises.

- Financial statement readers must recognize these influences and avoid unwarranted inferences based on the reported figures.

- Stock buybacks don't produce accounting gains and losses, but they can be used to artificially inflate a company's reported EPS.

- Preferred stock that has a mandatory redemption feature looks a lot like debt, so GAAP now requires it to be classified as debt in most cases.

- Some companies can pay dividends in excess of their retained earnings balance, but their ability to do so depends on state law.

- EPS numbers are adjusted for potential dilution from stock options, warrants, and convertible securities.

- GAAP now requires companies to record compensation expense when stock options are given to employees, but GAAP ignores the option value in traditional convertible debt.

- GAAP can understate interest expense when companies issue traditional convertible debt, but IFRS rules overcome this deficiency.

- While some rules for owners' equity accounting may seem arbitrary—and therefore insignificant—these financial statement items have a profound impact on lending agreements, regulation, and the cost of equity capital.

EXERCISES

E15-1

Understanding Shareholders' Equity **(LO 1, 3, 6, 7)**

Required:

1. What is the difference between preferred stock and common stock?

2. What is treasury stock?

3. Why does the SEC require companies to exclude redeemable preferred stock from shareholders' equity even when redemption is not mandatory?

4. Describe how the cost of stock-based compensation is determined?

5. Once the cost of stock-based compensation is determined, describe how the amount to be expensed in a given period is determined?

6. Explain the difference between *basic* and *diluted* earnings per share.

E15-2

Issuing common stock **(LO 5)**

Spridget Company has 1 million shares of common stock authorized with a par value of $3 per share, of which 600,000 shares are outstanding. The company received $7 per share when it issued shares to the public.

Required:

What is the book value of the Common stock par account and the Additional paid-in capital account?

The stockholders' equity section of Peter Corporation's balance sheet at December 31, 2014, follows:

E15-3

Retiring common stock **(LO 1)**

AICPA
ADAPTED

Common stock ($10 par value); authorized 1,000,000 shares, issued and outstanding 900,000 shares	$ 9,000,000
Additional paid-in capital	2,700,000
Retained earnings	1,300,000
Total stockholders' equity	$13,000,000

On January 2, 2015, Peter purchased and retired 100,000 shares of its stock for $1,800,000.

Required:

What is the balance in the Additional paid-in capital *and* Retained earnings accounts immediately after the shares were retired?

ForeEver Yours, Inc., a manufacturer of wedding rings, issued two financial instruments at the beginning of 2014: a $10 million, 40-year bond that pays interest at the rate of 11% annually and 10,000 shares of $100 preferred stock that pays a dividend of 7.5% annually. The preferred stock has a mandatory redemption feature that requires the company to repurchase all outstanding shares at par ($100 per share) in 40 years.

E15-4

Analyzing debt and redeemable preferred stock **(LO 3)**

Required:

Describe how each financial instrument will affect the company's balance sheet and income statement in 2014.

Warren Corporation was organized on January 1, 2014, with an authorization of 500,000 shares of common stock ($5 par value per share). During 2014, the company had the following capital transactions:

E15-5

Analyzing various stock transactions **(LO 1, 5)**

AICPA
ADAPTED

January 5	Issued 100,000 shares at $5 per share
April 6	Issued 50,000 shares at $7 per share
June 8	Issued 15,000 shares at $10 per share
July 28	Purchased 25,000 shares at $4 per share
December 31	Sold 25,000 shares held in treasury at $8 per share

Required:

What should be the balance in the Additional paid-in capital account at December 31, 2014?

Munn Corporation's records included the following stockholders' equity accounts:

E15-6

Determining how many shares **(LO 5)**

AICPA
ADAPTED

Preferred stock, par value $15, authorized 20,000 shares	$255,000
Additional paid-in capital—preferred stock	15,000
Common stock, no par, $5 stated value, 100,000 shares authorized	300,000

Required:

How many shares of preferred stock and how many shares of common stock have been issued?

Weldon Wire has issued 2,500,000 shares of $2 par common stock at an average price of $10 per share. Of these, 100,000 shares were repurchased during the year for $15 each and retired. Another 200,000 shares of the shares were repurchased for $17 each and are being held for later use. There were no other common stock transactions during the year.

E15-7

Treasury stock **(LO 1)**

AICPA
ADAPTED

Required:

Determine the balance in each of the following shareholders' equity accounts: Common stock—par; Additional paid-in capital; and Treasury stock.

E15-8

Determining stockholders' equity after a stock repurchase   **(LO 1, 5)**

AICPA
ADAPTED

Newton Corporation was organized on January 1, 2014. On that date, it issued 200,000 shares of its $10 par-value common stock at $15 per share (400,000 shares were authorized). During the period from January 1, 2014, through December 31, 2016, Newton reported net income of $750,000 and paid cash dividends of $380,000. On January 5, 2016, Newton purchased 12,000 shares of its common stock at $12 per share. On December 31, 2016, the company sold 8,000 treasury shares at $8 per share.

Required:

What is the book value of total shareholders' equity as of December 31, 2016?

E15-9

Stock dividends and retained earnings   **(LO 4)**

AICPA
ADAPTED

On December 31, 2014, the Stockholders' Equity section of Mercedes Corporation was as follows:

Common stock, par value $5; authorized 30,000 shares;	
issued and outstanding, 9,000 shares	$ 45,000
Additional paid-in capital	58,000
Retained earnings	73,000
Total stockholders' equity	$176,000

On March 1, 2015, the board of directors declared a 10% stock dividend and accordingly issued 900 additional shares. The stock's fair value at that time was $8 per share. For the three months ended March 31, 2015, Mercedes sustained a net loss of $16,000.

Required:

What amount should the company report as retained earnings on its quarterly financial statement dated March 31, 2015?

E15-10

Weighted-average number of shares   **(LO 6)**

Mason Manufacturing had 600,000 shares of common stock outstanding and 150,000 shares of $100 par value preferred stock outstanding January 1, 2014. An additional 120,000 shares of common stock were issued on August 1 and 24,000 common shares were repurchased and retired on December 1. Mason's preferred stock is not convertible into common shares.

Required:

Calculate the weighted-average number of common shares outstanding for purposes of computing Mason's 2014 basic earnings per share.

E15-11

Retained earnings transactions   **(LO 4)**

The Retained earnings account for Nathan Corporation had a credit balance of $800,000 at the end of 2013. Selected transactions during 2014 follow:

a. Net income was $130,000.

b. Cash dividends declared were $60,000.

c. Repurchased 100 shares of Nathan Corporation common stock, paying $20 per share. Each share has a $5 par value and was originally issued for $35.

d. Sold 20 shares of Nathan Corporation common stock for $22 each.

Required:

Calculate Nathan's retained earnings balance as of the end of 2014. What is the maximum dividend Nathan could have declared in 2014? Assume there are no legal or contractual restrictions that apply.

Effective April 27, 2014, Dorr Corporation's shareholders approved a two-for-one split of the company's common stock and an increase in authorized common shares from 100,000 shares (par value of $20 per share) to 200,000 shares (par value of $10 per share). The stock split shares were issued on June 30, 2014. Dorr's shareholders' equity accounts immediately before issuance of the stock split shares were:

Common stock, par value $20; 100,000 shares authorized;	
50,000 shares outstanding	$1,000,000
Additional paid-in capital	150,000
Retained earnings	1,350,000

Required:
After issuing the stock split shares, what are the balances of the Additional paid-in capital and Retained earnings accounts in Dorr's June 30, 2014, statement of shareholders' equity?

> **E15-12**
> Determining shareholders' equity after a stock split **(LO 5)**
>
> **AICPA**
> ADAPTED

Tam Company's net income for the year ending December 31, 2014, was $10,000. During the year, Tam declared and paid $1,000 cash dividends on preferred stock and $1,750 cash dividends on common stock. At December 31, 2014, the company had 12,000 shares of common stock issued and outstanding—10,000 had been issued and outstanding throughout the year and 2,000 were issued on July 1, 2014. No other common stock transactions occurred during the year, and the 5,000 shares of preferred stock are not convertible into common shares.

Required:
What should be the 2014 earnings per common share of Tam Company, rounded to the nearest penny?

> **E15-13**
> Computing basic EPS **(LO 6)**
>
> **AICPA**
> ADAPTED

Fountain Inc. has 5,000,000 shares of common stock outstanding on January 1, 2014. It issued an additional 1,000,000 shares of common stock on April 1, 2014, and 500,000 more on July 1, 2014. On October 1, 2014, Fountain issued 10,000 convertible bonds; each one had a $1,000 face value and paid 7% interest. Each bond is convertible into 40 shares of common stock. No bonds were converted during 2014.

Required:
What number of shares should be used in computing basic EPS and diluted EPS, respectively?

> **E15-14**
> Finding the number of shares for EPS **(LO 6)**
>
> **AICPA**
> ADAPTED

Information concerning the capital structure of the Petrock Corporation is as follows:

	December 31,	
	2013	**2014**
Common stock	90,000 shares	90,000 shares
Convertible preferred stock	10,000 shares	10,000 shares
8% convertible bonds	$1,000,000	$1,000,000

During 2014, Petrock paid dividends of $1 per share on its common stock and $2.40 per share on its preferred stock. The preferred stock is convertible into 20,000 shares of common stock. The 8% convertible bonds are convertible into 30,000 shares of common stock. The net income for the year ending December 31, 2014, was $285,000, and the company's income tax rate was 40%.

> **E15-15**
> Calculating earnings per share **(LO 6)**
>
> **AICPA**
> ADAPTED

Required:

1. What was basic EPS for 2014, rounded to the nearest penny?

2. What was diluted EPS for 2014, rounded to the nearest penny?

E15-16

Employee stock
options   **(LO 7)**

AICPA
ADAPTED

On July 18, 2014, Amos Corporation granted nontransferable options to certain key employees as additional compensation. The options permit the purchase of 20,000 shares of Amos's common stock at a price of $30 per share. On the grant date, the stock's market value was $42 per share. The options were exercisable beginning January 1, 2015, and expire on December 31, 2018. On February 3, 2015, when the stock was selling for $45 per share, all options were exercised.

Required:

How much compensation expense should Amos have recorded in 2014 and 2015 if the options are worth $17 per share on the grant date?

PROBLEMS / DISCUSSION QUESTIONS

P15-1

Identifying incentives for stock
repurchases   **(LO 2)**

Keystone Enterprises just announced record 2014 EPS of $5.00, up $0.25 from last year. This is the 10th consecutive year that the company has increased its EPS, an enviable record. Unfortunately, management fears that this string of EPS increases is about to be broken. Keystone is forecasting net income for 2015 and 2016 at $10 million each year, the same level earned in 2014. The company has 2,000,000 shares of common stock outstanding, no preferred stock, and no convertible debt.

Required:

1. How many common shares does Keystone need to buy back at the beginning of 2015 *and* 2016 to maintain EPS growth of $0.25 per share each year? (*Note:* Keystone will use excess cash from operations to pay for the stock.)

2. Explain why your answer to requirement 1 would change if the buybacks were to occur in the middle of each year.

3. Why do you think Keystone's management would be concerned about maintaining the company's record of EPS growth?

P15-2

Understanding convertible
debt   **(LO 8)**

Massey Coal just issued $50 million of convertible notes. Each note has a $1,000 face value, a stated interest rate of 2%, and matures in five years from the issue date. Investors have the option of holding each note to maturity or converting the note into 100 shares of Massey Coal common stock. Conversion is not permitted during the first two years after the issue date. The company received $50 million cash from investors when the convertible notes were issued.

Required:

1. Why were investors willing to pay $50 million for Massey's debt when the promised interest rate is only 2%?

2. Several analysts claim that Massey's incremental borrowing rate for a similar five-year note without the conversion option is 12%. Describe how analysts might have arrived at this borrowing rate from information typically found in a company's financial statements and notes.

3. Which interest rate—2% or 12%—would be used to compute Massey Coal's interest expense under U.S. GAAP, assuming cash settlement of conversion is not permitted. Which interest rate would be used under IFRS guidance?

The stockholders' equity section of Warm Ways Inc.'s balance sheet at January 1, 2014, shows:

Preferred stock, $100 par value, 10% dividend,	
50,000 shares issued and outstanding	$ 5,000,000
Common stock, $6 par value, 1 million shares issued	
and outstanding	6,000,000
Paid-in capital in excess of par	119,000,000
Retained earnings	50,000,000
Total stockholders' equity	$180,000,000

P15-3

Recording cash and stock dividends   **(LO 5)**

Warm Ways reported net income of $9,250,000 for 2014, declared and paid the preferred stock cash dividend, and declared and paid a $0.25 per share cash dividend on 1 million shares of common stock. The company also declared and distributed a 10% stock dividend on its common shares. When the stock dividend was declared, 1 million common shares were outstanding, and the market price of common stock was $135 per share.

Required:

1. Prepare journal entries to record the three dividend "events" that took place during 2014.

2. If the company's common stock was valued at $135 per share when the stock dividend was declared, what would the stock price be just after the dividend shares were distributed?

It's July 1, 2015, and the market price of Warm Ways' common stock (Problem P15-3) is $175 per share. There are 1.1 million common shares outstanding, and the Retained earnings account shows a balance of $45,000,000. Management wants to declare and pay a 20% common stock dividend, but this would mean halting the company's cash dividend payments because a 20% stock dividend would cause retained earnings to fall by $38,500,000 (that is, 20% × 1.1 million shares × $175 per share). This would leave a balance of only $6,500,000, far below the $25,000,000 minimum required for cash dividends as specified in the company's loan agreement. It would take several years to build up retained earnings so that Warm Ways could again pay cash dividends.

P15-4

Determining effect of splits and dividends on retained earnings   **(LO 5)**

The chief financial officer of the company has proposed two ways to distribute common shares and still manage to pay cash dividends:

- Option A: Split the stock 12 for 10.

- Option B: Increase the size of the stock dividend from 20% to 30%, and record the share distribution as a stock split.

Required:

1. How will these two approaches affect the company's retained earnings?

2. As a common stockholder, would you prefer a 20% stock dividend, a 12-for-10 stock split, or a 30% stock dividend? Why?

On January 1, 2012, when its $30 par-value common stock was selling for $80 per share, Gierach Corporation issued $10 million of 4% convertible debentures due in 10 years. The conversion option allowed the holder of each $1,000 bond to convert the bond into five shares of the company's $30 par-value common stock. Cash settlement upon conversion is not permitted. The debentures were issued for $10 million. Without the conversion feature, the bonds would have been issued for $8.5 million.

P15-5

Analyzing convertible debt   **(LO 8)**

AICPA
ADAPTED

On January 1, 2014, the company's $30 par-value common stock was split three for one. On January 1, 2015, when the company's $10 par-value common stock was selling for $90 per share, holders of 40% of the convertible debentures exercised their conversion options.

Required:

1. Following U.S. GAAP, prepare a journal entry to record the original issuance of the convertible debentures.

2. How much interest expense would the company recognize on the convertible debentures in 2012?

3. Prepare a journal entry to record the exercise of the conversion option.

4. Why do many companies use the book value method to record debt conversions?

P15-6

Cash-settled convertible debt   **(LO 8)**

Avnext Industries issues 10-year convertible notes at par for $10,000 on December 31, 2014. The notes mature in 10 years and are convertible into 400 shares of Avnext common stock at any time after January 1, 2019. Interest is paid annually at the end of each year at an interest rate of 2% of the principal amount (i.e., $200 per year). If investors exercise the conversion feature, Avnext either can deliver shares of common stock or make a cash payment equal to the market value of those shares. In the absence of the conversion feature, investors would have demanded a 6% return on an Avnext loan of similar terms.

Required:

[A] Using the bifurcation approach required by U.S. GAAP in this setting:

1. What are the fair values of the debt and equity components of Avnext's convertible notes? Round to the nearest dollar.

2. What journal entry would Avnext make to record the issuance of the convertible notes?

3. How much interest expense would Avnext recognize in 2015? In 2016?

4. What would be the carrying value of the convertible notes as of December 31, 2016?

5. Suppose investors opt to exercise the conversion feature on January 1, 2020, when Avnext common stock is trading at $30 per share. What is the cash settlement amount, and how much of this amount should be assigned to repurchasing the debt versus settlement of the conversion (equity) option? Round to the nearest dollar and assume that Avnext's borrowing cost at the conversion date is 5%.

6. What journal entry would Avnext make to record cash-settlement conversion of the notes on January 1, 2020?

[B] Using U.S. GAAP for traditional convertible debt instruments:

1. What journal entry would Avnext make to record issuance of the convertible notes?

2. How much interest expense would Avnext recognize in 2015? In 2016?

3. What would be the carrying value of the convertible notes as of December 31, 2016?

4. Suppose investors opt to exercise the conversion feature on January 1, 2020, when Avnext common stock is trading at $30 per share. What journal entry would Avnext make to record cash-settlement conversion of the notes on January 1, 2020? Round to the nearest dollar and assume that Avnext's borrowing cost at the conversion date is 5%.

P15-7

Computing EPS   **(LO 6)**

The Shareholders' Equity section of Holiday Roads Company's balance sheet shows:

	December 31, 2013	December 31, 2014
Preferred stock, $200 par value, 5% dividend, 20,000 shares issued and outstanding	$ 4,000,000	$ 4,000,000
Common stock, $2 par value	400,000	520,000
Paid-in capital in excess of par	19,600,000	26,800,000
Retained earnings	3,000,000	4,000,000
Total stockholders' equity	$27,000,000	$35,320,000

Net income for 2014 was $1,700,000, preferred stock dividends were $200,000, and common stock dividends were $500,000. The company issued 60,000 shares of common stock on July 1, 2014.

Required:

1. What is the company's basic EPS for 2014?

2. Suppose that Holiday Roads also had $500,000 of 10% convertible subordinated debentures outstanding at the beginning and end of 2014. Each $1,000 bond is convertible into 100 shares of common stock, cash settlement is not permitted, and the company's income tax rate is 34%. What is the company's diluted EPS for 2014?

3. What other types of securities in addition to convertible debt can affect the calculation of diluted EPS?

4. During 2013, Holiday Roads Company granted options to employees that allowed them to buy 50,000 shares at an exercise price of $10 per share, which was also the market price per share on the grant date. The options may be exercised beginning in 2016. The average market price per share of the company's shares in 2014 was $23. Building on requirement 2, what would be the company's diluted EPS for 2014 in light of both the convertible subordinated debentures and the employee stock options?

Tredegar Industries Inc. makes plastic films and molded plastic products and soft alloy aluminum extrusions, distributes business applications software, and provides proprietary chemistry services. A note to the company's annual report states:

P15-8

Setting limits on dividends **(LO 4)**

While certain of the Company's subsidiaries' debt facilities are outstanding, the Company's subsidiaries must meet specific financial tests on an ongoing basis, which are customary for these types of facilities. Except as provided by applicable corporate law, there are no restrictions on the Company's ability to pay dividends from retained earnings. However, the payment of cash dividends by the Company's subsidiaries to the Company are subject to certain restrictions under the terms of various agreements covering the Company's subsidiaries' long-term debt. Toledo, PDI, and Bal Crank [three of Tredegar's subsidiaries] are not permitted under each subsidiary's respective debt agreements to pay cash dividends. Assuming certain financial covenants are met, General Chemical [another subsidiary] is permitted to pay cash dividends of up to 50% of the net income (subject to certain adjustments) of General Chemical for the applicable period. Consequently, the Company's ability to pay cash dividends on Common Stock may effectively be limited by such agreements. At [year end] approximately $51,000 was available for dividend payments in accordance with these covenants.

The company's financial statements showed net income of $45,035, dividends of $3,176, and year-end retained earnings of $99,027. (All dollar amounts here and in the note are in thousands.)

Required:

1. Explain why and how lenders restrict a subsidiary's ability to pay dividends to the parent corporation.

2. What was Tredegar's dividend payout ratio?

3. What is the maximum amount of dividends the company could have paid to common stockholders in the year without violating the terms of its lending agreements?

4. Suppose that Tredegar's loan agreements contained no restrictions on dividend payments by subsidiaries or the parent company. What is the maximum legal amount of dividends the company could have paid to common stockholders?

5. Do contractual or legal restrictions on dividend payments seem to be influencing the company's dividend policy?

P15-9

Repurchasing stock and calculating EPS **(LO 2)**

Central Sprinkler Corporation manufactures and sells automatic fire sprinkler heads and valves, and it distributes components for automatic sprinkler systems. Selected information from the company's 2014 financial statements show:

	Years Ended October 31,			
($ in thousands except per share amounts)	**2011**	**2012**	**2013**	**2014**
Earnings available to common	$2,376	$4,018	$8,458	$3,763
Average common shares outstanding	4,752	5,023	3,383	3,330
EPS	$ 0.50	$ 0.80	$ 2.50	$ 1.13

In late December 2012, Central Sprinkler bought back 1,237,000 shares of common stock for $11,750,000.

Required:

1. What would EPS have been in 2013 and 2014 had the company not repurchased its common shares? Assume the stock buyback occurred on December 31, 2012, and notice that the company has an October 31 fiscal year-end.

2. Compare the company's profit performance in 2014 to earlier years, and comment on this comparison.

3. The stock buyback isn't the only reason that average common shares declined from 2012 to 2013. What else do you think could have contributed to this decline in average common shares?

P15-10

Preferred stock and credit analysis **(LO 3)**

AT&T Wireless Services was once one of the largest wireless communication—think "cell phones"—service providers in the United States. Information from its annual report to shareholders follows:

	December 31	
($ in millions)	**Year 2**	**Year 1**
Long-term debt	$ 6,705	$ 2,547
Preferred stock	7,644	3,000
Common stockholders' equity	19,281	21,887
Total stockholders' equity	$26,925	$24,887
Net income before interest and taxes	$972	$771
Interest expense	$386	$ 85
Long-term debt/total equity	0.25	0.10
Times interest earned	2.52	9.07

The company's (nonredeemable) preferred stock pays dividends at the rate of 8% annually.

Required:

1. Suppose that the increase in the preferred stock account was due to the issuance of new preferred shares at par on January 1, Year 2. What journal entry would the company make on the date to record the new preferred stock?

2. What journal entry would the company make to record preferred dividends for Year 2 and for Year 1?

3. Suppose that AT&T Wireless had issued 8% debt (at par) rather than *any* preferred stock. What general journal entry would the company make to record interest on the debt for Year 2 and for Year 1?

4. Compute the company's long-term debt-to-total-equity ratio and its interest coverage ratio for Year 2 and Year 1 *as if* AT&T Wireless had issued 8% debt rather than preferred stock.

(Continued)

5. Lenders generally do not restrict a company's ability to raise more equity capital. That's because the dollars raised from selling stock provide a cash cushion that protects the lender's debt claim. Under what conditions might lenders want to limit a company's ability to issue preferred stock?

6. How would the preferred stock be shown on the company's balance sheet if the shares contained a mandatory redemption feature?

Hanigan Manufacturing had 1,800,000 shares of common stock outstanding as of January 1, 2014, and 900,000 shares of 10% noncumulative (nonconvertible) preferred stock outstanding. The following events occurred during 2014:

P15-11

Calculating earnings per share **(LO 6)**

- On February 28, Hanigan sold 60,000 common shares.
- On May 15, Hanigan issued a 4% common stock dividend and paid cash dividends of $1,200,000 to common shareholders and $225,000 to preferred stockholders.
- On July 1, Hanigan repurchased and retired 6,000 common shares.
- On September 1, Hanigan issued $1,000,000 of convertible 10% bonds for par value. Each $1,000 bond certificate is convertible into 40 common shares. Cash settlement is not permitted.
- Under the terms of a separation agreement with its founder and former owner, Mike Hanigan, the company is obligated to issue Mr. Hanigan an additional 60,000 common shares if 2014 net income exceeds $5 million. No shares were issued as of December 31, 2014.
- Hanigan's net income for 2014 was $6,300,000 and the income tax rate was 40%.

Required:
Compute Hanigan Manufacturing's basic and diluted earnings per share for 2014.

Kadri Corporation reported basic EPS of $3.00 and diluted EPS of $2.40 for 2014. Its EPS calculations follow:

P15-12

Calculating EPS when the capital structure is complex **(LO 6)**

	EPS Calculation for 2014	
	Numerator	**Denominator**
Net income	$3,500,000	
Less dividend on 10% convertible preferred stock	(500,000)	
Weighted-average common shares outstanding		1,000,000
Basic EPS = $3.00	$3,000,000	1,000,000
Stock option dilution	—	33,334
Series A convertible debt dilution	240,000	250,000
Series B convertible debt dilution	300,000	200,000
10% Convertible preferred stock dilution	500,000	200,000
Diluted EPS = $2.40	$4,040,000	1,683,334

Kadri issued the convertible preferred stock at the beginning of 2014 and the Series A and Series B convertible debt at par in late 2013. No stock options were granted or exercised in 2014.

Required:
1. The convertible preferred stock has a $100 par value per share. How many preferred shares were issued, and what was the common stock conversion rate for each preferred share?

2. The Series B convertible debt pays interest at 10% annually, and Kadri's marginal income tax rate is 40%. How much Series B debt was outstanding, and what is the common stock conversion rate for each $1,000 face Series B bond?

3. What are the interest rate and common stock conversion rate for the $5 million par of Series A debt?

4. During the year, 50,000 shares were under option, and the average exercise price was $20 per share. What was the average market price of the company's common stock during 2014?

5. Explain why Series A debt carries a lower interest rate than Series B debt although both were issued at par on the same day in 2013.

P15-13

Analyzing shareholders' equity   **(LO 5)**

AICPA
ADAPTED

Trask Corporation, a public company whose shares are traded in the over-the-counter market, had the following shareholders' equity account balances at December 31, 2013:

Common stock	$ 7,875,000
Additional paid-in capital	15,750,000
Retained earnings	16,445,000
Treasury common stock	750,000

Transactions during 2014 and other information relating to the shareholders' equity accounts follow:

- As of January 1, 2014, Trask had 4,000,000 authorized shares of $5 par-value common stock; it had issued 1,575,000 shares of which 75,000 were held in treasury.

- On January 21, 2014, Trask issued 50,000 shares of $100 par value, 6% cumulative preferred stock at par in exchange for all of Rover Company's assets and liabilities. On that date, the net carrying amount of Rover's assets and liabilities equaled their fair values.

- On January 22, 2014, Rover distributed the Trask shares to its stockholders in a complete liquidation and dissolution of Rover. Trask had 150,000 authorized shares of preferred stock.

- On February 17, 2014, Trask formally retired 25,000 of 75,000 treasury common stock shares. The shares were originally issued at $15 per share and had been acquired on September 25, 2013, for $10 per share.

- Trask owned 15,000 shares of Harbor Inc. common stock purchased in 2013 for $600,000. The Harbor stock shares were trading securities. On March 5, 2014, Trask declared a property dividend of one share of Harbor common stock for every 100 shares of Trask common stock held by a shareholder of record on April 16, 2014. Harbor stock's market price on March 5, 2014, was $60 per share. The property dividend was distributed on April 29, 2014.

- On January 2, 2012, Trask granted stock options to employees to purchase 200,000 shares of the company's common stock at $12 per share, which was also the market price on that date. The options had a grant date fair value of $1.50 per share and are exercisable within a three-year period, beginning January 2, 2014. On June 1, 2014, employees exercised 150,000 options when the stock's market value was $25 per share. Trask issued new shares to settle the transaction.

- On October 27, 2014, Trask declared a two-for-one stock split on its common stock and reduced the per share par value accordingly. Trask shareholders of record on August 2, 2014, received one additional share of Trask common stock for each share of Trask common stock held. The laws of Trask's state of incorporation protect treasury stock from dilution.

- On December 12, 2014, Trask declared the yearly cash dividend on preferred stock, payable on January 11, 2015, to shareholders of record on December 31, 2014.
- On January 16, 2015, before the accounting records were closed for 2014, Trask learned that depreciation expense had been understated by $350,000 for the year ended December 31, 2013. The after-tax effect on 2013 net income was $245,000. The appropriate correcting entry was recorded on the same day.

Net income for 2014 was $2,400,000.

Required:

1. Prepare Trask's statement of retained earnings for the year ended December 31, 2014.
2. Prepare the shareholders' equity section of Trask's balance sheet at December 31, 2014.
3. Compute the book value per share of common stock at December 31, 2014.

Nike Inc. is one of the world's largest sellers of athletic footwear and athletic apparel. The following information is from Nike's annual report.

P15-14

Stockholders' equity
(LO 5)

Note 7: Redeemable Preferred Stock

NIAC is the sole owner of the Company's authorized Redeemable Preferred Stock, $1 par value, which is redeemable at the option of NIAC or the Company at par value aggregating $0.3 million.

Note 8: Common Stock

The authorized number of shares of Class A Common Stock, no par value, and Class B Common Stock, no par value, are 110 million and 350 million, respectively. Each share of Class A Common Stock is convertible into one share of Class B Common Stock. Voting rights of Class B Common Stock are limited in certain circumstances with respect to the election of directors.

From the Balance Sheet

Class A Convertible Common Stock—98.1 and 99.1 million shares outstanding at May 31, Year 3 and Year 2, respectively. Class B Common Stock—168.0 and 169.5 million shares outstanding at May 31, Year 3 and Year 2, respectively.

From the Statement of Cash Flow

	Years Ended May 31		
($ in millions)	Year 3	Year 2	Year 1
Cash provided by operations:			
Net earnings	$ 663.3	$ 589.7	$ 579.1
Adjustments	417.2	66.8	120.5
Net cash provided by operating activities	$1,080.5	$ 656.5	$ 699.6
Cash provided (used) by investing activities:	$ (302.8)	$(342.3)	$(440.0)
Cash used by financing activities:			
Proceeds from long-term debt issuance	$ 329.9	$ 0.0	$ 505.1
Reductions in long-term debt	(511.8)	(119.2)	(1.7)
Proceeds from exercise of stock options	59.5	56.0	23.9
Repurchase of stock	(226.9)	(157.0)	(646.3)
Dividends—common and preferred	(128.9)	(129.7)	(133.1)
Net cash provided (used) by financing activities	$ (478.2)	$(349.9)	$(252.1)

Required: Part A

1. How many shares of redeemable preferred stock were outstanding on May 31, Year 3? What is the par value of each share of preferred stock?

2. Suppose that Nike had sold 10,000 shares of preferred stock for $25 per share on June 1, Year 3. Prepare the journal entry to record this sale of preferred stock.

3. Assume the preferred stock described in requirement 2 pays a $0.10 per share annual dividend on May 15 each year. Prepare the journal entry to record the dividend payment on May 15, Year 3.

4. How many shares of common stock were outstanding on May 31, Year 3?

5. Explain why the number of shares outstanding might differ from the number of shares authorized or the number issued.

6. Why do some companies issue two classes of common stock?

7. Did Nike issue any common stock in the year ended May 31, Year 3? Why?

Required: Part B

Ignore your answers to all of Part A; instead assume the following hypothetical situation:

- Nike had 14,750,000 shares outstanding at the end of May Year 3. On this date, the balance in (a) the Common stock account was $147,500, (b) the Additional-paid-in capital account was $2,282,000, and (c) the Retained earnings account was $226,069,000.

- All cash dividends are paid in the year they are declared. Cash dividends in millions were $14.080, $240.830, and $0 in Year 6, Year 5, and Year 4, respectively.

- Net income in millions was $50.059, $49.589, and $45.080 for Year 6, Year 5, and Year 4, respectively.

- During the year ended May 31, Year 5, the company issued 17,250,000 common shares to the public as a stock dividend.

Determine the balances of Common stock, Additional paid-in capital, and Retained earnings accounts for the years ended May 31, Year 4, Year 5, and Year 6, respectively.

P15-15

Stock option accounting: Transitioning to current GAAP **(LO 6)**

The following excerpt is from Ball Corporation's 2006 annual report.

Effective January 1, 2006, the company adopted SFAS No. 123 (revised 2004), "Share-Based Payment," and elected to use the . . . Black–Scholes valuation model. Tax benefits associated with option exercises are reported in financing activities in the consolidated statements of cash flows beginning in 2006. Prior to January 1, 2006, expense related to stock options was calculated using the intrinsic value method under the guidelines of Accounting Principles Board (APB) Opinion No. 25, and has therefore not been included in the consolidated statements of earnings in 2005 and 2004. Ball's earnings as reported included after-tax stock-based compensation of $6.6 million and $12.5 million for the years ended December 31, 2005 and 2004, respectively. If the fair value based method had been used, after-tax stock-based compensation would have been $8.7 million in 2005 and $9.3 million in 2004. . . . The adoption of SFAS No. 123 (revised 2004) resulted in higher stock-based compensation in 2006 of $6.3 million compared to 2005.

Required:

1. Explain why Ball recorded $6.6 million of stock-based compensation expense in 2005 although the company was using the intrinsic value method.

2. What was the approximate fair value of the 2005 and 2004 stock option awards?

3. Some firms reduced the value of their 2006 stock option awards compared to earlier years or curtailed their use of stock options entirely. What is the accounting reason for these actions?

4. Does it appear that Ball reduced the value of its 2006 stock option awards?

5. Explain where Ball reported the cash flow statement item "tax benefits associated with option exercises" prior to the beginning of 2006.

The following excerpts are taken from the annual report of J. Crew Group, Inc.

P15-16

Distinguishing liabilities from equities **(LO 3)**

At January 29, 2005 and January 28, 2006, 92,800 shares of Series A preferred stock and 32,500 shares of Series B preferred stock were issued and outstanding. Dividends compound to the extent not paid in cash. . . . On October 17, 2009, Group is required to redeem the Series B preferred stock and to pay all accumulated but unpaid dividends on the Series A preferred stock.

[Under current GAAP, the company is required to classify as] long-term debt the liquidation value of Group Series B preferred stock and the related accumulated and unpaid dividends and the accumulated and unpaid dividends related to the Series A preferred stock since these amounts are required to be redeemed in October 2009. The preferred dividends related to . . . the Series B preferred stock and to the accumulated and unpaid dividends of the Series A and Series B preferred stock . . . are included in interest expense. The Series A preferred stock is only redeemable in certain circumstances (including a change in control at Group) and does not qualify for classification under SFAS No. 150. Accordingly, the dividends related to the Series A preferred stock are deducted from stockholders' deficit. (Edited for brevity.)

Required:

1. Explain why it makes sense that J. Crew Group is required to include its Series B preferred stock among long-term debt on the balance sheet.

2. Where on J. Crew's balance sheet was this debt shown before the current GAAP guidance on mandatorily redeemable preferred stock were issued?

3. Explain why it makes sense to include the dividends paid on Series B preferred stock as part of interest expense.

4. Where is the Series A preferred stock shown on the company's balance sheet?

5. Why does J. Crew use a different accounting treatment for Series A preferred stock and Series B preferred?

6. What impact (if any) has current GAAP guidance had on the popularity of mandatorily redeemable preferred stock as a corporate financing device?

CASES

Groupe Casino is a French multinational company that operates more than 9,000 multiformat retail stores—hypermarkets, supermarkets, discount stores, convenience stores, and restaurants—throughout the world. In January 2005, Casino issued €600 million of notes at a price of 101, meaning that the company raised €606 million cash by issuing these securities. Details of the note offering are described in C11-3 in Chapter 11.

C15-1

Groupe Casino: Determine whether it is debt or equity **(LO 5)**

Required:

- Casino management treated the notes as equity instruments for financial reporting purposes in accordance with International Financial Reporting Standards (IFRS). What specific IFRS guidance helps accountants and auditors distinguish between liabilities and equities?

- Do you concur with management's decision to treat the notes as equity instruments? Why?

- Suppose the notes were issued on January 1, 2005, that the first year's floating interest rate is 5%, and that interest is to be paid on December 31 of each year. Prepare the journal entries Casino would use to record (a) issuance of the notes on January 1, 2005; (b) interest expense for the year; and (c) the cash interest payment on December 31, 2005. Income tax considerations may be ignored.

- How would the Casino notes be treated under U.S. GAAP?

C15-2

Employee stock option accounting at Starbucks Corporation   (LO 7)

Starbucks Corp., the passionate purveyors of coffee and everything else that goes with a full and rewarding coffeehouse experience, included the following table in its 2009 annual report:

Total stock based compensation and ESPP expense recognized in the consolidated financial statements

		Fiscal Year Ended	
(in millions)	Sep 27, 2009	Sep 28, 2008	Sep 30, 2007
Stock option expense	$61.6	$57.6	$ 92.3
RSU expense	16.6	5.6	—
ESPP expense	5.0	11.8	11.6
Total stock-based compensation expense on the consolidated statements of earnings	$83.2	$75.0	$103.9
Total related tax benefit	$29.3	$24.0	$ 35.3

Starbucks maintains several share-based compensation plans that permit the company to grant employee stock options, restricted stock, and restricted stock "units" or RSUs. Starbucks also has an employee stock purchase plan ("ESPP") that allows participating employees to buy shares at a discounted price. At some companies, the discount can be as much as 15% lower than the prevailing market price.

Stock options to purchase Starbucks' common shares are granted at an exercise price equal to the market price of the stock on the date of grant. Most options become exercisable in four equal installments beginning one year from the date of the grant and expire 10 years from the date of grant.

Suppose Starbucks issues 100,000 employee stock options on January 1, 2013, and that one-fourth of the options vest in each of the next four years, beginning on December 31, 2013. For financial reporting purposes, the company elects to separate the total award into four groups (or tranches) according to the year in which each vests. Starbucks then measures the compensation cost for each vesting date tranche as if it was a separate award. The following table provides details about each vesting tranche:

Vesting Date	Shares Vesting	Fair Value per Option
Dec. 31, 2013	25,000	$2.00
Dec. 31, 2014	25,000	$3.20
Dec. 31, 2015	25,000	$4.80
Dec. 31, 2016	25,000	$7.00

Required:

1. Each tranche has the same exercise price—the market price of the stock on the grant date, or $23 on January 1, 2013. Explain why the option fair value increases with the vesting date.

2. Consider only the first option tranche vesting on December 31, 2013, and suppose that the price of Starbucks' common stock is $40 on that date. Determine the compensation expense that Starbucks would record in 2013 for this first option tranche. No stock options are exercised by employees that year.

3. Suppose that the price of Starbucks' common stock falls to $35 as of December 31, 2014. Considering only the first *two* option tranches, determine the compensation expense that Starbucks would record in 2014. No stock options are exercised by employees that year.

4. At the beginning of 2015, employees exercise 10,000 of the 2013 options. Employees hand over the 10,000 options along with $23 per option—the exercise price—and receive from the

company an equal number of shares. The price of Starbucks' common stock is $35 per share on the exercise date. Prepare the journal entry Starbucks will use to record this transaction.

5. Back in 2009, Starbucks' shareholders approved a management proposal to allow for a one-time stock option exchange program, designed to provide employees an opportunity to exchange certain outstanding but underwater stock options for a lesser amount of new options granted with lower exercise prices. Under this proposal, employees could exchange options granted with an exercise price greater than $19 and receive new options with an exercise price of about $15. A total of 14.3 million stock options were tendered by employees and 4.7 million of new stock options were granted. According to the company's financial statement note: "No incremental stock option expense was recognized for the exchange because the fair value of the new options, using standard employee stock option valuation techniques, was approximately equal to the fair value of the surrendered options they replaced." Explain why a company might offer employees the opportunity to exchange underwater stock options for new options with a lower exercise price.

6. Explain how management determined that only 4.7 million of new options would be granted in exchange for the 14.3 million options tendered. In other words, why might management be reluctant to grant 10.0 million of the new options?

Several years ago, RJR Nabisco Holdings Corporation (Holdings) offered for sale 93 million shares of its subsidiary RN-Nabisco Group. According to the prospectus, the estimated initial public offering price for RN-Nabisco common stock would be in the range of $17 to $19 per share. Holdings hoped to raise about $1.7 billion from the stock offering and to use the proceeds to reduce its debt burden. But investors weren't buying—at least not at the prospectus price—and Holdings scuttled the stock offer 23 days after it was first announced.

At the time, the Nabisco Group was one of the world's leading packaged foods businesses with sales of more than $6.7 billion. The Group's Nabisco Biscuit Division was the largest cookie and cracker manufacturer and marketer in the United States with eight of the nine top-selling brands.

Holdings was composed of the Nabisco Group and the Reynolds Group, which included the R.J. Reynolds Tobacco Company, the second largest manufacturer of cigarettes. The Reynolds Group's net sales as a percentage of Holdings' total consolidated net sales were 57%. Holdings was formed in 1989 when its predecessor company—RJR Nabisco, Inc. (RJRN)—was taken private in a leveraged buyout transaction. Holdings was taken public again in 1991 with the buyout group retaining 49% of Holdings' stock.

The plan at the time was to split off Nabisco Group from Reynolds Group and thereby improve the company's share price. Holdings had seen its stock price fall 36% that year for two reasons: R.J. Reynolds' earnings had been hurt by a brutal cigarette price war that began in early April, and investors had become increasingly concerned about the uncertainty over tobacco liability.

The Proposal

The Nabisco stock offered to the public would initially represent 25% of the equity of the Nabisco Group. The Reynolds Group would retain the balance of Nabisco's equity. Each outstanding share of common stock of Holdings would be redesignated into a common share of Reynolds stock, which was intended to reflect separately the performance of the Reynolds Group as well as the retained interest of the Reynolds Group in the Nabisco Group.

C15-3

RN-Nabisco Group: Calculating dividends and agency costs   **(LO 4)**

The offering prospectus described the company's dividend policy as:

The Board of Directors of Holdings currently intends to pay regular quarterly dividends on the Nabisco Stock in an aggregate annual amount equal to approximately 45% of the prior year's earnings of Holdings attributable to the outstanding Nabisco Stock. Consistent with this policy, Holdings currently intends to pay . . . an initial regular quarterly dividend of $0.13 per share of Nabisco Stock. While the Board of Directors does not currently intend to change such initial quarterly dividend rate or dividend policy, it reserves the right to do so at any time and from time to time. Under the Certificate of Incorporation and Delaware law, the Board of Directors is not required to pay dividends in accordance with such policy.

Dividends on the Nabisco Stock are limited by the Certificate of Incorporation and will be payable when, as and if declared by the Board of Directors out of the lessor of (i) the Available Nabisco Dividend Amount and (ii) funds of Holdings legally available therefore. Payment of dividends on the Nabisco Stock is also subject to the prior payment of dividends on the outstanding shares of Preferred Stock of Holdings (and any new class or series of capital stock of Holdings with similar preferential dividend provisions) and to restrictions contained in the Credit Agreements and certain other debt instruments of RJRN. . . . The "Available Nabisco Dividend Amount" is similar to that amount that would be legally available for the payment of dividends on Nabisco Stock under Delaware law if the Nabisco Group were a separate company, and will be increased or decreased as appropriate by, among other things, Holdings Earnings Attributable to the Nabisco Group. "Holdings Earnings Attributable to the Nabisco Group," for any period, means the net income or loss of the Nabisco Group during such period determined in accordance with generally accepted accounting principles (including income and expenses of Holdings allocated to the Nabisco Group on a substantially consistent basis). . . .

Holdings has never paid any cash dividends on shares of Common Stock. . . . The Board of Directors currently intends to pay future quarterly "pass-through" dividends on the Reynolds Stock with respect to the Reynolds Group's Retained Interest in the Nabisco Group. Holdings currently intends to pay . . . an initial quarterly pass-through dividend of approximately $0.03 per share of Reynolds Stock. . . . Subject to [certain limitations], the Board of Directors would be able, in its sole discretion, to declare and pay dividends exclusively on the Nabisco Stock or exclusively on the Reynolds Stock, or on both, in equal or unequal amounts, notwithstanding the respective amount of funds available for dividends on each series, the amount of prior dividends declared on each series or any other factor.

Required:

As a potential investor in Nabisco Group stock, what agency problems do you face that are not present when you buy common stock in most other companies?

COLLABORATIVE LEARNING CASE

C15-4

Classifying as equity or debt
(LO 3, 8)

 Collaborative

[A] Aon Corporation's Mezzanine Preferred Stock

In its 2002 annual report to shareholders, Aon Corporation described its mandatorily redeemable preferred stock as follows:

In January 1997, Aon created Aon Capital A, a wholly-owned statutory business trust, for the purpose of issuing mandatorily redeemable preferred capital securities (Capital Securities). The sole asset of Aon Capital A is $726 million aggregate principal amount of Aon's 8.205% Junior Subordinated Deferrable Interest Debentures due January 1, 2027.

Aon Capital A issued $800 million of 8.205% (mandatorily redeemable preferred) Capital Securities in January 1997. The Capital Securities are subject to mandatory redemption on January 1, 2027 or are redeemable in whole, but not in part, at the option of Aon upon the occurrence of certain events. . . . During 2002, approximately $98 million of the Capital Securities were repurchased on the open market for $87 million, excluding accrued interest. . . .

Aon's 2002 balance sheet showed the following amounts:

($ millions) **Liabilities and Stockholders' Equity**	**2002**	**2001**
Insurance premiums payable	$ 9,904	$ 8,233
Insurance policy liabilities	5,310	4,990
General liabilities		
General expenses	2,012	1,770
Short-term borrowings	117	257
Notes payable	1,671	1,694
Other liabilities	1,673	1,071
Total Liabilities	20,687	18,015
Redeemable Preferred Stock	50	50
Mandatorily Redeemable Preferred Capital Securities	702	800
Total Common Stockholders' Equity	3,895	3,465

Required:

1. Aon's capital securities are forms of preferred stock. Assume that Aon Capital A (the trustee) issued the preferred shares on January 1, 1997, for $800 million cash, the same day that Aon Corporation issued $800 million of its junior debentures to the trust. Describe the cash flows associated with these two transactions—that is, explain who received cash and who gave up cash in each case.

2. One year later (on December 31, 1997), Aon Corporation must pay 8.205% interest to debt holders, and Aon Capital A must pay an 8.205% dividend to preferred stockholders. Describe the cash flows associated with each of these payments—that is, explain who received cash, who gave up cash, and how much cash was exchanged.

3. Why did Aon Corporation create Aon Capital A?

4. For financial reporting purposes, Aon Corporation will issue consolidated financial statements that include the activities of Aon Capital A. In addition, GAAP at the time did not require liability treatment of mandatorily redeemable preferred stock. How did Aon Corporation show its cash interest payment on December 31, 1997?

5. Why does Aon Corporation's 2002 balance sheet show the Capital Securities in the "mezzanine" section between total liabilities and stockholders' equity?

6. Aon Corporation is an insurance company, so most of its liabilities relate to insurance policy premiums and policy liabilities. The company's debt includes Short-term borrowings and Notes payable. Compute Aon's debt-to-equity ratio for 2002 assuming that the Capital Securities are treated as part of equity. Repeat the calculation, this time assuming that the Capital Securities are part of debt. Which debt-to-equity ratio provides the most accurate measure of the company's true debt and equity position? Why?

[B] Cephalon Inc.'s Zero-Coupon, Zero Yield-to-Maturity Convertible Notes

Cephalon Inc. issued $750 million of zero-coupon convertible notes. Because the notes were issued at par, meaning that Cephalon received $750 million cash for the notes, they have a zero yield-to-maturity. Settlement in cash upon conversion is not permitted. Here is what Cephalon said about the notes:

We issued and sold in a private placement $750.0 million of Zero Coupon Convertible Subordinated Notes (the "Notes"). The interest rate on the Notes is zero and the Notes will not accrete interest. . . . The Notes are subordinate to our existing and future senior indebtedness. The Notes were issued in two tranches and have the following salient terms:

- $375.0 million of Zero Coupon Convertible Subordinated Notes due June 15, 2023 . . . are convertible prior to maturity, subject to certain conditions described below, into shares of our common stock at a conversion price of $59.50 per share (a conversion rate of approximately 16.8067 shares per $1,000 principal amount of notes). . . .

The Notes also contain a restricted convertibility feature that does not affect the conversion price of the notes but, instead, places restrictions on a holder's ability to convert their notes into shares of our common stock ("conversion shares"). A holder may convert the notes if one or more of the following conditions is satisfied:

- if, on the trading day prior to the date of surrender, the closing sale price of our common stock is more than 120% of the applicable conversion price per share (the "conversion price premium");
- if we have called the notes for redemption;
- if the average trading prices of the notes for a specified period is less than 100% of the average of the conversion values of the notes during that period . . . ;
- if we make certain significant distributions to our holders of common stock or we enter into specified corporate transactions.

Because of the inclusion of the restricted convertibility feature of the Notes, our diluted income per common share calculation does not give effect to the dilution from the conversion of the Notes until our share price exceeds the 20% conversion price premium or one of the other conditions above is satisfied.

Source: 10-Q filing for Cephalon Inc., June 2003.

Required:

1. Cephalon is a U.S. Company. What accounting entry did Cephalon make to record the $750 million proceeds received from issuing the notes? Over the next year, what other accounting entries (if any) related to these notes did the company make?

2. The notes mature in 2023, approximately 20 years from the date they were issued. At a 6% rate of annual interest, the present value of $1,000 to be received 20 years from today is only $311.805. (You might want to verify this conclusion.) Suppose that Cephalon's true cost of borrowing money is 6% per year. How much did note holders pay for Cephalon debt, and how much did they pay for the option to convert the notes into shares of common stock?

3. Suppose that Cephalon separated the notes into debt and equity components and then recorded each component separately. What accounting entry would the company make on the issue date to record the proceeds received from issuing the notes? Over the next year, what other accounting entries (if any) related to these notes would the company make?

4. Describe Cephalon's financial reporting advantages of issuing zero-coupon, zero yield-to-maturity notes rather than a more traditional debt instrument. Why aren't the notes included in the company's computation of diluted earnings per share?

5. If Cephalon were to issue those same notes today, would it still be able to use the accounting entries outlined in your answer to requirement 1?

[C] Avenet's Cash Settled Convertible Debt

Avenet Inc., a U.S. company, is a global provider of electronic parts, enterprise computing and storage products, and supply chain and logistics services for the electronic components industry. The company's 2009 annual report contained the following note:

The Financial Accounting Standards Board issued authoritative guidance which requires the issuer of certain convertible debt instruments that may be settled in cash (or other assets) on conversion to separately account for the debt and equity (conversion option) components of the instrument. The standard requires the convertible debt to be recognized at the present value of its cash flows discounted using the non-convertible debt borrowing rate at the date of issuance. The resulting debt discount from this present value calculation is to be recognized as the value of the equity component and recorded to additional paid in capital. The discounted convertible debt is then required to be accreted up to its face value and recorded as non-cash interest expense over the expected life of the convertible debt.

Required:

1. At the time this authoritative guidance was issued, Avenet had already issued $300 million of 2% Convertible Senior Debentures due in 2034. The debentures were issued at par several years earlier, and thus Avenet received the full $300 million cash at the issue date. What journal entry did Avenet make at the time to record the convertible debt issuance? How much interest expense would Avenet record each year?

2. Under the approach now required by GAAP for cash-settled convertible debt, Avenet says the debt discount to be recorded at the issue date would have been $50 million and that the nonconvertible debt borrowing rate at the date of issuance would have been 7%. What journal entry would Avenet make to record the convertible debt issuance under current GAAP? How much interest expense would Avenet record during the first full year?

3. If Avenet followed IFRS guidance rather than U.S. GAAP, which of the two accounting treatments would the company have used at the issue date?

4. Avenet decided to extinguish its 2% Convertible Subordinate Debentures just prior to adopting the new U.S. GAAP guidance (described above) for cash settled convertible debt. Why did the company decide to retire the debt early?

 mhhe.com/revsine6e

Remember to check the book's companion website for additional study material.

Intercorporate Equity Investments | 16

Companies often buy shares of other companies. The reasons for such purchases vary. The investment may be a passive one, whereby the investing company does not influence the operating decisions of the investee, but rather makes the investment to be part of a portfolio that is managed to return a profit, or simply to earn a return on funds that might otherwise sit idle. When the investment is a passive one, the investor's return comes from dividends and share price increases. The investor might instead take a more active role and seek to make improvements in the investee company's operations through, for example, representation on the board. The investment may even be of a majority interest, which could facilitate physical integration of the two firms in an attempt to derive "synergies." When a company has an active investment, the investor's return is likely to come from increased operating profits and growth.

> Synergies are ways in which two or more companies are more valuable when managed together than the sum of their values apart. Synergies may arise because of operating efficiencies that allow for more cost-effective production by, for example, closing some plants and operating the remaining plants at a greater proportion of capacity. They may also arise because of opportunities to market or distribute products together.

Share ownership generally entitles the investor-shareholder to vote at the company's annual shareholder meetings or on special matters that might come up during the year. Shareholders vote to elect company directors; to approve the company's outside auditor; and on proposed mergers and buyouts, compensation plan changes, and corporate charter amendments. Other shareholder proposals often address environmental, social, and political issues such as prohibiting the company from doing business in unfavored countries. Because the number of votes a shareholder may cast depends on the number of shares held, to a large extent, the investor's ownership proportion determines the degree to which it can influence the investee's decisions; that is, whether the investment is active or passive.

> Each share of **common stock** usually entitles the owner to one vote, but those who own **preferred stock** usually have no voting rights. There are exceptions. Some companies issue dual-class common stock (often denoted Common A and Common B) in which one class has voting rights and the other does not. In addition, some companies do issue voting preferred stock.

Under existing GAAP, the method of accounting for intercorporate investments depends on the degree to which the investor company is able to influence the operating decisions of the investee. And, because the proportion of shares held by the investor is generally related to its degree of influence, that proportion is an important factor, although not an absolute deciding factor, in determining the accounting method to be used.

LEARNING OBJECTIVES

After studying this chapter, you will understand:

1. How an investor's degree of influence over an investee company determines the accounting treatment of equity investments and why.
2. How fair value accounting is applied to securities held in trading and available-for-sale portfolios and how impairments are recorded.
3. How to apply the equity method and the fair value option.
4. What consolidated financial statements are, how they are prepared under the acquisition method, and how noncontrolling interests are measured and reported.
5. How goodwill arises and when it is considered impaired and written down.
6. How business combinations were previously accounted for under the purchase and pooling of interests methods and how the method used to record an acquisition in the past affects financial analysis, even today.
7. What variable interest entities (VIEs) are and when they must be consolidated.
8. How operations reported in foreign currencies affect the preparation of financial statements in U.S. dollars.
9. The major differences between IFRS and U.S. GAAP related to accounting for financial assets, consolidations, special purpose entities (SPEs) or VIEs, and joint ventures.
10. How to account for investments in debt securities.

Figure 16.1

FINANCIAL REPORTING
ALTERNATIVES FOR
INTERCORPORATE
EQUITY INVESTMENTS

Type of investment:	Minority Passive	Minority Active	Controlling
Level of influence:	No substantial influence	Substantial influence	Effective control
Level of ownership:	Less than 20%*	20%–50%*	More than 50%
Accounting:	Trading Securities: Fair value measurement with unrealized gains and losses reported in income statement	Equity method Fair value option permitted	Full consolidation Transactions completed 2009 or later: Acquisition Method
	Available-for-sale Securities: Fair value measurement with unrealized gains and losses reported in other comprehensive income		Transactions completed July 1, 2001 through 2008: Purchase Method Transactions completed prior to July 1, 2001: Purchase Method or Pooling of Interests**

* Presumptive ownership level. May be rebutted by evidence indicating level of influence is substantial even though ownership is below 20% or that level of influence is not substantial even though ownership exceeds 20%.

** For qualifying transactions completed through an exchange of shares.

We first discuss minority passive investments, in which the investor has no significant influence over the investee's operating decisions and usually owns less than 20% of the investee's voting shares. Then we consider minority active investments. In these cases, the investor does have influence over the investee, but not complete control. Ownership is typically between 20% and 50% of the voting shares. Then we analyze controlling investments, in which the investor holds more than 50% of the voting shares and therefore can unilaterally dictate policy, subject only to contractual and legal restrictions. We also consider the special reporting problems created by subsidiaries in foreign countries and some of the financial analysis issues that arise because companies that have made acquisitions at different points in time may have recorded those transactions differently as the rules for merger and acquisition (M&A) accounting have changed. Although this chapter primarily focuses on equity investments, we consider the accounting for investments in debt in the appendix.

Figure 16.1 summarizes the types of equity investments firms can make and the accounting methods applied in each case. We now consider each of those methods.

MINORITY PASSIVE INVESTMENTS: FAIR VALUE ACCOUNTING

Owning a small portion of a public company does not convey the power to elect directors or influence the company's operating policies, so it's safe to assume such an investment is made for speculation—that is, the investor hopes to earn a return from dividends and share price appreciation. Existing GAAP presumes that ownership of less than 20% of another company's voting shares constitutes a passive investment because an investment at such low levels seldom provides the investor with an opportunity to influence the investee's activities significantly. As Figure 16.1 shows, minority passive investments are classified on the investor's books in one of two ways. The classification depends on whether the investment is part of an actively managed portfolio intended to profit from near-term price swings.[1]

Passive equity investments that the investor intends to hold for a short time and that are purchased in an attempt to profit from near-term price changes are classified as **trading securities.** They are generally part of an actively managed portfolio designed to achieve trading gains.[2] Trading securities are generally shown on the balance sheet as current assets. Passive equity investments that are not trading securities are called **available-for-sale securities.** These securities may be classified as either current or noncurrent, depending on management's intended holding period.

Both trading and available-for-sale securities are initially recorded at cost—that is, the total amount paid for the securities, including any brokerage fees. At subsequent balance sheet dates, these investments are written up or down to their fair values, often referred to as *marked-to-market.* As discussed in Chapters 7 and 8, GAAP specifies three levels of fair value measurement. Level 1 fair value measurements are determined from prices in actively traded markets. Level 2 holdings are valued based on observable inputs such as quoted market prices for similar securities. Level 3 items are illiquid assets that must be valued using internal models (e.g., discounted expected cash flows) using unobservable inputs. Firms are required to disclose the portion of their trading and available-for-sale portfolios that are valued using each of the three levels of measurements. The subsequent illustrations assume that Level 1 measurements (market prices in actively traded markets) are readily available for all securities.

> Fair value accounting is *required* for marketable securities under FASB ASC Topic 320: Investments—Debt and Equity Securities, but is an *option* that a firm may elect for minority active (equity) investments and certain other types of assets and liabilities under ASC Topic 825: Financial Instruments. For further discussion of fair value measurement, see Chapters 7 and 8.

Trading Securities

Market price increases of trading securities are debited to a **Fair value adjustment account** that is *added* to the Trading securities asset account (reported at original cost). Market price decreases are credited to the same Fair value adjustment account and *deducted* from the Trading securities asset account. The offsetting credit or debit is made to the Unrealized gain or loss on trading securities account in the income statement. An example of fair value accounting for securities that Principal Financial Corporation purchased for **short-term speculation** follows:

Purchases and Sales of Trading Securities by Principal Financial Corporation

Security	Date Acquired	Acquisition Cost	Fair Value at December 31,			
			2014	2015	2016	2017
Company A common	1/1/14	$ 10,000	$11,000	$13,000	$ 14,000	$12,000
Company B preferred	1/1/14	20,000	18,000	17,000	18,000	*
Company C common	7/1/15	30,000	—	26,000	33,000	34,000
Company D common	7/1/15	40,000	—	41,000	37,000	30,000
		$100,000	$29,000	$97,000	$102,000	$76,000

*Company B preferred stock was sold on January 1, 2017, for $18,500.

---

[1] The reporting rules for noncontrolling passive investments are contained in FASB ASC Topic 320: Investments—Debt and Equity Securities.

[2] FASB ASC Paragraph 320-10-25-1: Investments—Debt and Equity Securities—Overall—Recognition—Classification of Investment Securities.

Let's first consider the entry to record the purchase of Company A common shares and Company B preferred shares on January 1, 2014:

DR Trading securities—Company A common	$10,000	
DR Trading securities—Company B preferred	20,000	
CR Cash		$30,000

Dividends on these securities are recorded as income when they are declared—if Company A declared dividends on December 15, 2014, and Principal's share of those dividends was $1,000, then the entry would be:

DR Dividends receivable	$1,000	
CR Dividend income		$1,000

When Principal Financial receives the cash dividend in January 2015, it will debit Cash for $1,000 and credit the Dividends receivable account for $1,000.

The 2014 year-end fair value adjustment requires two steps:

Step 1: The total fair value of all trading securities is compared to the total cost of the securities. Any difference becomes the *target balance* for the Fair value adjustment account.

Step 2: The Fair value adjustment account must be increased (or decreased) to equal its target balance, and then an unrealized gain (or loss) for the same amount must be recorded.

Principal Financial's 2014 year-end adjustment would be:

Step 1 Trading Securities Portfolio		Step 2 Fair Value Adjustment Account	
Total fair value	$ 29,000	$(1,000)	Target balance (CR)
− Total cost	(30,000)	-0-	Current balance
= Difference	$ (1,000)	$(1,000)	Adjustment needed (CR)

DR Unrealized holding loss on trading securities (income statement)	$1,000	
CR Fair value adjustment—trading securities		$1,000

Principal's December 31, 2014, balance sheet reports the trading securities at $29,000, the net of the investment costs and the fair value adjustment account.

Now let's look at the entry to record the purchase of Company C and Company D common stock on July 1, 2015:

DR Trading securities—Company C common	$30,000	
DR Trading securities—Company D common	40,000	
CR Cash		$70,000

Following the two-step process, Principal Financial's 2015 year-end fair value adjustment is:

Step 1 Trading Securities Portfolio		Step 2 Fair Value Adjustment Account	
Total fair value	$ 97,000	$(3,000)	Target balance (CR)
− Total cost	(100,000)	− (1,000)	Current balance (CR)
= Difference	$ (3,000)	$(2,000)	Adjustment needed (CR)

DR Unrealized holding loss on trading securities		
(income statement)	$2,000	
CR Fair value adjustment—trading securities		$2,000

This entry highlights why it is necessary to use the two-step procedure. Comparing the portfolio fair value to the *cost* of the underlying investments at each valuation date (as shown in Step 1), rather than comparing the total portfolio fair value at two successive dates, incorporates changes in the portfolio's composition at successive valuation dates.

The fair value adjustment for 2016 is:

Step 1 Trading Securities Portfolio		**Step 2** Fair Value Adjustment Account	
Total fair value	$ 102,000	$ 2,000	Target balance (DR)
− Total cost	(100,000)	− (3,000)	Current balance (CR)
= Difference	$ 2,000	$ 5,000	Adjustment needed (DR)

DR Fair value adjustment—trading securities	$5,000	
CR Unrealized holding gain on trading securities—		
(income statement)...............................		$5,000

When trading securities are sold, a *realized* gain or loss is recorded. The amount of the realized gain or loss is the selling price of the securities *minus* the fair value of the securities on the last balance sheet date. The original cost of the securities sold and the related portion of the Fair value adjustment account are removed from the accounts. This procedure is illustrated for the sale of Company B preferred stock on January 1, 2017:

> Using the fair value on the last balance sheet date in computing the realized gain or loss avoids double counting any unrealized gain or loss recorded in previous periods' income statements.

Computation of Realized Gain or Loss

Selling price of Company B preferred stock	$ 18,500
Fair value at 12/31/16 balance sheet date	(18,000)
Realized gain	$ 500

Entry to Record the Sale of Company B Common Stock

DR Cash	$18,500	
DR Fair value adjustment—trading securities	2,000*	
CR Realized gain on sale of trading securities		$ 500
CR Trading securities—Company B preferred..............		20,000

* $20,000 cost − $18,000 fair value at 12/31/16 = $2,000.

After this entry is recorded, the balances in the Trading securities account and the Fair value adjustment account are:

Trading securities account at cost ($100,000 − $20,000)	$80,000
Fair value adjustment account ($2,000 DR balance on 12/31/16 + $2,000 DR reversal from sale)	4,000
Trading securities at 12/31/16 fair value	$84,000

The fair value adjusting entry at the end of 2017 compares the target balance for the Fair value adjustment account to the balance that will appear in this account after the sale of the Company B preferred stock, as in the following computation:

	Step 1 Trading Securities Portfolio		Step 2 Fair Value Adjustment Account	
Total fair value	$ 76,000	$(4,000)	Target balance (CR)	
− Total cost	(80,000)	− 4,000	Current balance (DR)	
= Difference	$ (4,000)	$(8,000)	Adjustment needed (CR)	

DR	Unrealized holding loss on trading securities (income statement)	$8,000	
	CR Fair value adjustment—trading securities		$8,000

After this entry is recorded, the trading securities section of Principal Financial's balance sheet on December 31, 2017, would show trading securities at a $76,000 fair value, consisting of $80,000 of cost and a ($4,000) fair value adjustment.

Available-for-Sale Securities

Now assume that Principal Financial bought the securities described earlier because of their perceived **longer-term investment potential**—not for short-term speculation purposes. In this case, the securities would be classified as "available for sale." The entries to record the purchase, dividend, and fair value adjustment for available-for-sale securities are similar to the entries for trading securities.

The only significant difference when treating investment securities as "available for sale" rather than "trading" is that the ***mark-to-market adjustment is not included in net income. Instead, the upward or downward adjustment to reflect fair value for available-for-sale securities results in a direct credit or debit to a special owners' equity account.*** These unrealized gains or losses on available-for-sale securities are one of the Other comprehensive income components described in Chapter 2.

Returning to our example, the 2014 year-end downward fair value adjustment for Principal Financial's available-for-sale portfolio is:

DR	Other comprehensive income	$1,000	
	CR Fair value adjustment—available-for-sale securities		$1,000

As was the case with trading securities, a credit balance in the Fair value adjustment account is treated as a contra-asset account so that the net book value of the available-for-sale portfolio in the December 31, 2014, balance sheet is $29,000 ($30,000 cost − the $1,000 fair value adjustment). If fair values increase, as they did in 2016, the adjustment is effected by a debit to the Fair value adjustment account and a credit to Other comprehensive income.

GAAP excludes unrealized gains and losses on available-for-sale securities from net income because the securities are not held for active trading. Recording the debit or credit directly into owners' equity—rather than through net income—alleviates the potential for earnings volatility unrelated to eventual investment performance. When available-for-sale securities are later sold, the cumulative unrealized gain or loss is realized and included in net income. The realized loss on sale of Company B preferred stock that would be recorded in 2017 would be $1,500, which is the difference between the selling price ($18,500) and the *original cost* of these shares ($20,000). When gains and losses that arose in earlier periods are finally recognized in the income statement, the associated amounts are "recycled" out of Other comprehensive income. For example, the complete entry to record the sale of Company B preferred stock in 2017 is:

DR	Cash	$18,500
DR	Fair value adjustment—available-for-sale securities	2,000
DR	Realized loss on sale of available-for-sale securities	1,500
	CR Available-for-sale securities— Company B preferred stock.........................	$20,000
	CR Other comprehensive income	2,000

After this entry is recorded (and the Other comprehensive income account is closed out to Accumulated other comprehensive income) there will be no balance in Accumulated other comprehensive income related to the investment in Company B preferred stock nor will there be any Fair value adjustment related to that investment. The entire loss of $1,500 is recognized in 2017. In contrast, when we assumed the investment in Company B preferred stock was a trading security, the $1,500 loss was recognized across the entire holding period: ($2,000 loss in 2014, $1,000 loss in 2015, $1,000 gain in 2016, $500 gain in 2017).

Income Tax Effects

Fair value adjustments have income tax consequences but, because under income tax law gains and losses are not recognized until a security is sold, the tax effects are deferred. Let's consider the trading securities example first. In that example, Principal recorded a $1,000 loss in 2014. This loss reduced the company's pre-tax income but had no effect on 2014 taxable income, resulting in a temporary difference. The effect of this loss is to reduce 2014 income tax expense by $350 (assuming a 35% marginal tax rate) and to create a deferred tax asset of the same amount. The deferred tax asset arises because there is a $1,000 future deductible amount as a result of the temporary difference. In journal entry form, the tax effect is:

DR	Deferred tax asset	$350
	CR Income tax expense	$350

Principal does not actually make this journal entry separately. Rather, it is part of the company's overall tax entry. The journal entry notation above is simply telling us that in Principal's tax entry, the debit to Deferred tax asset is $350 higher (or the credit to it is $350 lower) and the debit to Income tax expense (assuming the company has a positive income tax provision) is $350 lower as a result of this particular item.

Now consider the available-for-sale case. Recall from Chapter 13 that when a transaction is reported as part of other comprehensive income rather than in net income, its tax effect is also reported in other comprehensive income, not in income tax expense. Therefore, the income tax effect of any entries to adjust the fair value of available-for-sale securities is also part of other comprehensive income. Like the situation for trading securities, the tax effect is a deferred tax effect because no gain or loss is reported for tax purposes until the security is sold, resulting in a temporary difference. The income tax effect (assuming a 35% income tax rate) of the $1,000 holding loss in available-for-sale securities would be:

DR	Deferred tax asset	$350
	CR Other comprehensive income	$350

This entry differs from the trading securities case in that the credit is to Other comprehensive income, not income tax expense. When combined with the original pre-tax entry to record the fair value adjustment, the result is a $650 ($1,000 − $350) reduction, net of tax, in Other comprehensive income in 2014, just as in the trading securities case there was a $650 reduction in net income.

In subsequent years, similar income tax consequences would be recorded. In 2015 Principal recorded an additional $2,000 unrealized holding loss, which would result in an increase in the deferred tax asset of $700 ($2,000 × 35%) regardless of the classification of the investment. In the trading securities case, Income tax expense would be reduced. In the available-for-sale securities case, the Other comprehensive loss would be reduced. In 2016 Principal recorded a $5,000 unrealized holding gain. Principal would record the following entries in the trading securities and available-for-sale cases for the income tax effects, which would again be part of the overall tax entry.

Trading Securities Case:

DR	Income tax expense		$1,750	
	CR	Deferred tax asset		$1,050
	CR	Deferred tax liability		700

Available-for-Sale Securities Case:

DR	Other comprehensive income		$1,750	
	CR	Deferred tax asset		$1,050
	CR	Deferred tax liability		700

Other-Than-Temporary Impairment of Available-for-Sale Equity Investments

The previous discussion illustrates the required accounting when fair value changes are considered temporary. Occasionally, the fair value of a security will decline for a reason that is judged to be "other than temporary." The meltdown in the credit markets that occurred in 2007–2008 and the related illiquidity of investments in mortgage-backed securities and collateralized debt obligations (see Chapters 7 and 8) provide a classic example of this sort of situation.

To determine whether a decline in value of an available-for-sale equity security is other than temporary, a firm considers the extent of the decline in value, the issuer's prospects and financial condition, as well as the investor's ability and intent to hold the investment until the value recovers. If the decline is deemed to be other than temporary, the security is written down to its fair value and a charge is taken against net income.

Suppose, for example, that Toews Corporation had previously made an investment in Carcillo Company common stock and classified the investment as available-for-sale. The original cost of the investment was $100,000 and as of December 31, 2013, the fair value was $90,000. Toews has no other available-for-sale securities. As of December 31, 2013, Toews has a $10,000 credit balance in the Fair value adjustment account and a $10,000 debit balance (before considering taxes) in Accumulated other comprehensive income. At December 31, 2014, the investment in Carcillo is worth only $60,000 and the impairment is deemed to be other than temporary, due to Carcillo's poor future prospects. Toews must record the impairment in its income statement in 2014 and reduce its cost basis to $60,000. The entry to record the impairment (before considering taxes) is:

DR	Impairment loss	$40,000	
DR	Fair value adjustment	10,000	
	CR Other comprehensive income		$10,000
	CR Investment in Carcillo Company common stock		40,000

Toews's balance sheet is now as if it had just purchased the Carcillo stock for $60,000. The subsequent accounting continues with the standard approach to available-for-sale securities, whereby changes in fair value are reflected in Other comprehensive income, unless there is another impairment that is deemed to be other than temporary.

Exhibit 16.1 provides an excerpt from a note in AIG's 2009 10-K report describing other-than-temporary impairment charges recorded on a variety of its investments.

RECAP

Trading securities and available-for-sale securities—the two types of minority passive equity investments—are carried at fair value on the balance sheet. The unrealized holding gain or loss on trading securities is run through net income in the period of the fair value change. Unrealized gains and losses on available-for-sale securities do not net affect net income in the period of the fair value change; instead these gains and losses are reported as Other comprehensive income (OCI), net of tax effects, and these amounts are closed out to a special owners' equity account—Accumulated other comprehensive income (AOCI). Other-than-temporary impairment of available-for-sale equity securities is reported as an adjustment to earnings.

MINORITY ACTIVE INVESTMENTS: EQUITY METHOD

When an investor has the ability to significantly influence the investee's decisions, it is said to have an active investment. Under GAAP, there is a presumption that an investor holding 20% or more of an investee's voting shares is able to significantly influence the investee's decisions. This presumption could be rebutted by evidence that the investor is unable to influence the investee. For example, the existence of a formal agreement that the investor not seek board representation or assist others in doing so after a failed takeover attempt would indicate a lack of ability to influence, even if ownership exceeded 20%.[3] The presumption that ownership

EXHIBIT 16.1	**American International Group (AIG): Excerpts from 2009 10-K Report**

Other-Than-Temporary Impairments

As a result of AIG's periodic evaluation of its securities for other-than-temporary impairments in value, AIG recorded impairment charges in earnings of $7.8 billion, $48.6 billion, and $4.6 billion in 2009, 2008, and 2007, respectively.

With the adoption of the new other-than-temporary impairments accounting standard on April 1, 2009, such severity loss charges subsequent to that date exclusively related to equity securities and other invested assets. In all prior periods, such charges primarily related to mortgage-backed, asset-backed and collateralized securities, corporate debt securities of financial institutions and other equity securities. Notwithstanding AIG's intent and ability to hold such securities until they had recovered their cost or amortized cost basis, and despite structures that indicated, at the time, that a substantial amount of the securities should have continued to perform in accordance with original terms, AIG concluded, at the time, that it could not reasonably assert that the impairment would be temporary.

below 20% indicates the investor does not have influence over the investee is also rebuttable. For example, if the investee's shares are widely held, an investor with, say, 18% ownership could have significant influence, which might be evidenced by its ability to gain a seat on the board of directors.

When the investor has significant influence, the simple accounting approach described for passive investments is no longer suitable. To see why, recall that the entry made on Principal Financial's books when an investee declared a dividend was:

DR	Dividends receivable	$1,000	
	CR Dividend income		$1,000

When the investor can significantly influence the investee's dividend policy, the minority passive accounting treatment would allow the investor to affect its own reported income by influencing dividend policy. For example, if the investor is able to cause the investee to raise its dividend, the higher dividend would immediately run through the investor's income statement.

To preclude this avenue for income manipulation, minority active investments are accounted for using the **equity method,** as indicated in Figure 16.1. Under the equity method, the investor records its initial investment in the investee at cost. Subsequently, the Investment account is increased for the investor's pro rata share of the investee's net income, and there is a corresponding credit to the Investment income account. In the case of a loss, the investor's Investment account decreases and there's a corresponding debit to the Investment loss account.

Because the investor's earnings are increased for its share of the investee's earnings each period, it would be inappropriate to record dividend distributions received from the investee as income too. This would "double count" the investee's earnings on the investor's books. Under the equity method, dividends from the investee reduce the Investment account. ***Thus, the net increase in the Investment account is the amount by which the investor's share of the investee's earnings exceeds its share of the investee's dividends declared.*** The intuition is that the equity method recognizes income on the investor's books when the investee creates its ability to pay dividends by earning a profit, not when it actually pays the dividend.

The following example illustrates the entries under the equity method.

On January 1, 2014, Willis Company purchases 30% of the outstanding common shares of Planet Burbank Inc. for $9 million. The book value and fair value of Planet Burbank's net assets (assets minus liabilities) is $30 million. Thus, Willis pays book value for its investment in Planet Burbank (30% × $30 million = $9 million). During 2014, Planet Burbank earns a $10 million net profit, and declares a $500,000 dividend on December 15, 2014. Under the equity method, Willis makes these entries:

January 1, 2014: Initial Investment in Planet Burbank

DR	Investment in Planet Burbank	$9,000,000	
	CR Cash		$9,000,000
(To record investment at cost.)			

---

[3] An investor that has significant influence but does not exercise it has not rebutted the presumption of ability to influence. To rebut the presumption, it must be the case that the investor *cannot* influence the investee, not simply that it *does not* influence the investee.

December 15, 2014: Investor's Share of Dividends Declared		
DR Dividend receivable from affiliate	$150,000	
CR Investment in Planet Burbank.		$150,000
(To reduce the investment account for dividends declared—30% of $500,000)		

December 31, 2014: Investor's Share of Earnings		
DR Investment in Planet Burbank.	$3,000,000	
CR Income from affiliate		$3,000,000
(To recognize 30% of Planet Burbank's total reported income of $10,000,000)		

The carrying value in the investment account at the end of the year would be:

Initial investment amount	$ 9,000,000
Plus: Willis's cumulative pro rata share of Planet Burbank's net income	3,000,000
Minus: Willis's cumulative pro rata share of dividends declared by Planet Burbank	(150,000)
Investment account carrying value	$11,850,000

The example shows how the equity method reduces the opportunity for income manipulation. Willis Company's income statement is affected only by its pro rata share of Planet Burbank's net income. ***Planet Burbank's dividend declaration—and subsequent payment—has no effect on Willis's income.*** Thus, while Willis could conceivably use its influence to increase Planet Burbank's dividends, doing so *would leave its income unchanged* **under the equity method.**

When Cost and Book Value Differ

In contrast to our Planet Burbank example, investors rarely buy shares at a price exactly equal to the book value of those shares. When the investor's cost differs from book value, a new issue arises.

To illustrate, let's return to Willis Company's purchase of Planet Burbank stock. Recall that Planet Burbank's book value is $30 million. Let's say that Willis paid $24 million for its 30% stake instead of $9 million. Why would Willis pay $24 million when the book value of the shares purchased is only $9 million (30% of $30 million)?

Before we answer that question, let's note that GAAP assumes transactions entered into between unrelated parties are at a fair price. That is, we assume Willis (and the seller) are both well informed about Planet Burbank's financial condition and prospects and the fact that they negotiated a price of $24 million is evidence per se that $24 million is a fair price for the shares. So, again, why would an informed buyer pay $15 million more than book value for this investment?

There are two reasons. First, Planet Burbank's books are prepared under GAAP, and reflect most balance sheet items at historical cost rather than at current value. As shown in Panel (a) of Exhibit 16.2, the fair value of Planet Burbank's *net* assets is $70 million, or $40 million greater than the $30 million book value (see the highlighted area). Sellers of Planet Burbank stock presumably know what the company's net assets are worth. On the basis of that knowledge, the asking price for the shares acquired by Willis Company will be greater than book value by $40 million × 30% = $12 million.

Willis paid $24 million, or $15 million more than book value. The difference between fair value and book value of inventories and fixed assets (see highlighted area) explains only $12 million of the disparity, leaving $3 million unexplained. The remaining disparity brings us

EXHIBIT 16.2   Willis Company: Equity Investment with Goodwill

Panel (a)

($ in millions)	Book Value	Fair Value	Difference	Investor's Share (30%)
Cash and receivables	$10	$10	$ 0	$ 0
Inventories (FIFO cost flow)	15	25	10	3
Depreciable assets (net of depreciation)*	25	55	30	9
Liabilities	(20)	(20)	0	0
Net assets	$30	$70	$40	$12

* Average remaining useful life of 10 years.

Panel (b)

($ in millions)

Analysis of Willis's investment cost over book value	
Cost of 30% investment	$24
30% of book value of Planet Burbank's net assets (30% × $30)	9
Excess of cost over book value of Willis's shares	$15
Amount of excess attributable to	
Inventories—30% × ($25 − $15)	$ 3
Depreciable assets—30% × ($55 − $25)	9
Remainder attributable to implicit goodwill	3
	$15

We often refer to the investee's net assets as separately identifiable to contrast them with goodwill. However, separately identifiable net assets could also include assets that are not actually recognized in the balance sheet. The most common such asset would be a patent or other intellectual property that was developed internally and, as a result of the accounting rules for research and development, have no cost reported in the balance sheet.

to the second reason why an informed buyer would knowingly pay a premium to acquire an investment in another company. **Goodwill** exists because thriving, successful companies are generally worth more than the sum of their individual net assets. Planet Burbank has developed a reputation for product quality, prompt service, and fair treatment of both employees and customers. Consequently, employees like to work for the company, and customers actively seek its products. The result is that Planet Burbank is exceptionally profitable—it earns a very large return on its investment base. The capitalized value of this earning potential is what gives rise to the remaining $3 million difference. This "extraordinary" earnings potential is called *goodwill*.

As Panel (b) of Exhibit 16.2 shows, we have now decomposed the amount Willis paid for its investment into three components: $9 million for its pro rata share of the book value of Planet Burbank's net assets, leaving a $15 million excess of cost over book value acquired; $12 million for its pro rata share of the excess value of Planet Burbank's separately identifiable assets of liabilities over their respective book values; and $3 million for goodwill.

When the cost of the shares acquired exceeds the underlying book value at the acquisition date, as it does in this case, the investor is required to amortize any excess that is attributable to separately identifiable assets and liabilities not having an indefinite life. For all practical purposes, this means all assets and liabilities other than goodwill and land. Amortization is recorded as a reduction (debit) to Investment income and a reduction (credit) to the Investment account. The rationale for amortizing the excess of the investor's cost over book value is that equity method accounting seeks to replicate the earnings the investor would report if it had purchased each of the investee's assets and liabilities individually. In the Willis example, Willis would have paid $9 million more than its share of book value for the depreciable assets, so its depreciation over the life of those assets would have been $9 million greater than the depreciation it "picks up" by incorporating its pro rata share of Planet Burbank's earnings.

Using the equity method, the entries based on the preceding set of facts, including that Planet Burbank earned $10 million and declared a $500,000 dividend in 2014, are:

January 1, 2014: Initial Investment in Planet Burbank

DR	Investment in Planet Burbank.........................	$24,000,000	
	CR Cash		$24,000,000

(To record investment at cost.)

December 15, 2014: Investor's Share of Dividends Declared

DR	Dividend receivable from Planet Burbank	$150,000	
	CR Investment in Planet Burbank....................		$150,000

(To reduce the investment account for dividends declared—30% of $500,000)

December 31, 2014: Investor's Share of Earnings

DR	Investment in Planet Burbank.........................	$3,000,000	
	CR Income from affiliate		$3,000,000

(To recognize 30% of Planet Burbank's reported net income of $10 million)

December 31, 2014: Amortization of Excess Cost over Book Value Attributable to Inventory and Depreciable Assets

DR	Income from affiliate................................	$3,900,000	
	CR Investment in Planet Burbank....................		$3,900,000

(To amortize excess cost per calculation below.)

	Excess Investment Cost	2014 Amortization
Amortization is computed as		
Attributed to inventory (all sold during the year)	$3,000,000	$3,000,000
Attributed to depreciable assets (over 10 years)	9,000,000	900,000
Attributed to goodwill (not amortized)	3,000,000	—
	$15,000,000	$3,900,000

The excess investment cost over book value attributable to inventory is assigned to inventory items on hand on January 1, 2014, when Willis purchased Planet Burbank's stock. This inventory is presumed to have been sold during 2014 under the FIFO cost flow assumption (see Chapter 9). The amount attributed to depreciable assets is amortized over the average remaining 10-year life of those assets. The amount attributed to goodwill is not amortized.

Under the equity method, Willis recognized an investment loss of $900,000 ($3,000,000 − $3,900,000) in 2014. The December 31, 2014, balance in the Investment in Planet Burbank account is $22,950,000 ($24,000,000 + $3,000,000 − $150,000 − $3,900,000).

Fair Value Option for Equity Method Investments

Firms may elect the fair value option for investments that would otherwise be accounted for under the equity method.[4] The election is irrevocable. Firms are allowed to elect the fair value option on **election dates,** which, for equity investments, include dates when one of the following events occurs: (1) the firm first acquires an investment that is eligible for equity method treatment; (2) the investment becomes subject to the equity method of accounting (e.g., investment goes from below 20% of the outstanding voting common stock to more than 20%); or (3) an investor ceases to consolidate a subsidiary (e.g., because the investor no longer holds a controlling interest) but continues to hold sufficient common stock to qualify for equity method treatment.

---

[4] FASB ASC Subtopic 825-10: Financial Instruments—Overall, and all Fair Value Option Subsections thereof.

Under the fair value option, unrealized gains and losses arising from changes in the investment's fair value are reported in the investor's income statement. The investor firm does not report its proportionate share of the investee profits and losses in earnings, and dividends received flow directly to earnings. Dividend distributions typically reduce the fair value of the investee's stock. So, increases in investor earnings from investee dividend distributions are likely to be offset by earnings decreases due to investment fair value declines.

Assets and liabilities measured at fair value must be reported in the balance sheet separately from other investments. This can be accomplished by separate line-item disclosure or by presenting the investment amounts in aggregate with parenthetical disclosure of the fair value amounts included in that line item.

To illustrate the fair value option, recall Willis Company's acquisition of 30% of Planet Burbank's common stock on January 1, 2014 (see Exhibit 16.2). Suppose Willis elects the fair value option for this investment at the acquisition date. As of December 31, 2014, the fair value of Willis's investment in Planet Burbank stock has increased to $30 million. In its 2014 income statement, Willis would report an unrealized gain from equity investment of $6 million ($30 million − $24 million) and as investment income its share of Planet Burbank's declared dividend ($150,000).[5] Willis's income statement would show no equity in Planet Burbank earnings, and no reduction in earnings for amortization of excess investment cost over Planet Burbank book values attributable to inventory or depreciable assets. Willis Company's December 31, 2014, balance sheet would show the Investment in Burbank stock at the $30 million fair value amount.

Under GAAP, a minority active equity investment, which generally involves an investment of between 20% and 50% of the investee, is accounted for under the equity method. The investor reports as income its pro rata share of the investee's net income, subject to any amortization of the excess cost of the purchase price over the investee's book value at the time the investment was acquired. The investment account increases when income is recognized under the equity method and decreases when dividends are received. Firms may elect the fair value option for minority active investments, in which case the investment is instead reported at fair value, with dividends received and fair value adjustments reported as income in the income statement.

CONTROLLING (MAJORITY) INTEREST: CONSOLIDATION

A majority-owned company may *not* be consolidated if effective control does not rest with the majority owner (parent). For example, if the majority-owned entity is in legal reorganization or in bankruptcy or operates under foreign exchange restrictions, controls, or faces other governmentally imposed uncertainties that cast significant doubt on the parent's ability to control the entity, consolidation is not deemed appropriate.*

* FASB ASC Paragraph 810-10-5-10: Consolidation—Overall—Scope and Scope Exceptions.

An entity that gains a **controlling financial interest** in another entity is referred to as the **acquirer** or **parent** company. Controlling financial interest is generally deemed to occur when one entity, directly or indirectly, owns more than 50 percent of the outstanding voting shares of another entity (**subsidiary**).[6] Under these circumstances, the subsidiary's financial statements are combined—line by line—with those of the parent using a process called **consolidation. Consolidated financial statements** are designed to cut across artificial corporate

---

[5] In order to ensure consistency, Willis should not record the income until the Planet Burbank stock is trading "ex dividend," meaning without the right to receive the dividend. At that point, Willis retains the right to receive the dividend, even if it sells its shares, and Planet Burbank's stock price should be lower by the amount of the dividend.

[6] FASB ASC Topic 810: Consolidation.

boundaries to portray the economic activities of the parent and the subsidiary as if they were one entity.

The procedures for recognizing and measuring the subsidiary's assets and liabilities and reporting **noncontrolling (minority) interest** in the subsidiary in consolidated financial statements have changed several times. Transactions accounted for under two previously permitted methods continue to be accounted for under those methods, so they cannot be ignored.

> When two companies form a **joint venture** and each company owns exactly 50% of the joint venture, neither of the "parent" companies consolidates the joint venture. Rather, each accounts for its investment under the equity method. Chapter 11 describes how this allows the joint venture entity to incur debt—usually guaranteed by the "parent" companies—but the debt does not appear on either parent's balance sheet because consolidation is not required. Intercorporate investment rules can be skillfully used to create off-balance-sheet assets and liabilities that impede accurate financial analysis.

The following sections describe the accounting required for current transactions, called the **acquisition method**, and the basics of how to prepare consolidated statements. We first examine a 100% acquisition and then an acquisition with a noncontrolling interest (i.e., where the parent acquires less than 100% of the subsidiary's voting stock). We then describe the previously permitted methods—the purchase method and the pooling of interests method—and highlight the key differences between the acquisition method and these methods.

> A noncontrolling interest is the equity interest in a subsidiary not attributable, directly or indirectly, to the parent. Prior to the issuance of pre-Codification *SFAS No. 141R* and *SFAS No. 160*, noncontrolling interests were referred to as *minority interests*.

Acquisition Method and Preparation of Consolidated Statements (100% Acquisition)

The acquisition method assigns the fair value of the consideration given to the acquired entity's identifiable net assets (assets minus liabilities) at the acquisition date. If the value of consideration given exceeds the fair value of the acquired entity's identifiable net assets, then goodwill is considered part of the acquisition cost. We use the following example, where the parent acquires 100% of the subsidiary's stock, to illustrate.

Assume that on December 31, 2013, immediately before acquiring Gaston Corporation on that date, the balance sheet of Alphonse Corporation (the acquirer or parent company) was as follows:

Assets

Current assets	$15,000,000
Fixed assets, net of accumulated depreciation	20,000,000
Total assets	$35,000,000

Liabilities and Stockholders' Equity

Current liabilities	$ 1,000,000
Common stock ($1 par)	28,000,000
Capital in excess of par	2,000,000
Retained earnings	4,000,000
Total liabilities and equity	$35,000,000

Alphonse paid $10 million cash to buy all of the outstanding shares of Gaston Corporation. After the transaction is recorded, Alphonse's current assets will be $10 million lower due to the payment of cash, and an investment account of $10 million will exist. See Exhibit 16.3 for both companies' balance sheets immediately after the acquisition.

Exhibit 16.3 illustrates Alphonse's consolidation of Gaston as of the acquisition date. We describe each step in the process. Note that the individual balance sheets of the two companies are *not* simply added together. As we will see, doing that would result in double counting.

Adjustments to the Consolidated Balance Sheet

Step 1: **Elimination of the Investment in Gaston Account against Gaston's Equity**
Alphonse paid $10 million for Gaston, a company whose *net* assets totaled only $8 million (assets of $8.5 million less liabilities of $0.5 million). Why did Alphonse pay more than the book value of the acquiree's net assets? An informed buyer would do so for two reasons: (1) the fair value of Gaston's individual assets was more than their combined book value (we assume this excess was $1.5 million here and was attributable to the fixed assets) and (2) goodwill, which is the remaining $0.5 million.

The factors comprising the $10 million acquisition value of Gaston are:

Recorded book value of Gaston's *net* assets	$ 8,000,000
Unrecorded difference between fair value and book value	
of Gaston's fixed assets ($8,000,000 − $6,500,000)	1,500,000
Unrecorded value of Gaston's goodwill	500,000
Acquisition value	$10,000,000

To see why we do not add the two balance sheets together to get the consolidated balance sheet, note that the $10 million Alphonse paid is already on its balance sheet (under Investment in Gaston in Exhibit 16.3). But, as we have just seen, $8 million of the acquisition cost represents the book value of Gaston's net assets, which also appears in Gaston's balance sheet. Simply adding the two balance sheets together would double count Gaston's net assets.

Now consider Alphonse's stockholders' equity accounts, comprised of $28 million (Common stock), $2 million (Capital in excess of par), and $4 million (Retained earnings). These stockholders' equity accounts represent the ownership interest in Alphonse's net assets, which include Alphonse's investment in Gaston. Gaston's stockholders' equity accounts, comprised of $6 million (Common stock) and $2 million (Retained earnings),

EXHIBIT 16.3	**Alphonse Company and Gaston Company:** **Acquisition Method—100% Ownership**

Worksheet for Preparing Consolidated Balance Sheet—Date of Acquisition

	Alphonse	Gaston	Adjustments and Eliminations Dr.	Adjustments and Eliminations Cr.	Consolidated Balance Sheet
Assets					
Current assets	$ 5,000,000	$2,000,000			$ 7,000,000
Fixed assets (net)	20,000,000	6,500,000	$ 1,500,000 (B)		28,000,000
Investment in Gaston	10,000,000	—		$ 2,000,000 (B) 8,000,000 (A)	—
Goodwill			500,000 (B)		500,000
	$35,000,000	$8,500,000			$35,500,000
Liabilities					
Current liabilities	$ 1,000,000	$ 500,000			$ 1,500,000
Stockholders' Equity					
Common stock	28,000,000	6,000,000	6,000,000 (A)		28,000,000
Capital in excess of par	2,000,000	—			2,000,000
Retained earnings	4,000,000	2,000,000	2,000,000 (A)		4,000,000
	$35,000,000	$8,500,000	$10,000,000	$10,000,000	$35,500,000

also represent ownership of Gaston's net assets. If the stockholders' equity accounts of the two companies were simply added together, ownership of Gaston would be counted twice—once as part of Alphonse's stockholders' equity and again as Gaston's stockholders' equity.

To avoid the double counting of both Gaston's net assets and the ownership interests in Gaston, Gaston's stockholders' equity accounts are eliminated against Alphonse's Investment in Gaston account. This is done opposite notation (A) in the Adjustments and Eliminations column in the consolidating worksheet in Exhibit 16.3. After this elimination, consolidated owners' equity is composed of only Alphonse's stockholders' equity accounts because these alone represent the consolidated entity's ownership.

Step 2: **Reclassification of the Remainder of the Investment in Gaston Account** The remaining balance in the Investment in Gaston account represents the amount of the acquisition value that is *not* reflected in Gaston's book values. As the acquisition value allocation shows, the $2 million remaining balance represents unrecorded fixed asset appreciation of $1.5 million and goodwill of $0.5 million. These amounts must stay on the consolidated balance sheet because Alphonse paid for them. However, they must be assigned to the items they actually represent: (1) an increase to fixed assets and (2) the acquisition of goodwill. These amounts are reclassified to the appropriate accounts in the Adjustments and Eliminations column of Exhibit 16.3 (next to notations B). After these adjustments are made, the Investment in Gaston account has been eliminated and thus does not appear in the consolidated column. Also, consolidated fixed assets have been increased by $1.5 million, and goodwill of $0.5 million is separately reported.

The process described here is solely for the purpose of preparing consolidated statements. The adjustments are not recorded on the books of the acquirer (parent company). However, they can also be expressed in journal entry form. For example, the entry to avoid double counting the book value of Gaston's net assets and its owners' equity is:

DR	Common stock	$6,000,000	
DR	Retained earnings	2,000,000	
	CR Investment in Gaston		$8,000,000

To avoid double counting Gaston's net assets and its owners' equity (adjustment notation [A] in Exhibit 16.3).

Similarly, reclassification of the remaining $2 million in the Investment in Gaston account to reflect the fair value of Gaston's fixed assets and acquired goodwill can also be expressed in journal entry form:

DR	Fixed assets	$1,500,000	
DR	Goodwill	500,000	
	CR Investment in Gaston		$2,000,000

To eliminate the remaining investment account balance and recognize the write-up of Gaston's Fixed assets (net), to fair value, and to recognize acquired goodwill (adjustment notation [B] in Exhibit 16.3).

After these adjustments, the last column of Exhibit 16.3 reflects the amounts reported in the consolidated balance sheet. Note that in this case, a 100% acquisition under the acquisition method, a new basis of accounting is established for the subsidiary's net assets (including goodwill)—they are reported at full fair value at the acquisition date.

Intra-entity Loans   Suppose that several months prior to the Gaston acquisition, Alphonse had borrowed $300,000 from Gaston that had not been repaid by the acquisition date of December 31, 2013. Under these circumstances, another adjustment is needed to consolidate the financial statements. ***This adjustment is necessary because Alphonse and Gaston are now part of the same economic unit.*** The ***Alphonse loan receivable*** on Gaston's books and the ***Gaston loan payable*** on Alphonse's books are not due from or due to outsiders. To include the intra-entity receivable and payable in the consolidated balance sheet would overstate both assets and liabilities by $300,000. That's why the following additional adjustment would be made in preparing the consolidated statements:

DR Loan payable—Gaston (on Alphonse's books)	$300,000	
CR Loan receivable—Alphonse (on Gaston's books)		$300,000
To eliminate the intra-entity loan from Gaston to Alphonse.		

There will also be eliminations and adjustments in the income statement, which are discussed later.

Acquisition Method with Noncontrolling Interests (Less Than 100% Acquisition)

The Consolidation Topic (ASC 810) embraces the economic unit concept for consolidation—a concept founded on the principle that the subsidiary's individual accounts should not be divided and measured differently along ownership lines. According to this view, a controlled company must be *consolidated as a whole* regardless of the parent's level of ownership. Authoritative accounting literature says that the parent must measure and recognize the subsidiary as a whole at **business fair value.** This means that under the acquisition method, the parent company includes in its consolidated financial statements 100% of the subsidiary's individual assets acquired and liabilities assumed at their *full fair values* determined as of the acquisition date, even when the parent owns less than 100% of the controlled subsidiary.

How is business fair value determined in the presence of a partial (less than 100%) acquisition? GAAP says business fair value is the sum of (1) the controlling interest fair value and (2) the noncontrolling interest fair value. Measurement of the controlling interest fair value is relatively straightforward—for the vast majority of cases, the value of the consideration transferred provides the best evidence of the controlling interest fair value. Measurement of noncontrolling interest fair value is more difficult because the noncontrolling shareholders are not parties to the transaction. One approach is to use the consideration paid by the parent for the controlling interest to impute a fair value for the acquired firm as a whole and then use the noncontrolling percentage of this imputed total acquired firm fair value to measure the noncontrolling interest fair value. For example, if the fair value of a 75% controlling interest is $240 million, then the imputed total business fair value would be $320 million ($240 million ÷ 0.75). The estimated noncontrolling interest fair value would be $80 million ($320 million × 25%).

> This approach for estimating the noncontrolling interest's fair value would not be appropriate if the parent pays a premium to secure sufficient shares to gain financial control. This can sometimes occur when the shares are being acquired from a single party that owns a large block of the acquiree's shares (e.g., 60%). In this case, the noncontrolling interest fair value is independently computed without regard to the consideration paid by the parent (e.g., by using the traded price of the shares not held by the major blockholder).

To illustrate the acquisition method with less than 100% ownership, refer to the data for the Alphonse and Gaston business combination underlying Exhibit 16.3. Assume instead, though, that Alphonse pays $8 million to acquire 80% of Gaston's outstanding shares. Assuming no premium was paid to gain control, Gaston's imputed total business fair value is $10 million

($8 million ÷ 0.80). Therefore, the fair value of the noncontrolling interest is $2 million (20% × $10 million). The factors comprising Gaston's value are:

($ in millions)	Controlling Interest	Noncontrolling Interest	Total
Recorded book value of net assets	$6.4	$1.6	$ 8.0
Unrecorded fixed assets	1.2	0.3	1.5
Goodwill	0.4	0.1	0.5
Total	$8.0	$2.0	$10.0

The worksheet to prepare the consolidated balance sheet of Alphonse and its 80%-owned subsidiary, Gaston, under the acquisition method is shown in Exhibit 16.4.

Entry (A) eliminates Gaston's equity accounts, which total $8 million. The portion pertaining to the 80% Alphonse owns is eliminated against the investment account. The other 20% sets up a Noncontrolling interest in Gaston. Entry (B) reclassifies the remainder of the investment account by increasing Alphonse's share (80%) of Gaston's net assets to fair value and also recognizing the goodwill attributable to Alphonse's controlling interest. Entry (C) recognizes the noncontrolling interest in the total business fair value of Gaston. In effect, it repeats entry (B) but for the *unacquired* portion of Gaston's net assets by adjusting to the fair value at the acquisition date and including goodwill.

After these adjustments, the net assets of the subsidiary (Gaston) are reported at acquisition date full fair value in the consolidated balance sheet. All of the acquired entity's goodwill is recognized and the noncontrolling interest in the net assets of the subsidiary is reported at fair value.

Although the noncontrolling interest is not an equity interest in Alphonse, it is an equity interest nonetheless in a portion of the consolidated net assets. As a result, GAAP requires

EXHIBIT 16.4	Alphonse and Gaston: Acquisition Method—80% Ownership

Worksheet for Preparing Consolidated Balance Sheet—Date of Acquisition

	Alphonse	Gaston	Adjustments and Eliminations Dr.	Adjustments and Eliminations Cr.	Consolidated Balance Sheet
Assets					
Current assets	$ 7,000,000	$2,000,000			$ 9,000,000
Fixed assets (net)	20,000,000	6,500,000	$ 1,200,000 (B) 300,000 (C)		28,000,000
Investment in Gaston	8,000,000	—		$ 1,600,000 (B) 6,400,000 (A)	—
Goodwill			400,000 (B) 100,000 (C)		500,000
Total assets	$35,000,000	$8,500,000			$37,500,000
Liabilities					
Current liabilities	$ 1,000,000	$ 500,000			$ 1,500,000
Stockholders' equity					
Common stock	28,000,000	6,000,000	6,000,000 (A)		28,000,000
Capital in excess of par	2,000,000	—			2,000,000
Retained earnings	4,000,000	2,000,000	2,000,000 (A)		4,000,000
Noncontrolling interest in Gaston				$ 1,600,000 (A) 400,000 (C)	2,000,000
Total stockholders' equity	34,000,000	8,000,000			36,000,000
Total liabilities and stockholders' equity	$35,000,000	$8,500,000	$10,000,000	$10,000,000	$37,500,000

that the noncontrolling interest be shown in the stockholders' equity section of the consolidated balance sheet.

Income Statement Consolidation

Exhibit 16.5 shows the worksheet for preparing the consolidated income statement for Alphonse and its subsidiary (Gaston) for the first year after acquisition in the 80% acquisition case. We additionally assume Alphonse sold goods to Gaston for $25,000, which Gaston resold to outside parties later in the year. The intra-entity sale between Alphonse and Gaston must be eliminated. To see why, suppose that Alphonse sold goods to Gaston on March 15, 2014, after the December 31, 2013, acquisition, and then Gaston resold all of these goods to outside customers before the end of the year. The facts follow:

INTRA-ENTITY SALE

	Alphonse's Sale to Gaston	Gaston's Resale to "Outsiders"	Total
Selling price	$25,000	$34,000	$59,000
Cost of goods sold	20,000	25,000	45,000
Gross profit	$ 5,000	$ 9,000	$14,000

Merely adding together the income statements of Alphonse and Gaston to form the consolidated income statement would result in double counting of sales and cost of goods sold. This would happen because neither Alphonse's $25,000 sale to Gaston nor the $25,000 of cost of goods sold on Gaston's income statement represents a transaction with outsiders. Therefore, the intra-entity sales transaction must be eliminated in preparing the consolidated income statement, as shown in Exhibit 16.5.

After this elimination, the consolidated income statement reflects only revenues realized from outsiders and costs paid to outsiders. The double counting of the intra-entity sales and cost of goods sold has been eliminated. Advanced accounting textbooks discuss the more complex situation where the inventory has not been resold to a third party by the end of the period.

We also assume the expected remaining life of Gaston's fixed assets at the acquisition date was 20 years. As a result, we amortize the portion of the excess acquisition value attributed to fixed assets ($1,500,000) over 20 years, resulting in $75,000 of amortization per year. Because the cost basis of the fixed assets in the consolidated balance sheet exceeds the cost basis of the fixed assets in Gaston's balance sheet, depreciation from a consolidated perspective would be understated without this adjustment.

The other adjustment that must be made made is to allocate the noncontrolling interest's share of Gaston's net income appropriately. Note that net income of $3,032,000 includes net income attributable to both the noncontrolling interest and Alphonse's shareholders. The portion of Gaston's earnings assigned to the 20% noncontrolling interests (($1,612,000 − $75,000) × 20% = $307,400, shaded) is then subtracted to arrive at net income attributable to the Alphonse shareholders.

Consolidated financial statements portray the parent company and its majority-owned subsidiaries as a single economic unit. But the individual balance sheets (and income statements) of each subsidiary and the parent are not simply added together. Instead, adjustments are made on the consolidated worksheet to avoid double counting internal business transactions as well as various balance sheet items. When the parent company acquires less than a 100% interest in a subsidiary, a noncontrolling (minority) interest in the subsidiary's net assets and income is created. Because the consolidated statements include the subsidiary's total assets, liabilities and net income, the noncontrolling shareholders' interest in these amounts must be reflected in the consolidated statements.

EXHIBIT 16.5	Alphonse and Gaston: Acquisition Method—80% Ownership

Worksheet for Preparing Consolidated Income Statement

First Year after Acquisition

	After the Acquisition		Adjustments and Eliminations		Noncontrolling Interest	Consolidated Income Statement
	Alphonse	Gaston	Dr.	Cr.		
Sales revenue	$ 25,000,000	$ 15,000,000	$ 25,000			$ 39,975,000
Cost of goods sold	(20,000,000)	(10,900,000)		$25,000		(30,875,000)
Gross profit	5,000,000	4,100,000				9,100,000
Selling, general, and administrative expenses	(2,500,000)	(1,500,000)	75,000			(3,925,000)
Interest expense	(200,000)	(120,000)				(320,000)
Tax expense	(805,000)	(868,000)				(1,673,000)
Consolidated net income	1,495,000	1,612,000				3,032,000
Net income attributable to noncontrolling interest	—	—			$307,400	(307,400)
Net income attributable to Alphonse shareholders	$ 1,495,000	$ 1,612,000	$100,000	$25,000	$307,400	$ 2,724,600

Accounting for Goodwill

As illustrated in the Alphonse and Gaston example, the acquisition method typically results in recognition of goodwill in the consolidated balance sheet. This goodwill is not amortized. Instead, goodwill is written down only when it is deemed to be impaired.[7] To test for impairment, firms must first allocate goodwill arising from an acquisition to one or more reporting units (e.g., segments) at the acquisition date. Once allocated, the two-step impairment test outlined in Figure 16.2 is applied at the reporting unit level. A two-step approach is necessary because goodwill is not separately identifiable. So, we must first determine if the reporting unit itself is impaired. If it is, then the second step establishes the amount of the goodwill impairment charge, if any.

In the first step, the reporting unit is considered impaired if the book value of its net assets (including allocated goodwill) exceeds its fair value. If the reporting unit is impaired, then the goodwill assigned to the reporting unit is compared to its **implied goodwill**, which is the amount of goodwill that would be recognized in a current transaction if the reporting unit were acquired at its fair value. The impairment charge is the difference between the goodwill reflected in the consolidated balance sheet and the implied goodwill. The following numerical example illustrates how to determine goodwill impairment under GAAP:

Examples of circumstances that would trigger impairment testing include:

- A significant adverse change in legal factors or in the business climate.
- A regulator's adverse action or assessment.
- Unanticipated competition.
- A loss of key personnel.
- A likelihood that a reporting unit or a significant portion of a reporting unit will be sold or disposed of.
- A significant asset group is being tested for recoverability.
- Recognition of a goodwill impairment loss in the financial statements of a subsidiary that is a component of a reporting unit.

FASB ASC Paragraph 350-20-35-30: Intangibles—Goodwill and other—Goodwill—Subsequent Measurement.

Fair value of a reporting unit refers to the price that would be received to sell the unit as a whole in an orderly transaction between market participants at the measurement date.* If the reporting unit is publicly traded, the stock price provides the best evidence of fair value. If stock prices are not available, fair values are determined using one or more other methods including discounted cash flow analysis or a multiple of earnings or some other performance measure such as revenues or earnings before interest, taxes, depreciation, and amortization.

* FASB ASC Paragraph 350-20-35-22: Intangibles—Goodwill and Other—Goodwill—Subsequent Measurement—Determining the Fair Value of a Reporting Unit.

---

[7] FASB ASC Section 350-20-35: Intangibles—Goodwill and Other—Goodwill—Subsequent Measurement.

Figure 16.2

GOODWILL IMPAIRMENT
TEST

Source: FASB ASC Topic 350:
Intangibles—Goodwill and other

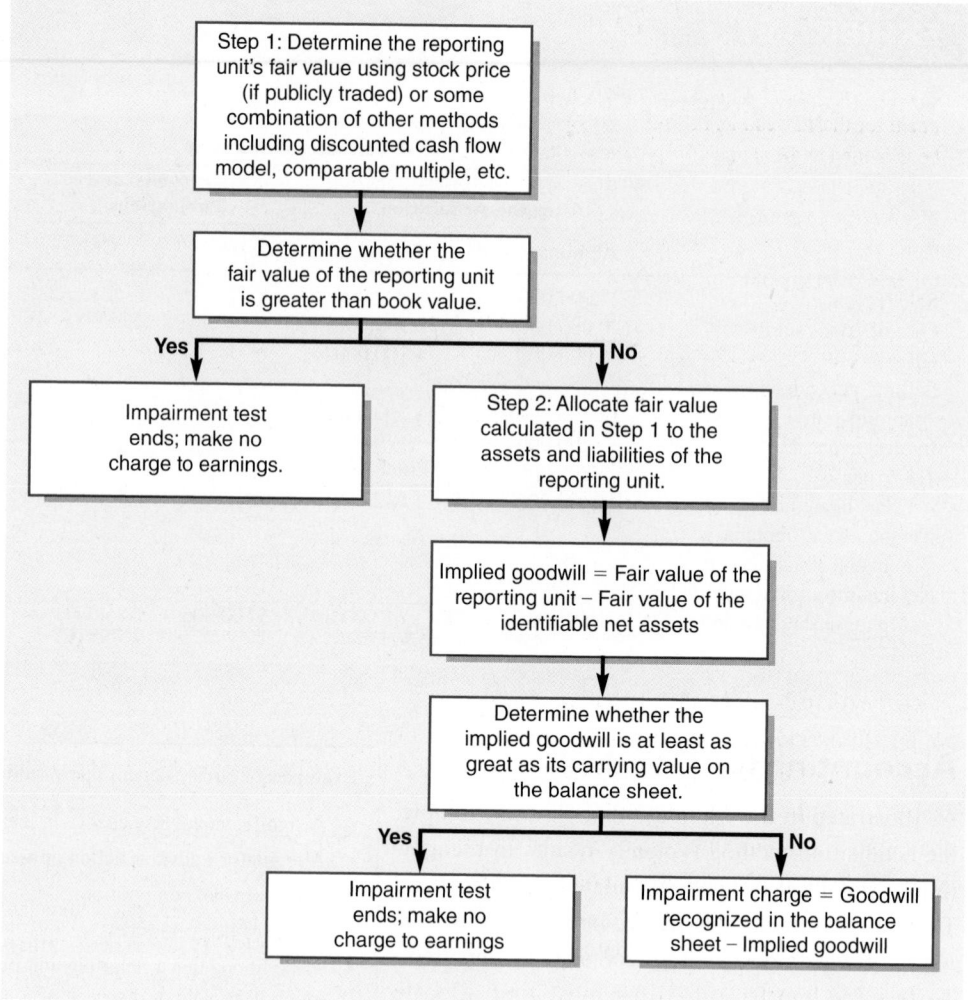

Assume that Aggressive Company acquires all of Slow Growth Company's outstanding voting stock early in 2014 for $100 million. On that date, Slow Growth's identifiable tangible and intangible net assets had a fair value of $80 million resulting in goodwill of $20 million. Aggressive assigned $15 million of the goodwill to reporting unit A and $5 million to reporting unit B. On December 31, 2014, Aggressive performs an impairment test and determines the following:

($ in millions)	Unit A	Unit B
(a) Fair value of reporting unit (including goodwill)	$60	$45
(b) Book value of reporting unit	75	35
(c) Is the reporting unit impaired?	Yes	No
(d) Sum of fair values of identifiable net assets of unit A, exclusive of goodwill	50	—
(e) Implied fair value of goodwill (a)–(d)	10	—
(f) Book value of goodwill	15	—
(g) Impairment charge (f)–(e)	$ 5	—

The accounting rules for determining goodwill impairment, together with the rather dramatic downturns in the stock market in 2002–2003 and 2008–2009, resulted in a significant number of firms reporting goodwill impairments totaling hundreds of billions of dollars.

The following excerpt from a special equity research report discusses the possible valuation implications of such write-downs:

> The facts and circumstances surrounding each goodwill impairment charge will need to be evaluated for their investment significance. The FASB rules require information about goodwill to be provided at the segment level, increasing the likelihood that the market will be cognizant of potential changes in fundamentals diminishing the value of goodwill. If the market is aware of this deterioration from other information, the impairment charge is unlikely to affect the company's stock price. However, if there is an impairment in a reporting unit that previously had been thought to have good fundamentals, it will be news to the market and could have a negative impact on stock price.[8]

Under current GAAP, goodwill is subject to a consideration of possible impairment. Financial statement users need to assess whether a goodwill impairment charge is a sign of a bad acquisition, a miscalculation of the value of the target (that is, the acquirer overpaid), or the result of an unexpected deterioration in the fundamentals of the business acquired.

PREVIOUS APPROACHES TO CONSOLIDATED STATEMENTS

As we mentioned earlier, the procedures for recognizing and measuring a subsidiary's assets and liabilities and reporting a noncontrolling (minority) interest in a subsidiary in consolidated financial statements have changed several times in the recent past. Although only the acquisition method is permitted for merger and acquisition (M&A) transactions entered into today, transactions originally accounted for under either of the other two methods—the purchase method and the pooling of interests method—continue to be accounted for under those methods. That is, the method applied depends on when the parent company acquired the subsidiary, not the date of the financial statements being presented. So, the effects of accounting methods that may no longer be applied to current transactions are still evident in current financial statements, making it important for analysts to understand the financial statement implications of all the approaches to M&A accounting, including those methods that are no longer permitted for current transactions.

Panel (a) of Figure 16.3 summarizes the three methods that have been used over the years to account for acquisitions. Until July 1, 2001, two methods were permitted. The pooling of interests method was permitted for transactions that met certain criteria, including that more than 90% of the voting common stock was acquired and that the transaction was consummated through an exchange of stock. The guiding principle behind the pooling of interests method was that the transaction was treated as if the two companies joined together to become a new entity, rather than that one of the companies acquired the other. The financial statements were restated retroactively as if the two companies had always been one. With this view of the transaction, there is no "purchase price." And, without a purchase price, there is no resetting of asset values to fair value or any recognition of goodwill. This feature of pooling of interests was viewed positively by many companies, especially because at the time that poolings were permitted, goodwill was subject to amortization. An acquiring company that had to recognize goodwill on an acquisition looked forward to up to 40 years of charges against earnings for goodwill amortization. As a result, many companies would structure transactions in a way to ensure pooling of interests could be applied. A 1995 study argued that in order to satisfy the

---

[8] "Goodbye, Goodwill," *Equity Research Special Report* (New York: Bear Stearns & Company, Inc., 2001).

Figure 16.3

M&A ACCOUNTING
RULES OVER TIME

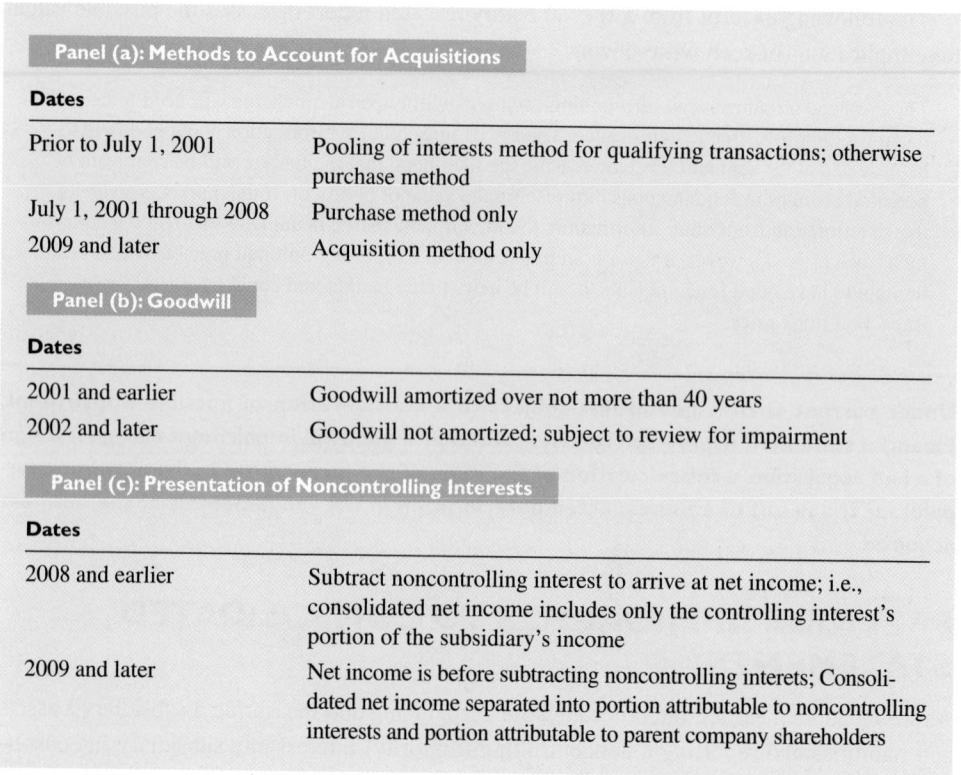

Panel (a): Methods to Account for Acquisitions

Dates	
Prior to July 1, 2001	Pooling of interests method for qualifying transactions; otherwise purchase method
July 1, 2001 through 2008	Purchase method only
2009 and later	Acquisition method only

Panel (b): Goodwill

Dates	
2001 and earlier	Goodwill amortized over not more than 40 years
2002 and later	Goodwill not amortized; subject to review for impairment

Panel (c): Presentation of Noncontrolling Interests

Dates	
2008 and earlier	Subtract noncontrolling interest to arrive at net income; i.e., consolidated net income includes only the controlling interest's portion of the subsidiary's income
2009 and later	Net income is before subtracting noncontrolling interets; Consolidated net income separated into portion attributable to noncontrolling interests and portion attributable to parent company shareholders

pooling of interests criteria for its 1991 acquisition of NCR, AT&T paid somewhere between $50 million and $500 million extra for the acquisition.[9]

Amid concerns that many transactions were being structured to qualify as poolings of interests even though they were clearly acquisitions of one company by another, not the merging of equals to form a new entity, the FASB banned poolings, effective July 1, 2001. However, any transactions completed prior to that date could be accounted for as poolings and did not have to be restated under purchase accounting, the only other acceptable method at the time. Many companies today have subsidiaries that were acquired in transactions accounted for as poolings of interests and, as a result, do not report goodwill related to those subsidiaries.[10]

Beginning July 1, 2001, only the purchase method was permitted. This method treated the transaction as an acquisition of one company by another, regardless of whether the consideration paid was in cash or stock. If the consideration was in stock, the purchase price was deemed to be the fair value of the stock given up in the transaction. Any excess paid above book value for the acquired company was attributed to specific assets and liabilities as well as to goodwill, in much the same way we did the allocation of excess cost for equity method transactions. Unlike under the acquisition method, fair value for the entire entity was not imputed from the purchase price when less than 100% was acquired. Rather, the step-up in values and recognition of goodwill only occurred on the portion of the assets acquired.

Importantly, through 2001 for calendar-year firms, goodwill was amortized over not more than 40 years. As shown in Panel (b) of Figure 16.3, goodwill is no longer amortized and has not been since 2002.[11] This change in the rules—the elimination of goodwill

---

[9] See T. Lys and L. Vincent, "An Analysis of Value Destruction in AT&T's Acquisition of NCR," *Journal of Financial Economics,* October–November 1995.

[10] The last major transaction to qualify for pooling treatment was Pepsico's acquisition of the Quaker Oats Company.

[11] Goodwill amortization was also eliminated for 2001 for acquisitions taking place after June 30 of that year.

amortization—made the elimination of the pooling of interests method more palatable to many companies. Although under the purchase method—the only acceptable M&A method remaining when poolings were eliminated—companies recognized goodwill on most transactions, the goodwill was not subject to amortization. Rather, it is subject to an annual review for impairment.

Effective January 1, 2009, for calendar-year firms, the purchase method was replaced with the acquisition method. The key difference between these two methods is that under the purchase method, assets were "stepped up" to their fair values and goodwill was recognized only on the portion of the company acquired. Under the acquisition method, the step-up in values and the recognition of goodwill is on the entire acquired company, even if less than 100% is acquired. For example, suppose Dale Corporation acquired 90% of Mara Inc. for $90 million. Mara's book value of equity at the acquisition date was $60 million. Under the purchase method, Mara's assets would be stepped up (including goodwill recognition) by $36 million, the excess cost Dale paid for its 90% interest ($90 million − $60 million × 90%). Under the acquisition method, Mara's assets would be stepped up (again including goodwill recognition) by $40 million, the inferred value of the entire entity ($90 million/0.90 = $100 million) less the entity's book value of $60 million.

The final change in financial reporting for business combinations and consolidations, shown in Panel (c) of Figure 16.3, relates to the presentation of noncontrolling interests in the income statement. Prior to 2009, the portion of a less-than-wholly-owned subsidiary's income that was attributable to the minority (noncontrolling) shareholders would be reported as an expense in the parent company's income statement, effectively reversing that portion of the subsidiary's net income that had been included in the consolidated numbers. The result was that consolidated net income would reflect only the parent company's share of the consolidated subsidiary's earnings. In the Dale and Mara example, Dale would include 100% of Mara's revenues and expenses in its income statement, but then remove the 10% it did not own with a line called "minority interest expense," resulting in Dale reporting consolidated net income that included only 90% of Mara's net income. Beginning in 2009 for calendar-year firms, consolidated net income is defined to include all earnings of a parent and its consolidated subsidiaries, even if the consolidated subsidiaries are not wholly owned. That net income is then allocated between the parent company shareholders and the noncontrolling interests (i.e., the minority shareholders of the subsidiary's stock). When the noncontrolling interests are subtracted from consolidated net income, the resulting amount is called consolidated net income attributable to parent company shareholders. As a result, the "bottom line" in an income statement today often is not consolidated net income, but rather consolidated net income attributable to parent company shareholders.

The following sections describe how the purchase method and the pooling of interests method differ from the acquisition method.

The Purchase Method

Under the purchase method, assets and liabilities are stepped up and goodwill is recognized only on the *acquired portion* of the subsidiary's asset and liability accounts. As a result, the subsidiary's assets and liabilities are not reported at their full fair values in the consolidated balance sheet. Rather, the subsidiary's net assets are valued at the parent's proportional interest in the net asset fair values plus the noncontrolling interest in the *book value* of the subsidiary's net assets at the acquisition date. Moreover, the noncontrolling interest equity is reported as the proportionate share of the subsidiary's net asset *book value*.

To illustrate how the purchase method works, we return to the example in the previous section where Alphonse acquires an 80% interest in Gaston by paying $8 million. The book value of Gaston's *total* net assets at the date of acquisition is $8 million ($8.5 million of assets minus $0.5 million of liabilities). The difference between the amount paid by Alphonse ($8 million) and its equity in the book value of Gaston's net assets (80% × $8 million = $6.4 million) is $1.6 million. If we again assume the excess of fair value over book value of all of Gaston's depreciable fixed assets is $1.5 million, then the $1.6 million difference is apportioned as follows:

Allocation of Excess Acquisition Cost:

Price paid by Alphonse for 80% interest in Gaston	$8,000,000
Book value of 80% of Gaston's net assets at acquisition (80% × $8,000,000)	6,400,000
Excess cost over book value of net assets acquired	$1,600,000
Excess attributed to Alphonse's share of the difference between fair value and book value of Gaston's fixed assets (80% × $1,500,000)	$1,200,000
Amount attributed to Gaston's unrecorded goodwill	400,000
Total excess cost assigned	$1,600,000

Immediately after this purchase combination, the worksheet to prepare the consolidated balance sheet of Alphonse and its 80%-owned interest in Gaston is as in Exhibit 16.6. The two adjustment and elimination entries reflected in the consolidated worksheet in Exhibit 16.6 are the same as elimination entries (A) and (B) shown for the acquisition method. But note that entry (C) is missing. That was the entry that recognized an additional $300,000 of fixed assets and $100,000 of goodwill to reflect the write-up to fair value of the noncontrolling shareholders' investment in Gaston, along with an additional $400,000 of noncontrolling interest.

EXHIBIT 16.6 | **Alphonse and Gaston: Purchase Method—80% Ownership**

Worksheet for Preparing Consolidated Balance Sheet—Date of Purchase

	Alphonse	Gaston	Adjustments and Eliminations Dr.	Adjustments and Eliminations Cr.	Consolidated Balance Sheet
Assets					
Current assets	$ 7,000,000	$ 2,000,000			$ 9,000,000
Fixed assets (net)	20,000,000	6,500,000	$1,200,000 (B)		27,700,000
Investment in Gaston	8,000,000	—		$1,600,000 (B) 6,400,000 (A)	—
Goodwill			400,000 (B)		400,000
	$ 35,000,000	$ 8,500,000			$37,100,000
Liabilities					
Current liabilities	$ 1,000,000	$ 500,000			$ 1,500,000
Noncontrolling (minority) Interest in Gaston				1,600,000 (A)	1,600,000
Stockholders' equity					
Common stock	28,000,000	6,000,000	6,000,000 (A)		28,000,000
Capital in excess of par	2,000,000	—			2,000,000
Retained earnings	4,000,000	2,000,000	2,000,000 (A)		4,000,000
	$35,000,000	$ 8,500,000	$9,600,000	$9,600,000	$37,100,000

The key differences between the consolidated balance sheet under the acquisition method and the purchase method are summarized in the table below.

	Acquisition Method	**Purchase Method**
Subsidiary net assets (assets – liabilities)	Valued at full fair value	Fair value of the controlling interest portion Subsidiary's book value for the noncontrolling interest portion
Goodwill	Valued at full fair value	Only recognized for the controlling interest portion
Noncontrolling equity interest	Noncontrolling interest portion of the subsidiary's total fair value of net assets	Noncontrolling interest portion of the subsidiary's book value of net assets

Figure 16.4 illustrates graphically how these alternative valuation approaches compare for Alphonse's acquisition of Gaston. Panel (a) (the one that looks like Colorado) illustrates the acquisition method. Note that *all* of the subsidiary's net assets are stepped up to the fair value implied by Alphonse's purchase of 80% of Gaston. The top four cells represent goodwill ($0.5 million) plus the step up of separately identifiable net assets ($1.5 million). The three cells at the right represent the noncontrolling interest. Note that the noncontrolling interest is valued at the value implied by the purchase price, even though the portion of the assets owned by the noncontrolling interest was not acquired. Panel (b) (the one that looks like Utah) represents the purchase method. The shape illustrates the mixed valuation approach. Gaston's net assets are valued partially at fair value and partially at the existing book value. Note that the

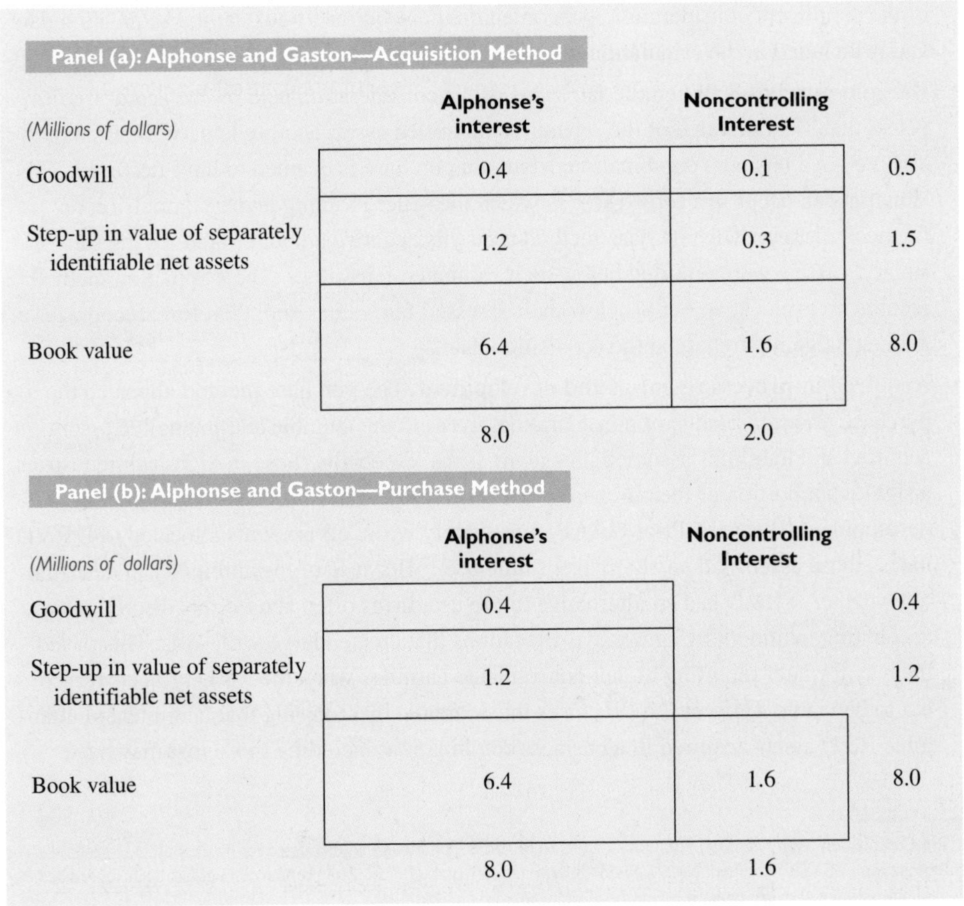

Figure 16.4

GRAPHICAL REPRESENTATION OF ACQUISITION AND PURCHASE METHODS

Panel (a): Alphonse and Gaston—Acquisition Method

(Millions of dollars)	Alphonse's interest	Noncontrolling Interest	
Goodwill	0.4	0.1	0.5
Step-up in value of separately identifiable net assets	1.2	0.3	1.5
Book value	6.4	1.6	8.0
	8.0	2.0	

Panel (b): Alphonse and Gaston—Purchase Method

(Millions of dollars)	Alphonse's interest	Noncontrolling Interest	
Goodwill	0.4		0.4
Step-up in value of separately identifiable net assets	1.2		1.2
Book value	6.4	1.6	8.0
	8.0	1.6	

noncontrolling interest is now only $1.6 million, which is 20% of the original book value of Gaston's net assets. Relative to the acquisition method, net assets are valued $0.4 million lower ($0.1 million related to goodwill and $0.3 million related to separately identifiable net assets) and the noncontrolling interest is correspondingly lower as well.

Besides adjustments of assets and liabilities to their fair values and the treatment of non-controlling interests, four items are treated differently under the purchase method than under the acquisition method. These differences are described below.

- **Direct combination costs.** Business combinations require several types of costly professional services. Examples include investment banking services, preparation of legal documents, and tax planning and accounting services. The purchase method considered these to be costs of making the acquisition. Therefore, these costs were capitalized in the Investment account. The increased purchase price resulted in an increase in the amount of goodwill recognized. The acquisition method treats these costs as payments for services which are expensed as incurred and reported in the consolidated income statement in the period of acquisition.

- **Contingent consideration.** Some business acquisitions provide for contingent consideration to be given to the acquired firm's shareholders if some future performance measures are met. For example, additional payments by the parent may be required if the subsidiary's profits reach a certain threshold within a short time following the acquisition. Under the purchase method, such contingent payments were accounted for as postcombination adjustments to the purchase price. The acquisition method treats contingent consideration as a negotiated component of the acquisition cost and, therefore, is treated as part of the fair value of consideration transferred at acquisition. This means that the estimated value of the contingent consideration is recorded on the acquirer's books at the acquisition date and is included in the calculation of goodwill acquired.

- **Bargain purchases.** When the fair value of the consideration paid by the acquiring firm is less than the fair value of the separately identified assets acquired net of liabilities assumed in a business combination, a bargain purchase is deemed to have occurred. This situation can occur in a forced sale in which the seller is acting under compulsion or financial distress. The purchase method used this negative amount to reduce the sub-sidiary's assets were reported below their estimated fair values. The acquisition method records no assets at amounts below their assessed fair values and, therefore, recognizes a gain on bargain purchase at the acquisition date.

- **Acquired in-process research and development.** The purchase method allocated the purchase price (fair value of consideration given) to the tangible and intangible assets acquired and liabilities assumed. For many firms, especially those in high-tech industries, a significant portion of the purchase price was allocated to in-process research and development (IPR&D). Prior GAAP immediately wrote off amounts allocated to IPR&D unless those assets had an alternative future use.[12] Because of the ambiguity in determin-ing whether IPR&D had an alternative future use, firms often abused this discretionary accounting treatment by aggressive allocations that created large write-offs. This paved the way for later reporting higher consolidated earnings when the R&D projects turned out to be viable. Current GAAP closes this loophole by requiring that tangible and intan-gible R&D assets acquired in a business combination, including those that may have

---

[12] Pre-Codification "Applicability of Statement No. 2 to Business Combinations Accounted for by the Purchase Method—An Interpretation of FASB Statement No. 2," FASB Interpretation No. 4. (1975). This pronouncement has been superseded but is available at www.fasb.org under pre-Codification Standards.

no alternative future use, be measured at fair value and recognized in the consolidated balance sheet at the acquisition date. These capitalized R&D costs are reported as intangible assets with indefinite lives subject to periodic impairment reviews (see Chapter 10).

Pooling of Interests

To see how pooling works and its financial statement effects relative to the acquisition method, let's return once more to the Alphonse and Gaston example from earlier in the chapter. Instead of acquiring a 100% ownership in Gaston with cash, assume that Alphonse exchanges 8 million shares of its own stock with a fair value of $10 million for all of Gaston's outstanding stock. Also assume this transaction meets all the requirements to qualify as a pooling of interests.

In a stock-for-stock exchange, the owners of both Alphonse and Gaston continue as equity investors in the newly merged corporation. This continuation of ownership interests in poolings contrasts sharply with what happens in a cash buyout. After a cash buyout, the acquired company's former shareholders have no further equity interest in the combined enterprise. Pooling-of-interests reporting rules treat the two formerly independent companies as though they have decided to join resources and "keep house together." Because both original ownership interests survive, no buyout is considered to have taken place. The consolidation of Alphonse's and Gaston's financial statements combines the book values of the two entities. As in acquisition and purchase accounting, however, intra-entity transactions and double-counted items must be eliminated as in Exhibit 16.7.

The entry to record the acquisition on Alphonse's books would use the *book value* of Gaston's net assets ($2,000,000 + $6,500,000 − $500,000) as the carrying amount in the investment account—that is,

DR	Investment in Gaston	$8,000,000	
	CR Common Stock		$8,000,000

The only adjustment needed here is the elimination of the Investment in Gaston account against Gaston's equity accounts. No other adjustments or reclassifications are needed

---

EXHIBIT 16.7 **Alphonse and Gaston Company: Pooling Method—100% Ownership**

Preparation of Consolidated Balance Sheet—Date of Acquisition

	Alphonse	Gaston	Adjustments and Eliminations Dr.	Adjustments and Eliminations Cr.	Consolidated Balance Sheet
Assets					
Current assets	$15,000,000	$2,000,000			$17,000,000
Fixed assets, net	20,000,000	6,500,000			26,500,000
Investment in Gaston	8,000,000	—		$8,000,000 (A)	—
	$43,000,000	$8,500,000			$43,500,000
Liabilities					
Current liabilities	$ 1,000,000	$ 500,000			$ 1,500,000
Stockholders' Equity					
Common stock	36,000,000	6,000,000	$6,000,000 (A)		36,000,000
Capital in excess of par	2,000,000				2,000,000
Retained earnings	4,000,000	2,000,000	2,000,000 (A)		4,000,000
	$43,000,000	$8,500,000	$8,000,000	$8,000,000	$43,500,000

because Alphonse's Investment in Gaston account equals Gaston's net book value of equity. That is why under pooling of interests there is no write-up of assets or recognition of goodwill.

Financial Analysis Issues—Acquisition Method and Purchase Method

The disclosure rules for business combinations accounted for under the acquisition or purchase methods complicate financial analysis. Trend analysis becomes difficult. Why? Because under U.S. GAAP, comparative financial statements are not retroactively adjusted to include data for the acquired company for periods prior to the acquisition. To illustrate, Panel (a) of Exhibit 16.8 presents comparative income statements from the 2007 annual report of Lincoln National Corporation, a holding company that operates multiple insurance, investment management, broadcasting, and sports programming businesses through subsidiaries. In April 2006, Lincoln National acquired a 100% interest in Jefferson-Pilot Corporation, a financial services and broadcasting holding company in an acquisition accounted for using the purchase method. Accordingly, Lincoln National's 2006 consolidated income statement includes the revenues and expenses of Jefferson-Pilot from the acquisition date (April 3) through December 31, 2006, Lincoln National's fiscal year-end. (See Panel (b) of Exhibit 16.8.) Under the rules of purchase accounting that existed at that time,[13] the 2005 numbers reported in Lincoln National's 2007 consolidated comparative income statement do not include any of Jefferson-Pilot's results for that year. However, Jefferson-Pilot's *full-year* revenues and expenses are included in Lincoln National's 2007 consolidated income statement numbers. ***Thus, the income statements over the three years are noncomparable—Lincoln National's 2007 statements include Jefferson-Pilot's results for 12 months, the 2006 statement reflects Jefferson-Pilot's performance for 9 months, and the 2005 statement excludes Jefferson-Pilot's results altogether!***

> Because the acquisition method also includes the operating results of the acquired subsidiary in consolidated income only from the date of acquisition, the same distortions in year-to-year growth rates described here for the purchase method also apply to the acquisition method.

To illustrate the problem of trying to perform time-series comparisons for a business combination, we use the operating revenue amounts in Panel (a) of Exhibit 16.8. The three-year operating revenue data from Lincoln National's consolidated statement of income, along with a computation of year-to-year growth in this measure is:

($ in millions)	2007	2006	2005
Operating revenue as reported in consolidated financial statements	$10,594	$8,962	$5,475
Rate of growth in operating revenue compared to prior year	18.2%	63.7%	

The computed growth rates are misleading because the basic operating revenue data—and all other items in the income statement—are noncomparable.

To aid interperiod comparisons, existing disclosure rules require a **pro forma** (meaning *as if*) note to the financial statements that gives information for key income statement items as if the acquisition had taken place on the first day of the *previous* fiscal year, in this case January 1, 2005. These pro forma note disclosures for Lincoln National (shown in Panel (c)

---

[13] Pre-Codification *SFAS No. 141,* para. 49.

EXHIBIT 16.8 · Lincoln National Corporation and Subsidiaries

Disclosures Subsequent to a Business Combination: Purchase Accounting

Panel (a)

Consolidated Statement of Earnings
($ in millions)

	2007	2006	2005
Revenue			
Insurance premiums	$ 1,945	$ 1,406	$ 308
Insurance fees	3,254	2,604	1,752
Investment advisory fees	360	328	256
Net investment income	4,384	3,981	2,702
Realized gain (loss)	(118)	(3)	(3)
Amortization of deferred gain on indemnity reinsurance	83	76	77
Other revenue and fees	686	570	383
Total revenues	10,594	8,962	5,475
Expenses			
Benefits and interest credited	5,152	4,170	2,332
Underwriting, acquisition, insurance and other expenses	3,284	2,790	1,981
Interest and debt expense	284	224	87
Total benefits and expenses	8,720	7,184	4,400
Income before federal income taxes	1,874	1,778	1,075
Federal income taxes	553	483	244
Income before cumulative effect of accounting changes	1,321	1,295	831
Income (loss) from discontinued operation, net of federal income taxes	(106)	21	—
Net income	$ 1,215	$ 1,316	$ 831

Panel (b)

Excerpts from Annual Report Note

On April 3, 2006, we completed our merger with Jefferson-Pilot by acquiring 100% of the outstanding shares of Jefferson-Pilot in a transaction accounted for under the purchase method of accounting prescribed by SFAS No. 141, "Business Combinations" ("SFAS 141"). Jefferson-Pilot's results of operations are included in our results of operations beginning April 3, 2006. As a result of the merger, our product portfolio was expanded, and we now offer fixed and variable universal life, fixed annuities, including indexed annuities, variable annuities, mutual funds and institutional accounts, 401(k) and 403(b) offerings, and group life, disability, and dental insurance products. We also own and operate television and radio stations in selected markets in the Southeastern and Western United States and produce and distribute sports programming.

Panel (c)

		Year Ended		
(in millions)	**2007**	**2006**		**2005**
Revenue	$10,594	$10,134		$9,559
	└─── 4.54% ───┘	└─── 6.00% ───┘		
Net Income	1,215	1,430		1,352
	└─── −15.03% ───┘	└─── 5.80% ───┘		

of Exhibit 16.8) reflect full-year results for Jefferson-Pilot in both 2006 and 2005. However, these pro forma data do *not* encompass all income statement items and do not include periods prior to 2005. Consequently, even with the note disclosure, it is usually not possible for analysts to make comparisons of *complete* income statements adjusted for the acquisition. This is a serious deficiency that destroys the comparability of the time-series financial statement data used by lenders and other financial analysts. Indeed, if the acquired company is large in relation to the acquirer, the consolidated financial statements seriously distort trends and other comparative data.

The pro forma rates of operating revenue growth for 2006 and 2007 were 6.0% and 4.5%, respectively—assuming that the combination had occurred at the beginning of 2005. These rates are much lower than the rates computed from the operating revenue numbers actually reported in the financial statements—63.7% and 18.2%. Also note in Panel (c) of Exhibit 16.8 how the sparseness of pro forma disclosures makes it possible to compare only one other income statement line item: bottom-line net income. The only way to overcome this problem is to gather past financial statement data for Jefferson-Pilot and consolidate its past results with those of Lincoln National (using appropriate assumptions about intra-entity sales and loans, of course). It's easy to obtain these data when the acquired company is publicly held. However, if it is not publicly held, these data may be difficult or even impossible to obtain.

For business combinations accounted for as poolings of interests (allowed until July 1, 2001), this comparability problem did not occur. That's because under pooling, all past financial statement data were retroactively consolidated to include both parties to the combination. Keep in mind, however, that while the pooling-of-interests approach overcame some income statement comparability problems, the reported financial data using this approach are still fraught with deficiencies.

Trend analysis under acquisition and purchase method accounting becomes difficult because U.S. GAAP comparative financial statements are not retroactively adjusted to include data for the acquired company for periods prior to the acquisition. In the year of the acquisition, the consolidated income statement includes the parent company results for the full year and the results of the subsidiary from the time the acquisition took place to the end of the year (that is, for the fraction of a year the parent owned the subsidiary). In the year following acquisition, the consolidated income statement includes the full year results for both the parent and the subsidiary. In the year prior to the acquisition, the income statement includes the results of the parent company only and does not include any of the subsidiary's results. This can lead to distortions in year-to-year growth rates in revenues and profits that statement users need to be aware of. Supplemental disclosures allow analysts to make adjustments to the reported numbers to make more valid comparisons, but only for selected statement items.

Financial Analysis Issues—Acquisition Method vs. Pooling of Interests

The pooling-of-interests method has been widely criticized. To help understand why, consider Exhibit 16.9, which highlights the differences in consolidated balance sheets that would result for Alphonse & Gaston Company, the combined organization, under acquisition versus pooling-of-interests accounting.

Prior to the acquisition, Gaston had a fair value of $10,000,000—the amount Alphonse was willing to pay. Acquisition accounting brings Gaston into the consolidated balance sheet at its fair value of $10 million. Under pooling-of-interests accounting, Gaston is shown in the consolidated balance sheet at its net book value of $8 million. The $1.5 million and $500,000 differences in fixed assets and goodwill, respectively, are shown in the "Difference" column in Exhibit 16.9. The other balance sheet differences are because Alphonse paid with cash in the acquisition method example and with stock in the pooling example.

EXHIBIT 16.9   **Alphonse and Gaston Company: Acquisition versus Pooling-of-Interest Method**

Comparative Consolidated Balance Sheets

	Acquisition Method	Pooling-of-Interests Method	Difference (Pooling minus Acquisition)
Assets			
Current assets	$ 7,000,000	$17,000,000	$10,000,000
Fixed assets, net	28,000,000	26,500,000	(1,500,000)
Goodwill	500,000	—	(500,000)
	$35,500,000	$43,500,000	$ 8,000,000
Liabilities			
Current liabilities	$ 1,500,000	$1,500,000	—
Stockholders' Equity			
Common stock	28,000,000	36,000,000	$ 8,000,000
Capital in excess of par	2,000,000	2,000,000	—
Retained earnings	4,000,000	4,000,000	—
	$35,500,000	$43,500,000	$ 8,000,000

Pooling critics argue that pooling permits acquiring companies to record acquisitions at artificially low amounts. In our example, Gaston is worth $10 million, and this is presumably the value that the sellers demanded. Therefore, the value of Alphonse stock that Gaston's shareholders received must have been $10 million. Despite this economic reality, the transaction is booked at $8 million under the pooling-of-interests method. Critics charge that this understatement distorts the balance sheet as well as subsequent income statements. The income in future years is affected because fixed assets are $1.5 million lower—the unrecorded difference between fair value and book value—under pooling than under acquisition accounting, so future depreciation expense will be lower. Similarly, because no goodwill exists under pooling, there is no potential goodwill impairment to reduce future earnings.[14] Both of these effects make income under pooling higher. Critics further charge that the lower pooling balance sheet numbers for gross assets and equity make rate-of-return ratios appear higher. That's because, under pooling, the denominator of both the return-on-assets and return-on-equity ratios is lower. Some critics suggest that these distortions are not accidental. They argue that the cosmetic statement effects of pooling explain its popularity among takeover-minded executives prior to July 1, 2001, when it was permitted under GAAP. Pooling provided an opportunity to buy companies and then record the acquisition on the books at artificially low numbers, thereby improving the appearance of subsequent financial statements.

> Enron, with the help of its chief financial officer, Andrew Fastow, set up a number of limited partnerships through which it engaged in billions of dollars of complex transactions to hedge fluctuating values in some of Enron's broadband telecommunications and other technology investments. Under existing reporting rules at the time, Enron was able to avoid consolidation of these VIEs, thereby keeping hundreds of millions of dollars of debt and losses off of their financial statements.

VARIABLE INTEREST ENTITIES

Enron's collapse in 2001 created a demand for increased disclosure and transparency about companies' interests in *special purpose entities (SPE)* or *variable interest entities (VIE)*. A VIE is a corporation, partnership, trust, or any other legal structure used for business purposes that either (a)

> Pre-Codification standards referred to these legal entities as special purpose entities (SPE). FASB ASC now refers to these as variable interest entities (VIE).

---

[14] At the time poolings were permitted, goodwill under the purchase method (the other permissible alternative at the time) was amortized, making future earnings charges a certainty.

does not have equity investors with voting rights or (b) has equity investors that do not provide sufficient financial resources for the entity to support its activities. VIEs are often formed to engage in what are called *structured financing arrangements,* which offer a company an opportunity to borrow money based on the value of a specific project or asset rather than on its own credit rating. Major uses of VIEs include synthetic leasing (see Chapter 12), securitizing loans and mortgages (see Chapter 8), selling receivables (see Chapter 8), and setting up **take-or-pay contracts** or **throughput arrangements.**

> For example, a company building a factory can borrow money based on the worth of the factory or on expectations of its future revenue.

> A *take-or-pay contract* is an "agreement between a purchaser and a seller that provides for the purchaser to pay specified amounts periodically in return for products or services. The purchaser must make specified minimum payments even if it does not take delivery of the contracted products or services."*
>
> For example, two companies may form an SPE with a nominal investment to build an oil refinery that both companies will use. The SPE borrows money to build the refinery with the note being guaranteed by one or both companies. Both companies agree to make minimum payments to the SPE each quarter in exchange for a specified number of barrels of refined oil on which they may or may not take delivery.
>
> A *throughput agreement* is an "agreement between a shipper (processor) and the owner of a transportation facility (such as an oil or natural gas pipeline or a ship) or a manufacturing facility that provides for the shipper (processor) to pay specified amounts periodically in return for the transportation (processing) of the product. The shipper (processor) is obligated to provide specified minimum quantities to be transported (processed) in each period and is required to make cash payments even if it does not provide the contracted quantities."*
>
> * FASB ASC Master Glossary.

The accounting for VIEs is complex and we only provide an overview here. In 2009, GAAP was amended to address the problem of off-balance-sheet entities generating significant losses for companies during the 2008 economic crisis. *The critical issue is determining when the sponsoring entity must consolidate a VIE.* GAAP requires a reporting (sponsoring) entity to consolidate a VIE if that company has a **controlling financial interest** in a VIE and, thus, is the VIE's primary beneficiary.[15] A company is deemed to have a controlling financial interest in a VIE if it has *both* of the following characteristics:

1. The power to direct the activities of the VIE that most significantly impact the VIE's economic performance.

2. The obligation to absorb losses of the VIE that could potentially be significant to the VIE or the right to receive benefits from the VIE that could potentially be significant to the VIE.

When these two conditions are met, the reporting entity (primary beneficiary) must consolidate the VIE using the acquisition method. A reporting entity must identify which activities most significantly impact the VIE's economic performance and determine whether it has the power (through voting rights or similar rights) to direct those activities. Only one reporting entity, if any, is expected to be identified as the primary beneficiary of a VIE and, therefore, to consolidate its activities.

> Although more than one reporting entity could have the characteristics in (2) above, generally only one reporting entity is likely to have the power to direct the activities of the VIE that most significantly impact its economic performance. Many joint ventures are VIEs with joint power. If each of the partners must consent to those activities that most significantly impact the VIE's economic performance, then GAAP would not require either party to consolidate the VIE.

Because the primary beneficiary is required to consolidate a VIE, financial statement users are provided with more complete information about the resources, obligations, risks, and opportunities facing the sponsoring firm. After the changes to the accounting guidelines in 2009, companies began consolidating numerous entities that had previously been off-balance-sheet. Because the consolidation of these entities increased both debt and assets, the debt-to-equity ratios for these companies increased. We discuss this issue within the context of a **securitization entity** in Chapter 8 (pages 437–439). The collateralized borrowing scenario in the Chapter 8 example is equivalent to what occurs in a consolidation.

---

[15] FASB ASC Paragraph 810-10-25-20: Consolidation—Overall—Recognition—Variable Interest Entities.

ACCOUNTING FOR FOREIGN SUBSIDIARIES AND FOREIGN CURRENCY TRANSACTIONS

Transactions denominated in foreign currencies pose a unique problem. Because these transactions must be presented in the financial statements in a different currency than the currency used to complete the transaction, the transaction must be translated into the home currency—the U.S. dollar in the case of a U.S. company. This problem is not unique to companies having foreign subsidiaries that need to be consolidated. Any company having transactions denominated in a foreign currency must translate the transactions. We address the issue here because the same approach to accounting for foreign currency transactions also applies to the translation of the financial statements of certain foreign subsidiaries.

Foreign Currency Transactions

Foreign currency transactions are business transactions denominated in a foreign currency. Examples include a U.S. company taking out a bank loan denominated in Norwegian kroner or purchasing inventory in the Netherlands on credit for a price expressed in euros. The accounting for foreign currency transactions depends on the type of asset acquired or liability incurred. Let's consider a foreign currency transaction that involves the acquisition of a **monetary asset**—that is, an asset such as cash or accounts receivable whose value is derived from the number of monetary units into which it is convertible.

Assume that on January 1, 2014, Yankee Corporation (a U.S. company) sells 100 units of its product to a U.K. customer for £10 per unit, or £1,000 total. Payment is due on April 1, 2014. On January 1, 2014, assume that £1 is worth $2 and that the per unit production cost incurred by Yankee is $8. Given this information, Yankee records the foreign currency transaction on its books in this way:

DR	Accounts receivable	$2,000	
	CR Sales revenue		$2,000

To record the receivable of £1,000 at its 1/1/14 U.S. dollar equivalent of $2,000.

DR	Cost of goods sold	$800	
	CR Inventory		$800

To record 100 units @ $8.

The receivable is denominated in pounds—which makes this a foreign currency transaction. Because Yankee keeps its books in dollars, the receivable must be reexpressed in home-currency units when preparing financial statements. The economically equivalent amount of U.S. dollars is found using the exchange rate in effect at the transaction date—£1 = $2. Although the receivable is initially reflected on the books at $2,000, in reality what the customer owes is £1,000, not $2,000.

Suppose that by the end of the quarter, the pound has fallen relative to the dollar, so that on March 31, 2014, the exchange rate is £1 = $1.80. At the current exchange rate, the receivable is worth only $1,800, so Yankee books the following entry when preparing its quarterly statements:

DR	Foreign exchange loss	$200	
	CR Accounts receivable		$200

To reduce the U.S. dollar value of a £1,000 receivable to $1,800.

Most liabilities are monetary because they are expressed in units of currency (for example, a Japanese yen account payable of ¥9,000,000) and will be settled using foreign currency monetary assets. However, a few liabilities are settled by using *nonmonetary* assets; this small class of liabilities is considered to be nonmonetary. Examples include estimated product warranty liabilities and customer deposits for products to be produced and delivered in future periods.

Yankee has a loss because it is owed pounds whose value in U.S. dollar terms has fallen. This loss is reflected in the income statement of the period in which the loss occurs. Monetary assets (such as accounts receivable) that arise from foreign currency transactions are shown in the financial statements at their dollar equivalent using ***the exchange rate in effect at the financial statement date.*** Monetary liabilities (such as accounts or bonds payable) are similarly translated using the exchange rate in effect at the statement date. The statement date exchange rate is referred to as the **current rate.**

Suppose that the exchange rate on April 1, 2014, when the receivable is paid, is still £1 = $1.80. The customer remits £1,000, which Yankee converts into dollars. The entry on Yankee's books is:

DR Cash	$1,800	
CR Accounts receivable		$1,800

To remove the receivable from the books. The initial $2,000 minus the 3/31/14 write-down of $200 equals the carrying amount of $1,800.

We next illustrate the accounting for a foreign currency transaction that involves a nonmonetary asset. Nonmonetary assets are items such as inventory, equipment, land, buildings, and trucks whose value is not derived from the right to receive cash.

Suppose that because of Yankee's growing volume of sales to U.K. customers it decides to purchase a warehouse in London to store inventory awaiting shipment to customers. It purchases a building on June 30, 2014, for £300,000; on that date, the exchange rate is £1 = $1.75. The building is recorded on Yankee's books at the U.S. dollar equivalent of the foreign currency transaction price at the purchase date:

DR Warehouse building	$525,000	
CR Cash		$525,000

To record the acquisition of the London warehouse at the U.S. dollar equivalent of the foreign currency transaction price: £300,000 × 1.75 = $525,000.

The subsequent accounting for nonmonetary assets acquired in a foreign currency transaction is identical to the accounting for nonmonetary assets acquired in the domestic currency. Specifically, the fixed asset's historical cost in dollars is used as the measurement basis in subsequent financial statements throughout the asset's life. Regardless of the pound's value relative to the U.S. dollar at year-end 2014, the London warehouse is still shown on Yankee's books at $525,000—that is, at its acquisition cost in dollars (minus depreciation, of course). Thus, to reflect the gross carrying amount of nonmonetary assets acquired in a foreign currency transaction, Yankee uses the exchange rate in effect at the time of the transaction. This rate is called the **historical exchange rate.**

 RE CAP

The accounting for assets and liabilities arising from foreign currency transactions depends on the nature of the item—that is,

1. **Foreign currency monetary assets and liabilities are remeasured using the current exchange rate in effect at the balance sheet date.**

2. **Foreign currency nonmonetary assets and liabilities are remeasured using the historical exchange rate in effect when the item was acquired or incurred.**

Foreign Subsidiaries

All majority-owned subsidiaries—foreign *and* domestic—must be consolidated using the methods described earlier in the chapter. However, there's an additional complication when consolidating foreign subsidiaries. The subsidiary's financial statements, which are expressed in foreign currency units, must first be *transformed* into the parent's currency units—U.S. dollars for a U.S. parent—before the consolidation process begins.

The transformation under U.S. GAAP specifies one of two procedures, depending on the foreign subsidiary's operating characteristics:[16]

1. Foreign subsidiaries that are mere extensions of the parent with no self-sufficiency are **remeasured** using the **temporal method.** For example, a European sales subsidiary of a U.S. seed company, which sells seed produced by the U.S. parent to European farmers and remits the sales proceeds back to the U.S. parent, would use the temporal method.

2. Foreign subsidiaries that are essentially freestanding units with self-contained foreign operations are **translated** using the **current rate method.** For example, a European manufacturing and sales subsidiary of a U.S. computer company, which buys parts in Europe, assembles the final product, and sells it to European businesses, would use the current rate method.

The procedure selected to transform subsidiary statements expressed in foreign currency units into the parent's currency units is called the **functional currency choice** because it is based on whether the currency in which the subsidiary effectively operates (i.e., the functional currency) is the local currency or the parent company's currency. What guides this choice is subtle;[17] foreign subsidiaries whose operations are not self-sufficient are considered to be effectively operating in the parent's currency (the U.S. dollar for a subsidiary of a U.S. company) while engaging in a series of foreign currency transactions. The transformation of the results to the parent's currency accordingly treats the financial results of these subsidiaries in the same way foreign currency transactions are treated. Freestanding subsidiaries follow a different approach because they are deemed to be effectively operating in the local currency and therefore not engaging in foreign currency transactions.

Accounting for Nonfreestanding Foreign Subsidiaries   To see what it means when we say that a foreign subsidiary is not freestanding, let's consider a U.S. company, Doodle Corporation, with a U.K. subsidiary called Dandy Ltd. Dandy serves as Doodle's U.K. marketing arm. Doodle manufactures a product in the United States using U.S. sourced materials and labor. Some of the production is shipped from the United States to the United Kingdom where it is sold to U.K. customers at a price denominated in pounds sterling. Product distribution and the collection of the receivables are coordinated by two U.K. employees of Dandy Ltd. Upon collection of the receivables, the pounds are remitted to the United States. This cycle is repeated as the pounds are converted into dollars, the dollars are used in the United States to manufacture more inventory, and some portion of the inventory is again shipped to the United Kingdom for sale to customers there. Dandy's only U.K. assets are (1) a small amount of cash to pay expenses, (2) inventory from Doodle that has not yet been shipped to customers, and (3) a building that serves as both a warehouse and an office for the two employees.

---

[16] FASB ASC Section 830-10-45: Foreign Currency Matters—Overall—Other Presentation Matters. Although our discussion centers on consolidation of a foreign subsidiary, the rules described here must also be used in conjunction with the equity method when the parent owns between 20% and 50% of a foreign company.

[17] See L. Revsine, "The Rationale Underlying the Functional Currency Choice," *The Accounting Review,* July 1984, pp. 504–14.

EXHIBIT 16.10	**Translation Exchange Rates under the Temporal Method**

Account Category	Rate Used
Balance sheet	
Monetary assets and liabilities	Current rate
Nonmonetary assets and liabilties	Historical rate
Income statement	
All revenue and expense accounts resulting in an immediate inflow or outflow of cash or recognition of a new asset (e.g., sales revenue creates an account receivable) or of a new liability (e.g., salary expense creates wages payable)	Rate at time of transaction
Expenses resulting in de-rcognition of an existing asset translated at the current rate (e.g., all expenses paid in cash)	Rate at time of transaction
Expenses resulting in de-recognition of an existing asset translated at the historical rate (e.g., depreciation de-recognizes a fixed asset, cost of goods sold de-recognizes inventory)	Historical rate

The situation described here is a classic illustration of a foreign subsidiary that is merely an extension of the parent. Dandy Ltd. is a marketing arm of Doodle rather than a viable, free-standing company. It is a conduit for administering foreign sales and has no independent life of its own.

Under GAAP, subsidiaries like Dandy Ltd. are treated as if they were created for the sole purpose of facilitating foreign currency transactions. Because such subsidiaries are conduits for foreign currency transactions, upon consolidation they are treated as if the parent company had engaged in the foreign transactions directly. That is, *the consolidated financial statements of a nonfreestanding subsidiary are identical to the financial statements that would have resulted had the subsidiary not existed and instead the parent had engaged in the foreign currency transactions directly.*

The temporal method achieves this effect in the financial statements by translating the subsidiary's foreign currency statements into U.S. dollars[18] using the exchange rates shown in Exhibit 16.10. The guiding principles behind these exchange rates are:

1. Monetary assets and liabilities are continuously revalued to the current rate at any point in time, whereas nonmonetary assets and liabilities are not revalued when exchange rates change.

2. When a transaction results in the recognition of a new asset or liability, the new asset or liability is valued (in U.S. dollar terms) using the exchange rate in effect at the time of the transaction and the corresponding revenue or expense is valued at the same amount.

---

[18] Authoritative accounting literature uses the term **remeasure** when describing the conversion from foreign currency units to home currency units under the temporal method. For simplicity, we ignore this nuance and refer to the process as *translation.*

3. When a transaction results in the de-recognition of an existing asset or liability, the corresponding U.S. dollar amount is removed from the balance sheet with a like amount treated as revenue or expense.

   a. If the de-recognized asset or liability was a monetary item, it was valued at the current rate at the transaction date (because it had been continually revalued) so the transaction date exchange rate is used to determine the amount of revenue or expense recognized.

   b. If the de-recognized asset or liability was a nonmonetary item, it was valued at the exchange rate in effect when the item was first recognized (i.e., the historical exchange rate), so the historical rate is used to determine the amount of revenue of expense to recognize.

To illustrate the temporal method, consider the following transactions for Dandy Ltd. during 2014.

1. On January 1, 2014, it receives inventory costing $800 from Doodle when £1 = $2, and sells those goods on credit for £1,000.
2. The pound falls to £1 = $1.80 on March 31, 2014. Dandy collects receivables of £1,000 on April 1, 2014, when £1 = $1.80.
3. Dandy purchases a building in London for £300,000 on June 30, 2014, when £1 = $1.75.

These transactions are identical to the foreign currency transactions entered into by Yankee Corporation directly in our earlier example. In Exhibit 16.11, we show the result of using the temporal method to translate Dandy Ltd.'s statements. The results under GAAP for Yankee's foreign currency transactions are displayed in the shaded column for comparison.

Comparing the Dandy statement numbers with those of Yankee in Exhibit 16.11 demonstrates that using the temporal method results in Dandy's statements being denominated in

EXHIBIT 16.11	Comparison of Temporal Method Results with Accounting for Foreign Currency Transactions			
	Temporal Method Translation			**Foreign Currency Transactions**
	Dandy Ltd. in £s	**Exchange Rate**	**Dandy Ltd. in $s**	**Yankee Corporation**
Income statement				
Sales	£ 1,000	1£ = $2	$ 2,000	$ 2,000
Cost of sales	400	1£ = $2	800	800
Gross profit	600		1,200	1,200
Foreign exchange loss*	—		200	200
Operating income	£ 600		$ 1,000	$ 1,000
Selected balance sheet accounts				
At 3/31/14				
Account receivable	£ 1,000	1£ = $1.80	$ 1,800	$ 1,800
At 4/1/14				
Cash	£ 1,000	1£ = $1.80	$ 1,800	$ 1,800
At 6/30/14				
Building	£300,000	1£ = $1.75	$525,000	$525,000

* Computed as:

Monetary asset on acquisition	£1,000 when 1£ = $2.00 =	$2,000
Monetary asset at March 31, 2014	£1,000 when 1£ = $1.80 =	1,800
Foreign exchange loss		$ 200

dollar figures that equal those of Yankee. This is no coincidence. ***Both Dandy and Yankee are considered to have engaged in identical foreign currency transactions, so the two sets of results must be equal.*** The temporal method achieves this result.

Accounting for Self-Contained Foreign Subsidiaries

When a foreign subsidiary and its parent operate independently, the translation of the subsidiary's financial statements into U.S. dollars uses the current rate method. To understand why, let's consider a self-contained subsidiary whose operations do not rely extensively on the parent.

A U.S. food company has a Swiss subsidiary formed by a capital infusion from the U.S. parent. Once the equity infusion was in place, the remainder of the Swiss subsidiary's long-term capital was raised using Swiss franc borrowing. The subsidiary engages in no transactions with the parent. Operations are entirely contained in Switzerland where the company hires employees, buys inventory, manufactures its product line, and sells to Swiss and other European customers. The Swiss operation plows back operating profits to expand into new product lines and to increase production capacity. While the parent may periodically receive dividends from the subsidiary, its investment remains until it either sells or liquidates the subsidiary.

For self-contained foreign subsidiaries, the effect of changes in exchange rates on future dollar cash flows is uncertain. Consider a rise in the Swiss franc. One possible effect of the rise is that it will make the subsidiary's products more expensive to foreign purchasers and could adversely affect profits. The rise in the Swiss franc also means that input purchases in other currencies are less expensive, so a favorable profit effect could ensue. The possibilities are many and depend on the subsidiary's individual characteristics and on those of the markets in which it operates. These possibilities include:

1. Does the subsidiary price its product sales in countries outside Switzerland in Swiss francs or in units of the foreign currencies?
2. Does the subsidiary adjust its Swiss franc selling price when the value of the franc rises or falls?
3. What proportion of the product input does the subsidiary purchase in Switzerland in francs?
4. Does the Swiss franc borrowing have a floating rate of interest that would be sensitive to exchange rate changes?

| See Chapter 2 for further discussion of Other comprehensive income components. |

These are only a few of the many possibilities that could influence the magnitude and direction of the effect of the exchange rate change on ultimate dollar cash flows from the subsidiary. ***Because the ultimate exchange rate effects on U.S. dollar cash flows are uncertain, U.S. GAAP requires such subsidiaries to be translated using the current rate method and that any debit or credit arising from translation "gains" or "losses" be reported as Other comprehensive income, which becomes part of Accumulated other comprehensive income in stockholders' equity.*** Under the current rate method, *all* asset and liability accounts are translated at the current exchange rate in effect at the balance sheet date and *all* income statement accounts are translated at the exchange rate that was in effect at the time of the transaction. In most cases, this means the weighted average exchange rate over the period can be used because it is common to assume transactions occurred evenly through the year. However, if there is a material transaction at a specific date (e.g., a large sale on a particular day) then the exchange rate on that date is used.

Because *all* asset and liability accounts in the balance sheet are translated at the *same* rate, the translated balance sheet asset and liability accounts have the same proportionality as the accounts expressed in foreign currency units. For example, the Swiss subsidiary's quick ratio derived from its Swiss franc statements will be identical to the quick ratio after the statements are translated into U.S. dollars using the current rate method. The current rate method provides a practical way to go from foreign currency units to dollars while still maintaining or very closely approximating the subsidiary's financial ratios. *Furthermore, by denying income statement recognition to the balancing debit or credit that arises from translation, the uncertain ultimate effect of exchange rate changes is explicitly carried forward.* Figure 16.5 is a diagram of the translation approach under FASB ASC Topic 820-10-30: Foreign Currency Matters—Overall—Translation of Financial Statements.

Ratio proportionality between foreign currency and translated dollar numbers is maintained *precisely* for any ratio for which the numerator and denominator are confined to a single statement. Examples include the current ratio—both balance sheet accounts—and gross margin ratio—both income statement accounts. This is true because the current rate method translates most accounts within a single statement at the same rate—weighted average rate for income statement items and end-of-year rate for balance sheet asset and liability items. For ratios that use numbers from both statements—for example, rate of return on assets—the current rate method does not maintain perfect proportionality. However, the difference between the "mixed-statement ratio" expressed in foreign currency and the translated ratio expressed in U.S. dollars is usually very small.

The figure shows that GAAP requires firms to categorize each of their foreign subsidiaries as either (1) a *nonfreestanding subsidiary*, whose activities are so closely integrated with the parent that they are considered to be engaging in foreign currency transactions on behalf of the parent or (2) a *self-contained subsidiary* with an independent or virtually independent operating existence of its own. For nonfreestanding subsidiaries, exchange rate movements have an immediately determinable effect on dollar cash flows; for this reason, translation gains and losses are run through the income statement. By contrast, self-contained subsidiaries are put into an income "holding pattern" because exchange rate movements have an indeterminate impact on the parent's ultimate dollar cash flows. Consequently, a *neutral* translation mechanism—the current rate method—is used for these subsidiaries, and the resulting equity debits or credits are reported in other comprehensive income rather than as elements of net income.

Exhibit 16.12 contains excerpts from the Pfizer Inc. 2012 annual report. Panel (a) of Exhibit 16.12 shows a portion of the note disclosure regarding foreign subsidiaries. Most of

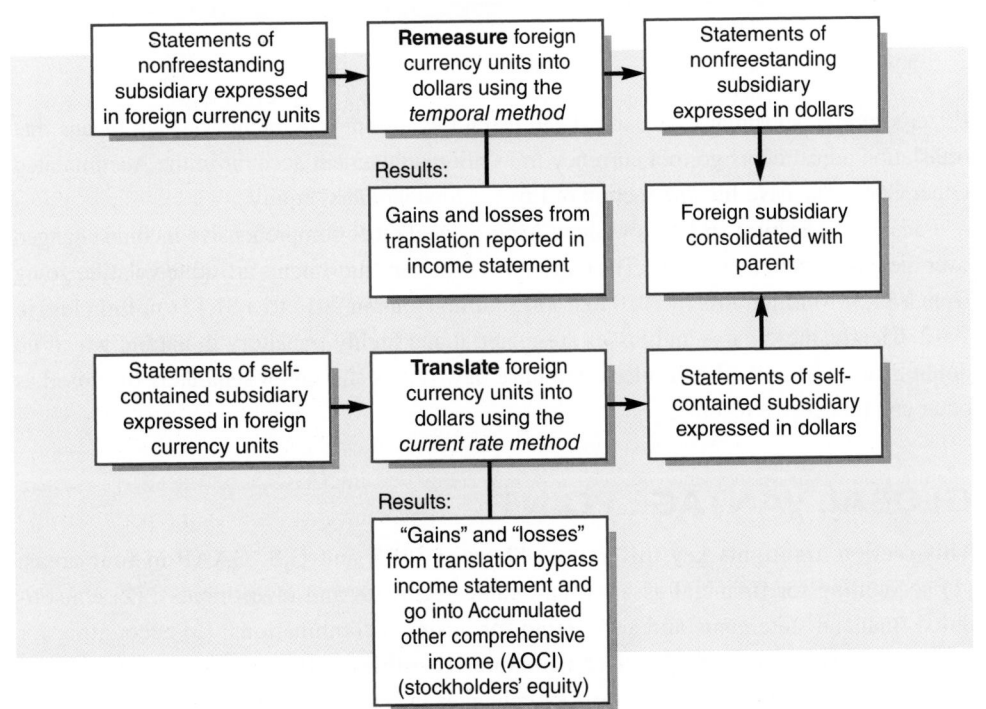

Figure 16.5

TRANSLATION APPROACH USED IN U.S. GAAP

FASB ASC Topic 830-10-30: Foreign Currency Matters—Overall—Translation of Financial Statements

EXHIBIT 16.12 — Pfizer Inc.

Panel (a): Foreign Currency Translation Note

For most of our international operations, local currencies have been determined to be the functional currencies. We translated functional currency assets and liabilities to their U.S. dollar equivalents at exchange rates in effect as of the balance sheet date and we translated functional currency income and expense amounts to their U.S. dollar equivalents at average exchange rates for the period. The U.S. dollar effects that arise from changing translation rates are recorded in Other comprehensive income/(loss). The effects of converting non-functional currency assets and liabilities into the functional currency are recorded in *Other deductions—net.* For operations in highly inflationary economies, we translate monetary items at rates in effect as of the balance sheet date, with translation adjustments recorded in *Other deductions—net,* and we translate nonmonetary items at historical rates.

Panel (b): Other Comprehensive Income (Expense)

The following table provides the changes, net of tax, in *Accumulated other comprehensive income/(loss):*

	Net Unrealized Gains/(Losses)			Benefit Plans		
(millions of dollars)	Currency Translation Adjustment and Other	Derivative Financial Instruments	Available-for-Sale Securities	Actuarial Gains/ (Losses)	Prior Service (Costs)/Credits and Other	Accumulated Other Comprehensive Income/ (Loss)
Balance, January 1, 2010	$ 3,550	$ 6	$ 269	$(3,367)	$ 94	$ 552
Other comprehensive income/(loss)[a]	(3,381)	(214)	(112)	(580)	295	(3,992)
Balance, December 31, 2010	169	(208)	157	(3,947)	389	(3,440)
Other comprehensive income/(loss)[a]	775	(153)	(111)	(1,173)	(27)	(689)
Balance, December 31, 2011	944	(361)	46	(5,120)	362	(4,129)
Other comprehensive income/(loss)[a]	**(1,121)**	**273**	**117**	**(990)**	**(103)**	**(1,824)**
Balance, December 31, 2012	**$ (177)**	**$ (88)**	**$ 163**	**$(6,110)**	**$ 259**	**$(5,953)**

[a] Amounts do not include foreign currency translation adjustments attributable to noncontrolling interests of $7 million loss in 2012, $45 million loss in 2011 and $5 million income in 2010.

As of December 31, 2012, we estimate that we will reclassify into 2013 income the following pre-tax amounts currently held in *Accumulated other comprehensive loss*: $4.7 million of the unrealized holding gains on derivative financial instruments; $609 million of actuarial losses related to benefit plan obligations and plan assets and other benefit plan items; and $62 million of prior service credits, primarily related to benefit plan amendments.

Pfizer's foreign subsidiaries are translated using the current rate method, which means that translation adjustments go to a currency translation adjustment account in the Accumulated Other Comprehensive Income section of Pfizer's Shareholders' equity.

Panel (b) of Exhibit 16.12 shows how Accumulated other comprehensive income changed over the most recent three years. The currency translation adjustments are quite volatile, going from a $3,381 million loss in 2010 to a $775 million gain in 2011 to a $1,121 million loss in 2012. Clearly, these gains and losses are material and highly transitory in nature, which no doubt is one reason the FASB elected to have these gains and losses separately disclosed as other comprehensive income.

 **International**

GLOBAL VANTAGE POINT

This section highlights key differences between IFRS and U.S. GAAP in four areas: (1) accounting for financial assets (marketable securities and investments); (2) consolidated financial statements and accounting for business combinations; (3) accounting for special purpose entities (SPEs) or variable interest entities (VIEs); and (4) accounting for joint ventures. We also briefly discuss key changes in accounting for financial instruments recently proposed in a FASB exposure draft designed to bring U.S. GAAP into greater alignment with IFRS.

Accounting for Financial Assets (Marketable Securities and Investments)

IFRS accounting for financial assets (along with other financial instruments) is contained in three pronouncements: *IAS 32,* "Financial Instruments: Presentation"; *IAS 39,* "Financial Instruments: Recognition and Measurement"; and *IFRS 7,* "Disclosures." Responding to criticisms of current recognition and measurement rules for financial instruments, the IASB has begun to replace *IAS 39* with *IFRS 9.* Phase 1 of this change deals with classification and measurement of financial assets and financial liabilities. The IASB issued *IFRS 9,* "Financial Instruments," in November 2009 (with an update in October 2010) to address classification and measurement of financial assets and financial liabilities, with transition required for fiscal years beginning on or after January 1, 2015. Originally, the IASB had intended adoption by 2013, but it delayed the transition date to allow constituents more time to prepare for the changes. Phase 2 deals with impairment methodology. The IASB is currently redeliberating its proposed guidance regarding impairment of financial assets after it received numerous comment letters from constituents voicing concerns over guidance proposed in a recent Exposure Draft. Phase 3 deals with hedge accounting. As of May 2013, the IASB is finalizing its deliberations and plans to issue revisions to *IFRS 9* with modified hedge accounting guidance. Because of the delayed implementation date for *IFRS 9,* we will discuss current guidance and anticipated guidance (after the 2015 transition) here.

Exhibit 16.13 highlights the current similarities and differences between U.S. GAAP and IFRS related to accounting for financial assets. Panel (a) summarizes classification, types of assets included, measurement bases, and where the unrealized gains and losses are reported for various financial assets; Panel (b) provides a summary of impairment testing. Key areas of difference between IFRS and U.S. GAAP are shaded.

Like U.S. GAAP, IFRS currently classifies financial assets into trading, available-for-sale (AFS), held-to-maturity, and equity-method investment categories. Fair value (FV) measurement is used for debt and equity securities held in the trading portfolio with FV unrealized gains/losses reported in income. For the available-for-sale category, there are three areas of difference between IFRS and U.S. GAAP. IFRS includes nonmarketable equity securities in this category if FV can be determined, and FV unrealized gains/losses are reported in Other comprehensive income (OCI) as is the case for other equity and debt marketable securities that are classified as AFS. U.S. GAAP does not allow nonmarketable *equity* securities to be included in the AFS category. Such assets are generally reported as other assets and measured at cost. IFRS differs from U.S. GAAP with respect to the treatment of unrealized gains and losses on financial assets with a foreign exchange component (e.g., securities held by a foreign subsidiary that are denominated in a foreign currency). IFRS isolates the unrealized gains and losses due to the foreign exchange component and reports this in income. Any remaining unrealized gain/loss is reported in OCI. U.S. GAAP does not isolate the portion due to foreign exchange adjustment and reports the entire FV unrealized gains/losses in OCI. Another difference between IFRS and U.S. GAAP relates to conventional loans and receivables. IFRS allows firms to include these financial assets in the AFS category if FV is determinable, and the related unrealized gains/losses are reported in OCI. U.S. GAAP does not permit conventional loans and receivables to be classified as AFS (see Chapter 8 for measurement and reporting of these items under U.S. GAAP).

EXHIBIT 16.13 U.S. GAAP vs. IFRS

Classification, Measurement, and Reporting of Financial Assets

Panel (a):

Classification		Assets Included		Measurement Basis and Where Unrealized Gains and Losses Are Reported	
U.S. GAAP	IFRS	U.S. GAAP	IFRS	U.S. GAAP	IFRS
Trading		Debt and marketable equity assets (no significant influence) intended to be traded		Fair value (FV) with unrealized holding gains/losses reported in income	
Available for sale (AFS)		Debt and marketable equity assets (no significant influence) not classified as trading or HTM		Fair value with unrealized holding gains/losses reported in OCI	
		Nonmarketable equity securities (no significant influence) are **not permitted** to be classified as AFS (Shown in Other assets section of balance sheet)	Nonmarketable equity securities (no significant influence) can be alternatively classified here if fair value is determinable. Otherwise, see other assets.	Generally measured at cost	Fair value with unrealized holding gains/losses reported in OCI
			Financial assets with foreign exchange components	Fair value with unrealized holding gains/losses reported in OCI	Fair value with unrealized holding gains/losses due to foreign exchange separately reported in income and the remaining unrealized holding gains/losses reported in OCI
		Conventional loans and receivables are **not** permitted to be classified as AFS	Conventional loans and receivables can be alternatively classified here as AFS. Otherwise, see loans/receivables (Chapter 8).	See Chapter 8.	Fair value with unrealized gains/losses reported in OCI
Held to maturity (HTM)		Debt assets intended to be held to maturity		Amortized cost using the effective interest method	
Equity-method investment		Equity assets with significant influence (> 20%) but not control (< 50%)		These assets are measured at cost and adjusted thereafter with the investor's share of post-acquisition earnings (equity method).	
				No fair value option	Firms can elect FV option

(continued)

EXHIBIT 16.13   **U.S. GAAP vs. IFRS** (continued)

Summary of Impairment Determination, Measurement, Reporting and Reversal

Panel (b):

Category	Impairment Determination		Impairment Measurement		Impairment Reporting		Impairment Reversal	
	U.S. GAAP	IFRS	U.S. GAAP	IFRS	U.S. GAAP	IFRS	U.S. GAAP	IFRS
AFS—debt	If fair value is less than the amortized cost basis and other-than-temporary impairment	If objective evidence of impairment	Amortized cost basis less fair value		Income for impairment due to credit losses	Income	Not permitted	Permitted in income if the reversal can be objectively related to an event occurring after the impairment was recognized
					OCI for impairment due to other factors	Income	OCI	
AFS—equity	If fair value is less than the cost basis and other-than-temporary impairment	If objective evidence of impairment	Cost basis less fair value		Income		Not permitted	
HTM—debt	If fair value is less than the amortized cost basis and other-than-temporary impairment	If objective evidence of impairment	Amortized cost basis less fair value	Amortized cost basis less the present value of estimated future cash flows discounted at the original effective interest rate	Income for impairment due to credit losses	Income	Not permitted	Permitted in income if the reversal can be objectively related to an event occurring after the impairment was recognized

Source: Adapted from the Ernst & Young Academic Resource Center, Financial Assets—lecture notes with permission of the Ernst & Young Foundation. Copyright 2010. All rights reserved.

When firms transition to *IFRS 9,* they will classify financial instruments based on both the entity's business model for managing the financial instruments and the contractual cash flow characteristics of the financial instruments. *IFRS 9* can lead to similar treatment to U.S. GAAP for financial assets. However, financial assets will default into one of two categories: (1) a financial asset to be measured at amortized cost or (2) a financial asset to be measured at fair value through profit or loss (i.e., net income). Conceptually, (1) is similar to the U.S. GAAP held-to-maturity category (See appendix to this chapter.) because *IFRS 9* allows this designation only if the business plans to hold the assets to collect contractual cash flows and the financial asset contractually provides principal and interest payments on regularly timed specified dates. All other assets that do not meet the criteria for (1) will default to (2), that is, measurement at fair value through profit or loss. Conceptually, (2) is similar to the U.S. GAAP trading security category. *IFRS 9* will provide an option to classify financial investments in the equity of other companies as instruments "not held for trading." If firms utilize this irrevocable election for specific investments, the fair value changes in the investments will flow to other comprehensive income instead of to net income. Conceptually, this option is similar to the U.S. GAAP available-for-sale security category.

Like U.S. GAAP, IFRS equity-method investments (equity ownership greater than 20%, but less than 50%) are initially reported at cost with subsequent adjustment for the investor's share of investee profits/losses reported in income (see discussion earlier in chapter). However, unlike U.S. GAAP, IFRS does not allow firms to use the fair value option for equity-method investments. The IASB plans to revisit its guidance for the equity method. The board notes that this method "is often criticised (because some constituents) question whether it provides helpful information to users, while others note the complexities and inconsistencies it creates when it interacts with other requirements in IFRS."

Panel (b) of Exhibit 16.13 summarizes key differences between IFRS and U.S. GAAP for impairment of financial assets. IFRS reports all impairment losses for AFS-debt securities in income regardless of the reason. If impairment is due to credit losses (e.g., issuing company becoming insolvent), U.S. GAAP reports the losses in income. Impairment losses due to other factors (e.g., markets for mortgage-backed securities collapsing) are reported in OCI. For AFS debt securities, IFRS allows reversal of impairment losses through income if the reversal can be tied to an event occurring after the impairment was recognized.[19] U.S. GAAP does not allow reversal of impairment losses due to credit losses, but increases in fair value on debt securities impaired for non-credit loss reasons are recorded in OCI as part of the normal fair value adjustment process described earlier in the chapter. Impairments of AFS equity securities are treated similarly under IFRS and U.S. GAAP.

For held-to-maturity debt securities, the measurement of impairment loss is somewhat different under the two sets of standards. U.S. GAAP measures the impairment loss as the difference between the amortized cost basis and the fair value of the security. IFRS compares the amortized cost to the present value of estimated future cash flows discounted at the original effective interest rate. Reversal of impairment losses through income is permitted under IFRS if the reversal can be tied to an event occurring after the impairment was recognized. U.S. GAAP does not permit firms to recognize reversal of impairment losses on HTM debt securities.

As of summer 2013, the IASB was redeliberating its March 2013 Exposure Draft that proposed to require firms to recognize immediately expected credit losses on financial assets. The Exposure Draft's objective was to provide financial statement users with more useful and

---

[19] The amount of reversal through income is limited to the amount of the original impairment loss.

timely information about potential credit losses on firms' financial assets. The proposal suggested that firms should have to report, each period, changes in the values of financial assets that are associated with changes in the credit quality of agents that determine the economics of the financial assets (e.g., loan borrowers). Currently, credit losses are not typically recognized until actual default has occurred on a financial asset.

Consolidated Financial Statements and Accounting for Business Combinations

For annual reporting periods beginning prior to January 1, 2014, IFRS guidance on accounting for business combinations and preparation of consolidated financial statements appears in *IAS 27 (amended),* "Consolidated and Separate Financial Statements"; *Standards Interpretations Committee (SIC) 12,* "Consolidation—Special Purpose Entities"; and *IAS 31,* "Interests in Joint Ventures." For annual reporting periods beginning after January 1, 2014, IFRS guidance will follow *IFRS 10,* "Consolidated Financial Statements," which was issued in May 2011. *IFRS 10* incorporates all the sources of guidance for consolidation into one standard, provides a revised definition of control so that a single control model can be applied to all entities, and enhances disclosures about consolidated and unconsolidated entities.

Generally, IFRS and U.S. GAAP are fairly well converged with respect to when consolidation is deemed necessary and the approach for measuring the subsidiary assets and liabilities on the consolidated balance sheet. However, there are a few areas of substantive difference.

IFRS and U.S. GAAP require a firm to consolidate entities it controls. IFRS defines control more broadly than does U.S. GAAP. Under IFRS, a firm is deemed to control another entity when it has the power to govern the financial and operating policies of that entity so it can obtain benefits from that entity's activities. For situations not involving special purpose entities (SPEs) or variable interest entities (VIEs), a firm is presumed to have control if it owns, directly or indirectly, more than 50% of the outstanding voting stock, which is the primary criteria used under U.S. GAAP for preparing consolidated financial statements. However, *IAS 27* requires a firm to assess the substance of its relationship with an investee, and if control is deemed to be exercised in the absence of majority ownership, then consolidation is still required. Thus, because the IFRS definition of control is much broader than that used in U.S. GAAP, it is possible to reach different conclusions regarding the need to consolidate.[20]

Under U.S. GAAP, a parent and a subsidiary are permitted to have different accounting policies. This is most likely to occur when the subsidiary is following some specialized industry guidance. However, under IFRS the accounting policies of the subsidiary must conform to those used by the parent. When differences exist, adjustments must be made in consolidation to conform the subsidiary's accounting policies to those of the parent.

Both U.S. GAAP and IFRS generally classify noncontrolling interest on the balance sheet in the stockholders' equity section shown separate from the equity of the parent. On the income statement, noncontrolling interest is shown as a deduction from total entity (parent + 100% subsidiary) consolidated earnings. Under U.S. GAAP and the acquisition method (described earlier in the chapter), the noncontrolling interest is measured at the full business fair value of the subsidiary at time of acquisition. This means that noncontrolling interest includes

---

[20] *IFRS 10* offers an exception to consolidation for specified investment entities. By definition, an investment entity (a) obtains funds from one or more investors for the purpose of providing investment management services; (b) has a business purpose focused entirely on investing funds for returns from capital appreciation and/or investment income; and (3) measures and evaluates the performance of substantially all of its investments on a fair value basis. *IFRS 10* states that an investment entity will measure an investment in a subsidiary at fair value through profit or loss (i.e., net income) in accordance with *IFRS 9* instead of consolidating the subsidiary.

the fair value of all reported subsidiary net assets and the relevant portion of any goodwill arising from the transaction. Under IFRS, firms can exercise a choice in initially measuring noncontrolling interest. One approach is to use the full business fair value as used in U.S. GAAP, which means that noncontrolling interest includes a portion of total goodwill that is recognized at date of acquisition. Alternatively, firms can elect to measure noncontrolling interest at the fair value of the *identifiable* net assets (i.e., those reported by the subsidiary) at the acquisition date, which excludes goodwill from the measurement of noncontrolling interest.

Accounting for Special Purpose Entities (SPEs) or Variable Interest Entities (VIEs)

Legal entities created to accomplish a narrow and well-defined objective (e.g., to effect a lease, research and development activities, or a securitization of financial assets) are referred to in IFRS as special purpose entities (SPE). U.S. GAAP refers to these entities as variable interest entities (VIE). These entities may take the form of a corporation, trust, partnership, or unincorporated entity. The primary accounting issue is determining when a reporting company must consolidate the activities of the SPE or VIE. As noted earlier in the chapter, U.S. GAAP requires the "primary beneficiary" to consolidate the activities of the VIE. A company is deemed to be the primary beneficiary if it has (1) the power to direct the economic activities that most significantly impact the VIE and (2) the obligation to absorb losses or the right to receive benefits considered potentially significant to the VIE.

Under IFRS, SPEs are consolidated when evidence indicates the reporting company "controls" the SPE. Under *SIC 12,* control is presumed if *any* of the following conditions exist:

- The SPE performs activities on behalf of the reporting company.
- The reporting company has decision-making powers over the activities of the SPE.
- The reporting company has the right to obtain the majority of the benefits of the SPE activities.
- The reporting company retains the majority of the residual or ownership risks related to the SPE or its assets.

When implemented, *IFRS 10* will consider that control has been established when the firm has (a) power over the investee; (b) exposure, or rights, to variable returns from its involvement with the investee; and (c) the ability to use its power over the investee to affect the amount of the firm's returns.

Because the criteria are different, the decision as to whether to consolidate the activities of a SPE or VIE can sometimes differ under IFRS vs. U.S. GAAP.

Accounting for Joint Ventures

IFRS accounting for joint ventures is set forth in *IFRS 11,* "Joint Arrangements." It states that a joint venturer shall recognize its interest in a joint venture as an investment using the equity method in accordance with *IAS 28,* "Investments in Associates and Joint Ventures," unless there is an exemption specified in that standard. This is generally similar to U.S. GAAP.

FASB Exposure Draft on Financial Instruments

As an outgrowth of joint deliberations with the IASB, the FASB recently issued an Exposure Draft of a proposed accounting standards update on accounting for financial instruments that has similarities to *IFRS 9*.[21] If adopted, this proposal would substantially change the accounting for financial assets to be more similar to *IFRS 9* in a number of ways, but with some key differences. This section outlines the key changes that are being proposed related to the accounting for financial assets.

The global financial crisis in 2007–2008 highlighted the ongoing concern that the existing accounting model for financial instruments is inadequate and often inconsistent in measuring seemingly similar instruments. For example, under existing U.S. GAAP, some debt instrument investments are measured at amortized cost (loans held for investment or held-to-maturity debt securities), some at lower of cost or market (loans held for sale), and some at fair value (debt securities held in trading portfolio). Moreover, impairments of financial assets are measured and reported differently depending on the category and instrument type. Investors, preparers, and high-level governmental bodies throughout the world urged the IASB and FASB to develop a single converged financial reporting model for financial instruments that would eliminate some of these inconsistent treatments and provide investors and regulators with relevant and transparent information about an entity's exposure to financial instruments. The main objective of the proposed standard is to provide financial statement users with a more timely and representative depiction of an entity's involvement with financial instruments, while removing some of the complexities that currently exist in accounting for these instruments.

Exhibit 16.14 summarizes the key differences between existing GAAP and what is being proposed in the FASB Exposure Draft as it relates to financial asset topics covered in this chapter. The proposal eliminates the current classifications of trading, available for sale, and held to maturity and replaces them with three classifications that describe the measurement basis and where the related fair value changes will be reported: (1) fair value net income (FV–NI); (2) fair value—OCI (FV–OCI); and (3) amortized cost. Thus, under the proposal, most financial assets other than equity investments where the investor exercises significant influence would be measured at fair value. For those debt securities that the reporting entity plans to hold for collection of contractual cash flows, the proposed guidance would require a reconciliation from amortized cost to fair value on the face of the balance sheet.

In a departure from current practice, most changes in fair value of financial assets would be recorded in net income under the FASB Exposure Draft. This would include fair value changes for equity securities, certain hybrid securities, and debt instruments that can contractually be prepaid in a way that the investor would not recover substantially all of its initial investment.[22] FV–OCI treatment is limited to debt instruments with the features noted in Exhibit 16.14. The Board believes that applying a consistent measurement model (FV) for all financial instruments will improve comparability across firms and consistency in how a firm accounts for different financial instruments. By presenting both fair value and amortized cost information for debt instruments that are being held for collection of the contractual cash flows, the Board believes that statement users can more easily incorporate either or both types of information into their analyses of the firm. We believe the proposals called for in this exposure draft will overcome many of the deficiencies and inconsistencies that currently exist for the reporting of financial instruments.

---

[21] "Recognition and Measurement of Financial Assets and Financial Liabilities," Financial Instruments—Overall (Subtopic 825-10) (Norwalk, CT: FASB, February 2013). This Exposure Draft can be accessed at www.fasb.org.

[22] Recall that *IFRS 9* provides an option to designate irrevocably an equity investment as FV-OCI. The FASB's proposed guidance would require, instead, that all equity investments be classified and measured as FV-NI, with a practicability exception only. This is a material difference across standards, which means these standards are not likely to be converged when implemented.

EXHIBIT 16.14 Summary of Proposed Changes in FASB Exposure Draft on Financial Instruments

Financial Asset Topics Covered in this Chapter

Accounting Issue	Current Approach	Proposed Approach in ED
Classification and measurement	Classification is based on entity's trading strategy Trading—Fair value with changes to income (FV-NI) Available for sale (AFS)—Fair value with changes to OCI (FV-OCI) Held to maturity (HTM)—Amortized cost	Three classification and measurement bases for *most* financial assets: • Fair value with changes to income (FV-NI) • Fair value with changes to OCI (FV-OCI) • Amortized cost
FV-NI items	Equity and certain debt securities based on entity's trading strategy (see above)	All *equity* securities, certain hybrid instruments, and financial instruments that can be contractually prepaid in such a way that the holder (investor) would not recover substantially all of its investment
FV-OCI items	Equity and certain debt securities based on entity's trading strategy (see above)	Primarily debt securities to be held until the end of the contract term
Amortized cost items	Certain debt securities expected to be held to maturity	Held-to-collect contractual cash flows where the contractual terms of the financial asset give rise on specified dates to cash flows that are solely payments of principal and interest
Unconsolidated equity investments with significant influence	Equity method with fair value option	If an investment is determined to be held for sale, it would be classified and measured at FV-NI. If not held for sale, it would be accounted for under Topic 323 (Investments—Equity Method and Joint Ventures)
Presentation	For many instruments, amortized cost reported on balance sheet and fair value reported in notes	Generally, both fair value and amortized cost (where applicable) values will be presented on the balance sheet for each investment
Impairment	Different impairment rules depending on the category and instrument type	Single impairment model. Only for FV–OCI instruments.
Reclassifications	Allowed but generally at fair value	Allowed only when the business model changes, which is expected to occur very infrequently

- Financial reporting for intercorporate equity investments depends on the degree to which the investor is able to influence the investee's operating decisions. Proportionate share size is a presumptive factor in assessing an investor's influence over an investee.

- When the ownership share is less than 20%, it is presumed that the investor cannot exert significant influence on the investee's decisions. These *minority passive investments* are shown at fair value on the balance sheet. Unrealized gains or losses on the trading portfolio are recorded on the income statement, and unrealized gains and losses on the available-for-sale portfolio are recorded as a component of other comprehensive income (OCI), which is closed out to a special stockholders' equity account, Accumulated other comprehensive income (AOCI).

- Other than temporary impairments of available-for-sale equity securities are recorded as an adjustment to net income.

- *Minority active investments* generally involve between 20% and 50% ownership and give the investor the ability to influence the investee's operating decisions significantly. The equity method is used to account for such investments whereby the investor records its proportionate share of the investee's profits and losses, net of any excess cost amortization, with a corresponding adjustment to the investment account.

- GAAP allows firms to elect the fair value option for equity investments. Unrealized gains and losses resulting from fair value changes are reported on the investor's income statement.

- Consolidated financial statements are required when one entity (parent) gains a controlling financial interest (more than 50% interest in voting common stock) in another entity (subsidiary). Prior to July 1, 2001, the purchase and pooling-of-interests methods were used to account for business combinations. From that date through 2008, only the purchase method was allowed. Beginning in 2009, the acquisition method must be used to account for all business combinations. The key differences between these three methods are: (1) how to measure the subsidiary's net assets (assets minus liabilities) at the acquisition date, (2) the amount of goodwill recognized, and (3) how the noncontrolling (minority) interests are measured and reported on the consolidated balance sheet.

- Goodwill is typically recorded in business combinations accounted for under the acquisition and purchase methods. Goodwill is subject to an annual impairment test. If goodwill is determined to be impaired, it is written down with an offsetting charge to consolidated earnings.

- The acquisition and purchase methods of accounting complicate financial analysis because none of the subsidiary's profit is included in consolidated earnings in the years prior to acquisition, a partial year's profit is included from the date of acquisition through the end of the year in the acquisition year, and 100% of the subsidiary's profits are included in the years following the year of acquisition. This approach distorts year-to-year growth rates in sales and profits.

- Enron's collapse brought about a demand for increased disclosure and transparency regarding companies' interests in *variable interest entities (VIE)*. A VIE is a corporation, partnership, trust, or any other legal structure used for business purposes that either (1) does not have equity investors with voting rights or (2) has equity investors that do not provide sufficient financial resources for the entity to support its own activities. GAAP requires a company to consolidate a VIE if that company has the power to direct the significant economic activities of the VIE and is subject to a risk of loss from the VIE's activities or is entitled to receive the benefits of the VIE that are potentially significant gains or losses to the VIE. A company that consolidates a VIE is called that entity's *primary beneficiary.*

- Before foreign subsidiaries can be consolidated, foreign currency amounts to be remeasured in U.S. dollars.

- Foreign subsidiaries that are mere extensions of the U.S. parent and have no self-sufficiency are remeasured using the *temporal method.* The temporal method treats the subsidiaries' business transactions as if they had been undertaken by the parent—but in the foreign currency.

- Foreign subsidiaries that are freestanding economic units are remeasured using the *current rate method.* This method provides an easy way to re-express foreign currency amounts in dollars while maintaining the proportionality of most of the subsidiary's financial ratios.

- There are a number of important differences between IFRS and U.S. GAAP: (1) measurement and reporting of financial assets; (2) how noncontrolling interests are measured on consolidated statements; (3) determining when SPEs or VIEs must be consolidated; and (4) accounting treatment for joint ventures.

APPENDIX

ACCOUNTING FOR INVESTMENTS IN DEBT SECURITIES

We saw in this chapter that investments in equity securities are classified as either trading securities or available-for-sale securities, depending on the purpose of the investment. Those same classifications are available for debt securities, as well, in addition to a third classification called *held to maturity.* Debt securities may be classified as held to maturity if the investor company has both the ability and the intent to hold the security until its maturity date. The held-to-maturity classification is not available for equity investments because those investments have no maturity date.

Held-to-Maturity Securities

Debt securities (e.g., bonds and notes) that a firm intends to hold to maturity are generally accounted for at amortized cost.[23] Interest income is recognized following the effective interest method (see Chapter 11), and the investment account is adjusted for the amortization of premium or discount in each period. No adjustments are made for changes in the fair value of debt securities in the held-to-maturity portfolio.

We illustrate the accounting for held-to-maturity debt investments with the following example. Assume that Principal Financial purchases a five-year $100,000 bond from Baker Company with a 7% coupon interest rate for $108,659 on January 1, 2014. The effective yield on this bond investment is 5%, meaning the discount rate that equates the $108,659 purchase price with the present value of the promised cash flows is 5%. The bond matures on December 31, 2018, and a $7,000 coupon payment is due at the end of each year. The following amortization table reflects interest income, amortization of bond premium, and amortized cost of the bond at each year-end. The table also shows the bond's fair value at each balance sheet

---

[23] FASB ASC Section 320-10-35: Investments—Debt and Equity Securities—Overall—Subsequent Measurement.

date. This information will be relevant when we extend the example to available-for-sale securities and trading securities.

Year-End	Interest	Premium Amortization	Amortized Cost	Fair Value
Jan. 1	—	—	$108,659	$108,659
2014	$5,433	$(1,567)	107,092	107,500
2015	5,355	(1,645)	105,447	105,000
2016	5,272	(1,728)	103,719	103,000
2017	5,186	(1,814)	101,905	102,000
2018	5,095	(1,905)	100,000*	100,000

* Before payment of principal on December 31, 2018.

The following entry would be made on January 1, 2014, to record the acquisition of the bond.

DR Investment in Bonds	$108,659	
CR Cash		$108,659

Principal makes the following entry on December 31, 2014, to record interest income and amortization of the bond premium.

DR Cash	$7,000*	
CR Interest Income		$5,433†
CR Investment in Bonds		1,567‡

* $100,000 × 7%
† $108,659 × 5%
‡ $7,000 − $5,433

Although, in general, held-to-maturity investments are accounted for at amortized cost, they are considered financial instruments, so firms may *elect* to use fair value accounting under the fair value option set forth in ASC 825-10-25 (Financial Instruemts—Overall—Recognition).

Available-for-Sale Securities

Investments in debt securities classified as available for sale are presented in the balance sheet at fair value, requiring an adjustment at each balance sheet date, much like there is an adjustment for equity securities. However, for debt securities, the investor applies the effective interest method just as it would for a held-to-maturity investment, and adjusts the amortized cost at each balance sheet date to the fair value. The adjustment is reported as part of other comprehensive income.

For example, suppose Principal Financial had classified its investment in the 7% Baker Company bonds as available for sale. It would have made the exact same entries in 2014—initially recording the investment at cost and then recording $5,433 of interest income, resulting in the amortization of $1,567 of bond premium. At December 31, 2014, the amortized cost of the bonds was $107,092, and that amount was reported as an asset on the balance sheet in the original example. The bonds had a fair value on that date of $107,500, so Principal makes an *additional* entry in order to present the bonds at fair value:

DR	Fair Value Adjustment—Available-for-Sale Securities	$408
CR	OCI—Unrealized gain or loss in fair value of available-for-sale securities.	$408

Note that although the bonds fell in value by $1,159 during 2014, the amortization of premium under the effective interest method ($1,567) reduced the book value of the bonds to $107,092, so an upward fair value adjustment of $408 is required to present the bonds at fair value on the balance sheet.

In subsequent periods, Principal Financial continues to account for the bonds under the effective interest method using the original amortization table. That is, it does not redo the amortization schedule based on the fair value at December 31, 2014. So, the interest income pattern in the income statements for the entire five-year life of the bonds will be identical to the interest income pattern under the held-to-maturity classification. In 2015, Principal would make the following entry to record the interest income under the effective interest method:

DR	Cash	$7,000
CR	Interest Income	$5,355
CR	Investment in Bonds	1,645

The above entry adjusts the Investment in bonds account to its amortized cost of $105,447 at December 31, 2015. The fair value on that date is $105,000, indicating that the balance in the Fair value adjustment account at December 31, 2015 needs to be a *credit* of $447. Because the account currently has a *debit* balance of $408, Principal Financial makes the following fair value adjustment entry at December 31, 2015:

DR	OCI—Unrealized gain or loss in fair value of available-for-sale securities	$855
CR	Fair Value Adjustment— Available-for-Sale Securities	$855

The result of this entry is that the Fair value adjustment account has a credit balance of $447 and the Investment in bonds is reported on the balance sheet, net of the Fair value adjustment, as $105,000 ($105,447 – $447).

When an available-for-sale investment is ultimately sold, the full amount of the gain or loss is recognized in the income statement and the related amount in Accumulated other comprehensive income is "recycled." For example, if at the end of 2015 Principal sold its Baker bonds for $105,000, it would have made the following entry, assuming it had already recorded the receipt of the interest payment at December 31, 2015, and the premium amortization and fair value adjustment for 2015:

DR	Cash	$105,000
DR	Fair Value Adjustment— Available-for-Sale Securities	447
DR	Loss on sale of bonds	447
CR	Investment in Bonds	$105,447
CR	OCI—Unrealized gain or loss in fair value of available-for-sale securities	447

This entry eliminates the Accumulated other comprehensive income balance, removes the bonds from the balance sheet, along with the associated fair value adjustment, and recognizes the entire holding period loss in the 2015 income statement.

Trading Securities

The accounting for trading securities is similar to available-for-sale securities, except that fair value adjustments are recognized in income rather than in OCI. Had Principal Financial classified the bonds as trading securities, there would have been a $408 gain reported in the income statement in 2014 and an $855 loss in 2015. Because gains and losses are recorded in the income statement each period as the bond's value fluctuates, there is no additional gain or loss recognized on the sale. Only the change in value during 2015 is recognized in 2015.

Other-Than-Temporary Impairments

In the chapter we saw that available-for-sale equity securities might incur an other-than-temporary impairment, in which case the investment is written down and an impairment charge is taken on the income statement. Other-than-temporary impairments can also occur with available-for-sale and held-to-maturity debt securities. Other-than-temporary impairments are not an issue for debt instruments classified as trading securities because these are already marked to fair value through the income statement.

For available-for-sale *debt securities,* if a firm intends to sell the security or it is more likely than not that the firm will be required to sell the security before recovery of its amortized cost basis less current-period credit loss, then the amount of impairment is recognized in earnings equal to the entire difference between the investment's amortized cost basis and its fair value at the balance sheet date. If a firm does not intend to sell the security and it is unlikely that the firm will be required to sell the security before recovery of its amortized cost basis less any current-period credit loss, then the other-than-temporary impairment is separated into the following two components:[24]

> Credit loss is the difference between the amortized cost basis of a debt security and the present value of expected cash flows for that security discounted at the effective interest rate implicit in the debt instrument when it was originally acquired.

a. The amount representing the credit loss
b. The amount related to all other factors

The portion of the impairment related to the credit loss is recognized in earnings. The portion of the impairment related to other factors is recognized in other comprehensive income. The previous amortized cost basis less the other-than-temporary impairment recognized in earnings becomes the new amortized cost basis of the investment. The new amortized cost basis is not adjusted for subsequent recoveries in fair value. However, the new amortized cost basis is adjusted for accretion and amortization as described in the following paragraph (see FASB ASC Paragraph 320-10-35-35).

Subsequent to the recognition of an impairment loss on debt securities, a firm continues to estimate the present value of cash flows expected to be collected over the life of the debt security. For debt securities for which the impairment was recognized in earnings (i.e., credit loss), the difference between the new amortized cost basis and the cash flows expected to be collected are recognized in earnings as interest income using effective interest amortization (see Chapter 11). For debt securities for which the impairment loss is due to other factors (i.e., not credit loss) subsequent increases and decreases (if not an other-than-temporary impairment) in the fair value of these available-for-sale securities are included in other comprehensive income.

---

[24] FASB ASC Paragraphs 320-10-35-35-34A to 35-34E: Investments—Debt and Equity Securities—Overall—Subsequent Measurement—Debt Securities: Determination of the Amount of Other-than-Temporary Impairment Recognized in Earnings and Other Comprehensive Income.

EXERCISES

The following data pertain to Tyne Company's investments in marketable equity securities. (Assume that all securities were held throughout 2014 and 2015.)

		Fair Value	
	Cost	12/31/15	12/31/14
Trading	$150,000	$155,000	$100,000
Available for sale	150,000	130,000	120,000

Required:

1. What amount should Tyne report as unrealized holding gain (loss) in its 2015 income statement?

2. What amount should Tyne report as net unrealized gain (loss) on available-for-sale securities at December 31, 2015, in its statement of stockholders' equity? Ignore tax effects.

During 2014, Rex Company purchased marketable equity securities as a short-term investment. These securities are classified as available for sale. The cost and fair values at December 31, 2014, follow:

Security	Cost	Fair Value
Company A—100 shares	$ 2,800	$ 3,400
Company B—1,000 shares	17,000	15,300
Company C—2,000 shares	31,500	29,500
	$51,300	$48,200

Rex sold 1,000 shares of Company B stock on January 31, 2015, for $15 per share, incurring $1,500 in brokerage commission and transaction taxes.

Required:

1. Ignoring income taxes, how much should Rex report as unrealized gain or loss on its available-for-sale securities at December 31, 2014, in the statement of stockholders' equity?

2. On the sale, Rex should report a realized loss of how much?

Information related to Jones Company's portfolio of trading securities at December 31, 2014, follows:

Aggregate cost of securities	$340,000
Gross unrealized gains	8,000
Gross unrealized losses	52,000

Jones reported a $10,000 credit balance in its Fair value adjustment—Trading securities account in its December 31, 2013 (prior year), balance sheet. Assume that it sold no trading securities during 2013 or 2014.

Required:

1. How much should Jones report as unrealized gain or loss on its 2014 income statement?

2. Prepare the journal entry that Jones would make to record the 2014 fair value adjustment to its trading portfolio.

In January 2014, Harold Corporation acquired 20% of Otis Company's outstanding common stock for $400,000. This investment gave Harold the ability to exercise significant influence over Otis. The book value of these shares was $300,000. The excess of cost over book value was attributed to an identifiable intangible asset, a patent, which was undervalued on Otis's balance sheet and had a remaining 10-year useful life.

For the year ended December 31, 2014, Otis reported net income of $90,000 and paid cash dividends of $20,000 on its common stock.

Required:

1. How much would Harold Corporation's income increase in 2014 as a result of its investment in Otis?

2. What is the carrying value of Harold's investment in Otis Company at December 31, 2014?

E16-4

Using the equity method **(LO 1, 3)**

AICPA
ADAPTED

Sage Inc. bought 40% of Adams Corporation's outstanding common stock on January 2, 2014, for $400,000. The carrying amount of Adams's net assets at the purchase date totaled $900,000. Fair values and carrying amounts were the same for all items except for plant and inventory, for which fair values exceeded the carrying amounts by $90,000 and $10,000, respectively. The plant has an 18-year life. All inventory was sold during 2014. During 2014, Adams reported $120,000 net income and paid a $20,000 cash dividend.

Required:

1. What amount should Sage report in its income statement from its investment in Adams for the year ended December 31, 2014?

2. What is the December 31, 2014, balance in the Investment in Adams account?

3. Assume that on January 2, 2014, when Sage acquired a 40% interest in Adams, it elected to account for this investment at fair value. If the fair value of Sage's investment in Adams is $470,000 on December 31, 2014, what amount should Sage report in its 2014 income statement for this investment under the fair value option?

E16-5

Using the equity method and fair value option **(LO 1, 3)**

AICPA
ADAPTED

Papa John's International, Inc., operates and franchises pizza delivery and carryout restaurants in domestic and global markets. In its December 30, 2012, 10-K filing with the SEC, Papa John's discloses the following relationship with a variable interest entity (VIE):

> Through February 2011, we had a purchasing arrangement with BIBP, a special-purpose entity formed at the direction of our Franchise Advisory Council, for the sole purpose of reducing cheese price volatility to domestic system-wide restaurants. BIBP was an independent, franchisee-owned corporation. BIBP purchased cheese at the market price and sold it to our distribution subsidiary, PJ Food Service, Inc. ("PJFS"), at a fixed price. PJFS in turn sold cheese to Papa John's restaurants (both Company-owned and franchised) at a set price. PJFS purchased $25.1 million of cheese for the three months ended March 27, 2011, and $153.0 million of cheese during 2010 from BIBP.

Required:

1. Discuss the primary business rationale for Papa John's purchasing arrangement with BIBP.

2. What criteria did Papa John's use to determine if it should consolidate BIBP in its financial statements?

3. Assuming that Papa John's consolidated BIBP, how were the intra-entity sales described above accounted for in the consolidation process?

E16-6

Determining business rationale and whether to consolidate a VIE; Intra-entity sales **(LO 4, 7)**

E16-7

Determining the value of goodwill   (LO 4, 5)

On April 30, 2014, Pound Corp. purchased for cash all 200,000 shares of the outstanding common stock of Shake Corp. for $20 per share. At April 30, 2014, Shake's balance sheet showed net assets with a $3,000,000 book value. On that date, the fair value of Shake's property, plant, and equipment exceeded book value by $300,000.

Required:

What amount should Pound report as goodwill on its April 30, 2014, consolidated balance sheet?

E16-8

Goodwill—acquisition method   (LO 4, 5)

AICPA
ADAPTED

On April 1, 2014, Dart Company paid $620,000 for all issued and outstanding common stock of Wall Corporation in a transaction properly accounted for under the acquisition method. Wall's recorded assets and liabilities on April 1, 2014, follow:

Cash	$ 60,000
Inventory	180,000
Property and equipment (net of accumulated depreciation of $220,000)	320,000
Goodwill (net of accumulated write-downs of $50,000)	100,000
Liabilities	(120,000)
Net assets	$540,000

On April 1, 2014, Wall's inventory had a $150,000 fair value, and its property and equipment (net) had a $380,000 fair value.

Required:

What is the amount of goodwill resulting from the business combination?

E16-9

Preparing consolidated financial statements   (LO 4)

AICPA
ADAPTED

On January 1, 2014, Pitt Company purchased an 80% investment in Saxe Company. The acquisition cost was equal to Pitt's equity in Saxe's recorded net assets at that date. On January 1, 2014, Pitt and Saxe had retained earnings of $500,000 and $100,000, respectively. During 2014, Pitt had net income of $200,000, which included its equity in Saxe's earnings, and declared dividends of $50,000. Saxe had net income of $40,000 and declared dividends of $20,000. No other intra-entity transactions between the parent and subsidiary occurred.

Required:

What should the consolidated retained earnings be on December 31, 2014?

E16-10

Determining consolidated retained earnings   (LO 4)

On January 1, 2014, Pack Corp. purchased all of Slam Corp.'s common stock for $500,000. On that date, the fair values of Slam's net assets equaled their book values of $400,000. During 2014, Slam paid cash dividends of $8,000. The following balance sheet and income statement accounts are reported on Pack and Slam's separate financial statements at December 31, 2014:

	Pack	Slam
Balance sheet accounts		
Investment in Slam	$552,000	$ 0
Retained earnings	780,000	250,000
Income statement accounts		
Equity in earnings of Slam	60,000	0
Net income	150,000	60,000

Required:

What amount of retained earnings will Pack report in its December 31, 2014, consolidated balance sheet?

Sea Company purchased 60% of Island Company's common stock for $180,000. On the acquisition date, Island's book value of net assets totaled $250,000 and the fair value of identifiable net assets totaled $275,000. The $25,000 excess of fair value over book value on the acquisition date is attributable to fixed assets. Sea appropriately uses the acquisition method to account for the business combination.

Immediately after acquisition, Sea Company's and Island Company's separate condensed balance sheets are as follows:

	Sea Company	Island Company
Other assets	$750,000	$320,000
Investment in Island Company	180,000	0
	$930,000	$320,000
Liabilities	$250,000	$ 70,000
Common stock	450,000	200,000
Retained earnings	230,000	50,000
	$930,000	$320,000

Required:

1. What is the dollar amount of the total assets in the consolidated balance sheet immediately after the acquisition?

2. What is the dollar amount of the noncontrolling interest in the consolidated balance sheet immediately after the acquisition? Assume that the noncontrolling interest fair value is imputed based on Sea's acquisition price.

E16-11

Consolidated balances using the acquisition method
(LO 4)

mhhe.com/revsine6e

On September 1, 2014, Cano & Company, a U.S. corporation, sold merchandise to a foreign firm for 250,000 euros. Terms of the sale require payment in euros on February 1, 2015. On September 1, 2014, the spot exchange rate was $1.30 per euro. At Cano's year-end on December 31, 2014, the spot rate was $1.28, but the rate increased to $1.33 by February 1, 2015, when payment was received.

Required:

1. What foreign currency transaction gain or loss should be recorded in 2014?

2. What foreign currency transaction gain or loss should be recorded in 2015?

E16-12

Recording transaction foreign exchange gain/loss **(LO 8)**

AICPA
ADAPTED

Stone has provided the following information on its available-for-sale securities:

Aggregate cost as of 12/31/14	$170,000
Unrealized gain as of 12/31/14	4,000
Unrealized losses as of 12/31/14	26,000
Net realized gains during 2014	30,000

Stone reported $1,500 in the contra-asset valuation account to reduce these securities to their fair value at December 31, 2013.

Required:

What amount should be debited as an unrealized loss to the stockholders' equity section of Stone's December 31, 2014, balance sheet as a result of 2014 fair value changes related to its available-for-sale securities? (Ignore taxes.)

E16-13

Accounting for available-for-sale securities
(LO 2)

AICPA
ADAPTED

E16-14

Fair value accounting for
trading securities   **(LO 2)**

Founded on January 1, 2014, Gehl Company had the following short-term investments in securities at the end of 2014 and 2015 (all were held in the "trading" portfolio):

Equity Security	Cost	2015 Fair Value
A	$ 96,000	$ 94,000
B	184,000	162,000
C	126,000	136,000

Required:

If the company recorded a $4,000 debit to its Fair value adjustment—Trading securities account at the end of 2015 as its fair value adjustment, what must have been the unrealized gain or loss recorded at the end of 2014?

E16-15

Eliminating intra-entity profit
(LO 4)

Pinto Inc. owns 100% of Scale Inc. The following information is from the 2014 income statements of Pinto and Scale:

	Pinto	Scale
Sales	$1,000,000	$600,000
Cost of goods sold	600,000	540,000
Gross profit	400,000	60,000
Depreciation expense	60,000	15,000
Other expenses	130,000	30,000
Income from operations	210,000	15,000
Gain on sale of equipment to Scale	16,000	0
Income before income taxes	$ 226,000	$ 15,000

Additional Information:

1. Pinto's reported sales revenue includes $200,000 of intra-entity sales to Scale. Scale sold three-fourths of this inventory to outside customers by the end of 2014. Pinto sells to Scale on terms similar those available to its outside customers.

2. Scale purchased equipment from Pinto for $60,000 on January 1, 2014. The equipment is depreciated using the straight-line method with no residual value and eight years of life remaining as of January 1, 2014.

Required:

1. How much intra-entity profit should be eliminated from Scale's inventory when preparing 2014 consolidated financial statements?

2. What amount of depreciation expense should be reported in the 2014 consolidated income statement?

E16-16

Consolidating sales and cost
of goods sold with intra-entity
transactions   **(LO 4)**

Pate Corp. owns 80% of Strange Inc.'s common stock. During 2014, Pate sold inventory to Strange for $600,000 on the same terms as sales made to outside customers. Strange sold the entire inventory purchased from Pate by the end of 2014. Pate and Strange report the following for 2014.

	Pate	Strange
Sales	$2,700,000	$1,600,000
Cost of sales	1,800,000	900,000
Gross profit	$ 900,000	$ 700,000

Required:

1. What amount should Pate report as sales revenue in its 2014 consolidated income statement?

2. What amount should Pate report as cost of sales in its 2014 consolidated income statement?

On July 1, 2014, Pushway Corporation issued 100,000 shares of common stock in exchange for all of Stroker Company's common stock. The Pushway stock issued had a market value of $500,000 on the date of the exchange. Following are the July 1, 2014, pre-acquisition balance sheets of Pushway and Stroker, plus fair value information for Stroker's assets and liabilities.

E16-17

Comparison of acquisition versus pooling method
(LO 4, 6)

mhhe.com/revsine6e

	Pushway	**Stroker**	
		Book Value	**Fair Value**
Assets			
Current assets	$300,000	$100,000	$100,000
Long-term assets	600,000	400,000	470,000
Total assets	$900,000	$500,000	$570,000
Liabilities			
Current liabilities	$200,000	$ 50,000	$ 50,000
Long-term liabilities	250,000	100,000	120,000
Total liabilities	450,000	150,000	$170,000
Stockholders' Equity			
Common stock	300,000	250,000	
Retained earnings	150,000	100,000	
Total stockholders' equity	450,000	350,000	
Total liabilities and equity	$900,000	$500,000	

Required:

1. Provide the journal entry Pushway recorded for the acquisition of Stroker, assuming Pushway used the acquisition method.

2. What amount will be shown on the July 1, 2014, consolidated balance sheet for the following:

   a. Total assets

   b. Total liabilities

   c. Total equity

3. Now assume the pooling method was used to record the acquisition. Complete requirements 1 and 2. (*Note to student:* Ignore the fact that the date in this problem would prohibit the use of the pooling method).

A wholly owned subsidiary of Ward Inc. has certain expense accounts for the year ended December 31, 2014, stated in local currency units (LCU) as follows:

E16-18

Translating foreign currency **(LO 8)**

AICPA
ADAPTED

	LCU
Depreciation of equipment (related assets were purchased January 1, 2012)	120,000
Provision for doubtful accounts	80,000
Rent	200,000

The exchange rates at various dates are as follows:

	Dollar Equivalent of LCU
12/31/14	$0.40
Average for year ended 12/31/14	0.44
1/1/12	0.50

Assume that the LCU is the subsidiary's functional currency and that the charges to the expense accounts occurred approximately evenly during the year.

Required:

What total dollar amount should be included in Ward's 2014 consolidated income statement to reflect these expenses?

E16-19

Reporting transaction foreign exchange gain/loss   **(LO 7)**

AICPA
ADAPTED

Lindy, a calendar-year U.S. corporation, bought inventory items from a supplier in Germany on November 5, 2014, for 100,000 euros, when the spot exchange rate was $1.40 per euro. At Lindy's December 31, 2014, year-end, the spot exchange rate was $1.38. On January 15, 2015, Lindy bought 100,000 euros at the spot exchange rate of $1.44 and paid the invoice.

Required:

How much foreign exchange gain or (loss) should Lindy report in its income statements for 2014 and 2015?

E16-20

Adjustments and eliminations for consolidation under acquisition method   **(LO 4)**

mhhe.com/revsine6e

On January 5, 2015, Alpha Inc. acquired 80% of the outstanding voting shares of Beta Inc. for $2,000,000 cash. Following are the separate balance sheets for the two companies immediately after the stock purchase, as well as fair value information regarding Beta Inc.:

	Alpha	Beta Book Value	Beta Fair Value
Assets			
Current assets	$1,750,000	$ 500,000	$ 500,000
Fixed assets, net	5,000,000	1,625,000	2,000,000
Investment in Beta	2,000,000	—	—
Total Assets	$8,750,000	$2,125,000	$2,500,000
Liabilities			
Current Liabilities	$ 250,000	$ 125,000	$ 125,000
Stockholders' Equity			
Common stock	7,000,000	1,500,000	
Capital in excess of par	500,000	—	
Retained earnings	1,000,000	500,000	
Total Stockholders' Equity	8,500,000	2,000,000	
Total Liabilities and Stockholders' Equity	$8,750,000	$2,125,000	

Required:

1. Prepare the entries for adjustments and eliminations required to prepare the consolidated balance sheet immediately after acquisition under the acquisition method.

2. Prepare the consolidated balance sheet immediately after acquisition.

On January 1, 2014, Chesapeake Corporation issued common stock with a fair value of $810,000 in exchange for 90% of Deardon Corporation's common stock. Following are the January 1, 2014, separate balance sheets of Chesapeake and Deardon immediately following the acquisition, plus fair value information for Deardon's assets and liabilities:

E16-21

Consolidated worksheet and balance sheet under acquisition method **(LO 4)**

mhhe.com/revsine6e

	Chesapeake	Deardon Book Value	Deardon Fair Value
Assets			
Current assets	$ 500,000	$ 400,000	$ 450,000
PP&E, net	800,000	800,000	775,000
Patent	100,000	—	75,000
Investment in Deardon	810,000	—	—
Total assets	$2,210,000	$1,200,000	$1,300,000
Liabilities			
Current liabilities	$ 400,000	$ 150,000	$ 150,000
Long-term liabilities	500,000	270,000	300,000
Total liabilities	900,000	420,000	$ 450,000
Stockholders' Equity			
Common stock	900,000	400,000	
Retained earnings	410,000	380,000	
Total stockholders' equity	1,310,000	780,000	
Total liabilities and equity	$2,210,000	$1,200,000	

Required:

1. Provide the adjustments and elimination entries needed to prepare the post-acquisition January 1, 2014, consolidated balance sheet under the acquisition method.

2. Prepare the January 1, 2014, consolidated balance sheet.

On January 1, 2014, Morrill, Inc., purchased at par value a bond issued by a German company for 5,000 euros. Morrill classifies this security in its available-for-sale (AFS) portfolio. On December 31, 2014, the fair value of the bond is 4,800 euros. The applicable exchange rates are:

E16-22

Financial asset denominated in a foreign currency **(LO 2, 9)**

- January 1, 2014: $1.30 = 1 euro
- December 31, 2014: $1.40 = 1 euro

Required:

1. Prepare the January 1, 2014, and December 31, 2014, journal entries, assuming Morrill uses U.S. GAAP to account for the bond investment. Ignore fair value adjustments for other securities in Morrill's AFS portfolio.

2. Repeat requirement 1 assuming Morrill uses IFRS.

3. Compare the effect on 2014 income and other comprehensive income (OCI) for U.S. GAAP and IFRS.

PROBLEMS / DISCUSSION QUESTIONS

P16-1

Equity method accounting
(LO 3)

On January 1, 2014, Figland Company purchased for cash 40% of Irene Company's 300,000 shares of voting common stock for $1,800,000. At the time, 40% of the book value of the underlying equity in Irene's net assets was $1,400,000; $50,000 of the excess was attributed to the excess of fair value over book value of inventory, which Irene accounts for using the first-in, first-out (FIFO) inventory method; and $150,000 was attributed to undervaluation of depreciable assets with an average remaining life of 10 years. The remainder was attributed to implicit goodwill.

As a result of this transaction, Figland can exercise significant influence over Irene's operating and financial policies. Irene's net income for the year ended December 31, 2014, was $600,000. During 2014, Irene paid $325,000 in dividends to its stockholders.

Required:

1. How much income would Figland report on its 2014 income statement for its investment in Irene?

2. What would be the balance in the Investment in Irene Company account on December 31, 2014?

P16-2

Accounting for trading
securities   **(LO 2)**

Second National Insurance Company provided this information for its trading securities portfolio:

| | | | | Fair Values | |
Security	Date	Acquisition Cost	12/31/13	12/31/14	12/31/15
Company A Common	1/15/13	$50,000	$60,000	$55,000	$58,000
Company B Common	6/30/13	30,000	25,000	13,000*	10,000
Company C Preferred	2/1/14	20,000	—	25,000	18,000
Company D Common	5/1/15	10,000	—	—	12,000

* Second National sold 50% of the Company B common shares for $14,000 on July 1, 2014. Fair values at December 31, 2014, and December 31, 2015, are for the Company B shares remaining in the trading portfolio.

Required:

1. Provide the journal entries to record the fair value adjustment on December 31, 2013. Assume that Second National uses an account entitled Fair value adjustment—trading securities to adjust the cost of the trading portfolio to year-end fair values. Show supporting calculations in good form.

2. Provide the entry to record the sale of Company B's common shares on July 1, 2014. Assume that the last fair value adjustment for these shares was on December 31, 2013.

3. Provide the journal entry and supporting calculations for the fair value adjustment on December 31, 2014.

4. Provide the journal entry and fair value adjustment on December 31, 2015.

5. What would the entry to record the sale of Company B common shares on July 1, 2014, have been if this security had been considered an available-for-sale security? Ignore tax effects.

On December 31, 2014, Pate Corporation acquired 80% of Starmont Corporation's common stock for $900,000 cash. Assume that the fair values of Starmont's identifiable assets and liabilities equaled book values on the acquisition date. Following are the December 31, 2014, separate balance sheets of Pate and Starmont immediately following the acquisition:

P16-3

Consolidated balance sheet and income statement under acquisition method **(LO 4)**

mhhe.com/revsine6e

	Pate	Starmont
Assets		
Current assets	$ 400,000	$ 300,000
Long-term assets	1,000,000	860,000
Investment in Starmont	900,000	—
Total assets	$2,300,000	$1,160,000
Liabilities		
Current liabilities	$ 300,000	$ 100,000
Long-term liabilities	900,000	170,000
Total liabilities	1,200,000	270,000
Stockholders' Equity		
Common stock	500,000	300,000
Retained earnings	600,000	590,000
Total stockholders' equity	1,100,000	890,000
Total liabilities and equity	$2,300,000	$1,160,000

The following are Pate's and Starmont's results of operations during 2015:

	Pate	Starmont
Sales revenue	$1,500,000	$1,000,000
Cost of goods sold	900,000	650,000
SG&A expenses	200,000	130,000

Additional Information:

- Included in these totals are intra-entity sales from Pate to Starmont totaling $100,000. Pate applies the same markup on sales to Starmont as to its other customers. Starmont sold all of this inventory to outside customers during 2015 for $150,000.

- There was no goodwill impairment during 2015.

- The applicable income tax rate is 35%.

Required:

1. Prepare the December 31, 2014, consolidated balance sheet under the acquisition method.

2. Prepare the consolidated income statement for the year ended December 31, 2015. Show the deduction for net income allocated to noncontrolling interest to arrive at net income—attributable to Pate shareholders.

On January 1, 2014, Newyork Capital Corporation purchased 30% of the outstanding common shares of Delta Crating Corp. for $250 million and accounts for this investment under the equity method. The following information is available regarding Delta Crating Corp.

P16-4

Equity method and fair value option **(LO 3)**

($ in millions)

Net identifiable assets at 1/1/2014 acquisition:	
Fair value	$ 700
Book value	500
2014 net income	100
2014 dividends declared and paid	30
2015 net income	80
2015 dividends declared and paid	20
12/31/2014 fair value (based on market value)	1,000
12/31/2015 fair value (based on market value)	1,200

Two-thirds of the difference between the book value and fair value of Delta's identifiable net assets at acquisition is attributable to depreciable assets having fair value greater than their book value and the remaining one-third is attributable to land having fair value in excess of its book value. The depreciable assets have an average remaining useful life of 10 years and are being depreciated by the straight-line method with zero residual value.

Required:

1. Provide the journal entries that Newyork Capital would make in 2014 and 2015 to account for its investment in Delta Crating under the equity method. Provide supporting details for all calculations needed.

2. Determine the carrying value of Newyork's Investment in Delta Crating account on December 31, 2014, and December 31, 2015, under the equity method.

3. Now assume that Newyork elected the fair value option for the equity method on the January 1, 2014, acquisition date. Repeat requirements 1 and 2.

4. Based on your answers, discuss the impact of the fair value option on Newyork's net profit margin in 2014 and 2015.

P16-5

Using acquisition versus purchase methods with goodwill **(LO 4, 5, 6)**

On January 1, 2014, Delta Inc. acquired 80% of Sigma Company's outstanding stock for $80,000 cash. Following are the balance sheets for Delta and Sigma immediately before the acquisition, as well as fair value information regarding Sigma's assets and liabilities:

	Delta Inc.	Sigma Company Book Value	Sigma Company Fair Value
Assets			
Cash	$ 91,000	$ 8,000	$ 8,000
Accounts receivable	19,000	15,000	9,000
Inventory	47,000	31,000	43,000
Land	12,000	5,000	12,000
Plant and equipment, net	66,000	35,000	51,000
Total	$235,000	$94,000	$123,000
Liabilities and shareholders' equity			
Accounts payable	$ 52,000	$35,000	$ 35,000
Long-term debt	66,000	15,000	15,000
Common stock			
Delta—5,000 shares, $1.00 par	5,000	—	
Sigma—4,000 shares, $0.50 par	—	2,000	
Additional paid-in capital	30,000	12,000	
Retained earnings	82,000	30,000	
Total	$235,000	$94,000	

Required:

1. Prepare the entry Delta would make to record the acquisition of Sigma under the **acquisition method.** Use the amount paid by Delta for its 80% interest to impute the total fair value of Sigma at acquisition.

2. Calculate the amount of goodwill that Delta will record as a result of acquiring Sigma.

3. Provide the adjustment and elimination entries Delta would make to prepare the consolidated balance sheet immediately after the acquisition.

4. Prepare the consolidated balance sheet for Delta immediately after its acquisition of Sigma Company.

5. Repeat requirements 1–4 under the **purchase method.** (*Note to student:* Ignore the fact that the date in this problem would preclude the use of the purchase method.)

Prince Corp. and Sprite Corp. reported the following balance sheets at January 1, 2014:

P16-6

Consolidating at acquisition: Acquisition vs. purchase method   **(LO 4, 5, 6)**

mhhe.com/revsine6e

	Prince	Sprite
Current assets	$30,000	$15,000
Noncurrent assets	55,000	25,000
Total assets	$85,000	$40,000
Current liabilities	$20,000	$10,000
Long-term debt	20,000	5,000
Stockholders' equity	45,000	25,000
Total liabilities and		
stockholders' equity	$85,000	$40,000

On January 2, 2014, Prince issued $36,000 of stock and used the proceeds to purchase 90% of Sprite's common stock. The excess of the purchase price over Sprite's book value of net assets was allocated 60% to inventory and 40% to goodwill.

Required:

Show the amounts that Prince will report on its January 2, 2014, consolidated balance sheet for the following items under (a) the acquisition method and (b) the purchase method. (*Note to student:* Ignore the fact that the date in this problem would preclude the use of the purchase method.)

1. Current assets.

2. Noncurrent assets.

3. Goodwill.

4. Current liabilities.

5. Noncurrent liabilities.

6. Stockholders' equity (controlling interest).

7. Stockholders' equity (noncontrolling or minority interest).

The following information is reported in the separate and consolidated balance sheets and income statements of Palace Corp. and its subsidiary, Show Corp., at December 31, 2014:

P16-7

Consolidating account balances with intra-entity transactions   **(LO 4)**

	Palace	Show	Consolidated (after eliminations)
Balance sheet accounts			
Accounts receivable	$ 58,000	$ 36,000	$ 80,000
Inventory	52,000	40,000	80,000
Investment in Show	120,000	—	—
Goodwill	—	—	30,000
Stockholders' equity	308,000	100,000	308,000
Income statement accounts			
Revenues	$350,000	$240,000	$510,000
Cost of goods sold	245,000	200,000	377,000
Gross profit	105,000	40,000	133,000
Equity in earnings of Show	16,000	—	—
Net income	$ 70,000	$ 20,000	$ 80,000

Additional Information:

During 2014, Palace sold goods to Show at the same markup on cost it uses for all sales. At December 31, 2014, Show had not paid for all of these goods and still held 50% of them in inventory.

Required:

1. What was the amount of intra-entity sales from Palace to Show during 2014?
2. What was the carrying amount of the inventory that Show purchased from Palace on the December 31, 2014, consolidated balance sheet?
3. How much did Show owe to Palace for intra-entity sales at December 31, 2014?
4. What percent of Show's stock does Palace own?

P16-8

Consolidating intra-entity sales   **(LO 4)**

On October 1, 2014, Pacer Corp. acquired all of Sunny Corp.'s outstanding stock for cash. The fair value of Sunny's net assets was less than the purchase price but more than the net carrying amount. During October 2014, Pacer sold goods to Sunny at a profit. At December 31, 2014, 40% of these goods remained in Sunny's inventory.

Required:

1. Specify reasons for preparing consolidated financial statements that present operating results, cash flows, and financial position as if a parent company and its subsidiaries were a single entity.
2. How will the acquisition affect Pacer's consolidated balance sheet at October 1, 2014?
3. What eliminations are required for the intra-entity sales when preparing consolidated financial statements at December 31, 2014?
4. What is the effect on Pacer's separate balance sheet immediately after the October 1, 2014, acquisition?

P16-9

Elimination entries and consolidated balance sheet   **(LO 4)**

mhhe.com/revsine6e

The following are the balance sheets for Plate and Salad immediately prior to Plate's September 1, 2014, acquisition of Salad:

	Plate	Salad
Assets		
Cash	$500,000	$100,000
Accounts receivable	50,000	20,000
Inventory	100,000	30,000
Land	50,000	10,000
Bldg. & equip. net	200,000	100,000
Total	$900,000	$260,000
Liabilities & equity		
Accounts payable	$ 40,000	$ 80,000
Bonds payable	200,000	–0–
Common stock & APIC	300,000	100,000
Retained earnings	360,000	80,000
Total	$900,000	$260,000

Consider the following cases:

Case 1

Plate buys 100% of Salad's common stock for $180,000 cash. The fair value of Salad's assets and liabilities equal their book value.

Case 2

Plate buys 100% of Salad's common stock for $210,000 cash. The fair value of Salad's land is $20,000 and of its buildings and equipment is $110,000. All other fair values equal book values.

Required:

1. Prepare the September 1, 2014, journal entry on Plate's books to record the acquisition of Salad.

2. Prepare the elimination entries needed to prepare a consolidated balance sheet immediately after the acquisition.

3. Prepare the consolidated balance sheet immediately after the acquisition.

Refer to the balance sheets of Plate and Salad in the previous problem. Assume that Plate buys 80% of Salad's common stock for $180,000 cash. The fair value of Salad's land is $20,000, the fair value of Salad's buildings and equipment is $110,000, and all other fair values equal book values.

P16-10

Elimination entries and consolidated balance sheet under acquisition versus purchase method **(LO 4, 6)**

mhhe.com/revsine6e

Required:

Provide answers to the following under (a) the acquisition method and (b) the purchase method. (*Note to student:* Ignore the fact that the date in this problem would preclude the use of the purchase method.)

1. Prepare the journal entry on Plate's books to record the acquisition of Salad.

2. Prepare the elimination entries needed to prepare a consolidated balance sheet immediately after the acquisition.

3. Prepare the consolidated balance sheet immediately after the acquisition.

On January 1, 2014, Pluto Company acquired all of Saturn Company's common stock for $1,000,000 cash. On that date, Saturn had retained earnings of $200,000 and common stock of $600,000. The book values of Saturn's assets and liabilities were equal to fair values except for the following:

P16-11

Eliminating entries and accounting for goodwill **(LO 4, 5)**

	Book Value	Fair Value
Equipment (net)	$200,000	$220,000
Land	250,000	300,000

Additional Information:

1. The equipment had an estimated remaining useful life of five years at acquisition.

2. Goodwill was not impaired at December 31, 2014, but was impaired by $25,000 at December 31, 2015.

3. Reported income for Pluto (excluding equity income from Saturn's earnings) and Saturn follows:

	Pluto	Saturn
Year 2014	$500,000	$200,000
Year 2015	$350,000	$100,000

Required:

1. Prepare the January 1, 2014, journal entry on Pluto's books to record the acquisition of Saturn.

2. Prepare the elimination entries needed to prepare a consolidated balance sheet immediately after acquisition.

3. Calculate consolidated income for 2014 and 2015.

AutoParts Heaven is a U.S. company whose operations include a large, 100% owned foreign subsidiary. The subsidiary's functional currency is the U.S. dollar. The local currency in the country where the foreign subsidiary operates is appreciating against the U.S. dollar. The subsidiary accounts for inventories using the FIFO method.

P16-12

Comparing translation effect on ratios **(LO 8)**

AICPA
ADAPTED

Required:

Compare each of the following ratios for the foreign subsidiary *in its functional currency after translation* to the same ratios *in the local currency before translation.* Briefly explain why each ratio differs.

1. Gross profit margin percentage.
2. Operating profit margin.
3. Net profit margin.

P16-13

Financial asset impairment and recovery **(LO 2, 8, 10)**

On January 1, 2014, Wilson Corporation acquired mortgage-backed securities (MBS) from National Financial for $10,000 and classified the investment in its available-for-sale (AFS) portfolio. On December 31, 2014, the MBS's fair value had declined to $7,000, and this decline was considered an other-than-temporary impairment. The $3,000 impairment during 2014 was attributed to:

- Credit losses–$1,000
- Other factors–$2,000

On December 31, 2015, the MBS's fair value recovered to $9,000. The $2,000 increase during 2015 was attributed to:

- Credit losses–$750
- Other factors–$1,250

Required:

1. Assume that Wilson follows U.S. GAAP. Prepare the journal entries to record:

- The January 1, 2014, purchase
- The December 31, 2014, impairment
- The December 31, 2015, impairment recovery

  Summarize the amounts that Wilson reports in income and other comprehensive income (OCI) during 2014 and 2015.

2. Repeat requirement 1 assuming Wilson follows IFRS.

3. Now assume that the MBS's value recovered to $11,000 on December 31, 2015. Explain how the $4,000 increase during 2015 will be allocated to income and OCI under (a) U.S. GAAP and (b) IFRS.

P16-14

Variable interest entities **(LO 7)**

In its 2005 annual report, Waste Management Inc. provided the following note to the financial statements:

> Financial Interest in Surety Bonding Company—During the third quarter of 2003, we issued a letter of credit to support the debt of a surety bonding company established by an unrelated third party to issue surety bonds to the waste industry and other industries. The letter of credit, which is valued at $24.8 million as of December 31, 2005, serves to guarantee the surety bonding company's obligations associated with its debt and represents our exposure to loss associated with our financial interest in the entity.
>
> As of December 31, 2005, $60 million of current assets, $6 million of long-term assets, $33 million of current liabilities, $22 million of long-term debt and $11 million in minority interest have been included in our Consolidated Balance Sheet.

Required:

1. Why did Waste Management have to include $60 million of current assets, $6 million of long-term assets, $33 million of current liabilities, $22 million of long-term debt, and $11 million in minority interest in its Consolidated Balance Sheet?

2. What percentage of Surety Bonding Company's equity was owned by Waste Management?

3. At the end of 2005, Waste Management reported $3,451 million in total current assets and $3,257 million in total current liabilities. Did Waste Management's accounting treatment with respect to the Surety Bonding Company increase or decrease Waste Management's current ratio? Why might an analyst or investor be confused by this accounting treatment when considering measures of short-term liquidity?

CASES

The disclosure rules for business combinations complicate financial analysis. Trend analysis becomes difficult because comparative financial statements are not retroactively adjusted to include data for the acquired company for periods prior to the acquisition.

For example, consider Shopko's acquisition of Pamida on July 6, Year 1. Excerpts from Shopko's Year 1 annual report highlight the revenue and earnings growth achieved in that year. In the president's letter, William Podany noted the following:

C16-1

Shopko: Business acquisitions and analysis of sales growth **(LO 6)**

For more than ten consecutive years we have achieved new records for revenues and this year we are pleased to report another year of record earnings.

The management's discussion and analysis (MD&A) section began with the following statement:

Consolidated net sales for fiscal Year 1 (52 weeks) increased $939.5 million or 31.8% over fiscal Year 0 weeks (52 weeks) to $3,898.1 million.

The details of the acquisition were disclosed in the following note in Shopko's Year 1 annual report:

On July 6, Year 1, the Company acquired all of the outstanding voting and nonvoting common stock of Pamida for $94.0 million in cash, $285.8 million in assumed debt and $138.6 million in assumed trade and other accrued liabilities. Pamida is a retail chain headquartered in Omaha, Nebraska, operating Pamida retail stores in 15 Midwest, North Central and Rocky Mountain states. In connection with the Pamida acquisition, the Company incurred special charges of $8.1 million for employee retention programs, elimination of administrative functions and various integration initiatives. The allocation of the purchase price of Pamida was based on estimated fair values at the date of acquisition.

This acquisition was accounted for under the purchase method of accounting and the allocation of the purchase price was based on fair values at the date of acquisition. Goodwill associated with the Pamida acquisition was approximately $186.6 million. The results of operations since the dates of acquisition have been included in the consolidated statements of earnings.

The following presents selected unaudited pro forma consolidated statement of earnings information that has been prepared assuming the Pamida acquisition occurred on January 1, Year 1, and January 1, Year 0, respectively:

	Fiscal Years	
($ in thousands, except per share data—unaudited)	**Year 1**	**Year 0**
Net sales	$4,181,567	$3,630,951
Earnings before extraordinary item	101,190	56,678
Diluted earnings per share before extraordinary item	3.54	2.14

Shopko's consolidated statements of earnings for the years ended December 31, Year 1, and December 31, Year 0, follow:

Consolidated Statement of Earnings

	Fiscal Years	
($ in thousands)	Year 1	Year 0
Revenues:		
Net sales	$3,898,090	$2,958,557
Licensed department rentals and other income	13,856	12,325
	3,911,946	2,970,882
Costs and Expenses:		
Cost of sales	3,047,930	2,296,085
Selling, general and administrative expenses	601,157	471,546
Special charges	8,068	5,723
Depreciation and amortization expenses	84,438	67,590
	3,741,593	2,840,944
Income from operations	170,353	129,938
Interest expense—net	(46,894)	(38,311)
Gain on sale of ProVantage stock	56,760	—
Earnings before income taxes, minority interest and extraordinary item	180,219	91,627
Provision for income taxes	71,800	35,991
Earnings before minority interest and extraordinary item	108,419	55,636
Minority interest	(2,463)	—
Earnings before extraordinary item	105,956	55,636
Extraordinary (loss) on retirement of debt, net of income taxes of $2,443	(3,776)	—
Net earnings	$ 102,180	$ 55,636

Note: At the time of this case, gains and losses on early retirement of debt received extraordinary item treatment and minority interest was subtracted in arriving at net earnings.

Required:

1. How should a financial statement user interpret the reference to 31.8% sales growth in the MD&A section?

2. Suppose you are asked to prepare a sales forecast for the year ended December 31, Year 2. Based on the information shown here, what is the best estimate of Shopko's sustainable growth in sales between the years ended December 31, Year 0, and December 31, Year 1? Explain your answer.

C16-2

City Holding Company: Accounting for available-for-sale securities   **(LO 2)**

City Holding Company is a multibank holding company headquartered in West Virginia. The company comprises multiple facilities located in West Virginia, Ohio, and Kentucky. The banking subsidiaries provide a full range of banking services and make investments in debt and equity securities under limitations and restrictions imposed by regulations of the Comptroller of the Currency.

Appearing on the following pages are City Holding Company's consolidated balance sheet and cash flow statement as well as selected note information pertaining to the available-for-sale securities for Year 2 and Year 1.

Using the information provided, determine responses to the questions that follow. Provide detailed support where appropriate.

(*Note:* Unrealized gains [losses] on available-for-sale securities are not recognized for tax purposes until the securities are sold. Accordingly, the tax effects of these unrealized gains [losses] are recognized as adjustments to the deferred tax liability [asset] accounts. Unrealized gains [losses] on available-for-sale securities are shown net of related tax effects as an adjustment to stockholders' equity. Assume that the all realized gains and losses reported in the note on page 1027 relate to available-for-sale securities. Transfers of securities from the held-to-maturity to available-for-sale category are recorded at fair value with the unrealized gain [loss] recorded in stockholders' equity.)

STRETCH

Required:

1. Determine the net before-tax unrealized holding gain (loss) on available-for-sale securities that City Holding recognized in Year 2. Assume no adjustments are made to the Unrealized holding gain (loss) account when securities are sold.

2. Assuming a 35% tax rate, determine the deferred tax amounts related to the net unrealized holding gains (losses) that were recorded in Year 2. Indicate whether the deferred tax amounts were a liability or an asset.

3. Prepare the entry that City Holding made at December 31, Year 2 to record the unrealized gain (loss) on available-for-sale securities and to adjust the related stockholders' equity account.

4. Prepare the entry that City Holding made to record sales and calls on available-for-sale securities in Year 2.

5. To the extent possible, explain the year-to-year change in the cost basis of the available-for-sale securities (from $377,013,000 on December 31, Year 1, to $436,070,000 on December 31, Year 2).

City Holding Company and Subsidiaries

Condensed Consolidated Balance Sheets

($ in thousands)	December 31	
	Year 2	Year 1
Assets		
Cash and cash equivalents	$ 129,318	$ 170,327
Investment securities available for sale, at fair value	445,384	383,552
Investment securities held to maturity, at amortized cost		
(approximate fair value at December 31 Year 2—$74,415)	72,410	—
Loans, net of allowance for loan losses	1,175,887	1,341,620
Other assets	224,912	220,796
Total assets	$2,047,911	$2,116,295
Liabilities		
Total deposits	$1,564,580	$1,691,295
Other liabilities	317,938	278,651
Total liabilities	1,882,518	1,969,946
Total Stockholders' Equity	165,393	146,349
Total liabilities and stockholders' equity	$2,047,911	$2,116,295

(*continued*)

City Holding Company and Subsidiaries *(continued)*

Condensed Consolidated Cash Flow Statement

	Years Ended December 31		
($ in thousands)	Year 2	Year 1	Year 0
Operating Activities			
Net income (loss)	$ 32,459	$ (8,015)	$ (38,373)
Adjustments to reconcile net income (loss) to net cash provided by operating activities:			
Depreciation and amortization, including goodwill impairment	7,370	9,791	53,128
Various adjustments for loan transactions	4,284	47,410	115,617
Realized investment securities (gains) losses	(1,459)	(2,382)	5,015
Other adjustments	9,409	(4,405)	12,242
Net cash provided by operating activities	52,063	42,399	147,629
Investing Activities			
Proceeds from maturities and calls of securities held-to-maturity	4,994	—	—
Purchases of securities held-to-maturity	(40,783)	—	—
Proceeds from sales of securities available for sale	348,052	262,241	51,606
Proceeds from maturities and calls of securities available for sale	165,014	171,546	32,417
Purchases of securities available for sale	(608,709)	(431,113)	(80,640)
Net decrease (increase) in loans	147,121	400,832	(64,191)
Other investing activities	(373)	(49,416)	(97)
Net cash provided by (used in) investing activities	15,316	354,090	(60,905)
Financing Activities			
Net increase (decrease) in deposits	(126,715)	(218,228)	128,171
Other financing activities	18,327	(98,562)	(246,379)
Net cash provided by (used in) financing activities	(108,388)	(316,790)	(118,208)
Increase (decrease) in cash and cash equivalents	(41,009)	79,699	(31,484)
Cash and cash equivalents at beginning of year	170,327	90,628	122,112
Cash and cash equivalents at end of year	$ 129,318	$ 170,327	$ 90,628

Notes to Consolidated Financial Statements
City Holding Company and Subsidiaries

Note Four: Investments

During Year 2, the Company initiated an investment strategy to invest in trust preferred securities issued by other financial institutions. Only those securities issued by financial institutions that satisfy various asset size, profitability, equity-to-asset ratio, and certain other criteria, as pre-established by management, are evaluated for potential investment. Securities acquired were predominantly investment grade or were reviewed and approved for investment by the Company's executive loans committee. As of December 31, Year 2, the Company had invested $40.75 million, classified as held-to-maturity, and $17.43 million, classified as available-for-sale, pursuant to this strategy.

Also during Year 2, the Company transferred debt securities with an estimated fair value of $37.14 million and an amortized cost basis of $36.03 million from the available-for-sale classification to the held-to-maturity category. Transfers of debt securities into the held-to-maturity category from the available-for-sale classification are made at fair value at the date of transfer. The unrealized holding gain of $1.11 million at the date of transfer is retained in the other comprehensive income section of stockholders' equity and in the carrying value of the held-to-maturity securities. Such amounts are amortized over the remaining life of the security.

The aggregate carrying and approximate market values of securities follow. Fair values are based on quoted market prices, where available. If quoted market prices are not available, fair values are based on quoted market prices of comparable financial instruments.

Available-for-Sale Securities

($ in thousands)		December 31, Year 2		
	Cost	Gross Unrealized Gains	Gross Unrealized Losses	Estimated Fair Value
U.S. Treasury securities and obligations of U.S. government corporations and agencies	$107,108	$5,607	$—	$112,715
Obligations of states and political subdivisions	22,687	804	—	23,491
Mortgage-backed securities	130,739	2,819	—	133,558
Other debt securities	51,591	101	(76)	51,616
Total debt securities	312,125	9,331	(76)	321,380
Equity securities	123,945	59	—	124,004
	$436,070	$9,390	$(76)	$445,384

Available-for-Sale Securities

($ in thousands)		December 31, Year 1		
	Cost	Gross Unrealized Gains	Gross Unrealized Losses	Estimated Fair Value
U.S. Treasury securities and obligations of U.S. government corporations and agencies	$202,422	$6,751	$ (318)	$208,855
Obligations of states and political subdivisions	64,609	1,426	(135)	65,900
Mortgage-backed securities	90,969	90	(1,519)	89,540
Other debt securities	6,089	161	—	6,250
Total debt securities	364,089	8,428	(1,972)	370,545
Equity securities	12,924	83	—	13,007
	$377,013	$8,511	$(1,972)	$383,552

Gross gains of $1.46 million were realized during Year 2 on sales and calls of securities. There were no gross losses realized during Year 2. Gross gains of $2.67 million and $105,000 and gross losses of $290,000 and $5.12 million were realized on sales and calls of securities during Year 1 and Year 0, respectively. Of the gross gains reported in Year 2, $1.35 million was directly attributable to two interest rate risk management processes utilized during the year. First, the Company reported $0.62 million in gains realized from the Company's investment in a mutual fund that generates capital gains, as opposed to interest income. Second, as further discussed in Note Five, the Company reported $0.73 million in gains realized from an investment transaction that entailed the short-sale of a high-coupon U.S. Treasury bond. Gross gains of $2.67 million in Year 1 include $1.62 million of gains realized from the Company's investment in a mutual fund during Year 1. The Company maintained an average balance of $46.25 million invested in the mutual fund during Year 1. This mutual fund generated capital gains, as opposed to interest income, which utilized capital loss carryforwards available to the Company for income tax purposes. The capital loss carryforwards were primarily generated by the gross securities losses recognized in Year 0. Gross losses of $5.12 million in Year 0 are comprised of losses the Company recognized on its investments in small business investment corporations.

The book value of securities pledged to secure public deposits and for other purposes as required or permitted by law approximated $158.11 million and $260 million at December 31, Year 2 and Year 1, respectively.

C16-3

Measurement and reporting of noncontrolling interest under acquisition method
(LO 4)

On December 31, 2009, Internet Capital Group (ICG) acquired 89% of the equity of Gov-Delivery for $19,670,000. This acquisition was accounted for under the acquisition method. In its 10-K filing with the SEC, ICG disclosed the following purchase price allocation to net assets and noncontrolling interest based on acquisition date fair values:

($ in thousands)	
Goodwill	$ 3,644
Customer lists (11-year life)	13,910
Trademarks/trade names (11-year life)	1,320
Technology (10-year life)	710
Other net assets	1,506
	21,090
Noncontrolling interest[1]	(1,420)
	$19,670

---

[1] ICG determined the noncontrolling interest of GovDelivery with consideration of discounts for lack of control and lack of marketability.

Required:

1. Locate the current accounting guidance in FASB ASC 805 for measuring noncontrolling interest in a subsidiary at the acquisition date. What is the basic measurement principle ICG must use to recognize the noncontrolling interest in GovDelivery at acquisition?

2. The accompanying note states that ICG valued the noncontrolling interest of GovDelivery *with consideration of discounts* for lack of control and lack of marketability. Discuss the appropriateness of this valuation technique with reference to current accounting standards.

3. Based on the above acquisition price allocation, estimate the amount of the discount applied to the noncontrolling interest valuation on the acquisition date relative to the acquired shares.

4. How will this acquisition affect ICG's consolidated income statement for the year ended December 31, 2009, and its consolidated balance sheet at December 31, 2009?

5. Explain the effect on future years' consolidated net income of the asset allocations listed in the table.

C16-4

Air Products: Joint ventures and off-balance-sheet effects
(LO 3)

Excerpts from the Year 2 annual report of Air Products and Chemicals, Inc., follow. The income statement and balance sheet are condensed but the note entitled "Summarized Financial Information of Equity Affiliates" is shown in its entirety.

The note provides information on several joint ventures that Air Products has entered into—primarily to incinerate municipal solid waste and generate electricity.

Air Products and Chemicals, Inc. and Subsidiaries

Consolidated Income Statement (Modified)

	Years Ended September 30	
($ in millions)	Year 2	Year 1
Sales and other income	$ 5,401.2	$ 5,857.8
Costs and expenses		
Cost of sales	3,827.7	4,243.3
Selling and administrative	715.1	752.1
Research and development	120.6	122.5
Other (income) expense, net	(37.1)	(5.5)
Operating income	774.9	745.4
Income from equity affiliates, net of related expenses	76.2	81.2
Gain on sale of U.S. packaged gas business	55.7	—
Gain on divestiture of interest in cogeneration facilities	—	101.6
Loss on early retirement of debt	—	(75.8)
Interest expense	122.3	191.2
Income before taxes and minority interest	784.5	661.2
Income taxes provision (benefit)	240.8	190.5
Minority interest in earnings of subsidiary companies	18.3	5.1
Net income	$ 525.4	$ 465.6

Consolidated Balance Sheets (Modified)

	September 30	
($ in millions)	Year 2	Year 1
Assets		
Total current assets	$ 1,909.3	$ 1,684.8
Investment in net assets of and advances to equity affiliates	484.2	499.5
Plant and equipment, at cost	10,879.8	10,226.5
Less accumulated depreciation	(5,502.0)	(5,108.0)
Plant and equipment, net	5,377.8	5,118.5
Goodwill	431.1	384.7
Other noncurrent assets	292.6	396.6
Total assets	$ 8,495.0	$ 8,084.1
Liabilities and Shareholders' Equity		
Total current liabilities	$ 1,256.2	$ 1,352.4
Long-term debt	2,041.0	2,027.5
Deferred income and other noncurrent liabilities	827.4	702.0
Deferred income taxes	725.6	778.4
Total liabilities	4,850.2	4,860.3
Minority interest in subsidiary companies	184.4	118.0
Total shareholders' equity	3,460.4	3,105.8
Total liabilities and shareholders' equity	$ 8,495.0	$ 8,084.1

Summarized Financial Information of Equity Affiliates

The following table presents summarized financial information on a combined 100% basis of the principal companies accounted for by the equity method. Amounts presented include the accounts of the following equity affiliates: Stockton CoGen Company (50%); Pure Air on the Lake, L.P. (50%); Bangkok Cogeneration Company Limited (48.8%); Daido Air Products Electronics, Inc. (49%); Sapio Produzione Idrogeno Ossigeno S.r.L. (49%); INFRA Group (40%); Air Products South Africa (50%); Bangkok Industrial Gases Company Ltd. (50.6%); INOX Air Products Limited (INOX) (49.4%); APP GmbH in WPS GmbH & CoKG (20%); DuPont Air Products Nanomaterials, LLC (50%); Island Pipeline Gas

(33%); Tyczka Industrie-Gases GmbH (50%); and principally other industrial gas producers. In the fourth quarter of Year 2, the company obtained control of San Fu after increasing its ownership interest from 48% to 70%. In the fourth quarter of Year 1, the company sold its 50% interest in Cambria CoGen Company and Orlando CoGen Limited. Amounts presented reflect the accounts of these companies for the periods during which the equity method was applied.

($ in millions)	Year 2	Year 1
Current assets	$ 732.6	$ 833.9
Noncurrent assets	1,148.7	1,391.0
Current liabilities	572.5	605.1
Noncurrent liabilities	452.2	620.3
Net sales	1,608.8	1,690.2
Sales less cost of sales	543.0	611.5
Net income	196.3	219.4

The company's share of income of all equity affiliates for Year 2, Year 1, and Year 0 was $88.7, $91.1 and $99.6, respectively. These amounts exclude $12.5, $9.9, and $12.0 of related net expenses incurred by the company. Dividends received from equity affiliates were $42.0, $44.9, and $49.7 in Year 2, Year 1 and Year 0, respectively.

The investment in net assets of and advances to equity affiliates at 30 September Year 2 and Year 1 included investment in foreign affiliates of $449.5 and $465.9, respectively.

As of 30 September Year 2 and Year 1, the amount of investment in companies accounted for by the equity method included goodwill in the amount of $69.6 and $77.2, respectively. Goodwill is no longer amortized, as discussed in Note 1.

Required:

1. What are some reasons companies give to justify entering into joint ventures?

2. Using the information provided, estimate what the effect on Air Products' return-on-assets ratio and debt-to-equity ratio would have been if its proportionate share of the joint ventures had been included as individual assets and liabilities on the consolidated balance sheet. For this purpose, use a 35% tax rate, and assume that Air Products' proportionate ownership in these equity affiliates averaged 45%.

www **.mhhe.com/revsine6e**

**Remember to check the book's companion website
for additional study material.**

Statement of Cash Flows | 17

Ode to Cash Flow
Though my bottom line is black, I am flat upon my back,
My cash flows out and my customers pay slow,
The growth of my receivables is almost unbelievable;
The result is certain—unremitting woe!
And I hear the banker utter an ominous low mutter,
"Watch cash flow!"[1]

A s this poem suggests, accrual earnings may not always provide a complete measure of enterprise performance and financial health. There are several reasons for this. Accrual accounting necessarily involves subjective judgments that can introduce measurement error and uncertainty into reported earnings. Examples include estimates of uncollectible receivables, useful lives of assets, and future pension and health care benefits. One-time write-offs and restructuring charges require subjective judgments that can adversely affect the quality of the reported earnings number as a reliable indicator of a company's long-run performance. Moreover, managers can readily manipulate accrual income by postponing discretionary expenditures for research and development or advertising or by purposeful last-in, first-out (LIFO) dipping.

For these reasons, analysts must scrutinize a firm's cash flows—not just its accrual earnings—to evaluate its performance and creditworthiness. A significant difference between accrual earnings and operating cash flow may be a "red flag" that signals distortions of reported profits or impending financial difficulties.

Equity analysts are interested in operating cash flows because a firm's value ultimately depends on the discounted present value of its expected future cash flows. Recent operating cash flows are sometimes used in conjunction with current earnings as a jumping-off point for generating forecasts of expected future operating cash flows. Thus, cash flows can provide useful information for assessing equity values.[2]

LEARNING OBJECTIVES

After studying this chapter, you will understand:

1. The major sources and uses of cash reported in the operating, investing, and financing sections of the statement of cash flows.

2. Why accrual net income and operating cash flow differ and the factors that explain this difference.

3. The difference between the direct and indirect methods of determining cash flow from operations.

4. How to prepare a statement of cash flows from comparative balance sheet data, an income statement, and other financial information.

5. Why changes in balance sheet accounts over a year may not reconcile to the corresponding account changes included in the statement of cash flows.

6. How operating cash flows can be distorted.

7. Differences between reporting interest and dividends received and interest and dividends paid on the statement of cash flows under IFRS rules vs. U.S. GAAP.

---

[1] H. S. Bailey, Jr., cited in R. Green, "Are More Chryslers in the Offing?" *Forbes,* February 2, 1981, p. 69.

[2] Research evidence that supports this assertion includes J. Rayburn, "The Association of Operating Cash Flow and Accruals with Security Returns," *Journal of Accounting Research,* Supplement 1986, pp. 112–33; P. Wilson, "The Relative Information Content of Accruals and Cash Flows: Combined Evidence at the Earnings Announcement and Annual Report Release Date," *Journal of Accounting Research,* Supplement 1986, pp. 165–200; P. Wilson, "The Relative Information Content of Accrual and Funds Components of Earnings after Controlling for Earnings," *The Accounting Review,* April 1987, pp. 293–322; and M. Johnson and D. Lee, "Financing Constraints and the Role of Cash Flow from Operations in the Prediction of Future Profitability," *Journal of Accounting, Auditing and Finance,* Fall 1994, pp. 619–52.

Chapter

FASB ASC Topic 230—
Statement of cash flows—
uses the term **net cash flows
from operating activities.**
Because they are widely
used in practice, we also use
the terms *operating cash
flows* and *cash flow from
operations* in this chapter.
They mean the same thing.

Commercial lenders monitor a firm's operating cash flows because such cash flows provide the resources for periodic interest payments and the eventual repayment of principal. Low or negative operating cash flows signal poor credit risks.

Investment bankers scrutinize operating cash flows before deciding whether to underwrite a debt or equity issue. They know that the ultimate purchasers of the securities will assess the attractiveness of the securities based, in part, on the firms' expected operating cash flows.

STATEMENT FORMAT

The Financial Accounting Standards Board (FASB) mandates that firms provide a **statement of cash flows** that explains the sources and uses of cash.[3] Firms are required to disclose cash flows generated (or used) from three distinct types of activities:

1. **Operating cash flows** result from events or transactions that enter into the determination of net income—that is, transactions related to the production and delivery of goods and services to customers. In effect, operating cash flows are a company's cash-basis revenues and expenses.

The International Financial
Reporting Standards (IFRS)
format for cash flow statements is similar to the U.S.
GAAP format. See "Cash
Flow Statements," *IAS No. 7*
(London: International
Accounting Standards
Committee, revised 1992).
Cash flows are classified by
operating, investing, and
financing activities.
Operating cash flows can be
reported using either the
direct method or the indirect
method, but the direct
method is preferred (paras.
18–20).

2. **Investing cash flows** result from the purchase or sale of productive assets such as plant and equipment, from the purchase or sale of marketable securities (government bonds or stocks and bonds issued by other companies), and from the acquisitions of other companies or divestitures.

3. **Financing cash flows** result when a company sells its own stock or bonds, pays dividends or buys back its own shares (treasury stock), or borrows money and repays the amounts borrowed.

Current U.S. GAAP allows firms the option of choosing between two alternative formats for presenting cash flows from *operating* activities: (1) the **direct method** and (2) the **indirect method.** Each of these alternative formats is illustrated on the following pages.

A fourth "section" consisting of a single line appears in the cash flow statements of companies having foreign operations. This item, called "Effect of exchange rates on cash and cash equivalents" (or some similar title) represents the change in the U.S. dollar amount presented for cash resulting from foreign currency holdings being revalued as exchange rates change. For example, a U.S. company with a European subsidiary holding euros would report a different cash balance at the end of the year than the beginning of the year even without any cash flows from its European subsidiary, if the exchange rate between the U.S. dollar and the euro changed.

The Direct Method

Exhibit 17.1 presents the fiscal 2012 (and comparative 2011) statement of cash flows for Golden Enterprises, a small snack food company, whose fiscal year ends June 1, 2012. The statement separates cash flows into operating, investing, and financing activities. For fiscal 2012, operating activities generated positive cash flow of \$5.747 million, while investing activities resulted in net cash outflow of \$4.992 million. The major investing outflow was to purchase property and equipment. The company had net cash outflow from financing activities of \$1.583 million with net outflows from debt repayments in excess of debt issuances (\$37.468 − \$36.640 = \$0.828 million) as a primary contributing source, along with \$1.467 million in

---

[3] FASB ASC Topic 230: Statement of Cash Flows.

EXHIBIT 17.1 — Consolidated Statement of Cash Flows (Direct Method)

Golden Enterprises, Inc. and Subsidiary
For the Fiscal Years Ended June 1, 2012 and June 3, 2011

	2012	2011
Cash flows from operating activities		
Cash received from customers	$135,839,804	$130,362,172
Interest income	7,353	4,439
Rental income	42,552	36,775
Other operating cash payments/receipts	63,968	144,371
Cash paid to suppliers and employees for cost of goods sold	(68,449,193)	(64,735,374)
Cash paid to suppliers and employees for selling, general, and administrative	(61,099,333)	(57,818,135)
Income taxes	(375,077)	(1,868,129)
Interest expense	(282,784)	(371,584)
Net cash provided by operating activities	5,747,290	5,754,535
Cash flows from investing activities		
Purchases of property, plant, and equipment	(5,214,408)	(5,559,183)
Proceeds from sale of property, plant, and equipment	222,755	96,916
Net cash used in investing activities	(4,991,653)	(5,462,267)
Cash flows from financing activities		
Debt proceeds	36,639,753	38,903,745
Debt repayments	(37,468,412)	(36,328,583)
Change in checks outstanding in excess of bank balances	712,031	(85,126)
Purchases of treasury shares	—	(36,960)
Cash dividends paid	(1,466,831)	(1,467,507)
Net cash (used in) provided by financing activities	(1,583,459)	985,569
Net (decrease) increase in cash and cash equivalents	(827,822)	1,277,837
Cash and cash equivalents at beginning of year	2,721,638	1,443,801
Cash and cash equivalents at end of year	$ 1,893,816	$ 2,721,638

Author note: Golden's 2012 fiscal year runs from June 4, 2011 to June 1, 2012.

dividend payments. As a result of its operating, investing, and financing activities, Golden Enterprises generated a net decrease in cash of slightly more than $825 thousand for fiscal 2012.

Golden Enterprises follows the direct method for presenting cash flows from operations. The direct method requires firms to report major classes of gross cash receipts (cash revenues) and gross cash payments (cash expenses). Note that Interest income and Interest expense are shown as components of cash flows from operating activities. This treatment is in accordance with GAAP reporting requirements, which classifies these two items as elements of cash flows from operating activities because cash flows from operating activities generally reflect the cash effects of transactions entering into the determination of net income.

> The minimum specific categories of cash inflows and cash outflows that are required to be reported under the direct method are:
>
> a. Cash collected from customers (including lessees and licensees).
> b. Interest and dividends received.
> c. Other operating cash receipts.
> d. Cash paid to employees and other suppliers of goods and services.
> e. Interest paid.
> f. Income taxes paid.
> g. Other operating cash payments.

EXHIBIT 17.2 Consolidated Statements of Income

Golden Enterprises, Inc. and Subsidiary
For the Fiscal Years Ended June 1, 2012 and June 3, 2011

	2012	2011
Net sales	$136,185,657	$131,047,850
Cost of sales	70,642,277	67,429,666
Gross margin	65,543,380	63,618,184
Selling, general, and administrative expenses	61,591,496	58,402,401
Operating income	3,951,884	5,215,783
Other (expenses) income:		
Gain on sale of assets	162,876	79,483
Interest expense	(282,784)	(371,584)
Other income	113,873	185,585
Total other income (expenses)	(6,035)	(106,516)
Income before income taxes	3,945,849	5,109,267
Provision for income taxes	1,738,226	2,094,499
Net income	$ 2,207,623	$ 3,014,768

Author note: Golden's 2012 fiscal year runs from June 4, 2011 to June 1, 2012.

Golden Enterprises discloses Cash received from customers of $135.840 million in fiscal 2012. This number differs from the accrual accounting sales revenue number of $136.186 million, which is reported in Golden's 2012 income statement shown in Exhibit 17.2. There are two possible reasons for this difference:

1. Some 2012 credit sales had not been collected in cash by year-end.
2. During 2012, cash was received for payment on accounts receivable generated from sales recognized in prior years.

The "Cash paid to suppliers and employees for cost of goods sold" of $68.449 million in Golden's 2012 cash flow statement (Exhibit 17.1) differs from the $70.642 million reported for Cost of sales in Golden's accrual-basis income statement (Exhibit 17.2). Similarly, "Cash paid to suppliers and employees for selling, general, and administrative" of $61.099 million and the $0.375 million of cash paid for Income taxes in the cash flow statement differ from the $61.591 million of Selling, general, and administrative expenses and the Provision for income taxes of $1.738 million reported in Golden's income statement.

Overall, Exhibits 17.1 and 17.2 show that Golden Enterprises generated positive operating cash flows of $5.747 million in fiscal 2012 while its accrual-basis net income was $2.208 million. Why is there a discrepancy between Golden's net income and operating cash flows? The answer is found in the reconciliation of net income to net cash provided by operating activities. This reconciliation explains the differences that cause net income to deviate from operating cash flow. This reconciliation for Golden Enterprises is shown in Exhibit 17.3.[4]

---

[4] This reconciliation schedule is required of all firms that use the direct method of presenting operating cash flows. See FASB ASC Paragraph 230-10-45-28: Statement of Cash Flows—Overall—Other Presentation Matters—Reconciliation of Net Income and Net Cash Flow from Operating Activities.

EXHIBIT 17.3	Consolidated Statements of Cash Flows (Indirect Method)

Golden Enterprises, Inc. and Subsidiary
For the Fiscal Years Ended June 1, 2012 and June 3, 2011

	2012	2011
Cash flows from operating activities		
Net Income	$2,207,623	$3,014,768
Adjustment to reconcile net income to net cash provided by operating activities:		
① Depreciation	3,303,353	3,174,956
② Deferred income taxes	557,576	1,329,868
③ Gain on sale of property and equipment	(162,876)	(79,483)
④ Change in receivables-net	(345,853)	(685,678)
⑤ Change in inventories	(161,169)	(94,964)
⑥ Change in prepaid expenses	48,956	(230,574)
⑦ Change in cash surrender value of insurance	176,177	364,240
⑧ Change in other assets	(151,239)	(167,256)
⑨ Change in accounts payable	(297,983)	186,036
⑩ Change in accrued expenses	(132,524)	138,626
⑪ Change in salary continuation plan	(100,324)	(92,506)
⑫ Change in accrued income taxes	805,573	(1,103,498)
Net cash provided by operating activities	$5,747,290	$5,754,535

Author note: Golden's 2012 fiscal year runs from June 4, 2011 to June 1, 2012.

The reconciliation of net income to net operating cash flow, in addition to being a required supplemental disclosure for companies using the direct method, comprises the operating section of the cash flow statement for companies using the indirect method. That is, the operating section of an indirect method cash flow statement is a reconciliation from net income to operating cash flow. Therefore, we discuss the reconciliation in the context of the indirect method cash flow statement.

The Indirect Method

The indirect method begins with accrual-basis net income and adjusts for the following:

- Items *included* in accrual-basis net income that *did not* affect operating cash flows in the current period, such as
  - Noncash revenues or gains (such as revenues earned but not received in cash and gains on the disposal of fixed assets).
  - Noncash expenses or losses (such as depreciation and amortization, provision for bad debt expense, and expenses accrued but not paid in cash).
- Items *excluded* from accrual-basis income that *did* affect operating cash flows in the current period, such as
  - Cash inflows (revenues) received but not recognized as earned in the current period (such as rent received in advance and collections on account).
  - Cash outflows (expenses) paid but not recognized for accrual accounting purposes in the current period (such as prepaid insurance and payments on account).

The overwhelming majority of public companies use the indirect method. Firms favor the indirect method because it relies exclusively on data already available in the accrual accounts. In addition, it characterizes cash flow in a way that many analysts find useful. For example, the change in inventory (a reconciling item in the indirect method cash flow statement) is useful information because it relates to expansion or contraction of inventory that can be placed in context depending on whether sales are growing or not. If sales are growing, an increase in inventory is expected. If sales are shrinking, an increase in inventory may signal obsolescence problems. Purchases of inventory (which are provided in a direct method cash flow statement) are less useful in addressing questions such as this one. Similarly, changes in accounts receivable may be more informative than cash collections.

We'll use Exhibit 17.3 to show how the indirect method reconciles accrual accounting net income ($2,207,623 in Exhibit 17.2) with cash flow from operations ($5,747,290 in Exhibit 17.1). Each of the reconciling items is discussed individually.

Items ① through ③ in Exhibit 17.3 represent amounts included in the accrual-basis net income figure *that did not have an operating cash flow effect*—that is, they did not cause cash flow from operations to increase or decrease during the year. Because they did not have a cash flow effect, the accrual-basis net income must be adjusted for these items to arrive at cash flows from operations.

① **Depreciation**   This is the most common indirect method adjustment. During 2012, Golden Enterprises made the following entry for depreciation:

DR Depreciation expense	$3,303,353	
CR Accumulated depreciation on fixed assets		$3,303,353

Although the debit reduced net income, the credit did not represent a cash outflow. Hence, this noncash expense caused net income to diverge from cash provided by operating activities. That's why depreciation expense must be added back to net income as a reconciling item under the indirect method.

② **Deferred Income Taxes**   Golden showed an increase in its deferred tax liabilities net of deferred tax assets of $557,576 in 2012. Golden's pre-tax book income exceeded its taxable income in 2012 due to a variety of temporary differences we discussed in Chapter 13. When this happens, the debit to income tax expense exceeds the taxes owed and paid in the current period. This increase in net deferred tax liabilities must be added to accrual-basis net income because the tax expense on Golden's income statement overstates the cash outflow for taxes in fiscal 2012.

③ **Gain on Sale of Property and Equipment**   This amount represents the excess of the selling price over book value of assets sold during the period. In 2012, Golden sold assets for a gain of $162,876. The gain increased net income, but it did *not* reflect the increase in cash flow from operations related to this transaction. The gain is considered a noncash addition to accrual income, so it must be subtracted from net income to arrive at cash flows from operations. The cash received from the transaction is shown later in the investing activities section. The amount reported there is the $222,755 actually received in cash.

Items ④ through ⑫ represent amounts that were included in the $2,207,623 net income

We can infer that the assets sold had a net book value of $59,399 by subtracting the gain of $162,876 from the $222,275 cash proceeds received on the sale. So, the entry to record the sale of assets was:

DR Cash	$222,275	
CR Assets (net of accumulated depreciation)		$59,399
CR Gain on sale		162,876

for which the net income effect either exceeds or falls below the cash flow effect. Because the net income effect and the cash flow effect differ, the following adjustments must appear in the reconciliation.

④ **Change in Receivables—Net**　During 2012, the amount in Golden's Accounts receivable (net of Allowance for uncollectibles) account increased by $345,853. This means that sales on account (accrual-basis revenue) were greater than cash collections on account (cash-basis revenue) in 2012. Accordingly, a subtraction must be made from the accrual-basis net income to arrive at cash provided by operating activities.

⑤ **Change in Inventories**　During 2012, the amounts in Golden's inventory accounts increased by $161,169, so inventory purchased exceeded the cost of inventory sold during the year. Let's temporarily assume that all inventory purchases were paid for in cash. (Adjustment ⑨ discusses changes in the Accounts payable account that corrects for noncash inventory purchases.) The inventory buildup means that cash outflow for inventory exceeded the accrual-basis Cost of goods sold on Golden's income statement. Thus, the increase in inventories must be subtracted from accrual-basis income to obtain cash flows from operations because the cash outflow for inventory exceeded the amount charged to expense under accrual accounting.

⑥ **Change in Prepaid Expenses**　Golden's Prepaid expenses decreased in fiscal 2012 by $48,956. This decrease represents cash payments for items such as insurance and rent that were below the amounts expensed on Golden's accrual-basis income statement. Because cash payments were below the accrual-basis expenses, Golden adds this decrease in prepaid expenses to accrual earnings to obtain cash flows from operations.

⑦ **Change in Cash Surrender Value of Insurance**　Golden carries life insurance policies on certain key executives in the firm. When it pays the premiums, part of the payment increases the cash surrender value of those policies. When policies are terminated, the company receives cash from the insurance company. During the year, Golden's balance sheet (not shown) shows a decrease in the Cash surrender value of life insurance of $176,177, which indicates that cash was received from termination of one or more of these policies. Golden treats this as an operating source of cash.[5]

⑧ **Change in Other Assets**　Golden's balance sheet shows a $151,239 increase in the Other asset account. This increase likely resulted in a credit (decrease) to one or more expense accounts on Golden's income statement. Because these reductions in expenses do not reflect the cash flow effect of these transactions, this amount is subtracted from Golden's accrual-basis earnings to arrive at the operating cash flows for the period.

⑨ **Change in Accounts Payable**　Golden's Accounts payable account decreased by $297,983 during the year. Thus, cash payments on account exceeded credit purchases on account by this amount. Because credit purchases (but not cash payments on account) are included as part of the Cost of goods sold on Golden's income statement, this decrease in accounts payable represents the excess of cash outflows for inventory during the period above the accrual-basis expense reported on the income statement. Hence, this amount is shown as a subtraction from accrual-basis earnings to arrive at cash flows from operations.

---

[5] An alternative and perhaps preferable method is to treat this as an investing source of cash inflows because the cash surrender value of life insurance policies could be viewed as a noncurrent investment. For a discussion of the issues surrounding this classification, see David McCann, "Key-Person Insurance: A Cash Flow Puzzle," April 4, 2012, CFO.com.

⑩ **Change in Accrued Expenses**   Accrued expenses represent expenses for items such as salaries, wages, and interest incurred in the current period but not paid. Golden's Accrued expenses (which reflects several liability accounts on its balance sheet) decreased by $132,524 during fiscal 2012. Because this decrease in accruals, which resulted in an offsetting credit to expense accounts on Golden's income statement, did not result in an inflow of cash, this amount is shown as a subtraction from accrual earnings to arrive at cash flows from operations for the year.

⑪ **Change in Salary Continuation Plan**   Golden has a salary continuation (pension) plan for certain key executives. This liability account is increased each year for the present value of increased retirement benefits earned during the year (which are reported as an expense on the accrual-basis income statement) and is decreased for the cash payments made to retired executives during the year. Golden's balance sheet shows a net decrease in current and noncurrent salary continuation liabilities of $100,324 for fiscal 2012, which implies that the cash payments for retirement benefits exceeded the amount recognized as expense on the accrual-basis income statement. Therefore, this amount is deducted from the accrual-basis income to arrive at cash flows from operations for the period.

⑫ **Change in Accrued Income Taxes**   This current liability account is increased for income taxes that are due for the period (with an offsetting debit to Tax expense on the accrual-basis income statement) and is reduced for cash payments made to the government for taxes in the current period. Golden's Accrued income taxes payable account increased by $805,573 in 2012. This implies that Golden's cash outflow for income taxes was less than the tax expense recorded on the accrual-basis income statement. Thus, this amount is added to accrual income to arrive at cash flows from operations for the year.

The direct and indirect methods for computing net cash provided by operating activities will result in the same number—$5,747,290 in Golden's 2012 annual report. Those who prefer the direct method justify their preference by claiming that this method discloses operating cash flows by category—inflows from customers, outflows to suppliers, and so on. They contend that this categorization facilitates cash flow predictions. For example, assume that an analyst expects product selling prices to increase by 6% in the ensuing year. The direct method's disclosure of cash received from customers could then be multiplied by 106% to construct next year's cash forecast. (There is no similarly easy way to incorporate the expectation of a 6% price increase in the indirect method approach.)

Analysis

Analysts who prefer the indirect method believe the size and direction of the items reconciling income to operating cash flow provide a rough yardstick for evaluating the quality of earnings. When a company reports high accounting income but simultaneously has low or negative cash flow from operations, this situation is considered a sign of low-quality earnings that are not sustainable. For example, if the excess of income over cash flow is accompanied by a large buildup in accounts receivable, this increase could indicate that the company is aggressively recognizing revenue. The receivables buildup may have occurred, for example, if a company shipped unwanted merchandise to distributors in an effort to inflate sales. Or the buildup could result from sales to customers with marginal creditworthiness that may never be collected.

Although the FASB allowed a choice between the direct and indirect methods for determining operating cash flows when it formulated current reporting requirements for the statement of cash flows, it anticipated that the vast majority of firms would use the indirect method. Because few firms were expected to use the direct method, the Board feared that users might find it difficult to compare the operating cash flows of firms using the direct method to that of firms using the indirect method. To address this comparability concern, GAAP requires firms using the direct method to provide a reconciliation between accrual earnings and operating cash flows such as the one that is presented by those firms using the indirect method. Golden

Enterprises' choice of the direct method explains why we have operating cash flow information for them under both methods.

Additionally, firms using the indirect method are required to disclose separately the amount of interest paid. Consequently, those who believe interest expense represents a cash flow from financing activities will always have sufficient information available to reclassify this item out of cash flows from operating activities for firms using the indirect method. However, GAAP does *not* require a separate disclosure of dividends and interest income *received*. Therefore, analysts who believe that these items should be classified as cash flows from investing activities will generally not have sufficient information to make this reclassification for firms that opt for the indirect method.

> GAAP also requires firms using the indirect method to separately disclose income taxes paid.

One additional difficulty confronting analysts using cash flow statement disclosures relates to the treatment of income taxes. Recall from Chapter 2 that intraperiod income tax allocation is followed in constructing the income statement—that is, the income tax expense associated with income from continuing operations is separately disclosed. Items not included in the computation of income from continuing operations (such as gains and losses from discontinued operations and extraordinary items) are reflected *net* of their associated income tax effects. Intraperiod income tax allocation facilitates predictions by statement users. The tax expense associated with the presumably recurring income from continuing operations is reported separately from the tax expense associated with items appearing below income from continuing operations. Unfortunately, GAAP does not treat cash outflows for income taxes in the same way. The entire amount of cash payments for income taxes is included in the Cash flows from operating activities section even though some of the taxes relate, for example, to gains on sales of assets whose gross cash flows are included in the Cash flows from investing activities section of the statement. The failure to differentiate tax cash flows by type (those pertaining to income from continuing operations versus other items) complicates forecasts of future cash flows. The FASB asserted that the allocation of taxes among the cash flow sections would be so complex and arbitrary that the benefits would not justify the costs. While this cost-benefit justification may be correct, the FASB provided no evidence to support its assertion.

RECAP

The statement of cash flows provides a summary of a firm's operating, investing, and financing activities that explains its change in cash position for the period. Operating cash flows can be presented using either the direct or indirect method. The direct method details major sources of cash receipts and major categories of cash expenditures. The indirect method begins with accrual earnings and adjusts for (1) items included in accrual-basis income that did not affect cash and (2) items excluded from accrual earnings that did affect operating cash flows.

Other Elements of the Cash Flow Statement

Let's return to Exhibit 17.1. Golden Enterprises' cash flow statement illustrates the typical range of items included in the Investing activities and Financing activities sections of the statement. The items included are relatively straightforward, and there should be no difficulties in interpreting these disclosures. For example, Golden shows investing cash outflows in 2012 for purchases of property, plant, and equipment of $5,214,408. Cash inflows from investing activities resulted from the sale of property, plant, and equipment of $222,755. Note that the *gross* inflows and outflows are both shown. That is, both purchases and sales of property, plant, and equipment are shown in the investing section, rather than a single net number.

Financing cash inflows resulted from the issuance of debt ($36,639,753); financing cash outflows were for debt repayment ($37,468,412), an increase in bank overdrafts ($712,031), and cash dividends paid ($1,466,831).

The net result of Golden's operating, investing, and financing activities for the year was a decrease in cash and cash equivalents of $827,822.

PREPARING THE CASH FLOW STATEMENT

The interrelationships among net income, cash flow, and assets and liabilities dictate how a cash flow statement for a period can be derived from the balance sheets at the beginning and end of that period. If a transaction giving rise to income or expense has a corresponding cash flow, there is no reconciling item in the indirect method cash flow statement because income and cash flow are equal. And, no assets (other than cash) or liabilities will change in value. In contrast, if a transaction results in a different amount of income and cash flow, one or more assets (other than cash) and liabilities must change in value. For example, if sales revenue outpaces collections, accounts receivable must increase by the difference. If cost of goods sold exceeds inventory purchases, inventory declines. When depreciation is taken, there is an expense with no cash flow, and fixed assets decrease. As a result, we can use the changes in all balance sheet accounts other than cash to derive the cash flow statement.

This section illustrates the procedures used to prepare a cash flow statement. Exhibit 17.4 provides comparative 2013–2014 balance sheet data, a 2014 income statement, and selected additional information for Burris Products Corporation. In the appendix to this chapter, we show the same example using a spreadsheet format to construct the analysis.

Reviewing the comparative balance sheets in Panel (a) of Exhibit 17.4 shows that the cash balance decreased by $8,000 during 2014. The purpose of a cash flow statement is to explain the underlying *causes* of this $8,000 change in the cash balance. Recall that the causes for change arise from operating, investing, and financing activities.

Constructing a cash flow statement requires the preparer to gather information like that in Exhibit 17.4. The three-step process that follows is then used to build the components of the statement.

Step 1: Identify the journal entry or entries that led to the reported change in each noncash balance sheet account.

Step 2: Determine the net cash flow effect of the journal entry (or entries) identified in Step 1.

Step 3: Compare the income statement effect of the entry (Step 1) with its cash flow effect (Step 2) to determine what cash flow statement treatment is necessary for each item.

This three-step approach is used to develop Burris's cash flow statement in Exhibit 17.5 using the indirect method of determining net cash flow from operating activities.

Cash Flows from Operating Activities

The Operating Activities section of the statement in Exhibit 17.5 begins with net income of $182,000. Under the indirect method, net income represents an initial rough approximation of the cash generated by operating activities. Starting the statement with net income presumes that revenues are ultimately collected in cash and that expenses represent cash outflows. In the long run, this approximation is basically correct. In any single period, however, accrual accounting net income will not equal that same period's cash flow from operating activities. The reason is that cash flows for some revenue and expense items occur either before or after accrual accounting revenue and expenses are recognized. The adjustment for these differences

EXHIBIT 17.4	Comparative Balance Sheets, 2014 Income Statement, and Additional Information

Burris Products Corporation

Panel (a)

	December 31,		Increase or
Comparative Balance Sheets	**2014**	**2013**	**Decrease**
Cash	$ 25,000	$ 33,000	$ 8,000 Decrease
Accounts receivable	171,000	180,000	9,000 Decrease
Inventory	307,000	295,000	12,000 Increase
Land	336,000	250,000	86,000 Increase
Buildings and equipment	1,628,000	1,430,000	198,000 Increase
Accumulated depreciation	(653,000)	(518,000)	135,000 Increase
	$1,814,000	$1,670,000	
Accounts payable	$ 163,000	$ 160,000	$ 3,000 Increase
Customer advance deposits	99,000	110,000	11,000 Decrease
Bonds payable	500,000	500,000	–0– —
Discount on bonds payable	(66,000)	(70,000)	4,000 Decrease
Deferred tax liability	100,000	94,000	6,000 Increase
Common stock	850,000	800,000	50,000 Increase
Retained earnings	168,000	76,000	92,000 Increase
	$1,814,000	$1,670,000	

Panel (b)

2014 Income Statement

Sales revenues	$ 3,030,000
Cost of goods sold	(2,526,625)
Depreciation expense	(158,000)
Sales commissions (all cash)	(34,000)
Interest expense	(44,000)
Gain on sale of equipment	17,000
Income before taxes	284,375
Income tax expense	(102,375)
Net income	$ 182,000

Additional Information

1. Equipment with a cost of $63,000 and a book value of $40,000 was sold for $57,000.
2. Cash dividends of $90,000 were paid in 2014.

between the timing of revenue and expense recognition and cash flow impact appear as the eight numbered items following the net income figure in Exhibit 17.5. We now explain each of these items.

① **Depreciation**   The income statement in Panel (b) of Exhibit 17.4 indicates that depreciation expense recognized during 2014 was $158,000. We use the three-step analytic approach, as follows:

Step 1: The journal entry that generated the account change was:

DR Depreciation expense	$158,000	
CR Accumulated depreciation		$158,000

EXHIBIT 17.5	**2014 Statement of Cash Flows**

Burris Products Corporation

Operating activities

Net income		$ 182,000
Adjustments to reconcile net income to net cash provided by operating activities		
① Depreciation	158,000	
② Gain on equipment sale	(17,000)	
③ Amortization of bond discount	4,000	
④ Deferred income taxes increase	6,000	
⑤ Accounts receivable decrease	9,000	
⑥ Customer advance deposits decrease	(11,000)	
⑦ Inventory increase	(12,000)	
⑧ Accounts payable increase	3,000	
		140,000
Net cash provided by operating activities		322,000
Investing activities		
② Equipment sale		57,000
⑨ Land purchase		(86,000)
⑩ Buildings and equipment purchase		(261,000)
Net cash used for investing activities		(290,000)
Financing activities		
⑪ Common stock issued		50,000
⑫ Dividend paid		(90,000)
Net cash used for financing activities		(40,000)
Net decrease in cash during 2014		$ (8,000)

Step 2: The journal entry appearing in Step 1 does not involve cash. Indeed, depreciation is unlike most other expenses because cash outflow often occurs *before* the expense recognition—that is, when the asset is initially purchased.

Step 3: Depreciation expense was included in the determination of net income (Step 1). But depreciation expense does not represent a cash outflow (Step 2) in the current period. Consequently, depreciation expense must be added back to net income to derive cash flow.

In short, depreciation expense is added back to accrual-basis income to obtain operating cash flows because it was included in the determination of net income even though it doesn't represent a cash outflow of the current period.

② **Gain on Equipment Sale** The net income number includes a $17,000 gain on the sale of equipment, as shown in Panel (b) of Exhibit 17.4. Using the same three-step approach, we arrive at the following:

Step 1: With the additional information disclosed below the income statement in Panel (b) of Exhibit 17.4, we can develop the following journal entry for the gain:

> Note that if the equipment originally cost $63,000 and its book value was $40,000, the accumulated depreciation must have been $23,000.

DR	Accumulated depreciation	$23,000	
DR	Cash	57,000	
	CR Equipment		$63,000
	CR Gain on sale		17,000

Step 2: The sale resulted in a cash inflow of $57,000. This cash inflow is the result of investing activities.

Step 3: Comparing the accrual accounting effect (Step 1) to the cash flow effect (Step 2) reveals three problems: (1) the recognized accrual gain ($17,000) does not correspond to the cash inflow ($57,000), (2) the $17,000 gain is included in income and thus would be categorized as an operating activities cash inflow unless adjustments are made, and (3) the $57,000 cash inflow from investing activities must be separately reflected in the statement.

The cash flow statement in Exhibit 17.5 reflects the information uncovered in Step 3. The $17,000 gain is subtracted from net income to arrive at cash flow from operating activities, and the $57,000 total cash received is correctly categorized and shown as a cash inflow from investing activities.

③ **Amortization of Bond Discount**   Panel (a) of Exhibit 17.4 discloses that the Discount on bonds payable account decreased by $4,000 during 2014. The three-step approach shows the following:

Step 1: Because the income statement reports interest expense as $44,000, the journal entry that led to the balance sheet change for discount on bonds payable was:

DR	Interest expense		$44,000	
	CR	Discount on bonds payable		$ 4,000
	CR	Cash		40,000

Step 2: Interest expense of $44,000 was subtracted in computing net income, although the cash outflow for the payment of interest in 2014 was only $40,000.

Step 3: Because the accrual accounting income statement charge for interest expense ($44,000) exceeds the cash outflow ($40,000), the $4,000 difference must be added back to net income in the operating activities section of the cash flow statement.

④ **Deferred Income Taxes Increase**   The deferred tax liability increased by $6,000, as shown in Panel (a) of Exhibit 17.4. The three-step approach shows the following:

Step 1: Because income tax expense for 2014 was $102,375, the journal entry for taxes in 2014 was:

DR	Income tax expense		$102,375	
	CR	Deferred tax liability		$ 6,000
	CR	Cash		96,375

Step 2: There is a disparity between the amount of the expense included in the determination of net income ($102,375) and the cash outflow to pay taxes ($96,375).

Step 3: Because the income statement expense is $6,000 more than the cash outflow, $6,000 must be added back in the Operating Activities section of the cash flow statement in Exhibit 17.5.

⑤ **Accounts Receivable Decrease**   Panel (a) of Exhibit 17.4 shows that during 2014 Accounts receivable decreased by $9,000. Following the three-step approach we obtain:

Step 1: If we assume that all 2014 sales were initially credit sales, the aggregate entry to record these sales would be:

DR	Accounts receivable	$3,030,000	
	CR Sales revenue		$3,030,000

If we assume that the only transaction causing a decrease in the Accounts receivable account is for collections on account, the $9,000 decrease during 2014 implies the following entry for cash collections:

DR	Cash	$3,039,000	
	CR Accounts receivable		$3,039,000

Step 2: Because Accounts receivable decreased, cash collections during the year ($3,039,000) must have exceeded the amount of revenues included in income ($3,030,000).

Step 3: The $9,000 excess of cash collections over accrual revenues must be added back to net income in Exhibit 17.5 to obtain net cash flow from operating activities.

⑥ **Customer Advance Deposits Decrease**   Burris Products Corporation requires cash payments from customers prior to the sale of special order custom merchandise. This advance payment represents a liability on the balance sheet. As the custom products are delivered to customers, the liability is reduced and revenue is recognized. During 2014, the amount of the liability decreased by $11,000, as shown in Panel (a) of Exhibit 17.4.

Step 1: The accounting entry that reflects the reduction in the advance payment liability during 2014 was:

DR	Customer advance deposits	$11,000	
	CR Sales revenues		$11,000

Step 2: Sales revenues were $11,000 higher due to the recognition of revenue related to previously received deposits. However, there was no corresponding cash flow effect this year because the cash flow arose in 2013 when the special products were ordered and paid for and the liability was recorded.

Step 3: Because revenues included in the computation of 2014 net income exceeded 2014 cash inflows by $11,000, this amount must be deducted in the operating activities section of the cash flow statement.

⑦ **Increase in Inventory**   When inventory increases during a period, the dollar amount of new inventory purchases exceeds the cost of goods that were sold.

Step 1: If we initially assume that all inventory is purchased for cash (we will relax this assumption in adjustment ⑧, which is discussed next), the two accounting entries giving rise to a $12,000 increase in inventory (see Panel (a) of Exhibit 17.4) are:

DR	Inventory	$2,538,625	
	CR Cash		$2,538,625
[$2,526,625 Cost of goods sold + $307,000 Ending inventory − $295,000 Beginning inventory]			

and

| **DR** | Cost of goods sold | $2,526,625 | |
| | **CR** Inventory | | $2,526,625 |

Note that the combined result of these two entries is a $12,000 increase in inventory.

Step 2: The cost of goods sold number that is subtracted in the computation of net income ($2,526,625) is $12,000 *lower* than the cash outflow to buy inventory.

Step 3: Because net income understates the cash outflow to acquire inventory, $12,000 must be deducted from income in Exhibit 17.5.

⑧ **Increase in Accounts Payable** Adjustment ⑦ for the increase in inventory was computed under the assumption that all inventory was purchased for cash. We assumed this because it makes it easier to see why an increase in inventory must be adjusted for when preparing a cash flow statement. We now relax this assumption because Panel (a) of Exhibit 17.4 shows that Accounts payable increased by $3,000 during 2014. A $3,000 increase in Accounts payable means that $3,000 of the $12,000 inventory increase during the year was not paid for in cash. Therefore, $3,000 is added to net income in the cash flow statement.

> There is another way to look at adjustments ⑦ and ⑧ that may make it easier for you to understand the accrual-to-cash adjustment. Together, adjustments ⑦ and ⑧ are designed to isolate the difference between accrual accounting's cost of goods sold measure and cash inventory purchases. Specifically:
>
> | | |
> |---|---:|
> | Accrual accounting cost of goods sold included in the determination of net income | $2,526,625 |
> | Add: Adjustment ⑦ (inventory increase) | 12,000 |
> | Equals: 2014 *total* inventory purchases | 2,538,625 |
> | Subtract: Adjustment ⑧ (payables increase) | (3,000) |
> | Equals: 2014 *cash* paid for inventory purchases | $2,535,625 |
>
> In combination, adjustments ⑦ and ⑧ subtract $9,000 from income, an amount equal to the difference between cost of goods sold ($2,526,625) and cash paid for inventory purchases ($2,535,625).

Cash Flows from Investing Activities

Turning to the investing activities section of Burris's cash flow statement (Exhibit 17.5), we see three transactions affected cash—one was a cash inflow and two were cash outflows.

② **Equipment Sale** This transaction was analyzed earlier when we adjusted accrual net income for the gain on sale of equipment. The $57,000 cash received when this equipment was sold represents an investing source of cash.

⑨ **Land** Panel (a) of Exhibit 17.4 indicates that the Land account increased by $86,000. The analysis here is straightforward.

Step 1: The journal entry that reflects this increase is

| **DR** | Land | $86,000 | |
| | **CR** Cash | | $86,000 |

Step 2: This transaction represents an outflow of cash of $86,000.

Step 3: The cash outflow is categorized as an $86,000 investment outflow.

⑩ **Buildings and Equipment Purchase** The Buildings and equipment account increased by $198,000 during 2014 (see Panel (a) of Exhibit 17.4). However, in computing the cash outflow that was incurred to acquire these fixed assets, we cannot simply use the $198,000 net account change. The reason is that some equipment was sold during 2014 (see preceding Item ②). Therefore, it is necessary to adjust the change in the Buildings and equipment account for the cost of the equipment sold to deduce the cost of the buildings and equipment purchased.

Step 1: When several items affect a particular account, it is useful to begin by reconstructing the account over the period being analyzed.

Buildings and Equipment

12/31/13 Balance	$1,430,000		
Building and equipment purchases (amount necessary to balance the account)	261,000	Reduction in account arising from sale of equipment (see discussion of Item ②)	$63,000
12/31/14 balance	$1,628,000		

The analysis reveals that the increase in the Buildings and equipment account due to purchases of assets was $261,000, resulting in the following journal entry:

DR Buildings and equipment $261,000
    CR Cash $261,000

Step 2: This transaction represents a cash outflow of $261,000.

Step 3: The outflow is categorized as a $261,000 investment cash outflow.

This adjustment illustrates that when constructing a cash flow statement, the analyst must be careful to look beyond just the net change in the account—he or she must also consider other known items that were added to or subtracted from the account during the period.

Cash Flows from Financing Activities

The financing section of Burris's cash flow statement in Exhibit 17.5 shows two other account changes during the period that had cash flow implications.

⑪ **and** ⑫ **Stock Sale and Dividend Paid** The increase in the Common stock account indicates additional capital was raised when new shares were sold. Furthermore, the additional information lists a $90,000 cash dividend (see Exhibit 17.5). The analysis of these items is straightforward:

Step 1: The stock sale journal entry was:

DR Cash $50,000
    CR Common stock $50,000

The dividend generated the following entry:

DR Retained earnings $90,000
    CR Cash $90,000

Step 2: The cash effects of these items are unambiguously indicated in the entries—that is, a $50,000 inflow for the new financing and a $90,000 dividend outflow.

Step 3: Both the $50,000 cash inflow and the $90,000 cash outflow are categorized as cash flows from financing activities.

To prepare a cash flow statement, (1) re-create the accounting entries that explain the changes in all noncash balance sheet accounts, (2) determine the net cash flow effect of the entry and the type of activity that generated or used the cash, and (3) compare the accrual accounting effect of the entry with the cash flow effect to determine what adjustments, if any, are needed to convert accrual earnings to cash flow from operations.

 RECAP

RECONCILIATION BETWEEN STATEMENTS: SOME COMPLEXITIES

Financial statement users frequently encounter situations in which changes in balance sheet accounts over the year do *not* reconcile to the corresponding account changes in the statement of cash flows. We'll demonstrate this discrepancy and explain why it happens using data from the H.J. Heinz Company's fiscal 2012 10-K report. The fundamental point of our analysis is this: ***While all accruals cause changes in balance sheet accounts, not all changes in operating balance sheet accounts (for example, receivables, inventory, and payables) are caused by accruals.*** Therefore, trying to infer accruals that affect income by analyzing changes in balance sheet accounts can be, and often is, misleading.

Exhibit 17.6 shows Heinz's statement of cash flows for the fiscal year ended April 29, 2012, and the previous fiscal year. Exhibit 17.7 shows data from Heinz's fiscal 2012 comparative balance sheet for two selected accounts— Inventory and Property, plant, and equipment. The operating activities section of Heinz's cash flow statement is prepared using the indirect method, and starts with fiscal 2012 accrual-basis net income of $939,908,000. Adjustments to reconcile net income to cash provided by operations are presented next. Notice that on the cash flow statement, the $60,919,000 change in inventory is added to accrual-basis income, implying that inventory decreased by this amount. However, the change in Inventory on Heinz's comparative balance sheet (Exhibit 17.7) shows a $122,195,000 decrease—a discrepancy of $61.276 million.

> The term *accruals* is used in a generic sense to include not only accrued revenues and accrued expenses but also deferred revenues and deferred expenses. So, *accrual adjustments* include situations in which the revenue or expense recognition under accrual accounting occurs both before and after the cash flow.

A similar discrepancy exists when trying to reconcile changes in Heinz's "Property, plant, and equipment" balance sheet account with information presented on its cash flow statement. Heinz's comparative balance sheets show a year-to-year increase in the Property, plant, and equipment account (before accumulated depreciation) of $41,846,000 (Exhibit 17.7). However, the "Investing activities" section of Heinz's statement of cash flows (Exhibit 17.6) shows fiscal year 2012 capital expenditures (implying an increase in Property, plant, and equipment) of $418,734,000—a difference of nearly $377 million.

> To understand why, review discussion on page 1044 for Item ⑦ in Exhibit 17.5 for Burris Products.

Why don't the changes in working capital accounts like Inventory and fixed asset accounts like Property, plant, and equipment shown on Heinz's balance sheet correspond with the amounts shown on its statement of cash flows? There are at least four reasons for these differences:

1. Asset write-offs due to impairment, corporate restructuring, or retirement,

2. Translation adjustments on assets and liabilities held by foreign subsidiaries,

3. Acquisitions of other companies, and

4. Simultaneous investing and financing activities not directly affecting cash.

EXHIBIT 17.6	Consolidated Statements of Cash Flows

H. J. Heinz Company and Subsidiaries

	Fiscal Years Ended		
($ in thousands)	April 29, 2012 (52 1/2 Weeks)	April 27, 2011 (52 Weeks)	April 28, 2010 (52 Weeks)
Operating activities			
Net income	$ 939,908	$1,005,948	$ 882,343
Adjustments to reconcile net income to cash provided by operating activities:			
Depreciation	295,718	255,227	254,528
Amortization	47,075	43,433	48,308
Deferred tax (benefit)/provision	(94,816)	153,725	220,528
Net losses on divestitures	—	—	44,860
Pension contributions	(23,469)	(22,411)	(539,939)
Asset write-downs from Fiscal 2012 productivity initiatives	58,736	—	—
① Other items, net	75,375	98,172	90,938
Changes in current assets and liabilities, excluding effects of acquisitions and divestitures:			
Receivables (includes proceeds from securitization)	171,832	(91,057)	121,387
② Inventories	60,919	(80,841)	48,537
Prepaid expenses and other current assets	(11,584)	(1,682)	2,113
Accounts payable	(72,352)	233,339	(2,805)
Accrued liabilities	(20,008)	(60,862)	96,533
Income taxes	65,783	50,652	(5,134)
Cash provided by operating activities	1,493,117	1,583,643	1,262,197
Investing activities			
③ Capital expenditures	(418,734)	(335,646)	(277,642)
Proceeds from disposals of property, plant and equipment	9,817	13,158	96,493
④ Acquisitions, net of cash acquired	(3,250)	(618,302)	(11,428)
⑤ Proceeds from divestitures	3,828	1,939	18,637
Sale of short-term investments	56,780	—	—
Change in restricted cash	(39,052)	(5,000)	192,736
Other items, net	(11,394)	(5,781)	(5,353)
Cash (used for)/provided by investing activities	(402,005)	(949,632)	13,443
Financing activities			
Payments on long-term debt	(1,440,962)	(45,766)	(630,394)
Proceeds from long-term debt	1,912,467	229,851	447,056
Net payments on commercial paper and short-term debt	(42,543)	(193,200)	(427,232)
Dividends	(619,104)	(579,618)	(533,552)
Purchases of treasury stock	(201,904)	(70,003)	—
Exercise of stock options	82,714	154,774	67,369
Acquisition of subsidiary shares from noncontrolling interests	(54,824)	(6,338)	(62,064)
Other items, net	1,321	27,791	(9,099)
Cash used for financing activities	(362,835)	(482,509)	(1,147,916)
Effect of exchange rate changes on cash and cash equivalents	(122,147)	89,556	(17,616)
Net increase in cash and cash equivalents	606,130	241,058	110,108
Cash and cash equivalents at beginning of year	724,311	483,253	373,145
Cash and cash equivalents at end of year	$ 1,330,441	$ 724,311	$ 483,253

EXHIBIT 17.7	Selected Accounts from Comparative Balance Sheets

H.J. Heinz Company and Subsidiaries

($ in thousands)	April 29, 2012	April 27, 2011	Changes in Account Balances*
Inventories			
Finished goods and work-in-process	$ 1,082,317	$ 1,165,069	
Packaging material and ingredients	247,034	286,477	
Total inventories	1,329,351	1,451,546	$(122,195)
Property, plant, and equipment accounts			
Land	81,185	85,457	
Buildings and leasehold improvements	1,009,379	1,019,311	
Equipment, furniture and other	4,175,997	4,119,947	
	5,266,561	5,224,715	41,846
Less: Accumulated depreciation	−2,782,423	−2,719,632	
Total property, plant, and equipment, net	$ 2,484,138	$ 2,505,083	$(20,945)

* Amounts without parentheses represent increases in accounts from 2011 to 2012, while amounts with parentheses represent decreases in accounts.

Discrepancies in Current Accruals

We'll use Heinz's inventory account to illustrate reasons for the discrepancy between working capital components of net accrual adjustments on the cash flow statement and changes in these accounts on the balance sheet. From Exhibit 17.7, the change in inventories from Heinz's comparative balance sheet is a decrease of $122.2 million while the inventory decrease implied by the accrual adjustment on Heinz's cash flow statement (Exhibit 17.6) is $60.9 million. Although a precise reconciliation is not possible, the primary factors causing the difference arise for the reasons explained next.

Write-Offs Due to Obsolescence and Restructuring   When inventories become obsolete (or fresh produce deteriorates, as can occur for Heinz) write-downs occur, which cause a reduction in inventory balances other than from sales. Inventory accounts, as well as property, plant, and equipment accounts, can also decrease because of corporate restructurings. Note 3 of Heinz's fiscal 2012 financial statements indicates the company took a $224.3 million pre-tax charge for "productivity initiatives." Of this amount, $58.7 million was a noncash charge for asset writedowns, and that amount appears as an addback in the cash flow statement (Exhibit 17.6). Although some of the asset writedowns undoubtedly were for property, plant and equipment, some may also have been for inventory, thereby explaining some of the difference between the change in inventory balances from the fiscal 2011 to the fiscal 2012 balance sheet and the inventory change reflected in the cash flow statement.

Foreign Currency Translation Adjustments   Heinz has numerous foreign subsidiaries whose statements are translated using the current rate approach described in Chapter 16. This method generates a potential discrepancy between the change in the inventory amount presented in the balance sheet and the statement of cash flows inventory change figure. This occurs because on the cash flow statement, inventory change is computed by comparing purchases with cost of goods sold, and if purchases exceed cost of goods sold, an inventory increase is indicated.

For simplicity, the translation may also be done using the weighted average rate of exchange in effect over the period.

This difference usually does not arise when *all* foreign subsidiaries are accounted for using the temporal method (Chapter 16). The reason is that under the temporal method, the U.S. dollar value of inventories is not adjusted for changes in the exchange rate. Inventory is always translated at the exchange rate in effect when it was purchased. The accounting matches the accounting that would have been used if the inventory had been purchased using U.S. dollars. Therefore, for firms whose subsidiaries all utilize the temporal approach, inventory change differences between the two statements usually do not arise.

Changes in inventories due to acquisitions do not create a corresponding accrual adjustment to cost of goods sold on the income statement. Therefore, changes due to these events would *not* be included as part of the inventory adjustment to accrual-basis income (Item ② in Exhibit 17.6) to arrive at operating cash flows.

To determine the inventory change for *foreign* subsidiaries, *translated* purchases and cost of goods sold are compared. Inventory purchases and cost of goods sold are translated into dollars using the exchange rates in effect at the times of the various transactions. In contrast, foreign subsidiaries' beginning inventories are translated at the beginning-of-period exchange rate while ending inventories are translated at the end-of-period exchange rate. The difference corresponds to the different nature of the two statements: The balance sheet reflects an *instant in time* (and thus uses the *exchange rate at that instant*); the cash flow statement uses a *series of exchange rates*. It should not be surprising therefore that the measures of inventory change on the two statements will differ.

Acquisitions Another reason why the inventory change on the two statements differs is because of acquisitions. The ending inventory number reported on the consolidated balance sheet includes the inventory of subsidiary companies acquired during the year, even though the beginning inventory excludes those subsidiaries' inventories. On the statement of cash flows, the increase in inventory due to acquisitions is reported as a component of Acquisitions, net of cash acquired in the Investing Activities section. ***Therefore, the inventory change figure in the Operating Activities section of Heinz's cash flow statement (Exhibit 17.6) excludes inventory changes arising due to acquisitions.***

The same factors explain discrepancies between changes in other working capital accounts on the balance sheet and accrual adjustments shown on the statement of cash flows.

Discrepancies Related to Property, Plant, and Equipment

Asset Impairments A portion of the discrepancy between the change in Property, plant, and equipment on Heinz's balance sheet (an increase of $41.8 million before accumulated depreciation shown in Exhibit 17.7) and the Capital expenditures on the cash flow statement ($418.7 million in Exhibit 17.6, Item ③) might be explained by asset impairment write-downs (see discussion in Chapter 10). The following excerpt is taken from Heinz's note on significant accounting policies related to property, plant, and equipment:

> The Company reviews property, plant, and equipment, whenever circumstances change such that the recorded value of an asset may not be recoverable. Factors that may affect recoverability include changes in planned use of the asset and the closing of facilities. The Company's impairment review is based on an undiscounted cash flow analysis at the lowest level for which identifiable cash flows exist and are largely independent. When the carrying value of the asset exceeds the future undiscounted cash flows, an impairment is indicated and the asset is written down to its fair value.

While there is no indication of an impairment charge for fiscal 2012, Heinz has recorded fixed asset impairment charges in the past.

Retirements and Reclassifications to Assets Held for Sale
During the year, Heinz may have sold or retired fixed assets that were not fully depreciated. Recall from Chapter 10 that the entry to record the retirement would take the following form:

DR Accumulated depreciation—plant and equipment	$XXX	
DR Loss on retirement	XXX	
CR Plant and equipment (for cost of assets retired)		$XXX

It is generally not possible for financial statement users to determine the exact dollar amount of the year-to-year change in fixed asset accounts due to retirements, although Heinz's Note 3 does indicate the company closed 8 factories during fiscal 2012 as part of its productivity initiatives. In addition, Heinz could have had property, plant and equipment reclassified to assets held for sale during the year, reducing the amount reported as property, plant and equipment.

Foreign Currency Translation Adjustment As noted already, Heinz translates the accounts of most of its foreign subsidiaries using the current rate approach. Accordingly, the Property, plant, and equipment accounts of these subsidiaries are translated using the current exchange rate—at the balance sheet date—between the dollar and the foreign currency. The rise (fall) of the functional currencies of these subsidiaries relative to the U.S. dollar would result in an increase (decrease) in the balance of the Property, plant, and equipment account that would not be reflected on the cash flow statement.

Acquisitions If Heinz had acquired companies during the year and those companies all owned property, plant, and equipment, should the portion of cash flow related to the cost of properties acquired be classified as Capital expenditures, or should it be included as a part of Acquisitions, net of cash acquired? Under current GAAP, capital expenditures reported on the cash flow statement contain only cash outflows made to acquire property directly. Cash outflows for property acquired as part of a business acquisition are classified under Acquisitions. The Investing Activities section of the statement of cash flow in Exhibit 17.6 shows that Heinz paid $3.25 million for acquisitions, net of cash acquired (Item ④), in fiscal 2012. However, additional disclosures in the 10-K indicate this payment was actually additional contingent consideration paid on a 2011 acquisition.

Simultaneous Noncash Financing and Investing Activities

Occasionally firms engage in investing and financing activities that cause changes in balance sheet asset and liability accounts even though they do not affect cash receipts or cash payments. Examples include (1) purchasing a building by incurring a mortgage loan to the seller, (2) acquiring an asset by entering into a capital lease, or (3) issuing stock for noncash assets in connection with a business acquisition. Current GAAP requires firms to disclose these noncash simultaneous financing and investing activities either in a narrative or in a schedule, which is sometimes included as a separate section of the statement of cash flows. Although there is no evidence in Heinz's fiscal 2012 10-K report that any of the balance sheet changes in property, plant, and equipment were acquired with noncash consideration, this is a fairly common situation.

Exhibit 17.8 provides the 2012 statement of cash flows for Amazon.com. The supplemental cash flow information (at the bottom of this statement) summarizes simultaneous financing and investing activities (highlighted) totaling $831 million that increased fixed asset accounts on Amazon's balance sheet but did not result in any cash flow.

The year-to-year changes in comparative balance sheet accounts may not coincide with the changes implied from amounts reported on the statement of cash flows. The factors contributing to these differences include (1) asset write-downs due to impairment or restructuring, (2) the translation of foreign subsidiary accounts using the year-end current exchange rate between the dollar and the foreign currency, (3) acquisitions of other companies, and (4) simultaneous noncash financing and investing transactions. Disclosures in notes, along with information in the income statement and in the operating activities section of the cash flow statement, are often helpful in reconciling some of these differences.

RECAP

EXHIBIT 17.8	Consolidated Statements of Cash Flows

Amazon.Com, Inc.

	Year Ended December 31,		
($ in millions)	**2012**	**2011**	**2010**
Cash and cash equivalents, beginning of period	$ 5,269	$ 3,777	$ 3,444
Operating activities			
Net income (loss)	(39)	631	1,152
Adjustments to reconcile net income (loss) to net cash from operating activities:			
Depreciation of property and equipment, including internal-use software and website development, and other amortization	2,159	1,083	568
Stock-based compensation	833	557	424
Other operating expense (income), net	154	154	106
Losses (gains) on sales of marketable securities, net	(9)	(4)	(2)
Other expense (income), net	253	(56)	(79)
Deferred income taxes	(265)	136	4
Excess tax benefits from stock-based compensation	(429)	(62)	(259)
Changes in operating assets and liabilities:			
Inventories	(999)	(1,777)	(1,019)
Accounts receivable, net and other	(861)	(866)	(295)
Accounts payable	2,070	2,997	2,373
Accrued expenses and other	1,038	1,067	740
Additions to unearned revenue	1,796	1,064	687
Amortization of previously unearned revenue	(1,521)	(1,021)	(905)
Net cash provided by (used in) operating activities	4,180	3,903	3,495
Investing activities			
Purchases of property and equipment, including internal-use software and website development	(3,785)	(1,811)	(979)
Acquisitions, net of cash acquired, and other	(745)	(705)	(352)
Sales and maturities of marketable securities and other investments	4,237	6,843	4,250
Purchases of marketable securities and other investments	(3,302)	(6,257)	(6,279)
Net cash provided by (used in) investing activities	(3,595)	(1,930)	(3,360)
Financing activities			
Excess tax benefits from stock-based compensation	429	62	259
Common stock repurchased	(960)	(277)	—
Proceeds from long-term debt and other	3,378	177	143
Repayments of long-term debt capital lease, and finance lease obligations	(588)	(444)	(221)
Net cash provided by (used in) financing activities	2,259	(482)	181
Foreign-currency effect on cash and cash equivalents	(29)	1	17
Net increase (decrease) in cash and cash equivalents	2,815	1,492	333
Cash and cash equivalents, end of period	$ 8,084	$ 5,269	$ 3,777
Supplemental cash flow information			
Cash paid for interest on long-term debt	$ 31	$ 14	$ 11
Cash paid for income taxes (net of refunds)	112	33	75
Property and equipment acquired under capital leases	802	753	405
Property and equipment acquired under build-to-suit leases	29	259	172

ANALYTICAL INSIGHTS: WAYS OPERATING CASH FLOWS CAN BE DISTORTED OR MANIPULATED

Healthy firms generate cash from their day-to-day operating activities. Firms that can't generate cash internally jeopardize their operations and risk loan default or bankruptcy. That is why an understanding of operating cash flows is so critical to assessing a company's financial health. Analysts watch operating cash flow for another reason—major discrepancies between accrual earnings and operating cash flows sometimes can be used to indentify instances in which earnings have been managed upward. Because cash flow from operations is such a carefully monitored number, firms have incentives to make this number look as strong as possible. Therefore, it is important for you to understand the ways in which operating cash flows can be distorted or even legitimately managed. In this section, we briefly review and illustrate some of the ways this can happen.

Changes in Working Capital Accounts

Changes in working capital accounts (excluding short-term debt) are one of the major sources and uses of operating cash flows. For example, collections on accounts receivable *increase* operating cash flows while payments on accounts payable or accrued expenses *decrease* operating cash flows. Two ways management can improve the short-run appearance of a firm's operating cash flows are to (1) accelerate the collection of receivables in the current period or (2) delay the payment of accrued expenses and accounts payable until after period-end. For example, receivables collection can be accelerated by offering special cash discounts or incentive programs to encourage customers to pay early. Payment of accounts payable can be extended beyond the normal collection period, but the firm may incur late payment fees by doing so. Thus, these improvements in operating cash flows are only temporary. So, large decreases in accounts receivable or large increases in accounts payable and accrued expenses should be viewed with a healthy level of skepticism because the impact on operating cash flows may not be sustainable. As demonstrated in Chapters 5 and 8, quarter-to-quarter changes in the number of days accounts receivable outstanding and of days accounts payable outstanding can be monitored to spot shifts in collection or payment policies that contribute to operating cash flow distortions.

> Days accounts receivable outstanding = 365/Accounts receivable turnover where Accounts receivable turnover = Net credit sales/Average accounts receivable; Days accounts payable outstanding = 365/Accounts payable turnover where Accounts payable turnover = Inventory purchases/Average accounts payable.

Accounts Receivable Sale (Securitization) versus Collateralized Borrowing

As you recall from Chapter 8, firms can accelerate the conversion of receivables into cash by selling (factoring) the receivables, securitizing the receivables, or borrowing against receivables pledged as collateral on the loan. You should be aware of how the cash flow statement reflects each transaction and you should monitor whether a firm has increased its use of one or more of these ways of accelerating the collection of cash from receivables during the period.

The accounting treatment for an accounts receivable sale either through factoring or securitization is determined by the criteria provided in the FASB Accounting Standards Codification (ASC) Topic 840: Transfers and Servicing. If the receivables transfer fails to qualify as a sale under GAAP, it is treated as a secured (collateralized) borrowing (see Chapter 8). The outstanding receivables remain on the company's balance sheet, and the loan proceeds received are shown as a *financing* cash inflow. Thus, receivable transfers that are secured borrowings have no effect on operating cash flows.

On the other hand, two things happen when the transfer qualifies as a true sale under FASB ASC Topic 840: (1) The accounts receivable are removed from the company's balance sheet and (2) the decrease in receivables is shown as an operating cash inflow on the cash flow statement.[6] Some analysts believe that classifying receivables sales as operating cash inflows provides a potentially misleading picture of sustainable cash flows from current operations.[7] The reason is that the outright sale or securitization of accounts receivable transfers what would be future operating cash flows into the current period. Accounts receivable that normally would be collected in the subsequent period and be recorded as operating cash inflow in that period are instead collected and reported as cash flows from operations in the current period. Although new receivables may be sold or securitized in the future period, these new receivables would serve only to replace those sold in the previous period. Only by increasing the amount of receivables sold or securitized in the subsequent period can the firm increase operating cash flows in the subsequent period. Clearly, financial statement users should monitor major changes in a firm's use of receivable sales and securitized transactions and be aware of how these changes can temporarily distort operating cash flows.

Capitalizing versus Expensing

Many recent accounting frauds involved improper capitalization of costs that instead should have been expensed. The poster child for this sort of accounting abuse was WorldCom's improper capitalization of line costs from 2001 to 2002 that resulted in an earnings overstatement of nearly $4 billion. WorldCom's operating cash flows over this time frame were also overstated because the improperly capitalized costs were treated as investing cash outflows on its cash flow statement. This type of distortion permanently boosts operating cash flow because amounts capitalized are later expensed as depreciation or amortization, which are non-

> Costs expensed on the income statement are treated as operating cash outflows to the extent that they are paid in cash.

cash income statement deductions that do not reduce cash flow from operations. Identifying improper capitalization of operating costs is difficult to spot. But one should be suspicious of significant increases in capital expenditures reported in the investing section of the cash flow statement that coincide with significant decreases in operating expenses as a percentage of sales (typically shown in the Selling, general, and administrative expenses account).

Software Development Costs

Computer software companies must expense all software development costs as incurred until the software reaches **"technological feasibility."** These costs are also treated as components of operating cash outflows on the cash flow statement.[8] Once technological feasi-

> Technological feasibility is established when the company has completed a detailed program design or a working model.

bility is achieved, software development costs are capitalized, and the corresponding cash

---

[6] FASB ASC Paragraphs for Cash Flows from Operating Activities and Investing Activities of Topic 230, Statement of Cash Flows, provide guidance on the cash flow statement reporting of receivable sales.

[7] See "Cash Flow Metrics and Cash Flow Statement Navigation Guide," *Accounting Issues* (New York: Bear Stearns, June 2006); and C. W. Mulford and K. Shkonda, "The Impact of Securitizations of Customer-Related Receivables on Cash Flow and Leverage: Implications for Financial Analysis," College of Management, Georgia Institute of Technology, June 2006.

[8] FASB ASC Section 985-20-25: Software—Costs of Software to be Sold, Leased, or Otherwise Marketed—Recognition.

flows are shown as investing activity outflows on the cash flow statement.[9] There are no bright-line GAAP criteria for determining when technological feasibility is achieved. So, firms can use their discretion to determine whether technological feasibility has been reached in ways that distort operating cash flows. By selecting a low threshold for technological feasibility, firms can move software development costs out of the operating section and into the investing section of the cash flow statement, thereby improving their operating cash flows.

Because the technological feasibility thresholds are likely to vary considerably across firms, some analysts believe the amount of capitalized software development costs should be deducted from operating cash flows to improve interfirm comparability of that number. We believe this to be a prudent adjustment to make when comparing the operating cash flow results of software development companies. If material, the amount of software development costs is typically disclosed as a line item in the investing section of firms' cash flow statement as illustrated by the excerpt from BMC Software's cash flow statement in Exhibit 17.9. Moving the amount of capitalized software development costs from the investing to the operating section of the cash flow statement not only improves interfirm comparability of operating cash flows but also corrects for a firm's attempt to improve operating cash flows by lowering the technological feasibility threshold in the current period relative to prior periods.

Capital versus Operating Leases

The accounting treatment for leased assets is another area that hinders interfirm comparability of operating cash flows. Recall from Chapter 12 the two ways to account for leased assets—the capital lease approach and the operating lease approach. These two alternative accounting methods have quite different effects on firms' cash flow statements. Under capital

EXHIBIT 17.9	**Capitalization of Software Development Costs**			

BMC Software

	Fiscal Year Ended March 31		
($ in millions)	Year 1	Year 2	Year 3
Cash flow from operations (as reported):	$ 606	$ 499	$ 502
Adjustment for capitalized software development costs	(88)	(53)	(62)
Revised cash flow from operations	518	446	440
Cash flows from investing:			
Purchases of property and equipment	(24)	(50)	(58)
Cash paid for technology acquisitions & other investments	(408)	(54)	(266)
Purchases of marketable securities	(134)	(322)	(191)
Proceeds from maturities/sales of marketable securities	404	229	331
Capitalization of software development costs	(88)	(53)	(62)
Other investing activities	1	2	11
Net cash used by investing activities:	$(249)	$(248)	$(235)

---

[9] Ibid.

> If material, these simultaneous financing and investing transactions are required to be disclosed in the Supplemental Cash Flow Information section of the cash flow statement as shown in Exhibit 17.8 for Amazon.com.

lease treatment, an asset and a liability equal to the present value of the minimum lease payments are recorded on the lessee's balance sheet at the inception of the lease. There is no immediate cash flow effect because the asset acquisition and capital lease obligation are considered to be a single simultaneous financing and investing transaction. Thus, the lease liability increase is not shown as a financing source of cash, nor is the leased asset increase recorded as an investing use of cash.

Under capital lease treatment, each lease payment comprises two elements: (1) an interest element and (2) a loan principal paydown amount as reflected in the following entry.

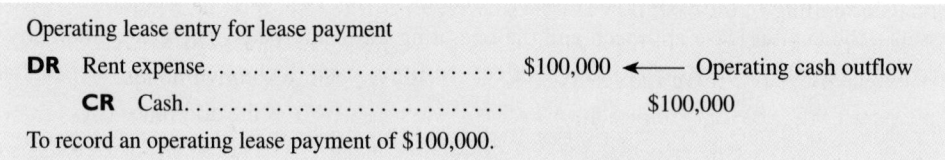

Capital lease entry for lease payment

DR	Interest expense	$60,000	⟵ Operating cash outflow
DR	Lease payable	40,000	⟵ Financing cash outflow
	CR Cash	$100,000	

To record a $100,000 lease payment of which $60,000 is interest and the remainder is a principal payment on the lease obligation.

The interest expense amount reduces earnings and operating cash flows. The principal repayment amount ($40,000) is a financing cash outflow (debt repayment). Therefore, only the interest expense component of the capital lease payment reduces operating cash flows.

For an operating lease, the lessee records no asset or liability on its balance sheet at the inception of the lease. It records the entire amount of each lease payment as rent expense and as an operating cash outflow as reflected in the following entry.

Operating lease entry for lease payment

DR	Rent expense	$100,000	⟵ Operating cash outflow
	CR Cash	$100,000	

To record an operating lease payment of $100,000.

> For a firm with a 10-year lease requiring a payment of $100,000 at the end of each year and using a 10% discount rate, the present value of the lease payments and the total difference in operating cash flows under capital versus operating lease treatment is $614,457.

Thus, the same lease under operating lease treatment reports lower operating cash flows in every year of the lease term relative to a firm that uses capital lease treatment for a lease with an identical payment schedule. The difference in operating cash flows in any given year is the portion of the lease payment attributed to principal repayment under capital lease treatment ($40,000 in the capital lease entry for lease payment). Over the life of the lease, the total difference in operating cash flows under capital versus operating lease treatment is the present value (as of the lease inception) of the minimum lease payments—firms using capital lease treatment record higher operating cash flows equal to this amount.

The proportion of leases treated as capital versus operating leases varies greatly across firms, even for firms within the same industry (see Exhibit 12.4 in Chapter 12). Firms' operating cash flows therefore also vary greatly, complicating the comparison of firms' operating cash flows. One approach to make the financial statement effects (including the operating cash flow effects) more comparable across firms that use varying amounts of operating versus capital leases is to use the data disclosed in lease notes to prepare a pro forma capitalization of operating leases. Following the procedures outlined in the appendix to Chapter 12, the present value of operating leases can be estimated as of the end of the current report year (Year t). Multiplying this amount by the interest rate used in computing the present value of the operating leases gives the portion of the next year's (Year $t + 1$) scheduled operating lease payment that would be considered interest under capital lease treatment. To adjust the reported operating cash flows in Year $t + 1$ for differences between operating and capital lease treatment, one adds back the total operating lease payments for that year (shown in the lease note) and deducts the amount of pro forma interest on the capitalized operating leases as just described. By making this adjustment, the operating cash flows of firms with varying proportions of operating to capital leases are made more comparable.

We use the data from the Whole Foods example in the appendix to Chapter 12 to illustrate this adjustment. The present value of Whole Foods' operating leases as of September 30, 2012, was $3.570 billion. Using an 8% discount rate, the amount of the fiscal 2013 scheduled operating lease payment of $309.1 million (see Exhibit 12.11) that would be considered pro forma interest under capital lease treatment is $285.6 million (8% × $3.570 billion). To illustrate the adjustment to Whole Foods' operating cash flows for capital versus operating lease treatment for fiscal 2013, we assume fiscal 2013 operating cash flows before the adjustment will be the same as in fiscal 2012 ($ in millions).

Whole Foods' operating cash flow for fiscal 2013 before adjustment (assume same as fiscal 2012)	$ 920
Add: Operating lease payment in fiscal 2013 (in 2012 lease note)	309
Subtract: Pro forma interest in fiscal 2013 if operating leases capitalized	(286)
Operating cash flow adjusted for capital lease treatment of operating leases	$ 943

Cash Flow Effect of Stock Option Expensing

Pre-Codification *SFAS No. 123(R),* "Share-Based Payment," effective January 1, 2006, for calendar year-end companies, significantly changed the accounting for stock option grants and the reporting of the cash flow tax benefits that firms receive from these grants.[10] Prior to adopting this standard, most firms did not expense stock option grants for GAAP purposes. However, firms do receive a tax deduction equal to the intrinsic value of nonqualified stock options when employees *exercise* the options. The intrinsic value is the difference between the market price of the firm's stock and the option's exercise price. The tax benefit is obtained by multiplying the intrinsic value at the exercise date by the statutory U.S. corporate tax rate, currently equal to 35%. For example, if an employee exercised 1,000 options at an option price of $40 per share when the stock was selling for $100, the company would receive a tax benefit in the year of *exercise* of $21,000 [35% × 1,000 × ($100 − $40)].

Prior to pre-Codification *SFAS No. 123(R),* these tax benefits were not reflected as a reduction to the company's GAAP tax expense in the income statement because there was no corresponding compensation expense reported in the income statement. Instead, the tax benefit was treated as an increase in Additional paid-in capital in the equity section of the balance sheet. Because the options exercised resulted in real cash savings by reducing the taxes otherwise payable, the tax benefit realized by the company was shown on the cash flow statement as an operating cash inflow. This treatment resulted in operating cash flow reflecting the amount of taxes actually paid in cash in the year that options were exercised.

Exhibit 17.10 illustrates how stock option tax benefits were reported in the cash flow statement prior to adoption *of pre-Codification SFAS No. 123(R)* for the exercise of 1,000 options assuming the market price of the stock at the exercise date was $100, the exercise price was $40, and the tax rate was 35%. The firm reported $50,000 of income under GAAP.

Before we present the cash flow statement effect of stock option exercises *following* the adoption of pre-Codification *SFAS No. 123(R),* let's review the measurement and reporting of stock options under this standard (see Chapter 15 for details). Companies are required to

---

[10] FASB ASC Topic 718: Compensation—Stock Compensation [pre-Codification *SFAS No. 123(R)*].

EXHIBIT 17.10	Cash Flow Statement Presentation of Stock Option Benefits in Year of Option Exercise *Before* Adoption of pre-Codification *SFAS No. 123(R)*

Cash flows from operating activities

Net income	$50,000
Change in deferred taxes	–0–
Tax benefit from exercised employee stock options	21,000*
Change in income taxes payable	–0–
= Operating cash flows	$71,000

* $1000 \times (\$100 - \$40) \times 35\% = \$21,000$

(1) measure the cost of employee services received in exchange for an award of equity instruments (such as stock options) based on the award's grant date fair value and (2) recognize this cost as compensation expense over the period during which an employee is required to provide services in exchange for the award, which is typically a vesting period of three to five years. The fair value at grant date is determined using an option pricing model such as the Black–Scholes or binomial models.

To illustrate the measurement and reporting of option expense under current GAAP, assume that an employee is granted 1,000 nonqualified stock options with an exercise price of $40 and a Black–Scholes fair value of $15 on the *grant* date. The options vest over three years. Also assume that during these three years, the company has income *before* employee option expense of $100,000 for both book and tax purposes. We assume a 35% tax rate throughout.

The stock option compensation expense the company would report in each of Years 1–3 is $5,000 ([1000 × $15]/3). Because nonqualified stock options are not deductible on the tax return until exercised, a deferred tax asset originates in Years 1–3 for the tax benefit related to the $5,000 compensation expense recorded on the company's GAAP financial statements (see Chapter 13 for discussion of temporary differences). The amount of the deferred tax asset recorded in each year is $1,750 ($5,000 × 35%). See Exhibit 17.11 for the cash flow statement presentation in Years 1–3.

EXHIBIT 17.11	Cash Flow Statement Presentation of Stock Option Benefits in Years 1–3 (Before Exercise) *Following* Adoption of pre-Codification *SFAS No. 123(R)*

Cash flows from operating activities

Net income	$ 96,750*
Add: Stock option expense (noncash expense)	5,000
Subtract: Increase in deferred tax asset (noncash reduction of tax expense)	(1,750)
Tax benefit from exercised employee stock options	–0–
Change in income taxes payable	–0–
= Operating cash flows	$100,000

* $100,000 Income before option compensation expense
 −5,000 Option compensation expense ($15,000/3 yrs.)
 +1,750 Deferred portion of current period's tax provision (35% × $5,000)
 $ 96,750 Reported GAAP income

EXHIBIT 17.12	Cash Flow Statement Presentation of Stock Option Benefits in Year of Option Exercise *Following* Adoption of pre-Codification *SFAS No. 123(R)*

Cash flows from operating activities

Net income	$ 50,000
Add: Tax benefit from exercised employee stock options	21,000*
Deduct: Excess tax benefit from exercised employee stock options ($21,000 − $5,250)	(15,750)†
Change in income taxes payable	–0–
= Operating cash flows	55,250
Cash flows from financing activities	
Excess tax benefit from exercised employee stock options	15,750

* $1000 \times (\$100 - \$40) \times 0.35 = \$21,000$

† $\$21,000 - (3 \times \$1,750) = \$15,750$

Note that the tax benefit recognized in the operating activities section of the cash flow statement is $21,000 − $15,750 = $5,250, which is the amount of the previously recorded deferred tax asset related to the option awards recognized in Years 1–3 (3 × $1,750). This is the reduction in deferred tax asset that occurs in the year of exercise.

When the employee *exercises* the option (assumed to be in Year 4), the company's tax savings in that year is $21,000 (1,000 × [$100 − $40] × 35%). Under the reporting rules of accounting for stock compensation, a tax benefit equal to the amount of the previously recognized deferred tax asset is reported in the *operating* section of the cash flow statement (3 × $1,750 = $5,250).The amount of tax benefit received in excess of the previously recorded deferred tax asset is considered an "excess tax benefit." This excess tax benefit ($21,000 − $5,250 = $15,750) is shown as a *financing* cash inflow on the company's cash flow statement rather than as an operating cash flow as was reported prior to pre-Codification *SFAS No. 123(R)* (see Exhibit 17.10).

The cash flow statement presentation of the company's tax benefits in the year of option *exercise* under pre-Codification *SFAS No. 123(R)* is shown in Exhibit 17.12. To provide comparability with Exhibit 17.10, we assume the company reports income of $50,000 for book and tax purposes and recognizes no stock option expense in the year.

Comparing Exhibit 17.12 and Exhibit 17.10 demonstrates the rather dramatic negative effect that changes in accounting for stock-based compensation have had on the reported operating cash flows of firms with significant option grants and exercises. Although year-to-year comparability is no longer a problem unless one is analyzing a cash flow history that goes back to 2005 or earlier, adjustments to operating cash flow would need to be made for longer analyses.

In this section, we describe ways that operating cash flows can be distorted or legitimately managed and how accounting alternatives can hinder interfirm comparisons of this number. Analysts and other financial statement users should be aware of the techniques for enhancing the comparability of operating cash flows both across firms and over time.

GLOBAL VANTAGE POINT

IAS 1, "Presentation of Financial Statements," requires firms to provide a statement of cash flows as part of a complete set of financial statements for each period for which financial statements are presented.[11] Requirements for the preparation and presentation of the statement

---

[11] "Presentation of Financial Statements," *IAS 1* (London: IASB, revised 2003).

of cash flows are set forth in *IAS 7*.[12] Like U.S. GAAP, IFRS rules call for the statement of cash flows to report changes in cash and cash equivalents broken down into three categories: operating, investing, and financing activities. IFRS rules permit entities that use bank overdrafts repayable on demand as part of their normal cash management activities to include those amounts as a component of cash and cash equivalents. U.S. GAAP does not allow bank overdrafts to be considered as cash and cash equivalents. Rather, overdrafts are considered borrowing and always classified as a financing activity.

IAS 7 allows entities to use either the direct or indirect method for presenting cash flows from operating activities. However, firms are encouraged, but not required, to use the direct method. A recent survey of 100 large foreign companies that follow IFRS reporting rules[13] reports that 9% of the firms surveyed used the direct method of reporting operating cash flows, which is a much higher percentage than for firms following U.S. GAAP (only 1%). Unlike U.S. GAAP, which requires firms that use the direct method to provide a reconciliation of net income to cash flows from operating activities (essentially the indirect method), IFRS rules do not *require* this additional disclosure, although many firms still provide it.

Reporting of Interest Received and Paid, Dividends Received and Paid, and Tax Refunds and Payments

As noted earlier in the chapter, U.S. GAAP requires entities to classify interest paid, interest and dividends received, and income tax receipts and payments as operating activities even when associated with an investing or financing transaction. Entities are also required to classify dividends paid as a financing activity. Under IFRS rules, nonfinancial firms are permitted to report interest and dividends received as either operating or investing activities and interest paid as either an operating or a financing activity. Dividends paid are typically classified as a financing cash flow because they are related to obtaining financial resources. But IFRS rules allow firms to classify dividends paid as a component of cash flows from operating activities in order to help users to determine the ability of an entity to pay dividends out of operating cash flows.[14] Cash flows from income taxes are to be reported separately as an operating activity unless they can be specifically identified with financing and investing activities.

Exhibit 17.13 presents the 2012 statement of cash flows and related note for Vodafone Group, PLC, a large international mobile telecommunications company headquartered in England. Panel (a) provides the body of the statement of cash flows broken down into operating, investing, and financing sections, while Panel (b) shows the details of operating cash flows under the indirect method presented in note 27. Several differences between IFRS and U.S. GAAP presentation are highlighted. Note that dividends received from associate companies and dividends received from investments are reported in the investing activities section (item ①). Interest received (item ②) is also shown as an investing activity. Unlike U.S. GAAP, which currently requires interest paid to be reported in the operating activities section, Vodafone reports interest paid in the financing activities section (item ③).

The alternative treatment of these items by firms following IFRS reporting is not all that uncommon. A recent AICPA survey of 100 large foreign companies that follow IFRS reporting shows that of those firms 33% reported interest received and 26% reported dividends received in the investing activities section of the cash flow statement, while 29% reported interest paid in the financing activities section.[15] You should be aware of these differences in cash flow reporting that currently exist between companies that follow U.S. GAAP versus IFRS reporting rules.

---

[12] "Cash Flow Statement," *IAS 7* (London: IASB, 1992).

[13] P. Walters, *IFRS Accounting Trends and Techniques* (New York: AICPA 2010).

[14] *IAS 7*, para. 34.

[15] P. Walters, *IFRS Accounting Trends and Techniques*, p. 487.

EXHIBIT 17.13   Consolidated Statement of Cash Flows

Vodafone Group PLC

Panel (a):

(amounts in £m)	For the Years Ended 31 March		
	2012	2011	2010
Net cash flow from operating activities	12,755	11,995	13,064
Cash flows from investing activities			
Purchase of interests in subsidiaries and joint			
ventures, net of cash acquired	(149)	(46)	(1,777)
Other investing activities in relation to purchase of subsidiaries	310	(356)	—
Purchase of interests in associates	(5)	—	—
Purchase of intangible assets	(3,090)	(4,290)	(2,134)
Purchase of property, plant and equipment	(4,762)	(4,350)	(4,841)
Purchase of investments	(417)	(318)	(522)
Disposal of interests in subsidiaries and joint			
ventures, net of cash disposed	832	—	—
Disposal of interests in associates	6,799	—	—
Disposal of property, plant and equipment	117	51	48
Disposal of investments	66	4,467	17
① Dividends received from associates	4,023	1,424	1,436
① Dividends received from investments	3	85	141
② Interest received	322	1,659	195
Taxation on investing activities	(206)	(208)	—
Net cash flow from investing activities	3,843	(1,882)	(7,437)
Cash flows from financing activities			
Issue of ordinary share capital and reissue of treasury shares	71	107	70
Net movement in short-term borrowings	1,206	(573)	227
Proceeds from issue of long-term borrowings	1,642	4,861	4,217
Repayment of borrowings	(3,520)	(4,064)	(5,184)
Purchase of treasury shares	(3,583)	(2,087)	—
Equity dividends paid	(6,643)	(4,468)	(4,139)
Dividends paid to non-controlling shareholders in subsidiaries	(304)	(320)	(56)
Contributions from non-controlling shareholders in subsidiaries	—	—	613
Other transactions with non-controlling shareholders in subsidiaries	(2,605)	(137)	—
③ Interest paid	(1,633)	(1,578)	(1,601)
Net cash flow from financing activities	(15,369)	(8,259)	(5,853)
Net cash flow	1,229	1,854	(226)

Panel (b):

27. Reconciliation of Net Cash Flow from Operating Activities

(amounts in £m)	2012	2011	2010
Profit for the financial year	7,003	7,870	8,618
Adjustments for:			
Share-based payments	143	156	150
Depreciation and amortisation	7,859	7,876	7,910
Loss on disposal of property, plant and equipment	47	91	101
Share of result in associates	(4,963)	(5,059)	(4,742)
Impairment losses	4,050	6,150	2,100
Other income and expense	(3,705)	16	(114)
Non-operating income and expense	162	(3,022)	10
Investment income	(456)	(1,309)	(716)
Financing costs	1,932	429	1,512
Income tax expense	2,546	1,628	56
Decrease/(increase) in inventory	24	(107)	2
Increase in trade and other receivables	(689)	(387)	(714)
Increase in trade and other payables	871	1,060	1,164
Cash generated by operations	14,824	15,392	15,337
Tax paid	(2,069)	(3,397)	(2,273)
Net cash flow from operating activities	12,755	11,995	13,064

As recently as May 2011, the IASB and FASB were jointly developing major proposed changes to the presentation of all the primary financial statements, including the statement of cash flows. If these changes had been adopted, they would have eliminated many of the differences noted above for the statement of cash flows, while altering the presentation format in several significant ways. A July 2010 Exposure Draft proposed that all firms use the direct method to present operating cash flows, with an indirect method reconciliation of operating income to operating cash flows in the notes to the financial statements. Both boards received a number of comment letters from constituents that provided negative feedback about the proposed changes. For example, the vice president and comptroller of Chevron Corporation wrote to FASB, in a letter dated October 25, 2010, "We strongly oppose the proposed requirement to use the direct method for the statement of cash flows. . . .We use an indirect method . . . and we understand nearly all preparers use the same approach. We have not heard from our financial statement users a demand for a direct statement of cash flows. . . . The information required to compile a statement of cash flows using the direct method is not readily available. The time, effort and cost required to compile the necessary data would be significant and likely far exceeds any perceived benefits."

The FASB's agenda now lists this project as "inactive," suggesting that the two boards do not currently plan to pursue the proposal any further.

SUMMARY

- The statement of cash flows provides information for assessing a firm's ability to generate sufficient cash to pay for operating expenses, capital improvements, and currently maturing obligations.

- Firms able to generate consistently strong positive cash flows from operations are considered better credit risks and benefit from a lower cost of capital.

- The two alternative methods for presenting the operating activities section of a cash flow statement are the direct and indirect methods.

- Most firms use the indirect method. It begins with net income and adjusts for depreciation, amortization, noncash gains and losses, and changes in noncash working capital accounts other than short-term debt, which cause net income to differ from operating cash flows for the period.

- You will frequently encounter situations in which the changes in noncash accounts shown on comparative balance sheets will not reconcile with the adjustments shown on the cash flow statement. These discrepancies are due to one or more of the following causes: (1) asset write-offs due to impairment, corporate restructuring, or retirement, (2) translation adjustments on assets and liabilities held by foreign subsidiaries, (3) acquisitions of other companies or operating units, and (4) simultaneous investing and financing activities not directly affecting cash. Failure to understand how these events cause balance sheet account changes to differ from changes in account balances shown on the cash flow statement can lead to incorrect interpretation of both statements.

- Operating cash flows can sometimes be distorted or legitimately managed. You should be aware of the ways this can occur and how to adjust reported operating cash flows to enhance the comparability of this important number across firms and over time.

- IFRS rules allow firms greater flexibility relative to U.S. GAAP in how interest and dividends received and interest and dividends paid are reported on the statement of cash flows.

WORKSHEET APPROACH TO INDIRECT METHOD CASH FLOW STATEMENT

This appendix describes a worksheet approach to creating cash flow statements. The methodology is identical to that described in the chapter in that it relies on analyzing the changes in all of the balance sheet accounts. However, the compact format and positive/negative notation for debits and credits makes this approach relatively easy to implement once one is comfortable with the concepts underlying the cash flow statement.

Exhibit 17.14 presents the worksheet. The top and bottom rows of the analysis present the balance sheets at the beginning and end of the period for which a cash flow statement is desired. Debit balances are shown as positive amounts and credit balances are shown as negative amounts. (This notation allows us to present "t-accounts" for each balance sheet account in a single column.) Using spreadsheet software and the positive/negative notation, it is easy to check that the balance sheets are input correctly by assuring that those two rows both sum to zero.

Once the balance sheets are input, the analyst must reconcile each of the balance sheet accounts *other than cash,* so that the entire change from the beginning balance to the ending balance is explained. Each change is placed in the column for that balance sheet item, again using positive/negative notation to represent debits/credits. The amounts are entered into rows that will correspond to line items in the cash flow statement.

It is useful to place a formula in a cell below each of the reconciliations that computes the amount that column is out of balance. When the cell shows a zero, the reconciliation of the corresponding column is complete. For example, before beginning the analysis, the common stock column would be out of balance by $50,000 because there is a $50,000 difference between the beginning and ending balances that has not been explained. When the analysis is complete, and the $50,000 stock issuance is entered into the common stock column, the out of balance amount is zero.

In each row of the cash column, there should be a formula that computes the *negative* of the sum of all the other cells in that row. So, for example, in the inventory increase line there is a $12,000 debit in the inventory column, reflecting an increase in the inventory balance. This resulted in inventory purchases exceeding cost of sales by $12,000 and therefore the negative reconciling item in the cash flow statement. The cash column, with appropriate subtotals for the various sections of the cash flow statement, becomes the basis for the cash flow statement.

Although most of the entries in the worksheet are self-explanatory, the analysis of buildings and equipment deserves some explanation. According to the original example, buildings and equipment having an original cost of $63,000 and a book value of $40,000 were sold for $57,000. The worksheet must result in a reversal of the $17,000 gain, which is included in the income statement, as a reconciling item in the operating section of the cash flow statement. We accomplish that by showing a $17,000 increase in the Buildings and equipment account, creating a negative $17,000 amount in the operating section of the cash flow statement. We then show proceeds on the sale of $57,000 in the investing section, corresponding to $80,000 minus $23,000 from the buildings and equipment and accumulated depreciation columns. Where does the $80,000 come from? It is equal to the original cost of $63,000 plus the $17,000 gain. So why do we add those amounts?

EXHIBIT 17.14 Cash Flow Statement Worksheet

Burris Products Corporation

DEBIT/(CREDIT) ($ in thousands)	Cash	Accounts Receivable	Inventory	Land	Buildings and Equipment	Accumulated Depreciation	Accounts Payable	Customer Advance Deposits	Bonds Payable	Discount on Bonds Payable	Deferred Tax Liability	Common Stock	Retained Earnings
Balance, December 31, 2011	33	180	295	250	1,430	(518)	(160)	(110)	(500)	70	(94)	(800)	(76)
Operating activities													
Net income	182												(182)
Depreciation	158					(158)							
Gain on equipment sale	(17)				17								
Amortization of bond discount	4									(4)			
Deferred income taxes increase	6										(6)		
Accounts receivable decrease	9	(9)											
Customer advance deposits decrease	(11)							11					
Inventory increase	(12)		12										
Accounts payable increase	3						(3)						
Net cash provided by operating activities	322												
Investing activities													
Equipment sale	57				(80)	23							
Land purchase	(86)			86									
Buildings and equipment purchase	(261)				261								
Net cash used for investing activities	(290)												
Financing activities													
Common stock issued	50											(50)	
Dividends paid	(90)												90
Net cash used for financing activities	(40)												
Balance, December 31, 2012	25	171	307	336	1,628	(653)	(163)	(99)	(500)	66	(100)	(850)	(168)
Unreconciled	0	0	0	0	0	0	0	0	0	0	0	0	0

We perform the analysis as if the sale had been recorded in two steps. First, the asset is written up to the amount at which it is to be sold. With a $17,000 gain to be reported, there would be a write-up of the asset as follows:

DR	Buildings and equipment	$17,000	
	CR Gain on sale of equipment		$17,000

Then the equipment is sold at its new, higher, book value of $57,000.

DR	Cash	$57,000	
DR	Accumulated depreciation	23,000	
	CR Buildings and equipment		$80,000

Although this is not the way the firm would have actually recorded the transaction, the net effect of these journal entries is equivalent to what the firm would have actually done:

DR	Cash	$57,000	
DR	Accumulated depreciation	23,000	
	CR Buildings and equipment		$63,000
	CR Gain on sale of equipment		17,000

By separating the entry into the two components as we did, we were able to create the cash flow statement appropriately, reversing any gain or loss in the operating section and showing the sale proceeds in the investing section. The trick is to think of first writing the asset up or down to the amount at which it was sold and then recording the sale at the revised book value.

A careful analysis of each of the columns in Exhibit 17.14 will reveal that the information in that column is identical to the information provided in the original analysis in the chapter. Exhibit 17.14 is not a different analysis but rather a different way to format the analysis, one that lends itself well to the use of spreadsheet software in order to reduce the amount of time (and the opportunity for arithmetic errors) involved in creating a cash flow statement.

EXERCISES

The income statement and statement of cash flows for ABC Equipment Company for 2014 are provided below.

E17-1

Deriving a direct method presentation of cash flow from operating activities **(LO 2, 3)**

ABC Equipment Company

Income Statement for the Year Ended December 31, 2014

($ in millions)

Sales	$81,860.0
Gain on the sale of marketable securities	83.2
Equity in earnings of affiliates	856.0
Total revenues and gains	82,799.2
Cost of goods sold	39,853.2
General and administrative expenses	22,280.8
Interest expense	11,549.2
Income tax expense	3,646.4
Total expenses	77,329.6
Net income	$ 5,469.6

ABC Equipment Company	

Statement of Cash Flows for Year Ended December 31, 2014

Operations	
Net income	$ 5,469.6
Adjustments for noncash transactions:	
Depreciation	2,656.0
Increase in deferred tax liability	328.0
Equity in undistributed earnings of affiliates	(188.4)
Gain from sale of marketable securities	(83.2)
(Increase) decrease in accounts receivable	298.4
(Increase) decrease in inventories	(795.6)
(Increase) decrease in prepayments	(161.2)
Increase (decrease) in accounts payable for inventory	135.6
Increase (decrease) in other current liabilities	(443.2)
Cash flow from operations	7,216.0
Investing	
Sale of marketable securities	199.2
Acquisition of marketable securities	(292.8)
Acquisition of property, plant, and equipment	(3,502.8)
Acquisition of subsidiaries	(178.0)
Cash flow from investing activities	(3,774.4)
Financing	
Common stock issued to employees	137.6
Repurchase of common stock	(403.6)
Dividends paid to stockholders	(971.6)
Additions to short-term borrowing	510.4
Additions to long-term debt	486.4
Payments on long-term debt	(1,905.6)
Cash flow from financing activities	(2,146.4)
Net change in cash	1,295.2
Beginning of year cash balance	2,027.2
End of year cash balance	$ 3,322.4

Supplemental Information:

Other current liabilities represent obligations for general and administrative expenses.

Required:

Derive a direct method presentation of cash flow from operating activities for ABC Equipment Company. Assume all depreciation is included in General and administrative expenses.

E17-2	Lino Company's worksheet for the preparation of its 2014 statement of cash flows included the following information:

Determining cash flow from operating activities **(LO 2)**

AICPA
ADAPTED

	December 31	January 1
Accounts receivable	$29,000	$23,000
Allowance for uncollectible accounts	1,000	800
Prepaid rent expense	8,200	12,400
Accounts payable	22,400	19,400

Lino's 2014 net income is $150,000.

Required:

What amount should Lino include as net cash that is provided by operating activities in the statement of cash flows?

An income statement for Hamilton Corporation follows:

E17-3

Calculating cash flows from operating activities, direct method   **(LO 2, 3, 4)**

Revenues from sales of products		$360,000
Cost of goods sold:		
Beginning inventory	$ 48,000	
Purchases	228,000	
Ending inventory	(168,000)	(108,000)
Depreciation expense		(48,000)
Gain on retirement of bonds		60,000
Uncollectible accounts expense		(6,000)
Salary expense		(42,000)
Insurance expense		(6,000)
Income tax expense		(36,000)
Net income		$174,000

Additional Information:

a. Decrease in accounts receivable (net of allowance for doubtful accounts), $36,000.

b. The prepaid insurance account increased by $4,800 during the year.

c. Included in salary expenses are salaries of $9,600 accrued at the end of the year; no salaries were unpaid at the beginning of the year.

d. The bonds payable had a book value of $240,000 at the date of retirement.

e. Increase in accounts payable, $21,000.

Required:
Prepare a schedule showing the net cash flows generated by the operating activities of Hamilton Corporation. Use the direct method.

During 2014, King Corporation wrote off accounts receivable totaling $25,000 and made sales, all on account, of $710,000. Other information about the company's sales activities follows:

E17-4

Determining cash collections from customers   **(LO 4)**

	Beginning of 2014	End of 2014
Accounts receivable	$170,000	$140,000
Allowance for uncollectible accounts	22,000	50,000

In addition, in February 2014, King accepted a $6,000 note from a customer whose account was overdue. King collected $2,300 on this note during December 2014.

Required:
Prepare a schedule showing the amount of cash collected from customers during 2014.

Karr Inc. reported net income of $300,000 for 2014. Changes occurred in several balance sheet accounts as follows:

E17-5

Determining cash flows from investing and operating activities   **(LO 1, 4)**

AICPA
ADAPTED

Equipment	$25,000 increase
Accumulated depreciation	40,000 increase
Note payable	30,000 increase

Additional Information:

1. During 2014, Karr sold equipment that cost $25,000 and had accumulated depreciation of $12,000, for a gain of $5,000.

2. In December 2014, Karr purchased equipment costing $50,000 with $20,000 cash and a 12% note payable of $30,000.

3. Depreciation expense for the year was $52,000.

Required:

1. In Karr's 2014 statement of cash flows, what should be the net cash from operating activities?

2. In Karr's 2014 statement of cash flows, what should be the net cash used in investing activities?

E17-6

Determining cash flows from investing and financing activities **(LO 1, 4)**

Superfine Company collected the following data in preparing its cash flow statement for the year ended December 31, 2014:

Amortization of bond discount	$ 1,000
Dividends declared	22,500
Dividends paid	19,000
Gain on sale of equipment	3,000
Proceeds from the sale of equipment	5,000
Proceeds from the sale of treasury stock (carrying amount $32,500)	37,500
Purchase of BAS Inc. bonds (par value $100,000)	90,000

Required:

Determine the following amounts that should be reported in Superfine's 2014 statement of cash flows.

1. What amount should Superfine report as net cash used in investing activities?

2. What amount should Superfine report as net cash provided by financing activities?

E17-7

Determining cash flow from investing activities **(LO 1)**

AICPA
ADAPTED

Alp Inc. had the following activities during 2014:

- Acquired 2,000 shares of stock in Maybel Inc. for $26,000.

- Sold an investment in Rate Motors for $35,000 when the carrying value was $33,000.

- Acquired a $50,000, four-year certificate of deposit from a bank. (During the year, interest of $3,750 was paid to Alp.)

- Collected dividends of $1,200 on stock investments.

Required:

In Alp's 2014 statement of cash flows, what amount would be shown for net cash used in investing activities?

E17-8

Relationship between balance sheet and statement of cash flows **(LO 4, 5)**

Selected financial statements for Ralston Company, a sole proprietorship, are as follows:

Balance Sheet as of December 31, 2013

Assets:	
Cash	$ 30,000
Equipment	36,000
Accumulated depreciation: equipment	(11,250)
Leased property	18,000
Total	$ 72,750
Liabilities and owner's equity:	
Lease liability	$ 18,000
Ralston, capital	54,750
Total	$ 72,750

Statement of Cash Flows for the Year Ended December 31, 2014

Cash flows from operating activities		
Collections from customers	$ 37,500	
Payments for salaries	(8,250)	
Payments for other expenses	(6,750)	
Net cash provided by operating activities		$ 22,500
Cash flows from investing activities		
Sale of equipment	5,250	
Purchase of land	(13,500)	
Purchase of investments	(22,500)	
Net cash used by investing activities		(30,750)
Cash flows from financing activities		
Payment on lease liability	(3,000)	
Issue of long-term notes	15,000	
Owner withdrawals	(12,000)	
Net cash from financing activities		–0–
Net decrease in cash		$ (8,250)

Additional Information:

a. During 2014, equipment having accumulated depreciation of $4,500 was sold for a $3,000 gain.

b. A $3,750 lease payment was made in 2014, reducing the lease liability by $3,000.

c. 2014 depreciation expense: on leased property, $3,000; on equipment, $8,250.

d. Net income for 2014, $14,250.

Required:
Using the provided data, prepare Ralston's December 31, 2014, balance sheet.

Metro Inc. reported net income of $150,000 for 2014. Changes occurred in several balance sheet accounts during 2014 as follows:

E17-9

Determining operating cash flow   **(LO 1, 2)**

AICPA
ADAPTED

Investment in Videogold Inc. stock, carried on the equity basis	$5,500 increase
Accumulated depreciation caused by major repair to projection equipment	2,100 decrease
Premium on bonds payable	1,400 decrease
Deferred tax liability (long term)	1,800 increase

Required:
Determine the reported net cash provided by operating activities for Metro in 2014.

Hoffman Engineering Company is a young and growing producer of pre-stressed concrete manufacturing equipment. You have been retained by the company to advise it in the preparation of a statement of cash flows. Hoffman uses the direct method in reporting net cash flows from operating activities. You have obtained the following information concerning certain events and transactions for the company during the year ended December 31, 2014:

E17-10

Statement of cash flows preparation   **(LO 1, 2, 3)**

AICPA
ADAPTED

a. The board of directors declared a $200,000 cash dividend on December 15, 2014, payable on January 15, 2015, to stockholders of record on January 5, 2015.

b. On August 27, 2014, Hoffman purchased $500,000 of its common stock on the open market.

c. Depreciation expense of $50,000 was included in the income statement.

d. The amount of net income for the year was $800,000, which included an extraordinary loss of $75,000 (see next item).

e. On June 1, 2014, a tornado caused an uninsured inventory loss of $75,000 ($115,385 loss, less tax benefit of $40,385). This extraordinary loss was included in the determination of net income (as indicated in item *d*).

f. Uncollectible accounts receivable of $20,000 were written off against the allowance for uncollectible accounts. Also, $35,000 of bad debts expense was included in net income; the same amount was added to the allowance for uncollectible accounts.

g. On August 1, 2014, a building and some land were purchased for $500,000. Hoffman gave in payment $100,000 cash, $150,000 market value of its unissued common stock, and a $250,000 mortgage note.

h. Hoffman realized a $5,500 gain on the sale of a machine. The machine originally cost $60,000, of which $25,000 was undepreciated at the time of the sale.

Required:
Write a brief explanation of how each of the items above should be disclosed in Hoffman's statement of cash flows for 2014. If any item is neither an inflow nor an outflow of cash, explain why it is not and indicate how the item should be disclosed, if at all, in Hoffman's statement of cash flows.

E17-11	During 2014, Xan Inc. had the following activities related to its financial operations:

Determining cash used in financing activities **(LO 1)**

AICPA
ADAPTED

Payment for the early retirement of long-term bonds payable (carrying value $370,000)	$375,000
Distribution in 2014 of cash dividend declared in 2013 to preferred shareholders	31,000
Carrying value of convertible preferred stock in Xan converted into common shares	60,000
Proceeds from sale of treasury stock (carrying value at cost, $43,000)	50,000

Required:
In Xan's 2014 statement of cash flows, how much should net cash used in financing activities be?

PROBLEMS / DISCUSSION QUESTIONS

P17-1	The management of Banciu Corporation provides you with the comparative analysis of changes in account balances between December 21, 2013, and December 31, 2014, appearing below.

Preparing a statement of cash flows under the indirect method **(LO 1, 2, 4)**

AICPA
ADAPTED

	December 31,	
	2014	**2013**
Debit balances		
Accounts receivable	$ 306,000	$ 327,600
Cash	174,000	223,200
Inventories	579,600	645,600
Leasehold improvements	104,400	104,400
Machinery and equipment	1,112,400	776,400
Patents	33,360	36,000
Securities held for plant expansion	180,000	–0–
Totals	$2,489,760	$2,113,200

(continued)

	December 31,	
	2014	**2013**
Credit balances		
Accounts payable	$279,360	$ 126,000
Accumulated amortization of leasehold improvements	69,600	58,800
Accumulated depreciation of machinery and equipment	499,200	446,400
Allowance for uncollectible accounts	19,200	20,400
Cash dividend payable	48,000	–0–
Common stock	600,000	600,000
Current portion of 6% serial bonds payable	60,000	60,000
Preferred stock	108,000	120,000
Retained earnings	506,400	321,600
6% Serial bonds payable—noncurrent portion	300,000	360,000
Totals	$2,489,760	$2,113,200

Supplemental Information:

a. The following table presents a comparative analysis of retained earnings as of December 31, 2013, and December 31, 2014.

	December 31,	
	2014	**2013**
Beginning balance	$ 321,600	$ 157,200
Net income	234,000	206,400
	555,600	363,600
Dividends declared	(48,000)	(42,000)
Premium on repurchased preferred stock	(1,200)	–0–
Ending balance	$ 506,400	$ 321,600

b. On December 10, 2014, the board of directors declared a cash dividend of $0.24 per share, payable to holders of common stock on January 10, 2015.

c. Purchased new machinery for $463,000. In addition, Banciu sold certain machinery it was no longer using for $57,600. The machinery cost $127,000 and had accumulated depreciation of $53,800 at the date of the sale. Banciu made no other entries in Machinery and equipment or related accounts other than for depreciation.

d. Purchased 120 preferred shares, par value $100, at $110 and subsequently canceled the shares. Banciu debited the premium paid to Retained earnings.

e. Paid $2,400 of legal costs in successful defense of a new patent, which it correctly debited to the Patents account. It recorded patent amortization amounting to $5,040 during the year ended December 31, 2014.

f. During 2014, Banciu wrote off accounts receivable totaling $3,600 as uncollectible.

g. During 2014, Banciu purchased $180,000 of securities that are being held for future plant expansion.

Required:

1. Prepare the entries (in general journal form) that would be entered into T-accounts needed to prepare a statement of cash flows from the data given. For example, the first entry would be

DR Cash (Operations—Net income) $234,000
   CR Retained earnings $234,000

2. Prepare a statement of cash flows for Banciu Corporation for 2014. Use the indirect method for presenting cash flow from operations.

The Barden Corporation's comparative balance sheets for 2014 and 2013 are presented below.

Barden Corporation

Balance Sheets

	December 31,		Increase
	2014	**2013**	**(Decrease)**
Assets			
Cash	$ 337,000	$ 246,000	$ 91,000
Accounts receivable, net	420,000	280,000	140,000
Marketable securities	15,000	–0–	15,000
Inventories	520,000	440,000	80,000
Land	650,000	400,000	250,000
Plant and equipment	1,160,000	1,266,000	(106,000)
Less: Accumulated depreciation	(180,000)	(200,000)	20,000
Total assets	$2,922,000	$2,432,000	$ 490,000
Liabilities and Stockholders' Equity			
Liabilities:			
Accounts payable	$ 660,000	$ 500,000	$ 160,000
Accrued wages	540,000	520,000	20,000
Long-term bonds (due 7/1/2020)	260,000	360,000	(100,000)
Total liabilities	1,460,000	1,380,000	80,000
Stockholders' equity:			
Common stock and			
Additional paid-in capital	966,000	760,000	206,000
Retained earnings	496,000	292,000	204,000
Total stockholders' equity	1,462,000	1,052,000	410,000
Total liabilities and stockholders' equity	$2,922,000	$2,432,000	$ 490,000

The income statement of Barden Corporation for the year ended December 31, 2014, is as follows:

Barden Corporation

Income Statement for the Year Ended December 31, 2014

Sales	$ 1,600,000
Gain on sale of marketable securities	2,000
Gain on extinguishment of debt	44,000
Total revenue and gains	1,646,000
Expenses:	
Cost of goods sold	720,000
Personnel costs	386,000
Depreciation	40,000
Loss on sale of equipment	8,000
Interest	32,000
Miscellaneous	16,000
Total expenses	1,202,000
Income before income taxes	444,000
Income tax expense	200,000
Net income	$ 244,000

Additional Information:

a. On January 11, 2014, Barden purchased land for $170,000 cash.

b. On January 23, 2014, Barden extinguished long-term bonds with a face value of $100,000.

c. On February 8, 2014, Barden issued 8,400 shares of common stock for cash. The stock was issued at $15 per share.

d. Barden purchased marketable securities for $30,000 on March 15, 2014; one-half of the securities were later sold on December 3, 2014.

e. On June 9, 2014, Barden issued 7,600 shares of common stock for land. The common stock and land had current market values of $80,000 at the time of the transaction.

f. On July 1, 2014, Barden declared and paid a $40,000 cash dividend.

g. On October 18, 2014, Barden sold equipment costing $106,000, with a book value of $46,000, for $38,000 cash.

Required:

Prepare a cash flow statement using the indirect method for operating activities.

The following are selected balance sheet accounts of Zach Corporation at December 31, 2014 and 2013, as well as the increases or decreases in each account from 2013 to 2014. Also presented is selected income statement information for the year ended December 31, 2014, as well as additional information.

P17-3

Determining amounts reported on statement of cash flows **(LO 1, 2, 4)**

AICPA
ADAPTED

Selected Balance Sheet Accounts

	2014	2013	Increase (Decrease)
Assets			
Accounts receivable	$ 34,000	$ 24,000	$10,000
Property, plant, and equipment	277,000	247,000	30,000
Accumulated depreciation	(178,000)	(167,000)	11,000
Liabilities and Stockholders' Equity			
Bonds payable	49,000	46,000	3,000
Dividends payable	8,000	5,000	3,000
Common stock, $1 par	22,000	19,000	3,000
Additional paid-in capital	9,000	3,000	6,000
Retained earnings	104,000	91,000	13,000

Selected Income Statement Information for the Year Ended December 31, 2014

Sales revenue	$155,000
Depreciation	33,000
Gain on sale of equipment	13,000
Net income	28,000

Additional Information:

- Accounts receivable relate to sales of merchandise.

- During 2014, equipment that cost $40,000 was sold for cash.

- During 2014, $20,000 of bonds payable were issued in exchange for property, plant, and equipment. There was no amortization of bond discount or premium.

Required:

Items 1 through 5, which follow, represent activities that will be reported in Zach's statement of cash flows for the year ended December 31, 2014. For each item, determine both the amount that should be reported in Zach's 2014 statement of cash flows and the section (operating, investing, or financing) in which the item should appear.

1. Cash collections from customers (direct method)
2. Payments for the purchase of property, plant, and equipment
3. Proceeds from the sale of equipment
4. Cash dividends paid
5. Redemption of bonds payable

P17-4

Preparing statement of cash flows under indirect method
(LO 1, 2, 3, 4)

Neighborhood Supermarkets is preparing to go public, and you are asked to assist the firm by preparing its statement of cash flows for 2014. Neighborhood's balance sheets at December 31, 2013 and December 31, 2014, and its income statement for the year ending December 31, 2014, appear below.

Neighborhood Supermarkets, Inc.

Balance Sheet

	December 31,	
($ in thousands)	2014	2013
Assets		
Current:		
Cash	$ 91,000	$ 59,351
Marketable securities	18,147	20,068
Accounts receivable, net	52,478	45,318
Inventories	228,515	187,433
Prepaid expenses	6,254	5,085
Total current assets	396,394	317,255
Property and equipment:		
Land	86,193	86,003
Buildings and improvements	417,954	417,954
Equipment	673,570	646,427
Leasehold improvements	139,418	136,589
Accumulated depreciation	(815,060)	(775,860)
Total property and equipment	502,075	511,113
Goodwill	35,162	15,722
Intangibles and other	3,843	4,124
Total assets	$ 937,474	$ 848,214
Liabilities		
Current:		
Accounts payable	$ 127,865	$ 95,128
Accrued expenses	30,227	28,173
Accrued self-insurance	21,998	23,344
Deferred revenue	6,731	6,920
Income taxes payable	484	738
Total current liabilities	187,305	154,303
Noncurrent:		
Notes payable	25,000	—
Postretirement benefit obligations	12,454	12,454
Deferred income taxes	22,544	20,357
Total noncurrent liabilities	59,998	32,811
Total liabilities	247,303	187,114
Stockholders' Equity		
Common stock	9,949	9,949
Retained earnings	826,473	795,473
Accumulated other comprehensive income	4,604	4,560
Treasury stock (at cost)	(150,855)	(148,882)
Total stockholders' equity	690,171	661,100
Total liabilities and stockholders' equity	$ 937,474	$ 848,214

Neighborhood Supermarkets, Inc.

Income Statement for the Year Ended December 31, 2014

($ in thousands)

Net sales	$2,516,364
Cost of sales	1,837,657
Gross profit	678,707
Depreciation expense	(47,201)
Amortization expense	(6,207)
Self-insurance expenses	(43,000)
Loss on sale of equipment	(60)
Operating, general, and administrative expenses	(486,665)
Income from operations	95,574
Gain on sale of marketable securities	208
Investment income	1,556
Income before provision for income taxes	97,338
Provision for income taxes	(35,107)
Net income	$ 62,231

Additional Information:

a. The only entries in retained earnings for 2014 were for net income and cash dividends.

b. During 2014, bad debt expenses of $906 were included in operating, general, and administrative expenses; no accounts were written off.

c. Adjusting marketable securities upward by $68 led to the increase of $44 in accumulated other comprehensive income, after considering the deferred tax effect of $24.

d. On July 1, 2014, Neighborhood Supermarkets bought land ($190) and equipment ($20,000), paying $10,190 in cash and issuing a $10,000 five-year note payable with interest at 6% payable annually. Accrued interest on the note was included in operating, general, and administrative expenses because the amount was deemed too immaterial to report separately.

e. No treasury stock was reissued during 2014.

f. Equipment costing $9,052 with a book value of $1,051 was sold for cash.

g. A much smaller competitor was acquired on December 31, 2014, for $34,890 cash and a 7%, $15,000 note that matures in two years. Neighborhood allocated the acquisition cost as follows: inventory, $5,500; intangibles, $5,926; equipment, $16,195; leasehold improvements, $2,829; goodwill, $19,440.

Required:

Use the indirect method to prepare Neighborhood Supermarkets' statement of cash flows for 2014. Use the worksheet approach from the appendix.

The balance sheets of Global Trading Company follow:

Balance Sheets as of December 31,

P17-5

Preparing and analyzing cash flow statement   **(LO 1, 2, 4)**

	2014	2013
Assets		
Cash	$120,000	$108,000
Accounts receivable	50,000	300,000
Less: Allowance for doubtful accounts	(20,000)	(30,000)
Inventory	80,000	250,000
Prepaid insurance	–0–	20,000

(continued)

	2014	2013
Property, plant, and equipment	500,000	500,000
Less: Accumulated depreciation	(450,000)	(400,000)
Goodwill	–0–	70,000
Total assets	$280,000	$818,000
Liabilities and Owners' Equity		
Accounts payable	$100,000	$ 22,000
Salaries payable	17,000	11,000
Bank loan	82,500	390,000
Capital stock	75,000	75,000
Retained earnings	5,500	320,000
Total liabilities and owners' equity	$280,000	$818,000

Additional Information:

- The company reported a net loss of $279,500 during 2014.

- There are no income taxes.

- Goodwill as of December 31, 2013, was part of an acquisition made during 2013.

- The company's bank provides a working capital loan to a maximum of 75% of net accounts receivable and inventory.

Required:

1. Prepare a statement of cash flows using the indirect method for the year ended December 31, 2014.

2. On the basis of available information, assess the financial performance of the company during 2014. In answering this part, consider both the net income and cash flows of the company. Also evaluate the future prospects of the company.

3. Assuming that the bad debt expense during 2014 was $55,000, calculate the amount of bad debts written off during the year. Further assume that the company collected $1,250,000 cash from its customers during 2014, and then compute the sales revenue for the year. You may assume that all sales are credit sales.

4. In answering this part, assume that Global uses the first-in, first-out (FIFO) inventory method. On December 31, 2014, the company purchased $35,000 worth of inventory on credit from a supplier. The transaction was inadvertently not recorded because physical possession was not obtained as of December 31, 2014. Discuss the effect of this omission on Global Trading Company's financial statements.

P17-6

Reconciling changes in balance sheet accounts with amounts reported in the cash flow statement **(LO 1, 2, 4)**

Excerpts from the financial statements of Publix Super Markets, Inc., and Stanley Black & Decker, Inc., are provided next.

Publix Super Markets, Inc.

Excerpts from Consolidated Balance Sheets as of December 29, 2012 and December 31, 2011:

(Amounts are in thousands)	2012	2011
Assets		
Current assets		
Cash and cash equivalents	$ 337,400	$ 366,853
Short-term investments	797,260	447,972
Trade receivables	519,137	542,900
Merchandise inventories	1,409,367	1,361,709

Reconciliation of Net Earnings to Net Cash Provided by Operating Activities for the Years Ended December 29, 2012, and December 31, 2011, and December 25, 2010:

	2012	2011	2010
Net earnings	$1,552,255	1,491,966	1,338,147
Adjustments to reconcile net earnings to net cash provided by operating activities:			
Depreciation and amortization	493,239	492,639	507,341
Increase in LIFO reserve	28,419	67,145	14,124
Retirement contributions paid or payable in common stock	304,285	291,240	275,547
Deferred income taxes	7,002	95,848	20,722
Loss on disposal and impairment of property, plant and equipment	24,855	13,734	19,896
Gain on AFS securities	(10,386)	(19,886)	(24,516)
Net amortization of investments	108,300	80,890	48,113
Change in operating assets and liabilities providing (requiring) cash:			
Trade receivables	22,517	(50,782)	16,165
Merchandise inventories	(76,077)	(70,277)	12,121
Prepaid expenses and other noncurrent assets	(3,374)	(15,635)	(8,054)
Accounts payable and accrued expenses	181,916	(51,741)	63,852
Self-insurance reserves	6,497	9,762	(13,494)
Federal and state income taxes	(41,153)	15,763	(5,113)
Other noncurrent liabilities	5,912	(9,479)	1,117
Total adjustments	1,051,952	849,221	927,821
Net cash provided by operating activities	$2,604,207	2,341,187	2,265,968

Stanley Black & Decker, Inc.

Excerpts from Consolidated Balance Sheet as of End of Fiscal 2012 and 2011:

	Fiscal	
($ in millions)	2012	2011
Assets		
Current assets		
Cash and cash equivalents	$ 716.0	$ 906.9
Accounts and notes receivable, net	1,538.2	1,445.0

Excerpt from Fiscal 2012 Income Statement:

Provision for doubtful accounts	$ 11.3

Operating Section of Consolidated Statement of Cash Flows

	For Fiscal Years		
($ in millions)	2012	2011	2010
Operating activities			
Net earnings attributable to common shareowners	**$ 883.8**	$ 674.6	$ 198.2
Adjustments to reconcile net earnings to cash provided by operating activities:			
Depreciation and amortization of property, plant and equipment	**237.9**	228.5	203.4
Amortization of intangibles	**207.4**	181.6	145.3
Inventory step-up amortization	**6.3**	0.8	173.5
Pretax (gain) loss on sales of businesses	**(384.7)**	16.2	—

(continued)

($ in millions)	For Fiscal Years		
	2012	**2011**	**2010**
Loss on debt extinguishment	**45.5**	—	—
Asset impairments	**10.8**	0.6	24.1
Stock-based compensation expense	**89.7**	68.9	85.1
Provision for doubtful accounts	**11.3**	15.9	10.6
Income tax settlements	**(48.6)**	(73.4)	(36.2)
Debt-fair value amortization	**(18.3)**	(34.1)	(37.9)
Other non-cash items	**(28.5)**	(12.2)	3.8
Changes in operating assets and liabilities:			
Accounts receivable	**(55.2)**	10.1	22.5
Inventories	**11.4**	(90.2)	35.3
Accounts payable	**109.1**	214.2	77.3
Deferred revenue	**(17.6)**	(6.0)	1.5
Accrued expenses	**24.2**	2.2	51.4
Other current assets	**(151.7)**	28.4	18.7
Long-term receivables	**(15.2)**	(21.1)	(14.6)
Defined benefit liabilities	**(107.0)**	(130.5)	(276.9)
Other long-term liabilities	**301.1**	(119.5)	39.2
Other long-term assets	**(145.5)**	43.9	15.0
Net cash provided by operating activities	**$ 966.2**	$ 998.9	$ 739.3

From Stanley Black & Decker's Accounts receivable note:

(Millions of Dollars)	**2012**	**2011**
Trade accounts receivable	$1,454.1	$ 1,356.7
Trade notes receivable	125.9	100.2
Other accounts receivables	24.4	41.7
Gross accounts and notes receivable	1,604.4	1,498.6
Allowance for doubtful accounts	(66.2)	(53.6)
Accounts and notes receivable, net	$1,538.2	$ 1,445.0
Long-term trade notes receivable, net	$ 146.4	$ 131.2

Required:

1. Reconcile the difference, if any, between the change in accounts receivable as reported in the statement of cash flows and the change in receivables based on the balance sheet value for each company.

2. Both companies report a small change in cash relative to their respective operating cash flow for 2012. Explain.

P17-7

Preparing cash flow statement—Indirect method
(LO 1, 2, 4)

AICPA
ADAPTED

Presented next are the balance sheet accounts of Bergen Corporation as of December 31, 2014 and 2013.

	2014	2013	Increase (Decrease)
Assets			
Current assets:			
Cash	$ 541,000	$ 308,000	$233,000
Accounts receivable, net	585,000	495,000	90,000
Inventories	895,000	780,000	115,000
Total current assets	2,021,000	1,583,000	438,000

(continued)

	2014	2013	Increase (Decrease)
Land	350,000	250,000	100,000
Plant and equipment	1,060,000	720,000	340,000
Accumulated depreciation	(295,000)	(170,000)	(125,000)
Leased equipment under capital lease	158,000	–0–	158,000
Marketable investment securities, at cost	–0–	75,000	(75,000)
Investment in Mason, Inc., at cost	180,000	180,000	–0–
Total assets	$3,474,000	$2,638,000	$836,000
Liabilities and Stockholders' Equity			
Current liabilities:			
Current portion of long-term debt	$ 159,000	$ –0–	$159,000
Accounts payable and accrued expenses	760,000	823,000	(63,000)
Total current liabilities	919,000	823,000	96,000
Note payable, long-term	300,000	–0–	300,000
Liability under capital lease	124,000	–0–	124,000
Bonds payable	500,000	500,000	–0–
Unamortized bond premium	16,000	18,000	(2,000)
Deferred income taxes	60,000	45,000	15,000
Common stock, par-value $20	640,000	600,000	40,000
Additional paid-in capital	304,000	244,000	60,000
Retained earnings	611,000	408,000	203,000
Total liabilities and stockholders' equity	$3,474,000	$2,638,000	$836,000

Additional Information:

- On January 2, 2014, Bergen sold all of its marketable investment securities for $95,000 cash.

- On March 10, 2014, Bergen paid a cash dividend of $50,000 on its common stock. No other dividends were paid or declared during 2014.

- On April 15, 2014, Bergen issued 2,000 shares of its common stock for land having a fair value of $100,000.

- On May 25, 2014, Bergen borrowed $450,000 from an insurance company. The underlying promissory note bears interest at 15% and is payable in three equal annual installments of $150,000. The first payment is due on May 25, 2015.

- On June 15, 2014, Bergen purchased equipment for $392,000 cash.

- On July 1, 2014, Bergen sold equipment costing $52,000, with a book value of $28,000 for $33,000 cash.

- On December 31, 2014, Bergen leased equipment from Tilden Company for a 10-year period. Equal payments under the lease are $25,000 due on December 31 each year. The first payment was made on December 31, 2014. The present value at December 31, 2014, of the 10 lease payments is $158,000. Bergen appropriately recorded the lease as a capital lease. The $25,000 lease payment due on December 31, 2015, will consist of $9,000 principal and $16,000 interest.

- Bergen's net income for 2014 is $253,000.

- Bergen owns a 10% interest in the voting common stock of Mason, Inc. Mason reported net income of $120,000 for the year ended December 31, 2014, and paid a common stock dividend of $55,000 during 2014.

Required:
Prepare a cash flow statement for Bergen using the indirect method for 2014.

<table>
<tr><td>**P17-8**</td><td colspan="2">A statement of cash flows for Friendly Markets, Inc., for 2014 appears below.</td></tr>
</table>

P17-8

Working backward from the
statement of cash flows
(LO 1, 2, 4)

A statement of cash flows for Friendly Markets, Inc., for 2014 appears below.

Operations

(1) Net income	$ 1,161,442
Adjustments for noncash transactions:	
(2) Depreciation and amortization	496,106
(3) Retirement contributions paid in common stock	256,110
(4) Deferred income taxes	27,018
(5) Loss on disposal of property, plant, and equipment	32,482
(6) Loss on sale of investments	6,801
(7) Net amortization of investments	15,625
Change in operating assets/liabilities providing (requiring) cash:	
(8) Trade receivables	(140,082)
(9) Merchandise inventories	2,302
(10) Prepaid expenses	(5,825)
(11) Accounts payable and accrued expenses	103,014
(12) Self-insurance reserves	(14,381)
(13) Federal and state income taxes	33,186
(14) Other noncurrent liabilities	24,434
Net cash provided by operating activities	1,998,232
Investing	
(15) Payment for property, plant, and equipment	(693,489)
(16) Proceeds from sale of property, plant, and equipment	4,150
(17) Payment for investments	(1,133,449)
(18) Proceeds from sale of investments	777,381
Net cash used in investing activities	(1,045,407)
Financing	
(19) Payment for acquisition of common stock	(629,453)
(20) Proceeds from sale of common stock	152,096
(21) Dividends paid	(325,295)
(22) Other, net	18,530
Net cash used in financing activities	(784,122)
Net increase in cash	168,703
Cash at beginning of year	201,813
Cash at end of year	$ 370,516

Required:

Prepare the worksheet entry that would be made to prepare a cash flow statement for each of
the numbered line items. For example, the worksheet entry for item (1) is as follows:

(1)	**DR**	Cash (operations—Net income)	$1,161,442	
	CR	Retained earnings		$1,161,442

P17-9

Preparing a statement of cash
flows—Indirect method
(LO 1, 2, 4)

AICPA
ADAPTED

Omega Corporation's comparative balance sheet accounts worksheet at December 31, 2014
and 2013, follow, together with a column showing the increase (decrease) from 2013 to 2014.

Comparative Balance Sheet Worksheet

	2014	2013	Increase (Decrease)
Cash	$ 800,000	$ 700,000	$ 100,000
Accounts receivable	1,128,000	1,168,000	(40,000)
Inventories	1,850,000	1,715,000	135,000
Property, plant, and equipment	3,307,000	2,967,000	340,000
Accumulated depreciation	(1,165,000)	(1,040,000)	(125,000)
Investment in Belle Company	305,000	275,000	30,000
Loan receivable	270,000	–0–	270,000
Total assets	$ 6,495,000	$ 5,785,000	$ 710,000

(continued)

	2014	2013	Increase (Decrease)
Accounts payable	$ 1,015,000	$ 955,000	$ 60,000
Income taxes payable	30,000	50,000	(20,000)
Dividends payable	80,000	90,000	(10,000)
Capital lease obligation	400,000	–0–	400,000
Capital stock, common, $1 par	500,000	500,000	–0–
Additional paid-in capital	1,500,000	1,500,000	–0–
Retained earnings	2,970,000	2,690,000	280,000
Total liabilities and stockholders' equity	$ 6,495,000	$ 5,785,000	$ 710,000

Additional Information:

- On December 31, 2013, Omega acquired 25% of Belle Company's common stock for $275,000. On that date, the carrying value of Belle's assets and liabilities, which approximated their fair values, was $1,100,000. Belle reported income of $120,000 for the year ended December 31, 2014. No dividend was paid on Belle's common stock during the year.

- During 2014, Omega loaned $300,000 to Chase Company, an unrelated company. Chase made the first semiannual principal repayment of $30,000 plus interest at 10%, on October 1, 2014.

- On January 2, 2014, Omega sold equipment for $40,000 cash that cost $60,000 and had a carrying amount of $35,000.

- On December 31, 2014, Omega entered into a capital lease for an office building. The present value of the annual rental payments is $400,000, which equals the building's fair value. Omega made the first rental payment of $60,000, when due, on January 2, 2015.

- Net income for 2014 was $360,000.

- Omega declared and paid cash dividends for 2014 and 2013 as follows:

	2014	2013
Declared	12/15/14	12/15/13
Paid	2/28/15	2/28/14
Amount	$80,000	$90,000

Required:
Prepare an indirect method statement of cash flows for Omega Corporation for the year ended December 31, 2014, using the worksheet method illustrated in the appendix to this chapter.

Rite Aid Corporation operates retail drugstores in the United States. It is one of the country's largest retail drugstore chains with 3,333 stores in operation as of March 3, Year 3. The company's drugstores' primary business is pharmacy services. The company also sells a full selection of health and beauty aids and personal care products, seasonal merchandise, and a large private brand product line.

P17-10

Operating cash flow impact of securitization   **(LO 2, 6)**

The following condensed information was extracted from Rite Aid's Form 10-K for the fiscal year that ended March 3, Year 3 (all dollars in thousands).

Consolidated Statements of Cash Flows—Operating Activities Section

	Year Ended		
	3/3/Year 3	3/4/Year 2	2/26/Year 1
Net Income	$ 26,826	$1,273,006	$ 302,478
Total noncash charges (credits)	379,715	(810,731)	129,729
Changes in operating assets and liabilities:			
Net proceeds from accounts receivable securitization	20,000	180,000	150,000
Accounts receivable	(39,543)	(51,494)	36,549
Net changes in other operating assets and liabilities	(77,853)	(173,616)	(100,310)
Net cash provided by operating activities	$309,145	$ 417,165	$ 518,446

Consolidated Statements of Operations

	Year Ended		
	3/3/Year 3	3/4/Year 2	2/26/Year 1
Revenues	$17,507,719	$17,270,968	$16,816,439
Costs and expenses			
Cost of goods sold	12,791,597	12,571,860	12,202,894
Selling, general, and administrative expenses	4,370,481	4,307,421	4,127,536
Store closing and impairment charges	49,317	68,692	35,655
Interest expense	275,219	277,017	294,871
Loss on debt modifications and retirements, net	18,662	9,186	19,229
(Gain) loss on sale of assets, net	(11,139)	(6,462)	2,247
	17,494,137	17,227,714	16,682,432
Income before income taxes	13,582	43,254	134,007
Income tax benefit	(13,244)	(1,229,752)	(168,471)
Net income	$ 26,826	$ 1,273,006	$ 302,478

Selected Data Pertaining to Accounts Receivable

	Year Ended		
	3/3/Year 3	3/4/Year 2	2/26/Year 1
Year-end Accounts receivable, net	$374,493	$354,949	$483,455
Allowance for uncollectible accounts at year-end	30,246	32,336	31,216
Additions to uncollectible accounts charged to costs and expenses	26,603	34,702	47,291

Accounts Receivable

The Company maintains an allowance for doubtful accounts receivable based upon the expected collectibility of accounts receivable. The allowance for uncollectible accounts at March 3, Year 3, and March 4, Year 2, was $30,246 and $32,336, respectively. The Company's accounts receivable are due primarily from third-party payors (e.g., pharmacy benefit management companies, insurance companies, or governmental agencies) and are recorded net of any allowances provided for under the respective plans. Since payments due from third-party payors are sensitive to payment criteria changes and legislative actions, the allowance is reviewed continually, and adjusted for accounts deemed uncollectible by management.

The Company maintains securitization agreements with several multiseller asset-backed commercial paper vehicles ("CPVs"). Under the terms of the securitization agreements, the Company sells substantially all of its eligible third-party pharmaceutical receivables to a bankruptcy remote Special Purpose Entity (SPE) and retains servicing responsibility. The assets of the SPE are not available to satisfy the creditors of any other person, including any of the Company's affiliates. These agreements provide for the Company to sell, and for the SPE to purchase these receivables. The SPE then transfers an interest in these receivables to various CPVs. Transferred outstanding receivables cannot exceed $400,000. The amount of transferred receivables outstanding at any one time is dependent upon a formula that takes into account such factors as default history, obligor concentrations, and potential dilution ("Securitization Formula"). Adjustments to this amount can occur on a weekly basis. At March 3, Year 3, and March 4, Year 2, the total of outstanding receivables that have been transferred to the CPVs were $350,000 and $330,000, respectively. The Company has determined that the transactions meet the criteria for sales treatment in accordance with (pre-Codification) SFAS No. 140 "Accounting for Transfers and Servicing of Financial Assets and Extinguishment of Liabilities."

Required:

1. Calculate cash collected from customers during fiscal Year 3.

2. Had Rite Aid *not* securitized receivables during Year 3, Year 2, and Year 1, what would its operating cash flows have been in each of these years? Do you believe that Rite Aid's operating cash flows were materially affected by its receivables securitization practices?

3. Calculate pre-tax operating income for Year 3, Year 2, and Year 1, and compare it to operating cash flows as originally reported and to operating cash flows assuming that Rite Aid did not securitize receivables. Compare both results and comment on the impact of Rite Aid's practice of securitizing receivables. (*Hint:* When calculating pre-tax operating income, include only items that relate to core business operations.)

CASES

Statements of cash flows are provided for three companies:

- Telstra Corporation Limited is an Australian telecommunications and media company, formerly owned by the Australian government and privatized in stages from the late 1990s. Telstra is the largest provider of local and long-distance telephone services, mobile services, dial-up, wireless, DSL, and cable Internet access in Australia.

- Seven Group Holdings Limited has a portfolio of businesses with a presence in industrial services, media, property, and other investments.

- First Solar, Inc., manufactures and sells solar modules with advanced thin film semi-conductor technology and designs, constructs, and sells photovoltaic (PV) solar power systems.

C17-1

Statement of cash flow differences under IFRS and U.S. GAAP **(LO 7)**

Telstra and Seven Group Holdings are both Australian companies and report under A-IFRS, the Australian version of IFRS. Australia, along with many European countries, was one of the initial adopters of IFRS, putting it into effect in 2005.

(*Note:* The Australian Accounting Standards Board has made certain amendments to the IASB pronouncements in making A-IFRS, however these generally have the effect of eliminating an option under IFRS, introducing additional disclosures or implementing requirements for not-for-profit entities, rather than departing from IFRS for Australian entities.)

Required:
Prepare a table like the one below and in each cell enter any reporting differences that you find between these three companies. Consider "reporting differences" to be any item found on more than one firm's statement of cash flows but reported in different sections.

	Telstra	Seven Group Holdings	First Solar
Operating section			
Investing section			
Financing section			

Telstra Corporation Limited and Controlled Entities

Statement of Cash Flows

	Year Ended 30 June			
	2012 $m	2011 $m	Change $m	Change %
Cash flows from operating activities				
Receipts from customers (inclusive of goods and services tax (GST))	**28,364**	27,389	975	**3.6**
Payments to suppliers and to employees (inclusive of GST)	**(17,491)**	(17,860)	369	**(2.1)**
Net cash generated by operations	**10,873**	9,529	1,344	**14.1**
Income taxes paid	**(1,597)**	(1,511)	(86)	**5.7**
Net cash provided by operating activities	**9,276**	8,018	1,258	**15.7**
Cash flows from investing activities				
Payments for:				
property, plant and equipment	**(3,006)**	(2,342)	(664)	**28.4**
intangible assets	**(942)**	(909)	(33)	**3.6**
Capital expenditure (before investments)	**(3,948)**	(3,251)	(697)	**21.4**
shares in controlled entities (net of cash acquired)	**0**	(36)	36	**(100.0)**
payments for associates	**(9)**	0	(9)	**(100.0)**
payments for other investments	**(18)**	0	(18)	**(100.0)**
Total capital expenditure	**(3,975)**	(3,287)	(688)	**20.9**
Proceeds from:				
sale of property, plant and equipment	**17**	16	1	**6.3**
sale of intangible assets	**2**	0	2	**100.0**
sale of shares in controlled entities (net of cash disposed)	**(9)**	288	(297)	**(103.1)**
sale of businesses (net of cash disposed)	**(2)**	14	(16)	**(114.3)**
sale of associates	**0**	23	(23)	**(100.0)**
Proceeds from finance lease principal amounts	**54**	74	(20)	**(27.0)**
Repayments of loans to jointly controlled and associated entities	**3**	2	1	**50.0**
Loans to jointly controlled and associated entities	**(443)**	0	(443)	**n/m**
Interest received	**117**	122	(5)	**(4.1)**
Settlement of hedges in net investments	**49**	96	(47)	**(49.0)**
Dividends received	**0**	41	(41)	**(100.0)**
Distributions received from FOXTEL Partnership	**108**	70	38	**54.3**
Net cash used in investing activities	**(4,079)**	(2,541)	(1,538)	**60.5**
Operating cash flows less investing cash flows	**5,197**	5,477	(280)	**(5.1)**
Cash flows from financing activities				
Proceeds from borrowings	**3,049**	2,340	709	**30.3**
Repayment of borrowings	**(2,224)**	(2,536)	312	**(12.3)**
Repayment of finance lease principal amounts	**(52)**	(61)	9	**(14.8)**
Staff repayments of share loans	**3**	8	(5)	**(62.5)**
Finance costs paid	**(1,154)**	(1,135)	(19)	**1.7**
Acquisition of non-controlling interests	**(37)**	0	(37)	**n/m**
Dividends paid to equity holders of Telstra Entity	**(3,475)**	(3,475)	0	**0.0**
Dividends paid to non-controlling interests	**(16)**	(14)	(2)	**14.3**
Net cash used in financing activities	**(3,906)**	(4,873)	967	**(19.8)**
Net increase in cash and cash equivalents	**1,291**	604	687	**113.7**
Cash and cash equivalents at the beginning of the year	**2,637**	2,105	532	**25.3**
Effects of exchange rate changes on cash and cash equivalents	**17**	(72)	89	**(123.6)**
Cash and cash equivalents at the end of the year	**3,945**	2,637	1,308	**49.6**

Seven Group Holdings Limited

Consolidated Cash Flow Statement

	2012 $'000	2011 $'000
Cash flows related to operating activities		
Receipts from customers	4,726,707	3,443,091
Payments to suppliers and employees	(4,819,946)	(3,447,287)
Dividends received from equity accounted investees	25,626	33,157
Other dividends received	38,798	31,372
Interest and other items of a similar nature received	4,371	7,621
Interest and other costs of finance paid	(109,677)	(58,487)
Income taxes received/(paid)	19,040	(38,341)
Net operating cash flows	**(115,081)**	**(28,874)**
Cash flows related to investing activities		
Payments for purchases of property, plant and equipment	(81,854)	(60,997)
Proceeds from sale of property, plant and equipment	9,587	1,689
Payments for purchase of intangible assets	(3,154)	(10,563)
Acquisition for non-controlling interests	(197,680)	—
Consideration for business combination, net of cash acquired	(422,461)	(44,093)
Proceeds from sale of subsidiary, net of cash disposed	164,028	—
Acquisition of equity accounted investees	(83,767)	(448,360)
Proceeds from sale of shares in equity accounted investees	1,989	300,586
Payments for other investments	(21,119)	(297,433)
Proceeds from sale of other financial assets	29,910	4,522
Other	2,010	(285)
Net investing cash flows	**(602,511)**	**(554,934)**
Cash flows related to financing activities		
Proceeds from issue of shares—Seven Group Holdings Limited	8,250	7,000
Proceeds from issue of shares—subsidiaries	2,000	159
Ordinary dividends paid	(110,488)	(109,948)
TELYS4 dividends paid	(33,209)	(34,222)
Proceeds from borrowings	1,933,575	1,347,215
Repayment of borrowings	(1,018,759)	(1,007,698)
Net financing cash flows	**781,369**	**202,506**
Net (decrease)/increase in cash and cash equivalents	**63,777**	**(381,302)**
Cash and cash equivalents at beginning of period	65,244	449,671
Effect of exchange rate changes on cash and cash equivalents	(1,272)	(3,125)
Cash and cash equivalents at end of the period	**127,749**	**65,244**

First Solar, Inc. and Subsidiaries

Consolidated Statements of Cash Flows

	Years Ended		
($ in thousands)	December 31, 2012	December 31, 2011	December 31, 2010
Cash flows from operating activities			
Cash received from customers	$ 3,231,268	$ 2,290,944	$ 2,458,088
Cash paid to suppliers and associates	(2,447,337)	(2,159,429)	(1,614,763)
Interest received	4,693	10,156	20,531
Interest paid	(19,916)	(14,229)	(7,610)
Income tax refunds (payments), net	21,543	(46,153)	(80,064)
Excess tax benefit from share-based compensation arrangements	(27,373)	(110,836)	(69,367)
Other operating activities	(669)	(3,916)	(1,323)
			(continued)

| | Years Ended | | |
	December 31, 2012	December 31, 2011	December 31, 2010
Net cash provided by (used in) operating activities	**762,209**	**(33,463)**	**705,492**
Cash flows from investing activities			
Purchases of property, plant and equipment	(379,228)	(731,814)	(588,914)
Purchases of marketable securities	(29,200)	(331,240)	(462,070)
Proceeds from sales and maturities of marketable securities	108,663	492,613	556,904
Payments received on notes receivable	—	—	61,658
Investment in note receivable, affiliate	(21,659)	—	—
Payments received on note receivable, affiliate	4,498	—	—
Purchase of restricted investments	(80,667)	(62,749)	(43,064)
Change in restricted cash	16,215	(23,154)	—
Sale of investment in related party	—	—	28,596
Acquisitions, net of cash acquired	(2,437)	(21,105)	(296,496)
Other investing activities	83	992	1,301
Net cash used in investing activities	**(383,732)**	**(676,457)**	**(742,085)**
Cash flows from financing activities			
Proceeds from stock option exercises	176	8,326	9,379
Repayment of borrowings under revolving credit facility	(1,305,000)	(450,000)	—
Proceeds from borrowings under revolving credit facility	1,375,000	550,000	100,000
Repayment of long-term debt	(178,842)	(33,796)	(27,879)
Proceeds from borrowings under long-term debt, net of discount and issuance costs	—	370,108	—
Excess tax benefit from share-based compensation arrangements	27,373	110,836	69,367
(Repayment of) proceeds from economic development funding	(6,820)	16,188	—
Other financing activities	(996)	(444)	(416)
Net cash (used in) provided by financing activities	**(89,109)**	**571,218**	**150,451**
Effect of exchange rate changes on cash and cash equivalents	**6,307**	**(21,368)**	**(12,668)**
Net increase (decrease) in cash and cash equivalents	295,675	(160,070)	101,190
Cash and cash equivalents, beginning of the period	605,619	765,689	664,499
Cash and cash equivalents, end of the period	**$ 901,294**	**$ 605,619**	**$ 765,689**
Supplemental disclosure of noncash investing and financing activities			
Property, plant and equipment acquisitions funded by liabilities	$ 62,344	$ 74,391	$ 88,977
Settlement of long-term debt	$ 4,802	$ —	$ —

C17-2

Lucky Lady Inc.: Preparing comprehensive statement of cash flows   **(LO 1, 2, 3, 4)**

The income statement for the year ended December 31, 2014, as well as the balance sheets as of December 31, 2014, and December 31, 2013, for Lucky Lady Inc. follow. This information is taken from the financial statements of a real company whose name has been disguised.

Income Statement

($ in thousands)	For the Year Ended December 31, 2014
Revenues	
Casino	$ 26,702
Rooms	2,897
Food and beverage	2,351
Other hotel/casino	5,066
Airline	20,784
Total revenues	57,800 *(continued)*

($ in thousands)	For the Year Ended December 31, 2014
Operating Expenses	
Casino	9,341
Rooms	1,016
Food and beverage	2,529
Other hotel/casino	5,777
Airline	20,599
Selling, general, and administrative (including bad debt expense of $3,855)	19,679
Depreciation expense	8,018
Hotel preopening expenses	45,130
Aircraft carrying value adjustment	68,948
Total operating expenses	181,037
Operating income	(123,237)
Nonoperating items:	
Interest income	12,231
Interest expense	(6,596)
Other, net	16
Income before taxes	(117,586)
Provision for income taxes	–0–
Net income (loss)	$(117,586)

Balance Sheets

($ in thousands)	December 31, 2014	December 31, 2013
Assets		
Cash	$ 211,305	$ 579,963
Gross accounts receivable	35,249	2,178
Less: Allowance for doubtful accounts	(4,733)	(1,531)
Prepaid expenses	11,755	1,219
Inventories	12,662	154
Total current assets	266,238	581,983
Gross property, plant, and equipment	953,796	471,506
Less: Accumulated depreciation	(86,512)	(21,796)
Pre-opening expenses	–0–	10,677
Other operating assets	26,601	21,116
Total assets	$1,160,123	$1,063,486
Liabilities and Stockholders' Equity		
Accounts payable	$ 14,181	$ 4,322
Accrued salaries and wages	8,194	945
Accrued interest on long-term debt	9,472	9,429
Other accrued liabilities	33,502	9,744
Construction payables	96,844	32,296
Current maturities, capital leases	1,830	289
Current maturities, long-term debt	1,573	–0–
Total current liabilities	165,596	57,025
Deferred revenues	10,784	–0–
Deferred income taxes	6,517	6,517
Long-term obligation, capital leases	14,044	162
Long-term debt	481,427	473,000
Total liabilities	678,368	536,704
Common stock	506	485
Capital in excess of par value	662,365	589,827
Common stock in treasury	(29,490)	(29,490)
Retained earnings (deficit)	(151,626)	(34,040)
Total stockholders' equity	481,755	526,782
Total liabilities and equity	$1,160,123	$1,063,486

Additional Information and Author Notes:

- *Aircraft valuation adjustment:* The company reduced the book value of its aircraft and related equipment to their expected recoverable values and recognized an aircraft carrying value adjustment in the 2014 income statement. [*Author Note:* You may treat this item as "extra" depreciation recorded during the year due to abnormal decline in the asset value.]

- *Property, plant, and equipment:* Includes land, buildings, aircraft equipment, furniture and fixture, equipment under capital lease, and so on. During 2014, the company acquired equipment under capital leases for $16,987,000. The company also sold equipment with a net book value of $2,501,000 for $684,000 cash. [*Author Note:* The gain or loss on this sale is combined with some other item in the income statement. Any other change in the gross book value of Property, plant, and equipment may be attributed to outright purchase of other equipment and building construction costs.]

- *Capital lease and long-term liabilities:* [*Author Note:* When preparing the cash flow statement, you may find it convenient to combine the current and long-term portions of each of these liabilities.]

- *Pre-opening expenses:* Pre-opening expenses include direct project salaries, advertising, and other pre-opening services incurred during the pre-opening period of the Lucky Lady Hotel. Such expenses were expensed upon opening the facility.

- *Stock offering:* The increases in Common stock and Capital in excess of par accounts are due to a common stock offering completed on August 17, 2014.

- *Laundry loan:* On June 16, 2014, the company obtained a $10,000,000 loan from a financial institution for a laundry facility in North Las Vegas, Nevada. As of December 31, 2014, $10,000,000 has been drawn down under the loan. Construction of the facility was completed in December 2014. The laundry provides the laundry and dry cleaning services for the Lucky Lady Hotel.

Required:

Using the indirect method, prepare the statement of cash flows for the year ended December 31, 2014, in as much detail as possible. For example, borrowing and repayment, if any, should be shown separately as financing inflow and outflow, respectively. Similarly, to the extent that information is available, separately disclose and explain the changes to each asset and each liability account that affected Lucky Lady's cash flows during 2014.

C17-3

Opus One, Inc.: Preparing and analyzing the cash flow statement **(LO 1, 2, 4)**

The following information is based on a real company whose name has been disguised. Opus One operates in a single business segment, the retailing and servicing of home audio, car audio, and video equipment. Its operations are conducted in Texas through 20 stores and two service centers. The information provided in the annual report has been combined and abbreviated.

Additional Information Regarding Year Ended June 30, 2014:

- The company did not declare or pay any cash or stock dividends during the year.

- The company reported a $7,377 loss from scrapping equipment with a book value of the same amount.

- The depreciation expense for the year was $2,265,735.

- The following breakdown is provided for the long-term debt:

	June 30,	
($ in thousands)	2014	2013
Long-Term Debt		
Term loan	$3,420,000	$ –0–
Mortgage note	534,475	555,455
Total	3,954,475	555,455
Less: Current installments	(681,716)	(21,348)
Long-term debt—current installments	$3,272,759	$534,107

Opus One, Inc.

Balance Sheet as of June 30, 2014 and 2013

	June 30,	
($ in thousands)	2014	2013
Current Assets		
Cash	$ 50,885	$ 19,481
Receivables	4,625,920	6,963,195
Less: Allowance for bad debts	(403,000)	(1,200,000)
Inventories	25,986,364	26,801,526
Prepaid expenses	455,875	710,058
Income taxes receivable	1,573,055	3,073,537
Noncurrent Assets		
Property and equipment	22,182,371	20,637,912
Less: Accumulated depreciation	(9,031,181)	(6,822,553)
Deferred tax asset, net	1,043,403	531,803
Goodwill	244,241	268,691
Total assets	$46,727,933	$50,983,650
Current Liabilities		
Revolving credit agreements	$ 4,810,398	$18,743,407
Accounts payable	11,054,418	7,951,545
Accrued liabilities	3,655,358	2,380,493
Current installments of long-term debt	681,716	21,348
Long-Term Liabilities		
Long-term debt minus current installments	3,272,759	534,107
Other liabilities and deferred credits	4,072,586	3,308,714
Total liabilities	27,547,235	32,939,614
Shareholders' Equity		
Common stock and additional paid-in capital	10,126,944	10,117,946
Retained earnings	9,053,754	7,926,090
Total shareholders' equity	19,180,698	18,044,036
Total liabilities and shareholders' equity	$46,727,933	$50,983,650

On February 26, 2014, the company obtained a $3,600,000 term loan from a bank due February 28, 2018.

Required:

1. Prepare a statement of cash flows for the year ended June 30, 2014, using the indirect approach.
2. On the basis of the cash flow statement, analyze Opus One's financial performance during the fiscal year 2014.

C17-4

Capitalizing software
development costs **(LO 6)**

ESCO Technologies Inc. and Take-Two Interactive Software, Inc., both capitalize software development costs in accordance with their respective policies as summarized here. The condensed financial information that follows was extracted from each company's fiscal 2007 Form 10-K (all dollars are in thousands). Full financial statements for each company may be accessed at www.sec.gov.

ESCO Technologies Inc.

ESCO Technologies Inc. and its wholly owned subsidiaries are organized into three reporting units: Communications, Filtration/Fluid Flow, and RF Shielding and Test. The Communications unit is a proven supplier of special purpose fixed network communications systems for electric, gas, and water utilities, including hardware and software to support advanced metering applications. The Filtration unit develops, manufactures, and markets a broad range of filtration products used in the purification and processing of liquids. The Test unit provides its customers with the ability to identify, measure, and contain magnetic, electromagnetic, and acoustic energy.

Statement of Cash Flow Data Affected by Software Capitalization Policies

	Years Ended September 30,		
	2007	**2006**	**2005**
Net cash provided by operating activities	$ 45,263	$ 58,626	$ 68,556
Cash flows from investing activities:			
Acquisition of businesses, net of cash acquired	(8,250)	(91,968)	—
Capital expenditures	(19,503)	(9,117)	(8,848)
Additions to capitalized software	(30,094)	(27,977)	(8,342)
Net cash used by investing activities	$(57,847)	$(129,062)	$(17,190)

Selected Other Financial Statement Items

	Years Ended September 30,		
	2007	**2006**	**2005**
Total current assets	$260,350	$207,257	
Net property, plant, and equipment	78,277	68,754	
Goodwill	149,466	143,450	
Capitalized software, net	65,700	45,200	
Other intangible assets, net	11,542	14,002	
Other assets	10,772	10,031	
Total assets	$576,107	$488,694	
Amortization of capitalized software	7,700	3,300	
Net earnings	$ 33,713	$ 31,280	$43,544

Condensed Note Disclosure: Capitalized Software

The costs incurred for the development of computer software that will be sold, leased, or otherwise marketed are charged to expense when incurred as research and development until technological feasibility has been established for the product. Technological feasibility is typically established upon completion of a detailed program design. Costs incurred after this point are capitalized on a project-by-project basis in accordance with (pre-Codification) *SFAS No. 86.* Costs that are capitalized primarily consist of external development costs. Upon general release of the product to customers, the Company ceases capitalization and . . . amortizes the software development costs over a three- to seven-year period based upon the estimated future economic life of the product.

Take-Two Interactive Software, Inc.

Take-Two Interactive Software, Inc., is a global publisher, developer, and distributor of interactive entertainment software, hardware, and accessories. Its publishing segment develops, markets, and publishes software titles for leading gaming and entertainment hardware platforms.

Statement of Cash Flow Data Affected by Software Capitalization Policies

	Years Ended October 31,		
	2007	2006	2005
Operating activites			
Net Income (loss)	$ (138,406)	$ (184,889)	$ 35,314
Adjustments to reconcile net income (loss) to net cash provided by (used for) operating activities:			
Amortization and write-off of software development costs and licenses	109,891	147,832	81,959
Other adjustments, net	54,499	89,728	43,573
Changes in assets and liabilities, net of effect from purchases and disposal of businesses:			
Software development costs and licenses	(163,859)	(143,248)	(138,609)
Other changes in assets and liabilities, net	73,830	133,939	17,743
Net cash (used for) provided by operating activities	$ (64,045)	$ 43,362	$ 39,980
Investing activities			
Payments for purchases of businesses, net of cash acquired	(5,795)	(191)	(37,753)

Selected Other Financial Statement Items

	Years Ended October 31,		
	2007	2006	2005
Current assets			
Software development costs and licenses	141,441	85,207	
Other current assets	357,082	459,666	
Total current assets	498,523	544,873	
Software development costs and licenses, net of current portion	34,465	31,354	
Other noncurrent assets	298,155	292,579	
Total assets	$ 831,143	$ 868,806	
Net income (loss)	$(138,406)	$(184,889)	$35,314

Condensed Note Disclosure: Software Development Costs

We utilize both internal development teams and third-party software developers to develop the titles we publish.

We capitalize internal software development costs (including stock-based compensation, specifically identifiable employee payroll expense, and incentive compensation costs related to the completion and release of titles), third-party production and other content costs, subsequent to establishing technological feasibility of a software title. Technological feasibility of a product includes the completion of both technical design documentation and game design documentation. Amortization of such capitalized costs is recorded on a title-by-title basis in cost of goods sold (software development costs) using (1) the proportion of current year revenues to the total revenues expected to be recorded over the life of the title or (2) the straight-line method over the remaining estimated useful life of the title, whichever is greater.

We frequently enter into agreements with third-party developers that require us to make advance payments for game development and production services. . . . We capitalize all advance payments to developers as software development. On a product-by-product basis, we reduce software development costs and record a corresponding amount of research and development expense for any costs incurred by third-party developers prior to establishing technological feasibility of a product. We typically enter into agreements with third-party developers after completing the technical design documentation for our products and therefore record the design costs leading up to a signed developer contract as research and development expense. We also generally contract with third-party developers that have proven technology and experience in the genre of the software being developed, which often allows for the establishment of technological feasibility early in the development cycle. In instances where the documentation of the design and technology are not in place prior to an executed contract, we monitor the software development process and require our third-party developers to adhere to the same technological feasibility standards that apply to our internally developed products.

Prior to establishing technological feasibility, we expense research and development costs as incurred.

Required:

Some analysts believe the amount of capitalized software costs should be subtracted from operating cash flows to improve interfirm comparability and to correct for a firm's possible attempt to improve operating cash flows by lowering the technological feasibility threshold in the current period relative to prior periods. Consider this possibility when responding to requirements 1 and 2.

1. Make any needed adjustment to Take-Two's statement of cash flows to improve interfirm comparability of its operating cash flows.

2. Make any needed adjustment to ESCO Technologies' statement of cash flows to improve interfirm comparability of its operating cash flows.

3. What is the likely impact of any adjustment(s) you made in requirements 1 and 2 on an analysis of operating cash flows?

4. What impact do ESCO's software capitalization policies have on the company's net income as reported for fiscal 2007? (*Hint:* Compare to income assuming that ESCO expenses all software development costs when incurred. Assume a marginal income tax rate related to the software development costs of 35%. Do not adjust income tax expense related to any elements of pre-tax income other than software development costs.)

5. Compare Take-Two's and ESCO Technologies' policies with respect to establishing technological feasibility and comment on the impact of these policies on reported net income.

6. Re-create summary journal entries for the fiscal 2007 activity in Take-Two's Software development costs and licenses account. Do your entries reconcile with the information reported on Take-Two's cash flow statement? If not, offer a plausible explanation for any discrepancy. (*Hint:* Combine both current and noncurrent balance sheet items related to software development costs and licenses.)

**Remember to check the book's companion website
for additional study material.**

Appendix

TIME VALUE OF MONEY

Cash is an economic resource. When firms borrow cash—for example, take a two-year bank loan—they are renting the use of that economic resource for the two-year term of that loan. The lender's charge for renting its cash to the borrower is **interest.**

Interest is an important concept because many business transactions involve borrowing, lending, or investing. Because of interest, a dollar amount invested today increases (or accumulates) to a higher amount in the future. The amount that that dollar grows to in the future is the **future value.** Similarly, because of interest, a dollar amount that will be received in the future—say, two years from now—is less valuable than that same dollar amount in hand today. Calculating today's value of a future dollar amount is called **discounting.** The result of that discounting calculation is the **present value** of that future dollar amount.

The time at which cash inflows and cash outflows occur determines the ultimate future value or the present value of those flows. Correctly valuing these flows is necessary to represent properly the value of the assets, liabilities, revenues, and expenses arising from various business transactions.

> The concepts of present value and future value are totally driven by the role of interest. These concepts are unrelated to the buying power of money—inflation or deflation—which is a distinct and separate topic that we do not discuss in this appendix.

Future Value

Assume that Alice Han's parents give her a $1,000 check for her twenty-first birthday. She wants to invest the money for graduate school, which she will attend in two years. Three local banks advertise that their savings accounts pay 6% interest per year, although how that interest is computed differs among them. Bank A pays 6% **simple interest** on the cash in a depositor's savings account. *Simple interest* means that each year's interest is computed on the original amount invested, which is called the **principal.** So, interest each year would be $1,000 × 0.06, or $60. At the end of two years, the account at Bank A will have a future value of $1,120, calculated as:

$$\text{Future value with simple interest} = \$1{,}000 + \$60 + \$60 = \$1{,}120$$

Bank B pays 6% compound interest on savings accounts. **Compound interest** means that interest is paid not just on the in itial principal but also on the interest that has been earned each period to date. So, the accumulated amount would be computed as follows:

Date	Interest Calculation	Accumulated Amount
Initial principal		$1,000.00
Year 1	$1,000 × 0.06 = $60.00	$1,060.00
Year 2	$1,060 × 0.06 = $63.60	$1,123.60

> Future value with interest compounded annually = $1,123.60

Bank B has compounded the interest annually; that is, interest is computed only once a year.

Bank C pays 6% interest compounded semiannually. This means that interest is computed every six months at a rate of 3%. The accumulated amount is:

Date	Interest Calculation	Accumulated Amount
Initial principal		$1,000.00
Year 1—First 6 months	$1,000 × 0.03 = $30.00	$1,030.00
—Last 6 months	$1,030 × 0.03 = $30.90	$1,060.90
Year 2—First 6 months	$1,060.90 × 0.03 = $31.83	$1,092.73
—Last 6 months	$1,092.73 × 0.03 = $32.78	$1,125.51

> Future value with interest compounded semiannually = $1,125.51

Because most business transactions use compound interest, so will our examples. The formula for computing compound interest is

$$FV = PV(1 + r)^n$$

Where:

FV = future value

PV = present value

r = interest rate per compounding period

n = number of compounding periods

For simplicity, let's assume that interest is compounded annually. So, the compounding period is a year. Using the formula to compute the future amount of a $1,000, two-year deposit in Bank B:

$$FV = \$1,000(1 + 0.06)^2$$
$$FV = \$1,123.60$$

Of course, $1,123.60 equals the same future amount computed previously by the earlier more tedious calculation.

Present Value

As you just saw, if interest is compounded annually at 6%, the future value of $1,000.00 after two years is $1,123.60. This means that $1,123.60 to be received two years in the future is equivalent to $1,000 today—its present value—when the interest rate is 6% per year. To be sure you understand this concept of present value, we'll look at it from another perspective.

Assume that Alice Han's parents, knowing that she wanted to enroll in graduate school in two years, gave her a choice of birthday gifts:

- $1,000 cash immediately.
- $1,123.60 to be received in exactly two years.

Which option should she choose? If she is determined to spend the money for graduate school (that is, she doesn't need the cash immediately) and if she knows that 6% per year is the prevailing interest rate, *she should be indifferent between the two options.* Here's why. If she chooses the $1,000 today, she could put it in a savings account at Bank B at 6% per year compounded annually where it would accumulate to $1,123.60 in two years.[1] So, the two alternative gift amounts are identical at 6% per year compounded annually. *Being indifferent between $1,000 today and $1,123.60 in two years means that the present value of $1,123.60 due in two years is $1,000 at a 6% interest rate compounded annually.*

By rearranging the formula for computing compound interest, we can represent this notion of present value:

$$FV = PV(1 + r)^n$$

Solving this formula for *PV*, we find the present value:

$$PV = \frac{FV}{(1 + r)^n}$$

Table 1 at the end of this appendix shows the present value factors for various compounding periods and various interest rates per period. These present value factors result from solving the present value equation for *PV.* This table provides the factor for computing the present value of a dollar to be received *n* periods in the future at interest rate *r.* (A portion of that table is reproduced here for convenience.)

Using Han's two gift options as a concrete example, we can show you how to use Table 1. Look at the intersection of the Period 2 row and the 6% column (denoted *PV* 2, 6%) and you will see the number 0.89000 (highlighted). This number is the factor that represents the present value of a dollar to be received at the end of two years at a 6% per period **discount rate.**

TABLE 1 (Selected Excerpts) **Present Value of $1**

$$PV = \frac{1}{(1 + r)^n} = (1 + r)^{-n}$$

(n) Periods	2%	3%	4%	5%	6%	7%	8%	9%	10%	11%	12%	15%
1	0.98039	0.97087	0.96154	0.95238	0.94340	0.93458	0.92593	0.91743	0.90909	0.90090	0.89286	0.86957
2	0.96117	0.94260	0.92456	0.90703	0.89000	0.87344	0.85734	0.84168	0.82645	0.81162	0.79719	0.75614
3	0.94232	0.91514	0.88900	0.86384	0.83962	0.81630	0.79383	0.77218	0.75132	0.73119	0.71178	0.65752
4	0.92385	0.88849	0.85480	0.82270	0.79209	0.76290	0.73503	0.70843	0.68301	0.65873	0.63552	0.57175
5	0.90573	0.86261	0.82193	0.78353	0.74726	0.71299	0.68058	0.64993	0.62092	0.59345	0.56743	0.49718

[1] For simplicity, we focus on annual compounding and ignore the possibility of depositing money in Bank C.

Discount rate is what the interest rate is called when computing present values.

To verify this, notice that if 89¢ were invested at 6% compounded annually for two years, it would accumulate to:

Date	Interest Calculation	Accumulated Amount
Initial principal		$0.89
Year 1	$0.89 × 0.06 = 0.0534. Then, $0.89 + 0.0534	=$0.9434
Year 2	$0.9434 × 0.06 = 0.0566. Then, $0.9434 + 0.0566	=$1.00

We use table factors throughout the text so that students can see how amounts are calculated and be prepared for exams that rely on tables. These calculations can also be done easily in Excel or with a financial calculator.

Because 0.89000 is the present value factor for one dollar, the present value for $1,123.60 (Alice's parents' second birthday choice amount) is $1,123.60 × 0.89000 = $1,000. So, you see how Table 1 helps us verify that the two gift amounts have identical present values.

Careful examination of Table 1 reveals two general characteristics of present value computations. First, looking *down any column,* you can see that the numbers become smaller. For example, in the 6% column, the number in the Period 3 row is 0.83962, which is smaller than 0.89000—the number in the Period 2 row. This illustrates that the further in the future is the dollar flow, the smaller is its present value. Second, looking to the right *across any row,* the numbers again become smaller. For example, in the Period 2 row, in the 7% column, the number 0.87344 is smaller than 0.89000—the number in the 6% column. This illustrates that the higher the discount rate is (7% versus 6%), the smaller the present value of $1 is. Why? Because the higher the discount rate is, the smaller is the amount that must be invested at r% to equal $1 in n periods. At 7%, only 87.344¢ must be invested to equal $1 in two periods, whereas at 6%, 89¢ must be invested to equal $1 in two periods.

Present Value of an Ordinary Annuity

Jacquie Henderson has just won the state lottery's $100,000 Bonanza. The winnings are paid out in four equal installments. Each $25,000 installment is mailed to the winner on the one-year anniversary of the lottery drawing beginning 365 days from now. Jacquie understands that the discounted present value of the prize is less than $100,000 and wishes to compute its exact value using a discount rate of 5%. One way she can do this is to list each of the four payments separately and use the present value factors from Table 1. Doing it this way, the computation is:

Payment Number	Payment Amount	Present Value Factor	Present Value
1	$25,000	0.95238	$23,809.50
2	25,000	0.90703	22,675.75
3	25,000	0.86384	21,596.00
4	25,000	0.82270	20,567.50
Total			$88,648.75

As the computation shows, the present value of the advertised $100,000 prize is only $88,648.75. Notice that the $25,000 undiscounted dollar amount received each period is the

TABLE 2 (Selected Excerpts)   Present Value of an Ordinary Annuity of $1

$$PVOA = \left(1 - \frac{1}{(1 + r)^n}\right)/r$$

(n) Periods	2%	3%	4%	5%	6%	7%	8%	9%	10%	11%	12%	15%
1	0.98039	0.97087	0.96154	0.95238	0.94340	0.93458	0.92593	0.91743	0.90909	0.90090	0.89286	0.86957
2	1.94156	1.91347	1.88609	1.85941	1.83339	1.80802	1.78326	1.75911	1.73554	1.71252	1.69005	1.62571
3	2.88388	2.82861	2.77509	2.72325	2.67301	2.62432	2.57710	2.53129	2.48685	2.44371	2.40183	2.28323
4	3.80773	3.71710	3.62990	3.54595	3.46511	3.38721	3.31213	3.23972	3.16987	3.10245	3.03735	2.85498
5	4.71346	4.57971	4.45182	4.32948	4.21236	4.10020	3.99271	3.88965	3.79079	3.69590	3.60478	3.35216

same. When each payment in a series is the same dollar amount, the series is called an **annuity.** When each payment is made at the *end* of each period, as in our example, that payment series is an **ordinary annuity** (also called an **annuity in arrears**).

To compute the present value of an ordinary annuity, it isn't necessary to compute the present value of each payment separately as we just did. Instead, Table 2 of the appendix provides present value factors for ordinary annuities of various lengths at selected discount rates. A portion of Table 2 is reproduced here for convenience.

Notice in Table 2 that the intersection of the Period 4 row and the 5% (denoted *PVOA* 4, 5%) column contains the factor 3.54595 (highlighted). This number is simply the sum of the four present value factors we just used in the lottery computation. Specifically:

Payment Number	Present Value Factor
1	0.95238
2	0.90703
3	0.86384
4	0.82270
Total	3.54595

So, you see that 3.54595 is the present value of an ordinary annuity of $1.00 each period for four periods. To determine the present value of an ordinary annuity of $25,000 each period for four periods, we multiply 3.54595 times $25,000. The product, $88,648.75, is identical to the number we just computed more tediously for the present value of Jacquie Henderson's lottery winnings.

Present Value of an Annuity Due

Let's return to the lottery example and assume now that Henderson receives the first lottery check immediately. The next three checks follow at one-year intervals, that is, at the start of each of the next three periods. When each payment is made at the *beginning* of the period, as we now assume in this example, that payment series is an **annuity due** (also called an **annuity in advance**).

To determine the present value of the lottery winnings when the payout is an annuity due, we can again compute from Table 1 the present value at 5% of each of the $25,000 checks, remembering that the present value factor for the first payment received *today* is 1.0000:

Payment Number	Payment Amount	Present Value Factor	Present Value
1	$25,000	1.00000	$25,000.00
2	25,000	0.95238	23,809.50
3	25,000	0.90703	22,675.75
4	25,000	0.86384	21,596.00
Total			$93,081.25

When the lottery payments are made at the start of the year rather than at the end of the year (that is, an annuity due rather than an ordinary annuity), the present value of those payments is higher—$93,081.25 versus only $88,648.75 for the ordinary annuity.

Tables for computing the present value of an annuity due are also available; see Table 3 of this appendix. A portion of Table 3 is reproduced here for convenience.

The highlighted present value factor at the intersection of the Period 4 row and the 5% column (denoted *PVAD* 4, 5%) is 3.72325. Multiplying 3.72325 times $25,000 yields $93,081.25, the answer we just computed. And, if you have suspected that the 3.72325 factor is simply the sum of 1.00000 + 0.95238 + 0.90703 + 0.86384, your suspicion is not only correct but also you understand annuities, discount rates, and present value.

TABLE 3 (Selected Excerpts) Present Value of an Annuity Due of $1

$$PVAD = 1 + \left(1 - \frac{1}{(1 + r)^{n-1}}\right)/r$$

(n) Periods	2%	3%	4%	5%	6%	7%	8%	9%	10%	11%	12%	15%
1	1.00000	1.00000	1.00000	1.00000	1.00000	1.00000	1.00000	1.00000	1.00000	1.00000	1.00000	1.00000
2	1.98039	1.97087	1.96154	1.95238	1.94340	1.93458	1.92593	1.91743	1.90909	1.90090	1.89286	1.86957
3	2.94156	2.91347	2.88609	2.85941	2.83339	2.80802	2.78326	2.75911	2.73554	2.71252	2.69005	2.62571
4	3.88388	3.82861	3.77509	3.72325	3.67301	3.62432	3.57710	3.53129	3.48685	3.44371	3.40183	3.28323
5	4.80773	4.71710	4.62990	4.54595	4.46511	4.38721	4.31213	4.23972	4.16987	4.10245	4.03735	3.85498

*Please visit our website (**www.mhhe.com/revsine6e**) for a spreadsheet template that can be used to find present value factors for interest rates not shown in this appendix.*

TABLE I		Present Value of $1													

$$PV = \frac{1}{(1+r)^n} = (1+r)^{-n}$$

(n) Periods	2%	3%	4%	5%	6%	7%	8%	9%	10%	11%	12%	15%	16%	17%
1	0.98039	0.97087	0.96154	0.95238	0.94340	0.93458	0.92593	0.91743	0.90909	0.90090	0.89286	0.86957	0.86207	0.85470
2	0.96117	0.94260	0.92456	0.90703	0.89000	0.87344	0.85734	0.84168	0.82645	0.81162	0.79719	0.75614	0.74316	0.73051
3	0.94232	0.91514	0.88900	0.86384	0.83962	0.81630	0.79383	0.77218	0.75132	0.73119	0.71178	0.65752	0.64066	0.62437
4	0.92385	0.88849	0.85480	0.82270	0.79209	0.76290	0.73503	0.70843	0.68301	0.65873	0.63552	0.57175	0.55229	0.53365
5	0.90573	0.86261	0.82193	0.78353	0.74726	0.71299	0.68058	0.64993	0.62092	0.59345	0.56743	0.49718	0.47611	0.45611
6	0.88797	0.83748	0.79031	0.74622	0.70496	0.66634	0.63017	0.59627	0.56447	0.53464	0.50663	0.43233	0.41044	0.38984
7	0.87056	0.81309	0.75992	0.71068	0.66506	0.62275	0.58349	0.54703	0.51316	0.48166	0.45235	0.37594	0.35383	0.33320
8	0.85349	0.78941	0.73069	0.67684	0.62741	0.58201	0.54027	0.50187	0.46651	0.43393	0.40388	0.32690	0.30503	0.28478
9	0.83676	0.76642	0.70259	0.64461	0.59190	0.54393	0.50025	0.46043	0.42410	0.39092	0.36061	0.28426	0.26295	0.24340
10	0.82035	0.74409	0.67556	0.61391	0.55839	0.50835	0.46319	0.42241	0.38554	0.35218	0.32197	0.24718	0.22668	0.20804
11	0.80426	0.72242	0.64958	0.58468	0.52679	0.47509	0.42888	0.38753	0.35049	0.31728	0.28748	0.21494	0.19542	0.17781
12	0.78849	0.70138	0.62460	0.55684	0.49697	0.44401	0.39711	0.35553	0.31863	0.28584	0.25668	0.18691	0.16846	0.15197
13	0.77303	0.68095	0.60057	0.53032	0.46884	0.41496	0.36770	0.32618	0.28966	0.25751	0.22917	0.16253	0.14523	0.12989
14	0.75788	0.66112	0.57748	0.50507	0.44230	0.38782	0.34046	0.29925	0.26333	0.23199	0.20462	0.14133	0.12520	0.11102
15	0.74301	0.64186	0.55526	0.48102	0.41727	0.36245	0.31524	0.27454	0.23939	0.20900	0.18270	0.12289	0.10793	0.09489
16	0.72845	0.62317	0.53391	0.45811	0.39365	0.33873	0.29189	0.25187	0.21763	0.18829	0.16312	0.10686	0.09304	0.08110
17	0.71416	0.60502	0.51337	0.43630	0.37136	0.31657	0.27027	0.23107	0.19784	0.16963	0.14564	0.09293	0.08021	0.06932
18	0.70016	0.58739	0.49363	0.41552	0.35034	0.29586	0.25025	0.21199	0.17986	0.15282	0.13004	0.08081	0.06914	0.05925
19	0.68643	0.57029	0.47464	0.39573	0.33051	0.27651	0.23171	0.19449	0.16351	0.13768	0.11611	0.07027	0.05961	0.05064
20	0.67297	0.55368	0.45639	0.37689	0.31180	0.25842	0.21455	0.17843	0.14864	0.12403	0.10367	0.06110	0.05139	0.04328
25	0.60953	0.47761	0.37512	0.29530	0.23300	0.18425	0.14602	0.11597	0.09230	0.07361	0.05882	0.03038	0.02447	0.01974
30	0.55207	0.41199	0.30832	0.23138	0.17411	0.13137	0.09938	0.07537	0.05731	0.04368	0.03338	0.01510	0.01165	0.00900
35	0.50003	0.35538	0.25342	0.18129	0.13011	0.09366	0.06763	0.04899	0.03558	0.02592	0.01894	0.00751	0.00555	0.00411
40	0.45289	0.30656	0.20829	0.14205	0.09722	0.06678	0.04603	0.03184	0.02209	0.01538	0.01075	0.00373	0.00264	0.00187

TABLE 2	Present Value of an Ordinary Annuity of $1

$$PVOA = \left(1 - \frac{1}{(1 + r)^n}\right)/r$$

(n) Periods	2%	3%	4%	5%	6%	7%	8%	9%	10%	11%	12%	15%	16%	17%
1	0.98039	0.97087	0.96154	0.95238	0.94340	0.93458	0.92593	0.91743	0.90909	0.90090	0.89286	0.86957	0.86207	0.85470
2	1.94156	1.91347	1.88609	1.85941	1.83339	1.80802	1.78326	1.75911	1.73554	1.71252	1.69005	1.62571	1.60523	1.58521
3	2.88388	2.82861	2.77509	2.72325	2.67301	2.62432	2.57710	2.53129	2.48685	2.44371	2.40183	2.28323	2.24589	2.20958
4	3.80773	3.71710	3.62990	3.54595	3.46511	3.38721	3.31213	3.23972	3.16987	3.10245	3.03735	2.85498	2.79818	2.74324
5	4.71346	4.57971	4.45182	4.32948	4.21236	4.10020	3.99271	3.88965	3.79079	3.69590	3.60478	3.35216	3.27429	3.19935
6	5.60143	5.41719	5.24214	5.07569	4.91732	4.76654	4.62288	4.48592	4.35526	4.23054	4.11141	3.78448	3.68474	3.58918
7	6.47199	6.23028	6.00205	5.78637	5.58238	5.38929	5.20637	5.03295	4.86842	4.71220	4.56376	4.16042	4.03857	3.92238
8	7.32548	7.01969	6.73274	6.46321	6.20979	5.97130	5.74664	5.53482	5.33493	5.14612	4.96764	4.48732	4.34359	4.20716
9	8.16224	7.78611	7.43533	7.10782	6.80169	6.51523	6.24689	5.99525	5.75902	5.53705	5.32825	4.77158	4.60654	4.45057
10	8.98259	8.53020	8.11090	7.72173	7.36009	7.02358	6.71008	6.41766	6.14457	5.88923	5.65022	5.01877	4.83323	4.65860
11	9.78685	9.25262	8.76048	8.30641	7.88687	7.49867	7.13896	6.80519	6.49506	6.20652	5.93770	5.23371	5.02864	4.83641
12	10.57534	9.95400	9.38507	8.86325	8.38384	7.94269	7.53608	7.16073	6.81369	6.49236	6.19437	5.42062	5.19711	4.98839
13	11.34837	10.63496	9.98565	9.39357	8.85268	8.35765	7.90378	7.48690	7.10336	6.74987	6.42355	5.58315	5.34233	5.11828
14	12.10625	11.29607	10.56312	9.89864	9.29498	8.74547	8.24424	7.78615	7.36669	6.98187	6.62817	5.72448	5.46753	5.22930
15	12.84926	11.93794	11.11839	10.37966	9.71225	9.10791	8.55948	8.06069	7.60608	7.19087	6.81086	5.84737	5.57546	5.32419
16	13.57771	12.56110	11.65230	10.83777	10.10590	9.44665	8.85137	8.31256	7.82371	7.37916	6.97399	5.95423	5.66850	5.40529
17	14.29187	13.16612	12.16567	11.27407	10.47726	9.76322	9.12164	8.54363	8.02155	7.54879	7.11963	6.04716	5.74870	5.47461
18	14.99203	13.75351	12.65930	11.68959	10.82760	10.05909	9.37189	8.75563	8.20141	7.70162	7.24967	6.12797	5.81785	5.53385
19	15.67846	14.32380	13.13394	12.08532	11.15812	10.33560	9.60360	8.95011	8.36492	7.83929	7.36578	6.19823	5.87746	5.58449
20	16.35143	14.87747	13.59033	12.46221	11.46992	10.59401	9.81815	9.12855	8.51356	7.96333	7.46944	6.25933	5.92884	5.62777
25	19.52346	17.41315	15.62208	14.09394	12.78336	11.65358	10.67478	9.82258	9.07704	8.42174	7.84314	6.46415	6.09709	5.76623
30	22.39646	19.60044	17.29203	15.37245	13.76483	12.40904	11.25778	10.27365	9.42691	8.69379	8.05518	6.56598	6.17720	5.82939
35	24.99862	21.48722	18.66461	16.37419	14.49825	12.94767	11.65457	10.56682	9.64416	8.85524	8.17550	6.61661	6.21534	5.85820
40	27.35548	23.11477	19.79277	17.15909	15.04630	13.33171	11.92461	10.75736	9.77905	8.95105	8.24378	6.64178	6.23350	5.87133

| TABLE 3 | | Present Value of an Annuity Due of $1 | | | | | | | | | | | | |

$$PVAD = 1 + \left(1 - \frac{1}{(1 + r)^{n-1}}\right)/r$$

(n) Periods	2%	3%	4%	5%	6%	7%	8%	9%	10%	11%	12%	15%	16%	17%
1	1.00000	1.00000	1.00000	1.00000	1.00000	1.00000	1.00000	1.00000	1.00000	1.00000	1.00000	1.00000	1.00000	1.00000
2	1.98039	1.97087	1.96154	1.95238	1.94340	1.93458	1.92593	1.91743	1.90909	1.90090	1.89286	1.86957	1.86207	1.85470
3	2.94156	2.91347	2.88609	2.85941	2.83339	2.80802	2.78326	2.75911	2.73554	2.71252	2.69005	2.62571	2.60523	2.58521
4	3.88388	3.82861	3.77509	3.72325	3.67301	3.62432	3.57710	3.53129	3.48685	3.44371	3.40183	3.28323	3.24589	3.20958
5	4.80773	4.71710	4.62990	4.54595	4.46511	4.38721	4.31213	4.23972	4.16987	4.10245	4.03735	3.85498	3.79818	3.74324
6	5.71346	5.57971	5.45182	5.32948	5.21236	5.10020	4.99271	4.88965	4.79079	4.69590	4.60478	4.35216	4.27429	4.19935
7	6.60143	6.41719	6.24214	6.07569	5.91732	5.76654	5.62288	5.48592	5.35526	5.23054	5.11141	4.78448	4.68474	4.58918
8	7.47199	7.23028	7.00205	6.78637	6.58238	6.38929	6.20637	6.03295	5.86842	5.71220	5.56376	5.16042	5.03857	4.92238
9	8.32548	8.01969	7.73274	7.46321	7.20979	6.97130	6.74664	6.53482	6.33493	6.14612	5.96764	5.48732	5.34359	5.20716
10	9.16224	8.78611	8.43533	8.10782	7.80169	7.51523	7.24689	6.99525	6.75902	6.53705	6.32825	5.77158	5.60654	5.45057
11	9.98259	9.53020	9.11090	8.72173	8.36009	8.02358	7.71008	7.41766	7.14457	6.88923	6.65022	6.01877	5.83323	5.65860
12	10.78685	10.25262	9.76048	9.30641	8.88687	8.49867	8.13896	7.80519	7.49506	7.20652	6.93770	6.23371	6.02864	5.83641
13	11.57534	10.95400	10.38507	9.86325	9.38384	8.94269	8.53608	8.16073	7.81369	7.49236	7.19437	6.42062	6.19711	5.98839
14	12.34837	11.63496	10.98565	10.39357	9.85268	9.35765	8.90378	8.48690	8.10336	7.74987	7.42355	6.58315	6.34233	6.11828
15	13.10625	12.29607	11.56312	10.89864	10.29498	9.74547	9.24424	8.78615	8.36669	7.98187	7.62817	6.72448	6.46753	6.22930
16	13.84926	12.93794	12.11839	11.37966	10.71225	10.10791	9.55948	9.06069	8.60608	8.19087	7.81086	6.84737	6.57546	6.32419
17	14.57771	13.56110	12.65230	11.83777	11.10590	10.44665	9.85137	9.31256	8.82371	8.37916	7.97399	6.95423	6.66850	6.40529
18	15.29187	14.16612	13.16567	12.27407	11.47726	10.76322	10.12164	9.54363	9.02155	8.54879	8.11963	7.04716	6.74870	6.47461
19	15.99203	14.75351	13.65930	12.68959	11.82760	11.05909	10.37189	9.75563	9.20141	8.70162	8.24967	7.12797	6.81785	6.53385
20	16.67846	15.32380	14.13394	13.08532	12.15812	11.33560	10.60360	9.95011	9.36492	8.83929	8.36578	7.19823	6.87746	6.58449
25	19.91393	17.93554	16.24696	14.79864	13.55036	12.46933	11.52876	10.70661	9.98474	9.34814	8.78432	7.43377	7.07263	6.74649
30	22.84438	20.18845	17.98371	16.14107	14.59072	13.27767	12.15841	11.19828	10.36961	9.65011	9.02181	7.55088	7.16555	6.82039
35	25.49859	22.13184	19.41120	17.19290	15.36814	13.85401	12.58693	11.51784	10.60857	9.82932	9.15656	7.60910	7.20979	6.85409
40	27.90259	23.80822	20.58448	18.01704	15.94907	14.26493	12.87858	11.72552	10.75696	9.93567	9.23303	7.63805	7.23086	6.86946

Index